"WE THE PEOPLE" AND OTHERS

*Duality and America's Treatment
of its Racial Minorities*

"WE THE PEOPLE" AND OTHERS

Duality and America's Treatment of its Racial Minorities

BENJAMIN B. RINGER

TAVISTOCK PUBLICATIONS
NEW YORK AND LONDON

First published in 1983 by
Tavistock Publications
in association with Methuen, Inc.
29 West 35th Street, New York NY 10001
and Tavistock Publications Ltd
11 New Fetter Lane, London EC4P 4EE

First published as a Social Science Paperback in 1985

© 1983 Benjamin B. Ringer

Typeset in Linotron 202 by
Graphicraft Typesetters Limited, Hong Kong
Printed in the United States of America

Library of Congress Cataloging in Publication Data
Ringer, Benjamin B. (Benjamin Bernard), 1920–
"We the People" and others.

"In association with Methuen" – T.p. verso.
Bibliography: p.
Includes indexes.
1. United States – Race relations.   2. Racism – United
States – History.   3. United States – Colonial influence.
I. Title.
E184.A1R49   1983   305.8'00973   83-470

0-422-78180-0
ISBN 0-422-60160-8 (SSP)

British Library Cataloguing in Publication Data
Ringer, Benjamin B.
"We the people" and others: duality and
America's treatment of its racial minorities.
1. Race discrimination – United States –
History   2. Racism – United States – History
I. Title
305.8'00973   E184.A1

0-422-78180-0
ISBN 0-422-60160-8 (SSP)

CONTENTS

BOOK THREE THE EXTENSION OF DUALITY AND THE ENCOUNTERS OF OTHER RACIAL MINORITIES

To my wife,
Elinor Lawless

PREFACE

HYLAN LEWIS

Professor Ringer's study of America's duality – the existence of two fundamental entities that have been defined and are still being defined in complex ways by race, culture, law, and class – a Plural Terrain and a People's Domain – is at once an extraordinary and an important achievement. This is a fresh analysis of the much-studied problem of the manner in which race compounds the classic tension between democracy and equality in American society.

This work is a product of the 1960s in that the significant impetus for it came from questions raised by the effective but not fully decisive assault of the Civil Rights Movement on America's duality, and in particular on the racial creed that is the basis of the Plural Terrain. Reflections on the achievements and the frustrations of that period raised in an acute fashion insistent questions about changes in the quality of participation of racial and ethnic minorities in American society; the consequences of those changes; and efforts of observers and scholars to conceptualize and explain the processes involved. Professor Ringer uses historical analysis both to illuminate contemporary issues and to cue and challenge current research on race and class in other parts of the world, as well as the United States. The central thesis:

> "Through ... colonial conquest, subjugation and forcible importation of nonwhites ... the white European has characteristically imposed upon the nonwhite a racially-segmented Plural Societal Structure which he has dominated through the raw exercise of power. And in his quest for a permanent abode, he has characteristically created a colonist society in his own racial, religious and national image for himself and his fellow whites. The character of these dual structures, their linkage and relationships have varied with the national identity

of the white European, the racial identity of the nonwhite, proportions of each race, and historical circumstances. Accordingly, the way in which this duality has been imprinted in ... various societies is problematic and merits detailed study."
(Ringer 1982:85–6)

The focus on duality and race has important linkages to the writings of numerous scholars and observers of the United States from Tocqueville to Myrdal, and beyond. And it has significance as well for the very recent literature devoted to inequality that has been spurred in large measure by a "race-conscious affirmative action policy ... unlike the race-conscious policies of the ... [past]" (Ch.12:556).

Professor Ringer describes the making, the institutionalizing and the variable lessening of racial inequality in the United States for native Americans or Indians, blacks, Chinese, Japanese, and Puerto Ricans. In describing the historical workings of duality in Virginia, he notes that the dualities that evolved in the other southern colonies bore some similarity to the duality already fashioned in Virginia and that those in New England and the Middle Atlantic took on a distinctive character and quality of their own. The description of the various ways in which the United States and its regions have sought to resolve the historic duality and to build a monistic society in this country supports the cautionary conclusion:

"The United States seemed to have come closer in the 1960s to resolving its historic duality than had any of the other 'Colonist-Colonialist' societies in which the white European had become the numerical majority. It dismantled the legal-normative foundations of its Plural Society and granted its racial minorities access to and legal equality within the People's Domain.... [However] many of the inequities imprinted from the duality of America's past are still deeply engraved in its institutional arrangements."
(1982:Postscript:6–7)

The course of duality in the United States has been shaped significantly by international affairs – including the imperative of trade, war and the threats of war, and by the changes in the domestic labor market. This duality is demonstrated clearly in immigration policies and practices. They reveal in both symbolic and concrete ways the issues and human stakes involved in the palpable racial dimension that is part of a paradoxical mixture. They are a metaphor of America's duality. And speaking of metaphors and race, Professor Ringer deftly examines the fallacies in the immigrationist model, the limitations of the colonial analogy, and the relevance of is-it-race-or-is-it-class controversy when they are invoked to describe the status and to project the future of blacks and other nonwhite minorities. While acknowledging the major influence of the colonial perspective on his own formulations, he sees "it neither necessary to transport the entire vocabulary of colonialism nor to transplant its baggage of details onto the

American scene" (1982:28). And further on the race versus class issue: "we conclude that race has not declined in significance as a factor affecting the fate of the middle-class black in the economic sector; it has merely been *transformed*" (1982:Ch.12:556–57).

The duality framework has great potential for comparative studies of the dialectics of ongoing racial and ethnic stratification in all parts of the world. It is useful for the examination of time and regional variations in the structuring of race and ethnic relations in the United States of America and in a very timely way for the understanding of much of the ferment and change in practically all other countries of North and South America, and in Europe, Asia, Africa, and Australia as well. It is as relevant to the historical understanding of the racial correlates of European expansion and modernization as it is to the clearer comprehension of the stakes and issues, the dangers and the opportunities, in today's racial, religious, and political hotspots – for example, those in England and Ireland as well as the United States; in South Africa, Rhodesia, and Ethiopia and in various parts of the Near East, including Israel, Lebanon, and Iran.

The answers to the questions that all nations face – Who are "We the People?" and How is eligibility to the People's Domain determined? – have been shaped, and are being constantly modified in small and sometimes large ways in the United States by "various paradoxes and ambiguities." These appear in the Constitution, laws, court decisions, administrative rulings, and customs. The descriptions of "the historical encounters of blacks and other minorities with American society" emphasize that paradoxes and ambiguities with reference to race and equality have been wittingly built into a system of white dominance; and that every racial or nationality group that has been the victim of discrimination and oppression in the United States has actively fought against these. One result has been that democracy and equality insofar as nonwhite racial categories are concerned have followed zig-zag and uneven courses. Thus, the experience with the American system of duality presents a fascinating mixture of optimism and pessimism about race, politics, and human nature, and an uncertain future for the United States.

Forty years ago, Gunnar Myrdal's classic characterization of race relations in the United States as "An American Dilemma" appeared (Myrdal 1944). In many ways, Professor Ringer has built upon Myrdal's work. In doing so, he has extended coverage by developing an analytical model that includes other nonwhite American minorities in addition to blacks; and further the framework he has developed permits comparative analysis. And in a distinctive and very useful way, he forces the important realization that the treatment of blacks and other nonwhite minorities in the United States historically and now is the result of efforts to compartmentalize the society under white dominance; and further to sustain the dual system in the face of attacks on it by nonwhites that the system itself permits or cannot defend itself against. American Dilemma? American Paradox? There is a difference. Professor Ringer shows that recognition of the difference is important for understanding and for public policy.

BOOK ONE

THE HISTORICAL FRAMEWORK
FOR AMERICA'S DUALITY

I

INTRODUCTION

The American Creed and the optimism of the early 1960s

By the early 1960s the United States seemed to be fulfilling finally to its various ethnic and racial minorities the promise of the American creed with its "ideals of the essential dignity of the individual human being, of the fundamental equality of all men, and of certain inalienable rights to freedom, justice, and a fair opportunity" (Myrdal 1944:4). (For a more elaborate discussion of the American creed, see Chapter 7.) The disparity between the creed's ideals and actual practice about which Myrdal wrote in *An American Dilemma* seemed to be rapidly closing for all. The greatest strides had obviously been made by the progeny of the white immigrant minorities who landed in America about the turn of the century. A half century later their descendents had attained a level of achievement, acculturation, and acceptance that far exceeded anything their first-generation progenitors could have imagined. No longer locked out of the various institutional environments by discriminatory practices and policies to the extent that the first generation had been, they made remarkable progress occupationally and educationally and became as Americanized in their way of life as those of longer-standing American stock.

No one was prepared however to paint the same kind of picture of acceptance and mobility for any of the nonwhite minorities, except perhaps for the Japanese-Americans, who were beginning to show a remarkable rise by the early 1950s in the face of their earlier adversity. Certainly the blacks had experienced no such rise. Few denied that they still bore the especially onerous burdens of a racial creed in the South which confronted them with a virtually solid wall of discrimination and exclusion. Even in the North, most observers agreed, blacks encountered more discrimination than did the white immigrants and their offspring, but this was viewed only as a matter of quantitative degree and not a qualitative kind of difference as in the South.

Further, most observers, particularly those who were white, were convinced that it was just a matter of time before the blacks in the North would be able to benefit in full from the American creed. Indications of their progress – not very substantial to be sure – were already there. Myrdal, himself, saw great hope for the black in the North, which he believed had a much clearer commitment to the American creed than did the South. Other observers, such as Kristol, have even referred to the northern black, most of whom had arrived after World War I, as "like the immigrant [of] yesterday" (Kristol 1966:50). He, and others like him, have been convinced that the acceptance and amalgamation of the black into American society would follow the linear path forged by the white immigrant.

Even the racial situation in the South, then in the tightening grip of the civil rights movement, seemed on the verge of losing its "special" regional character and of moving into the mainstream of American life, presumably to be regulated by the American creed, as Myrdal had predicted. Did not the policy pronouncements from Presidents Truman to Kennedy sound as though they had been taken verbatim from Myrdal's *An American Dilemma*?

Scholarship during this period lent credence to this optimistic view. It reflected the conviction of a number of social scientists that the American creed was finally fulfilling its potential as the consensual value framework for the kind of America that the Founding Fathers hoped they were establishing through the Declaration of Independence and the Constitution. In fulfilling this potential, the scholars believed, the creed was ridding America of beliefs and practices abhorrent to its basic character and that were "sick" reminders of man's baser nature. As evidence, they could point to nationwide opinion polls conducted by The American Jewish Committee since World War II. The results showed that prejudiced opinions and negative stereotypes of Jews and other ethnic minorities were markedly on the decline and becoming less respectable. In addition, the Harris polls revealed an upsurge of willingness on the part of white America to accord the basic rights and tenets of the American creed to black Americans even though, on a personal level, white Americans still wished to keep blacks at a distance.

Analytic and systematic studies in depth shared the premise that prejudice and discrimination were irrational and aberrant responses in a society whose core value system was the American creed. For example, the classic studies of the authoritarian personality conducted in the early 1940s by Horkheimer, and Adorno *et al.* (1950) at the University of California concluded that prejudice served important psychic and emotional functions for "sick" personalities; hence their need to scapegoat ethnic and racial minorities. Other observers applied the label of abnormality and even of sickness to their studies of hate groups from the Ku Klux Klan to the Asiatic Exclusion League. Perhaps the largest component of the American society stamped by various scholars with the label of abnormal and aberrant was the Deep South, with its Jim Crow societal structure built on the racial creed of black difference and inferiority. So convinced were many scholars, from Dollard (1949), and Park (1950), to Myrdal, that the racial situation in the South was alien to an America dedicated to the normal workings of Myrdal's American creed, that they grafted the concept *caste* onto their vocabulary of race as a label for this regionally residual network of black-white relations.

Thus, from a variety of directions, students of American race and ethnic relations concluded by the early 1960s that the American creed was the generative source for an assimilative and acculturative process that had ultimately transformed these minorities from alien and unacceptable to Americanized and functioning parts of the dominant society. Thereby, assimilation became the conceptual cornerstone for an optimistic theory. It was first put forth by Robert Ezra Park in the form of a race relations cycle whose inevitable outcome was amalgamation and absorption of the racial or ethnic group into the American society (Park 1950). In the early 1960s Milton Gordon undertook a major overhaul of the theory (Gordon 1964). He offered an elaborate reconceptualization of the assimilative process which he divided into a number of sub-processes. Each had its own inner dynamics, momentum, and rate of progression, depending on external and internal resistances to change.

In his reformulation, Gordon left no doubt that he believed his conceptual paradigm fit the experiences of the various ethnic and racial minorities in America. He conceded each of the minorities might be at a different stage of a specific assimilative sub-process. For example, he stated,

> "unusually marked discrimination, such as that which has been faced by the American Negro, if it succeeds in keeping vast numbers of the minority group deprived of educational and occupational opportunities and thus predestined to remain in a lower-class setting, may indefinitely retard the acculturation process [cultural assimilation] for the group." (Gordon 1964:78)

He insisted this produced merely a temporary delay in the process. "Even in the case of the American Negro, however, from the long view or perspective of American history, this effect of discrimination will be seen to have been a delaying action only; the quantitatively significant emergence of the middle-class Negro is already well on its way" (Gordon 1964:78).

The urban riots of the mid- and late 1960s and the emergence of the colonial analogy

Even as Gordon's volume began to reach the bookstores by the mid-1960s, race riots erupted in various western and northern cities of America. Within a few years their full fury sent shock waves that not only disrupted the civic and political fabric of the American society, but also played havoc with the state of knowledge and theory in the field of ethnic and race relations. At the least, they undermined the optimistic projections of scholars based on the American creed. Even more they laid bare to a number of scholars the inadequacy of the conceptual assimilative paradigms constructed by Gordon and others. In short, the urban riots raised overwhelming doubts in the minds of these scholars that America's historical encounter with its racial minorities, particularly the black, could be adequately subsumed under the same conceptual and theoretical model that applied to America's historical encounter with its white immigrant minorities.

In addition the urban riots ripped apart the notion that the black problem was confined to the regionally aberrant South. The riots showed for those who would see that it was and always has been a national problem. Once the black revolution turned to northern cities, it exposed the frozen edifice of historic and contemporary racial discrimination and segregation that had long lain invisible to the eyes of the white community. In short, it showed that the racial creed and racism were much more deeply embedded parts of the normal structure of our total society than we had wanted to believe.

From the volcanic eruptions of the 1960s, a political rhetoric was articulated by the more militant of the black leaders. Its ideological themes were black nationalism, black separatism, and black power. Its axiomatic foundation was the premise that blacks had never had and never would have the benefits and protection of the American creed, Declaration of Independence, or Constitution and as a result they were doomed to continued exploitation as a subordinated and segmented racial group in white America.

Rejecting the concept of caste (in terms reminiscent of what Cox had said almost twenty years before), these ideologists likened the fate of blacks and other nonwhite minorities in America to the colonialized people of the Third World who had been subjugated by the whites but had never accepted the legitimacy of their subjugation – something which presumably is done by members of a caste system. In sum, the colonial analogy surfaced in the ideological heat of the 1960s as the rallying cry for Malcolm X, later for Carmichael and the Black Panthers.

The analogy also caught the imagination and attention of scholars such as Blauner (1972), Allen (1970), Tabb (1970), Pinkney (1976), and others who sought to apply it to a reexamination of the black experience in America, thereby bestowing upon it a respectability it lacked while still a product of the streets. From the ferment of the 1960s, then, emerged an alternative perspective and model for viewing the historical encounters of blacks and other nonwhite minorities with the American society. It has failed, however, to make any headway among the more orthodox assimilationist American creed scholars, almost all of whom are white. They have dismissed – frequently with contempt – the analogy as having no scholarly or analytic value. They have even refused to look with an open mind at the uncomfortable questions this approach has raised, which might unsettle their beliefs.

As a result, scholars of ethnic and race relations in America have been aligned for the past decade or so on either side of a deep "theoretical" divide that has evoked verbal warfare more frequently associated with an emotional conflict over religious dogma than with an intellectual controversy over competing scientific theories. And yet, despite this deep cleavage, both approaches, in our judgment, share a common flaw. They have sought to transmute into full explanations of America's encounter with its racial minorities what are essentially only partial explanations. In doing so, each side has oversimplified and distorted this encounter and has failed to recognize its complexity.

The duality of America's encounter with its racial minorities

This study offers a different approach. Its basic premise is that America's response to and treatment of its racial minorities have had a dual character which no single explanatory model can capture. This duality, we contend, is deeply rooted in America's past and is built into its structural and historical origins. It derives from the twofold processes of colonization and colonialization that were generated by the white European's conquest and settlement of the New World. First, the Spanish conquistador shaped his version of the duality in Hispaniola, New Spain, and other areas of the New World. A century later the English developed their version in Virginia and later in the other twelve colonies.

As colonists, the English created a society whose institutions were molded in their racial, religious, and national image. They took particular pride in the structure of self-governance they built, first in Virginia and later in the other colonies. In each instance the people of the colonist society had certain basic rights and immunities, but only the white colonist could be part of the people. This colonist heritage found expression in the Declaration of Independence and the Constitution as the thirteen colonies were transformed into a federated nation-state. Through this heritage, the sovereignty of the people was reaffirmed in both the political state and in the national community. In each, "We the People" were to share various rights and immunities and were to be defined as citizens. Within the Domain of the People, universalistic, egalitarian, achievement-oriented, and democratic norms and values were to be the ideals. In the words of Myrdal, the American creed was to symbolize its legal-normative environment (Myrdal 1944). Membership in this People's Domain, though, was confined, as in the colonist society, to whites.

As colonialists, the English subjected the nonwhites with whom they came into contact to violence, force, and fraud; and they subjugated, killed, or drove them off. The Indians, for example, were overwhelmed by force of arms, deprived of their land and resources, and treated as a conquered subject or inhuman enemy. Blacks were involuntarily brought into the colonies to work as slaves and treated as a dehumanized chattel property.

The relations between the whites and each of the nonwhite groups were crystallized and stabilized even in the colonial days into a structure akin to what Furnivall labeled a "Plural Society" in his study of tropical dependencies (Furnivall 1956). This plural structure, particularly as it related to slavery and the blacks, emerged unscathed by the writing of the Declaration of Independence, the Constitution, and the promulgation of the American creed. In fact it was legitimized by the Constitution, and if anything became even more firmly established after colonist America became the United States of America.

As a result, the nonwhite races, particularly the blacks and Indians, were not only excluded from the newly-created People's Domain of the Constitution, but their treatment continued much in the manner of America's colonialist past. They were to continue to be exploited for their labor (the blacks), to be deprived of their land (the Indians), and in general to be treated as conquered subjects or property. The structure of relations between the whites and each of the other races continued in the colonialist model of a "Plural Society." Its normative environment was still defined by a racial creed which stressed the separateness of the races and the inferiority of the nonwhite.

In this manner, the Founding Fathers and the Constitution perpetuated and sanctified the Manichean dualism that had derived from the period of the colonies. On a higher and visible level, they transformed the colonist society of white America into a nation-state rooted in the rights and sovereignty of the people and regulated by the normative code of the American creed. On a lower and less visible level, they legitimated and perpetuated virtually untouched the plural society of a racially bifurcated colonialist America regulated by the normative code of a racial creed.

The two structural models were reaffirmed by the New Nation and set in their distinctive institutional terrains where they coexisted for a long period of time, each evolving according to its own inner dynamics and with its own separate creedal statement. Nevertheless, from the very beginning of the New Nation their coexistence was uneasy, for their fates were inextricably linked in several ways. The whites, for example, were the superordinate masters of the plural society, and the citizens and the elected officials of the People's Domain. In effect, they could move freely between the two systems and did so to protect their position, privilege, and property in both. The southern white plantation owner, for example, was particularly skilled in these maneuvers before the Civil War. He adroitly used his command of legal and extralegal resources and powers in both systems to keep the black in his "place" in the plural society.

In turn, the black, despite his position in the plural structure, was not explicitly forbidden from gaining access to the People's Domain by the Founding Fathers. In writing the Constitution for the Domain, the Founding Fathers avoided any racial references; only naturalization was confined by explicit statutory decrees to the white. From the beginning of the New Nation, blacks and their supporters* continually challenged the legitimacy of the plural society that prevented them from gaining access to the People's Domain and/or from enjoying all of its rights and immunities as guaranteed by the Constitution and the American creed.

In sanctifying both societal models, the Founding Fathers set the stage for what turned out to be in succeeding generations a herculean struggle between the two for the control of the destiny of nonwhite minorities. And it is the basic contention of this study that America's historic treatment of its racial minorities has been both an expression and product of the dialectical tension and struggle between these two models.

The historical background of the New Nation's duality is the focus of the first book of this study. But before we examine this background, we introduce in Chapter 2 the concept "plural society" that was first used by J.S. Furnivall (1956) and later by other scholars to describe the racially segmented societal structures that were products of the colonial conquest and domination of other races by the white Europeans. We contend that such structures were first created in the New World as a result of its colonial conquest by white Europeans. At the same time, though, the white European also built colonist societies in his own image. The net result was that the processes of colonialization and colonization imprinted a duality in the New World from almost the moment the first European set foot on it. The nature of this duality, however, varied with the national identity of the European. For example, the Spanish conquistador shaped and created a different type of duality from that of the English settler.

---

*Interestingly, white abolitionists joined northern blacks in challenging the legitimacy of the southern variant of the plural society (slavery), but most failed to join them in seeking to dismantle the northern variant.

Our concern is primarily with the version constructed by the English settler in Virginia, described in Chapter 3; however, we comment briefly on the Spanish version in Appendix A. In Chapter 4 we examine how the duality that stamped Virginia and the other twelve colonies was perpetuated and reinforced as the colonies were transformed into a federated nation-state and was given the imprimatur of legitimacy by the New Nation. We conclude Book One with a chapter on the Indian. Although pushed beyond the perimeter of the white society, the Indian's colonialist encounter with the whiteman shaped the frontier experience of the American society from the time the English settler first set foot in Virginia to almost a hundred years after the New Nation had come into existence.

Government policy as an expression and instrument of America's duality

Once the New Nation was formed, the struggle over its duality frequently spilled over into violence and bloodshed, from lynch mobs and riots to warfare along the frontiers and even between the States. Perhaps the most significant arena in which the struggle has been historically joined has been the Supreme Court of the United States. From the beginning of the New Nation to the present, the Court has had to weigh in balance this duality to determine whether a particular version of a plural society was in accord with the Constitution, the basic law of the People's Domain and also the supreme law of the land. Its record through the early 1940s was highly favorable to the whites. In effect, it legitimized most of the plural structures imposed by them on various racial minorities and gave these structures the protection of the law of the land as seen in such decisions as Dred Scott (1857), Civil Rights (1883), and Plessy-Ferguson (1896) [black]; The Cherokee Nation v. The State of Georgia (1831) [Indian]; Fong Yue Ting (1893) [Chinese]; Ozawa (1922) and Korematsu (1943) [Japanese]; and the Insular Cases (1901) [Puerto Rico]. In doing this the Court frequently invented concepts or adopted those invented by the other two branches of government for the same purpose to characterize the particular plural structure it had sanctified: such as domestic dependent nation (Indian), unincorporated Territory of the United States (Puerto Rico), alien ineligible to citizenship (Chinese and Japanese), and chattel/property (black).

Yet on occasion, the Court acted, even by the end of the nineteenth century, to curb some of the more obnoxious efforts by whites to extend the reach of the plural society: Yick Wo v. Hopkins (1886) and Wong Kim Ark (1898) [Chinese]; Strauder v. West Virginia (1880), Guinn v. United States (1915), and Buchanan v.

Warley (1917) [black]. Not until the mid-1940s did it make any real effort to delegitimize the plural structures. It dealt, for example, a major blow to a cornerstone of the northern variant in Shelley v. Kraemer (1948). The most telling blow was its Brown decision (1954) and its later decisions in the early 1960s on the sit-in cases. These rulings undercut the legitimacy of the southern variant and its racial creed and thereby ushered in the second period of reconstruction for America.

Whereas the Supreme Court could only give the stamp of legitimacy or illegitimacy to plural structures that were already created and brought to its attention through lawsuits, Congress and the President were instrumental at various periods of time in creating new plural structures and arrangements. For example, Congress took the initiative in 1790 in denying naturalization or access to the People's Domain to any nonwhite (it extended this access to black aliens in 1870). Thereby, it confined the Chinese and later the Japanese to a segregated "plural" existence within the plural terrain of America. But beginning in the 1880s it went further and denied them the right even to enter the plural terrain through the Exclusion Act of 1882 and the Immigration Act of 1924. At one point, Congress went so far as to try to drive out Chinese aliens already here through the Geary Act of 1892. Then in 1900, it created for Puerto Rico a new kind of "plural" status. Instead of incorporating it as a Territory of the United States, Congress made it, through the Foraker Act, into the first legally constituted colonial dependency of the United States.

Presidents have also taken the initiative in building plural arrangements. For example, President Jackson pushed hard for the Indian removal policy that drove the Cherokees west of the Mississippi, in the infamous "trail of tears". President Wilson extended Jim Crow segregation into the federal civil service, and President Roosevelt signed the executive order that authorized the military to put the Japanese, including those of American citizenship, into concentration camps during World War II.

In pendulum-like swings, similar to those of the Supreme Court, both Congress and the President have also acted at other times to dismantle features of the plural structures and finally the structures themselves. In so doing they extended the reach of the People's Domain to various racial minorities, and finally to all of them. For example, Congress overrode the objections of President Andrew Johnson after the Civil War and ushered in the first period of reconstruction. Congress passed wide-ranging civil rights legislation and the three great reconstruction amendments which gave nonwhites some of the rights and immunities of the People's Domain (although only as a result of the second period of reconstruction, almost 100 years later, did they gain the full rights and immunities).

For the next seventy-five years, Congress did nothing of any significance, until 1952 when the otherwise reactionary McCarran Act eliminated the racial requirement for naturalization and thereby allowed Japanese and other Asian aliens to gain access to the People's Domain. Later in the 1950s it passed the first civil rights act. The zenith of the pendulum swing was reached in 1964 and 1965 when, this time under the leadership, not opposition, of a President Johnson, Congress passed the Civil Rights and Voting Rights Acts. The result was to make illegal the plural structures in the South and elsewhere and to dismantle many of their institutional structures and supports, which the Supreme Court had merely delegitimated twelve years before. So the nation for the first time in its entire history extended the promise of full membership in the People's Domain under the legal-normative umbrella of the American creed to persons of all races. Yet the strongly embedded petrified effects of the now illegal plural structures were not dislodged by these actions. Instead they continued to rut the paths of most nonwhites and to limit their chances and opportunities in the People's Domain.

Even before Congress expressed any renewed interest in the 1950s in opening up the People's Domain to nonwhites, presidents, beginning with Franklin D. Roosevelt, had already taken action through executive orders to open up sectors of the People's Domain to nonwhites, particularly to blacks. Roosevelt started it by establishing the Fair Employment Practices Committee (FEPC) and by announcing a policy of nondiscrimination in employment for government contracts during World War II. For the next thirty years, during five subsequent presidential administrations, this policy was given structure and substance primarily through successive executive orders, until it emerged as the Affirmative Action Program under Johnson and was given its full set of teeth for effective enforcement under Nixon.

This book, then, views those in positions of authority in the executive, legislative, and judicial branches of government, primarily at the federal level but occasionally on the state or local level, as the principal actors in the politico-historical drama of the duality of America's treatment of its racial minorities. These leaders' actions and policies are not the only subject of our concern. We are also interested in their definitions and reconstructions of the "realities" in which these actions were taken and decisions made. This means, in effect, examining the words used in these reconstructions in order to assess the extent to which they were in accord with the rhetoric and language of the domain of "We the People" or with that of a plural society. We have therefore concentrated heavily in this book on the primary data of judicial opinions, congressional hearings, reports and debates, and presidential messages and statements of policy in addition to the formal laws, treaties, executive orders, and the like. Certain statutes such as the Exclusion Acts, the Foraker Act, and the Immigration Act of 1924 are crucial to our thesis. As a result, we devote considerable time to the legislative process in order to re-create the ideological atmosphere and climate of opinion in which these deliberations were held. The purpose is to have the actors write the manifest details of the script.

The encounters of four racial minorities with America's duality

The range of behaviors, beliefs, and reconstructions of the governmental actors are examined in Books Two and Three within the framework of a specific racial minority's encounter with America's duality over time. Four such encounters are studied in depth. No two are exact replicas of each other. Each of the four highlights significant – if not qualitatively – different facets and contexts of America's duality. Together they give a relatively full view of the dialectical tensions and the historical struggle between the two societal constructs: "We the People" and the plural society.

As we have seen, the racial encounter that from early colonial days has been, and still is, at the heart of this struggle is that of the black with white America. No other encounter has played as direct and dramatic a part in the creation, growth, and institutionalization of America's duality. It was on the back of the enslaved black that the white settler constructed his first comprehensive model of a plural society. After the abolition of slavery, the southern white built a second and almost as comprehensive a model with Jim Crow legislation, again on the backs of the black. He even succeeded in constructing for a decade a third model after the Supreme Court's Brown decision in 1954. The northern white, who had abolished slavery much earlier, developed his own distinctive versions both before and after the Civil War.

In addition, the two great constitutional challenges to the legitimacy of the racial creed and its plural structures that resulted in the first and second periods of reconstruction were direct outgrowths of the black-white encounter. In view of its centrality for the emergence, perpetuation, and (hopefully final) demise of America's duality, we devote to this encounter the seven chapters of Book Two.

Book Three covers three other racial encounters with America's duality. Each encounter has had a distinctive character, and each reflects the extension of America's duality into one of two institutional areas that were not officially imprinted with it prior to the establishment of the New Nation. The first extension was into the realm of immigration which came under the sway of America's duality through the 1790 statute that confined naturalization to free white persons. Almost a century later the statute was used effectively to deny citizenship and membership in the People's Domain to Chinese and Japanese immigrants. It became the nub around which a web of coercive and arbitrary legal and political restrictions was spun. Parts One and Two of Book Three compare and contrast the experience of the two immigrants from Asia as they struggled to carve what turned out to be an unstable niche in the plural terrain of the American society.

The second extension transformed America into an imperialist power in its relations with territorial acquisitions. Until it obtained Puerto Rico, the New Nation treated each acquisition as part of a colonizing function in which the new territory would eventually become another state in the Union and its people would in the interim be protected by the Constitution. With the Foraker Act, the United States legitimized a colonializing role for itself and established Puerto Rico as its first colonial dependency. But even as it was elaborating upon this status for the island, the United States was enmeshing the relationship of the Puerto Ricans to the People's Domain and Constitution of the American society with ambiguities and confusions and was bestowing upon them some of the rights and immunities of membership in a colonist society. This is examined in Part Three of Book Three.

In sum, we hope that by the end of this extensive and detailed historical analysis of America's encounters with its racial minorities we will have established the significance of duality as a construct for understanding these encounters. What is more, we firmly believe, as we suggest in the Postscript, that this construct can be applied meaningfully as a framework for comparative analysis wherever the white European generated the dual processes of colonization and colonialization.

2

THE COLONIALIST HERITAGE
AND THE
PLURAL SOCIETY

Introduction

Columbus' first voyage to the New World in 1492 launched white Europeans on four and a half centuries of colonial conquest and expansion that eventually extended to all the continents of the world. From the Americas to Africa and Asia they conquered and subjugated nonwhite races and imposed upon each a system of exploitation for economic and political gain. In some instances, as in the Spanish conquest of New Spain and Peru, they took land and its resources away from the native populations and harnessed them to this exploitative system as a labor force. In other instances, as in the English conquest of North America, they drove the native populations from their land and resources and then imported as a work force an enslaved nonwhite population from other lands. In each case the Europeans, beginning with the Spanish and English in the New World, created through the force of arms colonial societal structures hierarchically segmented along racial lines. They stood astride these structures as colonialist elite, consolidated their hold on the channels of political and economic power, and monopolized the major instruments of control and coercion.

In his research on the tropical dependencies of Burma and Netherlands East Indies, J.S. Furnivall adopted the label "plural society" to describe these structures (Furnivall 1956). Since then, the concept has been applied to studies of colonialism in the Caribbean, South America, and Africa, and one scholar, Kammen, has even applied the construct to his study of colonial British America (Kammen 1972). In this chapter we shall examine the construct as it was developed by Furnivall and as it was later reconceptualized and respecified by others, including M.G. Smith (1965), Rex (1970), Fanon (1968), and van den Berghe (1967). We shall then look at the "sojourner" elite who stand perched atop a colony that remains nothing more than a colonialist plural society. By means of this theoretical voyage, we shall be elaborating a conceptual framework for our subsequent analysis of America's colonialist heritage. Like the white Europeans in the various societies described in this chapter, the English too – though at a much earlier date – imposed a network of coercive legal, political, and economic constraints and a harness of racial subordination and segmentation on nonwhite minorities first in the thirteen colonies and later in the New Nation that were similar to those of a plural society. As a result, the construct, we contend, can be usefully applied to an examination of America's colonialist heritage. At the end of the chapter, however, we shall comment on our need to modify some of the distinctive features of the construct, inasmuch as the English in America, unlike their counterparts and other white Europeans in most of the societies described in this chapter, did more than build a colonial plural society. They also built a permanent colonist society for themselves.

J.S. Furnivall and the plural society

Furnivall stressed the profound impact of western political control and capitalism upon traditional societies, those organized around personal authority, custom, and a self-subsistent economy. According to Furnivall, the introduction of western law and administration, particularly when it was accompanied by direct rule as was British control of Burma, tended to undermine and virtually destroy the organic native society which was built around the village, its headmen, and customary rules and procedures. The indirect rule of the Dutch in the Netherlands East Indies allowed the normative system of the native to continue to function, but only under the domination of the western legal system. Even there, the organic basis of the native society underwent disruption and fragmentation.

The unleashing of capitalistic economic forces, Furnivall continued, also contributed to the dissolution of a collective will and a societal solidarity by undermining the traditional economy and by fostering a "market mentality" of self-interested quest for individual gain. This was particularly true under the direct rule of the British in Burma. Under the indirect rule of the Dutch in the East Indies, economic forces were somewhat held in check by customary procedures and traditions which allowed an occasional expression of collective concern and will.

In breaking down the traditional sources of solidarity, these colonialist societies created a "consensual" vacuum, for they failed to generate any common social will of their own. As a result, they became fragmented into racial segments. Each segment lived, by and large, unto itself behind its territorial, cultural, and social boundaries and met the others only as political and economic necessity warranted. In short, they were transformed, according to Furnivall, into plural societies.

"In Burma, as in Java, probably the first thing that strikes the visitor is the medley of peoples – European, Chinese, Indian and native. It is in the strictest sense a medley, for they mix but do not combine. Each group holds by its own religion, its own culture and language, its own ideas and ways. As individuals they meet but only in the market-place, in buying and selling. There is a *plural society* [author's italics], with different sections of the community living side by side, but separately, within the same political unit." (Furnivall 1956:304)

What further fragmented these plural societies, according to Furnivall, was the fact that "even in the economic sphere there is a division of labour along racial lines. Natives, Chinese, Indians and Europeans all have different functions, and within each major group subsections have different functions."

This pattern, he insisted, was to be found throughout the Tropical Far East: whether the dependency was under "Spanish, Portugese, Dutch, British, French or American rule," or whether the native populations were "Filipinos, Javanese, Malays, Burmans or Annamese;" or "whether the objective of the colonial power has been tribute, trade or material resources; under direct rule and under indirect. The obvious and outstanding result of contact between East and West has been the evolution of a plural society" (Furnivall 1956:304–5).

Furnivall feared that collective social will and action were also disappearing within these racial segments, not merely between them. He saw a breakdown in relations within these segments and an inexorable process of atomization taking place which transformed the segments from communities into "crowds:"

"In all accounts of the modern tropics we read of the collapse of corporate tribal or village life and the atomization of society. In the foreign sections the individual stands even more alone; even among the Indians caste loses its validity, and in every census in Burma it has been found impossible to compile useful returns of Indian castes. Among the Indian immigrants in South Sea Islands one may even find mixed marriages between Moslems and Hindus. Europeans often deplore the isolation of the individual in their own section. Men are continually on the move; they form business acquaintances but not friends; there are no children in the home; the club and not the home is the centre of social life, and all look more or less eagerly to going 'home' on retirement. Each section in the plural society is a crowd and not a community." (Furnivall 1956:307)

What produced this atomization and segmentation? According to Furnivall, the unleashing of capitalistic economic forces with their emphasis on self-interest and profit raised mammon to the level of a common deity and placed people, even of the same racial group, into a competitive relation with each other. As a result, these people came to resist banding together for the collective whole and were turned instead into an atomized mass intent upon the pursuit of their self-interest in the marketplace. The marketplace, then, rather than a consensual value scheme, bound them together, but the marketplace also mirrored in sharp outline the basic tensions and conflict generically related to a plural society.

Furnivall offered a graphic description of this process in his research on Burma. He showed that the Burmese had become a propertyless people. They had lost their land and were now nothing more than "sharecroppers." They resented their present status and directed their anger against those whom they believed responsible for their plight. They were particularly hostile toward the Indian middlemen who were moneylenders and merchants. A lesser target for their antipathy was the white colonialist. He was too far up the pyramid of political and economic power for them to have the same kind of abrasive contact with him that they had with the middlemen.

Persuasive and dramatic as Furnivall's description was of the plural societies of Burma and also of Indonesia, his claim that racial segments of the two societies had become so fragmented and their internal relations so atomized that they were incapable of collective action seemed to be contradicted by other conclusions he also drew. For example, in another section of the book, he referred to the survival of social and religious customs and traditions within the various racial segments as though they were still functioning as a collective umbrella for the segment. He also mentioned growth of nationalistic forces within some of these segments. Accordingly, it would appear that despite the economic self-interest and its atomizing effect on the internal group relations, some ties of a non-economic nature continued to bind the persons into a cohesive whole in at least some of the racial segments.

Another point that merits mention is Furnivall's contention that the plural society need not remain a totally coercive, exploitative system as was the case in Burma under the British; it may also develop paternalistic features as was the case in the Netherlands East Indies. There, the Dutch pursued a policy whereby the dependent population was protected from excessive economic exploitation. The Dutch implemented this policy through the use of indirect rule and through the setting up of special categories of professionals and administrators whose function was to see that the needs of the subject populations did not go entirely unheeded.

M.G. Smith and the cultural segmentation of the plural society

As can be seen by the title of his book *The Plural Society in the British West Indies* (1965), M.G. Smith adopted Furnivall's concept, but he did more. He elaborated the concept and applied it to a wider range of societal situations than did Furnivall.

To Smith the crucial feature of the plural society was its division into separate social and cultural sections, each of which was characterized by a distinctively different system of basic institutions: "This basic institutional system embraces kinship, education, religion, property and economy, recreation, and certain sodalities" (Smith 1965:82). These differences, according to Smith, organized the society into a hierarchically arrayed mosaic of total communities, each capable of providing for its members the entire range of life experience.

His most detailed illustration of a plural society was Jamaica. It consisted, he stated, of three layered sections; a small white section was at the top; at the bottom was a black section which included about four-fifths of the population; and in between, a brown section.

"The white section which ranks highest locally represents the culture of mid-twentieth century West European society. It is the dominant section, but also the smallest, and consists principally of persons reared abroad from early childhood. The black or lowest section may include four-fifths of the population, and practices a folk culture containing numerous elements reminiscent of African societies and Caribbean slavery. The brown intermediate section is culturally and biologically the most variable, and practices a general mixture of patterns from the higher and lower groups.... Thus the culture of the middle section includes coexistent institutional alternatives drawn from either of the two remaining traditions, as well as those forms which are peculiar to itself."

(Smith 1965:163–64)

Smith then went on to describe in elaborate detail the basic institutional differences among the various sections.

Smith agreed with Furnivall that a plural society lacked a common institutional framework and a common value-belief system that embraced all sections and classes within the society. Smith also recognized, as did Furnivall, that a plural society required the existence of some mechanism by which order and control could be maintained. Accordingly, he argued, the society depended on an overall governmental structure, whose control was in the hands of the dominant cultural section as was the control over the economic means of production.

"Even in a plural society, institutional diversity does not include differing systems of government. The reason for this is simple: the continuity of such societies as units is incompatible with an internal diversity of governmental institutions. Given the fundamental differences of belief, value, and organization that connote pluralism, the monopoly of power by one cultural section is the essential precondition for the maintenance of the total society in its current form. In short, the structural position and function of the regulative system differ sharply in plural and other societies. Institutionally homogeneous societies develop a variety of institutional motivations toward conformity with social norms; institutionally split societies lack these common motivations and tend to rely correspondingly on regulation. The dominant social section of these culturally split societies is simply the section that controls the apparatus of power and force." (Smith 1965:86)

Smith insisted, however, that each of the subordinated sections did not merely rely upon control by the dominant section. Each possessed its own internal system of control and status that reflected its own traditions and values which frequently were not in accord with those of other sections.

"The distribution of status within each cultural section rests on common values and criteria quite specific to that group, and this medley of sectional value systems rules out the value consensus that is prerequisite for any status continuum. Thus the plurality is a discontinuous status order, lacking any foundation in a system of common interests and values, while its component sections are genuine status continua, distinguished by their differing systems of value, action and social relations." (Smith 1965:83)

In short, Smith recognized that within each of the cultural sections a sense of dignity and of worth developed which frequently ran counter to that which the dominant section sought to impose upon the society as a whole.

Smith eventually addressed himself to two questions: How did these plural societies originate? What perpetuated them? His answers were somewhat ambiguous. First he rejected Furnivall's thesis that plural societies "were limited to the modern colonial tropics and were products of Western economic expansion" (Smith 1965:88). He insisted that "the Norman conquest of Britain, and the Roman conquest before it, certainly established plural societies, and there are many other instances that cannot be attributed to Western economic activity" (Smith 1965:89). Smith then went on to enumerate plural societies of the past. As he did, he stated:

"Modern economic forces may account for colonial pluralities, but these are not the only ones. Perhaps the most general answer to this question of origin is migration, which also accounts for the development of ethnic minorities. This migration may be forced, as in Habe Maradi or West Indian slavery, or semivoluntary as in the movement of indentured East Indian labor into the West Indies, or voluntary as in the British penetration of Kenya and Burma, or the Dutch colonization of South Africa. It may involve conquest and consolidation, but this is not always the case." (Smith 1965:89)

One might take exception to Smith's tendency to underplay conquest as a basic generative source for plural societies. For example, he might have added to the category of conquest a plural society created by the transport of slaves or subjugated peoples of another race into its midst.

In stressing cultural segmentation, Smith sought to avoid the overly deterministic view that inextricably linked the emergence of plural societies with racial differences. In other words, he wished to deflate the notion that wherever you have a racially differentiated society you are likely to have a plural society. He insisted that not all multiracial societies became plural societies; instead they might remain heterogeneous societies, or they might form "a common homogeneous society as for instance among the Hausa Fulani of northern Nigeria" (Smith 1965:89).

However, in trying to mute a deterministic view, he overstated the case. For even he recognized the fact that "modern plural societies are multiracial, and that these racial groups tend also to be culturally distinct" (Smith 1965:89). But, he insisted, in some instances these imputed racial differences were the result of social definition and not of biological origin and as such expressed symbolically the basic cultural divisions of that society. Accordingly, he continued, a plural society may be characterized by

"culturally distinct groups that belong to the same racial stock expressing their differences in racial terms. This seems to be the case in Guatemala, Haiti and among the Creole folk and elite of the British West Indies. History provides us with many other examples, such as the Normans and Anglo-Saxons, the English and the Scots or, most recently and most elaborately, the Nazi ideology. Race differences are stressed in contexts of social and cultural pluralism. They lack social significance in homogeneous units. As the Caribbean slave literature shows most clearly, the function of racism is merely to justify and perpetuate a pluralistic social order." (Smith 1965:89)

Finally, Smith emphasized even more than Furnivall did the coercive control that the dominant section exercised over the other sections of the plural society. This control, he admitted, might go unchallenged through much of the society's history, but it would nevertheless produce an uneasy calm between the subordinated and dominant sections. In time political consciousness might develop within some of the subordinated sections and express itself in nationalistic longings and ultimately in a challenge to the status quo through violence, rebellion, and revolution.

> "Since the plural society depends for its structural form and continuity on the regulation of intersectional relations by government, changes in the social structure presuppose political changes, and these usually have a violent form. In desperation, the subordinate cultural section may either practice escapist religious rituals or create a charismatic leadership as the organ of sectional solidarity and protest. This sort of leadership develops only where people are desperate in the face of overwhelming odds. We have numerous examples of charismatic leadership in the West Indies."   (Smith 1965:91)

In view of this potential, Smith saw an inherent instability in the structure of a plural society.

John Rex and the dual colonial societies

The third theorist, John Rex, concurred with Furnivall on the racially plural character of the colonial society and on the role of conquest in its creation. However, he placed even greater emphasis than did Furnivall on the unequal distribution of power and privilege that produced a hierarchical arrangement among the various racial segments in the colonial plural society.

Rex also agreed with Furnivall and Smith in their contention that the colonial society lacked an overall value-belief system which could integrate the various segments and strata in society into a unified whole, as in the caste system.

> "The important thing when we turn our attention to colonial society is the absence of over all value-consensus, the fact that one stratum or segment dominates the others, and that one of the dimensions on which the various segments or strata have to be differentiated concerns the degree to which they are legally free and capable of controlling their own economic destiny. In this sense we should say that power is an extremely important factor in colonial societies. If such distinctions are really viable, however, we should say that our concept of power is a zero-sum concept, since quite clearly the more one group has the less is available to the other."   (Rex 1970:69)

As a result, Rex continued, the colonial society had to rely heavily on a political and governmental structure in order to bring the parts of the society together; and its ruling racial elite had to depend upon control of the instruments of coercion to insure compliance. Further, Rex attributed, even more than Furnivall and Smith did, a similar unifying function to economic institutions; he also viewed coercion as the major mechanism of control in the economic order.

In effect, Rex stressed, even more emphatically than the other two, the power differentials within the colonial society and the potential for coercive, exploitative, and conflictual relations contained therein. However, he recognized that relations between dominant and subordinate segments in the colonial society might under some conditions become relatively harmonious. In fact, one of the major distinctions he drew was between colonial societies "structured in terms of class conflict" and those structured "in terms of a particular kind of estate order" (Rex 1970:78).

The former situation is likely to arise, according to Rex, "where there is a large settler population including farmers and employed workers living in a colonial context," as in the case of South Africa and Algeria. In such instances, he continued, "the farmer and settler element amongst the settlers is likely to form a class in something like the Marxian or Weberian sense and defend its interests not merely in the market but in the political sphere. Native labour is thus forced into a position of having less control over the means of production and is potentially a separate class." In this manner, racial and class divisions mutually reinforce each other, and the ensuing struggle between the two groups assumes the form of "a conflict between physically distinguishable groups acting in terms of their material interests" (Rex 1970:74).

Such an "ethno-Marxist" struggle is unlikely to develop in colonial societies where the settler population is either small or virtually non-existent or where alien ethnic and racial groups perform the function of "middlemen" or "secondary capitalists." In such situations peaceful accommodation may come to characterize relations between the various segments. Rex called the resulting societal structure a colonial estate system or an ethnically plural estate system.

"The social structure which is maintained in societies of this kind under colonial rule is sociologically speaking a little difficult to classify. The fact that the groups of differing national or ethnic origin which constitute the population are also in some degree occupationally specialised is suggestive of a caste or estate system of some kind. Yet it is as clear that there is no common ideology or value system in such a society, as it is that all groups participate in, and are united by the same economy. It would perhaps be best to refer to a society of this kind by some special term like colonial estate system or ethnically plural estate system. Again the use of such a term might serve to draw attention to the fact that more is at stake than merely the cultural and institutional differences between the component groups in the population."   (Rex 1970:75–6)

According to Rex, stability in such a society is maintained as long as it remains under the protection of the colonializing power, particularly if the power pursues a policy of benevolent paternalism in its relations with the colony. Furnivall clearly agreed with this in his obvious preference for the paternalistic rule of the Dutch in the East Indies to the more coercive rule of the British in Burma. We shall have more to say about paternalistic race relations later, but first let us turn to Fanon who emphasized even more than Rex did the ethno-Marxist character of the struggle between the colonized and colonialist.

Frantz Fanon and "ethno-Marxism"

More a radicalized ideologist and man of action than a scholarly observer, Frantz Fanon nevertheless developed penetrating insights into the working of the colonial society. His work added significant dimensions to the conceptual framework of the plural society, although this was a term he never adopted. His major contribution was his effort in *The Wretched of the Earth* (1968) to adapt a Marxian mode of analysis to the colonial situation, the result of which made him an "intellectual hero" to the Third World and to the Black Nationalist Movement in the United States. Marx, though, was not Fanon's only inspirational model. As a practicing psychiatrist, he was also greatly influenced by the work of Freud; pivotal features of his "theory" show this influence.

Fanon accepted in broad outlines Marx's conflict theory of society and his thesis that historically this conflict has been expressed in a struggle between the powerful and the powerless, the haves and have nots. Fanon took exception, however, to Marx's contention that the generative source for this conflict was in the economic arena while the political arena was merely part of the derivative superstructure built from the particular economic foundations of the society. Fanon insisted that the reverse was true in the colonial society. He argued that the struggle in that society derived from its conquest by an alien race and continued to be fought in the political arena, as the white colonialist imposed upon the colonized nonwhite control over the instruments of coercion and government and used this control to exploit the economic resources and wealth of the colony. In short, political domination led to economic domination.

According to Fanon, Marx's contention that the basic cleavage in society was between the economic class which owned and controlled the means of production and the economic class which did not had to be modified in any analysis of the colonial society. There, the basic cleavage was between a white colonialist race who had seized the colony's economic wealth and the nonwhite colonized race who was dispossessed. "In the colonies the economic substructure is also a superstructure. The cause is the consequence; you are rich because you are white, you are white because you are rich" (Fanon 1968:40). In short, the interlocking of race and class, according to Fanon, was the result of the drive by the racially dominant group to monopolize all sources of power in the colonial society.

To Fanon the rule of the white colonialist was even more repressive than the rule of the bourgeoisie under the capitalism Marx wrote about. The colonialist lacked any of the national, cultural, and territorial interests and values which the bourgeoisie ostensibly shared with the subordinated classes in capitalist society and by which they were able to claim legitimacy for their rule and to appeal for the loyalty and support of the subordinated classes. (Fanon acknowledged Marx's belief that this appeal to "false consciousness" was bound to fall on deaf ears eventually.) As a result, the colonialist elite had to rely heavily and continually on the use of force and violence to keep the colonized in line. In turn, the colonized, according to Fanon, were even more estranged, antagonistic, and resistant to colonialist rule than was the proletariat to the rule of the bourgeoisie. Thus, relations between the two in the colonial society, Fanon contended, were more tense, more raw, more conflictual, and based more on naked power than were relations between dominant and subordinate classes under capitalism.

If the inevitable result for Marx of the growing antagonism and disenchantment of the subordinated groups to the rule of the elite under capitalism was an eventual drive for revolutionary change, then, Fanon insisted, conditions were even riper for such change in the colonial society. He agreed with Marx that this drive would be spearheaded by some – not by all – segments of the subordinated groups, but he differed in his choice of the revolutionary vanguard. Marx had insisted, for example, that the vanguard was to consist of that particular class of dispossessed who bore a special relationship to the unfolding technology of society; under captalism, it would be the industrial proletariat. Fanon, however, located his vanguard elsewhere. He was convinced that virtually all of the occupational strata in the towns and cities had been contaminated by the colonialist. They had accepted "economic crumbs" from the table of the colonialist, had sought to adopt his values, and had become soft on the issue of colonialist rule. Even the proletariat occupied a favored position under colonialism and had identified their interests too closely with those of the colonialist. Fanon exempted the town lumpen-proletariat from this contaminating influence and considered them one of the major allies of the vanguard. (Marx had contemptuously dismissed the lumpen-proletariat as having any effective role in the revolution.) The vanguard itself, according to Fanon, were the peasantry who lived in the hinterland under a traditional system of authority far from the "siren song" of the colonialist way of life.

The peasantry, Fanon opined, did not automatically develop revolutionary ardor. For this to happen they had to go through stages similar to those posited by Marx for the proletariat. According to Marx, in the early stages of the introduction of machinery into the factory system, the proletariat – egged on by the capitalist – fought among themselves as they competed for the scarce jobs. Similarly, Fanon argued, rivalry and dissension rent the ranks of the peasantry along ethnic and tribal lines as they were encouraged by the colonialist to fight among themselves in their struggle for survival and as they began to displace aggression built up by the exploitative colonial system onto other peasants.

In time, Marx postulated, the proletariat would stop fighting among themselves as they came to recognize their common interests and needs, and from this would develop a class consciousness and solidarity. The peasantry, according to Fanon, were also destined to attain a similar level of cohesion, but, unlike the proletariat of Marx, their solidarity was to be organized around a collective identification with emergent nationalism and not around an emergent class consciousness. Finally, both proletariat and peasantry would be ready for being molded, through effective political leadership, into an organized and disciplined vanguard of the revolution.

Fanon recognized that for Marx passage from one stage to the next was inextricably linked to the elaborating technological changes and processes of capital accumulation within the capitalistic economy. These changes, according to Marx, exacerbated relations between the various classes, with the capitalist class growing ever more powerful though declining in size and the proletariat becoming ever more powerless and propertyless though expanding in size. Thus the objective conditions of the classes generated the tensions and strains which literally forced the proletariat to become subjectively aware of their situation, and as their class consciousness grew they became increasingly convinced that the future was theirs. Revolution involved cognitive and rational processes that made the exploited class subjectively aware of the nature of their rational interest; it was accordingly a rational outcome to an organic process which literally "compelled" the exploited to act against the exploiter. Revolution was in effect the product of a dynamic set of forces internal to the economic-technological system and the end result of a summatory and cumulative process.

The colonial society, Fanon acknowledged, had neither the technological nor the industrial development of the capitalist society which could generate the kind of internal dynamic that according to Marx linked one stage to the next. It was instead a society whose elite was externally imposed and for whom political instruments of control were uppermost. Therefore Fanon was obliged to view the revolutionary process as the unfolding of political processes in which stages could be identified but which lacked any propelling force that provided the momentum for the next stage.

In the absence of a Marxian dynamic in the institutional system of the colonial society, Fanon found in the psychoanalytic theories of Freud a functionally equivalent "psychic" dynamic. According to Fanon, the collective psychic and libidinal energies of the peasantry became transformed under the repressive rule of the colonialist into a seething volcano of violent emotions and action that under appropriate political channeling propelled the revolutionary process from one stage to another.

The primordial response of the peasant to the violently repressive, dehumanizing colonial system, Fanon claimed, was anger, resentment, and hatred of the colonialist: "The settler keeps alive in the native an anger." But in its initial stages, "the native is trapped in the tight links of the chains of colonialism," and was accordingly deprived of an outlet for his mounting anger against the colonialist. In short, fear of violent retribution prevented the native from expressing his anger openly and directly against the white colonialist.

Unable to direct his anger against the "real" target of his oppression, the native, Fanon insisted, displaced his anger onto his fellow natives.

"The native's muscular tension finds outlet regularly in bloodthirsty explosions – in tribal warfare, in feuds between septs, and in quarrels between individuals.... While the settler or the policeman has the right the livelong day to strike the native, to insult him and to make him crawl to them, you will see the native reaching for his knife at the slightest hostile or aggressive glance cast on him by another native; for the last resort of the native is to defend his personality vis-à-vis his brother."   (Fanon 1968:54)

The native, Fanon continued, also deflected his anger from the colonialist by concentrating on a magical and mythological superstructure populated by malevolent spirits of frightening proportions. "The supernatural, magical powers reveal themselves as essentially personal; the settler's powers are infinitely shrunken, stamped with their alien origin. We no longer really need to fight against them since what counts is the frightening enemy created by myths. We perceive that all is settled by a permanent confrontation on the phantasmic plane" (Fanon 1968:56).

Periodically, Fanon argued, the natives sought to exorcise the evil spirits and to relieve themselves of the mounting internal pressures of unrelieved violence and anger through dance and community rituals.

"There are no limits ... in the huge effort of a community to exorcise itself, to liberate itself, to explain itself ... for in reality your purpose in coming together is to allow the accumulated libido, the hampered aggressivity, to dissolve as in a volcanic eruption. Symbolical killings, fantastic rides, imaginary mass murders –

all must be brought out. The evil humors are undammed, and flow away with a din as of molten lava." (Fanon 1968:57)

Despite these various efforts to drain off this molten core of suppressed libidinal energies, Fanon insisted, the brutal repressions of the colonialist regime continually refueled it so that it retained, if not expanded, its potential for volcanic violence. The arrival among the peasantry of radicalized and politicized nationalists from the town who were seeking to escape the dragnet of the colonial police set the stage for the next phase of the revolutionary process.

"From the beginning, the peasantry closes in around them and protects them from being pursued by the police. The militant nationalist who decides to throw in his lot with the country people instead of playing at hide-and-seek with the police in urban centers will lose nothing. The peasant's cloak will wrap him around with a gentleness and firmness that he never suspected.... [In this way] the men coming from the towns learn their lessons in the hard school of the people; and at the same time these men open classes for the people in military and political education. The people furbish up their weapons; but in fact the classes do not last long, for the masses come to know once again the strength of their own muscles and push the leaders onto prompt action. The armed struggle has begun." (Fanon 1968:126–27)

In sum, Fanon insisted, "the meeting between these militants with the police on their track and these mettlesome masses of people who are rebels by instinct ... can produce an explosive mixture of unusual potentiality" (Fanon 1968:127). In this fashion the natives become politicized and shift their attention from parochial concerns onto a growing national consciousness in which they join with others of their own kind. And the volcanic libidinal energies they had previously displaced on scapegoats now become channeled into sluices of revolutionary action and political violence against the colonialist oppressor. The revolutionary ardor soon spreads to the lumpenproletariat in the towns and the stage is set for the final assault on the colonialist.

For our purposes Fanon's scenario for revolution is less pertinent than is his analysis of the conflictual character of the racially segmented colonial society. He emphasized even more than the plural theorists the coercive rule of the white colonialist and left no doubt that in time the colonized would rise in revolutionary wrath. He treated any policy of harmonization and paternalism by the colonialist as sheer sham and fraud and any responsiveness to this policy by segments of the colonized as examples of Marxian false consciousness. Thus its naked brutality was the only truth about colonialism with which Fanon wished to deal.

Pierre L. van den Berghe and paternalistic race relations

The theorists we have already discussed all left some room in their plural theories for the development of a normative overlay and code that would mitigate some of the harsh coerciveness of the colonial society. Van den Berghe made this code central to the type of race relations he labelled paternalistic. According to van den Berghe, this code defined rights and obligations of dominant and subordinated strata to each other and was structured on a "master-servant" or "parent-child" relation. It accepted without question the right of the dominant group to rule, and it maximized the distance between ruler and ruled "by an elaborate and punctilious etiquette involving nonreciprocal terms of address, sumptuary regulations, and repeated manifestations of subservience and dominance" (van den Berghe 1967:27).

In turn, the master class was presumed to have certain obligations toward the subordinated strata. Its dealings with this strata were to be motivated by more than exploitative self-interest; they were also to be conditioned by concern over the welfare and the need to protect the subordinated group. According to the dominant group, the subordinated strata needed this because they were incapable of taking care of themselves; they were regarded "as childish, immature, irresponsible, exuberant, improvident, fun-loving, good-humored, and happy-go-lucky; in short as inferior but lovable as long as they stay in 'their place'" (van den Berghe 1967:27).

In effect, benevolent paternalism was the normative model for the society. However, the extent to which paternalism was indeed practiced by ruling groups varied. In some societies paternalism was built into the very fabric of the society as in the case of the caste system in India; in other societies it was primarily expressed through public and administrative policy as in the case of the Dutch East Indies; in still others it extended into legal, religious, and other major societal institutions as in the case of colonies in the New World conquered by Spain and Portugal. And in still other societies the paternalistic code operated on the more informal level of relations between master and slave as in the case of the South before the Civil War. However, no matter how narrowly or widely defined were the institutional or other areas of society in which the paternalistic code in fact operated, it served as the idealized model for the society as a whole of what relations between dominant and subordinated groups should be like. So significant did van den Berghe consider this paternalistic model that he identified it as one of the two basic systems of race relations in society; the other was the competitive type of race relations.

The extent to which the subordinated strata accepted this view of the world and of themselves also varied within and between societies. The caste system represented the most extreme case of general consensus built usually around a commonly shared religious set of beliefs; even the lower castes presumably accepted their inferior status as fitting and proper. Within colonial societies, conformity to the paternalistic code was also found among the subordinated groups. They knew how to defer to the master, to act servilely, to conform to his demands, and to play the part of a "carefree child." However, the extent to which they inwardly accepted the validity of the paternalistic system and the truth of their own innate inferiority is a question still being argued. In those societies which Rex would label as "colonial estate" societies, the process of "sambofication" may have spread fairly extensively throughout the lower groups; however, in virtually all colonial societies it could be expected that behavioral conformity to the code was much more widespread than were inner feelings and convictions about the validity of the code. The cost of expressing negative or hostile convictions through non-conforming behavior was just too high, given the generally repressive character of the society. (For a more detailed comparison between caste and colonial plural societies, see Chapter 7.)

In effect, the presence of a normative overlay on the colonial society may have mitigated some of its harsher features; the paternalistic code may have facilitated accommodation and varying degrees of harmony between strata; and in the case of the caste system it may even have provided for an integrated and stable structure. Yet in most instances the code functioned as a veneer for what was essentially a repressive, coercive system in which fear and resentment were inherent features – though overt conflict may have been less frequent.

The colonialist as a sojourner elite

Having forcibly "created" the colonial plural society, the white European stood at its pinnacle of power and privilege. He superimposed his own political, economic, and social institutions on whatever traditional base there was and retained in his own hands the ultimate instruments of coercion and power. He introduced and installed administrative procedures and structures that enhanced his control. He created elite role models which were patterned in his own image and style and he introduced schemes of status evaluation with himself at the top.

In effect, much of his energy was devoted to securing and maintaining his political, economic, and social dominance in the colony. As such he became obsessed with his elite status and where he could, as in the plantation colonies, he attempted to construct an aristocratic style of life with its elaborate codes of etiquette. As Freyre (1946) and Frazier (1957) stated, the plantation house became the center of the life style; and the development of the leisure class à la Thorstein Veblen, its hope.

The style of life was modeled after that of the social elite in the metropolitan country, but in the colonies it became something different. It was characterized by a greater ostentatiousness, flamboyance, and display of wealth. This contrast in the use of wealth was made evident in the metropolitan country such as in England where some of the absentee owners of plantations set up residence. The colonial style of life was also characterized by a combination of fastidiousness and crudity and by a veneer of gentility over a foundation of cruelty. John Stedman graphically described these paradoxical features in his account of a planter's day in the eighteenth century (Stedman 1806:48–51).

The European elite in many of the colonies adopted what can best be described as a sojourner's philosophy. Even after generations in the colony, the elite professed a longing to return to the metropolitan country; as Eric Williams (1944) reported in his study of the British West Indies, the elite neither spiritually nor physically lost its ties with the home country. Whenever and wherever possible they returned home for visits and retirement.

As a result, members of the European elite frequently saw themselves as transients in the colony; someday they would leave. Mederic-Louis-Elie Moreau de Saint-Mery described in his account of the French settler in Saint Domingue (1797) the pervasiveness of this attitude among the second-generation children of the original settlers. They had been sent back to the homeland for their education and were even more alienated from the colony after their return.

"Settlers enriched through well-planned agriculture now sought other occupations for their children. They had to be sent to France to acquire an education appropriate to their future state. Those who came back to the island brought with them tastes which could not be satisfied there. Sometimes they could not give up penchants already strongly confirmed; or perhaps they were ashamed of the simple customs of their parents. Hence, their aversion toward their birthplace, a kind of lassitude in which they viewed themselves only as transients in a country where they were sometimes forced to stay for their entire lives. Hence, their unconcern for the good and prosperity of a country which they wished to extract only the means of living far away. Hence, the high price paid for pleasures which were multiplied merely because they failed to bring satisfaction."   (Mederic-Louis-Elie Moreau de Saint-Mery 1797:55)

Memmi brought the special relationship between colonialist and home country into the twentieth century in his observations on the French in Algeria (1965). He viewed the close identification with the homeland as an inextricable part of being a colonialist. "In order that he may subsist as a colonialist, it is necessary that the mother country eternally remain a mother country. To the extent that this depends upon him, it is understandable if he uses all his energy to that end" (Memmi 1965:62).

The mother country then helped the white colonialist to establish his identity and to legitimize his privileged position in the colony. In effect, he sought the source of his grandeur in his connection with the mother country and expressed an exaggerated patriotism for a mother country which he had transformed in his mind into a myth and an illusion.

> "Having assigned to his homeland the burden of his own decaying grandeur, he expects it to respond to his hopes. He wants it to merit his confidence to reflect on him that image of itself which he desires (an ideal which is inaccessible to the colonized and a perfect justification for his own borrowed merits). Often by dint of hoping, he ends up beginning to believe it. . . . The colonialist appears to have forgotten the living reality of his home country. Over the years, he has sculptured, in opposition to the colony, such a monument of his homeland that the colony necessarily appears coarse and vulgar to the novitiate."
>
> (Memmi 1965:59–60)

Memmi offered two major reasons for this glorification of homeland ties. First it reaffirmed the privileged position of the colonialist in the colony. Second, it further dissociated the colonialist from the colonized by emphasizing a tie which the latter did not and could not share.

This was only one of the ways in which the colonialist sought to increase the gulf between himself and the colonized. In word and deed, he widened this gap and avoided any kind of contact that might convey the notion of equality to the colonized. His primary concern was to reaffirm his own superiority and to emphasize the inferiority of the colonized. As such, he virtually barricaded himself behind the boundaries of his own group and symbolically at least wrapped a mantle of invisibility around the colonized so that his privileged position did not have to be disturbed.

Despite his efforts to isolate himself, the colonialist nevertheless had to come to terms with his extreme dependence on the native population. Memmi believed that the colonialist only reluctantly faced the fact that his own fate was inextricably tied up with that of the colonized. According to Lowenthal, the response of the colonialist as slave-master in the British West Indies to this dependence was shame and tyranny:

> "The discrepancy between the slave-master's authority and his circumstances was for him a source of aggravation and shame. He found himself dependent on

his slaves at every point – for livelihood, for safety, for comfort, even for companionship. Power encouraged a taste for tyranny: the typical planter was 'a petty monarch, as capricious as he is despotic.' Yet the galling recognition of dependency on a despised inferior helps to explain why whites often described their lives in terms of slavery."   (Lowenthal 1972:38)

Memmi however went further. He was convinced that recognition of this dependence compelled the colonialist to degrade and to dehumanize the colonized.

"With all his power he must disown the colonized while their existence is indispensable to his own. Having become aware of the unjust relationship which ties him to the colonized, he must continually attempt to absolve himself. He never forgets to make a public show of his own virtues, and will argue with vehemence to appear heroic and great. At the same time his privileges arise just as much from his glory as from degrading the colonized. He will persist in degrading them, using the darkest colors to depict them. If need be, he will act to devalue them, annihilate them. But he can never escape from this circle. The distance which colonization places between him and the colonized must be accounted for and, to justify himself, he increases this distance still further by placing the two figures irretrievably in opposition; his glorious position and the despicable one of the colonized."   (Memmi 1965:54–5)

The dual response of the colonialist to his homeland and to the colonized reflected his limited commitment to the colony itself. Despite efforts through church missions, schools, and public media to diffuse his values and beliefs throughout the colony, the sojourner colonialist did not see himself constructing anything resembling a national community within the colony. He did not view the colony as a collective entity toward which he had civic responsibilities and with which he could identify. In other words he was not prepared to share certain kinds of ties and equalities that such common membership might imply with the colonized; to do so would "destroy the principle of his privileges."

"This rejection of the colony and the colonized seriously affects the life and behavior of the colonized. But it also produces a disastrous effect upon the colonialist's conduct. Having thus described the colony, conceding no merits to the colonial community, recognizing neither its traditions, nor its ways, he cannot acknowledge belonging to it himself....

It is not the dryness of the country or the lack of grace of the colonial communities which explain the colonialist's rejection. It is rather because he has not adopted it, or could not adopt it, that the land remains arid and the architecture remains unimaginative in its functionalism. Why does he do nothing about town planning, for example? When he complains about the presence of a bacterially infected lake at the gates of the city, of overflowing sewers or poorly functioning utilities, he seems to forget that he holds the power in the government and should assume the blame. Why does he not direct his efforts in a disinterested manner, or is he unable to? Every municipality reflects its inhabitants, guards their immediate and future welfare and their posterity. The colonialist does not plan his future in terms of the colony, for he is there only temporarily and invests only what will bear fruit in his time. The true reason, the principal reason for most deficiencies is that the colonialist never planned to transform the colony in the image of his homeland, nor to remake the colonized into his own image! He cannot allow such an equation – it would destroy the principle of his privileges."   (Memmi 1965:68–9)

Conclusion

This description of the white European as a sojourner elite resonates throughout the literature on the plural society. Such resonance reflects the almost exclusive preoccupation of the scholars of the plural society with the white European as colonialist. They have failed, however, to give due weight to those historical situations of expansion and conquest where the white European did more than create a plural society on the shoulders of nonwhites who were either indigenous or involuntarily imported into the territory. In those areas the white European also assumed the role of colonist and founded a permanent settlement in which he created a society whose institutions were molded in his racial, religious, and national image and with which he closely identified. In those settings he dominated the plural structure and defined his status as a permanently established, not as a sojourner, elite. At the same time he viewed himself as the people of the colonist society. His rights and immunities in both structures stood in sharp contrast to those of the racial groups that comprised the subjugated strata of his colonialist plural society.

Whereas this dual colonialist-colonist role rarely characterized the white European's conquest and subjugation of most of South Asia and Africa, it was clearly imprinted in his conquest of the New World during the first centuries of European expansion. The character of the duality, though, varied markedly with the national identity of the white European. For example, the conquistador from Spain, who launched the era of European expansion with his mission of discovery and conquest in the New World, constructed a duality that differed significantly from that which was built by the English colonialist-colonist who followed him into the New World a century later.

In the next chapter we shall examine the version of duality created by the English in Virginia. Only passing reference will be made to the version constructed by the Spanish conquistador. For a fuller description of the duality he imprinted on Hispaniola, the reader is referred to Appendix A.

3

THE DUAL PROCESSES
OF COLONIALIZATION AND
COLONIZATION:
THE ENGLISH IN VIRGINIA

Introduction

In building their colonial societies in the New World, the English did not follow the example set by the Spanish conquistador one hundred years earlier in his conquest of Hispaniola (see Appendix A). They did not construct their colonial societies on the backs of the subjugated Indians as a captive labor force, though several small-scale but unsuccessful attempts did occur. Instead they fought the Indian for his land and resources and, once they defeated him, they forced him to move beyond the perimeter of the societies they constructed. In short, except for the early days when trade with the Indian was important for the survival of the English settler, the Indian played virtually no significant role in the internal functioning of the colonial society, but a crucial role in defining its frontier. (We shall examine this role in Chapter 5.)

Thus, when under the aegis of the Virginia Company of London the English founded their first successful colony on the Atlantic Coast at Jamestown, they had to rely initially on their own labor to realize their colonial objectives of economic gain. And in the process they built a colonist society in their own image. Only later did they turn to a labor force of captive nonwhites, imported as slaves from abroad, and build on their backs a colonial plural society. Their colonist society came before and not after their racially segmented colonialist society. In this respect too they differed from the Spanish conquistador (see Appendix A).

In this chapter we shall examine the processes of colonization and colonialization and the dual structures they created in Virginia.

Early abortive efforts at colonization

By the time England took notice of the New World in the sixteenth century, Spain had already established its dominance. Its empire extended from the northern boundaries of New Spain to the tip of South America, and its fleet controlled the seas and protected the flow of bullion to Spain and trade with its colonies. England's earliest ventures into the New World in the sixteenth century amounted to little more than slashing attacks against Spanish shipping and raids against Spanish towns by buccaneers like Sir Francis Drake and John Hawkins. "But the buccaneer was not a colonizer. Sir Francis Drake or John Hawkins never tried to establish colonies. They were adventurers for whom profit, patriotism, and religious zeal could be combined in a sea war against the Spanish empire" (Lang 1975:107).

Other Englishmen attempted to do what Columbus failed to do. They tried to find a passage to the East Indies and China through a northwest route to the Arctic:

> "but little came of these undertakings, other than the final discovery of the Hudson Strait, and the painful conclusion that a road to the East, at least by the north-west or north-east, was for the time being too costly in terms of life and money. It was left to Drake in 1577 to find a route to the Moluccas by the south-west. In the process he became the first Englishman to circumnavigate the globe."
>
> (Graham 1970:16)

Not until the 1580s, however, was a serious attempt made at colonization by an Englishman, Sir Gilbert Humphrey. His first attempt in 1578, largely financed by individual contributions, ended in failure. Five years later Humphrey succeeded in organizing a smaller expedition and in July 1583 he reached Newfoundland where he found some fishermen of mixed nationalities. He claimed the territory in the name of Queen Elizabeth and issued several proclamations. Beyond that nothing was accomplished, for none of his men elected to stay behind as he sailed for England. On his way back, the ship on which he sailed sank, and he drowned.

The most noteworthy feature of his second voyage was his pioneering use of the trading company to finance his expedition. Those who contributed to his Merchant Adventurers were to gain trade privileges and a grant of land. Adventurers who also joined the expedition were to receive a double share of land. "Thus, as a means of securing funds the preliminary steps for the organization of a trading company were taken which might traffic and colonize within the vast domain that Sir Humphrey had received, but no rights of government appear to have been expressly conferred on the company" (Osgood 1957:10).

A year later Sir Walter Raleigh, who had accompanied Humphrey on his first voyage and was his vice admiral on the second, though his ship never left England, received a royal charter similar to that which Humphrey had received six years before. A year later his first expedition of 107 men landed at Roanoke Island, North Carolina. And "like all colonizers of his generation, who were imitating Spain while they were fighting her, Lane [the colony's civilian governor] considered the two chief objects of his enterprise to be the discovery of a gold mine and of a route to the South Sea" (Osgood 1957:18). As a result he and his men searched the various waterways in the area for signs of the two. Relations with the Indians which were initially friendly deteriorated rapidly as the behavior of the colonists aroused their suspicions. Open warfare broke out, and though the colonists defeated the Indians through their superior firepower, they lost an important source for supplying their foodstuff. Faced with the danger of famine, further attacks by the Indians, and even destruction by the Spaniards, the English abandoned Roanoke a year after they first arrived and returned to England.

Determined to benefit from this failure, Raleigh financed his second expedition in a manner similar to that employed by Humphrey. He organized a group of London merchants into an adventurers' association which would share the profits in exchange for underwriting the venture. According to the terms of the charter of incorporation,

> "all who became members of the corporation should enjoy freedom of trade with any colony which Raleigh should thereafter found in America, and be exempt from all rents and subsidies, as well as from all duties and customs . . . the strength of the mercantile element in the undertaking was increased, and a borough government was expressly provided for the colony. Raleigh retained for himself the title of 'chief governor of Virginia.'"   (Osgood 1957:21)

John White was made governor. Approximately 150 colonists, including several women, reached Roanoke in July 1587, but despite all the precautions taken, this colony too failed. It literally vanished without a trace.

Jamestown and the Virginia Company of London

Despite these setbacks, colonial aspirations for England were kept alive by a small group of merchants and noblemen, a number of whom were related to the earlier generation of seamen and discoverers. They subsidized private voyages of discovery for the purpose of obtaining more information about the coastline of North America and about "the value of the fisheries and fur trade available there, the resources of the region in timber and other naval stores" (Osgood 1957:24). With this information they hoped to rekindle interest in colonization; one enterprising captain even brought back five Indians whom he "taught enough words to praise the climate and richness of their country, a feat worthy of the ingenuity of modern realtors" (Wright 1959:54).

So effective were these efforts in arousing interest among commercial circles that by 1606 the leading members of this group successfully petitioned King James I for a charter "'to make Habitation, Plantation, and to deduce a Colony of sundry of our People into that Part of *America* commonly called VIRGINIA.'" Obviously fearful of any collision with the interests of Spain, the King stipulated that such a colony should be located on territories "'which are not actually possessed by any *Christian* Prince or People.'"

The King's charter also authorized the Virginia Company to divide itself into two companies: the London and the Plymouth. The former was to include "'certain Knights, Gentlemen, Merchants and other Adventurers, of our city of *London* and elsewhere;'" the latter, to include a similar category of persons "'of our Cities of *Bristol* and *Exeter*, and of our Town of *Plymouth*, and of other Places'" (Commager 1963:8). In addition, the London Company was granted permission to establish the first Colony of "Plantation and Habitation" on the coast of Virginia between the 34th and 41st degree latitude; the Plymouth Company, permission to establish the second colony between the 38th and 45th degree latitude.

Each colony was to be governed locally by a council of thirteen; in England a Council of Virginia, also consisting of thirteen members, was to be appointed by the King to oversee the entire operation. Further, the charter stipulated that all of the King's subjects who settled in a colony as well as their offspring born there were to retain their rights as Englishmen: "'[they] shall HAVE and enjoy all Liberties, Franchises, and Immunities, within any of our other Dominions, to all Intents and Purposes, as if they had been abiding and born, within this our Realm of *England* or any other of our said Dominions'" (Commager 1963:10).

The colonial success of Spain was clearly in the mind of the English King in the attention he paid to the mining of gold and other precious metals. Accordingly, he authorized the local councils "'to dig, mine, and search for all Manner of Mines of Gold, Silver, and Copper, as well within any part of their said several Colonies, as for the said main Lands on the Backside of the same Colonies'" (Commager 1963:9). The only requirement was that a fifth of the yield of gold and silver and one-fifteenth of the yield of copper be reserved for the King.

The councils were also granted the right to regulate trade with the colonies and the "'Power and Authority to take and surprise, by all Ways and Means whatsoever, all and every Person and Persons, with their Ships, Vessels, Goods and other Furniture, which shall be found trafficking, into any Harbour or Harbours, Creek or Creeks, or Place, within the Limits or Precincts of the said several Colonies and Plantations, not being of the same Colony'" (Commager 1963:9–10), unless these British subjects or strangers paid a graduated set of charges.

Intent upon replicating the success of the Spanish in Mexico and Peru and upon discovering the elusive route to the East, the Virginia Company of London recruited

"a motley group numbering slightly more than one hundred men in search of adventure rather than homes in the wilderness.... Only a few of the first immigrants looked upon Virginia as a place of permanent abode. They still had the Elizabethan dream of quick riches from gold and precious stones. The majority of the adventurers were denominated 'gentlemen,' and hardly more than a quarter could be described as artisans and laborers."   (Wright 1958:55)

Osgood disputed these figures. He claimed that listings for the Jamestown settlement show that "from one-third to one-half bore the designation of gentlemen, while the rest were artisans and laborers" (Osgood 1957:34). But neither scholar disputed the fact that most showed "small inclination for the drudgery of cutting trees and tilling the soil" (Wright 1959:56). Osgood reported that Captain John Smith estimated that "only about one-fourth of the settlers were vigorous workers" (Osgood 1957:54).

Sloth, however, was not alone in cutting down the numbers available for work; disease was an equally if not more important factor. And death shriveled drastically the total number available for anything. The net result was that the Jamestown colony founded in South Virginia in May 1607 barely survived the early years of travail. The second colony established by the Plymouth Company three months later at Sagadahoc in North Virginia was not so fortunate; it was abandoned within several years. To make matters worse dissension among the members of the Jamestown council magnified the factionalism and internal tension in the Jamestown colony and only the emergence of Captain John Smith "as a dominant spirit capable of enforcing discipline and organizing the group into something approaching a civil society" (Wright 1959:56) enabled it to avoid total internal collapse. What also helped the colony to survive its early days was trade with the Indians: "it brought to Jamestown supplies of food without which its continued existence would have been impossible, it opened up friendly relations with the natives, and it facilitated and encouraged discovery" (Osgood 1957:40).

The charter of 1609 and authoritarian control

By 1609 the leaders of the Virginia Company of London had become so alarmed at the structural and other defects revealed by the first year's experience in the colony

that they sought remedies on a relatively broad front. First, they petitioned the
King for a new charter which would basically revamp the Company's governance
structure in England and in Virginia. The new charter did this and gave the new
organizational structure the title "The Treasurer and Company of Adventurers
and Planters of the City of London for the first Colony in Virginia." It authorized
the Company to expand or contract its membership of planters and adventurers at
will. It replaced the royal council of the 1606 charter with another council and
treasurer of enhanced authority to control the affairs of the Company and of the
colony.

The internal affairs of the colony were now to be centralized under a governor
with the colony council reduced to a consultative role. The general authority of
the Company expanded even further in the third charter of 1612 which also
granted the right to elect the previously crown-appointed members of the council.

"The effect of this was to make it a permanent administrative body within the
company, wholly subject to its control like any other standing committee. By
virtue of this change the patentees came to have the power of directly governing
the colony, though of course, like all other corporations, they were subject to
the sovereign control of crown and parliament."   (Osgood 1957:57–8)

At the same time the charter of 1612 made the council accountable to a general
court of all members of the Company who were to meet on a fairly regular basis.

Once the charter of 1609 was proclaimed, the Company began a vigorous
campaign to attract new members and to augment its treasury. It sold shares of
stock to adventurers who merely invested their money and had no intention of
emigrating to the colony. It also recruited planters who merely had their and their
families' labor to invest in the colony, but this time the Company carefully
screened for the kind of planter it wanted. No longer interested in those seeking
gold, the Company now concentrated its search for "the husbandsman or artisan,
reared in the Protestant faith, and honest in his past life." As a result a markedly
distinctive class division separated those who invested their money in the
Company from those who were to invest their labor: "the active adventurers
represented the nobility, clergy, and merchants, while the planters were being
drawn to a large extent from the lower classes" (Osgood 1957:59).

The Company was also convinced that it knew what had gone wrong during the
early years in the colony and what had remained sound in its approach to the
colony. With respect to the latter, it decided to continue for another seven years
the corporate economic arrangement it had instituted in 1606.

"There should be no landholding or trading by individuals, but the company
should, as formerly, provide all necessities and receive all products. In the
meantime, such dividends as the business would warrant should be declared for

the benefit of the adventurers, and the planters would be guaranteed their
support."   (Osgood 1957:58)

The reason why this arrangement did not seem to work in the early days, the
Company insisted, was due to the slothfulness and lack of discipline among the
early colonists. Accordingly it instructed the newly appointed Governor Gates to
wield a strong hand, to demand discipline and hard work from the colonists, and
to punish severely any slothful or rebellious behavior. He was also told to
continue "with great vigor" the plantation system of "working [the colonists] in
gangs under officials as overseers, eating at common tables and living in common
barracks" (Osgood 1957:64).

By late Spring of 1609 the Company was prepared to put its new plan into
operation. It assembled 500 planters, including some women, and nine ships and
sent them off to Virginia with Sir Thomas Gates as "sole and absolute governor."
Unfortunately a severe storm battered the nine ships as they approached the
Bahamas. One ship sank; another with the governor aboard was wrecked on the
Bermudas; the remaining seven – their supplies badly damaged by the storm –
finally limped into Jamestown with 200 colonists aboard.

When Gates finally reached Jamestown almost a year later with 150 colonists, he
met the bedraggled survivors of a settlement that was teetering on the edge of
oblivion. Only sixty had weathered a year of famine and disease that equalled if
not exceeded that experienced in the first year of the colony. What had made
matters even worse was the deterioration in relations with the Indians. They had
cut off trade with the colony and were engaged in what Brown (1898:113) called
"a war of extermination."

Gates decided to evacuate the settlers and to concede that another experiment in
English colonization had proved to be a failure. But almost as soon as he set sail,
he met Delaware's ships at the mouth of the river and returned with them to
reestablish the colony. "Thus the most serious crisis in the history of Virginia – far
more serious in its nature than that which resulted in Lane's return from Roanoke
– was passed, and a repetition of the experiment in colonization on the James river
was insured" (Osgood 1957:68).

Almost immediately the Company's plan of administration was put into
operation. A military-like structure of governance replaced the other; presumably
it would remedy the sloth and lack of discipline that allegedly caused the failure of
the Company's earlier colonization experiment. Under the new structure the
governor was to wield virtually absolute power; he was to consult with a body of
councillors, almost all of whom were to be given military titles; and he was to be
guided by a detailed written code of conduct to be drafted after the fashion of the
military regulations in force in the Netherlands.

"According to this code, freedom of action within the colony was to be reduced to a minimum. The colony was to be regarded and treated as an absolute unit. The traditional forces of military discipline, severe penal enactments, and strict religious observance were brought to bear, to repress disorder and direct the productive energies of the settlement."   (Osgood 1957:70)

Violation of the code elicited serious punishments; death, for example, could be decreed for any of twenty crimes. Persistent neglect of labor was to be punished by galley service from one to three years; and relatively minor infractions by whippings.

Under Governor Dale this mold of the military was shaped to a fine turn and imposed for six long years on the daily life of the colonists.

"The instructions of Dale show it to have been the intention to order all activities of the colonists according to military routine. The governor at Jamestown, as well as at each outlying plantation, was to perform the double duty of military commander and overseer. The same was true of all the officers under him, and they all bore military titles. The ordinary colonist was plainly told that he was both soldier and husbandman, and the rigid discipline of the former calling was to dominate the latter. A strict watch and system of training was to be maintained, and at appointed times the soldier was to lay down his gun in order to take up the spade or other tool. The day was so divided that the hours of labor in the morning continued from six to ten o'clock, and in the afternoon from two until four. These periods began and closed with the beat of drum, and at their close all the settlers were marched to the church to hear prayers. Under the supervision of officers all tools were taken day by day for use from the storehouse and returned thither again.... To train husbandmen in Virginia who should have the regularity and persistence of soldiers was the aim of the managers of the system."   (Osgood 1957:71–2)

Thus the colonist in Virginia was deprived of the contractual rights he theoretically had as a member of the London Company.

"As a planter absent in Virginia he could not sit nor have a voice in the councils of the Company; he was entirely dependent on the Company's good faith for the performance of its obligations, and had recourse to no means to enforce their performance. He was kept by force in the colony, and could have no communication with his friends in England. His letters were intercepted by the Company and could be destroyed if they contained anything to the Company's discredit. He was completely at the mercy of the edicts of arbitrary governors, and was forced to accept whatever abridgment of his rights and contract seemed good to the Governor and the Company. His true position was that of a common servant working in the interest of a commercial company. In lieu of his support, or of his transportation and support, he was bound to the service of this company for a term of years. Under the arbitrary administration of the Company and of its deputy governors he was as absolutely at its disposal as a servant at his master's. His conduct was regulated by corporal punishment or more extreme measures."

(Ballagh 1895:26)

By the time Dale left for England in 1616 he had created a regimented and orderly society in which tasks seemed to be getting done. In addition, the colony had expanded with six more settlements established along the lower and middle course of the James river. Its livestock and produce had increased. Even tobacco had begun to be produced.

The cost for these accomplishments appeared, however, to be exceedingly high. Dissatisfaction was rife among the colonists; morale was very low. As a result, productivity never reached the level the Company hoped for. In addition some colonists became so disaffected that they sought to escape despite the specter of the severe punishment that awaited them if they were caught. Some managed to return home; others made it to the Indians; still others made it to the Spanish.

Word of the oppressive regime got back to England despite the Company's concerted efforts to prevent this from happening. Consequently too few Englishmen emigrated to Virginia during this period to offset the toll that pestilence and disease were continuing to take of the colony's inhabitants. As a result, the population declined precipitously so that by April 1616 only 351 were left of a total of 1650 who had been sent to Virginia; the rest had either died (1000) or returned to England (300). As quoted in Brown, John Rolfe, who accompanied Governor Dale to England, characterized the survivors as "a small number to advance so great a worke" (Brown II 1964:782).

Thus ended the seven-year period of a corporate economic arrangement and authoritarian rule. It had begun with the optimistic promise by the Company that the colonist was to be accorded the same status as an adventurer. Only he would contribute his labor to the joint enterprise; the adventurer, his money. Both were to share in the profits of the Company at the end of the seven-year period. Only there were no profits to be shared at the end of a period during which most planters were in what Ballagh (1895) called a state of servitude to the Company. However, approximately one-third of the planters, those of "superior qualities," received special concessions by 1614; they were afforded the first private holdings, leases of three acres each.

"Those who received them were called farmers, and paid an annual rent into the common store of two and one-half barrels of corn for each male worker. They were exempted from all labor for the community, save during one month in the year, and that not in seed-time or harvest."   (Osgood 1957:75)

Though the end of the seven-year experiment with joint management seemed at hand with the departure of Dale, its demise was delayed by the arrival of Argall as governor. He sidetracked the Company's preparations to deliver on its promise of seven years before: a division of land to adventurers and planters alike on the basis of the shares they held. In perpetuating the system, though, the governor did not seek to enhance the value of the Company's assets.

"Instead, both the lands and trade of the company were recklessly exploited for the benefit of the governor and his friends. The 'ancient colony men,' who were entitled to their freedom, and the laborers from the common garden were kept at work as the governor directed, and largely for his personal advantage."
                    (Osgood 1957:77)

Brought home on charges, the governor was found guilty of some by the Company court; no definite decision seemed to have been reached on the others. Though some scholars consider the governor's behavior as more of a symptom than as a cause of the malaise the Company was going through, agreement seems general that "the significance of his administration appears in the fact that it delayed the process of economic transition in the colony for two years" (Osgood 1957:79). Further his case became the cause célèbre that fueled an open revolt in the ranks of the adventurers in London against the policies of the top administration. Their opposition led to an irresistible demand for reform and reorganization. The Treasurer bowed to this demand and worked closely with the leader of the opposition, Sir Sandys, in reshaping the policies of the Company. The scope and character of the reforms rank in importance with those of 1609 and 1612; and as in the earlier years, they came only after the Company had gone through a period of disarray and dissatisfaction with the lack of profits and progress.

The reforms of 1618

The new statement of policy focused primarily on three major areas of concern. First was an expression of alarm at the growing dependence of the colony on the production of one crop, tobacco. It was felt that the colony had to diversify its crops, particularly the production of corn, in order to become self-sufficient, and to expand the production of other crops that could be used in trade with England.

The second and primary area of concern was the question of land allocation and tenure which had been sidetracked by the Argall administration. One recommendation was that public lands be reestablished "in the hope of some financial benefit thereby for the Company" (Craven 1964:54). These lands, to encompass an area of 3000 acres in each of the four boroughs into which the older holdings of Virginia were divided, were "to be farmed for the profit of the joint-stock by tenants sent at Company's expense.... The tenants were entitled to one half the profit of their labors. The remainder, after the deduction of a fifth of it for the payment of bailiffs and overseers, was to be the Company's share" (Craven 1964:54–5). Large tracts of Company land were also to be set aside for officials in the various boroughs, and they too were to be tilled by tenants sent for the purpose from England on a "tenants by halves" basis. Other land was to be set aside in each borough for the construction of churches, and 10,000 acres for the construction of a college in one of the boroughs.

A second recommendation which was of particular interest to the colonists in Virginia was the set of proposals regarding the question of land tenure. Special consideration was given to the "ancient planters," those who came to Virginia before the departure of Governor Dale in 1616 and who presumably suffered through the authoritarian regime of that day. If they had come at their own expense, they were to receive 100 acres as the land equivalent of the £12 10s invested by the earlier adventurers. They were also to receive an additional grant of the same size if they had also invested money as a shareholder. If they had come at Company expense, they were to receive 100 acres at an annual quit-rent of two shillings at the expiration of their seven years' service on the public land.

Those who came after 1616 were to receive lesser grants. If they paid their own way, they were to be given 50 acres at an annual quit-rent of one shilling. If they came at Company expense, they were first "to complete a seven year term of service on the Company's land, during which time they were entitled to one half the profit of their labor" and then they would receive 50 acres at an annual rent of a shilling.

> "For the encouragement of all necessary trades it was [also] ordered that any tradesman who preferred to follow his trade should be allowed a dwelling house and four acres of land to be held in fee simple so long as he, or his heirs, continued to ply their trade in the said house. A free rent of four pence was to be paid in return for this grant."
>
> (Craven 1964:57)

Another recommendation involved the development and status of private plantations organized "by associated groups of adventurers in the Company to be farmed for their own benefit separate and apart from the projects of the common joint-stock." Special patents were to be issued by the Company "conveying to the patentees large contiguous areas of land with the privilege of farming the grant as a private plantation ... by 1618 several projects of this kind were under way, of which there were three general types" (Craven 1964:57–8). Over the next five years, approximately fifty patents for private plantations were granted by the Company.

The third major area of concern had to do with the governance and control of the colony. First, the Company decided to abolish martial law, a vestige of its authoritarian past that had proved so objectionable to adventurers and planters, and to substitute English common law for it. In addition, the Company decided to make available to the colonists an institutional channel similar to that which the adventurers already had in London; it would give the colonists some voice in the governance of the Company too. However, instead of being labeled a company court as was the London channel, it was to be called a legislative assembly. In this manner the one-sided flow of policy and action by Company officials and adventurers in London who had little firsthand knowledge of conditions in Virginia might be balanced by a return flow of information and resolutions from an officially convened body of colonists in Virginia. The structure of this legislative body was subsequently worked out; it was to consist of two groups.

"First, a Council of State, the members of which were listed as chosen by the Company in London, was to act as a permanent advisory body to the governor. The larger council, to be known as the General Assembly, was to consist of the Council of State and two burgesses chosen by the inhabitants from every town, hundred, or 'other particular plantation.' It was to be assembled by the governor once a year, and no oftener except upon 'very extraordinary and important occasions.' It had the power to treat and conclude 'of all emergent occasions concerning the public,' and to make, ordain, and enact such general laws and orders for the welfare of the colony as should from time to time seem necessary."   (Craven 1964:74)

The General Assembly of 1619

Within a year of making these proposals, the administration was out of office, and Sandys had taken over the post of Treasurer of the Company. Coincidentally, the day following the election, Sir George Yeardley, who had the strong support of Sandys, arrived in Virginia after a voyage of almost three months to take over the office of governor. He carried with him the instructions for implementing the various reforms formulated the previous winter. Almost immediately he issued a proclamation

" 'That all those that were resident here before the departure of Sir Thomas Dale (April 1616) should be freed and acquitted from such publique services and labours which formerly they suffered, and that those cruel laws by which we had so long been governed by those free laws which his Majesties subjects live under in Englande.'" (Brown 1898:312)

He then declared that in order "'that they might have a hand in the governing of themselves,'" a General Assembly was to be convened annually; the governor and his council would be present as well as "'two Burgesses from each Plantation *freely to be elected by the inhabitants thereof*; this Assembly to have power to make and ordaine whatsoever lawes and orders should by them be thought good and proffittable for our subsistence'" (Brown 1898:312).

On August 9 1619 the General Assembly became a reality as it was called to order in a church in Jamestown. Present were the governor, his council of state, and twenty-two burgesses elected from eleven boroughs, hundreds, or plantations. After prayers were said, a controversy erupted over the seating of burgesses from several plantations; finally all but two were seated.

During the next several days the Assembly endorsed the Company's plans for the allocation of lands; in several instances it showed even greater concern than did the Company in espousing the rights of ancient planters. In addition,

"a good many laws of sundry sorts were passed, namely: relative to the Indians, the treatment of them, trading with them, educating and converting them, etc.; to affairs of the church; to planting corn, mulberry-trees, silk flax, English flax, anise seed, vines, tobacco, etc.; to land patents, landlords, tradesmen, mechanics, tenants, servants, etc.; to 'the Magazin,' trading etc.; to the general conduct of affairs, private and public, in the colony; and 'against Idleness, Gaming, drunkeness and excesse in apparell.'" (Brown 1898:320)

In its closing days, the Assembly also petitioned the Company in England to give the Assembly the right to veto orders for the colony enacted by the courts and council in England just as the courts and council had the authority to veto enactments from the General Assembly in Virginia. In short, "something like legislative equality with the court of the Company in England was sought" (Osgood 1957:94). The General Assembly also requested that any of its actions be deemed binding in the colony until or unless official word to the contrary came from London. (The various petitions and enactments were sent for approval to the Company in London where they were taken under advisement by Sandys; whether they were ever officially approved by the Company is in doubt.)

Thus ended the first session of the legislative body set up in Virginia for the planters that paralleled in function and structure the legislative body previously set up for the adventurers in London. A symmetrical design for governance had finally been achieved for the Company at each geographic end of its operations.

Ostensibly this would facilitate the reciprocal flow of communications and expressions of need within Company channels and thereby create a more effective and efficient design for control and policy-making in the Company.

But something more than an institutional mechanism for Company control and decision-making had been created in Virginia. The colonists had also been given an identity as a body of people organized into and unified as a political community. The General Assembly, as "the first popular representative legislative assembly ever held within the limits of the present United States" (Brown 1898:315), was to symbolize this political unity, but even more it was to serve as its instrument for generating and maintaining law and order within the territorial limits of the political community.

Even the Company recognized that it had created in the General Assembly a political instrument of territorial control. This is evident in the following stipulation in its 1621 ordinance for Virginia, which Commager and others have insisted is an exact reproduction of the lost 1619 ordinance authorizing the convening of the first assembly.

> "'And this General Assembly shall have free Power to treat, consult, and conclude, as well of all emergent Occasions concerning the Publick Weal of the said Colony and every Part thereof, as also to make, ordain, and enact such general Laws and Orders, for the Behoof of the said Colony, and the good Government thereof, as shall, from time to time, appear necessary or requisite.'"   (Commager 1963:14)

Who was to be included as part of the People in the political community of these early years cannot be clearly determined due in large measure to the ambiguity of the term inhabitants which Governor Yeardley used to identify those eligible to vote for the burgesses of the 1619 assembly. Some scholars believe that all whites, even the indentured servants voted; others, however, believe that membership in the political community of this time was largely if not exclusively confined to whites "free" of servitude to the Company or to individuals.

The rise and fall of Sandys' campaign for colonization and the dissolution of the Virginia Company

Even before the first General Assembly formally convened in Jamestown, Sandys launched in London a major campaign to inject new vigor into the colonization project. He bemoaned the fact that from 1616 to 1618 when the Company was still under the control of his predecessor, the planter population in Virginia had barely increased from 350 to 400, of whom only 200 were able to "set hand to husbandry."

Sandys had pamphlets and tracts published and widely distributed which sought to redeem the low status of Virginia's reputation in the public's mind. Once again the virtues of Virginia were extolled: its fertile soil and bountiful game. Prospective adventurers were enticed with the promise of quick returns, and prospective colonists who worked Company lands were promised adequate provisions, equipment, and shelter. They would also enjoy half the profits of their labor and after seven years' service they would be free to take over their own plot of land.

So successful was this campaign that during the succeeding four-year period, Sandys was able to secure the emigration of over 4000 settlers. In the first year alone, a total of 1261 sailed for Virginia; the expenses of 871 were borne by the Company although only 650 actually settled on its land. The rest were sent to private plantations. Sandys even included ninety single women as the first installment in a plan to ship prospective brides to the colony in order to insure its permanence and stability by anchoring it to a familial life. Another hundred were to be shipped the second year along with 700 men at Company expense, most of whom were to labor on the general land of the Company. He also solicited funds from affluent citizens of London for sending a number of orphans and other dependent children to Virginia as apprentices and servants. They too would be allowed some acreage after completion of a seven-year term of service. Sandys even recruited some criminals and delinquents for the settlement, although he maintained that most of those whom he had recruited for settlement were "choice men born and bred to labor and industry" (Craven 1964:98).

Sandys was determined that the labor of these settlers would not contribute to the colony's lopsided dependence on the production of tobacco. Accordingly he sought to set limits on the amount that could be produced by individual colonists as well as by the private plantations. He was particularly intent upon securing an adequate food supply, particularly through the production of corn. But he wanted more. He also wanted to secure a solid place for Virginia in the trade of England. He was confident that that would happen if Virginia were to produce goods and staples for which there were "a constant and steady market at home" (Craven 1964:104). Thus he encouraged colonists to experiment with a variety of different products. He was particularly interested in developing iron, silk, and wine industries, and he even imported craftsmen from the various European countries to assist in these endeavors.

Sandys also threw his strong support behind the political development of Virginia just described. In addition, he even undertook the development of a code of general regulations based on English law which would serve in the words of the Company as a legal-normative framework for "'such a form of government [in

Virginia] as might be to the greatest benefit and comfort of the people; and thereby all injustice, grievances, and oppression might be prevented, and kept off as much as possible from the Colony.'" Bruce viewed "this successful effort of the Company to supply a framework of written laws for the preservation of an ordered government in Virginia, the protection of its interests, and the advancement of its general prosperity" as comparable "in spirit, if not in lasting results . . . [to] the drafting of the Federal Constitution by the fathers of the Republic" (Bruce II 1910:248).

Within a few years, most of Sandys' ambitious programs and grandiose schemes for the colony seemed on the verge of collapse; only those for the political structure seemed to survive intact. His call for new colonists, for example, had enticed so many that he could not deliver on his promises of adequate supplies and equipment. As a result, they proved a drain on the resources of the colony which could not absorb the marked increase in numbers. To make matters even worse, Sandys' program for diversifying agriculture in order to obtain a large and dependable food supply for the colony failed as more of the colony's resources were devoted to the production of tobacco. The net result was that the threat of disease and famine did not diminish and the rate of mortality continued at a high and virtually intolerable level. And in 1622 an almost fatal blow was struck at the colony's flagging energies: the Indians rose up and massacred hundreds of colonists. The survivors of these catastrophic events numbered no more than 2500 by 1624.

As conditions were worsening in Virginia, and as factionalism rent the Company in London, Sandys came under increasing attack. He even incurred the enmity of the King who forbade his reelection in 1620 to the office of Treasurer; despite this ban Sandys continued to wield primary power behind the scenes until 1624. As news of the colony's misfortunes filtered back and the danger of economic collapse and bankruptcy for the Company loomed, Sandys' opponents and enemies petitioned the King for an investigation of the Company's affairs. Within a year after the investigation, the King rebuffed efforts to reorganize the Company. He subsequently withdrew the Company's charter, and on May 13 1624 he proclaimed that Virginia would henceforth become part of "Our Royal Empire."

The colonist society: the bases of solidarity

THE POLITICAL COMMUNITY AS A FRAMEWORK FOR CONSENSUS

Though the colonists seemed to express ambivalent feelings about the demise of the Company, they expressed no such ambivalence in their determination to retain the political society that had been created five years before under the Company's aegis. Accordingly their representatives set out to persuade a King who had little faith in popular government, and at a session of the General Assembly early in 1624 – even before the official termination of the Company – they petitioned the King to retain a role for the General Assembly and council in the governance of the colony and not to entrust the governor with the autocratic authority of earlier years.

Their pleas seem to have had little effect as the King and his advisors appeared determined to curb the General Assembly and to centralize control in the hands of the governor. However, before any final plan could be drawn up, the King died, and the issue was held over for the new King. Four years later King Charles I authorized the convening of a General Assembly to debate the single issue of a levy on the import of tobacco; a year later he sent instructions for the convening of a "Grand Assembly" to approve the building of a protective wall for defence against the Indians.

> "The calling of such 'conventions' in 1628 and 1629 may well have seemed to the governor and the planters a sufficient precedent for a continuation of the practice every year and for the reassumption of law-making powers, because from this time on, with the possible exception of the year 1636 – for which no record can be found – annual assemblies were held and laws passed. There is no reason to doubt that these assemblies assumed all the rights and privileges of regular representative bodies and followed each its own variety of parliamentary practice." (Andrews 1934:199)

These were, however, little more than *ad hoc* arrangements to which the King may have given an unofficial nod but which in fact had no legal standing. According to Andrews, the planters sought through petition and other form of subtle pressure to induce the King to bestow legitimacy on this arrangement, and after ten years they finally succeeded. Not until his instructions to Governor Wyatt in January 1639 can it be documented that the King gave his formal and official consent to the practice of convening an annual assembly. In these instructions he ordered the governor

> "'as formerly once a year or oftener, if urgent occasion shall require, to summon the burgesses of all and singular plantations there, which together with the governor and council shall have power to make acts and laws for the government of that plantation, correspondent as near as may be to the laws of England, in which assembly the governor was to have a negative voice as formerly.'" (Andrews 1934:204)

In this manner the King, after fifteen years of indecision, reaffirmed the legitimacy and permanence of the political society and its structure of governance constructed by the Virginia Company almost two decades earlier, now that Virginia was a royal colony. As such,

> "a precedent was set according to which the people of any royal colony were assured of their right to share in the making of laws, the levying of taxes, and the taking into consideration those many other things, chiefly of a local and prudential nature, that meant most to men two and three hundred years ago. As the result of fifteen years indecision on the part of the crown and of action on the part of the colony, the principle was finally laid down that a royal colony should be, in part at least, a self-administering community, with a governor and council appointed in England and a representative assembly chosen by the freemen or freeholders in the colony."   (Andrews 1934:204–5)

To the Virginia colonists however, the King's decision signified more than a victory for self-government. It also meant that the primordial and politically generated consensual framework that bound the colonists to each other as a people and as a community in their organizational relationship to the Virginia Company would now apply to their territorial relationship to the Crown. As such it meant the reaffirmation of a structure that had already begun to be venerated as a sacred symbol of the collective whole, much as it continued to be viewed as an instrument for serving the people's secular political and economic interests. In the words of Wertenbaker, "the champions of the people were the Burgesses. The small planter, the tradesman, the freedman looked to them for protection against any infringement of their liberties or disregard of their interests by King, Governor, or Council" (Wertenbaker 1957:20). In short the "people" of this early period included all white male colonists, except those who were indentured, and all the people were expected to participate in the election of the burgesses; by 1645 voting had become a solemn duty; "anyone failing to do so without proper excuse was heavily fined" (Bruce II 1910:410) – a penalty that persisted throughout the colonial period.

For all but one of the next twenty-five years, all freedmen had what was tantamount to a "sacred duty" to participate in the political process. In 1670 however, the House of Burgesses, labeled the Long Assembly because its members stayed in office for fourteen years (well beyond their elected terms), bowed to the sustained seven-year pressure of Governor Berkeley and voted to restrict suffrage to freeholders and housekeepers. Six years later in 1676, the Governor under pressure of the Bacon Rebellion dissolved the Long Assembly, only to have the new assembly repeal the restrictive suffrage. Three years later with the defeat of the rebellion, property qualifications were imposed once again and remained in effect throughout the colonial period.

Just as casting a ballot was deemed a sacred obligation of the voter, the task of governing was similarly deemed by the ruling elite. And by the late seventeenth century when the elite came to be dominated by a "plantation aristocracy," the duty to govern assumed the character of a "religious calling."

"It was generally accepted in Virginia in those days that the ruling planters of good family had a prescriptive right to become ruling Burgesses, always, of course, provided they had earned the good opinion of their less substantial neighbors.... [Thus] Virginia was governed by its men of property. There was no family of substance without its members in the Governor's Council, the House of Burgesses, the county court or other governing bodies; and there was no governing body of the colony that was not dominated by the men of substance."

(Boorstin 1958:118–19)

RELIGION AS AN AXIS OF COLONIST SOLIDARITY

Unlike their political ties and interests which evolved serendipitously into a primary source of solidarity, the shared religious ties and interests of the Virginia colonist were expected from the very beginning to serve a similar function. Thus, in its instructions to the colony's president and council in 1606, the Company called upon them to provide "'with all diligence, care and respect ... that the true word and service of God and Christian faith be preached, planted and used ... according to the doctrine, rights and religion now professed and established within our realm of England'" (Bemiss 1957:15).

Any attempt by colonists to pursue any other religion, the Company continued, was to be punished severely. In building this internal moral and religious order, the Company insisted, the colonists were also to use the Anglican faith in the proselytization and conversion of the heathen Indian, a charge explicitly made by King James in his charter of 1606.

Three years later, driven by the near demise of the colony into a fundamental revamping of its structure of governance, the Company not only centralized authority but also instructed the newly appointed governor in much greater detail than it had the council in the past to rely heavily on religion for creating the kind of moral solidarity that would hopefully help to curb the sloth and lack of discipline deemed responsible for the near-collapse of the colony.

Sir Thomas Dale, the prime architect of the system of authoritarian control instituted by the Company from 1609 to 1616, carried out with great zeal the Company's instructions on religion. He interwove religious and secular obligation into a system of divine and martial law that compelled strict conformity from the colonist, else he faced severe punishment.

> "The duty was imposed upon every officer to see that 'God was served;' and each was commanded to set the example to all persons under him by a regular attendance at morning and evening prayers. Whoever omitted going to church was punished for the first offence by the loss of his day's allowance; for the second, by a severe whipping; and for the third, by his condemnation to the galleys for a period of six months. Profanation of God's name by an unlawful oath was, for the second offence, to be punished with a bodkin's thrust through the tongue; and for the third, with death; and the penalty of death also was to be paid by whoever stole one of the sacred articles belonging to the church building."   (Bruce I 1910:12–13)

Sir Thomas viewed as his most satisfying accomplishment the success he had in imposing this code of religious conduct on the colony, and he expressed hope in a letter to a clergyman in London that he would receive his reward for what he had done "'from Him in whose vineyard I labour, whose Church with greedy appetite I desire to erect'" (Bruce I 1910:12).

But what Sir Thomas had created for the Company was a far cry from the theocratic society the Pilgrims and Puritans were subsequently to build in Massachusetts. Even in Dale's world religious values and beliefs did not become the generating center for organizing all other institutional facets of life in the colony or for transmuting the ordinary churchgoing of the colonists into a community of sectarian believers who would gladly endure the various hardships, controls, and other sacrifices in order to build their "City of God." Instead Dale's religious code was viewed by most colonists as part of the general system of repression and constraint by which he sought to impose the rule of the Company. In other words, religion was being used as an instrument of control by the wielders of political power.

The subsequent dismantling of Dale's authoritarian regime did not basically alter the service function of religion for the colony's political system of control. The General Assembly of 1619, for example, clearly established itself as the temporal governing body of the Church; it also adopted "the Constitutions and Canons Ecclesiastical" of the Church of England as the basic code for the Church of Virginia. However, in the absence of a hierarchical church structure, certain pragmatic reinterpretations of the code had to be made. Thus the Assembly took a much more active role in the formulation of the church code than would have been the case if a "diocesan organization or ecclesiastical synod" had been in existence: "the enactments of the General Assembly in so far as these were concerned with ecclesiastical matters [took] the place of canons which normally should have been enacted by a diocesan organization or ecclesiastical synod" (Brydon 1947:68).

However, unlike the canons passed by a church organization, the enactments of the General Assembly also had the force of civil law. Thus religion and civil law were intermingled in the workings of the legislature. In 1619, for example, the General Assembly devoted considerable attention to the religious and moral conduct of the colonists and legislated "'against Idleness, gaming, drunkenness and excesse in apparell'" (Brown 1898:320). It also spelled out the obligations of ministers to conduct services and to monitor the moral conduct of their parishioners, insisting too that all ministers meet once a quarter to review recommendations for excommunication. The Assembly required regular church attendance of the laity as well, with a forfeit of three shillings everytime the lay person "shall transgress the Law."

So heavily involved had the Assembly become in church affairs that by 1632 in its first codification of enactments and orders passed in earlier sessions approximately one-third of the laws dealt explicitly with church matters and the religious duties of the clergy and parishioners; still others dealt with the moral conduct of parishioners.

Pivotal as the Assembly had become by the 1620s in establishing overall church policy, basic structural deficiencies in the governance and operation of the churches of Virginia manifested themselves, particularly with the dissolution of the Virginia Company in 1624. At this juncture had the King placed Virginia under the umbrella of the Church of England by making it a diocese or the special respondent of an Anglican bishop, then the history of the Church of Virginia might have been entirely different. Instead the Virginia colonists were thrown on their own resources; accordingly they elaborated a governance structure that brought the church even more than in the past under the political system of control.

At the base of the structure was the parish which served as "a distinct and separate ecclesiastical unit" and secondarily as a "subsidiary civil unit" for the people living within its territorial boundaries. In each parish, according to the assembly laws enacted in the 1630s, a vestry of generally twelve laymen was to be elected as its governing body in temporal affairs. With respect to its church-related responsibilities, the vestry "had authority to buy land for churches, churchyards and glebe farms, to erect church buildings and to build glebe-houses as residents for ministers" (Brydon 1957:13). It was also charged with the laying of a parish levy for paying various expenses, including the salary of the minister. By 1643 the vestry assumed its most important responsibility, that of selecting the minister himself. After a trial period, the minister presumably was to be presented to the Governor for induction, which under the laws of the Church of England was tantamount to giving him permanent tenure in his post; "no rector could be forced out of a parish after induction except after an ecclesiastical trial by the bishop or his commissary" (Brydon 1957:16). In the absence of such officials in the colony, only the governor had the authority to unseat him, which vestrymen charged he would be unlikely to do. To avoid the tenure issue, vestries in Virginia developed the stratagem of appointing ministers for only one year at a time and thereby of never having to present them to the governor for induction. As a result, a minister despite repeated renewals of his contract always remained at the mercy of his vestry. Lay control of church affairs was thus securely entrenched at the local level.

In addition, the vestry also assumed a number of civil duties.

"These duties were mainly based upon human relationships and needs and were developed usually out of duties performed by the Church in England. The duty performed by churchwardens in English parishes of presenting certain offenders to ecclesiastical courts was adopted from the first in Virginia and extended into the wider duty of presenting to the civil court of the county all offenders against the moral law. The duties of seeking and providing for the aged and the sick poor, as well as that of taking charge of orphaned children and all illegitimate ones, and of binding them out as apprentices to masters and mistresses who would give them homes and teach them to read and write, were considered as naturally belonging under the sphere of the Church and to be performed by the vestry. Gifts and bequests either of money or land, for the care of the poor, or for the education of poor children, were, as a general rule, made to the vestries of the parishes."   (Brydon 1947:94−5)

In sum, the vestry was located at the very center of power in the parish that linked the Church to the local system of political control. What insured this linkage was the fact that vestrymen were drawn from the socially established, the affluent, the land-owners, and the influential. Even more, a number were active in the even larger system of political control.

"Many vestry-men enjoyed the further distinction of being members of the county court, the House of Burgesses, or the Executive Council. It does not seem strange to discover that even so powerful an individual as the Governor himself was generally at great pains to be conciliatory in his bearing towards the vestries, not only because they had practical control of their communities, and, through their representatives, of the colonial Assembly, but also because their family connections in England were often able to affect favourably his standing with the persons to whom he owed his appointment, and upon whose good will his continuance in office depended."   (Bruce I 1910:62−3)

Thus the vestry became in time an important part of the total fabric of political control in the colony. As such, service in the vestry shared with service in the burgesses some of the sacred qualities of a calling. At the same time the vestry's close linkage with the Church insured that the latter would continue to "serve" the colony's political system.

Virginia as a colonist society: yeomen planters and indentured servants

LAND POLICIES AND THE HEADRIGHT

Just as the demise of the Virginia Company did not basically alter the political and religious structures built under its aegis, so were its land policies largely retained with the advent of royal control. Thus the rights of individual planters and private corporations to lands allocated under the Company's "Great Charter of 1618" were reaffirmed. The King was even prepared to honor the rights of former stockholders in the Company to take up 100 acres of land for each share that they had failed to convert in the past, but few took advantage of his offer. The land owned by the Company, however, was taken over by the Crown, and cultivation of this "public estate" no longer played the role in the economy of the colony that it had in the days of Company control. Instead the economy and land of the colony were increasingly placed in the hands of the individual planters; even the large land grants given to the private corporations were in time to dissolve into small separate holdings.

Other land policies that the King retained also played a part in bringing this about. For example, the Crown continued the practice of awarding land patents for meritorious service to "ministers, political officials, physicians, sea captains, and various other individuals" (Robinson Jr 1957:31) much as the Company had in the past. Charles II extended this practice to include his servants and others who aided him in the Restoration. Another form of service which the King continued to reward had to do with settling on and fortifying the frontier. Generous offers of land and tax exemptions were made, particularly after the Indian massacres of 1622 and 1644, to those who would man and maintain the forts along the frontier. Those who accepted these offers tended to be military men.

But the policy that "became the principal basis for title to land in the seventeenth century" (Robinson Jr 1957:32) and the single most important influence in populating the colony and in structuring its economy was the granting of land under a headright provision. As first formulated in the company's "Great Charter of 1618" and subsequently reaffirmed by the King, the provision was meant to stimulate immigration to the colony at the same time that it endeavored to maintain some sort of balance between population and land use. Thus anyone who brought settlers to the colony was entitled to a grant of 50 acres for each person, including himself, who stayed three years and a day. In Virginia only those who paid their own way or financed the transportation of others benefited from this headright grant; the immigrant whose fare was financed did not.

According to Wertenbaker, the flow of immigrants was relatively large and continuous during the rest of the seventeenth century under the terms of the headright provision. The rate stayed at a relatively constant 1500 to 2000 per year; occasionally it dropped to 1200 to 1300 during particularly bad tobacco years. As a result, "considerably more than 100,000 persons migrated to the colony in the years that elapsed between the first settlement at Jamestown and the end of the century" (Wertenbaker 1959:36).

As we have already seen, most of the early immigrants were wiped out by disease, famine, and war with the Indians. As a result, the census of 1625 revealed only 1227 survivors, but the combined effects of continuing migration, of declining mortality rates, and of an increasing birth rate enhanced the growth of the population, first at a gradual rate then at a rapidly rising rate. In 1634, for example, the total population in Virginia was approximately 5000; in 1649, 15,000, and in the 1690s, 70,000.

LAND AND THE YEOMAN PLANTER

The average size of the land grants made during the early part of the period following the dissolution of the Company was relatively small. From 1626 to 1632, for example, the average grant for the period ranged between 100 to 300 acres; for the next twenty years the annual average hovered around the 450 mark; after mid-century to the end of the century the average grant grew to approximately 600 to 700 acres. Some large grants were also awarded through these periods; but in only three of the twenty-five years before the midcentury did the largest grant exceed 5000 acres; the largest in most years was closer to 2000 or 3000 acres. From 1650 to 1700, grants of over 5000 acres were made in virtually every year for an approximate total of ninety-four.

A number of these land patents granted under the headright provision were held by such persons as sea captains, merchants, and others who did not intend to work the land themselves. They functioned more or less as "middlemen" who sold part or all of their holdings to others. Thus the average size of the plantation actually under cultivation during this period was smaller than the average land patent. Wertenbaker confirmed this in his comparison of land transfers and land patents.

"It is clear, then, that the size of the average patent in the Seventeenth century is not an indication of the extent of the average plantation.... Over and over again in the records of various land transfers it is stated that the property in question had belonged originally to a more extensive tract, the patent for which was granted under the headright law." (Wertenbaker 1959:49)

In examining still other "records of the time that deal with the distribution of land – deeds, wills, transfers, tax lists, inventories," Wertenbaker drew the overall conclusion that

"the average plantation, especially in the Seventeenth century, so far from vieing with the vast estates in existence in certain parts of America, was but a few hundred acres in extent.... One can find in this no evidence of the fabled barons of colonial Virginia, but only of a well established class of small proprietors." (Wertenbaker 1959:45–6)

"Thus vanishes the fabled picture of Seventeenth century Virginia. In its place we see a colony filled with little farms a few hundred acres in extent, owned and worked by a sturdy class of English farmers. Prior to the slave invasion which marked the close of the Seventeenth century, and the opening of the Eighteenth, the most important factor in the life of the Old Dominion was the white yeomanry." (Wertenbaker 1959:59)

Wertenbaker estimated that 90 percent of all freeholders during this period comprised this "sturdy, independent class of small farmers" (Wertenbaker 1959:54).

The crop they concentrated most of their energies on was tobacco which became "the life and soul of the colony" (Herndon 1957:50). The farmers raised and sold it for a market whose vicissitudes gravely affected their life circumstances. Most however cushioned themselves against starvation by raising foodstuff for their personal consumption – a practice which the Company had such great difficulty in establishing among the early colonists – but they could not cushion themselves against the need for money to pay for goods, equipment, seed, taxes, and the like. Thus the disastrous market slump of 1639 threatened the survival of many, but the relatively good years which characterized much of the first half of the seventeenth century enabled many of the yeoman class to build a small surplus for extending somewhat their holdings, for improving their relatively modest living conditions, and for extending their influence in the vestries and House of Burgesses.

In addition, the tobacco producers of this period were yet to feel the full impact of the British colonial policy then being evolved. The cornerstone of this policy was to be the shipment of all tobacco to England so that then it could be transshipped elsewhere upon payment of a levy to the Crown. During the first half of the century this regulation was not fully enforced.

"Thus Virginia contrary to the wishes of the mother country and in defiance of her regulations, enjoyed for its staple product in the years prior to 1660, a world market. Whether by direct trade or by re-exportation from England a goodly share of the annual crop was consumed in foreign countries, a share which had it been left in England to clog the market, would have reacted disastrously upon all concerned."   (Wertenbaker 1959:70)

LABOR AND THE INDENTURED WHITE SERVANT:
FROM SERVITUDE TO FREEDOM

According to Wertenbaker and other scholars, the relatively small size of the landholdings during the seventeenth century was not due to any serious shortage of land, for much had become available through conquest and purchase from Indians. Instead it was the limited number of hands that were available to work the land that made large holdings economically unfeasible.

This scarcity of labor had plagued the colony from its earliest days. As we have already seen, the Virginia Company's initial attempts to solve the problem involved transportation of planters at Company expense to the colony where they were to work the Company's land for seven years, after which they would share in the division of land. A division of land was subsequently carried out through the provisions of the charter of 1618. The charter also set aside other Company land which was to be worked at half shares by tenants who would be transported at Company expense; after seven years the tenant could stay or go elsewhere "at his own will and pleasure." By 1620 the Company tried still another approach for obtaining labor for the colony. It transported at Company expense "'one hundred servants to be disposed among the old *Planters*, which they greatly desire, and have offered to defray their charges with very great thankes.'" According to Smith, "except for the arrangements concerning the young women, this is the first clear example we have of the characteristic transaction of the [indentured] servant trade: a colonist paying a lump sum to the importer, and thereby acquiring full right and title to the services of the immigrant" (Smith 1947:12–13).

He concluded "it was under the auspices of the Virginia Company that the customs and habits of indentured servitude were established essentially in the forms which became so familiar to later colonial history" (Smith 1947:8). But the Company, as we have already seen, did more; its 1618 charter also established the headright system for all persons who "'during the next seven years after Midsummer Day 1618 shall go into Virginia with intent there to inhabite. If they continue there three years or dye after they are shiped there shall be a grant made of fifty acres for every person upon a first division'" (Robinson Jr 1957:33).

As a result by the time the Company was dissolved both "indentured service" and the "headright system" had become firmly established in Virginia and inextricably linked together in practice. For example, in a study of headright lists from 1623 to 1637, approximately three out of four immigrants on those lists arrived in the colony under terms of an indenture. Wertenbaker's estimate was roughly four out of five for most of the seventeenth century (Wertenbaker 1959).

Under terms of the typical indenture that developed with the demise of the Company, a person voluntarily contracted to bind himself over to a master for a specified period of time ranging from two to eight years, during which time he would "serve the master in such employments as the master might assign.... In return the master undertook to transport the servant to the colony, furnish him with adequate food, drink, clothing, and shelter during his service, and perhaps give him a specified reward when his term [of contract] was ended" (Smith 1947:17).

Until 1640 these relationships were primarily regulated by customary procedures and practices that had evolved from the experience of the Company with its planters. Reflecting the relatively benign normative atmosphere created by the Sandys administration and the General Assembly of 1619, the rights and immunities of the person of the indentured servant were almost indistinguishable from those of the person of the freeman early in this period.

"In the early period, like a freeman, he was liable to military service in behalf of the state. He enjoyed rights of trade, except with the Indians, and could acquire property. His testimony was always received in court, unless he was a convict, and he was a valid witness to contracts. His religious instruction was provided for in the same manner as that of freemen. The courts carefully guarded his contract and effected speedy redress of his grievances. He might sue and be sued, and had the right of appeal to the supreme judiciary of the colony."

(Ballagh 1895:44)

After 1640 statutory law began to replace custom as the regulatory system for indenture, and the scales began to tip in favor of the master. Thus, corporal punishment and the adding of time to the length of service of the servant became standard operating procedure for dealing with the recalcitrant or runaway servant, whereas they had been used only occasionally prior to 1640. Despite the corrosion of some of their rights, the servants nevertheless retained other basic ones, a number of which were extended beyond those of the early period. By 1705, for example, a mantle of legal protection enveloped the status of white indentured servants. Their rights and immunities were spelled out in perhaps even greater detail than before. Their masters were obliged to provide them with "wholesome and competent diet, clothing, and lodging, by the discretion of the county court; and [the master] shall not, at any time, whip a christian white servant naked, without an order from a justice of the peace" (Hening III 1823:448).

Servants could seek redress in the courts "without the formal process of an action" against any failure of the master to live up to the terms of the labor contract. Further, only the court could approve any extension of the original term of indenture: "no master or owner of any servant shall during the time of such servant's servitude, make any bargain with his or her said servant for further service, or other matter or thing relating to liberty, or personal profit, unless the same be made in the presence, and with the approbation, of the court of that county where the master or owner resides" (Hening III 1823:450). The servants were also to retain possession of their own personal property and were to be cared for by their masters if they "fall sick or lame during the time of service."

At the conclusion of his term of indenture, the freedom dues that the indentured servant was to receive became more clearly spelled out and fixed.

> "The servant's claim to freedom dues recognized by the custom of the country and enforced by the courts was at first only a general one and not specific, the amount granted varying according to the will of the master or of the court in which it was sued for, unless it had been specified in the contract. A clause was inserted in the act of 1705 confirming this right and making it thereafter certain in amount. Every male servant was to receive upon his freedom 'ten bushels of indian corn, (sic) thirty shillings in money or the value thereof in goods, and one well fixed musket ... fuzee of the value of twenty shillings at least;' a woman servant, fifteen bushels of indian corn and forty shillings in money or value."
>
> (Hening III 1823:62)

Once the indentured servant completed his term of service, the way was open for him to join the other freemen as part of the colonist society. Though his freedom dues in Virginia did not include any grant of land, whether as part of the headright or any other provision, most expected to obtain a tract of land. The General Court of Virginia encouraged them in this expectation, for in an order issued in 1627 it stated:

> "'The Court, taking into consideration that the next ensueing year there will be many tenants and servants freed unto whom after their freedom there will be no land due, whereby they may without some order taken to the contrary settle and seat themselves ... have ordered that the Governor and Council may give unto the said servants and tenants leases for terms of years such quantities of land as shall be needful.'"
>
> (Wertenbaker 1959:62)

Thus the atmosphere in the colonist society was favorable to the acquisition of land by the freedmen and in time most acquired some. As a result, by 1635 graduates of the indenture system comprised 30 to 40 percent of all landowners, and this figure remained stable through 1660. Another result of the constant flow of these graduates into the freedman society of Virginia was to reduce over time the relative importance of indentured servants in the colony. Thus despite the constancy of the stream of servants entering Virginia in the seventeenth century, they dropped from being 40 percent of the population in 1625 to approximately 15 percent in 1670. By 1708 their percentage was almost invisible as the flow of indentured servants to Virginia had virtually ceased.

Not only did a significant number of freedmen become freeholders by 1660, but some even rose to positions of political importance and power during this period. In the General Assembly of 1629, 7 of the 44 Burgesses had been indentured as recently as 1624: "Whether there were other members who came over under terms of indenture but secured their freedom before 1624, we have no means of determining" (Wertenbaker 1959:74). By 1652 the figure rose to approximately one out of four Burgesses, but later in the century the figure dropped markedly as the colonist society of Virginia became increasingly transformed.

Thus until 1660 many of the freedmen were absorbed into the colonist society of the yeoman planter. They faced no insurmountable barriers and shared with the freemen a chance to get a stake in the land and even to rise to positions of influence, in the political structure as Burgess and in the religious structure as vestryman. Thus in many respects, according to Wertenbaker,

"in the first half century of its existence Virginia was the land of opportunity. The poor man who came to her shores, whether under terms of indenture or as a freeman, found it quite possible to establish himself as a person of some property and consideration. We may imagine the case of the servant who had completed his term and secured his freedom at any time during the third decade of the Seventeenth century. As we have seen, it was an easy matter for him to secure a small patch of land and the tools with which to cultivate it. By his unassisted efforts, if he applied himself steadily to the task, he could produce a good crop of tobacco, consisting perhaps of some 400 pounds. This he could sell to the merchants for from two shillings to six pence a pound, or a total of from £10 to £40.... When we take into consideration the fact that the planter produced his own food, and that out of the proceeds of his tobacco crop he paid only his taxes and his bills to the English importers, it is evident that he had a goodly margin of profit to lay aside as working capital." (Wertenbaker 1959:71)

Virginia as a colonialist society: black slavery and the white aristocratic elite

Even as the colonist society was being constructed, the seeds for the development of a racially segmented colonialist society were also being sown. For in 1619 – the

landmark year for the emergence of the political system of the colonist society –
the first group of blacks, twenty in all, were set ashore in Jamestown by a Dutch
sea captain to be sold to the labor-hungry planters. Their numbers grew only
gradually during the next several decades. By mid-century they could still be
counted in the hundreds. In 1670 they reached an estimated 2000 in contrast to
6000 white indentured servants.

During much of this period, their legal status was ambiguous and ill-defined and
the character of their treatment unclear. Some scholars, including Ballagh (1895)
and Franklin (1952), have maintained that most blacks were treated in the manner
of the white indentured servants; both had to serve a finite period of servitude.
Other scholars such as Bruce (1910) have insisted that from the beginning the
servitude of most blacks was in perpetuity. Despite this ambiguity and lack of
clarity, judical decisions during this period increasingly set double standards in the
treatment of the races and pointed to a growing debasement of the black. For
example, in a case involving runaways in 1640 the court merely imposed a sentence
of several more years of indenture on the white servants involved, but a lifetime of
slavery on the one black. In another case decided the same year a black woman
servant was to be whipped and the white man merely to do public penance for
having "begotten [her] with child." A further case also decided in 1640 revealed
that despite the growing corrosion of the rights of the black, he retained some of
the rights of the white. Thus a black servant successfully petitioned the court that
he be granted the right to purchase the freedom of his young child so that the
child "'should be made a christian and be brought up in the fear of God and
in the knowledge of religion taught and exercised by the church of England'"
(Higginbotham Jr 1978:25).

Not until 1659, however, was there any statutory allusion to the black as slave.
This appeared in a law which reduced duties on merchants who "shall import any
Negro slaves" to the colony. The following year statutory recognition was
obliquely given to bondage in perpetuity for a black slave. It was enacted "'that in
case any English servant shall run away in company with any Negroes who are
incapable of making satisfaction by addition of time that the English so running
away shall serve for the time of the Negroes' absence as they are to do for their
own by a former act'" (Higginbotham Jr 1978:34). The next year white
"Christian" servants who ran away with any black slave were made liable for the
loss of the slave if the latter managed to escape capture or died during the escape
attempt.

Having given statutory legitimacy to slavery, the legislature then proceeded in
the next decade or so to clarify certain ambiguities in the status of the black slave.
For example, in 1667 the legislature sought to dispel any lingering doubts about
the legal standing of a baptized black slave. (In 1624 a Virginia court had actually

ruled that a black "was qualified as a free man and Christian to give testimony, because he had been 'Christened in England 12 years since'" (Higginbotham Jr 1978:21).) It stipulated "that *baptism does not alter the condition of the person as to his bondage of freedom; masters freed from this doubt may more carefully propagate Christianity by permitting slaves to be admitted to that sacrament*" (Higginbotham Jr 1978:36–7).

Two years later the legislature took note in the preamble to a law that the practice of adding years of service to "refractory" white indentured servants was not an effective punishment for refractory black slaves. Accordingly, it recognized the need for "violent meanes" to keep them in line, and so it released the white slave owners from any criminal liability for "the casual killings of slaves" that might result from such punishment "since it cannot be presumed that propensed malice (which alone makes murther Felony) should induce any man to destroy his own estate" (Higginbotham Jr 1978:36).

By 1671 considerable sentiment had developed in the colony to place the black slaves completely outside the pale of human society and to treat them as "sheep, horses, and cattle" in the transmission of wealth from generation to generation of white owners. The legislature endorsed this sentiment, in principle, in a law it enacted "for preservation, improvement, or advancement of the estate and interest of such orphants" (Hening II 1823:288), but it left to the courts to determine in a particular case the precise kind of property the black slave should be designated as: real or personal.

Thirty-four years later, in 1705, the legislature sought to end all ambiguities about the property status of black slaves. It stipulated that henceforth they "shall be held, taken, and adjudged, to be real estate (and not chattels;) and shall descend unto the heirs and widows of persons departing this life, according to the manner and custom of land of inheritance, held in fee simple." Unsold slaves, however, "in the possession of such merchant, or factor, or of their executors, administrators, or assigns, shall, to all intents and purposes, be taken, held, and adjudged, to be personal estate, in the same condition they should have been in, if this act had never been made" (Hening III 1823:333). (Twenty-two years later in 1727 the legislature extended the concept of slaves as chattel property to other acts of exchange.)

Thus by the first decade of the eighteenth century, the black slave had been completely dehumanized and transmuted into a piece of property. As such he was completely under the domination of the white master. Fearful though that the black slave would not submit readily to this subjugation, the Virginia legislature elaborated in 1705, as it had begun to earlier, a network of coercive controls that would forcibly keep the slave in a state of submission. Thus it not only reaffirmed the waiving of criminal liability for any master who inadvertently killed a slave in the act of punishing him; it also authorized the slaying of runaway slaves under certain conditions; however, "for every slave killed, in pursuance of this act, or put to death by law, the master or owner of such slave shall be paid by the public" (Hening III 1823:461).

In addition, the legislature forbade any slave from going "armed with gun, sword, club, staff, or other weapon" or from leaving his plantation "without a certificate of leave in writing, for so doing, from his or her master, mistress, or overseer." Further,

> "all horses, cattle, and hogs, now belonging, or that hereafter shall belong to any slave, or of any slaves mark in this her majesty's colony and dominion, shall be seised and sold by the church-wardens of the parish, wherein such horses, cattle, or hogs shall be, and the profit thereof applied to the use of the poor of the said parish."   (Hening III 1823:459–60)

In short, "by 1705, Virginia had rationalized, codified, judicially affirmed its exclusion of blacks from any basic concept of human rights under the law" (Higginbotham Jr 1978:58). The web of coercive constraint and oppression that had been spun over the half century finally stripped them of any residual rights and dignities they may have clung to from the earlier days of ambiguity.

In the meantime, as we have seen, the very act of 1705 that tightened the vise of restrictive control around the black slave limited the controls around the white indentured servant and spelled out in bold detail the latter's rights and immunities during and after completion of his indenture. What in effect started early in the seventeenth century as a legal distinction measured primarily in quantitative terms of length of service became by the turn of the eighteenth century an unbridgeable gulf that separated two qualitatively different kinds of relationships to the white colonist. For example, servitude for the indentured white servant was but a transitional stage of limited bondage that ended in full access to and membership in the white colonist society. Contrastingly, servitude for the black meant permanent exclusion from the white colonist society and the creation of a colonialist relationship of exploitation and coercion with a white master. So profitable did this colonialist system of enslaved labor become for the white master that it replaced in time the colony's earlier dependence on the more costly and less malleable system of indentured labor. Thus by the middle of the eighteenth century, the flow of indentured white servants to Virginia was reduced to a mere trickle while the stream of black slaves had broadened to a torrent. In 1730 for example, they numbered 30,000 or 26 percent of the total population of Virginia; sixty years before they constituted a mere 5 percent.

FROM A YEOMAN TO AN ARISTOCRATIC WHITE ELITE

After 1660, the fortunes of the yeoman class of planters began to decline significantly. The turning point, according to Wertenbaker (1959), was King Charles II's determination to enforce rigorously the Navigation Acts. Accordingly all tobacco and other products from the British colonies were to be shipped to England in English vessels manned primarily by Englishmen. There the products would be subject to a levy and consumed at home or transshipped elsewhere. No longer would tobacco producers be able to sell their products directly on foreign markets.

The result was a ruinous glut on the tobacco market in England and a sharp decline in prices. This produced great hardship for the small yeoman planter and for the indentured servant who had completed his term of service. Wertenbaker estimated that only 5 or 6 percent of the indentured servants of this period became independent planters: "the Navigation Acts brought to a dead halt the process of molding freedmen and other poor settlers into a prosperous yeomanry" (Wertenbaker 1959:99).

Even though prosperity returned to the tobacco markets by the early 1680s, the small planters failed to share in it, for the price remained too low to afford them a sufficient margin of profit to accumulate a working capital.

> "He [the planter] could not, as he had done a half century earlier, lay aside enough to purchase a farm, stock it with cattle, hogs and poultry, perhaps even secure a servant or two. Now, although no longer reduced to misery and rags as in the years from 1660 to 1682, he could consider himself fortunate if his labor sufficed to provide wholesome food and warm clothing."
>
> (Wertenbaker 1959:123)

In short, he could not afford to expand his production beyond what he could produce himself, otherwise he faced the prospect of ruinous debts; even adding an indentured servant might prove too costly for him to bear, and few could afford the initial capital outlay for a black slave whose forced labor might eventually reduce his costs. Thus only the large planter with a work force of slaves could produce a large enough volume of tobacco at reduced costs to make a substantial profit.

So it was that the economics of the tobacco market by the turn of the eighteenth century increasingly favored the large planter with a work force of slaves. Small planters unable to compete were forced to sell their land; indentured servants could not afford to buy land at the completion of their service. As a result, both began to leave Virginia for the unchartered lands of the west; by the turn of the century the exodus reached flood proportions.

Not all of the yeoman planters left however; a number remained. Some sought salvation through cultivating higher priced tobacco; others joined the ranks of slave owners with the purchase of one or two slaves. However by the first decade or so of the eighteenth century, the yeoman planter who may have employed several indentured white servants was replaced by the large slave-owning plantation owner as the elite of the colonist society of Virginia. Some "had already laid the foundations of their fortunes in vast land grants acquired before 1700," and by mid-century they surfaced as the mainstay of Virginia's aristocratic elite. "The 'best' families tended to intermarry and by mid-century probably not more than a hundred families controlled the wealth and government of the colony" (Boorstin 1958:103).

Within a short period of time, then, the influence of this elite radiated into the major institutional arenas of the colonist society. Bolstered by the restrictive suffrage laws of the 1670s they did not so much alter the basic institutional structure of the white colonist society as to make it their own. As we have seen, they approached their political responsibilities, even more than did the yeoman elite, in the manner of a religious calling and their religious responsibilities in the manner of a political calling. In the words of Boorstin, "never did a governing class take its political duties more seriously: power carried with it the duty to govern" (Boorstin 1958:111). "'Self-government' in eighteenth century Virginia – in religious no less than in civil matters – was, of course, self-government by the ruling planters on behalf of their servants and neighbors. The parish was their elementary school in the political arts" (Boorstin 1958:129).

Even as members of the aristocratic elite espoused in the political arena of the colonist society the ideological virtues of republicanism, self-government, liberty, and freedom in Virginia's relations with England, they stood as white masters atop a racially segmented colonialist structure they had built on the backs of the enslaved black. Unlike their counterparts in the West Indies who were an absentee "sojourner" elite, they exercised active control over the plural structure they had built, masterminded the code of law which dehumanized the black slave, and transmuted him into a piece of property, and at the same time they represented the people of the colonist society with whom they identified.

By mid-eighteenth century this aristocratic elite presided over a dual societal structure, one which they inherited from the yeoman elite, the colonist, and the other which they had created, the colonialist plural. They saw no logical contradiction between the two, for in the colonist society they were dealing with the "People;" in the colonialist, with "Things." In Chapter 6 we shall examine further the role of the planter elite after the white colonist society of Virginia and of the other twelve colonies became the United States of America.

4

DUALITY AND THE TRANSFORMATION
OF THE THIRTEEN COLONIES
INTO A FEDERATED NATION-STATE

Introduction

Within 125 years of the founding of Jamestown, the last of the other twelve colonies was established. All thirteen reflected aspects of their British heritage, but each responded to the process of colonization in its own distinctive manner and constructed its own version of a white colonist society from this heritage. All thirteen colonies also legalized slavery, but each experienced the process of colonialization differently and created its own variant of a colonial plural society from the foundation of the enslaved black. Regional patterns also evolved. As a result, the dual societal structures that developed in the later southern colonies resembled in part those already fashioned in Virginia while those that evolved in New England and the Middle Atlantic took on a different character and quality.

Initially each of the thirteen white colonist societies functioned as separate entities. Their primary contact was with England; their relations with other colonies, either non-existent or competitive. Slowly, however, cooperative ties between the colonies began to develop and, with increasing opposition to British policy after mid-eighteenth century, they rapidly evolved an elaborate network of relations, while holding fiercely onto their distinctive identities. Even with the successful conclusion of the Revolution, the colonies still sought to maintain as much of their autonomy as possible under the Articles of Confederation. But with the enactment of the Constitution, the thirteen white colonist societies were changed into a federated nation-state in which the white colonist became the people and citizenry of the new nation. During this period the colonial plural societies built on the labor of the enslaved black flourished and became increasingly stable and entrenched in the South. In the North these structures retained their racial and legal character, though the labor of the enslaved black was not central to their economies. All of these plural structures, however, survived the transformation of the thirteen colonies into a nation-state and were given the stamp of legitimacy by the supreme law of the New Nation, the Constitution. Several years later the first Congress with many of the Founding Fathers in attendance made manifest its intention of keeping the people of the United States racially pure by enacting naturalization legislation for whites only. And approximately seventy years after that Chief Justice Taney made explicit in his opinion on the Dred Scott case the Founding Fathers' fundamental belief in the black, enslaved and free, as a race apart in need of forceful control by the whites. He also made manifest their intention of confining membership in the People's Domain of the New Nation to the white race only.

In this manner the duality built into the institutional fabric of the thirteen colonies from virtually their beginnings became part of the new nation and was sanctified by the Constitution and early statutes. In this chapter we shall examine the transformation of the colonies into a nation-state and the Manichean dualism that was carried over from the past and imprinted on the new nation.

British influence in colonist America

As mother country, Britain played an important role in the affairs of colonist America. Its influence was felt in a variety of ways, physically through its chosen agents and symbolically through its past and present effects on the lifestyle of the colonists. As James Truslow Adams says:

> "With England herself the relations of the colonists were of the closest sort and embraced every field of political, economic and social life, although the closeness of these relations varied to some extent in the different colonies. She was not merely the source of protection, the seat of power, the center of empire, but was still 'home' in the speech of all Americans of English descent."
>
> (Adams 1927:24)

Despite this pervasive influence, time and distance made the government of England seem a remote presence; this allowed the colonists to do things fairly much their own way on a day-to-day basis. Thus from the earliest days most colonies carved out broad areas of self-governance; they developed local legislative bodies which zealously guarded their self-defined autonomy. On a number of occasions this pitted them against the royal governor who was appointed by the Crown and even against the English government itself. There was a continuing struggle over who had the right to rule and over what jurisdiction this right extended. As a result the question of legitimacy became an increasingly central issue between the colonies and England as the eighteenth century moved closer to the revolutionary period.

The problematic relation that developed between the colonies and England over the right to rule was but part of a broader historical ambiguity that has puzzled scholars for many years. What precisely was the influence of England on the colonist institutions and way of life? Answers have varied from one extreme to another. Some "Imperial scholars" have insisted that colonist life in America was primarily a "reflection" of British life. Other scholars such as Turner (1920) lean heavily on an environmental interpretation: they believe that colonists constructed a set of institutions uniquely their own because of the need to adapt to new environmental conditions; and at most these institutions had only a vestigial connection with those of England.

Somewhere in between fall such historians as Boorstin (1958). He believes that Britain provided the models for the institutional life of the colonies but that these models were drastically transformed in their contact with the realities of the colonial experience. There, they took on a pragmatic and practical bent:

"America began as a sobering experience. The colonies were a disproving ground for utopias. In the following chapters we will illustrate how dreams made in Europe – the dreams of the zionist, the perfectionist, the philanthropist and the transplanter – were dissipated or transformed by the American reality. A new civilization was being born less out of plans and purposes than out of the unsettlement which the New World brought to the ways of the Old."

(Boorstin 1958:1)

Boorstin contends that, in Massachusetts, American Puritanism had "none of the speculative vigor of English Puritanism" nor was it concerned with the finer points of theology or of ideas generally. Instead it was much more involved in the practical application of religion "to everyday life and especially to society" and in building a strong and viable community. Thus the American Puritans "were concerned less with the ends of society than with its organization and less with making the community good than with making it effective, with insuring the integrity and self-restraint of its leaders, and with preventing its government from being oppressive" (Boorstin 1958:29–30).

In Georgia, General Oglethorpe had the dream of building a welfare society according to an elaborately detailed blueprint of philanthropy and charity. This dream, though, became overly authoritarian and dogmatic in its execution and finally foundered on the practical exigencies of life in the colonies and on the individualized needs of the colonist.

In Virginia, Boorstin continues, the colonist came close to realizing his dream of becoming a new kind of English country gentleman. In the process he became a planter capitalist and built an aristocratic way of life with its dedication to public service on the backs of enslaved labor.

Kammen takes issue with Boorstin's thesis. He contends:

"His [Boorstin's] approach, however intriguing, depends upon certain assumptions about early modern Europe, about the role and success of ideas there, about the nature (or absence) of ideas in America, and about the peculiar powers of New World environments to defeat the best laid plans of mortal men."

(Kammen 1972:16)

Kammen argues against these assumptions in some detail and concludes that Boorstin has overstated the influence of the new environment in transforming the colonists' English ways and understated the continuing influence of England on them.

"In many significant ways the colonies became more rather than less English in the century after 1660. In certain cases this occurred consciously, as part of an imitative process. In other spheres it occurred involuntarily, either because the colonies yielded to pressures from Parliament and the Privy Council, or because both England and America were subjected to common forces of change. Perhaps historians have been too eager to discern patterns and processes in colonial affairs that were uniquely American. If provincial legislatures were dominated by the politics of land distribution, Stuart and Georgian parliaments were deeply concerned with pressures of land enclosure. If interest groups and interest politics were unstable in the colonies, they were scarcely less so in England."

(Kammen 1972:29)

British America as a dual society

While the extent and degree of British influence on colonial life and institutions is still being actively debated, one fact remains unchallenged. The early colonists came primarily from England. They comprised the majority of inhabitants in all thirteen colonies except Pennsylvania where they constituted a plurality, not a majority, of the population.

Even more important, the English colonists monopolized virtually all positions of power and privilege in the colonies. As a result, they in fact built and shaped the societies that emerged in the colonies. Whatever they did was obviously influenced by environmental factors, by their British heritage, and by the active intervention of Britain itself, but in the final analysis they made the choices and constructed the societies.

The results were quite varied. Most of the thirteen colonies showed marked differences in origins, history, style, and structure. They also developed their own governmental institutions and so for all intents and purposes each became a distinctive society. We have already suggested some of the ways that Massachusetts, Virginia, and Georgia differed. The list could easily be expanded. Connecticut and Rhode Island were largely settled by those who were dissatisfied with or expelled from Puritan Massachusetts. New York and New Jersey were first settled by the Dutch and, even after the English took them over as crown colonies, the Dutch influence remained, particularly in the New York City area. Pennsylvania was largely influenced by the Quakers who found it difficult to reconcile their religious principles with the exercise of effective political control. Lord Baltimore tried to make Maryland into a haven for the persecuted Catholic and passed the first Toleration Act in 1649. The proprietors of the Carolinas tried to impose a plan of government patterned after the ideas of John Locke, only to have it fail within short order.

So, in small and large ways the colonies developed their distinctive styles. And in the early days they developed in relative isolation, one from the other: the major tie was with England and not with other colonies. During the colonial period, therefore, America consisted of not one society, but of a plurality of societies. Each was jealous of its own integrity and autonomy, and not infrequently during the colonial period found itself in open conflict with neighboring colonies over boundaries, trade, and other issues over which neighboring countries have struggled throughout much of European history. In effect, America was very much a "Balkanized" country during the colonial period.

Diversity and heterogeneity characterized most colonies internally as well. By 1780 they had substantial minorities of inhabitants who came from countries other than from England proper. Even in Massachusetts – the most ethnically homogeneous colony – one out of five residents by 1780 was not an Englishman. Most of these were Scots and Scotch Irish, each of whom comprised about 10 percent of the population. At the other extreme, Pennsylvania – one of the most ethnically heterogeneous of the colonies – had almost as many Germans as Englishmen (32 percent and 35 percent respectively). In addition, almost one out of five of its population was either a Scot or Scotch Irish, each group comprising about 10 percent of the population.

Falling between the two in ethnic heterogeneity were the other colonies, some of which attracted virtually the same minorities as the above. For example, the Scotch-Irish comprised about 10 percent of the population in the Carolinas and Georgia. In addition to Pennsylvania, the Germans were also attracted to New York, New Jersey, and Maryland; in each colony they comprised about 8 percent of the population. The Dutch favored New York and New Jersey where they became 15 percent of the population; by 1780 the French had become about 10 percent of the population in Delaware, but a number of them were also distributed through the Middle Atlantic colonies.

Most colonies were even more fragmented in the religion of their inhabitants than in their national origins. For example German immigrants to Pennsylvania and elsewhere were not merely Lutherans or members of the German Reformed Church, but also included substantial numbers of Moravians, Mennonites, and other pietistic sects. The English were likewise divided into a number of denominations: the congregationalists, Anglicans, Quakers, Methodists, and so on. The other nationalities were relatively homogeneous in their religious preferences: the Scotch and Scotch-Irish being predominantly Presbyterian, the Dutch being Dutch Reformed. Despite these marked variations, the fact remained that most were within the confines of the Protestant religion. Very few colonists were Catholics or Jews; even by 1780, only about 1 percent of the population or about 25,000 were the former, and 5000 the latter.

The racial composition of the colonies also varied significantly. In 1780 the New England colonies were almost exclusively white; blacks comprised less than 1 percent of the population in Massachusetts and Connecticut and approximately 5 percent in Rhode Island. The proportion was higher in the Middle Atlantic colonies. While blacks comprised just over 2 percent of the population in Pennsylvania, in New York, New Jersey, and Delaware they were from 8 to 10 percent of the population. In the South, however, blacks had already become a substantial proportion of the population. They were about one-third of the population in Maryland, North Carolina, and Georgia; about two-fifths in Virginia; and over half in South Carolina.

Still another major source of difference within various colonies were those of region. Perhaps the most profound of these regional differences was that between frontier and the more civilized tidewater coastal areas. The population in each area faced strikingly different life circumstances and accordingly developed contrasting lifestyles and political and economic interests.

What accentuated the effect of these differences in the various colonies was the fact that they clustered together in the same people. Thus the Scotch-Irish was also Presbyterian and likely to be a frontiersman. The Englishman, however, was never a Presbyterian; instead he was an Anglican, Congregationalist, or Quaker. Although he was frequently on the frontier, he was also even more likely to live in the coastal region. On the other hand the German was never a Presbyterian or Anglican but instead was a Lutheran, Moravian, or from some other sect. He tended to live with others of his kind in the farming regions between the frontier and the coastal region.

Thus one kind of difference reinforced another so that many people differed from each other on all three counts of nationality, religion, and region. This clustering of difference magnified the gap between the various population groups within various colonies. So impressed was Kammen by this internal segmentation of the various colonies that he has applied to them the concept of plural society (Kammen 1972).

However, Kammen considered the segmentation as quite different from that which characterized other plural societies, such as those of the Caribbean about which Smith wrote (Smith 1965). In colonist America relations between segments were not stabilized; each was isolated from the other and arranged in some hierarchical order. The segments were engaged in a competitive struggle for position and power and this struggle created a relatively fluid situation in the various colonies. Thus in Pennsylvania the Scotch-Irish frontiersmen fought with the Quakers who were in power particularly over the issue of defense of the frontier. A similar conflict arose between these frontiersmen and the tidewater English in the Carolinas. Erikson shows that even in Massachusetts, which seemed to have the greatest stability, Puritans were constantly contending with religious or other outsiders in order to maintain the sanctity of their community (Erikson 1966).

In effect, Kammen labels colonial America as being an unstable plural society, in contrast to the stable plural societies of the Furnivall and Smith type (Furnivall 1956; Smith 1965). According to Kammen, a major source of instability was the rampant sectarianism of colonial America. He is convinced that sectarianism preceded denominationalism in American history and that "sects and factions tend to be unstable and impermanent, they lack the longevity, institutional apparatus, and coalition qualities of denominations and parties. Sects fluctuate, fragment and feud among themselves" (Kammen 1972:65). The mobility of the colonial population and the increasing migration into the colonies also contributed to the fluidity of the colonial societies.

In the final analysis, however, Kammen is talking about white colonist America. It had the fluidity and instability to which he refers, but it also had something else, which raises questions about his labeling it a plural society. It had, to use Kammen's words, "a fairly complex governmental apparatus" (Kammen 1972:58) in which the white colonist shared certain basic rights and immunities. In effect, the white colonist, in the early days of most colonies, participated as freeman or freedman in the structure of governance, particularly in the election of legislative assemblies, and developed deeply embedded beliefs about the right of self-governance; later suffrage was restricted to freeholders in various colonies but these still comprised a sizable proportion of the population.

Thus, despite the "distinct cleavages amongst diverse population groups" (Kammen 1972:60) which he pointedly states kept colonist America in a state of fluidity, instability, and heterogeneity, Kammen nevertheless concedes that the colonists comprised a "polity" who shared a political framework in which they claimed the right as a people to have their collective voices heard in the governance of the colony. Occasionally violence – as in the case of Bacon's Rebellion – sorely tested this framework, but did not destroy it.

With the white colonists comprising a polity and a people in each of the thirteen colonies, it is evident that two of the defining features of a plural society as delineated by the various theorists discussed in Chapter 2 were missing. The two features were the presence of coercive unilateral and arbitrary control by the culturally or racially dominant segment and the absence of any integrative institutional or consensual value framework. Kammen, though he nods briefly in the direction of these theorists, pays scant attention to their definitions and caveats. He dismisses them with the statement that to engage in what he calls "conceptual archeology of the social sciences" would not be very instructive, "particularly since the digging thus far has thrown up more rubble than it has revealed eternal foundations" (Kammen 1972:59). Accordingly he concludes, "I am most comfortable with an ordinary-language definition in which 'plural society' connotes a polity containing distinct cleavages amongst diverse population groups" (Kammen 1972:60).

In accepting this definition Kammen comes close to paraphrasing the definition of pluralism in Webster's *Third New International Dictionary*: "a state or condition of society in which members of diverse ethnic, racial, religious or social groups maintain an autonomous participation in the development of their traditional culture or special interest *within the confines of a common civilization* [author's italics]." Both definitions, in effect, focus on diversity in the presence of and not in the absence of a unifying framework. And as such they resemble more closely the concept of a pluralistic society as it has evolved in the literature on ethnicity in America than that of a plural society as it has evolved in the literature on colonialism and race. We conclude that what Kammen has described for us is a white colonist America that was an "unstable pluralistic society" and not an "unstable plural society." But when we turn to racially segmented colonial America, we find that we have no quarrel with Kammen's use of the word unstable, at least for the early years.

In Virginia, for example, we have already seen that only until the sixth decade of the seventeenth century was there any ambiguity over the legal status of the black; after that there was none, as his servitude in perpetuity was given both legislative and judicial sanction. By the end of the seventeenth century the importation of black slaves had increased markedly, so that by 1730 they comprised more than one-fourth of Virginia's population. In addition, blacks did not passively accept their enslavement:

"[they] gave evidence of being restive under their yoke and began conspiring to rebel against their masters. In the following decades there was open discontent among the slaves in several sections of the colony. In 1687 a plot was uncovered in the Northern Neck in which the slaves, during a mass funeral, had planned to kill all the whites in the vicinity in a desperate bid for freedom. By 1694 lawlessness among the slaves had become so widespread that Governor Andros complained that there was insufficient enforcement of the code."

(Franklin 1952:73)

The code to which Governor Andros referred had become increasingly elaborated in detail and design, increasingly exacting in enforcement, and increasingly harsh and severe in punishment, as we saw in Chapter 3. Thus, by the end of the colonial period relations between black slave and white master in Virginia had become relatively stabilized, but only because a massive apparatus of coercion and repression had been perfected by the whites to keep the slave in subjection. Except for sporadic outbursts such as the Nat Turner rebellion, the slaves had little recourse but to submit.

Much the same pattern repeated itself in the other southern colonies: "Just as everywhere else the increase in the number of Negroes in Maryland and their proclivity to lawlessness called forth the enactment of stringent laws designed to keep order among the blacks" (Franklin 1952:75).

Perhaps the most repressive system was developed in South Carolina where blacks became a majority of the population by the end of the colonial period. Only Georgia prevented the entry of slaves at first because its proprietors were "determined to keep slavery out of the colony" (Franklin 1952:82). By 1750, however, they were no longer able to resist the pressure and petitions of white settlers. Accordingly they repealed the prohibition against slaves. Their efforts to provide some legal protection for the slaves collapsed as a stringent slave code patterned after that of South Carolina was adopted in 1755.

By the end of the colonial period, then, the whites in the southern colonies had consolidated their control over the black slaves through a system of legal repression, constraint, and physical coercion. The gulf between white and black had become insurmountable and a system of stable racial segmentation had been created that resembled the segmentation to be found in the more orthodox plural societies that Furnivall (1956) had described in Southeast Asia, that Smith (1965) had described in the Caribbean, and along with Kuper (1969) in Africa. In effect, a relatively stable colonialist plural society had developed in the southern colonies that separated white from black.

On a smaller scale a relatively similar pattern developed in the middle colonies of New York and New Jersey. Although blacks did not quite reach 10 percent of the population in either colony by the end of the colonial period, both developed black codes. However, New York's response was much more repressive than was New Jersey's in view of the greater restlessness and violent reaction of the blacks against slavery there. In Pennsylvania slavery was a milder institution, primarily because of the work of the Quakers. In its early days while under the authority of Pennsylvania, Delaware's reaction to slavery was equally mild, but later on it followed the path of the southern colonies.

Perhaps the mildest version of slavery and also the fewest number of blacks were to be found in the New England colonies. Although the New Englander profited greatly from the slave trade, he brought relatively few slaves into his colonies. Even so slave codes emerged near the end of the seventeenth century. They were neither as elaborate nor as harsh as were those in the southern colonies, but they nevertheless reinforced the separate and inferior status of the black.

However, even as a freedman the black in Massachusetts and in other New England colonies was not able to shed this separate and inferior status. As Greene comments, "Strictly speaking, they [the free blacks in New England] were not free for they were proscribed politically, economically and socially" (Greene 1968:298). He then cites a variety of ways in which they were subject to constraints and their rights were proscribed. He could have multiplied his examples many times over. He could have mentioned, for example, the restrictions imposed by the selectmen of Boston in 1723. They had been charged by "the freeholders and Inhabitants of the Town at their Annual meeting in March last" to prepare "Articles for the Better Regulating [of] Indians, Negros and Molattos within this Town" (Record Commissioners of the City of Boston 1883:173). Accordingly, the selectmen forbade the "free Indian Negro or Mulatto" from bearing any kind of arms, from drinking alcoholic beverages during specified days, from receiving goods or wares, or from entertaining any servants or slaves. In addition, "every free Indian Negro or Mollato Shal bind out, all their Children at or before they arrive to the age of four years to Some English master, and upon neglect thereof of the Select men or Overseers of the Poor Shal be Empowered to bind out all Such Children till the age of Twenty one years" (Record Commissioners of the City of Boston 1883:173–74).

Greene also states that the free black was deprived of basic legal and political rights. "Nowhere in New England could free Negroes serve on juries.... Full citizenship was withheld from them, and although taxed as other free persons, they could not vote" (Greene 1968:299–300). He acknowledges that some scholars maintain that the free black could vote in various parts of New England, but he categorically denies that there is any evidence to support that any ever did.

However, when it comes to defining the kind of legal and political status the free black did enjoy in the New England colonies, Greene offers an ambiguous reply.

All he says is that "Legally, the freedmen held an intermediate status somewhat higher than that of the slaves, but palpably lower than that of free white persons" (Greene 1968:299). Had he looked back to the words of Chief Justice Taney in his opinion on the Dred Scott case in 1857, Greene would have found a clearly defined conception of what the Chief Justice presumed to be the legal and political status of the free black.

According to the Chief Justice, blacks whether free or enslaved were never meant to be part of the people in any of the thirteen colonies. They were always meant to be under the control and the domination of the white. This state of affairs, he declared, continued into the making of the Constitution.

> "They [freed or enslaved blacks] were at that time [still] considered as a subordinate and inferior class of beings, who had been subjugated by the dominant race, and whether *emancipated* [author's italics] or not, yet remained subject to their authority, and had no rights or privileges but such as those who held the power and the Government might choose to grant them."
>
> (60 US 1857:404–5)

Taney insisted, in other words, that freedom added little to the political and legal status of the black. He was still not treated as a person, but only as a colonialized subject.

This formulation opens up a challenging avenue of inquiry that we propose to pursue in the future. It suggests that the Virginia model of duality which was built on the backs of the enslaved black was complemented by another model that was forged in Massachusetts and in other New England colonies. This model harnessed the black as freedman to a system of coercive control dominated by the whites, who were simultaneously constructing their colonist society with its People's Domain. Should there be merit to this conjecture, it will also be interesting to determine if the Massachusetts model of duality rather than that of Virginia served as a prototype for the version of duality that characterized the northern states from the abolition of slavery through the enactment of the Reconstruction Amendments.

We therefore contend that the thirteen colonies created two different kinds of pluralized societies, and not one as suggested by Kammen. One kind, a pluralistic society, reflected the instability and fluidity that operated within white colonist America. The other kind, a plural society, reflected the stabilized structure of repression that had come to characterize relations between black and white by the end of the colonial period. There seems to be no doubt that one version was built on the back of the enslaved black. The intriguing question still to be determined is whether or not another version was built on the shoulders of the freed black.

The struggle with England and the growth in intercolonial cooperation

The dramatic transformation of colonist America into a federated nation-state has been examined and reexamined by historians and other scholars. Our purpose in this section is not to detail the already detailed, but merely to highlight certain features of the process as it affected the dual versions of society in the thirteen colonies.

As Adams and others have indicated, each individual colony during the seventeenth and eighteenth century was preoccupied with its relations with England and not with its relations with other colonies (Adams 1927). To the extent possible, each colony went its own way. However, the colonies could not completely avoid having something to do with each other. They were increasingly becoming economically interdependent and on occasion cooperated with each other in the frontier wars against the Indians. They even made several attempts at federation and unity such as the New England Confederation of 1643 to 1684 and the Albany Convention of 1754. More frequently, though, they were at odds with each other over trade, boundaries, and territorial expansion.

Many scholars agree that this state of affairs continued into the early 1760s, when a series of events helped shift the attention of the colonies from that which divided them toward similar interests and problems that they shared. The precipitating cause of this shift was the increasingly stringent policies and actions of England as it sought to reassert its authority over the colonies.

The colonists grumbled over the first series of such measures and sought to circumvent their more onerous provisions. But they did not perceive even these provisions as a basic threat to what until then had been "a compromise between imperial control and colonial self-government; between the principle of authority and the principle of liberty" (Morison 1965:181).

The passage of the Stamp Act in 1765 changed all that. According to Jensen, it "transformed American opposition to British policies" (Jensen 1968:98). It evoked a massive wave of protest and violence in the colonies and brought to the fore a new generation of militant political leaders.

The crisis produced, in effect, "the first spontaneous movement toward colonial union that came from Americans themselves" (Morison 1965:187). At the behest of Massachusetts, nine colonies sent delegates to a congress in New York in October 1765. The meeting adopted a declaration of rights and a statement of grievances and sent petitions as loyal subjects of the Crown to the King and to Parliament. However,

"the declaration and petitions of the Stamp Act Congress were of little practical importance, for they were ignored in England and they did not reflect either

opinion or action on the local level in America. The great significance of the
Stamp Act Congress was that it was the first official meeting of delegates from
colonial legislatures and as such it was a precedent for future action."

(Jensen 1968:124)

Further the crisis also produced a prototypic revolutionary organization in the
form of the Sons of Liberty.

"At first there was no formal organization and the name was used by various
groups whether the purpose was the passage of resolutions or the tearing down
of a house. By the end of 1765, however, the Sons of Liberty were well-
organized action groups in several colonies led by men who were willing to use
force to achieve their ends when defeated in the realm of legal political action."

(Jensen 1968:146)

In sum, the Stamp Act crisis was "a political 'great awakening' which stirred
Americans as nothing before in their history" (Jensen 1968:153).

The act itself was repealed on March 1766, but Parliament did not budge on its
right to tax the colonies and reaffirmed its position in the Declaratory Act of 1766.
In 1767 Parliament passed the Townshend Acts, which forbade the New York
legislature from passing laws until it obeyed the Quartering Act, established an
American board of customs, and imposed taxes in the form of import duties to be
collected in American ports.

The reaction of the colonies was swift and predictable. Massachusetts was joined
by all other colonies but New Hampshire "in making a constitutional protest
against the Townshend Acts" (Jensen 1968:264). At the same time a boycott of
British imports was proposed. The campaign met with limited success and
collapsed within months after Parliament repealed all but the import duty on tea.
A mood of tranquility seemed then to prevail. The propertied classes, in particular,
expressed a nostalgia for the good old days of harmonious relations between the
mother country and the colonies. The respite, however, was relatively shortlived.
Restive under the tea tax and England's favoritism toward the East India
Company, Boston finally acted in 1773, and the celebrated Tea Party took place.
This goaded Britain into passing a series of acts in 1774 which the colonies labeled
the Intolerable Acts. The Boston port, for example, was to be shut until restitution
was made for the destroyed tea; private homes could be commandeered for the
quartering of troops; the Massachusetts charter was to be changed by concentrating power in the hands of the royal governor and his appointed councils at the
expense of the elected officials; and trials of representatives of the royal government could be conducted in England and not merely in Massachusetts.

As the British reply became increasingly repressive, opposition congealed in the colonies; and with the closing of their ranks, the Committees of Correspondence, present in virtually all colonies by 1774, took on an enhanced importance. They served as the primary network of communications between colonies. Virginia used its committee to make inquiries of other colonies about convening a congress. The idea gained support and in September 1774 the First Continental Congress was convened in Philadelphia. The delegates were selected in a variety of ways "by legislature, by colony-wide conventions, by New York City, and by certain New York counties" (Jensen 1968:483). Whatever their mode of selection, they nevertheless defined themselves as representatives of their individual colonies and were very much concerned with protecting its interests. To most delegates their home colony appeared to them as Massachusetts appeared to John Adams when he used the statement "our country" to refer to Massachusetts.

Despite the clash of interests and loyalties between colonies, the delegates "were determined to present a united front to the world, no matter how sharply they divided in their secret sessions." They saw themselves as having "been forced to meet together, some willingly and some reluctantly, by what many viewed as a greater threat from Britain than ever before. As members of Congress, therefore, they were forced to act as Americans, to define American rights, and to devise means for defending themselves" (Jensen 1968:484). In effect, they introduced a new dimension into the colonial scene: that of a national framework for deliberation and policy-making. "In agreeing to meet in a continental congress, Americans, whether they knew it or not, consented to a major political revolution, for they transferred the debate over the theories and policies from the local to what was in effect the 'national' level" (Jensen 1968:486).

However, they were not yet prepared to accept the concept of a national government or parliament which would have united them into a common political framework under the Crown. By a narrow margin the delegates voted to table the Galloway plan, which would have done just that, and never dealt with it again.

Instead, after much debate, Congress voted a "Declaration of Rights stating that Americans were entitled to all English liberties and cited a number of acts of Parliament of the past ten years which violated that principle" (Morison 1965:208). Congress then adopted the Association which was to bring about the non-importation, non-exportation, and non-consumption of British goods through a series of progressive steps and deadlines. To implement the agreement local agencies were to be set up in each colony. Congress dissolved itself in October 1774 and decided to meet again in 1775.

By the time the Second Continental Congress met in May 1775, the battles of Lexington and Concord had taken place. The colonies were in an uproar over these events, and public opinion was overwhelmingly in favor of fighting the

British. This opinion was expressed in committees, legislatures, street meetings, newspapers, correspondence, and the like.

Even as Congress began its deliberations, news reached it of the attack on Fort Ticonderoga and Crown Point by New Englanders. Thus events as well as sentiment were forging an answer to the first major question Congress had to face: should the colonies submit to the British demands or resist them? The answer was resist, but Congress in its early deliberations insisted that the resistance be defensive in nature. The colonies were to protect themselves and their rights against British attack but were not to engage in offensive or overly provocative actions.

Eventual reconciliation with Britain was the manifest policy of Congress. It even made several attempts to make this posture of loyalty known to the King, but they went unheeded. At the same time Congress became involved in the details and problems of a united defense. In June it created the continental army, appointed George Washington its commander-in-chief, and sought ways of financing its operation. In doing so, Congress

"made an irrevocable commitment to a war and to the direction of it ... [and] assumed two essential functions of a sovereign government although it lacked the power to tax and the power to coerce and was dependent upon the will of the individual colonies for its very existence. Congress, in fact, had no real power except the power to persuade Americans to support its policies."

(Jensen 1968:613)

While urging the war against Britain, Congress also became increasingly involved in affairs between the colonies. Intercolonial rivalry had not stopped with the conflict. Ethan Allen's capture of Fort Ticonderoga, for example, had exacerbated relations between New York and New Hampshire and Connecticut. Congress sought to compromise the dispute. In this manner Congress had to mediate and to reconcile contending claims of colonies over borders, trade, and other issues in dispute throughout the entire war period.

In addition, civil order was breaking down in a number of the colonies. The problem became especially acute in Massachusetts when the elected provincial congress severed its relations with the royal governor and his council and sought to reinstitute the abrogated Charter of 1691. This move was opposed by the propertyless, the westerners, and the radicalized leaders, all of whom wanted a basic change in the format of civil government. To relieve the mounting pressure, the provincial congress, comprised primarily of the propertied classes, turned to the Continental Congress for instructions. It contended that the issue was of general concern to all the colonies and that advice was needed from Congress. In

June Congress supported the position of the colonist establishment in Massachusetts and reaffirmed the Charter of 1691. Shortly thereafter Congress went further. It provided a general model for all such transformations, a model which invariably favored the propertied classes.

Congress also took on other functions of a sovereign government. It set up a department of Indian affairs and sought to negotiate treaties with various tribes. It also sent diplomatic agents to several European countries. Much of this structure and many of these functions of sovereignty were set in motion while Congress was still operating under the policy of loyalty to the Crown. However, by the end of 1775 this policy became increasingly tenuous. Events were rapidly catching up with it. The war had been on for almost a year. The Crown and Parliament had rejected the colonial petitions and the pleas of its own members such as Pitt and Burke and had moved toward even more repressive legislation. By the end of December, Parliament had passed the American Prohibitory Act which cut off all trade with the colonies and called upon the royal navy to enforce the act.

Early in 1776 congressional sentiment started to shift perceptibly. The publication of *Common Sense* by Thomas Paine in January 1776 helped set the stage, but news in late February of the Prohibitory Act and of the transport of an army of 25,000 to the colonies was the catalyst. At the least it brought into the open the issue of independence and increased the ranks of its proponents. For the next four months the public debate on independence intensified and popular feelings swelled. In the meantime members of Congress were involved in complex but frequently subtle maneuvers on the issue. Proponents were confronted by the task of transforming popular feelings into legislative action. Part of the task was getting the provincial assemblies of the colonies to instruct their delegates to the Continental Congress to support independence.

Colonist America becomes an independent federated state

By May the tide had turned. Proponents of independence won an indirect skirmish on the issue by a narrow victory on the preamble for a resolution that had been passed earlier on internal governance of colonies. However it was not until June that the issue was fully joined. Richard Henry Lee of Virginia offered three resolutions:

> "That these United Colonies are, and of right ought to be, free and independent States, that they are absolved from all allegiance to the British Crown, and that all political connection between them and the State of Great Britain is, and ought to be, totally dissolved."

"That it is expedient forthwith to take the most effectual measures for forming foreign Alliances."

"That a plan of confederation be prepared and transmitted to the respective Colonies for their consideration and approbation."   (Jensen 1968:688)

A great debate ensued and lasted for several days. Although proponents seemed to be in the majority, they decided to postpone final consideration until July 1, in order to avoid what appeared to be an irretrievable split on the issue. In the interim three committees were appointed: one was to prepare a declaration of independence; the second, to draft articles of confederation; the third, to make plans for foreign alliances.

By July 1 all colonies but New York gave positive instructions to their congressional delegates for independence, but it still took two attempts before Lee's resolutions were adopted on July 2 by the delegates from twelve colonies. (The New York delegates abstained because their instructions did not permit them to seek anything other than reconciliation with England; their personal preferences, though, were for independence.) On July 4 the delegates unanimously endorsed the Declaration of Independence which had been largely prepared by Thomas Jefferson.

Of special significance for our purpose is the basic principle that is enunciated in the Declaration: namely that political authority is rooted in the consent of the people who share certain equalities and certain inalienable rights.

"We hold these truths to be self-evident – that all men are created equal; that they are endowed by their Creator with certain inalienable rights; that among these are life, liberty, and the pursuit of happiness. That, to secure these rights, governments are instituted among men, deriving their just powers from the consent of the governed;"   (Declaration of Independence 1776:4)

The Declaration concluded with the statement:

"We, therefore, the representatives of the United States of America, in general Congress assembled, appealing to the Supreme Judge of the world for the rectitude of our intentions, do, in the name and by the authority of the good people of these colonies, solemnly publish and declare that these united colonies are, and of right ought to be, free and independent States; that they are absolved, from all allegiance to the British crown, and that all political connection between them and the state of Great Britain, is, and ought to be, totally dissolved, and that, as free and independent States, they have full power to levy war, conclude peace, contract alliances, establish commerce, and do all other acts and things which independent States may of right do."

(Declaration of Independence 1776:17–19)

With the kinds of functions and powers being claimed for each of the states, it would appear that the thirteen colonies were not merely being transformed into thirteen states, but into thirteen distinct nation-states. The history of the next eleven years indicates how close to realization this became.

In July 1776 the committee appointed to deal with Lee's third resolution made its report to Congress. Congress was slow in reacting to the recommendations on confederation, and not until November 1777 did Congress adopt the Articles of Confederation in their final form. By 1779, twelve of the thirteen states had ratified the Articles. Maryland held out until March 1781; she insisted that certain territorial issues involving Virginia be settled first before she joined.

As Morison states,

"the adoption of the Articles made no perceptible change in the federal government because it did little more than legalize what the Continental Congress had been doing. That body was now taken over as the Congress of the Confederation; but Americans continued to call it the Continental Congress since its organization remained the same."   (Morison 1965:279)

The basic premise of the Articles was the preservation of the independence and sovereignty of the states. As such the federal government was to have only those powers which the colonies believed should belong to the King and Parliament. Two important powers were, accordingly, withheld: the power to raise money and the power to regulate commerce. In many respects the federal government had

"some of the outward seemings of a government ... [and] ... many of its responsibilities, [yet] ... it was not a government.... It could ask for money but not compel payment; it could enter into treaties but not enforce their stipulations; it could provide for raising of armies but not fill the ranks; it could borrow money but take no proper measures for repayment; it could advise and recommend but not command."   (McLaughlin 1905:50–1)

The net result was that the framework of political unity that the colonies were prepared to accept in order to preserve their own independence and sovereignty soon proved inadequate for the task of governing a federated structure. Even strengthening this framework proved virtually impossible because of the stipulation that amendments to the Articles required unanimous approval of the states.

The weaknesses of the structure became quickly evident as the Congress had literally to scrounge for funds with which to operate and to pay war debts. It resorted to loans from France and Holland, but soon these sources ran dry as repayments could not be made. Even an effort to obtain authority to impose a modest import tax foundered as first one state and then another refused to agree to it; similarly efforts to obtain the proportionate share that a state had agreed to contribute to the federal government produced meager results.

Further, as the pressures of the war subsided, intercolonial rivalry renewed with increased vigor. Even though the Articles provided for federal machinery to adjudicate disputes between states, the struggle over boundaries and trade intensified. States even began to levy high tariffs against each other's goods. Thus the dream of a confederation that imposed few restrictions on the sovereignty of the states proved unworkable; and yet it is unlikely that the states would have been prepared for the next step in the formation of a federal government without having experienced this experiment in confederation first.

While its inherent weaknesses were finally its undoing, the Confederation did have a number of important accomplishments. For example, the Articles spelled out a number of functions for the federal government that were retained in its subsequent revision. What had been missing, though, under the Articles was the power to carry through these functions.

The most significant and lasting contribution of the Confederation was its policy on new territories as formulated in the Northwest Ordinance of 1787; two years later the ordinance was reaffirmed by the First Congress under the Constitution with only the following minor modification: the President was to assume the functions relegated to Congress in the earlier bill. Despite Chief Justice Taney's opinion in 1857 (which we shall examine later), the ordinance served as a general model for future legislation that dealt with governance of any newly acquired land granted territorial status prior to eventual incorporation as a State in the Union. (Puerto Rico was the first newly acquired land to be denied territorial status. The significance of this will be explored in a later chapter.)

The ordinance established two grades of territorial governance. The first was entirely appointed by Congress in the 1787 bill, and by the President with the advice and consent of the Senate in the 1789 revision. At the top was a governor appointed for a three-year term; also appointed were a court consisting of three judges and other civil and military officials.

Once the population of the territory reached 5000 free male adults, the inhabitants were to elect representatives to a general assembly for two-year terms with one representative for every 500 inhabitants. After the total number of such legislators reached twenty-five, the legislature was to determine how many more were to be added to the assembly. Further, a legislative council consisting of five members was to be appointed by the President (in the 1789 version) from a list of nominees prepared by the general assembly. The council and assembly were also to elect jointly a delegate to Congress who would have the right to debate but not to vote on legislation. Together with the governor still an appointee, the two bodies and the delegate constituted the second grade of territorial governance.

The ordinance also stipulated that important articles of what came to be known as the Bill of Rights under the Constitution were to be incorporated in the "compact between the original States and the people and States in the said territory, and forever remain unalterable, unless by common consent" (US Public Statutes at Large I:52). Accordingly, freedom of religion, trial by jury, no cruel or unusual punishment, the right of private property and contract were guaranteed. Slavery and involuntary servitude were banned except for those who had been convicted and were being punished for their crimes. This stipulation on slavery, however, was not binding on subsequent territorial acquisitions; those who allowed slavery were also admitted to the Union. In fact, Congress sought to placate both the South and the North by maintaining through legislative action a balance in the admission of free and slaveholding territories into the Union. As we shall see, the Supreme Court upset this stratagem in its 1857 Dred Scott decision.

The constitutional convention: the restructuring of the federal government through compromise

Criticism of the ineffectual federal government mounted during the 1780s. Several efforts to convene general conventions to amend the Articles proved abortive, but in 1786 an opportunity developed from an improbable set of circumstances. Enthusiastic over the success of a cooperative trade arrangement that it had worked out with Maryland and Pennsylvania, Virginia passed a resolution at the urging of Madison which invited all states to send delegates to a convention at Annapolis "'to consider how far a uniform system in their commercial regulations may be necessary to their common interest and their permanent harmony'" (McLaughlin 1905:181).

Delegates from only five states showed up at the convention in 1786; nothing could be done on the expressed purpose of the conference, but delegates decided to take bold action. They adopted unanimously a report by Alexander Hamilton which described the critical state of affairs under the Confederation and recommended a convention of delegates from all the states "'to take into consideration the situation of the United States, to devise such further provisions as shall appear to them necessary to render the constitution of the federal government adequate to the exigencies of the Union'" (McLaughlin 1905:182).

Congress waited until February 1787 before acting on the recommendation and in its call for a national convention it restricted its purpose to "'revising the articles of confederation'" (McLaughlin 1905:183). Delegates from twelve states assembled in Philadelphia in May 1787; only Rhode Island refused to attend. Strikingly different from the elected members of the Confederation Congress, many of whom were mediocre and uninspiring by 1787, the delegates to the convention were by and large an accomplished and gifted group of relatively young men.

Many were among the cultural and intellectual leaders of the time, and most were committed to an effective national government. Hofstadter describes this linkage of knowledge and power among the early national leaders:

"When the United States began its national existence, the relationship between intellect and power was not a problem. The leaders *were* the intellectuals. Advanced though the nation was in the development of democracy, the control of its affairs still rested largely in a patrician elite: and within this elite men of intellect moved freely and spoke with enviable authority. Since it was an unspecialized and versatile age, the intellectual as expert was a negligible force; but the intellectual as ruling-class gentleman was a leader in every segment of society – at the bar, in the professions, in business, and in political affairs. The Founding Fathers were sages, scientists, men of broad cultivation, many of them apt in classical learning, who used their wide reading in history, politics, and law to solve the exigent problems of their time. No subsequent era in our history has produced so many men of knowledge among its political leaders as the age of John Adams, John Dickinson, Benjamin Franklin, Alexander Hamilton, Thomas Jefferson, James Madison, George Mason, James Wilson and George Wythe."   (Hofstadter 1964:145)

It was evident within three days after the convention opened that the delegates were not going to be content with merely patching up the Articles of Confederation; instead they were intent upon building a new structure from the experience that had been gained from the Confederation. Early in the deliberations, Virginia presented a series of resolutions, largely reflecting the inspirational and intellectual leadership of James Madison, which became "the basis of the convention's work, and formed the foundation of the new Constitution" (McLaughlin 1905:192). One of these resolutions stated "'that a *national* Government ought to be established consisting of a *supreme* Legislative, Executive and Judiciary'" (McLaughlin 1905:196). The dominant institution would be the national legislature which would appoint members of the other two. The legislature was to consist of two houses, membership in which would be apportioned according to population. Representatives to the lower house would be elected; they would in turn elect the members of the upper house.

The Virginia Plan was vigorously debated; a number of its features were passed fairly early, but in the process it had become evident that the major cleavage dividing the convention was not that between delegates loyal to the Articles and those in favor of a "national government" but that between delegates from large and those from small states. The latter became increasingly concerned that they were going to become powerless under the Virginia Plan. Accordingly, in June 1787 they struck back with the New Jersey Plan which called for revising and improving the Articles of Confederation. The plan would retain the one state and one vote feature for Congress, but it would expand the functions of Congress to include taxation and increase its powers of enforcement. The New Jersey Plan was defeated, and the Virginia Plan was brought back to the floor. However, the controversy between the delegates from the large and small states became so intense that at several occasions the proceedings were in danger of breaking down. Finally in mid-July the convention adopted the Connecticut compromise which broke the deadlock. The compromise stipulated that the House of Representatives was to be elected by the citizenry of a state, the numbers to be based on the proportion of the national population in that state. The Senate was to include two members from each state who were to be elected by their legislature. The compromise took much of the steam out of the large and small state controversy, but other issues remained, chief among which were those that divided the North and the South.

Finally on September 17 1787 the work was completed and the Constitution was passed. Only 39 of the 55 delegates approved and signed the document. But to give the matter the appearance of unanimity Gouverneur Morris devised the following as the last sentence: "Done in Convention by the unanimous consent of the States present." The ninth state (New Hampshire) ratified the Constitution in 1788 and it thereby became the supreme law of the land.

The Constitution and the formation of a nation-state

The Constitution established the construct of a federal government that was no longer dependent on the goodwill of the states. It was sovereign and supreme within its sphere of jurisdiction, and this sphere was what the Constitution spelled out in detail. Activities and functions that were not specified were left to the states as stipulated in the Tenth Amendment: "The powers not delegated to the United States by the Constitution, nor prohibited by it to the States, are reserved to the States respectively, or to the people." In effect, what was created were two governmental structures, each charged with its own area of responsibilities, neither of which could be subordinated to the other. In this "the states are co-equally sovereign within the sphere of their reserved powers; in no sense are they subordinate corporations as the British insisted that the colonies must be" (Morison 1965:312).

Both structures derived their authority and legitimacy from the consent of the people and each bore a direct relationship to the people. As a result, each person who was part of the people possessed a dual citizenship. First they were "citizens of the general government;" and "second ... citizens of their particular states"

(McLaughlin 1905:243). James Wilson of Pennsylvania expanded on this notion during one of the debates at the convention.

> "'The General Government was meant for them in the first capacity; the State Governments in the second. Both Governments were derived from the people – both meant for the people – both therefore ought to be regulated on the same principles. The same train of ideas which belonged to the relation of the Citizens to their State Governments were applicable to their relation to the General Government and in forming the latter, we ought to proceed, by abstracting as much as possible from the idea of the State Governments.'"
>
> (McLaughlin 1905:243)

To insure that the sovereignty of the people would be respected and not subordinated to either governmental structure, the Bill of Rights was added to the Constitution. It carved out a sphere of rights that was the preserve of the people as individuals and that could not be encroached upon by the state or federal governments.

The Constitution thus serves as the unifying framework for this triadic division of functions and rights. It serves as "the supreme law of the land" and thereby becomes the ultimate means for guarding the boundaries that define the spheres of rights and powers of federal and state governments and of the people, and prevent these from being breached.

In creating the Constitution and the federal government, the Founding Fathers constructed a viable political framework for the development of a transcendent identity that would bind the peoples from the various states into a nation and national community. Some scholars trace the beginning of an American identity to the colonial period. Adams, however, doubts any such identity existed at the beginning of the 1700s:

> "At the opening of the eighteenth century there was no fully differentiated American life, no American people. There was merely a loose group of English colonies in the West Indies and on the American continent. The latter possessed, it is true, certain fundamental institutions in common and were subject to certain common influences, but as yet they were without any common consciousness, common culture or even a vague premonition of a common destiny."
>
> (Adams 1927:24)

Merritt in his study of colonial newspapers from the five cities of Boston, New York, Philadelphia, Williamsburgh, and Charleston concludes that there was a steady increase in collective self-referent symbols from the beginning of the study period in 1735 to its end in 1775 (Merritt 1966). He does not see any overly dramatic effect of specific events on this trend. Further he reports that most of these collective self-referent symbols used the term American either implicitly or explicitly, and the percentage that did also increased from 1735 to 1775. Thus only two out of five collective referents were to America in 1735, but by 1775 they were three out of five.

Other scholars, however, place greater emphasis on the impact of events on the emergence of an American identity. Few, though, consider events before the Stamp Act crisis of the 1760s of any significance. The cumulative effect of subsequent events which culminated in the Revolution is what is viewed by a number of scholars, including Nevins (1969), Knollenberg (1960), and so on, as decisive in stimulating the growth of American nationalism and identity. It is evident that, for much of the colonial period, the American identity had to compete with loyalty to Great Britain and even more importantly to loyalty to one's colony.

The extent and degree to which the colonists identified themselves as British and felt strong loyalties to the home country and Crown has still to be ascertained. However, there is little doubt that the attachment was real and significant for many. Ties were exceptionally strong with the British style of life and culture, which served as models for so much of colonial life. Colonists even expressed pride as British subjects in the successful exploits of the Empire; perhaps this feeling peaked at the British victory in the French and Indian War.

But with the succession of harsh measures and policies beginning with the Stamp Tax, many colonists became increasingly estranged from the British government, but they did so without questioning their basic ties to Britain and the Crown. In fact, they opposed these policies in the name of their rights as Englishmen. And as we have already seen, even after the Revolutionary War began, the Continental Congress still clung to the hope of reconciliation with Britain. As the war dragged on and independence was declared, anti-British hostility and sentiments correspondingly grew. In fact, it may be surmised that the cohesion of the colonies during this period was more a function of anti-British sentiment than the growth of American nationalism. However, even at this juncture it proved impossible for many colonists to give up their British identity; it is estimated that about one-third remained loyal to the Crown.

Unquestionably the colonist's strongest attachment was to his own colony. And it was this attachment that proved the greatest obstacle to the development of a national identity. However, for a period of time the growth of both identities followed a parallel course. The same events and experience that made the colonists aware that they needed each other and helped build intercolonial cooperation also intensified their sentiments and attachment to their own colony. The events of the 1760s, that led to and through the continental congresses and the Revolutionary War, reinforced awareness of being part of a larger intercolonial scheme but rarely at the expense of intracolonial loyalties and attachment. In fact it is open to question how many colonists developed any real sentiments or loyalties to this more abstract entity. Some significant groups did, as for example the officers of the Continental Army, intellectual and other popular leaders, and various working class and frontier groups. Even within these groups, however, many still opted for reconciliation with Britain until the Declaration of Independence; after that they became the primary exponents of American nationalism.

Even during the late eighteenth century, intercolonial cooperation seemed all too frequently at cross purposes with the interests of one's colony. On such occasions few hesitated: loyalty to one's colony was paramount. The conflict between the two identities peaked during the period of the Articles of Confederation; the very way in which the Confederation was structured made it inevitable that national interest would clash with those of the states and that in such clashes the state's interest would win. Only by experiencing the consequences of this failure at federated government were the states then prepared to try to do something about it: it took the initiative of a nationalistic elite to convert this opportunity into the writing of the Constitution. And even during the convention, loyalties to and interests of the states continually intruded into the deliberations. In fact, delegates deleted the term "national" from the final draft of the Constitution.

Thus, it is open to question how widely or deeply held was any sense of American identity at the time of the constitutional convention. That the experience with the Articles of Confederation enhanced interest in a more national structure of government cannot be denied, but how much sentiment was attached to this transcendent identity in these early days is debatable. Too much of the political, economic, and social structuring of life was organized first around the individual colony and then the state for the individual to develop a viable sense of identification with the nation. However, once the Constitution established the legal and governmental framework, America became increasingly a nation which was able to evoke sentiment and loyalty from its inhabitants. Lipset describes the role that George Washington, Federalists, and intellectual elite played in forging the sense of national identity once the Constitution was enacted (Lipset 1963).

The sovereignty of the people

A further contribution of the Founding Fathers was their basing the entire political system on the sovereignty of the people. Political authority was legitimate only to the extent that it governed by the consent of the people.

Interestingly many of the Founding Fathers were in fact distrustful of the people. They were frightened by what they considered to be the "tyranny of democracy" or the excesses of popular action that they saw at various times during the Revolution. Consequently they built a number of controls into the Constitution which made the people's voice indirect in the selection of members of the Senate and even the President, and several steps removed from the legislative process itself.

In a number of ways, the people they had in mind were a relatively abstract concept, quite removed from the flesh and blood people of the street. The people of the Constitution were to have a number of clearly spelled-out rights. As stated in the Bill of Rights and also the Constitution, they were to have access to and the protection of the legal and judiciary system. They were granted the right of trial by jury of their own peers; they did not have to testify against themselves; they were guaranteed due process of law and also the protection of their property. Further, they were granted the right of access to and participation in the political system. They were guaranteed the right "to petition the Government for a redress of grievances" (*The Constitution of The United States of America with the Amendments* 1872:21) and to vote directly for members of the House of Representatives and indirectly for members of the Senate and the President. Most were eligible to stand for public office.

And finally the people had rights which would allow them to interact freely with whomever they wished in their communities. They could worship as they pleased and with whomever they pleased. They could assemble peaceably and say what was on their mind without fear of legal and political authority and also publish the newspapers they wanted. In addition they could remain "secure in their persons, houses, papers and effects, against unreasonable searches and seizures" (*The Constitution of the United States of America with the Amendments* 1872:21). In effect, the rights of the people transcended the legal and political system and included the national community as well.

In this manner then the sovereignty of the people was reaffirmed in both the political state and in the national community. In both they shared equally in the various rights and were in effect citizens of both. In sum, according to the Constitution and the Founding Fathers: the people are the citizens of the United States.

However, as we shall shortly see, the Founding Fathers were not quite accurate. They excluded a whole category of persons whom they did not define as people. Accordingly, we contend that to get a more accurate reading of what actually took place in the United States then the above statement should be revised to read: the citizens are the people of the United States.

In constructing a framework from which America as a nation could develop, the Founding Fathers were able to build on a number of other things that Americans already shared in common. America was for all intents and purposes a Protestant country. Despite the separation of church and state on the national level and the denominational differences, the values of Protestantism – both in its religious and secularized version à la Weber – suffused the nation and were an important part of the shared value system. Humphrey stresses the importance that religious forces played "in the formation of a national spirit and even in the shaping of national institutions according to models furnished by prior American efforts at ecclesiastical organization" (Humphrey 1965:4).

In addition Americans shared a common language and a common cultural and political heritage from the colonist period. What is more, Americans had already experienced what it was like to be part of a whole larger than the individual colony or state: they had been part of the British imperial system. In other words, cultural and other features of American life that were shared in common reinforced the attempt of the Founding Fathers to build a consensual framework for the development of a nation.

Despite this, it would be a mistake to conclude that at the time of the constitutional convention Americans shared so much in common that what the Founding Fathers produced was an expression of this consensus. America was still very much a pluralistic society (as defined by Kammen) so that the Founding Fathers had to contend continually with the ways Americans differed from each other. Accordingly, what they produced was largely a result of compromise.

Dualism and biformities in the American system

In the final analysis, then, the history of the constitutional convention is the history of a group of men who sought to come to terms with a number of polarities and contradictions in the America of that day, and in the process made compromises and thereby created a number of dualisms. As we have already mentioned, they based the entire political structure on the sovereignty of the people, and yet they were fearful of giving the people too much power. Accordingly they hedged the democratic principle with an aristocratic principle by devising structural and other constraints that would give the "better classes" more of a voice in the system. The net result was democratic elitism or popular aristocracy, as Kammen phrases it (Kammen 1972).

The Founding Fathers were very much committed to the principle of equality and they sought to insure equality of access to and treatment in the legal and political systems. However, they also sought to preserve the rights of private property and the freedom of the individual to pursue his own interests within the framework of the law, which in fact perpetuated and magnified basic inequalities between the people. Lipset considers the dual values of equality and individual achievement as of cardinal importance in the societal system that the Founding Fathers constructed (Lipset 1963).

They recognized the need for a stronger federal government than the one established by the Articles of Confederation, but they also wished to perpetuate the strong colonist tradition of local and state government. Accordingly they devised a dual sphere of political authority for both and thereby gave rise to the concept of dual citizenship for the American people.

They were concerned about the concentration of too much authority in one body and so they created a dual legislative structure: a House of Representatives and a Senate. They solved the struggle between large and small states by devising a dual mode of representation. The Senate was to have an equal number of representatives from each state; the House, to have a number proportionate to the population of a state. In addition they created a system of checks and balances so that each branch of the federal government – the legislative, executive, and judiciary – would have its circumscribed sphere of powers.

Kammen considers dualism and the paradoxical coupling of opposites as a core feature of American history and experience. He believes that "biformity," the term he adopts, has come to be part of the national style on several levels:

> "Collective individualism is only one among a large cluster of biformities which express the contradictory tendencies of our contrapuntal civilization. There are also the conservative liberalism of our political life, the pragmatic idealism of our cerebral life, the emotional rationalism of our spiritual life, and godly materialism of our acquisitive life."   (Kammen 1972:116)

He traces this American tendency toward biformity to the heritage of an unstable colonist society in its relationship to England and also to the effort of the Founding Fathers to impose a "new network of institutions and assumptions [in 1789] upon well established older ones" (Kammen 1972:91).

Among the biformities that America has experienced, Kammen alludes to the ethnic diversity of the colonist period and also to the immigration since then of millions of people from different national, religious, and ethnic groups.

> "In nineteenth- and twentieth-century America, the most obvious biformity born of pluralism would be the bilingual condition known as hyphenated Americanism, defined in the following manner by *The Random House Dictionary of the English Language*: 'noting a naturalized citizen of the US believed to be ambivalent in his loyalty: so called because of the tendency to style himself according to his former and present nationalities, using a hyphen: e.g. "German-American."'"   (Kammen 1972:95)

The racial biformity: perpetuation of the colonialist plural society

Kammen also treats with the racial biformity of the American experience, but he deals with it as just another biformity that Americans have experienced. What he fails to recognize is its qualitative difference from the others. All the other biformities that he alludes to are dualisms that were either built into the political and national framework created by the Founding Fathers or were dualisms experienced by different subgroups, including the national, religious, and ethnic minorities, who were part of this framework. However, the racial biformity expressed a crucial boundary in the American society. On one side were the whites who were part of the national political system that the Founding Fathers had created. On the other side were the nonwhites, principally the blacks, who were not. And it is to a consideration of this subgroup that we shall now turn.

The transformation of the colonies into a nation-state was an experience that only included the white Americans. Black America was almost totally excluded from the transformation; its presence intruded into the process at several strategic points, but the net result was to reaffirm and to consolidate its status as a subjugated people.

The struggle with England that culminated in the Revolutionary War set forces in motion that disturbed somewhat the established pattern of subjugation of the blacks. This took several different forms. Some white colonists, particularly the Quakers, sought to equate the oppression of the colonists with the oppression of the blacks: the linkage of the two fates did not gain many white converts. Some blacks, however, such as Crispus Attucks, threw themselves into the struggle as though the struggle was also theirs, but not many did so.

In general whites were not in favor of having the blacks fight on their side; they were worried about what might happen once the blacks got guns. In fact in November 1775 General Washington issued an order forbidding the enlistment of blacks, free or slave, into the continental army. The order was subsequently modified, in part because the Royal Governor of Virginia issued a proclamation that he would free those slaves who joined the British army. A number of slaves responded. This sent waves of alarm through Virginia; accordingly Washington modified his policy to allow free blacks to enlist. As the war dragged on, an increasing number of states liberalized their policy and admitted blacks into their militia. At first the policy only included free blacks, but later it included slaves as well. A number of blacks responded and by the end of the war they comprised somewhat less than 2 percent of the armed forces; most of them were from the North.

Many of the states freed the slaves who served in the war. In addition, the

Revolutionary War generated some anti-slavery sentiment and also interest in anti-slave societies, particularly among the Quakers. The anti-slavery momentum continued long enough to have most northern states abolish slavery by the end of the eighteenth century – states which had had a 150-year old heritage of slavery. "Perhaps the high water mark of the post-war anti-slavery movement was reached in 1787 when the Congress added to the Northwest Ordinance the provision that neither slavery nor involuntary servitude should exist in the territory covered by the Ordinance" (Franklin 1952:140). Even this bill had a provision that protected the interests of the slave states; it stipulated the return of any slaves who might seek refuge in the territory.

However, these relatively minor gains affected the lives of only a handful of blacks and modified only the legal face of relations with the blacks in the northern states. But when the issue was confronted on a national level at the Constitutional Convention, the result was reaffirmation of the subjugated status of the black.

THE CONSTITUTIONAL CONVENTION AND THE LEGITIMATION OF SLAVERY

Nowhere in the Constitution is slavery explicitly mentioned or approved, but it surfaces indirectly in three sections. The first instance has to do with the apportionment of representatives according to population numbers. Black slaves are to be counted as three-fifths of a person; the reference, though, is not to black slaves but to "all other persons." The second instance grants slave states the right to import slaves until 1808 without interference from the federal government. In this case too, slaves are not referred to directly; instead Article 1, Section 9 states "The migration or importation of such persons as any of the States now existing think proper to admit shall not be prohibited by the Congress prior to year one thousand eight hundred and eight." And finally Article 4, Section 2(3) was written expressly for the return of fugitive slaves, but it made no direct reference to slaves. It says "No person held to service or labor in one State, under the laws thereof, escaping into another, shall in consequence of any law or regulation therein, be discharged from such service or labor, but shall be delivered up on claim of the party to whom such service or labor may be due."

The first two provisions were the subject of debate and the products of sectional compromise. For example, several times during the proceedings delegates from Georgia, South and North Carolina warned that their states would refuse to ratify the Constitution if there was any "meddling with the importation of negroes" (The Federal Convention of 1787 II:364). They applauded the initial report of the Committee on Detail that recommended that "migration or importation of such persons as the several States shall think proper to admit … shall … [not] be prohibited" (The Federal Convention of 1787 II:183).

Faced with the prospect of this proposal's defeat, they agreed with delegates from four other states to recommit this clause. A committee of eleven was appointed and instructed to find some middle ground. Two days later the committee proposed that Congress be prohibited from acting against such migration "prior to the year 1800" (The Federal Convention of 1787 II:400). The next day a delegate from South Carolina moved to amend the proposal by prohibiting legislative action "until the year 1808" (The Federal Convention of 1787 II:409). After some debate his amendment passed by the vote of 7 to 4.

The three-fifths figure or federal ratio was not in itself a major topic of controversy at the Convention. It had already been arrived at as a product of sectional compromise during the days of the Articles of Confederation when the issue of tax revenues for the government was under consideration. At that time the North favored counting slaves on a one-to-one basis with whites in determining the taxable wealth of the South. The South wanted to exclude them. The federal ratio was the compromise, although agreement was never reached on raising revenues for the government.

In the Constitutional Convention the federal ratio was introduced early in the proceedings on June 11 as part of a resolution for apportioning *representation of each of the States* [in the first branch of the national legislature] ... *from the number of its free inhabitants, and of every other description three fifths to one free inhabitant*" (The Federal Convention of 1787 I:205). It was overwhelmingly approved 9 to 2 without any debate.

A month later, though, on July 11, debate erupted on the federal ratio during consideration of a resolution for conducting a census "of the free inhabitants of each State, and three fifths of the inhabitants of other description" in order to ascertain "the alterations that may happen in the population and wealth of the several States" (The Federal Convention of 1787 I:575). This time the South vigorously favored counting slaves on a one-to-one basis with whites in determining the population base for allocating representation. For example,

"Mr Butler [of South Carolina] insisted that the labour of a slave in S. Carola. was as productive and valuable as that of a freeman in Massts., that as wealth was the great means of defence and utility to the Nation they are equally valuable to it with freemen; and that consequently an equal representation ought to be allowed for them in a Government which was instituted principally for the protection of property, and was itself to be supported by property."

(The Federal Convention of 1787 I:580–81)

In turn, the North opposed the inclusion of any slaves as part of the population base. In his rebuttal, for example, Wilson of Pennsylvania queried "on what principle the admission of blacks in the proportion of three-fifths could be explained. Are they admitted as Citizens? Then why are they not admitted on an equality with White Citizens? Are they admitted as property? Then why is not other property admitted into the computation?"

(The Federal Convention of 1787 I:587)

In a close vote three northern states joined with three southern states to vote down the federal ratio, 6 to 4.

Overnight the pressure for compromise grew. Early in the debate the next day a delegate from North Carolina, for example, warned that his state "would never confederate on any terms that did not rate them [the blacks] at least as 3/5. If the Eastern States meant therefore to exclude them altogether, the business was at an end" (The Federal Convention of 1787 I:593).

The federal ratio was accordingly reinstated in an oblique fashion through a resolution that stipulated "that representation ought to be proportional according to direct Taxation." The resolution also provided for a census that would be used "to ascertain the alteration in the direct Taxation which may be required from time to time by the changes in the relative circumstances of the States." This census was to "be taken within six years from the first meeting of the Legislature of the United States and once within the term of every Ten years afterwards of all the inhabitants of the United States in the manner and according to the ratio recommended by Congress in their resolution of April 18 1783" (The Federal Convention of 1787 I:590–91). (This was the resolution in which the federal ratio was approved under the Articles of Confederation.) The vote on the resolution was 6 to 2 with Massachusetts and South Carolina delegations divided on the vote.

From that point on the federal ratio was never really contested, and, in the final version of the clause on representation, the federal ratio no longer had to be inferred from the 1783 date. It was stated openly and explicitly as being involved in the apportionment of both direct taxes and representation.

Although a number of delegates from the northern states entered into the debate on the two provisions, neither provision imposed any obligation on their home states to demonstrate any active support for slavery. The provisions merely gave the stamp of constitutional legitimacy to the status of slavery as practiced within the borders of the various southern states.

The third provision, however, did impose such obligations on the northern states and in doing so gave "a nationwide sanction to property in slaves" (Robinson 1971:228). Yet, on this provision the delegates from the northern states were curiously mute. True, several did make comments when the first draft of the provision was offered from the floor by delegates from South Carolina late in August; these delegates were seeking "further securities for their peculiar property" (Robinson 1971:228). Accordingly, they moved "to require fugitive slaves and servants to be delivered up like criminals" (The Federal Convention of 1787 II:443). The proposal met with some discussion. "Mr Wilson [delegate from Pennsylvania]: This would oblige the Executive of the State to do it, at the public expence. Mr Sherman [delegate from Connecticut] saw no more propriety in the public seizing and surrendering a slave or servant, than a horse" (The Federal Convention of 1787 II:443).

The two delegates from South Carolina withdrew their proposal and returned the next day with a revised version that avoided the points of contention of the previous day. This version was adopted without debate or dissent and subsequently, after several stylistic changes by the Committee of Style, was incorporated as Section 2 of Article 4 of the Constitution. (The only change of any significance was the deletion of the adverb *justly* from the phrase describing the claims of the person who sought the return of the laborer.)

The joy with which the delegates from the southern states greeted this action is evident in the words of the delegates from North Carolina. In their report to the Governor of their state, they declared that "The Southern States have also a much better Security for the Return of Slaves who might endeavor to escape than they had under the original [Articles of] Confederation" (The Federal Convention of 1787 III:84).

The failure of any of the delegates from the northern states to object to this provision has puzzled scholars such as Robinson (1971). He takes it as evidence that blacks, even free blacks, had no spokesmen to represent their interests either in government or at the Convention; the white spokesmen were casually indifferent to their plight.

"It may be harsh to belabor Northern delegates for not foreseeing the abuses to which fugitive-slave acts were later put. Nevertheless, the casual way in which this clause – so full of peril to Negroes, both bond and free – was adopted tells volumes about the plight of black men in a nation governed by whites. The United States was a miserable place for Negroes, in part because, while Southerners were zealous to keep Negroes enslaved, Northerners cared only superficially, if at all, about the rights, welfare, and happiness of free Negroes. The careless language of the fugitive-slave clause reveals better than anything else in the Constitution that the fundamental problem for blacks in the union was that the government was in no way answerable to them, and white Americans in general did not hold them in just regard."

(Robinson 1971:229–30)

Robinson, we feel, fails to follow through on the logic of his own explanation. Blacks had no one to represent their interests not because "[white] Northerners cared only superficially " for their rights, but because these Northerners did not believe that blacks had any rights or should have any in the People's Domain of the North. As such, we conclude, the northern delegates, much more through deliberate design than through casual indifference, were signalling to the blacks that they were not welcome in the North and that they were not to see the North as a haven of freedom. The inaction of these delegates suggests, in effect, that what we have earlier called the Massachusetts model of duality may have indeed become firmly imprinted in the North by the time of the Constitutional Convention.

In the final analysis, then, by adopting the three provisions the Convention made the federal government a party to the perpetuation of the slave system. It was to forgo its right to regulate commerce and immigration by doing nothing for twenty years to prevent importation of slaves. At the same time it was to protect the rights of the slave owner by seeing to it that fugitive slaves who crossed state lines were returned to him. In effect, the Convention not only failed to abolish slavery throughout the land as repugnant to the goals of a society based on the sovereignty of the people, but it even helped extend the reach of slave states beyond their borders into other areas. In so doing, the Convention endowed the slave system – albeit indirectly – with an aura of legitimacy as being in accord with the supreme law of the land. The net result, it can be argued, is that the Convention sanctified not one but two models of society. On the "visible" level of the Constitution is the society built on the concept of the sovereignty of the people and on the rights of the governed. And on the "invisible" level of the Constitution is the society built on the concept of "unequal rights" and on the enslavement of subjugated "other persons."

The Dred Scott decision: the ideology of duality made visible

Almost seventy years later what was treated obliquely by the Founding Fathers was made explicit and incorporated into the supreme law of the land. In its decision on *Dred Scott v. John F. A. Sandford* the United States Supreme Court rejected a writ in error filed by Dred Scott, a black born a slave, from a suit he had earlier instituted in the Circuit Court of the United States for the district of Missouri. In his suit he had claimed that he and his family were entitled to their freedom because prior to their involuntary return to Missouri and subsequent sale to their present owner, they had lived for two years with their former owner, an army surgeon, at a military fort in the northern part of the Louisiana Territory which Congress had decreed in 1818 was to be free of slavery. His own suit for freedom was bolstered, he insisted, by the fact that even before that period, when he was still unmarried, he had lived with this former owner for two years in the State of Illinois, which had abolished slavery.

EXCLUSION OF THE FREED AND ENSLAVED BLACK FROM
THE PEOPLE'S DOMAIN

In his opinion, Chief Justice Taney declared that, even before the substantive issue raised by the writ could be decided, a prior question had to be answered by the Court. Did Scott have the right to bring suit in a court of the United States? He would have this right, the Chief Justice stated, if he were part of the people of the United States.

> "The words 'people of the United States' and 'citizens' are synonymous terms, and mean the same thing. They both describe the political body who, according to our republican institutions, form the sovereignty, and who hold the power and conduct the Government through their representatives. They are what we familiarly call the 'sovereign people,' and every citizen is one of this people, and a constituent member of this sovereignty." (60 US 1857:404)

Thus, the fundamental question facing the Court, he argued, was whether Scott as a black man could become part of the people:

> "Can a negro, whose ancestors were imported into this country, and sold as slaves, become a member of the political community formed and brought into existence by the Constitution of the United States, and as such become entitled to all the rights, and privileges, and immunities, guarantied by that instrument to the citizen? One of which rights is the privilege of suing in a court of the United States in the cases specified in the Constitution." (60 US 1857:403)

The Chief Justice's answer to this more or less rhetorical question was that blacks even if emancipated cannot and do not "compose a portion of this people" nor are they "constituent members of this sovereignty." In other words, "they are not included, and were not intended to be included, under the word 'citizens' in the Constitution, and can therefore claim none of the rights and privileges which that instrument provides for and secures to citizens of the United States" (60 US 1857:404). He then went on, as we saw earlier in this chapter, to define them as "a subordinate and inferior class of beings" who required the control of the whites.

The whites' attitude toward the blacks, he then attempted to show, was deeply rooted in the early days of European expansion, as reflected in the "public history of every European nation," particularly the English.

> "They [the blacks] had for more than a century before [the Revolution] been regarded as beings of an inferior order, and altogether unfit to associate with the white race, either in social or political relations; and so far inferior, that they had no rights which the white man was bound to respect; and that the negro might justly and lawfully be reduced to slavery for his benefit. He was bought and

sold, and treated as an ordinary article of merchandise and traffic, whenever a profit could be made by it. This opinion was at that time fixed and universal in the civilized portion of the white race. It was regarded as an axiom in morals as well as in politics, which no one thought of disputing, or supposed to be open to dispute; and men in every grade and position in society daily and habitually acted upon it in their private pursuits, as well as in matters of public concern, without doubting for a moment the correctness of this opinion."

(60 US 1857:407)

The thirteen colonies shared this conviction, he continued; all had laws of slavery and even the emancipated black was viewed as an inferior being. The Chief Justice then reported the laws banning interracial marriage in Maryland (1717) and Massachusetts (1705).

"We give both of these laws in the words used by the respective legislative bodies, because the language in which they are framed, as well as the provisions contained in them, show, too plainly to be misunderstood, the degraded condition of this unhappy race. They were still in force when the Revolution began, and are a faithful index to the state of feeling towards the class of persons of whom they speak, and of the position they occupied throughout the thirteen colonies, in the eyes and thoughts of the men who framed the Declaration of Independence and established the State Constitutions and Governments. They show that a perpetual and impassable barrier was intended to be erected between the white race and the one which they had reduced to slavery, and governed as subjects with absolute and despotic power, and which they then looked upon as so far below them in the scale of created beings, that intermarriages between white persons and negroes or mulattoes were regarded as unnatural and immoral, and punished as crimes, not only in the parties, but in the person who joined them in marriage. And no distinction in this respect was made between the free negro or mulatto and the slave, but this stigma, of the deepest degradation, was fixed upon the whole race."   (60 US 1857:409)

The Founding Fathers who wrote about the general rights of man and the rights of people in the Declaration of Independence and in the Constitution, he contended, were immersed in the beliefs about the blacks.

"They perfectly understood the meaning of the language they used, and how it would be understood by others; and they knew that it would not in any part of the civilized world be supposed to embrace the negro race, which, by common consent, had been excluded from civilized Governments and the family of nations, and doomed to slavery. They spoke and acted according to the then established doctrines and principles, and in the ordinary language of the day, and no one misunderstood them. The unhappy black race were separated from the white by indelible marks, and laws long before established, and were never thought of or spoken of except as property, and when the claims of the owner or the profit of the trader were supposed to need protection." (60 US 1857:410)

He then referred to the two clauses in the Constitution "which point directly and specifically to the negro race as a separate class of persons, and show clearly that they were not regarded as a portion of the people or citizens of the Government then formed" (60 US 1857:411). (As we have seen, these gave implicit sanction for the continuation of slave trade until 1808 and for the return of fugitive slaves even if they escaped into a state which had abolished slavery.)

Congress soon gave evidence of its agreement with the "construction of the Constitution that we have given," he continued; two of the laws it passed almost as soon as it came into existence under the Constitution are "particularly worthy of notice, because many of the men who assisted in framing the Constitution, and took an active part in procuring its adoption, were then in the halls of legislation, and certainly understood what they meant when they used the words 'people of the United States' and 'citizen' in that well-considered instrument" (60 US 1857:419). The first, a naturalization law enacted by the First Congress in March 1790, confined the right of becoming citizens to aliens who were "free white persons." (We shall examine this law in greater detail in the next section.) The second law passed in 1792 limited enrollment in the militia to the "free able-bodied white male citizen."

Even the abolition of slavery in some states, claimed the Chief Justice, was done for the convenience and benefit of the white rather than of the black, and in those states that banned slavery after the adoption of the Constitution blacks were not accorded the full rights and immunities of citizenship. He quoted legislative examples from Massachusetts, Connecticut, New Hampshire, and Rhode Island. He then referred to the conclusion of Chancellor Kent in his Commentaries published in 1848: namely, "in no part of the country except Maine, did the African race, in point of fact, participate equally with the whites in the exercise of civil and political rights" (60 US 1857:416).

Thus he concluded that:

"upon a full and careful consideration of the subject, the court is of opinion, that, upon the facts stated in the plea in abatement, Dred Scott was not a citizen of Missouri within the meaning of the Constitution of the United States, and not entitled as such to sue in its courts; and, consequently, that the Circuit Court had no jurisdiction of the case, and that the judgment on the plea in abatement is erroneous." (60 US 1857:427)

Having disposed of the matter of jurisdiction, the Chief Justice then turned to Scott's claim that he and his family should be given their freedom because of their stay in the territory in which Congress had prohibited slavery. Appendix B offers a detailed discussion of this part of Taney's opinion.*

The Constitution and the dual societal systems

Through its Dred Scott decision, the United States Supreme Court stripped away the fiction of "other person" that had been devised by the Founding Fathers to mask the term "black slave" in the Constitution, and in doing so the Court explicitly labeled him as property just as the various southern states had already done. Chief Justice Taney's opinion, though, went beyond clarifying the Founding Fathers' conception of the black slave as property; he maintained that the Founding Fathers did not consider even the emancipated black as worthy of being part of the sovereign people of the Constitution and of sharing the full rights and immunities of citizenship in the People's Domain.

Small wonder then that black social scientists view the Constitution in a light opposite from that of white social scientists. The latter as represented by such eminent scholars as Commager (1963 and 1968), Morison (1965), and Nevins (1969) see the Constitution as a remarkable testimony to enlightened and rational government by and for the people; the former as represented by John Hope Franklin view the Constitution as an instrument that legitimized repression and enslavement:

> "The fathers of the Constitution were dedicated to the proposition that 'government should rest upon the dominion of property.' For the Southern fathers this meant slaves, just as surely as it meant commerce and industry for the Northern fathers. In the protection of this property, the Constitution had given recognition to the institution of human slavery, and it was to take seventy-five years to undo that which was accomplished in Philadelphia in 1787.
> The adoption of the Federal Constitution marks the end of an era not only in

---

*Chief Justice Taney's opinion on the role of the Constitution in new territories serves as an important conceptual setting for our discussion of Puerto Rico in a later chapter. Taney's thesis which cast the protective mantle of the Constitution around the introduction of America's duality into new territories would have produced the exactly opposite result had it prevailed at the time of the acquisition of Puerto Rico almost forty years later. The island would have escaped being enmeshed in this duality and thereby avoided becoming America's first colonial dependency, for it would have had to be given territorial status under the protection of the Constitution with the view toward eventual statehood in the Union. Passage of the thirteenth amendment at least thirty years before would have made moot the question of slavery in the island.

the political history of the United States but in the history of the American Negro as well. With British domination at an end and stable government established, Americans could no longer lay the onus for slavery at the door of the Mother Country. They proudly accepted the challenge and responsibility of their new political freedom by establishing the machinery and safeguards that insured the continued enslavement of the Negro. Ironically enough, America's freedom was the means of giving slavery itself a longer life than it was to have in the British empire. New factors on the horizon were about to usher in a new day for slavery as the old day passed away." (Franklin 1952:143)

In conclusion, then, the Constitution perpetuated and sanctified the Manichean dualism that had evolved early in the history of the thirteen colonies. On a higher and more visible level, it transformed the unstable pluralistic society of white colonist America into a nation-state that was rooted in the rights and sovereignty of the people. On a lower and more invisible level it sanctified and perpetuated the stable plural society of racially segmented colonial America. It placed this society under the control of the political authority, primarily of the states but also of the federal government, but excluded it from the national community of people. It was a society of the nether world; it had a coherence and logic of its own, a dominant class of white masters and a subjugated class of slaves who were defined as "other persons" in the Constitution but as property in state law, though in neither instance were they ever to be part of the people of the national community.

The two societal systems were set on parallel tracks, each evolving according to its own inner dynamics. They were linked in crucial ways. The whites were the masters of the nether plural society and also citizens of the nation-state. In effect, they could move freely between the two systems and protect their position and property in both; only the blacks as slaves remained isolated in the nether society. Even the emancipated black was largely confined to this nether society, though in some states he attained some of the rights but not the status of citizen or of full membership in the People's Domain.

So sharp was the distinction between these two systems that van den Berghe applies the same term to America for much of its history that he applied to South Africa of today. "My central thesis is that, with the early development and later florescence of racism in the United States, this republic has been, since its birth and until World War II, a 'Herrenvolk Democracy'" (van den Berghe 1972:211).

Naturalization and the free white alien

Approximately seventy years elapsed after the adoption of the Constitution before Chief Justice Taney wrote his "authoritative unmasking" of the duality built into the document; within two years of its enactment, the First Congress, which included a number of the Founding Fathers, had already acted to exclude all but the white race from membership in the People's Domain of the new nation. It did this by preventing all but free white aliens from becoming citizens. The matter-of-fact way in which this took place merits examination; accordingly we propose to conclude this chapter with a review of the deliberations in Congress as it wrote the first naturalization bill and subsequently revised it five years later.

THE FIRST NATURALIZATION ACT

In mid-January 1790 at the behest of President Washington, who proposed it in his address at the opening of the second session of the First Congress, a committee of three was appointed in the House of Representatives to recommend a uniform rule of naturalization. Almost three weeks later the committee presented to the House the first clause of such a bill. It stipulated

> "that all free white persons,* who have, or shall migrate into the United States, and shall give satisfactory proof, before a magistrate, by oath, that they intend to reside therein, and shall take an oath of allegiance, *and shall have resided in the United States for one whole year* shall be entitled to all rights of citizenship, except being capable of holding an office under the State or General Government, which capacity they are to acquire after a residence of two years or more."   (US Congress, Debates and Proceedings 1790:1109)

In the ensuing two-day debate no argument arose over the racial restriction; the only topic that was debated was length of residence. This was precipitated by an amendment proposed by one of the committee members to delete the one year requirement. He argued that aliens could own lands in their own right almost as soon as they came to this country and "there was a seeming contradiction in making them freeholders, and, at the same time, excluding them from the performance of duties annexed to that class of citizens" (US Congress, Debates and Proceedings 1790:1115–116). A congressman from Virginia supported his motion on the ground that

> "We shall be inconsistent with ourselves, if, after boasting of having opened an asylum for the oppressed of all nations, and established a Government which is the admiration of the world, we make the terms of admission to the full enjoyment of that asylum so hard as is now proposed. It is nothing to us,

---

*It took almost 100 years before the full impact of this phrase was felt. It revitalized America's historic duality at a time when the vestigial effects of Reconstruction were still muting it. And it spun a web of duality around a new category of nonwhites, the yellow immigrant from Asia, particularly from China, and later from Japan – a web from which he only recently escaped.

whether Jews or Roman Catholics settle amongst us; whether subjects or Kings, or citizens of free States wish to reside in the United States, they will find it their interest to be good citizens, and neither their religious nor political opinions can injure us, if we have good laws, well executed."

(US Congress, Debates and Proceedings 1790:1110)

Other congressmen, however, opposed the amendment; most of them were against the committee's one-year requirement as being too short. Several argued that too easy naturalization would attract the vagrants, paupers, and other undesirables from Europe. Another insisted that the country needed farmers, artisans, and the like to build its wealth and resources, but without any residence requirements a class of

"European merchants, and factors or merchants ... [will] come with a view of remaining so long as will enable them to acquire a fortune, and then they will leave the country, and carry off all their property with them. These people injure us more than they do us good, and, except in this last sentiment, I can compare them to nothing but leeches. They stick to us until they get their fill of our best blood, and then they fall off and leave us."

(US Congress, Debates and Proceedings 1790:1117)

Others argued that a period of probation was necessary to test the sincerity, character, and knowledge of the alien. As one congressman stated, "some kind of probation, as it has been termed, is absolutely requisite, to enable them to feel and be sensible of the blessing [of republicanism]." The "them" he was referring to were the many Europeans whose "sensations [were] impregnated with the prejudices of education, acquired under monarchical and aristocratical Governments, [which] may deprive them of that zest for pure republicanism, which is necessary in order to taste its beneficence with that gratitude which we feel on the occasion" (US Congress, Debates and Proceedings 1790:1117).

By the next day sentiment for a residency requirement had grown sufficiently strong that the amendment was withdrawn by its author. Not even the one-year requirement seemed to satisfy the representatives. As a result the bill was recommitted to a newly constituted committee of ten. Two weeks later a revised bill was reported that extended the residency requirement in the United States to two years, but only one year in a state. The bill retained the racial restriction though now it was worded,

"that any alien, being a free white person, who shall have resided within the limits and under the jurisdiction of the United States for the term of two years, may be admitted to become a citizen thereof, on application to any common law court of record, in any one of the states wherein he shall have resided for the term of one year at least.... [The applicant was also required to submit] proof to the satisfaction of such court, that he is a person of good character and taking the oath or affirmation prescribed by law, to support the constitution of the United States, which oath or affirmation such court shall administer; and the clerk of such court shall record such application, and the proceedings therein; and thereupon such person shall be considered as a citizen of the United States."

(US Public Statutes at Large I:103)

The bill passed both houses and was signed into law on March 26 1790.

THE TITLED NOBILITY AS A THREAT TO THE PEOPLE'S DOMAIN

Almost five years later, the House of Representatives took up once more a bill to establish a uniform rule of naturalization. In the ensuing debate no argument again arose over the racial restriction that was carried over from the earlier bill, "any alien being a free white person." Also only a brief exchange occurred at the very end of its deliberations as it extended the residency requirement to five years in the United States while retaining the one-year residency in a state or territory.

But almost three days were spent on an issue that agitated southern congress-men in particular: the disruptive effect of the immigration from Europe of titled nobility on the "equalitarian republicanism" of the People's Domain of the new nation. To forestall this effect, a congressman from Virginia offered an amendment that proposed as finally enacted:

"In case the alien applying to be admitted to citizenship shall have borne any hereditary title, or been of any of the orders of nobility, in the kingdom or state from which he came, he shall, in addition to the above requisites, make an express renunciation of his title or order of nobility, in the court to which his application shall be made; which renunciation shall be recorded in the said court."

(US Public Statutes at Large I:414)

The first day of debate was relatively short and involved a brief exchange between the congressman from Virginia and one from Massachusetts. The latter stated that he "was averse to titles as any man in the House, but he did not like to make any laws against them. An alien might as well be obliged to make a renunciation of his connections with the Jacobin club. The one was fully as abhorrent to the Constitution as the other." The Virginia congressman replied "that if a thing be implied in the Constitution, where is the harm of expressing it? This is said to be implied in the Constitution, and therefore it is needless to express it. Now this was one of the very best arguments which could be thought of in favor of the motion. At the time when the Constitution was made, nobody could foresee the strange turn which affairs have taken, or that there might be a danger from an innundation of titled fugitives." Later he expressed regret that the debate had turned on the Jacobins, but he insisted "both these and the persons with titles were dangerous to the country" (US Congress, Debates and Proceedings 1795:1031–32). Another part of the proposed bill would deal with the danger from the Jacobins, he continued; his motion was meant to deal with the nobility.

The next day the Virginia congressman formally presented his resolution and offered a lengthy defense of it. He argued that "a revolution is now going onward, to which there is nothing similar in history. A large portion of Europe has already declared against titles, and where the innovations are to stop, no man can presume to guess" (US Congress, Debates and Proceedings 1795:1034). He then expressed fear that without such a law "fugitive nobility" would flock into the United States and soon begin to exercise undue influence on the political process. The congressman from Massachusetts again indicated his uneasiness with the motion. Madison however agreed with it. "It is very probable that the spirit of Republicanism will pervade a great part of Europe. It is hard to guess what numbers of titled character may, by such an event, be thrown out of that part of the world. What can be more reasonable than that when crowds of them come here, they should be forced to renounce everything contrary to the spirit of the Constitution" (US Congress, Debates and Proceedings 1795:1035).

Another congressman concurred heartily with the motion. He insisted that "titles only give a particular class of men a right to be insolent, and another class a pretence to be mean and cringing." Thus, "mischievous effects" will result if such men are allowed to retain their titles and become citizens. It is therefore necessary for them to renounce their titles if they want to be citizens. For "equality is the basis of good order and society, whereas titles turn everything wrong" (US Congress, Debates and Proceedings 1795:1035).

One Southerner however expressed his regret that the issue was raised. He feared that the public might misinterpret the motion and assume that "there was a real danger of the establishment of nobility or aristocratic orders in this country; and that those who voted against this motion were friendly to such a change in our political system: and that those who voted for it were the only true patriots" (US Congress, Debates and Proceedings 1795:1036). He scoffed at the notion of any such danger, for he said foreign titles by themselves meant nothing without privileges being attached to such titles, and "they [the foreigners] in fact can have no privilege among us in consequence of any foreign title; but must exist in perfect equality in all social rights with the rest of our citizens" (US Congress, Debates and Proceedings 1795:1038).

He then turned to what he identified as his Virginia colleague's "strongest reason why a foreign nobleman could not become a good citizen: ... the superiority which he had been accustomed to exercise over his fellow men, and the servile court he had been accustomed to receive from them. It was, then, the corrupting relation of lord and vassal, which rendered him an unfit member of an equal Republican Government." The logic of this argument, he continued, might also be "applied to the existing relation of master and slave in the Southern country, (rather a more degrading one than even that of lord and vassal) [and might be used] to prove that the people of that country were not qualified to be members of our free Republican Government." But he insisted, this would be contrary to fact. For,

> "Though in that house the members from the State of Virginia held persons in bondage, he was sure that their hearts glowed with a zeal as warm for the equal rights and happiness of men, as gentlemen from other parts of the Union where such degrading distinctions did not exist. He rejoiced, that, notwithstanding the unfavorable circumstances of his country in this respect, the virtue of his fellow-citizens shone forth equal to that of any other part of the nation."
> (US Congress, Debates and Proceedings 1795:1038)

Shortly thereafter, the congressman from Massachusetts, who was also unhappy with the Virginian's motion, took advantage of the linkage between aristocracy and slavery that had just been made and proposed an amendment to the Virginian's amendment. As formally worded the next day, it stated, "and also, in case such alien shall, at the time of his application [for citizenship], hold any person in slavery, he shall in the same manner renounce all right and claim to hold such person in slavery" (US Congress, Debates and Proceedings 1795:1041).

No sooner had he made the motion than the climate of the debate was transformed from calm and peaceable to heated and bitter. The congressman from Virginia immediately rose and objected strongly to the amendment. He said, that "he was sorry to see slavery made a jest of in that House. He understood this to be intended as a hint against members from the Southern States. It had no proper connection with the subject before the house. He had therefore no scruple in voting against it. It was calculated to injure the property of gentlemen." He then expressed how much he personally detested slavery "but from the existing state of the country, it was impossible at present to help it. He himself owned slaves. He regretted that he did so, and if any member could point out a way in which he could be properly freed from that situation, he should rejoice in it" (US Congress, Debates and Proceedings 1795:1039). He then insisted that slavery was actually declining in the South.

Madison also defensively echoed these sentiments, and said it was bad taste to bring the issue before the House. Another Southerner protested that the congressman from Massachusetts really believed that "possessors of slaves were unfit to hold any Legislative trust in a Republican Government;" another "read a clause of the Constitution prohibitory of proposing an abolition [to slavery] for many years to come. He then asked how gentlemen in the face of an express article of the Constitution, could propose an amendment like that." And a third remarked heatedly "To propose an abolition of slavery in this country would be the height of madness. Here the slaves are, and here they must remain" (US Congress, Debates and Proceedings 1795:1040).

The final day of debate began with an expression of keen disappointment about the slavery amendment by another Southerner. He explained that he had always respected the congressman from Massachusetts and thought he was joking when he first proposed the amendment. However, when the congressman persisted, the speaker continued, he felt obliged to speak out in protest.

> "This amendment not only tends to irritate the minds of members, but of thousands of the good citizens in the Southern States, as it affects the property which they have acquired by their industry. Thus it cools their affections towards the Government, as they will find that one part of the Government is about to operate on their property in an indirect way. The gentleman dare not come directly forward, and tell the House that men who possess slaves are unfit for holding an office under a Republican Government."
>
> (US Congress, Debates and Proceedings 1795:1042)

Any review of the past struggle for independence, he added, would reveal that representatives from the South "partake more of the Republican spirit than the members from the Eastern States." He then condemned the amendment for reflecting "more of monarchical or despotic principles than anything which he had seen for some time. What right had the House to say to a particular class of people, you shall not have that kind of property which other people have? This was the language of the motion, and he considered it as highly unjust" (US Congress, Debates and Proceedings 1795:1042).

In a conciliatory gesture, the congressman from Massachusetts offered to withdraw his amendment if no "yea-or-nay" vote were taken on the Virginian's original amendment. He explained that he had made his motion because supporters of that amendment wanted to hold its opponents "up to the public as aristocrats." As a result, he had decided "as a retaliation" to hold them up "to the same public as dealers in slaves" (US Congress, Debates and Proceedings 1795:1043). He made no mention of any intention to undo the system of slavery within this country. The congressman from Virginia joined in this reconciliation.

Calm was restored to the discussion as the pros and cons of the original amendment were debated. But when the congressman from Massachusetts discovered that a vote was to be taken on the Virginian's resolution, he insisted that his was to be voted on too. In the showdown his slavery amendment was defeated overwhelmingly, 63 to 28, and the Virginian's amendment won by almost as big a margin, 59 to 32 despite the negative vote from the congressman from Massachusetts.

Five days later the House passed the amended bill which also included the stipulation in two other sections that an alien at the time of his application for citizenship must "absolutely and entirely renounce and abjure all allegiance and fidelity to every foreign prince, potentate, state or sovereignty whatever, and particularly by name, the prince, potentate, state or sovereignty, whereof he was before a citizen or subject" (US Public Statutes at Large I:414); a less intense version of the above was included in a third section.

The Senate received the bill on January 9 1795 and six days later seemed on the verge of eliminating the racial restriction, for a motion was made to amend the first section of the bill so that it would exclude the phrase "free white persons" in the following manner: "That no alien shall hereafter become a citizen of the United States, or any of them, except in the manner prescribed in this act." Consideration of the bill was postponed until the next day; by then the phrase resurfaced and the only revisions were to change citizen of the United States to "citizen of any of the United States" and to add "and not otherwise" after "following conditions." Accordingly the clause read: "That any alien, being a free white person, may be admitted to become a citizen of any of the United States, on the following conditions, and not otherwise." The final version of the bill that became law on January 29 1795 restored the phrase "citizen of the United States" and read "That any alien, being a free white person, may be admitted to become a citizen of the United States, or any of them, on the following conditions, and not otherwise" (US Public Statutes at Large I:414).

The phrase "white persons" remained on the statute books for 157 more years or until the McCarran Act of 1952. It survived an effort to strike it from the naturalization laws during reconstruction. As a concession to the spirit of the time, aliens of African nativity and descent were also made eligible for citizenship; immigrants from Asia were not. Consequently, these, particularly those who came from China and Japan, bore the brunt of the racist heritage of America's colonialist past as they too became enmeshed in the country's duality during the last part of the nineteenth century and through the first half of the twentieth. We shall undertake a detailed examination of this encounter in Book Three.

5

THE AMERICAN INDIAN
AND THE FRONTIER

Introduction

So far we have concentrated on the role of the black in the exploitative colonial system that the English settler built. Our story of the creation of this system would be incomplete if we did not now return to a fuller examination of the settler's encounter with the first nonwhite he confronted in the New World, the Indian. From the Indian he wrested through force and fraud the land upon which he constructed his dual colonialist-colonist societal system. However, unlike the Spanish conquistador who forcibly dragged the Indian into the very center of his dual system as its major source of labor, the English settler sought systematically to push the Indian out of his. As a result, his struggle with the Indian took place along the everchanging territorial perimeter of the societal system he was building, and the struggle lasted for almost 300 years, well beyond the transformation of the thirteen colonies into the New Nation. In short, white America's encounter with the Indian played a crucial role in the shaping of its frontier experience that began early in the seventeenth century and ended in the late nineteenth and, to the extent that Turner's frontier thesis is valid (Turner 1920), this encounter supplemented the one with the black in searing duality and racial biformism into the institutional structure of white America as a whole.

However, unlike the black or any other racial minority, the Indians faced white America initially as independent and sovereign nations with whom treaties were signed and between whom boundaries were drawn. Even as their power waned and that of white America waxed along the frontier, the illusion of sovereign independence was maintained. By early nineteenth century, though, their claim to territorial autonomy and integrity was rejected by the United States government, and they were tagged with the ambiguous label of "domestic dependent nation" by the Supreme Court. And when the last battle was finally fought along the frontier in the late nineteenth century, they became a conquered people and a racially distinctive segment in a structure of oppressive administrative control under the United States government. They had, in other words, become part of the duality internal to the American society, much as the black and nonwhite alien already had.

In this chapter we shall describe and analyze this process with particular attention to the role that government policy and action played in bringing the transformation about but, unlike our earlier chapters, we shall not stop with the creation of the New Nation. Instead we shall bring the process of transformation up to the near present. But first let us turn to an examination of Turner's frontier thesis.

Frederick Turner and the American frontier

In his classic work on American history, Frederick Turner repeatedly stresses the importance of the frontier in the development of American institutions and society and of the character of its people (Turner 1920). He argues that the growth of America for 300 years was along successive frontier lines. "In the course of the seventeenth century the frontier was advanced up the Atlantic river courses, just beyond the 'fall line,' and the tidewater region became the settled area" (Turner 1920:4). "The fall line marked the frontier of the seventeenth century; the Alleghanies that of the eighteenth; the Mississippi that of the first quarter of the nineteenth; the Missouri that of the middle of this century (omitting the California movement); and the belt of the Rocky Mountains and the arid tract, the present frontier" (Turner 1920:9).

According to Turner, Americans have had to return over and over again to primitive conditions to cope with each successive frontier. "American social development has been continually beginning over again on the frontier. This perennial rebirth, this fluidity of American life, this expansion westward with its new opportunities, its continuous touch with the simplicity of primitive society, furnish the forces dominating American character" (Turner 1920:2–3). Turner contends that the frontier experience, rather than the European origins of the settlers, stamped the emerging American society and accounts for the special brand of democracy, individualism, ambition, innovativeness, materialism, and pragmatism that have come to characterize its institutions, ethos, and the character of its people.

In advancing his thesis at the turn of the twentieth century, Turner did much to turn around the thinking in American history. For a generation or more, he dominated American historiography; his students scurried all over to examine facets of the frontier experience. In more recent years his thesis has come under increasing challenge. A number of scholars have questioned the priority that Turner places on the frontier and have raised doubts about some of his interpretations; but few have discounted in its entirety his thesis that the frontier was a significant feature of the American experience.

Our purpose is not to argue the merits of either side in the debate, but to develop the following premise: to the extent that the frontier played an important part in the American experience, then to that extent the encounter with the Indian was of critical significance; for this encounter primarily defined the character and meaning of the frontier experience.

Turner recognizes the importance of the encounter with the Indian in the successive frontier experiences. In fact, he states that each involved an intense struggle with the Indian. "Each [of the successive frontiers] was won by a series of Indian wars" (Turner 1920:9). He is also impressed by the number and variety of Indian techniques and cultural traits that were adopted by the white frontiersman which enabled him to survive in the wilderness (while in turn the Indians became dependent on the white man's material culture):

> "The wilderness masters the colonist. It finds him a European in dress, industries, tools, modes of travel, and thought. It takes him from the railroad car and puts him in the birch canoe. It strips off the garments of civilization and arrays him in the hunting shirt and the moccasin. It puts him in the log cabin of the Cherokee and Iroquois and runs an Indian palisade around him. Before long he has gone to planting Indian corn and plowing with a sharp stick; he shouts the war cry and takes the scalp in orthodox Indian fashion. In short, at the frontier the environment is at first too strong for the man. He must accept the conditions which it furnishes, or perish, and so he fits himself into the Indian clearings and follows the Indian trails."   (Turner 1920:4)

Turner illustrates at some length the impact of the Indian on the frontier life of the New England colonist: "there are clear evidences of the transforming influence of the Indian frontier upon the Puritan type of English colonist" (Turner 1920:45). He mentions the adoption by the colonist of snowshoes and moccasins among other things, and in the armed struggle with the Indian "the frontier fighter adapted himself to a more open order, and lighter equipment suggested by the Indian warrior's practice" (Turner 1920:40).

On a more general level, Turner views the encounter with the Indian as having a decisive effect on "nationalizing" the white colonist and frontiersman. It reinforced a sense of common danger and facilitated the development of a common defense. In effect, the encounter was instrumental in the development of a common defense. In effect, the encounter was instrumental in the development of intercolonial cooperation in the early days of the frontier, and in orienting the frontiersman and pioneer toward the federal government for protection in the later days of the frontier:

"The effect of the Indian frontier as a consolidating agent in our history is important. From the close of the seventeenth century various intercolonial congresses have been called to treat with Indians and establish common measures of defense. Particularism was strongest in colonies with no Indian frontier. This frontier stretched along the western border like a cord of union. The Indian was a common danger, demanding united action. Most celebrated of these conferences was the Albany congress of 1754, called to treat with the Six Nations, and to consider plans of union. Even a cursory reading of the plan proposed by the congress reveals the importance of the frontier. The powers of the general council and the officers were, chiefly, the determination of peace and war with the Indians, the regulation of Indian trade, the purchase of Indian lands, and the creation and government of new settlements as a security against the Indians. It is evident that the unifying tendencies of the Revolutionary period were facilitated by the previous cooperation in the regulation of the frontier. In this connection may be mentioned the importance of the frontier, from that day to this, as a military training school, keeping alive the power of resistance to aggression, and developing the stalwart and rugged qualities of the frontiersman." (Turner 1920:15)

In the final analysis, however, Turner omits the implications of the encounter with the Indian when he articulates the permanent effects of the frontier experience on the American society and character; as we have already seen, he merely focuses on the virtues of the frontier experience. Had he given the encounter with the Indian its due weight, he would have had to include a number of negative effects of the frontier experience.

For one, the hatred of the Indian was a pervasive feature of frontier life. As Turner himself comments, "the Massachusetts frontiersman like his western successor hated the Indians; the 'tawney serpents' of Cotton Mather's phrase were to be hunted down and scalped in accord with law" (Turner 1920:46). This hatred was obviously fed by the constant anxiety and fear that the Indian would attack and kill; what compounded this worry was the alienness and strangeness of the Indian. The frontiersman and pioneer deemed him a savage, both biologically and culturally inferior to the white man, and in many respects not even human. Thus a deep-abiding racial and cultural antipathy and prejudice was part of the frontier heritage.

This frontier view made it easier to justify the use of force and fraud in dealings with the Indians. Some scholars have argued that violence was just as much part of the frontier life as were democracy and individualism. However, violence of white man toward white man was generally viewed as antisocial, and in time strenuous efforts were exerted by the frontier society to curb its use. By contrast, violence of white man toward Indian was viewed as legitimate and was normatively approved by the frontier society: a popular theme was, "The only good Indian is a dead Indian." Thus the violence of the frontier was more than a behavioral response to the conditions of life; it was also a value response to the Indian and was positively sanctioned as long as the target was the "less-than-human" Indian. This too was part of the heritage of the frontier.

In much the same manner was fraud legitimized in dealings with the Indian. Cheating and deceiving the Indian were part of the frontier way of life. These responses elicited neither guilt nor shame from the white man, but were frequently treated by the frontiersman as a "right."

In sum, the frontiersman and pioneer were bearers of a bifurcated value system. In their relations with their fellow white, they positively valued things that are deemed virtues in human society; in their relations with Indians, they positively valued things that are generally deemed vices in human society. Thus the frontier society had a schizoid character which Turner failed to capture. This split – clearly following the line of division between the races – highlights the basic paradox of the frontier. The very experience that Turner contended was instrumental in the development of democracy and individualism on the frontier was also instrumental in the development of a racist and, in the final analysis, a "colonialist" orientation toward the Indian. This duality is the central meaning of the frontier heritage in America.

*   *   *

Merely offering a general appraisal of the frontier's reaction to the Indian does not do full justice to an understanding of the encounter between white man and Indian; it merely sets the stage.

The history of successive frontiers to which Turner alludes covers about 300 years of American history. During that period the Indians were transformed from independent sovereignties to subjugated plural segments of the American society. The rest of this chapter will be devoted to an examination of how this came about. Understanding the process requires that we enlarge the framework of our analysis. We shall continue to be interested in the stress and turmoil of the frontier, but our prime attention will be directed toward the role that governmental policy and action played in this transformation of the Indian.

The confrontation between the colonist and the savage but sovereign Indian

When they landed on the American shores, most English colonists met a racially different group of people for the first time in their lives. Their initial reactions to the Indians were tentative and not entirely unfriendly. They were impressed with the hospitality of the Indians but explained it as the working of the colonist's own God "who temporarily imbued the Indian with kindness" (Washburn 1971:33), or as the cunning stratagem of a savage who was inherently treacherous. In effect, most early colonists viewed the Indian as a "strange creature." They were suspiciously tolerant of him but were equally convinced that he was a heathen who was a religious and racial inferior. A few colonists such as John Smith openly expressed friendly feelings and helped give rise to the "noble savage" theme that has surfaced on occasion as an alternate view of the Indian.

Before long this relatively benign encounter was shattered by the outbreak of fierce and bloody hostilities. The Indians reacted against the injustices they experienced and began to attack the settlements. For Virginia the turning point was the "massacre of 1622;" for Massachusetts it was the Pequot War of 1637 and the King Philip's War of 1676. These Indian attacks

> "provided the English with the 'bloody shirt' needed to justify hostilities against the natives whenever convenient. Up until that time it was necessary to see malice in good will or to cite occasional Indian violence against small groups of settlers. Now the English could point to a full-scale war directed against all the settlements and carried out with terrible effects." (Washburn 1971:36)

In this manner then "the Virginia Company seized on the Massacre to order a war against the Indians, dispossession of those near the settlements, and as a gesture of mercy, the enslavement rather than slaughter of the younger people of both sexes. The company's instructions were hardly necessary. The governor and council had already initiated a policy of exterminating the neighboring Indians" (Washburn 1971:37). In many other ways this episode was a prototypic example of the kinds of treatment that white America has generally accorded the Indian. It involved signing a treaty which "lulled" the natives "into a sense of false security," which the colonists had no intention of keeping. Further "on one occasion poison was placed in the wine offered to the Indians on the conclusion of a peace treaty" (Washburn 1971:37). In this manner then fraud and treachery were deemed normal part of the intercourse with the Indian, as reflected in the following statement:

> "When chided by the company for their 'false dealing,' the council in Virginia replied that 'wee hold nothinge injuste, that may tend to theire ruine, (except

breach of faith). Stratagems were ever allowed against all enemies, but with these neither fayre Warr nor good quarter is ever to be held, nor is there any other hope of theire subversione, who ever may inform you to the Contrairie.'"

(Washburn 1971:37)

Thus the pattern was established in the earliest days of colonial America for the combined use of force and fraud in the treatment of the Indians. To justify this response, the Indians were increasingly characterized treacherous barbarians.

"A wide assortment of contemporary records reveals that the seventeenth-century colonials, who helped mold early Indian policy, generally considered themselves superior to the aborigines. The first settlers' writings often record that they were repelled by Indian religion, Indian sexual mores, Indian illiteracy, and Indian ideas of dress, personal modesty, and adornment. There are frequent portrayals of Indians as depraved savage brutes, as impious rascals who lived in filth and ate nasty food. Even Francis Parkman, one of the first serious students of the Indians, portrayed him in colonial history as a Stone Age savage whose homicidal fury in war gave him a demoniac character."

(Jacobs 1972:110)

And yet despite the alleged barbarism of the Indians, England and the colonists did not perceive them as an undisciplined and unorganized primitive; instead they were viewed as having attained a rudimentary level of societal and political organization and as being a sovereign people. From the earliest days of settlement Indians were presumed to be organized into distinctive state societies (somewhat in the image of "minor European states") with which diplomatic negotiations could be conducted and treaties concluded.

"European statesmen anticipated that they would be dealing with political states akin to their own experience: kingdoms, sultanates, khanates, chiefdoms, and kindred systems organized with a central authority able to rely upon military force. The conquistadores had reported civilized societies of this sort (while portraying themselves in the conquering role of Julius Caesar or Pompey). In like manner, the Virginians regarded Powhatan as a 'king;' James I crowned him by proxy, and Rolfe's marriage to his daughter was expected to consolidate an alliance with a minor power in a fashion familiar to continental diplomacy."

(Wax 1971:42)

However, England and the colonists were not prepared to accept the notion that the Indian had a very high level of societal organization. Despite the fact that many of the Woodland tribes whom the colonists encountered lived in villages, engaged in agricultural pursuits, and were part of a relatively complex societal and political system, the colonists persisted in defining all Indians as nomadic hunting tribes with no settled habitation who had a frivolous and wasteful relationship to the land and resources they occupied.

This conception proved extremely useful to colonists and to later Americans as well. They argued that such wasteful land use had to give way to the needs and demands of a superior civilization which knew how to use the land more effectively. (The fact that the opposite was probably true did not prevent the colonists from using this theme to help justify their cavalier treatment of the Indians through force and fraud.)

The military situation faced by the early colonists, however, did not permit easy realization of their aims. Despite the technological superiority of their arms, they were confronted by a powerful and numerous adversary whose own interests and wishes could not be readily dismissed. Accordingly, the colonists could not merely drive the Indian off his land and seize the land through the right of conquest. Instead, they were obliged to take into account the claims of the Indian to the land; they sought to do this through acts of purchase and the signing of treaties. Engaged in extensive negotiations with the Indian, the colonists employed the various devices of diplomatic intercourse and sought to obtain at minimal cost the land (and also the furs) they coveted. They legitimated the entire transaction through the signing of formal treaties.

> "The facts of the power relationship in the early seventeenth century resulted in an elaborate diplomatic exchange between the English and the Indians in the New World. No sweeping claims to legal title – such as the Spanish Requirement – were read to the Indians. Rather, the head of each English settlement – whether it was Plymouth or Jamestown – dealt with the Indians who could affect his purpose in the manner of one independent power dealing with another. Threats, cajolery, bribery, force, persuasion, gifts – in sum, all the tools of international relations – were used to facilitate English purchase of, or occupation of the lands to which they aspired. De facto agreements were reached which – if the speculative legal claims of European sovereigns were meaningful – would have been totally unnecessary. The two realms coexisted."
>
> (Washburn 1971:41–2)

As part of the elaborate ceremonials of diplomatic exchange, gift-giving took on special symbolic significance, but as in the case of the treaties, gift-giving had a different meaning for each party:

> "From the Indian point of view, it is possible to see such presents as 'tribute' given by the Europeans to the Indians as 'protection money' to insure that the

Indians did not exercise their power against the white men. From a European point of view, however, the presents were often thought of as symbolic of the dependence of the Indians upon the Europeans and as a practical method of arming auxiliaries against a common foe. There is an element of truth in both Indian and English points of view. Certainly the presents of guns, ammunition, clothes, useful articles of iron and items of personal decoration such as paint, silver gorgets, hawks bells and the like, came to be expected and sometimes demanded by the Indians as a right due them in exchange for their neutrality or aid. On the other hand, it is also true that the Europeans obtained good will, loyalty and military service in exchange for what was regarded in Indian cultural terms as the evidence of a true friendship and alliance."   (Washburn 1971:48)

In the early days both parties met at these negotiating sessions as they did on the battlefield as virtual equals. Neither could overwhelm the other nor enforce its will entirely at the expense of the other. According to Washburn, the watershed year for the Indians in Virginia and in New England was 1675. After that their negotiating strength started to wane under the combined onslaught of numbers and military power of the English. "The fact that that year marks the outbreak of two significant Indian wars – King Philip's War in New England and Bacon's Rebellion in Virginia – during which the Indian power was demonstrably reduced – is not without significance. With their newly acquired predominance of numbers and weapons, the English could disregard justice and exercise mere force" (Washburn 1971:42).

However, the Indian made his presence and power both felt and feared during much of the eighteenth century in the Northeast. Indian affairs were a continuing concern of high priority to most colonial legislatures; each sought to pursue its own policies from defense of the frontier to punitive actions against the Indians, from treaty negotiations to open hostilities. Most colonies took a narrow, harsh, and ethnocentric view of the situation. They were convinced that the Indians were treacherous savages who were bent on widespread destruction of the colonists and therefore had to be pushed back mercilessly. Little attention was paid to the needs and grievances of the Indians and to the injustices visited upon them. A few colonies such as Pennsylvania under the Quakers or Rhode Island under Roger Williams were prepared to give serious consideration to the complaints and needs of the Indians and to protect their interests and rights, and to live up to the terms of treaties which were negotiated between "equals."

In time, however, even these colonies were unable to withstand the unrelenting pressure from the frontiersmen, land speculators, and fur traders. These groups were generally in the vanguard of those who sought to force the Indian to sign a treaty in which he "sold" substantial tracts of land to the colonial governments.

They were also in the vanguard of those who, even after a treaty was signed, infiltrated into the land presumably accepted as still belonging to the Indian by the colonial government. This set the stage for a new confrontation between Indian and colonial government in the near future, and a repeat of the process once again.

The response of the Indian to these repeated incursions was frequent and violent raids on frontier establishments. On occasion the response took on the character of a major military campaign. Under the leadership of such dynamic and skillful chiefs as Pontiac or King Philip, Indians launched widespread and concerted attacks against the frontier that spread destruction and threatened the survival of the white settlers. But in time these campaigns failed; the Indians were beaten back, and the white frontier advanced once again.

Not until the middle of the eighteenth century did England seek to wrest from the colonies primary control over Indian affairs. The precipitating factor was the clash of imperial interests between France and England. The two countries competed vigorously for the loyalty and support of Indian tribes. Their efforts were intensified even more when open warfare broke out between the two.

Accordingly, England adopted an Indian superintendency plan that was patterned after Edmond Atkins' proposal.

"Two imperial superintendents were to be appointed; these should be vested by Parliament with full authority and be provided with the financial resources necessary for carrying out their duties. The northern superintendent was to have jurisdiction over the Iroquoian confederacy and its allies, and his southern counterpart was to govern British relations with the southern tribes, the Cherokee and their Muskhogean brothers.

One of the first duties of the superintendents would be to negotiate a series of treaties with all the principal Indian nations that would bind them to the British. The Indians were to agree to trade only with the English, and new trade regulations were to be established by law to protect the natives from abuses. Indian commerce was to follow a regular procedure with licensed traders, fixed prices, and standard weights and measures. In addition, heavy penalties were to be imposed on any trader who allowed Indians to become drunk. All spirits given to the warriors had to be 'temper'd' with water." (Jacobs 1972:66)

In this manner

"the British Crown in 1754 took over from the colonies the power of dealing with Indians, under this imperial policy: The tribes were independent nations, under the protection of the Crown; Indian lands were inalienable except through voluntary surrender to the Crown; and any attempt by an individual or group, subject to the Crown, or by a foreign state, to buy or seize lands from Indians, was illegal."   (Collier 1947:197)

One other feature of British policy was added several years later which also became a cornerstone of subsequent American policy: the notion of Indian country or land which was to be the preserve of the Indian. This policy developed from the upheavals that beset the frontier after the defeat of the French. Under the leadership of Pontiac, the Indians threatened the entire wilderness frontier along the northern line of white settlement. Under the pressure of these events, England rushed through a policy decision which it had been considering for some time as a decisive way of dealing with the grievances of the Indians: "Conciliation of the Indians was of prime importance; British officials knew that justice in the treatment of the Indians was a prerequisite and that this justice demanded strong measures to restrain, if not prevent, the encroachment on the Indian lands" (Prucha 1962:15).

Accordingly, the Proclamation of 1763 was issued; it drew a boundary line along the Appalachian watershed beyond which white settlers were not to go, at least temporarily.

> "The Proclamation of 1763 did not represent a fully worked out western policy and was at best a framework upon which such a policy could be built. The boundary line idea was definitely settled upon; there seems to have been no disagreement about it, although there may well have been different reasons for it in the minds of different men. But the line described in the Proclamation was temporary, to stand only until more definite agreements could be made with the Indians, new lands purchased by the government, and distinct boundaries run by the surveyors."   (Prucha 1962:20)

Intent as England was on a just policy for the Indian and on the adherence to the terms of treaties with the Indians, its efforts to implement this policy, though significant and sincere, proved unequal to the task. Its own royal governors and military men followed their own bent; the colonies did not unite in support of these policies and frequently undermined them, and the frontiersmen, traders, and land speculators kept pressing ahead. As a result encroachment continued and sharp dealings with the Indians flourished. Both British policy and treaties therefore proved ineffectual; they were unable to stabilize the situation or to prevent encroachment on tribal lands. In effect, policy, treaties, and even the military response of Indians provided at best just a temporary respite in the unrelenting pressure for the acquisition of land and resources.

Early governmental policy of the United States and the sovereign Indian

With the coming of the Revolutionary War, the colonies were confronted by a crisis in their relations with the Indians. They were no longer bound by the Imperial policy toward the Indians, and England was making good use of this fact in its negotiations with the tribes. England argued that only the presence of Imperial policy had prevented the colonies from further depredations of the Indian country; without England the colonies would once again engage in their *laissez-faire* practice of encroachment and displacement; only a military victory over the colonies would stop the recurrence of this practice. So persuasive were the English that many tribes rallied to their side and fought against the colonists.

In turn, the colonists were so concerned about the threat of Indian warfare that, despite the zeal with which they guarded the autonomy of the individual colony, they were prepared to accept the idea of a general policy for securing peaceful relations with the Indians. And so in 1775 "the Continental Congress inaugurated a federal Indian policy." It created three geographical departments and appointed a commissioner for each.

> "The commissioners were to treat with the Indians 'in the name, and on behalf of the united colonies;' they were to work to preserve peace and friendship with the Indians and, in the quaint understatement of the report, 'to prevent their taking any part in the present commotions.' Agents were to be appointed by the commissioners to spy out the conduct of the British superintendents and their agents and to seize any British agents who were stirring up the Indians against the Americans." (Prucha 1962:28)

When it came to the regulation of trade and management of Indian affairs, proponents of federal control had a more difficult time. The advocates of state control continually sought to amend the proposals. This was particularly true of proposals that dealt with Indians living within the borders of a state; less opposition was expressed toward federal control of Indians in territorial areas. Eventually a provision was passed and incorporated in the Articles of Confederation that reaffirmed the principle that the federal government had "the sole and exclusive right and power of . . . regulating the trade and managing all affairs with the Indians, not members of any of the states" (Prucha 1962:30). This power was, however, seriously compromised by a further provision that gave the states the right to regulate Indian affairs within their own borders. The consequent ambiguity plagued relations with the Indians for the next ten years; some states such as New York and North Carolina went their own way. They encroached on Indian land and signed separate treaties.

However, despite the ambiguity,

"the debates over the Articles of Confederation and the subsequent practice under this frame of government nevertheless did gradually clarify one element of Indian relations. The concept of the Indian Country was strengthened. Not only was the Indian Country that territory lying beyond the boundary lines and forbidden to settlers and to unlicensed traders; but it was also the area over which federal authority extended. Federal laws governing the Indians and the Indian trade took effect in the Indian Country only; outside they did not hold."

(Prucha 1962:31)

With the coming of peace, the victorious Americans were even less sanguine in their approach to the Indians than they were before. They were intent upon punishing them for having sided with the British and sought to treat them as subjugated nations.

"The United States in these first treaties after the Revolution thought it was dealing with conquered tribes or nations. Although Congress spoke of liberality toward the vanquished and realized that some moderation of claims might be necessary to avoid renewal of fighting, its commissioners dictated the boundary lines and offered no compensation for the ceded lands. To this high-handed arrangement the Indians, abetted by the British, continued to object. They had never asked for peace, they insisted, but thought that the Americans desired it, and they had no idea that they were to be treated as conquered peoples."

(Prucha 1962:34)

What troubled the Indians was not merely this policy of expropriation, but also the fact that further encroachments on their land were taking place even as the ink on the treaties was drying. As a result, by 1786 most tribes in the Northwest were ready to repudiate the peace treaties and open up hostilities.

Threatened by an explosion of fury along the frontier, Congress recognized that the New Nation could ill afford hostilities: its survival as a nation might be at stake. Accordingly, Congress reexamined its policies and in 1786 enacted the first of several laws which were presumably to insure justice for the Indian and guarantee their rights and property against encroachment. A most solemn statement of good intention and faith was inscribed in the Northwest Ordinance of 1787.

"The utmost good faith shall always be observed towards the Indians, their lands and property shall never be taken from them without their consent; and in their property, rights and liberty, they shall never be invaded or disturbed, unless in just and lawful wars authorized by Congress; but laws founded in justice and humanity shall from time to time be made, for preventing wrongs being done to them, and for preserving peace and friendship with them."

(Prucha 1962:37)

In addition, land was not to be taken away arbitrarily from the Indian; instead it was to be purchased as before. The major proponent of reinstituting the principle of buying the land was Henry Knox, secretary of war under the Articles of Confederation.

"Knox came to realize that agreements with the Indians based upon the right of conquest did not work and that adherence to such a policy would continually endanger the peace of the frontier. The British and colonial practice of purchasing the right of the soil from the Indians was the only method to which the Indians would peaceably agree, and Knox urged a return to that policy. To establish claims by the principle of conquest would mean continuous warfare. He recommended, therefore, that the lands ceded by the northwest Indians be compensated for and that future cessions be acquired by purchase. By the treaties signed at Fort Harmar on January 9, 1789, with the Six Nations and the northwest Indians, the lands granted to the United States at Fort Stanwix and Fort McIntosh were paid for. Small as the payments were, they marked the abandonment of the policy that the lands from the Indians were acquired by right of conquest."

(Prucha 1962:40)

Further, efforts were made to put some teeth into enforcement of the ordinances and treaties, but in the final analysis the federal government was not prepared to go beyond a certain minimum in controlling the excesses of the states and of the individual frontiersmen. As a result, encroachment continued and treaties were grossly violated.

Indian affairs were not a major topic of debate in the Constitutional Convention as they had been in the Continental Congress and in the promulgation of the Articles of Confederation. The reason may well be that the principle of federal control over Indian affairs had already been fought and won in the promulgation of the Articles. What was still needed was a clear-cut resolution to the ambiguities in the Articles which allowed the individual states to retain an indeterminate amount of authority in their hands.

However, even at the Constitutional Convention it was difficult to obtain a clear-cut statement affirming that the federal government had sole responsibility for dealings with the Indians. What finally emerged was a prepositional phrase that was appended to the commerce clause as part of the section of the Constitution defining the powers vested in Congress. Accordingly, under Article I, Section 8, Congress was "To regulate Commerce with foreign Nations, and among several states, and with the Indian Tribes" (*The Constitution of The United States with the Amendments* 1872:8).

These few words plus other powers delegated to the federal government such as treaty-making became the basis upon which Congress established the primacy of its authority in Indian affairs and upon which it came to exercise "what amounts to plenary power over the Indian tribes" (Prucha 1962:43).

Under the leadership of George Washington, Congress passed a series of laws that reaffirmed its hegemony over Indian affairs. In the process the United States government sought to hammer out a policy of conciliation and negotiation with the Indian tribes. It reaffirmed their integrity as distinctive nations and rejected the solution of absolute conquest. It agreed to seek peaceful and harmonious relations with the Indians through treaties and gave solemn assurances that the terms of the treaties would be strictly adhered to, including protection of the new boundaries from further encroachment.

> "Having waived the right of conquest, it [the US government] determined to compensate the Indians fairly for lands given up and to protect them in the lands they still retained. The Indians' wants would be cared for by a government-fostered trade, and presents would be freely used when necessary to smooth the road toward solid friendship."
>
> (Prucha 1962:44)

Within the next ten years a series of acts were passed which sought to give this policy the force of law. In 1790, for example, a law was passed which "declared the purchase of lands from the Indians invalid unless made by a public treaty with the United States" (Prucha 1962:45). It also "provided for the licensing of traders;" provision was even made for the "punishment of murder and other crimes committed by whites against the Indians in the Indian Country" (Prucha 1962:46). In 1793 even more inclusive legislation was passed. In 1796 the concept of Indian country was first introduced into statute laws.

In this manner the US government sought to construct a protective legal environment around its treaties with the Indians in Indian country so that its promises and guarantees could be honored or at least its good faith would become visible. In so doing it reaffirmed the distinctive separateness of the Indian nation and sought to reduce contact and communication between the two to officially designated channels and agents, whether these were Indian agents, military officials, or officially licensed traders. The obvious intent of these provisions was to provide breathing space and time from the relentless pressures of the moving frontier; it created the illusion of two plural societies coexisting side by side.

At still another level, the United States government sought to pursue a policy which would in theory at least bring the Indian into American society – albeit not in an equal but in an inferior position. This was the "civilizing" policy that was pursued with special vigor by Thomas Jefferson during his presidency. According to its advocates, the Indians were savages at a low level of civilization who could be and were to be guided and if necessary pushed into the ways and virtues of the higher civilization of the white American. The more optimistic spokesmen for this point of view – particularly during the early days of the policy – were convinced that this could be done in a relatively short period of time; the more pessimistic advocates – and this group grew increasingly large during the latter days of the policy – were not so sure; an increasing number of this group became convinced that the Indians were biologically inferior and could never rise to the heights of civilization or could do so only after countless generations.

The path to civilizing the Indian seemed quite clear. He had to adopt the white man's religion, but even more generally he had to give up his aboriginal ways. Specifically this meant settling down, giving up the nomadic way of life of hunting and fishing, and becoming farmers and residents of permanent villages. In addition, the Indian had to learn the value of private property and the virtues of the white man's language and education. In sum he had to adopt the white man's values, occupations, and way of life and look with disdain on his former existence as a savage.

No matter how lofty their conceptualization nor how sincere and serious their design, both sets of policies proved within a short period of time to be relatively ineffective, and at times even disastrous. For example, encroachment on Indian country continued in a relentless manner despite laws and treaties. Frontiersmen pushed into the country; unscrupulous traders and land speculators continued to cheat and to exploit the Indians. In general, tension and conflict marked most of the boundaries between Indian country and white settlement.

Efforts were made by the United States government to enforce the law and to live up to the treaties. On occasion army units were sent to clear out scattered settlers from Indian country; some individuals were even punished for cheating and killing peaceful Indians. But there were limits beyond which the government was not prepared to go in enforcing the terms of the treaties against its own citizens; it was not prepared, for example, to evict large concentrations of settlers who were illegally in Indian country, nor to punish interlopers with the severity that their crimes would have called for had they been committed against white citizens and not against Indians.

Further the government itself was split into factions on the issue of the "sanctity" of treaties and on the general question of treatment of the Indians. Some were convinced that the Indians deserved no better fate than extermination or at the least being driven from the land. As a result, efforts to enforce the treaties were frequently neutralized and an air of resigned inaction replaced any firm resolve.

Many of the Indians on the other hand were not prepared either to accept the encroachments as inevitable or to stand by passively while they were taking place. They reacted violently and open warfare erupted; white settlers were slain in a bloody conflict of no holds barred. The most serious of these conflagrations occurred in the Northwest territory during the 1790s and around the time of the War of 1812 when Tecumseh rallied the Indians in a bloody struggle against the whites.

In turn the United States government would launch punitive expeditions against the Indians on behalf of the beleaguered frontiersmen who were in general illegally ensconced in Indian territory. Despite occasional military defeats, the US government would eventually overwhelm the Indians and would then renegotiate a new treaty in which Indians would be reimbursed for "voluntarily" ceding the contested land. They would once again receive guarantees from the government concerning the sanctity of their rights to the remaining Indian country.

And so the cycle would repeat itself: encroachment by frontiersmen, violent reaction by the Indians, punitive response by the US government, eventual defeat of the Indian, and renegotiation of a new "permanent" treaty with the purchase of the disputed land. Throughout the history of the encounter with the Indian, an estimated 400 treaties were signed, most being renegotiations of previously broken treaties.

The civilizing policy of the government produced in the final analysis equally limited, if not ill-fated results. Although various presidents of the United States, most notably Jefferson, gave voice to this policy and set aside governmental funds for its implementation, missionary agencies assumed much of the active leadership in seeking to convert the Indian from savagery to civilization. With the ever increasing support of the federal government, they frequently combined both facets of civilizing the Indian: the religious and the secular.

The missionaries preached and proselytized among the Indians. They established schools within the Indian country for the education of the young; later some established schools outside the Indian country in order to isolate the young Indian more completely from his tribal environment. The missionaries and governmental officials also sought to intervene in the tribal society and attempted to restructure its institutional character and above all to make farmers of the Indians.

The relative success of these efforts is still being argued. It is evident that many Indian tribes adopted features of this civilizing process. They became Christians and also skilled in aspects of the white man's technology. Some, such as the Cherokees, even became farmers and adopted significant institutions of the white man. In general, however, no matter how much or how little they absorbed, most

Indian tribes refused to give up their identity, their basic way of life and institutions, and their claims to land and treaty rights. Those individual Indians who did leave the tribal environment and settle among the whites frequently became the victims, not the beneficiaries of the civilizing process. They became "marginal men" in the full meaning of Stonequist's (1937) term and sank quickly into a state of personal and social disorganization.

The forcible removal of the Indian to the West as a domestic dependent nation

By the late 1820s and early 1830s a series of crises virtually dismembered established governmental policy toward the Indian and fundamentally transformed the character of the relationship between government and Indian. These upheavals literally sent shock waves through the entire governmental system and produced a constitutional crisis of no mean proportion. Perhaps the crisis that did most to generate these profound effects was the confrontation between the Cherokee Indians and the State of Georgia.

What precipitated this confrontation was the decision by the Cherokee Indians, who were largely located in Georgia, to set themselves up as a separate "nation-state." The General Council, which came into existence as the central legislative body for the Cherokees in 1820, convened a constitutional convention in 1827 consisting of delegates democratically elected from each of eight districts. The convention adopted a constitution; its preamble was as follows:

"'We, the Representatives of the people of the Cherokee Nation, in Convention assembled, in order to establish justice, ensure tranquility, promote our common welfare, and secure to ourselves and our posterity the blessings of liberty; acknowledge with humility and gratitude the goodness of the sovereign Ruler of the Universe, in offering us an opportunity so favorable to the design, and imploring His aid and direction in its accomplishment, do ordain and establish this Constitution for the government of the Cherokee Nation.'"

(Every 1966:84–5)

The constitution "defined the boundaries of the Nation as 'embracing the land solemnly guaranteed and reserved forever to the Cherokee Nation by the Treaties concluded with the United States'" (Every 1966:85). The governmental structure was patterned after that of the United States.

"There was provision for separate legislative, executive and judicial department. The legislature, termed the General Council, consisted of two houses, a

> National Committee composed of two members from each district and a National Council of three members from each, in both cases elected for two-year terms. Each house had a veto power over the enactments of the other. Executive power was vested in Principal Chief to be elected by the General Council to serve for four years. There was provision for a Supreme Court, circuit courts and district courts."   (Every 1966:85)

This action by the Cherokees was neither impulsive nor poorly thought through. It was the logical outcome of a sequence of actions over a ten-year period that modified their traditional form of government in favor of a more "modern Americanized" version. The decision to embark on this course of modernization was the result of fateful encounters that the Cherokees had had with "civilization." As recently as 1819, they were obliged to cede another sizable portion of land to the United States government; in addition, they had just heard of the hardships and disappointments that a band of Cherokees had experienced in migrating westward.

> "It was not until the twin crisis of 1817–19, the migration of a significant portion of the nation to the Arkansas coupled with a new urgency in American demands for the cession of more land, that their more perceptive leaders began to realize that were their people to be saved from extinction a more effective form of government must be devised. Having once embarked upon this total departure from Indian political dogma Cherokee progress was as remarkable as that made by the inspired designers of a more effective American government during the period from the First Continental Congress through the Confederation to the Constitutional Convention."   (Every 1966:78)

The Cherokees were fully prepared to take these political steps because they had already taken similar steps in other areas of their life. They had within the space of one generation shifted dramatically from "savagery" to "civilization." They had responded enthusiastically to the opportunities for education and schooling offered to them by various missionaries who had gained their confidence. They had even invented a written language by the 1820s, and most had become Christianized.

> "This extraordinary widening of the Cherokee intellectual horizon had been accompanied by an equally extraordinary metamorphosis in Cherokee manners, customs, occupations and living conditions. More and more Cherokee families were descending from their isolated mountain glens to cultivate river bottom farms. More and more Cherokee youths were becoming blacksmiths, carpenters, masons. An 1826 count of Cherokee property disclosed 22,000 cattle, 7600 horses, 46,000 swine, 726 looms, 2488 spinning wheels, 172 wagons, 2943

plows, 10 saw mills, 31 grist mills, 62 blacksmith shops, 8 cotton machines, 18 schools, 18 ferries and many roads. The ambitious young Cherokee who once had dreamed of the number of scalps he might take or horses he might steal was now dreaming in terms of a two-story brick house, a hundred slaves and a 500 acre plantation."   (Every 1966:53)

In effect, the Cherokees by the end of the 1820s were ready to put to the test what Jefferson and others had preached: namely that acceptance of the Indian would depend upon his becoming civilized. Subsequent events showed that America was not prepared to practice what it preached or deliver on its promises.

The State of Georgia took the opportunity offered by the action of the Cherokees in 1827 to renew its campaign to dislodge the Cherokees from their land. Ever since 1802 Georgia had continually prodded the federal government to live up to its agreement with the state. At that time Georgia had given up its claims to western lands; in exchange the federal government had promised to arrange in due time "for the conveyance to Georgia of title to all remaining Indian lands within the state's borders" (Every 1966:104). The federal government had on occasion sought to apply pressure on the Indians to cede further land to Georgia, but to little avail.

In 1827 Georgia risked a military confrontation with the federal government over the validity of a treaty negotiated with the Creek Indians. President Adams threatened military intervention over Georgia's precipitate implementation of the suspect treaty but backed down. And Georgia won its point.

Once having disposed of the Creek, Georgia turned its attention to the Cherokees. In 1829 Georgia took a decisive step; it passed a bill that gave it extraordinary powers over the Cherokees. Its major provisions were:

"1. Confiscation by the state of Cherokee land for the purpose of its erection into counties and early distribution among white owners. . . .

2. Abolition of the authority of the Cherokee government, the nullification of all Cherokee laws and the exclusive subjection of all Cherokee residents to state jurisdiction.

3. Prohibition of the meetings of the Cherokee Council and of all other gatherings of Cherokee for any purpose, including religious.

4. Punishment by imprisonment of all Cherokee who advised other Cherokee to refuse to migrate.

5. Abrogation of all contracts between Indians and white unless they had been witnessed by two whites.

6. Denial of the right of any Cherokee to testify in court against any white."
                                                        (Every 1966:144)

Georgia's action was taken at a time when the United States congress was actively debating a bill of profound significance in the treatment of the Indian. The Indians were to be removed from eastern United States and resettled west of an Indian Line beyond the Mississippi River. The proposal was first submitted to Congress during the Monroe administration of 1825, but nothing much happened. It was revived in Congress by a Georgia congressman in 1827 in which he made explicit reference to the Cherokees, but once again nothing happened.

The election of Andrew Jackson to the presidency in 1828 dramatically changed the situation. Despite his protestations of personal friendliness to the Indian, Jackson – who had gained his reputation as a frontier fighter – was determined to push through the expulsion of the Indian from the East. Accordingly, the issue assumed a high priority in the deliberations of the Congress that was convened after the election. Jackson in his message to Congress not only insisted upon passage of a removal bill but also focused his attention on the Cherokee claim of sovereignty. He stated categorically, "'I informed the Indians inhabiting parts of Georgia and Alabama that their attempt to establish an independent government would not be countenanced by the Executive of the United States, and advised them to emigrate beyond the Mississippi or submit to the laws of those States'" (Every 1966:122).

The debate over the Indian removal bill was long and bitter; it evoked considerable emotion and argument throughout the country; public opinion was deeply divided. The cause of the Cherokees, which had become inextricably interwoven in the debate, evoked great sympathy and support, particularly in the North. Even liberal humanitarians who earlier supported the removal policy because they thought this was the only way to insure the survival of the Indian "savage" from the incursion of civilization were troubled by the plight of the highly "civilized" Cherokees; many shifted their views and rallied behind opposition to the bill. But despite the opposition, the bill finally passed by a narrow margin in both houses of Congress and finally became law in May 1830.

Failing to gain favorable governmental action, despite widespread public support, the Cherokee Indians then sought redress against Georgia through the federal courts. In its famous decision of 1831, the Supreme Court turned down their request for an injunction. Examination of the grounds upon which the decision was made reveals quite clearly how anomalous the status of the Indian had become in his relationship to the national policy of the United States.

In his opinion Chief Justice John Marshall reiterated the premise that the Indians were indeed a distinctive nation and political community:

"The counsel for the plaintiffs have maintained the affirmative of this proposition with great earnestness and ability. So much of the argument as was intended to prove the character of the Cherokees as a state, as a distinct political society, separated from others, capable of managing its own affairs and governing itself, has in the opinion of a majority of the judges, been completely successful. They have been uniformly treated as a state from the settlement of our country. The numerous treaties made with them by the United States recognize them as a people capable of maintaining the relations of peace and war, of being responsible in their political character for any violation of their engagements, or for any aggression committed on the citizens of the United States, by any individual of their community. Laws have been enacted in the spirit of these treaties. The acts of our government plainly recognize the Cherokee nation as a state, and the courts are bound by those acts." (30 US 1831:16)

Chief Justice Marshall, however, took strong exception to the plaintiffs' contention that this fact of nationhood necessarily meant that they were "a foreign state in the sense of the constitution" (30 US 1831:20). He argued,

"Indian territory is admitted to compose a part of the United States. In all our maps, geographical treatises, histories and laws, it is so considered. In all our intercourse with foreign nations, in our commercial regulations, in any attempt at intercourse between Indians and foreign nations, they are considered as within the jurisdictional limits of the United States, subject to many of those restraints which are imposed upon our own citizens.... [The Indians] acknowledge themselves in their treaties to be under the protection of the United States; they admit that the United States shall have the sole and exclusive right of regulating the trade with them, and managing all their affairs as they think proper; ... Though the Indians are acknowledged to have an unquestionable, and heretofore unquestioned right to the lands they occupy, until that right shall be extinguished by a voluntary cession to our government; yet it may well be doubted whether those tribes which reside within the acknowledged boundaries of the United States can with strict accuracy, be denominated foreign nations."

(30 US 1831:17)

Accordingly he labeled the Indians as "domestic dependent nations" (30 US 1831:17) as distinct from independent foreign nations. He continued:

"They occupy a territory to which we assert a title independent of their will, which must take effect in point of possession, when their right of possession ceases. Meanwhile they are in a state of pupilage; their relation to the United States resembles that of a ward to his guardian.

They look to our government for protection; rely upon its kindness and its power; appeal to it for relief to their wants; and address the president as their great father. They and their country are considered by foreign nations, as well as by ourselves, as being so completely under the sovereignty and dominion of the

United States, that any attempt to acquire their lands, or to form a political connexion with them, would be considered by all as an invasion of our territory, and an act of hostility."

(30 US 1831:17)

The distinction that Marshall made was of critical significance. A foreign independent nation has a right to seek redress from state and federal governmental actions in federal courts. This right is explicitly stipulated in the Constitution. Marshall, however, argued that such a right did not explicitly exist in the Constitution for a domestic dependent nation. Accordingly, he and the Court dismissed the suit claiming that the federal courts had no jurisdiction in the case.

In effect, the Indians suffered a fateful decision in 1831 comparable to that the blacks came to suffer in 1857. Both groups were defined as being within the territorial boundaries of the government of the United States and subject to its laws. But neither could seek nor obtain legal redress because they were neither part of the people of the United States nor sufficiently independent of the people to warrant separate consideration.

The Supreme Court modified its position somewhat in the following year in a case brought by several white missionaries against Georgia. The missionaries had been arrested and convicted in Georgia under provision of a state law passed in 1831 which forbade whites from residing among the Cherokees without a special license. Not only did the Supreme Court find in behalf of the missionaries, but it also declared Georgia's laws against the Cherokees as unconstitutional because they trespassed on an area of legislation reserved for the federal government by the Constitution.

Georgia refused to abide by the Supreme Court decision and thereby provoked a constitutional crisis with the Court, which the Court lost. What prevented the situation from escalating into a general constitutional confrontation with the federal government as a whole was the refusal of the executive branch under Jackson to back up the Supreme Court. The President's goal was in the final analysis no different from that of Georgia; both wanted the Indians to leave the East. The President differed from Georgia only in seeking to soften the harshness of Georgia's repressive measures. Despite this difference, Georgia had its way and continued its campaign of repression and terror to force the Indians from their land. In a short period of time, Georgia had succeeded in converting a fairly affluent group of people into homeless paupers. However, it still took the United States government several more years before it succeeded in getting the Cherokees to migrate. Finally in 1838 the infamous "trail of tears" took place and the Cherokees were expelled from the East.

Thus ended in a brutal manner a major act in the drama between Indian and white man that had lasted for 200 years. During that period that Indians had been inextricably interwoven in the fate of the white man as the latter sought to build a nation-state. They represented the frontier, and the frontier was for several hundred years but a short distance from the very heart of civilized America.

During that period, particularly in the early days, the white man could not avoid the presence of the Indians. He might cheat them, take their land through force or fraud, but he still had to deal directly with them for they were neither few in number nor weak in military force. Thus treaty-making was in many ways an adaptive response to the realities of the situation that existed at the time. Confronting each other initially as near equals, the scales of power inexorably tipped toward the white man, but not enough to make him disavow the policy of treaty-making for generations. The rivalry among the various colonial powers, France, England, and Spain, helped perpetuate the strategic role of the Indians, many of whom played the part of Simmel's *tertius gaudens* and used the situation to further their own interest. The concept of the Indian tribe as a sovereign nation was reinforced by the policy and practice of treaty-making. As the strength and numbers of the white man grew, the treaties that his government signed were rarely kept for long, but the illusion persisted that the United States and the Indian tribes were independent coexisting nations.

The events of the 1830s shattered this illusion beyond repair and laid bare the naked power situation. The Indians had become too weak to pursue an independent course; they had become dependent on the policy and action of United States government. The latter in turn was no longer prepared to countenance the presence of the Indians within the heart of the American nation that at the time was east of the Mississippi River. Instead they forcibly expelled the Indians to the then "uncivilized" West. In effect, they sought to make the Indian invisible at the center.

This decision served to highlight the paradoxical dualism that had come to characterize Indian-white relations. At the level of final authority the white man had clearly demonstrated his power over the Indians through his federal government. They were to be subject to the exercise of his law and were defined as well within the jurisdiction of his authority. In effect, despite minor challenges in the future, the issue had for all intents and purposes been settled: no matter where the Indian might live, it was part of the territory over which the political state (the US government) claimed overall authority. Even the Cherokees did not contest this as they rebuilt their nation in Oklahoma.

However, within this political state, the Indians were not to be randomly distributed; instead they were to be confined to the area beyond the boundary that clearly separated the territory of the people of the United States or of the national community from the uncivilized and wild periphery of the political state. Within this area the Indians were to be permitted the status of a "quasi-nation." Treaties were to be signed as though the Indians still constituted a state society, but the terms of the treaties were heavily weighted in favor of the white man's government. In effect, what was left was a shadowy remnant of the "myth of sovereignty."

The West and the quasi-nationhood of the Indian

Within their territory, the Indians were once again promised integrity and autonomy – up to a point – and their claims to the land reaffirmed. The mechanism for making these promises was still the treaty. Elaborate ceremonies took place as the Indian and the agents of the United States government solemnly signed protocols in a manner not too different from that of numerous generations before. But the content and terms of these treaties revealed the dramatic change in status of the Indians. The land that was being set aside for their reservations was increasingly devoid of productive viability; it had neither the game nor fish for their traditional means of livelihood nor the fertility of soil which would permit them to become agriculturists. Thus the economic base was increasingly cut out from under them. As a result they became more and more dependent upon the supplies, goods, and annuities provided by the US government through treaty. In this way the mechanism originating from the premise that the two parties to the transaction were independent and autonomous became an instrument for converting one of the parties into an increasing state of dependence; however, without this mechanism, the conversion to dependence and impotence would probably have taken place more rapidly and more completely than it did, as subsequent events proved. Further, in making a treaty, the white man had to listen to the Indian's definition of his needs and interests although the white man could and frequently did reject them.

A number of Indian tribes did not submit meekly or passively to the changed circumstances. They reacted vehemently as the boundaries of civilization pressed more and more into Indian territory. As a result, violence erupted frequently; savagery knew no bounds as each party confronted the other in struggles in which no quarter was given or asked. Death and destruction were thus constant features of the frontier life of both white and Indian; and dehumanized hatred and passion, its heritage.

And so in many ways the "winning of the West" was a replay of the earlier encounter between Indian and white in the East, but it was in most respects an epilogue to the earlier drama; and the outcome of the earlier drama had already determined the outcome of the epilogue. The Indians could do little but delay their final subjugation. Active opposition to the encroachments of the white did have some positive consequences for the Indian. Not only did it reaffirm his sense of pride and self-respect but it also enabled him to exact better terms in treaties, even after defeat. One of the most striking examples is the contrast between the treatment of the Poncas with that of the Sioux. The Poncas, a small tribe with a history of peaceful relations with the United States, were forcibly removed in 1877 by the US government from their reservation which they had occupied for years because of a treaty that had been signed with the more warlike Sioux which gave them that territory. The results were disastrous for the Ponca, many of whom died in the forced march from their reservation. In time, however, the Sioux did not fare much better. They fought bitterly to defend their Black Hills against the encroachment of the whites; they even defeated General Custer; but they were finally overwhelmed and forced to cede much of their treasured land.

As the dependence of the Indian tribes on the government grew – particularly as they were forced onto reservations without viable means of livelihood – so grew the bureaucratic structure that was charged with the responsibility of implementing government policy and with discharging the obligations that the government had incurred through its treaties. In 1849 the Bureau of Indian Affairs was taken out of the Department of War and placed in the Department of the Interior. It was enlarged as the number of tribes it had to administer increased. In the 1860s a Board of Indian Commissioners was appointed to advise the Bureau and to improve the liaison with the public.

From its beginning, administration of Indian Affairs was enmeshed in politics, corruption, and exploitation. While a number of Bureau agents worked heroically and unselfishly to fulfill the obligations to the Indians and to meet their needs, the system itself literally invited greed and corruption. The lure was the monies and supplies that the Bureau dispensed to the tribes. These attracted unscrupulous contractors and agents who would short weight and shortchange the Indians. Politicians were also quick to recognize the value of these positions for patronage. A whole industry of patronage and corruption emerged full bloom as an integral part of the administration of Indian Affairs. In addition, the perennial hunger for more Indian land guaranteed that the entire network of relations with the Indians would be mired in a cesspool of avarice, greed, and exploitation of the Indian.

Periodically efforts were undertaken to reform the administration of Indian Affairs, but these too had little lasting effect on the internal working of the bureaucratic machinery. In 1869, for example, President Grant placed in the hands of church bodies the responsibility for nominating Indian agents and other personnel and for generally supervising activities in selected reservations. Before long, the various denominations began to squabble among themselves; their efforts at reform proved generally inadequate. Within ten years church supervision of Indian Affairs was abandoned. In the late 1870s Secretary of Interior Carl

Schurz made a major effort to overhaul the administrative machinery, but he too had only limited success.

The demise of the Indian as quasi-nation: the end of treaty-making

What was having growing effect was the mounting pressure for a basic change in Indian policy. "As the Indians became militarily impotent, and their condition could no longer be concealed in a secluded wilderness, critics and reformers of Indian policy increased in numbers and energy" (Wax 1971:52). The first casualty of this movement was the long-established policy of treaty-making.

In 1871 Congress abolished it in favor of direct legislation for the Indian. Much of the pressure for this move came from those who felt treaties had become inconvenient and unnecessary for negotiation; the Indians had become so powerless. In this manner was dispelled any lingering notion about the sovereignty of the tribes. Also, an important channel of communication with the tribes was closed, for direct legislation did not include consultation with the Indians. Some friends of the Indians nevertheless felt that such congressional action would afford greater protection for the Indians than did treaties. The abandonment of the policy, however, did not foreclose "legislative agreements" with some tribes. This functional equivalent to a treaty was worked out with the Sioux in 1876. But in general abandonment of the policy meant that the government had accepted without qualification the view that Indians had become nothing more than its wards and its supplicants. Such a view reinforced the already prevailing notion that the government knew best what was good for the Indians and did not have to consult with them.

The allotment policy: converting the Indian into an atomized plural mass

Not content with undermining the last vestiges of political autonomy of the Indian, many reformers were convinced that the tribal system was primarily at fault for keeping the Indian in a chronic state of "savagery" and poverty. Accordingly, they breathed new life into the Jeffersonian vision of civilizing the Indian through making him a farmer and making him appreciate the virtue of owning his own land. They attacked the vulnerable core of the traditional system, the tribal title to communal property, and advocated allotting each Indian a plot of land for his own use. They did this with honorable intentions but without much regard to what the Indian himself wanted:

"These reformers were not really knowledgeable about the Indian, or even interested in learning how the Indian thought or what he desired. They were motivated by an objective concern: that the Indian be dealt with honestly and fairly, and assisted in becoming a moral being exactly like themselves. Seeing that the reservation system as it was then established had not protected the Indians in their property or assisted them in becoming self-sufficient farmers, the reformers became advocates of a policy of allotment in severalty. They reasoned that if reservation lands were made into individual property rather than the congregate property of the tribe, their owners would share the rights and protections that Anglo-Saxon legal codes give to landholders. Moreover, they believed that if the lands were allotted to individual Indians as private property, then these persons would be motivated to cultivate the lands and progress in the status of civilized and Christian men."   (Wax 1971:53-4)

The drive toward a policy of allotment in severalty was enthusiastically joined by many land speculators and frontier groups who saw in such a policy an opportunity to get hold of substantial portions of the reservation property. By 1887 these combined forces were successful in passing the Dawes Act (the General Allotment Act). The friends of the Indians did manage to include in the law a stipulation that the allotment could not be sold for twenty-five years; during that time it would be held in trust by the United States government. This presumably was to protect the naive Indian from the unscrupulous white.

What the law tried to do in effect was to impose a new institutional arrangement on the Indian which would obliterate his traditional system. All hostilities with the Indians had virtually ceased by this time, and they had indeed become a conquered people. The hope was that the Indian could be persuaded to adopt this new arrangement; if he could not, then coercion would be used. It was as though the Indian was being told that his way of life could no longer be tolerated; instead he would have to change his ways to conform to the standards of the larger society. Entry into that society would depend upon his meeting three conditions: (1) he become the owner of a piece of property; (2) he become a farmer; and (3) he divorce himself from the tribal way of life. If he were to do these things he could look forward to being treated like anyone else under law and the courts and to becoming a citizen of the United States. In fact, Section 6 of the Dawes Act stipulated:

"That upon the completion of said allotments and the patenting of the lands to said allottees, each and every member of the respective bands or tribes of Indians to whom allotments have been made shall have the benefit of and be subject to the laws, both civil and criminal, of the State or Territory in which they may reside; and no Territory shall pass or enforce any law denying any such Indian within his jurisdiction the equal protection of the law. And every Indian born within the territorial limits of the United States to whom allotments shall have been made under the provisions of this act, or under any law or treaty, and every Indian born within the territorial limits of the United States who has voluntarily taken up, within said limits, his residence separate and apart from any tribe of Indians therein, has adopted the habits of civilized life, is hereby declared to be a citizen of the United States, and is entitled to all the rights, privileges, and immunities of such citizens, whether said Indian has been or not, by birth or otherwise a member of any tribe of Indians within the territorial limits of the United States."   (US Statutes at Large 1887 XXIV:390)

For approximately fifty years – from 1888 to 1934 – the allotment system was at the center of government policy toward the Indians; during that period the allotment practices and procedures were modified by various legislative acts; the major legal modification was the granting of permission under certain conditions to the leasing of allotted land. But despite these modifications, the policy remained unchanged: Indian land was to be carved into smaller privately owned parcels.

The consequences of this policy for the Indian over the years were disastrous. According to a report by the House of Representatives in 1934, the Indians had lost 90,000,000 acres of their land over the fifty year period in which the allotment system was in operation. These acres had mostly been put on the market under the legal provisions that stipulated that unallotted land could be put up for sale, and the proceeds put aside for Indian purposes. Whites had bought most of the acres. Other acres had been originally part of the allotment to individual Indians but despite the presumed legal safeguards they had fallen into the hands of whites through fraud or other devices. As a result of these various depredations, by the end of the allotment period, an estimated 65 percent of territory that was Indian land at the beginning of the period was lost to the Indians.

Further a major goal of the policy, namely the conversion of Indians into farmers, fell far short of realization. In large measure, this was because much of the land to which Indians were finally able to retain title was not suitable for farming; nothing much could be grown. The more desirable lands had fallen into the hands of whites. In addition, in the early days the government failed to provide sufficient funds for farming equipment and for effective training of the Indians in the ways of agriculture. As a result, many Indians had neither the tools nor the knowhow to become farmers. Further, the practice of leasing land owned by Indians became increasingly widespread despite some inadequate legal and administrative restrictions of the practice. Thus the Indian leased his property to whites and then tried to get along on the usually meager rentals – payments which frequently kept him just on the border of starvation.

The allotment system did, however, come close to realizing one of its professed goals; it systematically undermined the tribal system. Traditional authority lost its economic and financial base through its hold on tribal property. The policy itself became a source of controversy and cleavage. Although most Indians were against it, some of the younger halfbreeds were for it while the older fullbloods were unalterably opposed. The government played the former group against the latter and thus kept the internal structure of authority in a state of ferment. Further the governmental agency did what it could to dismantle Indian culture and traditions. The net result was widespread social and personal disorganization – a climate of anomie pervaded many of the tribes.

One of the chief beneficiaries of this period was the governmental bureaucracy, the Bureau of Indian Affairs. It increasingly assumed an autocratic and paternalistic posture and was convinced that it knew what was best for the Indian. A scathing indictment of its activities during that period was made in a report prepared by the Office of Indian Affairs in 1938.

"While treaties and wars had failed to break down the internal organization and culture of the Indian tribes, the allotment policy brought with it a growing roster of white superintendents, farm agents, teachers, inspectors and missionaries who superseded Indian leaders and to a large extent succeeded in destroying Indian culture. There was developed a system of closed reservations ruled autocratically by the Indian Bureau.... This autocratic rule was carried out under an ever-increasing number of uncorrelated statutes; a never codified and vast body of administrative regulations; and the personal government of Indian agents who were politically appointed." (Cohen 1942:28)

The basic premises underlying bureaucratic practice and policy were the presumed incompatibility between Indian "savagery" and American "civilization," and the presumed irreconcilability between the role of citizen with that of tribal member. Accordingly, it was determined that the Indian could only become a member of the American national community if he divested himself of his culture and identity as an Indian. The fact that the Indian did not particularly wish for these "benefits" made no real difference; it merely meant coercion not persuasion would be necessary.

The above report describes this bureaucratic approach graphically:

"The guiding concepts in what may be called the autocratic phase of the Federal policy toward Indians were the destruction of all Indian tribal bonds, the effacing of Indian languages and cultural heritages, the forcing of the Indian as an individual to become identified with and lost in the white life, and the breaking of tribal, communal and even family landholdings into individual allotments of farm, timber and grazing lands."   (Cohen 1942:28)

In effect, the thesis of the allotment period was that the only basis of acceptance into the national community for the Indian was his being transformed into an occupational-class group acculturated into the values of the dominant society. To the extent that he retained his distinctive tribal ways and identity, to that extent he was doomed to remain a pariah ethnoracial group dependent on the largess of the host society but excluded from membership in it. The program of the allotment period, then, was to transform (forcibly if necessary) the Indian from an ethnoracial group to an occupational-class category. The fact that in the latter status the Indian would still be doomed to poverty as he was in the former was deemed irrelevant; at the least he would be in the system. The gravest miscalculation of this period was the vacuum that was created for the Indians with the undermining of their traditional system. Accordingly, many were transformed into an impoverished atomized mass, their pariah plural identity remaining intact.

Reconciliation of tribal identity and citizenship

During the early 1920s the philosophy behind the allotment program was significantly modified. Whereas in the past perpetuation of the tribal status of the Indian was deemed incompatible with the full rights of citizenship, Congress changed that in 1924. It granted citizenship to all Indians born within the boundaries of the United States. Felix Cohen estimates that this law affected only about one-third of the Indians; approximately two-thirds having already acquired citizenship through the allotment program, special treaties, and statutes. The law, however, resolved the anomalous status of the non-citizen Indian. He had been

"barred from the ordinary processes of naturalization open to foreigners.... The naturalization laws applied only to free white persons and did not include Indians, who were regarded as domestic subjects or nationals. As members of domestic dependent nations, owing allegiance to their tribe, they were analogized to children of foreign diplomats, born in the United States."

(Cohen 1942:154–55)

In 1856 the Attorney General of the United States succinctly described the subject status of the Indian:

"'The fact, therefore, that Indians are born in the country does not make them citizens of the United States.

The simple truth is plain, that the Indians are the *subjects* of the United States,

and therefore are not, in mere right of home-birth, citizens of the United States.'"
(Cohen 1942:155)

So many questions and doubts had arisen about the policy toward the Indians by the middle of the 1920s that an exhaustive survey of their economic and social conditions was commissioned by the Department of Interior from the Institute for Government Research. Its report, which was completed in 1928, was extremely critical of the allotment system, of the workings of the Bureau of Indian Affairs, and in general of the entire manner in which relations with the Indians were being conducted. The researchers were appalled at the poverty, the social and personal disorganization of the Indian, and his poor health and education. They made a number of recommendations, including the need to strengthen the family and communal life of the Indian and to encourage Indian participation in his own affairs.

In many respects the Institute's report furnished the guidelines for the fundamental change and redirection of the Indian policy that occurred in the early 1930s. This change was incorporated in the Indian Reorganization Bill of 1934; its purposes were stated as follows:

"(1) To stop the alienation, through action by the Government or the Indians, of such lands, belonging to ward Indians, as are needed for the present and future support of these Indians.

(2) To provide for the acquisition, through purchase, of land for Indians, now landless, who are anxious and fitted to make a living on such land.

(3) To stabilize the tribal organization of Indian tribes by vesting such tribal organizations with real, though limited, authority, and by prescribing conditions which must be met by such tribal organizations.

(4) To permit Indian tribes to equip themselves with the devices of modern business organization, through forming themselves into business corporations.

(5) To establish a system of financial credit for Indians.

(6) To supply Indians with means for collegiate and technical training in the best schools.

(7) To open the way for qualified Indians to hold positions in the Federal Indian Service."
(Cohen 1942:84)

Under the vigorous leadership of the Indian Commissioner John Collier, the allotment policy of the past fifty years was brought to an end. It had sought to "assimilate" forcibly the Indian into the American society by destroying his tribal life and culture, but now Indian life and culture was to be revitalized. Further, under the allotment system the tribal system was treated as alien to the American society; now it was to become integrated into that society and was to serve as a mediating link between the individual Indian and the larger society. Under the new policy the Indian was to have a voice on matters of concern to him and to his way of life, and the tribal council was to serve as the mechanism for collective decision-making and self-government. In effect, the tribe was legitimized as a plural segment *within* the larger society. It regained the legitimacy it had during the treaty-making period: then it was treated as a political nation and community outside the host society. During the allotment period the tribe not only lost its status as a distinctive nation but was also viewed as alien to and incompatible with the larger society.

The relegitimation of the tribe symbolized the new policy orientation in which the Indian was to have a voice in his own affairs and in which Indian interests and needs were to play a larger role than they had in the past in governmental action. During the early years of the new policy, efforts were made to build up the land base of the Indians; by 1938 several million acres had been added. However, the structure of self-government was largely patterned after the white man's, and the Bureau of Indian Affairs, with the departure of Collier, sought to circumscribe the voice of the Indians on their affairs. Consequently, dissatisfaction with the internal structure of authority grew over the years among factions in the tribe.

Termination policy: the struggle over the guardian role of the government

After World War II, pressures once again grew to sell Indian land under the patent fee provisions of the allotment program. Even more significantly an attack was mounted in Congress and elsewhere against the guardianship role of the federal government. These people generally argued in the name of equality of treatment. Some of their arguments were: the Indians should be treated like everyone else, their ward status branded them as inferior and as children; to become and to be treated as mature adults, Indians would have to stand on their own feet and compete with everyone else on equal terms. The attack then was not against the tribal system as such, as it had been in the allotment period, but against the protective environment which the federal government had constructed around the Indian and his tribe. What the advocates of terminating the trustee role of the government failed to recognize was the historical validity of this arrangement. Trusteeship, payment of annuities, preservation of the integrity of the tribe and reservation were in large measure part of the treaty obligations assumed by the United States government in exchange for land and peace with the Indians. The normative framework of relations with the Indian obviously atrophied with the ever-increasing powerlessness of the Indian. The net result was that by mid-twentieth century the normative framework which had been set in an earlier period presumably between "equals" had become transmuted into a "parent-child" relationship in the eyes of the powerful white. Professing to act in behalf of his "ward," the dominant white was actually tiring of his historical obligation, and he wished to abandon his old responsibilities without assuming new ones.

By the Eisenhower administration congressional sentiment for a termination policy reached such a point that it was merely a matter of time before legislation in support of such a policy would be enacted. The rhetoric in behalf of such legislation was in the best tradition of the Constitution and of the Republic. The Indians were to be treated as part of the people of the United States. This was the sentiment expressed in the preamble to the House Concurrent Resolution No. 108 which passed both Houses of Congress in 1953 and set the tone for subsequent legislative.

> "Whereas it is the policy of Congress, as rapidly as possible, to make the Indians within the territorial limits of the United States subject to the same laws and entitled to the same privileges and responsibilities as are applicable to other citizens of the United States to end their status as wards of the United States, and to grant them all the rights and prerogatives pertaining to American citizenship; and whereas the Indians within the territorial limits of the United States should assume their full responsibilities as American citizens."
>
> (US Congressional Record (83:1) 1953:9968)

The resolution then went on to declare that at the earliest possible time a number of designated tribes "should be freed from Federal supervision and control and from all disabilities and limitations specially applicable to Indians" (US Congressional Record (83:1) 1953:9968).

The first termination bill passed Congress in 1954 and was directed at the Menominee tribe of Wisconsin. "The tribe was to be 'free' of federal control by December 31, 1958. The act, ostensibly developed by mutual agreement of the Menominees, the Congress, and the Bureau, was called a 'monumental step' and a 'recognition of the accomplishments of the Menominees in handling their affairs' in the Bureau's annual report" (Washburn 1971:92). Five other termination laws were passed in 1954. These involved selected tribes in Oregon, Utah, and Texas. The results of the termination policy proved catastrophic for several of the tribes, particularly for the Menominees who had attained a level of economic well-being and self-sufficiency under the old policy.

> "In the ten years, following the passage of the termination act, Gary Orfield concluded, none of the major goals of the termination policy were realized. A major goal was to give the Indians full control over their property, both personal and collective. By the time of termination, virtually no trace of this

intention to grant economic freedom remained. The Menominees were given more than ample responsibility but they gained no significant new freedoms. The high burden of taxes thrust upon the Indians, the high cost of government services, the low profits of the tribal saw mill, combined to place the Menominees into a worse position than they occupied before termination."

(Washburn 1971:95–6)

By the end of the 1960s the implementation of the termination policy ground to a halt; the government promised a new approach to Indian affairs. It would put more substance and wherewithal into the formal structure of self-government and give Indians more latitude "to manage their own affairs on their reservations and not be governed like colonial subjects by Department of the Interior bureaucrats with yes-and-no power over everything that was important" (Josephy Jr 1973:18). In addition, the government would maintain its special relationship with the Indian and continue to fulfill its contractual obligations as trustee.

In 1970 President Nixon even sent a special message to Congress outlining his new program. He declared that the "policy of forced termination is wrong" just as too much "federal paternalism" was also wrong. He continued "only by clearly rejecting both of these extremes can we achieve a policy which truly serves the best interests of the Indian people. Self-determination among the Indian people can and must be encouraged without the threat of eventual termination. In my view, in fact, that is the only way that self-determination can effectively be fostered." He then proposed a number of specific policies "in which the Federal Government and the Indian community play complementary roles." He insisted that "we have turned from the question of *whether* the Federal government has a responsibility to Indians to the question of *how* that responsibility can best be fulfilled. We have concluded that the Indians will get better programs and that public monies will be more effectively expended if the people who are most affected by these programs are responsible for operating them" (US Congressional Record (91:2) 1970: 23134–3136).

Promising beginnings were made in implementing this new program, but before too long it too foundered under the combined onslaught of vested interests in Congress, in the western states, in private industry and in government bureaucracy. However, the militance of young Indians roiled the lapse into indifference. In 1972, for example, their organization, the American Indian Movement, led a caravan to Washington DC to protest injustice and broken promises. A year later they took over the Wounded Knee reservation in South Dakota and engaged in a violent confrontation with federal officials that lasted for several months. In 1975 Menominee Indians seized a vacant church facility in Wisconsin.

By the end of the 1970s the tactics of confrontation declined markedly as the federal courtroom became increasingly the stage upon which activist Indians have sought with modest success to pursue their drive for "'self determination' and 'sovereignty'" (Raines 1979:22). They have been intent upon making white America live up to its treaties of the past. As a result, according to Raines, "the drive for economic power has become the main thrust of Indian activism throughout the nation – in the Rocky Mountain coal fields, along the salmon rivers of the Northwest and on vast Eastern tracts where, after almost 200 years of silence, Indians stunned and infuriated whites by claiming 'aboriginal title'" (Raines 1979:21).

Their goal, in short, is to stop the historic drift that has converted Indians into a relatively "undigested" impoverished plural segment of the national community. They wish to revitalize Indian tribes and to transform them into a new version of Chief Justice Marshall's construct. In the words of the chairman of the Navajo Nation and of the Council of Energy Resources Tribes, Indian tribes should be "'dependent, yet *sovereign*,' [author's italics] nations within the United States" (Raines 1979:22).

In the wings, however, stand many whites who see their interests threatened by the favorable court decisions. Some are prepared to renew the discredited termination policy; others would go so far as to wipe out all the historical claims of the Indians derived from past treaties. That is where the matter stands now. Many Indians view the future with foreboding.

BOOK TWO

THE BLACK ENCOUNTER
WITH AMERICA'S DUALITY

As we have seen in Book One, the duality created by the white settler in Virginia and later reaffirmed by the Founding Fathers of the New Nation was formed in the crucible of slavery. This "peculiar institution" that arrayed black slave against white master indelibly stamped the New Nation's subsequent struggle with its duality and made the black the central nonwhite figure in a racial drama. Accordingly, to study America's duality and its historical transformations is to study the historical encounter between black and white. Book Two, therefore, is devoted exclusively to this encounter as it shaped and was shaped by America's continuing struggle with its duality, from the formation of the New Nation until today, both in the South and in the North.

6

FROM SLAVERY TO ENTRY INTO THE PEOPLE'S DOMAIN AND THE FIRST PERIOD OF RECONSTRUCTION

Introduction

Nowhere and at no time in American history was the Manichean dualism that was sanctified and stabilized by the Constitution more in evidence than in the antebellum South. On the one side stood a fully elaborated plural societal structure whose racial segmentation was built on slavery, organized around the plantation, and governed by black codes. On the other side stood the People's Domain, whose sovereignty was guaranteed by the supreme law of the land under a creed derived from the Declaration of Independence, but whose rights and immunities applied to whites only. The linchpin between the two structures was a planter elite who dominated both and who also succeeded in clamping its values and interests on both. Thus, white supremacy and control came to be the leitmotif not only of the plural structure but of the People's Domain as well. In this manner the fates of the two systems were inextricably linked: survival of the one required the survival of the other.

In the North, slavery had been disavowed by the early nineteenth century, but its heritage of black subordination and inferiority indelibly stamped the plural edifice of racial segmentation, discrimination, and exclusion that was then justified on more purely racial and racist grounds. This edifice, though, never attained the organic closure of the plural structure of the South. As a result, blacks were not completely locked out of the People's Domain of the North as the enslaved blacks were in the South; they were able to drive a slim wedge into it even though most whites treated them as interlopers who did not belong in the company of the people.

The Civil War brought America face-to-face with its structural dualism, and for the brief period of the radical reconstruction it seemed to be reshaping this dualism into a single Domain of the people, in which blacks would have full rights of access and membership, North and South. But soon this reshaping collapsed and the dualism reappeared in a somewhat different form but still deeply entrenched in the American society.

In this chapter we shall examine the racial segmentation of the antebellum days, South and North, and its relationship to the People's Domain in each region, and we shall conclude with an analysis of the impact of the first period of reconstruction on this structural dualism.

Slavery and the plantation system

As we have already described in Chapter 4, slavery was not confined to any single region in the colonial period; it was widely accepted and – to at least a minimal extent – practised in virtually all the colonies. This continued through the Revolutionary War period. Slavery did not become firmly rooted in the North and within several decades after the Revolutionary War was abolished there. But the fact nevertheless remains that for well over a hundred years of America's early history slavery had a national presence. The possible significance of this heritage for the North will be explored later; in the meantime we shall focus our attention on the system of slavery that was nourished and flourished in the South for almost a century beyond the Revolutionary War.

THE PLANTER CLASS AS THE ELITE OF THE PEOPLE
AND THE SYSTEM OF SLAVERY

The ownership of slaves, according to Stampp (1956), was confined to only one-fourth of the white population in the South, and even within this small segment, the typical slaveowner possessed few slaves; only a handful of whites owned fifty or more:

"If membership in the planter class required the ownership of at least twenty slaves, the 'typical' slaveholder of 1860 certainly did not belong to it. For 88% of the owners held less than that number, 72% held less than ten, and almost 50% held less than five. Not only was the 'typical' slaveholder not a planter, but the 'typical' planter worked only a moderate-sized gang of from twenty to fifty slaves. The planter aristocracy was limited to some ten thousand families who lived off the labor of gangs of more than fifty slaves. The extremely wealthy families who owned more than a hundred slaves numbered less than three thousand, a tiny fraction of the southern population."(Stampp 1956:30–1)

This relatively small group of large slaveowners dominated the slave economy; they owned most of the slaves.

"It does not follow that most of the slaves therefore lived on small agricultural units, for by 1860 slaves were heavily concentrated in the hands of a few owners. Only one-fourth of them belonged to masters who owned less than ten. Considerably more than half of them lived on plantation units of more than twenty slaves, and one-fourth lived on units of more than fifty. That the majority of slaves belonged to members of the planter class, and not to those who operated small farms with a single slave family, is a fact of crucial importance concerning the nature of bondage in the antebellum South."

(Stampp 1956:31)

By the same token this planter elite also dominated the white community. It controlled the major instruments of economic power. Most of the non-slaveholding whites of the middle and lower classes were dependent on it directly or indirectly for jobs and business. The planter elite also controlled the channels of credit and investment and were primarily responsible for the prevailing agrarian character of the southern economy.

The planter elite and its representatives also monopolized and controlled the southern political and social life. They successfully transplanted a set of values and interests of immediate and vital significance to a small slaveowning class onto the community as a whole. In joining the two they made it seem that the preservation of the peoplehood of the white community under the Constitution required the preservation of the slave system.

As a result, spokesmen from the South frequently argued inside and outside of Congress that their rights under the Constitution were being impugned by attacks against slavery. John C. Calhoun, for example, a major defender of slavery in Congress, argued eloquently that the Constitution protected the rights of states to deal with issues of moment within their own boundaries. Accordingly, he contended that the federal government is obliged to respect the jurisdiction of states in these matters. He even went so far as to articulate these sentiments in a set of resolutions which he offered to Congress in 1838. Of special interest is the one on the rights of a state to preserve the institution of slavery.

"IV. *Resolved* That domestic slavery, as it exists in the Southern and Western States of this Union, composes an important part of their domestic institutions, inherited from their ancestors, and existing at the adoption of the Constitution, by which it is recognized as constituting an important element in the apportionment of powers among the States, and that no change of opinion or feeling, on the part of the other States of the Union in relation to it, can justify them or their citizens in open and systematic attacks thereon, with the view to its overthrow; and that all such attacks are in manifest violation of the mutual and solemn pledge to protect and defend each other, given by the States respectively, on entering into the constitutional compact which formed the Union, and as such are a manifest breach of faith, and a violation of the most solemn obligations."

(Blaustein and Zangrando 1968:102)

In this manner exclusion of a whole category of persons from the community of people became an integral part of the community's definition of itself. The slave system was not merely a substructure or an appendage of the small strata of the white elite but was inextricably interwoven in the entire fabric of the society. The entire white community used it as a mirror for reflecting the common peoplehood of the whites and for distinguishing the boundaries of the people (the white) from the instruments of the people (the black).

THE PLANTATION AS A TOTAL INSTITUTION

In many ways then "the road to power (in the South) lay through the plantation" (Genovese 1965:19). It provided access to all the forms of dominance – economic, political, and social. It was in effect the generative source of power in the total societal structure of the South. Perhaps the venerated plantation aristocrat of Virginia seemed a more desirable model of this dominance than did the rough-hewed plantation parvenu of the Southwest, but both were at the top of the heap, no matter from which perspective it was viewed.

And yet despite this paramount role of the plantation in the total society, it was also a relatively self-contained institution that was reinforced by law and custom and was for all intents and purposes a microcosm of the society itself. Within its boundaries the white master and his overseers ruled with an iron fist that was frequently veiled in velvet. His slaves were his property with whom he could do as he willed; the law gave him a wide range of discretionary power.

The economic function obviously played a crucial role in life on the plantation. The slaves provided the labor and were divided into work groups, both field and domestic. Their overseers were occasionally blacks and at the top was the towering figure of the white master. Unlike many of the Caribbean and Brazilian plantations, the southern plantation was generally run by a resident planter, and not by an employed manager for an absentee planter. Increasingly the crop that was produced for sale in the early 1800s was cotton; earlier it had been tobacco and in some regions of South Carolina it was still rice.

Scholars have disagreed sharply over the character and effectiveness of the plantation economy. Genovese has insisted that the economy was pre-capitalistic, that it retained many quasi-feudalistic features, that plantation owners were driven by non-economic goals of honor and prestige and not merely by economic goals of profit, that labor productivity of slaves was low, and that in general the plantation was a relatively ineffective and inefficient mode of economic organization (Genovese 1965).

Elkins disagrees with Genovese's emphasis; he claims that the plantation was organized along capitalistic lines and its central goal was the drive for profit (Elkins 1963). Perhaps the most unqualified support for a capitalistic interpretation of the slave and plantation economy has come from two cliometricians, Fogel and Engerman (1974). They sought to apply sophisticated quantitative and statistical methods to historical analysis by processing "large quantities of numerical data" (Fogel and Engerman 1974:4). Such data included the original schedules of information by census takers of 1850 and 1860, business records, and family papers of large plantation owners. "The wills and other legal documents of the estates of planters have been particularly valuable" (Fogel and Engerman 1974:8). The authors conclude that their quantitative analysis has been a major breakthrough in historical analysis and has produced results that contradict some of the most widely held notions about the slave system and the plantation. For example, they insist that contrary to what other scholars have said,

> "the slave system was not economically moribund on the eve of the Civil War. There is no evidence that economic forces alone would have soon brought slavery to an end without the necessity of a war or some other form of political intervention. Quite the contrary; as the Civil War approached, slavery as an economic system was never stronger and the trend was toward even further entrenchment."   (Fogel and Engerman 1974:4)

Through their findings, Fogel and Engerman construct a portrait of the large plantation owner as much more the enlightened and rational capitalist than was the wont of most early historians. "Far from being cavalier fops, the leading planters were, on the whole, a highly self-conscious class of entrepeneurs" (Fogel and Engerman 1974:201). These planters were well informed on the latest developments of technological innovations in agriculture; they kept up-to-date on the scientific agricultural literature of the day; they organized agricultural societies and continually discussed the problems of labor management.

According to the authors, the planters sought self-consciously to apply this knowledge to the running of their plantations and to the taking maximum advantage of the economics of large scale production. The net result of these efforts was to make large plantations into "the first large, scientifically managed business enterprises" and the plantation owners into "the first group to engage in large-scale, scientific personnel management" (Fogel and Engerman 1974:208).

In a variety of ways, the planters sought to maximize the efficiency and effectiveness of the various factors of production. According to the authors, they did not recklessly abuse the land. They sought to fertilize it and, when over time the land's fertility was depleted, they added capital machinery to maintain its output.

The planters paid particular attention to the factor that supplied the labor for their plantations: the slave. Defined as part of his capital, the slaves were not to be treated overly cruelly or inhumanly; the planter had invested too much in this valuable piece of property not to make sure that its productive life was extended as long as possible. The major goal of the planter was to mold his slaves into "a highly disciplined, highly specialized, and well-coordinated labor force" (Fogel and Engerman 1974:203). To accomplish this he relied on a combination of incentives and force. The authors spend considerable time in describing the kinds of incentives and prizes the planter used to increase productivity and to raise the morale of his work force, but much less time in describing the role of force. At times they make work on the plantation seem like fun and games; they also treat relatively gently the use of whipping as a means of instilling discipline. Throughout their discussion runs the theme: the planter is not going to do anything to destroy his valuable piece of property and is going to do everything to make him a willing and effective part of his work force. Thus the planter becomes more than just an enlightened capitalist in the portrait painted by the authors; he is also a human relations expert in the best tradition of the industrial sociology school of the 1920s. In other words, he finds it to his best self-interest as a capitalist to treat his workers humanely and to be concerned with their welfare, and this treatment of the workers gives him his competitive advantage.

> "This feature of plantation life – the organization of slaves into highly disciplined, interdependent teams capable of maintaining a steady and intense rhythm of work – appears to be the crux of the superior efficiency of large-scale operations on plantations, at least as far as field work was concerned. It is certainly the factor which slaveowners themselves frequently singled out as the key to the superiority of the plantation system of organization."
>
> (Fogel and Engerman 1974:204)

The response of the slaves themselves fits very much this picture of a viable and basically benign enterprise. The authors stress repeatedly that the slaves were engaged in all kinds of occupations on the plantation. Contrary to what many other scholars have maintained, the slaves filled most of the supervisory and managerial positions on the plantation. In other words, they were a highly skilled and competent work force. So impressed by this conclusion are the authors that they use it in a slashing attack on scholars who have claimed low productivity and incompetence for the slaves. Fogel and Engerman insist that most of these scholars – even those professing anti-slavery sentiments – had bought the racist argument of black inferiority; they had accepted the notion that blacks were incompetent because they were little more than children biologically.

The authors have greater difficulty with the thesis of such scholars as Elkins (1963) and Stampp (1956). The latter relate the low productivity of the slave to his day-to-day resistance to being a slave. We shall discuss this more fully later, but Fogel and Engerman contend that Stampp "overestimated the cruelty of the slave system" (Fogel and Engerman 1974:231). They fault him with failing "to acknowledge that ordinary slaves could be diligent workers, imbued like their masters with a Protestant ethic, or that, even though they longed for freedom, slaves could strive to develop and improve themselves in the only way that was open to them" (Fogel and Engerman 1974:231-32).

Thus Fogel and Engerman make the slave a willing and active participant in the capitalistic world of the plantation; he too is imbued with the work ethic just as is the slaveowner. In this manner the authors round out their picture of planter and slave as economic men in the best tradition of Adam Smith and transform the plantation into a thriving, harmonious, capitalistic institution.

Important as the empirical findings are and will be of cliometricians like Fogel and Engerman in rethinking the economics of the slave period, serious questions can be raised about the adequacy of these findings as explanations of the total slave and plantation system. For scholars, no matter what their approach, generally agree that the plantation was more than an economic institution where slaves and masters acted merely as rational economic men. It was also a political system in which a structure of authority was clearly defined and in which coercion and pressure were inextricably built into the system, as they are in all political systems. The plantation was a place where a complex scheme of life prevailed, where the entire range of human activities was experienced, from the religious to the social and familial, and where an elaborate normative system sharply defined the roles and statuses of slave and master. Frazier calls the plantation that emerged under such conditions a social institution.

"Where the authority of the white planters developed beyond mere physical coercion and the lives of planters and workers became intertwined in a web of social relationships, the plantation became a social institution. As a social institution, the plantation has had its peculiar culture and a system of social control based upon traditions and customs."   (Frazier 1957:236)

SLAVERY AS A SYSTEM OF REPRESSIVE PATERNALISM

A number of scholars have raised questions in recent years about the character of slavery in the various countries of the New World; they have debated the relative harshness of the system in these countries. Some such as Freyre (1946) contend that there was basically no difference. Slavery was equally cruel in virtually all countries; the absolute power of the master lent itself to brutality and violence against the slave.

Other scholars most notably Tannenbaum (1946), Elkins (1963), and Hoetink (1967) argue differently. They state that the system of slavery in the Iberian-controlled countries, as in Brazil, was less harsh than that in the Anglo-Saxon-dominated countries, as the Southern United States. Tannenbaum and Elkins insist that the Church and Crown imposed limits on the master's control over the body and soul of his slave. According to Tannenbaum, the Church insisted upon the right of access to the slave soul, which made him the equal of other men in his spiritual being. The Crown insisted on certain traditional rights for the slave and demanded certain residual powers over the relationship between master and slave. As a result legal and other institutional constraints were imposed upon the absoluteness of the master's control of his slaves. The slave's rights to manumission and to family life therefore received some form of legal and other protection.

In Anglo-Saxon countries neither Church nor Crown had any prior experience with slavery. The Church in particular developed no overriding claim to the slave's soul, and the Crown accepted the market definition of the slave as a commodity. Accordingly the government was disinclined to interfere with the workings of capitalistic enterprise, and the legal system reflected this "hands off" policy. The result was virtually unrestricted and unrestrained control of the master over his property. The courts and law supported the master in this interpretation and gave him a wide range of discretionary power in his treatment of the slave.

Hoetink agrees that the slave system in the Iberian-controlled countries was less harsh, but he disputes the Tannenbaum-Elkins interpretation (Hoetink 1967). He contends that the historical mixing of people in Portugal and Spain made the elite and other classes familiar with racially different people and that over time their standards of beauty and tolerance reflected this intermingling. As a result, the encounter of this elite with the native peoples and slaves in the New World did not elicit repugnance and disgust; the compatible somatic norm images helped reduce barriers and social distance and increased the likelihood of miscegenation, human interaction, and empathy between owner and slave.

The colonists from Anglo-Saxon countries had no such historical experience with racially different peoples. Accordingly, the native group and slaves were viewed as a strange and alien collection of creatures; most colonists were unable to see themselves as engaging in normal human intercourse with such people. The gulf between the two was virtually unbridgeable. The colonists saw the slave and native as a dehumanized instrument of the colonist's will toward whom normal displays of human decency and feeling were unwarranted and with whom one had as few human and humane dealings as possible.

Genovese does not basically dispute the Tannenbaum-Elkins thesis that the legal and political institutions reinforcing slavery in the Anglo-Saxon countries were much more repressive than were those of Latin America; however, he argues that in practice the gap between the two was much narrower than suggested by the thesis.

"Much of Hispanic law was unenforced; not every Jesuit father consistently defended the faithful; government officials could be and often were corrupt or indifferent. On the other hand, much of the arbitrariness of American slavery was mitigated by community pressure and the prevalent patriarchal ideology."

(Genovese 1968:337)

Genovese contends that the slaveowning class sought to construct from its base of absolute power a social and ideological world of benevolent paternalism. (It is difficult to determine the extent to which he agrees that this class actually succeeded in doing so.) Its authority over the slave was to be total and final; it could decree life as well as death. However, its power was to be tempered with sentiment and kindliness as a father's power is tempered in his relation with his child. Only the slave as child was never to be accorded the right of eventual adulthood, as was presumably the right of the planter's child. Accordingly the slave was doomed to treatment as a perennial child; only the master knew what was best.

From premises such as these, writers such as Fitzhugh (1850) and Phillips (1968) drew a romanticized version of slavery. They were convinced that the plantation represented a superior moral and social order in which master and slave cared for each other and were united in bonds of sentiment and loyalty. This benevolent paternalism, even according to Genovese (1968), was primarily a product of traditions that stemmed from the non-economic, quasi-feudalistic character of the plantation. Were it predominantly a capitalistic enterprise then the barbarism of dog-eat-dog and the brutality of the strong exploiting the weak would prevail; the slave would in effect become a brutalized and terrorized piece of property.

Fogel and Engerman (1974) take exception to this point of view. As we have already seen, they define the plantation system as essentially a capitalistic enterprise; it is run by an enlightened entrepeneur who recognizes that it is to his best self-interest to treat his slaves benevolently. Thus Fogel and Engerman see the treatment of slaves as an example of rational paternalism and not as an example of traditional paternalism à la Genovese, Phillips, and others.

In general, the notion of slavery as a viable economic and moral order has attracted a number of scholars. They are not merely content with saying that a deeply-rooted functional interdependence tied master to slave which in itself would serve to limit the harsh treatment of the slave: the master could not afford to ill-treat most of his slaves else his capital investment would suffer – though he might maim or kill a few as examples to the rest. They go further. They see the plantation society as a normatively regulated system whose solidarity is pegged to the morally and socially responsible behavior of the white master; sentiment and attachment to his slaves limit the exercise of his awesome naked power.

Many other scholars reject this conception of the slave society in the South. They view the society as an essentially repressive and exploitative political system which was rooted in fear, coercion, and the dehumanization of the slave. Stampp describes in measured tones the preoccupation of the slaveholders with the problem of control and discipline of the slaves. Their goal was to produce a perfect slave who would bend completely to the will of the master. To accomplish this at least minimally, the masters had to undertake a systematic campaign to break the spirit of the slave. Stampp summarizes the various steps that were recommended by those who wrote on slave management: "Here, then, was the way to produce the perfect slave: accustom him to rigid discipline, demand from him unconditional submission, impress upon him his innate inferiority, develop in him a paralyzing fear of white men, train him to adopt the master's code of good behavior, and instill in him a sense of complete dependence. This, at least, was the goal" (Stampp 1956:148). Stampp argues that the "goal was seldom reached." The slaveholders were unable to mold or to socialize the black into the "perfect" slave who would automatically do his master's bidding. Accordingly they had to rely on a pervasive system of control and surveillance to get the slave to do what the master wanted him to do or to keep the slave in line. A variety of incentives was employed and persuasion was not an infrequent device. But at the hub of the system of control was the use of physical force and coercion. Physical punishment became part of the accepted routine on the plantation: "the whip was the most common instrument of punishment – indeed it was the emblem of the master's authority. Nearly every slaveholder used it, and few grown slaves escaped it entirely" (Stampp 1956:174).

Concerted efforts were made to use physical force and the whip as a rational means of control and not as an expression of rage or emotion. Accordingly individual slaveholders developed sets of rules as guidelines for the punishment of their slaves. These rules included how many lashes, for which offenses, with what kind of whip, and under what conditions. (Slaves were not to be whipped when the master or overseer was in a state of rage or intense anger.) In addition the community at large looked with askance at masters who were overly brutal: "A master who gave some thought to his standing in the community certainly wished to avoid a reputation for inordinate cruelty" (Stampp 1956:179).

And yet, despite the various constraints, the system lent itself to a dehumanization of relations between even the kindly master and his slave. As Stampp says,

"One of the inherent tragedies of slavery was that a humane master's impulse to be kind to his slaves was severely circumscribed by the inescapable problem of control. He could indulge only the most obsequious of them, and only within the bounds of essential discipline" (Stampp 1956:162–63). More significantly the system permitted the brutal and sadistic master a license to indulge in cruelty far in excess of anything he would dare do in ordinary society. Even the average slaveholder – neither intentionally brutal nor sadistic – could not resist taking advantage on occasion of the absolute power he wielded over his slaves; he might beat one or more capriciously and arbitrarily as the whim or frustration seized him:

> "Cruelty, unfortunately, was not limited to the mentally unbalanced. Men and women, otherwise 'normal,' were sometimes corrupted by the extraordinary power that slavery conferred upon them. Some made bondsmen the victims of their petulance.... Others who were reasonably humane to most of their slaves made the ones who annoyed them beyond endurance the targets of their animosity. Still others who were merely irresponsible, rather than inherently brutal, made slaves the objects of their whims. In other words, masters were seldom consistent; they were apt to be indulgent or harsh depending upon their changing moods, or their feelings toward individual slaves. In truth, said one Southerner, 'men of the right stamp to manage negroes are like Angels visits few and far between.'" (Stampp 1956:182)

Basic as physical force was to the functioning of the slave society, it was kept within bounds during periods of normalcy; but in periods when the whites felt threatened by rumors or the reality of slave uprisings, such as the Nat Turner rebellion, physical force by whites literally knew no bounds. Such situations unleashed fear, anger, hatred, and violence among the whites. No longer was the black seen as a child; he became a savage animal that had to be severely punished, maimed, or killed. Stampp (1956) and Aptheker (1956 and 1962) describe in detail the brutality of the white reaction to real or perceived threats from the blacks.

Though such black uprisings were relatively infrequent in the South, the fear of such uprisings was pervasive and ever-present among the whites. As a result, whites were likely to overreact to minor incidents and to resort to punitive force against the black at the slightest provocation. Thus whatever may have been the extent of benevolent paternalism in the slave system, not far beneath its surface flourished an extensive apparatus of coercion and force that gave the system its basic character and order.

Elkins goes so far as to draw a comparision between the slave system in the South and the concentration camps in Nazi Germany (Elkins 1963). He disclaims any intention of identifying one with the other or even of treating them as analogous, but he does spend considerable time in describing the process by which the Nazis systematically used the repressive and coercive structure of the concentration camp to undermine the self-hood of the inmates, to infantilize them, and to transform them finally into craven and subservient "children." Elkins argues that the plantation system accomplished much the same thing with the slaves.

Suggestive as Elkins' thesis is, it fails to recognize that the Nazis had much greater total control over the environment and behavior of the inmates than the slaveholders had over the slaves. Thorpe alludes to this in his criticism of Elkins:

"Several observers have written of the manner in which the Nazis thought of and sought to operate the concentration camps with the same organizational and administrative emphases as are found in the most modern factory. Absence of the mid-twentieth century level of organizational knowledge and efficiency was a major factor which kept plantation slavery from being as dehumanizing as was the case with concentration camps. It is not without justification that modern man uses the word 'totalitarianism' to describe this century's mass state."

(Thorpe 1971:90)

As a result of this total control, Bettelheim (1943) has shown that the Nazis were able to conduct continuous surveillance of the inmates, to regulate in minutest detail their day-to-day, hour-to-hour behavior, to resort to a continuous campaign of repression and degradation of the individual, and to pit one inmate against the other so that each stood completely alone against the repressive machinery without the support or companionship of his fellow inmates. The net result was pulverization of the self and the infantilization of the inmates.

Thorpe (1971) and Genovese (1968) argue that the plantation owner was not able to maintain such total control over the slave's environment. Despite the owner's efforts to approximate such control, the slave was able to escape into his own world during the evening and perhaps part of the day. Within this world, slaves lived and worked together, developed cooperative and mutually supportive relations, and created a communal solidarity which protected them from the repressive system. As an expression of this solidarity, slaves developed their own modes of communication and culture, which provided even greater distance between themselves and the white masters.

The masters sought to penetrate this solidarity through surveillance and through networks of informers; in turn the slaves tried to offset this by developing features of their communal life that resembled a secret society. However, too much of the life activity and life space of the slave was exposed to and controlled by the white master and his overseers to permit the development of an overly complex communal life for the slave. Certainly he was unable to politicize his communal ties and to organize them effectively as a means of protest and resistance against the slave system.

THE SLAVE'S RESPONSE: ACCEPTANCE OR REJECTION

One of the most controversial issues in the current debate over the system of slavery in the South is the response of the slave to the system. As we might expect, scholars who have stressed the benevolent paternalism of the system have been inclined to emphasize the conforming tendencies of the slaves. Few have gone so far as the earlier white historian Phillips (1968) in portraying the slaves as contented and happy with their lot; they argue that the slaves at the least had accommodated themselves to the system and were not an overly discontented group. Fogel and Engerman (1974) are among the recent recruits to this point of view. In their preoccupation with showing the high level of competence and efficiency of slave labor, they press the point of view that the slave was a functioning and motivated part of the system. They reject emphatically Stampp's contention that the slaves were troublesome and alienated from the system (Stampp 1956).

Disagreeing sharply with this kind of interpretation are those scholars who characterize slavery as a coercive and harsh system of exploitation. They view the slaves as generally dissatisfied with their status and even on occasion openly resistant and rebellious. Such black scholars as DuBois (1910), Woodson (1922) and Brawley (1921) have argued this thesis for a long time; Aptheker (1956 and 1962) was one of the earliest white exponents of this point of view. More recently other scholars have joined the ranks and have raised questions about the slave's adaptation to the plantation system.

No definitive statement can be made on the response of the slave; and perhaps none will ever be possible, for the people who could answer the question have died. And yet it may be possible to piece together some of the evidence and to reconstruct significant features of the probable response of the slave.

The idyllic portrait of the slaves as a uniformly happy and contented group painted by southern writers in the past has been more or less discarded by many recent scholars of slavery. Most agree that some subgroups of slaves received preferential treatment under the system and were therefore favorably disposed toward it. Such groups included slaves who worked in the plantation house, not the field, who were skilled artisans, or who were overseers or performed other supervisory functions. The rest were probably characterized by varying degrees of alienation and dissatisfaction.

In other words, if an opinion survey had been taken then and the respondents guaranteed anonymity, the probability is that few would have expressed a favorable opinion at their enslaved status. Most would have expressed an unfavorable opinion, with perhaps a few being relatively indifferent about the whole thing. Evidence of the extent of disaffection with the system is emerging through letters and diaries, slowly come to light as an increasing number of scholars rummage through the past for relics of the lives and thoughts of slaves.

Whatever their private opinions may have been, it is obvious that the cost to the slaves of expressing negative opinions openly and acting upon them was extremely high. The slaves were well aware of the ready resort to the whip by the white master – even without any provocation by the slave. They were also well aware of the brutal treatment of runaways, of "uppity" and recalcitrant slaves, to say nothing of the treatment of those slaves who were presumed to be implicated in uprisings. Consequently we could only expect the most hardy slaves with intense negative sentiments and convictions to be prepared to pay the price of expressing their feelings in behavior; most of the others could be expected to withhold their opinions from the ears of the whites and to behave in ways not in accord with their feelings.

But the matter did not stop there. The whites expected their slaves to behave in ways which demonstrated that the slaves liked their status and respected and loved their masters. Over time an elaborate etiquette and a set of sharply defined roles had developed which clearly marked the inferior status of the slaves and which defined the kind of obsequious behavior they were to express. As a result, each generation of slaves did not have to invent the appropriate behavior; they merely had to learn the scenario that had already been set. In this manner the slaves could make the learning process a cerebral affair of rote memory and response and detach their inner feelings from the learning process.

Thus the role provided the slave with a protective mask. All the white saw was the behavior, not the private and inner self of the slave – the self which he might reveal only to his most trusted friends and family. One of the significant indicators of the separation of the public role from the private self is the eventual development of *double entendre* language among the slaves. Several observers have noted the widespread use of language symbols and forms that were designed to convey one set of meanings to the white master but in fact meant something quite different to his fellow slaves.

The question that has troubled a number of scholars, such as Pettigrew (1980) and Elkins (1963), has been the long-term effect on the slave's personality of his continually having to perform this public role. Both believe that the brand of inferiority that stamped the public role had to penetrate the private world of the self of the slave and make him define himself as inferior. In other words the personality of the actor tended to become indistinguishable from the role he was playing. Elkins calls the process the "Sambofication" of the slave. This question too has become the subject of considerable controversy.

However, it is well to bear in mind that members of virtually all groups that are or have been racial or ethnic minorities in a society have to contend with the stamp of inferiority imposed on them from the dominant society and with the danger of this stamp seeping into their private views of themselves. Few members of minorities have been able to escape fully the psychological ramifications of this definition, but the extent to which this societal brand permeates and pervades the person's definition of self depends upon the extent to which the minority group has been able to build a protective environment around itself. Historically minorities that have had a communal and cultural life of their own and an ethnocentric definition of their group have fared better in withstanding the brand of inferiority from the outside, but even they have not been entirely immune from the brand's psychological ramifications.

The issue of the "Sambofication" of the slave then turns back onto the prior question we have raised with respect to the concentration camp analogy: How successful were the slaves in building a protective environment between themselves and the repressive slave system? As we have already indicated, Thorpe takes issue with Elkins; he is convinced that the slaves had enough "elbow room," to use his words, to withstand the infantilizing and "Sambofying" pressures of the system (Thorpe 1971). We agree that there was much more elbow room than Elkins concedes to the slave, but how much more remains open to question.

Despite the reluctance of most slaves to pay the price of overt disobedience, they resorted to "safe" ways of expressing their displeasure. They would slow down their work, manhandle tools and animals, feign illness, and in general seek to exasperate the master in a variety of ways. The Bauers summarize the various kinds of day-to-day resistance they were able to cull from the the materials they studied:

> "The patterns of resistance to slavery studied in this paper are: (1) deliberate slowing up of work; (2) destruction of property, and indifferent work; (3) feigning illness and pregnancy; (4) injuring one's self; (5) suicide; (6) a possibility that a significant number of slave mothers killed their children."
>
> (Bauer and Bauer 1971:57)

In their attempt to stress the high level of skill and productivity of slave labor, Fogel and Engerman (1974) reject the notion that slaves manipulated their labor to protest their slave status. Stampp, however, recognizes that the pride in their work that many slaves had posed a dilemma for them; he argues that many of these slaves nevertheless resorted to poor and slovenly work on occasion to express their dissatisfaction.

"The masses of slaves, for whom freedom could have been little more than an idle dream, found countless ways to exasperate their masters – and thus saw to it that bondage as a labor system had its limitations as well as its advantages. Many slaves were doubtless pulled by conflicting impulses: a desire for the personal satisfaction gained from doing a piece of work well, as against a desire to resist or outwit the master by doing it badly or not at all. Which impulse dominated a given slave at a given time depended upon many things, but the latter one was bound to control him at least part of the time. Whether the master was humane or cruel, whether he owned a small farm or a large plantation, did not seem to be crucial considerations, for almost all slaveholders had trouble in managing this kind of labor. ... The element of conscious resistance was often present too; whether or not it was the predominant one the master usually had no way of knowing. In any case, he was likely to be distressed by his inability to persuade his slaves to 'assimilate' their interest with his. 'We all know,' complained one slaveholder, that the slave's feeling of obligation to his master 'is of so flimsy a character that none of us rely upon it.'"

(Stampp 1956:97–8)

These patterned evasions served as covert symbols of protest which were relatively safe and would not lead to excessive physical discipline. In fact, the whites took these acts as further evidence of the innate inferiority of the slaves – a belief that protected the slaves from the consequences of their own acts.

Still to be explored fully is the extent to which the slave culture developed lines of hidden protest which only the blacks themselves understood. We have already mentioned the significance of the patois that slaves developed which had a double level of meaning. Further study is needed of the covert protest contained in the spirituals and slave folklore.

Fanon in his work on Algeria indicates other avenues of approach (Fanon 1968). He shows how certain acts and objects can become symbols of protest and be misinterpreted by the masters. In Algeria during the French occupancy, for example, Algerians perpetuated the tradition of veils for women. The French took this as a sign of their backwardness. Fanon on the other hand calls it a silent means of protest against the French and a way for the Algerians to reaffirm their personal integrity and dignity. Once the revolution began, the Algerians no longer needed this symbol of protest and reaffirmation; women quickly discarded their veils in order to fight as equals with their men. Fanon offers a similar interpretation of the ownership of radios. During the French occupancy, Algerians considered it a sign of distinction and honor not to own a radio; during the revolution stocks of radios were depleted because the radio no longer represented a symbol of French domination and was urgently needed for effective communciation during the revolution.

In addition to these covert expressions of protest, overt slave uprisings did occur in the South, the most famous being that of Denmark Vesey and Nat Turner. However, scholars generally agree that such uprisings were much more infrequent in the South than in Latin America. Aptheker, however, has sought to challenge the conception that the southern slave was docile (Aptheker 1956 and 1962). He has enumerated an extensive list of slave disturbances and uprisings which he concludes demonstrates the active resistance of blacks to their subjugation throughout the period of slavery – an issue which we have already indicated has yet to be resolved.

We can conclude that the system of slavery was the most extreme case of racial segmentation in American history. It approximated the kind of closed plural society which Furnivall wrote about (Furnivall 1956). It shut the black slave completely out of the human community and treated him as a conquered subject. The system did not develop the kind of harmony and solidarity that the white southerners and some scholars claim it did. It was a system of coercion and stressful relations mitigated by a veneer of paternalism that on occasion bred sentimental ties between slave and master or at the least bred a sense of responsibility of master for the slave.

The free black and the antebellum North

So much attention has been paid by scholars to the system of slavery in the South that by contrast the status of the black in the antebellum North seems sorely neglected. As a result, we do not find the same rich lode of materials and studies. However, in recent years some scholars such as Litwack (1961), Fredrickson (1971), Jordan (1974), Greene (1968), and others have taken a new look at the situation of the black in the antebellum North. Their conclusions point in the same general direction: while slavery eventually took on a regional character, the subordination of the black and racial segmentation of society knew no regional boundaries and were deeply embedded features of the nation as a whole.

THE LEGAL STATUS OF THE FREE BLACK IN THE NORTH

For approximately one hundred years the northern colonies retained the institution of slavery; however, few whites actually owned slaves and the practice was largely confined to a few states like New York and New Jersey. But despite these limits, slavery was legally sanctioned in all colonies and exhaustive slave codes were promulgated in most. Further the slave was closely identified with the black, and the two were viewed as virtually interchangeable. Both were deemed inferior species who could never be expected to share the rights and virtues of the white man. Thus the slave-black duality became institutionally anchored in the early formation of the North and became part of its heritage.

The gradual abolition of slavery after the Revolutionary War may have done away with the right of one person to own another as a piece of chattel property, but it did not basically alter the prevailing conception and treatment of the black. He may no longer have been enslaved but he was not thereby welcomed as an equal into the political community of the white people of the Constitution. In fact, his legal status became ambiguous, and he was ensconced in a no man's land outside the boundaries of both the slave system and the white community. He was in many respects more harshly treated than he was under the somewhat protective environment of slavery. As Litwack states:

"Legal and extralegal discrimination restricted northern Negroes in virtually every phase of existence. Where laws were lacking or ineffectual, public opinion provided its own remedies. Indeed, few held out any hope for the successful or peaceful integration of the Negro into a white-dominated society. 'The policy, and power of the national and state governments, are against them,' a Philadelphia Quaker wrote in 1831. 'The popular feeling is against them – the interests of our citizens are against them.'"   (Litwack 1961:64)

The range of legal restrictions that the free black faced was formidable. It included immigration into the state, political suffrage, justice in the courts, interracial marriage, use of public transportation and facilities, and so forth. Some of these restrictions were more widely adopted than others. Of particular note were laws barring entry of free blacks. "Nearly every northern state considered, and many adopted, measures to prohibit or restrict the further immigration of Negroes" (Litwack 1961:64). Particularly prone to adopt such legislation were newly admitted states and territories. Illinois, Indiana, and Oregon included in their constitution provisions barring the immigration of blacks. Ohio also adopted such legislation, which stipulated that black immigrants "post a $500 bond guaranteeing their good behavior;" they were also required "to produce a court certificate as evidence of their freedom" (Litwack 1961:72). The older established states also considered such legislation. Most such as Massachusetts and Pennsylvania failed to pass it, but some such as Connecticut imposed barriers to the entry of the black.

Much more pervasive were the legal efforts to curtail or to deny suffrage to the free black.

"By 1840, some 93 per cent of the northern free Negro population lived in states which completely or practically excluded them from the right to vote. Only in

Massachusetts, New Hampshire, Vermont and Maine could Negroes vote on an equal basis with whites. In New York, they could vote if they first met certain property and residence requirements. In New Jersey, Pennsylvania and Connecticut, they were completely disfranchised, after having once enjoyed the ballot." (Litwack 1961:75)

Litwack comments that the denial of the vote to the black was frequently coupled with the extension of the right to vote to the white man. "In several states the adoption of white manhood suffrage led directly to the political disfranchisement of the Negro" (Litwack 1961:75). In a number of states the issue was vigorously debated for a number of years. The result was virtual disfranchisement of the blacks particularly in the new states.

"From the admission of Maine 1819 until the end of the Civil War, every new state restricted the suffrage to whites in its constitution. In New Jersey and Connecticut, where no racial distinctions had appeared in the original constitutions, the legislatures limited the suffrage to whites, and subsequent constitutions incorporated the restrictions." (Litwack 1961:79)

In 1838 Pennsylvania followed suit; New York accomplished virtually the same result by retaining property qualifications for the blacks while eliminating them for the whites.

Not only did the black face legal restrictions in his right to vote, but he was also confronted by serious barriers in his pursuit of justice in the courtroom.

"No state questioned a Negro's right to legal protection and a redress of injuries, but some added significant qualifications. Five states – Illinois, Ohio, Indiana, Iowa, and California – prohibited Negro testimony in cases where a white man was a party and Oregon forbade Negroes to hold real estate, make contracts, or maintain lawsuits. Under these circumstances, an Oregonian protested, the colored man 'is cast upon the world with no defense; his life, liberty, his property, his all, are dependent on the caprice, the passion, and the inveterate prejudices of not only the community at large but of every felon who may happen to cover an inhuman heart with a white face.' But this, nevertheless, was the Negro's judical plight in a large part of the North and West." (Litwack 1961:93)

Thus the free black retained certain abstract rights to justice in the North, but in practice he was denied their realization – either fully or partially. In many states he could not serve on juries; he could not testify against whites though black slaves could testify against him. He was much more likely than a white to be arrested for wrongdoing and to be dealt with severely in the court of law.

In effect the black as free man bore heavily and directly the cost and brunt of the legal system that the whites had constructed for the political community of the people, but he benefited in only meager fashion from the protection that it afforded to the people as citizens. As such he stood fully exposed to its coercive constraints: he was neither citizen nor slave.

White Southerners were well aware of the treatment of the black in the North and they used their knowledge with telling effect in the increasingly heated debates over the extension of slavery to new territories. They pointed to the hypocrisy of the North in its opposition to the extension of slavery and sarcastically alluded to the self-righteous fraudulence of its congressional representatives. Calhoun even went so far as to use the results of the 1840 census to prove the superiority of the southern treatment of the black slave over the northern treatment of the free black.

However, the legal status of the free black was even more clouded and restricted in the South than it was in the North. This was also true at the level of the federal government where the free black was not only deprived of basic rights of citizenship but also denied the more limited rights of the alien immigrant who wanted to become a citizen.

In general, the legal status of the free black remained relatively unclear and ambiguous at the federal level during much of the antebellum period. As a result, contradictory policies were usually pursued in the various executive departments of the government – usually to the detriment of the black. The confusion seemed to come to an end with the Dred Scott decision of 1857. All blacks – freed and slave – were to be excluded from the polity of the United States, none could ever be citizens. However, within a few years the situation became once again indefinite, for the Civil War had begun.

WHITE SUPREMACY AND SEGREGATION OF THE BLACK

In the North as in the South, the black faced a community sentiment that overwhelmingly favored white supremacy. Accordingly, most whites saw themselves as the "People of the Constitution;" they had the rights, the power, and the authority. They had come to oppose slavery, not out of any particular sympathy for the black but out of concern for their own interests. In fact, they viewed the black as an interloper who did not properly belong in the company of the people. More specifically they labelled him an inferior and degraded being. They spread these stereotypes publicly and privately and elaborated upon them. "Newspapers and public places prominently displayed cartoons and posters depicting his (the Negro's) alleged physical deformities and poking fun at his manners and customs"

(Litwack 1961:99). In this manner then anti-black sentiment permeated the atmosphere of much of the North. As Tocqueville comments, "Race prejudice seems stronger in those states that have abolished slavery than in those where it still exists, and nowhere is it more intolerant than in those states where slavery was never known" (Tocqueville 1969:343).

This widespread and intense sentiment among whites was expressed in concerted efforts through legal and extralegal means to keep the black out of their communities and, if he gained entry, to subordinate and to separate him from the white community. Tocqueville describes the pressures for segregation that were exerted against the black.

"The Negro's son is excluded from the school to which the European's child goes. In the theaters he cannot for good money buy the right to sit by his former master's side; in the hospitals he lies apart. He is allowed to worship the same God as the white man but must not pray at the same altars. He has his own clergy and churches. The gates of heaven are not closed against him, but his inequality stops only just short of the boundaries of the other world. When the Negro is no more, his bones are cast aside, and some difference in condition is found even in the equality of death.

So the Negro is free, but he cannot share the rights, pleasures, labors, griefs, or even the tomb of him whose equal he has been declared; there is nowhere where he can meet him, neither in life nor in death."   (Tocqueville 1969:343)

The net result was a racial segmentation of many northern communities, with the blacks treated as an inferior pariah group to be kept apart from the whites. They lived in the worst sections of town. They were employed in the most menial jobs and were continually contending with want and poverty. And no matter where they went they were buffeted by exclusion and discrimination.

Perhaps some of the most pervasive and persistent attempts to keep the black out or, once in, to keep him in his place occurred in the Northwest – the region in which slavery was barred from the beginning not, as it turned out, to grant equality to the black but to reduce the likelihood of his presence there.

"The Northwest comprised the seven states of Ohio, Indiana, Illinois, Michigan, Wisconsin, Minnesota and Iowa. In 1861 it was a stronghold of white supremacy. As the nation girded for war, state constitutions and statutes reflected the racism that flourished in the region. The severity of the discriminatory legislation varied, but every state imposed legal disabilities upon its black residents. All seven states limited service in the militia to white males and barred Negroes from the suffrage. In Illinois and Indiana there were no provisions for the education of colored children, and Negroes were not recognized as competent witnesses in court trials when a white person was a party to the case. Iowa and Ohio excluded Negroes from jury service. Interracial marriages were forbidden in Michigan, Ohio, Indiana and Illinois. Ohio denied Negroes the benefits of poor relief and provided for racially segregated public schools. Exclusion laws carrying severe penalties prohibited Negroes from settling in Indiana, Illinois and Iowa."

(Hoover 1968:160)

On a number of occasions the efforts to keep the black in his place erupted in violence. Wade (1968) writes about the race riots that beset Cincinnati in 1829 and forced a significant number of blacks to migrate to Canada. New York City had its share of violence, the most notorious being the draft riots of 1863. Philadelphia was the site of an even greater number of riots: "Between 1832 and 1849, Philadelphia mobs set off five major anti-Negro riots" (Litwack 1961:100). And so in a number of communities the blacks periodically faced the wrath and violence of the whites. In sum, there was a frequently harsh and brutal character to the confrontation between black and white in the North – a confrontation in which the black was forcibly reminded of his pariah and outsider status.

THE COLONIZATION MOVEMENT

Opposed to the continued enslavement of the black but at the same time convinced that the emancipated black had no real place in white society, a number of white Northerners sought to resolve this dilemma by proposing the colonization of the black in Africa and elsewhere. To accomplish this purpose, they established the American Colonization Society in 1817. Supported by the white clergy and segments of the Federalist party, the Society took as its first major step the establishment of a colony for blacks in Liberia, Africa. And with that act it spread its doctrine far and wide throughout America in true missionary style.

Special attention was paid to the white Southerner. He was warned of the ever-present "danger of slave unrest and rebellion" (Fredrickson 1971:8) and advised that the best course of action was to free his slaves eventually and to ship them to the African colony. In the meantime the free blacks should be sent as a precautionary measure. In the North, the whites were entreated to rid themselves of a cancerous social problem by supporting the movement. Much of the literature of the movement reinforced the stereotype of the black; he was deemed inferior and degraded. However most white colonizationists did not accept a simple biological determinism as an explanation for black incapacities; they were much more likely to be environmental determinists. They were convinced that the cause of the black's "fallen" condition in America was slavery and his inability to compete in white society. If he were colonized, they believed, he would reassert his identity and gain personal and social competence and "salvation."

The response of the blacks to the colonization appeal was extremely meager. Few accepted the invitation to emigrate; only an estimated 1400 reached Liberia in this period. But what is even more significant is the generally negative and hostile reaction of the black community as a whole. Quarles (1969) describes at length the intense opposition to colonization that was generated among the black leadership as the Society came into being. Only a small handful saw merit in the scheme.

Opposition to the plan also manifested itself in the 1820s among the white slaveholders in the Deep South. They denounced any efforts to obtain federal subsidies for the movement. In addition, some white abolitionists in the North had second thoughts on the matter. Led by William Lloyd Garrison, they increasingly denounced the movement after 1830. Consequently by the mid-1830s enthusiasm for the movement faded away and it became relatively quiescent.

In the 1850s the colonization movement revived. Such events as the Fugitive Slave Act and the pending Dred Scott decision cast a pall on hopes for a future for the emancipated black in America. Accordingly colonization as a viable solution for the black problem gained momentum. Sites other than Liberia were recommended such as in the Caribbean and Latin America. A number of northern states reaffirmed their support for colonization; some even set aside funds to encourage the project. But even more significant was the support the movement attracted from influential newspapers and political leaders. Some abolitionists rethought their opposition; moderates on race relation favored it. Most notably Abraham Lincoln supported the plan and was still actively in favour of colonization during the early days of the Civil War.

However, despite its renewed vigor, the colonization program never achieved much. Blacks – though somewhat more sympathetic to its appeal in the 1850s than they were in the 1820s – were still overwhelmingly opposed to the plan. And relatively few emigrated. It is estimated that only about 10,000 blacks migrated to Liberia during the whole period and several more thousand to other areas such as Haiti. The colonization scheme was the white man's solution to the black problem and not the black's.

Meager though its results, the colonization scheme represents a significant ideological statement of the plural character of racial America at the time. It states, in effect, that even with emancipation the blacks could not expect to become part of the people of the United States; they were doomed to remain an inferior and degraded stratum of outsiders who would never attain the rights and equalities of insiders. The colonizationists were convinced that the blacks had to go elsewhere to establish themselves as a people.

THE WEDGE INTO THE DOMAIN OF THE PEOPLE

Despite their pervasive subordination, segmentation, and segregation, blacks of the North were not as completely locked out of the Domain of the People as were the enslaved southern blacks. Although most northern states sought to curtail their rights and to deny them effective membership in the people, even in these states they were able to maintain certain residual rights. In other states such as Massachusetts they were able to gain a broader range of rights, including that of voting. As a result, the northern black was slowly able to carve out a presence for himself in the outer boundaries of the People's Domain and to win grudgingly from the whites a shadowy and tentative acceptance of the legitimacy of his presence. This meant that he could do things that were absolutely forbidden to the enslaved black.

> "Although a victim of racial proscription, he could – and on several occasions did – advance his political and economic position in the antebellum period; he could and did organize and petition, publish newspapers and tracts, even join with white sympathizers to advance his cause; in sum he was able to carry on a variety of activities directed toward an improvement of his position."
>
> (Litwack 1961:ix)

Thus the history of this period marks the beginning of organized black protest within the framework of the People's Domain. In 1827 the first black newspaper, *Freedom's Journal*, was published in New York City. Its first editorial stressed the newspaper's intent to pursue the cause and interest of the black, both freed and enslaved. In 1830 a national convention of blacks met for the first time and passed a series of resolutions in support of the blacks who had emigrated from Cincinnati to Canada because of the draconian laws that were being enforced against them in the city. A year later another convention met in Philadelphia consisting of delegates from five states, and so began a series of annual conventions in which the blacks addressed themselves to the wrongs they were experiencing in white society. The 1832 convention, for example, "resolved to raise money for Negro refugees in Canada, to form Negro temperance societies, to boycott slave-made products, to petition state and national legislatures against slavery and discrimination, to employ a Negro lecturer on the question of Negro rights, and to continue the efforts for an industrial school" (Aptheker 1962:133).

The convention was just one of the mechanisms the blacks developed to mount a protest against their treatment in society. They relied on a whole panoply of devices from organizations, rallies, pulpit, to the press. Only in recent years have scholars come to recognize the extent of black activism in this period.

However, the audience for these activities would have largely remained their fellow blacks, had not the protest movement become linked with the white abolitionist movement that had become revitalized by Garrison in the 1830s. This gave black abolitionists access to a much wider audience and, even though some of these audiences proved hostile, many of them were visibly affected by the appeals of such former slaves as Douglass, Brown, and Tubman. Much more frequently, white abolitionists carried out their activities among white audiences themselves; in this manner they extended the scope of the protest movement by reaching segments of the white society to which the blacks had no access.

Despite the linkage, relations between black and white abolitionists were frequently strained. Although Garrison became a hero to blacks, many white abolitionists were viewed with distrust. What particularly annoyed the black abolitionists was the various anti-black themes that seemed to be woven into the white movement. Some of these were: the general acceptance of the stereotype of the black as an inferior; the movement's lack of concern for the status and life circumstances of the free black; the susceptibility of some of the white abolitionists to the colonizationist movement; the white abolitionists' reluctance to cooperate jointly with the black abolitionists and to define them as equals. In effect, the black abolitionists resented the fact that they "were largely excluded from decision-making positions in the organized anti-slavery societies." Despite this limitation "through their lecturing, writing, and activities in the Underground Railroad, they played a central role in the fight against slavery" (Bracey, Meier, and Rudwick 1971:2).

The first period of reconstruction and the confrontation with racial biformism

The end of the Civil War ushered in a critical ten-year period which witnessed America's first major confrontation with its racial biformism. By the middle of the period this confrontation seemed on the verge of reshaping this dualism into a single Domain of the People. For a brief period this happened, but then the reshaping collapsed and the biformism resumed, entrenched even more deeply in the American society.

Presidential reconstruction: reconciliation and the Union

Even as the Civil War was in progress, President Lincoln pondered over the course of action that he would take with the defeat of the secessionist states. He was determined to reconstruct the Union, under the Constitution, with as little social and political upheaval as possible. From his first inaugural speech on, Lincoln had forcefully stated that, "'no State upon its own mere motion can lawfully get out of the Union; that resolves and ordinances to that effect are legally void'" (Commager 1968:386). Lincoln argued in his message to a special session of Congress in July 1861 that

> "'The States have their status in the Union, and they have no other legal status. If they break from this, they can only do so against law and by revolution. The Union, and not themselves separately, procured their independence and their liberty. By conquest or purchase the Union gave each of them whatever independence or liberty it has. The Union is older than any of the States, and in fact it created them as States.'"
>
> (Commager 1968:394)

Accordingly, Lincoln did not view the Civil War as a struggle between two distinctive political sovereignties; it was instead an effort by the federal government to put down a domestic insurrection being waged by disloyal segments of the population. "'Acts of violence, within any State or States, against the authority of the United States, are insurrectionary or revolutionary, according to circumstances'" (Commager 1968:386).

Lincoln was therefore committed to the punishment of the disloyal and rebellious segments of the population and to the restoration of the control of the state governments to those who were loyal "to the old relationship between the southern states and the Union." This was his basic conception of reconstruction. "This task, he thought, belonged to the President, not to Congress" (Stampp 1972:27–8). During the intervening years he sought to implement this policy through the formation of loyal governments in Virginia, Tennessee, Louisiana, and Arkansas. In each case he depended heavily on the support of those who had been Whigs in earlier years.

In December 1863 Lincoln brought together the various strands of his policy with a proclamation of amnesty and reconstruction. He reaffirmed his authority over reconstruction through the pardoning power of the president and restated his contention that "'a rebellion now exists whereby the loyal State governments of several States have for a long time been subverted, and many persons have committed and are now guilty of treason against the United States'" (Commager 1968:430). He laid down the conditions under which persons within these rebellious states could gain pardons and regain their rights of property and citizenship. They had to take an oath of allegiance (only those who occupied positions of military and governmental leadership in the rebellious states were excluded from the general provisions of the amnesty). Further, Lincoln decreed that state governments could be reestablished with full authority under the Constitution where at least 10 percent of the qualified voters of 1860 took the oath of allegiance.

Lincoln adhered in basic respects to his plan for reconstruction until the time of his assassination, even though Congress had expressed its displeasure with the plan's conciliatory character through passage of the Wade-Davis Bill of 1864. Unable to override the presidential veto of the bill, Congress refused to seat the representatives and senators from the states that had met Lincoln's conditions of reconstruction. Whether or not Lincoln might have changed his terms for reconstruction had he lived is a question still being debated.

Determined as he was to restore the Union, Lincoln did not have as firm a set of convictions toward slavery or the black. In his exchange of letters with Horace Greeley in 1862, Lincoln clearly indicated his paramount concern was the Union. He contended that the issue of slavery was of only secondary importance and that he would take that side of the issue that would best promote the cause of the Union.

> "'My paramount object in this struggle *is* to save the Union, and is *not* either to save or destroy Slavery. If I could save the Union without freeing *any* slave, I would do it; and if I could save it by freeing *all* the slaves, I would do it; and if I could do it by freeing some and leaving others alone, I would also do that. What I do about Slavery and the colored race, I do because I believe it helps to save this Union; and what I forbear, I forbear because I do *not* believe it would help to save the Union.'"   (Commager 1968:418)

Having clearly established his priorities, Lincoln never pressed very hard on the issue of slavery. Although he had concluded by the 1850s that slavery was a moral evil, he never joined the ranks of the committed abolitionists to make the struggle for the Union interchangeable with the struggle for emancipation of the slave. Instead he was inclined to view the latter instrumentally; policy on slavery was to be used as a means of promoting the struggle for the Union. Even the Emancipation Proclamation of 1863 can be read in this vein. It was a proclamation to be applied only to areas in the South still under rebellion and not to those under federal control. As Stampp says, "Lincoln's proclamation was not one of his great state papers, for its appeal was not to the rights of man or to any other external principles but only to military necessity. Indeed, it may be said that if it was Lincoln's destiny to go down in history as the Great Emancipator, rarely has a man embraced his destiny with greater reluctance than he" (Stampp 1972:44).

Even with the Proclamation, Lincoln did not embrace total abolition of slavery. In his message to Congress in December 1862, he was still prepared to accept the notion that slavery continued to be a legitimate issue of debate among the friends of the Union. (Lincoln, however, rejected any voice for the enemies of the Union in this debate.) Accordingly, he advocated compromise as the most effective solution for the diversity of opinion among the friends of the Union on the issue of slavery.

"'Among the friends of the Union there is great diversity of sentiment and of policy in regard to slavery and the African race amongst us. Some would perpetuate slavery; some would abolish it gradually and with compensation; some would remove the freed people from us; and some would retain them with us; and there are yet other minor diversities. Because of these diversities we waste much strength in struggles among ourselves. By mutual concession we should harmonize and act together. This would be compromise, but it would be compromise among the friends and not with the enemies of the Union.'"

(Commager 1968:404)

With this in mind, Lincoln presented a proposal for a gradual process of compensated emancipation which would be concluded by the turn of the twentieth century. He argued that

"'The (length of) time spares both races from the evils of sudden derangement – in fact, from the necessity of any derangement – while most of those whose habitual course of thought will be disturbed by the measure will have passed away before its consummation. They will never see it. Another class will hail the prospect of emancipation, but will deprecate the length of time. They will feel that it gives too little to the now living slaves. But it really gives them much. It saves them from the vagrant destitution which must largely attend immediate emancipation in localities where their numbers are very great, and it gives the inspiring assurance that their posterity shall be free forever.'"

(Commager 1968:404)

In addition, Lincoln also restated his earlier proposal for voluntary colonization of the freed slaves in areas outside the United States. "'Congress may appropriate money and otherwise provide for colonizing free colored persons with their own consent at any place or places without the United States'" (Commager 1968:404).

By 1865 Lincoln took a firmer position on abolition of slavery as a condition for peace with the rebellious South. He urged those forming loyal governments in Arkansas, Louisiana, and Tennessee to incorporate emancipation of the slave within their constitutions. In his last public address in April 1865, he applauded the efforts of the 12,000 loyal voters in Louisiana to bring that state into a "proper practical relation with the Union."

"'Some twelve thousand voters in the heretofore Slave State of Louisiana have sworn allegiance to the Union, assumed to be the rightful political power of the State, held election, organized a State government, adopted a Free State constitution, giving the benefit of public schools equally to black and white, and enpowering the Legislature to confer the elective franchise upon the colored man.'"

(Commager 1968:450)

However, the legislature did not in fact enfranchise the black. Lincoln took cognizance of this. Although he did not object, he expressed his preference for enfranchising "'the very intelligent'" and "'those who serve our cause as soldiers.'" Further, he expressed his approval of the fact "'that this (Louisiana) legislature has already voted to ratify the Constitutional Amendment recently passed by Congress, abolishing slavery throughout the nation'" (Commager 1968:450).

Despite these modifications, Lincoln did not take a position for unqualified emancipation for the slaves nor for their enfranchisement as a precondition for peace. He retained the conviction as did most of his fellow Northerners that the blacks were indeed inferior and that they could never gain complete equality with the whites. Stampp draws this conclusion. He states, "As long as the Negroes remained in America, he (Lincoln) doubted that white men would give them citizenship and equal rights and he did not ask white men to do so." Accordingly, "Lincoln never abandoned his hope that the great mass of Negroes could be persuaded to leave the country." Stampp, however, believes that Lincoln might have changed his mind had he lived. "Had Lincoln lived to the end of his second administration, he would have been forced to accept the presence of the Negro in his country as a permanent fact; and, given his flexibility, he would doubtless have discovered a more constructive policy than colonization. That he had failed to do so before his death, however, is clear enough" (Stampp 1972:47–8).

Congressional opponents of Lincoln's reconstruction policies were convinced that Johnson would join them in overturning these policies once he took office. They drew this conclusion from Johnson's past record and utterances as a public official in Tennessee and Washington. He had bitterly opposed the southern rebellion and had denounced the wealthy plantation owners as traitors who had misled the average white Southerner.

By the end of May 1865 these critics realized that they had misjudged the new President. He issued an amnesty proclamation which resembled in basic details that promulgated by Lincoln two years earlier. He would "grant to all persons who have, directly or indirectly, participated in the existing rebellion, except as hereinafter excepted, amnesty and pardon, with restoration of all rights of property, except as to slaves ... but upon the condition, nevertheless, that every such person shall take and subscribe the following oath." The oath stipulated that the person would "henceforth faithfully support, protect and defend the Constitution of the United States, and the union of the States thereunder ... [and] all laws, and proclamations which have been made during the existing rebellion with reference to the emancipation of slaves."

Even the classes that were excepted from the proclamation were similar to those excepted by Lincoln. The major difference was that Johnson included as an excepted class. "All persons who have voluntarily participated in said rebellion and the estimated value of whose taxable property is over twenty thousand dollars" (US Statutes at Large 1866 13:758–59). Lincoln had provided for no such excluded class. Despite his exclusion of these classes from the general amnesty, Johnson announced liberal procedures for granting pardons to members of the excepted classes on an individual basis.

Johnson also issued a second proclamation on the same day which described the procedure for the formation of loyal state governments. The President would appoint a provisional governor

"whose duty it shall be, at the earliest practicable period, to prescribe such rules and regulations as may be necessary and proper for convening a convention, composed of delegates to be chosen by that portion of the people of said state who are loyal to the United States, and no others, for the purpose of altering or amending the constitution thereof; and with authority to exercise, within the limits of said state, all the powers necessary and proper to enable such loyal people of the State to restore said State to its constitutional relations to the federal Government, and to present such a republican form of state government as will entitle the state to the guarantee of the United States therefor, and its people to protection by the United States against invasion, insurrection and domestic violence." (US Statutes at Large 1866 13:760)

The proclamation further stipulated that

"no person shall be qualified as an elector, or shall be eligible as a member of such convention, unless he shall have previously taken and subscribed the oath of amnesty as set forth in the President's Proclamation ... and is a voter qualified as prescribed by the constitution and laws of the State ... in force immediately before ... the date of the so-called ordinance of secession.... [The convention would then] prescribe the qualification of electors, and the eligibility of persons to hold office under the constitution and laws of the state, – a power the people of the several states composing the Federal Union have rightfully exercised from the origin of the government to the present time." (US Statutes at Large 1866 13:760)

After that an election would be held for the governor, state legislature, and members of congress.

Johnson was convinced that his plans for the South would result in a restructuring of the white power structure. He was sure that the less affluent whites shared his belief that the white affluent class, particularly the plantation owner, was responsible for dragging the South into the rebellion. Accordingly, he was confident that all he had to do was to create the opportunity for these less affluent whites by excluding the affluent class from the electorate. The less affluent, would then disown the plantation class and assume control of the reconstructed society. In this manner, he believed, the small white farmer, yeoman, and bourgeoisie would create an agrarian society in which they were dominant. The black for all intents and purposes was disregarded in his scheme of things. True, Johnson demanded abolition of slavery as one of the conditions of a state's being considered to have been rehabilitated, but "beyond this, he thought the federal government had no jurisdiction; questions of education, social relationships, and civil and political rights must be settled by individual states" (Stampp 1972:77). Thus, the fate of the black was thrown back into the hands of the reconstructed states; they were to have virtually a blank check on issues of suffrage, education, and work.

As word of Johnson's benign reconstruction policies filtered through the South, its initial hostility toward the president dissipated and he became a hero. Persons in the excepted classes sought in droves to gain pardons on an individual basis; these were readily granted. State conventions were hurriedly convened. They generally accepted the three conditions that Johnson had laid down: repudiation of the Confederate debt, abolition of slavery, and repeal of the laws of secession. Several tried to modify the slavery provision by retaining the right for future compensation, but this provision was quickly eliminated.

The conventions completed their tasks within several months and elections were held for state officials and congressional representatives. So rapid had the "reconstruction" process taken place that by December 1865 Johnson announced to Congress that his reconstruction program had been completed successfully. He proclaimed that the South had been returned to its proper relationship with the Union and the Constitution, and he urged that the new senators and representatives from the South be seated in Congress.

The reconstructed South that Johnson was prepared to accept mirrored in many respects the South that had fought the war. The white planter class had reasserted its dominance and many of the civilian and military leaders of the rebellion had come back into power and had taken over the reins of government as elected officials in many of the states. Johnson's dream of a society dominated by the yeoman class failed to materialize and the antipathy which he insisted pervaded this class's attitude toward the antebellum political, economic, and social elite proved to be a myth.

Nowhere were the efforts of the white Southerners to retain as much of the past as they could more manifest than in their treatment of the blacks. While grudgingly consenting to the abolition of slavery, they sought to build a structure of legal constraint and overt repression which would control the black and keep him in a state of subjugation and subservience. Within a short period of time, the newly reconstructed states had passed black codes. These laws varied in severity from state to state, but in general they sought to regulate such matters as employment, vagrancy, and civil and criminal rights and penalties. All seemed to pay some lip service to the new freedom of the emancipated slave and to spell out areas of rights previously forbidden to the black. He could now sue and be sued, bear witness in court, become legally married, and even sign a contract as a free laborer. But each new right was so severely hemmed in by restrictive conditions that the black remained for all intents and purposes relatively unprotected under the law.

For example, he was given the right to own personal property in Mississippi, but he was constrained from renting or leasing "any lands or tenements except in incorporated cities or towns, in which places the corporate authorities shall control the same" (Commager 1968:452). He could legally marry but not intermarry. He could bear witness in court against a black but only under certain conditions against a white.

The most serious and comprehensive restrictions were placed against the slave's newly won right to work as a free laborer. While manifestly accepting the right of the freedman to contract his labor with whomever he wished, the codes bore down heavily on the obligation of the freedman to fulfill his contract – even if he had to be forced to do so. The black code of Louisiana clearly stipulated:

"Sec. 2. Every laborer shall have full and perfect liberty to choose his employer, but when once chosen, he shall not be allowed to leave his place of employment until the fulfillment of his contract . . . and if they do so leave, without cause or permission they shall forfeit all wages earned to the time of abandonment."

(Commager 1968:455)

The payment of fines was not considered to be enough of a punishment, so the black was to be returned forcibly to his employer to complete his term of service. This is evident in the Mississippi code.

"Sec. 7. . . . Every civil officer shall, and every person may, arrest and carry back to his or her legal employer any freedman, free negro, or mulatto who shall have quit the service of his or her employer before the expiration of his or her term of service without good cause; and said officer and person shall be entitled to receive for arresting and carrying back every deserting employe aforesaid the sum of five dollars, and ten cents per mile from the place of arrest to the place of delivery; and the same shall be paid by the employer, and held as a set-off for so much against the wages of said deserting employe:"   (Commager 1968:453)

Carl Schurz, who was commissioned by President Johnson to survey the situation in the South*, condemned the codes as trying to impose a new form of bondage on the black. He compared this new bondage to the peonage of Mexico and to the serfdom of Europe.

> "Peonage of the Mexican pattern, or serfdom of some European pattern, may under that clause (of the code) be considered admissible; and looking at the legislative attempts already made, especially the labor code now under consideration in the legislature of South Carolina, it appears not only possible, but eminently probable, that the laws which will be passed to guard against the dangers arising from emancipation will be directed against the spirit of emancipation itself."   (Schurz 1969:34)

Schurz was convinced that these codes reflected the general sentiment of the white Southerners. The latter had reluctantly accepted the abolition of slavery, but they were not prepared to give up their control of the black. They were intent upon developing a new form of servitude.

> "The emancipation of the slaves is submitted to only in so far as chattel slavery in the old form could not be kept up. But although the freedman is no longer considered the property of the individual master, he is considered the slave of society, and all independent State legislation will share the tendency to make him such. The ordinances abolishing slavery passed by the conventions under the pressure of circumstances, will not be looked upon as barring the establishment of a new form of servitude."   (Schurz 1969:45)

To retain this control, the white Southerners were prepared to use force and coercion. They were not going to allow the disruption of the normative system that "harmonized" relations between black and white under slavery to frustrate this control. Accordingly they resorted to terror and violence. Blacks were killed and maimed; they were forcibly kept out of some places and forcibly kept in others. Schurz and others have described in detail the victimization of the black during this period.

This combined onslaught of legal and extralegal instruments of repression prevented the black from experiencing in any significant way the freedoms which he presumably had just acquired. He enjoyed certain minimal legal rights against his fellow black; but against the white, virtually none. He was denied any political rights and access to the Domain of the People. He was also denied entry into institutions that might eventually allow him to gain access to the Domain of the People; for example, he was to be kept illiterate and unschooled.

---

*Johnson sought to discredit Schurz's report when he became aware of Schurz's critical assessment of the situation in the South.

In effect the reconstructed South succeeded in returning to "a modified form of involuntary servitude" (Stampp 1972:80). Only now it had to rely more heavily on coercion and force than in the past; for its antebellum normative system, built on the paternalism of the white and the submissiveness of the black, had been seriously uprooted with military defeat and the abolition of slavery. Thus, the black remained outside the Domain of the People as a "propertyless rural laborer under strict controls, without political rights, and with inferior legal rights" (Stampp 1972:79).

Congressional reconstruction and entry of the black into the Domain of the People

The erosion of congressional support for Johnson's reconstruction policies was virtually complete by the end of 1865. By the precipitousness with which he organized governments in the southern states and by his uncompromising behavior, Johnson undercut his support among the moderate Republicans and moved them into an accord with the Radical Republicans. The accord was solidified by the provocative and frequently violent action in the southern states.

The net result was that Congress and the President were pitted against each other with respect to the treatment of the South. The President insisted that the process of reconstruction was finished and that the newly reconstructed states should take their "rightful" place in the Union and Congress under the Constitution. Congress rejected this contention; it insisted that the South had still to be restored to its constitutional relationship with the Union and, until such time as it was, the South was to be subject to the rules and regulations prescribed by Congress.

Stampp contends that the central issue which divided the President and Congress was "the place of the free Negro in American society. This was the question that the radicals and Johnsonians always came to sooner or later. Between them they gave shape to the debate – its terms, its form, its assumptions – that has raged with varying degrees of intensity ever since" (Stampp 1972:87).

While scholars may dispute Stampp's contention and may question the sincerity of the Radical Republicans' advocacy of the rights of the black, the fact nevertheless remains that the status of the black was a primary item, both open and hidden, on the agenda of the momentous series of acts that Congress passed over the next several years. These acts established the legal and normative framework for the period of the radical reconstruction. They emerged from the work of the joint committee of fifteen senators and representatives which served as the generative source and repository for the congressional reconstruction.

The first major act that survived a presidential veto and became law was the Civil Rights Act of April 1866. The primary effect of this act was to reverse the Dred Scott decision of 1857 and to confer citizenship upon the blacks. However, a number of congressional leaders expressed concern about the constitutionality of the measure; accordingly steps were taken almost immediately to transform the act into a constitutional amendment. Thus the Fourteenth Amendment was proposed in June 1866 and finally proclaimed in July 1868.

Section One of the amendment clearly conferred citizenship in the national community to the black. It stipulated that citizenship was to be a function of birth or naturalization and that membership in the national domain entitled the person to the full protection of the Constitution and of the Bill of Rights. The extent to which such protection was also to apply to state citizenship and not merely to national citizenship remained to be determined by the Supreme Court in future decisions:

> "Section 1. All persons born or naturalized in the United States, and subject to the jurisdiction thereof, are citizens of the United States and of the State wherein they reside. No State shall make or enforce any law which shall abridge the privileges or immunities of citizens of the United States; nor shall any State deprive any person of life, liberty, or property, without due process of law; nor to deny any person within its jurisdiction the equal protection of the laws."
> (*The Constitution of the United States of America with the Amendments* 1872:24–5)

The amendment dealt only tangentially with political rights. Section 2 stated that the number of representatives in Congress for a state could be curtailed proportionate to the number of adult male citizens not given the vote in federal elections. Section 3 excluded certain categories of Confederates from holding federal office; however, Congress could remove this disability by a two-thirds vote.

In his veto of the original Civil Rights Act, President Johnson took strong exception to the preferential treatment that he alleged the act gave to the black. He complained that ill-prepared blacks would become citizens overnight by virtue of birth in this country, while patient domicile aliens who were slowly learning the ways of citizenship would still have to wait for it. "'The bill in effect proposes a discrimination against large numbers of intelligent, worthy, and patriotic foreigners, and in favor of the Negro, to whom, after long years of bondage, the avenues to freedom and intelligence have just now been suddenly opened'" (Commager 1968:466).

However, Johnson reserved his most caustic criticism for the bill's presumed encroachment on the rights of the state to govern without interference within its own boundaries and to define the terms and conditions of citizenship within its own borders as distinct from terms and conditions of citizenship in the nation as a whole. Johnson argued that to have the federal government become the agency for extending the rights of the black would be a radical departure from the established relationship between state and federal government and would in effect provide the black with preferential treatment that had never been given to the whites.

> "'In all our history, in all our experience as a people living under Federal and State law, no such system as that contemplated by the details of this bill has ever before been proposed or adopted. They establish for the security of the colored race safeguards which go infinitely beyond any that the General Government has ever provided for the white race. In fact, the distinction of race and color is by the bill made to operate in favor of the colored and against the white race. They interfere with the municipal legislation of the States, with the relations existing exclusively between a State and its citizens, or between inhabitants of the same State – an absorption and assumption of power by the General Government which, if acquiesced in, must sap and destroy our federative system of limited powers and break down the barriers which preserve the rights of the States. It is another step, or rather stride, toward centralization and the concentration of all legislative powers in the National Government. The tendency of the bill must be to resuscitate the spirit of rebellion and to arrest the progress of those influences which are more closely drawing around the States the bonds of union and peace.'"   (Commager 1968:468)

Once again the opposing priorities of President and of Congress were affirmed. The former would preserve the sanctity of the rights of the states, even if this meant continued exclusion of the black from the Domain of the People. The latter would extend the boundaries of the Domain of the People to include membership for the black, even if this meant a basic restructuring of past relations between state and federal government. Such congressional leaders as Sumner were convinced that the imperative Congress faced was to bring the Constitution and governmental practice into fuller accord with the promise of the Declaration of Independence. Sumner in particular insisted that the Declaration was the legitimating source for the Constitution.

> "'This was the document which declared the purposes of the United States as a nation, and nothing had happened when the Constitution was made to alter those purposes and principles. [Accordingly,] ... the Constitution must be interpreted by the Declaration. I insist that the Declaration is of equal and co-ordinate authority with the Constitution itself.... Whenever you are

considering the Constitution, so far as it concerns human right, you must bring it always to that great touchstone; the two must go together and the Constitution must never be interpreted in any way inconsistent with the Declaration.'"

(Brock 1963:267)

If changes in established governmental practices and relations are required to do so, then he and the other congressional leaders had no qualms about making these changes.

By June 1866 the joint committee on reconstruction issued its report after extensive hearings on the state of affairs in the South. It concluded "that the so-called Confederate States are not, at present, entitled to representation in the Congress of the United States" (Commager 1968:470) and agreed that the President did not have the authority to control the process of reconstruction. In July Congress passed a revised version of the Freedmen's Bureau Bill which had previously been vetoed, but now Congress was able to override a second veto.

By the autumn of 1866 the issue of who had the authority over reconstruction was bitterly joined by the President and Congress. The President looked to the congressional elections of 1866 as a way of solidifying support for his position and accordingly launched a harsh and hard-hitting campaign against his congressional opponents. But the results dealt a catastrophic blow to his hopes. The Radical Republicans gained the kind of endorsement that they needed to assert their control over reconstruction. Why the results of the election turned out as they did still remains largely a puzzle.

Even though many Northerners expressed indignation over the brutality of southern authorities toward the black, this was probably not a decisive factor in the vote. For, as we have already seen, the Northerners themselves did not treat the black well. Most northern states had highly discriminatory laws against the blacks, and Northerners showed no great interest in redressing the historical wrongs done to the black, as evidenced by the bitter struggles that developed in their legislatures over passage of the Fourteenth Amendment.

What probably built the Northerner's anger to fever pitch was the open arrogance of many of the officials of the newly reconstructed state governments. A number were reported in northern newspapers and elsewhere as talking and acting as though the South had won the war; others, as flaunting their confederate loyalties and symbols. These reports from the South did not reach dispassionate and inattentive ears. War wounds were still too fresh in the North; too many northern solders had died to allow the survivors to forgive or to forget quickly. It would therefore seem reasonable to conclude that the North was not prepared to treat the South as lightly as the President seemed intent upon doing. Small wonder then that the electorate supported the Radical Republicans. They were responding to the Republican advocacy of a harsh reconstruction for the South more than to its advocacy of the rights of the blacks.

Once the election results were in, Congress under the leadership of the Radical Republicans moved quickly to establish its control over reconstruction. It was intent upon achieving a basic restructuring of the political system of the South. At the heart of its program was the role of the black. Stampp leaves no doubt about the importance of the black to the Radical Republican's plan for reconstruction.

> "The radicals, to reconstruct the South on a firm foundation, would throw out the Black Codes, which were hardly designed to prepare the Negroes for freedom anyway, give the Negroes civil rights and the ballot, and get white men accustomed to treating Negroes as equals, at least politically and legally. Aid to the freed men was thus at the very heart of radical reconstruction; it was this aspect of the program, and little else, that justified designating as radicals the Republican leaders in Congress. Their attempt to give full citizenship to southern Negroes – in effect, to revolutionize the reaction of the two races – was the great 'leap in the dark' of the reconstruction era."   (Stampp 1972:122)

Some Radical Republicans like Thaddeus Stevens would have extended the restructuring of the South to its economic system as well. They would have divided much of the land into smaller parcels and distributed them among the freedmen, but the efforts to legislate land redistribution soon came to naught, and Congress confined much of its attention to the restructuring of the political system of the South.

As it first major step in this direction Congress sought to dismantle the structure of civil government in the southern states that had already won the endorsement of the President. In the First Reconstruction Act of March 1867 the eleven rebel states were divided into five military districts. Each was placed under the command of a brigadier-general who was to enforce the law and was to insure public peace and order. He was also authorized to supervise an election of delegates who would meet in convention to write a constitution for a new state government which was in conformity with the Constitution of the United States. The right to vote for the delegates was to be bestowed on all adult males "of whatever race, color or previous condition, who have been resident in said State for one year previous to the day of such election, except such as may be disfranchised for participation in the rebellion or for felony at common law" (US Statutes at Large 1868 14:429).

For Congress to approve the newly written constitution it had to meet certain conditions. Chief among these was the following: the constitution had to provide an elective franchise similar to that stipulated for the election of the delegates; no bar to voting because of race or color; it had to be ratified by a "majority of the persons voting on the question of ratification who are qualified as electors for delegates" (US Statutes at Large 1868 14:429).

Even with such approval the new state government still had to do certain things before it would be admitted to full membership in the federal government. It had to enact the Fourteenth Amendment to the United States Constitution, and only when the amendment was ratified by enough states in the Union so that it became part of the Constitution would the individual state be granted full membership. It would then be

> "entitled to representation in Congress, and senators and representatives shall be admitted therefrom on their taking the oath prescribed by law.... [However] until the people of said rebel States shall be by law admitted to representation in the Congress of the United States, any civil governments which may exist therein shall be deemed provisional only, and in all respects subject to the paramount authority of the United States at any time to abolish, modify, control or supersede the same."   (US Statutes at Large 1868 14:429)

Three weeks later Congress passed the Second Reconstruction Act. This act elaborated on the procedures the military commanders were to follow in registering voters for the proposed election of delegates to the constitutional conventions; it introduced an oath that all registrants were to affirm. The act also spelled out in greater detail the processes by which the constitutional convention was to be convened and stipulated the conditions under which Congress would consider a constitution as having been duly ratified and would thereby admit the civilly governed state into the political community. President Johnson vetoed both acts; in his veto messages he vehemently denounced the "bondage of military domination" which he argued was being clamped on states that had already met the requirement for being readmitted into the Union. He bitterly complained in his first veto message that Congress had usurped its authority and was seeking to impose a radically new structure on the South for no other reason than to bring the black into the political community. In so doing, he argued, Congress was violating the rights of the states and intruding into an area which the Constitution had reserved for the states.

> "'The purpose and object of the bill – the general intent which pervades it from beginning to end – is to change the entire structure and character of the State governments and to compel them by force to the adoption of organic laws and regulations which they are unwilling to accept if left to themselves. The Negroes have not asked for the privilege of voting; the vast majority of them have no idea what it means. This bill not only thrusts it into their hands, but compels them, as well as the whites, to use it in a particular way....

Without pausing here to consider the policy or impolicy of Africanizing the southern part of our territory, I would simply ask the attention of Congress to that manifest, well-known, and universally acknowledged rule of constitutional law which declares that the Federal Government has no jurisdiction, authority, or power to regulate such subjects for any State. To force the right of suffrage out of the hands of the white people and into the hands of the negroes is an arbitrary violation of this principle.'"   (Commager 1968:484)

In his second veto message, Johnson made an even more determined attack on black suffrage as the focal feature of congressional reconstruction. He argued that Congress was prepared to upset traditional relations between state and federal government in order to force states whose constitutions were fully in accord with the requirements of the law of the land into a state of military occupation and was also prepared to impose a new definition of what it means to be loyal to America – all for the sake of giving the black the right to vote.

"'In all these States there are existing constitutions, framed in the accustomed way by the people. Congress, however, declares that these constitutions are not "loyal and republican," and requires the people to form them anew. What, then, in the opinion of Congress, is necessary to make the constitution of a State "loyal and republican"? The original act answers the question: It is universal negro suffrage – a question which the Federal Constitution leaves exclusively to the States themselves. All this legislative machinery of martial law, military coercion, and political disfranchisement is avowedly for that purpose and none other. The existing constitutions of the ten States conform to the acknowledged standards of loyalty and republicanism.'"   (Commager 1968:490)

Johnson continued his slashing response by arguing that adoption of black suffrage as a major criterion for a state's membership in the political community would require expelling most of the northern states, for they too exclude the black from suffrage. He concluded that if Congress were to be consistent, it would have to extend reconstruction to these states too.

"'If in the exercise of the constitutional guaranty that Congress shall secure to every state a republican form of government universal suffrage for blacks as well as whites is a *sine qua non*, the work of reconstruction may as well begin in Ohio as in Virginia, in Pennsylvania as in North Carolina.'"

(Commager 1968:491)

Congress disregarded Johnson's advice and overrode both vetoes, and in July passed the Third Reconstruction Act which further clarified certain ambiguities in the earlier acts. However, Johnson refused to desist in his opposition. In fact he was encouraged by relative lack of public support in the North for military rule and black suffrage. The election returns of 1867 showed a swing toward the Democratic party and significant opposition to amendments and laws in favor of black suffrage. These results so invigorated the President that he launched an even more strident attack on black suffrage. He was convinced that the intent of the reconstruction laws was to saddle black domination on the South. "'It is not proposed merely that they (the negroes) shall govern themselves, but that they shall rule the white race, make and administer State laws, elect Presidents and members of Congress, and shape to a greater or less extent the future destiny of the whole country'" (Cox and Cox 1973:92).

The President then asked "Would such a trust and power be safe in such hands?" He answered with a resounding no, not merely because blacks had been kept down so long and had not learned the skills of government, but primarily because they were inferior to the white man.

> "'No independent government of any form has ever been successful in their (negroes') hands. On the contrary, wherever they have been left to their own devices they have shown a constant tendency to relapse into barbarism.... The great difference between the two races in physical, mental, and moral characteristics will prevent an amalgamation or fusion of them together in one homogeneous mass. If the inferior obtains the ascendancy over the other, it will govern with reference only to its own interests – for it will recognize no common interest – and create such a tyranny as this continent has never yet witnessed.'" (Cox and Cox 1973:92–4)

Johnson was convinced that survival of the political system in America depended upon continuation of white control; and that universal suffrage for the black spelled disaster. "'Of all the dangers which our nation has yet encountered, none are equal to those which must result from the success of the effort now making to Africanize the half of our country'" (Cox and Cox 1973:94–5).

Thus Johnson opposed full membership of the black in the political community. In this he would retain the historical dual track that was built into the Constitution but with certain modifications. He would legitimate the blacks' presence in the Domain of the People but as wards who needed to be protected and socialized into the ways of the superior white race.

> "'I repeat the expression of my willingness to join in any plan within the scope of our constitutional authority which promises to better the condition of the negroes in the South, by encouraging them in industry, enlightening their minds, improving their morals, and giving protection to all their just rights as freedmen. But the transfer of our political inheritance to them would, in my

opinion, be an abandonment of a duty which we owe alike to the memory of
our fathers and the rights of our children.'"   (Cox and Cox 1973:94)

The stance of the President expressed more clearly than anything else could the
deeply embedded barriers within the Constitution to the enfranchisement of the
black. His exclusion from the Domain of the People had been reaffirmed by the
Dred Scott decision of 1857, and it was reinforced by the constitutional rights of
each individual state to authority over affairs within its boundaries. Confronting
this issue head on provoked a constitutional crisis of no mean proportion. It set
President and Congress at loggerheads with each other and produced a thrust
toward legislative supremacy in the central government that had few historical
precedents.

The net result was an estrangement between President and Congress that could
not be healed. By the time President Johnson had made his December declaration,
Congress had already passed the Tenure of Office Act and Command of the Army
Act which sought to curb the presidential power. Within a few short months
impeachment proceedings were set in motion. Although Johnson escaped impeachment by one vote, his influence on governmental affairs waned and Congress
was able to continue its reconstruction program virtually unchallenged.

In March of 1868 it passed the fourth and last of its Reconstruction Acts. This
modified the ratification requirements of the second Reconstruction Act. A new
state constitution could now be accepted by a majority of those voting and not
merely by a majority of the registered voters. In this manner Congress sought to
prevent what had happened in Alabama in 1868 when enough registered white
voters stayed away from the polls and thereby defeated the new constitution.

With these four acts, Congress rounded out its legal and normative framework
for reconstructing the southern states. Its goal was to reshape completely the
political structure of the states so that they would become "loyal and republican"
members of the Union. This was to be accomplished in part by curbing and
"delegitimating" the power of the established political elite, but most of all by
admitting the black to full membership in the political community and by making
him a part of the people.

Thus black suffrage was the keystone to the kind of political society that many
Radical Republicans were trying to create in the South. Within several years,
however, many of these Republicans realized that it was not enough to base black
suffrage on simple legislative acts, which could be reversed by simple majorities in
future Congresses. Accordingly they mounted a drive for a constitutional
amendment. What finally passed Congress in 1869 and became a constitutional
amendment in 1870 fell far short of the legislation of 1867. There, universal
suffrage was mandated irrespective of race and color; the Fifteenth Amendment

merely stipulated that suffrage could not be denied or abridged because of race or color.

> "Section 1. The right of citizens of the United States to vote shall not be denied or abridged by the United States or by any State on account of race, color or previous condition of servitude.
>
> Section 2. The Congress shall have power to enforce this article by appropriate legislation."
>
> *(The Constitution of the United States of America with the Amendments* 1872:26)

To the Coxes this represented a retreat from the 1867 legislation.

> "The amendment in some respects did represent a retreat from the 1867 legislation, first in theory but later in practice. The 1867 law had mandated the vote to black men in ten Southern states; for them, the amendment merely meant that it could not be taken away because they were black. This left the door open to evasion through property, literacy, and poll tax requirements, devices widely used in the South after 1890."   (Cox and Cox 1973:105)

Despite this inherent limitation, the amendment produced almost immediate results. Its effect, though, was not confined to the South; "in eleven Northern and five Border States where black men had no right to vote in 1869, the Fifteenth Amendment, negative in form, meant a positive grant of suffrage" (Cox and Cox 1973:105).

The enactment of the Fourteenth and Fifteenth Amendments, according to Brock, "cut off the old constitution from the new." They laid the foundations for a legal-normative challenge to the duality built into the old Constitution. However, for the next century efforts were made to corrode this foundation and to circumscribe the institutional span of the amendments. Yet despite these efforts, Brock continues, "the great amendments were in the Constitution and could not be removed; their day was to dawn in the twentieth century and upon them was to be built the yet incomplete edifice of racial equality" (Brock 1963:264–65).

In the early 1870s Congress passed three acts to enforce and to implement the amendments. Their primary purpose was to protect and to implement black suffrage and to punish the violent response of many white Southerners. In fact the third act was labelled the Ku Klux Klan Act, and its goal was to curb the extralegal means of force and violence that found expression in the organization that had recently come into being. The effectiveness of these laws remains open to debate, but they were further expressions of Congress's intent to press ahead with its reconstruction program.

The high-water mark of congressional action was reached in the Civil Rights Act of 1875. It sought to expand the boundaries of civil rights from voting to places of public accommodation and transportation.

"Whereas it is essential to just government we recognize the equality of all men before the law, and hold that it is the duty of government in its dealings with the people to mete out equal and exact justice to all, of whatever nativity, race, color, or persuasion, religious or political; and it being the appropriate object of legislation to enact great fundamental principles into law: Therefore,

Be it enacted, That all persons within the jurisdiction of the United States shall be entitled to the full and equal enjoyment of the accommodations, advantages, facilities, and privileges of inns, public conveyances on land or water, theaters, and other places of public amusement; subject only to the conditions and limitations established by law, and applicable alike to citizens of every race and color, regardless of any previous condition of servitude."

Section 4 extended equal rights to service on the jury.

"Sec. 4. That no citizen possessing all other qualifications which are or may be prescribed by law shall be disqualified for service as grand or petit juror in any court of the United States, or of any State, on account of race, color or previous condition of servitude;"   (US Statutes at Large 1875 18, 3:335–36)

However, Radical Republicans were balked in their efforts to pass an Enforcement Bill to insure the implementation of the Civil Rights Bill. And with that ended for all intents and purposes significant legislative action on racial equality that had begun with the Act of 1866. It would take almost another century before any concerted effort would be attempted by Congress to build on these foundations.

RADICAL RECONSTRUCTION IN THE SOUTH

By directing its attention toward both the top and the bottom of the hierarchy of power in the southern states, Congress sent profound reverberations through the entire political structure of the states and produced an almost "revolutionary" reallocation of political power for at least a short period of time. Significant segments of the established white elite were disfranchised for their earlier association with the Confederacy. They found themselves on the outside looking in on the political system – at least temporarily. By 1872 virtually all were back in the system and in the saddle shortly thereafter. However, Congress did little to disturb the economic power that inhered in these groups. For a while it had toyed with the idea of a major program of land redistribution for the freedmen, but it never did anything substantial about taking land away from the plantation owners.

Accordingly these groups still retained primary control of property and of the means of production in the South. What is more they still stood at the top of the status system. In fact their prestige and social influence were enhanced within the white community by the "martyrdom" they suffered from the congressional acts. They took on the guise of sanctified heroes. They were sanctified in the sense that they were held to be relatively blameless for what was wrong or was going wrong in the South, despite the fact that they had presided over the wrecking of the South and were still largely in command of its resources. They were heroes in the sense that they represented the glories of the South that had been overrun but was still viewed as a bastion of the superior white civilization.

Small wonder that this group lost little of its *de facto* power with disfranchisement and little of its zeal for reasserting its right to legitimate political power. As such it stood at the center of a structure of extralegal power that was prepared to exert coercion and force to gain its ends and to cow the black. The elite members of this group may not have actually run or even belonged to groups such as the Ku Klux Klan or Knights of the Camelia, which mushroomed during this period, but they provided the spiritual and moral guidance and justification for the widespread resort to violence and terror. (A reasonable question might arise as to how this group would have fared had they had to bear directly the responsibility which was theirs for the economic and social miseries of the South, instead of being able to displace these responsibilities on to others. At the least such historians as Dunning (1907) and Burgess (1902) might have been less inclined to make heroes of them.)

The new white leadership group that took control of the political structure for part or all of the decade from 1867 to 1877 in the former states of the Confederacy was identified with the Republican party and was drawn from two segments of the population.

One of these segments consisted of Northerners who had migrated to the South. Historians such as Dunning and Burgess have seen no reason to dispute the contention of the conservative southern whites in castigating these Northerners as opportunists and outsiders who had come to feed on the carcass of the South. The opprobrious label of carpetbagger was attached to these persons. Stampp agrees that some may have been of this ilk, but he argues that this was in fact a polyglot group of people, many of whom did not deserve the opprobrious label.

"Few of the carpetbaggers came to the South originally for the purpose of entering politics; many of them arrived before 1867 when political careers were not even open to them. They migrated to the South in the same manner and for the same reasons that other Americans migrated to the West. They hoped to buy cotton lands or to enter legitimate business enterprises: to develop natural resources, build factories, promote railroads, represent insurance companies, or engage in trade. A large proportion of the carpetbaggers were veterans of the Union Army who were pleased with the southern climate and believed that they had discovered a land of opportunity. Others came as teachers, clergymen, officers of the Freedmen's Bureau, or agents of the various northern benevolent societies organized to give aid to the Negroes. These people went south to set up schools for Negroes and poor whites, to establish churches, and to distribute clothing and medical supplies. They were of all types – some well trained for their jobs, others not. Seldom, however, can they be dismissed as meddlesome fools, or can the genuineness of their humanitarian impulses be doubted."

(Stampp 1972:159)

The greatest venom, however, was directed toward the other segment from whom the new white leadership was drawn: the native-born Southerner. This group were defined as renegades and deserters who were prepared to destroy the white southern society that spawned them. They were labeled scalawags who were the lowliest of the low. Stampp takes issue with the broad stereotypic brush that made into a homogeneous group what in fact was a heterogeneous collection of people. "All scalawags were not degraded poor whites, depraved poor whites, depraved corruptionists or cynical opportunists who betrayed the South for the spoils of office" (Stampp 1972:160). They were also drawn, he insists, from the Unionists, the newly emerging industrial and business classes, and upper-class Southerners who had been affiliated with the Whig party before the Civil War.

However heterogeneous the carpetbaggers and scalawags may have been, they nevertheless comprised only a small fraction of the white southern population and provided accordingly only a modest white constituency for the Republican party.

Among the blacks, the situation was markedly different. From being locked out of the political system, they were suddenly thrust into its very heart through enfranchisement. Franklin estimates that approximately 700,000 or about 17 percent of the black population qualified as voters (Franklin 1961). DuBois offers a more detailed breakdown by state of the registration by race that took place under the reconstruction acts (DuBois 1935). In almost all of the states the ratio of black to white registrants was higher than would be expected from the racial proportions of the total population in the state. The only significant exception was Alabama where the ratio of black to white registration was much lower than would be expected from the population ratios.

In some states such as South Carolina, Mississippi, and Louisiana the blacks comprised an overwhelming majority of the registered voters – approximately 60 percent. In the other states they consisted of half or a sizable minority of the registered voters.

In effect, virtually overnight the blacks became a political force of no mean significance. Alone, they had neither the numbers, resources, experience, nor organization to take over the political system, contrary to what Dunning and Burgess have said. Accordingly they were receptive to alliances and even leadership from the white community. The most natural alliance would seem to have been with the poor whites, whose own poverty, illiteracy, and powerlessness generally matched that of the black. Had this coalition developed, then the full revolutionary potential of the radical reconstruction might have been realized in the South; the struggle for power would have taken on more of a class character à la Marx than a racial character. The result might have been a basic reallocation of economic and not merely political power. (It is of course reasonable to question whether Congress would have continued on its path of radical reconstruction if this coalition had occurred, with the potential threat it posed to basic property rights.)

DuBois saw the revolutionary Marxist potential in the developing situation of the black in the South.

> "Among Negroes, and particularly in the South, there was being put into force one of the most extraordinary experiments of Marxism that the world, before the Russian revolution, had seen. That is, backed by the military power of the United States, a dictatorship of labor was to be attempted and those who were leading the Negro race in this vast experiment were emphasizing the necessity of the political power and organization backed by protective military power."
>
> (DuBois 1935:358)

To realize this potential, DuBois was convinced that the black and white laboring classes would have to unite. But this failed to materialize. "This union of black and white labor never got a real start." In fact, DuBois attributes the final collapse of black reconstruction to the uniting of the white upper and lower classes. "The final move which ... led to the catastrophe of 1876, was a combination of planters and poor whites in defiance of their economic interests; and with the use of lawless murder and open intimidation" (DuBois 1935:352). What DuBois could have said even more forcefully is that the racial cleavage in the South fractured the working and poorer classes and aligned the poor whites with the planters and Conservative parties and the Ku Klux Klan. Only in areas where blacks were not present in any significant numbers did the poor whites express antagonism to the planter class and show some friendliness to Radical Republicanism – Johnson's Tennesseans showed some such inclination.

Some of the white planters also realized the potent political force that the black electorate represented and sought to persuade and to cajole the black into supporting the Conservatives against the Republicans. They stressed the paternalistic ties that presumably characterized relations between white masters and black slaves during the antebellum days. They insisted that the white planters were still interested in the welfare of the black and knew what was best for him – unlike the whites from the North who just wanted to exploit him. For a period of time these appeals made inroads into the ranks of the blacks, particularly in those areas where relations between the two had been relatively harmonious before the rebellion.

However this alignment did not last long. It broke down as the white response took on an uglier character with night riders spreading terror among the blacks and with the Conservative parties stridently calling for the disfranchisement of the black. The net result was that the white planters lost any lingering credibility they may have had among the blacks and the Conservative parties came to be defined almost universally by the black as agents of reaction whose primary goal was to take away the gains that the blacks had made or were going to make.

Alienated as they were from the Conservative parties and "mainstream" southern whites, the blacks were prepared to forge meaningful political links only with those whites who also supported Radical Republicanism. To the average white Southerner this linkage further intensified the hatred and antipathy that he already felt toward the carpetbaggers and scalawags and solidified his conception of these whites as traitors and outsiders. His response literally propelled them to the periphery of the white southern society. They were shunned, physically assaulted, and in many ways reminded of their marginal status. Despite such treatment, these whites were able to stake a major claim to political power and were the major officeholders during this period. They relied heavily on the black as their political base and also on the civil and military branches of the federal government.

To enlarge their base of active support among the blacks, the white Republicans sought to adapt the machinery of the Union League to the southern situation. As Franklin says, "The results produced the nearest thing to a real organization that the Republicans ever had in the South" (Franklin 1961:124). He contends that the League met with a measure of success in its program of political education for the black. To the extent that it was successful, to that extent it helped connect the newly enfranchised black, who was mostly illiterate, untutored, parochial, and a political innocent, to the structure of political party and government. In the process it hammered home the connection between the black's self-interest and freedom and the Republican party. In effect, the League helped to penetrate the cloistered and isolated local environment of the black and tied him to the larger political world. It provided the black with an important political education.

Understandably the League soon became a target of criticism and abuse from the Conservative whites.

"The League was accused of voting the freedmen like 'herds of senseless cattle.' Some chapters of the League were even accused of committing acts of violence against the former Confederates. Whatever their offenses happened to be, they were greatly exaggerated by the excited and outraged whites who were disfranchised by the same legislation that placed the vote in the hands of the freedmen. As the League's program of political education met with a measure of success, the opposition increased its objections and called for countermeasures to destroy the political power that was being put into the hands of the Negroes."   (Franklin 1961:125–26)

The League was finally destroyed by the Ku Klux Klan through violence and intimidation; however Franklin contends that the organization was already on the decline before the fatal blows were struck. "It had no long-range program, even in the area of politics, for the Negroes of the South. By the time it completed its initial task of political education in connection with launching the new Radical governments, the leaders of the League themselves were interested in other things" (Franklin 1961:126).

Although the black provided the broad electoral base for the Republican party, he was not a passive instrument of the white Republican. He developed in a short time his own indigenous political leadership. Some blacks had never been out of the South; others were northern-bred and educated. A number had already gained experience through their espousal of black causes and participation in various black conventions. Others like Beverly Nash of South Carolina rose from the rank and file of the poor illiterate freedmen and gained their experience in the crucible of the reconstruction itself.

Occupationally, "most of the Negro leaders were ministers. A fair number taught school. Some were employees of the Freedman's Bureau or another federal agency. Here and there one found a Negro who had been trained in the law. There were, of course, farmers; and there were some artisans engaged in a variety of occupations" (Franklin 1961:89).

In the early stages of radical reconstruction a number were elected delegates to constitutional conventions. Examination of the membership of the conventions for the various states for 1867 and 1868 reveals that blacks comprised one-half or more of the membership in only two states, Louisiana and South Carolina; they were between 20 and 50 percent of the membership in two more states, Florida (40 percent) and Virginia (24 percent); and were less than 20 percent but at least 10 percent in the rest. White Northerners were the majority in four states: Alabama (55 percent), Arkansas (52 percent), Georgia (74 percent), and North Carolina (75 percent). None of the three groups had a majority in Florida or Virginia. Data about the breakdown between the two white groups are not available for Texas (Franklin 1961:102).

Once the state governments were established, a number of blacks were elected to public office and appointed to governmental positions. However, contrary to the assertions of Dunning and Burgess they neither monopolized political power nor dominated the political system of this period. Franklin states categorically:

"Negroes were not in control of the state governments at any time anywhere in the South. They held public office and, at times, played important parts in the public life of their respective states. But it would be stretching a point to say that their roles were dominant, and it would be hopelessly distorting the picture to suggest that they ruled the South."   (Franklin 1961:133)

The blacks had their greatest strength in the three states where they comprised a large majority of the voter registrants: South Carolina, Mississippi, and Louisiana. But even in South Carolina where they displayed their greatest political strength, they were only able to control the lower house until 1874; during this period the whites retained control of the upper house and the governor was always white. There was however a liberal sprinkling of blacks throughout the rest of the administration; for example two of the lieutenant governors, several cabinet members, and a judge were black.

In Mississippi blacks comprised only about one-third of the members of the first reconstruction legislature. John R. Lynch, black speaker of the house in 1872, reported the relatively low percentage of blacks in other public office. He estimated that only 5 percent of the officials on the county level were black, and only one of seven state officers were black until 1873 when three of the seven were black.

A similar picture emerges for Louisiana. A number of blacks were "prominent and influential but they never approached a dominant position in public affairs" (Franklin 1961:134). For example, there were forty-two blacks in the first legislature, but they were a minority as were those in succeeding legislatures. Blacks served in other important public offices such as lieutenant governor, secretary of state, superintendent of education, and state treasurer.

In other states where blacks were not the majority of voter registrants, they played a lesser role in public and political life than in the first three states. They neither attained as high a public office in the state government nor had as many members in the legislatures. Nevertheless they comprised a not insignificant minority in many of the legislatures: for example, they were one-seventh of the membership in the North Carolina legislature and about one-third of the membership in the first Alabama legislature.

On the federal level sixteen blacks served in Congress between 1869 and 1880. Two represented Mississippi in the Senate; the rest were elected to the House.

"South Carolina sent six Negroes to the House of Representatives, the largest number from a single state. But they were not all in the House at one time.

Alabama was second with three. Georgia, Florida, Mississippi, North Carolina, and Louisiana sent one each. Most of these men had some experience in public service before going to Congress."   (Franklin 1961:137)

In many respects then, the political party became the major vehicle by which blacks gained access to a higher position in society. Compared with a few short years earlier when they were locked out of the political arena both as voters and officeholders, blacks had now become a potent force. They became the major constituency of one of the parties and also supplied a significant number of contenders for political office. The situation was not unlike that recounted in Greek mythology when Athena emerged full grown from the head of Zeus.

This transformation had a tremendous impact on the plural character of southern society. Prior to the Civil War, blacks were primarily the property of the whites; accordingly they had the status of things which were completely outside the Domain of the People. The racial cleavage was then along the boundary of the People's Domain with the black categorically denied entry into it and the whites comfortably within it. President Johnson's reconstruction policies did not disturb the situation much. All that he really insisted on was that slavery be abolished, but he did not require any affirmation of the status of the black, either as a person or as a member of the political community. As a result, the southern states – some more reluctantly than others – abolished slavery and thereby eliminated the status of black as thing. However, most tried to bar him from assuming the status of person in the political and public domain. These states reaffirmed their constitutional right to determine the conditions and qualifications for being a member (citizen) within its political boundaries. They enacted black codes which reinstituted a form of "legalized slavery" and which sought to exclude to the extent possible the freedmen from membership in the political domain. In effect, the black was no longer a *thing*, but he was still a *non-person*.

The radical reconstruction changed that. The black was now defined as a person, admitted to full membership in the Domain of the People and given access to political office. This was a transformation imposed from the outside by congressional mandates and sustained by the presence of military and civilian representatives from this outside agency.

Most southern whites resisted and resented this reconstruction of their political society. They had done their utmost in the past to keep the black out of their political domain. Now they had to view him not merely as a political equal but also as a legitimate claimant for political power and office. Many whites were still not prepared to accept the first, the black as citizen, and virtually all were driven to paroxysms of rage at the notion of the black as legitimate claimant for political power and office.

Accordingly, these whites aligned themselves on the opposite side of the political fence from the black and his "minority white allies." They comprised the constituency for the Conservative and later Democratic parties. In the earlier days of the radical reconstruction when their party suffered significant disabilities either through the disfranchisement policy of Congress or through other restrictions, they had also organized extralegal counterparts of their political party.

Thus, a revolutionary transformation occurred in the character of the racial segmentation of southern society. The traditional mode of the racial segmentation had, for the moment at least been, broken. No longer were blacks and whites on opposite sides of the boundaries of the Domain of the People with the blacks defined as non-persons and whites as persons. Both groups were inside the domain where they remained "pluralized" and segmented. But now they were both competing for political power and office, instead of political power being monopolized by only one. However, racial segmentation and separation were in some respects even more intensified and antagonistic than before. The ideology of paternalism of the antebellum days became less palatable to many southern whites, as their monopoly of political power was threatened and waned under the impact of reconstruction. They were much more prepared to shed the velvet glove of paternalism for the iron fist of force to reassert their authority. As a result, the response of many whites took on an ugly and raw character, which further destroyed the normative bridges that had been built between the two races and that had softened the impact of the coercive system. On the other hand blacks were much more preoccupied with moving out of their subordinated status and securing economic and political gains than they were in seeking to control or even to get even with the whites. One example of this response is the frequent rejection by elected black officials of efforts by other white state legislators to add further barriers to the enfranchisement of former confederate officials.

While racial segmentation persisted, its relationship to the structure of power had shifted. No longer did one side, the whites, possess all the sources and expressions of power; in fact for a few short years political power shifted to the other side, the blacks, whereas economic and social power remained as it had always been with the whites. Both the symbol and vehicle for this restructured segmentation was the political party: the Republican versus the Conservative parties. The political party thereby served as a vertical axis which sliced the political domain into two racial sub-communities, each competing for the instruments of government: the one community under a temporary handicap of constraints from external sources of authority but still in possession of the basic social and economic resources of the society; the other sub-community having the temporary benefit of these external supports but under the profound handicap of having always been the exploited strata of powerless "non-persons."

The political dominance of the Radical Republicans lasted for a few brief years – somewhat longer in some states than in others. To the established white community, the constituency for the conservative party, this period was viewed as an abomination, as a gross miscarriage of human virtue and justice. This point of view has come down to the present with the stamp of historical authenticity through the writings of such major interpreters of the period as Dunning and Burgess. Burgess, an ex-confederate himself, virtually discarded all pretense to dispassionate analysis. He viewed radical reconstruction as a repressive and coercive attempt to destroy the traditional authority of the white as sanctioned by the Constitution through placing "the worst" instead of "the best" in power.

> "It was the most soul-sickening spectacle that Americans had ever been called upon to behold. Every principle of the old American policy was here reversed. In place of government by the most intelligent and virtuous part of the people for the benefit of the governed, here was government by the most ignorant and vicious part of the population for the benefit, the vulgar, materialistic, brutal benefit of the governing set."   (Burgess 1902:263–64)

Burgess unleashed a particularly emotional attack against black domination of state governments. He labeled it a form or barbarism which threatened to rip asunder the fabric of civilization and culture.

> "But there is no question, now, that Congress did a monstrous thing, and committed a great political error, if not a sin, in the creation of this new electorate. It was a great wrong to civilization to put the white race of the South under the domination of the negro race. The claim that there is nothing in the color of the skin from the point of view of political ethics is a great sophism. A black skin means membership in a race of men which has never of itself succeeded in subjecting passion to reason, has never, therefore, created any civilization of any kind. To put such a race of men in possession of a 'state' government in a system of federal government is to trust them with the development of political and legal civilization upon the most important subjects of human life, and to do this in communities with a large white population is simply to establish barbarism in power over civilization. The supposed disloyalty, or even the actual disloyalty of the white population will not justify this."   (Burgess 1902:133–34)

Dunning offered a more dispassionate critique of what has been called "Negro rule"; however, he too painted a picture of gross maladministration: "the inefficiency, extravagance, and corruption of the radical southern state governments" (Dunning 1907:204).

According to both historians, the South was saved only as the "decent southern white Democrats, their patience exhausted, organized to drive the Negroes, carpetbaggers, and scalawags from power, peacefully if possible, forcefully if necessary. One by one the southern states were redeemed, honesty and virtue triumphed, and the South's natural leaders returned to power" (Stampp 1972:8).

In recent years this view of the reconstruction period has been challenged by a number of historians. As Stampp says, these revisionists do not disclaim the Dunning interpretation in its entirety. They agree that there was corruption, extravagence, and incompetency in the radical governments. They argue, though, that it was not as prevalent nor as vicious as the white critics have painted. Further they insist that these practices were in accord with the general climate of the times under the Grant administration. Even Dunning acknowledges this as he alludes to the Tweed ring in New York City, but he goes on to say, "The really novel and peculiar element in the maladministration in the South was the social and race issue which underlay it, and which came to the surface at once when any attempt at reform was instituted" (Dunning 1907:209).

However, the story of radical reconstruction is more than this. As Stampp states, "High taxes, mounting debts, corruption, extravagance, and waste, however do not constitute the complete record of the radical regimes" (Stampp 1972:176). What characterized the record of the radical governments was their reformist nature. Although the redistribution of land was a constant demand of the freedmen, no concerted effort was made at confiscation; no legislation was passed which threatened private property. In this the freedmen showed little appetite for a revolutionary reallocation of economic resources. However, they did show considerable interest in civil rights. The constitutions they helped to design extended equality to all groups in society. The freedmen figuratively dragged a number of white legislators dependent upon their support into reluctant acceptance of laws which were in accord with the federal legislation on civil rights.

In addition, the radical government sponsored with strong black support significant social and class legislation whose goal was the improvement of the lot of the poor, both white and black. They built hospitals and institutions for the poor. They restored the physical damage of the war by constructing roads, railroads, and public buildings. They sought to establish free public schools without pressing too hard on the question of racial integration. According to DuBois, the three major accomplishments of these governments were: "1. Democratic government 2. Free Public Schools 3. New social legislation" (DuBois 1910:18).

In effect the radical governments sponsored ambitious programs of social and public welfare, but unfortunately on a tax base that was inadequate for the purpose. Consequently the public debt mounted astronomically. This is where the extravagance primarily lay, and not in the private gain for the officeholder as many critics have contended. Whereas the final assessment of the legislative goals and actions of this period has yet to be done, Stampp and other revisionist historians come away with a more positive evaluation of this period than has traditionally been made.

"Finally, granting all their mistakes, the radical governments were by far the most democratic the South had ever known. They were the only governments in southern history to extend to Negroes complete civil and political equality, and to try to protect them in the enjoyment of the rights they were granted. The overthrow of the governments was hardly a victory for political democracy, for the conservatives who 'redeemed' the South tried to relegate poor men, Negro and white, once more to political obscurity. Near the end of the nineteenth century another battle for political democracy would have to be waged; but this time it would be, for the most part, a more limited version – for whites only. As for the Negroes, they would have to struggle for another century to regain what they had won – and then lost – in the years of radical reconstruction."

(Stampp 1972:184–85)

The post-reconstruction era and the creation of a new plural society in the South

By 1877 the radical reconstruction had come to an end. In that year Louisiana, Florida, and South Carolina were finally "redeemed" and the Conservative and Democratic parties once again took over political control of all of the southern states. This was also the year of the Compromise by which President Hayes removed the few remaining federal troops from the South.

Dramatic and intense as this period had been, it covered only a relatively short span of time. Radical governments were in power in most of the states for only an average of three and a-half to four years; only in the above three states were they in office for approximately a decade. However, the impact of this historic episode reverberated throughout the South for decades. It had jarred open the doors of a racially closed society and allowed a category of previously defined non-persons to gain access to the legal and political system and some measure of power within it.

"Redemption" did not produce an instant dismantling of the normative and legal structure that had been created nor an immediate expulsion of the black presence from the political community. DuBois shows that a number of the state constitutions written during the reconstruction were barely altered during the first twenty years of the redemption period: Virginia's remained unchanged for approximately thirty-two years; South Carolina's for twenty-seven years.

"Even in the case of states like Alabama, Georgia, North Carolina, and Louisiana, which adopted new constitutions to signify the overthrow of Negro rule, the new constitutions are nearer the model of the Reconstruction document than they are to the previous constitutions. They differ from the Negro constitutions in minor details but very little in general conception.

Besides this there stands on the statute books of the South today law after law passed between 1868 and 1876, and which has been found wise, effective, and worthy of preservation."   (DuBois 1910:21)

DuBois offers this argument to show how thoughful and constructive the work of the black and white radicals had been, but equally if not more significant is the support his data give to Woodward's thesis that the "redeemed" South did not rush pellmell into destroying the apparatus built in reconstruction and into slamming shut the door that had been opened to the black (Woodward 1957).

Woodward argues that for approximately twenty years after redemption began the South was in a state of instability and ferment. The old order had been disrupted by the Civil War and reconstruction and the forces that had been unleashed by reconstruction retained a momentum that carried them well into the period of redemption. Thus the civil rights laws which the federal and various state governments had enacted created a normative environment that was not immediately destroyed with redemption. Woodward contends that blacks and whites shared public facilities and displayed a marked degree of civility in their contacts with each other in these public places. For example, they ate in the same restaurants without incident, rode in the same public conveyances without overt tension, and in general participated and interacted with each other in public environments which were still under the control of the normative heritage from the reconstruction. Much of his evidence comes from journals and observations of travelers from the North and abroad who were surprised at what they saw.

Woodward also insists that the black continued to have some political clout after the reconstruction. Once the coalition of white radical republicans and blacks started to come apart, other segments of the white community started to compete with each other for the votes of the blacks. These efforts were intensified as agrarian and industrial unrest engulfed sections of the South during the 1880s and particularly the 1890s, and exacerbated class cleavages among the whites. Thus the struggle for political power between the Bourbons and the Populists or their forerunners the Greenbackers, Independents, and the like carried over into a contest for the black vote.

Perhaps the Bourbons were the more successful in appealing for the black vote. They emphasized the paternalism of the past and sought to convince the black that they had always been his benevolent patron who would take care of him. The Bourbons were even prepared to accept a role – albeit a subordinate one – for the black in the public domain.

"The conservatives acknowledged that the Negroes belonged in a subordinate role, but denied that subordinates had to be ostracized; they believed that the Negro was inferior, but denied that it followed that inferiors must be segregated or publicly humiliated. Negro degradation was not a necessary corollary of white supremacy in the conservative philosophy." (Woodward 1957:29)

The Bourbons were even prepared to offer the black some political office to keep him in line and to use him as a counterbalance against the challenge of the disaffected white lower classes. In turn segments of these disaffected white classes also sought alliances with the black voter. Perhaps the most sustained effort was in the early days of the populist movement. Led by the early Tom Watson, the Populists

"fancied themselves as exponents of a new realism on race, free from the delusions of doctrinaire and sentimental liberalism on the one hand, and the illusions of romantic paternalism on the other. There was in the Populist approach to the Negro a limited type of equalitarianism quite different from that preached by the radical Republicans and wholly absent from the conservative approach. This was an equalitarianism of want and poverty, the kinship of a common grievance and a common oppressor." (Woodward 1957:42–3)

Some headway was made in these efforts toward working-class unity.

"In the opinion of Henry Demarest Lloyd, the Southern Populists gave 'Negroes of the South a political fellowship which they have never obtained, not even from their saviors, the Republicans.' Certain it is that the Negroes responded with more enthusiasm and hope than to any other political movement since their disillusionment with radical Republicanism. It is altogether probable that during the brief Populist upheaval of the 'nineties Negroes and native whites achieved a greater comity of mind and harmony of political purpose than ever before or since in the South." (Woodward 1957:46)

Woodward concludes that in general the South was a relatively open public and political society during this period, with the black a functioning part of it. He cautions, however, against an exaggerated view of the interracial harmony during this period. He emphasizes that coexisting with and even overshadowing the harmony were forces of repression and violence that sought to push the black out of the public and political society of the day. Terror and lynching reached a peak in the 1880s, and by the end of the century the forces of discrimination and exclusion had triumphed and for all intents and purposes the black was expelled from the People's Domain. A new variant of the plural society was thereby created. The new variant however was not a mere replication of the plural model of the antebellum days; it had many new constitutive components, which we shall examine in the next chapter.

7

THE DUAL PLURAL SOCIETIES: JIM CROWISM IN THE SOUTH AND RACIAL SEGMENTATION IN THE NORTH

Introduction

By the turn of the twentieth century, a new version of a plural society was constructed in the South that stamped black-white relations for the next half century. This version was built on legal and institutional grounds differing significantly from those of the older slavery version. And it required a series of Supreme Court decisions to reconcile these grounds with the great reconstruction amendments and to establish thereby the legitimacy of the new plural society. The court decisions also provided a protective shield for the kind of *de facto* plural society that subsequently evolved in the North as whites sought to counter the mass movement of blacks northward during World War I.

These transformations, North and South, generated an atmosphere of fear and tension between the races, as blacks expressed resentment at the dilution and loss of the rights to and in the People's Domain that they had won during reconstruction under the American creed, and balked at the dictates of the plural structures under their racial creed. As a result, to keep blacks in line whites in the South resorted to legal and extralegal repression and pogrom-like violence that even exceeded the level found during slavery. In the North, tensions between the races erupted into violence and riots and kept black-white relations in a state of chronic rawness; however, the increasing segmentation of the races in places of work and residence minimized direct contact and therefore kept overt conflict within certain bounds.

In this chapter we shall first examine the series of Supreme Court decisions that furnished the legal scaffolding for the plural structures in the South and in the North during this fifty-year period. Next, we shall look at each of these structures in detail, first in the South then in the North; and then we shall analyze the patterning of violence and riots that these structures provoked.

The Supreme Court and the erosion of the black's civil and political rights

Even as the whites in the South were mounting their drive to force blacks out of the People's Domain and to construct a new plural society, they might not have succeeded to the extent they did had not a series of Supreme Court decisions bestowed legitimacy on most of their efforts. However, just as the new plural society took a while to unfold in the South so did the process of its legitimation extend over a period of time. The process began while the legacy from the reconstruction was still affecting the political system of the South, and it ended with the virtually complete neutralization of the gains that the blacks had made through the Fourteenth and Fifteenth Amendments and through congressional and state legislative action of the radical reconstruction.

What proved to be a major cornerstone in the process of legitimation was the Supreme Court decision in the Slaughter House Cases in 1873. These cases "involved neither racial discrimination nor Negroes. At issue was the constitutionality of a Louisiana statute granting to one particular slaughterhouse syndicate the exclusive monopoly in butchering livestock in the New Orleans area" (Blaustein and Zangrando 1968:247). The plaintiffs, the Butchers' Benevolent Association of New Orleans, contended that the legislative grant violated their rights under the Fourteenth Amendment.

The Supreme Court found in favor of the defendants. In doing so, it etched in bold detail the distinctions between national and state citizenship. Justice Miller argued in his opinion for the Court that this distinction was explicitly drawn in the first clause of the first section of the amendment. He then went on to make two basic observations:

"The first observation we have to make on this clause is, that it puts at rest both the questions which we stated to have been the subject of differences of opinion. It declares that persons may be citizens of the United States without regard to their citizenship of a particular State, and it overturns the Dred Scott decision by making *all persons* born within the United States and subject to its jurisdiction citizens of the United States. That its main purpose was to establish the citizenship of the negro can admit of no doubt. The phrase, 'subject to its jurisdiction' was intended to exclude from its operation children of ministers, consuls and citizens or subjects of foreign States born with the United States.

The next observation is more important in view of the arguments of counsel in the present case. It is, that the distinction between citizenship of the United States and citizenship of a State is clearly recognized and established. Not only may a man be a citizen of the United States without being a citizen of a State, but an important element is necessary to convert the former into the latter. He must reside within the State to make him a citizen of it, but it is only necessary that he should be born or naturalized in the United States to be a citizen of the Union.

It is quite clear, then, that there is a citizenship of the United States, and a citizenship of a State, which are distinct from each other, and which depend upon different characteristics or circumstances in the individual."

(83 US 1873:73–4)

Justice Miller then proceeded to delineate some of the privileges and immunities attached to each type of citizenship. Although he asserted that the present case did not require an exhaustive listing of the privileges and immunities of national citizenship, he suggested "some which owe their existence to the Federal government, its National character, its Constitution, or its laws."

"One of these is well described in the case of *Crandall v. Nevada*. It is said to be the right of the citizen of this great country, protected by implied guarantees of its Constitution, 'to come to the seat of government to assert any claim he may have upon that government, to transact any business he may have with it, to seek its protection, to share its offices, to engage in administering its functions. He has the right of free access to its seaports, through which all operations of foreign commerce are conducted, to the sub-treasuries, land offices, and courts of justice in the several States.' And quoting from the language of Chief Justice Taney in another case, it is said 'that *for all the great purposes for which the Federal government* was established, we are one people with one common country, *we are all citizens of the United States*;' and it is, as such citizens, that their rights are supported in this court in *Crandall v. Nevada*." (83 US 1873:79)

Justice Miller then argued that adoption of the amendments was not intended "to destroy the main features of the general system." They were not intended to disrupt the basic separation in jurisdictions between the state and national governments; they were to function through them. He elaborated his argument by saying:

"Under the pressure of all the excited feeling growing out of the war, our statesmen have still believed that the existence of the States with powers for domestic and local government, including the regulation of civil rights – the rights of person and of property – was essential to the perfect working of our complex form of government, though they have thought proper to impose additional limitations on the States, and to confer additional power on that of the Nation." (83 US 1873:82)

The net result of this decision was to reaffirm the claim of the state over conduct of its own internal affairs, including civil rights, and over definition of the basic terms of citizenship within its boundaries. The amendments and Constitution imposed certain constraints on what these terms might be; however, the decision posed a serious threat to the kind of federal control over civil rights which Congress had envisaged. This threat was more fully realized in later decisions.

Thus began the steady rollback by the Supreme Court of federal authority over civil rights. Taking his cue from the Slaughter House Cases, Chief Justice Waite articulated even more clearly the judicial conception of two distinct citizenships in his opinion on the case of United States v. Cruikshank in 1876.

"We have in our political system a government of the United States and a government of each of the several States. Each one of these governments is distinct from the others, and each has citizens of its own who owe it allegiance, and whose rights, within its jurisdiction, it must protect. The same person may be at the same time a citizen of the United States and a citizen of a State, but his rights of citizenship under one of these governments will be different from those he has under the other *Slaughter-House Cases*." (92 US 1876:549)

The major significance of this case is that it introduced restraints not only on the national government, but also on the state governments in interceding on civil rights matters.

"This case established the principle that the Fourteenth Amendment guarantees the rights of citizens only against encroachments by the *states*, and not against the actions of private individuals. In addition, it held that the violation by a private person of the civil rights of another could only be a crime when it interfered with an act connected with *national* citizenship."
(Blaustein and Zangrando 1968:255)

Thus the dual realms of the state and private individual provided the Supreme Court with a two-pronged argument for pushing back the boundaries of federal authority in civil rights. This dual attack was used effectively in nullifying the Civil Rights Act of 1875, the high-water mark of reconstruction legislation.

The Supreme Court was confronted in 1883 with five suits against private individuals who were charged with violating the Civil Rights Act of 1875 by denying to individual blacks admission to hotels and theaters or access to accommodations on a public conveyance. One of these incidents took place in the

West; another, in the North; the others, in the South. The suits were dealt with by the Supreme Court under the general rubric of Civil Rights Cases.

In his opinion for the majority, Justice Bradley denied that Congress had the constitutional authority to legislate racial equality in the area of public accommodation, conveyance, or facilities. He based his conclusion on the dual curbs to federal authority that had evolved from such earlier decisions as Cruikshank and Slaughter House: the rights of states and those of private individuals.

Justice Bradley did not dispute the premise that the Fourteenth Amendment gives Congress the authority to void and to correct state legislation that "impairs the privileges and immunities of citizens of the United States, or which injures them in life, liberty or property without due process of law; or which denies to any of them the equal protection of the laws."

But he argued that the Amendment

"does not invest Congress with power to legislate upon subjects which are within the domain of State legislation; but to provide modes of relief against State legislation, or State action of the kind referred to. It does not authorize Congress to create a code of municipal law for the regulation of private rights; but to provide modes of redress against the operation of State laws, and the action of State officers executive or judicial, when these are subversive of the fundamental rights specified in the amendment."   (109 US 1883:11)

Thus Justice Bradley insisted that the Fourteenth Amendment does not give Congress the right to legislate directly on the civil behavior of the individual, but the Civil Rights Act does just that. "In other words, it steps into the domain of local jurisprudence, and lays down rules for the conduct of individuals in society towards each other, and imposes sanctions for the enforcement of those rules, without referring in any manner to any supposed action of the State or its authorities" (109 US 1883:14).

Justice Bradley then addressed himself to the contention that the congressional legislation was authorized under the Thirteenth Amendment. He raised the question of any similarity between discrimination in public places and servitude. "Can the act of a mere individual, the owner of the inn, the public conveyance or place of amusement, refusing the accommodation, be justly regarded as imposing any badge of slavery or servitude upon the applicant, or only as inflicting an ordinary civil injury, properly cognizable by the laws of the State, and presumably subject to redress by those laws until the contrary appears?" (109 US 1883:24).

He rejected outright the first alternative.

"It would be running the slavery argument into the ground to make it apply to every act of discrimination which a person may see fit to make as to the guests he will entertain, or as to the people he will take into his coach or cab or car, or admit to his concert or theatre, or deal with in other matters of intercourse or business. Innkeepers and public carriers, by the laws of all the States, so far as we are aware, are bound, to the extent of their facilities, to furnish proper accommodation to all unobjectionable persons who in good faith apply for them. If the laws themselves make any unjust discrimination, amenable to the prohibitions of the Fourteenth Amendment, Congress has full power to afford a remedy under that amendment in accordance with it."   (109 US 1883:24–5)

Justice Bradley concluded that these types of discriminations by white individuals should be treated by blacks as part of the normal inconveniences of being included in the domain of the ordinary citizen. They should not seek special treatment under the law but should instead be content with the "ordinary modes" by which the rights of the citizen are protected.

"When a man has emerged from slavery, and by the aid of beneficent legislation has shaken off the inseparable concomitants of that state, there must be some stage in the progress of his elevation when he takes the rank of a mere citizen, and ceases to be the special favorite of the laws, and when his rights as a citizen, or a man, are to be protected in the ordinary modes by which other men's rights are protected. There were thousands of free colored people in this country before the abolition of slavery, enjoying all the essential rights of life, liberty and property the same as white citizens; yet no one, at that time, thought that it was any invasion of his personal status as a freeman because he was not admitted to all the privileges enjoyed by white citizens, or because he was subjected to discriminations in the enjoyment of accommodations in inns, public conveyances and places of amusement. Mere discriminations on account of race or color were not regarded as badges of slavery."   (109 US 1883:25)

Whereas the earlier decisions laid the groundwork for the legitimation of the new plural society in the South, the capstone for its legitimation was laid by the Plessy v. Ferguson decision of 1896. Blaustein argues that this decision created a "novel doctrine. It represented a substantial departure from what the Court had said and done in the first cases following the passage of the Civil Rights Acts" (Blaustein and Zangrando 1968:294). Perhaps this was indeed the legal character of the case; and yet sociologically it was consistent with the earlier decisions. The Slaughter House decision had declared that the State had primacy over the national government in civil rights matters within its own boundaries; the Cruikshank-Civil Rights decisions declared that neither federal nor state government should intervene in private expressions of discrimination. Now the Plessy v. Ferguson decision declared that the predilections and prejudices of the white members of the community could receive the support of state law without running afoul of the

Fourteenth Amendment as long as the law conformed to the doctrine of "separate but equal." The net result was that state law could now be used to sustain a racially bifurcated society which would be viewed as legitimate by the supreme law of the land.

The state law whose constitutionality was being contested was the Louisiana Railways Accommodations Act of 1890. This act, one of the early examples of what came to be known as Jim Crow law, called for segregation of white and black into presumably equal accommodations on railroad trains.

> "'Sec. 1. *Be it enacted by the General Assembly of the State of Louisiana*, that all railway companies carrying passengers in their coaches in this State, shall provide equal but separate accommodations for the white, and colored races, by providing two or more passenger coaches for each passenger train, or by dividing the passenger coaches by a partition so as to secure separate accommodations;'" (Blaustein and Zangrando 1968:297)

Homer Adolph Plessy refused to ride in the designated colored coach and was arrested under the provisions of the law. He subsequently "instituted an action to restrain enforcement of the statute on the grounds that it violated the Thirteenth and Fourteenth Amendments. Ferguson, the defendant, was the Louisiana judge designated to conduct the trial of Plessy on criminal charges" (Blaustein and Zangrando 1968:295).

The Supreme Court decided that the Louisiana law was constitutional. In his opinion for the Court, Justice Brown argued that "A statute which implies merely a legal distinction between the white and colored races – a distinction which is founded in the color of the two races, and which must always exist so long as white men are distinguished from the other race by color – has no tendency to destroy the legal equality of the two races, or reestablish a state of involuntary servitude" (163 US 1896:543).

He further contended that the Fourteenth Amendment was meant "to enforce the absolute equality of the two races before the law, but in the nature of things it could not have been intended to abolish distinctions based upon color, or to enforce social, as distinguished from political equality, or a commingling of the two races upon terms unsatisfactory to either" (163 US 1896:544).

He concluded that the issue before the Court was not the legal or political equality of the black; that he claimed was protected by the Fourteenth Amendment and by recent decisions of the court. Instead he argued that the issue before the Court was the relationship between law and social policy: whether the statute of Louisiana was a reasonable exercise of the police power of the state and was "enacted in good faith for the promotion for the public good, and not for the annoyance or oppression of a particular class" (163 US 1896:550).

Justice Brown answered his own question in the affirmative. He argued that,

"In determining the question of reasonableness, it [the state] is at liberty to act with reference to the established usages, customs and traditions of the people, and with a view to the promotion of their comfort, and the preservation of the public peace and good order. Gauged by this standard, we cannot say that a law which authorizes or even requires the separation of the two races in public conveyances is unreasonable, or more obnoxious to the Fourteenth Amendment than the acts of Congress requiring separate schools for colored children in the District of Columbia, the constitutionality of which does not seem to have been questioned, or the corresponding acts of state legislatures."

(163 US 1896:550–51)

Justice Brown insisted that such a law merely makes manifest and sanctions the racial divisions already built into the structure of the community. He denied that "the enforced separation of the two races stamps the colored race with a badge of inferiority. If this be so, it is not by reason of anything found in the act, but solely because the colored race chooses to put that construction upon it" (163 US 1896:551).

Thus he accepted the basic thesis generally attributed to William Graham Sumner (1940) that laws should conform to the mores and to the sentiments of the community. Elaborating on the other side of this thesis, Justice Brown repudiated the use of law to change community sentiment or to insure "social equality" between the races. Thus he rejected the argument that "social prejudices may be overcome by legislation" or that "enforced commingling of the two races" may secure equal rights for the black. "If the two races are to meet upon terms of social* equality, it must be the result of natural affinities, a mutual appreciation of each other's merits and a voluntary consent of individuals" (163 US 1896:551).

As a final justification for his theme, Justice Brown used a lower court decision to hammer home his point that social equality cannot be achieved through "laws which conflict with the general sentiment of the community upon whom they are designed to operate" (163 US 1896:551). He concluded,

"Legislation is powerless to eradicate racial instincts or to abolish distinctions based upon physical differences, and the attempt to do so can only result in accentuating the difficulties of the present situation. If the civil and political

---

*Justice Brown and the Supreme Court never clearly defined what they meant by or included in the term "social;" however, the term obviously meant more to them than interpersonal or social relations. In fact, the Court only treated in specific detail what it meant by the legal and political as the realm in which the rights of blacks as citizens were protected by the Constitution. It left, by inference at least, the rest of the societal system both as a community and as a network of economic, educational, social, and other institutions to be included in the residual category that the Court called the "social."

rights of both races be equal one cannot be inferior to the other civilly or politically. If one race be inferior to the other socially, the Constitution of the United States cannot put them upon the same plane." (163 US 1896:551–52)

In his classic dissent, Justice Harlan acknowledged the dominance of the white race in this country. "And so it is, in prestige, in achievements, in education, in wealth and in power" (163 US 1896:559). However, he argued that,

"in view of the Constitution, in the eye of the law, there is in this country no superior, dominant, ruling class of citizens. There is no caste here. Our Constitution is color-blind, and neither knows nor tolerates classes among citizens. In respect of civil rights, all citizens are equal before the law. The humblest is the peer of the most powerful. The law regards man as man, and takes no account of his surroundings or of his color when his civil rights as guaranteed by the supreme law of the land are involved." (163 US 1896:559)

Thus he rejected outright the contention that any legislative body or judicial tribunal "may have regard to the race of citizens when the civil rights of those citizens are involved," (163 US 1896:554) and he viewed with great dismay the decision of the Supreme Court on the Louisiana law. He was convinced that it would permit the use of state law by the dominant whites to superimpose upon the framework of equality that was guaranteed by the Constitution a doctrine of racial inequality that would relegate the black to an inferior status and would corrode the framework of equality itself.

"The present decision, it may well be apprehended, will not only stimulate aggressions, more or less brutal and irritating, upon the admitted rights of colored citizens, but will encourage the belief that it is possible, by means of state enactments, to defeat the beneficent purposes which the people of the United States had in view when they adopted the recent amendments of the Constitution, by one of which the blacks of this country were made citizens of the United States and of the States in which they respectively reside, and whose privileges and immunities, as citizens, the States are forbidden to abridge."

(163 US 1896:560)

According to Justice Harlan, the net result would be the intensification and exacerbation of hostility and cleavage between the races at a time when the

"destinies of the two races, in this country, are indissolubly linked together, and the interests of both require that the common government of all should not permit the seeds of race hate to be planted under the sanction of law.... What can more certainly arouse race hate, what more certainly create and perpetuate a feeling of distrust between these races, than state enactments, which, in fact, proceed on the ground that colored citizens are so inferior and degraded that they cannot be allowed to sit in public coaches occupied by white citizens? That, as all will admit, is the real meaning of such legislation as was enacted in Louisiana."   (163 US 1896:560)

In this manner did Justice Harlan take issue both explicitly and implicitly with the premises of the Court's decision. He defined racial equality as indivisible, not to be divided as the Court had done into the legal, which the Constitution protected, and the social, which was fair game for state legislation. Further, he demolished Justice Brown's argument that enforced separation did not brand the blacks inferior. And finally he expressed great alarm at the probable consequences this decision would have for the future. "In my opinion, the judgment this day rendered will, in time, prove to be quite as pernicious as the decision made by this tribunal in the *Dred Scott case*" (163 US 1896:560).

Justice Harlan concluded his opinion with a remarkably prescient statement:

"If laws of like character [to the statute of Louisiana] should be enacted in the several States of the Union, the effect would be in the highest degree mischievous. Slavery, as an institution tolerated by law would, it is true, have disappeared from our country, but there would remain a power in the States, by sinister legislation, to interfere with the full enjoyment of the blessings of freedom; to regulate civil rights, common to all citizens, upon the basis of race; and to place in a condition of legal inferiority a large body of American citizens, now constituting a part of the political community called the People of the United States, for whom, and by whom through representatives, our government is administered. Such a system is inconsistent with the guarantee given by the Constitution to each State of a republican form of government, and may be stricken down by Congressional action, or by the courts in the discharge of their solemn duty to maintain the supreme law of the land, anything in the constitution or laws of any State to the contrary notwithstanding."   (163 US 1896:564)

The racially segmented South

JIM CROWISM

Justice Harlan's fears did not take long to be realized and with a speed and scope that even he could not have anticipated. By the first decade of the twentieth century the southern states were saturated with Jim Crow laws of virtually every size and kind. They were no longer confined to train accommodations, which was the prevailing form of Jim Crow law until 1900, but extended into every kind of public mode of transportation. In time these laws included virtually all forms of public facility, from toilets and water fountains to theaters and boarding houses. In the final analysis, almost every point of public contact – and even private contact as in the case of sexual and marital relations – came under scrutiny of Jim Crow laws. Segregation was decreed at work, in places of residence and of amusement, in the various institutional settings of schools, hospitals, and the like. As Woodward states, "The mushroom growth of discriminatory and segregation laws during the first two decades of this century piled up a huge bulk of legislation. Much of the code was contributed by city ordinances or by local regulations and rules enforced without the formality of laws" (Woodward 1957:82). He goes on to say that these laws do not convey the full extent and prevalence of segregation and discriminatory practices in the South. The practices often anticipated and sometimes exceeded the laws. He concludes with the statement that "there is more Jim Crowism practiced in the South than there are Jim Crow laws on the books" (Woodward 1957:87).

Thus was re-created a racially segmented society where the blacks were once again relegated to a subordinated and subjugated status. Segregation and discrimination were the keystones of the new plural society. Further, the new society did not have the ameliorating grace of the paternalism and the personal relationships between black and white that characterized the antebellum version of the plural society. It depended heavily on the coercive arm of the law and where necessary a vigilantism of community sentiment; it thereby sought to draw a sharp line between black and white without exception and spread the authority to maintain this line to a variety of public officials, bureaucrats, and ordinary white citizens.

"Barring those disappearing exceptions, the Jim Crow laws applied to *all* Negroes – not merely to the rowdy, or drunken, or surly, or ignorant ones. The new laws did not countenance the old conservative tendency to distinguish between classes of the race, to encourage the 'better' element, and to draw it into a white alliance. Those laws backed up the Alabamian who told the disfranchising convention of his state that no Negro in the world was the equal of 'the least, poorest, lowest-down white man I ever knew;' but not ex-Governor Oates, who replied: 'I would not trust him as quickly as I would a negro of intelligence and good character.' The Jim Crow laws put the authority of the state or city in the voice of the street-car conductor, the railway brakeman, the bus driver, the theater usher, and also into the voice of the hoodlum of the public parks and playgrounds. They gave free rein and the majesty of the law to mass aggressions that might otherwise have been curbed, blunted or deflected."

(Woodward 1957:93)

The net result was the development of an openly coercive structure of control by which the whites sought to force the subjugation and segregation of the black. The blacks were pushed out of the institutional and public environments of the white and were expected to develop their own lifestyle within the crevices and cracks that remained. Their segregated facilities were built from the crumbs left over from the table of the whites.

Paralleling these developments in the social realm were the concerted efforts to strip the black of his legal and political rights and to drive him out of the political and public Domain of the People. Unable to launch a frontal attack on these rights because of the Fourteenth and Fifteenth Amendments, the white Southerner devised successful circumventions. The basic model was provided by the Mississippi Constitution of 1890. It introduced the "understanding clause" which required that each person had to understand and interpret sections of the new state constitution in order to qualify as a voter. The local registrar was to be the judge of whether he passed or not; this provided the loophole for allowing whites to become certified at whatever level of literacy and for blocking certification of even the most educated black. The legality of the constitution was contested before the US Supreme Court in the case of Williams v. Mississippi, but in 1898 the Court affirmed its legality.

This decision permitted virtually all the southern states to copy this subterfuge for the disfranchisement of the black and to invent others. Thus, Louisiana went a step further and introduced the "grandfather clause" which stipulated that:

"No male person who was on January 1st, 1867, or at any date prior thereto, entitled to vote under the Constitution or statutes of any State of the United States, wherein he then resided, and no son or grandson of any such person not less than twenty-one years of age at the date of the adoption of this Constitution, and no male person of foreign birth, who was naturalized prior to the first day of January, 1898, shall be denied the right to register and vote in this State by reason of his failure to possess the educational or property qualifications prescribed by this Constitution;"   (Blaustein and Zangrando 1968:313)

In general the states also added poll taxes, property and literacy qualifications to their armory of disfranchisement devices. The effectiveness of these efforts to drive the black out of the political domain was not immediately apparent, but within a few years they had virtually depleted the ranks of the black voters.

"The effectiveness of disfranchisement is suggested by a comparison of the number of registered Negro voters in Louisiana in 1896, when there were 130,334, and in 1904, when there were 1342. Between the two dates the literacy, property and poll-tax qualifications were adopted. In 1896 Negro registrants were in a majority in twenty-six parishes – by 1900 in none."

(Woodward 1957:68)

CASTE AS THE RACIAL MODEL

By the first decade of the twentieth century the mold of black-white relations in the South had hardened and set; it lasted for almost a half century. The decisive feature of this mold was the pervasive inequality that segregated and subordinated the black and that kept him permanently in an inferior status to the white. The term that was popularly used to characterize this system of racial inequality was caste. The term was adopted by a number of social scientists. Robert Ezra Park used the concept: "the social order which emerged with the abolition of slavery was a system of caste – caste based on race and color" (Park 1950:181). By the 1930s, when a series of field studies were conducted in the South, the term had become a generally accepted label for the black-white situation. For example, Dollard's monograph on his research in Southerntown in the 1930s was entitled *Caste and Class in a Southern Town* (1949). Davis and the Gardners' book *Deep South* (1941) carried the subtitle *A Social Anthropological Study of Caste and Class.* And Myrdal in his classic study, *An American Dilemma* (1944), devoted a chapter in his book to "Caste and Class."

What these and other observers generally recognized was that the character of the inequality between the two races was significantly different from the character of the inequality within each race: hence the term caste to describe the interracial inequality and the term class to describe the intraracial inequality. Myrdal points to the distinction between the two: *"A man born a Negro or a white is not allowed to pass from the one status to the other as he can pass from one class to another. In this important respect, the caste system of America is closed and rigid, while the class system is, in a measure, always open and mobile"* (Myrdal 1944:668).

Among the leading proponents of these terms were the social scientists who worked with or were inspired by W. Lloyd Warner of the University of Chicago. Their version of the two concepts focused on the social bases and character of the two kinds of inequalities. According to Davis and the Gardners, the keystone of the caste system is its endogamous character.

"The practice of endogamy is the most significant social control in any caste situation. In Old City it is the most rigidly enforced aspect of Negro-White relations and carries more emotive content than any other. While some individual Negroes may achieve a high economic position, receive recognition of their high intellectual abilities, or may even occasionally transgress the rules of deference, no Negro may ever marry a white person. All other rules may be, and at times are, broken; this one never. Thus, social mobility between the white and Negro societies becomes impossible, for there can be no legal family life involving a Negro and a white. The two in-marrying groups are perpetuated as *castes* whose differences are regarded as inherent, 'in the very nature of things.'"   (Davis, Gardner, and Gardner 1941:24–5)

The class system, according to the authors, may also be characterized by a high degree of in-group marriage, but it nevertheless permits "a certain proportion of interclass marriage between lower and higher groups" (Davis, Gardner, and Gardner 1941:9).

The second distinctive feature of the caste system, according to the authors, is the absence of any "opportunity for members of the lower group to rise into the upper or for the members of the upper to fall into the lower one." In effect, the gulf between the two is virtually unbridgeable; each remains encloistered behind the boundaries of its own kind. By contrast, the class system both encourages and permits social mobility and provides "mechanisms . . . by which people move up and down the vertical extensions of the society" (Davis, Gardner, and Gardner 1941:9).

The authors recognize that the two types of stratification seem to operate on dialectically opposed principles, and yet "they have accommodated themselves to each other in the southern community we are examining" (Davis, Gardner, and Gardner 1941:10). The authors spend considerable time on the nature of this accommodation: specifically the operation of the class system within and not across the boundaries of each caste. However, they recognize that the white caste virtually controls the political, economic, and social resources of the community; not all whites, though, have equal control over these resources and this inequality underlies the class system in the white caste. The few crumbs of these resources that filter into the black community are also unequally distributed among the blacks, and this inequality becomes the basis for the class system in the black caste.

The interplay between the opposing principles of class and caste poses some interesting questions; but before we address any of these, we shall examine more fully the application of the concept caste to black-white relations in the South and assess the fitness of the concept.

The term caste conveyed more than the notion of racial endogamy and segmentation to Park and the others; it also conveyed the notion of peaceful accommodation and stability. They were convinced that black and white relations had once again become orderly and stabilized after the interruption of the Civil War and reconstruction. As Park says, "So firmly was the system of caste fixed in the habits and custom – what Sumner calls the mores – of both races in the South that all the social disorganization incident to the Civil War and Reconstruction were not sufficient wholly or suddenly to destroy it" (Park 1950:181). However, few were prepared to argue that relations between black and white were either as stable or as harmonious as they had been in the antebellum days. But neither were they prepared to argue that orderly relations between the two had broken down significantly.

At the heart of the caste system, according to these scholars, was an elaborate code of etiquette and beliefs that reinforced and justified the subordinate status of the blacks. Doyle describes how the South sought to restore the code of etiquette of slavery days after the reconstruction.

"It was natural, and hence not unexpected, that the South would revert to the antebellum code as far as possible. For patterns of behavior, hitherto regulating the contacts of the races, had been fixed in habit and custom, and persons had come to expect and to accept those observances as just, right, and proper. Hence, even though the basis of ceremonial control underlying the relative peace of slavery was, perhaps, not at the time understood, it was nevertheless felt that the antebellum system of relations was a good one."   (Doyle 1971:136)

Davis and the Gardners and Dollard take the codes and creeds into the 1930s and show empirically how they served as the normative framework for the caste system in the southern community. The creed emphasized the inherent inferiority of the black, his childlike behavior and unsocialized nature, and the consequent need of responsibility by the white for the black. Davis and the Gardners conclude that the creed provides Old City with "a commonly shared body of beliefs about the status and capabilities of Negroes. This body of beliefs constitutes an ideological system which is used to justify the social relationships between the superordinate whites and the subordinate Negroes" (Davis, Gardner, and Gardner 1941:20).

The code of etiquette prescribed in detail the kinds of deferential behavior the black was to exhibit in the presence of the white:

"According to the dogma, and to a large extent actually, the behavior of both Negroes and white people must be such as to indicate that the two are socially distinct and that the Negro is subordinate. Thus, the Negro, when addressing a white person, is expected to use a title such as 'Sah,' 'Mistah,' 'Boss,' etc., while the white must never use such titles of respect to the Negro but should address him by his first name or as 'Boy.' . . . This deferential behavior goes beyond the mere observance of certain formalities; it extends to what the Negro may say and how he may say it. Under no circumstance may he contradict a white person except as a very humble offering of his opinion; and if the white man persists in his statements, the Negro must agree. In no event may he say or even insinuate that a white is lying. If the white is wrong, it can only be a mistake, never a deliberate untruth. Furthermore, under no provocation may the Negro curse white people, whatever the white may do or say to him. He must never express his antagonism through profanity or violence."

(Davis, Gardner, and Gardner 1941:22–3)

The caste system according to Davis and the Gardners was not only expressed in the beliefs and codes that regulated individual behavior but was deeply imbedded in the institutional arrangements as well. The authors elaborate in detail on the "operation of the caste controls in the distribution of economic and political power" (Davis, Gardner, and Gardner 1941:44) and their pervasive influence in organizing institutional life generally. "All social structures in the society operate to reinforce the caste system – associations, churches, the courts, even the schools and the Negro class system – for none of these challenges the fundamental separate, endogamous nature of the two caste groups" (Davis, Gardner, and Gardner 1941:44–5). According to these and other observers, the caste system defined a comprehensive and inclusive order of relations between black and white that was made into a cohesive whole by an elaborate and all-embracing normative and institutional framework.

To most of these observers the system seemed to function fairly smoothly; most blacks and whites seemed to conform to its basic dictates. There was little difficulty in providing evidence in support of this thesis for the whites. Most whites subscribed wholeheartedly in sentiment and behavior to the creed, conventions, and etiquette of the caste system. Dollard emphasizes the economic, sexual, and prestige gains accruing to the white caste (Dollard 1949). Even the poor whites were shown to experience significant social and psychological gains from their identification with the theme of white supremacy; accordingly they were among its most vigorous advocates.

The picture that these observers drew with respect to the black was less clear. Virtually all were impressed with the extent that the blacks conformed "with some enthusiasm" to the caste rules in situations of contact with the whites. Most recognized however that this kind of response was demanded by the caste rules.

"Not only must the Negro observe these rules of deferential speech and conduct, but he must observe them wholeheartedly and with no apparent reservations. It is not enough that he should conform reluctantly to the expected modes of behavior. He must show that he accepts them as proper and right; he must conform willingly and cheerfully." (Davis, Gardner, and Gardner 1941:23)

Further these observers were aware that failure to conform exposed the black to serious sanctions from the white.

"The tendency among students of culture to consider such acts as tipping the hat, shaking hands, or using 'Mr' as empty formalisms is rebuked by experience in the South. When we see how severely Negroes may be punished for omitting these signs of deference, we realize that they are anything but petrified customs; our illusion to the contrary occurs because we are not accustomed to think in terms of the emotional value of such forms. In Southerntown the use of 'Mr' as a white-caste mark and the omission of it in speaking to Negroes have great emotional value. The Negroes know that to omit the 'Mr' in referring to a white man would always mean that the addressee could enforce his right in some uncomfortable way. The main fact is that behind deference from the Negroes is the demand for deference by the whites and the ability to secure it by force if it is not willingly given."   (Dollard 1949:178–79)

Small wonder then that various observers have stressed the widespread tendency of blacks to accommodate themselves to the caste system. They saw little evidence of overt aggression by blacks against the system or against whites. According to Dollard, such accommodation produced three major kinds of gains for the lower class black: "first, greater ability to enjoy the sexual freedom possible in his own group; second, greater freedom of aggression and resentment within his own group; and third, the luxury of his dependence relationship to the white caste. All these types of freedom represent primitive biological values and none of them is constrained to the degree customary in white middle-class society" (Dollard 1949:391–92).

The precise meaning of this accommodative behavior has been a topic of considerable discussion even among those observers who have adopted the term caste for the black-white situation in the South. Some have argued that the accommodative behavior of the black was primarily an expression of his acceptance of the system. They have argued that most blacks had come to identify with and to relate themselves to the caste system, had internalized its basic values, and had accepted the legitimacy of the white's claim to superiority and supremacy. However, virtually no one has been prepared to project an image, similar to that projected by Phillips about the antebellum period (Phillips 1968), of the black as "happy and contented with his lot" and as expressing attitudes of "love and loyalty" to the white man (Dollard 1949:186). Dollard asserts that such attitudes characterized the response of many blacks "long after emancipation" (Dollard 1949:186), but eventually they diminished. What remained as the true heritage from slave days and persisted until the time of his study was a "dependent and submissive" attitude:

"These attitudes in turn are socially transmitted and are visible in large numbers of Negroes today, especially those living still under plantation condition. Very little external force is needed to maintain them. One may say that subservience is an attitude corresponding to the limited conditions of safety for slaves, that it has been built into the personalities of individual Negroes, and that thereafter it is culturally transmitted from one generation to the next."   (Dollard 1949:186)

In effect, Dollard paints a picture of a relatively passive, not active, acceptance of the caste system by the black.

Dollard seeks to connect this response to his theory of frustration and aggression. According to this theory, the experiencing of frustration leads to acts of aggression, but these acts may be expressed in a variety of ways. They may be expressed directly against the object of frustration. In the case of blacks, they may "become overtly aggressive against the white caste; this they have done, though infrequently and unsuccessfully in the past" (Dollard 1949:253). The more usual response for the blacks has been to "suppress their aggression" and to "supplant it with passive accommodative attitudes." Dollard contends that the latter "was the slavery solution and it still exists under the caste system" (Dollard 1949:253), but he leaves unclear exactly what he means.

For example, he indicates that accommodative attitudes were adaptive responses to the coercive system that engulfed the black as he was brought into the United States as a slave. Undoubtedly the black experienced a high degree of frustration, only to find that overt expression of aggression against the white resulted in death or severe punishment. Consequently to survive, he had to suppress aggression and take on a submissive attitude. In time, according to Dollard, the slave adjusted himself to the situation. "Once accommodation was a fact, other incentives could make themselves felt, such as loyalty and pride. The result of force and routine was in the end a change in Negro character; these factors formed character and resulted in the accommodated Negro, i.e. the one who had made his choice to live rather than die in fruitless resistance" (Dollard 1949:254).

If this personality transformation and social adjustment did indeed occur, then it can be argued that the feelings of acute frustration must have diminished so that the pervasive submissive attitude was no longer merely an indirect product of acutely experienced frustration but derived from these other sources as well, such as transformed personality, alternative types of gratification, etc. Following the path of Dollard's logic, we might thereby infer that the angers and resentments of the black against the white became buried even more deeply in his psyche as his expectations and aspirations settled more and more on sheer survival and on remembering his place in the scheme of things. His submissive attitude would become increasingly detached from the "frustration-aggression" syndrome.

Such a state of affairs may have developed and continued over time, but even Dollard recognizes that the reconstruction period disturbed whatever equilibrium had developed and introduced new elements into the situation. Reconstruction raised the hopes and expectations of the black and made him less willing to accept his position. Dollard asserts, "During the reconstruction period, the news was circulated adequately to the masses of Negroes that there were some people who did not accept the caste situation as inevitable; the result has been that the perfection of the slavery accommodation has broken down and many Negroes are able to see the class and caste gains quite clearly, even though they do not formulate them in technical language" (Dollard 1949:252).

Black hopes and aspirations were obviously dashed with the reimposition of white supremacy and Jim Crowism on the black. Once again the latter had to adopt a passive accommodative attitude. But this time – much more clearly than under slavery – these attitudes would have to be expressions of suppressed aggression if Dollard's thesis is sound, for, as Dollard himself says, "We may believe, then, that Negroes will perceive the caste and class distinctions as a chronic frustration situation. In such a situation we should expect aggression from them" (Dollard 1949:252). But Dollard realizes that overt aggression would lead to dire consequences; consequently, he reports that the more general reaction was for aggression to be suppressed and to be supplanted by passive accommodative attitudes. Thus it may be concluded that the post-reconstruction caste system reintroduced a close linkage between submissive attitude and the "frustration-aggression" syndrome with an added dimension: each component was near or at the surface of consciousness of the black. He was more acutely aware than in the past of his frustration, of his anger stemming from the frustration, and of his submissive behavior by which he avoided the kind of punitive response from the whites that their awareness of his underlying anger would otherwise have elicited.

What Dollard recognizes as compounding the sense of frustration of the blacks is their exclusion from the People's Domain. They "cannot in these days ignorantly accept their 'place' as once they could" (Dollard 1949:68). The reason why is fairly clear to Dollard. The Negroes have come to "share sufficiently in American society to want to be fully human in the American sense" (Dollard 1949:70). Thus the individual "Negro shares inevitably the values of the dominant group and aspires to full participation in it" (Dollard 1949:68).

The rooting of the claim among blacks that they have a legitimate right to membership in the larger society and to its rewards was obviously a post-slavery phenomenon. It was nurtured and flourished in the reconstruction period and obviously survived – if not grew – during the repression of the Jim Crow society.

It seems reasonable to suppose that the presence of these values and expectations would serve to limit the extent to which blacks would accept wholeheartedly the premises and values of the caste system, and the extent to which they would subscribe to its pervasive beliefs about their inferiority and subordinated position in life. What probably kept these expectations alive and offered some hope for their fulfillment for at least some blacks during this period was the operation of the very class system that the various observers have noted. While the whites maintained control over most of the economic and other resources, some seeped into the black community and provided the basis for the development of a small middle and upper class. These classes became in all probability the guardians among the blacks of the values of individual achievement and reward and were covertly or overtly resentful of the caste stigmata imposed by the white. (One indirect piece of evidence of this is the anger these classes have characteristically expressed against the lower-class blacks for displaying the kind of personal behavior that seemed to confirm the white's stereotype of the black as inferior, delinquent, and childlike.)

With such diametrically opposed values and beliefs competing for their attention, blacks in the post-slavery South were not as prepared to accept either emotionally or intellectually their subordinated status as they were in slavery, nor as likely as they were under slavery to share the sentiments of whites, as stated by Davis and the Gardners, that the system as a whole was legitimate, right, and in accord with the will of God.

As a result, customs and mores, which to Sumner, Park, and others reflected shared sentiments and values, could no longer be relied on as the major mechanism for regulating the caste system as they had under slavery. Instead law and force, according to Park, became the major devices for shoring up the system:

> "The caste system as it had existed [in slavery] was maintained not by law but by a body of customs that was more or less self-enforcing. One evidence of the change in race relations, as a result of emancipation, was the efforts of the southern communities to enforce by statute racial distinctions and discriminations which it was difficult or impossible to maintain by custom and tradition.
>
> Most of the racial conflicts and controversies in the southern states during Reconstruction and after seem to have had their origin in the caste system, and in the efforts to maintain it by law and force when it was no longer sustained by the inertia of tradition and the force of public opinion."　　　(Park 1950:185)

Doyle also describes the expanded role that law came to play in support of the caste system: the multivarious Jim Crow laws in all the southern states were the product of legislative efforts to reaffirm the caste system (Doyle 1971).

Even with the imposing apparatus of law and custom behind them, the whites during this period expressed a nervousness about the stability of white and black relations. As Myrdal indicates they felt the need for constant vigilance and they closed ranks against any sign of black insubordination.

"Southern whites feel a caste solidarity that permits no exception: some of them may not enforce the etiquette against all Negroes in all its rigor, but none will interfere with another white man when he is enforcing his superiority against a Negro. A white man who becomes known as a 'nigger lover' loses caste and is generally ostracized if not made the object of violence. Even a Southern white child feels the caste solidarity and learns that he can insult an adult Negro with impunity."

(Myrdal 1944:677)

Accordingly the whites maintained and honed an apparatus of coercion against the blacks; whippings, lynchings, and other terroristic acts were not uncommon activities. Any indication of black restiveness under the caste restrictions were met by a prompt exercise of force. Davis and the Gardners describe in detail the white reaction to any sign of black discontent.

"Periodically there seems to develop a situation in which a number of Negroes begin to rebel against the caste restrictions. This is not an open revolt but a gradual pressure, probably more or less unconscious, in which, little by little, they move out of the strict pattern of approved behavior. The whites feel this pressure and begin to express resentment. They say the Negroes are getting 'uppity,' that they are getting out of their place, and that something should be done about it. Frequently, the encroachment has been so gradual that the whites have no very definite occurrence to put their hands on; that is, most of the specific acts have been within the variations ordinarily permitted, yet close enough to the limits of variation to be irritating to the whites. Finally, the hostility of the whites reaches such a pitch that any small infraction will spur them to open action. A Negro does something which ordinarily might be passed over, or which usually provokes only a mild punishment, but the whites respond with violence. The Negro victim then becomes both a scapegoat and an object lesson for this group. He suffers for all the minor caste violations which have aroused the whites, and he becomes a warning against future violations. After such an outburst, the Negroes again abide strictly by the caste rules, the enmity of the whites is dispelled, and the tension relaxes. The whites always say after such a outburst: 'We haven't had any trouble since then.'"

(Davis, Gardner, and Gardner 1941:48–9)

Under the circumstances it is difficult to describe the caste system, particularly after reconstruction, as constituting a harmonious system in which black and white shared common values and sentiments. Myrdal for one does not subscribe to this view though he uses the concept "caste." He states, "The caste distinctions are actually gulfs which divide the population into antagonistic camps. And this is a conscious fact to practically every individual in the system" (Myrdal 1944:677).

In view of such inherent instability and dissonance, it is not surprising to find that a number of scholars, particularly black scholars, reject the characterization of the racial system in the South as a caste system. Perhaps the most penetrating and incisive criticism comes from Oliver Cromwell Cox, who engages in a wide-ranging attack on this characterization in his book *Caste, Class and Race* (1970). Cox takes as his model of a caste system the one found in India, and he claims that the "modern caste school of race relations" had this as its basic model too, even though the school professes to believe that the caste concept can be applied to a variety of other societies as well. Cox contends that the standard he is using to assess the black-white situation in the South is therefore the same standard used by the school. He takes the school to task for exaggerating the resemblances of the two systems and for papering over the fundamental differences between them so that it can label the southern situation a caste system. Cox takes it upon himself to show the inappropriateness of the label for the South by pinpointing a variety of crucial ways in which the caste system in India differs qualitatively from the race relations system in the South.

Basically he argues that both systems are based on inequality, but in the caste system in India this inequality is organically integrated into a system of values and relationships that provide a *"natural*, socially accepted, peaceful status ordering of the society"* (Cox 1970:431). Accordingly "the caste system may be thought of as a social order in stable equilibrium" (Cox 1970:433); it has an organic character in which the parts are harmoniously interrelated and the whole unified by a consensual value scheme of a religious nature. "In attempting to explain their social systems, most peoples will seek some sort of justification in religious terms; it is a way of achieving divine sanction for the social fact. The Hindus, more than any other people of comparable magnitude, have been able to couch their social behavior in a religious frame of reference" (Cox 1970:436).

According to Cox, each caste accepts its own position in the scheme of things and is governed by a complex normative structure that reinforces its sense of worth and sanctifies its present status. "In the caste system each caste knows or assumes that it knows its place" (Cox 1970:450). Learning and education are monopolized by the highest caste; however "in the caste system, an individual is naturally limited by his caste dharma, and the idea of education serving as a means of broadening the functional scope of the individual is anomalous" (Cox 1970:438).

Endogamy is practiced and accepted as a basic value by each caste.

"Endogamy among castes in India is a basic trait. A group cannot function within the Brahmanic system if its social area of choice of partners in marriage is undefined. The caste is a truly endogamous social entity. The prohibitions against outmarriage are not a reaction to similar actions of some other castes; they are the most reliable means available to the caste for protecting its heritage. Furthermore, the social heritage of low castes is to them as important as that of high castes is to the latter." (Cox 1970:447)

According to Cox, the economic and occupational arrangements in the caste system also contribute to its basic stability. "The theory of production which obtains in the caste system is founded upon hereditary group specialization and co-operation. It maintains that the most satisfactory economic system is one in which each group has a specified occupation rendering service on a sort of intergroup barter basis" (Cox 1970:439).

The racial system in the United States, according to Cox, is built on an entirely different set of principles from that of a caste system and is expressed in a different setting and structure of relations. It lacks the organic character of the caste system and is instead a coercive system of "subordination and superordination" which is based on "a power relationship in which definite aims and ends of each [racial] group are opposed" (Cox 1970:431).

The dominant white group has sought to impose a value-normative framework on relations between the races which would reaffirm its claim to superiority and keep the subordinated black group in its place. However, it has failed to gain the loyalty and acceptance of the blacks to this normative system and accordingly has had to rely heavily on force, coercion, and fraud to maintain its control over and its exploitation of the subordinated racial group for economic and political gain. This has produced an inherent instability in the system.

What has compounded this instability is the fact that the racial system in the South is set into a larger societal system whose value-normative framework is built on the principle of equality and achievement. Cox asserts that many blacks identify with and relate themselves to this broader framework. "Unlike castes in India, Negroes in America have been seeking to increase their participation and integration in the dominant culture. Cessation of such striving is an inseparable feature of the caste system" (Cox 1970:441). Thus the blacks, even in the South, desire to break down the barriers to upward mobility that the whites have imposed; they desire educational and job opportunities and aspire to higher status; their goal is eventual assimilation into the larger society.

In this manner Cox sets the stage for a critical assault on the work of various scholars who have applied the term caste to the racial situation in the South. He takes issue with Park on a number of matters, but perhaps the most significant for our purposes is his attack on Park's presumption of harmony and stability in relations between the races through his emphasis on etiquette and the mores as primary regulatory mechanisms for the caste system. Cox repeats his argument that the blacks do not accept the caste values and that the so-called caste mores are only shared by the whites, not the blacks. Accordingly the whites cannot rely on the sentiments and loyalty of the blacks for maintaining their control but instead have to rely on force.

> "The white ruling class is, to be sure, determined to keep the Negro exploitable, but it dares not rely upon 'the mores' to do this. It must exercise 'eternal vigilance' in maintaining an ever-present threat of interracial violence if it is to continue its exploitative social order. The Southern racial system 'lives, moves, and has its being' in a thick matrix of organized and unorganized violence."
>
> (Cox 1970:472)

Cox concludes that under such circumstances the racial system "in America could never become stabilized" (Cox 1970:473) and must therefore remain "in a state of continual unrest" (Cox 1970:470).

Cox also challenges the major premises of what he calls the "modern caste school of race relations" of which "Professor W. Lloyd Warner is the admitted leader" (Cox 1970:489). He argues that despite the relative lack of agreement and clarity in the school's concept of caste, it seems to focus on endogamy as a critical essence of its concept. Cox insists that endogamy characterizes many groups in society: "endogamy may be an isolator of social classes, castes, tribes, sects, millets, or any other social groups which think they have something to protect" (Cox 1970:494). Thus, he continues, "the final test of caste is not endogamy but the social values which endogamy secures.... Endogamy is not the essence of caste; if there is an essence of caste, endogamy merely bottles it up" (Cox 1970:494). He also contends that in-group marriage is a positive value only to the whites; the blacks have no such positive valuation of endogamy. They marry within their group primarily as an adaptive response to the situation.

Cox aims his major thrust against the underlying thesis of the "caste school" that "the dichotomized racial system in the South becomes a natural type of social ranking" (Cox 1970:501) in a single societal framework. He argues that unlike the caste society in India which "carries within itself no basic antagonisms ... the social aims and purposes of whites and Negroes are irreconcilably opposed. If such a situation could be termed a society at all, it must be a society divided against itself." He elaborates upon this by saying:

> "The caste system of India is a minutely segmented, assimilated social structure; it is highly stable and capable of perpetuating itself indefinitely. Castes in India

constitute a natural status system in one society, while Negroes and whites in the South tend to constitute two status systems, i.e., two social-class systems in two societies that are in opposition.... Negroes and whites in the Deep South do not constitute an assimilated society. There are rather two societies. Thus, we may conceive of Negroes as constituting a quasi or tentative society developed to meet certain needs resulting from their retarded assimilation. Unlike the permanence of a caste, it is a temporary society intended to continue only so long as whites are able to maintain the barriers against their assimilation. It provides the matrix for a universe of discourse in which members of the group give expression to their common sympathies, opinions, and sentiments, and in which their primary social institutions function. The political and economic structure is controlled by another and larger society to which the whites are assimilated and toward which all Negroes are oriented."   (Cox 1970:502–04)

Thus the dual structure described by Cox stands in striking contrast to the orderly and integrated arrangement of the divisions of a caste system; however it bears close resemblance to the racial segmentation of a plural society as defined by Furnivall (1956). In fact, what Cox seems to have done generally in his critique of the concept caste is to describe the structure of race relations in the South in terms similar to those used by Furnivall in his description of the plural society. In both formulations the racial groups function as distinctive communal and sub-societal entities; boundaries between them are clear and impenetrable and the gulf between them deepened and widened by mutual mistrust and antagonism. Further the various racial groups stand in a relatively "naked" power relationship to each other. The dominant racial group seeks to impose on the subordinated groups a value-normative structure which would legitimize its dominance but largely fails in its efforts. Accordingly the race relations society of Cox and the plural society of Furnivall lack the consensual value scheme and shared sentiments that would transform them into integrated caste societies. Instead the dominant racial group in each type of society depends upon its monopolization of governmental, political, and economic power to maintain control over the subordinated groups and to impose its version of law and order on the society as a whole. As a result, coercive compliance (to use Rex's phrase) becomes the major mechanism for regulating relations between the various parts of the society; its unity is sustained because it is essentially a state society and not an organically organized community of castes.

In repudiating the concept of caste, Cox does more than offer the plural society as an alternative way of dealing with the racial segmentation of the South. He frequently addresses himself to another societal model which he locates at the backstage of southern society just as the plural society occupies the forestage and dominates the scene. Cox recognizes that the backstage model is presently inoperative for the blacks, but he argues that it nevertheless exercises a powerful pull on them. Blacks experienced this model briefly during the reconstruction, and it still functions for them on the national level as an expression of the people as defined by the Constitution and extended to the blacks through the Fourteenth and Fifteenth Amendments.

When he says, "Unlike castes in India, Negroes in America have been seeking to increase their participation and integration in the dominant culture" (Cox 1970:441), or "Negroes are moving away from a condition of extreme white domination and subjection to one of normal citizenship" (Cox 1970:498), Cox is obviously not referring to their coming to terms with the plural society that subjugates them but rather to their orientation toward and identification with the broader societal model of the people, which serves as a backdrop for their hopes and aspirations. Its presence – even as a backstage abstraction for the blacks – has prevented the plural society from developing the internal stability that it might otherwise have developed and has thereby made it impossible for the whites to close the circle on the plural society and convert it into a caste society.

The dual creeds: the American creed and the racial creed

The character of the larger societal model of the people to which Cox alludes was for Myrdal the focus of his classic study of the black. In the introduction to his book, *An American Dilemma* (1944), Myrdal states that the problem of the black in America can only be understood and analyzed if it is located in the value-normative framework that describes and defines the basic ideals of America as a nation and as a people. This system of ideals Myrdal calls the American creed and he links its development to the struggle of America for nationhood and independence. "These ideals of the essential dignity of the individual human being, of the fundamental equality of all men, and of certain inalienable rights to freedom, justice, and a fair opportunity represent to the American people the essential meaning of the nation's early struggle for independence" (Myrdal 1944:4).

The tenets of this creed have been

"written into the Declaration of Independence, the Preamble of the Constitution, the Bill of Rights and into the constitutions of the several states. The ideals of the American Creed have thus become the highest law of the land. The Supreme Court pays its reverence to these general principles when it declares what is constitutional and what is not. They have been elaborated upon by all national leaders, thinkers and statesmen. America has had, throughout its history, a continuous discussion of the principles and implications of democracy, a discussion which, in every epoch, measured by any standard, remained high, not only quantitatively but also qualitatively. The flow of learned treatises and popular tracts on the subject has not ebbed, nor is it likely to do so."

(Myrdal 1944:4–5)

Thus the American creed represents to Myrdal a set of high ideals that is identified with the American people as a nation and is legitimated as the supreme law of the land by the Constitution as interpreted by the Supreme Court. Myrdal is convinced that Americans are almost universally conscious of the creed and accept it as a valid and idealized normative standard and framework for the governance and treatment of the people.

"As a result of this for more than two hundred years continuing hammering of these ideals of the essential dignity of the individual human being, of the fundamental equality of all men, and of certain inalienable rights to freedom, justice and fair opportunity, they had become highly conscious to all Americans, including, as the author of *An American Dilemma* could then observe, the oppressors as well as the oppressed. In spite of all the conspicuous and systematic, gross failure of compliance, America, of all countries I know, had come to have the most explicitly formulated system of general ideals in reference to human interrelations, shared, on one level of valuations, by all its citizens."

(Myrdal 1974:8)

Myrdal argues that even the blacks have been included under the canons of the American creed. He leaves no doubt about their historical acceptance of the creed, and he suggests, largely through inference, that white America, even in the South, has long felt that the American creed ought to apply in some way to the black, although Myrdal is unclear as to exactly when this inclusion came about historically.

This inclusion serves as one horn of what Myrdal identifies as an American dilemma. The other horn arises from the great disparity between ideals and practice. In his book Myrdal devotes much of his attention to the discriminatory and exploitative treatment of the black and to the subordinated and inferior position to which the black has been relegated. However, the dilemma to which Myrdal alludes is not manifestly an expression of the tension between the creed and practice, but between the creed and another set of beliefs and values which have grown up around the inferior status of the black and have served to justify the white man's exploitative and discriminatory treatment of him.

"The 'American Dilemma,' referred to in the title of this book, is the ever-ranging conflict between, on the one hand, the valuations preserved on the

general plane which we shall call the 'American Creed,' where the American thinks, talks, and acts under the influence of high national and Christian precepts, and, on the other hand, the valuations on specific planes of individual and group living, where personal and local interests; economic, social, and sexual jealousies; considerations of community prestige and conformity; group prejudice against particular persons or types of people; and all sorts of miscellaneous wants, impulses, and habits dominate his outlook."   (Myrdal 1944:xlvii)

As evident in the above quotation and throughout most of his work, Myrdal leaves no doubt of his conviction that the set of beliefs which is predicated on the presumed innate inferiority of the black is connected with "narrow economic, social, or sexual interests and jealousies" (Myrdal 1944:9). These beliefs reflect the prejudices, antipathies, and selfishness of various groups and individuals; Myrdal even states that they may be of even greater importance than the American creed in the day-to-day behavior of people and groups. However, he contends that these beliefs have not been elevated to statements of a normative code by the whites who hold them, but have instead become transmuted into presumptive factual statements of reality. Thus one order of belief and valuation, the American creed, is used to define a higher order of what ought to be; and the other, used to justify a lower order of what presumably is.

"Through this process, beliefs become distorted. People succeed in believing what they want to believe, what serves the 'purpose' of the underlying valuations on the lower level. A scientific scrutiny of people's beliefs – for instance the stereotyped beliefs among white people of certain inherited racial traits of blacks – shows not only that these beliefs are regularly mistaken but also that they are systematically twisted so as to serve the needs of rationalization of their behavior, when it deviates from the ideals on the higher level. The beliefs also show blind spots of unnecessary ignorance and, on the other hand, an often astonishing eagerness to acquire knowledge, when it is opportune for their urge to rationalize their behavior."   (Myrdal 1974:9)

Myrdal believes that only the set of values he calls the American creed has been legitimated by the legal-normative order of the larger society; the other represents the prejudicial and exploitative character and interests of the white for which he has not sought legal and normative legitimacy.

"The white man can humiliate the Negro: he can thwart his ambitions; he can starve him; he can press him down into vice and crime; he can occasionally beat him and even kill him; but he does not have the moral stamina to make the Negro's subjugation legal and approved by society. Against this stands not only the Constitution, which could be changed, but also the American Creed which is firmly rooted in the Americans' hearts."   (Myrdal 1974:10)

Many of the early reviewers of Myrdal's work found themselves in agreement with his conceptualization of the American creed. In fact, Frank Tannenbaum literally waxed rhapsodic over the idealistic character of American values. What is more he left no doubt that he believed the American creed expressed the consensual value scheme that undergirds America as a nation.

> "Since the ideals that dominate American life are believed in by all groups – the conservatives as well as the liberals, the 'old aristocrats' and the new immigrants, all worship at the same shrine – the American credo belongs to no special sect, caste, or class, and it is this 'spiritual convergence' which makes 'the nation great' and holds the promise of an even 'greater future.'"
>
> (Tannenbaum 1944:326–27)

Kimball Young also accepted the American creed as a basic statement of American values; however he contended that the disparity between ideals and practice was not confined to black-white relations,

> "as Myrdal at times seems to imply. It is but a phase of the larger dichotomy between our idealistic morality and the intense aggressiveness found in our competitive individualism. For example such a separation is found in the world of ordinary business and professional struggles, in the contrast between our political principles and the every day operations of machine politics."
>
> (Young 1944:327–28)

Other observers, however, have raised reservations about Myrdal's conceptualization. For example, in a recent essay, Lyman does not seriously challenge Myrdal's conception of the American creed as expressing a set of general values of the American society, but he complains about the primacy that Myrdal gives to this set of values over others. "For Myrdal the American Creed is *the* national ethos, a basic and dominant set of values which takes precedence over all others. Myrdal specifically rejects a pluralistic image of values and any conception of equal competition among values" (Lyman 1973:111).

The significance of Lyman's critique will be examined later; in the meantime let us turn to another kind of criticism that some observers have made: namely, that Myrdal is too Weberian in his emphasis on the role of values in society. Cox, for example, would emphasize class conflict and interests à la Marx. However, it is unclear whether Cox finally rejects or accepts the idea of a unified value-normative framework for the American society. At the least, he seems to accept the notion that there is an abstract and stereotyped set of values about which the various groups and classes agree but which each interprets to its own self-interested satisfaction. These beliefs and values derive from the Declaration of Independence and the Constitution which "have become national symbols, like the flag" (Cox 1970:513). But Cox argues that "it is quite another thing, however, to say that the content of these documents is accepted even as a creed by the whole people" (Cox 1970:513). Cox contends that there is too much ignorance and selfish interest for the necessary commitment and sentiment to have developed.

He suggests that under certain conditions the Constitution might develop into a viable legal-normative system which could unite the American society as a whole and thereby provide the basic legal framework for something akin to the American creed: "And yet the Constitution is so ample in its scope what with certain amendments and abrogations it may become the fundamental law of a consummate democracy" (Cox 1970:514).

What Cox seems only belatedly to realize is that Myrdal's conception of the American creed is more than a moral code which Americans share; it is also a code of legal rights and immunities for those who are defined as the people of the United States.

This legal-moral character of the American creed raises an important question which Myrdal and the others do not come to grips with directly: namely, what is the historical relevance of the American creed as a legal-normative framework for the treatment of the black? As we have already shown in the last two chapters, the blacks, and not merely those who were enslaved, were effectively excluded from the category of the people as defined by the Constitution and Declaration of Independence until the passage of the Fourteenth and Fifteenth Amendments during the radical reconstruction period. Whatever lingering doubts there may have been about such exclusion were clearly settled by the Dred Scott decision of 1857. Consequently for much of America's early history the blacks were not included in the moral and legal community of people to whom the American creed applied.

Myrdal himself recognized the fundamental cleavage between the world to which the American creed applied and the world in which most blacks of this period lived: the world of slavery. "Human slavery, in spite of all rationalization, was irreconcilably contrary to the American Creed. The South had to stand before all the world as the land which, in modern times, had developed and perfected that ignominious old institution" (Myrdal 1944:220).

One of the consequences of this cleavage, according to Myrdal, was to spare the antebellum planter the same kind of "embarrassing moral conflict" that his peer of today might experience. For, "slavery then was a lawful institution, a part of the legal order, and the exploitation of black labor was sanctioned and regulated. Today the exploitation is, to a considerable degree, dependent upon the availability of extra-legal devices of various kinds" (Myrdal 1944:220). In other words, the white Southerner in the antebellum days was able to separate his treatment of the black from the dictates of the American creed; today he is not able to do so readily; therefore he is more likely to experience guilt and moral conflict.

Consequently it can be argued that the period of the radical reconstruction marked the true beginning of the inclusion of the blacks in the community of the people and the true beginning of their being accorded the moral and legal rights of the American creed. Congress had done this by forcibly imposing the radical reconstruction on a reluctant South and by passing amendments to the Constitution. The Supreme Court had done this by refraining from a premature overruling of the basic cornerstones of the congressional reconstruction.

The blacks were brought into the moral and legal community of the American people; the American creed came to apply to them as it applied to the whites. For a short while it appeared that the American creed would be the only legal-normative code sanctioned by the Constitution and legitimated by the Congress and the Supreme Court for regulating black-white relations.

The inclusion of the black within the American creed, however, did not dissipate the widely held beliefs about black inferiority among the whites, particularly in the South. Myrdal describes the pervasive persistence of these racist beliefs even down through the period of his study, but he insists that they were never legitimized morally and legally by the American society as it had legitimized the American creed; instead they always remained expressions of parochial, selfish, and primordial interests of whites. Lyman takes issue with Myrdal on this matter:

> "It is perfectly possible in theory and reasonable on the basis of the evidence to postulate that racism is not a lower and local set of values but rather a complex value premise equal in every respect to that of the American Creed. Myrdal's original theoretical approach should have forced him to consider this at least *as a possibility*, since in his formal report on methods he explicitly enunciates the proposition of competing values. Moreover, the evidence presented in the report itself on the political, economic, social, sexual, and personal aspects of racism would seem to bear out such a hypothesis." (Lyman 1973:113)

Pertinent as Lyman's comments are, he fails to address the issue in the terms that Myrdal does. Nowhere does Myrdal deny the long and unsavory historic record of racist beliefs in American society as Lyman seems to imply he does; but Myrdal does deny that these beliefs have ever been affirmed as part of the legal-normative order of the American society as a whole, thereby acquiring the kind of legitimacy that the American creed has. It is at this level that Myrdal's thesis can be challenged.

Myrdal is well aware that within twenty years of the reconstruction and the constitutional adoption of the American creed for the blacks, the South had constructed an imposing legal edifice of Jim Crowism. It was built on the foundation of racist beliefs, and it sought to neutralize the effects of the American creed on black-white relations. Myrdal, however, treats this edifice as though it were merely a local or regional manifestation. In so doing he fails to recognize the crucial role that the Supreme Court played in legitimizing it and thereby making it part of the legal-normative code of the nation as a whole and not merely of the region. As we have already seen, the Supreme Court did this through a series of critical decisions that spanned a quarter of a century. These decisions effectively eroded the institutional reach of the Reconstruction amendments.

By accepting the principle of racial difference and "social inequality" as part of the supreme law of the People's Domain, the Supreme Court in effect endowed the racial beliefs of the white man with a status and sanctity that they did not have before. During the period of radical reconstruction, only the American creed served as the basis for the legal-normative code of the People's Domain. Racial beliefs were popularly expressed and widely held, but as Myrdal maintains they were transmuted into presumptive statements of fact and were not part of the legal-normative code of the people (Myrdal 1944). Even prior to reconstruction, the American creed was the sole basis for the legal-normative code of the people; the racial beliefs and values that were expressed in law and through decisions of the Supreme Court applied to a category of beings who were excluded from the Domain of the People and treated as chattels or non-persons subject to the authority of the state. The language of the Dred Scott decision indicated that the blacks were viewed as inferior beings close to savagery and in need of the "protection" of the whites. This judicial legitimation of racist beliefs reinforced the conception of the black as unfit for citizenship and therefore ineligible to receive the privileges and immunities of the American creed. Thus the racist creed was viewed as dealing with a lower order of beings; and the American creed, with a higher order of people in the American society.

The re-legitimation of the racial creed during the post-reconstruction period was a different kind of thing; it now applied to blacks who had gained membership in the higher order of the people and who were presumably to be governed as were the whites by the tenets of the American creed. Thus, the new racial doctrine, which was a thinly disguised version of the old racist creed, gained a level of respectability that it had not had before. Supported by the legal and moral authority of the Supreme Court and Constitution, it became part of the legal-normative framework of the people and as such could compete on relatively equal terms with the American creed as a guideline for policies on and treatment of the "Negro problem."

The history of the American society from the post-reconstruction period until recently witnessed the dynamic tension between the two creeds, as adherents of each sought to foster and to enact policies and legislation that bore the stamp of their creed. In no instance, however, was either able to eradicate completely the presence of the opposing principle.

In the South for example, the racial creed gained preeminence during this period, for most southern states quickly realized the significance of the Supreme Court decisions. They sought to extend the social realm into as many reaches of society as they could so that the racial doctrine of separateness could be applied without breaching the limit defined by the Supreme Court as the realm of the political and legal, which was still protected by the American creed. Some states breached this limit frontally and were set back by adverse court rulings. Others discovered bypasses to this realm by such devices as "grandfather" and "understanding" clauses; for all intents and purposes they succeeded in a *de facto* manner in once again pushing the blacks out of the People's Domain. But these successes proved vulnerable in time as the Supreme Court never quite abandoned the principle, which for a period seemed more fictional than real, that the blacks had become part of the people through the Fourteenth and Fifteenth Amendments and that at the least in theory their political and legal rights were to be protected by the American creed.

In the North the struggle between the two creeds was much more complex and complicated. On the surface the American creed seemed to be the dominant force as Myrdal implies, but in many ways the racial creed also made its presence felt. And it is to an examination of the interplay between the two creeds in the North that we shall now turn.

The North: the social realm as a *de facto* plural society

By excluding the "social realm" from the protection of the federal government under the Fourteenth Amendment and by approving the doctrine of "separate but equal" for this realm, the Supreme Court set forth a legal-normative framework that affected race relations for over a half a century, not only in the South but in the North and in the rest of the country as well. One of its profound consequences was to legitimize the policy and practice of racial differentiation and segregation within the community and within social and economic institutions and to sanction inequality for the black in the North as well as in the South. The result was the nourishing and embellishing of an infrastructure of exclusion, segregation, and discrimination which already had deep roots in the North, and the developing of a *de facto* plural society within the boundaries of the social realm.

Another profound consequence of the Supreme Court decisions was to place within the hands of the state governments the authority to legislate directly on the civil rights of individuals in the social realm. The South, as we have already seen, responded by enacting Jim Crow laws which transformed it into a *de jure* plural society. Many northern states seemed to follow the opposite path, the one leading in the direction of the American creed and equality. But this legislative intent was so narrowly defined and circumscribed that it had little impact on the prevailing infrastructure of racial segregation and discrimination, which was in accord with the sentiment of the white community and with the main features of the law of the land as interpreted by the Supreme Court.

STATE LAW AND EQUALITY

As Litwack and others have shown, the heritage of anti-black sentiment was deep and widespread in the North, even as the Civil War ended and reconstruction began (Litwack 1961). Many states had laws on their books that severely restricted the rights and life circumstances of the blacks. The struggle over the passage of the Fourteenth and Fifteenth amendments in Ohio and other northern states bears further witness to the strength of the anti-black feelings in the North. And yet the North had also spawned abolitionism, was the fount of Radical Republicanism, and had supported the imposition of a harsh reconstruction program on the South which favored the black.

Thus, by the reconstruction period, the North was becoming even more than the South the arena for the struggle between the American and racial creeds. After the reconstruction period the North was even more caught in the dialectical struggle between the two creeds. The schizoid character of its response fits more closely what Myrdal calls the American dilemma than the less schizoid response of the South during this period (Myrdal 1944).

For example, despite widespread anti-black feeling a number of northern states gave fuller expression in this period to basic tenets of the American creed than they had in the past. After the Supreme Court declared the Civil Rights Act of 1875 unconstitutional in 1883, they took advantage of the authority vested in states by the Supreme Court on civil rights and passed public accommodation laws modeled on the now defunct federal civil rights act. In 1884 four states passed such laws (Connecticut, Iowa, New Jersey, and Ohio); seven more did so in 1885 (Colorado, Illinois, Indiana, Michigan, Minnesota, Nebraska, and Rhode Island). By the late 1890s four others added such laws to their books: Pennsylvania (1887), Washington (1890), Wisconsin (1895), and California (1897).

Prior to this period only three states had enacted laws on public accommodations. Massachusetts was the first. In 1865 it banned "distinctions or restrictions based on race or color in any licensed place of public accommodation" (Konvitz and Leskes 1961:155). In 1874 New York became the "second state to enact a civil rights law with a statute prohibiting race distinctions at inns, public conveyances on land and water, theaters, other places of amusement, common schools, public institutions of learning, and cemeteries" (Konvitz and Leskes 1961:156). Almost at the same time Kansas passed a similar law. Thus by 1900 eighteen states had enacted public accommodation laws. Not until the 1950s was there a further upsurge in the passage of such laws by states.

> "The wording of all the early state statutes is essentially the same: all persons (citizens in Alaska, California, and Ohio) within the jurisdiction of the state, regardless of race, color, or previous condition of servitude, are entitled to the full and equal advantages facilities and privileges of the various places of public accommodation, resort, or amusement listed. Individuals who defy the law are subject to fine or imprisonment (criminal sanction) or are responsible in damages to the party aggrieved (civil sanction). In some states both remedies are available but an action for one bars an action for the other. Places listed in the various state laws include inns, taverns, restaurants, eating houses, boarding houses, cafes, chophouses, lunch counters, hotels, motels, saloons, soda fountains, ice cream parlors, bathhouses, barber shops, theaters, concert and music halls, skating rinks, bicycle rinks, churches (Colorado), public meetings (Massachusetts), elevators (Illinois), public conveyances, colleges and universities, schools and places of public instruction, places of public amusement, resort or entertainment, places where refreshments are served, and public places kept for hire, gain, or reward."   (Konvitz and Leskes 1961:157–58)

For years the significance of these laws rested on their symbolic value as representations of the American creed rather than on their impact on practices in the public domain. For enforcement was sporadic and selective where infractions were treated as violations of the penal code; and the aggrieved party had to be prepared for a costly and difficult court trial where the remedy was civil. Even if he lost a specific case, a violator would still find it paid to pursue discriminatory practices.

> "Owners of places of public accommodation tend to regard the occasional fine or civil penalty which they are forced to pay for violations of civil rights laws as a kind of 'license fee' for the privilege of continuing to practice discrimination. Because actions based on the civil rights statutes are rarely instituted, and when instituted are frequently lost or compromised, the 'fee' is not deemed exorbitant."   (Konvitz and Leskes 1961:178)

The effectiveness of these statutes was even more severely limited by the strict interpretations that the courts placed on them. Konvitz and Leskes argue that "three principal grounds have been used to justify strict construction of civil rights laws: (1) such statutes are in derogation of the common law; (2) they are penal in nature; and (3) they impose restrictions on the control or management of private property" (Konvitz and Leskes 1961:159).

Of special significance is the last ground for it points up once again the reluctance of the courts to enter into the domain of private rights and property. Accordingly, the courts took a narrow and literal view of the "public places" that were covered by the statutes. Only if the law specifically denoted a place as public did the courts say it was included under the statute; otherwise they were reluctant to do so even if their logic seemed strained. For example,

"when two Negroes who were refused service in a New York Saloon because of their color, sued under the New York Civil Rights Law in 1917, the court of appeals applied the strict construction principle to rule that a saloon was 'closer to a tobacco and cigar shop' than to a restaurant, and hence not a 'place of public accommodation within the letter or spirit of the statute.'"

(Konvitz and Leskes 1961:161)

In effect the realm of the private became a vast residual category that included everything not specifically defined by law as public. For many years then discriminatory treatment in this arena and also in such arenas as employment, housing, and the like were viewed as within the rights of the private and social domain of the individual.

Even for those installations defined as public accommodations, the laws functioned as potential inconveniences to owners and operators and not as compelling constraints upon their behavior. Not until the 1940s and 1950s were efforts made to strengthen the enforcement machinery of these laws. New Jersey was only the first of the various states to place the enforcement of its public accommodations laws under the jurisdiction of an administrative agency of the state. No longer did the individual minority person have to proceed on his own; he had the authority of a state agency behind him.

Further, not until the 1940s and 1950s was there any significant extension of the areas of civil rights to be covered by state law. Most notable were the laws on fair employment practices; prior to the 1940s only thirteen states had any law on discrimination in employment. The post-1940 laws also established administrative mechanisms for enforcement that subsequently became the model for the implementation of civil rights legislation generally. Laws against discrimination in housing did not appear until even later: the 1950s.

Ineffective as the public accommodation laws were for much of their history, they nevertheless represented an important effort to salvage some of the gains for racial equality of the reconstruction period at a time when the Supreme Court and the state governments in the South were moving precipitously in the direction of emasculating these gains. What makes their enactment even more astounding is the fact that the forces of racial reactionism, discrimination, and inequality were also actively tapping the historical structure of racism in the North and threatening to engulf the North as it had the South. Thus it can be stated that these laws served as a wedge of equality into the social realm which was itself being increasingly defined in terms of racial separation and inequality in the North and the South under a legal-normative environment sanctioned by the Supreme Court.

THE COMPETITIVE STRUGGLE FOR RESOURCES AND THE "PLURALIZED" MARKETPLACE

Introduction

The absence of an articulated system of Jim Crow laws in the North meant that monopolization of societal resources and control of the social realm by the whites could not depend as fully and directly on the authority of the state and laws as it did in the South and therefore could not be as effectively sustained. Further, the urban character of the black-white encounter in the North made it less likely that a system of caste-like inequality could be stabilized there as it was in the South where black-white relations were set in a rural economy.

In eschewing a juridical-legal approach, whites in the North did not thereby accord the blacks full membership in the social realm nor allow them to compete equally with whites for privilege, power, and position in this realm, despite the laws on public accommodation. In fact, they treated the blacks as a pariah group and relied heavily on their control of the social realm for effectively curbing the black as a competitive threat for these resources. They did this in large measure by superimposing the creed of racial differentiation and segmentation on the work-ings of the allocative machinery in society and thereby reaffirming their historic claim that blacks were unworthy of full and equal membership in the social and economic Domain of the People.

The whites carved up the marketplace for jobs and residence into plural segments and forced the black to compete primarily in those segments of the market which could only lead to inferior jobs and residences, the more desirable segments being more or less monopolized by the whites. What gave legitimacy to the northern whites' "pluralization" of the marketplace was the legal framework created by the Supreme Court through its decisions which culminated in its legitimation of the "separate but equal" doctrine as the law of the land. In short this framework provided a protective umbrella for policies and practices of whites – severally and collectively – in the marketplace and in the community, whose goal was to keep blacks out of their private environments of work and residence. The decisions of various lower courts throughout this period helped reaffirm the rights of the white citizen to his private realm of property, contract, and discrimination.

Residential segregation and the ghetto

During the early post-reconstruction period, relatively few blacks lived in the North; by 1900 only about one out of ten lived there. This proportion had grown slowly from 1860 at which time 7.6 percent of blacks lived in the North. And for the next ten years beyond 1900 an additional 1 percent of the blacks lived in the North.

Unlike the South, blacks in the North were heavily concentrated in urban areas; they showed a preference for the larger cities. In 1890, for example, Philadelphia had the largest concentration of blacks in the North. In fact only three other cities throughout the country had a larger number than Philadelphia: Washington, New Orleans, and Baltimore. New York and Chicago had the next largest number in the North. However, in each northern city, including Philadelphia, blacks comprised an extremely small part of the total population: less than 2 percent in New York, Chicago, and Boston and less than 4 percent in Philadelphia and Cincinnati.

By 1900 New York had virtually caught up with Philadelphia; both had witnessed a substantial numerical increase to over 60,000 blacks. Chicago had almost doubled its blacks to 30,000; but in all instances they still comprised a small percentage of the population. In 1910 New York had even more blacks than Philadelphia, 92,000 to 84,000 respectively; Chicago was a distant third, 44,000.

During this period – from 1880 to 1910 – the residental distribution of blacks within the northern cities showed, according to Weaver, a pattern of neighborhood clustering which was not as pervasively segregative as it became in later years.

"Negroes in northern cities usually lived in clusters in racially mixed neighborhoods, and there were so few colored people in most northern cities before 1915 that a few such concentrations were adequate to accommodate most of them; consequently, these clusters were seldom found in all parts of the city."

(Weaver 1948:9–10)

In Philadelphia, for example, DuBois identified the four major wards in which blacks primarily resided in 1896 (DuBois 1967). In none of them did the black comprise more than 30 percent of the population. Within the seventh ward, which had the greatest number of blacks, significant concentrations of blacks were found in some neighborhoods, particularly in the poorer sections, but rarely to the complete exclusion of working-class whites. Less dense clusters of blacks were interspersed in other neighborhoods which included significant numbers of working-class whites. In the high rent areas, even the more affluent blacks tended to be excluded.

Ovington describes a similar pattern for Manhattan in 1905 (Ovington 1969). She identified five neighborhoods of concentration of the black. No neighborhood was exclusively black. All had clusters; some streets were virtually dominated by blacks but, in almost all, enclaves of other ethnic groups, Jewish or Irish, were to be found. The pattern was not random dispersal of individuals from the various ethnic and racial groups, but distinctive enclaves, set side by side in a common environment. In general the areas were poor, rundown, and congested.

Drake and Cayton allude to the emergence of the Black Belt after the second fire in Chicago in 1874; it was "sandwiched between a well-to-do white neighborhood and that of the so-called 'shanty Irish'" (Drake and Cayton 1962:47). However Weaver contends that, throughout the early years of the twentieth century, Chicago too followed the pattern of clustering but not complete separation. "Yet as recently as 1910, in no area of Negro concentration were Negroes more than 61 per cent of the population; more than two-thirds of the colored people lived in sections less than 50 percent Negro, and a third were in areas less than 10 percent Negro" (Weaver 1948:15).

With World War I the situation changed dramatically. A massive migration began, pouring increasing numbers of blacks into industrial northern cities. Virtually overnight the black population in many of these localities doubled and quadrupled. Detroit, for example, experienced a 600 percent increase from 1910 to 1920. The increase for Cleveland was 300 percent; for Chicago, 150 percent; for New York, 60 percent; and for Philadelphia, 59 percent. Hauser estimates that between 1910 and 1920 the "net migration of blacks out of the South totaled 454,300" (Hauser 1971:41). The net result was that by 1920 a number of industrial cities in the North had black populations that exceeded 30,000. Each of the three with the largest number of blacks – which were as they were in 1910: New York, Philadelphia, and Chicago respectively – had black populations exceeding 100,000.

Similar to the pattern of other immigrant groups, the Negro migrants moved into areas already identified as Negro sections.

"At first, the new arrivals filled up the run-down housing which more affluent residents, black and white, had abandoned. Even though the most inadequate facilities were rapidly pressed into use, the supply soon was exhausted, and the pressure of the increasing numbers required expansion in other directions. The Negro areas, starting from the established colored sections, not only filled up but began to spread. Whites began to flee before the never-ending stream of Negro migrants. Enterprising realtors, anticipating inflated prices, commissions and rentals often manipulated the evacuation of whites by crying 'Wolf.'"

(Weaver 1948:29)

The impact of this expansion on the surrounding areas was dramatic and overwhelming. Resembling a tidal wave, it engulfed these areas as whites sought to flee.

"In the process of this expansion, not only were tens of thousands of whites displaced from neighborhoods where they had long lived, but the wave of invasion was so strong that churches, community centers and other facilities were soon surrounded by a new racial group. Schools underwent a transformation in the color composition of their pupils; merchants found their clients made up of a new racial and often a lower economic group. All of this was a shock. It was sudden, too."

(Weaver 1948:29–30)

As a result, relations between the races became increasingly strained and raw as whites sought to counter what they considered to be threats to their life space. Weaver reports "at least 26 race riots in American cities in 1919" (Weaver 1948:30). In time the whites developed a variety of policies and techniques whose goal was to contain the blacks within the boundaries of their own territorial area; consequently whatever may have been the natural tendencies of blacks to live among their own kind, these tendencies were compellingly reinforced by white policies and techniques of containment.

Municipal ordinances as an unconstitutional expression of state action

Whites in northern cities were too late to adopt an instrument that had been used in San Francisco in 1890, in Louisville in 1912, and in Baltimore, Richmond, and Atlanta in 1912 and 1913; namely municipal ordinances to enforce residential segregation. According to these ordinances, neighborhoods were to be zoned as white or black depending upon the character of the racial majority living there. No one could move into a neighborhood designated for the other race; and members of the other race currently residing in the neighborhood had to get out.

In the 1917 case of Buchanan v. Warley, the Supreme Court reversed the judgment of the Kentucky Court of Appeals and declared the Louisville ordinance unconstitutional. The defendants had argued that the ordinance was in accord with the "separate but equal" doctrine of the Plessy-Ferguson decision of 1896 (the Kentucky Court of Appeals agreed with this contention) and was a constitutional exercise of police power in the social realm of society.

"It is said such legislation tends to promote the public peace by preventing racial conflicts; that it tends to maintain racial purity; that it prevents the deterioration of property owned and occupied by white people, which deterioration, it is contended, is sure to follow the occupancy of adjacent premises by persons of color."   (245 US 1917:73)

Justice Day in his opinion for the Court declared that the defendants as well as the Kentucky Court of Appeals were in error in insisting that the Plessy-Ferguson doctrine applied to the Louisville ordinance. What was at issue, he argued, was not "the social rights of men" but their "fundamental rights in property" which are protected by the statute of 1866 and the Fourteenth Amendment.

"The statute of 1866, originally passed under sanction of the Thirteenth Amendment, 14 Stat. 27, and practically reenacted after the adoption of the Fourteenth Amendment, 16 Stat. 144, expressly provided that all citizens of the United States in any State shall have the same right to purchase property as is enjoyed by white citizens. Colored persons are citizens of the United States and have the right to purchase property and enjoy and use the same without laws discriminating against them solely on account of color.... These enactments did not deal with the social rights of men, but with those fundamental rights in property which it was intended to secure upon the same terms to citizens of every race and color.... The Fourteenth Amendment and these statutes enacted in furtherance of its purpose operate to qualify and entitle a colored man to acquire property without state legislation discriminating against him solely because of color."   (245 US 1917:79)

In rendering his opinion, Justice Day did not dismiss the professed social objectives of the ordinance as either undesirable or unconstitutional. In several instances he expressed doubt whether the ordinance would or could achieve some of these objectives:

"It is the purpose of such enactments, and it is frankly avowed it will be their ultimate effect, to require by law, at least in residential districts, the compulsory separation of the races on account of color. Such action is said to be essential to the maintenance of the purity of the races, although it is to be noted in the ordinance under consideration that the employment of colored servants in white families is permitted, and nearby residences of colored persons not coming within the blocks, as defined in the ordinance, are not prohibited."   (245 US 1917:81)

However he does not state what his position would be if he believed that the ordinance would indeed realize these goals.

Further, Justice Day did not basically question the use of segregation as a device for promoting public peace, and he lauded the goal of preserving public peace, but in this case, he insisted, the social goals clash with fundamental constitutional guarantees of the rights of property and therefore have to be set aside.

> "It is urged that this proposed segregation will promote the public peace by preventing race conflicts. Desirable as this is, and important as is the preservation of the public peace, this aim cannot be accomplished by laws or ordinances which deny rights created or protected by the Federal Constitution.
>
> We think this attempt to prevent the alienation of the property in question to a person of color was not a legitimate exercise of the police power of the State, and is in direct violation of the fundamental law enacted in the Fourteenth Amendment of the Constitution preventing state interference with property rights except by due process of law. That being the case the ordinance cannot stand." (245 US 1917:82)

In this manner the Supreme Court sought to clarify part of the ambiguous boundary between the social realm, in which the state had the right to act in racial matters, and the legal-constitutional realm, in which the state was prohibited from acting by the Fourteenth Amendment. It fixed, in effect, another limit to the right of the state to legislate racial separatism in the social Domain of the People. It stipulated that the state cannot arbitrarily override the rights of the individual – whether black or white – to own, use, or control private property; it did not, however, question or deal with the basic legitimacy of racial separation in the social domain or with the constitutionality of other kinds of legal sanctions for such separation.

Despite this decision, New Orleans subsequently enacted a similar ordinance which was also declared unconstitutional. Even Chicago toyed seriously with the idea of enacting a similar ordinance after the Supreme Court decision had been rendered, but it was tabled before final action could be taken.

Restrictive covenants and the private realm of discrimination

While thwarted in their efforts to use legislative remedies, whites were quickly able to transmute the primary obstacle to their efforts – the right of private property – into a major legal support for implementing residential segregation in the community. They did this by getting together and drafting agreements in which they mutually consented to refrain from selling or leasing their houses and property to blacks (in some instances to other racially and ethnically "undesirable" people as well) for a specified period of time. These agreements were deposited with the appropriate municipal authorities and had the binding effects of a legal contract which could be enforced by courts of law. Weaver views these restrictive covenants as direct heirs of the aborted efforts to legislate segregation through ordinance.

> "Following the lead of San Francisco, which adopted a race segregation ordinance in 1890 (aimed at the Chinese), cities in several southern and border states attempted to establish racial zones by ordinance. All were declared unconstitutional. In order to accomplish the same end and still not run afoul of the law, race restrictive housing covenants were hit upon."   (Weaver 1948:231)

Thus the courts took over from the state legislature the role of legally sanctioning the territorial separation of the races in the social domain.

For the next quarter of a century, racial covenants became a "principal instrument for effecting residential segregation in northern and border states" (Weaver 1948:231). They spread throughout most of the northern and western cities that were experiencing significant in-migrations of blacks. Chicago was perhaps one of the most pervasive users of the covenants; it is estimated that at one time they covered approximately 80 percent of its residential area. Other pervasive users were Los Angeles, Columbus, Philadelphia, and, as a latecomer, Detroit.

Typically the network of covenants was most extensive in white neighborhoods immediately contiguous to areas of black concentration. However, covenants were also widely used in medium and high-income neighborhoods in urban and suburban areas far removed from the black ghettos.

The effectiveness of the covenants varied inversely with their distance from the black ghettos. Weaver argues that at the most they merely delayed the expansion of black ghettos immediately beyond their boundaries as the inexorable pressure of increasing numbers of blacks made outward expansion inevitable. In the areas further removed from the black ghettos, covenants were much more successful in keeping the black out.

> "Racial covenants in new subdivisions and in medium- and high-income districts removed from the Black Belt are a more lasting impediment to Negro occupancy. In the case of new subdivisions this is due, in part, to the fact that the degree of coverage is extremely high. In the case of high-rent areas removed from the Black Belt, covenants are effective chiefly because they are a deterrent to the *individual* colored family that attempts to break them."
> (Weaver 1948:237–38)

A number of legal challenges were mounted against racial covenants from its earliest days but to no avail. Loren Miller describes briefly the history of these challenges in state courts:

"Beginning with Louisiana in 1915, appellate courts in sixteen states and the District of Columbia had held that courts did not violate constitutional guarantees by enjoining sale or occupancy of property on racial grounds. Included in that list of states were California, New York, Ohio, Michigan, Illinois, Colorado, Wisconsin and Kansas, to list some of the more 'liberal' jurisdictions." (Miller 1971:140)

The matter reached the Supreme Court in 1926 in the case of Corrigan v. Buckley. In his opinion, Justice Sanford dismissed the defendants' contention that the covenant should be voided because it was contrary to the Fifth, Thirteenth, and Fourteenth Amendments. He stated that the issue was the rights of individuals and not limitation "upon the powers of the General Government" (Fifth Amendment); nor a "condition of enforced compulsory service of one to another" (Thirteenth Amendment); nor "State action of a particular character" (Fourteenth Amendment). He continued "It is obvious that none of these Amendments prohibited private individuals from entering into contracts respecting the control and disposition of their own property; and there is no color whatever for the contention that they rendered the indenture void" (271 US 1926:330). Accordingly, the Court declined jurisdiction because "neither the constitutional nor statutory questions relied on as grounds for the appeal to this Court have any substantial quality or color of merit, or afford any jurisdictional basis for the appeal" (271 US 1926:331). It let stand the plaintiff's bill for an injunction which would prevent the white and black defendants from completing the transaction for the sale of a house which was covered by the covenant.

Thus the Supreme Court confirmed the contractual right of individuals to discriminate in the private domain which could be legally enforced in the courts. Not until 1948 in the case of Shelley v. Kraemer did the Supreme Court introduce significant curbs on the exercise of this right. It did not, however, disturb the earlier decision that reaffirmed the right of propertyholders to engage voluntarily in restrictive covenants. In his opinion for the Court, Chief Justice Vinson declared that there is no constitutional "shield against merely private conduct, however discriminatory or wrongful" (334 US 1948:13). What has become "firmly embedded in our constitutional law," since the Court's decision on the *Civil Rights Cases*, according to Vinson, is the principle that the Fourteenth Amendment inhibits "only such action as may fairly be said to be that of the States" (334 US 1948:13).

Under these strictures, Vinson contended,

"the restrictive agreements standing alone cannot be regarded as violative of any rights guaranteed to petitioners by the Fourteenth Amendment. So long as the purposes of those agreements are effectuated by voluntary adherence to their terms, it would appear clear that there has been no action by the State and the provisions of the Amendment have not been violated." (334 US 1948:13)

Having dismissed the private domain of discriminatory behavior as a constitutional issue, Vinson then focused on the role of the courts in enforcing these private agreements. He argued that "the action of state courts and judicial officers in their official capacities is to be regarded as action of the State within the meaning of the Fourteenth Amendment." This proposition, he insisted, "has long been established by decisions of this Court" (334 US 1948:14).

"The short of the matter is that from the time of the adoption of the Fourteenth Amendment until the present, it has been the consistent ruling of this Court that the action of the States to which the Amendment has reference includes action of state courts and state judicial officials. Although, in construing the terms of the Fourteenth Amendment, differences have from time to time been expressed as to whether particular types of state action may be said to offend the Amendment's prohibitory provisions, it has never been suggested that state court action is immunized from the operation of those provisions simply because the act is that of the judicial branch of the state government."

(334 US 1948:18)

Vinson therefore concluded that the state courts in seeking to enforce restrictive agreements, as in the cases under consideration, were functioning as agents of the state within the meaning of the Fourteenth Amendment.

"We have no doubt that there has been state action in these cases in the full and complete sense of the phrase. The undisputed facts disclose that petitioners were willing purchasers of properties upon which they desired to establish homes. The owners of the properties were willing sellers; and contracts of sale were accordingly consummated. It is clear that but for the active intervention of the state courts, supported by the full panoply of state power, petitioners would have been free to occupy the properties in question without restraint."

(334 US 1948:19)

Accordingly the Court ruled that judicial enforcement of restrictive covenants was in violation of the Fourteenth Amendment. In Vinson's words,

"We hold that in granting judicial enforcement of the restrictive agreements in these cases, the States have denied petitioners the equal protection of the laws and that, therefore, the action of the state courts cannot stand. We have noted that freedom from discrimination by the States in the enjoyment of property rights was among the basic objectives sought to be effectuated by the framers of the Fourteenth Amendment. That such discrimination has occurred in these cases is clear. Because of the race or color of these petitioners, they have been denied rights of ownership or occupancy enjoyed as a matter of course by other citizens of different race or color. The Fourteenth Amendment declares 'that all persons, whether colored or white, shall stand equal before the laws of the States, and, in regard to the colored race, for whose protection the amendment was primarily designed, that no discrimination shall be made against them by law because of their color....' Only recently this Court had occasion to declare that a state law which denied equal enjoyment of property rights to a designated class of citizens of specified race and ancestry, was not a legitimate exercise of the state's police power but violated the guaranty of the equal protection of the laws.... Nor may the discriminations imposed by the state courts in these cases be justified as proper exertions of state police power."   (334 US 1948:20–1)

The structure of discrimination and the dual housing market

Until the late 1940s, a legal-normative environment was sustained in the North that legitimized policies and practices of massive discrimination against the black in the housing market. Although explicit legislative action was precluded, individuals and organizations could act severally or collectively in an overtly discriminatory manner without running afoul of the law or of the courts. As a result, the widespread sentiment and prejudice against the blacks could be acted upon with relative impunity and without creating any significant strain between the mores and the law. What made this discriminatory behavior even more respectable, according to Weaver, was the leading role that middle and upper income groups played in trying to keep blacks out of their neighborhoods through restrictive covenants or other means.

Where covenants emerged, Weaver contends that they were not merely the expressions of spontaneous neighborhood sentiment, but were instead "carefully, and often expensively promoted" (Weaver 1948:249). Weaver identifies the property owners' or neighborhood improvement associations and the developers of subdivisions as the two groups which were most active in promoting these agreements. He describes several expensive campaigns that such groups undertook to convince individual property owners that they should join restrictive agreements.

Where covenants did not emerge, real estate operators assumed an even greater strategic role in the creation of segregated neighborhoods. In many instances they deliberately steered blacks away from white neighborhoods: "the practices of real estate operators have been an effective deterrent to colored peoples' moving into new neighborhoods, since many realtors have entered into 'gentlemen's agreements' not to sell or rent to Negroes in areas outside existing colored districts" (Weaver 1948:215).

Reinforcing the pattern of residential segregation was the action of governmental agencies. Most noteworthy were the policies and practices of the Federal Housing Administration. According to Weaver, it succeeded in doing for the executive branch of the state what the Supreme Court had ruled was unconstitutional for the legislative branch of the state: namely the fostering of racially segregated housing. The agency did this by including racially segregated criteria in guidelines to its "valuators" for rating applications for housing loans in various areas. It stipulated that an area should be given a high rating if covered by restrictive covenants and deed restrictions which would protect the area from "undesirable encroachment and unharmonious use."

Weaver argues,

"These instructions have a dual significance. They have been effective in accelerating the spread of racial covenants to vacant and newly subdivided areas. Most important, they have put the Federal Government's stamp of approval upon residential segregation and racial covenants. Not only has that brought comfort and support to the manipulators and proponents of racial covenants, but it has also permitted real estate operators, builders and developers to absolve themselves of responsibility for the exclusion of colored people from most new housing. With the FHA *Manual* in operation, they were able to and often did cite its provisions as the reason for barring Negroes from the bulk of new housing that was constructed from 1934 to 1940. What the Supreme Court said was unconstitutional when attempted through municipal zoning, what property owners' associations have been able to accomplish only at great expense and imperfectly, the Federal Housing Administration encouraged and facilitated."

(Weaver 1948:72−3)

The outcome of these concerted and pervasive efforts to restrict access of blacks to white neighborhoods was the creation, according to several scholars, of a dual housing market which carved out mutually exclusive territories for each race. Whites avoided buying or renting residences in black areas, but their options were so widespread and varied that they virtually monopolized the more desirable living areas in the cities and suburbs. Blacks were confined to relatively few circumscribed areas of inferior housing and facilities, but the pressure of numbers pushed them into contiguous white areas which frequently were quickly vacated by the whites as the blacks moved in. The Taeubers describe the racially bifurcated housing situation.

"The concept of the dual housing market is helpful in explaining certain facets of the relationship between race, residence, and income. It can be assumed that the supply of housing for non-whites is restricted in terms of both number of units and quality of units. For non-whites, then, demand is high relative to supply, and this situation is aggravated by the rapidly increasing urban Negro populations. Housing within Negro areas can command higher prices than comparable housing in white residential areas. Furthermore, there has been a continual need for Negro housing, which has been met by transferring property at the periphery of Negro areas from the white housing market to the Negro housing market. The high demand among Negroes for housing, combined with a relatively low demand among whites for housing in many of these peripheral areas, makes the transfer of housing from whites to Negroes profitable."

(Taeuber and Taeuber 1965:25)

By fostering a dual market, the whites in the North were instrumental in creating a territorially segmented society along racial lines. They did so by controlling the terms and conditions of the housing market for blacks, which served to reinforce the inferiority and isolation of the black in spatial terms. In many respects, these efforts to control the machinery of the market became as much a trademark of the discriminatory practices of the North as was the legal Jim Crowism of the South. This will become even more evident in our later discussion of the labor market and blacks in the North.

The expansion of the ghetto and bifurcated racial domains

Even as the dual housing market was being institutionalized, more and more blacks were pouring into the northern urban areas. According to Hauser, the net migration of blacks out of the South between 1920 and 1930 almost doubled that between 1910 and 1920: 749,000 and 454,300 respectively. During the depression years, between 1930 and 1940, the net migration slowed to 347,500. But during and after World War II it accelerated to about three times the rate of the depression period. Between 1940 and 1950 the net migration reached 1,244,700 and increased somewhat between 1950 and 1960 to 1,457,000.

"Six states in the North and West (California, Illinois, Michigan, New York, Ohio, and Pennsylvania) absorbed 72 per cent of all Negro net in-migration between 1910 and 1950. Between 1950 and 1960, the same six states absorbed 68 percent of all net in-migration of nonwhites" (Hauser 1971:41). Within these states the largest cities witnessed the greatest growth in their black population. For example, the black population in New York, which has had the largest number through the years, grew from 150,000 in 1920 to over 400,000 by 1940 and exceeded one million by 1960. Chicago showed an almost equally spectacular growth. Blacks numbered somewhat over 100,000 in 1925, over 250,000 in 1940 and over 800,000 in 1960. Philadelphia, which had more blacks than Chicago did in 1920 (134,000 to 109,000), grew at a slower rate. By 1940, Philadelphia had 250,000 and by 1960 somewhat over half a million. Detroit showed the most sensational growth of all. Starting with only 5000 blacks in 1910, Detroit witnessed an eightfold jump by 1920 to 40,000 blacks; by 1940 not quite another fourfold jump to 150,000; and by 1960 another threefold increase to 480,000. Cleveland also witnessed a massive growth in its black population: from 8000 in 1910 to 34,000 in 1920, to 84,000 in 1940, and to 250,000 in 1960.

Within these cities, the blacks moved into the already established black ghettos and produced a density of population that far exceeded that for the whites. Woofter (1928) shows that in 1925 the density of the black population per acre was one and a half times that of the whites in New York; more than two times in Chicago; almost five times that of the whites in Philadelphia. The pressure of numbers forced the boundaries of the black areas into the contiguous white areas. The Duncans (1957) describe the process of invasion and succession that occurred. But even as the boundaries were expanding, a process of racial homogenization was taking place on either side of the boundary which magnified the racially bifurcated character of the city. The Taeubers describe quantitatively the trend toward increasing segregation through an index they constructed (Taeuber and Taeuber 1965). From 1910 to 1950, Chicago moved on an index of segregation from 66.8 to 79.7; Cleveland from 69.6 to 86.6; Philadelphia from 46.0 to 74.0; and Pittsburgh from 44.1 to 68.5.

As the black enclaves became increasingly devoid of whites and the white areas increasingly devoid of blacks, the percentage that blacks comprised of the total population also increased. In 1910, blacks comprised 1.9 percent of the population of New York City; by 1960, they were 10.5 percent. In Chicago the percentage rose from 2 to 14.4; in Philadelphia from 5.5 to 15.5; in Detroit from 1.2 to 14.9; and in Cleveland from 1.5 to 14.9.

The critical turning point for these cities occurred in the 1960s; from a relatively small minority in the urban population the blacks became major segments of the population. By 1970 they comprised 21.2 percent of the population in New York; 32.7 percent of the population in Chicago; 33.6 percent of the population in Philadelphia; 43.7 percent of the population in Detroit; 38.3 percent of the population in Cleveland; and 20.2 percent of the population in Pittsburgh. In Newark, New Jersey, and Gary, Indiana they became a majority of the population by 1970.

In effect, the relatively small enclaves of blacks had become transformed in large urban centers of the North into major territorial domains that dominated the inner city. In this manner, the historical trends of segregation came to full bloom by the 1970s and converted city after city into territorially bifurcated societies.

Racial segmentation and the world of work

The territorial segmentation of the blacks in the North has had its parallel in their segmentation at the bottom of the occupational structure. They have had to struggle continually against a legal and a market system that has placed them in a competitive disadvantage in the struggle for jobs and employment. Historically, they even lost ground to immigrant groups that also came in at the bottom but soon moved on to better jobs and positions. The only mobility most blacks experienced was lateral into more marginal jobs or downward into even more menial and lower-paying jobs. Bloch emphasizes the difference in the occupational experiences of the two groups:

"Usually, in an open class society such as is generally ascribed to the United States, vertical mobility is possible, and has taken place, as is exemplified by the successive waves of immigrants and their offspring who have attained varying degrees of such mobility. Each new wave of immigrants has replaced the longer established immigrants on the lower rungs of the social ladder. However, the historical progress of the immigrant has not applied to the Afro-American. The latter's failure to achieve upward mobility can be linked, chiefly, to a continuing pattern of social and economic discrimination." (Bloch 1969:ix)

In effect, blacks have functioned as a perennial underclass in the North as they have in the South. Most have been confined to the bottom rungs of the occupational ladder for generations; only a few have escaped and made it up the ladder. Bloch argues that the historic subordination of the black has produced a pattern of social and economic discrimination mutually reinforcing each other in a circle of discrimination which restricts the mobility of the black and keeps him at the bottom of the occupational structure. Bloch, however, fails to recognize the importance of the legal-normative order as a source of continuing legitimation for this historic subordination and circle of discrimination.

Despite the continuing and historic underclass status of the black, changes occurred over time in the occupational positions held by the blacks in the North. Bloch, for example, argues that the black was not always confined to a narrow range of menial occupational roles in the North. He states that the "'freedom of entry' into most occupations [for blacks] reached its zenith [in the North] after the close of the Colonial period" (Bloch 1969:19). The widespread shortage of labor and the fact that the "Northern economy was based primarily on commerce, manufacturing and small scale agriculture" opened up a variety of occupational roles for the blacks. "They performed a multiplicity of tasks: as barbers, carpenters, cabinetmakers, sawyers, blacksmiths, printers and maritime workers." They were also put to work on farms "on the production of foodstuffs and dairy products and in sheep raising" (Bloch 1969:20). DuBois estimates "that between 1790 and 1820 a very large portion, and perhaps most, of the artisans of Philadelphia were Negroes" (DuBois 1967:33). However, most blacks performed these roles as slaves and not as freemen. Thus the benefits of their labors went to their masters who frequently hired them out for profit.

But even under the protected environment of slavery, pressures mounted early in the North from white workers to eliminate or to restrict employment of blacks in the crafts or trades. Under these pressures, the occupational status of free blacks in New York and Pennsylvania deteriorated markedly; many could no longer find jobs in the work in which they had gained skills. This is evident in a report prepared in 1838 by the Pennsylvania Society for Promoting the Abolition of Slavery on "Trades of Colored People in the City of Philadelphia and Districts." According to this study, 1600 blacks out of a population of about 10,000 claimed to have a trade. The most frequent trade for women was that of dressmaker; for men, that of barber; in addition competence was claimed in a variety of skills by one or more members of each sex. Despite these claims, substantial numbers could not find employment in their chosen field. "Less than two-thirds of those who have trades follow them" (Bacon 1856:15). The report concludes that many were "compelled to abandon their trades on account of the unrelenting prejudice against color" (Bacon 1856:15).

By the 1850s fewer than 5 percent of the gainfully employed blacks were in the crafts in New York City. Almost four out of five were employed in menial and personal service jobs. Their five major occupations were laborers, servants, mariners, barbers, and coachmen. One commentator wrote in the 1850s about the blacks in New York City,

> "'As tradition of servitude and the continuing stigma of inferiority prevented most Negroes from pursuing skilled trades, they followed the only course open to them: common labor and various service trades.... Some two thousand colored persons were servants, laundresses, cooks, and waiters – over half of all the gainfully employed Negroes.'" (Bloch 1969:33)

Throughout this period the blacks were able to achieve some prominence in several of the domestic and personal service occupations. They served as coachmen, butlers, cooks, and waiters in the homes and restaurants of the rich and provided an array of services for hire as freedmen which they had been forced to offer without pay as slaves. This access to the affluent white classes gave some blacks in New York, Philadelphia, and, to a certain extent, Boston an opportunity to go into business for themselves. They opened up catering establishments and, for a period of time during the nineteenth century, blacks dominated the industry which provided a protected environment for the employment of blacks as waiters and other personnel. As late as the 1890s, DuBois identified sixty-five caterers in Philadelphia. By then catering was no longer controlled by the black, who once again found himself vulnerable in competition with the white man.

Decisive in the northern black's competitive struggle for survival in the nineteenth century was his encounter with the white immigrant. Scholars such as Bloch have concluded that the influx of white immigrants served to displace the blacks from occupational gains that they may have made as freedmen prior to this influx or that they would have made had they been the only source of manual labor during the rapid industrial expansion of the North during the nineteenth century. For example, even in the area of personal service, blacks were forced out of the better jobs in the more affluent homes and in the firstrate hotels and restaurants. They had to become increasingly content with jobs as waiters and cooks in secondrate establishments and in less affluent homes. In effect, they experienced a dual kind of marginalization. They were pushed into increasingly marginal and menial jobs in the personal service industry and could only find employment in the marginal establishments in the industry. At the same time, the blacks were blocked from entering the expanding mainstream industrial occupations by the flow of white immigrants, at virtually every level of skill. Thus the blacks could only find jobs in industries peripheral to the main industrial thrust of the American economy at the time.

The process was repeated with each new wave of immigration. In each period the immigrants, most of whom had not previously been exposed to anti-black sentiments, quickly adopted these sentiments in the competitive struggle with blacks. Despite being victims of oppression themselves, they soon came to share with other white Americans the conviction that blacks were not the equal of any white and were, therefore, not entitled to the same rights and immunities as the whites in the social and economic Domain of the People. In turn, the blacks sought to undermine the competitive position of the white immigrant by stressing the latter's alien and un-American behavior, but this had little effect on stemming the blacks' lessening fortunes. Thus the racial cleavages prevented any effective working-class solidarity from developing among whites and blacks at the bottom of the occupational ladder. In fact, these cleavages polarized the labor market and raised serious doubts about the rights of the black to be treated as an equal in the competition for jobs even at the bottom of the ladder. What magnified the vulnerability of the blacks was their numerical weakness. Even in those occupations in which they clustered, they comprised only a small proportion of the work force for that occupation. Accordingly, they were easily overwhelmed by the numerical strength of the white groups. As Ovington stated, "This enormous difference in the proportion of colored workers to white must never be forgotten in considering the labor situation North and South. We cannot expect in the North to see the Negro monopolizing an industry which demands a larger share of workers than he can produce, nor need we admit that he has lost an occupation when he does not control it" (Ovington 1969:77).

In the early nineteenth century the racial struggle was primarily between blacks and Irish. The latter tried to force the black off the waterfront and from construction jobs. The Draft Riots of 1863 etched sharply the ugly overtones of the racial encounter and the unceasing efforts to push the blacks ever deeper into their pariah status.

"No matter how low any white ethnic group's social status was, it was usually higher than that of the Afro-American, with the former being given economic preference in the labor market. In other words, 'the newcomers from Europe had to be provided for,' even if it was to be at the expense of the indigenous colored American. This was the case even when the bulk of immigrants had little or no prior occupational skill for the jobs. This contention has merit when viewed longitudinally. Thus, the 1870 Census of Occupations for New York City revealed that foreigners constituted at least 50 percent of the mariners, 90 percent of the laborers, 74 percent of the launderers, and about 80 percent of the shoemakers." (Bloch 1969:37–8)

Toward the end of the nineteenth century, the old immigrants were replaced at the bottom of the occupational ladder by the new immigrants from Southern and Eastern Europe, but the pressure against the black knew no surcease. Blacks were further displaced in some occupations and forced into ever more marginal positions in others. In an issue of *Annals of the American Academy of Political and Social Science*, the declining fortunes of the black from 1865 to 1910 were graphically described:

"'Fifty years ago, the waiter in New York ... was usually a man of color, as was the barber, the coachman, the caterer, or the gardener. True enough, he had little opportunity to rise above such menial occupations, but with the growth of a humanitarian, if rather apologetic attitude toward the Negro, engendered by the great conflict which had brought about verbal abolition of slavery ... it [was] possible that the Negro's status in New York ... would have been rapidly and permanently improved, industrially, as well as in civic recognition, had not the current immigration which had been retarded for a decade or two during the Civil War and preceding the agitation, started with the renewed force on the cessation of conflict ... The European immigrant soon outstripped his Negro rival for employment and the respect of the American ... [the white immigrant] looked and still looks upon the Negro with the contemptuous eye of an easy victor over a hopelessly outnumbered weak and incompetent foe.'" (Bloch 1969:43)

By the turn of the century almost three out of five blacks in New York City were in domestic and personal service. Within this occupational category, they were greatly overrepresented in jobs as servants, waiters, stewards, and janitors. No longer, though, were they disproportionately barbers, bootblacks, or caterers. Approximately three out of ten of the blacks were in trade and transportation. Within this occupational category they greatly exceeded their expected proportion of the population in such jobs as porters, helpers in stores, and hostlers; however, no longer were they disproportionately boatmen or longshoremen as they had been in earlier years. Fewer than one out of ten were in manufacturing and fewer than one out of twenty in any professional occupation. Within the last category blacks were only overrepresented proportionately as actors, musicians, and clergymen.

DuBois found a generally similar occupational picture for blacks in Philadelphia at the turn of the century (DuBois 1967). Over three out of five men were in the domestic and personal service industry and almost three out of ten were in the trade and transportation industry.

The outbreak of World War I with its profound effect on immigration produced a dramatic change in the job market for blacks. First, the burgeoning needs of the rapidly expanding industries of the North and the shrinking stream of white immigrants created a widespread shortage of labor that markedly increased the number of jobs available for blacks. So many were needed that the demand could not be met by the indigenous black population of the North or by the modest population increases from the South of the past. Accordingly, a massive migration was triggered and thousands upon thousands of blacks streamed northward, not merely to the older centers of black concentration but to the new industrial centers of the North as Pittsburgh, Detroit, and Cleveland.

Second, these jobs were not in the peripheral or service areas of the economy to which the black had been traditionally confined; instead they were in the mainstream industrial life of the North, for no longer were masses of white immigrants blocking the way. Accordingly, by 1930 manufacturing became the second most important source of employment for blacks; only domestic and personal service exceeded it – no longer by a vast margin but only by about 13 percent. Approximately 43 percent worked in domestic service – a sharp decline from earlier decades and 31 percent worked in manufacturing – a marked increase from earlier decades.

Within the manufacturing sector, greatest gains in employment were made in the iron and steel industry.

"Among the first to feel the need for laborers, steel factories sent agents to recruit Negro workers in the South not only during the Great War, but also during the recrudescence of business in 1923. As a result, thousands of Negroes were drawn into these factories, and the number of Negroes, negligible in such plants in 1910, increased unexpectedly in some instances from 30 to 150 percent." (Greene and Woodson 1970:249)

In Pittsburgh alone, steel workers "increased from less than 100 in five plants in 1910 to 16,900 in 23 plants in 1923—21 percent of all steel workers in the district" (Johnson 1928:131).

Almost as remarkable was the growth of blacks in the automobile industry. "In 1914, there was less than 1,000 Negroes in all the automobile factories of Detroit" (Greene and Woodson 1970:257). Within four years "the number of Negroes in the plants had increased to between 12,000 and 15,000. According to an authority, writing in 1920, there were 25,800 Negro workers in automobile factories distributed throughout the automobile centers of the country" (Greene and Woodson 1970:257–58). Other industries that experienced marked increases in black employment were meat packing, shipbuilding, railroad and car shops, and the manufacture of chemical and allied products.

Within these industries blacks were almost exclusively confined to the most menial and unskilled jobs and had to perform work "which was dirty, unpleasant or backbreaking" (Northrup and Rowan 1970:4). Accordingly, they were more likely to be employed in certain branches of these industries than in others. In the steel industry, for example, they were much more heavily concentrated in the blast furnace division than in rolling mills or steel works. "It is not surprising that the Negro was highly represented in the blast furnace area of the industry. This part of the industry contains a great deal of the hot, dirty, heavy work that Negroes were thought to be eminently qualified to perform" (Northrup and Rowan 1970:260). In the automobile industry the blacks were primarily concentrated in the foundries. "In many large plants the foundry is known as a 'black department.' In general, foundry occupations are the most undesirable in the industry ... hot, dirty, and demand exceptional strength. The accident rate is higher in the foundry than any other department" (Northrup and Rowan 1970:52)

In addition, blacks were also employed disproportionately as sanders and sprayers in the paint department; "again these were (and are) undesirable jobs, arduous and unpleasant. And, of course, Negroes were widely used as janitors, porters, laborers, cafeteria bus boys, etc" (Northrup and Rowan 1970:52). Within the rubber industry prior to World War II, blacks "were almost always confined to janitorial and laboring jobs, and in the hot, dirty work in the then nonmechanized compounding room, which in some plants was known as the 'Black Department'" (Northrup and Rowan 1970:402).

In general then the black became an important part of the labor supply for unskilled jobs in a number of industries in the North. Johnson reported in 1928 that blacks provided nationally "21 percent of the building laborers, 24 percent of the chemical laborers, 60 percent of the tobacco workers, 14 percent of the iron and steel laborers, 89.5 percent of the turpentine laborers, 39 percent of the saw and planing mill unskilled hands, 16 percent of the blast furnace and rolling mill unskilled hands" (Johnson 1928:132).

However, even in the market for manual labor, the blacks retained their separate and unequal status. Their needs for jobs and security were filled only after those of the white workers; they were the last hired and the first fired. Blacks served as a fluid industrial reserve that was figuratively appended to the larger labor market and could be tapped as the fortunes of white employers and workers varied. As a result, the employment of blacks was extremely sensitive to the fluctuations of the business cycle. They benefited greatly by the industrial expansion of World War I and its aftermath. According to Ross, the 1920s "represented a high point of prosperity for the Negro in the Northern cities. Most Negroes were working and unemployment was no higher than among whites" (Ross 1967:14). However, the 1930s dealt a devastating blow to any occupational gains the blacks had made. "The burden of the Depression fell heaviest upon Negroes because they were located at the bottom of the occupational pyramid, because they were concentrated in industries sensitive to the business cycle, and because they were subject to sharper discrimination in a period of job scarcity" (Ross 1967:14–15).

Once again blacks suffered displacement from their jobs; this time the displacement was from unemployed whites and not from first-generation immigrants as in the nineteenth century. Ross comments that "displacement was concentrated in the traditional Negro jobs – waiters, porters, housemaids, elevator operators, railroad laborers, etc. In industries such as steel, automobiles, meat-packing, and coal mining, temporary layoffs and work staggering were more customary than outright discharge" (Ross 1967:15). As a result, the percentage of blacks employed in manufacturing in the North dropped to 18 percent by 1940.

Even the coming of World War II did not immediately benefit the black. The reserve of unemployed white workers was first tapped for employment in the booming defense and armament industries; only later through a combination of governmental pressure and an increasingly acute labor shortage were blacks able to enter in large numbers into the war economy. However, they "did gain substantially from the secondary expansion of consumer and service industries; they were in heavy demand for the less-skilled tasks in the construction of airports, military bases, arsenals, and other military projects; and they found many additional jobs in industries that had traditionally employed them, such as iron and steel, chemicals, sawmills, and meat-packing" (Ross 1967:16). By the end of the 1940s employment in manufacturing equalled once again its relative importance during the 1920s; three out of ten blacks in the North were so employed. This figure increased somewhat by 1960 (34 percent) and then dropped to 29 percent by 1970.

Entry into mainstream industry did not basically alter the fact that blacks were largely confined to a limited number of onerous jobs. They were locked out of a whole range of white collar and professional occupations; only a few were able to slip into skilled jobs. Accordingly, they could only compete for poor paying jobs and frequently had to work at an even lower rate of pay than the white worker. As such they were rarely able to move far from the poverty line. Frequently unemployed or underemployed, they experienced want and poverty directly during much of their life. Thus they became part of the hard core of the underclass of the poor in the city.

The apex of black employment, according to Ross, was reached during the Korean war; since then "retrogression rather than progress" has marked the black's course of employment (Ross 1967). Since the late 1950s his lot has been aggravated by the rapid growth of automation, which has eliminated many of the unskilled and marginal jobs traditionally filled by the black. As a result, increasing numbers of blacks have become expendable and relegated to the ranks of the permanently unemployed.

In effect the impact of the various technological and industrial changes of the past several decades has been to raise the specter of displacement once again for the blacks. This time, though, the displacement into the reserve army of the unemployed will come from machines, not from white men. In addition, these changes have sharpened the segmentation of the labor market. According to Peck and others,

"labor in the US may be moving into a dual economy. In the main economy, fairly stable employment with regular income rises guaranteeing higher living standards may continue to be available for those who remain in it. But in the marginal economy centered upon low-level service trades and occupations, employment is unstable, wages are low, and the standard of living is depressed."

(Peck 1968:215)

Conclusion

The history of the blacks in the northern industry has been that of a group that has faced fully the exploitative and coercive powers of the marketplace and of the employer. The terms and conditions of their work have been almost entirely determined by external forces against which they have been virtually powerless and unprotected. Whatever sensibilities an employer may have had about the human qualities and needs of his worker, these have rarely been brought into play in the employer's treatment of his black workers. Even outside the world of work, the black has been defined as an inferior and as less than a human being. Accordingly, the racial stigmata that the blacks bear in the society-at-large have intensified and reinforced the depersonalizing and alienating forces at work in the marketplace and have completed their transformation into dehumanized objects which can be treated with impunity and without human regard by the employer. Thus, the blacks have come close to fulfilling what Marx had forecast for the proletariat generally under capitalism: its conversion into an alienated and depersonalized commodity subject to ruthless exploitation by the capitalist.

What is more the blacks have had to face these exploitative forces virtually alone, without support from the white workers. In fact, their isolation has been compounded by the treatment of the white workers, who have sought to stunt the competitive threat of the black by blocking his entry into job markets defined by the whites as theirs. As a result where access has been gained – as in the case of steel, coal mining, or other industries – the blacks have frequently entered as strikebreakers or scabs during periods of industrial conflict. These episodes have further exacerbated tensions and strains between the workers. One of the ugliest confrontations between the two races was in East St Louis in 1919, where a riot erupted that culminated in the death of a number of blacks.

Perhaps the most widespread and sustained attempt by white workers to exclude and to isolate the black as a competitive threat have been in and through various crafts unions that formed part of the American Federation of Labor. Officially, the AFL proclaimed under the leadership of Gompers a policy of non-discrimination in 1890; persons were not to be excluded from membership because of race or color. However, this policy soon gave way to the principle of autonomy which reaffirmed the practice by local unions of excluding blacks from membership or of relegating them to segregated auxiliary locals which confirmed their inferior status. In effect, the crafts unions mirrored the discriminatory practices of the communities in which they functioned and effectively kept the blacks out of the market for craft jobs.

The blacks fared better in the United Mine Workers and in the industrial unions that were organized under the banner of the Congress of Industrial Organizations during the 1930s. But even here they were frequently confronted by discriminatory practices on the local level which effectively curbed their participation in unions as equals and reinforced their subordinated and segmented status in the marketplace.

THE IMMIGRANT ANALOGY AND THE NORTHERN MIGRATION OF BLACKS

To many social scientists the northward migration of blacks during and after World War I bore a striking resemblance to the earlier flow of white immigrants from Europe. Both groups of migrants were seen as unlettered and unskilled menials who crowded into urban ghettos and had to start at the bottom of the occupational ladder. In 1966, for example, Irving Kristol pursued this comparison in an article that he entitled "The Negro is Like the Immigrant Yesterday." A few years earlier Glazer and Moynihan had written, "These American (Negroes) of two centuries are as much immigrant as any European immigrant group, for the shift from the South to New York is as radical a change for the Negro as that faced by earlier immigrants" (Glazer and Moynihan 1963:26). This thesis continues in popularity among those scholars who have in the past several decades focused their attention on white ethnicity. It has been seriously challenged and discarded by other scholars who have concentrated during the same period on racial minorities. (We shall examine in Chapter 12 the alternative thesis that has gained popularity among the latter.)

According to the proponents of the immigrant analogy, both groups of migrants lived initially in poverty and followed a style of life that was alien to the larger society. Accordingly they elicited anger and resentment from members of the established society who deemed their behavior disruptive to the public, social, and moral orders. Kristol describes in vivid detail the parallel response of hostility both to the immigrant of yesterday and to the urban black of today and the massive discrimination both faced on the job and housing markets (Kristol 1966).

By concentrating on the existential situation at the time of entry, these analysts seem intent on making the point that the white immigrant was no better off than the black, or its converse that the black was no worse off than the white. To support their case, these writers have no difficulty in showing the extreme hardship and contempt the white immigrants had to bear upon their arrival in a new world where people like themselves were first making their way. However, to make a similar point about the blacks, these analysts have virtually had to divest the blacks of any past history in the North and to treat their northward migration as though it took place on a blank tablet. Obviously Glazer, Kristol, and the others are aware of an earlier presence of blacks in the North, but they dismiss this presence as irrelevant to their thesis because they claim the numbers were too few to make a difference.

Yet whether few or many, the fact of their presence poses a serious challenge to the thesis of similar starting points for black and white immigrants. As we have seen, the blacks were already a fixed underclass in the North at the time of the white immigrant's arrival, their status having been determined by the distinctive kind of duality imprinted in the North from colonial days on and legitimated by the Supreme Court prior to the Civil War and again later in the post-reconstruction period. The Irish immigrant of the pre-Civil War days quickly learned the nature and meaning of this duality and used it in his competitive struggle with the blacks for jobs and housing. He saw himself as superior to the black and accepted the premise that the black did not have the same rights as he in any of the realms of the People's Domain. In a similar fashion the post-reconstruction immigrant from Eastern and Southern Europe benefited from the re-legitimation of the duality both North and South by the Supreme Court.

Ironically even as the white immigrants were benefiting from the duality, they almost became its victims. This was particularly true of the immigrants from Southern and Eastern Europe. They were caught in the web of discrimination that was an expression of this duality. In addition, they faced a concerted effort on the part of scientific and political circles in the dominant society to attach the label of race to them – a stigma whose function was to clamp the duality as securely on them as it already was clamped on blacks and other nonwhites.

These efforts successfully barred the white immigrants from mainstream occupations and restricted their access to institutions of higher learning. But, the anti-immigrant forces failed to block their membership in the People's Domain. For, despite the scope of their opposition, these forces had to admit that the immigrants were white – albeit, according to them, an inferior subspecies of whites. And in being white, the immigrant's right of membership was protected by the law of 1790.* Further, by the second decade of the twentieth century the number of immigrants had increased sufficiently to make them a political force to be reckoned with in New York and in other large cities.

Even in the economic sphere, white immigrants, particularly those of East European Jewish extraction, were able to bypass the barriers. A number of East European Jews, for example, took advantage of America's expanding economy and became entrepreneurs in high-risk, low-capital business ventures, particularly in the garment industry. Their rapid rise from poverty to respectability has been trumpeted by the immigrant analogists as a model for all ethnic and racial groups. These observers have primarily attributed the success of the Jews to the strength of their inner communal and personal values and traits, and to the benign working of the American creed which provided the legal-normative support for the individual effort and achievement of the immigrant. These observers have failed, however, to give due weight to what Steinberg insists was crucial to their success: the set of urbanized occupational skills that they brought with them as part of their social and cultural baggage (Steinberg 1981). These skills, according to Steinberg, found a ready market in America's expanding economy. As a result, the East European

---

*Determined to remedy this "defect," the anti-immigrant forces shifted the battleground to immigration policy itself in the early decades of the twentieth century. If they could not keep the white immigrant from the People's Domain, then they were going to try and bar him from entering the country. Even on this front, though, these forces were not as successful as they were with the nonwhite Asians; but they still managed to saddle the "inferior" subspecies of whites with discriminatory immigration quotas.

Jew who decided to strike out on his own in the garment industry was able to tap a skilled labor supply which only he and his fellow ethnic entrepreneurs were in a position to exploit and to monopolize through the common language, the cultural and ethnic ties they shared. This gave him a competitive edge in the marketplace where he sold his product to customers who were primarily of the larger society and not of the impoverished ethnic group. In this manner, he gained access to the resources and wealth of the dominant society and began his rapid ascent on the ladder of success.

Only for a brief historical moment was the black in a comparable situation. Interestingly, this moment took place in the nineteenth and not in the twentieth century. For approximately four decades of that century, as we have seen, black entrepreneurs played an important role in the catering industry in Philadelphia and in New York City. They served a white elite that fashioned its tastes after the Southern plantation owner, and they exploited their fellow blacks as a skilled work force in the field of personal service. The brief moment came to an end by the last two decades of the century as the tastes of the white elite shifted toward the cuisine of the European aristocracy and as the white immigrant pushed the black service worker out of the fashionable into the secondrate hotels. As a result by the turn of the century blacks were once again experiencing a double marginality: marginal jobs in marginal establishments in the field of personal service.

The northward migration during and after World War I did indeed mark the opening of a new job market for blacks – without however, altering the basic outlines of the duality long imprinted on the North. In other words, blacks were finally allowed into the manufacturing sector but only in its most menial and unskilled jobs. What is more, whites at virtually all levels soon expressed concern at this influx and sought to breathe new life and vitality into the duality of the North. They solidified their virtually monopolistic control of the dual labor and housing markets with the general blessing, once again, of the courts.

As a result, blacks remained anchored to the lower reaches of the manufacturing and other sectors of the economy. And for decades they functioned as an industrial reserve à la Marx that in recent years has become increasingly expendable as the economy itself has undergone dramatic technological and organizational changes. Under the circumstances few blacks have been able to follow the path of upward mobility that Kristol and the other immigrant analogists predicted they would (Kristol 1966). These observers tend to interpret this as basically a failing of the blacks themselves. According to their way of thinking, if the blacks were to develop the necessary personal and communal resources – which some doubt they will – they should be able to overcome any obstacle and should eventually be able to make their way up the occupational and societal ladder as did the white immigrant. For these analysts insist that whatever differences in historical barriers the two groups may have had to face in their struggle upward, the differences are merely those of degree and not of kind. Both are, in their view, members of a society governed by the American creed which values individual achievement and effort over group prejudice.

It is readily evident that to sustain this thesis these observers have had to draw a sharp distinction between the North and the South. They are prepared to concede, for example, that the heritage of slavery and Jim Crowism so pervaded the South that the black was relegated to an inferior "caste" position from which he has only in recent years been able to escape. The North, however, according to these observers, followed a different path. While prejudice against the black may have been widespread as was prejudice against the white immigrant, neither form of prejudice received the sanction of statutory law, at least after the Civil War; it merely remained an expression of private and communal sentiment.

Only the American creed, they insist, has been embodied in the legal-normative framework of the North, much as it was the only creed to be embodied in the Constitution of the New Nation by the Founding Fathers. These analysts have in effect given the Myrdallian thesis a regional home. (It is interesting to note that even Myrdal himself was convinced that the North was committed to the American creed in a way in which the South was not.) In espousing this thesis these observers have failed, as did Myrdal, to read accurately and fully the historical record of America's mistreatment of its racial minorities and of the sanctification of this mistreatment in the supreme law of the land.

As we have so often repeated, duality was imprinted in the legal-normative fabric of the American society from its very beginnings and was not merely an aberration of one region. In time each region developed its own distinctive version of this duality. Each version in turn affected the life circumstances of blacks and of other nonwhite races in ways qualitatively different from those experienced by any white, including the non-Protestant immigrant. As a result, to say "today's black is like yesterday's immigrant" is to utter an interesting metaphor that has little historical relevance. Perhaps closer to the historical mark is a metaphor that can be articulated from Rex's observations (1973). Namely, the northernbound black is like the colonial immigrant of yesterday who left the colony to live in the metropolitan society which had its own colonial heritage. This will be examined further in Chapter 12.

Racial violence and riots

During the first two decades of the twentieth century, the basic instability in the relations between whites and blacks became increasingly evident. Whites in the

South had succeeded in imposing a repressive system of control on the blacks, but beneath the surface tranquility of law and order lurked coercion and violence, which the whites were prepared to use to maintain their control. They were particularly alerted to signs of restlessness and disaffection among the subordinated blacks and to any invasion of the personal and societal domains that the whites defined as rightfully theirs. Accordingly, the whites were prepared to deal harshly with violations of what Grimshaw calls the "accommodative relationship of superordination-subordination" (Grimshaw 1969:7) and of the code of white supremacy.

The most visible and graphic symbol of this exercise of naked power and control was lynching. During the post-reconstruction period lynching mounted steadily and peaked during the 1890s; however, the numbers remained substantial for the next several decades. From 1889 to 1918 an estimated 2400 blacks were lynched in the South; another 115 in the rest of the country. Georgia and Mississippi led the nation with 360 and 350 respectively; Louisiana, Texas, and Alabama followed with 264, 263, and 244 respectively.

The most frequent incidents to provoke violence were a rumored or real murder of a white or a rumored or real rape of a white woman. Typically the incident merely brought to a head the strain and tension that had been building between black and white, as whites became more edgy and angry at signs of discontent among blacks with the accommodative relationship and at signs of the blacks' breaching the boundaries of their subordination. As such, "lynchings [frequently] focused the hostilities of a mob, often of riot proportions, in a single human object, who became a symbol, an actor in a violent racial drama" (Mitchell 1970:31–2). Not infrequently the hatred and violence generated among the whites in and through the act of lynching flowed over the scene of the lynching into the areas of residence, play, and work of the blacks. A number would be beaten, maimed, and some even killed; their homes pillaged and burned as the mob action of the whites spread terror and destruction. More frequently the lynching would remain an isolated instance of mob action which would soon dissipate but the memory of which would serve to intimidate the blacks for a long time after. On other occasions, mass violence of the whites exploded without an initial lynching but with a prior build-up of tension, not infrequently the product of manipulation and agitation by segments of the white population.

One such eruption occurred in Atlanta in 1906. Before the outbreak the white newspapers had been competing with each other for weeks in leveling sensational charges of a crime wave engulfing the city. One paper in particular printed graphic accounts of white women being assaulted by black men (few of these charges were ever actually substantiated). This inflammatory campaign precipitated several days of violence in which whites ravaged the city, bludgeoned and shot blacks, at least a dozen of whom were killed.

Another even more violent outbreak had taken place in Wilmington, North Carolina, in 1898. Whites under the leadership of the Democratic party were determined to rid the community of any vestiges of a black presence in the political system. Accordingly they conducted a particularly inflammatory political campaign in which they proclaimed the sanctity of white womanhood, and death to the black violators of its virtue. They also organized a vigilante committee to intimidate the black and succeeded thereby in winning a decisive victory at the polls. Two days later a mob of white citizens burned down a black newspaper, and launched a general reign of terror among the blacks. Many were slain; estimates ranged from 20 to over 100. Once again blacks were unable to resist the inexorable wave of white violence.

The one-sided character of these violent episodes approximated what Myrdal calls "terrorization or massacre." He further identified them as "magnified, or mass lynching" (Myrdal 1944:566). Waskow accepts Myrdal's designation of "mass lynchings" and argues that these events were "analogous to the East European 'pogrom'" (Waskow 1967:9). Accordingly he adopts the term "pogrom" for characterizing such one-sided occurrences. Grimshaw, however, places a broader regional label on such eruptions; he calls them "southern-style" race riots. According to him, there are three distinguishing characteristics to these riots.

First, the precipitating incident involves a violation of the "sacred" code of white supremacy, a basic tenet of which is "protection of white Southern womanhood" (Grimshaw 1969:107). The classic instance of this is the charge of rape of a white woman by a black man. "A second characteristic of Southern riots is a pattern of non-resistance on the part of the minority population" (Grimshaw 1969:107), or at most only minimal and ineffectual efforts at self-defense. The third characteristic is the "re-establishment of earlier accommodative patterns with the white community firmly in a superordinate position" (Grimshaw 1969:113). Thus, whatever are the real or imagined incursions of the black into the domains of the whites, they are repelled through violence and the subordinated status is reaffirmed, with the black at least for the time being cowed into submission.

> "This pattern – a gradual build-up of tension through assault, however moderate, on the *status quo*, followed by a real or imagined incident in which the very tenets of white supremacy were questioned and sharp reprisals in force against the Negro populace culminated in re-assertion of white dominance – occurred in all major color violence in the American South in the nineteenth and early twentieth centuries."
>
> (Grimshaw 1969:113)

The post-World War I period witnessed the outbreak of a number of these riots in the South. The outbreak in Tulsa, Oklahoma in 1921 was perhaps the worst; in fact Grimshaw singles it out as a classic example of the southern-style riot. Others included Charleston, South Carolina (1919), Longview, Texas (1919), and Knoxville, Tennessee (1919).

Such one-sided encounters, however, have not been confined to the South. The North has also had its share of them. In fact from the colonial period until the second decade of the twentieth century, most racial outbreaks in the North bore a striking resemblance to Grimshaw's southern-style riot and Waskow's pogrom. For example, Joel Headley (1970) describes in vivid detail the lynching fever that gripped a white mob in New York City in 1741 and resulted in the burning and hanging of hundreds of blacks. The Philadelphia riots of the 1830s and the Cincinnati riot of 1841 also had the one-sided character. Waskow identifies the New York draft riots of 1863 as an "almost pure example of a 'pogrom'" (Waskow 1967:9). At the turn of the century (1908) the riot in Springfield, Illinois represents an equally pure example of the southern-style riot. An alleged rape of a white woman triggered a violent mob reaction which spilled over into a carnage of black life and property. Waskow also identifies the Omaha, Nebraska outburst of 1919 as a pogrom. The precipitating event was once again the alleged rape of a white woman by a black man, and the result was mob action against the black population.

Thus the North was not immune to the same forces that operated in the South to keep the black in line and to prevent him from real or imagined incursions into the domains of the white man. Particularly in such border cities as Springfield and Cincinnati, many whites, a number of whom had migrated from the South, accepted the full panoply of the code of white supremacy; elsewhere in the North whites were less immersed in the code's full ideological embellishments and not as inclined to sanctify it in its entirety. They were nevertheless convinced that blacks were not the equals of whites and were therefore not entitled to the same kind of access to place and position.

However, unlike the white Southerners who had developed a dependence upon the black that went back centuries, the white Northerners were not readily reconciled to his actual presence in their communities. In some localities as in the Northwest, his was a relatively new presence. In others, as in New York and Philadelphia, he had been around a long time though in relatively small numbers. But irrespective of the area he was defined a "troublesome presence" by many whites and any increase in his numbers constituted a cause for alarm. It was as though the blacks had been grafted onto the community as an alien unintegrated pariah group, and they remained in that status no matter how long they were in the community. Whites, even the immigrant who arrived later in these communities than the black, were inclined to treat blacks as perennial newcomers and transients who had no real or permanent claim or stake in the community and its resources. As a result, virtually every white group, no matter how recent their own arrival in the community, felt that they had superior claims to position and space than the black. In some instances, this meant that they were prepared to push the black out of space and position that the black had already occupied, as in the case of New York and other cities of the Northeast. In other cases, the whites were prepared to resist any real or imagined incursion by the black into territories and positions that the whites considered their own.

Underlying the various eruptions in the North was therefore a prior history of tension between blacks and whites. Not infrequently the strain was generated from a competitive struggle for jobs which both reflected and expressed the alienation and inequality between white and black. Hofstadter and Wallace describe the background of the New York City draft riots of 1863:

> "Racial and economic tensions had been closely linked since the 1840s. Before then, Negroes had virtually controlled some occupations: longshoremen, hod carriers, brick makers, barbers, waiters, and domestic servants. The Irish influx, particularly after 1846, led to a sharp struggle between the blacks and the newcomers, which the Irish won. Many blacks could find no employment but strike breaking, which often led, particularly on the docks, to violence. Existing animosities were made more severe by the Emancipation Proclamation. Anti-war Democrats told white workers that the freed slaves would all come north and take their jobs."   (Hofstadter and Wallace 1970:211)

In Omaha, racial tensions had been exacerbated by the confrontation between white unions and black laborers. "White trade-union leaders were bitter about the recent use of Negroes to break strikes by meat packers and teamsters; and although the local NAACP had urged Negroes to support union labor, the workingmen's bitterness was often directed at the Negroes as well as at their employers" (Waskow 1967:110).

Once violence erupted during this period, there was little the black in the North could do but to seek refuge and to escape the carnage. He may have been even more disposed than his southern peers to fight back and to resist. But he was too few in numbers to do so effectively. He was extremely vulnerable, individually and collectively, to the attacks of marauding whites as he traveled on buses and streetcars through white areas on his way to and from work. He could not even find protection in his own residential enclaves, let alone mobilize his fellow blacks for effective defense; for his areas of residence did not have the population concentrations and territorial size that might have dissuaded intruders. Accordingly, there was nothing to discourage the violent onslaughts of white mobs on his neighborhoods.

The mass migrations of blacks during and after World War I dramatically altered the numerical balance in northern cities and expanded markedly the points of contact and potential conflict between blacks and whites. Coupled with the generally unsettling effects the war itself had on race relations, these population changes aggravated racial tension in many areas and produced violent confrontations in some. Particularly violent was the year 1919 when an estimated twenty-five riots broke out throughout the country; they erupted in such widely separated places as Washington, DC, Knoxville, Tennessee, Omaha, Nebraska, and Elaine, Arkansas.

Several of these outbreaks signaled a significant departure from the historical pattern of one-sided pogroms: the blacks did not passively submit; they fought back. Evidence of this response was already apparent in the East St Louis Riot of 1917; it manifested itself even more clearly in the Washington, DC riot of 1919 as blacks sought to mount a defense of their neighborhoods and even to engage in lightning sorties into white areas. However, the outbreak which Grimshaw and Waskow agree most closely approximated a two-sided riot during this period took place in Chicago in 1919.

Prior to the outbreak, racial tension had been growing steadily as increasing numbers of blacks poured into Chicago. They pressed steadily against the geographical boundaries that had confined them to established black slums. In some areas as in the North and South sides of Chicago, blacks and whites had accommodated to each other and developed what the Chicago Commission on Race Relations called "adjusted neighborhoods." Most other bordering neighborhoods, however, were "non-adjusted" as whites sought to resist the entry of blacks or to dislodge those already there.

Tensions had grown markedly in the contested neighborhoods before the riot; bombings of black homes had become a regular occurrence; in fact twenty-four such bombings had taken place during the three-week period before the riot. Tension and hostility also spilled over into parks, playgrounds, and other public recreational facilities where the more typical response had been separation and mutual avoidance.

Further, the mass influx of blacks into industrial and manufacturing firms at the lowest level of jobs brought blacks increasingly into work environments in which whites predominated. The Commission report claimed that in many of these environments relations between the two races were relatively amicable. In addition the report emphasized that the competitive struggle for jobs between the two was not intense, for "the demand for labor was such that there were plenty of jobs to absorb all the white and Negro workers available. This condition continued even after the end of the war and demobilization" (The Chicago Commission on Race Relations 1922:2–3).

However, even the Commission report recognized that periods of industrial conflict strained and exacerbated relations between black and white worker. For management took advantage of the exclusionary and discriminatory practices used by white unions against blacks and hired them to break strikes such as those that took place in the stockyards in 1904 and 1916. The practice was especially in vogue during 1919 – a year of general labor unrest and strikes in the Chicago area as well as in the rest of the country. As a result, relations between black and white workers were further corroded and were enveloped in an atmosphere of mutual suspicion and distrust by the time of the riot.

The riot itself was precipitated by an incident along a boundary that had been tacitly set previously by blacks and whites in order to allow each exclusive use of a section on a public beach. Several blacks allegedly violated the boundary on July 27; this led to a stone-throwing fracas between the races. A young black boy who had been innocently swimming nearby was caught in the middle and drowned. Rumor had it that he was killed by stones thrown by a white man (the coroner's jury ruled later that he had died from fright, his body revealing no evidence of being struck by a stone). This led to a confrontation with a white police officer who refused to arrest a white man whom several blacks had identified as the one who had killed the boy. As a result, according to the Commission report, "the Negroes in the crowd began to mass dangerously. At this crucial point the accused policeman arrested a Negro on a white man's complaint. Negroes mobbed the white officer, and the riot was under way" (The Chicago Commission on Race Relations 1922:4).

A week of active rioting was followed by six days of returning to normalcy. According to the Commission, "in the seven days, rioting was not continuous but intermittent, being furious for hours, then fairly quiescent for hours. The first three days saw the most acute disturbance" (The Chicago Commission on Race Relations 1922:7–8).

The Commission further reported that "the main areas of violence were thoroughfares and natural highways between the job and the home" (The Chicago Commission on Race Relations 1922:9). Particularly vulnerable were blacks, most of whom had to travel through white areas to work. A number of those killed and beaten were trapped in streetcars. Several whites were also killed as they made their usual trek to work through black areas. Further, isolated families living in areas predominantly occupied by the opposite race were targets of violence, not generally by their immediate neighbors but by strangers organized to commit mayhem.

Particularly unsettling were the "automobile raids carried on by young [white] men crowded in cars, speeding across the deadline at Wentworth Avenue and the 'Black Belt,' and firing at random. Crowded colored districts, with people sitting on front steps and in open windows, were subjected to this menace. Strangely enough, only one person was killed in these raids, Henry Baker, Negro" (The Chicago Commission on Race Relations 1922:18).

A major form of retaliation by blacks was sniping from windows at the raiding automobiles. In general their response was of a defensive nature; on occasion blacks sallied into white areas, but rarely in the organized mob-like fashion of the whites, who were frequently led by members of gangs and "athletic clubs." The final toll of the riots was 38 dead, of whom 23 were black and 15 white. Approximately 500 more were injured, two-thirds of whom were black, and over 1000 were left homeless and destitute.

To Grimshaw the Chicago riot represented more than just a two-sided affair; it also represented a significant change in the conditions and terms of an overt conflict between black and white (Grimshaw 1969). Unlike the southern-style riot, protection of "sacred values" was not the focal preoccupation of whites. They were not primarily goaded into action because a white woman had allegedly been raped or because the sanctity of white supremacy had been challenged. Instead the whites were driven into the streets to protect what they deemed were their vital secular interests. The blacks were seen as threatening to invade and to take over their neighborhoods, parks, and jobs. Thus the whites were convinced that they were merely standing guard and warding off unwarranted invasions of their respective domains. These whites, however, shared with the whites of the southern-style riot the following basic premise: blacks were not entitled to the same kind of access and treatment as were whites. Their claims were deemed of lesser account.

In turn, blacks were much less prepared to accept the white man's premise in the Chicago riot than they were under conditions of the southern-style riot. Even the black fresh from the South and its Jim Crow regulations was soon prepared to stand up for his private rights on streetcars and elsewhere and to respond to appeals by local politicians. However, this did not basically alter the firm grip that whites had on space, position, and power in Chicago, but it did rub raw relations with the whites in contiguous areas. Consequently in time the whites, as in the case of the southern-style riots, forcibly asserted their claims, though they may not have actually initiated the riot, and sought to push the blacks out of their domains through mass action; but unlike the southern-style riot they were not able to run roughshod over the blacks, for the blacks fought back.

Finally, the Chicago riot did not cow the black into submission. Unlike the southern-style riot the status quo ante was not restored at the end of the riot, and blacks did not entirely retreat behind the boundaries of earlier accommodative arrangements in "peaceful and passive" submission. Instead, according to Grimshaw, the Chicago riot "was followed by other disturbances of lesser magnitude, and Chicago has continued to be characterized by social tensions between the two racial groups and by continued assaults by Negroes upon the accommodative structure. Minor violence continued to occur in Chicago through the forties and fifties following the Second World War, and only major changes in the policing of the city prevented the occurrence of a major interracial disaster." (Grimshaw 1969:114)

In this manner Grimshaw lists the major differences between the Chicago riot and the southern-style riot. These differences demonstrate to Grimshaw that the Chicago episode represented a different kind of riot phenomenon. It is to him "an almost 'ideal-typical'" example of what he calls the "Northern-style riot." Elements of this kind of riot had already been evident in the East St Louis riot of 1917, but it received its fullest expression in Chicago and then almost a quarter of a century later in the Detroit riot of 1943. In the latter riot more than in the one in Chicago, the focal clash in secular interests between the two groups was over jobs; however, Rudwick places special emphasis on the competitive struggle over jobs in all three cities.

"In all three cities, unskilled whites manifested tension after they considered their jobs threatened by Negroes. There was also concern because migrants had overburdened the housing and transportation facilities. Everywhere, efforts of Negroes to improve their status were defined as arrogant assaults, and whites insisted on retaining competitive advantages enjoyed before the Negro migration.

Economic conflict was inevitable because the industrial corporations had employed Negroes not only to supplement white labor but also to crush strikes and destroy unions. Negroes had helped to break the 1904 and 1916 strikes in the Chicago stockyards, and a generation later near Detroit, a strike erupted at the Ford River Rouge plant where Negro and white workers were 'pitted against each other.' However, nowhere was the relationship between labor strife and race rioting more clearly and directly evident than in East St. Louis. The July violence occurred shortly after the Aluminum Ore Company workers lost a strike that began when union sympathizers were replaced by Negroes."

(Rudwick 1964:218)

Although Grimshaw's northern-style riots were primarily confined to the North from World War I through the 1940s, several violent encounters that erupted in the South during the period included significant features that resembled the northern riots. One of the more notable took place in Elaine, Arkansas in 1919. The precipitating incident was a violent attempt by whites to disrupt efforts of black sharecroppers to organize a union for protection of their economic interests.

This led to several days of violence in which blacks actively sought to protect their lives and property. The blacks were finally no match for the whites; many more blacks than whites were killed and wounded. The Washington, DC riot of 1919, as we have already mentioned, also witnessed an active defense by the blacks; in addition, underlying the conflict was a clash between the economic interests of blacks and whites. Thus, even in the South following World War I, violent confrontations between blacks and whites were less and less the one-sided pogroms of earlier years.

8

THE SECOND
PERIOD OF RECONSTRUCTION
AND THE LAW

Introduction

Following the first period of reconstruction, blacks had to struggle for more than fifty years in an institutional and legal-normative environment, particularly in the South, that reaffirmed the racial creed and the inequalities of a plural society and that severely restricted their access to and enjoyment of the rights and immunities of the American creed and of the People's Domain. Now and then, early in this period, isolated governmental actions kept alive hope for expansion of the American creed. This was particularly true of several Supreme Court decisions that limited the extent to which whites could obliterate the legal and political rights of the blacks under the Fourteenth and Fifteenth Amendments. Specifically, basic rights of blacks to a fair trial were sustained, and grandfather clauses that furthered the disfranchisement of blacks were declared unconstitutional.

However, not until the 1940s was the incidence of governmental action enough to make any dent on the pattern of racial segmentation and discrimination. Here again the Supreme Court led the way with its rulings on white primaries, residential covenants, and the like. Also significant was the entry of the executive branch of the federal government into the arena. Roosevelt took the first step by setting up the wartime Fair Employment Practices Committee (FEPC) and by introducing a nondiscriminatory clause in government contracts. Truman expanded the role of the federal government further with his executive order establishing The President's Committee on Civil Rights and with his subsequent order integrating the military establishment. Even Congress made several attempts to pass anti-lynching and other civil rights legislation, but these foundered against the resistance of the still powerful southern legislators.

Significant as some of these governmental measures proved to be, they were still of a piecemeal nature. They failed to shake the basic foundations of the plural society or to reverse in any significant manner the tide of racial inequality and discrimination. The turning point came with the Supreme Court decision on school desegregation in 1954. That decision marked the beginning of a general delegitimation of the racial creed as part of the supreme law of the land and ushered in the second period of reconstruction. For the next fifteen years America witnessed a general attempt by the various branches of government to dismantle the institutional and legal-normative underpinnings of a racially segmented plural society and to reaffirm the original intention of the reconstruction amendments for full membership and equality of blacks in the People's Domain. The significance and meaning of this transformation of governmental policy and action will be described in this chapter and in Chapter 9.

The Supreme Court and the delegitimation of racial segmentation and the racial creed

THE REAFFIRMATION AND EXTENSION OF RIGHTS IN THE LEGAL-POLITICAL REALM

Even as the Supreme Court in the late nineteenth century was making its landmark decisions which legitimated the racial segmentation of the social realm, it revealed its intention to preserve some of the rights and immunities of the blacks in the legal-political realms that were manifestly protected by the reconstruction amendments.

Jury service and discrimination

One of the areas of special concern was the exclusion of blacks from jury selection and panels. As early as 1880 the Supreme Court overturned a West Virginia statute in Strauder v. West Virginia which explicitly excluded blacks from jury service. In his opinion, Justice Strong applied the criteria from the Slaughter House Cases which stipulated that discriminatory actions by the state were forbidden by the Fourteenth Amendment.

"Is not protection of life and liberty against race or color prejudice a right, a legal right, under the constitutional amendment? And how can it be maintained that compelling a colored man to submit to a trial for his life by a jury drawn from a panel from which the State has expressly excluded every man of his race,

because of color alone, however well qualified in other respects, is not a denial
to him of equal legal protection?"   (100 US 1880:309)

In view of this state action, he insisted, the black defendant had been denied his
constitutional rights.

> "The Fourteenth Amendment makes no attempt to enumerate the rights it is
> designed to protect. It speaks in general terms, and those are as comprehensive
> as possible. Its language is prohibitory; but every prohibition implies the
> existence of rights and immunities, prominent among which is an immunity
> from inequality of legal protection, either for life, liberty, or property. Any
> State action that denies this immunity to a colored man is in conflict with the
> Constitution."   (100 US 1880:310)

However, in another case decided the same day, Virginia v. Rives, the Court
revealed its intention of keeping the implications of the Strauder decision within
narrow bounds. The Court ruled that where a state does not have exclusionary
statutes on its books as in the case of Virginia, the mere absence of blacks from
juries was not to be treated as prima-facie evidence of discriminatory state action.
Instead, the burden of proving that such action was discriminatory rested with the
defendant. Further, the Court decided that in the absence of exclusionary statutes,
the black defendant had to exhaust remedies in the state courts before he could
turn to federal courts. The Court, however, did accept the argument that behavior
bearing on jury selection by a state official represents action by the state and not
merely that of a private individual.

The Supreme Court followed this narrow interpretation for the next fifty years.
As a result, all-white juries flourished throughout the South, for the burden of
proving the practice as discriminatory state action, in the absence of an explicit
statute, proved almost impossible. Not until the Scottsboro cases in the early
1930s did the Court liberalize its construction and accept proof of longstanding
exclusion from jury service as prima-facie evidence of discriminatory state action
against blacks.

In his opinion in the case of Norris v. Alabama, Chief Justice Hughes stated:

> "We think that the evidence that for a generation or longer no negro had been
> called for service on any jury in Jackson County, that there were negroes
> qualified for jury service, that according to the practice of the jury commission
> their names would normally appear on the preliminary list of male citizens of
> the requisite age but that no names of negroes were placed on the jury roll, and
> the testimony with respect to the lack of appropriate consideration of the
> qualifications of negroes, established the discrimination which the Constitution
> forbids. The motion to quash the indictment upon that ground should have
> been granted."   (294 US 1935:596)

By 1940 the Supreme Court elaborated still further the grounds upon which it would find discriminatory action by the state. Merely professing lack of discriminatory intent was no longer sufficient justification by jury commissioners for their exclusion of blacks from service. They would also be held accountable if they merely limited their panels to persons they knew. Thus, in Smith v. Texas, the Court ruled that commissioners could not exclude blacks merely because they had no personal acquaintanceship with any. As Justice Black said in his opinion for the Court:

"Where jury commissioners limit those from whom grand juries are selected to their own personal acquaintance, discrimination can arise from commissioners who know no negroes as well as from commissioners who know but eliminate them. If there has been discrimination, whether accomplished ingeniously or ingenuously, the conviction cannot stand."   (311 US 1940:132)

The Court went further in Cassell v. Texas (1950). It instructed the jury commissioners to go beyond their circle of personal acquaintances and "to familiarize themselves fairly with the qualifications of the eligible jurors of the county without regard to race and color" (339 US 1950:289). Even judges were put under a similar constraint. They were not to exclude blacks from grand jury service because they were outside the range of people the judge knew or because community traditions demanded their exclusion (Eubanks v. Louisiana 1958).

Over the years, the Court was tending to shift the burden of proof from the defendant to the state once it could be established that blacks had not served on juries for a number of years. Under these circumstances, the state would have to demonstrate that the exclusion was *not* the result of discrimination; otherwise, the Court would rule in favor of the defendant. Justice Black alluded to this in his opinion for the court in Patton v. Mississippi:

"It is to be noted at once that the indisputable fact that no Negro had served on a criminal court grand or petit jury for a period of thirty years created a very strong showing that during that period Negroes were systematically excluded from jury service because of race. When such a showing was made, it became a duty of the State to try to justify such an exclusion as having been brought about for some reason other than racial discrimination. The Mississippi Supreme Court did not conclude, the State did not offer any evidence, and in fact did not make any claim, that its officials had abandoned their old jury selection practices."   (332 US 1947:466)

Failure of the state to explain this practice then became grounds for overturning the conviction.

"We hold that the State wholly failed to meet the very strong evidence of purposeful racial discrimination made out by the petitioner upon the uncontradicted showing that for thirty years or more no Negro had served as a juror in the criminal courts of Lauderdale County. When a jury selection plan, whatever it is, operates in such a way as always to result in the complete and long-continued exclusion of any representative at all from a large group of Negroes, or any other racial group, indictments and verdicts returned against them by juries thus selected cannot stand." (332 US 1947:468–69)

Despite these decisions, the Court remained wary about automatically equating racial exclusion with discrimination. As recently as 1965 it was still inclined to give the state the benefit of the doubt if it could show that such exclusion was not entirely the result of its efforts. Thus, we find that in McSwain v. Alabama the Court ruled on behalf of the prosecuting attorney who was able to show that the exclusion of Negroes was in part a result of the way the established peremptory challenge system worked; defense lawyers joined forces on occasion with the prosecuting attorney in striking blacks from jury service, despite their names being on the panel.

By the 1970s the Court was prepared to go somewhat beyond cases in which blacks were totally excluded and to deal with cases where blacks were significantly underrepresented on juries and panels according to the numbers who were eligible to serve in the population as a whole. However, the results have been mixed in such cases. The Court has not been able to develop a consistent rationale to guide its deliberations. Bell comments:

"While, as these cases indicate, judges are willing to rely on intuitive notions of probability in deciding whether the absence of blacks from the jury selection process can be attributed to racial discrimination, they are much more reluctant to apply more advanced mathematical techniques, which are necessary in jury cases where blacks are neither entirely excluded nor included on only a token basis. In these 'underrepresentation' cases, courts have not been able to articulate a rationale that defines what is meant by the oft stated notion that *some* blacks should have been chosen, when in fact some blacks *were* chosen." (Bell Jr 1973:966)

The early Court decisions were important in that they established limits, though feeble, to the complete erosion of the legal rights of blacks to service on juries and to being judged by their peers. Only in recent years has the Court added substance to these rights, but full parity with whites is still to be achieved, particularly in the South.

Voting discrimination and the white primary

After reconstruction, southern blacks were increasingly driven from the political arena so that by the turn of the twentieth century only a fraction of those who had voted twenty years earlier continued to do so. Southern whites accomplished this almost total disfranchisement without enacting laws which explicitly revoked black suffrage, for even they were aware that such laws would be overturned by the Supreme Court as contrary to the Fifteenth Amendment. Instead they resorted to indirection and adopted such devices as literacy tests and poll taxes (to say nothing of the extralegal means of coercion). One of the more ingenious devices was the grandfather clause which effectively neutralized any poor showing on literacy tests for whites but not for blacks.

In 1915 the Oklahoma version of this clause written as an amendment to the state constitution came under judicial review. The amendment ostensibly required a literacy test of all potential voters; they had to be able to read and write sections of the state constitution. However, the amendment went on to say: "But no person who was, on January 1, 1866, or at any time prior thereto, entitled to vote under any form of government, or who at that time resided in some foreign nation, and no lineal descendant of such person, shall be denied the right to register and vote because of his inability to so read and write sections of such constitution."

In Guinn and Beal v. United States, the Supreme Court acknowledged that the grandfather clause

"contains no express words of an exclusion from the standard which it establishes of any person on account of race, color, or previous condition of servitude prohibited by the Fifteenth Amendment.... [Despite this,] the standard itself inherently brings that result into existence since it is based purely upon a period of time before the enactment of the Fifteenth Amendment and makes that period the controlling and dominant test of the right of suffrage."

(238 US 1915:364–65)

Accordingly, the Court concluded that the grandfather clause violated the Fifteenth Amendment and was therefore unconstitutional. The Court did not, however, question the validity of the literacy test requirement, provided it applied to all citizens. Further, the Court went out of its way to emphasize that the state government still retained the basic power over suffrage, whatever limitation on this power might be imposed by the Fifteenth Amendment.

"(a) Beyond doubt the Amendment does not take away from the state governments in a general sense the power over suffrage which has belonged to those governments from the beginning and without the possession of which power the whole fabric upon which the division of state and national authority under the Constitution and the organization of both governments rest would be without support and both the authority of the nation and the State would fall to the ground. In fact, the very command of the Amendment recognizes the possession of the general power by the State, since the Amendment seeks to regulate its exercise as to the particular subject with which it deals."

(238 US 1915:362)

Oklahoma sought to bypass the decision by enacting a statute in 1916 that left out the objectionable clause but added a provision that retained its effect. The new clause stated that all those who voted in 1914 when the grandfather clause was still in operation would be permanently enfranchised; the rest were required to register within a twelve-day period or face permanent disfranchisement. The net result was relatively minimal black registration.

This more sophisticated version of the grandfather clause was allowed to stand until 1939 when it too was declared in violation of the Fifteenth Amendment (Lane v. Wilson). The other restrictive devices had even longer life. For example, poll taxes were not abandoned until enactment of the Twenty-fourth Amendment in 1964, and literacy tests were not significantly modified until passage of the Federal Voting Rights Act of 1965.

Although most devices for disfranchisement were already in place by the early twentieth century, the all-white primary was not added to the list until the early 1920s. According to Loren Miller, it then became the single most effective instrument used to prevent Negroes from playing a significant role in southern elections after the 1920s. "By rule or resolution, southern Democratic parties prohibited blacks from voting in their primary elections, in which local, state, and federal officials were nominated. Nomination was tantamount to election in the one-party South, and the exclusion of Negroes meant that they were disfranchised for all practical purposes" (Miller 1966:294).

What paved the way for the all-white primary was the Supreme Court ruling in Newberry v. United States (1921) that Congress did not have the constitutional authority to regulate primaries as it had to regulate congressional elections. Texas immediately seized the opportunity offered by this decision and enacted a statute in 1924 which restricted participation in primaries to whites only: "In no event shall a negro be eligible to participate in a Democratic party primary election held in the State of Texas" (273 US 1927:540).

In 1927 the Supreme Court ruled unanimously in Nixon v. Herndon that the statute was unconstitutional, not because it violated the Fifteenth Amendment but because it violated the Fourteenth Amendment, which explicitly forbade any state from overtly and explicitly acting in a racially discriminatory manner against the black. Texas lost no time in repealing the 1924 statute, and in passing another which circumvented the restriction on explicit state action by placing responsibility for devising membership qualifications in the hands of the State Executive Committee of each political party. In turn, the State Executive Committee of the Democratic Party adopted a resolution that only white Democrats could participate in its primaries.

Five years later in 1932 the Supreme Court ruled once again against Texas, this time by the narrowest of margins: 5 to 4. The Court maintained that the statute had made the Executive Committee a representative or agent of the state; as a result, the Committee's action in establishing racially discriminatory qualifications was tantamount to state action in a constitutionally forbidden area.

Undaunted, Texas again sought to circumvent the ruling of the Court. It moved to eliminate any manifest link between the state and the political party in the conduct of primaries by repealing any statutes on the matter. In turn, the Democratic party converted itself into a private voluntary association at its convention and proceeded to restrict categorically its membership to whites.

When this arrangement was challenged in Grovey v. Townsend in 1935, the Supreme Court

"unanimously accepted the constitutionality of this new loophole on the grounds that the *State of Texas was not involved*, that the private group referred to was not a 'creature of the state' but a *voluntary association* that had acted on its own. This appeared to settle the matter at issue, for 'private persons or groups cannot violate the Fourteenth Amendment,' since there was no state action *per se*."   (Abraham 1972:331)

In drawing this conclusion, the Court was merely applying the finding of its Newberry v. United States decision that primaries were of a different character than general elections. In 1941 the Court changed its mind. In United States v. Classic, a case involving fraud in a Louisiana primary, not the voting rights of blacks, the Court determined that "Section 4 of the Constitution's Article One in fact authorized Congress to regulate *primaries* as well as *elections* because 'primaries' in the words of the Constitution were tantamount to 'elections' and, being an integral part of the election machinery, were subject to Congressional regulations" (Abraham 1972:331). In assessing the significance of this ruling in his opinion on a later case, Justice Reed stated: "By this decision the doubt as to whether or not such primaries were part of 'elections' subject to federal control, which had remained unanswered since Newberry v. United States . . . was erased" (321 US 1944:660).

The Court decision in the Classic case had no immediate effect on the Texas primaries, but three years later in Smith v. Allwright (1944) the Court alluded to the case as having altered the basic premise upon which the decisions in the

Grovey v. Townsend case had been made. Then the primary was viewed as separate from a general election, but since the Classic case,

> "it may now be taken as a postulate that the right to vote in such a primary for the nomination of candidates without discrimination by the State, like the right to vote in a general election, is a right secured by the Constitution. By the terms of the Fifteenth Amendment that right may not be abridged by any State on account of race. Under our Constitution the great privilege of the ballot may not be denied a man by the State because of his color."   (321 US 1944:661–62)

Once having adopted this position, the Court was no longer prepared to treat the primaries as the private preserve of political parties nor to treat the political party as merely a voluntary association which had the invariable right to determine the qualifications for voting in a primary. The Court therefore ruled that the statutes that had set up the general procedures for the primary election had in effect made the political party "which is required to follow these legislative directions an agency of the State in so far as it determines the participants in a primary election. The party takes its character as a state agency from the duties imposed upon it by state statutes; the duties do not become matters of private law because they are performed by a political party" (321 US 1944:663).

In this manner the Court justified the application of the same test for discriminatory action by the state or its agencies in primaries as it had in general elections. Justice Reed emphasized this in his opinion:

> "When primaries become a part of the machinery for choosing officials, state and national, as they have here, the same tests to determine the character of discrimination or abridgement should be applied to the primary as are applied to the general election. If the State requires a certain electoral procedure, prescribes a general election ballot made up of party nominees so chosen and limits the choice of the electorate in general elections for state offices, practically speaking, to those whose names appear on such a ballot, it endorses, adopts and enforces the discrimination against Negroes, practiced by a party entrusted by Texas law with the determination of the qualifications of participants in the primary. This is state action within the meaning of the Fifteenth Amendment."
>
> (321 US 1944:664)

As a result, according to Justice Reed, a state cannot nullify the constitutional rights of citizens to participate in the election of officials without restriction because of race "through casting its electoral process in a form which permits a private organization to practice racial discrimination in the election. Constitutional rights would be of little value if they could be thus indirectly denied" (321 US 1944:664). Accordingly, the Court overruled its Grovey v. Townsend decision and declared the Texas primary law in violation of the Fifteenth Amendment.

Identifying what seemed to be a vulnerable link between law and the political party as agent of the state in the Allwright decision, South Carolina repealed all of its state laws and one constitutional provision dealing with the conduct of primaries. It hoped that this would eliminate the legal basis for considering the Democratic party an agent of the state and would thereby enable the party to hold primaries as a private undertaking of a voluntary association. This would in turn presumably allow the party to exclude blacks without violating the Fourteenth and Fifteenth Amendments. The plan was struck down in a federal circuit court; the judge observed that "no election machinery can be upheld if its purpose or effect is to deny to the Negro, on account of his race or color, any effective voice in the government of his country or the state or community wherein he lives" (Tresolini and Shapiro 1970:596). The Supreme Court refused to review the decision in Rice v. Elmore (1948).

By 1953 it became evident that the Supreme Court was determined to eliminate any effort by a state or its white citizens, no matter how longstanding or ingenious, to "privatize" any portion of the electoral process in order to exclude blacks. The issue was fully and finally joined in the test of the preprimary primary of the Jaybird Democratic Association of Fort Bend, Texas. The Association had been organized as a private voluntary association in 1889 with membership confined to whites. Prior to the regular primary of each general election, the Jaybird Association would have its own preprimary election which was confined to its white membership. Invariably, winners of the preprimary primary would go on to win the regular Democratic primary unopposed and subsequently the general election.

After the Smith v. Allwright decision of 1944, blacks were able to vote in both the regular primaries and general elections, but were still excluded from the preprimary primary. In 1953 in Terry v. Adams, the Supreme Court ruled that this exclusion was unconstitutional. In his opinion reporting the judgment for the Court, Justice Black extended the Allwright doctrine from the primary to the preprimary primary; both were viewed as integral parts of an electoral process that was protected by the Fifteenth Amendment:

"The only election that has counted in this Texas county for more than fifty years has been that held by the Jaybirds from which Negroes were excluded. The Democratic primary and the general election have become no more than the perfunctory ratifiers of the choice that has already been made in Jaybird elections from which Negroes have been excluded. It is immaterial that the state does not control that part of this elective process which it leaves for the Jaybirds to manage. The Jaybird primary has become an integral part, indeed the only effective part, of the elective process that determines who shall rule and govern in the county. The effect of the whole procedure, Jaybird primary plus Democratic primary plus general election, is to do precisely that which the Fifteenth Amendment fobids – strip Negroes of every vestige of influence in selecting the officials who control the local county matters that intimately touch the daily lives of citizens." (345 US 1953:469–70)

Black based his argument almost exclusively on the ground that the Fifteenth Amendment forbade racial discrimination in "any election in which public issues are decided or public officials selected." This is so "whether the voting on public issues and officials is conducted in community, state or nation. Size is not a standard" (345 US 1953:468–69).

Missing from his opinion is any significant reference to the "agency of the state" doctrine that figured so prominently in earlier court decisions. The action of the Association was unconstitutional, according to Black, because it introduced discrimination into the electoral process and not because the Association was acting either directly or indirectly as an agent of the state. In this way, Black erased the distinction in the electoral process between discrimination by a state and that by a private group; both were forbidden.

General overview of the Supreme Court and the legal-political realm

So we find that virtually as soon as white reaction against the reconstruction amendments began to grow and to flourish, particularly in the South, the Supreme Court was prepared to place limits on what whites could legally do to deprive the blacks of benefits from these amendments in the legal and political domains. But for years these limits were defined by the Court in a very narrow and literal fashion. They were viewed as being exceeded only if a state passed statutes which explicitly and directly violated the legal and political rights of the black, as in the case of Strauder v. West Virginia, or if a state approved legislation whose particular and discriminatory character was so immediately transparent that its racist purpose could not be disguised, despite claims of universal applicability, as in the case of the grandfather clauses.

Only in recent years has the Court been prepared to move more decisively into the thicket of actions by the state which have discriminatory consequences but no professed legislative intent to produce these consequences. For example, the Court's rulings on jury service over the past quarter of a century have increasingly eschewed manifest legislative intent and treated as prima-facie evidence of state discrimination any continuous history of exclusion or marked underrepresentation of the black. Further, the Court has expressed greater willingness to curb the power of the state in areas which were formerly deemed its sacrosanct bailiwick. Thus in its decisions in the white primary cases, the Court not only entered an area of state jurisdiction that it had always treated gingerly but also extended its rulings to include all elections and primaries and not merely those conducted for federal office. In Gomillion v. Lightfoot (1960) the Court even went so far as to overturn a state law that expressed the efforts of white citizens and officials to gerrymander blacks out of their city.

Even more significantly, the Court extended the scope of state responsibility for eliminating overt and covert discriminatory practices and policies within the legal and political domain. As early as 1880, the Court refused to confine its standard of state responsibility merely to explicit legislative enactments which were discriminatory in character. It also insisted that discriminatory actions of state officials were not to be treated as those of private individuals and citizens which are excluded from constitutional constraint, but were instead to be treated as behaviors of agents of the state and therefore subject to constitutional control.

Years later the Court expanded the concept of agent or agency of the state to include political parties and voluntary associations that had been charged with electoral responsibilities by the state. In this manner the Court effectively countered the efforts of various states to evade their constitutional responsibilities to blacks in the legal-political domain by transferring some of their functions and activities to the private realm and private organizations which are free of such constitutional constraints. In the process, the Court sharpened the distinction between private and state spheres of action while broadening the concept of state accountability.

Yet, despite the increased resolve of the Supreme Court during the 1940s, its decisions were of a patchwork nature and only of limited effect, particularly in the South. They pushed back the more extreme encroachments on the legal and political rights of the blacks, but left virtually untouched the underlying normative base that legitimized the unequal treatment of blacks and anchored them to an inferior and subordinated status. In other words, even as the Court was seeking to apply nondiscriminatory and universalistic standards in the legal-political domain, it still accepted racial segmentation as the "law of the land" in the other major institutional environments of the social realm. The Court could not treat decisively or even effectively with the massive and continuing flow of racial inequities in the legal-political domain as long as it was not prepared to root out their generating source in the social realm. Only as the Court began systematically to delegitimize racial segmentation and the racial creed in this realm during the 1950s was the stage set for a general assault on the institutionalized and normatively sanctioned racial inequalities and injustices in all the societal domains. We shall now turn to an examination of the process of delegitimization, which started slowly but then gained momentum in the 1950s and 1960s.

THE DESEGREGATION OF THE SOCIAL REALM

Having adopted in 1896 the doctrine of Plessy v. Ferguson as the "law of the land," the Supreme Court in effect provided whites, particularly in the South, with a legal-normative foundation and scaffolding for legitimizing their racial creed and for constructing a plural society in which races were to be kept apart in the various institutional environments of the social realm. And yet in promulgating this doctrine, the Supreme Court attached an important condition: the segmentation of the social realm must be based on equal availability of public resources and facilities to each race. For the next half a century, though, the whites in the South conveniently ignored the *equal* part of the "separate but equal" doctrine and concentrated all their energies on the *separation* of the races. Even the Supreme Court seemed more intent in the first several decades after the decision on reaffirming and amplifying the principle of racial separation; it paid little attention to the question of equal facilities. Only later did the question of equality become a significant concern for the Court, and not until the 1950s was it prepared to reexamine its basic position on the issue of separation itself. Nowhere is the history of the Court's metamorphosis on the "separate but equal" doctrine more dramatically revealed than in the sphere of education.

Education and the metamorphosis of the "separate but equal" doctrine

In articulating the "separate but equal" doctrine, the Supreme Court did not merely apply it to public transportation facilities, the contested setting of the Plessy-Ferguson case, but to virtually every institutional setting in the social realm, including education. In the early years the Court employed the standard mechanically, rarely if ever seeking to establish independently whether the segregated facilities were indeed equal. It tended to accept the state's version of the situation and to rubber stamp the lower court's holdings on the matter.

This is evident in Cummings v. Richmond Board of Education which arose three years after Plessy-Ferguson. The black plaintiffs had opposed the Board's conversion of the only black high school into several elementary schools for black children. They argued that their constitutional rights had been violated because the Board continued to operate a high school for white children. Accordingly, they asked for an injunction to close the white high school until equal facilities were available for black children. In turn, the Board argued that its action was not motivated by race prejudice nor was it intended to result in any overall reduction in funds for the education of black children; it merely involved, the Board said, a reallocation of resources because of the numbers of elementary-school children that had to be accommodated.

The Court unanimously rejected the plaintiffs' demand. In his opinion for the Court, Justice Harlan did not raise any question about the validity of the "separate but equal" doctrine despite the fact that he had written his classic dissent against it three years earlier. In addition, he avoided the issue of equal facilities as the plaintiffs had defined it (if there is a white high school there should also be a black one) or the issue as it might have been defined at the initial allocation of tax funds (did the black educational facilities as a whole receive an equal or fair share of tax funds collected for educational purposes?). Instead Justice Harlan merely took issue with the plaintiffs' request for an injunction; he did not see how the educational needs of black children would be served by depriving white children of theirs. He also dwelt at length on the reasons that the Board had offered for its action without once questioning their face validity.

> "It was impossible, the Board believed, to give educational facilities to the three hundred colored children who were unprovided for, if it maintained a separate school for the sixty children who wished to have a high school education. Its decision was in the interest of the greater number of colored children, leaving the smaller number to obtain a high school education in existing private institutions at an expense not beyond that incurred in the high school discontinued by the Board."   (175 US 1899:544)

In short, the Court was reluctant to question the judgment of the state in an area primarily under its jurisdiction.

> "We may add that while all admit that the benefits and burdens of public taxation must be shared by citizens without discrimination against any class on account of their race, the education of the people in schools maintained by state taxation is a matter belonging to the respective States, and any interference on the part of Federal authority with the management of such schools cannot be justified."   (175 US 1899:545)

Justice Harlan then went on to mention one exception to this rule: if and only if there is a "clear and unmistakable disregard of rights secured by the supreme law of the land," can federal authority intervene (175 US 1899:545).

Justice Harlan insisted that this case did not involve such an exception. In coming to this conclusion, he relied heavily on what the state courts had said.

"The state court did not deem the action of the Board of Education in suspending temporarily and for economic reasons the high school for colored children a sufficient reason why the defendant should be restrained by injunction from maintaining an existing high school for white children. It rejected the suggestion that the Board proceeded in bad faith or had abused the discretion with which it was invested by the statute under which it proceeded or had acted in hostility to the colored race." (175 US 1899:545)

In this manner the Court virtually renounced any kind of active or independent role for itself in overseeing the application of the "separate but equal" doctrine to public educational facilities. It gave the states almost free rein to do what they wished provided the state courts were prepared to certify, which they almost invariably were, that the state actions did not violate the constitutional rights of the blacks. As a result, southern states received virtually a blank check to pursue their Jim Crow policies with little concern or regard for the question of equal facilities.

By 1908 the Supreme Court even went so far as to allow the state to extend its reach into private educational institutions and to impose segregation upon an institution even against the latter's wishes and policy. In Berea v. Kentucky the Supreme Court affirmed Kentucky's right to forbid Berea College from pursuing its policy of teaching black and white children in integrated classrooms. It based its finding on the premise that the college, like other private educational institutions, was a corporate creature of the state and therefore subject to its control. Such control, the Court contended, was not in violation of the college's grant if it merely required that students from different races were to be taught at different times.

Justice Harlan took strong exception to the ruling. In a bitter dissent, reminiscent of the one he had registered on the Plessy-Ferguson decision, he argued that the state had violated the Constitution by invading the realm of private action and behavior which had been deemed sacrosanct by the Founding Fathers: "Have we become so inoculated with prejudice of race that an American government, professedly based on the principles of freedom, and charged with the protection of all citizens alike, can make distinctions between such citizens in the matter of their voluntary meeting for innocent purposes simply because of their respective races?" He continued with a blistering attack on racial policies of which the logical outcome would be a legally imposed plural society whose institutional environments would be racially segmented:

"Further, if the lower court be right, then a State may make it a crime for white and colored persons to frequent the same market places at the same time, or appear in an assemblage of citizens convened to consider questions of a public or political nature in which all citizens, without regard to race, are equally interested. Many other illustrations might be given to show the mischievous, not to say cruel, character of the statute in question and how inconsistent such legislation is with the great principle of the equality of citizens before the law."

(211 US 1908:69)

In the final analysis, however, Justice Harlan was not protesting against the segregation of public schools, only private schools.

Within the guidelines set by the Supreme Court, southern states pursued their policies of segregation in public and private schools, paying little attention to the issue of equality of facilities. The major thrust of these actions was to separate black from white children, but in 1927 the Court extended the racial doctrine to include other nonwhite minorities in the category of the colored. In Gong Lum v. Rice, the Court rejected the petition by a Chinese father to have his daughter enrolled in a white high school. In so doing, it reaffirmed the decision of the Supreme Court of Mississippi upholding the state constitution of 1890 which provided for separate schools for "children of the white and colored races." According to the state court, "this provision of the [state] Constitution divided the educable children into those of the pure white or Caucasian race, on the one hand, and the brown, yellow and black races, on the other, and therefore that Martha Lum of the Mongolian or yellow race could not insist on being classed with the whites under this constitutional division" (275 US 1927:82). As a result, the court concluded, Martha Lum could not attend a white school; she had to attend a colored school.

In concurring with the decision of the state court, the Supreme Court wrapped a mantle of legitimacy around the categorical separation of whites from all nonwhites. Not only was it legally permissible to exclude the blacks from the privileged environments of the whites but also to exclude the yellow, brown, and other nonwhite races. As such, the Court forged into a common mold what had been expressed historically as distinctive strands of racism and racial segmentation in the American society against individual racial minorities. Thus was made manifest once again the general character of America's racially bifurcated nature: whites were on one side of the racial divide, firmly ensconced with the rights and privileges of the People's Domain; all nonwhites, not merely some, were on the other side of the racial divide, treated historically as outsiders or even non-persons whose claims to the People's Domain were minimally acknowledged.

Not until the late 1930s was the Supreme Court prepared to probe beyond the states' version of the "separate but equal" doctrine and to come to an independent assessment of the matter. Its decision on Missouri ex rel Gaines v. Canada marked a significant reversal in the usual direction of its rulings on educational matters.

It overturned the decisions of the Missouri courts. (This departure from past precedent did not escape the exasperated attention of Justice McReynolds in his vigorous dissent.)

At issue in this case was the refusal of university officials to admit a black college graduate to the School of Law at the State University of Missouri. They conceded that he had the necessary qualifications but they nevertheless rejected his application; they claimed that it was "'contrary to the constitution, laws and public policy of the State to admit a negro as a student in the University of Missouri'" (305 US 1938:343). Taking cognizance of the fact that Missouri had no law school for blacks, they advised him to apply for aid under a statute that provided support for a student to attend a university in an adjacent state if a particular facility was not available in Missouri.

The petitioner refused the offer and sued instead for admission to the law school. He contended his constitutional rights had been denied. The state courts rejected his petition, but the Supreme Court agreed that his rights had been violated under the equal protection clause of the Fourteenth Amendment. The Court contended that the state had failed to provide an equivalent facility for the black student as it had for the white student. In view of this, the state could not shift its responsibility to other states; its constitutional obligation was to deal with the matter internally. In his opinion for the Court, Chief Justice Hughes elaborated on this thesis:

> "The basic consideration is not as to what sort of opportunities other States provide, or whether they are as good as those in Missouri, but as to what opportunities Missouri itself furnishes to white students and denies to negroes solely upon the ground of color. The admissibility of laws separating the races in the enjoyment of privileges afforded by the State rests wholly upon the equality of the privileges which the laws give to the separated groups within the State. The question here is not of a duty of the State to supply legal training, or of the quality of the training which it does supply, but of its duty when it provides such training to furnish it to the residents of the State upon the basis of an equality of right. By the operation of the laws of Missouri a privilege has been created for white law students which is denied to negroes by reason of their race. The white resident is afforded legal education within the State; the negro resident having the same qualifications is refused it there and must go outside the State to obtain it. That is a denial of the equality of legal right to the enjoyment of the privilege which the State has set up, and the provision for the payment of tuition fees in another State does not remove the discrimination."
>
> (305 US 1938:349–50)

Nowhere in his opinion did Chief Justice Hughes raise any question about the validity of the principle of separate racial facilities; but he raised for the first time the issue of equality of these facilities and made the question of standards a viable part of the "separate but equal" doctrine. By linking the two components together, he let it be known that failure of the state to meet the standard of equality could serve as grounds for the Court's breaching the walls of separateness. Thus he concluded that "the petitioner was entitled to be admitted to the law school of the State University in the absence of other and proper provision for his legal training within the State" (305 US 1938:352).

The Supreme Court's position was reaffirmed ten years later in Sipuel v. Oklahoma. There too the issue of equality was narrowly pegged to the state's granting access to a type of educational facility that was available for whites only. By 1950, the Supreme Court was prepared to go beyond this narrow focus. In Sweatt v. Painter, it sought to assess the relative merits of two segregated facilities: one for blacks that had just come into being, the other for whites that had been in existence for a long period of time.

The case had actually begun four years earlier when the black petitioner had been rejected for admission to the University of Texas Law School. In the absence of a law school for blacks, the state court recognized that the petitioner's constitutional rights à la Gaines had been violated but it did not grant him immediate relief; instead, the court continued the case for six months to give the state time to construct a law school for blacks. Having done so, the state obtained a dismissal of the case. The petitioner, however, refused to register in the new facility claiming that it was inferior to the law school for whites. Accordingly, he applied for a writ to allow him to attend the Texas law school. The Texas Supreme Court affirmed the findings of the lower courts and denied the petitioner's application. In turn, the United States Supreme Court "granted certiorari ... because of the manifest importance of the constitutional issues involved" (339 US 1950:632).

By the time the Court rendered its decision an even better law school than the first had opened for blacks. Chief Justice Vinson took note of this in his opinion for the Court. He insisted, though, that the issue before the Court was not the relative merits of the two black schools, but the relative equality between the white and even the better of the two black schools. With this in mind, he contended "we cannot find substantial equality in the educational opportunities offered white and Negro law students by the State." He then went on to list the objective and physical characteristics of the white school that were superior to those of the black school: "number of the faculty, variety of courses and opportunity for specialization, size of the student body, scope of the library, availability of law review and similar activities" (339 US 1950:633–34).

However, even more significant than these objective characteristics, Chief Justice Vinson insisted, were the intangible and qualitative features that the white school possessed which the black school did not.

"What is more important, the University of Texas Law School possesses to a far greater degree those qualities which are incapable of objective measurement but which make for greatness in a law school. Such qualities, to name but a few, include reputation of the faculty, experience of the administration, position and influence of the alumni, standing in the community, traditions, and prestige."

(339 US 1950:633)

Since it was evident that the black law school lacked these qualities, Vinson concluded that "it is difficult to believe that one who had a free choice between these law schools would consider the question close" (339 US 1950:634).

Chief Justice Vinson did not stop with merely contrasting the internal characteristics of the two institutions; he went on to compare the access to and experience with environments, people, and institutions each school provided its students which would be important in due course in the performance of their professional roles as lawyers.

"The law school, the proving ground for legal learning and practice, cannot be effective in isolation from the individuals and institutions with which the law interacts. Few students and no one who has practiced law would choose to study in an academic vacuum, removed from the interplay of ideas and the exchange of views with which the law is concerned. The law school to which Texas is willing to admit petitioner excludes from its student body members of the racial groups which number 85% of the population of the State and include most of the lawyers, witnesses, jurors, judges and other officials with whom petitioner will inevitably be dealing with when he becomes a member of the Texas Bar."

(339 US 1950:634)

Concluding, therefore, that the education which the petitioner would receive in the black law school would be grossly inferior to that in the white law school, Chief Justice Vinson held on behalf of the Court, that "the Equal Protection Clause of the Fourteenth Amendment requires that petitioner be admitted to the University of Texas Law School" (339 US 1950:636).

On the same day, the Supreme Court issued another ruling which further elaborated on the doctrine of equality of facilities. In McLaurin v. Oklahoma State Regents, the Court was faced, according to Chief Justice Vinson who wrote the opinion for this case too, "with the question whether a state may, after admitting a student to graduate instruction in its state university, afford him different treatment from other students solely because of his race" (339 US 1950:638).

The black appellant had several years earlier been denied admission to the University of Oklahoma to pursue a doctorate in education on the grounds that state statutes required segregated facilities. He obtained relief from a district court which cited the Gaines and Sipuel cases. In turn, the state legislature amended its statutes to permit blacks to attend white institutions of higher learning, if similar courses of instruction were not available in black institutions. They added, however, the important provision that within these institutions the program of instruction was to be conducted on a segregated basis. Accordingly, after being admitted, the black appellant "was required to sit apart at a designated desk in an anteroom adjoining the classroom; to sit at a designated desk on the mezzanine floor of the library, but not to use the desks in the regular reading room; and to sit at a designated table and to eat at a different time from the other students in the school cafeteria" (339 US 1950:640).

The appellant's attempt to remove these restrictions was first rejected by the district court on the ground that such treatment did not violate the Fourteenth Amendment. During his appeal to the Supreme Court, the University modified the more obvious features of its segregated treatment, such as removing a "Reserved For Colored" sign in the classroom and allowing the appellant to sit in a segregated row of the classroom itself. In short, it retained what it called "merely nominal" forms of separation (339 US:640).

The Supreme Court nevertheless ruled that the state and the institution had handicapped the appellant in the pursuit of his education. Their restrictions, though seemingly nominal, "impair and inhibit his ability to study, to engage in discussions and exchange views with other students, and, in general, to learn his profession" (339 US 1950:641). The Court concluded that these state-imposed restrictions produced a situation of inequality that could not be constitutionally sustained:

> "The conditions under which this appellant is required to receive his education deprive him of his personal and present right to the equal protection of the laws.... We hold that under these circumstances the Fourteenth Amendment precludes differences in treatment by the state based upon race. Appellant, having been admitted to a state-supported graduate school, must receive the same treatment at the hands of the state as students of other races."
>
> (339 US 1950:642)

In his opinion, Chief Justice Vinson acknowledged that the appellant might be "in no better position when these restrictions are removed, for he may still be set apart by his fellow students." However, Justice Vinson considered this to be "irrelevant" for the matter before the court. He continued,

> "There is a vast difference – a Constitutional difference – between restrictions imposed by the state which prohibit the intellectual commingling of students, and the refusal of individuals to commingle where the state presents no such

bar.... The removal of the state restrictions will not necessarily abate individual and group predilections, prejudices, and choices. But at the very least, the state will not be depriving appellant of the opportunity to secure acceptance by his fellow students on his own merits."   (339 US 1950:641–42)

In approaching the issue of equality as it did, the Vinson Court did more than just bring into focus the equal part of the "separate but equal" doctrine. It also gave the realization of equality a priority that under certain conditions even exceeded that for maintaining segregation. Thus the Court ordered the breaching of the walls of segregation in the name of equality for the individual black in the law school cases. Even more, the opinions of the Vinson Court contained the seeds of a judicial interpretation that would ultimately question the inherent compatibility of equality with segregation. In this regard, the Court found the black law schools inferior to the white school because in part they lacked the intangible and qualitative features of the latter – features which the former would probably never possess as long as their special position in the larger society was reinforced by segregation. Further, in also ordering the end of the segregated treatment of a black appellant in a white university, the Court was saying in effect that the constitutional rights of the individual to be treated equally could not be realized under the internal conditions of separateness that the institution had imposed.

And yet the Vinson Court disclaimed any intention of dealing with the basic validity of the doctrine of separateness itself. In fact, it deliberately set for itself the task of dealing with the more limited issue of equality and resisted any effort to broaden its task to include the entire doctrine of "separate but equal." In his opinion on the Sweatt case, Chief Justice Vinson made this position of the Court clear and manifest:

"Broader issues have been urged for our consideration, but we adhere to the principle of deciding constitutional questions only in the context of the particular case before the Court. We have frequently reiterated that this Court will decide constitutional questions only when necessary to the disposition of the case at hand, and that such decisions will be drawn as narrowly as possible.... Because of this traditional reluctance to extend constitutional interpretations to situations or facts which are not before the Court, much of the excellent research and detailed argument presented in these cases is unnecessary to their disposition."   (339 US 1950:631)

However, even with this disclaimer, the Vinson Court had nevertheless set the stage for a major confrontation with the central issue of separateness. This confrontation was to begin just two years after the Sweatt and McLaurin decisions as five lower court cases bearing on the issue of segregation in the public schools reached the Supreme Court. By June 1952, the two cases from Kansas (Brown v. Board of Education) and South Carolina (Briggs v. Elliot) were set for oral argument in the fall. Before that could take place, the Court decided to group with them a case from Virginia (Davis v. County School Board of Prince Edward County) and another from Delaware (Gebhart v. Belton). The fifth case from the District of Columbia (Bolling v. Sharpe) was to be argued immediately after the other four. Oral arguments for the five cases were scheduled for December 1952.

Four of the cases involved direct constitutional challenges of state segregation laws on the grounds that they violated the equal protection clause of the Fourteenth Amendment. The fifth case challenged the federal government's policy of segregated public schools in the District of Columbia on the grounds that the policy violated the due process clause of the Fifth Amendment (the Fourteenth Amendment not being applicable to actions by the federal government, only to actions by state governments). In each case the black petitioner not only relied on legal arguments but also stressed expert testimony from social scientists on the negative psychological and social effect of segregation on black children. Except for the Delaware case, the black petitioners lost in the lower federal courts; however, in the South Carolina and Virginia cases, the courts required that the states improve the educational facilities of the blacks so that they were more nearly equal to those of the whites. In the Delaware case the state courts did not follow the same kind of equalization approval; instead they ordered the immediate admission of the black children into white schools.

Despite the submission of voluminous briefs and records and ten hours of oral argument, in December the Supreme Court concluded that it needed still more information. Accordingly, it ordered in June 1953 that the case be argued again, and it requested the opposing counsel to direct their attention to five questions. In particular, the Court wanted Counsel to examine the historical record and circumstances at the time of the congressional approval and state ratification of the Fourteenth Amendment. Specifically, the Court wanted to know:

"1. What evidence is there that the Congress which submitted and the State legislatures and conventions which ratified the Fourteenth Amendment contemplated or did not contemplate, understood or did not understand, that it would abolish segregation in public schools?

2. If neither the Congress in submitting nor the States in ratifying the Fourteenth Amendment understood that compliance with it would require the immediate abolition of segregation in public schools, was it nevertheless the understanding of the framers of the Amendment

(a) that future Congresses might, in the exercise of their power under section 5 of the Amendment, abolish such segregation, or

(b) that it would be within the judicial power, in light of future conditions, to construe the Amendment as abolishing such segregation of its own force?"

Anticipating ambiguous results, the Court then asked: "3. On the assumption that the answers to questions 2 (a) and (b) do not dispose of the issue, is it within the judicial power, in construing the Amendment, to abolish segregation in public schools?" The remaining two questions requested Counsel's advice on the manner in which the Court decision should be implemented if the Court should decide that "segregation in public schools violates the Fourteenth Amendment" (345 US 1953:972–73).

Several months before the rearguments were to be heard, Chief Justice Vinson died and his place was taken by Warren. Accordingly, the Warren Court heard the reargument that lasted three days in early December 1953. Not until May 17 1954 was the first decision rendered. In his opinion for a unanimous Court, Chief Justice Warren declared in Brown v. Board of Education that the search of the historical record by Counsel and the Court had proved inconclusive and that the general legislative intent of Congress and the states with regard to segregation in the schools could not be determined.

> "The most avid proponents of the post-War Amendents undoubtedly intended them to remove all legal distinctions among 'all persons born or naturalized in the United States.' Their opponents, just as certainly, were antagonistic to both the letter and the spirit of the Amendments and wished them to have the most limited effect. What others in Congress and the state legislatures had in mind cannot be determined with any degree of certainty."   (347 US 1954:489)

The reason for this ambiguity, Chief Justice Warren conjectured, was the rudimentary state of public education at the time. The South had taken only its first faltering steps toward public education. "Education of white children was largely in the hands of private groups. Education of Negroes was almost nonexistent, and practically all of the race were illiterate. In fact, any education of Negroes was forbidden by law in some states." Even in the North, public education was in an undeveloped stage. "The curriculm was usually rudimentary; ungraded schools were common in rural areas; the school term was but three months a year in many states; and compulsory school attendance was virtually unknown. As a consequence, it is not surprising that there should be so little in the history of the Fourteenth Amendment relating to its intended effect on public education" (347 US 1954:490).

To Warren, the "separate but equal" doctrine was also not an accurate reading of these origins; in the early years the Court proscribed "all state-imposed discriminations against the Negro race" (347 US 1954:490). Only years later did the doctrine emerge and transform the Court's approach to the Fourteenth Amendment.

However, even if the historical record were clearer, it is doubtful that Chief Justice Warren would have based his opinion on an elaboration of the past. For he explicitly stated, "we cannot turn the clock back to 1868 when the Amendment was adopted, or even to 1896 when *Plessy v. Ferguson* was written." Instead he argued, "we must consider public education in the light of its full development and its present place in American life throughout the Nation. Only in this way can it be determined if segregation in public schools deprives these plaintiffs of the equal protection of the laws" (347 US 1954:493).

In assessing its role today, he concluded,

> "education is perhaps the most important function of state and local governments. Compulsory school attendance laws and the great expenditures for education both demonstrate our recognition of the importance of education to our democratic society. It is required in the performance of our most basic public responsibilities, even service in the armed forces. It is the very foundation of good citizenship. Today it is a principal instrument in awakening the child to cultural values, in preparing him for later professional training, and in helping him to adjust normally to his environment. In these days, it is doubtful that any child may reasonably be expected to succeed in life if he is denied the opportunity of an education. Such an opportunity, where the state has undertaken to provide it, is a right which must be made available to all on equal terms."
> (347 US 1954:493)

Chief Justice Warren, however, was not prepared to focus only on the issue of equality as the Vinson Court had done, thereby bypassing the issue of segregation itself. The Chief Justice did not dispute, for example, the findings presented to the Court that black and white school facilities were being equalized "with respect to buildings, curricula, qualifications and salaries of teachers and other 'tangible' factors" (347 US 1954:492). However, he insisted that the Court in its earlier decisions had agreed that equality of educational opportunity involved more than just tangible factors.

> "In *Sweatt v. Painter, supra*, in finding that a segregated law school for Negroes could not provide them equal educational opportunities, this Court relied in large part on 'those qualities which are incapable of objective measurement but which make for greatness in a law school.' In *McLaurin v. Oklahoma State Regents, supra*, the Court, in requiring that a Negro admitted to a white graduate school be treated like all other students, again resorted to intangible

considerations – 'his ability to study, to engage in discussions and exchange views with other students, and, in general, to learn his profession.'"

(347 US 1954:493)

The Chief Justice seemed to be saying that the Vinson Court by focusing on the question of intangibility had in effect raised doubts – at least implicitly – about the compatibility of equality with segregation, but had failed to follow through on the logic of its own decisions. Now however, the Warren Court was prepared to follow through on this logic and to say explicitly that "in the field of public education the doctrine of 'separate but equal' has no place. Separate educational facilities are inherently unequal" (347 US 1954:495).

To Justice Warren this conclusion was not merely a rational extension of the Vinson Court's earlier decisions but also a logical outcome from the most advanced thinking and research in psychology and other social sciences. Thus, he alluded to negative psychological and social effects that stem from segregating schoolchildren from their peers because of race. Such separation "generates a feeling of inferiority as to their status in the community that may affect their hearts and minds in a way unlikely ever to be undone." He then quoted a finding in the Kansas case by a court which nevertheless felt compelled to rule against the black plaintiffs:

"Segregation of white and colored children in public schools has a detrimental effect upon the colored children. The impact is greater when it has the sanction of the law; for the policy of separating the races is usually interpreted as denoting the inferiority of the negro group. A sense of inferiority affects the motivation of a child to learn. Segregation with the sanction of law, therefore, has a tendency to [retard] the educational and mental development of negro children and to deprive them of some of the benefits they would receive in a racial [ly] integrated school system."

(347 US 1954:494)

In the final analysis, the Warren Court found that segregation deprived the black plaintiffs of the "equal protection of the laws guaranteed by the Fourteenth Amendment" (347 US 1954:495). This ruling disposed of the four cases. In the fifth case, Bolling v. Sharpe, the Court also held for the petitioners. It declared that segregation in the public schools of the District of Columbia violated the due process clause of the Fifth Amendment and therefore the federal government had to desegregate the schools just as the states had to under the Brown ruling.

The Court did not attempt to deal with the question of implementation until a year later, at which time it took note of the complexity of the problem and the wide range of situations and conditions that would have to be dealt with among the multiplicity of school systems in the country. Accordingly, it gave district courts jurisdiction over the matter "because of their proximity to local conditions and the possible need for further hearings" (349 US 1955:299). It instructed these courts "to take such proceedings and enter such orders and decrees consistent with this opinion as are necessary and proper to admit to public schools on a racially nondiscriminatory basis with all deliberate speed the parties to these cases" (349 US 1955:301).

The outcry against the decision was bitter, intense, and widespread throughout the South. A group of southern congressmen even issued a manifesto in 1956 which advocated resistance, preferably lawful, to the ruling. They denounced the decision "as a clear abuse of judicial power. It climaxes a trend in the Federal Judiciary undertaking to legislate, in derogation of the authority of Congress, and to encroach upon the reserved rights of the States and the people" (Blaustein and Zangrando 1968:451).

In addition, a constitutional crisis was provoked by the governor of Arkansas in 1957 when he sought to interpose the state forcibly between the schools and the federal judiciary, thereby preventing implementation of a desegregation plan to which the school board of Little Rock had agreed. President Eisenhower reluctantly intervened by federalizing the national guard, and the Supreme Court unanimously denied the request by the school board to delay implementation of the plan. The Court expressed great concern at this turn of events in Cooper v. Aaron because "it raises questions of the highest importance to the maintenance of our federal system of government. It necessarily involves a claim by the Governor and Legislature of a State that there is no duty on state officials to obey federal court orders resting on this Court's considered interpretation of the United States Constitution" (358 US 1958:1). The Court vigorously and unanimously rejected this contention and reaffirmed the primacy of the Court as "supreme in the exposition of the law of the Constitution" (358 US 1958:18).

Even with the successful fending off of this constitutional threat, the Supreme Court was still to face patterns of evasion, delay, and avoidance that lasted for years as at least ten southern states sought to sidetrack desegregation. By the end of the 1960s even the Supreme Court became impatient with the pace of implementation and sought to speed it up; however by then all states including Mississippi had accepted at the least some form of token desegregation. The struggle, however, took on another complexion as it turned northward.

Despite the gargantuan obstacles of its effective implementation, the historic significance of the Brown decision was that it became the touchstone for the pervasive judicial delegitimation of state-imposed racial segmentation in the major institutional environments of the social realm. Of particular significance was its impact in the area of public facilities and transportation.

Public facilities and transportation

From the time they served as the original setting for the court case to the mid-twentieth century, transportation carriers have been the most visible and public symbol of the Plessy v. Ferguson principle. For most of this period, as with educational facilities, the prevailing emphasis was on the separate part of the "separate but equal" doctrine. This was also the firm policy of the Interstate Commerce Commission, despite its professed goal under law of maintaining nondiscrimination in common carriers. Beginning in 1940, though, the Supreme Court began to pay more attention to the equal part of the doctrine. Thus in Mitchell v. United States, the Court ordered equal treatment for black passengers who had paid for pullman accommodations. In Henderson v. United States (1946) the Court voided the efforts of a railroad company to maintain arbitrary barriers for separating black from white passengers in the dining car – a position similar to that taken four years later in the McLaurin case. Piecemeal as such efforts were to insure equal treatment on interstate carriers, they were virtually absent with respect to intrastate carriers.

After 1954 the entire situation changed dramatically. Citing the Brown case, the Interstate Commerce Commission reversed its policy and ordered the end of segregation on public conveyances in interstate commerce. In 1960 the Supreme Court extended this ban to restaurants in interstate bus terminals in Boynton v. Virginia. The assault against segregation on interstate carriers was launched during the Montgomery Alabama bus boycott. In 1956 the Supreme Court affirmed in Browder v. Gayle the district court's decision that state statutes and city ordinances requiring segregation on public carriers violated the due process and equal protection clauses of the Fourteenth Amendment. In its ruling the lower court had explicitly stated:

> "We cannot in good conscience perform our duty as judges by blindly following the precedent of Plessy v. Ferguson, supra, when our study [of the law] leaves us in complete agreement with the Fourth Circuit's opinion . . . that the separate but equal doctrine can no longer be safely followed as a correct statement of the law. In fact, we think that Plessy v. Ferguson has been impliedly, though not explicitly, overruled." (142 Federal Supplement 1956:717)

By 1962 the Court treated the desegregation of carriers in a matter of fact manner, no longer the subject of dispute and contention. In Bailey v. Patterson, the Court stated in no uncertain terms: "We have settled beyond question that no State may require racial segregation of interstate or intrastate transportation facilities. The question is no longer open; it is foreclosed as a litigable issue" (369 US 1962:33).

In a similar vein, the Court has ruled since 1954 that state and local laws that require segregation in the use of public facilities are unconstitutional. In rapid succession it struck down laws and policies of segregation in public parks, beaches, municipal golf courses, cafeterias, auditoriums, and the like. Typical of the new normative atmosphere that had been created by the Brown decision was the opinion of the Court of Appeals in the 1955 case of Dawson v. Baltimore. The Court had just struck down desegregation in the public parks of Baltimore. In explaining its decision, the Court said:

"It is now obvious, however, that segregation cannot be justified as a means to preserve the public peace merely because the tangible facilities furnished to one race are equal to those furnished to the other. The Supreme Court expressed the opinion in Brown v. Board of Education of Topeka. With this in mind, it is obvious that racial segregation in recreational activities can no longer be sustained as a proper exercise of the police power of the State; for if that power cannot be invoked to sustain racial segregation in the schools, where attendance is compulsory and racial friction may be apprehended from the enforced commingling of the races, it cannot be sustained with respect to public beach and bathhouse facilities, the use of which is entirely optional."

(220 Federal Reporter, Second Series 1955:387)

The Supreme Court and other parts of the federal judiciary trod more warily in their approach to segregation in privately owned facilities which had public functions or served the public, but even here significant inroads were made into the private sphere of discrimination that has traditionally been treated as inviolable under the Constitution.

The restructuring of the boundaries of the private realm of discrimination

In its 1883 decision on the Civil Rights Cases, the Supreme Court carved out an area of discriminatory practice and policy that was not subject to the restraints of the Fourteenth Amendment: the private realm of individual and group behavior. The Court did this by severely restricting the role of the federal government in implementing the nondiscriminatory goals of the amendment. It stipulated that the federal government could engage in corrective actions against the discriminatory acts of state governments but was forbidden from intervening directly with the conduct and behavior of private individuals and groups in the political community. Chief Justice Vinson succinctly described the source and character of this distinction in his opinion on the Shelley v. Kraemer case of 1948:

"Since the decision of this Court in the *Civil Rights Cases*, the principle has become firmly embedded in our constitutional law that the action inhibited by

the first section of the Fourteenth Amendment is only such action as may fairly
be said to be that of the States. That Amendment erects no shield against merely
private conduct, however discriminatory or wrongful." (334 US 1948:13)

While the decision in the Civil Rights Cases staked out the terrain of permissible
discriminatory action, the Plessy-Ferguson decision of 1896 added a crucial
dimension to the private sphere of discrimination. Through its endorsement of
racial segmentation, the Court made much more explicitly available to discriminatory practice and policy within the private sphere the protective shield of the state
and its courts of law. In so doing, the Court gave both practice and policy a legal
and moral authority that enhanced their respectability and legitimacy and enabled
them to resort to the machinery of the state for support and strength.

As a result, most territorial and institutional environments both North and
South became honeycombed with discriminatory policies and practices. In the
South these were given the force of law through enactments of state legislatures.
Thus Jim Crow statutes virtually permeated every nook and cranny of the
community and gave full expression and support to the mores and to the
sentiments of the white population. In the North, however, these discriminatory
policies and practices were primarily expressions of private agreements and
behaviors of individuals and groups that were frequently upheld as proper and
binding in courts of law (as in the case of restrictive covenants) and as proper and
desirable by the dominant white community. In addition, governmental policies
were frequently mindful of these private predilections and prejudices, as in the
case of the Federal Housing Administration policies.

The period from the 1890s to the mid-1940s was characterized by repeated
attempts of the whites to expand the sphere of the private in order to defeat court
decisions that had struck down certain state laws and actions as violative of the
Fourteenth Amendment. One of the most notable of these efforts was the attempt
by Texas to "privatize" primaries so as to neutralize a Supreme Court ruling
against the all-white primary. As we have already seen, the Court first accepted
this "privatization" of the primary in 1935, but by 1944 it changed its mind and
declared it unconstitutional. Another historic example was the mushrooming of
restrictive covenants, particularly in northern cities from the second decade on, as
a response to the decision by the Supreme Court that state and municipal
governments could not legislate residential segregation. These private agreements
by whites sought to keep blacks out of neighborhoods and were treated by the
courts as any other enforceable contractual arrangement until the late 1940s.

By the 1940s, the Supreme Court began to render decisions that significantly
altered the scope and force of the private right to discriminate. It did this primarily
by redefining in two significant ways the relationship between state action and

private behavior. First, the Court shifted the boundaries between the two and categorized actions and relations as "quasi-state" which it had formerly treated as merely private. Second, and perhaps even more important, it withdrew the machinery of the state from shoring up and supporting the private sphere of discrimination.

Transmuting the private into state action

Interestingly the Court handed down two decisions in the same year, 1944, that bore directly on redefining private actions as state actions. One of the decisions had to do with the white primaries of Texas. In Smith v. Allwright, a case that we have already discussed at length, the Court declared that primaries could no longer be treated as the private preserve of the political party acting as a private voluntary association. Instead, the Court determined that henceforth primaries were to be viewed as integral parts of the electoral process – a process that is protected by the Constitution – and that political parties were to be treated as agents of the state because they had been charged with "quasi-governmental" functions by the state in the running of the primary.

The other decision had to do with the legal responsibilities of a union which had been elected under terms of the Railway Labor Act to be the exclusive bargaining representative for a class of railway firemen (Steele v. Louisville & Nashville RR Co). As bargaining representatives, the union gained the authority to negotiate contracts with management that affected all workers and not merely its own members. Thus black employees, who comprised a substantial minority of the work force, were affected by the terms of any agreement even though they were barred from membership in the union itself.

In its ruling the Court did not dispute the right of the union to define itself as a private voluntary association and therefore to determine the eligibility and qualifications of its membership, even to the extent of excluding blacks. But in taking the role of exclusive bargaining agent, Chief Justice Stone insisted in his opinion for the Court, the union had been "clothed" by Congress through the Railway Labor Act "with power not unlike that of a legislature which is subject to constitutional limitations on its power to deny, restrict, destroy or discriminate against the rights of those for whom it legislates and which is also under an affirmative constitutional duty equally to protect those rights" (323 US 1944:198).

As a result, Chief Justice Stone continued,

"So long as a labor union assumes to act as the statutory representative of a craft, it cannot rightly refuse to perform the duty, which is inseparable from the power of representation conferred upon it, to represent the entire membership of the craft. While the statute does not deny to such a bargaining labor organization the right to determine eligibility to its membership, it does require the union, in collective bargaining and in making contracts with the carrier, to represent non-union or minority union members of the craft without hostile discrimination, fairly, impartially, and in good faith. Wherever necessary to that end, the union is required to consider requests of non-union members of the craft and expressions of their views with respect to collective bargaining with the employer and to give to them notice of and opportunity for hearing upon its proposed action."   (323 US 1944:204)

Even though the Court did not place the issue in the context of a constitutional challenge to racial discrimination as Justice Murphy would have liked it to do, it nevertheless provided a defense with its principle of fair representation for the protection of the rights and interests of the black workers against the arbitrary actions of the union. The latter did not have the license to function merely as a private organization; it had to assume the responsibilities of a "quasi-governmental" agency.

In 1961 the Court transferred still another significant set of behaviors and relationships from the private sphere of permissive discrimination to the domain of forbidden state action in the case of Burton v. Wilmington Parking Authority. At issue was the discriminatory policy and practice of an incorporated privately owned restaurant which was located in an auto parking building owned and operated by the Wilmington Parking Authority, an agency of the State of Delaware. The Authority had leased the property to the restaurant for twenty years and provided virtually all the services of a landlord for a tenant.

The private owner had contended that in barring blacks from his restaurant he was acting in a "purely private capacity" under his lease and that his action was not that of the Authority and could not therefore be defined as state action under terms of the Fourteenth Amendment (365 US 1961:716).

The Supreme Court of Delaware had agreed with his argument, but the United States Supreme Court disagreed and overturned the state court's ruling. In his opinion for the Court, Justice Clark indicated that the specific leasing agreement signed between corporation and state created a condition of continuing close interdependence and mutual benefit between the two. For example,

"The land and building were publicly owned. As an entity, the building was dedicated to 'public uses' in performance of the Authority's 'essential governmental functions.' The costs of land acquisition, construction, and maintenance are defrayed entirely from donations by the City of Wilmington, from loans and revenue bonds and from the proceeds of rentals and parking services out of which the loans and bonds were payable. Assuming that the distinction would be significant,... the commercially leased areas were not surplus state property, but constituted a physically and financially integral and, indeed, indispensable part of the State's plan to operate its project as a self-sustaining unit. Upkeep and maintenance of the building, including necessary repairs, were responsibilities of the Authority and were payable out of public funds."

(365 US 1961:723–24)

In view of the degree of state involvement in the leasing arrangement, Justice Clark insisted that the state could have and should have required the restaurant "to discharge the responsibilities under the Fourteenth Amendment imposed upon the private enterprise as a consequence of state participation." However, he continued, merely because the state had not done so does not discharge it of its responsibility in the matter, for by failing to do what it should have done in the first place the Authority, and through it the state, "elected to place its power, property and prestige behind the admitted discrimination." Such a situation is not acceptable to the Court: "no state may effectively abdicate its responsibilities by either ignoring them or by merely failing to discharge them whatever the motive may be" (365 US 1961:725).

As a result, Justice Clark concluded, "By its inaction, the Authority, and through it the State, has ... made itself a party to the refusal of service." This is because "the State has so far insinuated itself into a position of interdependence with Eagle that it must be recognized as a joint participant in the challenged activity, which, on that account, cannot be considered to have been so 'purely private' as to fall without the scope of the Fourteenth Amendment" (365 US 1961:725).

Justice Clark realized that by introducing the concept of "state action" to leasing arrangements between the state and private individuals and organizations, the Court was opening up to constitutional challenge a bewildering thicket of relationships in which the state had some involvement. Accordingly, he cautioned against viewing the present decision as providing a universal standard for all such cases; instead he insisted that each case would have to be decided on its merits. Thus he concluded, "Specifically defining the limits of our inquiry, what we hold today is that when a State leases public property in the manner and for the purpose shown to have been the case here, the proscriptions of the Fourteenth Amendment must be complied with by the lessee as certainly as though they were binding covenants written into the agreement itself" (365 US 1961:726).

By 1972 the Court began to place stringent limits on the application of the Burton principle to state licensing and leasing arrangements. In Moose Lodge No. 107 v. Irvis, the Court decided that the refusal of the lodge to serve food and liquor to a black was a private act of discrimination, despite the fact that it was licensed by a state agency, the Pennsylvania State Liquor Board, to sell liquor. The black appellee had contended such licensing involved significant state involvement in the lodge's affairs; for to get and to keep the license, the lodge was obliged to conform to extensive regulations of the board. In view of the continuing surveillance and control by the state agency, the black appellee concluded that the discriminatory act of the lodge had been transmuted from a private into a state action "for the purposes of the Equal Protection Clause of the Fourteenth Amendment" (407 US 1972:165).

The Court disagreed. In his opinion for the Court, Justice Rehnquist argued that connections between state and individuals have become so vast and varied that to hold that any such connection transformed a private discriminatory act into a state act would be to erase the distinction between the two spheres. "Since state-furnished services include such necessities of life as electricity, water, and police and fire protection, such a holding would utterly emasculate the distinction between private as distinguished from state conduct set forth in *The Civil Rights Cases, supra,* and adhered to in subsequent decisions" (407 US 1965:173).

Consequently, Justice Rehnquist contended, a more stringent requirement would have to be imposed; the relationship between state and private party would have to be similar to that of the Burton case in order to have a private discriminatory act transformed into a state action. Such a condition, the Justice insisted, did not prevail in the present case. "Here there is nothing approaching the symbiotic relationship between lessor and lessee that was present in *Burton.*" In that case the "Eagle was a public restaurant in a public building;" in this case the "Moose Lodge is a private social club in a private building" (407 US 1965:175).

In this manner the Court has sought to preserve a protective wall for the private sphere of permissible discriminatory practice and policy even though some relationship with the state may be sustained. The matter, though, is still far from being resolved.

Withdrawing the machinery of the state from support of the private sphere

In 1948 the Supreme Court added to the "state action" approach another line of judicial reasoning that altered even more dramatically and pervasively the relationship between the private sphere of discrimination and the state. The landmark case was Shelley v. Kraemer, which we have discussed at length already. Once again the Court did not dispute the right of the individual to discriminate. It even reaffirmed the right of individual property holders to agree voluntarily to restrictive covenants which bar racial and other minorities from residence in a neighborhood; however, the Court stipulated that such property holders could no longer turn to the courts to enforce these private agreements if one or more of the covenanters should change their mind and sell their property to members of such minorities. In the words of Chief Justice Vinson, who wrote the opinion for the Court, "the action of state courts and judicial officers in their official capacities is to be regarded as action of the State within the meaning of the Fourteenth Amendment" (334 US 1948:14). In this manner the Court withdrew the judicial machinery of government as a means of redress or support for the private realm of discrimination.

Five years later the Court even went so far as to deny the right of a white covenanter to bring a suit for damages in civil court against a white co-covenanter who broke the agreement by selling his property to a black. In his opinion for the Court, in Barrows v. Jackson (1953) Justice Minton identified as the central issue "whether a court's awarding damages constitutes state action under the Fourteenth Amendment." He answered in the affirmative.

> "To compel respondent to respond in damages would be for the State to punish her for her failure to perform her covenant to continue to discriminate against non-Caucasians in the use of her property. The result of that sanction by the State would be to encourage the use of restrictive covenants. To that extent, the State would act to put its sanction behind the covenants. If the State may thus punish respondent for her failure to carry out her covenant, she is coerced to continue to use her property in a discriminatory manner, which in essence is the purpose of the covenant. Thus, it becomes not respondent's voluntary choice but the State's choice that she observe her covenant or suffer damages. The action of a state court at law to sanction the validity of the restrictive covenant here involved would constitute state action as surely as it was state action to enforce such covenants in equity, as in *Shelley, supra*."   (346 US 1953:254)

Important as the Shelley decision was, the ruling that probably did most to restructure fundamentally the relationship between the machinery of the state and the private sphere of discrimination was the Brown decision. Prior to the decision, executive and legislative branches of state government had been able to bring to bear the power and authority of the law in supporting the racial segmentation of the major institutional environments of the social realm. Such laws bestowed an aura of respectability on the practices and policies of discrimination that private individuals and groups pursued in these environments and gave these practices and policies a strength and compelling force that they would not otherwise have had. This mutual reinforcement between law and private practice was most manifest in the South, in the North the "national" presence of the doctrine of "separate but equal" compensated in part for the absence of supportive state laws in providing a benign legal-normative environment in which the private sphere of discrimination could flourish.

With the Brown decision, the Court drove an ever-widening wedge between the state and private sphere of discrimination. The latter was increasingly deprived of instruments of legal and police control that it had been able to rely upon in the past. This is clearly evident in the sit-in cases that flooded the courts of the South in the early 1960s.

Beginning spontaneously in a dime store in North Carolina in 1960, sit-in demonstrations spread rapidly and widely throughout the South for the next several years. A major target was private facilities, particularly restaurants, which excluded blacks from their premises or made available separate and inferior accommodations to them. Students would enter the private premises, sit peaceful-ly though stubbornly at a counter or tables reserved for whites, and refuse to leave. Many owners and managers of these private facilities would view these actions as violating their property and private rights and would call the police who would arrest the students on grounds that they had broken a law or ordinance against trespassing or disturbing the peace. Countless students were convicted on these grounds; and their convictions were upheld in the state courts. The Supreme Court, though, reversed a number of these convictions.

Of particular interest are three major grounds for these reversals, which clearly highlight the efforts of the Court to detach still further the machinery of the state from the private sphere of discrimination. Perhaps the most obvious of these grounds surfaced in Peterson v. City of Greenville, a case in which ten students were arrested in 1960 for violating the trespass statute of South Carolina. Prior to the arrest they had seated themselves at a lunch counter – the only section of this particular department store reserved for whites only – and had refused to leave. The manager subsequently informed them that they could not be served at the same counter as whites without violating local customs and a municipal ordinance which declared: "'It shall be unlawful for any person owning, managing or controlling any hotel, restaurant, cafe, eating house, boarding-house or similar establishment to furnish meals to white persons and colored persons in the same room, or at the same table, or at the same counter'" (373 US 1963:246).

The Court unanimously reversed the conviction on the ground that the discriminatory policy that was being infringed did not derive from a private party only but was instead a mandate imposed upon the private party by the state through a municipal ordinance. Whether or not the manager would have still acted the same way in the absence of the law was irrelevant according to the Court; the pertinent fact was that the law required that he act the way he did. In effect, Chief Justice Warren concluded for the Court.

"The convictions had the effect, which the State cannot deny, of enforcing the ordinance passed by the City of Greenville, the agency of the State. When a state agency passes a law compelling persons to discriminate against other persons because of race, and the State's criminal processes are employed in a way which enforces the discrimination mandated by that law, such a palpable violation of the Fourteenth Amendment cannot be saved by attempting to separate the mental urges of the discriminators."   (373 US 1963:248)

In a second case decided at the same time, Lombard v. Louisiana, the Court did not allow the absence of a state law or municipal ordinance to prevent it from coming to virtually the same conclusion as in the Peterson case and from reversing a sit-in conviction. The Court determined that the behavior and statements of public officials produced an atmosphere of coercion similar to the presence of a law. In the words of Chief Justice Warren, "a State, or a city, may act as authoritatively through its executive as through its legislative body.... Consequently, the city must be treated exactly as if it had an ordinance prohibiting such conduct.... The official command here was to direct continuance of segregated service in restaurants, and to prohibit any conduct directed toward its discontinuance" (373 US 1963:273). Accordingly, the Court concluded that the discriminatory behavior of the manager had been constrained by the state and could not be treated as a privately determined act; the behavior therefore entered the constitutionally forbidden territory of state action.

In the first series of sit-in cases that reached it in 1961, the Court had to deal with a somewhat different situation. Only the discriminatory behavior of private parties was at issue; no link with state law or policy was alleged. Specifically, in each of the three cases that had been consolidated into Garner v. Louisiana, a manager had refused to serve black students at a food counter reserved for whites. Upon their refusal to vacate their seats, the manager had called the police who arrested the students under a disturbance of peace statute.

The Court was particularly interested in determining the extent to which the behavior of the students violated the terms of the statute. In his opinion for the Court, Chief Justice Warren concluded: "that these records contain no evidence to support a finding that petitioners disturbed the peace, either by outwardly boisterous conduct or by passive conduct likely to cause a public disturbance." By arresting the petitioners, Warren continued, the police had in effect substituted "their own opinions" of what the law interdicts for what it actually does interdict. They assumed "it was a breach of the peace for the petitioners to sit peacefully in a place where custom decreed they should not sit. Such activity, in the circumstances of these cases, is not evidence of any crime and cannot be so considered either by the police or the courts." As a result, the Court overturned the convictions and held "that these convictions violated petitioners' rights to due process of law guaranteed them by the Fourteenth Amendment to the United

States Constitution" (368 US 1961:173–74). Thus, even where his discriminatory behavior was purely private and not state-linked, the owner of a private facility was to face certain constraints after Brown. He could not automatically turn to the police to enforce his policy of discrimination, since refusal to obey his wishes could no longer be treated by itself as evidence of any legal wrongdoing.

While concurring with the majority in the Garner case, Justice Douglas wrote a separate opinion in which he decried the limited basis on which the majority had made its ruling. He would have played down the issue of disturbing the peace and focused instead on the fundamental constitutional question: Was the discriminatory action of the manager protected by the Constitution as within the private sphere of behavior, or was it forbidden by the Constitution as state action? Justice Douglas answered without hesitation: "state action." He contended that so pervasive was the policy of segregation throughout the legal system of Louisiana that

"though there may have been no state law or municipal ordinance that *in terms* required segregation of the races in restaurants, it is plain that the proprietors in the instant cases were segregating blacks from whites pursuant to Louisiana's custom. Segregation is basic to the structure of Louisiana as a community; the custom that maintains it is at least as powerful as any law. If these proprietors also choose segregation, their preference does not make the action 'private,' rather than 'state,' action. If it did, a miniscule of private prejudice would convert state into private action. Moreover, where the segregation policy is the policy of a State, it matters not that the agency to enforce it is a private enterprise."   (368 US 1961:181)

Further, Justice Douglas continued, restaurants and other corporate enterprises cannot be treated as just another species of private property. Instead they are affected with public interest; their actions have public consequences which have a significant impact on the community at large. This is apparent, Douglas insisted, in the degree of control that the state maintains over these enterprises through licensing procedures and the like. Such control places the enterprise on a footing different from that of the private home. "One can close the doors of his home to anyone he desires. But one who operates an enterprise under a license from the government enjoys a privilege that derives from the people. Whether retail stores, not licensed by the municipality, stand on a different footing is not presented here. But the necessity of a license shows that the public has rights in respect to those premises (368 US 1961:185). Accordingly, Douglas concluded, "Those who license enterprises for public use should not have under our Constitution the power to license it for the use of only one race. For there is the overriding constitutional requirement that all state power be exercised so as not to deny equal protection to any group" (368 US 1961:184–85).

Three years later Justice Douglas shifted markedly the weight of his argument in a separate opinion in Bell v. Maryland. Once again he agreed with the decision of the majority but took issue with the grounds for its decision. Unlike his earlier opinion, he no longer stressed the linkage between the state and the discriminatory policies and practices of a business enterprise; in fact, in the case at hand, Baltimore had just passed an ordinance opposing discrimination in public accommodations. Instead Justice Douglas concentrated on the public character and responsibilities of private enterprises which he said made them qualitatively different from the private property or home of a person.

"The problem in this case, and in the other sit-in cases before us, is presented as though it involved the situation of 'a private operator conducting his own business on his own premises and exercising his own judgment' as to whom he will admit to the premises.

The property involved is not, however, a man's home or his yard or even his fields. Private property is involved, but it is property that is serving the public. As my Brother Goldberg says, it is a 'civil' right, not a 'social' right, with which we deal. Here it is a restaurant refusing service to a Negro. But so far as principle and law are concerned it might just as well be a hospital refusing admission to a sick or injured Negro, . . . or a drugstore refusing antibiotics to a Negro, or a bus denying transportation to a Negro, or a telephone company refusing to install a telephone in a Negro's home.

The problem with which we deal has no relation to opening or closing the door of one's home. The home of course is the essence of privacy, in no way dedicated to public use, in no way extending an invitation to the public. Some businesses, like the classical country store where the owner lives overhead or in the rear, make the store an extension, so to speak, of the home. But such is not this case. The facts of these sit-in cases have little resemblance to any institution of property which we customarily associate with privacy."

(378 US 1964:252–53)

The public character of these enterprises, Justice Douglas insisted, imposed upon them constitutional responsibilities which are absent for the private individual. Accordingly, he would deny such corporate enterprises the right to discriminate against one class of customers because of race, and even more emphatically he would make it unconstitutional for these enterprises to turn to the police and courts to enforce their discriminatory practices.

To affirm the right of the corporation, he concluded,

"to refuse service to anyone 'it' chooses and to get the State to put people in jail who defy 'its' will [under the private shield or private action] *would make corporate management the arbiter of one of the deepest conflicts in our society*: corporate management could then enlist the aid of state police, state prosecutors, and state courts to force *apartheid* on the community they served, if *apartheid* best suited the corporate need."   (378 US 1964:263–64)

The Court has chosen not to follow the path that Justice Douglas outlined; it continues to view "state-related" actions as the key to the Fourteenth Amendment. Over the years it has of course elaborated the conception of "state-related" far beyond the literal definition that it employed in the 1880s. What Justice Douglas proposed more aptly describes the path that the executive and legislative branches of government began to follow in the 1950s and 1960s. Since then they have brought under control of public authority an increasingly larger sphere of private action and behavior that have significant public consequences. At the same time, the two branches of government have taken a more active role in the regulation of "state-related" actions in the area of racial discrimination.

Congressional affirmation of racial equality and the American creed

INTRODUCTION

Significant as its decisions were in delegitimizing and withdrawing the support of the state from the racial creed, the Supreme Court could do little more than set the legal-normative stage for a fuller extension of the mantle of the American creed to the black and for an affirmation of his claims to the rights and immunities of the People's Domain. But the Court had neither the power nor the authority to translate these claims into public policy and actions which would have the full force of the government behind them. Only the executive and legislative branches of government could give body and substance to these claims and provide for their realization as affirmative expressions of law and policy in and for the political community. In this section we shall examine the legislative response to the racial imperatives that were first enunciated by the Supreme Court. (The executive response will be considered in the next chapter.)

From being the primal governmental force behind the drive for equality for the blacks during the first period of reconstruction, Congress became the most resistant to doing anything about civil rights and abdicated any semblance of responsibility and leadership to the judiciary and executive branches. For well over eighty years after the high point of its aggressive leadership during reconstruction, namely the passage of the Civil Rights Act of 1875, Congress failed to enact any legislation whatsoever on civil rights. Efforts to pass anti-poll tax and anti-lynching laws in the 1930s and 1940s proved abortive under the sustained obstructionist tactics of southern legislators and under the indifference of many Republican congressmen.

THE VOTING RIGHTS ACTS OF 1957 AND 1960

Three years after the Brown decision, however, Congress enacted the first of a series of laws that dramatically renewed the promise of the first reconstruction to gain for racial minorities full membership in the People's Domain under the American creed. The first, enacted in 1957, was a relatively modest attempt to deal primarily with the voting and to a lesser extent the legal rights of blacks. Its historical significance derives primarily from its being the first congressional bill on civil rights in over three-quarters of a century rather than from the substantive remedies it proposed or achieved.

One of the major provisions of the act was the establishment of a nonpartisan Civil Rights Commission whose major function was to "investigate allegations in writing under oath or affirmation that certain citizens of the United States are being deprived of their right to vote and have that vote counted by reason of their color, race, religion, or national origin; which writing, under oath or affirmation, shall set forth the facts upon which such belief or beliefs are based" (US Statutes at Large 71, 1957:635). The act also authorized the appointment of an additional assistant Attorney General to strengthen the civil rights activities of the Department of Justice. Further, it authorized the Attorney General to institute in behalf of the United States "civil action or other proper proceeding for preventive relief, including an application for a permanent or temporary injunction, restraining order, or other order" (US Statutes at Large 1957 71:637) against any person who threatens or actually interferes with the voting rights of another person. And finally the act also prescribed nondiscriminatory qualifications for the selection of federal jurors.

Within a short period of time, the inadequacies of the act became readily apparent. It did little to alter the disfranchisement of the blacks in the South. To defeat the purposes of the bill, southern officials destroyed or damaged voting and registration lists; in this way they sought to hamper investigations by the Civil Rights Commission and the Department of Justice. Despite the obviousness of these attempts at obstruction, only one suit was brought by the federal government against election registrars before January 1959. In its first report, the Civil Rights Commission described the pervasive evasions of the law in the South and the wide range of tactics used to obstruct its implementation.

As a result, by 1959 pressures began to mount for additional legislation. President Eisenhower recommended a modest and limited seven-point civil rights program, and Congress began to consider legislation. Berman, in his book *A Bill Becomes a Law* (1966), presents a detailed account of the tortuous process by which a new civil rights bill wended its way through Congress. He describes the success of congressional leaders in putting a leash on the efforts of the more liberal congressmen to push for a strong bill and in outmaneuvering the solid bloc of southern congressmen who resorted to any delaying and obstructionist tactic they could devise to abort the passage of any law. The outcome was a bill whose mere passage was acclaimed a triumph by congressional leaders but which was viewed as weak and ineffectual by liberals and blacks. Thurgood Marshall remarked caustically, "The Civil Rights Act of 1960 isn't worth the paper it's written on" (Berman 1966:135). Even the southern congressmen did not seem too upset by the result; in fact Senator Byrd of Virginia referred to the outcome as a victory for the South.

The most controversial provision of the bill was the granting of authority to district courts to appoint voting referees who would determine for the court whether a person has been "deprived of or denied under color of law the opportunity to register or otherwise to qualify to vote" despite his having the necessary qualifications under state law.

> "Upon receipt of such report, the court shall cause the Attorney General to transmit a copy thereof to the State attorney general and to each party to such proceeding together with an order to show cause within ten days, or such shorter time as the court may fix, why an order of the court should not be entered in accordance with such report. Upon the expiration of such period, such order shall be entered unless prior to that time there has been filed with the court and served upon all parties a statement of exceptions to such report."
>
> (US Statutes at Large 1960 74:90–1)

Another provision of the bill required that state officials retain for twenty-two months after any election for federal office all records and papers "relating to any application, registration, payment of poll tax, or other act requisite to voting in such election" (US Statutes at Large 74, 1960:88) and make them available to the Attorney General. The law also extended the powers of the Civil Rights Commission and provided criminal penalties for obstructing court orders in school desegregation cases and for "flight . . . to avoid prosecution, or custody, or confinement after conviction, under the laws of the place from which he flees, for willingly attempting to or damaging or destroying by fire or explosive any building, structure, facility, vehicle, dwelling house, synagogue, church, religious center, or educational institution, public or private" (US Statutes at Large 1960 74:86).

In the final analysis, the act of 1960 was only a slight improvement over the act of 1957; both were of greater symbolic than factual significance for the cause of civil rights. They represented the end of complete inaction by Congress and the breaching of the solid wall of resistance to civil rights legislation erected by a coalition of conservative Republicans and southern Democrats.

THE CIVIL RIGHTS ACT OF 1964

Three years later Congress again took up the issue of civil rights. There was little to indicate in the early stages of its deliberations that anything more than a modest bill would be produced. Even the administration's proposals were tentative and limited in scope. However, events in the South dramatically changed the situation. What particularly shifted the sense of urgency and priority was the brutal confrontation of police with peaceful black demonstrators in Birmingham, Alabama, which evoked a nationwide outcry. Shortly thereafter, in June 1963, President Kennedy was compelled to federalize the national guard to prevent Governor Wallace from obstructing a court order to admit two black students to the University of Alabama. (These events are discussed in detail in Chapter 11.)

In a nationwide address that evening the President described what he had done and then went on to say in terms reminiscent of Myrdal's analysis of the American dilemma: "This nation was founded by men of many nations and backgrounds. It was founded on the principle that all men are created equal, and that the rights of every man are diminished when the rights of one man are threatened" (Blaustein and Zangrando 1968:484). As Americans, he continued, blacks were entitled to share all of these rights and to enjoy full membership in the People's Domain; instead they had had to endure massive inequities, discrimination, and indignities which had kept them on the outside and in a state of relative unfreedom. "One hundred years of delay have passed since President Lincoln freed the slaves, yet their heirs, their grandsons, are not fully free. They are not yet freed from the bonds of injustice; they are not yet freed from social and economic oppression" (Blaustein and Zangrando 1968:486).

The solution, he insisted, required legislative and legal action. "It is better to settle these matters in the courts than in the streets, and new laws are needed at every level" (Blaustein and Zangrando 1968:485). But, he continued, "law alone cannot make men see right. We are confronted primarily with a moral issue. It is as clear as the American Constitution. The heart of the question is whether all Americans are to be afforded equal rights and equal opportunities; whether we are going to treat our fellow Americans as we want to be treated" (Blaustein and Zangrando 1968:485).

In this manner the President posed the central issue of Myrdal's American dilemma: the disparity between ideal and practice. He then developed in vivid detail the urgent need to do something about bridging the gap. He warned that the blacks were growing increasingly impatient. "The fires of frustration and discord are burning in every city North and South. Where legal remedies are not at hand, redress is sought in the street in demonstrations, parades, and protests, which create tensions and threaten violence – and threaten lives" (Blaustein and Zangrando 1968:486).

As a result, the President continued, America was facing "a moral crisis as a country and a people. It cannot be met by repressive police action. It cannot be left to increased demonstrations in the streets. It cannot be quieted by token moves or talk." Instead the crisis required immediate action "in the Congress, in your state and local legislative body, and above all, in all of our daily lives" (Blaustein and Zangrando 1968:486). The President went on to propose a far-ranging program of legislation, which completely dwarfed the limited set of proposals that he had submitted earlier to Congress.

Shortly after his speech, he sent to Congress a comprehensive set of proposals. Galvanized into action by these proposals, the congressional committees of both houses expanded and strengthened them. Berman describes in detail the turning of the tide in Congress and the concerted drive to enact a strong civil rights bill. Unlike 1960, the Southerners, not the liberals, were put almost immediately on the defensive. With the assassination of President Kennedy the momentum for such a bill became inexorable despite a four-month filibuster in the Senate. The outcome was the comprehensive Civil Rights Act of 1964.

In line with the earlier laws, the 1964 act sought to strengthen the political rights of blacks by forbidding various discriminatory practices and devices through which they had been disfranchised. Title I stipulated that universalistic criteria had to be applied to all persons in determining qualifications for voting in state and federal elections; further, literacy tests had to be impartially and universally given to all persons if they were to be required as part of the procedure for qualifying to vote; and minor errors and omissions were not adequate grounds for depriving anyone of the right to vote. Congress also requested the Secretary of Commerce in Title VIII to compile registration and voting statistics in geographic areas designated by the Commission on Civil Rights. The voting provisions, however, were not so much more stringent than those in the earlier bills as to mark a distinct break with the past; in fact they were generally so ineffective that another law devoted exclusively to voting was put on the congressional docket for the next year.

What made the act of 1964 so distinctive was the scope of its treatment of segregation and discrimination in the major institutional environments of the social realm. The act built on the foundations that had been laid almost a decade earlier by the Supreme Court in its historic rejection of the "separate but equal" doctrine of Plessy-Ferguson. Only what had then been expressed by judicial decision as a set of negative constraints against segregation and discrimination was now transformed by legislative enactment into a set of positive imperatives for desegregation and nondiscrimination.

Within the social realm the act clearly applied to those institutions and activities that were supported financially and otherwise by public and state sources. Title III, for example, dealt with the desegregation "of any public facility which is owned, operated, or managed by or on behalf of any State or subdivision thereof, other than a public school or public college as defined in section 401 of title IV hereof." It authorized the Attorney General "to institute for or in the name of the United States a civil action in any appropriate district court of the United States against such parties and for such relief as may be appropriate, and such court shall have and shall exercise jurisdiction of proceedings instituted pursuant to this section" (US Statutes at Large 1964 78:246.)

Title IV dealt with desegregation of public educational facilities. It authorized the Commissioner of Education "to render technical assistance" to appropriate governmental units, school boards, and the like "in the preparation, adoption, and implementation of plans for the desegregation of public schools." It also authorized the Commissioner to establish institutes "for special training designed to improve the ability of teachers, supervisors, counselors, and other elementary or secondary school personnel to deal effectively with special educational problems occasioned by desegregation." The Commissioner could award grants to school boards for the training of teachers and other school personnel and for employing specialists to advise on problems of desegregation. He was also charged with undertaking a survey within two years on "the lack of availability of equal educational opportunities for individuals by reason of race, color, religion, or national origin in public educational institutions at all levels in the United States, its territories and possessions, and the District of Columbia" (US Statutes at Large 1964 78:247). Finally, the Attorney General was also authorized to contribute to the process. He could initiate civil action wherever "meritorious" complaints were brought to his attention to achieve redress for persons whose rights under the law were being denied by school authorities.

Title VI extended provisions of the act to all federally assisted programs. It stipulated that "no person in the United States shall, on the ground of race, color, or national origin, be excluded from participation in, be denied the benefits of, or be subjected to discrimination under any program or activity receiving Federal financial assistance" (US Statutes at Large 1964 78:252). Failure to comply with this provision was grounds for terminating such assistance by governmental departments and agencies, after appropriate notice was given.

The act of 1964 also moved into institutional terrains of the social realm that had been previously placed within the sphere of private discrimination and behavior by the Supreme Court decision of 1883 and therefore out of reach of legislative action. Title II, for example, dealt with discrimination in places of public accommodation: "All persons shall be entitled to the full and equal enjoyment of the goods, services, facilities, privileges, advantages, and accommodations of any place of public accommodation, as defined in this section, without discrimination or segregation on the ground of race, color, religion, or national origin" (US Statutes at Large 1964 78:243). Included in its definition were such establishments as inns, hotels, and motels; also "any restaurant, cafeteria, lunchroom, lunch counter, soda fountain, or other facility principally engaged in selling food for consumption on the premises" and thirdly "any motion picture house, theater, concert hall, sports arena, stadium, or other place of exhibition or entertainment" (US Statutes at Large 1964 78:243).

To avoid the kind of court challenge that overturned the Civil Rights Act of 1875, Congress did not stake its primary claim to legislate in this area on the Fourteenth Amendment. It salvaged from the Fourteenth Amendment, however, what had been retained by the Court in its Shelley v. Kraemer ruling: namely, state action could not be used to enforce private acts of discrimination. Accordingly, Section 202 reads: "All persons shall be entitled to be free, at any establishment or place, from discrimination or segregation of any kind on the ground of race, color, religion, or national origin, if such discrimination or segregation is or purports to be required by any law, statute, ordinance, regulation, rule, or order of a State or any agency or political subdivision thereof" (US Statutes at Large 1964 78:244).

Instead of the Fourteenth Amendment, Congress was placing primary emphasis on its constitutional authority to regulate commerce between states. It defined commerce as

"travel, trade, traffic, commerce, transportation, or communication among the several States, or between the District of Columbia and any State, or between any foreign country or any territory or possession and any State or the District of Columbia, or between points in the same State but through any other State or the District of Columbia, or between points in the same State but through any other State or the District of Columbia or a foreign country."

(US Statutes at Large 1964 78:243)

Accordingly, Title II stipulated that its constraints against discrimination applied to the various establishments listed in Section 201 that catered to interstate travelers or that sold services or products which moved between states, such as food, gas, films, and the like. (The Supreme Court subsequently accepted this line of reasoning in finding Section 201 constitutional in Heart of Atlanta Motel v. United States [1965].)

However, to make doubly sure that Title II did not stray into the constitutionally protected sphere of private discrimination, Congress clearly stated that "The provisions of this title shall not apply to a private club or other establishment not in fact open to the public, except to the extent that the facilities of such establishment are made available to the customers or patrons of an establishment within the scope of subsection (b)" (US Statutes at Large 1964 78:243–44). Congress even exempted any establishment that catered to the public if it is "located within a building which contains not more than five rooms for rent or hire and which is actually occupied by the proprietor of such establishment as his residence" (Blaustein and Zangrando 1968:529).

Perhaps the most virginal legislative terrain which the act of 1964 entered was the economic sphere of employment and jobs. Even during the days of the first reconstruction Congress had not ventured into this realm of private decision and market behavior. In the intervening years whatever action on the federal level had been taken came from court decision or executive order, not congressional enactment.* The act of 1964 therefore, marked a significant point of entry for congressional intervention into the workings of the labor and occupational markets as they produced and reinforced racial discrimination and inequality. In its Title VII, Congress articulated "equal employment opportunity" as the normative base for the operation of these markets and thereby made it unlawful for the principal actors in these markets to discriminate because of race, color, religion, sex, or national origin.

A major target for these normative constraints was the employer of labor services. He was informed that it was unlawful

"(1) to fail or refuse to hire or to discharge any individual or otherwise to discriminate against any individual with respect to his compensation, terms, conditions, or privileges of employment, because of such individual's race, color, religion, sex, or national origin; or (2) to limit, segregate or classify his employees in any way which would deprive or tend to deprive any individual of employment opportunities or otherwise adversely affect his status as an employee, because of such individual's race, color, religion, sex, or national origin."   (US Statutes at Large 1964 78:255)

Labor unions were also put on notice that they too would be engaging in "an unlawful employment practice" if they were

---

*Action on the state level antedated federal action by almost twenty years. New York passed the first fair employment practices law in 1945; by 1960 at least fifteen other states had done so too. The effectiveness of most of these laws left much to be desired before the entry of the federal government into the field. Since then, significant improvement has been noticed in the results on the state level.

"(1) to exclude or to expel from its membership, or otherwise to discriminate against, any individual because of his race, color, religion, sex, or national origin; (2) to limit, segregate or classify its membership or to classify or fail or refuse to refer for employment any individual, in any way which would deprive or tend to deprive any individual of employment opportunities, or would limit such employment opportunities or otherwise adversely affect his status as an employee or as an applicant for employment, because of such individual's race, color, religion, sex, or national origin; or (3) to cause or attempt to cause an employer to discriminate against an individual in violation of this section."

(US Statutes at Large 1964 78:255–56)

Both labor and management were also warned that

"it shall be an unlawful employment practice for any employer, labor organization, or joint labor-management committee controlling apprenticeship or other training or retraining, including on-the-job training programs, to discriminate against any individual because of his race, color, religion, sex, or national origin in admission to, or employment in, any program established to provide apprenticeship or other training."   (US Statutes at Large 1964 78:256)

And finally, employment agencies were also instructed that it was unlawful "to fail or refuse to refer for employment, or otherwise to discriminate against, any individual because of his race, color, religion, sex, or national origin, or to classify or refer for employment any individual on the basis of his race, color, religion, sex, or national origin" (US Statutes at Large 78, 1964:255–56).

To provide a vehicle for enforcing the provisions of Title VII, Congress created the Equal Employment Opportunity Commission (EEOC). The Commission was empowered to receive and to investigate complaints of unlawful employment practices. It was also charged with seeking to eliminate the bases of the complaints through conciliation and conference. Failing in this, the Commission could merely appear as a friend in court for the aggrieved party in a civil action or could request civil action by the Attorney General if a pattern or general practice of discrimination appeared to underlie the specific grievance. In 1972 Congress expanded the powers of the Commission. It would thenceforth bring civil action itself against the offender in the district court and also seek temporary or preliminary relief pending the final disposition of the charge. If the offending party was a governmental unit, the Commission had to rely on the Attorney General to bring the necessary court action. (The legal and administrative path which the commission has taken in the pursuit of the goal of equal employment opportunity will be examined in Chapter 10.)

In turn, in Section 706 (g) the courts were given the authority to enjoin the offending party "from engaging in such unlawful employment practice, and [to] order such affirmative action as may be appropriate, which may include reinstatement or hiring of employees, with or without back pay (payable by the employer, employment agency, or labor organization, as the case may be, responsible for the unlawful employment practice)" (US Statutes at Large 1964 78:261). (In 1972 Congress gave the courts even broader latitude in determining the kind of equitable relief they might deem appropriate.)

In many respects then, the provisions of the Civil Rights Act of 1964 moved well beyond the legal and political realms of the People's Domain and extended into the major institutional environments of its social realm. No longer were the two realms to be governed by two different sets of standards: the racial and the American creeds; instead they were to have a common and unified legal-normative framework based on racial equality and the American creed.

To facilitate realization of this goal, Congress not only created the Equal Employment Opportunity Commission, but also established the Community Relations Service under Title X. The major function of the Service was to defuse situations; of potential racial conflict and to aid groups and communities

> "in resolving disputes, disagreements, or difficulties relating to discriminatory practices based on race, color, or national origin which impair the rights of persons in such communities under the Constitution or laws of the United States or which affect or may affect interstate commerce. The Service may offer its services in cases of such disputes, disagreements, or difficulties whenever, in its judgment, peaceful relations among the citizens of the community involved are threatened thereby, and it may offer its services either upon its own motion or upon the request of an appropriate State or local official or other interested person."   (US Statutes at Large 1964 78:267)

Congress did not, however, alter in any significant manner its earlier charge to the agency it had created in 1957, the Civil Rights Commission. It modified procedures somewhat; it also broadened existing functions with authority to serve as a national clearinghouse for information on the denial of civil rights and to investigate voting frauds as well as denials of the right to vote; and it extended the life of the Commission for four years with a final report required as of January 31, 1968.

THE VOTING RIGHTS ACT OF 1965

Significant as it was for opening up new institutional territories to legal-normative control, the Civil Rights Act of 1964 broke no new ground in implementing the political rights of the blacks. It merely reduced the difficulties in pursuing what still remained the primary remedy for voting discrimination: namely, case-by-case litigation through the courts. As a result, it had almost as little impact as had the earlier acts of 1957 and 1960 on the registration and voting of blacks.

> "According to estimates by the Attorney General during the hearings on the Act [of 1965], registration of voting-age Negroes in Alabama rose only 14.2% to 19.4% between 1958 and 1964; in Louisiana it barely inched ahead from 31.7% to 31.8% between 1956 and 1965; and in Mississippi it increased only from 4.4% to 6.4% between 1954 and 1964. In each instance, registration of voting-age whites ran roughly 50 percentage points or more ahead of Negro registration."   (Blaustein and Zangrando 1968:575)

In 1965 Congress once more focused its attention on voting discrimination and with the active and intense encouragement of President Johnson passed the Voting Rights Act of 1965. Wary again of the possible court challenges to the constitutionality of the act, Congress left no doubt as to which constitutional umbrella it thought would best protect the act from such a challenge. The title of the bill read: "To enforce the fifteenth amendment to the Constitution of the United States, and for other purposes" (US Statutes at Large 1965 79:437). (The Supreme Court accepted this line of reasoning in its decision upholding key sections of the law in South Carolina v. Katzenbach, 1966.)

What followed was a detailed and complicated series of provisions that at times bordered on technical obtuseness and over-elaboration; yet the substance of these provisions produced a fresh and innovative break with the past. The act shifted the primary instrumentality of enforcement from litigation, the courts, and voting referees to direct action, the executive branch, and federal examiners. It authorized the appointment of federal examiners by the Civil Service Commission for states and other political subdivisions in which the Attorney General had instituted court proceedings to enforce the guarantees of the Fifteenth Amendment. These examiners were to prepare and to maintain lists of persons qualified to vote in federal, state, and local elections. Such lists were to be transmitted on a regular basis to appropriate state or local election officials who were then required to place the names on the official voting list, subject to an expeditious challenge procedure. In turn, the examiners were obliged to "issue to each person whose name appears on such a list a certificate evidencing his eligibility to vote."

During an actual election, the examiner was also authorized to assign observers to polling places "for the purpose of observing whether persons who are entitled to vote are being permitted to vote," and to places where votes are tabulated "for purpose of observing whether votes cast by persons entitled to vote are being properly tabulated" (US Statutes at Large 1965 79:441).

States and political subdivisions were to be among those earmarked for such examiners if the Director of Census had determined that "less than 50 percentum of the persons of voting age residing therein were registered on November 1, 1964 or that less than 50 percentum of such persons voted in the presidential election of November 1964" (US Statutes at Large 1965 79:438) and if literacy or other tests were used as a qualifying measure for voting. In addition, the Attorney General had to certify for any of these states and subdivisions that

"(1) he has received complaints in writing from twenty or more residents of such political subdivision alleging that they have been denied the right to vote under color of law on account of race or color, and that he believes such complaints to be meritorious, or (2) that in his judgment considering among other factors, whether the ratio of nonwhite persons to white persons registered to vote within such subdivision appears to him to be reasonably attributable to violations of the fifteenth amendment or whether substantial evidence exists that bona fide efforts are being made within such subdivision to comply with the fifteenth amendment."   (US Statutes at Large 1965 79:440)

Within these designated areas the act of 1965 also suspended tests or other devices used to qualify a person as a voter. As defined by law,

"the phrase 'test or device' shall mean any requirement that a person as a prerequisite for voting or registration for voting (1) demonstrate the ability to read, write, understand, or interpret any matter, (2) demonstrate any educational achievement or his knowledge of any particular subject, (3) possess good moral character, or (4) prove his qualifications by the voucher of registered voters or members of any other class." (US Statutes at Large 1965 79:438–39)

The effect of the law was both dramatic and widespread. In its 1975 report the US Commission on Civil Rights stated:

"Minority political participation has increased substantially in the 10 years since enactment of the Voting Rights Act. There are more minority citizens registered, voting, running for office, and holding office than at any time in the Nation's past. Though the potential of minority political participation has yet to be realized, the progress of the last 10 years is striking. A large part of this progress is due directly or indirectly to the impact of the Voting Rights Act. Minority citizens are no longer politically invisible."

                    (US Commission on Civil Rights 1975:39)

As evidence of the law's impact, the commission reported that "More than 1 million new black voters registered in the seven covered Southern states* between 1964 and 1972, increasing the percentage of eligible blacks registered from about 29 percent to over 56 percent" (US Commission on Civil Rights 1975:40–1).

Six years later the chairman of the Subcommittee on Civil and Constitutional Rights of the House Committee on the Judiciary offered a similar assessment of the act at the beginning of hearings for its extension. He said, "unquestionably, the Voting Rights Act is the most important civil rights bill enacted by the Congress. Its sometimes dramatic successes demonstrate that it has been the most effective tool for protecting voting rights" (Subcommittee on Civil and Constitutional Rights of the US House Committee on the Judiciary 1981:1).

He then went on to present statistics that showed that the gap in voting registration between whites and blacks had declined from 44 per cent in 1965 to 23 per cent in 1980. "Prior to 1965, the percentage of black registered voters in the now covered States was 29 percent, registered whites stood at 73 percent. In 1980, it is estimated that approximately 57 percent of eligible black voters were registered in these States and just under 80 percent of whites were registered." He also added that "in 1968, less than one-half percent of all elected officeholders in the covered States were black; by 1980, the percentage had increased to 5.6 percent" (Subcommittee on Civil and Constitutional Rights of the US House Committee on the Judiciary 1981:1).

Despite these impressive gains, however, much still remains to be done to erase the continuing inequities from the past. This became the rallying cry in the successful battle in 1982 to extend key sections of the Voting Rights Act, particularly its preclearance enforcement provisions.

THE FAIR HOUSING ACT OF 1968

Having enacted in less than a decade civil rights legislation for most of the institutional areas in the political and social realms of the People's Domain, Congress finally turned to what some observers had labeled the "most sensitive" institutional area of all: that of housing. This has proved to be the last major area in which Congress has ventured civil rights action.

Not since the first reconstruction had Congress done anything in this area. At that time it stipulated as part of the Civil Rights Act of 1866 that "'All citizens of the United States shall have the same rights, in every State and Territory, as is

---

*The seven states were Alabama, Georgia, Louisiana, Mississippi, North Carolina, South Carolina, and Virginia.

enjoyed by white citizens thereof to inherit, purchase, lease, sell, hold, and convey real and personal property'" (Emerson, Haber, and Dorsen 1967:2050). Little was done to implement this provision in succeeding years. Courts interpreted it as applying only to restrictive state action, but left untouched restrictive covenants between private individuals; it backed the enforcement of these covenants with the power of the state until the landmark decision of Shelley v. Kraemer in 1948. Even after that, restrictive covenants were treated as legitimate parts of the constitutionally protected sphere of private discrimination and action.

Thus, only in the late 1960s did Congress seriously attempt to move into an institutional terrain that had been viewed as sacrosanct by the courts, let alone by the white homeowners and real estate interests. After several years of struggle and intense lobbying by its opponents, Congress finally passed the Fair Housing Act of 1968. The provisions of the act applied stage by stage to different kinds of dwellings and housing units so that by 1970 an estimated 80 percent of all housing was covered by the law. For example, the law applied immediately upon enactment to dwellings owned or subsidized by the federal government such as public housing and urban renewal projects. On January 1 1969 coverage extended to multiple unit dwellings, excluding those of fewer than five rooms or units that were owner-occupied, and to other dwellings that were owned and operated by persons in the business of selling or renting dwellings. As of January 1 1970, the law also applied to privately owned single-family houses that were sold or rented by a real estate broker or agent whose sale was publicly advertised in one or more of the media. Only private owners who did not resort to either in the sale or rental of their house were exempt from the provisions of the law.

The act made it unlawful to discriminate in the sale or rental of a dwelling "because of race, color, religion or national origin" (US Statutes at Large 1968 82:83). It forbade ethnic and racial references in public announcements and advertising for the sale or rental of dwellings. It also sought to curb "block busting." In addition, the act made it unlawful for any financing agency

> "to deny a loan or other financial assistance to a person applying therefor for the purpose of purchasing, constructing, improving, repairing, or maintaining a dwelling, or to discriminate against him in the fixing of the amount, interest rate, duration, or other terms or conditions of such loan or other financial assistance, because of the race, color, religion, or national origin of such person."   (US Statutes at Large 1968 82:83)

(A prohibition against sex discrimination was added in the Housing and Community Development Act of 1974.)

Authority and responsibility for administering and enforcing the act were placed in the hands of the Secretary of Housing and Urban Development. He was to seek voluntary compliance with the law through educational and informal conciliatory action.

In many respects, the long-term significance of the act has lain in its symbolic stand against discrimination in housing more than in its substantive accomplishments. In its 1974 report, for example, the US Commission on Civil Rights pointed to the limited enforcement provisions as a major flaw in the statute.

> "In the event of a refusal to comply with its provisions, the statute only authorizes HUD [Department of Housing and Urban Development] to use the informal methods of conference, conciliation, and persuasion. These methods have proved inadequate to bring about prompt compliance with the law."
>
> (US Commission on Civil Rights 1974:328)

The effects of the flaw, the commission stressed, were compounded by the relatively poor performance of the department, particularly by its failure "to make maximum use of its powers to bring about compliance" (US Commission on Civil Rights 1974:329). It also faulted other federal agencies for their reluctance to assume their responsibilities under the law. Accordingly, the commission concluded that despite any positive steps that the department and the other agencies may have taken, "the steps have not gone nearly far enough to have a major impact on racial, ethnic, and sex discrimination. The positive actions they have taken have generally been either superficial or incomplete and have had little impact on the country's serious housing discrimination problem" (US Commission on Civil Rights 1974:328).

Approximately six years later, the Carter administration undertook a belated but concerted effort to strengthen the enforcement features of the act. The bill easily passed the House of Representatives in June 1980 but foundered in the Senate in the wake of a filibuster. A coalition of Republicans and conservative Democrats – shades of the past and harbinger of the near future – defeated a vote on cloture in the waning days of the session, and the bill was withdrawn.

In a post mortem on the defeat, according to Martin Tolchin of *The New York Times*, "Senator Robert C. Byrd of West Virginia, the majority leader, referring to the influx of Republicans and conservatives in the next Congress, told the Senate that the failure to end the filibuster meant that 'it will be many years until a truly decent fair housing bill can be enacted'" (Tolchin 1980:138).

SUMMARY

Within a decade Congress had completed the process of transforming the racial creed from a legitimate to an illegitimate code of behavior – a process that had been initiated years earlier by the Supreme Court. However, unlike the Court,

Congress did not confine the transmutation to actions of the state and/or its agencies, but extended it also to actions of public consequence by individuals and organizations in the major institutional environments of the political and social realms of the People's Domain. In so doing, Congress explicitly and clearly affirmed the right of blacks to share with whites equality of access, opportunity, and treatment within these environments. In effect, Congress had mandated that all the major institutional environments of the People's Domain were to be governed under a common legal-normative framework based on racial equality and the American creed. Thus, the normative task begun in the first period of reconstruction seemed finally to have come to fruition during the height of the second period of reconstruction.

9

THE SECOND
PERIOD OF RECONSTRUCTION
AND EXECUTIVE POLICY

Introduction

Important as congressional action was in establishing the legal-normative framework for the second period of reconstruction, the president and executive branch of government have played an even more significant role in determining the direction and character of the governmental response to the struggle for civil rights during the twentieth century. For example, during the past two decades of congressional action, they have been instrumental in defining the legislative situation and in setting the tone and style of the congressional reaction. Even after Congress passed the civil rights acts, the executive branch was able to place its interpretive stamp on implementation of these laws, for the executive branch, not Congress, translates the abstract statements of law into detailed guidelines for administrative action and enforcement. This stamp is likely to be most pronounced where the law contains inherent ambiguities and contradictions as did the Civil Rights Act of 1964. The Equal Employment Opportunity Commission (EEOC), a creature of Title VII of the act, for example, has wended its way through the act's ambiguities by adopting an administrative direction and policy that many of its critics decry as being contrary to what Congress intended. (This will be examined in Chapter 10.)

Presidents have not merely been administrators of congressional enactments; they have also charted independent courses of policy and action through the vehicle of the executive order, which has the force of law. In the area of civil rights, for example, presidents have used this instrument to establish policy for the treatment of racial minorities within the government establishment itself and by parties having contractual ties with the government. Thus in the early twentieth century President Wilson used this vehicle to graft onto the bureaucratic structure of the federal government a policy of racial segregation and discrimination lasting for approximately three decades. Since World War II, the executive order has been used to achieve the opposite results. Beginning with Roosevelt, each succeeding president has issued orders and/or has sponsored changes within the executive branch of which the cumulative effect has been to create the administrative machinery to pursue a policy directly contrary to that of Wilson. In the process, what started with Roosevelt as a policy of nondiscrimination in government contracts and employment has become transformed into a policy of equal employment opportunity and affirmative action.

This chapter will examine presidential policy from Wilson to Nixon on treatment of racial minorities and will treat the executive order as a primary vehicle for the expression of this policy. We shall be particularly interested in the history of the past forty years, which have witnessed the change from nondiscrimination to affirmative action. Contributing significantly to this history for at least the past decade have been the EEOC and the federal courts. We shall examine their involvement in the process in the next chapter.

Wilson: ascendancy of Jim Crowism in the government establishment

Scholars generally agree that Taft was the first president in the twentieth century to move openly and consequentially in the direction of Jim Crowism and racial segmentation in the federal establishment. He refused, for example, to appoint blacks to post offices or other federal offices in the South for fear that their presence would offend whites, despite the fact that blacks had served in these posts for years. In addition, he introduced segregation into the workings of the census bureau by insisting that census takers only interview members of their own race.

These steps were the mere beginnings of a policy of segregation and racial separation that flourished more fully and widely in the next presidential administration. Many observers point to the Wilson administration as representing the high-water mark in this century for executive support of a racially bifurcated and segmented society. For example, Davis says "The administration of Woodrow Wilson was the most unfortunate the negro federal worker ever experienced" (Davis 1946:65). Van Riper echoes this sentiment: "The period from 1913 to 1931 deserves to be considered the most critical period in the recent history of Negro federal civil employment" (Van Riper 1958:242). A black observer of the day, Kelly Miller, bitterly denounced President Wilson in a pamphlet as seeking to impose a caste system on the federal service.

Meier and Rudwick do not agree that Wilson's administration represented the peak of Jim Crowism, despite the fact that it flowered during that period. Instead they insist that Wilson neither initiated the policy (Taft and to a lesser extent Theodore Roosevelt did) nor did he bring it to the heights that Coolidge did. "Ironically the climax of this process came not under Woodrow Wilson, who had been born in the South, but during the administration of Calvin Coolidge, the most Yankee of presidents" (Meier and Rudwick 1967:184).

Whatever may be the merits of Meier and Rudwick's statement, the fact remains that Jim Crowism became a distinctive mark of the Wilson administration, despite his assurances to the contrary to black leaders during the political campaign for the election of 1912. Almost immediately upon taking office, several of his cabinet members from the South instituted policies of segregation in their departments; none had had such a policy since the Civil War. Specifically restrictive measures were introduced into the Treasury and Post Office Departments and the Bureau of Engraving and Printing. Meier and Rudwick describe the various forms that racial separation took: "Negroes were commonly required to work in separate rooms, or in a separate section of a larger room in which whites also worked. Segregated lockers and lavatories were also widespread. Most pervasive of all, apparently, was the practice of segregated lunchrooms" (Meier and Rudwick 1967:179). In addition, federal positions that had traditionally been filled by blacks went to whites, such as Register of Treasury, Customs Collector for the District of Columbia, and Auditor of the Navy, and a clean sweep was made of black political appointees in the South.

Wilson saw no contradiction between his repressive and restrictive policies on race, which he justified on the grounds of racial harmony and humanitarianism, and the lofty and progressive goals of his New Freedom. In his first inaugural address, he committed his administration to social justice and to concern for the well-being and needs of the ordinary member of the "body politic." Apparently he did not view blacks as part of that "body politic."

> "'The firm basis of government is justice, not pity. These are matters of justice. There can be no equality or opportunity, the first essential of justice in the body politic, if men and women and children be not shielded in their lives, their very vitality, from the consequences of great industrial and social processes which they cannot alter, control, or singly cope with. Society must see to it that it does not itself crush or weaken or damage its own constituent parts. The first duty of law is to keep sound the society it serves. Sanitary laws, pure food laws, and laws determining conditions of labor which individuals are powerless to determine for themselves are intimate parts of the very business of justice and legal efficiency.'" (Commager II 1968:84)

Black leaders, on the other hand, were painfully aware of the contradiction. As a black editor complained in the *New York Amsterdam News* on October 3, 1913:

"'When the Wilson Administration came into power, six months ago, it promised a "new freedom" to all people, avowing the spirit of Christian Democracy,.... But on the contrary we are given a stone instead of a loaf of bread; we are given a hissing serpent rather than a fish'" (Link 1956:248). Thus was exemplified once again in the acts and words of Wilson a curious paradox of American history: the periodic linkage between liberalism on matters of concern to the larger white society with reactionism on matters of concern to racial minorities.

The incubus of discriminatory racial policies that infected the executive branch during the Wilson administration also pervaded the legislative branch which was under the firm control of white Southerners;

> "During the first Wilson administration nearly two dozen anti-Negro measures were introduced in the House and Senate, 'the greatest flood of bills proposing discriminatory legislation against Negroes' ever to come before the Congress. They ran the gamut from Jim Crow transportation regulations and armed forces enlistment to prohibition of miscegenation, civil service, segregation, and repeal of the Fifteenth Amendment. Their sponsors were southerners, and they made little or no progress, with only the miscegenation bill being reported by a committee."　　　　　　　　　　　　　　　　　　　　　　　(Weiss 1970:133)

The outcry of blacks and liberal white Northerners and the pressures of the war intervened to keep the segregationist policies of Wilson from pervading all departments of the federal government, but the pattern had been set and it continued with minor variations through succeeding administrations. Some scholars say the practice declined somewhat during the 1920s. They cite the increased number of blacks in the employ of government and allude to Hoover's termination of segregation in the Department of Commerce while he was still its secretary. As we have already seen, Meier and Rudwick claim the opposite; they contend that the practice of segregation expanded to such departments as the Interior and the Register of Treasury, and that it peaked during the Coolidge period. In fact, they say that "the 1920s ended with the problem of the Treasury Department untouched, some segregated work units existing in the Interior Department and the general prevalence of jim crow lavatories, locker rooms and cafeterias" (Meier and Rudwick 1967:183).

Roosevelt: modest beginnings of an executive policy

Blacks did not fare much better in the early days of the New Deal. Discriminatory policies were still followed by a number of departments and agencies in their internal and external relations with blacks. As we have already seen in Chapter 7, the Federal Housing Administration supported restrictive covenants and zoning restrictions against blacks until the late 1940s. The practices of the Home Owners Loan Corporation and the Federal Home Loan Bank virtually shut off loans to black applicants. The Tennessee Valley Authority (TVA) only hired blacks as unskilled labor but refused to include them in its training programs. Most New Deal work and relief agencies relied on local officials to dispense jobs and relief; consequently blacks received much less than they should have, particularly in the South.

And yet, despite the record of discriminatory treatment, many blacks overcame their initial reservations about Roosevelt, which were reflected in the low percentage who voted for him in 1932, and endorsed him for the election of 1936. In part, this turnabout stemmed from the fact that some of the welfare and work benefits of the New Deal had filtered down to the blacks despite the discrimination and the reluctance of President Roosevelt to espouse publicly the cause of the black. In part it stemmed from the fact that Mrs Roosevelt and Secretary of the Interior Ickes had gained the respect of the blacks by their open and fervent advocacy of black rights and causes. The Secretary had eliminated segregationist policies that had been traditional for his department and had brought young and promising blacks into positions of responsibility. From these blacks and others President Roosevelt had assembled what came to be known as his "black cabinet" to advise him on policies and matters of concern to blacks.

Not until 1940, however, did these individual and unofficial strands of goodwill coalesce into an explicit statement of policy. As part of its platform for the 1940 election, the Democratic party included for the first time in the twentieth century a plank on the rights of the black. It made the following promise: "'We shall continue to strive for complete legislative safeguards against discrimination in Government service and benefits, and in national defense forces. We pledge to uphold due process and the equal protection of laws for every citizen regardless of race, creed or color'" (Bergman 1969:491). By the election of that year Roosevelt fulfilled part of the promise. He issued an executive order that forbade racial discrimination in personnel policies for employment in the federal government. His executive order anticipated by nineteen days passage of the Ramspeck Bill which also forbade discrimination for those employed in the federal government "on the basis of race, color and creed in fixing salaries, in allocating positions to grades, and in making transfers, promotions, and other personnel decisions" (Rosenbloom 1971:126).

Under pressure from black leaders and A. Phillip Randolph, President of the Brotherhood of Sleeping Car Porters, who threatened a mass protest against discrimination in Washington, Roosevelt took another step to fulfill the promise of 1940. In June 1941 he issued Executive Order 8802 that reaffirmed "'the policy of the United States that there shall be no discrimination in the employment of workers in defense industries or government because of race, creed, color, or national origin.'" He also said in the order, "'I do hereby declare that it is the duty of employers and labor organizations in furtherance of said policy and of this order, to provide for the full and equitable participation of all workers in defense industries, without discrimination because of race, creed, color, or national origin'" (Blaustein and Zangrando 1968:358).

Accordingly, the President ordered all governmental departments and agencies to make sure that their vocational and training programs for defense production did not discriminate. In addition, he stipulated that "'all contracting agencies of the Government of the United States shall include in all defense contracts hereafter negotiated by them a provision obligating the contractor not to discriminate against any worker because of race, creed, color, or national origin'" (Blaustein and Zangrando 1968:359). And finally he established a Committee on Fair Employment Practice (FEPC) in the Office of Production Management to oversee the terms of the order. The committee, however, had no authority to enforce the provisions of the order, merely to investigate complaints of discrimination and to seek redress through moral persuasion.

In December 1941 Roosevelt issued another order (9001) authorizing the War and Navy Departments and the US Maritime Commission to enter into defense contracts under Title II of the just approved "Act to Expedite the Prosecution of the War Effort." The President ordered these departments not to discriminate in their choice of contractors and to incorporate a nondiscrimination provision in all the contracts that they signed.

In May 1943, Roosevelt amended Order 8802 with Executive Order 9346. He increased the Committee on Fair Employment Practices to six members and placed it in the Office for Emergency Management. In addition, he ordered that all contracting agencies and departments of the federal government, not merely those of the military, were to include in their contracts a provision which obligated the contractor and subcontractor not to discriminate against any employee or applicant for employment because of race, creed, color, or national origin.

The FEPC continued to operate throughout World War II but it faced constant harassment from Congress. Specifically, Congress hobbled the work of the committee by mandating congressional approval for its funding and then by systematically reducing its funds to a trickle. Despite the efforts of Truman, who had by then become president, to transform the committee into a permanent agency by statute, the FEPC was dissolved by the end of 1945. Its factual accomplishments were meager, but its symbolic value great; for it was the pioneering venture in the area of fair employment. While the committee itself was allowed to die, the policy of nondiscrimination that gave birth to it remained as a vestigial provision in government contracts. As we shall see later, this provided Truman with the rationale for setting up another version of the FEPC five years later under a different name.

Truman: a turning point in executive policy in civil rights and nondiscrimination

Despite his failure to get Congress to act on the FEPC, President Truman remained attentive to the pleas of black leaders that his administration do something to blunt the postwar tide of mounting violence and lynching against blacks in the South. Aware that nothing could be done with Congress, Truman issued Executive Order 9808 in December 1946 that established the President's Committee on Civil Rights. In his charge to the committee, the President deplored "the action of individuals who take the law into their own hands and inflict summary punishment and wreak personal vengeance" and insisted that "all possible steps be taken to safeguard our civil rights." Accordingly, he authorized the committee "to inquire into and to determine whether and in what respect current law-enforcement measures and the authority and means possessed by federal, state, and local governments may be strengthened and improved to safeguard the civil rights of the people" (Blaustein and Zangrando 1968:374). As its final act, the committee was to prepare a report of its findings and a statement of its recommendations "with respect to the adoption or establishment by legislation or otherwise, of more adequate and effective means and procedures for the protection of the civil rights of people of the United States" (Blaustein and Zangrando 1968:375).

By the end of October 1947 the committee submitted its report, "To Secure These Rights," to the President. In many respects the report was set in the conceptual framework of Myrdal's American dilemma. Like Myrdal, it asserted that the disparity between American ideals and practices had corroded the moral sensibilities of whites and undermined the confidence of the victimized blacks in the American creed. "The pervasive gap between our aims and what we actually do is creating a kind of moral dry rot which eats away at the emotional and rational bases of democratic beliefs. There are times when the difference between what we preach about civil rights and what we practice is shockingly illustrated by individual outrages" (The President's Committee on Civil Rights 1947:139–40). This, the report insisted, has continued for too long: *The United States can no longer countenance these burdens on its common conscience, these inroads on its moral fiber*" (The President's Committee on Civil Rights 1947:141). The report then offered two additional reasons "for believing that the time for action is now"

(The President's Committee on Civil Rights 1947:131). One was economic: "*The United States can no longer afford this heavy drain upon its human wealth, its national competence*" (The President's Committee on Civil Rights 1947:146). The other was international: "*The United States is not so strong, the final triumph of the democratic ideal is not so inevitable that we can ignore what the world thinks of us or our record*" (The President's Committee on Civil Rights 1947:148).

The report concluded with a comprehensive set of recommendations that ranged across the entire spectrum of racial discrimination and segregation and were classified under six general headings. A number of these recommendations were primarily addressed to the federal government. For example, the government was asked to strengthen: in Section I, the machinery for the protection of civil rights; in Section II, the right to safety and security of the person; in Section III, the right to citizenship and its privileges; in Section IV, "the right to freedom of conscience and expression." Section V was addressed primarily to state governments in the areas of employment, education, housing, and health services; in turn, Congress was asked to pass a federal fair employment practices act and to enact a public accommodations law. In general, this section insisted on "the elimination of segregation, based on race, color, creed, or national origin, from American life" (McCoy and Ruetten 1973:90). Section VI was addressed primarily to the American people, not to the government; it recommended "a long-term campaign of pubic education to inform the people of the civil rights to which they are entitled and which they owe to one another" (McCoy and Ruetten 1973:91).

The report provided the President with an ideational and ideological approach, framework, and substance that he was soon to employ in his ambitious legislative and executive program for civil rights. He prepared the groundwork in his State of the Union address in January and followed up with a message to Congress on February 2 1948 in which he submitted his recommendations for legislation. According to McCoy and Ruetten, "The February 2 message was historic, if only because it represented the first occasion upon which an American president had dispatched a civil rights message to Congress" (McCoy and Ruetten 1973:99).

In his message Truman reaffirmed the basic tenets of the American creed and argued as Myrdal and his own committee had done before that the disparity between ideal and practice had created a moral and legal dilemma for America whose resolution required action by the federal government. The President then made ten recommendations for legislative action, many of them derived directly from the report of his committee. He organized these recommendations under the six headings that the committee had used. Of particular interest to civil rights advocates were his recommendations that a permanent FEPC be established and that voting rights be protected. In addition, he proposed such additional measures as establishment of a permanent Commission on Civil Rights, federal protection against lynching, the prohibition of discrimination in interstate transportation facilities, and the like.

The administration, however, did not seek immediate passage of the bill in Congress. It allowed the bill to be put on the shelf for that session and thereby blunted the pressure for action. However, the dramatic and successful floor fight for a strong civil rights plank at the Democratic presidential convention thrust the issue once again onto center stage. Truman, having survived the struggle for the nomination, added to the momentum on July 26 by issuing two executive orders: the first (9980) dealt with fair employment practices in the executive branch; the second (9981) with the desegregation of the armed forces (we shall return to these orders shortly). Truman did not continue to press hard on the civil rights issue during the early part of the campaign, but by its end he hammered relentlessly on the issue in speeches in the big cities of the Northeast. So impressed were blacks and other minorities with his record and with what he said that they voted overwhelmingly for him and thereby provided the margin in key states for his upset victory over Dewey.

Once elected, Truman made it clear in his State of the Union Address that he was going to push, as part of his Fair Deal program, for passage of the civil rights legislation that he had previously presented to Congress in his message of February 1948. However he had virtually no success with Congress. Those few pieces of legislation that managed to squeak through the House, such as the anti-poll tax bill in 1949 and the modest FEPC bill of 1950, died in the Senate from the combined onslaught of the filibuster and of the coalition of southern Democrats and midwestern Republicans. As a result, the Truman administration, despite its efforts, wrote no civil rights legislation of any real consequence during its tenure of office; and yet it compiled an impressive record of governmental actions, not merely words.

Frustrated by the intransigence of Congress, Truman relied heavily on two other governmental avenues of decision and action: the courts and the executive office. For example, during the middle and late 1940s when the Supreme Court effectively stemmed and reversed the tide of its own history of restrictive civil rights decisions, President Truman was responsible for the appointment of the chief justice, Vinson, whose Court rendered these landmark decisions. Truman also chose for the Court, somewhat later, Clark, whose commitment to civil rights had already been demonstrated during his tenure as attorney general. In addition, government attorneys were instructed to file briefs of *amicus curiae* in many of these cases, including Shelley v. Kraemer, Sweatt, McLaurin, and so on. In the Henderson case the Solicitor General even went so far as to reject a motion prepared by the Interstate Commerce Commission "to affirm the position that segregation of Negroes in diners was not discriminatory" (McCoy and Ruetten

1973:218); he then filed an *amicus curiae* brief for Henderson. On the virtual eve of his departure from office, Truman had government attorneys intervene in the first set of hearings in the Supreme Court on the school desegregation cases. The Attorney General, McGranery, filed an *amicus curiae* brief that hit hard against practices of racial discrimination and segregation and that recommended the overturning of the Plessy-Ferguson doctrine. A year later the new Attorney General Brownell, in the Eisenhower administration, failed to match the eloquence and decisiveness of McGranery in the re-hearing before the Court. He even avoided mentioning the government's position on Plessy-Ferguson; only during the oral arguments was its position elicited by the Court. No such ambiguity had existed in the Court arguments conducted by the Truman appointee.

While his influence on the Supreme Court was necessarily limited and indirect, as president Truman was able to exercise direct control over the policies and programs of the executive branch of the federal government. The executive branch therefore became the primary vehicle for the realization of his commitment to civil rights. He issued executive orders and did other things to effectuate changes in policies and practices of discrimination and segregation in its various branches. Observers generally agree that the most impressive and lasting achievement of this kind in the Truman administration was the desegregation of the armed forces.

Issued in July 1948 – during the early phase of the presidential campaign as we have already noted – Executive Order 9981 declared that the policy of the President was to be "'equality of treatment and opportunity of all persons in the armed forces without regard to race, color, religion, or national origin'" (Blaustein and Zangrando 1968:385). To implement this policy, Truman established the President's Committee on Equality of Treatment and Opportunity in the Armed Services under the chairmanship of Charles H. Fahy. The committee was authorized to examine "'the rules, procedures, and practices of the armed services in order to determine in which respect such rules, procedures, and practices may be altered or improved with a view to carrying out the policy of this order'" (Blaustein and Zangrando 1968:386).

The committee received the close cooperation of the Secretary of Defense who issued a directive to the various secretaries of the armed forces in April 1949 to the effect that the policy of the National Military Establishment was "equality of treatment and opportunity for all persons in the Armed Services without regard to race, color, religion, or national origin" (Blaustein and Zangrando 1968:387). He then listed three ways in which this overall policy was to be realized:

> "'(1) To meet the requirements of the Services for qualified individuals, all personnel will be considered on the basis of individual merit and ability and must qualify according to the prescribed standards for enlistment,

attendance at schools, promotion, assignment to specific duties, etc.

(2) All individuals, regardless of race, will be accorded equal opportunity for appointment, advancement, professional improvement, promotion, and retention in their respective components of the National Military Establishment.

(3) Some units may continue to be manned with Negro personnel; however, all Negroes will not necessarily be assigned to Negro units. Qualified Negro personnel shall be assigned to fill any type of position vacancy in organizations or overhead installations without regard to race.'"

(Blaustein and Zangrando 1968:387)

Within eighteen months, the committee accepted the plans for desegregation that the air force and navy had prepared. However, the army resisted desegregation and procrastinated in preparing plans for its implementation that were acceptable to the committee. Not until the Korean War did *ad hoc* integration occur in some combat units, but even then an overall policy of integration was not worked out for the Far Eastern Command until 1951. Two more years elapsed before the policy became general throughout the army. By 1954, the army claimed that all units were integrated except for an occasional small group that was in the process of being assigned.

Less effective and impressive were the results of the other executive order issued on that same day in July. Order 9980 reaffirmed the President's commitment to employment without discrimination in the federal government. It set up a network of fair employment officers in the various executive agencies and departments who were to hear grievances and to seek redress through consultation. At the summit of this network, the order placed a Fair Employment Board that was to be in the Civil Service Commission. The board was to coordinate the program and to hear appeals; it was also supposed to bring agency practices into line with board policy through consultation with the various government agencies and through moral persuasion. However, the board had to operate in a much less clearly defined context than the Fahy committee. For example, the institutional environment in which the board had to operate did not have the same clear-cut structure of authority as did the environment for the Fahy committee, nor did it face as clear-cut a case of policies and practices of overt segregation.

Instead, the board was confronted with a myriad of agencies, each with its own sphere of authority and with its own set of racial policies and practices; in fact, many professed policies of nondiscrimination though their practices were suspect. Further, the leadership of the board was not as effective as that of the Fahy committee, and its budget and staff were considerably smaller. As a result, the board compiled a very undistinguished record.

Pleased as the civil rights advocates were with the issuance of these executive orders, they viewed them as mere beginnings. They especially wanted the re-creation of something akin to the FEPC. Throughout his administration the President continually sought to satisfy this demand by calling on Congress to pass the necessary legislation, but he was reluctant to act on his own through an executive order, particularly in view of the legislative restraints which Congress had earlier imposed on the FEPC and which were still on its books.

As the pressures mounted during the Korean War, the President sought to placate his critics by issuing a series of orders from February through October 1951 in which he reaffirmed the policy of nondiscrimination for executive departments and stipulated that all of their contracts must contain a nondiscriminatory provision. The orders applied first to the Departments of Defense and Agriculture and later to the Department of the Interior.

In December 1951, Truman finally overcame his misgivings and issued Executive Order 10308, which established The President's Committee on Government Contract Compliance. In a statement that accompanied the order, Truman said:

"The purpose of this order is to secure better compliance by contractors and subcontractors with certain provisions now required in their contracts with the United States Government. For nearly ten years it has been mandatory to include in such contracts a clause obligating the contractor to practice nondiscrimination in the performance of his contract. The clause specifically forbids discrimination because of race, creed, color, or national origin; relates to the various aspects of employment; and extends to subcontracts as well as to original contracts."

(The President's Committee on Government Contract Compliance 1953:6)

The committee was authorized to examine and to study rules, procedures, and practices of contracting agencies as they related to the compliance with the nondiscrimination provision. It was also to confer with and advise officers of the contracting agencies on how to set up effective procedures, but it had no power of enforcement, nor was it even authorized to receive complaints of discrimination. Only the contracting officers were to handle such matters and then only by persuasion.

In its final report in 1953, the committee claimed to have had some effect on the practices of contracting agencies in the government. It cited, for example, the fact that prior to its existence only two of the twenty-eight agencies it studied had made more than a token effort to obtain compliance from contractors. Many had not even bothered to insert the nondiscrimination clause in their contracts; nor had they assigned any personnel to oversee compliance. As a result, few complaints were received or processed, and the provision was a dead letter for all intents and purposes.

With the committee in existence, virtually all contracting agencies inserted the provision in their contracts and made an effort to set up some sort of machinery for complaints and compliance. The committee, however, did not seek to exaggerate its accomplishments; instead it dwelled on the basic inadequacy of the entire compliance procedure including its own role, and on the superficial treatment accorded complaints of discrimination by contracting agencies. It claimed that contracting agencies were inclined to feel that "a sufficient inquiry had been made by sending a representative to the plant to ask what apparently amounted to the simple question – 'Are you discriminating against Negroes?' When the obvious answer 'No' was recorded, the inquiry was considered closed by the agency" (The President's Committee on Government Contract Compliance 1953:29).

Accordingly, the committee made a lengthy set of recommendations. Their primary focus was on the inadequacies of the process and procedures for receiving complaints and securing compliance; their primary purpose, to make the bureaucratic structure more effective and efficient in the realization of the basic goal of nondiscrimination. For example, the committee would centralize the receiving, investigating, and conciliating of complaints of discrimination and place the responsibility in the hands of a permanent government agency, preferably the Department of Labor. The primary responsibility for enforcement of the provision would remain with the contracting agencies.

Further, the committee recommended a fundamental revision of the nondiscriminatory clause in the government contracts so that the obligations of the contractor would be spelled out with more clarity and detail; it offered an example of such a revised clause. The nondiscriminatory provision should also be given the same weight and importance as any other provision in a government contract – "the nondiscrimination provision must be rated equally with other government contract provisions" (The President's Committee on Government Contract Compliance 1953:29) – and should be adopted as a standard provision in all federal grants in aid and loan programs.

In addition, the committee would streamline, standardize, and tighten the complaint and compliance process and procedures within the various contracting agencies. It would also make available to contracting agencies more coercive and compelling instruments of control. Where compliance, for example, could not be obtained through persuasion and conciliation, then the agency should be authorized to terminate the contract, to seek an injunction, and/or to disqualify the party from further contracts. "Liquidated damages to obtain conformance" and arbitration might be additional legislative remedies to be sought.

So perceptive and farsighted was the committee in its recommendations that succeeding presidential administrations relied on one or more of them to plug various gaps in the program. Consequently, by the time President Johnson took over the administration of the program, many of the committee's recommendations had already been incorporated in its bureaucratic structuring and functioning; he adopted most of what remained. Thus it is evident that, as early as 1953, the basic requirements for an effective program of nondiscrimination in government contracting had already become visible. The will to act on these requirements, though, took a long time to materialize.

Interestingly, an equivalent of the phrase "affirmative action," which took on such a controversial meaning during the Johnson administration, was first used by the committee in another area of recommendation: that bearing on manpower policy and training. The committee used the phrase to goad a bureaucratic agency into acting more boldly and positively in the implementation of the policy of nondiscrimination:

"5. THE COMMITTEE RECOMMENDS THAT THE BUREAU OF EMPLOYMENT SECURITY TAKE A MORE AFFIRMATIVE STAND ON THE POLICY OF NONDISCRIMINATION IN THE PERFORMANCE OF ITS MISSION.

The Committee urges the Bureau of Employment Security to act positively and affirmatively to implement the policy of nondiscrimination in its functions of placement counseling, occupational analysis and industrial services, labor market information, and community participation in employment activities. It should intensify its efforts to obtain maximum placement of minority group workers in jobs appropriate to their skills and to eliminate the use of discriminatory job orders by employers. It also should maintain a system of records to measure adequately the results of its efforts to persuade employers to abandon discriminatory requests for applicants." (The President's Committee on Government Contract Compliance 1953:72–3)

In sum, the Truman years represented a major turning point in the struggle for civil rights. Until then no administration had sought to challenge, head on, the basic premises of the racial creed, which had a "sanctified presence" in the various institutional environments of the society. But beginning in the mid-1940s, both the executive and judiciary branches of the federal government took important first steps in the delegitimation of the racial creed that finally took place almost a decade or so later. They pioneered the way for the future. The President, though, had an even tougher row to hoe than the Court. He had to face an intransigent Congress that refused to legislate anything in civil rights, impatient racial minorities that were no longer prepared to wait, and a white majority, particularly in the South, that was prepared to fight every step of the way to guard its privileges. Consequently, Truman may in fact have accomplished very little, but his administration set important bench marks for the future and his words and actions made visible the commitment of a president to civil rights for the first time in the twentieth century. As McCoy and Ruetten say, Truman "was the first president to have a civil rights program, the first to try to come to grips with the basic problems of minorities, and the first to condemn, vigorously and consistently, the presence of discrimination and inequality in America" (McCoy and Ruetten 1973:352).

Eisenhower: modest elaboration of a policy of nondiscrimination

The executive branch during the Eisenhower administration played a less dramatic and innovative role in the field of civil rights than did the other two branches of government. The Supreme Court, for example, announced early in the President's first term the momentous Brown decision that overturned the Plessy-Ferguson doctrine and opened the door to the second period of reconstruction. Congress in turn passed during Eisenhower's second term its first legislation on civil rights since the first period of reconstruction.

In each of these events, the executive branch played an important though backstage role. As we have already seen, Eisenhower's Attorney General Brownell prepared an *amicus curiae* brief at the re-hearing in the Brown case. His approach was not as forthright nor as unambiguous as that of Truman's Attorney General, but he nevertheless supported desegregation of the schools. Further, Eisenhower may have been unhappy with the Court's decision and may have given it little public support, but he nevertheless used the powers of the presidency to enforce the school desegregation decision of the Court in Little Rock when the governor of Arkansas sought to block its implementation by interposing the power of his state. (This is discussed in detail in Chapter 11.) (In the 1960 Civil Rights Act he even had punitive measures included against those who would impede the implementation of a court order.

With respect to civil rights legislation, President Eisenhower defined the parameters in which Congress acted. He offered relatively modest proposals on voting rights for the 1957 and 1960 bills and opposed stringent enforcement provisions and the extension of civil rights legislation to other institutional areas of society

Within the executive branch, the President also pursued a policy of moderations. During his tenure in office, he undertook no strikingly new initiatives in the area of civil rights. Instead, he built generally upon the foundations that Truman had laid earlier. In the case of the desegregation of the military for example, he consolidated the gains of the Truman administration and then pushed on until the policy and practice were general throughout the defense establishment. Similarly, he retained the basic outlines of Truman's approach to nondiscrimination in government contracting; the modest modifications were also largely along the lines recommended by the Truman committee.

President Eisenhower created his own version of the Committee on Government Contract Compliance in August 1953. He replaced Truman's Order 10308 with his own 10479 and shortened the committee's name to Committee on Government Contracts. The committee was to be more than a study and advisory group as Truman's had initially been set up to be. It was authorized to receive complaints of discrimination, but it did not have the authority to investigate or to act on them; instead it was required to transmit these complaints to the appropriate government contracting agency for study and action. The contracting agency was obliged, however, to inform the committee of its final disposition of the complaint.

In effect, a small step had been taken in the direction that Truman's group had recommended but the committee was still far from being the centralized agency that the earlier body had envisioned. Even the way the committee was structured kept it from becoming centralized. Instead of being located in the Department of Labor as the Truman group had recommended, it was designed as an interdepartmental committee of fourteen whose membership consisted largely of the heads of various departments, including that of Labor; its chairman was Vice President Nixon.

Within a year the committee revised drastically the nondiscrimination clause in government contracts along the lines suggested by the Truman group. It replaced the vague general statement with a detailed listing of the various aspects of employment in which discrimination was forbidden: "employment, upgrading, demotion, or transfer; recruitment or recruitment advertising; lay-off or termination; rates of pay or other forms of compensation and selection for training, including apprenticeship" (The President's Committee on Government Contracts 1955:14). Further, the contractor was obliged to post this revised nondiscrimination clause "in conspicuous places" for his present and prospective employees. These changes took on the force of law through Executive Order 10557 which Eisenhower issued in September 1954.

Although its authority was limited to reviewing the actions of contracting agencies on complaints, the committee was able to exercise a degree of influence on the complaint and compliance process that the Truman committee had not. It kept a record of all complaints that were received and it required an accounting by the contracting agency of its disposition of a case. During the years of its existence, the number of complaints increased fourfold from 65 in 1954 to 244 in 1969. Of the total 888 cases, however, only 258 were carried to a successful resolution in which the committee endorsed the agency's action. Most of the others (383) were thrown out because the committee disclaimed jurisdiction (for example, the company about which the complaint was lodged might not be a government contractor) and because of incomplete information. The remainder (247) were still in the process of being acted upon.

The committee also encouraged the contracting agencies to do compliance surveys; over 1500 were conducted during its tenure. Occasionally and with considerable fanfare, the committee would report that a given company had agreed to hire more blacks or other racial minorities and/or to comply generally with the nondiscrimination clause. As an example, the committee's report, "Five Years of Progress 1953–1958," is replete with photographs of individual blacks who had benefited from the program, with short written descriptions of companies that had cooperated with the program, and with glowing accounts of the success of the program.

The committee even embarked on an ambitious series of informational and educational meetings and conferences for businessmen, labor leaders, and others to increase awareness of and compliance with its program. Its efforts yielded significant gains in publicity and in public relations but produced meager results in compliance with the nondiscrimination clause. For, lacking any power of enforcement, the committee had to rely on what the contracting agencies would do to insure compliance. The answer was that they did very little. Agencies assigned responsibility for obtaining compliance from contractors to personnel who were already responsible for gaining compliance on the other provisions of the contract. The personnel had both the interest and skill for doing the latter, but rarely for doing the former. In fact, many resented what they deemed to be an additional burden. The committee tried to remedy the situation by preparing a field manual and by conducting training sessions on occasion, but the situation barely improved during its term of office.

As a result, no real effort at enforcement was attempted. In no instance, for example, were any contracts cancelled or withheld because of noncompliance nor was any other sanction applied during the years the committee functioned. In assessing the overall effectiveness of the Eisenhower and Truman committees, the Southern Regional Council concluded in 1961 that "The Government Contract Committee and its predecessor seem to have accomplished little to arrest discrimination in employment" (Southern Regional Council 1961:33).

In January 1955 President Eisenhower placed his stamp through Executive

Order 10590 on still another mechanism Truman had created for monitoring discriminatory employment practices. He replaced Truman's Fair Employment Board with The President's Committee on Government Employment Policy. The committee was charged, as was its predecessor, with eliminating discriminatory practices in federal employment. To assist the committee, each government agency and department was required to appoint an employment policy officer who would investigate complaints and would seek resolution of the problem at the departmental level. The committee was to function as a board of review and appeal; its findings, though, were to be treated as advisory and not binding by the department.

During its tenure, the committee conducted a number of surveys of black employment in federal jobs, principally in five cities. It noted a gradual increase in employment from 1956–60. The committee also ran educational and instructional programs to familiarize the employment policy officers with its procedures and to indoctrinate them with the importance of their position. Lack of interest in implementing the policy of nondiscrimination was a chronic problem the committee faced with these officers, similar in many ways to the chronic problem the Government Contract Committee faced with its departmental compliance officers.

On the average, 200 complaints were processed annually from 1955 to 1960. Of the five-year total of 1053 complaints, only 173 produced a finding of discrimination or of corrective action without such a finding. Some of the complaints (81) were not investigated because of incomplete information by the complainant; the rest (799) were dismissed with findings of no discrimination. Of these, only 189 complainants expressed satisfaction with the investigation or withdrew their complaints; the rest neither replied nor withdrew their complaints upon being informed of the decision.

The committee itself received only 225 or 21 percent of all the complaints for review and an advisory opinion, the rest being settled at the departmental level. In 33 of the 225 referrals, the committee disagreed with the findings of the department; it determined that discrimination had been present and recommended corrective action. In general, however, the committee went along with the findings of the department.

Overall, The President's Government Employment Committee resembled his Government Contract Committee in conception and operation. Both were modest improvements over the earlier Truman versions, but each was tethered by policies of caution and moderation and by an ineffectual administrative machinery that was grossly inadequate for the task of handling complaints of individual discrimination or of insuring compliance with its policy of nondiscrimination.

Kennedy: laying the normative groundwork for affirmative action

In the early days of his administration, President Kennedy continued Eisenhower's policy of restraint and moderation in his dealings with Congress over civil rights legislation. However, he very quickly revealed that he was prepared to take important new initiatives in the province under his direct control, the executive branch. In March 1961 almost as soon as he took office, he established the President's Committee on Equal Employment Opportunity under Executive Order 10925. This committee was to combine the functions of the two Eisenhower committees: the one on Government Contracts and the other on Government Employment Policy. Both were abolished, and the two executive orders establishing them revoked.

The intent of the President was evident in the preamble to his order. Unlike those in the earlier orders of Truman and Eisenhower, his did not confine itself merely to reaffirming the constitutional obligation of the government to eliminate policies and practices of discrimination. It emphasized the positive obligation of the government to "insure equal opportunity for all qualified persons" – this to be done by "positive measures" and not by trivial actions:

> "Whereas it is the plain and positive obligation of the United States Government to promote and insure equal opportunity for all qualified persons without regard to race, creed, color, or national origin, employed or seeking employment with the Federal Government and on government contracts; and

> Whereas it is the policy of the executive branch of the Government to encourage by positive measures equal opportunity for all qualified persons within the Government."   (Preamble to Executive Order 10925, March 6, 1961)

Accordingly, Kennedy strengthened the committee to the extent that its authority was more akin to that proposed by Truman's committee than that actually wielded by the Truman and Eisenhower committees. No longer was the committee merely a study group as in Truman's case or an advisory group without power to impose its will on what contracting agencies did as in Eisenhower's case. It became the focal policy-making body for the program and was given the powers to implement its policies.

The contracting agencies still retained primary responsibility for investigating and processing complaints and for obtaining compliance from the contractors. In all of their activities, the contracting agencies were obliged to follow the rules, regulations, and orders of the committee and to keep the committee informed of their activities and actions. In addition, the committee was no longer removed from direct contact with the field of action and therefore entirely dependent on the contracting agencies for information. It could investigate directly the employment practices of government contractors or cause to have such an investigation made by the appropriate contracting agency. The committee could also receive complaints from employees directly and cause to have these complaints investigated by the appropriate contracting agency. Both parties – agency and committee – were required to keep each other informed of their activities. Further, the committee served as a board of appeals in the complaint process with the power to impose its will on the contracting agency. In short, the committee became the central hub of the program. Its chairman was Vice President Lyndon Johnson; its vice chairman, the Secretary of Labor; its other members included the heads of the major governmental departments and agencies.

The order also reaffirmed the basic obligation of contractors and subcontractors "not to discriminate against any employee or applicant for employment because of race, creed, color, or national origin." The order subsequently repeated the itemized list of activities that had been previously adopted by the Eisenhower committee in which discrimination was forbidden. Significantly, the listing is preceded by a sentence that appears for the first time in any of the executive orders: "The contractor will take *affirmative action* [author's italics] to ensure that applicants are employed, and that employees are treated during employment without regard to their race, creed, color, or national origins" (Executive Order 10925 1961, Section 301(1)). The phrase affirmative action remains undefined throughout the order, but it is evident from the additional obligations that the President imposes on the contractors (and subcontractors) that he wishes at the least for more assertive action on their part in carrying out the nondiscriminatory provisions of this order.

As in the earlier orders, the contractors (and subcontractors) were to post their nondiscrimination policy in conspicuous places. In addition, they were to announce their policy in all solicitations and advertisements for employees and to send notices of their policy to any labor union with which they had an agreement. They were also to submit to investigations by the appropriate contracting agency and the committee; their books and all records could be inspected. In addition, contractors and subcontractors had to file compliance reports with the government. Finally, a labor union might also be required to sign a statement that it did not discriminate.

Failure to comply with nondiscrimination clauses or the rules, regulations, and orders of the committee or contracting agencies could have extremely serious consequences for the contractor or subcontractor. None of the earlier executive orders by Truman or Eisenhower had spelled out as wide-ranging and severe a set of penalties and sanctions for noncompliance. Perhaps the most severe was the threat to cancel, terminate, or to suspend the contract in whole or in part, and to bar the contractor or subcontractor from future contracts with the government. In addition, the committee or contracting agency could recommend that the Department of Justice initiate injunctive proceedings if the violation of the nondiscrimination provision was substantial and material or start criminal proceedings if false information was involved. The least severe of the penalties would be to publish the names of contractors, subcontractors, and unions that failed to comply.

None of these sanctions, however, could be imposed until the committee or contracting agency attempted to resolve the matter through conciliation and conferences.

As one of its primary tasks the committee set out to overhaul and to strengthen the processing of complaints. It spelled out a set of rules and regulations in much more explicit detail than the earlier committees had, and it retained a central role for itself in the process. While primary responsibility remained with the contracting agency, the committee was to be kept informed at each stage of the process. It would review the findings and disposition of the agency and serve as a board of appeal at the end. Further, the process of complaints was to be expedited and completed within sixty days. Perhaps most important of all, the committee sought to discard the long-standing practice of having the same person serve the dual role of monitoring the nondiscrimination provision along with all the other provisions of the contract; the ineffectiveness of this arrangement had long been apparent. Accordingly, the committee sought to have the agencies recruit specialized personnel who were both interested and skilled in dealing with problems of discrimination. By 1963, a number of these specialists were appointed to the staffs of the agencies and were working in all phases of the complaint process.

So immediate was the improvement in the administrative processing of complaints that within its first nine months the committee processed the equivalent of 60 percent of the total number of complaints that the Eisenhower committee had processed in its seven years of operation. In addition, almost one half of the 641 cases were resolved. Among these resolved cases, ninety-one were dismissed because the committee lacked jurisdiction (for example, the complainant's employer was not a government contractor). Sixteen others were dismissed because the complainant had failed to provide the necessary information for the investigation. However, among the complaints carried to final disposition, 60 percent resulted in corrective action. In short, at each level of complaint processing and action, the Kennedy committee had begun to function almost immediately with greater effectiveness and efficiency than had the Eisenhower committee during its entire existence. As a result, toward the end of its term of office, the Kennedy committee had processed over twice as many complaints (2111) within two and one-half years as the Eisenhower had in its seven years (1042).

Improving the processing of complaints, however, did not in itself answer a basic question that had plagued the earlier committees as well: How compliant with the nondiscrimination clause of the government contract were contractors against whom registered complaints had not been lodged? The Kennedy and earlier committees recognized that many of these contractors were probably engaged in discriminatory practices not too different from those of the small number of contractors against whom complaints had been registered. Thus the absence of complaint did not necessarily mean the presence of compliance. And yet the committees had to proceed on the assumption that in the absence of a specific complaint or other information a contractor was adhering to a policy of nondiscrimination because he had signed his name to the government contract.

As we have already seen, the Eisenhower committee had recognized the need for additional information on compliance and had therefore resorted to an *ad hoc* procedure of conducting surveys and re-surveys among a limited number of contractors, frequently by mail. Aware of the limitations of this voluntary *ad hoc* procedure, President Kennedy discarded it in Section 302 of his executive order and made it obligatory for contractors and subcontractors generally to file compliance reports with the appropriate contracting agency "which will be subject to review by the Committee upon its request. Compliance Reports shall be filed within such times and shall contain such information as to the practices, policies, programs, and employment statistics of the contractor and each subcontractor, and shall be in such form, as the Committee may prescribe" (Executive Order 10925 1961, Section 302 [a]).

The Kennedy committee took about a year to translate the President's charge into a design for compliance reporting and review. During the year, extended discussions were held with various government departments; the final product was a detailed set of rules and regulations and a questionnaire for the collection of information. The committee mandated that annual reports were to be filed by prime contractors and first-tier subcontractors whose contracts were $50,000 or more. In June 1963 the President issued Executive Order 11114 extending the authority to those involved in construction contracts who received financial assistance of some kind from the federal government; they too had to file annual reports.

The report consisted of answering a relatively simple set of questions. One question, for example, asked "Has a company-wide employment policy been established with procedures put into effect to assure that equal opportunity is given to all persons without regard to race, color, creed, or national origin?" Of primary significance, however, were the items that elicited information on the numbers of persons from specified racial minorities employed at each occupational level of the firm and also on the total number of all employees at each level. In effect, the committee wanted to determine the proportion of the work force from a given minority at each occupational level. In turn, the committee was to register, tabulate, collate, and machine process all reports for distribution to the contracting agencies.

From the very beginning the committee viewed the task of developing such a reporting system as one of its most important tasks. In fact, in the report on its first nine months in office, the committee said:

"The development of a compliance reporting system for all Government contractors and subcontractors may prove to be among the most significant steps taken in 20 years of Federal antidiscrimination effort. Although the nondiscrimination clause has been a standard clause in Government contracts since 1941, Executive Order 10925 provides for the first time the mandatory filing of periodic reports by Government contractors reflecting employment policies and practices as a condition of performance under a government contract.

The compliance reporting program developed by the Committee is the first reporting program designed to review systematically the effect of the nondiscrimination provision of Government contracts and to assess the impact of such provisions on the effective utilization of minority group manpower."

(The President's Committee on Equal Employment Opportunity 1962:41)

By the spring of 1962, the committee had received its first wave of reports, and by June 1963, the committee had reports from over 10,000 establishments representing 4.2 million workers. Its 1963 report provided statistical summaries of these data. The committee estimated that eventually approximately 38,000 companies in non-agricultural industries would be covered. Since some of these companies owned several establishments, this would mean separate reports from about 50,000 establishments with 15.5 million employees – or approximately one-third of the non-agricultural workforce in America.

So impressed did the committee become with the potential usefulness of the compliance reporting system by the time it issued its 1963 report that it spelled out the multiple functions that the system could serve:

"The compliance reporting system is designed to provide:
1. A means of assessing the impact of the non-discrimination provision on Government contractors and for measuring progress in opening up equal job opportunities to minority group persons.

2. A manpower profile of the work force of the nation affected by Government contracts.

3. An analysis of employment patterns of minority groups in the work force.

4. An analysis of situations affecting the under-utilization of the manpower potential of such minority groups.

5. An effective tool to be used by the employers themselves, in assessing the effect of their employment policies on minority group persons.

6. An instrument to be used by the Federal contracting agencies in administering the nondiscrimination program and for promoting the practice as well as the principle of equal employment opportunities among Government contractors.

7. A means for an affirmative approach to be taken by the Government, by management, by labor, by the community, and by organizations and individuals to eliminate practices and conditions which disadvantage considerable segments of our nation's population only because of reasons of race, creed, color, or national origin."

(The President's Committee on Equal Employment Opportunity 1963:15)

In effect, the committee recognized that in mandating a reporting system it had taken an essential first step in the development of an effective program of compliance; however, it failed to take any of the other necessary steps. Specifically, it faltered and equivocated in constructing the kind of evaluational and enforcement machinery that could effectively use the data from the reporting system.

Perhaps the weakest link in the chain was the reluctance of the committee to use the arsenal of penalties and sanctions that the President had made available to it in his executive order. In no instance was a contract terminated or a contractor debarred from future government contracts. Instead, the committee relied almost exclusively on persuasion and exhortation and voluntary compliance. In particular it promoted its Plans for Progress program under which companies voluntarily agreed to abide by a policy of nondiscrimination and to develop a plan for implementing equal opportunity within their organizations. The committee even drew up a model plan that could be adopted by companies with the following preamble:

"This company recognizes that the national policy enunciated by the President of the United States that all persons are entitled to equal employment opportunity regardless of their race, creed, color, or national origin, is in keeping with the best traditions and spirit of the American way of life. Adherence to such a policy, moreover, is essential if all of the Nation's human resources are to be effectively utilized."

(The President's Committee on Equal Employment Opportunity 1963:111)

The committee viewed the program as being eminently successful. It took considerable pride in the numbers and in the importance of the firms that joined. By mid-1963, for example, 115 companies including such corporate giants as General Motors and IBM, with a total of 5.5 million employees, had signed up. Further, the committee was pleased at what appeared to be authentic efforts by companies such as Lockheed to implement their Plan for Progress and by the results of a nationwide study in 1963 of ninety-one companies with Plans for Progress. The study showed a slight increase in the number of nonwhites in the total work force and in their proportionate representation at most higher occupational levels, particularly at that of the salaried white collar worker.

Other observers in the early 1960s were much less sanguine about the effectiveness of the program. They pointed to the fact that many of the proclaimed Plans for Progress were little more than letters of general intent not to discriminate without any detailed plan for implementation. Also, the Southern Regional Council found evidence of general ineffectualness in its study of twenty-four participating firms with plants of offices in the Atlanta area. Only seven of the firms demonstrated any concerted or affirmative effort to comply with their program; the other seventeen showed few signs of carrying out the plans to which they had agreed. In a number of instances, top management had made little or no attempt to implement the promises it had made; as a result, middle and lower management frequently professed indifference to or ignorance of the Plan for Progress their company had signed. Black organizations such as the National Association for the Advancement of Colored People (NAACP) tended to take a jaundiced view of the program. Not only did they believe that voluntary compliance could never be as effective as mandatory compliance, but they also believed that the option of voluntary compliance through the Plans for Progress program was being used by many companies to avoid any meaningful compliance at all.

Whatever may be the final assessment of the merits of its Plans for Progress program, the committee itself recognized that voluntary programs had only a supplemental function to play; they were no substitutes for mandatory compliance and vigorous enforcement. And yet the committee never did mount such a mandatory effort; it never really got such efforts off the ground.

In failing to opt for vigorous enforcement, the committee also revealed its reluctance or inability to come to grips clearly and decisively with what it meant by compliance or non-compliance with the dual contractual requirement of nondiscrimination and affirmative action among contractors who neither had complaints of discrimination lodged against them nor had participated in Plans for Progress. Accordingly, the committee was prepared to accept verbal assurances of nondiscrimination and to view askance only those occupational situations where a pattern of long-term exclusion of blacks and other racial minorities was evident. The committee had even more trouble with the phrase affirmative action. It used the phrase in so many different ways that it took on the character of a sponge when applied to contractors. In the course of its multiple usage, the phrase soaked up virtually every shade of non-negative action and intent, both verbal and behavioral, from active recruitment and training of blacks to merely keeping the door to employment from being entirely shut. Small wonder that the committee proceeded in an *ad hoc* manner with these contractors. It neither offered them nor imposed upon them meaningful and universal standards of compliance; consequently its relations with these contractors were tenuous and undefined during its lifetime.

As a result, the phrase affirmative action as applied to these contractors, served more as a slogan for the future than as an operationally defined requirement for the present. This is evident in the report the committee prepared on its first nine months in office. Among the seven significant steps that the committee said it had taken, the phrase affirmative action or affirmative steps appears prominently in statements on five of these steps. Only one, however, refers to affirmative steps taken by contractors. These are contractors against whom complaints had been lodged or who had joined the Plans for Progress program; no other contractors are mentioned. Another item refers to affirmative steps taken by unions. Two of the remaining items concentrate on what the government is doing to lay the groundwork for the building of effective affirmative action programs among contractors. "*Agencies are developing manpower capability for effective operation of affirmative action programs with government contractors.*" "*The Compliance Report system of the Committee will provide for the first time, information on minority group employment necessary for the development of affirmative action programs on a broad scale*" (The President's Committee on Equal Employment Opportunity 1962:3). A third reference to the government emphasizes the "*affirmative steps*" it has taken "*to insure equal opportunity for all employees and applicants for employment*" (The President's Committee on Equal Employment Opportunity 1962:1).

In another section of the report, the committee no longer juxtaposed what the government agencies were doing with what affirmative action programs were about. Instead, it came to define what the government agencies had done and were doing as *ipso facto* what affirmative action was operationally at that time.

"In issuing this Order (10925), President Kennedy emphasized the necessity of using *affirmative action* to achieve the objectives of this policy and specifically indicated that such efforts should be made by all departments and independent agencies of the Government, not simply by the Committee itself.

This is the new note in intent and method of Executive Order 10925 that was absent from previous Executive Orders affecting employment practices in the Federal establishment. It has placed heavier responsibilities on Government agencies and the Committee for more expeditious achievement of the goal while at the same time opening new avenues for effective cooperative action among agencies and Committee for reaching the policy aims of the President in a more efficient and harmonious way. It has also more specifically prescribed the division of labor between the various Federal departments and agencies, on the one hand, and the Committee staff on the other."

(The President's Committee on Equal Employment Opportunity 1962:5)

Thus Kennedy's committee seemed to have a clearer picture of the kind of affirmative role the government should play in implementing the program of equal employment opportunity than the kind of affirmative role contractors should play.

Johnson: building the bureaucratic machinery for affirmative action

Having successfully shepherded the Civil Rights Act of 1964 and the Voting Rights Act of 1965 through Congress, President Johnson rounded out the extraordinary record in civil rights of his first two years in office by issuing Executive Order 11246 in September 1965. The order abolished Kennedy's Committee on Equal Employment Opportunity and did what the Truman committee had recommended fifteen years earlier. It centralized the authority for carrying out the policy of nondiscrimination and equal employment opportunity in government contracts and placed it in the hands of the head of an established and powerful part of the administrative mainstream of the executive branch, the Department of Labor. (Similarly the other major responsibility of Kennedy's committee was also shifted to an established administrative branch of the government; the Civil Service Commission was to oversee the program of nondiscrimination in federal government employment.)

By doing what he did, President Johnson had in effect accepted a basic premise of the earlier Truman committee. To be effective, the agency responsible for the contractor program had to occupy a strategic position as an integral part of the bureaucratic system of government. Otherwise, it would have neither the kind of access to or leverage on those parts of the system upon which it had to rely heavily for the actual carrying out of its policies and directives. This was clearly evident in the fifteen years that had elapsed since the Truman committee's recommendation. Each presidentially appointed committee since then had very little success in getting the contracting agencies in the various government departments to do what the committee believed should be done to monitor government contractors and to enforce its policies in dealing with them. The agencies did not pay too much attention, in large measure, because they viewed these committees as appendages that had been grafted onto the main bureaucratic structure of government without the kind of administrative continuity, power, and machinery that would make the committee's authority stick.

Johnson's order also gave the Secretary of Labor more direct control over and contact with the complaint and compliance process than Kennedy's order had given his committee. Whereas Kennedy's committee could only cause a complaint to be investigated, the Secretary of Labor could investigate complaints directly. The Secretary could also demand a wider range of factual information from government contractors than the Kennedy committee could. The Secretary merely had to afford the contractor with an opportunity for a hearing before penalties were imposed; Kennedy's committee was obliged to hold such hearings. Further, the Secretary had the authority to rescind the debarment of a contractor; no mention of such authority was made in the Kennedy order.

Beyond these basic administrative and structural changes, the Johnson order did not alter in any significant way the set of policies and procedures that had already been laid out by the Kennedy order. Contractors were still to "take affirmative action to ensure that applicants are employed, and that employees are treated during employment, without regard to race, color, religion, sex, or national origin" (Executive Order 11246 1965:Section 202 [1]). (The Kennedy order used 'creed' instead of 'religion' and did not include 'sex'.) The responsibilities of the contractor were spelled out in much the same precise terms as they had been in the Kennedy order; however, in their compliance reports, contractors were also to include specific information on their employment policies and to add any other factual information that the Secretary of Labor or the contracting agency might require.

Johnson's order adopted the entire range of penalties and sanctions that had been included in the Kennedy order. It only added the following provision in view of the recent passage of the Civil Rights Act of 1964: The Secretary or appropriate contracting agency may "recommend to the Equal Employment Opportunity Commission or the Department of Justice that appropriate proceedings be instituted under Title VII of the Civil Rights Act of 1964" (Executive Order 11246 1965: Section 209 [3]). In effect, Johnson's order added little to the arsenal of sanctions and penalties already listed in Kennedy's Order 10925 and its subsequently amended version. Johnson's order also absorbed most of the provisions of Kennedy's Order 11114 that had set forth nondiscrimination provisions in federally assisted construction contracts.

In the final analysis then, whatever were the features of the Kennedy program on equal employment opportunity that Johnson sought to change in his executive order, these did not include the basic normative framework of general goals, policy, and sanctions. This framework was incorporated in its almost exact form in the Johnson order. Only the administrative and structural mechanisms for translating the normative framework into an operational system of rules and actions were dramatically changed. President Kennedy provided the normative foundation and scaffolding upon which Johnson sought to build an effective and efficient bureaucratic structure that would fulfill the promise of the contractor program.

Within a month after the issuance of the executive order, the Secretary of Labor established the Office of Federal Contract Compliance (OFCC) under his general supervision. The office, under a director, was charged with carrying out the responsibilities assigned to the Secretary in Parts II, III, and IV of the executive order. It was also to develop and to recommend to the Secretary rules and regulations for the implementation of the purposes of the order, to coordinate its activities bearing on Title VII of the Civil Rights Act of 1964 with the EEOC and Department of Justice, and finally to provide regular reports to the Secretary.

Moving at a rate that the US Commission on Civil Rights called in its report in 1971 "slow and inauspicious," the OFCC spent its first year in organizing itself and in trying to make some headway on the problem of contract compliance. In this, the office differed strikingly from the earlier committees. It never gave the problem of individual complaints the priority that the committees had; instead, it always viewed the matter of contract compliance as its central concern.

From the beginning the office operated on the assumption that the problems of compliance were qualitatively different for contracts involving construction than for those involving supplies and services. Accordingly, it set up two units, Procurement Contract Compliance (later called Supplies and Services) and Construction Contract Compliance, and it developed different administrative arrangements and compliance procedures and processes for each. For example, from its earliest years, the OFCC has stressed regular compliance reviews of each nonconstruction contractor as the most effective means of spurring minority employment; in the case of construction, the OFCC has from the beginning sought to develop "area plans" which focused on improving "minority construction employment within an entire labor market or metropolitan area" (US Commission on Civil Rights 1971:53). The first plans were developed for St Louis, San Francisco, Cleveland, and Philadelphia. Each of the plans subsequently faltered. The first Philadelphia plan, for example, was declared illegal by the Comptroller General; the others accomplished little because of general lack of enforcement.

From its start, the office operated under severe handicaps. It was grossly understaffed. In 1966 it had only 40 full-time employees, 39 of whom were stationed in Washington, DC. By mid-1968 it still had only 40 full-time employees, 36 of whom were still in Washington, DC, and one part-time employee. In the meantime, its budget increased from less than one-half million to over one million, and it was authorized to fill sixty-nine positions. With so many positions vacant, the OFCC did not have the manpower to perform certain basic functions such as monitoring the work of contracting and compliance agencies. In addition to its manpower problem, the office also lacked any firm sense of direction or purpose and was unable to translate for over two years the general objectives of the Johnson order into a clear and detailed set of rules and regulations. Instead it puttered along on a patchwork basis with the rules and regulations that had been promulgated by Kennedy's committee.

What contributed significantly to the sense of drift and inaction of the office was its evident difficulty in defining and in specifying in precise and meaningful terms what affirmative action was to mean to it, to the contracting agencies, and to the contractors. It was content to talk in vague generalities about results. This is evident in a statement made by the Director of OFCC in January 1967 in the *Report of 1967 Plans for Progress Fifth National Conference*, January 23–4 1967:

> "'Affirmative action is going to vary from time to time, from day to day, from place to place, from escalation to escalation. It depends upon the nature of the area in which you are located, it depends upon the kinds of people who are there, it depends upon the kind of business that you have. There is no fixed and firm definition of affirmative action. I would say that in a general way, affirmative action is anything that you have to do to get results.'"
>
> (US Commission on Civil Rights 1971:51)

In the absence of central direction and control, many of the agencies devised their own versions of affirmative action. Some even saw no conflict between certain kinds of segregation and discrimination and their definition of affirmative action and contract compliance. Many were lax and even negligent in collecting compliance reports from contractors. Much of the data that were collected were therefore outdated and useless for assessing current employment policies and practices.

Compounding the ineffectiveness of the OFCC's activities was its "failure to impose sanctions on known non-complying contractors" (US Commission on Civil Rights 1971:52). Despite its professed preference for compulsory implementation in contrast to the voluntarism of its predecessors, the OFCC failed in its early days to follow a policy of vigorous enforcement. Not until May 1968 did it send its first notices of debarment to contractors.

"At that time there had not been a single cancellation or termination because of a contractor's discriminatory policies. Furthermore, only two non-complying contractors had been sued or recommended for suit; the administrative authority to suspend contractors from Government business during pending of hearings has never been used; only one hearing had been held by a contracting agency since the start of the compliance program."

(US Commission on Civil Rights 1971:52–3)

In effect, the office failed in its first few years, as had the Kennedy committee before it, to use the arsenal of sanctions and penalties that the executive orders had given it.

By the spring of 1968, under a new director, the OFCC dispelled some of the uncertainty and drift that had beset it and developed a more positive and firm sense of purpose. Even as it took its first decisive steps in enforcement in May of 1968, the OFCC also issued that month its first comprehensive code of rules and regulations explicitly addressed to the general goals and purposes of Johnson's Executive Order 11246. Thus, what Johnson had started during the first year of his elected term of office was finally brought to fruition in the last year of his administration.

The new code retained virtually intact several of the basic features of the older code. For example, the equal opportunity clause that was to be incorporated in all government contracts was virtually a verbatim replication of the Kennedy committee's; however, the new code added an exact copy of the notices on equal employment opportunity that contractors and subcontractors were to post. Also virtually unchanged were the procedures for filing and processing complaints of discrimination by individuals. The new code, however, extended the deadline for filing from 90 to 180 days and gave a more detailed set of instructions of the kind of case record that the contracting or compliance agency was to compile as part of its investigation of the complaint.

The new code also reaffirmed the structural innovations that had been adopted with Johnson's Order 11246 and that had already produced dramatic changes in the administrative set-up of the program. Authority was to remain with the Director of the Office of Federal Contract Compliance under the general direction of the Secretary of Labor. The new code did not merely restate that fact. It spelled out in great detail the extent of the Director's authority, and made him a more pivotal figure in the entire program than his counterparts had ever been in the past. He had more to say and to do than they in the formulation and implementation of policy and guidelines, in the monitoring of the activities of contracting and compliance agencies, and in direct dealings with contractors. He was given greater authority than in the past to enter into virtually every phase of the complaint and compliance process, to oversee the workings of the various agencies, and to review and even to reverse their decisions and actions.

Despite its expansion of the powers of the central office, the new code retained a cardinal feature of the past; contracting and compliance agencies were to have primary responsibility for obtaining compliance from contractors. The new code, however, spelled out in greater detail than in the past what the duties and powers of the agencies and of their contract compliance officer were to be. It enhanced their authority in the awarding of government contracts. For example, they had to approve the compliance status of the prospective contractor before the contract could be officially awarded; formerly they were likely to be kept completely out of the negotiations. At the same time, the code clearly indicated that the agency and compliance officer were not to have the same degree of autonomy and independence as in the past. As we have already said, their actions and decisions were to come under the continuing scrutiny and general direction of the Director of OFCC.

Whereas the basic administrative changes had already been implemented by the time the new code was published, the code itself made manifest a profound shift in programmatic and procedural priorities from all earlier codes. The Kennedy code, for example, continued the central preoccupation of previous codes with developing the process and procedure for handling complaints. It built a fairly elaborate complaint structure and it also did something the earlier codes neglected to do: it paid some, though not very much, attention to the problem of compliance. Johnson's code went even further and reversed the order of priority. For example, his code added little of any significance to the Kennedy version of the complaint process, but it built a more substantive structure of compliance on the rudimentary foundations laid by the earlier code.

The new code did not basically alter the compliance reporting procedure of the Kennedy version. It merely added a number of significant details such as the precise form to be used, the date for filing the report, and examples of other kinds of information that might be required from contractors. The new order did alter substantively the procedure for compliance review. For example, it replaced the vague general statement of purpose of Kennedy's code with a more detailed and direct one. In the older code the focus was on the implementation of equal employment opportunity in general: "The purpose of compliance reviews shall be to ascertain the extent to which the Orders are being implemented by the creation of equal employment opportunity for all qualified persons in accordance with the national policy" (The President's Committee on Equal Employment Opportunity, *Federal Register* 1963: Subpart B, 60–1.20).

In the Johnson code, implementation of both nondiscrimination and affirmative action in specified contexts of employment practice and policy were to be the dual targets of compliance reviews:

"The purpose of a compliance review is to determine if the prime contractor or subcontractor maintains nondiscriminatory hiring and employment practices and is taking affirmative action to ensure that applicants are employed and that employees are placed, trained, upgraded, promoted, and otherwise treated during employment without regard to race, creed, color, or national origin."
(Office of Federal Contract Compliance *Federal Register* 1968:
Subpart B, 60–1.20)

The new code also shed the humble and apologetic reassurance of the older one that compliance reviews "are not intended to interfere with the responsibilities of employers to determine the competence and qualifications of employees and applicants for employment" (Office of Federal Contract Compliance, *Federal Register* 1968: Subpart B, 60–1.20). It stated firmly that these reviews were to be an integral part of invigorated and strengthened enforcement proceedings that would apply sanctions and penalties where needed. The new code also signified the added importance which it now attached to compliance reviews by making them part of the heading of Subpart B, even before the phrase complaint procedures in the title: "*General Enforcement: Compliance Review and Complaint Procedure.*"

And finally, the new code established significant new bench marks for compliance reviews. Prime responsibility for such reviews was to be in the hands of the various compliance agencies, under the general direction of the OFCC which could also conduct its own reviews. Contractors were put on detailed notice that such reviews were going to be taken seriously and that deficiencies uncovered by them had better be remedied within a reasonable period of time. However, outside of these general bench marks, several years elapsed before the Director of the OFCC issued a detailed set of instructions and guidelines as to the precise procedures for such compliance reviews.

In many other respects the new code shifted away from the former emphasis on persuasion and voluntary compliance to a more overt and concerted preoccupation with enforcement. In the very first paragraph of Subpart A, 60–1.1, it added a sentence missing from the earlier versions: "Failure of a contractor or applicant to comply with any provision of the regulations in this part shall be grounds for the imposition of any or all of the sanctions authorized by the order." The compliance procedure that we have already outlined reflects this stiffening attitude. In addition, the new code no longer relied merely on informal hearings to gain voluntary compliance as did the earlier codes; it instituted formal hearings as well for assessing the degree and kind of non-compliance and for determining the kind of sanction or penalty to be levied. Thus, the process of enforcement took on a more formal and legal character.

Perhaps the most dramatic change in the code was the new ground that it broke in elaborating and specifying that contractors would have to do concretely towards meeting the dual requirements of nondiscrimination and affirmative action. For the first time, for example, contractors were officially notified that segregated facilities and conditions of work for employees were forbidden. The contractor "may neither require such segregated use by written or oral policies nor tolerate such use by employee custom. His obligation extends further to ensuring that his employees are not assigned to perform their services at any location, under his control, where the facilities are segregated" (Office of Federal Contract Compliance, *Federal Register* 1968: Subpart A, 60–1.8).

Of equal, if not of greater significance was the groundwork that the new code laid for translating the generalized commitment to affirmative action that Kennedy had been the first to espouse into a distinctive set of operational demands and requirements for contractors. Thus, each prime contractor or subcontractor who had fifty or more employees and a contract of $50,000 or more was henceforth required to develop in writing an affirmative action program for each of his establishments.

To develop a "satisfactory affirmative action program," the code stated, the contractor would first have to identify and to analyze "the problem areas inherent in minority employment" and to evaluate the "opportunities for utilization of minority group personnel." Such an evaluation was to include the following:

1. "An analysis of minority group representation in all job categories."
2. "An analysis of hiring practices for the past year, including recruitment sources and testing, to determine whether equal employment opportunity is being offered in all job categories."
3. "An analysis of upgrading, transfer, and promotion for the past year to determine whether equal employment opportunity is being afforded."
   (Office of Federal Contract Compliance, *Federal Register* 1968: Subpart C, 60–1.40)

In addition to the evaluation and analysis, the contractor was also to describe in his program the "specific steps" he would take to "guarantee equal employment opportunity keyed to the problems and needs of members of minority groups." If his analysis showed "deficiencies" in his program, he was also supposed to spell out how he proposed to correct these deficiencies through "the development of specific goals and time tables for the prompt achievement of full and equal employment opportunity" (Office of Federal Contract Compliance, *Federal Register* 1968: Subpart C, 60–1.40).

The contractor was also to prepare a report annually which assessed the results of his program during the year and revised and updated the original plan on the basis of these results. All of the documents, including the original plan, were to be made available to the OFCC and to the appropriate compliance agency and were to become part of the compliance review of the contractor.

In this manner then, the code outlined what it labeled as the "necessary prerequisite(s) to the development of a satisfactory affirmative action program," but it did not go beyond these preliminaries. Nowhere did it attempt to define what it meant by a satisfactory program, what its essential ingredients would be, or what criteria would be used to distinguish between a satisfactory and an unsatisfactory program. This was left to the Nixon administration. And yet in doing what it did, the Johnson administration had taken an important first step in coming to grips with these matters. It had set the basic direction and design for transforming Kennedy's vague and general normative goal of affirmative action into an operational set of procedures and processes.

Nixon: operationalizing the policy of affirmative action

Breaking with the precedent set by the past five administrations, President Nixon did not seek to place his own distinctive stamp during his term of office on the policy of nondiscrimination and affirmative action in government contracts. Unlike the other presidents, he never issued an executive order that was to supercede completely the order of his predecessor; in other words, he never revoked Johnson's Order 11246. However, Nixon did replace Part I of Order 11246 with his Order 11478 of August 1969. Part I had dealt with nondiscrimination in government employment; Nixon's order "called for affirmative action programs for equal opportunity at the agency level under general supervision of the Civil Service Commission; establishment of complaint procedures at each agency with appeal to the Commission and promulgation of regulations by CSC" (Executive Order 11246, Part One as amended by President Nixon's Executive Order 11478 1969).

Outside of this modification, the Nixon administration retained virtually intact the heritage of the past: the normative goals of Kennedy and the structural framework of Johnson. Within the general parameters of this heritage, however, the Nixon administration did not keep its rudimentary procedural plumbing but developed instead a much more finely honed and effective set of bureaucratic instrumentalities and supplied a number of "capstones" to administrative procedures and processes whose basic direction had already been set in the Johnson administration.

In mid-1969 and early 1970 the OFCC underwent several important organizational changes. First, it was transferred from the jurisdiction of the Office of the Secretary to that of the Wage and Labor Standards Administration (now called the Employment Standards Administration). Second, the office was reorganized internally to provide for a more efficient execution and coordination of activities among the OFCC headquarters, its eleven regional offices, and the various contracting and compliance agencies.

However, before this internal restructuring took effect, the OFCC, under the combined leadership of its relatively new director and the Assistant Secretary of the Wage and Labor Standards Administration, both of whom were black, launched in the fall of 1969 major programmatic and procedural initiatives that added key elements to the structure of affirmative action that the office had been building.

Perhaps the most important of these elements was the development of external standards onto which contractors could peg the goals of their affirmative action programs and by which they could assess their effectiveness. The pioneering venture in this matter was the Philadelphia plan.

As early as 1967, the OFCC had sought to develop in Philadelphia an affirmative action program for construction projects financed in part or whole by the federal government. Somewhat over a year later the pre-award requirement that contractors commit themselves to increased minority employment was ruled as illegal by the Comptroller General. As a result, the program was temporarily shelved until a new version was formulated in June 1969. Again, the Comptroller General ruled the plan was illegal, this time because it presumably gave preferential treatment to one racial group over another. The Attorney General, however, stepped in and ruled in September 1969 that the plan was legal and that "his opinion should be the basis of future action by OFCC and the contracting agencies" (US Commission on Civil Rights 1971:63).

Accordingly, the Philadelphia plan was resuscitated and put into effect in September. As in the case of the 1967 version, the 1969 plan was addressed to increasing the employment of minorities in eight construction trades that pursued pervasive and systematic discriminatory and exclusionary practices. Other than this similarity, the two plans had little in common. In the 1967 version, for example, the contractor merely had to agree to increase the number of minority members in each of these trades; no uniform standards were defined or applied. As a result, the contractors differed greatly in what they did. Many even sought to avoid entirely implementation of the plan. The outcome was a meager increase in the representation of the minorities in these trades.

In the 1969 plan, each contractor was obliged to "set specific goals of minority manpower utilization" for meeting certain "definite standards" that were to be uniformly established and applied within each trade. A timetable for reaching these goals was to be included in the written affirmative action program that each contractor was to submit with his bid. These standards would not pinpoint a fixed proportion for minority manpower utilization within a trade but would instead define a percentage range which would be determined by the OFCC from its study of such factors as:

"1. The current extent of minority group participation in the trade.
2. The availability of minority group persons for employment in such trade.
3. The need for training programs in the area and/or the need to assure demand for those in or from existing training programs.
4. The impact of the program upon the existing labor force."

(US Department of Labor 1969:401:253)

Within three months the OFCC completed its study of the four factors and set up a series of graduated standards to be applied in each of four years. Thus, the ironworkers, for example, were to attain an average range of minority group employment of 5–9 percent in the first year; of 11–15 percent in the second year; of 16–20 percent in the third year; and of 22–26 percent in the fourth year. A contractor was expected to comply with these standards as they were transformed into goals for his own affirmative action program. Failure to meet his goals, however, did not automatically subject a contractor to penalties or sanctions if he could show that he had engaged in "good faith" efforts to broaden his base of recruitment. Such efforts might include enlisting the aid of community organizations in recruitment, participating in training programs, and so forth.

Once the Philadelphia plan was launched, the OFCC announced a three-point plan for the construction industry throughout the nation. First, voluntary "hometown" agreements would be sought from unions, employers, and minority groups in an area on the standards to be set for minority employment in a trade. Second, the OFCC would provide the local parties with whatever technical assistance it could in arriving at these agreements. Third, failure of the parties to produce a hometown solution would result in imposition of a Philadelphia-type plan on the area by the government. Early in 1970, the OFCC undertook a nationwide program for hometown solutions in eighteen target cities. By the end of the fiscal year, ten area plans were in effect; two of them had been imposed by the government, including the one for Philadelphia.

The Philadelphia plan also served as a pilot project for another major initiative by the OFCC in the late fall of 1969 that soon proved of even greater moment than its pilot. At that time, the OFCC submitted to the heads of federal agencies its first version of Order No. 4 which adopted some of the basic features and approaches of the Philadelphia plan for application to non-construction contracts. The order underwent several revisions and experienced a number of delays before it was finally put into effect at the end of 1971 as Revised Order No. 4.

This order, however, did not merely replicate for non-construction contracts what the Philadelphia plan had done for construction contracts. It went well beyond the plan in elaborating a code of regulation and procedure for the development and implementation of affirmative action programs. It could also trace its origins back beyond the Philadelphia plan to the ancillary statement on affirmative action programs in the Johnson code of 1968. The new code, for example, retained the requirement that contractors conduct an analysis of the utilization of minority group members and women in the various job categories, one of the major innovations of the 1968 code. But unlike the earlier code which for all intents and purposes stopped with this internal analysis, the revised order broke new ground already charted by the Philadelphia plan. It introduced an external set of standards by which the contractors could evaluate their internal utilization of minorities and women: were they employing too few, too many, or just the right number in a given job classification? The central concern of the revised order was, however, with the question of too few, particularly as it related to the better job. *Underutilization* became the pivotal term in the evaluative scheme constructed by the order and was defined "as having fewer minorities and women in a particular job classification than would reasonably be expected by their availability." The order also specified what the term "availability" was to mean operationally; it listed eight components, with most of the eight referring to aspects of the local labor market or situation external to the contractor's facility:

"(1) In determining whether minorities* are being underutilized in any job classification the contractor will consider at least all of the following factors:

(i) The minority population of the labor area surrounding the facility;

(ii) The size of the minority unemployment force in the labor area surrounding the facility;

(iii) The percentage of the minority work force as compared with the total work force in the immediate labor area;

(iv) The general availability of minorities having requisite skills in the immediate labor area;

(v) The availability of minorities having requisite skills in an area in which the contractor can reasonably recruit;

*These factors were also to be taken into account in determining whether women were being underutilized.

(vi) The availability of promotable and transferable minorities within the contractor's organization;

(vii) The existence of training institutions capable of training persons in the requisite skills; and

(viii) The degree of training which the contractor is reasonably able to undertake as a means of making all job classes available to minorities."

(Office of Federal Contract Compliance *Federal Register* 1971:
Subpart B 60–2.11)

In introducing external standards of evaluation, the revised order enabled contractors to do more systematically what they could only do impressionistically under the 1968 code: namely, pinpoint deficiencies in their work force in the utilization of minorities and women whom the order labeled as "members of an 'affected class' who, by virtue of past discrimination continue to suffer the present effects of that discrimination" (Office of Federal Contract Compliance, *Federal Register* 1971: Subpart A, 60–2.1). As a result, the further requirement in both codes that the contractors seek to remedy these deficiencies by setting up goals and timetables took on a much fuller and more exact meaning in the 1971 version than it could in the 1968 code. The latter, for example, merely made a passing reference to goals and timetables without any further explanation. In 1971, the revised code developed the terms in greater detail under the subsection heading Subpart B, 60–2.12, *Establishment of Goals and Timetables* (Office of Federal Contract Compliance, *Federal Register* 1971). The first sentence reiterates the close linkage between the two terms and the utilization analysis of the contractor: "The goals and timetables developed by the contractor should be attainable in terms of the contractor's analysis of his deficiencies and his entire affirmative action program." Thus, "goals, timetables, and affirmative action commitments must be designed to correct any identifiable deficiencies." Consequently, "goals should be significant, measurable, and attainable," and "should be specific for planned results, with timetables for completion." However, goals should not be treated as "rigid and inflexible quotas which must be met," but should be regarded as "targets reasonably attainable." Thus, "in establishing the size of his goals and the length of his timetables, the contractor should consider the results which could reasonably be expected from his putting forth every good faith effort to make his overall affirmative action program work." Thus, "good faith effort" was to be a key consideration – as it was in the Philadelphia plan – in judging the actions of the contractor, particularly where the goals and timetables might not be adequate to remedy the deficiencies.

The Revised Order No. 4 required much more than the above in the contractor's affirmative action program. It insisted that top management enunciate or reaffirm a policy of equal employment opportunity and see to it that the policy be vigorously applied in all personnel and other organizational decisions and action. Accordingly, the order stipulated that top management should inform all levels of authority of the seriousness of its intentions and should disseminate its policy to all ranks within the organization as well as to unions and other groups outside of it.

In this manner the contractor was to stamp out all vestiges of overt discrimination and bias in the policies and practices of his organization. The order also addressed itself to the ferreting out of the more hidden discriminatory practices and biases that might have become so embedded in the organizational structure of the contractor that they had become part of the ordinary routines and definitions of the job and of personnel decisions and actions. The contractor was accordingly instructed to examine carefully organizational structures and processes with a view to ridding them of these hidden "contaminants" which may have deflected them from their original purposes and functions. He was to "conduct detailed analyses of position descriptions to insure that they accurately reflect position functions, and are consistent for the same position from one location to another." He was also to "validate worker specifications by division, department, location or other organizational unit and by job category using job performance criteria." He should pay special attention to "academic, experience, and skill requirements to insure that the requirements in themselves do not constitute inadvertent discrimination. Specifications should be consistent for the same job classification in all locations and should be free from bias as regards race, color, religion, sex, or national origin, except where sex is a bona fide occupational qualification." In addition, the contractor was to "evaluate the total selection process to insure freedom from bias and, thus, aid the attainment of goals and objectives." This would include such things as "application forms, interview procedures, test administration, test validity, referral procedures" and the like. In particular, he was to abide by the requirements of the OFCC order in the validation and standardization of employee testing and other selection procedures that went into effect in October 1971. In addition, "all personnel involved in the recruiting, screening, selection, promotion, disciplinary, and related processes should be carefully selected and trained to insure elimination of bias in all personnel actions" (Office of Federal Contract Compliance, *Federal Register* 1971: Subpart C, 60–2.24).

To oversee the carrying out of the multiple facets and functions of the affirmative action program, the order required that an executive of the contractor "be appointed as director or manager of the company Equal Opportunity Programs." This person "should be given the necessary top management support and staffing to execute the assignment" (Office of Federal Contract Compliance,

Federal Register 1971: Subpart C, 60–2.22). In addition, the contractor should develop "internal audit and reporting systems to measure effectiveness of the total program." In this connection, "the contractor should monitor records of referrals, placements, transfers, promotions, and terminations at all levels to insure nondiscriminatory policy is carried out." He should also "require formal reports from unit managers on a schedule basis as to degree to which corporate or unit goals are attained and timetables met,... review report results with all levels of management, [and] ... advise top management of program effectiveness and submit recommendations to improve unsatisfactory performance" (Office of Federal Contract Compliance, *Federal Register* 1971: Subpart C, 60–2.25).

The third major initiative that the OFCC took in late 1969 was the issuance of Order No. 1 which reduced the number of compliance agencies from twenty-six to fifteen and redefined the basis on which contractors of supplies and services were to be assigned to these fifteen compliance agencies. Previously they had been assigned to agencies that had a predominant financial involvement with a contractor through its contractual awards. With the order, assignments were to be made on the basis of the Standard Industrial Classification (SIC) Code. Thus the compliance agency of the Department of Defense, which had compliance responsibility for more contracts than any other agency, was to handle such industries as textile and apparel, primary metal and fabricated metal products, motor vehicles, aircraft and guided missiles, and miscellaneous manufacturing, and the like. The Office of Civil Rights of the Department of Health, Education, and Welfare was to be responsible for such industries as health, legal, educational, and social services, museums, human resources programs, and the like.

In addition, the order set a target for annual compliance reviews of 50 percent of all contractor facilities assigned to a compliance agency. Most agencies had barely done 10 percent annually; the numbers of reviews increased perceptibly in 1969, but few if any agencies to this day have ever reached the 50 percent figure.

While the target may have proved unrealistic, the OFCC revealed in the issuance of the order a significant shift in its approach to the compliance review process. Prior to 1969, the OFCC merely required each agency to submit an annual memorandum on its plans for performing the compliance function during the coming year; a number of agencies even failed to comply with this request.

With the order, the OFCC became more actively involved in monitoring the compliance review process and in developing guidelines and standardized procedures for conducting the reviews. By January 1972 the OFCC had drafted a comprehensive set of standardized procedures for evaluation of the performance on non-construction contractors and issued it as Order 14 to heads of federal agencies. The order was implemented in July 1972 and subsequently revised, reissued, and codified as Revised Order 14 in May 1973; a further revision was made a year later.

The revised order set forth a number of steps in the compliance review process. As the first step, the agency was to conduct, on a routine basis, desk audits of a contractor's affirmative action program, including a work force analysis, and of the extent to which he had sought to implement the program in "good faith." Once a desk audit was finished, the next step was an on-site review for these contractors who had not had one within two years or whose program and/or progress on his program was not deemed acceptable in the audit. The on-site review was to delve much more systematically and deeply than could the desk audit into the contractor's policies and practices in recruiting and utilizing minorities and women. They were to be compared with nonminority workers in all contexts, from recruitment, placement, promotion, wages, and salaries to termination. The central focus was on the adequacy of the contractor's program and on the extent and degree to which he was making "good faith" efforts to meet the current goals and timetables of his program.

If the compliance officer required more time to complete his analysis of the data from the on-site review, he could continue it with an off-site analysis. Upon completion of the analysis, the compliance officer was to schedule an exit conference with the contractor in order to go over the findings of the analysis and review. Any deficiencies that had been uncovered were to be itemized and a written commitment obtained from the contractor specifying the dates when corrective action would be completed. Where more time was needed for study, the commitment was to be obtained later. The contractor could also request a hearing to reconsider the recommendation or orders of the compliance agency.

The entire sequence of reviews from desk audit to exit conference was to be completed within sixty days. At its end, the compliance agency was obliged either to notify the contractor of his being in compliance or to issue a notice requiring the contractor to show cause within thirty days why enforcement proceedings or other appropriate action to insure compliance should not be instituted.

As the various key elements from Orders 1, 4, and 14 were fitted into the administrative machinery, the effect was almost immediate in broadening the sweep and scope of the activities of the OFCC and of the various compliance and contracting agencies. During the fiscal year of 1970, for example, the OFCC distributed its first version of Order 4 and conducted training conferences for personnel of compliance agencies to familiarize them with the new standards. It also held several industry-wide seminars on the order. During the year, the Annual Report of the Department of Labor stated that 6000 compliance reviews were conducted and ten area plans were in effect in the construction industry.

By the end of the fiscal year of 1971, Order 14 had already been distributed to heads of federal agencies and a conference was held for policy level personnel from all compliance agencies to discuss review procedures. During the year, compliance reviews jumped fivefold and totalled 31,000, of which 16,000 were of non-construction firms and 15,000 were of construction firms. In addition, 300 contractors were given notices to show cause in thirty days why enforcement proceedings should not be instituted against them, and four notices of proposed debarment were actually issued. Further, by the end of the fiscal year, twenty-seven volunteer hometown plans were in operation; four others were imposed by the labor department and one by the courts.

By the end of the fiscal year of 1972, Revised Order 4 had been issued as well as the regulations on testing and national guidelines for compliance reviews of construction firms. During the year, 23,000 compliance reviews were made; twenty-three hometown plans plus one imposed by the labor department were added to those already in existence. In addition, 640 contractors received show cause notices; eight received notices of proposed debarment, and two were actually debarred.

By the end of the fiscal year of 1973, compliance reviews increased to the level of 1971; 31,000 were conducted of which 22,000 were with supply and service firms and 9000 with construction firms. Six additional voluntary hometown plans were developed, bringing the total to fifty-six. In addition, 775 contractors received thirty-day notices. One of the most significant developments that occurred during the year was the agreement reached through the combined efforts of the Departments of Labor and Justice and the Equal Employment Opportunity Commission with AT&T, Bethlehem Steel, and Delta Airlines on affirmative action programs and back wages for thousands of minority and women employees. According to a statement from the Department of Labor, "These should provide models for civil rights agreements for years to come" (US Department of Labor 1973:30).

In the fiscal year of 1974, compliance reviews returned to the level of 1972; 23,000 were conducted, including 15,000 with supply and service firms and 8000 with construction firms. In addition, 700 contractors received show cause notices. Further, the development of seven hometown and two imposed plans brought the total of construction compliance plans to 70 by the end of the fiscal year. Audits were made of 61 plans; most revealed "good faith" efforts toward realization of goals, but mandatory hiring goals were imposed on twenty-one localities where efforts were lagging. Another major event of the year was agreement with nine steel companies and the steelworkers union "to provide equal employment opportunity and back wages for thousands of workers discriminated against because of race or sex. The agreement with the Departments of Labor and Justice and the Equal Employment Opportunity Commission provided $31 million in back wages to approximately 40,000 black, Spanish-surnamed, and women employees at 249 plants" (US Department of Labor 1974:23). Another agreement was signed with AT&T on back pay for managerial employees.

By the end of the fiscal year of 1975, Revised Order 14 was fully implemented with approximately 90 percent of the compliance reports completed. However, the total number of reviews remained at the 1974 level; 22,750 were conducted, with 12,450 among supply and service contractors and 10,300 among construction contractors; 500 contractors received thirty-day notices and four firms were actually debarred. Only one additional hometown plan was added to the construction compliance plans; thus the construction program was still short of its original goal of 102.

Early in the fiscal year of 1976, the OFCC was enlarged to include affirmative action programs for the handicapped and for veterans. Its name was changed to Office of Federal Contract Compliance Programs (OFCCP). Two years later the OFCCP took over, in a major reorganization, "the day-to-day responsibility for enforcement" that had until then been performed by compliance agencies "scattered" throughout various departments of the federal government; in 1977 the number of such agencies had been reduced to eleven. The goal of this consolidation was to produce a "more efficient enforcement activity and more responsiveness on the part of the program to the needs of the people it affects" (US Department of Labor 1978:52)

By the fiscal year of 1979 "OFCCP's staff of about 200 grew to over 1300 employees in a nationwide network of 81 offices in 63 cities" (US Department of Labor 1979:45). As the first signs of success of this consolidation, the OFCCP reported that nearly all of its enforcement statistics for the fiscal year 1980 were "substantially higher than those for the previous year." For example, "OFCCP conducted over 3000 compliance reviews of federal contractors in locations where over 900,000 persons are employed. The agency also investigated 1640 complaints of discrimination." In 1979, the first year of consolidation, the figures were 2400 compliance reviews and 1550 investigations of complaints. In addition, "financial commitments made by federal contractors in settlements with the department are nearly twice as large as those for the previous fiscal year. A total of 670 employers committed $16.2 million to equal employment opportunity and affirmative action, of which $9.9 million went into back pay awards to 5100 women, minorities, disabled persons and veterans" (US Department of Labor 1980:53–4).

An overview: the bureaucratic evolution of affirmative action over three decades

In conclusion, we have found that it took approximately thirty years for the policy of nondiscrimination in government contracts, as first enunciated by President Roosevelt, to develop the kind of administrative machinery, procedural codification, and normative translation that enabled it to become something more than an abstract statement. This thirty-year evolution cut across six presidential administrations, Republican and Democratic alike. Each administration added something to the process; however, what Democratic presidents added was strikingly different from what Republican presidents added. Normative formulations and re-formulations, for example, took place primarily during Democratic administrations as seen in Roosevelt and Truman being the first to enunciate the nondiscrimination policy and in Kennedy's transformation of the policy into affirmative action and equal employment opportunity. Basic structural foundations were also laid while the Democrats were in power as in the case of Roosevelt's and Truman's first use of a committee as the central organ of the program and of Johnson's placing the program in the Department of Labor. Constrastingly, Republican administrations increased the effectiveness of the procedural machinery that was devised to function within the normative and structural framework inherited from the Democrats. Accordingly, Eisenhower gave his committee more authority than Truman had given his. Nixon honed an effective bureaucratic apparatus within the normative parameters of Kennedy and the structural parameters of Johnson. Republican presidents implemented more effectively than Democratic presidents what the latter had in fact started.

Overall progress toward an effective administrative instrumentality was snail-like, and the cumulative effects of the actions of the various administrations were modest for most of the policy's history. Even Kennedy's normative reformulation of the policy and Johnson's structural transformation did not initially speed up the process. They served, though, as blueprint and generating source for the burst of energy that propelled the program into the 1970s. With the addition of key procedural elements under the Nixon administration, the blueprint became fully operational, and a bureaucratic machine was perfected. The machine subsequently developed an almost inexorable momentum of its own – despite the ideological opposition of President Nixon – and implemented with a marked degree of success the policy first enunciated three decades before.

10

THE EQUAL EMPLOYMENT
OPPORTUNITY COMMISSION
AND THE COURTS

Introduction

Crucial as the internal changes and elaborations were for the evolution of the government contract program, its character, scope, and rate of growth were also significantly influenced by developments external to it. Of particular importance were the actions and decisions of two organs of government. One derived its basic authority from the legislative branch; the other, from the judiciary branch. Thus we find that the Equal Employment Opportunity Commission (EEOC), a creation of Title VII of the Civil Rights Act passed by Congress in 1964 and made even stronger by Congress in its Equal Employment Opportunity Act of 1972, and the federal courts, including the Supreme Court, have been largely responsible for developing a body of procedure, precedent, and law that have vitally affected the operation of the contract program and the pursuit by government of equal employment opportunity and affirmative action generally.

However, as this program developed effectiveness and teeth, it became increasingly the object of public controversy. A complex matter, it was reduced to the oversimplified issue of affirmative action versus quotas.

In the first section of this chapter we shall examine the legal and administrative framework constructed by the EEOC and legitimized by the federal courts that shored up the government program, and in the second section we shall analyze the opposition to the program that has been spearheaded by academicians.

The legal scaffolding for affirmative action

ESTABLISHING PRIORITIES: THE BAN ON "PREFERENTIAL TREATMENT" V. AFFIRMATIVE RELIEF

By the time the EEOC had become a functioning entity, the government contract program had already shifted its emphasis from nondiscrimination to affirmative action for equal employment opportunity and had reshuffled its priorities from complaint processing to compliance reporting and review. In turn, the EEOC was obliged by the very nature of its legislative mandate to focus primarily on charges of unlawful discrimination against an employer by individual employees and applicants. The law further stipulated that where charges were substantiated the EEOC could seek to change the unlawful practices of the employer, not merely to redress the specific wrong against the individual complainant. As a first step, conciliation was to be tried; if that failed, legal remedies could be pursued. In the early days the EEOC could not appear as a party in any such legal action; it could only support the individual complainant as a friend in court, or under certain conditions it could turn to the Attorney General to initiate court action. After 1972, however, it could become a party to such action. Further, the law also authorized the judge in Section 706(g) of Title VII of the Civil Rights Act 1964 to "enjoin the respondent from engaging in such unlawful employment practice, and order such affirmative action as may be appropriate, which may include reinstatement or hiring of employees, with or without back pay (payable by the employer, employment agency, or labor organization, as the case may be, responsible for the unlawful employment practice)" (US Statutes at Large 1964 78:263). In 1972, this provision was amended to enlarge the range of options available to the court in ordering affirmative relief.

Thus, Title VII inextricably linked the EEOC and the federal courts in probing the virginal federal territory of legally proscribed discrimination in employment, in working out the parameters, meanings, and diverse manifestations of unlawful discrimination, and in devising remedies and relief for those persons, as individuals or as a class, who have borne the brunt of unlawful discrimination.

Manifest as the authorization was in Section 706(g) for the EEOC and courts to seek redress, still another section of Title VII, Section 703(j), imposed serious constraints on what if anything could be done to redress past discrimination. It forbade the granting of

"preferential treatment to any individual or to any group because of the race, color, religion, sex, or national origin of such individual or group on account of an imbalance which may exist with respect to the total number or percentage of persons of any race, color, religion, sex, or national origin employed by any employer, referred or classified for employment by any employment agency or labor organization, admitted to membership or classified by any labor organization, or admitted to, or employed in, any apprenticeship or other training program, in comparison with the total number or percentage of persons of such race, color, religion, sex, or national origin in any community, State, section, or other area, or in the available workforce in any community, State, section, or other area." (US Statutes at Large 1964 78:257)

The EEOC quickly resolved the apparent contradiction in the law by opting for Section 706(g) of Title VII and not for Section 703(j). It decided in its first year that its primary function was not merely to curb policies and practices of unlawful discrimination so that nondiscrimination would prevail in the future, but also to provide immediate relief for those who have suffered ill effects from these policies and practices of discrimination

"Negro discrimination is generally discrimination against a class. Certainly, where a pattern of previous discrimination is established, the Commission felt it should not be diffident about seeking effective relief for those who have been its victims.

When a finding of such discrimination is made in accordance with the provisions of Title VII, should not the remedy require specific results – immediate hiring and promotion of Negroes in appropriate cases – rather than procedures that offer them equal opportunity in the future?"
(Equal Employment Opportunity Commission 1966:8)

Several district courts disputed the EEOC interpretation in their rulings. In writing the court's opinion on Griggs v. Duke Power Co. in 1968, District Judge Gordon insisted that "Congress intended the Act [the Civil Rights Act of 1964] to be given prospective application only. Any discriminatory employment practices occurring before the effective date of the Act, July 2, 1965 are not remedial under the Act" (292 Federal Supplement 1968:247). Similar sentiments had already been expressed in another lower court decision. In US v. Sheet Metal Workers, March 1968, District Judge Meredith wrote,

"The Civil Rights Act of 1964 was not intended to penalize unions or others for their sins prior to the effective date of the Act. It is prospective only. Neither was it passed to destroy seniority rights in unions or in business. The Act specifically forbids a union or a business from giving preferential treatment to Negroes to correct an existing imbalance of whites. In order to be a violation of the Act, there must be an intentional pattern and practice of discrimination and not an isolated instance of discrimination. There is no pattern or practice of discrimination in this case since the effective date of this Act."

(280 Federal Supplement 1968:730)

Both of these decisions, however, were reversed upon appeal, and federal courts came to support generally the position of the EEOC. They ruled that Section 703(j) did not prevent affirmative relief against the present effects of past discrimination. In the 1970 Appeals Court reversal of a district court ruling in US v. IBEW that had taken the line of the lower court in the Sheet Metal Workers case, Judge Edwards emphasized that Section 703(j) should not be treated in isolation from the basic purposes of the law and from those sections of the law that referred to remedial action and court proceedings; to do otherwise, he maintained, would nullify the stated aims of the Civil Rights Act.

"We believe this section [703(j)] prohibits interpreting the statute to require 'preferential treatment' solely because of an imbalance in racial employment existing at the effective date of the Act. But we also believe that its prohibition must be read in conjunction with the fundamental purposes of the statute . . . and in conjunction with the section providing for affirmative relief [through 'civil actions by the Attorney General' where the 'pattern or practice' of racial discrimination is evident.]

When the stated purposes of the Act and the broad affirmative relief authorization above are read in context with . . . [Section 703(j)] we believe that section cannot be construed as a ban on affirmative relief against continuation of effects of past discrimination resulting from present practices (neutral on their face) which have the practical effect of continuing past injustices.

Any other interpretation would allow complete nullification of the stated purposes of the Civil Rights Act of 1964. This could result from adoption of devices such as a limitation of new apprentices to relatives of the all-white membership of a union, . . . or limitation of membership to persons who had previous work experience under union contract, while such experience was racially limited to whites, . . . or administration of qualification examinations which had no objective standards and which produced unexplained discriminatory results." (428 Federal Reporter, Second Series 1970:149–50)

Thus, in time, the federal courts did not treat Section 703(j) as unrelated to Sections 706(g) or 707; they sought to reconcile the former's proscription of preferential treatment with the latter's stipulation of remedial and affirmative action. By 1973 the courts determined that remedial action even to the extent of "preferential quota hiring" held a higher priority than did the proscription. In a bellwether case, US v. Lathers, Local 46, the US Court of Appeals in New York applied the principle that had been enunciated by the US Supreme Court in a voting rights case in 1965: "'[t]he Court has not merely the power but the duty to render a decree which will so far as possible eliminate the discriminatory effects of the past as well as bar like discrimination in the future' (Louisiana v. United States, 380 US 145, 154 ... (1965))" (471 Federal Reporter, Second Series 1973:413).

At the same time the Appeals Court did insist that the power of affirmative relief, broad as it was, was not unlimited: "The only limitation on the broad powers of affirmative relief is that restricting preferential quota hiring." As such, the Court articulated the principle that "quotas [preferential treatment] merely to obtain racial balance are forbidden quotas to correct past discriminatory practices are not" (471 Federal Reporter, Second Series 1973:430).

Federal courts have varied in the literalness with which they have drawn the distinction between lawful and unlawful preferential treatment. The US Appeals Court in New York in particular has generally opted for a narrow interpretation and has been inclined to introduce qualifications and conditions in its decisions. This is evident in its "solomon-like" rulings in the case of Kirkland v. Department of Correctional Services. First, the Court reaffirmed the lower court's decision that an examination and selection procedure for the position of sergeant was discriminatory and had to be revised in accordance with the EEOC guidelines. The Court also supported the lower court's decision that interim appointments could be made on a preferential basis: one out of every four promotions was to be black and Hispanic until the combined percent of black and Hispanic sergeants was equal to the combined percent of black and Hispanic correction officers. But the higher court reversed the lower court's ruling that this arrangement should be made permanent, even after the selection procedures had become job-related and free of discriminatory elements.

In explaining the Court's reversal of the permanent arrangement, Judge Van Graafeiland declared:

"The benefits of such order are not limited to the plaintiff class. Its quota requirements are based upon a shifting and rapidly expanding racial base, wholly unrelated to the consequences of any alleged past discrimination. It provides for appointment according to race without regard to the individual applicant's standing on a job-related examination and, indeed, without regard to whether the benefited Black or Hispanic received a passing grade. It completely ignores the statutory requirements and constitutional purpose of the New York Civil Service Law and constitutes court-imposed reverse discrimination without any exceptional or compelling governmental purpose."

(520 Federal Reporter, Second Series 1975:430)

By the mid-1970s it was evident that the federal courts were still seeking to clarify the boundaries between lawful and unlawful preferential treatment and quotas under Title VII. Until recently this preoccupation did not seem to have any relevance for statistical goals and quotas set under the affirmative action programs developed by the Office of Federal Contract Compliance (OFCC) under Executive Order 11246. For in 1971 the US Court of Appeals in Philadelphia had ruled in a case brought by the Contractor Association of Eastern Pennsylvania against the OFCC that the constraints imposed by Section 703(j) of Title VII against preferential treatment did not apply to the statistical goals set up under the Philadelphia plan for the utilization of minority manpower in various crafts by the OFCC under Executive Order 11246. The Court concluded that

> "[the] Civil Rights Act of 1964 provision stating that nothing should be interpreted to require any employer or labor organization to grant preferential treatment to any individual or group because of race [Section 703(j)] is a limitation only upon that title of Act dealing comprehensively with discrimination in employment [Title VII] and not upon any other remedies, state or federal."   (442 Federal Reporter, Second Series 1971:160)

Since the mid-1970s an increasing number of reverse discrimination suits have been filed by white males against affirmative action programs sponsored by the OFCC on the grounds that they violated various provisions of Title VII. One suit finally reached the Supreme Court in 1979.

That suit began in 1976 when a white employee, Brian F. Weber, brought a class action against the Kaiser Aluminum and Chemical Corporation and the US Steelworkers of America in the US District Court for the Eastern District of Louisiana. He alleged that an affirmative action plan, that was part of a master collective agreement between the two organizations, discriminated against him and other similarly situated white employees in violation of Title VII.

Under the plan which had been "designed to eliminate conspicuous racial imbalances in Kaiser's then almost exclusively white craftworkforce," (443 US 1979:198) black hiring goals for each plant were to be met by recruiting enough blacks to in-plant craft training programs so that their numbers in each plant's craft work force would in time be "equal to the percentage of blacks in the respective local labor forces" (443 US 1979:198). At one particular plant, Gramercy, Kaiser selected trainees "on the basis of seniority, with the proviso that at least 50 percent of the new trainees were to be black until the percentage of black skilled craftworkers in the Gramercy plant [less than 2 per cent] approximated the percentage of blacks in the local labor force [39 per cent]" (443 US 1979:199).

"During 1974, the first year of the operation of the Kaiser-USWA affirmative action plan, 13 craft trainees were selected from Gramercy's production work force. Of these, seven were black and six white. The most senior black selected into the program had less seniority than several white production workers whose bids for admission were rejected. Thereafter one of those white production workers, respondent Brian Weber (hereafter respondent), instituted this class action in the United States District Court for the Eastern District of Louisiana."   (443 US 1979:199)

The district court ruled in favor of the plaintiff in June 1976. In his opinion for the court, Judge Gordon took cognizance of the fact that the agreement was not made under terms of Title VII but was made instead to satisfy regulations issued by the OFCC and to avoid "vexatious litigation by minority employees" (415 Federal Supplement 1976:765). He insisted, however, that once the Civil Rights Act was passed, the terms of Title VII superceded those of any other governmental program or policy on nondiscrimination in employment and established "unequivocal prohibitions against racial discrimination against *any individual*" (415 Federal Supplement 1976:769).

Under Title VII, he agreed, affirmative action programs may be permitted as remedies for past discriminatory practices, but only if ordered by the judiciary. Title VII, he continued, forbids such action by employers on their own initiative

"because relief of this nature should be imposed with extreme caution and discretion, and only in those limited cases where necessary to cure the ill effects of past discrimination, the courts alone are in a position to afford due process to all concerned in determining the necessity for and in fashioning such relief. Further, the administration of such relief by the courts tends to assure that those remedial programs will be uniform in nature and will exist only as long as necessary to effectuate the purposes of the Civil Rights Act."

(415 Federal Supplement 1976:767–68)

In this case, the judge argued, such affirmative action was not even necessary because there was no record of past discrimination against the blacks anywhere in the company that would require remedial action. The blacks were in effect in their "rightful place in the plant" (415 Federal Supplement 1976:769).

The Court of Appeals affirmed the lower court decision, but on *certiorari* the US Supreme Court reversed the two. In his opinion for the Supreme Court, Justice Brennan took a position exactly opposite to that of the district court judge. He declared that Title VII did not forbid voluntary agreements between employers and unions on bona fide affirmative action plans that seek "to eliminate traditional patterns of racial segregation" (443 US 1979:201).

To come to any other conclusion, he insisted,

> "would 'bring about an end completely at variance with the purpose of the statute' and must be rejected ... Congress' primary concern in enacting the prohibition against racial discrimination in Title VII of the Civil Rights Act of 1964 was with 'the plight of the Negro in our economy ... (443 US 1979:202). [It saw as the] crux of the problem ... [the need] to open employment opportunities for Negroes in occupations which have been traditionally closed to them,' ... and it was to this problem that Title VII's prohibition against racial discrimination in employment was primarily addressed ... (443 US 1979:203).
>
> Given this legislative history, we cannot agree with respondent that Congress intended to prohibit the private sector from taking effective steps to accomplish the goal that Congress designed Title VII to achieve. The very statutory words intended as a spur or catalyst to cause 'employers and unions to self-examine and to self-evaluate their employment practices and to endeavor to eliminate, so far as possible, the last vestiges of an unfortunate and ignominious page in this country's history,' ... cannot be interpreted as an absolute prohibition against all private, voluntary, race-conscious affirmative action efforts to hasten the elimination of such vestiges. It would be ironic indeed if a law triggered by a Nation's concern over centuries of racial injustice and intended to improve the lot of those who had 'been excluded from the American dream for so long,' ... constituted the first legislative prohibition of all voluntary, private, race-conscious efforts to abolish traditional patterns of racial segregation and hierarchy."   (443 US 1979:204)

In writing the law, Brennan conceded, Congress was mindful of the objections of those who feared that Title VII might "lead to undue 'Federal Government interference with private business because of some Federal employee's ideas about racial balance or racial imbalance'" (443 US 1979:206). For that reason, he acknowledged, Congress wrote Section 703(j) with its stipulation that "nothing contained in this title shall be interpreted to require any employer,... labor organization,... subject to this title to grant preferential treatment to any individual, or to any group because of race" (443 US 1979:205fn). Yet, he continued, in failing to add the verb "permit" after the verb "require" Congress again revealed its intention not "to limit traditional business freedom to such a degree as to prohibit all voluntary, race-conscious affirmative action" (443 US 1979:207).

Justice Brennan agreed that limits might be imposed on those plans, but he added "We need not today define in detail the line of demarcation between permissible and impermissible affirmative action plans. It suffices to hold that the challenged Kaiser-USWA affirmative action plan falls on the permissible side of the line . . . [because] the purposes of the plan mirror those of the statute" (443 US 1979:208).

He then went on to offer other reasons why the plan was acceptable.

"The plan does not unnecessarily trammel the interests of the white employees. The plan does not require the discharge of white workers and their replacement with new black hirees. . . . Nor does the plan create an absolute bar to the advancement of white employees; half of those trained in the program will be white. Moreover, the plan is a temporary measure; it is not intended to maintain racial balance, but simply to eliminate a manifest racial imbalance. Preferential selection of craft trainees at the Gramercy plant will end as soon as the percentage of black skilled craft workers in the Gramercy plant approximates the percentage of blacks in the local labor force." (443 US 1979:208)

Justice Brennan acknowledged that the Court's decision had bypassed consideration of the "petitioners' contention that their affirmative action plan represented an attempt to comply with Exec. Order No. 11246" (443 US 1979:209 fn). The Court's decision also failed to deal with the linkage between Title VII and Executive Order 11246. These matters were not relevant, Brennan argued because the "Kaiser-USWA plan does not involve state action. . . . The only question before us is the narrow statutory issue of whether Title VII *forbids* private employers and unions from voluntarily agreeing upon bona fide affirmative action plans" (443 US 1979:200).

It is evident that these matters have yet to be decided by the Court, and that the issue of reverse discrimination has still to be dealt with in a definitive manner.

DEFINING UNLAWFUL EMPLOYMENT PRACTICES: CONSEQUENCES AND STATISTICAL IMBALANCE

Just as Title VII treats the question of remedial action in an ambiguous manner, so does it fail to specify clearly the defining features of an unlawful employment practice. It merely states in Section 703, for example, that certain kinds of behaviors by the employer are unlawful if they are linked directly to the employee's race, color, religion, sex, or national origins. It fails to say, however, whether this behavioral linkage to race must be purposefully intended by the employer or must merely manifest itself – intended or not – in discriminatory results for the employee.

The EEOC opted very early in its history for the latter approach to unlawful employment practices. It contended

"that to prove a violation of Title VII one need not prove that there was a specific intent to discriminate; a violation may be established on proof that the conduct it complained of had the foreseeable effect of denying persons equal employment opportunity.... [Thus] certain employment practices may be in violation of Title VII not because they constitute disparate *treatment* but because they produce unjustifiably disparate *effect*."

(Equal Employment Opportunity Commission 1968:12)

As happened with remedial action, several courts soon challenged the EEOC's interpretation and insisted that intention, not merely discriminatory results, had to be evident for a practice to be deemed unlawful. This position was clearly expressed in the decision of the Federal Court of Appeals of the Fourth Circuit in Griggs v. Duke Power Co. This case involved a class action suit brought by black employees under Title VII against the company's educational and testing requirements for employment, transfer, and promotion. The employees claimed that these requirements produced disproportionately negative results for blacks and thereby continued the effects into the present of the past discriminatory practices that the company had actively pursued prior to 1965. Present policies of the company, the plaintiffs conceded, were nondiscriminatory in nature.

The Appeals Court did not dispute the basic facts as outlined by the plaintiffs nor their claim that Title VII applied to present effects of past discrimination; in so doing the Court rejected the lower court's ruling that Title VII did not apply to such effects. (This has already been pointed out in the previous section of this chapter.) However, the Appeals Court concluded that the company had not deliberately adopted these requirements to continue these effects. It offered six reasons for this conclusion. These effects, then, were the unintended byproducts, the Court maintained, of a company effort to pursue a valid business purpose. (As we shall see later, the Supreme Court subsequently questioned whether the testing and educational requirements of the company did indeed serve a valid business purpose.) Accordingly, the Court ruled against all the black plaintiffs but those who had been hired prior to the imposition of the educational requirement and were accordingly subject to the discriminatory policies then in effect.

In a strong dissenting opinion, Judge Sobeloff took exception to the importance that the majority had attached to intention in their decision. He argued that to give legal sanction to discriminatory behavior merely because evidence of manifest intent is absent is to perpetuate the kinds of subterfuges that have historically plagued enforcement of nondiscrimination in the legal-political realm. Such subterfuges have frequently hidden the real discriminatory intent behind a mask of neutrality.

"The pattern of racial discrimination in employment parallels that which we have witnessed in other areas. Overt bias, when prohibited, has ofttimes been supplanted by more cunning devices designed to impart the appearance of neutrality, but to operate with the same invidious effect as before. Illustrative is the use of the Grandfather Clause in voter registration – a scheme that was condemned by the Supreme Court without dissent over half a century ago. Guinn v. United States, 238, U.S. 347 . . . (1915)."

(420 Federal Reporter, Second Series 1970:1238)

To avoid such subterfuges, Judge Sobeloff continued, the Court must not become bogged down with the question of intent but must instead deal merely with the consequences of discrimination and only allow those consequences to stand if they can be justified by the standard of business necessity. In the case at hand, the Judge insisted, the Court's interpretation of that standard has to be found wanting, for the Court had inappropriately substituted a general and vague version of that standard for the precise job-related version advocated by the EEOC.

The black plaintiffs appealed the decision and, in its first ruling on a case under Title VII, the Supreme Court reversed the Appeals Court decision in March 1971. In his opinion for the Court, Chief Justice Burger did not probe into the underlying motives of the company as Judge Sobeloff had. He was even prepared to accept the finding of the district and Appeals Courts that the company was not guilty of any discriminatory intent in its testing and educational requirements, though he did note its past history of discrimination. In exonerating the company, Chief Justice Burger did not thereby conclude as had the lower courts that the disparate testing and educational results were merely the product of fortuitous and selective factors unrelated to racial discrimination. Instead, he traced them to the discriminatory forces operative in the larger society, particularly those bearing on education. He said, "petitioners have long received inferior education in segregated schools" (401 US 1971:430).

He went on to say that the Supreme Court had already recognized the importance of such factors in perpetuating discriminatory results. Specifically, in Gaston County v. United States (1969), he continued, the Court had ruled that the policies of segregation and discrimination practiced in North Carolina imposed an inferior educational system on the black. As a result, blacks could not be expected to pass a literacy test for voting registration to the same extent as whites because of this racially induced difference. Therefore, the Court had concluded that the literacy test was unconstitutional because it perpetuated racially discriminatory practice and thereby "would abridge the right to vote indirectly on account of race" (401 US 1971:430).

The implication of this decision for the case at hand, Chief Justice Burger insisted, was not that everyone was to be guaranteed the same kind of universal right in employment as in voting: "Congress did not intend by Title VII, however, to guarantee a job to every person regardless of qualifications. In short, the Act does not command that any person be hired simply because he was formerly the subject of discrimination, or because he is a member of a minority group" (401 US 1971:430–31).

But what the voting decision and Title VII do mean for employment is, Chief Justice Burger continued, that the path to jobs should not be littered by present or residues of past discriminatory practices whether these be in society generally or in the company in particular. "What is required by Congress is the removal of artificial, arbitrary, and unnecessary barriers to employment when the barriers operate invidiously to discriminate on the basis of racial or other impermissible classification" (401 US 1971:431). Thus, he argued, Congress enacted Title VII "to achieve equality of employment opportunities and remove barriers that have operated in the past to favor an identifiable group of white employees over other employees. Under the Act, practices, procedures, or tests neutral on their face, and even neutral in terms of intent, cannot be maintained if they operate to 'freeze' the status quo of prior discriminatory employment practices" (401 US 1971:429–30). Accordingly, he continued, "good intent or absence of discriminatory intent does not redeem employment procedures or testing mechanisms that operate as 'built-in headwinds' for minority groups and are unrelated to measuring job capability" (401 US 1971:432). In view of this, he concluded, "Congress directed the thrust of the Act to the *consequences* of employment practices, not simply the motivation" (401 US 1971:432). As a result, "the Act proscribes not only overt discrimination but also practices that are fair in form, but discriminatory in operation" (401 US 1971:431). The only exception is an employment practice that can be shown to be related to "job performance." "The touchstone is business necessity" (401 US 1971:431).

Having received judicial support for its position that consequences not intent distinguished the unlawful from the lawful employment practice, the EEOC concentrated increasing attention in investigating and resolving complaints that dealt with what was euphemistically called "systemic discrimination, that is discrimination through employment policies which appear to be neutral on their face but which, in fact, operate to the disadvantage of a protected group" (Equal Employment Opportunity Commission 1972:8); by 1972 a majority of its "cause" decisions were of this nature.

One of the two major kinds of discrimination that the EEOC has identified as "systemic" has to do with the racially neutral employment practice or policy that perpetuates the effects of past discrimination, primarily by penalizing an employee "because he lacks something which the employer denied him in the past because of his race, sex, national origins, or religion, etc" (Equal Employment Opportunity Commission 1972:8). The EEOC has found, for example, that transfer, promotion, and seniority practices and policies of a company are particularly susceptible to this form of discrimination. In one case, for example, that reached the courts, Quarles v. Philip Morris, Inc., a district court ruled that a departmental seniority system discriminated against black employees who had sought to transfer from the only department in which they could work prior to 1965 because of the company's former policy of segregation to a much more desirable department which company policy had opened to blacks after 1965. In making this transfer, the black employee was obliged, however, to start at the bottom of the seniority list in the new department; his years of accumulated service in the first department were thereby lost.

In another case, Jones v. Lee Way Motor Freight Inc., the Federal Court of Appeals of the tenth circuit ruled that a no-transfer policy of the company, nondiscriminatory on its face, was an unlawful employment practice because it confined long-term black employees to jobs which the company's past policy of segregation had assigned to them, and thereby prevented them from moving into more desirable jobs which were no longer arbitrarily closed to them.

In most of these cases, the EEOC had no difficulty in validating the company's historic record of discrimination through written and other materials. To supplement this record, the EEOC would, as the occasion warranted, look at the past numerical distribution of minorities in various departments: their absence or presence in disproportionately large or small numbers would pinpoint those departments which excluded them or kept their numbers to a minimum as well as those to which they were primarily assigned. Such statistical evidence took on even greater importance for the EEOC in its assessment of the present effects – direct or indirect – of past policies and practices of discrimination. Particularly where the latter had been replaced by neutral practices and policies or did not seem to be directly applicable, as with seniority and transfer policies, their data comprised the only solid evidence of the radiating residual effects of past discrimination. As a result, the EEOC garnered statistical data wherever possible and used evidence of numerical imbalances "to infer the existence of a pattern or practice of discrimination" (Equal Employment Opportunity Commission 1970:8) and accepted it as prima facie evidence of discriminatory behavior, intended or otherwise.

The courts were generally supportive of the commission's position on statistical evidence. In Jones v. Lee Way (1970), Judge Breitenstein concluded that racial imbalance between city and line drivers established "a prima facie case that during the 1964–1968 period, race was a factor in staffing the two driver categories" despite the company's protestation that it had never discriminated against blacks.

"In the case at bar, the statistics show that at no time between July 1, 1964, and March 1, 1968 did the company employ a single Negro line driver in spite of the fact that there were between 353 and 542 men in that category. Although all city drivers during this period, were not Negroes, all Negro drivers were city drivers. The line driver group is sufficiently larger than the city driver group that approximately 80% of the white drivers are in the line category. In short, there were no Negro line drivers; most whites were line drivers; and all Negroes were city drivers.

In the light of the large number of line drivers, the statistics establish a prima facie case that during the 1964–1968 period, race was a factor in staffing the two driver categories.... Nothing in the record leads us to believe that the situation was any different in preceding years. The company's conclusory claims that it has never discriminated against Negroes in hiring line drivers do not overcome this prima facie case."   (431 Federal Reporter, Second Series 1970:247)

In accepting the principle that statistical distributions could be used as prima facie evidence of racial discrimination, the courts were aware that they were not charting a new course in virginal territory. They had already accepted the principle almost forty years before in the Supreme Court's formulation of the "exclusionary principle" in the jury service case of Norris v. Alabama. The Supreme Court, however, had not come to this principle easily or without a great legal struggle. For over fifty years after it had declared a West Virginia statute unconstitutional in Strauder v. West Virginia, as we saw at the beginning of Chapter 8, the Court was prepared to accept as prima facie evidence a state's declaration that it neither discriminated nor excluded blacks from jury service as long as no exclusionary law was on its statute books as had been the case in West Virginia. As a result, the burden of proving otherwise rested with the black plaintiff. His task had proved virtually impossible, no matter what statistical evidence he might have been able to bring to bear.

In the Title VII cases, however, several courts have imposed more rigorous statistical requirements for a prima facie showing than has been true in the jury service cases. In his opinion on Dobbins v. Local 212 IBEW, District Judge Hogan insisted that statistical comparisons should not be made to entire populations but only with those portions of the populations that have the particular skills under dispute.

"In some fields a prima facie case of pattern and practice is made out on a showing that given privileges are exercised only, or for the greater extent, by Ws [whites] and that there is in the area a substantial N [Negro] population and that there have been repeated attempts by Ns to exercise such rights. Such is certainly true in the education and voting fields. However, we deal here with a 'craft' union. It is one thing to presume or assume, prima facie-wise or otherwise, that a significant number of a group have the qualifications for schooling or voting, or jury service. It is another thing to assume, prima facie-wise or otherwise, that because a certain number of people exist, be they W or N, that any significant number of them are lawyers or doctors, or merchants, or chiefs – or to be concrete, are competent plumbers or electricians or carpenters....

To make out a prima facie case for class purposes, as distinguished from individual purposes, the plaintiff has the burden of showing the existence of a significant number of members of the group possessing the basic skill in the particular trade involved. The plaintiffs have shown the existence of some members of the class who are skilled and who have applied and as to those it has established a case. We cannot assume and do not assume from that there are other members of the group similarly qualified."

(292 Federal Supplement 1968:445–46)

In the final analysis, however, the importance and relevance of statistical evidence for demonstrating the kind of systemic discrimination that results from past discriminatory practices has varied with the case. In some cases, it has been crucial to any demonstration of past or present discriminatory effects. In others, it has had little or no relevance as the evidence was derived from other kinds of data and sources.

Such varying relevance of statistical data does not hold, however, for the second type of systemic discrimination to which the EEOC alludes, for this is operationally defined only in terms of statistical or numerical imbalances. Thus, what the EEOC calls "impact discrimination" refers to negative or undesirable consequences of policies and practices that disproportionately affect racial minorities and women but that cannot be demonstrably linked to purposeful past or present acts of discrimination. This does not necessarily mean that such a linkage does not exist, merely that it cannot be demonstrated or proved; but neither does it mean that such a linkage in fact exists. The disparate outcome may stem from neutrally selective, not discriminatory, factors. An inherent ambiguity therefore characterizes most instances of "impact discrimination;" the EEOC has chosen to bypass this ambiguity by focusing on the disparate outcome and by placing the burden on the employer of proving that the disparate outcome is not the result of an unlawful employment practice. The employer in turn does not have to prove what the EEOC has already been unable to prove, the presence or absence of discriminatory intent or practice; instead, he may resort to the "touchstone (of) business necessity" with which the courts have provided him as a legally valid justification for the imbalance.

Employee complaints over manifestly racially neutral and universally applied testing procedures and schooling requirements have provided the EEOC with its most frequent and important example of "impact discrimination." Characteristically, the commission has found that a disproportionately larger number of blacks and other racial minorities than white males are disqualified by such procedures and requirements for jobs and promotions. To deal with the situation, the EEOC issued guidelines for employee testing and other selection procedures under the authorization of Section 703(h) of Title VII which stated, "nor shall it be an unlawful employment practice for an employer to give and to act upon the results of any professionally developed ability test provided that such test, its administration or action upon the results is not designed, intended, or used to discriminate because of race, color, religion, sex, or national origin" (420 Federal Reporter, Second Series 1970:1240).

The guidelines stipulated that such procedures had to be tied in clearly and precisely with specific requirements and features of a job and had to be predictive of actual job performance. Only if an employer's selection procedures met these requirements, the commission stated, would it accept any numerical racial imbalance that might result from its procedures as a lawful outcome; otherwise the imbalance itself would be treated as prima facie evidence of an unlawful employment practice.

The EEOC's approach to selection procedures was soon challenged in the courts in the classic case of Griggs v. Duke Power Co., which we have already dealt with in another context.

In his 1968 opinion for the district court, Judge Gordon directly contradicted the EEOC's view of Section 703(h).

"Nowhere does the Act require that employers may utilize only those tests which accurately measure the ability and skills required of a particular job or group of jobs. Nowhere does the Act require the use of only one type of test to the exclusion of other non-discriminatory tests. A test which measures the level of general intelligence, but is unrelated to the job to be performed is just as reasonably a prerequisite to hiring and promotion as is a high school diploma. In fact, a general intelligence test is probably more accurate and uniform in application than is the high school education requirement.

The two tests used by the defendant were never intended to accurately measure the ability of an employee to perform the particular job available. Rather, they are intended to indicate whether the employee has the general intelligence and overall mechanical comprehension of the average high school graduate, regardless of race, color, religion, sex, or national origin. The evidence establishes that the tests were professionally developed to perform this function and therefore are in compliance with the Act.

The Act does not deny an employer the right to determine the qualities, skills, and abilities required of his employees. But the Act does restrict the employer to the use of tests which are professionally developed to indicate the existence of the desired qualities and which do not discriminate on the basis of race, color, religion, sex, or national origin." (292 Federal Supplement 1968:250)

Accordingly, the court ruled that "the tests in use by the defendant at its Dan River Station are professionally developed ability tests within the meaning of Section 703(h) of the Act and are not administered, scored, designed, intended, or used to discriminate because of race or color" (292 Federal Supplement 1968:251).

The court also ruled in favor of the high school education requirement that the company had instituted almost ten years before the passage of the Civil Rights Act of 1964. Justice Gordon, speaking for the court, concluded that the requirement "has a legitimate business purpose and is equally applicable to both Negro and white employees similarly situated" (292 Federal Supplement 1968:251).

The Appeals Court basically reaffirmed the district court's conclusions in 1970. However, in his opinion for the Court, Judge Boreman spent even more time than did Judge Gordon of the district court in seeking to show that the educational requirement "did have a genuine business purpose and that the company initiated the policy with no intention to discriminate against Negro employees who might be hired after the adoption of the educational requirement. This conclusion would appear to be not merely supported, but actually compelled by the following facts:" (420 Federal Reporter, Second Series 1970:1232). He then went on, as we have indicated elsewhere, to list six reasons for the conclusion.

With respect to the testing requirements, the Appeals Court agreed with the district court in ruling that such tests need not be "job-related" despite the argument by the EEOC that "the interpretation given a statute by an agency which was established to administer the statute is entitled to great weight" (420 Federal Reporter, Second Series 1970:1234). Judge Boreman contended that, "At no place in the Act or in its legislative history does there appear a requirement that employers may utilize only those tests which measure the ability and skill required by a specific job or group of jobs. In fact, the legislative history would seem to indicate clearly that Congress was actually trying to guard against such a result"

(420 Federal Reporter, Second Series 1970:1235). Judge Boreman modified this conclusion significantly in a footnote: "This decision is not to be construed as holding that *any* educational or testing requirement adopted by *any* employer is valid under the Civil Rights Act of 1964. There must be a genuine business purpose in establishing such requirements and they cannot be designed or used to further the practice of racial discrimination" (420 Federal Reporter, Second Series 1970:1235).

In reversing the decisions of the lower courts in 1971, the Supreme Court took an exactly opposite tack on the issue and in many ways accepted the basic reasoning of Judge Sobeloff in his Appeals Court dissent. In his opinion for the Court, Chief Justice Burger argued:

> "On the record before us, neither the high school completion requirement nor the general intelligence test is shown to bear a demonstrable relationship to successful performance of the jobs for which it was used. Both were adopted, as the Court of Appeals noted, without meaningful study of their relationship to job-performance ability. Rather, a vice president of the company testified, the requirements were instituted on the Company's judgment that they generally would improve the overall quality of the work force.
>
> The evidence, however, shows that employees who have not completed high school or taken the tests have continued to perform satisfactorily and make progress in departments for which the high school and test criteria are now used ... (401 US 1971:431–32).
>
> The facts of this case demonstrate the inadequacy of broad and general testing devices as well as the infirmity of using diplomas or degrees as fixed measures of capability."   (401 US 1971:433)

According to the Chief Justice, if the testing and educational requirements had indeed measured job capability and performance, then the fact that they also disqualified a disproportionate number of blacks would not have prevented the Court from ruling them lawful under the standard of business necessity. But since they failed to meet this standard, the Court deemed them unlawful even though the company did not intend to have the requirements produce discriminatory results.

> "The Act proscribes not only overt discrimination but also practices that are fair in form, but discriminatory in operation. The touchstone is business necessity. If an employment practice which operates to exclude Negroes cannot be shown to be related to job performance, the practice is prohibited." (401 US 1971:431)

Chief Justice Burger also dismissed the claim of the company that its general intelligence tests were in accord with the provision of Section 703(h) that "authorizes the use of 'any professionally developed ability test' that is not 'designed, intended, or *used* to discriminate because of race ....' (emphasis added)" (401 US 1971:433). He contended that courts have to give great weight to the contrary interpretation of the EEOC which has enforcement responsibility for the statute and "has issued guidelines interpreting Section 703(h) to permit only the use of job-related tests. The administrative interpretation of the Act by the enforcing agency is entitled to great deference.... Since the Act and its legislative history support the Commission's construction, this affords good reason to treat the Guidelines as expressing the will of Congress" (401 US 1971:434).

The Chief Justice concluded his opinion with the following statement:

"Nothing in the Act precludes the use of testing and measuring procedures; obviously they are useful. What Congress has forbidden is giving these devices and mechanisms controlling force unless they are demonstrably a reasonable measure of job performance. Congress has not commanded that the less qualified be preferred over the better qualified simply because of minority origins. Far from disparaging job qualifications as such, Congress has made such qualifications the controlling factor, so that race, religion, nationality, and sex become irrelevant. What Congress has commanded is that any tests used must measure the person for the job and not the person in the abstract."

(401 US 1971:436)

Five years later in Washington v. Davis, the Supreme Court enlarged the validating criterion to include training course performance. Thus, a test or examination could be treated as lawful even if it produced a racial imbalance provided the test was predictive of performance in the training program for a job; whether or not performance in the training program was predictive of later job performance was deemed irrelevant.

LIMITING THE GRIGGS PRINCIPLE: SENIORITY SYSTEMS AND SECTION 703(H) OF TITLE VII

Within six years after the Griggs ruling, the Supreme Court rendered a decision, in International Brotherhood of Teamsters v. United States and Equal Employment Opportunity Commission (May 31 1977), that imposed a serious qualification in the application of the Griggs principle by which an employment practice, fair or neutral in form, is deemed unlawful if it perpetuates the effects of past discrimination.

The case in point had to do with a seniority system anchored to bargaining units; the plaintiffs contended that the system, though neutral on its face, was unlawful because it compounded the effects of past and present company policies and practices that discriminated in the hiring of blacks for the more desirable line driver jobs. The lower courts agreed with the plaintiffs that the system violated the

Griggs principle. In the words of Justice Stewart, who wrote the opinion for the Supreme Court:

"The linchpin of the theory embraced by the District Court and the Court of Appeals was that a discriminatee who must forfeit his competitive seniority in order finally to obtain a line driver job will never be able to 'catch up' to the seniority level of his contemporary who was not subject to discrimination. Accordingly, this continued, built-in disadvantage to the prior discriminatee who transfers to a line-driver job was held to constitute a continuing violation of Title VII, for which both the employer and the union who jointly created and maintain the seniority system were liable."   (431 US 1977:344–45)

In reversing the decision of the lower courts, the Supreme Court did not dispute the finding that the company was guilty of discriminatory practices nor did it challenge the statistical imbalance data that the government used to support its charges. In short, the Court agreed with the lower courts that "the Government had proved a prima facie case of systematic and purposeful employment discrimination, continuing well beyond the effective date of Title VII" (431 US 1977:342).

Under the circumstances, Justice Stewart remarked,

"the seniority system in this case would seem to fall under the *Griggs* rationale. The heart of the system is its allocation of the choicest jobs, the greatest protection against layoffs, and other advantages to those employees who have been line drivers for the longest time. Where, because of the employer's prior intentional discrimination, the line drivers with the longest tenure are without exception white, the advantages of the seniority system flow disproportionately to them and away from the Negro and Spanish-surnamed employees who might by now have enjoyed those advantages had not the employer discriminated before the passage of the Act. This disproportionate distribution of advantages does in a very real sense 'operate to "freeze" the status quo of prior discriminatory practices.'"   (431 US 1977:349–50)

But, Justice Stewart insisted, the legislative history of Title VII and the "explicit" terms of Section 703(h)* indicate that Congress intended to extend a degree of immunity to seniority systems that were truly neutral:

---

*Those terms are: "Notwithstanding any other provision of this title, it shall not be an unlawful employment practice for an employer to apply different standards of compensation, or different terms, conditions, or pivileges of employment pursuant to a bona fide seniority or merit system, or a system which measures earnings by quantity or quality of production or to employees who work in different locations, provided that such differences are not the result of an intention to discriminate because of race, color, religion, sex, or national origin."

"In sum, the unmistakable purpose of Section 703(h) was to make clear that the routine application of a bona fide seniority system would not be unlawful under Title VII. As the legislative history shows, this was the intended result even where the employer's pre-Act discrimination resulted in whites having greater existing seniority rights than Negroes. Although a seniority system inevitably tends to perpetuate the effects of pre-Act discrimination in such cases, the congressional judgment was that Title VII should not outlaw the use of existing seniority lists and thereby destroy or water down the vested seniority rights of employees simply because their employer had engaged in discrimination prior to the passage of the Act."   (431 US 1977:352–53)

Not all seniority systems, the Justice continued, were thereby immunized by Section 703(h). They must not be themselves the product of an intention to discriminate. Thus merely because a seniority arrangement perpetuates pre-Act discrimination does not preclude its being "bona fide" as the EEOC would have it unless it is also rooted in the very discriminatory practices which it helps to preserve.

"To accept the [Government's] argument would require us to hold that a seniority system becomes illegal simply because it allows the full exercise of the pre-Act seniority rights of employees of a company that discriminated before Title VII was enacted. It would place an affirmative obligation on the parties to the seniority agreement to subordinate those rights in favor of the claims of pre-Act discriminatees without seniority. The consequence would be a perversion of the congressional purpose. We cannot accept the invitation to disembowel [Section] 703(h) by reading the words 'bona fide' as the Government would have us do. Accordingly, we hold that an otherwise neutral, legitimate seniority system does not become unlawful under Title VII simply because it may perpetuate pre-Act discrimination. Congress did not intend to make it illegal for employees with vested seniority rights to continue to exercise those rights, even at the expense of pre-Act discriminatees."   (431 US 1977:353–54)

All earlier cases that had been decided under the Quarles standard, Justice Stewart argued in a footnote, failed to meet this test, because the seniority systems were themselves "racially discriminatory" or had their "genesis in racial discrimination" (431 US 1977:346 fn). But the seniority system in this case, Justice Stewart continued, meets the test in a number of ways and is therefore bona fide and lawful. For example,

"It applies equally to all races and ethnic groups. To the extent that it 'locks' employees into non-line-driver jobs, it does so for all. The city drivers and servicemen who are discouraged from transferring to line driver jobs are not all

Negroes or Spanish-surnamed Americans; to the contrary, the overwhelming majority are white. The placing of line drivers in a separate bargaining unit from other employees is rational, in accord with the industry practice, and consistent with National Labor Relations Board precedents. It is conceded that the seniority system did not have its genesis in racial discrimination, and that it was negotiated and has been maintained free from any illegal purpose. In these circumstances, the single fact that the system extends no retroactive seniority to pre-Act discrimination does not make it unlawful."   (431 US 1977:355–56)

In view of the lawfulness of the seniority system, the Court concluded, employees who were only discriminated against before Title VII of the Civil Rights Act of 1964 went into effect were not entitled to any remedy. Those who experienced discrimination after that date were, but the relief accorded them could not extend retroactively beyond the effective date of the Act. To obtain such relief, the Court decided, the person did not have to demonstrate that he actually applied for the position, but he had to show that he "actually wanted it" and that he possessed "the requisite qualifications."

Clearly perturbed by the Court's decision, the EEOC sought to confine its scope and applicability in a memorandum that officially defined and delineated the agency's position on the ruling. The EEOC declared that a seniority system would be protected under Section 703(h) "only if it was instituted prior to the effective date of Title VII (July 2, 1965) and only if the evidence shows that there was no discriminatory intent in the genesis or maintenance of the system" (The Bureau of National Affairs 95, *Labor Relations Reporter*: 235). The commission clearly indicated that it would not include under the Court ruling collective bargaining agreements "which prohibit transfer from one unit to another" (The Bureau of National Affairs 95, *Labor Relations Reporter*: 235 fn).

But even more significantly, the EEOC stated that it would subject the intent of a company in setting up or maintaining a seniority system to a searching inquiry and would rely on a variety of behavioral and other indicators to infer such intent. Where such indicators revealed directly or indirectly that a discriminatory intent was present, then the seniority system would be viewed as falling outside the protective pale of Section 703(h) and would therefore be deemed unlawful.

"In examining possible discriminatory intent, the Commission will review all available evidence, including the respondents' collective bargaining history and employment practices. Where unions or units were previously segregated, discriminatory intent in the institution of a unit seniority system will be inferred. When a unit seniority system is in effect and the employer or union is made aware that it is locking in minorities or females, discriminatory intent will be inferred if the system is maintained or renegotiated when an alternative system is available. Grievances, EEOC charges, and charges filed with other compliance agencies are among those factors which should make respondents aware of the lock-in effect of a system."

(The Bureau of National Affairs 95, *Labor Relations Reporter*: 235)

However, no matter how successful the EEOC may be in limiting the effects of the Court's ruling, it nevertheless stands that the Court has introduced an important qualification in the universal application of the Griggs principle under Title VII. Whether this is but the beginning of the corrosion of this principle remains to be seen.

THE EQUAL EMPLOYMENT OPPORTUNITY COMMISSION AND THE OFFICE OF FEDERAL CONTRACT COMPLIANCE: STRESSFUL COMPLEMENTARITY

By its original ruling in the Griggs case, the Supreme Court not only gave the EEOC the go-ahead to continue applying its guidelines on testing and selection procedures to the cases before it, but it also opened the door for the OFCC to adopt these guidelines, albeit modified somewhat to fit the particular legal and other needs of its affirmative action programs. This is reported in a footnote to the order that described the precise code of regulation in the *Federal Register*: "this order and the Guidelines on Employee Selection Procedures, issued earlier by the Equal Employment Opportunity Commission (35, *Federal Register*, 12333, August 1, 1970) are intended to impose the same basic requirements on persons and contractors covered by each of them" (Office of Federal Contract Compliances, *Federal Register* 1971:fn1).

Thus, a major procedural link was forged between the two agencies, but by then another significant connection had also developed. In May 1970 they signed a memorandum of agreement which dampened the festering tension and competitive rivalry between them by establishing a working relationship built on a basic division of function. The agreement shifted to the EEOC the primary responsibility for investigating individual complaints that had been filed with both agencies. In turn, the OFCC was to institute compliance proceedings against any government contractor who was being investigated by the EEOC because of an employee complaint filed against him. Thus, one agency was to concentrate on compliance reviews; the other, on the investigation and review of individual complaints. In May 1974 the agreement was revised and a much more elaborate framework of cooperation and interdependence was developed. Both agencies were to exchange and to share materials on cases pending before each and were to keep each other fully informed on the progress of such cases. Even more clearly spelled out than in the earlier memorandum was the division of function between the two: complaint investigation and review by the EEOC; compliance reviews by the OFCC. In addition, both agencies agreed to strive for mutually consistent procedures and policies to enhance the "full coordination of their activities. Therefore it is the intention of the agencies to develop mutually compatible investigative procedures and compliance policies including minimum standards of remedy. The parties will designate members of a task force to develop such standards, which will commence meetings as soon as possible after the signing of this Memorandum" (Office of Federal Contract Compliance 1974, *BNA FEP Manual:* 401:271–73).

The agreement was basically reaffirmed in 1978. In the final analysis, both agencies have come to recognize the need for uniform policies and procedures as their joint areas of activities and jurisdictions have increasingly overlapped. This recognition, however, has not completely eliminated the residue of tension between the two that has persisted from the early days. Their stressful complementarity highlights the fact that both agencies have grown from different historic origins. As we have already noted, the OFCC was a creation of executive policy that took thirty years of bureaucratic development to reach its present form; contrastingly, the EEOC was a creature of congressional action whose subsequent structure and shape were influenced and legitimated by rulings of federal courts.

The controversy over affirmative action and quotas

THE ACADEMIC ASSAULT AGAINST QUOTAS

Even during the formative years of the EEOC's policy on "preferential treatment" and the OFCC's on affirmative action programs, various segments of the public expressed uneasiness and concern over the direction the two agencies were taking. But not until 1972 did the inchoate uneasiness coalesce and erupt into a public outcry led by members of the academic community. What had set the stage for the outcry was the OFCC's issuance of Revised Order No. 4 in 1971, but what had actually triggered it off was the concerted effort by the Office of Civil Rights of HEW (US Department of Health, Education, and Welfare) to apply the order to universities and colleges. Now they too would have to submit written affirmative action programs with goals and timetables for the recruitment of racial minorities to positions in which they were underutilized.

The academic reaction was intense and reverberated through the media, through periodicals such as *Commentary* and *Public Interest*, through books such as Glazer's *Affirmative Discrimination* (1975), and through groups specially organized to combat the program. The Committee on Academic Nondiscrimination and Integrity led by three nationally known academicians spearheaded the drive. The attacks against affirmative action generated the emotion and passion of a religious crusade and persist even today.

And yet, despite the intensity of the reaction, it is difficult to estimate how many academicians have ever actively or even passively supported the anti-affirmative action movement. But it is clear that leadership in the movement has been drawn from what Kadushin (1974) calls the "Social Science-Literary Circle" in his study of the elite intellectuals. This circle includes white academicians who were liberal on civil rights during the early 1960s but who became increasingly less so by the end of the decade. As a result, their views on racial matters have tended to find increasing favor in conservative circles. This is evident in the May 22 1973 issue of the *US Congressional Record* (93.1), in which former Senator Buckley, the conservative Republican from New York, not only had his speech printed but also had reprinted articles and speeches of "liberal" academicians whose views on the issue were similar to his. In recent times, several of these "liberals" have come to call themselves "neo-conservatives."

The principal target of these critics was the "goals" and "timetables" of affirmative action programs. Only the critics called them "quotas" and insisted that there was no difference between the two terms. For example, Hook writing in *Freedom at Issue* scoffed at the effort of the Assistant Director for Public Affairs, Office of Civil Rights, HEW, to distinguish between the two concepts. He dismissed the notion that goals were more flexible than quotas and merely required "good faith" efforts, not compulsory fulfillment. He argued, "Quotas are numerical goals. A 'quota of 20%' is equivalent to 'a numerical goal of 20%.' The expressions are interchangeable" (Hook 1973:16438). He and others also rejected the later efforts by the director of the office to elaborate upon the distinction between the terms. The director had contended that "level of expectancy," "honest guesses," and "targets" described the "predictive aspect" of the terms goals as applied to affirmative action programs much better than did the term "quotas" (Pottinger 1972:27).

RACIAL IMBALANCE AND SYSTEMIC DISCRIMINATION

So preoccupied have many critics been with denouncing the evils of quotas that they have glossed over a requirement imposed by both government agencies and courts for the promulgation of statistical goals and timetables. These are to be developed only where a prior condition of racial imbalance can be shown to exist. In the case of the OFCC and its compliance agencies, goals and timetables are, accordingly, to be established only for jobs in which affected classes are shown to be underutilized. In the case of the EEOC, such goals and timetables may be used as one of the options for remedying a condition of racial imbalance that has been found to exist through investigation of a complaint filed with the commission.

Some critics are evidently not aware of this requirement. As a result, their denunciation of quotas has the ring of a sermon against universal sin; it fails to address itself to the problem for which quotas have been defined as an answer. Most critics, however, are aware of this stipulation, and many of those who profess to have had a liberal stance in the early days of the civil rights movement are even prepared to acknowledge that such imbalances may stem in part from intentional acts of discrimination. Where such acts can be proved, they favor remedial action on a case-by-case basis. As Glazer states unequivocally, "I oppose discrimination; I fully support the law.... Where the EEOC takes up a case of discrimination and gets a job and compensation for the victim, I applaud it" (Glazer 1975:66–7).

But Glazer goes on to maintain that such cases of "discrimination" comprise only a fraction of the workload of government agencies. "The fact is that much of the work of the government agencies has nothing to do with discrimination. One may review these enormous governmental reports and legal cases at length and find scarcely a single reference to any act of discrimination against an individual" (Glazer 1975:67).

What he is really saying is that most instances of racial imbalance with which the government is dealing do not "fit" *his* definition of discrimination. But, since he cannot deny the existence of these cases of racial imbalance, he explains them away in part as being the products of market or "natural" forces and factors of competition and selection.

> "Economists, labor market analysts, and sociologists have devoted endless energy to trying to determine the various elements that contribute to the distribution of jobs of minority groups. Some of the relevant factors are: level of education, quality of education, type of education, location by region, by city, by part of metropolitan area, character of labor market at time of entry into the region or city, and many others. These are factors one can in part quantify."
>
> (Glazer 1975:63)

Glazer then goes on to mention another factor that seems to loom even larger in his causal explanation of racial imbalance: the internal characteristics of the minority, its "taste or, if you will, culture" (Glazer 1975:63). Elsewhere he refers to "life style." Hook (1973) extends the same mode of analysis to the disproportionately low number of women in professional occupations. He explains this primarily in terms of women's identification with and commitment to their domestic roles and of their corresponding reluctance to pursue careers in the occupational marketplace. And there are also the critics who have resurrected the intelligence test and who interpret the racial differences in scores on these tests in terms of hereditary capabilities and capacities.

For Glazer and the other critics, then, racial imbalance is the product of discrimination only if it corresponds to *their* definition of discrimination. The key to their definition is *intent*. Where there is no apparent intent, they are eager to look elsewhere for an explanation of the persistence of racial imbalance. They are, in other words, extremely reluctant to accept even the possibility that racial imbalance can be a surviving and viable consequence of past discriminatory policies and practices.

As a result, they are inclined to look askance at the phrase "systemic discrimination" which the EEOC devised to cover this type of imbalance and have great difficulty with the phrase "institutional racism." This is evident in the way Glazer deals with the phrase in his book, *Affirmative Discrimination*. He treats it disdainfully as a residual term. "It is obviously something devised in the absence of clear evidence of discrimination and prejudice." He expresses incredulity at the notion that, "It [institutional racism] suggests that, without intent, a group may be victimized;" for, he argues, "Racism, in common understanding, means an attitude of superiority, disdain, or prejudice toward another person because he is of another race, and a philosophy or ideology that justifies such attitudes on the basis of the inferiority – genetic, cultural, moral, or intellectual – of a race." He then attempts to turn the phrase against its users: "The rise of the popularity of the term 'institutional racism' points to one happy development, namely, that racism pure and simple is less often found or expressed." He concludes with a discussion of the way the phrase is used to label all cases of racial imbalance. He objects to this: "Each institutional form of exclusion must be judged in its own terms" (Glazer 1975:69). And yet even as he illustrates his point, Glazer reveals his deep-seated resistance toward defining as racist or discriminatory any act or policy that does not express intent and design as well. Consequently the term "institutional racism" remains for him a slogan and a fanciful piece of rhetoric.

In rejecting "institutional racism" and "systemic discrimination" as valid characterizations of the American society, Glazer and the other critics are not merely expressing their opposition to a particular version of the present, but are also questioning the general validity of the version of the historical past which such a conceptualization implies. They reject the notion that until recently the American society as a whole had features of a plural society with such a markedly rigid and institutionalized segmentation of the races and that it denied blacks full membership in the People's Domain and confined them to the lowest rungs of the occupational order. The critics do agree, however, that until recently the South fitted this mold in its treatment of the blacks. But they are equally convinced that this was a regional aberration which has increasingly disappeared since 1965.

Elsewhere in the American society, the critics insist that blacks did not face the same kind of legal and institutionalized restrictions and segmentation; their treatment in effect was not qualitatively different from that afforded to the white immigrants. In fact, Glazer in his book intertwines the fates of the two in the North. Both faced intense discrimination and prejudice from the majority group, which Glazer continually interprets in social-psychological terms as expressions of the fears of the majority that they were losing their country. Glazer even concedes that blacks have had to face somewhat more of this hostility than the white immigrants and for a longer period, but he insists that these differences were matters of degree, not of kind. What is even more important for his thesis is his contention that even in the economic and occupational spheres the differences are disappearing. He makes a great deal of the narrowing of the income gap between blacks and whites in a highly selective group: families where both husband and wife work.

With such a version of the past and present racial situation, small wonder that Glazer and his fellow critics reserve their greatest sense of outrage for the decision by the EEOC and the federal courts to treat racial imbalance as prima facie evidence of an unlawful employment practice and for the policy of the OFCC to insist upon goals and timetables as remedies for the underutilization of affected classes. They consider such a decision and policy as flagrant examples of preferential treatment which, according to their interpretation, is unqualifiedly forbidden by Title VII of the Civil Rights Act of 1964. In addition, these critics are convinced that the decision and policy also violate the true intent of the Constitution, even though the Supreme Court has ruled otherwise. For, as Glazer says, "public policy must be exercised without distinction of race, color, or national origin" (Glazer 1975:221). Or, as Hook maintains "HEW knows that morally its case is lost if it involves a quota system or the barbaric notion that we can atone for past injustices towards innocent victims by present injustices to innocent victims" (Hook 1973:16437).

Thus it can be concluded that their version of the past and present encounters of racial minorities with the American society provides Glazer and his fellow critics with a logical and reasonable argument for their opposition to quotas and affirmative action programs. What it fails to do is to provide them or anyone else with a truly valid statement of the reality it purports to represent. For example, their version distorts and oversimplifies the historical character of these racial encounters.

As we have repeatedly demonstrated in this book, these encounters have been so complex that they require more than one mode of interpretation or one conceptual model for fitting the data together. Thus, as we have already spelled out in detail in Chapter 7, the immigrant analogy alone does not suffice as an explanation of the black experience in the North and, on a more general level, neither does the classical assimilationist theory adequately account for the historical encounters of racial minorities in America.

Further, these critics' version of events also distorts and oversimplifies the historical development of affirmative action programs. Glazer, for example, mentions in passing some of the historical antecedents of the present program from President Roosevelt's executive orders on nondiscrimination in government to Kennedy's and Johnson's on affirmative action and equal employment opportunity. He does so, however, in the space of less than one paragraph. What he and his fellow critics have failed to do is to examine systematically and in detail the historical record as we have done. Had they done so, they might have concluded, as we have, that the present affirmative action program did not burst into its present form overnight but was instead the end product of a thirty-year evolutionary process that gave bureaucratic substance and form to what was initially a mere abstract and vague policy of the executive branch of government. As we saw in the previous chapter, this process flowed through Republican and Democratic administrations alike with the former implementing what the latter had started. Throughout its early history the results were minimal, but the quest for increased effectiveness continued. Not until Kennedy reformulated the normative goals and Johnson supplied the basic structural components was a bureaucratic machinery finally in place that could do the job. Its initial efforts were still relatively inconsequential, and only as the Nixon administration refined the procedural mechanisms further and supplied such missing capstones as standards for assessing the underutilization of affected classes was the program able to achieve a level of effectiveness that had long been its goal.

Viewed in this manner, the decision of the OFCC to establish statistical goals and timetables takes on a significance and meaning different from that espoused by its critics. The decision can be seen as organically related to the struggle by the OFCC and its predecessors to overcome a long history of ineffectualness through the development of procedures and standards that would transform it into an effective instrument of policy.

Such an interpretation directly contradicts that proffered by Glazer and others. They treat the imposition of statistical goals as having no coherent connection with the past and as being entirely a product of capricious and arbitrary decision-making by bureaucrats, intent upon flexing their muscles.

And just as they have misread the historical development of the policy of statistical goals, so in many respects have Glazer and his fellow critics given an overly simple and one-sided interpretation to the ban on preferential treatment as stated in Section 703(j) of Title VII. According to them, Congress intended this ban to take precedence over any other consideration, and they insist that the courts and the EEOC have circumvented this intention by ordering quotas as remedies for situations of racial imbalance.

What they fail to realize is that, in early decisions on this provision, several lower courts followed almost to the letter their singularly simple line of reasoning. As we have already seen, these courts went so far as to forbid any remedies for discriminatory action because they said such remedies ran afoul of the preferential treatment clause. Only as the issue reached higher courts was this simplistic interpretation of the law challenged. Higher courts took note of the fact that Congress had built into the law contradictory provisions. On the one hand, Section 703(j) forbade preferential treatment; on the other, Section 706(g) stipulated various kinds of relief for past discriminatory action which might give the aggrieved person or class preferential treatment in the future. Thus the courts increasingly defined their role as balancing these conflicting equities and as clarifying an ambiguous situation created by congressional action. In order to resolve this dilemma, they determined that remedial action for past discrimination did not constitute preferential treatment and did not accordingly fall under the proscription of Section 703(j).

Finally, because Glazer and the other critics have so narrowly and rigidly construed the definition of discrimination, they have failed to grasp the significance and meaning of the reach of the past into the present. Specifically, they have discounted the continuing effects of past policies and practices of discrimination even after these public policies have been manifestly abandoned. They have dismissed – often contemptuously – the efforts of the EEOC and the courts to grapple with the matter and have treated as mere rhetoric the labeling of such situations as systemic discrimination or institutional racism.

And yet as policies and practices of overtly intended discrimination have become increasingly things of the past in industry and elsewhere, the EEOC and the courts have had to confront on an ever larger scale the lingering effects of such policies and practices, let alone the effects of policies that have merely masked their discriminatory intent. They have observed how institutional arrangements and mechanisms perpetuate the consequences of these past discriminatory policies even though such arrangements may never have been manifestly devised for that purpose.

Interestingly, in early cases of this sort, the lower courts adhered to the same kind of narrow definition of discrimination as presently advocated by Glazer and the others. They ruled that, in the absence of explicit intent by the employer, practices and policies could not be deemed legally discriminatory even if they had a disproportionately negative effect on racial minorities and/or created racial imbalances in his work force. However, as these and other cases wended their way through the higher courts, the courts discarded this simplistic approach and began to savor the full complexity of the problem to the extent of identifying and weighing the neutral institutional mechanisms that reinforced the discriminatory effects of the past. In the process, they moved increasingly toward a definition of discrimination that stressed consequences – as finally enunciated and legitimized by Justice Burger in the Griggs decision – and they cumulatively carved out the operational meanings of systemic discrimination and institutional racism in a variety of specific contexts. And in this way the Griggs principle was articulated, stating that employment practices, though neutral or fair in form, are unlawful if they perpetuate the effects of past discrimination. (A major exception to date is the limitation imposed by Section 703(h) of Title VII on applying the principle to seniority systems.)

Behind the specificity of the courts' focus, however, loomed a more general premise, shared by the commission, that the debilitating effects of past discrimination were not merely confined to individual enterprises but were also spread throughout the societal system by a variety of neutral and not so neutral institutional mechanisms. In the Griggs decision, for example, Justice Burger traced the poor performance on tests of racial minorities to the inferior schooling they received because of past policies of segregation and discrimination in education.

Added to this was an awareness by the EEOC and the courts that discriminatory effects were also being perpetuated throughout the occupational system by policies and practices that were professedly neutral but which masked a prejudicial intent. As we have already seen, Judge Sobeloff, in dissenting with the Appeals Court decision in the Griggs case, drew a sharp parallel between some of the practices in the employment sector and the long history of legal and political discrimination of blacks in the South that was a thinly disguised attempt to subvert the constitutional ban on such discrimination. However, neither he nor others who made similar references ever meant that the continuing discriminatory effects in employment were necessarily as much a function of masked intention as was true of the history of such effects in the legal and political spheres.

With such a view of the present, it is understandable why the courts also accepted the premise of the EEOC that employment situations which differentially affected racial minorities or reflected a racial imbalance were more probably than not linked to this persisting structure of discrimination, whether through overt or masked intention or through neutral mechanisms. Accordingly, the EEOC and the courts established as a matter of evidentiary procedure that, where such situations of racial imbalance were found, the employer would have to bear the burden of proving that such a link did not exist.

Obviously Glazer and the other critics have been unable to accept this premise and procedure, for to do so would undermine their own interpretation of the present. But in his rejection of the premise and procedure, Glazer reveals once again that he cannot break out of his theoretical mold. The situation must be defined in terms of subjective intent. Accordingly, he attributes to those who support the premise the belief

> "that there is such a deeply ingrained prejudice in whites, leading to discrimination against blacks and other minorities, that it can be assumed prejudice is the operative cause in any case of differential treatment, rather than a concern about qualifications. To this assumption there can be no answer. One can only, as an individual, search one's own motives and actions, and those of the institutions and bodies with which one is involved."   (Glazer 1975:68)

Since he denies the factual pervasiveness of such an attitude, citing results from public opinion polls as proof, Glazer is in effect saying that the premise and procedure of the EEOC and the courts are based on a distorted version of reality and are therefore "mythic" in character. And with the rapid rolling back of prejudice that he believes is happening, he is equally convinced that any remaining situations of racial imbalance are less likely than ever to be the result of overt discriminatory intent, or even covert intent, and more likely to be the product of "natural" forces of selection and competition. Under the circumstances he would completely re-orient the evidentiary procedure of the EEOC. Instead of the employer, it would be the employee or EEOC who would have to bear the burden of proof. Thus Glazer would require that the latter prove discriminatory intent on the part of the employer in a case of racial imbalance; in the absence of such proof, racial imbalance would be deemed a product of "innocent forces."

By imputing to the EEOC and courts a definition of the situation that is actually his, not theirs, Glazer once again distorts and oversimplifies their position, this time on their rationale for the policy on racial imbalance. They make no claim, for example, as he says they do, that a deep and abiding race prejudice saturates the feelings of white Americans, although they probably believe that such prejudice is more prevalent among white Americans than Glazer would like to believe. But they have contended that persistence of systemic discrimination and institutionalized racism into the present make it probable that any given situation of racial imbalance is a product of this persistence and that therefore this imbalance should be treated as prima facie evidence of discrimination.

It can accordingly be concluded that the academic opponents of affirmative action programs fail to comprehend the complexity and persistence of the historic and present-day structure of racial discrimination and inequality in America. They prefer to read and to interpret this history in terms similar to those they use for the history of white immigrants. As a result, they see no reason why the normative model that gave the latter access to full membership in the American society should not apply to the racial minorities as well. They firmly support policies of nondiscrimination as being an intrinsic part of the American creed and condemn affirmative action programs with their statistical goals as falling beyond the pale of the American creed, both morally and constitutionally.

Seligman contends, "For a democratic society to systematically discriminate against 'the majority' seems quite without precedent. To do so in the name of nondiscrimination seems mind-boggling" (Seligman 1973:16456). Hook argues "[a quota system] is never *morally legitimate*, particularly when we are on record as being opposed in principle to discrimination on grounds of race, religion, sex, or national origin (except when these are justifiably among the qualifications, e.g. sex for certain kinds of dancers or officers for women's detention centers, religion for service in houses of worship, etc.)" (Hook 1973:16438). Even the then-Senator Buckley joins the chorus. He alludes to the affirmative action program with its goals as contrary to the aims of the civil rights movement: namely, the achievement of a color-blind society.

> "The notion of affirmative action plans designed to achieve precise goals is inherently vicious, inherently discriminatory. It flies in the face of everything that the civil rights movement has sought to achieve – a society in which every human being is judged on his merits as a human being, a society that is truly color blind, a society that applies a single set of standards for employment and advancement irrespective of the accident of birth."   (Buckley 1973:16432)

But if these critics were to rid themselves of their moral and historical preconceptions and were instead to read and to understand more accurately the distinctive character of the racial encounters in America, then they would in all probability realize that the institutionally engrained discriminatory effects of America's past as a plural society cannot be remedied by merely dismantling that society and its racial creed. More is needed, in effect, for fulfilment of the American creed with its normative goal of equal access and opportunity than merely opening up to all the institutional doors of the People's Domain. That something more includes affirmative action programs – included, that is, at least until such time as the effects of America's dualistic past have been truly erased.

MERITOCRACY AND AFFIRMATIVE ACTION

Despite the compelling case for affirmative action programs, their critics might still score a telling blow if their fears were justified that these programs also pose a serious threat to meritocracy, excellence and competence. Then, the use of affirmative action as even a transitional policy could be called into serious question. The programs do this, these critics contend, by imposing extrinsic, ascriptive group standards and criteria upon a system that presumably operates rationally and objectively to allocate position and rewards on the basis of individual achievement and merit. As Hook complains, "criteria of selection will not be personal merit alone but will reflect *group* membership largely beyond the power of individuals to alter, and for which they cannot and should not be held responsible" (Hook 1973:16437).

Raab places the issue in a broader normative framework. What distinguishs democratic from aristocratic and racist societies, he argues, is the conferring of status on the basis of individual performance and achievement and not on the basis of ancestral, racial, or other ascriptive characteristics. To impose the latter characteristics upon a democratic society, as would be the case with affirmative action programs, would be to blur the distinction between the two.

> "One of the marks of the free society is the ascendance of performance over ancestry – or, to put it more comprehensively, the ascendance of achieved status over ascribed status. Aristocracies and racist societies confer status on the basis of heredity. A democratic society begins with the cutting of the ancestral cord. This by itself does not yet make a humanistic society or even a properly democratic one. There is, for example, the not inconsiderable question of distributive justice in rewarding performance. But achieved versus ascribed status is *one* inexorable dividing line between a democratic and an undemocratic society. This is the aspect of democracy which represents the primacy of the individual, and of individual freedom. It has to do with the belief that an individual exists not just to serve a social function, but to stretch his unique spirit and capacities for their own sake: 'the right of every man not to have, but to be his best.'"
>   (Raab 1973:16448)

In view of their forebodings, these critics predict that under a policy of affirmative action, qualifications and standards will be tampered with and progressively lowered so that group quotas can be met; excellence and competence will accordingly be sacrificed as the less qualified and less capable are brought into the system. The outcome, they conclude, will be mediocrity, in harness or worse and a system functioning with marked ineffectualness and inefficiency.

Overwrought as these critics seem, they cannot be dismissed as readily on this issue as they were on their version of the historical experience of racial minorities. For historically the impact of race and also of ethnicity, with their principles of particularism, traditionalism, ascriptiveness, and expressiveness, has posed problems and difficulties for the functioning of meritocratic and bureaucratic structures, with their principles of universalism, rationalism, achievement-orientation, and instrumentalism. However, the way these critics pose the problem would seem to suggest that the meritocratic system they are so fiercely defending is free of such problems. The image they project is of a utopian structure that does what it should. It allocates positions and distributes rewards according to an impersonal, objective, and rational assessment of the individual's merit. Accordingly, they treat the system as though it already is "a fully automated, self-correcting, and foolproof computer which sorts individuals into occupational slots and differentially rewards them according to a mathematical formula, rationally and objectively derived, quantitatively described and universalistically and impersonally applied" (Ringer 1976:25).

What the critics fail to realize is that, even before the advent of affirmative action programs, the meritocratic system that they are defending did not function in the objective and rational manner that they would like to believe it did and should. In an article for *Society* magazine early in 1976, this author identified a number of non-rational and subjective components contained in the system. He concluded that, unlike the presumed effects of affirmative action programs, these components did not favor the disadvantaged racial and ethnic minorities but instead favored the already advantaged racial and ethnic groups and tilted the system even more in their direction.

> "They [the critics of affirmative action] fail to realize that merit is a dynamic system in which people make decisions about its vital features. What is to be defined as technical competence? What should be the criteria of evaluation? How is an individual to be scored on each of the criteria? How should these scores be weighted? The hope, of course, is that these decisions will be rational and objective and will lead to the goal of excellence and merit. But the fact is that these decisions contain so many subjective and non-rational elements which reinforce the positions of those people who are already favored. As a result, the merit system operates like a political system and not like the self-regulatory economic market system of Adam Smith."　　　　　　　　(Ringer 1976:25)

Just as the critics of affirmative action tend to overstate the virtues of the meritocratic system presently in operation, so do they understate the extent to which the EEOC, OFCC, and the federal courts are concerned with its survival and effectiveness. The critics act as though these agencies were so intent upon imposing racial quotas that they would even be prepared to accept destruction of the meritocratic system if that were necessary to achieve these results. Quite the contrary, these agencies and the courts believe that what they are doing will, in the long run, rid the system of its encrustations, subjectiveness, and racial biases and inequities, and transform it into a more effective and efficient meritocracy. Their ultimate goal is a meritocratic society which might not differ significantly from that espoused by their critics, but with racial inequities eliminated not masked.

In the interim they have used the meritocratic model of a bias-free economy in setting standards for "good faith" efforts by employers to reduce racial imbalances in their work forces. Thus, the OFCC requires that the contractor conduct in the work force analysis for his affirmative action program a detailed study of "position descriptions to insure that they accurately reflect position functions" (Federal Register 36(234) 1971: Section 60–2.24a) and that he "validate worker specifications by division, department, location, or other organizational unit and by job category using job performance criteria" (Federal Register 36(234) 1971: Section 60–2.24b). The OFCC is saying, in effect, that the contractor has to eliminate any technically irrelevant "barnacles" that have attached themselves to various jobs by confining his job descriptions merely to those qualities intrinsically linked to job performance itself.

Even the most ardent advocate of meritocracy should not find fault with these instructions for bringing jobs more in line with their technical purpose and function, but the OFCC has more than increased efficiency in mind. It is convinced that many of the encrusted features of jobs are discriminatory in nature and consequence. Thus, to return a job to its "technical purity" would be to improve the prospects of racial minorities in and for these jobs.

A similar effort to reconcile the principles of racial equity and meritocracy can be seen in the EEOC's guidelines on employee testing and other selection procedures which have also been adopted by the OFCC. These guidelines stipulate that testing and selection procedures have to be specific to the qualifications and requirements for a given job and must be predictive of performance in it. Accordingly, an employer has to prove that this is indeed true of his procedures if they have produced a racial imbalance in any given job.

The proof, however, has not been easy to come by; it requires rigorously prescribed validation studies. If the employer's procedures can be validated, then the imbalance is allowed to stand. If they cannot be validated, then his testing and selection procedures have to be changed to reduce the racial imbalance and to bring the procedures more in line with the specific requirements for the job.

The EEOC obviously expected that in relatively few instances of racial imbalance would an employer's procedures meet the strict validation requirements. Even if not one such instance materialized, the fact would remain that the EEOC has set a limiting condition on its efforts to remedy racial imbalance. It has given precedence to the continued functioning of a proven meritocratic procedure even at the expense of redress of racial imbalance. This limiting condition was given legal expression and legitimacy by Chief Justice Burger when he said in the Griggs case that "business necessity" was the "touchstone" by which an employer could successfully counter the prima facie evidence of racial imbalance.

Thus, in principle at least, the EEOC's guidelines would seem to be in accord with the best tradition of a meritocratic system, and yet Glazer for one does not even reveal an awareness that this might be so. Instead, he merely pounces on the inconvenience and cost of validation studies and ridicules the premise that such studies can be done for many job qualifications and skills.

Relevant as his critical remarks may be, Glazer lets them stand in mid-air. He merely talks about the problems and limitations of validation studies in a vacuum, and nowhere addresses himself to their purpose of making testing procedures more predictive of job performance – a matter of fundamental concern to a truly meritocratic system. In effect, he fails to see or to acknowledge any link between these validation studies, no matter how faulty the conception, and the underlying meritocratic design of which they are a part.

In fact, contrary to what Glazer and the other critics say, government agencies and federal courts have been seeking to reconcile the principles of racial equity and meritocracy. Their present priority is racial equity, but they have not lost sight of their ultimate goal: a meritocratic society in which the basic racial inequities of the past have been resolved and equality of opportunity is a reality. Accordingly, the courts in particular view the present policy and program of affirmative action and statistical goals as of finite duration and not a permanent fixture, but how long is temporary is an open question.

To say that the government agencies and courts have been seeking to reconcile broadly the two principles is not to suggest that they have managed to do so successfully in particular instances. Critics of affirmative action, despite their obvious partisanship, have indeed raised several important objections and questions. Hook, for example, complains that government agencies in seeking to implement their job-related dictum for testing and selection procedures tend to stress minimal and not maximal performance requirements (Hook 1973). As a result, he argues, the least effective, instead of the most effective, incumbent of an occupational role becomes the model for recruitment. This is disastrous, he continues, for organizations like the university which are presumably built on excellence.

Glazer's scathing remarks about validation studies point to another area of concern. The government agencies may indeed have adopted too rigid and too literal an approach to such studies. Thus, tests of behavioral skills that can be quantified are much better able to meet these validation standards than are those of more qualitative skills or characteristics.

On an even more general level, Hook and Raab may be a little too quick to absolve specific white groups of today from any responsibility for past inequities to racial minorities, but they point to a question that has yet to be answered: How can the cost of redressing the continuing effects of past racial inequities be shared by whites so that no specific individual or group has to bear more than a proportionate share of the cost? Relevant as the answer would be for affirmative action programs, it would be of even greater consequence for other programs and policies that have been set up to relieve persisting inequities such as the busing remedy for school segregation.

THE ISSUE OF EFFECTIVENESS

And finally these critics have questioned the effectiveness of the affirmative action programs. Glazer and Sowell are convinced, for example, that the programs have accomplished nothing (Glazer 1975; Sowell 1976). (In fact, Glazer says that he might set aside his objections to the program if he thought it would accomplish anything.) Both critics have apparently overlooked or have discounted data that could raise doubts as to the validity of their conclusions. In its Tenth Annual Report, for example, the EEOC records significant progress for blacks in white collar and professional occupations in private industry from 1966 through 1974. During that period blacks virtually tripled their proportionate representation in the work force for professional and managerial positions: from 0.9 percent to 2.9 percent for the managerial category and from 1.3 percent to 3.1 percent for the professional category. In addition, they more than doubled their representation in sales and clerical jobs: from 2.4 percent to 5.5 percent for sales and from 3.5 percent to 9.0 percent for clerical. Further, their representation almost doubled in the technician category (from 4.1 percent to 7.3 percent) and in craft jobs (from 3.6 percent to 6.9 percent) (Equal Employment Opportunity Commission 1975:19, Table 1).

Despite these increases, the proportion of blacks in the work force for unskilled and service jobs did not undergo any significant reduction. It declined from 21.2 percent to 20.4 percent for the unskilled and increased slightly for the service workers from 23.1 percent to 23.7 percent.

Suggestive as this evidence is as a counter to the Glazer and Sowell assertions, it is still too fragmentary to be treated as conclusive proof of the effectiveness of affirmative action programs. These critics would insist that the changes would have happened even without the programs. Consequently, a much more systematic and carefully designed assessment has to be made. Individual studies such as Hudson's (1978) of IBM have gone part of the way toward meeting this requirement. Ironically, the data for a broad-gauged assessment are probably sitting in raw form in the files of the OFCC. Each year government contractors have to report how they are faring in reaching their goals. By now enough of these reports have been accumulated for each contractor to provide a definitive statement on work force changes that have occurred since the inception of affirmative action programs.

In general then, a number of important problems have yet to be resolved. But only the government agencies and federal courts are carrying the primary burden of grappling with these problems. Academicians are too inclined to stand on the sidelines immobilized by the obsession with quotas; they shrink from their responsibility to provide creative intellectual leadership on the matter. But unless they join forces with agencies and courts and do so soon, a critical historical opportunity may be lost for America to rid itself finally of the vestiges of its heritage as a plural society and to become finally one people under the American creed.

I I

THE RESURGENT PLURAL
SOCIETY AND THE
CIVIL RIGHTS MOVEMENT
IN THE SOUTH

Introduction

As the Supreme Court progressively whittled away at the legal-normative foundations of the plural society in the 1940s, the unease that had seeped into black-white relations with the coming of World War II began to fester and to smolder; tensions between the races mounted. The chief battleground was the South, although the North did not escape the strain, as evidenced by the riots in Detroit and Harlem in 1943. White Southerners in particular felt threatened by the unfolding events. They were determined to protect their privileged position and were prepared to resort to repression and violence, both legal and extralegal, to do so. In turn, southern blacks were becoming increasingly dissatisfied and bitter under the constraints of the racial creed, but they primarily confined their resentment to further withdrawal from direct contact with whites and to private acts and expressions of discontent. Direct challenges to the racial creed and to the plural system during this period came primarily from blacks based in the North. The National Association for the Advancement of Colored People (NAACP), for example, shouldered prime responsibility for the ever-increasing numbers of court cases against the system. Even the 1947 "journey of reconciliation" into the border South, a harbinger of the freedom rides of the future, was sponsored and carried through by northern-based black organizations, the Congress of Racial Equality (CORE), and the Fellowship of Reconciliation, as a test of the 1946 Supreme Court decision banning segregation on interstate buses.

Yet, despite these rumblings, the whites retained firm control of the situation. They were secure in their monopoly of legal and political authority in local and state governments in the South and in the continuing Supreme Court affirmation of the racial creed and segmentation as constitutional. For, despite its pecking away at features of the Plessy-Ferguson doctrine in the 1940s, the Court retained more or less intact the doctrine's fundamental principle of "separation." Thus the doctrine continued to serve as the linchpin that connected state and local law, and custom of the South, with the law of the land. As a result, the local and state governments could bring to bear as constitutionally lawful and legitimate the full force of their coercive power and legal authority to enforce the racial creed and to shore up the plural structure of the South. The two sovereignties – state and federal – reinforced each other.

In 1954, however, the Court withdrew the linchpin in its Brown decision from one area of the social realm, the educational. In so doing, it not only stripped the racial creed of its constitutional mantle but also imposed constitutional restraint on the states that they desist from enforcing the creed. As a result, the two sovereignties confronted each other over the racial issue in a manner unprecedented since the Civil War. Each represented more clearly than ever a different facet of the duality which America had precariously balanced for much of its history: the state government with its championing of a plural society and racial creed and the federal government with its championing of the People's Domain and the American creed.

The confrontation grew in scope and intensity for almost fifteen years as it extended into other institutional areas of the social realm and into the deeper reaches of the South. The southern whites mounted massive resistance along a broad front. Even where they were obliged to retreat they delayed as much as they could and fought fierce rearguard actions. They might have succeeded in permanently blunting the thrust of the courts had not the southern blacks mobilized themselves and launched what Dr Martin Luther King, Jr called the "Negro revolution." The revolution under the charismatic leadership of King provided a grass roots challenge to state law that kept the Supreme Court busy in delegitimizing the racial creed in one institutional area after another; but equally if not more significantly it supplied the momentum and pressure that eventually pushed a reluctant Congress and President into renouncing categorically the racial creed as having any legal standing whatsoever within any sovereignty or public realm of the People's Domain and in placing the entire domain under a single legal-normative framework: the American creed.

In this chapter we shall examine the response of southern whites and blacks to the accelerating confrontation between the two sovereignties and between the racial and American creeds, and we shall explore the meaning and significance of the black revolution and the role of its most articulate spokesman and leader, Dr Martin Luther King, Jr.

Southern white resistance: the fight to preserve the plural society

Whatever may have been the prior state of tension and restiveness among southern whites about their relations with the black, the Brown decision quickly crystallized these into widespread and intense expressions of fear and anger. While officials in some border states took almost immediate steps to comply at least in part with the desegregation ruling, most other white Southerners, particularly those of the Deep South, from elected state and local officials to private citizens, were determined to resist and to defeat the court ruling.

REBIRTH OF THE DOCTRINE OF INTERPOSITION AND NULLIFICATION

Some of the state legislatures launched a frontal assault against the ruling. They questioned the constitutionality of the Court's action and resurrected the doctrines of interposition and nullification, first articulated by Jefferson and Madison and later used by southern states as legal justification for their secession from the Union in 1860. According to the doctrine,

> "the central government is nothing more than a compact between and among the several sovereign states, and ... each state has the right to determine the constitutionality of any act of federal authority. In declaring a federal act unconstitutional, a state would be interposing its sovereignty between the central government and the state's own citizens – hence the term interposition."
>
> (Blaustein and Ferguson 1962:242)

The first bill on interposition was introduced into the Virginia general assembly in January 1956. It declared that

> "the action of the Supreme Court of the United States in holding that the states cannot provide separate but equal facilities for children of different races constitutes an unlawful and unconstitutional assumption of power which does not exist. An agency created by a document to which sovereign states were parties cannot lawfully amend the creating document when that document clearly specifies in Article V thereof the manner of amendment."
>
> (Race Relations Law Reporter February 1956:253)

Accordingly, such an action by the Supreme Court, the bill continued, "poses a clear and present threat to the several states and to their citizens. Tyranny goes from one excess to even greater ones" (Race Relations Law Reporter February 1956:253). Therefore, the bill concluded, Virginia is "under no obligation to

accept supinely an unlawful decree of the Supreme Court of the United States"
(Race Relations Law Reporter February 1956:253).

Almost three weeks later the general assembly passed a joint resolution in lieu of
the original bill that repeated the bill's argument that the Supreme Court ruling
constituted "a deliberate, palpable, and dangerous attempt by the court itself to
usurp the amendatory power that lies solely with not fewer than three-fourths of
the States." The resolution then went on to reaffirm in no uncertain terms the
doctrine of interposition:

> "The General Assembly of Virginia, mindful of the resolution it adopted on
> December 21, 1798, and cognizant of similar resolutions adopted on like
> occasions in other States, both North and South, again asserts this fundamental
> principle: That whenever the Federal Government attempts the deliberate,
> palpable, and dangerous exercise of powers not granted it, the States who are
> parties to the compact have the right, and are in duty bound, to interpose for
> arresting the progress of the evil end for preserving the authorities, rights and
> liberties appertaining to them."   (Race Relations Law Reporter April 1956:446)

The resolution, however, stopped short of calling for nullification of the Supreme
Court decision – an action that had one hundred years earlier led to the Civil War.
Instead it called on its "sister states" to support passage of a constitutional
amendment that would "settle the issue of contested power." Until then the
resolution concluded "we pledge our firm intention to take all appropriate
measures honorably, legally, and constitutionally available to us to resist this
illegal encroachment upon our sovereign power" (Race Relations Law Reporter
April 1956:447).

Asked two weeks later to clarify the legal standing of the resolution, the
Attorney General of Virginia insisted that the resolution was a

> "declaration of right invoking and interposing the sovereignty of the State
> against the exercise of powers seized in defiance of the creating compact;
> powers never surrendered by the remotest implication but expressly reserved
> and vitally essential to the separate and independent autonomy of the States. It is
> an appeal of last resort against a deliberate and palpable encroachment transgres-
> sing the Constitution."   (Race Relations Law Reporter April 1956:464)

He agreed, however, that it was not "within the power of (a) the General
Assembly of Virginia by resolution, or (b) the people of Virginia in convention
assembled by ordinancy to legally nullify, in whole or in part, the said [Supreme
Court] decision or to thereby suspend for any period of time its enforcement in
Virginia" (Race Relations Law Reporter April 1956:464). He concluded "the
resolution is not one of nullification. Its plain terms negate the concept of

nullification. The Court embraced that doctrine in its most far-reaching implication when it nullified basic provisions of the Constitution of the United States. The resolution is one of interposition with resort to constitutional processes for relief" (Race Relations Law Reporter April 1956:462).

Within two months five other states – all from the Deep South – passed resolutions similar to that of Virginia. They reaffirmed the doctrine of interposition but refrained from a head-on collision with the Supreme Court over the issue of nullification. Most, however, indicated in a variety of ways that they would nevertheless not pay much attention to the ruling, labeling it "null and void and of no effect."

In March 1956, as we have already noted in Chapter 8, all the congressional members but three from eleven southern states joined the controversy and issued a strong protest in the form of a "Declaration of Constitutional Principles," also known as the "Southern Manifesto." The manifesto vigorously condemned the Supreme Court ruling as violating the constitutional intent of the Founding Fathers and as therefore being "'a clear abuse of judicial power.... It climaxes a trend in the Federal Judiciary undertaking to legislate, in derogation of the authority of Congress, and to encroach upon the reserved rights of the States and the people'" (Blaustein and Zangrando 1968:451).

In addition, the manifesto continued, the Supreme Court decision upset the way of life built over the years by people in many states on the basis of the Plessy-Ferguson principle. As a result,

> "'this unwarranted exercise of power by the Court, contrary to the Constitution, is creating chaos and confusion in the States principally affected. It is destroying the amicable relations between the white and Negro races that have been created through 90 years of patient effort by the good people of both races. It has planted hatred and suspicion where there has been heretofore friendship and understanding.'"   (Blaustein and Zangrando 1968:452)

In view of this, the signers of the manifesto argued, the decision of the Supreme Court must be opposed as an encroachment "'on rights reserved to the States and to the people, contrary to established law, and to the Constitution,'" and the states must be supported in their declared intention "'to resist forced integration by any lawful means'" (Blaustein and Zangrando 1968:452).

By 1957 the controversy had escalated from mere rhetoric and "resolutions" to a constitutional crisis of major significance as the governor of Arkansas challenged the authority of the Supreme Court with the military forces of his state. He did this by ordering out the national guard to forestall implementation of a desegregation plan worked out by the Little Rock school board in compliance with court decrees. In promulgating his order the Governor skirted the issue of interposition and focused instead on his authority to protect public order and peace. According-ly, he justified his action by saying, "it has been made known to me, as Governor, from many sources, that there is imminent danger of tumult, riot, and breach of the peace and the doing of violence to persons and property in Pulaski County, Arkansas" (Race Relations Law Reporter October 1957:937).

Unable to avoid this thinly veiled challenge to federal authority, President Eisenhower retreated from his oft-expressed determination to have as little to do as possible with the school desegregation controversy. He condemned the actions of the Governor in a statement issued in September 1957. In it, he contended that the "powers of a state government may not be used to defeat a valid order of a Federal court.... [A governor may not use the] pretext of maintaining (domestic) order," for which he has primary responsibility, in order to "interpose military force or permit mob violence to occur so as to prevent the final order of a Federal court from being carried out." If a governor, however, "interposes" such an "obstruction of justice" or permits "mob violence" so that the law cannot be enforced "by the ordinary course of judicial proceedings, the obligation of the President under the Constitution and law is inescapable. He is obliged to use whatever means may be required by the particular situation" (Race Relations Law Reporter October 1957:929–30).

Accordingly, the President ordered out federal troops, federalized the national guard, and charged them with enforcing the federal court orders. They went to protect the nine black children who were to be admitted to the high school. However, fearful of community hostility, the school board petitioned the courts for delay in implementing its desegregation plan for the high school. The petition was unanimously denied by the Supreme Court in Cooper v. Aaron. In its decision, the Court took direct aim at the doctrine of interposition and nullifica-tion. Citing historic opinions from Chief Justice Marshall's for a unanimous Court in Marberry v. Madison (1803) to Chief Justice Hughes' for an equally unanimous Court in Sterling v. Constantin (1932), the Court declared in no uncertain terms:

"Article VI of the Constitution makes the Constitution the 'Supreme Law of the Land' ... [and] makes it of binding effect on the States, 'any Thing in the Constitution or Laws of any State to the Contrary notwithstanding.' Every state legislator and executive and judicial officer is solemnly committed by oath taken pursuant to Art. VI, cl. 3, 'to support this Constitution'.... No state legislator or executive or judicial officer can war against the Constitution without violating his undertaking to support it.... [To have it otherwise would mean] 'that the fiat of a state Governor, and not the Constitution of the United States, would be the supreme law of the land; that the restrictions of the Federal Constitution upon the exercise of state power would be but impotent phrases.'"

(358 US 1958:18–19)

The confrontation at Little Rock demonstrated to even the most ardent segregationists among state officials that in any showdown the forces available to the state were no match for those available to the federal government. The Florida legislature took cognizance of this in its memorial to the United States Congress in October 1957. It warned that the arbitrary use of this power by the President as in the case of Little Rock could lead to destruction of the union and to a dictatorship.

> "WHEREAS if the President of the United States is permitted to exercise the power to determine the method of enforcing a federal decree, and thereby to invoke military rule because of the inconvenience attendant in the proper use of constitutional processes, the states will have been destroyed; and the indestructible union of indestructible states established by the Constitution of the United States will have ceased to exist, and in its stead the President will have created, without jurisdiction or authority from the people, a dictator form of government, possessing total, unrestricted power."
> (Race Relations Law Reporter December 1957:1173)

Accordingly, the legislature demanded that Congress censure the President for his resort to military force in Little Rock which it likened to Hitler's use of storm troopers.

> "WHEREAS the President of the United States, without the request, consent, and in the absence of the Governor ordered federal troops to occupy a portion of the sovereign state of Arkansas, and such troops through the exercise of brute force and with the high-handed tactics reminiscent of Hitler's storm troopers declared their intention to rule the citizenry therein, and thereby succeeded to maliciously and unnecessarily enjoin the inherent and inalienable rights and powers of the citizens thereof." (Race Relations Law Reporter December 1957:1172)

In December the Texas legislature passed its version of censure which demanded that the President desist from such actions in the future. Georgia's legislature echoed Florida's storm trooper charge in its resolution of censure in January 1958; the resolution inveighed against the President for "arbitrary and illegal action unprecedented in the annals of history" (Race Relations Law Reporter April 1958:357).

Recognition of the superior physical power of the federal government did not prevent other confrontations from happening. These, though, were relatively infrequent and were at most minor skirmishes, as in Alabama and Mississippi, although several persons were killed in the latter encounter. In each instance, state officials expressed their outrage at what they perceived as threats to the sovereignty of their state. In the censure resolution passed after the Meredith incident at the University of Mississippi in 1962, for example, the state legislature decried "the invasion of the sovereign state of Mississippi by several hundred United States Marshals and some 15,000 Federal troops with orders to force, intimidate, and crush [the] state's ability and willingness to protect its sovereignty" (Race Relations Law Reporter Winter 1962:1248).

In each instance, though, the state officials were obliged to retreat. They had overplayed their defiance and as a result had provoked into retaliation a power vastly superior to theirs that rendered moot any thought of a Civil War replay of outright nullification and secession. Most state officials were fully aware of this and tried not to overstep those limits that would precipitate a head-on collision with the executive power of the federal government. But within these boundaries they pressed relentlessly for full exercise of their rights of sovereignty and continually reaffirmed the doctrine of interposition as a symbolic expression of these rights. They took advantage of their factual control of public educational resources and facilities within their state to pursue a policy of *de facto* nullification, which still managed to avoid a direct legal confrontation with the full power of the presidency.

NULLIFYING THE EFFECTS OF THE BROWN DECISION

A number of southern states threatened to dismantle their public school systems if they were forced to desegregate. South Carolina, for example, repealed the law providing for a "liberal system of free public schools for all children" and then enacted a law that would close a public school if it were under court order to integrate. Mississippi repealed various sections of its code that required compulsory education. Louisiana amended its compulsory attendance law so as to provide for its suspension where integration of a school was required by court order. Various counties in Virginia in 1956 suspended funding of public schools that were to be integrated. Georgia provided for suspension of the compulsory attendance law upon a proclamation from the governor. After Little Rock, both Texas and Virginia authorized school boards to close their schools if a military presence had been ordered by the federal government to impose integration.

As an alternative to desegregated public schools, a number of states sought to provide support and sustenance for segregated private schools. The most extreme example of this was Georgia's efforts to lease its public school facilities and properties to private schools. In addition, Georgia also underwrote a program of tuition grants for students who wished to transfer from public to private schools. Other states such as North and South Carolina, Virginia, and the like also followed the example of tuition grants, particularly for students whose public schools were under court order to desegregate. The various states also sought to ease the personnel problems of these private schools. Georgia, for example, allowed teachers in certain privately operated schools to become part of the state teachers' retirement system and also continued retirement benefits to teachers and other public school employees who accepted jobs in private non-sectarian schools.

In addition to restrictive policies on the funding of public schools, various states such as Virginia and Georgia also developed elaborate schemes of avoidance, evasion, and delay to circumvent the implementation of the Brown decision. Most of these schemes followed the historic path clearly mapped by years of circumventing Supreme Court rulings on jury service and voting rights of blacks. In other words, they avoided explicit reference to racial segregation but devised "neutral procedures" that perpetuated it.

Perhaps the most popular and successful of these devices, which withstood court challenges, were the pupil assignment laws. These laws manifestly classified students merely on the basis of performance in scholastic aptitude and achievement tests. In fact they perpetuated the racial discrimination that was the heritage of inferior segregated schooling for the blacks. Further, such laws also gave local school boards wide discretion in placing students. As a result, they could resort to other "neutral devices" to keep black and white students completely apart if the testing procedures failed to do so. In Florida, for example, school boards were obliged to consider the following:

"In designating the school to which pupils may be assigned there shall be taken into consideration the available facilities and teaching capacity of the several schools within the country, the effect of the admission of new students upon established academic programs, the suitability of established curriculum to the students enrolled or to be enrolled in a given school, the scholastic aptitude, intelligence, mental energy or ability of the pupil applying for admission and the psychological, moral, ethical, and cultural background and qualification of the pupil applying for admission as compared with other pupils previously assigned to the school in which admission is sought."

(Race Relations Law Reporter October 1956:925)

Education was not the only institutional area of the plural society that various states sought to protect from actual or expected incursion of federal authority in the immediate post-Brown era. Harried by the Interstate Commerce Commission and court decisions on interstate carriers, Georgia, Mississippi, and Louisiana enacted laws that required segregation for waiting rooms and other facilities and intrastate carriers. Alabama and South Carolina joined them in reaffirming the policy and practice of segregated public recreational facilities. They authorized the governor to close the facilities or to sell them to private interests if the former policy could not be sustained.

Perhaps the most elaborate post-Brown reaffirmation of the plural society came from the legislature of Louisiana. Staking its claims on its police power, the legislature was convinced that even its segregated school system could be protected by this power from the Brown ruling. Accordingly, it pushed for an amendment to the state constitution in 1954 that explicitly stated:

"All public elementary and secondary schools in the State of Louisiana shall be operated separately for white and colored children. This provision is made in the exercise of the state police power to promote and protect public health, morals, better education, and the peace and good order in the State, and not because of race. The Legislature shall enact laws to enforce the state police power in this regard."   (Race Relations Law Reporter February 1956:239)

(The Supreme Court dismissed this contention in later court proceedings.)

The high-water mark of the legislature's aggressive efforts to sustain and to foster a plural society was perhaps reached during the summer of 1956. By the end of May it had clearly signalled its intention to assert its authority even more strongly than before. As an opener, it passed an interposition resolution that condemned "encroachment upon the police powers reserved to the State." It also renewed its mandate to the Joint Legislative Committee to carry on "the fight to maintain segregation of the races in all places of our life in accordance with the customs, traditions, and laws of our state" (Race Relations Law Reporter August 1956:755). By the middle of June the legislature followed the example of Georgia and Mississippi and required segregated washrooms and other facilities for passengers of intrastate carriers. In July it went even further than that and required separate facilities for white and black employees generally.

Perhaps most significantly of all, it extended in June the umbrella of its police powers to protect racial segregation in all public recreational facilities whether run by the state or by its political subdivisions.

"AN ACT: In the exercise of the police power of the State of Louisiana, to provide that all public parks, recreation centers, playgrounds, community centers and other such facilities at which facilities for swimming, dancing, golfing, skating or other recreational activities are conducted shall be operated separately for members of the white and colored race in order to promote and protect public health, morals and the peace and good order in this State; to provide penalties for the violation of this act and to repeal all laws and parts of laws in conflict herewith."   (Race Relations Law Reporter August 1956:732)

By July the legislature even went so far as to ban interracial participation in athletic events or social functions and to require separate seating of white and black spectators.

After this apex was reached, the legislature continued to pass laws affirming segregation, but these laws increasingly took on a defensive character as adverse court rulings, federal legislation, and pressures from the blacks took their toll. By the early 1960s Louisiana was fighting the same kind of rearguard action as were the other southern states. It too repealed its compulsory school attendance laws, provided tuition grants for students to attend private schools, and in general struggled to counteract the growing pressure against its plural society.

THE ASSAULT AGAINST THE "ALIEN PRESENCE" OF THE NAACP

Even as the various southern states were organizing the defense of their plural society against the challenge of the Supreme Court and the occasional action of the President, they launched a withering campaign against "the enemies" in their midst whom they were convinced came from the outside and were threatening to subvert the peace and quiet of their society. Their chief target was the NAACP, whose legal challenges, they maintained, had opened the door for the Supreme Court and had also triggered disquiet in the traditionally "harmonious" relations between the races. Accordingly, the various states directed their anger at the NAACP and sought to neutralize, if not destroy, its effectiveness.

One approach that Alabama pioneered and other states such as Texas and Virginia followed was to label the NAACP as an alien presence, thereby subjecting it to a stringency of regulation that such a presence may be legally required to endure. Alabama insisted that the organization register as a foreign corporation doing business with the state and that it comply with all state laws respecting registration and place of business.

Upon the NAACP's refusal to register, the state obtained a temporary restraining order which enjoined the organization from further activity in Alabama. The state then added the stipulation that the NAACP must also submit certain books, papers, and other documents including a membership list. Upon the NAACP's continued refusal to comply, the court held it in contempt and levied a fine that amounted to $100,000. In his opinion Judge Jones dealt neither with the substance nor merits of the NAACP's contention that the state law had been mistakenly and maliciously applied to it in violation of its rights under the higher law of the federal constitution. He made no mention of a conflict in the jurisdictions of two sovereignties; instead he merely defined the issue in terms of the laws and jurisdiction of one sovereignty, Alabama. As a result, the judge failed to perceive the NAACP as a group seeking to conform to one set of laws rather than to another; instead he viewed it as a selfish and contemptible criminal whose defiance of the rule of law threatened the very foundations of civilized society.

"The court cannot permit its orders to be flouted. It cannot permit a party, however wealthy and influential, to take the law into his own hands, set himself up above the law, and contumaciously decline to obey the orders of a duly constituted court made under the law of the land and in the exercise of an admitted and ancient jurisdiction. If this were allowed, there would be no government of law, only the government in a particular case of the litigant who elected to defy the court for his own private and selfish ends."

(Race Relations Law Reporter October 1956:918)

In 1958 the United States Supreme Court reversed some of the actions of the Alabama court. For example, it dissolved the fine and affirmed the right of the NAACP not to disclose its membership, but it referred back to the state courts the foreign corporation issue for determination on its merits. The state court responded in December 1961 by reaffirming its designation of the NAACP as a foreign corporation and by finding that the organization had grossly violated the law regulating such corporations. Accordingly, the NAACP was permanently enjoined from engaging in any activities vital to its survival in Alabama. The banned activities ranged from soliciting membership and contributions and collecting membership dues to conducting any kind of business in Alabama. As a result, the NAACP was effectively barred from doing anything in Alabama for the next several years. In 1964 the Supreme Court set the injunction aside on the grounds that it violated the First Amendment. Only then were the constitutional arguments of the NAACP vindicated and was the organization able to resume its activities in Alabama.

No other southern state succeeded quite as effectively as Alabama in neutralizing the NAACP. Even those who also used the foreign corporation gambit, such as Texas and Virginia, fell short of the mark, in part because the state courts did not take the same across-the-board hardline as did the Alabama court. But most states succeeded in significantly harassing and disrupting the work of the organization and in sapping its morale and strength in the state. South Carolina, for example, developed one of the more telling devices. It passed a law in 1956 that made it illegal for any state agency, school district, county, or municipality to employ a member of the NAACP. By 1957, under pressure of court cases, the law was repealed and replaced by one that merely required questions on organizational membership to be included on all applications for employment in government. The revenue commissioner of Georgia followed another tack. He sought to obtain the books, papers, and other records of the NAACP under the pretext of assessing its tax liabilities for the past and present.

But perhaps the technique most widely used to hobble the NAACP was a direct attack on its litigative activities in the state. In order to do this, a number of states including Georgia, South Carolina, Tennessee, and Virginia resurrected "barratry" as a viable category of crime and tailored their definition to apply more closely to the activities of the NAACP. Tennessee, for example, defined barratry in a 1957 law as "the offense of stirring up litigation;"

"'Stirring up litigation' means instigating or attempting to instigate a person or persons to institute a suit at law or equity; 'Instigating' means bringing it about that all or part of the expenses of the litigation are paid by the barrator or by a person or persons (other than the plaintiffs) acting in concert with the barrator, unless the instigation is justified."

(Race Relations Law Reporter April 1957:503)

(What the NAACP did was never defined as "justified.") In its version, South Carolina would penalize for barratry "any person who shall willfully solicit or incite another to bring, prosecute, or maintain an action at law or in equity, in any court having jurisdiction within this state" and who exhibits five other behavioral characteristics. These behavioral characteristics were then drawn to bear a relatively close fit to the kinds of things that the NAACP would do. These included having "no direct and substantial interest in the relief thereby sought," engaging in the action with the "intent to distress or harass any party to such action, and supporting directly or indirectly the litigation" (Race Relations Law Reporter April 1957:502).

Punishment could be exceptionally severe for an organization found guilty of the crime. South Carolina, for example, stipulated that "Any corporation or unincorporated association found guilty of barratry shall be forever barred from doing any business or carrying on any activity within this State, and in the case of a corporation, its Charter or Certificate of Domestication, shall be summarily revoked by the Secretary of State" (Race Relations Law Reporter April 1957:502). Tennessee echoed the same sentiment: "If the corporation be a foreign corporation, its certificate of authority to transact business in Tennessee shall be revoked by the District Attorney General of the district in which the offense is committed" (Race Relations Law Reporter April 1957:504). Again, the target was the NAACP.

"Barratry" was not the only legal weapon the states used in their efforts to control the litigative activities of the NAACP. Some enacted laws specifically directed toward litigation over school desegregation. Arkansas, for example, required in a 1957 law the registration of organizations promoting school desegregation by legislation or litigation. Such organizations were obliged to keep detailed and extensive records of contributions and contributors as well as of expenditures and of those who received its funds. Tennessee also passed a bill in 1957 that required registration of any organization,

> "which engages as one of its principal functions or activities in the promoting or opposing in any manner the passage of legislation by the General Assembly in behalf of or opposition to any race or color or whose activities cause or tend to cause racial conflicts or violence, or who or which is engaged or engages in raising or expending funds for the employment of counsel or payment of costs in connection with litigation in behalf of any race or color, in this state."
> (Race Relations Law Reporter April 1957:499)

Virginia had earlier set forth a similar requirement in Chapter 32 of its 1956 Extra Sessions Acts.

Varied as the attacks were against the NAACP, all seemed to share the same mythical conception of the society which was being defended. According to this view, the South had long been a society of peace and repose in which white and black had lived in harmony and mutual regard. Into this scene of tranquility had intruded the NAACP, intent upon disrupting and subverting this solidarity and quiet. The state, accordingly, had to render the organization ineffective so that the past equilibrium could be restored – something which the blacks, not merely the whites, presumably wanted and to which both were entitled.

Such a state of "interracial harmony and tranquility" was presumably the goal of the 1957 Tennessee law which required the registration of the NAACP and other organizations concerned with legislation and litigation on racial matters and "whose activities cause or tend to cause racial conflict or violence." As stated in its preamble, the purpose of the bill was "to promote interracial harmony and tranquility and to that end to declare to be the public policy of the State that the right of all people to be secure from interracial tension and unrest is vital to the health, safety, and welfare of the state" (Race Relations Law Reporter April 1957:498). Virginia described in similar terms the purpose of one of its laws requiring registration of persons and organizations engaged in the desegregation controversy.

> "An Act to promote interracial harmony and tranquility and to that end to declare it to be the public policy of the State that the right of all people to be secure from interracial tension and unrest is vital to the health, safety, and welfare of the State; to require registration of persons and organizations in promoting or opposing legislation in behalf of a race or color, or advocating racial integration or segregation, or whose activities tend to cause racial conflicts or violence."
> (Race Relations Law Reporter October 1957:1021)

An even more clearly delineated version of the disruptive role of the NAACP is spelled out in the South Carolina Law that denied employment in governmental jobs to members of the NAACP. As stated in the preamble, the NAACP has disturbed the peace and tranquility between the races and has threatened the ever-increasing progress of racial understanding. It has done this in part by indoctrinating blacks "with the belief that they are the subject of economic and social strangulation which will forever bar Negroes from improving their station in life and raising their standard of living to that enjoyed by the white race." In this and other ways, the preamble continues, "the NAACP is so insidious in its propaganda and the fostering of those ideas designed to produce a constant state of turmoil between the races, that membership in the organization is wholly incompatible with the peace, tranquility, and progress that all citizens have a right to enjoy" (Race Relations Law Reporter August 1956:752).

WHITE SOLIDARITY, ORTHODOXY, AND THE CITIZENS' COUNCIL

The rapid mobilization of the machinery of state government against the Brown ruling was neither fortuitous nor contrived. It was the natural and logical outcome of the widespread anger and resentment that surged through the southern white communities, particularly in the Deep South. Many whites reacted to the ruling as though "a way of life is being swept from under them – a way of life for which the race issue has become symbolic" (Vander Zanden 1965:21). Accordingly, "they have chosen to take their stand upon the race issue."

In the process, the whites feverishly reaffirmed their heritage of the past. Phoenix-like, the symbols and rhetoric of the Confederacy blossomed full-flood. Passions of defiance and threats of interposition, nullification, and even secession spewed venomously into the channels of intercourse, public and private. Silver vividly illustrated the linkage between the mythical past and the desegregation crisis in Mississippi and describes how the cult of the past came to represent symbolically the kind of orthodoxy which the "closed society" of Mississippi imposed on its people during the crisis. "Today the closed society of Mississippi imposes on all its people acceptance of an obedience to an official orthodoxy almost identical with one developed in the middle of the nineteenth century" (Silver 1966:22).

On a more general level, Vander Zanden alludes to the connection between the southern white struggle against integration and the resurrection of the past:

"The Old South has become a legend – its memories boundless – but above all other memories rises that of the Confederacy. Robert E. Lee and his army are immortalized men: 'their beards unkempt, their uniforms torn and patched with clumsy hands, their feet upon the ground, devoted men, ironsides after the fashion of Cromwell's army two hundred years before, their commander second only to God himself.' It was a 'Golden Age.'" (Vander Zanden 1965:21)

Vander Zanden goes on to say that in their interpretation of this legendary history, southern whites have carefully juxtaposed their version of the past racial situation with that of today. In the golden age of the Confederacy, they insist, blacks were treated well and were happy. No outside agitators disrupted the pervasive racial harmony, and the state of affairs between the races today would continue to be harmonious if such agitation were eliminated.

"It was a 'Golden Age' in which Negroes were happy, white people were dedicated to making them happier, and in which no such thing as racial conflict existed. It is the wishful preservation of an order that allegedly would continue to exist except for the interference of malevolent elements. It is a fantasy of a happy 'southern way of life' in which everything used to be all right."
(Vander Zanden 1965:22)

Gestated by a groundswell of resentment and the refertilization of a mythology, numerous groups and organizations, small and large, came into being as instruments of resistance and defense throughout the South. Vander Zanden estimates that "110 resistance organizations mushroomed from the Potomac to the Rio Grande" (Vander Zanden 1965:25).

The most effective and important of these were the Citizens' Councils which took shape in Yazoo, Mississippi in the summer of 1954. Started by a man who was inspired by Judge Tom Brady's book *Black Monday*, that bitterly assailed the Brown ruling, the Citizens' Council movement spread rapidly throughout Mississippi. In the words of a recruitment pamphlet, the Council sought to organize "white Americans who have pride in their white race and forethought for their posterity" (Association of Citizens' Councils 1954:4). By November 1954, the Association of Citizens' Councils estimated that Councils had been set up in 110 towns in Mississippi with a total white male membership of 25,000. Within a year or so the movement had spread throughout most of the states in the black belt region of the Deep South. By 1956 it is estimated that Alabama had fifty-two chapters with 65,000 members. Georgia and Louisiana also had their full share. However, it is likely that total membership for all of the Councils never exceeded 250,000.

Though never a mass movement, the Councils made up for their limited numbers by their access to seats of influence and prestige. Leadership was primarily recruited from the prominent, educated, and the well-to-do; their membership drawn from the moderately well-off, middle-of-the-road white

Southerner who was not identified with the fanatic extremism of the Ku Klux Klan. As a result, the Councils forged strong ties between the wielders of governmental and political power and the social and economic elite of the community. In Mississippi, in particular, they were a force to be reckoned with at each level of government and of the community. Their power is said to have reached its peak during the Ross Barnett administration as governor. He had wrapped the mantle of the Council around himself either as a member or as a close ally in his third attempt at the governorship; his victory enhanced their fortunes.

The goal of the Councils was to prevent any form of integration in their state or in any of their local communities. This was announced in no uncertain terms in the pamphlet that the Association of Citizens' Councils for Mississippi prepared for the recruitment of new members: "The Citizens' Council is the South's answer to the mongrelizers. *We will not be integrated*! We are proud of our white blood and white heritage of sixty centuries" (Association of Citizens' Councils 1954:2).

The Association insisted in its pamphlet that the plural society it was seeking to preserve was not merely a parochial product of the South but was anchored in the heritage of America as a nation. The Association evoked the names of the Founding Fathers in defense of its position.

"If we are bigoted, prejudiced, un-American, etc., so were George Washington, Thomas Jefferson, Abraham Lincoln, and our other illustrious forebears who believed in segregation. We choose the old paths of our founding fathers and refuse to destroy their ancient landmarks to appease anyone, even the internationalists."   (Association of Citizens' Councils 1954:3)

Even the image that the Association projected of the Councils was in accord with the best democratic traditions of the nation as a whole.

"The Citizens' Council is the modern version of the old-time town meeting called to meet any crisis by expressing the will of the people. The right to peaceably assemble to petition for a redress of our grievances is guaranteed in the first one of our Bill of Rights in the Constitution of the United States of America. The only reliable prophet for the future is the past, and history proves that the Supreme Power in the government has always been Public Sentiment."

(Association of Citizens' Councils 1954:1)

Accordingly, the Association viewed the Citizens' Councils as an instrument of public persuasion. "The Citizens' Council simply provides the machinery for mobilizing, concerting and expressing public opinion" (Association of Citizens' Councils 1954:1). As such, the Association argued, the Citizens' Council forswore the use of violence and even promised to maintain the peaceful and paternalistic relations of the past with the blacks. This is further evident in the words of the

Association: "We intend to prevent integration legally and thus prevent violence, friction, and racial hatred. We intend to carry on the peaceful relations we have had with our colored citizens, to help them help themselves and to try to help instill in them a sense of pride in their race as we have in ours" (Association of Citizens' Councils 1954:5).

Respectable and restrained as their view of themselves was, the Councils were prepared to use a vast arsenal of coercive instruments of control and pressure. They resorted to economic boycotts and sanctions by which they would deprive blacks and the few recalcitrant whites of jobs, credit, and goods and services. They constantly applied political pressure against officeholders and became the primary arbiters of public morality and behavior.

Silver paints a grim portrait of the control the Council came to exercise over Mississippi (Silver 1966). According to him, it was instrumental in clamping a rigid orthodoxy upon the people and was the prime mover in the creation of the contemporary version of the closed society in Mississippi. Deviation from the norms grafted from the Confederacy was not tolerated; transgressors, both black and white, were dealt with summarily. The Council even pushed back the boundaries of the recent gains of the blacks in the People's Domain. Voter registration lists were combed, and challenges mounted against blacks already on the lists. Pressures were also intensified against blacks who were otherwise qualified to vote, and fewer of them showed up at the polls than had done so earlier.

If the fine line between peaceful persuasion and violence was frequently blurred by the Citizens' Council, no such blurring characterized the actions of other organizations such as the Ku Klux Klan. They openly embraced extralegal and violent measures and were prepared to resort to any and all means to protect the plural society. They too had mushroomed in the immediate aftermath of the Brown ruling, but not to the extent that the Citizens' Councils had. The Klan, for example, claimed to have gained 100,000 new members and 500 new chapters from 1954 to 1958. It nevertheless remained in the shadow of the Council during this period, having neither the respectability nor influence of the latter.

In this manner, a fearsome juggernaut was constructed by southern whites in state and community to oppose the implementation of the Brown decision. Led by the respectable and influential, it professedly kept to a peaceful path of persuasion which, given its command of community resources, public opinion, and machinery of state, was awesome enough. But it also had as its allies organizations and segments of the population that were prepared to resort to physical force. Thus, never far below the surface of peaceful control lurked the threat of violence, which became an increasing reality as racial tensions and conflict intensified by the early 1960s.

The juggernaut flourished in a climate of white opinion that remained overwhelmingly opposed to the Brown ruling years after it was handed down. This is evident in the results of a nationwide poll taken in 1959 – five years after the Brown decision. As many as 96 percent of white Protestants from the Deep South expressed disapproval of racial integration of public schools even though "the United States Supreme Court has ruled that racial segregation in public schools is illegal." And 75 percent of their counterparts from the Border South also disapproved, in contrast to only 27 percent of white Protestants in the rest of the nation.

However, despite this near unanimity of opinion among Deep Southerners, evidence of actual or potential fissures in this solid front was manifest in their responses to another question. Even among those who disapproved strongly of racial integration, only one-half were prepared to have public schools closed permanently to resist it. Another quarter would countenance only a temporary closing of the schools; the remaining quarter said no or were uncertain. The latter responses were in the majority among those who merely disapproved of racial integration. Less than one out of five of this group favored permanent closing of the public schools.

In other words, Deep Southerners varied markedly in the price they were prepared to pay for resisting integration. Not many would go so far as to sacrifice permanently their public schools. Consequently, what appeared at first as a general consensus of opinion in 1959 would in time erode as the ante was raised for holding that opinion. However, in 1959 even the potential for such erosion seemed just a straw in the wind. The solid front of white resistance was still intact, although several shifts in tactics and strategies had already been forced by court decisions. And yet there was growing evidence, including the results of the above-mentioned poll, that, as the real costs mounted through the combined and increasing pressure of external and internal forces, the solid front of white resistance would prove vulnerable and start to crumble.

The civil rights movement and the "black revolution"

INTRODUCTION

Throughout the early years of their struggle against the Brown decision, the white Southerners had reassured themselves that their struggle was entirely with forces and enemies external to their society: the Supreme Court, the NAACP, northern liberals and northern blacks, and so on. They were confident that most southern blacks were not part of this cabal. They firmly believed that these blacks were still contented with their lot and still accepted the basic values of the plural society. Consequently, the whites justified much of their counteraction to the Brown ruling as an effort to restore the racial tranquility and harmony of the past and to prevent contamination of the innocent southern blacks from outside agitation. Even as the southern blacks began to stir against the reinforced constraints of the plural society, southern whites persisted with the myth of the outsider. Only belatedly did they realize that southern blacks had become the energizing source for the assault on the plural society.

MONTGOMERY AND DR MARTIN LUTHER KING, JR: PROLOGUE TO THE CIVIL RIGHTS DRAMA

The southern blacks made their collective presence felt for the first time in a confrontation in 1955 with the whites of Montgomery, Alabama over segregation on buses. Long nettled by their treatment on buses and by the arbitrary and humiliating manner in which the police and local authorities backed this treatment, the blacks of Montgomery rose in spontaneous indignation over the arrest of Rosa Park. They refused *en masse* to ride the buses and organized themselves into a disciplined movement. Spearheading the movement was the Montgomery Improvement Association, set up by community leaders, predominantly from the Church, and at the head of the entire structure stood Dr Martin Luther King, Jr. He had been thrust into a position of leadership by the turn of events and was no longer merely a pastor of a single church but the uncontested leader of the entire black community.

Dr King set the tone for the movement in his speech to an overflowing crowd at a mass meeting called at the end of the first day of the successful boycott. He said: "We are here this evening to say to those who have mistreated us so long that we are tired – tired of being segregated and humiliated; tired of being kicked about by the brutal feet of oppression." He then went on to insist that blacks had no alternative but to protest. He continued, "For many years, we have shown amazing patience. We have sometimes given our white brothers the feeling that we liked the way we were being treated. But we come here tonight to be saved from that patience that makes us patient with anything less than freedom and justice" (King 1958:61–2). He then entreated his audience to stay off the buses and to urge others to do likewise. But he insisted that force should not be used, only persuasion. In this manner he unveiled a strategy of peaceful persuasion that was soon to be elaborated into a more general philosophy of nonviolent resistance. He anchored the strategy in the Christian doctrine of love. "Our actions must be guided by the deepest principles of our Christian faith. Love must be our regulating ideal. Once again we must hear the words of Jesus echoing across the centuries: 'Love your enemies, bless them that curse you, and pray for them that despitefully use you'" (King 1958:62).

For twelve months the boycott continued. During this period, the white officials mounted increasing pressure to break it. At first they were the prisoners of their own myths about the blacks. They were convinced that the blacks were neither discontented nor energetic enough to sustain the boycott. Accordingly, they expected it to collapse within a few days. When it did not, they invited black leaders, including King, to "negotiations." However, they rejected as a violation of law and custom any modification of the segregated seating arrangement on buses, even though the proposed plan of the blacks did not basically alter the arrangement itself; instead they urged the blacks to become law-abiding citizens by giving up the boycott.

In a subsequent meeting King took strong exception to this white line of argument.

> "We have been talking a great deal this morning about customs.... It has been affirmed that any change in present conditions would mean going against the 'cherished customs' of our community. But if the customs are wrong, we have every reason in the world to change them. The decision which we must make now is whether we will give our allegiance to outmoded and unjust customs or to the ethical demands of the universe. As Christians we owe our ultimate allegiance to God and His will, rather than to man and his folkways."
>
> (King 1958:117)

With the breakdown of negotiations, the white officials stepped up their counter-measures. They tried without success to breed dissension and disunity among the blacks by circulating false rumors of peace and of malfeasance by King and other leaders of the movement. In addition, the police engaged in a campaign of surveillance and harassment; they issued traffic summonses for real and imaginary violations. Shortly thereafter, the officials dusted off an old state law against boycotts and began mass arrests. King was also arrested, convicted, and fined. Even as these actions were under way, the Citizens' Council and the Ku Klux Klan stepped up their pressure. King's home was bombed, and threats on life and property were omnipresent. But as King commented, the whites

> "did not know the Negroes with whom they were dealing. They thought they were dealing with a group who could be cajoled or forced to do whatever the white man wanted them to do. They were not aware that they were dealing with Negroes who had been freed from fear. And so every move they made proved to be a mistake. It could not be otherwise, because their methods were geared to the 'old Negro,' and they were dealing with a 'new Negro.'"   (King 1958:150)

The blacks even counterattacked in May 1956 with a suit in federal court against bus segregation as violative of the Fourteenth Amendment.

But the most difficult days were yet to come for the blacks, despite an early ruling by the lower court in their favor. In the summer their unity was almost sundered by the resignation of an official of the movement who charged abuse of power, mismanagement of funds by various officials. The charges proved unfounded and the accuser even retracted his statement. A residue of tension nevertheless remained. And finally, in October, city officials seized on a legal strategy that threatened the survival of the boycott. They sought to obtain an injunction against the continued operation of the car pool and transportation system that blacks had devised to offset the boycott. They also sued for damages for the loss of revenue from the bus boycott.

King recognized the potency of this threat and feared that the end of the boycott might be in sight. He was reluctant to break the news about the injunction to his followers:

> "The evening came, and I mustered up enough courage to tell them the truth. I tried, however, to end on a note of hope. 'This may well be,' I said, 'the darkest hour just before dawn. We have moved all of these months with the daring faith that God was with us in our struggle. The many experiences of days gone by have vindicated that faith in a most unexpected manner. We must believe that a way will be made out of no way.' But in spite of these words, I could feel the cold breeze of pessimism passing through the audience. It was a dark night – darker than a thousand midnights. It was a night in which the light of hope was about to fade away and the lamp of faith about to flicker. We went home with nothing before us but a cloud of uncertainty."   (King 1958:158–59)

King's fears might well have been realized if the injunction had been granted, for the white community, with a few exceptions, seemed determined to crush the boycott and was increasingly prepared to throw the full weight of its legal and extralegal power into the battle. However, before the hearing on the injunction was completed, the Supreme Court announced its decision. It affirmed the lower court ruling that local and state laws requiring segregation on buses were unconstitutional. This ended the hearing and for all intents and purposes the legal battle over the boycott, but the conflict was still not over. For, after a few days of peaceful integration, white extremists launched a reign of terror. This resulted in a suspension of bus services for almost a week. They subsequently resumed during daytime hours only.

So ended the bus boycott. A small fragment had been chipped from the edifice of the plural society of Montgomery, but the edifice as a whole remained fairly intact for the next number of years. In fact the whites reaffirmed the policy of segregation in institutional areas other than public transportation, but no longer could they delude themselves about black contentment and support of their plural society.

Though the victory may have been limited in scope, the Montgomery boycott forged in the crucible of protest a "hammer-anvil" strategy that eventually corroded in its entirety the legal-normative foundations of the plural society of the South. Henceforth, demonstrations and protests by blacks in the burgeoning civil rights movement would hammer these foundations against the anvil of federal authority where they would be made malleable and eventually pounded out of shape. On one level, the pressure by the blacks would force a confrontation between the plural society and the federal judiciary on a scale and scope that the NAACP could never have achieved alone in the normal course of events. On another level, the pressure would also be instrumental in forcing the executive and legislative branches of the federal government to construct the kind of anvil of federal authority by the mid-1960s that could encompass the broad sweep of the plural society and not merely its bits and pieces.

Alone, however, black pressure as witnessed in Montgomery was no match for the consolidated strength of white resistance, just as the federal judiciary by itself proved to be no match either for this resistance in the Deep South in the years immediately following the Brown decision. Until the mid-1960s then, the federal judiciary and the black protest movement needed each other to make any kind of significant dent in the wall of white resistance in the Deep South.

Beyond pioneering the "hammer-anvil" strategy, the Montgomery boycott also served as a prologue to the civil rights drama that was soon to be enacted in the South. Its immediate role was as a model for other bus boycotts. Even as the Montgomery boycott was still in effect, blacks in Tallahassee, Florida had also refused to ride their city's buses. They subsequently obtained favorable court rulings requiring desegregation of the buses, but city and state authorities sought to thwart the rulings. Only after a period of violence was order restored and bus service resumed on an integrated basis, just a few days before the final resumption of service in Montgomery. Birmingham, Alabama and Atlanta, Georgia also witnessed concerted efforts by blacks to hammer local ordinances on bus segregation against the anvil of the Supreme Court ruling outlawing bus segregation.

As the first confrontation over the issue, the Montgomery boycott was also the first to demonstrate that the audience for the unfolding civil rights drama would not merely be local and regional, but would be national as well. Initially treated as a local event and only incidentally reported in the national press and television, the boycott had been transformed into a national event by the time King's house was bombed. Subsequently it was covered regularly in the national media with special coverage at critical junctures of the boycott such as at King's arrest. King stressed the importance of locating the struggle in a national framework in a postscript he appended to his account of the boycott, *Stride Toward Freedom* (1958). In addition, he gave high priority to recruiting white northern liberals for supporting roles in the civil rights struggle.

"Another group with a vital role to play in the present crisis is the white Northern liberals. The racial issue that we confront in America is not a sectional but a national problem. The citizenship rights of Negroes cannot be flouted anywhere without impairing the rights of every other American. Injustice anywhere is a threat to justice everywhere. A breakdown of law in Alabama weakens the very foundations of lawful government in the other forty-seven states. The mere fact that we live in the United States means that we are caught in a network of inescapable mutuality. Therefore, no American can afford to be apathetic about the problem of racial justice. It is a problem that meets every man at his front door. The racial problem will be solved in America to the degree that every American considers himself personally confronted with it. Whether one lives in the heart of the Deep South or on the periphery of the North, the problem of injustice is his problem; it is his problem because it is America's problem."   (King 1958:199)

The Montgomery boycott catapulted Dr King onto the center stage of the embryonic civil rights movement in the South, certified his credentials as a bona fide black leader from the region, and shaped his approach to the movement through the ordeal by fire he had just experienced. And as the first major step into this broader framework, King met in January 1957 with approximately 100 other black leaders from the South, mostly churchmen, and established the first civil rights organization to be formed in the South, the Southern Christian Leadership Conference (SCLC).

Within a few years the SCLC spread affiliates throughout the South until they numbered approximately eighty-five in 1963; the headquarters remained in Atlanta, Georgia. However, as Clark has observed,

"One cannot understand SCLC solely in terms of its organization, which is amorphous and more symbolic than functional.... To understand this organization one has to understand King, because SCLC *is* Martin Luther King, Jr. King is a national hero, a charismatic leader, portrayed in America and through the world as a man of quiet dignity, a personification of courage in the face of racial danger."   (Clark 1966:612)

The initial goal of the SCLC was to implement through nonviolent resistance the Supreme Court ruling against bus segregation. Before long it branched out into a wider range of civil rights activities and worked with other civil rights leaders and organizations on a broad front. Not until 1962, though, did the SCLC seek to apply the lessons of Montgomery in a general nonviolent assault on segregation in a community, Albany, Georgia. According to King, the results were disappointing: "months of demonstration and jailings failed to accomplish the goals of the movement" (King 1964:43). Despite this, the protest did make a dent in the plural structure of the community. "City authorities had been obliged to close down facilities such as parks, libraries, and bus lines to avoid integration. The authorities were crippling themselves, denying facilities to the white population in order to obstruct our progress" (King 1964:44).

In many respects Albany proved a trial run for King's massive campaign against Birmingham, Alabama the following year. For King Birmingham was the acid test of the theory of nonviolent direct action. As he commented, "The challenge to nonviolent, direct action could not have been staged in a more appropriate arena. In the summer of 1963 an army brandishing only the healing sword of nonviolence humbled the most powerful, the most experienced, and the most implacable segregationists in the country.... Faith in this method had come to maturity in Birmingham" (King 1964:45–6). (The significance of the Birmingham campaign for the struggle against the plural society will be discussed later in this chapter.)

THE STUDENT NONVIOLENT COORDINATING COMMITTEE AND THE SIT-IN DEMONSTRATIONS: MOBILIZING THE GRASS ROOTS

Even before King and the SCLC moved boldly in Albany and Birmingham, another shock wave thundered through the plural society of the South and threatened its internal stability in a way it had not been threatened before. The wave began inauspiciously and spontaneously in Greensboro, North Carolina in February 1960 with the decision by four freshmen of AT&T College to sit patiently and at length at a lunch counter reserved for whites in protest at the policy of segregation. Within weeks the idea spread like a tidal wave to other college campuses throughout the South primarily, but elsewhere as well. Within weeks, sit-ins were organized in as many as fifteen different cities in five southern states. By September 1961, over 70,000 students, mostly black, had taken part in some form of sit-in; and 3600 of them had been arrested. The movement, however, did not confine itself to lunch counter sit-ins. "Within months the original sit-in notion had been generalized to wade-ins at segregated beaches, read-ins at segregated libraries, kneel-ins at segregated churches, walk-ins at segregated theaters and amusement parks" (Waskow 1967:227).

In May 1961, the movement was augmented by a "freedom ride" campaign initiated by the Congress of Racial Equality (CORE). On that date an interracial group of thirteen left Washington, DC for travel through the South on interstate buses to test compliance with an earlier Supreme Court ruling banning segregation in interstate carriers and facilities.

At the center of the burgeoning sit-in movement was the Student Nonviolent Coordinating Committee (SNCC). It also played a major role in carrying on with the "freedom rides" after they had exploded into violence and rioting in Alabama. The SNCC had come into being some three months after the Greensboro sit-in at a conference convened at Shaw University in Raleigh, North Carolina. Supported from the beginning by King, the SNCC had adopted formally at its May meeting the principle of nonviolent direct action, as is evident in the first few sentences of its statement of purpose:

> "'We affirm the philosophical or religious ideal of non-violence as the foundation of our purpose, the pre-supposition of our faith, and the manner of our action. Non-violence as it grows from Judaic-Christian traditions seeks a social order of justice permeated by love. Integration of human endeavor represents the first step towards such a society.'"   (Zinn 1965:34)

Though couched initially in religio-philosophical terms, nonviolence functioned increasingly for the SNCC as a secularized political strategy that was sorely tested in the citadels of the Deep South, Mississippi and Alabama. Only for King did nonviolence retain throughout the same religio-philosophical character.

The SNCC eschewed any formal bureaucratic structure and never became a membership organization; instead it retained a functional and federated looseness that was oriented toward action and field work. Despite its title, it never became a closely knit coordinating agency. As Zinn comments, "for SNCC, even after it had a large staff, its own office, and money for long-distance phone calls, managed to maintain an autonomy in the field, an unpredictability of action, a lack of overall planning which brought exasperation to some of its most ardent supporters, bewilderment to outside observers, and bemusement to students itself" (Zinn 1965:38).

What its adherents may have lacked in bureaucratic skills, they more than made up in their determination and courage. As Clark wrote, "the SNCC 'kids' in their worn denims brought new verve, drive, daring, and enthusiasm – as well as the brashness and chaos of youth – to sustain the dynamism of direct-action civil rights tactics" (Clark 1966:616). They penetrated the deepest reaches of the plural society of the Deep South and entered the lives of the poorest blacks in small towns and villages as no other civil rights group had. They became closely involved with these people and lived and worked among them. As a result, they generated a groundswell of enthusiasm that energized the entire civil rights movement.

Clear-cut victories were won in a number of cities in the Border South. Business and political leaders in Nashville, Tennessee and San Antonio, Texas, for example, came to terms. Four national chain stores announced in October the integration of lunch counters in about 150 stores in 112 cities predominantly of the Border South. In the Deep South, however, particularly in Mississippi, the SNCC and the movement came up against a well-organized and highly solidified opposition spearheaded by a police and governmental authority that was determined to beat them back. Students were arrested and jailed on a variety of charges from disturbing the peace to trespass. Many suffered brutal treatment at the hands of the police, but even more vulnerable to attack were the local blacks of the community, who were intimidated and threatened with violence and death if they cooperated with the young people of the SNCC.

The history of this period in the Deep South is written in the slowly elaborating network of contact and trust between student and local black within an environment of white violence and repression. Zinn reports that the first efforts by the SNCC to mobilize local blacks in Mississippi proved abortive. "For SNCC the McComb days of 1961 had been a quick and ugly rebuff" (Zinn 1965:101). Its efforts at "direct action ran head-on into the stonewall of absolute police power" (Zinn 1965:77). As a result, few blacks were prepared to risk the full fury and wrath of the white and those who did soon found themselves jailed, brutalized, some even killed. The same atmosphere of terror and fear enveloped the SNCC's voter registration drive; as a result, no one registered.

A year later the SNCC was much more successful in its Greenwood drive. From the beginning it confronted a repressive campaign of white pressure and violence, but slowly it gained access to and the confidence of local blacks – its food campaign helping immeasurably. As a result, a number of the blacks joined demonstrations, waited in line to be registered for voting, despite their vulnerability to white repression. However, the whites remained as firmly as ever in control of the plural society, willing and able to use instruments of coercion and violence. They rebuffed forcefully and effectively efforts to change the ways of their society. They even prevented blacks from voting in the regular gubernatorial election. Zinn recognizes this but he nevertheless insists that the black response throughout Mississippi at this time suggested that "the 'Mississippi iceberg' was beginning to crack. The evidence was not yet in changes in the social structure of the state, but in the people who emerged slowly, as rocks appear one by one out of a receding sea" (Zinn 1965:93).

By 1963 a milestone was reached in the emerging solidarity of the black. The SNCC along with other civil rights organizations in the Council of Federated Organizations (COFO) decided to offer the blacks of Mississippi an alternative to the regular gubernatorial election from which they were excluded. Accordingly, they prepared a "freedom ballot" for distribution among blacks throughout the state. Included on the ballots were the names of the regular gubernatorial candidates plus those of a black and his running mate, a white minister. About

83,000 blacks turned in their ballots at churches and other designated places; all but 500 voted for the black candidate and his running mate.

Thus was "invented a new form of creative disorder" (Waskow 1967:264), that made visible to black and white alike the growing solidarity of the blacks and their increased willingness to challenge the plural society. And yet, as a symbol of this challenge, the freedom ballot highlighted more than ever the continuing vitality of the plural society. The ballot may have provided blacks with an institutional form parallel to that available to the white, but it could not disguise the fact that the white's version still factually controlled the apparatus of power and the state, while the black version was merely a dramatic gesture.

By April 1964 another parallel political institution – the Mississippi Freedom Democratic Party – was formed which etched in even more graphic outlines the boundaries of the persisting plural society of Mississippi. Ostensibly open to all Democrats of voting age, the Freedom party attracted few whites and many blacks, as the SNCC and other members of the COFO mounted a major effort to register them in the new as well as the old party. This drive became a major activity of the Mississippi Summer Project for which over 1000 students, teachers, lawyers, and ministers, many of them white and from the North, had volunteered. (The project also developed another institutional parallelism: freedom schools in which blacks could learn about their history and their political, social, and economic problems in the state and nation, just as whites learned about their history in their schools.)

So successful were these efforts that the Freedom party developed a statewide precinct and county structure similar to that of the regular Democratic party. It also held, beginning in July, precinct and county elections as did the regular party for delegates to a statewide convention. There, a state delegation was selected to challenge the delegation from the regular party for seats at the forthcoming Democratic National Convention in Atlantic City. The challenge sparked a major controversy in the credentials committee at the convention. The outcome of which was a compromise offer of two seats-at-large for the Freedom party and the imposition of a loyalty oath on the regular delegation. The Freedom party rejected the offer and staged a sit-in of several days' duration in the seats vacated by the members of the regular delegation who had refused to take the oath. All this was played out before a national television audience of millions. As Waskow comments, "the Freedom Party argued by their deeds the case for bringing a major infusion of creative disorder not merely to peripheral institutions like restaurants and schools, but to the heart of political power in the United States, to the party system itself" (Waskow 1967:275).

In mobilizing southern black sentiment and in unleashing the kind of "creative disorder" they did, the SNCC, the COFO, and the other civil rights organizations intensified tensions and strains within the plural society of the Deep South to such an extent that its very stability, let alone survival, seemed at stake to its white officials, both state and local. Accordingly, these officials turned their attention to shoring up the internal defenses of their society. Specifically they strengthened the criminal code and penalties against trespass and disturbing the peace and enacted laws against picketing and assembly, as did Americus, Georgia, Talladega, Alabama, and Ederton, North Carolina. Perhaps the most comprehensive tailoring of the criminal code to fit the specific features of civil rights protest and demonstrations took place in Louisiana in 1963. The state government amended a number of acts in the criminal code to apply specifically to what was going on in the streets. Thus, the crime of resisting an officer was extended "to include congregating with others on a public street and refusing to move on when ordered to do so by an officer" (Race Relations Law Reporter Summer 1963:699). And the crime of disturbing the peace was extended to refusal to leave on demand the property of another: "molesting or disturbing a religious exercise after being requested to leave; and congregating in a noisy manner in streets, avenues, and highways, or around the entrance of public buildings or in parks" (Race Relations Law Reporter Summer 1963:697). In addition, fines and jail terms were doubled for each of the specified crimes in the code. In 1964, Mississippi also undertook a comprehensive revision of its criminal code to make it more directly applicable to civil rights demonstrations.

In building their defenses during this period, the white authorities revealed clearly that they had given up the myth that their enemies were merely outsiders. Too many of their own blacks were expressing strong sympathy for the civil rights movement to be disregarded, and the numbers were increasing. As a result, the white authorities no longer drew their line of defense merely to separate the plural society from the outside world but also to separate the black from the white segment of the plural society itself.

Under attack as they were, the whites of the Deep South nevertheless remained in command of the instruments of control and coercion and would have been able to cow the blacks into submission eventually if the entire drama were not being played out on the national stage as well. Most civil rights leaders and southern blacks realized this and were fully aware that they could not, in the final analysis, muster by themselves the resources and power to break the mold of the plural society in the various citadels of the Deep South, no matter what their gains might be in the border areas. Accordingly, they sought to apply the "hammer-anvil" strategy through constantly reaffirming the linkage between their struggle and the American creed and Constitution. They did this by regularly forcing confrontations between the law of the plural society and the law of the Constitution. As students were tried and convicted under local laws, regularly as clockwork their cases were appealed until some reached the docket of the United States Supreme Court. And as we have seen in earlier chapters, the Court overturned a number of these convictions in a series of crucial decisions on grounds that the legal basis of the plural society, its racial creed, was constitutionally invalid and that the machinery of the state was to be divorced from enforcement of this creed in the plural society.

The hammer-anvil thrust of the Supreme Court rulings and the black demonstrations had little immediate effect in the Deep South. In fact it seemed to intensify the resolve of those in authority, both in the state and in the local communities, to resist the threat to their plural society. Accordingly, the Court rulings were largely ignored and black demonstrators continued to bear the full brunt of police and legal action. Only the occasional physical intervention of the executive branch of the federal government, as in Little Rock, the freedom rides in Alabama, and at the University of Mississippi, prevented a decisive defeat for the opponents of the plural society.

BIRMINGHAM: THE CRUCIBLE OF THE "REVOLUTION"

By 1963 King was prepared to challenge the plural society frontally in one of its major strongholds of white intransigence, Birmingham, Alabama. He was convinced that success in this confrontation would alter significantly the balance of forces in the Deep South.

> "We believed that while a campaign in Birmingham would surely be the toughest fight of our civil rights careers, it could, if successful, break the back of segregation all over the nation. This city has been the country's chief symbol of racial intolerance. A victory there might well set forces in motion to change the entire course of the drive for freedom and justice."   (King 1964:54)

Accordingly, months were spent in planning and preparing for the assault on the plural structure of Brimingham. The four basic demands were to be:

> "1. The desegregation of lunch counters, rest rooms, fitting rooms, and drinking fountains in variety and department stores.
> 2. The upgrading and hiring of Negroes on a nondiscriminatory basis throughout the business and industrial community of Birmingham.
> 3. The dropping of all charges against jailed demonstrators.
> 4. The creation of a bi-racial committee to work out a timetable for desegregation in other areas of Birmingham life."   (King 1964:102–3)

Delayed until the end of a run-off election for major, the campaign began with a low-key but well organized series of sit-in demonstrations in large department and drug stores. Soon it escalated into disciplined daily street demonstrations and a boycott of the downtown merchants. As the numbers of volunteers grew, the campaign spread to "kneel-ins at churches; sit-ins at the library; a march on the county building to mark the opening of a voter-registration drive" (King 1964:69). In the early stages most of the participants were mature adults; toward the end of April, King decided to recruit younger people. Colleges and high schools in the area were canvassed, and within a short period the average age of the volunteers had dropped perceptibly. Thus, by the end of April the campaign was pushing ahead vigorously on its varied fronts; its ranks had swelled to overflowing; and in its vanguard were high school and college students.

The reaction of the local authorities to the campaign was for a period of time firm but not brutal. As the first sit-ins began, about three dozen demonstrators were arrested for violating a city ordinance against trespassing. Within a few days, daily mass street demonstrations started, and many others were jailed for parading without a permit. By the end of the first week hundreds had been arrested by police who showed a restraint that impressed King. On April 10, the city took a decisive step; it obtained a temporary injunction against the demonstrations until the right to demonstrate had been argued in court. King, after "prolonged and prayerful consideration" decided to defy the injunction: "Two days later, we did an audacious thing, something we had never done in any other crusade. We disobeyed a court order" (King 1964:70).

As an expression of this resolve, he and Ralph Abernathy led the first demonstration after the date of the injunction. ("I intended to be one of the first to set the example of civil disobedience" (King 1964:71).) Both were arrested along with many others and spent eight days in jail, at least one of which King spent in solitary confinement. After their release, the arrests multiplied as the pace of the demonstrations was stepped up. They peaked in the first week of May. By then the police under Bull Connor abandoned their restraint and acted brutally to suppress the demonstrations. They turned pressure hoses and police dogs loose on the crowds and wielded their clubs in fierce assault. The result was an ugliness too well known to Americans and to people all over the world. The newspapers of May 4 carried pictures of prostrate women, of policemen bending over them with raised clubs, of children marching up to the bared fangs of police dogs, and of the terrible force of pressure hoses sweeping bodies into the streets.

"This was the time of our greatest stress, and the courage and conviction of those students and adults made it our finest hour. We did not fight back, but we did not turn back. We did not give way to bitterness. Some few spectators, who had not been trained in the discipline of nonviolence, reacted to the brutality of the policemen by throwing rocks and bottles. But the demonstrators remained nonviolent."

(King 1964:100)

Most of the other whites in Birmingham, opposed as they were to the demonstrations, nevertheless did not do what their peers had done at other times and in other places. They did not violently confront the blacks in the street or resort to widespread acts of terror or reprisal. This surprised and heartened King.

> "Strangely enough, the masses of white citizens in Birmingham were not fighting us. This was one of the most amazing aspects of the Birmingham crusade. Only a year or so ago, had we begun such a campaign, Bull Connor would have had his job done for him by murderously angry white citizens. Now, however, the majority were maintaining a strictly hands-off policy. I do not mean to insinuate that they were in sympathy with our cause or that they boycotted stores because we did. I simply suggest that it is powerfully symbolic of shifting attitudes in the South that the majority of the white citizens of Birmingham remained neutral through our campaign. This neutrality added force to our feeling that we were on the road to victory."   (King 1964:100–01)

At the same time the white leaders were dead set against entering into any negotiations with the blacks. Even as the white business community began to hurt badly by the end of April, white resistance persisted. Only the patient and insistent urging of an official of the United States Department of Justice brought the two sides around a table. Even then, nothing happened until the violent confrontation between police and demonstrators during the first week of May. By May 10, an agreement was finally signed that encompassed the four demands of the blacks.

The agreement signified that the civil rights movement had reached a significant turning point in the Deep South. For the first time, blacks were able to marshal enough internal strength to force whites of influence and authority in a citadel of the plural society to come to terms on a general agreement. Earlier sit-in demonstrations had succeeded in wrenching a narrower agreement that was confined to lunch-counter desegregation in Atlanta, a community that did not have the antediluvian reputation of Birmingham. And still earlier, Montgomery had required a favorable Supreme Court ruling to insure the victory of the blacks in the bus boycott.

Yet, despite this show of strength, the blacks of Birmingham were not strong enough to sustain their victory alone. For upon the signing of the agreement the Ku Klux Klan and other white extremists rallied their forces, and a day later they bombed the home of King's brother and the motel in which King had been staying. Rioting erupted as the blacks responded to this violence. They tangled with the Alabama state police who had been called in by Governor Wallace to quell the riots forcibly. Peace was restored only after President Kennedy announced that federal troops were being sent to bases near Birmingham and that preparations were being made to federalize the Alabama national guard. Thus, a federal presence, which had earlier opened up the channels of communication between the parties during the struggle, now became instrumental in stabilizing the situation. But even then the situation remained tense, and white resistance did not end.

One month later, Governor Wallace heightened the tension in Alabama by defying a court order which admitted two blacks to the University of Alabama. Once again the exercise of federal authority by President Kennedy staved off a challenge by the forces of white resistance and reestablished an uneasy equilibrium. Three months later, violence by white extremists exploded anew in Birmingham as the first tentative efforts to desegregate the public schools under court decree began. Their most brutal assault was the Sunday bombing of a black church in which four girls were killed. The violence rekindled rioting among the blacks who fought on the streets with the local police. This time the President did not exercise his authority directly, but he expressed his outrage at the bombing in a public statement and dispatched two federal officials to Birmingham to prod white and black leaders into an interracial dialogue to relieve the tensions. In effect, the victory of May did not defeat the forces of white opposition which fought fiercely then and later to dislodge any wedge from the walls of the plural society. Only the exercise of executive authority by the President, or the visible presence of this authority, was able to hold the counterattack at bay. Even the authority of the federal courts was generally not enough to do so alone; it needed the backing of the executive branch of govenment.

The drama of Birmingham was not confined to the city itself; it was also performed throughout the entire period on a national stage provided by the visual and printed media. Early in the struggle, King had to contend with unfavorable reactions from press and public alike. He was castigated for starting his campaign just after the election of a moderate mayor without waiting to assess the new mayor's policies and actions. He was also labeled an outsider and criticized for his advocacy of civil disobedience, particularly after an injunction had been issued.

King took cognizance of these charges and in his famous letter from the Birmingham jail he sought to answer them one by one as they had been raised in an earlier public statement by eight clergymen from Alabama. However, as April wore on, press and public sentiment turned markedly toward the blacks. White and black organizations offered their support; national appeals for bail funds for the jailed demonstrators were quickly met. But perhaps the watershed of public opinion was reached in the first week of May as the photographs mentioned earlier flashed throughout the nation. In commenting upon the impact of these events, King said, "In the face of this resolution and bravery [by the blacks], the moral conscience of the nation was deeply stirred and all over the country, our fight became the fight of decent Americans of all races and creeds" (King 1964:100).

By the summer of 1963, the happenings in Birmingham triggered a nationwide response. King calls Birmingham "a fuse – it detonated a revolution" (King 1964:114). Mass demonstrations broke out in towns and cities throughout the country, from Savannah, Georgia in the Deep South and Cambridge, Maryland in the Border South, to Detroit, Michigan in the North. In a number of places, whites joined the ranks of the protesters, more so in the North than in the South, but the protesters remained predominantly black. A number of the demonstrations, particularly in the South, erupted into violence and rioting; deaths occurred, including the murder of Medgar Evers, an NAACP official of Jackson, Mississippi, and of William Moore, a white postman on a solitary civil rights march through Alabama.

THE MARCHES ON WASHINGTON AND SELMA: THE EPILOGUE TO THE BLACK-WHITE COALITION

The events of the summer of 1963 crested in late August when approximately a quarter of a million people from various parts of the country gathered in Washington, DC for a "march for jobs and freedom." The march brought together for one historical moment in time the divergent strands of the civil rights movement, its various leaders, and organizations. At the head stood A. Phillip Randolph whose threat of a similar march twenty years earlier had pressured President Roosevelt into setting up the first FEPC. Also in the front ranks were the leaders of the major black civil rights groups: Dr Martin Luther King, Jr (SCLC), Roy Wilkins (NAACP), Whitney Young (Urban League), James Floyd McKissick (CORE), John Lewis (SNCC), and Bayard Rustin. Thus was represented visually for the entire nation to see a solidarity in the black civil rights movement that frequently seemed absent in the competitive rivalries among leaders and organizations in the day-by-day struggle.

The march, however, was more than an intraracial affair. It included an estimated 60,000 whites and received strong and vigorous support from the three major religious faiths. Among Protestants the march was endorsed by a wide range of denominations and organizations, from the National Council of the Churches of Christ, the American Baptist Convention, and the United Presbyterian Church, to individual congregations and clergy of the Methodist and Lutheran Churches. Within the Catholic Church, pastoral letters were read urging support for racial justice and the march, and representatives from several of the archdioceses were sent to the march. Jewish organizations, secular and religious, vigorously promoted the march and sent many of their people to Washington. Dr Joachim Prinz, of the American Jewish Congress, was one of the day's chairmen. So impressed was King with the outpouring of religious support that he commented, "One significant element of the march was the participation of the white churches.

Never before had they been so fully, so enthusiastically involved [in the civil rights movement]" (King 1964:123).

Representatives from these major religious organizations joined the black leaders in the front ranks of the march. Also in front was Walter Reuther of the United Automobile Workers Union, but conspicuously absent from the ranks was any representative from the American Federation of Labor and Congress of Industrial Organizations (AFL-CIO), which had refused its support.

Whites and blacks joined together in a display of interracial harmony and amity over the issue of racial justice that had never been seen before and was to be seen but once more – in a lesser fashion – in Selma, Alabama. As Waskow comments, "The March on Washington was in many ways the high point of 'gladness' in the civil rights movement of the 1960s, and also the high point of coalition between the various elements in the country, white and black, that supported the demand for racial equality" (Waskow 1967:236).

The march ended with a mass meeting before the Lincoln Memorial where a number of demands were made, including a call to Congress and the President for comprehensive civil rights legislation, for training and jobs programs, for fair employment practices laws, and the like. The highlight of the meeting was a stirring speech by Dr Martin Luther King, Jr entitled "I Have a Dream." In it he gave voice to the major hopes and goals of the civil rights movement at that time.

He first reminded his audience that even though the Emancipation Proclamation was signed 100 years ago,

> "we must face the tragic fact that the Negro is still not free. One hundred years later, the life of the Negro is still sadly crippled by the manacles of segregation and the chains of discrimination. One hundred years later, the Negro lives on a lonely island of poverty in the midst of a vast ocean of material prosperity. One hundred years later the Negro still languishes in the corners of American society and finds himself an exile in his own land."   (King 1963:356)

In other words, blacks were still being excluded from the People's Domain that the Founding Fathers had designed through the "magnificent words of the Constitution and the Declaration of Independence" (King 1963:356). The Founding Fathers, King insisted, had not intended this, for when they uttered these words they were in effect "signing a promissory note to which every American was to fall heir. This note was a promise that all men would be guaranteed the inalienable rights of life, liberty, and the pursuit of happiness" (King 1963:356).

America, he continued, "has defaulted on this promissory note insofar as her citizens of color are concerned . . . [but] we refuse to believe that the bank of justice is bankrupt. We refuse to believe that there are insufficient funds in the great vaults of opportunity of this nation. So we have come to cash this check – a check that will give us upon demand the riches of freedom and the security of justice" (King 1963:356).

But, King declared, America can no longer delay in cashing the check for,

"it would be fatal for the nation to overlook the urgency of the moment and to underestimate the determination of the Negro. This sweltering summer of the Negro's legitimate discontent will not pass until there is an invigorating autumn of freedom and equality. Nineteen sixty three is not an end but a beginning.... The whirlwinds of revolt will continue to shake the foundations of our nation until the bright day of justice emerges."   (King 1963:356–57)

The blacks must move ahead firmly and unswervingly against all opposition until they have realized their full rights; but, in the process, he demanded,

"Let us not seek to satisfy our thirst for freedom by drinking from the cup of bitterness and hatred. We must forever conduct our struggle on the high plane of dignity and discipline. We must not allow our creative protest to degenerate into physical violence. Again and again we must rise to the majestic heights of meeting physical force with soul force. The marvelous new militancy which has engulfed the Negro community must not lead us to a distrust of all white people, for many of our white brothers, as evidenced by their presence here today, have come to realize that their destiny is tied up with our destiny and their freedom is inextricably bound to our freedom. We cannot walk alone."
                                                                 (King 1963:357)

He ended his speech on an optimistic note. "I say to you today, my friends, that in spite of the difficulties of the moment I still have a dream. It is a dream deeply rooted in the American dream. I have a dream that one day this nation will rise up and live out the true meaning of its creed: 'We hold these truths to be self-evident; that all men are created equal'" (King 1963:358).

In his concluding paragraph he reaffirmed his hope that some day people of all races and creeds "will be able to join hands and say in the words of the old Negro spiritual, 'Free at last! Free at last! Thank God Almighty, we are free at last!'" (King 1963:359).

Thus King sketched the full credo of the civil rights movement in relatively few, simple, and dramatic words that kept his audience transfixed. Blacks were to press resolutely ahead through nonviolent direct action until the walls of racial segmentation and segregation crumbled and they were able to gain full rights of membership in the People's Domain under the American creed as promised by the Constitution and the Declaration of Independence.

Two years later, in March 1965, the epilogue to the drama of interracial unity and harmony that had climaxed in Washington was played out in Selma, Alabama.

Two months before, King had launched a voter registration drive with mass demonstrations. These had been met forcibly by the police, and at least one black was killed. Police violence crescendoed and reached its peak in a brutal assault on a column of marchers who were going from Selma to Montgomery to present a petition to Governor Wallace for the rights of blacks to vote.

The sight on television of police clubbing defenseless marchers and spraying them with tear gas aroused intense indignation throughout the nation. The anger was compounded several days later by a violent attack on three white Unitarian ministers, one of whom died from his injuries. Protest marches were spontaneously organized in a number of northern cities; resolutions of protest were passed by Connecticut and New Jersey legislatures; and demands for federal intervention and protection flooded the White House.

Two weeks later at least 3000 people started on a second march from Selma to Montgomery. This time the local blacks under King were joined by whites, including clergymen from the three faiths and union leaders, and by black civil rights leaders and others, many of whom had flown in from other parts of the country. The marchers were protected by the Alabama national guard that had been federalized by President Johnson. Relatively few walked the entire distance, but four days later they were joined at the end of their march in Montgomery by approximately 40,000 blacks and whites who had come from all over the country.

And thus ended the last major expression of interracial unity in the civil rights movement. Some whites were also present the following year in the march from Memphis, Tennessee to Jackson, Mississippi that several hundred people, under the joint sponsorship of the CORE, the SNCC, and the SCLC, had resumed for James Meredith, who had been shot earlier while attempting this pilgrimage alone. Thousands of others joined these people at the end of the march in Jackson.

However, the march had little historical relevance as another example of interracial amity; instead, its relevance stems from its having given birth to a phrase that almost immediately came to symbolize a parting of the ways between black and white in the civil rights movement. The phrase was uttered by Stokely Carmichael (SNCC) at a mass meeting in Greenwood, Mississippi during the course of the march. In the midst of a speech attacking racial injustice in Mississippi, he proclaimed, "What we need is black power!" The phrase "black power" was instantly picked up by the marchers and became the regnant slogan of the march and, in later months, of a considerable part of the black protest movement generally. Carmichael had also opted during the planning for the march for black participation only, but had reluctantly agreed, primarily through the urgings of King, to interracial participation. The significance of this turn of events became more evident as black protest moved to the northern ghettos. (We shall examine this in the next chapter.)

CIVIL RIGHTS LEGISLATION AND THE FINAL ASSAULT ON THE LEGAL
FRAMEWORK OF THE PLURAL SOCIETY

As the civil rights movement stepped up pressure against the citadel of the plural society, it became increasingly evident that even with the support of the Supreme Court no more than modest wedges could be driven into the plural society and no more than local victories – spectacular though some might be – could be won. Only the executive and legislative branches of the federal government were capable of a direct and final assault against the legal-normative framework of the plural society.

Thus, the ultimate goal of the hammer-anvil strategy became increasingly delineated in broad and bold terms. The legal fabric of the plural society had to be forced eventually against the anvil of federal authority generally, not merely of the courts specifically, by a hammer whose toughness and strength would be tempered not merely through the pressure of increasing demonstrations but also through the forging of a national coalition of blacks and whites.

Early manifestations of this strategy were already evident during the Eisenhower administration. For example, the passage of the Civil Rights Acts of 1957 and 1960, though confined to voting, was obviously speeded along by the Montgomery bus boycott of 1955 and the sit-in demonstration of 1960. However, not until 1963 in Birmingham were all the major components of the strategy finally in place. As a result, the executive branch of government was forced to take a stand and to exercise a boldness of leadership it had not intended. As we have already seen, early in 1963 President Kennedy was still inclined to do little more than modestly improve earlier civil rights legislation and even that not too aggressively. Berman comments on the sense of drift that pervaded the early stages of hearings on civil rights in the house sub-committee: "an air of complete unreality prevailed, for there could be no action without firm support from the Kennedy Administration, and that support was not forthcoming" (Berman 1966:14). The Kennedy administration even voiced criticism of King's campaign in Birmingham as it was launched in April 1963.

But once the events of Birmingham began to unfold and the cruel and repressive behavior of the police surfaced during the first week of May, President Kennedy could no longer stand on the sidelines as a neutral spectator. He immediately dispatched the head of his Civil Rights Division to mediate the controversy. Within a week an agreement was worked out and the President applauded it at his news conference that day. Two days later he ordered several thousand troops to bases near Birmingham and made plans to federalize the national guard in order to meet the violence and bombings from white extremists that had erupted shortly after the agreement was signed.

But the real watershed in Kennedy's posture on civil rights was to take place several weeks later in his confrontation with Governor Wallace over a court order to admit two blacks to the University of Alabama. He overwhelmed the governor's defiance of the order through a show of federal force. That night he delivered before a nationwide television audience his most dramatic and far-ranging attack on racial injustice, segregation, and discrimination and committed himself openly to strong and comprehensive legislation on civil rights. One week later, he spelled out his legislative proposals in a special message to Congress and reaffirmed his determination to see the matter through. And thus was the omnibus Civil Rights Act of 1964 truly born. Ironically Kennedy's own death provided the final impetus for its early passage in 1964: as President Johnson said in an address to a joint session of Congress five days after the assassination, "'No memorial oration or eulogy could more eloquently honor President Kennedy's memory than the earliest possible passage of the civil rights bill for which he fought so long'" (Berman 1966:48).

Somewhat over a year later, President Johnson was himself caught in the middle of a voter registration drive begun by King in Selma, Alabama. Johnson intervened personally as the brutality and violence of the police sent waves of indignation throughout the nation, but he failed to gain the support of Governor Wallace for a peaceful resolution to the problem. A week later the President announced at a televised news conference that he would submit a Voting Rights Bill to Congress that would have the teeth missing from all earlier voting rights laws. He also provided troop protection for the celebrated second march from Selma to Montgomery. Thus, the passage of the two most important civil rights acts of the twentieth century can be directly linked to the pressures of the civil rights movement and of a nationwide reaction against brutality by legally constituted authority.

EPILOGUE: DR MARTIN LUTHER KING'S "WHERE DO WE GO FROM HERE?"

In a somber appraisal of the civil rights struggle a year after the signing of the Voting Rights Act of 1965, Dr King acknowledged that it had advanced America well beyond where it was at the end of the first period of reconstruction. It had even shaken the normative foundations of the plural society, but he cautioned that much more was still to be done. For, he insisted, only the first phase had been completed in the struggle by the black for equality. What had been accomplished was to grant the black the right to be treated "with a degree of decency, not of equality. White America was ready to demand that the Negro should be spared the lash of brutality and coarse degradation" (King 1967:3). In short, the black could no longer be deprived self-righteously or legitimately by the white society of the rights and immunities of membership in the People's Domain or denied the legal right of access to the major institutional terrains of that Domain.

However, these civil rights victories, Dr King maintained, cost America very little and required, in fact, very little sacrifice from the white.

"The practical cost of change for the nation up to this point has been cheap. The limited reforms have been obtained at bargain rates. There are no expenses, and no taxes are required, for Negroes to share lunch counters, libraries, parks, hotels, and other facilities with whites. Even the psychological adjustment is far from formidable. Having exaggerated the emotional difficulties for decades, when demands for new conduct became inescapable, white Southerners may have trembled under the strain but they did not collapse.

Even the more significant changes involved in voter registration required neither large monetary nor psychological sacrifice. Spectacular and turbulent events that dramatized the demand created an erroneous impression that a heavy burden was involved."   (King 1967:5)

But now America, King argued, would have to face the deeply entrenched and massive historical consequences of these generations of racial discrimination, exploitation, and segregation: the searing and widespread poverty and destitution of the black masses and their lack of education and occupational skills. To meet this challenge, he insisted, America would have to resort to large-scale allocation of resources and funds and a shifting of national priorities. It might even have to give the black "special treatment" in order to give him his historical "due." For, "a society that has done something special *against* the Negro for hundreds of years must now do something special *for* him, in order to equip him to compete on a just and equal basis" (King 1967:90).

This would not come cheaply, King continued; thus, "the real cost lies ahead.... The discount education given Negroes will in the future have to be purchased at full price if quality education is to be realized. Jobs are harder and costlier to create than voting rolls. The eradication of slums housing millions is complex far beyond integrating buses and lunch counters" (King 1967:5–6).

White America, King declared, has shown increasing resistance to moving into the next phase of the black quest for equality and justice and to bearing the cost of meeting this challenge. As evidence of this, he referred to the violence of whites that he had personally experienced in his marches in Chicago, to the white "backlash" in elections in California, Maryland and elsewhere, and to the fracturing of the white-black civil rights coalition. He was particularly disturbed over the growing disaffection of white liberals with the civil rights struggle, for he considered them the key to bringing the rest of white America around to facing up to its responsibilities to the black. He recognized their unease to be in part due to the escalating violence in the streets and to the expanding popularity of black power slogans among blacks, but he insisted that behind their withdrawal was their greater preference for order than for justice. He called on them to keep the increasing tension in proper historical perspective. "It is important for the liberal to see that the oppressed who agitates for his rights is not the creator of tension. He merely brings out the hidden tension that is already alive" (King 1967:91).

But above all, he was fearful that whites generally, the liberals included, wanted to preserve their advantaged position and to maintain the status quo.

"The persistence of racism in depth and the dawning awareness that Negro demands will necessitate structural changes in society have generated a new phase of white resistance in North and South. Based on the cruel judgment that Negroes have come far enough, there is a strong mood to bring the civil rights movement to a halt or reduce it to a crawl. Negro demands that yesterday evoked admiration and support, today – to many – have become tiresome, unwarranted, and a disturbance to the enjoyment of life. Cries of Black Power and riots are not the causes of white resistance, they are consequences of it."

(King 1967:11−12)

Dr King also expressed great concern at the direction the struggle was taking among blacks: the increasing role of violence and the burgeoning popularity of the black power slogan. He hoped to counter this by reaffirming the viability of his strategy of nonviolent direct action; and, to this end, he sought to remind blacks not to underestimate what it had accomplished in the struggle in the South:

"The historic achievement is found in the fact that the movement in the South has profoundly shaken the entire edifice of segregation. This is an accomplishment whose consequences are deeply felt by every Southern Negro in his daily life. It is no longer possible to count the number of public establishments that are open to Negroes. The persistence of segregation is not the salient fact of Southern experience; the proliferating areas in which the Negro moves freely is the new advancing truth.

    The South was the stronghold of racism. In the white migrations through history from the South to the North and West, racism was carried to poison the rest of the nation. Prejudice, discrimination and bigotry had been intricately embedded in all institutions of Southern life, political, social, and economic. There could be no possibility of life-transforming change anywhere so long as the vast and solid influence of Southern segregation remained unchallenged and unhurt. The ten-year assault at the roots was fundamental to undermining the system. What distinguished this period from all preceding decades was that it constituted the first frontal attack on racism at its heart."   (King 1967:13−14)

But now he recognized that the battleground had to include also the North: "Concentration of effort in the large Northern cities can no longer be postponed in favor of Southern campaigns. Both must now be sustained" (King 1967:19). To mount such a formidable undertaking, he called for organized unity among blacks with strategic reliance on mass nonviolent demonstrations whenever and wherever necessary. He also pleaded with them to avoid violence:

> "The American racial revolution has been a revolution to 'get in' rather than to overthrow. We want a share in the American economy, the housing market, the educational system, and the social opportunities. This goal itself indicates that a social change in America must be nonviolent. If one is in search of a better job, it does not help to burn down the factory. If one needs more adequate education, shooting the principal will not help. If housing is the goal, only building and construction will produce that end. To destroy anything, person or property, cannot bring us closer to the goal that we seek."   (King 1967:130)

Despite his urgings, black protest in the North took a more militant and radicalized direction during the 1960s. In the next chapter we shall examine the response of the urban black in the North to the racial struggle.

12

THE *DE FACTO* PLURAL SOCIETY
AND BLACK MILITANCE
IN THE NORTH

Introduction

At no period during the twentieth century did racial injustice and inequality seem more like a regional problem than from the end of World War II until the early 1960s. For just as the states in the Deep South moved to consolidate and to reaffirm the legal basis of white supremacy and the plural society during this period, particularly after the Brown ruling, so many states in the other parts of the country seemed to move in the opposite direction toward a society of racial equality. They enacted a wide range of nondiscriminatory legislation for the major institutional environments of the social realm.

For example, prior to this period only a few laws had been passed by a handful of states for any of these environments, except possibly for that of public accommodations. Even in that area, once the flurry during the first reconstruction had subsided and eighteen states had passed laws on public accommodations no other state added similar legislation to its books until the 1950s. Then in rapid succession Oregon, Montana, and New Mexico rekindled the legislative process that eventuated by the mid-1960s in public accommodation laws for virtually every state but those from the Deep South. In other institutional areas such as employment, approximately a dozen states had a scattering of statutes that proscribed discrimination in specific fields of work, such as civil service and public utilities, but none had a comprehensive fair employment practices law until the mid-1940s. Then New York passed the first such state law; New Jersey, Massachusetts, and Connecticut came next; and by 1960 the total reached seventeen states. Even more virginal was the area of housing and residential dwellings, for not until 1949 when Connecticut acted did any state prescribe a remedy for discrimination in public housing project; prior to that only several had even a "toothless" law against such discrimination. In 1955 New York was the "first state to ban discrimination in certain types of housing which receive mortgage repayment guarantees from the Federal Housing Administration, the Veterans Administration or any other governmental agency" (Konvitz and Leskes 1961:237). But not until 1959 was the first fair housing law passed at the state level that prohibited discrimination in private housing. Only five states had passed such a law by 1961, but by then a number of others outside the South had passed some version of the earlier and more selective housing acts. Thus by the early 1960s a fabric of nondiscriminatory laws had been widely woven into the major institutional areas of most states of the North and West, but for most states the fabric was less than a decade old.

Also supportive of the view that the North had decisively parted normative company with the South over the race issue was the response of northern white liberals to the mounting civil rights crisis in the South in the late 1950s and early 1960s. More than any other white group in America they represented the national conscience to which King had appealed and the moral conscience which Myrdal had much earlier insisted was essential for resolving America's racial dilemma (Myrdal 1944). These liberals were very much behind the civil rights laws being enacted in the states of the North and West at this time. Many even joined forces with blacks in an interracial coalition, which marched in Washington, Selma, and elsewhere and which spearheaded the drive for congressional action on the civil rights legislation of the mid-1960s. These liberals seemed to have taken upon themselves the role of racial gatekeeper and advocate who would escort the black into full membership in the various realms of the People's Domain under the American creed, first in the North and later hopefully in the South.

However, by the mid-1960s a series of racial disturbances and riots ripped through cities of the North and West and stripped away the optimism of the liberal and the veneer of racial equality with which the legal codes of many of these states had just been coated. They laid bare the petrified boundaries of racial segmentation and white dominance that had long been embedded in the major institutional environments of the social realm. This northern version of a plural society had frozen most blacks to the bottom of the occupational class ladder and had confined them to the black ghettos in slum areas. Long nourished and legitimized by the racial creed and the "separate-but-equal" doctrine of the Supreme Court, the plural structure had lost its *quasi de jure* status by the mid-1960s with the delegitimation of the creed and doctrine in 1954 and with the passage of state laws on nondiscrimination and racial equality, but it still seemed as viable as ever as a *de facto* system of racial segmentation and inequality.

The urban riots, however, did more than make visible the underlying *de facto* plural structure. They also energized, politicized, and radicalized the subsequent black challenge to white dominance and to the plural structure. Much of this challenge came to view racial inequality and the historical exclusion of the black from full membership in the People's Domain and from the benefits of the American creed as an inevitable and permanent feature of a white society. Accordingly, it moved ideologically toward separatism and nationalism and reconceptualized the historical encounter of blacks with white America in terms of a colonial analogy.

In this chapter we shall examine the catalytic function of the urban riots and the radicalization of the black challenge to white dominance and the plural structure. We shall pay particular attention to three of the major contributors to the ideological expression of this radicalization: Malcolm X and his black nationalism, Stokely Carmichael and his black power, and the Black Panther party and its revolutionary nationalism. We shall assess the adequacy of the colonial analogy as an explanation of the black's encounter with the American society, and we shall then look at the neocolonialist interpretation for the emergence of the new black middle class and for the growing impoverishment of the black masses. We shall conclude with an evaluation of the most recent attempt by a black sociologist to account for these same phenomena.

The urban riots

THE SEQUENTIAL PATTERNING OF THE RIOTS

By the mid-1960s the fuse that King had lit in Birmingham detonated explosions in cities of the North, Midwest, and Far West, as increasing numbers of blacks began to take to the streets in some form of public protest. During 1963 these protests remained for the most part relatively limited in scope and nonviolent in nature. In Detroit, for example, thousands marched and demonstrated against racial discrimination and in support of King's Birmingham campaign. In Chicago well over 200,000 black students boycotted public schools in protest against *de facto* segregation; a much smaller number did the same in Boston. In New York City demonstrations for jobs were conducted daily during the summer at various construction sites for public buildings. Arrests were made as black pickets lay down in the path of trucks to stop work on the sites, but no violence was reported. In Philadelphia, however, a similar demonstration for jobs at a construction site for a public school developed into an open clash between white workers and black pickets.

With the summer of 1964 the politics of the street began to erupt more frequently into violence. The initial explosion of the summer was triggered in mid-July by the killing of a black teenager by a white policeman in Harlem. Rallies and riots followed upon each other as blacks vented their anger and hostility against the police. The rioting tapered off within three days but not before more than a hundred blacks were injured and at least one killed. By the fourth night the rioting spread to the Bedford Stuyvesant area in Brooklyn where a pitched battle was fought between black youths and police. Again, like the Harlem riot, over a hundred people were injured and at least one killed but, unlike Harlem, looting of shop stores was a central feature of the Brooklyn outburst. Almost a week after the Harlem explosion began on July 24, blacks in Rochester, New York reacted violently to the arrest of a black at a street dance in the ghetto and virtually engulfed the police, who had to call for state police reinforcement to extricate themselves. For two nights rioting continued; order was only restored with the calling in of the national guard. Over 300 people were hurt and four killed.

Another arrest triggered two nights of rioting in early August in Jersey City; forty-four persons were hurt. A week later a similar incident set off several nights of disorder in Elizabeth and Patterson, New Jersey where approximately fourteen persons were hurt. In mid-August the violence shifted to the Midwest, a suburb of Chicago. Again an arrest was the precipitating event. In this instance a black woman had been arrested on the complaint of a white store owner that she had stolen a bottle of liquor. Angered by the owner's alleged manhandling of the woman, blacks focused their attack on the store, eventually setting it on fire. For two nights disturbances continued with over fifty people being injured. The final outbreak of the summer took place at the end of August in Philadelphia. Again an arrest, this time for a traffic offense, led to confrontation between the blacks and the police. For several nights rioting and looting on a scale not hitherto witnessed in any of the disturbances ravaged the city; approximately 350 people were hurt, including 67 policemen.

Thus the summer of 1964 witnessed a series of confrontations between blacks and police on the streets of a number of cities, but these proved to be minor skirmishes in contrast to the massive confrontation that exploded in Watts in August 1965. The Watts riot started, as did the earlier ones, with a relatively routine traffic arrest. The incident soon turned ugly as a gathering crowd of blacks began to vent its anger over the allegedly excessive use of force by the police. Rocks were thrown, cars were overturned and set afire, and white motorists were beaten. But not until the following evening after a day of relative calm did the black response escalate into full-scale rioting. By the next day the disorders had spread throughout the entire black area and took an increasingly devastating toll of life and property over the next several days.

A central target of the rioters was business and commercial establishments. They firebombed and wiped out scores of these stores and buildings and smashed windows and looted *en masse* many others. Over 500 buildings were ravaged in this manner, at an estimated cost of 35 to 100 million dollars in damages.

The streets of Watts soon took on the appearance of a battlefield as rocks and gunfire were exchanged between rioters and police. By Friday August 13, the national guard was called in and a curfew ordered by the governor. Almost without hesitation, guardsmen began to fire at anyone suspected of being a sniper. That night the riot reached its peak of fury and violence under a hail of bullets, firebombs, and rocks. Watts had become a battlefield.

By late Saturday the number of guardsmen swelled to almost 14,000, and slowly their massive show of force succeeded in restoring some semblance of control. By August 21, enough order had been reestablished so as to permit the withdrawal of the national guard. The cost in human lives was great. Thirty-four persons were killed, thirty-one of whom were blacks, and many hundreds were injured. No white civilians were killed, despite the fact that a number were attacked and injured. Three white officials were killed in the line of duty, although only one of them was killed from the gunfire by blacks.

The impact of Watts was so profound and traumatic that it sent shock waves throughout the nation and marked the beginning of the end of a mythological innocence about the historical character and meaning of the black encounter in the North; no longer would this encounter be seen in the same simplistic, optimistic, and liberalistic terms. (We shall discuss this more fully later.) As the Kerner commission stated, "The Los Angeles riot, the worst in the United States since the Detroit riot of 1943, shocked all who had been confident that race relations were improving in the North, and evoked a new mood in Negro ghettos across the country" (The National Advisory Commission on Civil Disorders 1968:20).

This new mood and resolve of the blacks in the North blossomed in 1966 through disorder, demonstration, and riot to the extent that the Kerner commission observed, "The events of 1966 made it appear that domestic turmoil had become part of the American scene" (The National Advisory Commission on Civil Disorders 1968:20). By spring another flare-up erupted in Watts, again precipitated by an arrest, but the subsequent riot was only a pale version of the previous year's, though two people were killed – one black, the other white – and twenty-six others were injured.

Much more serious was the rioting that broke out in Chicago in the middle of July. Triggered by a minor police action – the turning off of a water hydrant which was being used to cool youngsters during an extended hot spell – the disorder soon escalated into a full-scale rampage of looting, arson, rock-throwing, and gunfire. Order was restored only after the national guard moved in, but not before two blacks were killed and many more injured.

Racial conflict in Chicago extended beyond the ghetto border at the end of July, as Dr King led a series of street demonstrations and marches against racial segregation in housing through predominantly white suburbs. Whites attacked the marchers, and at least three were injured. The demonstrations continued until the end of August when King reached an agreement with local officials on ending discrimination in the renting and selling of houses.

In Cleveland, Ohio rioting broke out on July 18 in the Hough section of the black ghetto and was not quelled until four nights later by the national guard. Four blacks were killed, two by law officers and the other two by a white sniper and a group of white "vigilantes" outside the riot area; over 100 buildings were firebombed and many were totally destroyed.

Toward the end of September, the worst rioting in the history of San Francisco erupted over the shooting of a black youth by a white policeman in a car theft incident. Over a three-day period, at least fifty people were injured, close to 400 were arrested, and damages from looting and arson ran well over $150,000. All in all, according to the Kerner commission, "forty-three disorders and riots were reported during 1966. Although there were considerable variations in circumstances, intensity, and length, they were usually ignited by a minor incident fueled by antagonism between the Negro population and the police" (The National Advisory Commission on Civil Disorders 1968:21).

Urban rioting and civil disturbances continued to gain momentum during 1967 so that by the end of the first nine months, according to the Kerner commission, 164 disorders had broken out throughout the country. Eight of these disorders were defined as "major" by the commission because they possessed the following four characteristics: "(1) many fires, intensive looting, and reports of sniping; (2) violence lasting more than two days; (3) sizeable crowds; and (4) use of National Guard or Federal forces as well as other control forces" (The National Advisory Commission on Civil Disorders 1968:65). Thirty-three others were defined as "serious but not major;" and the remaining 123, as of "minor" significance.

Though the disorders of 1967 first erupted in the South, only one of the southern disorders, that in Tampa, Florida, developed into a major disturbance; of the other seven major disturbances, three took place in the East; and four, in the Midwest.

The first of these seven broke out in Cincinnati during the second week of June. The precipitating event was the arrest of a black for carrying a placard on the street protesting the murder conviction of another black. Its background was a history of growing tension between blacks and local authorities over discriminatory treatment in the courts, in the job market, and by government officials and police. The riot itself did not generate full fury until the second night with its barrage of rocks and bottles, firebombings, looting, desultory gunfire, and massive street confrontations between police and blacks. Order was slowly restored with the arrival of the national guard, but not until one person was killed, and sixty-three others were injured. Over 400 were arrested and property damage exceeded a million dollars. A distinctive feature of this riot was the number of whites caught up in its vortex. A white motorist was the one person to be slain, and over four out of five persons reported injured were white.

Two weeks later the second major altercation of the North erupted in Buffalo, New York. By the second night well over a thousand blacks were roaming the streets, smashing windows, setting fires, throwing rocks, and on occasion firing guns. By its end, sixty-eight people were hurt, some of whom were white passersby, over 200 were arrested, and damage exceeded $100,000.

Dwarfing by far the confrontations in Cincinnati and Buffalo was the third major riot of the North; it erupted in Newark, New Jersey on July 13. Triggered spontaneously by the arrest of a black cab driver, the riot brought to the surface the long smoldering resentment and anger of blacks against discriminatory treatment, and also brought to a head a long intensifying struggle between black and white over control and allocation of resources and power in the community, from jobs and the location of a medical center, to control of the board of education. Unlike most of the earlier riots, the black militants sought actively to articulate these concerns symbolically and politically on the streets. Even cries of "black power" were heard, but the militants were unable to channelize the spontaneous and randomized street response into a disciplined and organized movement. Instead, large bands of rioters roamed the city, particularly through the principal business district, firebombing stores, smashing their windows, and looting their merchandise. Gunfire and sniping also occurred at sporadic intervals.

By the third day, the national guard bolstered the ranks of local law enforcement officials but, instead of dampening the violence, the reinforced body helped transform Newark for the next few days into a battlefield. According to the Kerner commission, the guardsmen, police, and state troopers, nervous and without effective liaison and leadership, all too frequently unleashed massive fire power against buildings and other sites at the slightest suspicion of sniping; on occasion they wound up firing at each other.

For six days Newark was ravaged. Twenty-three people were killed, including twenty-one blacks and two whites – one a detective and the other a fireman. Over 1200 people were injured and an even greater number were arrested. Property damage exceeded ten million dollars, of which 80 percent was due to looting and other stock loss. Damage to buildings and fixtures was in the neighborhood of two million dollars.

Within several days of its inception, the tensions and unease had spread from Newark to other communities in northern New Jersey. Local authorities in Jersey City, Elizabeth, and Englewood sought to offset the mounting black discontent by beefing up police patrols and by proclaiming a "get tough" policy. This did not prevent the outbreak of disorderly incidents, the more serious being in the latter two communities. None of these incidents, however, reached the level of violence and destruction that exploded in Plainfield several days after the Newark riot began. The Plainfield rioting peaked three days after the first outburst, which was triggered by the shooting of a young black by a white police officer who was then beaten to death by a crowd of enraged young blacks. A special note of fear was added to the Plainfield disturbances by the seizure of forty carbines by blacks and by the subsequent rumor that they were to be used in the melee. Sporadic gunfire and sniping did occur, but the threat of massive retaliation never materialized. In turn, the police cordoned off the area, and two days later the national guard conducted a house-to-house search of the area to no avail; no carbines were found. Unlike Newark, though, law enforcement officials showed restraint in their use of firepower; only once during the riot was it reported that they had engaged in a general firing of their guns.

The climactic disturbance of that summer took place in Detroit from July 23 to July 27; its ferocity, violence, and destructiveness exceeded even that of Watts or of any other urban riot that came after Watts. In many respects the black ghetto in Detroit was transformed into a combat zone: more firepower was unleashed there than in Newark or Watts, and as the riot subsided the ghetto resembled an occupied country with tanks, armored personnel carriers, and troops patrolling the streets.

The riot began, as did many of the other, with a confrontation between police and local blacks. This time it was an early morning raid on all illegal drinking club that triggered the disturbance. Not expecting the more than eighty patrons they found there, the police were too few in number to complete the raid speedily; as a result a large and restless crowd had collected around the club by the time the last of the patrons had been driven off in a police wagon. Within several hours, thousands of blacks were roaming the streets, and by late morning widespread window smashing and looting were reported as well as the first instances of firebombing. However, not until early afternoon was it evident that a full-scale riot was in the making. By then the crowds had turned increasingly belligerent as rumors of police brutality swept through them. The crowds pelted the police and firemen with rocks, bottles, and other objects; looting escalated as did firebombing.

By late afternoon the police had virtually lost control of the situation; the mayor sent a formal request to the governor for the national guard. Several hours later he also announced a curfew and the governor shortly after that proclaimed a "state of public emergency." By early morning 800 state police officers and 1200 national guardsmen had joined the Detroit police on the streets, with 8000 more guardsmen on their way. The mayor also solicited assistance from the federal government, but the governor balked at declaring the state of insurrection that he thought was demanded by the United States Attorney General as a condition for federal assistance. After several hours, the matter was resolved short of such a declaration; the President dispatched paratroopers to a base near Detroit, and later that evening he federalized the Michigan national guard and authorized the use of paratroopers in the city.

Though the governor may have refused to proclaim a state of insurrection, Detroit took on the character of a city under siege as guardsmen and, later, paratroopers in trucks, jeeps, tanks, and personnel carriers poured into the city. By the time they began to patrol the streets, sniper fire had already become part of the scene, although the first instance of sniping was not reported until several hours after the mayor's curfew proclamation. So worried and obsessed with the dangers of sniper fire did the police and guardsmen – neither of whom had any training in riot control – become that they frequently brought to bear massive firepower at the merest rumor of a sniper in the vicinity. The Kerner commission report describes graphically instances where a random or accidental shot, not infrequently by a guardsman himself, triggered a massive fusillade of cannon, machine gun, and rifle fire, at times to the fatal detriment of an innocent bystander. As a result, police and guardsmen accounted for seven of every ten deaths resulting from the riots. Only the paratroopers maintained rigid discipline under the firm leadership of their commanding officer; they fired relatively few rounds of ammunition. As a result, only one riot death was due to their action.

Report of sniping mounted steadily during the riot so that by the third day they reached well over 800. As these reports proliferated, the pressure on law enforcement officers to uncover the snipers became intense. Homes were broken into. Searches were made on the flimsiest of tips. A Detroit newspaper aptly proclaimed: "'Everyone's Suspect in No Man's Land'" (The National Advisory Commission on Civil Disorders 1968:59).

The actual incidence of sniping was obviously a mere fraction of the number reported as sniping, but the exact figure is still unknown. However, it is evident that fewer than one out of ten riot deaths was caused by the rioters themselves. In addition, 22 of the 27 persons charged with sniping had charges against them dismissed at preliminary hearings; two others had their charges dismissed later. In other words, sniper fire accounted for only a small portion of the total firepower that ravaged the area; most came from the guns of the police and guardsmen.

The final cost in human lives and property exceeded that for any other urban riot. Forty-three persons – 33 black and 10 white – were killed. Of the 43, 18 died of gunshot wounds, including 11 black citizens, 4 white citizens, 1 white guardsman, 1 white fireman, and 1 black private guard. Injuries were sustained by countless hundreds, and over 700 persons were arrested. Initially, damage estimates exceeded $500 million but these were later scaled down. "The city assessor's office placed the loss – excluding business stock, private furnishings, and the buildings of churches and charitable institutions – at approximately $22 million. Insurance payments, according to the State Insurance Bureau, will come to about $32 million, representing an estimated 65 to 75 percent of the total loss" (The National Advisory Commission on Civil Disorders 1968:61).

Within a day of the riot's onset, the violence of Detroit spread to a number of surrounding communities in Michigan. For two days, arson, looting, and gunfire erupted in Flint, Grand Rapids, Pontiac, and Saginaw. None, however, was more than a minor disturbance as compared to Detroit, although two blacks were killed in Pontiac and 400 people were injured in Grand Rapids.

Even as the Michigan disturbances were subsiding, disorders broke out in other cities of the North and continued to do so for the next month in such diverse places as Syracuse, New Haven, Providence, and Wichita. The most serious of these disturbances exploded in Milwaukee on July 31. So widespread were the firebombing, looting, and sniper fire that a state of emergency was proclaimed, a curfew was imposed, and the national guard was called in. The toll of the riot was four people dead, approximately 100 injured, and over 500 arrested. Property damage exceeded $200,000.

The last major outbreak of urban disorders followed the assassination of King in April 1968. Within days violence spread to 110 cities and widespread looting, arson, and gunfire were reported. By the time the disturbances had run their course, 34 blacks and 5 whites had been killed. Twenty-five of the slain died of gunshot wounds, 10 died in fires, and 4 from other causes. The police killed 11 of those slain by gunfire, 9 were shot by unknown persons, and 5 by private citizens. In addition to the 39 who were slain, well over 2500 people were injured and more than 14,000 were arrested. National guardsmen and federal troops were deployed by the thousands in more than a dozen cities, and property damage exceeded $45 million.

The disorders reached their crescendo in Chicago and Washington, DC from April 5 to 7. Eighteen people lost their lives in the two cities alone (11 in Chicago and 7 in Washington) and 1000 more in each city were injured. Property damage ran into the millions as widespread looting and firebombing ravaged the area. Both guardsmen and federal troops were called in, and curfews were imposed. Lesser disturbances erupted in such places as Pittsburgh, New York City, and Kansas City. Even the two cities, Detroit and Newark, that had been devastated by the summer riots of 1967 were touched – albeit slightly – by the tidal wave of disorders.

Once the disturbances of April had run their course, only a few minor outbreaks as in Salisbury, Maryland and Louisville, Kentucky in May marred the uneasy quiet that descended over the cities of the North and South. For all intents and purposes the cycle of urban racial riots had drawn to a close.

THE RIOTS AS RADICALIZED STREET PROTEST

The national alarm over the urban riots spawned major governmental efforts to study and to explain them. The first investigation was conducted by a commission set up by Governor Brown of California in August 1965 and headed by John McCone, to investigate the Watts riot. The second and even more comprehensive study was undertaken by the National Advisory Commission on Civil Disorders established by President Johnson on July 29 1967 and headed by Otto Kerner, former governor of Illinois. A third was a commission set up by Governor Hughes of New Jersey to examine the Newark riot of 1967.

In its pioneering effort to explain the urban riots, the McCone commission defined the problem in the traditional terms of law and order versus criminal and deviant behavior. With this as its frame of reference, the commission concluded that the Watts riot was caused by a small number of blacks – estimated at 2 percent of the local black population – who were not only alienated from the larger society but who were also unable to fit into the black community. In other words, according to the commission the rioters included the uprooted, the drifters, the unemployed, and the uneducated. They were, in short, the "riff-raff" of society whose chronic "despair" was broken by the "momentary relief" of "mass violence." But this "relief," the commission continued, was "a formless, quite senseless, all but hopeless violent protest – enjoyed in by a few but bringing great distress to all" (The Governor's Commission on the Los Angeles Riots 1965:5). In the final analysis "the rioters seemed to have been caught up in an insensate rage of destruction" (The Governor's Commission on the Los Angeles Riots 1965:1) which erupted spontaneously without planning or effective leadership.

The larger society, the McCone commission argued, has to bear its share of responsibility for nurturing the social pathologies and discriminatory practices that have led to the personal disorganization, anger, frustration, and anomie of the rioter; for schools, government, public welfare, and business have failed to address themselves effectively to the problem.

The commission found little fault with the conduct of law enforcement agencies during the riot. It recognized that blacks were highly critical of the performance of the agencies, but the commission gave short shrift to the black charge of police brutality. Instead it expressed concern with the charge itself "for there is a real danger that persistent criticism will reduce and perhaps destroy the effectiveness of law enforcement."

What was needed, according to the commission, was a better understanding between police and blacks: "We call for a better understanding by the law enforcement agencies of Negro community attitudes and, on the other hand, a more widespread understanding within the Negro community of the value of the police and the extent to which the law enforcement agencies provide it with security" (The Governor's Commission on the Los Angeles Riots 1965:29).

To the commission the police and law were agencies of the community, both expressing and protecting its peaceful solidarity against violence, chaos, and anarchy, and therefore must never be "rendered impotent" (The Governor's Commission on the Los Angeles Riots 1965:29).

The commission also dismissed consumer exploitation as a factor in the riots. It found no evidence "that there was a vengeance pattern to the destruction of stores in the curfew area, that it was a retribution on merchants who were said to 'take from the area but put nothing back into it'" (The Governor's Commission on the Los Angeles Riots 1965:70). In a similar vein, the commission rejected a conspiratorial interpretation for the riot: "There is no reliable evidence of outside leadership or preestablished plans for the rioting" (The Governor's Commission on the Los Angeles Riots 1965:22).

The commission report was issued in December 1965, and almost immediately its basic findings and interpretations were widely challenged. At the very heart of the criticism was the contention that the commission "completely misunderstood the character and implications of the Los Angeles riots" (Fogelson 1969:116). Though sympathetic to the plight of the black in the slums, according to the critics the report had nevertheless approached the matter and defined the problem entirely from the perspective of the established white authority and the dominant white middle class. It had, in other words, made no effort to look at the situation and to define it as the blacks themselves might have. As a result,

> "They [the commissioners] brought to their task assorted preconceptions about violence, law enforcement, ghettos, and slums, preconceptions which they share with others of their class and race. These preconceptions – they emerge clearly from the hearings and, less so, from the report – prevented the commission from perceptively analyzing the evidence and correctly interpreting the riots. For they filtered the testimony and other information received by the commissioners and enabled them to draw conclusions based on the flimsiest material while ignoring more substantial but less reassuring data."   (Fogelson 1969:118)

What was at the root of these shortcomings, according to the critics, was the failure of the commission to collect the kinds of data that would have allowed it, had it so chosen, to address itself to the black point of view. Such data were collected after the riots by the Institute of Government and Public Affairs of

UCLA in personal interviews with black residents of Watts and black riot arrestees, two of the seven basic populations the Institute surveyed in its various studies.

The results of the survey struck a serious blow at the commission's thesis that the riot was the handiwork of a small number of "riff-raff" who were marginal to and out of step with the black community. According to the study, at least seven times as many people actively participated in the riots than were projected to have participated by the commission; the figure jumped from the commission's 2 percent of the black residents to 15 percent in the survey. The study also showed that young people were much more active than older people; men, more active than women. Suggestive findings on the relationship between riot participation and education, occupation, and length of residence in Watts also pointed away from the "riff-raff" theory. However, not until the publication of the Kerner commission report on the 1967 riots did a definitive portrait of the riot participant emerge which finally laid to rest this theory of the McCone commission.

Having made a concerted effort to obtain systematic data from the blacks in a way that the McCone commission never had, the Kerner commission was able to delineate in striking detail the differences between the black as riot participant and bystander.

> "The typical rioter in the summer of 1967 was a Negro, unmarried male between the ages of 15 and 24. He was in many ways very different from the stereotype. He was not a migrant. He was born in the state and was a lifelong resident of the city in which the riot took place. Economically his position was about the same as his Negro neighbors who did not actively participate in the riot.
>
> Although he had not, usually, graduated from high school, he was somewhat better educated than the average inner-city Negro, having at least attended high school for a time.
>
> Nevertheless, he was more likely to be working in a menial or low status job as an unskilled laborer. If he was employed, he was not working full time and his employment was frequently interrupted by periods of unemployment."
>
> (The National Advisory Commission on Civil Disorders 1968:73)

The riot participant was therefore not the kind of drifter, deviant, illiterate, and societal reject that the McCone commission had portrayed him as.

What is more, the riot participant was not alone in his response to the situation, as the McCone commission insisted. He operated in a sympathetic milieu of fellow blacks. This is the conclusion of Sears and McConahay in their analysis of data from the Watts survey. They estimate that about one out of three blacks in the curfew area (31 percent) were "active spectators to the disturbance" in which an additional one out of seven (15 percent) were actively participating. The spectators "were on the streets, close enough to see crowds of people, and stores being looted and burned. It seems clear that they formed permissive, if not actively supportive, audience for the rioting. The proportion in the crowds who actively opposed the rioting was very small" (Sears and McConahay 1970:279–80).

They elaborated on the scope of black community support for the riot in the conclusion to their analysis:

> "The picture portrayed by these data is one of widespread community involvement in the riot, though it does not rule out the possibility that certain acts were the work of a small minority. But it must be emphasized again that a majority of the area's inhabitants were involved in the incidents, at one level or another. Further, our data imply that the burning and looting of places of business, if not the shooting and rock throwing, took place in open view of and with the passive consent (if not approval) of a majority of the Negro community."
>
> (Sears and McConahay 1970:279–80)

Somewhat over two years after release of the McCone Commission report, the Kerner commission found in its fifteen-city survey that black support for the urban riots had not diminished; in fact it may well have increased. According to the survey, a majority of the respondents expressed sympathy for their fellow blacks who joined the riots, though they themselves would refuse to do so.

In their analysis of survey data from black and white residents of the curfew zone of Watts, Tomlinson and Sears scuttled still another major conclusion of the McCone commission – that the rioting was an irrational and senseless act of rage and destruction (Tomlinson and Sears 1970). They reported that a majority of the black respondents were convinced that the Watts riot had a broader purpose and goal; the white respondents were even more convinced that it had none. Its purpose, according to most blacks, was to protest against the racial discrimination and unfair treatment of blacks and the oppressive and exploitative conditions of their life and to call society's attention to these problems. The blacks were also quite sanguine about the outcome of this protest. They believed it would make whites more aware of and sympathetic to the problems of blacks. The majority of whites were of the opposite opinion: they were convinced that the riot would only hurt the cause of the black, that it would make whites less sympathetic to their problems, and that it would increase the gap between the races.

Later in the Kerner commission survey, most blacks continued to define the riots as protests against unfair conditions and to emphasize their beneficial effects on the struggle of rights for the blacks. White respondents were much less inclined than those in the Watts survey to define the urban riots as protest; almost as many viewed the riots as an exercise in lawless looting as viewed them as protest. Most of the white respondents, however, retained the conviction of their Watts counterparts that the riots hurt the cause of black rights.

In defining the Watts disturbance as a protest, many black residents expressed misgivings about applying a term to it that conveyed the notion of inchoate violence. As a result, almost as many of them referred to the disturbance as a "revolt," "revolution," or "insurrection" as referred to it as a "riot." However, even those who used a revolutionary term were not prepared to view the disturbance as a planned uprising masterminded by radicals and extremists. Instead they saw it, as did the McCone commission, as a spontaneous, spur-of-the-moment explosion.

The blacks were also inclined, in the Kerner commission survey, to stress the unplanned character of the 1967 disturbances. Many whites, however, were convinced by then that the urban riots were planned and were the handiwork of radicalized extremists. They had bought a conspiratorial theory that the McCone commission had earlier rejected.

Though in basic agreement with the McCone Commission's characterization of the disturbance as unplanned and spontaneous, black residents of Watts disagreed vigorously with the commission's further characterization of the spontaneous outburst as randomized and unfocused behavior. They insisted that the violence of the riot was highly selective in its expression and focus. It was directed, they claimed, primarily against two targets: the police and white merchants of the area.

The police were singled out because of the history of maltreatment and brutality that the blacks claimed to have experienced at their hands. Raine (1970) reports that seven out of ten of the black respondents in the survey of curfew zone residents complained that local police used insulting language and also arbitrarily routed and frisked blacks; four out of ten claimed actually to have witnessed such scenes. These indignities suffered at the hands of the police, the black respondents claimed, were at the heart of black estrangement from the police in Watts. Blauner places these complaints in a broader framework:

> "What the Negro community is presently complaining about when it cries 'police brutality' is the more subtle attack on personal dignity that manifests itself in unexplainable questionings and searches, in hostile and insolent attitudes toward groups of young Negroes on the street, or in cars, and in the use of disrespectful and sometimes racist language – in short, what the Watts man quoted above called 'police harassment.'" (Blauner 1969:177)

Similar sentiments were voiced by black respondents in the fifteen-city survey by the Kerner commission. Specifically, they were much more likely than white respondents to agree with the following statements: "the police don't show respect for people and use insulting language;" "the police frisk or search people without good reason;" "the police rough up people unnecessarily when they are arresting them or afterward." Young blacks in particular expressed these opinions; further, almost all of them claimed to have had a similar experience with the police as described in the statement or to have known someone who had such an experience.

The Kerner commission did not dismiss the views of the blacks as "paranoid" or based on a "misinterpretation of fact" as did the McCone commission according to Blauner. Instead, the Kerner commission agreed that there were grounds for the black reaction, but not to the extent that blacks seemed to believe. The commission believed that of equal if not greater significance was the role of the policeman in the ghetto as

> "a symbol not only of law, but of the entire system of law enforcement and criminal justice.
>
> As such, he becomes the tangible target for grievances against shortcomings throughout the system: against assembly-line justice in teeming lower courts; against wide disparities in sentences; against antiquated correctional facilities; against the basic inequities imposed by the system on the poor – to whom, for example, the option of bail means only jail."
>
> (The National Advisory Commission on Civil Disorders 1968:157)

In the final analysis, the commission concluded, "The policeman in the ghetto is the most visible symbol, finally, of a society from which many ghetto Negroes are increasingly alienated" (The National Advisory Commission on Civil Disorders 1968:157).

An even more visible target than the police for the anger of the blacks in Watts was the local merchant. This is evident in the responses of blacks to the Institute survey. Also examination of the topography of the riot shows a selective patterning to the firebombing, looting, and destruction of buildings and property. The McCone commission argued that this selectivity was confined to broad categories of structures. It observed, for example, that libraries, schools, and other public buildings as well as industrial plants, banks, and private residences were generally spared while retail establishments, particularly apparel, furniture, liquor, and foodstores bore the brunt of the black fury. The commission insisted, however, that such establishments were attacked on a random basis, without regard to the race of the owner. Other observers such as Rustin (1969), Blauner (1969), and Fogelson (1969) vehemently disagreed with this conclusion, as did the Kerner commission in its study of the 1967 riots. All agreed that the most vulnerable to attack were white-owned establishments that had gained a long-term reputation for low-quality merchandise and for usurious credit and outlandish pricing policies and practices.

The McCone commission defined these actions against the merchants almost exclusively in the legal terms of the established society and condemned them as manifestations of antisocial deviant behavior. In other words, the perpetrators had willfully broken the legal code of society and in the process had regressed to the irrational and "animal-like" level of the delinquent and criminal. This was true, according to the commission, of the firebombing and of looting the stores; both expressed the anomic rootlessness and lawlessness of a socially and personally disorganized segment of society.

The other observers and the Kerner commission were less preoccupied with society's legal assessment of the action and more with the blacks' definition of the situation. With this change in frame of reference, the normative burden also shifted. The blacks did not see themselves as engaging in antisocial and irrational behavior, but as expressing their normative outrage against the white merchants whom they saw as siphoning off the resources and funds of the black community and as cheating and robbing them out of the full value of their dollars. Thus, in burning and destroying his property, they saw themselves as punishing the white merchant for his transgression; in looting his store, as redressing an inequity.

Quarantelli and Dynes elaborate upon this thesis as it bears on looting during the urban disturbances. They reject outright McCone's contention that looting is an expressive act by an antisocial and normless individual; instead they make much of its "widespread, collective, and public" character (Quarantelli and Dynes 1971:292), the community support its receives, and the selective targets against which it is directed. Accordingly, they see looting as a social act which expresses shared sentiments and an emergent community consensus. As this consensus evolves, looting takes on a normative character that involves a redefinition of property rights and norms. In short, the black community is no longer prepared to accept – at least temporarily – the societally sanctioned norms of property; it believes that the white merchants have forfeited their claims to their property. Quarantelli and Dynes conclude that through this redefinition the black community is delivering still another message of protest to the white society. It is calling for "social change, particularly with regard to the distribution of valued resources in communities" (Quarantelli and Dynes 1968:137).

The two scholars fail to take their argument a step further and to specify the grounds for this particular type of protest – grounds that become evident in the words of the blacks. The looters are to be supported, according to the blacks, because they have just claims to the property that they have taken; as such they are merely reclaiming some of the "surplus value" of their wage labor – to paraphrase Marx – that they had lost to the white merchants as a result of usurious and exploitative sales practices. By "expropriating the expropriators," according to an even more radicalized interpretation, looters are pursuing "street socialism" and seeking to redistribute the consumption wealth of the community.

Building from this more radical view of the situation, Blauner elaborated the thesis that the urban riots were indeed of an insurrectional and revolutionary character. He compared them to the uprisings of native populations against their white oppressors in colonial societies.

> "The gulf between Watts and affluent Los Angeles is disturbingly similar to that between 'natives' and their colonial masters. The Afro-American's alienation from the institutions and values of the larger society was made clear during the revolt. The sacredness of private property, that unconsciously accepted bulwark of our social arrangements, was rejected. Black people who looted, apparently without guilt, generally remarked that they were taking things that 'really belonged' to them anyway. The society's bases of legitimacy and its loci of authority were attacked. Law and order were viewed as the white man's law and order. Policemen were the major targets, police activity the main issue, because uniformed law enforcement officers represent the most crystallized symbols and the most visible reality of colonial domination." (Blauner 1972:209)

Thus to Blauner the riots represented the total alienation of blacks from the larger society; its "guiding impulse was not integration with American society but an attempt to stake out a sphere of control by moving against that society" (Blauner 1972:209).

Fogelson also saw a broader significance to the urban disturbances. He even compared them to the riots of the proletariat against factory machines in the early days of the industrial revolution, but he rejected the revolutionary interpretation of Blauner and other radical observers who "contend that Negroes, by looting and burning stores have struck at the essence of capitalism, the institution of private property. And by challenging the police and assaulting patrolmen, they have refused to acknowledge the legitimacy of the governmental system" (Fogelson 1968:34).

Instead, Fogelson argued, the urban riots were a politicized collective protest "against the system's abuses and not the system itself."

> "The Negroes looted to acquire goods most Americans deem their due and burned to even the score with unscrupulous white merchants; they did not attempt to undermine property rights in general. Also, they assaulted patrolmen to express specific resentments against the local police and not, as the Negroes' respect for the National Guard indicates, over disaffection with public authority." (Fogelson 1968:34)

The Kerner commission's interpretation is basically in accord with that of Fogelson's.

"The central thrust of Negro protest in the current period has aimed at the inclusion of Negroes in American society on a basis of full equality, rather than at a fundamental transformation of American institutions. There have been elements calling for a revolutionary overthrow of the American social system or for a complete withdrawal of Negroes from American society. But these solutions have had little popular support. Negro protest, for the most part, has been firmly rooted in the basic values of American society, seeking not their destruction but their fulfillment."

(The National Advisory Commission on Civil Disorders 1968:113)

As further evidence of continued black support of the American creed and society, the commission alluded to its survey findings in fifteen cities which showed marked support by blacks for integration and interracial harmony; at the same time, though, blacks expressed widespread discontent with the discriminatory treatment and abuse they experienced within the system. The Kerner commission warned that continued failure to deal frontally and definitively with the historically ingrained racial inequities and discrimination would fan the separatistic tendencies among blacks and the exclusionist and repressive responses of whites, even rekindling violent racial confrontations.

As it is, the commission emphasized, "Our nation is moving toward two societies, one black, one white – separate and unequal" (The National Advisory Commission on Civil Disorders 1968:1). And if this trend were to continue, the commission concluded, the consensual value framework of the American society would eventually be fractured beyond repair and the nation would be split irrevocably into two racially "separate societies" at loggerheads with each other. But the commission was hopeful that measures would finally be taken to prevent this from happening.

Malcolm X and the radicalization of the black struggle in the North

INTRODUCTION

Although the urban riots were less than the revolutionary upheavals of Blauner, they nevertheless were far more than the lawless outbursts of the McCone commission and in certain respects even more than the collective protests of the Kerner commission. They injected a note of radical urgency into the growing racial struggle in the North and "trained" a whole new generation of militant black leaders who subsequently transformed the language in which and the grounds upon which the struggle was to be waged. This cadre of leadership never succeeded in gaining control over what remained essentially a spontaneous series of urban outbursts. But as the riots unfolded the cadre came increasingly to the fore as the translators of the political meaning and significance of the disturbances, and as the architects of an ideological scaffolding that grew to compelling stature among the black intelligentsia after the riots and changed the terms of the debate over the future of the black in America. Its key conceptual components were black nationalism and the colonized status of the blacks in America; its pivotal slogan, black power.

Even as the urban rumblings of the black in the North were first being felt, the ideological character of the emerging mood of militancy was already being shaped by Malcolm X who had become a national figure by 1960. Though his dramatically evolving career was cut short by assassination, his charismatic presence made such a profound impression on a nascent generation of young militant northern black leaders that even in death his stature as a legendary hero continued to grow.

MALCOLM X AND THE BLACK MUSLIMS

In his early years of hustling, Malcolm X honed to a sharp edge the mental and physical skills and cunning needed for survival in the ghetto jungle. But even more he developed a finely tuned resonance for and understanding of the feelings, frustrations, and angers of the black ghetto residents which he never lost. However, not until his total and dramatic conversion to the Nation of Islam did he move beyond his private sphere of personal experience and response into a broader world of ideas and larger meanings. In the process he absorbed the religio-moral *Weltanschauung* and eschatology espoused by Elijah Muhammed as basic Black Muslim dogma.

The central theme of this dogma was the evil character and brutal nature of the white man. He was the devil incarnate, a creature of historical hybridization who had enslaved and subjugated the "original man," the black and his fellow nonwhite. This hegemony, however, would be doomed, according to Muhammed, if the blacks were to unite in a common front under Black Muslim leadership and were to "take the offensive and carry the fight for justice and freedom to the enemy" (Lincoln 1961:85). The methods, terms, and time of this coming confrontation were not spelled out by Muhammed and the Black Muslims; whether the white man was eventually to destroy himself or to be destroyed in a struggle with the blacks and other nonwhites of the world remained unclear.

For the present and immediate future, however, Muhammed and the Black Muslims "demand absolute separation of the black and white races" (Lincoln 1961:87), not, however, along the historical lines of the segregated subordination and dependency of the black but along the lines of autonomy and independence for the black as a people. Thus, the plural structure of society would be transformed from that based on white dominance to that based on equalness between the races. Either as separate nations, separate states, or separate people, the Black Muslims are prepared to have this transformation come about by stages: "the economic, and political links, for example, need not be severed immediately – but all personal relationships between the races must be broken *now*. Economic severance, the next major step, is already under way, and political severance will follow in good time" (Lincoln 1961:87–8).

As this took place, the Black Muslims were convinced, the "Lost-Nation-in-the-West" would become re-purified,

> "ideologically, morally, and above all, biologically. Only when this has been done can the black people of America assume their rightful place of dignity and leadership among the triumphant black nations of the world. The United Front of Black Men, therefore, will countenance no interracial dallying. The intelligent Black Man must look beyond today's personal whimsies to the building of the Black Nation of tomorrow."   (Lincoln 1961:89–90)

With this dogma as his primer, Malcolm X began to apply his prodigious intellectual and emotional energies to the advancement of the cause. He soon rose to the rank of minister and spread the gospel from pulpit and platform coast to coast. So successful were his efforts that within a decade he was largely instrumental in transforming what was essentially a small sect into an important force within the black community.

However, despite his growing influence, until 1959 Malcolm X remained essentially a parochial figure within the black ghetto. In that year he burst forth onto the national stage and was a controversial public figure from that time on. Malcolm X attributed this metamorphosis to the nationwide airing of the television program on the Black Muslims, "The Hate That Hate Produced," which he said "was edited tightly into a kaleidoscope of 'shocker' images" (Malcolm X 1965a:238). The public response was immediate and angry; much of its spleen was vented against him as a primary purveyor of anti-white sentiments. Even the members of the black establishment joined the chorus of outrage.

Once discovered by the mass media, Malcolm X remained in its spotlight until his death. Few of his public appearances and utterances remained unreported and many were the invitations he received for interviews and talk shows and panels. But he complained that the primary purpose of the media for this exposure was to distort what he said and to portray him as a villain and a black racist. However, even as controversy increasingly swirled around him and as an unsympathetic press plagued him, the demand for his appearance escalated to such an extent that he was forever on the move from one place to the next. He was particularly popular on college campuses; both black and white students flocked to his speeches. His mass rallies in the black ghetto also grew to enormous size. And so by the early 1960s Malcolm X emerged as the leading black leader of the northern ghetto, overshadowed only by the towering stature of Dr Martin Luther King, Jr.

Throughout this period, Malcolm X did not stray far from the basic tenets of the Nation of Islam, and he constantly sought advice and guidance from Elijah Muhammed. In his autobiography he insists that he never forgot his personal and spiritual debt to Muhammed during this period and remained a loyal and dedicated follow even as he was gaining a public luminescence himself. However, even at this juncture it was evident that he was starting to chafe at the constraints imposed by the orthodox doctrine of Muhammed. He was particularly restless over Muhammed's policy of aloofness from and non-involvement in the unfolding struggle of the blacks in America. By 1963 he began to talk less about the religio-moral character of the dogma and more about its socio-political implications. In turn, his rapid rise to prominence had made him a target of envy and resentment among various leaders of the Nation, apparently including Muhammed. By mid-1963 the rift had become evident and Malcolm X found himself increasingly isolated among the leadership. His remarks about the Kennedy assassination triggered his suspension, but it soon became evident, he says in his autobiography, that the suspension was not to be of temporary duration.

THE BREAK WITH THE BLACK MUSLIMS AND HIS SUBSEQUENT DEVELOPMENT

In March 1964 Malcolm X formally left the Nation of Islam. In his Declaration of Independence, he renounced Muhammed's policy of abstention and declared his intention "to be very active in every phase of the American Negro struggle for *human rights*" (Malcolm X 1965b:20). But at this juncture he still decided to retain a religiously based organization as the vehicle for promulgating and disseminating his ideas and program. Accordingly, he announced the formation of a new mosque in New York City, the Muslim Mosque, Inc. "This," he claimed, "gives us a religious base, and the spiritual force necessary to rid our people of the vices that destroy the moral fiber of our community." However, unlike Muhammed, he was prepared to adapt his mosque to the needs of secularized clientele. "Many of our people aren't religiously inclined, so the Muslim Mosque, Inc. will be organized in such manner to provide for the active participation of all Negroes in our political, economic, and social programs, despite their religious or non-religious beliefs" (Malcolm X 1965b:21).

Within a month, Malcolm X left on a pilgrimage to Mecca; he also visited a number of African nations. The journey profoundly affected his thinking on a number of fundamental issues. It jarred loose several of the key ideological pegs that still linked him to his Black Muslim past, from the categorical condemnation of whites as devils to the nature of the racial struggle itself. He also began to emphasize the need for a non-religious instrumentality to forge the racial unity that the struggle required and the need to place the struggle on the international stage.

Upon his return to the United States, Malcolm X initiated almost immediately efforts to create such an instrumentality, and by the end of June he announced the formation of the Organization of Afro-American Unity (OAAU), "patterned after the letter and spirit of the Organization of African Unity" (Breitman 1967:105). Its statement of basic aims and objectives "*resolved* to reinforce the common bond of purpose between our people by submerging all of our differences and establishing a non-religious and non-sectarian constructive program for human rights" (Breitman 1967:106).

Within several weeks Malcolm X served notice of his intention to use the organization as an instrumentality for internationalizing the struggle. Specifically he was able to arrange an invitation to the Cairo meeting of the Organization of African Unity as representative of the Organization of Afro-American Unity. At the conference he was formally recognized as an observer which allowed him, in his own words, "to represent the interests of 22 million African-Americans whose *human rights* are being violated daily by the racism of American imperialists" (Malcolm X 1965b:73). As an observer, he was permitted to submit a memorandum to the conference in which he entreated the African nations to support the racial struggle in America and to back efforts to bring the cause of the American black before the United Nations.

Although he failed to win the conference's backing for the United Nations proposal, he nevertheless succeeded in obtaining a resolution from the conference which expressed deep concern over the racial discrimination being practiced in the United States and made an urgent appeal to "*the government authorities in the United States of America to intensify their efforts to ensure the total elimination of all forms of discrimination based on race, color, or ethnic origin*" (Malcolm X 1965b:84).

He stayed on in Africa even after the conference was over to expand his contacts with the African nations and people. For the next several months he toured and spoke in at least fourteen different countries. According to two black leaders from the SNCC who also happened to be visiting several of these countries during this period, "'*Malcolm's impact on Africa was just fantastic. In every country he was known and served as the main criteria for categorizing other Afro-Americans and their political views*'" (Malcolm X 1965b:85).

Upon his return to the United States in November 1964, he plunged immediately into the racial struggle in the North. He spoke before black audiences, principally at rallies sponsored by the OAAU, before white audiences, at rallies sponsored primarily by the militant labor forum. He also appeared on radio and television panel shows, talked with young civil rights workers from the South, and despite the bombing of his house felt obliged to appear at a scheduled public meeting. In sum, for the few short months between his return and his assassination in February 1965, he engaged in an ever-mounting crescendo of activity and became the lightning rod of the embryonic mood of black militancy.

Malcolm X's own articulation of this mood underwent a dramatic transformation from the time of his split with the Black Muslims until his death. Breitman insists that this period can be divided into two phases of ideational and ideological development for Malcolm X. First, Breitman says, was a transitional period that lasted from the time of the split until his return from Africa at the end of May 1964; it found Malcolm X grappling – almost in a trial-and-error fashion – with his own thoughts and seeking to formulate his own independent stance on the racial struggle. According to Breitman, "in this transition period Malcolm inevitably made mistakes. He made some false starts and had to retrace his steps. He said and did things which he himself later called errors; in other cases he did not publicly call them errors but he changed positions he had taken in the transition" (Breitman 1967:22–3). After he returned from Africa, according to Breitman, Malcolm began to fashion a more distinctive, coherent, and radicalized approach to the racial struggle that was still in the process of development at the time of his assassination. In the process he reshaped some of the axioms he had absorbed as a Black Muslim without entirely discarding them.

BLACK SEPARATISM AND NATIONALISM

Nowhere was the reshaping process more evident than in Malcolm X's approach to black separatism and solidarity. Even in his last several months as a Black Muslim, he continued to advocate its orthodox doctrine of separatism. In a speech in December 1963 he said, "'The only lasting or permanent solution is complete separation on some land that we can call our own.'" He then repeated Muhammed's proposal that blacks go "'*back to our homeland* where we can live in peace and harmony.'" He insisted, however, that the American government would have to underwrite the costs of this transportation. Failure to do this, he continued, would oblige the American government "'to set aside some separate territory here in the Western Hemisphere, where the two races can live apart from each other, since we certainly don't get along peacefully while we are here together.'" The size of the land would have to be in accord with the size of the black population: "'If our people number one-seventh of America's total population, then give us one-seventh of this land. We don't want any land in the desert, but where there is rain and much mineral wealth'" (Breitman 1967:57).

White America would also be expected to subsidize this transition for a quarter of a century and to make reparations: "'After 400 years of slave-labor, we have some '*back pay*' coming, a bill owed to us that must be collected.'" If white America refused to do this, it would face the wrath of God, for "'if America waits for Almighty God himself to step in and force her into a "just settlement," God will take this entire continent away from her; and she will cease to exist as a nation'" (Breitman 1967:58).

Although his threat of an Armageddon expressed a basic religious tenet of the sect, Malcolm X had already, even as a Black Muslim, begun to translate the terms of this Armageddon into political and revolutionary terms and to transmute the religio-moral solidarity that the Muslims sought for the blacks into a secular-political solidarity which he labeled black nationalism. In a speech in Detroit in November 1963, he scoffed at the notion that the nonviolent civil rights movement was producing a "Negro revolution." All that it was gaining, he said, was some desegregated facilities, but "that's not revolution. Revolution is based on land. Land is the basis of all independence. Land is the basis of freedom, justice, and equality" (Malcolm X 1965b:9).

Getting this land involved bloodshed and violence, not "loving your enemy, [for] ... revolution is hostile, revolution knows no compromise, revolution overturns and destroys everything that gets in its way.... A revolutionary wants land so he can set up his own nation, an independent nation. These [civil rights] Negroes aren't asking for any nation – they're trying to crawl back on the plantation" (Malcolm X 1965b:9–10).

This quest for a nation was called nationalism, but each quest had its own racial expression. What the whites did in the American, French, and Russian Revolutions expressed "white nationalism;... All the revolutions that are going on in Asia and Africa today are based on what? – black nationalism. A revolutionary is a black nationalist. He wants a nation." Malcolm X then concluded with a ringing declaration, "If you're afraid of black nationalism, you're afraid of revolution. And if you love revolution, you love black nationalism" (Malcolm X 1965b:10).

Four months later in his Declaration of Independence, Malcolm X began to shift his priorities. He still professed to believe that despite his having left the Black Muslims. "Mr Muhammed's analysis of the problem is the most realistic and that his solution is the best one." Accordingly, he still believed that "the best solution is complete separation, with our people going back home, to our own African homeland" (Malcolm X 1965b:20). But he declared that that was a long way off in the future, whereas what was important now was the meeting of the needs of the blacks here. He elaborated on these needs in an interview with A.B. Spellman:

"'we must eat while we're still here, we must have a place to sleep, we must have clothes to wear, we must have better jobs, we must have better education; so that although our long-range political philosophy is to migrate back to our African homeland, our short-range program must involve that which is necessary to enable us to live a better life while we are still here'" (Breitman 1967:60).

To achieve these goals for the present, he publicly and privately embraced black nationalism for himself, his platform, and his organization, whereas four months earlier he had merely talked about it as a detached observer might. Now he said, "Our political philosophy will be black nationalism. Our economic and social philosophy will be black nationalism. Our cultural emphasis will be black nationalism" (Malcolm X 1965b:21). Ten days later he spelled out in a speech in Cleveland what he meant by the various forms of black nationalism.

"The political philosophy of black nationalism means that the black man should control the politics and the politicians in his own community; no more.... The economic philosophy of black nationalism is pure and simple. It only means that we should control the economy of our community. Why should white people be running all the stores in our community? Why should white people be running the banks of our community? Why should the economy of our community be in the hands of the white man? Why? If a black man can't move his store into a white community, you tell me why a white man should move his store into a black community.... The social philosophy of black nationalism only means that we have to get together and remove the evils, the vices, alchoholism, drug addiction, and other evils that are destroying the moral fiber of our community. We ourselves have to lift the level of our community, the standard of our community to a higher level, make our own society beautiful so that we will be satisfied in our own social circles and won't be running around here trying to knock our way into a social circle where we're not wanted."

(Malcolm X 1965b:38–9).

In this manner Malcolm X became increasingly preoccupied with elaborating the dimensions of racial solidarity and with raising the banner of black nationalism as a rallying cry for the racial struggle. He retained this emphasis for the rest of his life, although by 1965 he seemed to be searching for a more universal way of defining "the overall philosophy which I think is necessary for the liberation of the black people in this country" (Malcolm X 1965b:213).

Even as his preoccupation with black nationalism grew, toward the end of what Breitman called his transition period Malcolm X seemed to lose interest in a physical return to Africa for the black even in the long run. And by the time he returned from Mecca, he had become convinced that blacks "should stay and fight in the US for what was rightfully theirs" (Breitman 1967:63). His "return to

Africa" theme accordingly took on an increasingly different meaning so that by December 1964 it had become transmuted from a physical return to a spiritual and cultural return. In short, he resurrected Africa as a symbolic and cultural national homeland for the American black.

> "And I believe this, that if we migrated back to Africa culturally, philosophically, and psychologically, while remaining here physically, the spiritual bond that would develop between us and Africa through this cultural, philosophical, and psychological migration, so-called migration, would enhance our position here, because we would have our contacts with them acting as roots or foundations behind us. You will never have a foundation in America. You're out of your mind if you think that *this* government is ever going to back you and me up in the same way that it backed others up. They'll never do it. It's not in them."
>
> (Malcolm X 1965b:210–11)

FROM CATEGORICAL ANTI-WHITISM TO OUTSPOKEN ANTI-CAPITALISM

Significant as Malcolm X's break with the Muslims was in shifting his priorities on separatism and black nationalism, it had no immediate effect on his attitude toward another Muslim maxim. He continued to accept its categorical rejection of the white. But even as a Muslim, he primarily voiced this rejection in secular and political terms and not in the religio-moral terms of the sect, though he accepted its labeling of the white as evil incarnate. (In fact, one of his favorite public expressions was "white devils," a phrase for which he was criticized by Muhammed.) Thus, he talked as a Muslim about the evil oppression and exploitation that the white man had visited upon the black not only in America but throughout the world. He even introduced the notion that white colonial conquest was the link that bound the fates of the blacks of America with the fate of blacks in other countries. Typically his condemnation of white oppression remained during this period on a general and even abstract level without much attention to its underlying political and economic structuring.

With his break with the Muslims, Malcolm X began to focus more on this structuring of the white man's domination of the black in America. He referred more frequently and aggressively to its colonial character and origins. In a speech in New York in April 1964, for example, he proclaimed, "America is a colonial power. She has colonized 22 million Afro-Americans by depriving us of human rights. She has not only deprived us of the right to be a citizen, she has deprived us of the right to be human beings, the right to be recognized and respected as men and women. In this country the black can be fifty years old and he is still a 'boy'" (Malcolm X 1965b:50–1).

He also addressed himself to the monopolization by the whites of societal power, its resources, and its instruments of coercion. But until his trip to Mecca he saw this institutional apparatus of control and coercion as a creature and handmaiden of the white race in its categorial and universal exploitation and domination of the black race.

His trip to Mecca jarred dramatically his views and treatment of the racial issue. He was impressed, according to a letter he wrote in April 1964, with the

> "sincere hospitality and the overwhelming spirit of true brotherhood as is practiced by people of *all colors and races* here in this ancient holy land, the home of Abraham, Muhammed and all the other prophets of the Holy Scriptures. For the past week I have been utterly speechless and spellbound by the graciousness I see displayed all around me by people *of all colors*."
>
> (Malcolm X 1965b:59)

He attributed this interracial amity that he experienced to the "true" religion of Islam, not to the Black Muslim variant or to Judaeo-Christianity. "True Islam removes racism, because people of all colors and races who accept its religious principles and bow down to the one God, Allah, also automatically accept each other as brothers and sisters, regardless of differences in complexion" (Malcolm X 1965b:60). He concluded with the hope that the spirit of Islam might yet "remove the 'cancer of racism' from the heart of the white American, and perhaps in time to save America from imminent racial disaster, the same destruction brought upon Hitler by his racism that eventually destroyed the Germans themselves" (Malcolm X 1965b:60).

As for himself, Malcolm X vowed in a speech in Chicago several days after his return not to engage any longer in

> "sweeping indictments of one race.... In the future, I intend to be careful not to sentence anyone who has not been proven guilty. I am not a racist and do not subscribe to any of the tenets of racism. In all honesty and sincerity it can be stated that I wish nothing but freedom, justice, and equality: Life, liberty, and the pursuit of happiness – for all people. My first concern is with the group of people to which I belong, the Afro-Americans, for we, more than any other people, are deprived of these inalienable rights."
>
> (Malcolm X 1965b:59)

His trip to Africa also caused him to shift toward an institutional interpretation for racism. He was particularly struck during the course of his travels with the fact "'that most of the countries that have recently emerged into independence have turned away from the so-called capitalistic system in the direction of socialism, So out of curiosity, I can't resist the temptation to do a little investigating wherever that particular philosophy happens to be in existence or an attempt is being made to bring it into existence'" (Breitman 1967:32–3).

By the time he returned to America, Malcolm X was fairly well convinced that racism and capitalism were inextricably linked and that whites who believed in capitalism had to believe in racism too. This was evident in the tenor of his response to a question that was raised soon after his return from Africa. "Most of the countries that were colonial powers were capitalist countries, and the last bulwark of capitalism today is America. It's impossible for a white person to believe in capitalism and not believe in racism. You can't have capitalism without racism" (Malcolm X 1965b:69).

His anti-capitalism grew in strength and intensity until he identified it pointedly and insistently as the primary source of oppression and exploitation throughout the world. In a dramatic metaphor he likened it to a vulture that was no longer capable of sucking the blood of the strong, only that of the weak and helpless and was therefore doomed to eventual destruction.

> "'It is impossible for capitalism to survive, primarily because the system of capitalism needs some blood to suck. Capitalism used to be like an eagle, but now it's more like a vulture. It used to be strong enough to go and suck anybody's blood, whether they were strong or not. But now it has become more cowardly, like the vulture, and it can only suck the blood of the helpless. As the nations of the world free themselves, then capitalism has less victims, less to suck, and it becomes weaker and weaker. It's only a matter of time in my opinion before it will collapse completely.'" (Breitman 1967:37–8)

Hastening the end of capitalism, Malcolm X continued to believe, would be an Armageddon. When queried in a radio interview about the Armageddon in January 1965, Malcolm X no longer referred to it in the racial terms that he had as a Black Muslim. In fact, he explicitly rejected Muhammed's characterization of the struggle: "I don't think that it will be based upon the color of the skin, as Elijah Muhammed taught it." Instead, he continued, it would be "a clash between the oppressed and those that do the oppressing. I believe that there will be a clash between those who want freedom, justice, and equality for everyone and those who want to continue the systems of exploitation" (Malcolm X 1965b:216). A month later he repeated a similar theme at Columbia University: "It is incorrect to classify the revolt of the Negro as simply a racial conflict of black against white, or as a purely American problem. Rather, we are today seeing a global rebellion of the oppressed against the oppressor, the exploited against the exploiter" (Malcolm X 1965b:217).

However, even as Malcolm X moved toward a "class" analysis of capitalist exploitation and oppression, he remained alert to the continuing overlay of racial cleavage upon the structural faults of capitalism. Race and class, he believed, could and would mutually reinforce each other much as Fanon claimed they would in his theory of "ethnoMarxism" (Fanon 1968). As a result, Malcolm X prophesied that white Europeans and Americans would continue to express and to organize their exploitative class interests in racial terms; consequently, he believed that what is essentially a struggle between classes would be transformed into a war between the races. This is evident in a later segment of the previously mentioned radio interview: "I do think you'll find that the European powers, which are the former colonial powers, if they're not able to readjust their thinking of superiority toward the darker skinned people, whom they have been made to think are inferior, then the lines can be easily drawn – they can easily be lumped into racial groups and it will be a racial war" (Malcolm X 1965b:216).

THE UNKEPT PROMISE OF THE CONSTITUTION AND THE AMERICAN CREED

Even as his call for a radical transformation of the American society grew more insistent, Malcolm X expressed a modicum of faith in its underlying value-normative framework. For example, in his "black revolution" speech delivered a month after his break with the Muslims, he contended that things might be different in America if blacks were accorded in full measure the rights guaranteed to them under the Constitution and the American creed. They would then be able to bring to bear the balance of power they held in the country in a basic realignment of the political system and in the wiping out of segregationism.

> "If the Negro in this country were given what the Constitution says he is supposed to have, the added power of the Negro in this country would sweep all of the racists and the segregationists out of office. It would change the entire political structure of the country. It would wipe out the Southern segregationism that now controls America's foreign policy, as well as America's domestic policy." (Malcolm X 1965b:57)

If this were to come to pass, America would be "the only country in history in a position to bring about a revolution without violence and bloodshed" (Malcolm X 1965b:56).

He concluded, however, that white America was determined not to let this come to pass. As a result, the blacks would have to struggle mightily for the implementation of the rights that were already theirs constitutionally. And since these rights already belonged to them, they had no reason, he insisted, to be grateful for any modest gains that may have been made in the civil rights movement: "How can you thank a man for giving you what's already yours? How then can you thank him for giving you only part of what's already yours? You haven't even made progress, if what's being given to you, you should have had already. That's not progress" (Malcolm X 1965b:31). However, he felt that such gains were an illusion at best; for he firmly believed that no progress in civil rights had been made since the Civil War. In his "black revolution" speech he elaborated on this theme of no progress.

> "He [the black man] doesn't see any progress that he has made since the Civil War. He sees not one iota of progress because number one, if the Civil War had freed him, he wouldn't need civil rights legislation today. If the Emancipation Proclamation, issued by that shining liberal called Lincoln, had freed him, he wouldn't be singing 'We Shall Overcome' today. If the amendments to the Constitution had solved his problem, his problem wouldn't still be here today. And if the Supreme Court desegregation decision of 1954 was genuinely and sincerely designed to solve his problem, his problem wouldn't be with us today."   (Malcolm X 1965b:52–3)

This was the situation, he contended, because the black man could not expect to get what was rightfully his if he had to rely on the legislative acts of the class of "criminal whites" who deprived him of his rights in the first place.

> "When you go to Washington, DC, expecting those crooks down there – and that's what they are – to pass some kind of civil rights legislation to correct a very criminal situation, what you are doing is encouraging the black man, who is the victim, to take his case into the court that's controlled by the criminal that made him the victim. It will never be solved in that way." (Malcolm X 1965b:53)

As a result, if the blacks expected anything to be done, they would have to take it upon themselves resolutely and aggressively. They would have to organize their energies and resources under the slogan of black nationalism into a potent political force, and even to be prepared to defend themselves by violence if necessary against the agents and forces of repression that would forcibly deny them that which was rightfully theirs.

> "If you don't take this kind of stand, your little children will grow up and look at you and think 'shame.' If you don't take an uncompromising stand – I don't mean go out and get violent; but at the same time you should never be nonviolent unless you run into some nonviolence. I'm nonviolent with those who are nonviolent with me. But when you drop that violence on me, then you've made me go insane, and I'm not responsible for what I do. And that's the way every Negro should get. Any time you know you're within the law, within your legal rights, within your moral rights, in accord with justice, then die for what you believe in. But don't die alone. Let your dying be reciprocal. This is what is meant by equality. What's good for the goose is good for the gander."
>
>   (Malcolm X 1965b:33–4)

FROM CIVIL RIGHTS TO HUMAN RIGHTS: INTERNATIONALIZING
THE STRUGGLE

Malcolm X recognized that such a course of action would be difficult for the black to follow alone; whether the path was the "ballot or the bullet," the black would need powerful allies to help him in his travail. To gain such allies, Malcolm X insisted,

> "We need to expand the civil rights struggle to a higher level – to the level of human rights. Whenever you are in a civil rights struggle, whether you know it or not, you are confining yourself to the jurisdiction of Uncle Sam. No one from the outside world can speak out in your behalf as long as your struggle is a civil rights struggle. Civil rights comes within the domestic affairs of this country. All of our African brothers and our Asian brothers and our Latin-American brothers cannot open their mouths and interfere in the domestic affairs of the United States. And as long as it's civil rights, this comes under the jurisdiction of Uncle Sam."   (Malcolm X 1965b:34)

By placing the struggle on the world stage and focusing on human rights, blacks in America would no longer constitute a minority as they did in America and have to act on a stage that was controlled by the whites. As a result, they would no longer have to settle for the role of the "underdog" and for a "begging, hat-in-hand, compromising approach." Instead they would become part of a world-wide movement in which "the dark man outnumbers the white man." ("On the world stage the white man is just a microscopic minority.") As a result, the black man could use "a different approach in trying to struggle for his rights." With such an approach, "he doesn't beg. He doesn't thank you for what you give him because you are only giving him what he should have had a hundred years ago. He doesn't think you are doing him any favors" (Malcolm X 1965b:52).

To Malcolm X, however, the emphasis on human rights was more than a stratagem to enlarge the cohort of allies and to get the United States before the bar of nations and the United Nations. It also represented the ultimate and transcendent goal of the racial struggle in which integration and separatism were merely specific means and in which civil rights was merely a lower order of rights.

> "All of our people have the same goals, the same objective. That objective is freedom, justice, equality. All of us want recognition and respect as human beings. We don't want to be integrationists nor do we want to be separationists. We want to be human beings. Integration is only a method that is used by some groups to obtain freedom, justice, equality, and respect as human beings. Separation is only a method that is used by other groups to obtain freedom, justice, equality, or human dignity.

Our people have made the mistake of confusing the methods with the objectives. As long as we agree on objectives, we should never fall out with each other just because we believe in different methods or tactics or strategy to reach a common objective.

We have to keep in mind at all time that we are not fighting for integration, nor are we fighting for separation. We are fighting for recognition as human beings. We are fighting for the right to live as free humans in this society. In fact, we are actually fighting for rights that are even greater than civil rights and that is human rights."

(Malcolm X 1965b:51)

His trip to Mecca reinforced and intensified his commitment to this approach. More than ever he concentrated his energies on efforts to place the racial struggle on a world stage and to have international forums, including the United Nations, condemn American racism. He also used the independence movement in Africa as a constant inspirational reference and model for the American scene and rarely failed to allude to it in his public addresses from then on. And with growing intensity, he connected the domestic to the international scene through the universal struggle for human rights. His transcendent goal remained, as he had articulated before his trip to Mecca, a society in which human rights were respected for all and in which "freedom, justice, and equality" were realized for everybody. But after his trip he was prepared to add another dimension to his vision of the future: the prospect of an eventual brotherhood between the races. As he emphasized in early 1965, "I say again that I'm not a racist, I don't believe in any form of segregation or anything like that. I'm for brotherhood for everybody, but I don't believe in forcing brotherhood upon people who don't want it" (Malcolm X 1965b:177). But even more this Utopian society took a specific form and substance in his mind before he was killed. It was to be a socialist society.

THE TRANSFORMATION OF THE REPRESSIVE SOCIETY AND THE RIGHT OF SELF-DEFENSE

Closely woven into Malcolm X's drive to internationalize the racial struggle following his African trip was his deepening conviction that America had become an even more repressive society than before. By this he not only meant the mushrooming violence against the civil rights movement in the South but also the violent confrontations with the police that were beginning to erupt in the North. He likened Harlem, for example, to "a police state; the police in Harlem, their presence is like occupation forces, like an occupying army. They're not in Harlem to protect us; they're not in Harlem to look out for our welfare. They're in Harlem to protect the interests of the businessmen who don't even live there" (Malcolm X 1965b:66).

Shortly after the bombing of his house in February 1965, he launched a particularly scathing attack against the repressive character of white America.

"America is a society where there is no brotherhood. This society is controlled primarily by the racists and segregationists who are in Washington, DC, in positions of power. And from Washington, DC, they exercise the same forms of brutal oppression against dark-skinned people in South and North Vietnam, or in the Congo, or in Cuba, or any other place on this earth where they are trying to exploit and oppress. That is a society whose government doesn't hesitate to inflict the most brutal form of punishment and oppression upon dark-skinned people all over the world."   (Malcolm X 1965b:163)

He even raised the specter of racial genocide.

"This is how the [white] man does it, and if you don't wake up and find out how he does it, I tell you, they'll be building gas chambers and gas ovens pretty soon – I don't mean those kind you've got at home in your kitchen – [and] . . . you'll be in one of them, just like the Jews ended up in gas ovens over there in Germany. You're in a society that's just as capable of building gas ovens for black people as Hitler's society was."   (Malcolm X 1965b:168)

He also treated with growing acerbity the disparity between the American creed and its racial practices. In an appeal to African heads of state, he charged that this disparity made America worse than South Africa because the latter at least did not try to disguise its outright racism by preaching one thing and practicing another as America did.

"America is worse than South Africa, because not only is America racist, but she also is deceitful and hypocritical. South Africa preaches segregation and practices segregation. She, at least, practices what she preaches. America preaches integration and practices segregation. She preaches one thing while deceitfully practicing another.
    South Africa is like a vicious wolf, openly hostile towards black humanity. But America is cunning like a fox, friendly and smiling, but even more vicious and deadly than the wolf."   (Malcolm X 1965b:75)

In addition, he assailed the Civil Rights Act of 1964 as perpetuating this deceitful hypocrisy. "This propaganda maneuver is part of her [America's] deceit and trickery to keep the African nations from condemning her racist practices before the United Nations, as you are now doing as regards the same practices of South Africa" (Malcolm X 1965b:76). Several months later Malcolm X intensified his attack against the act as "only a valve, a vent that was designed to enable us [blacks] to let off our frustrations. But the bill itself was not designed to solve our problems" (Malcolm X 1965b:151). In other words, he concluded, the act was designed merely to siphon off the explosive potential expressed on the streets of the urban ghettos and not to get at its underlying causes.

Just as he grew more impatient with white America after his trip, so did Malcolm X become more critical of the black civil rights leaders. He intensified his attack against their policy of nonviolence at a time when white violence was growing. He also labeled them Uncle Toms for their too ready willingness to compromise with the white power structure. He insisted that their efforts were bound to fail. "Black people in 1965 will not be controlled by these Uncle Tom leaders, believe me; they won't be held in check, they won't be held on the plantation by these overseers, they won't be held on the corral, they won't be held back at all" (Malcolm X 1965b:155).

The increasing radicalization of Malcolm X convinced him more than ever that the future of the black rested in a dramatic transformation of the American society. He was still prepared for the foreseeable future, however, to work within the system toward this goal. Accordingly, he advocated political action for the black that was not tied to either political party: "In my opinion, we should reserve our political action for the situation at hand, in no way identifying with either party or selling ourselves to either party, but taking political action that's for the good of human beings and that will eliminate these injustices" (Malcolm X 1965b:202)

However, he became less sanguine that this course of action would lead to the "bloodless revolution" that he had talked about before his trip to Africa. Instead he foresaw the increased risk and danger of violence and bloodshed. But he vigorously denied the charge by the press that he was "a teacher, a fomentor of violence." He said, "That is a lie. I'm not for wanton violence," but then he added, "I'm for justice" (Malcolm X 1965b:366).

And in the name of justice, Malcolm X insisted that the blacks had to act aggressively if they wanted to achieve their just claims to equality and first-class citizenship. In fact, he proclaimed in a speech at the end of 1964, he and his fellow blacks would prefer to achieve their just claims through peaceful and legal means, but they had been and were unable to do so despite the fact that the Constitution, courts, and American creed seemed to be on their side. As a result, he contended, blacks would have to take matters in their own hands and push aggressively for the full realization of their civil and human rights.

"There's only one way to be a first-class citizen. There's only one way to be independent. There's only one way to be free. It's not something that someone gives to you. It's something that you take. Nobody can give you freedom. Nobody can give you equality or justice or anything. If you're a man, you take it. If you can't take it, you don't deserve it. Nobody can give it to you. So if you and I want freedom, if we want independence, if we want respect, if we want recognition, we obey the law, we are peaceful – but at the same time, at any moment that you and I are involved in any kind of action that is legal, that is in accord with our civil rights, in accord with the courts of this land, in accord with the Constitution – when all of these things are on our side, and we still can't get it, it's because we aren't on our own side."   (Malcolm X 1965b:111)

In pressing for their rights, Malcolm X argued, blacks would never initiate violence or illegal action, for they would be striving to fulfill the purposes of the law. He repeated this message early in 1965 as he talked about going to Mississippi for a voter registration drive. "We don't intend to break the law, but when you're trying to register to vote you're upholding the law" (Malcolm X 1965b: 153). But the whites, he contended, would be intent on thwarting the purposes of the law and would resort to violence as they had done continually in the past. Under the circumstances blacks would be entitled to defend themselves, by arms if necessary. "It's the one who tries to prevent you from registering to vote who's breaking the law, and you've got a right to protect yourself by any means necessary. And if the government doesn't want civil rights groups going equipped [with guns], the government should do its job." And he announced in no uncertain terms, *"we intend to go prepared"* (Malcolm X 1965b:153). (His assassination within a month prevented him from ever carrying out his intention.)

In this manner, Malcolm X reaffirmed his general commitment to the principle of self-defense: "I feel that when the law fails to protect Negroes from whites' attack, then those Negroes should use arms, if necessary to defend themselves" (Malcolm X 1965a:366). But since he expected such a failure to be general, he viewed the right of self-defense as bestowing legitimacy to violence as a natural and logical extension of the blacks' drive for justice and equality.

"I *am* for violence if nonviolence means we continue postponing a solution to the American black man's problem – just to *avoid* violence. I don't go for nonviolence if it also means a delayed solution. To me a delayed solution is a non-solution. Or I'll say it another way. If it must take violence to get the black man his human rights in this country, I'm *for* violence." (Malcolm X 1965a:367)

In many ways, then, Malcolm X had reached what might be called a quasi-revolutionary stance by the time of his death. He was for a forceful if not violent fulfillment of the rights of the black within the American society. He had even begun to question whether such rights could ever be realized under a capitalist structure, but he seemed to stop short of endorsing the Marxist doctrine of revolution. Under this doctrine, particularly as it was developed by Fanon (1968), violence is a legitimate tool of the oppressed in its revolutionary attempt to overthrow the existing capitalist order, including its legal-normative structure. Even at his death, Malcolm X still saw the black challenge as legitimized by the existing legal-normative code of the American society and his resort to violence as justified by the right to self-defense under the code. Thus, a basic transformation of the American society could occur, while its legal-normative code might remain intact. In short, Malcolm X seems to have retained vestiges of his notion that a "bloodless revolution" might still be possible. Whether or not he might in time have fully adopted a version of the Marxist doctrine of revolution as Fanon did, given his increasingly anti-capitalistic bent, cannot of course be answered; but Breitman thinks he would have.

Carmichael, black power, and black nationalism

INTRODUCTION

In articulating a mood of rage and militancy that was just beginning to be expressed on the streets of northern black ghettos, Malcolm X was treated by many black leaders, to say nothing of the white leaders, as a dangerous and fanatical heretic. They insisted that he represented at best only a small extremist fringe of the black community and that he was out of touch with the mainstream of black sentiment and thought. However, they feared his charismatic presence; therefore they strove mightily to quarantine him and thereby to prevent his ideas from contaminating the unfolding civil rights movement with its strategy of nonviolence. In general these leaders were satisfied that they had contained his influence; for, even though Malcolm X had attained widespread popularity among the black masses in the northern ghettos by the time of his death, the battleground was still primarily in the South.

Six months after Malcolm X's death, Watts exploded. Its spontaneous violence challenged the virtual monopoly that the moderate civil rights leaders had in defining the terms and strategies of the black protest movement. It paved the way for a vocabulary of militance and separatism to become a legitimate part of the language of protest. As violence erupted in city after city, this rhetoric of militance became louder and louder. Finally, in Mississippi in 1966, Stokely Carmichael fused the call for militance and separatism into a simple slogan black power, that captured the imagination of the black. As a result, from that time on the phrase "black power" came to dominate the language of protest, and Carmichael assumed the leading role as its interpreter.

THE EXPLOSIVE IMPACT OF THE BLACK POWER SLOGAN AND EFFORTS TO MAKE IT RESPECTABLE

Once having been proclaimed and enthusiastically embraced, by young urban blacks in particular, the slogan sent shudders through white America and elicited tirades of anger and laments of dismay each time it was repeated in the mass media. Among whites the slogan conjured up an image of massive and wanton destruction and violence by blacks that would spill over the boundaries of the ghettos into white neighborhoods and would take the form, at its worst, of guerrilla warfare in city streets. These fears and anxieties were fed by the rapid spread of the urban riots through 1967 and 1968, with their climactic fury in Newark and Detroit, and by the mounting crescendo of militant rhetoric. As a result, many white liberals withdrew from the civil rights struggle and cut off their financial support.

Blacks leaders of established civil rights organizations also expressed their misgivings about the slogan. Some did applaud its call for racial solidarity and pride, while deploring with the others its strategy of separatism and self-defense. In an advertisement placed in newspapers throughout the nation in the fall of 1966, the heads of the NAACP and Urban League joined other black leaders in taking issue with these features of the slogan and in reaffirming their commitment to integration and to nonviolence. Similarly, King expressed his serious reservations about the use of the phrase as a rallying cry for black protest. In fact, he prevented it from being used for that purpose during the march through Mississippi when it had first been enunciated. He was particularly unhappy with its implied rejection of nonviolence and integration. ("I cannot see how the Negro will be totally liberated from the crushing weight of poor education, squalid housing, and economic strangulation until he is integrated, with power, into every level of American life" (King 1967:62).) He professed to find virtue, however, in its call for pride and solidarity among blacks and in its distress with the current life circumstances and conditions of the blacks. But in the final analysis he considered it a nihilistic cry of despair that expected defeat and not victory for the black protest movement.

Similarly, Bayard Rustin found little to object to in the phrase "in its simplest and most innocent guise" as an "effort to elect Negroes to office in proportion to Negro strength within the population," but he was strongly opposed to its separatistic and violent themes as espoused, he claimed, by Carmichael and to its rejection of the kind of coalition politics needed for a successful civil rights movement. As a result, he concluded, "I would contend that 'black power' not only lacks any real value for the civil rights movement, but that its propagation is positively harmful. It diverts the movement from a meaningful debate over strategy and tactics, it isolates the Negro community, and it encourages the growth of anti-Negro forces" (Rustin 1948:466).

BLACK POWER AND THE ETHNIC ANALOGY

Mindful of the agitated response of the white community and established black leaders, Carmichael wrote in an article in a New York publication, shortly after he had sprung the phrase, that black power posed no violent racist threat to whites. He said, "Black people do not want to 'take over' this country. They don't want to 'get Whitey;' they just want to get him off their backs, as the saying goes" (Carmichael 1971:28). In fact, he continued, "The white man is irrelevant to blacks, except as an oppressive force. Blacks want to be in his place, yes, but not in order to terrorize and lynch and starve him. They want to be in his place because that is where a decent life can be had" (Carmichael 1971:29).

Accordingly, Carmichael insisted that the purpose of black power was to forge unity and solidarity among blacks, to instill in them a sense of pride and confidence in who they were and in what they could do:

> "Only black people can convey the revolutionary idea that black people are able to do things themselves. Only they can help create in the community an aroused and continuing black consciousness that will provide the basis for political strength.... Black people must do things for themselves, they must get poverty money they will control and spend themselves, they must conduct tutorial programs themselves so that black children can identify with black people."
>
> (Carmichael 1971:27)

With such solidarity, Carmichael argued in the same article, blacks would be better able to cope with the oppressive and exploitative environment imposed upon them by the white society and to gain control over their life circumstances and destiny. Under such circumstances, black power would mean "the creation of power bases from which black people can work to change statewide or nationwide patterns of oppression through pressure from strength – instead of weakness" (Carmichael 1971:21). It would, in other words, give blacks a kind of political leverage that they presently lacked. He offered as a model for such leverage the SNCC's experience in the Alabama county elections of 1966. In those elections, he said, the SNCC had succeeded in running slates of candidates from an independent freedom organization whose ballot symbol was the black panther; so near victory had it come in Loundes County that its organization there was able to qualify as an official party in Alabama, the Loundes County Freedom party.

What Carmichael was offering was a version of black power that would convert blacks into a potent political force but would still operate within the system, posing no violent revolutionary threat to it. It would, as he was to say a year later, recognize "the ethnic basis of American politics as well as the power-oriented nature of American politics. Black Power, therefore, calls for black people to consolidate behind their own, so that they can bargain from a position of strength" (Carmichael and Hamilton 1967:47). This would be in accord with the basic character of the American society, for,

> "*before a group can enter the open society, it must first close ranks.* By this we mean that group solidarity is necessary before a group can operate effectively from a bargaining position of strength in a pluralistic society. Traditionally, each new ethnic group in this society has found the route to social and political viability through the organization of its own institutions with which to represent its needs within the larger society."
>
> (Carmichael and Hamilton 1967:44)

This ethnic version of black power placated some of the white critics and even gained the support of white liberals. Danzig (1966), for example, saw it as a way for blacks to move through collective action into the mainstream of American society. Some moderate black civil rights leaders, as we have already seen, also responded favorably, as did King, to the ethnic elements of black power; several even grafted the slogan onto their own vocabulary of protest. As a result, the phrase lost in time some of its stinging terror as it gained the respectability of an ethnic analogy.

However, even as he was enunciating this ethnic version, Carmichael never intended to convey the notion that the black experience in America was analogous to that of the white immigrant and ethnic. Quite the contrary, he distinguished the two experiences both categorically and dramatically. Even in the article in which he elaborated certain features of the ethnic version of black power, he left no doubt about the difference in the treatment of the two: "Whereas most of the [white] people who settled this country came here for freedom or for economic opportunity, blacks were brought here to be slaves" (Carmichael 1971:25). This historical difference, he maintained, has produced a colonized status for the blacks in which they have been oppressed, exploited, and deemed inferior by the white, the immigrants included.

> "[These] colonies of the United States – and this includes the black ghettos within its borders, North and South – must be liberated. For a century, this nation has been like an octopus of exploitation, its tentacles stretching from Mississippi and Harlem to South America, the Middle East, southern Africa, and Vietnam; the form of exploitation varies from area to area but the essential

result has been the same – a powerful few have been maintained and enriched at the expense of the poor and voiceless colored masses." (Carmichael 1971:22–3)

Further, the kind of solidarity Carmichael envisioned for the black even in his ethnic version bore in fact only a faint resemblance to that which characterized the white immigrant group historically. His conception involved a totalness of control of the life circumstances and destiny of the black and expressed a degree of alienation from the dominant society which exceeded anything that all but the most sectarian white immigrant ever sketched for his group. In fact, what Carmichael was calling for was not the retrospective solidarity of the white immigrant but the prospective solidarity of Malcolm X's black nationalism.

BLACK POWER AND BLACK NATIONALISM

Carmichael soon addressed himself openly to this fact. Unlike his co-author Hamilton who continued to pursue the ethnic analogy, Carmichael soon moved to an openly nationalistic version of black power and black solidarity. He acknowledged his debt to Malcolm X and frequently framed his responses in terms reminiscent of the words of Malcolm X. But in certain respects he went even further in the kind of solidarity he advocated for the black ghetto. By the time he made his speech at Morehouse College in 1970, he envisioned the black ghetto transformed into a "quasi-nation-state" with full control over its major institutions: "we must seek to take over all of the political institutions inside our community: the police station, the judicial system, the board of education, the welfare system" (Carmichael 1971:207).

In short, Carmichael had become more fully convinced than ever that blacks could not expect to find full justice and equality within the American society as presently constituted. He had concluded, as Malcolm X had before him, that capitalism and racism were closely interwoven and he began to stress more than ever the colonized status of the black, repeatedly referring to the black ghettos as internal colonies. Added to this was his growing conviction that "America is showing the internal contradictions of capitalism Marx speaks about" (Carmichael 1971:208), and was rushing pellmell toward fascism; this he opined boded ill for the blacks.

"She [America] is obviously divided. Now what we know about white folks is that they're always united around one question – *us*. On the question of race, white America is a monolithic structure. Therefore, since the country must move to fascism in order to avoid internal collapse, we must not allow the white leaders of this country to use us for the justification of that fascism."

(Carmichael 1971:208)

As a result, Carmichael saw this kind of black solidarity as furnishing a protective umbrella against the growing reactionarism of white America. He foresaw no overwhelming resistance by whites to abandoning their outposts in the ghetto colony. If necessary, however, Carmichael would have blacks resort to guerilla warfare to achieve this goal.

But even more, this political decolonization of the ghetto represented to Carmichael a stage in a broader revolutionary process that was to be guided by a political ideology that contained "the three necessary ingredients" of class, race, and land: "if we're to talk about ideology – we must speak to the problem of class, against capitalism; we must speak to the problem of race, against racism; and we must speak to the problem of land" (Carmichael 1971:198).

Marx, according to Carmichael who claimed to be a student but not a disciple of his work, had correctly identified the generating source of class formation and conflict in the capitalist societies – the relationship of people to the means of production. At the top of the structure of power is the capitalist "who owns and controls the means of production" (Carmichael 1971:192) and coercively exploits and oppresses those who do not. Beneath the capitalist, Carmichael continued, is a stratum of bourgeoisie who serve as his lackeys. "On the bottom of Marx's analysis, of course, you have the urban proletariat, the workers, the peasants, the factory workers, the landless, misdirected masses. According to Marx these are the people who will lead the inevitable class struggle" (Carmichael 1971:194).

Yet, Carmichael continued, this had not materialized in many countries because Marx failed to "deal with the question of race; and in the twentieth century we see that race has not only become a phenomenon with the proportions of a class structure, but in many cases it has itself become an entity and a class unto itself" (Carmichael 1971:192).

Thus differences of race generally prevented those who were in the same class level from joining forces in the pursuit of their common class interests. Carmichael said this was true on each class level, except that of the capitalist, all of whom were white: "If you understand this definition [of capitalist] according to Marx, then you will know that there is no such thing as a black capitalist anywhere in the world today" (Carmichael 1971:193). A few blacks however were among the bourgeoisie, the lackey class of the capitalist. Even in that class white and black were unable to unite, despite the fact that

"it is in the interest of the capitalist to have the white lackeys and the black lackeys come together because they are the ones who are going to fight for him. Yet the capitalists in this country are incapable of bringing them together, again because of the question of race. Because, according to Karl Marx, the white lackeys of capitalism and the black lackeys of capitalism should come together because it is the class interest that binds these people together, and since they have the same class interest, they should come together, but they do not because of race." (Carmichael 1971:193–94)

Most disturbing of all for the Marxian thesis was the fact that, even among the proletariat who were to lead the class struggle, racial differences undermined class solidarity. "We have seen that poor whites and poor blacks are incapable of coming together in this country, or when they do come together, we see it is the white man who benefits and having gained what he wants he turns against the black man. We have seen that time and time again. All coalitions of the two groups have always worked to the disadvantage of the black man" (Carmichael 1971: 194). As examples, Carmichael then pointed to the populist movement, the labor movement, and in recent times the coalition between the Black Panther party and the Peace and Freedom party.

Thus, Carmichael concluded, blacks faced the dual inequities of class and race, neither of which could be reduced to the other. Their two basic problems were

"capitalism and racism. Some people in our community say that if you eliminate capitalism, you will automatically eliminate racism. I say this is not true. While I agree that capitalism reinforces racism and racism reinforces capitalism, it is nonsensical to say that if we got rid of capitalism we would automatically get rid of racism. There are many so-called communist and socialist societies in the world today that are rampant with racism. I don't argue about which came first, whether capitalism produced racism or vice versa, but I say that racism today, even if it *were* produced by capitalism, has taken on such proportions, such institutions, that it has become an entity unto itself, and it must be dealt with as a separate entity." (Carmichael 1971:192)

To rid themselves of their oppression, Carmichael insisted, blacks in America should not try to rely on any alliance along class lines, given their historical experiences with the whites. Instead they should seek to develop a sense of self-sufficiency and also forge common bonds and a coalition along racial lines with the nonwhite people of the Third World. If they were to do this, they would become a force for revolutionary change.

The goal of this revolutionary change was not to be the means of production as phrased in Marxian terms but was to be land as phrased in Malcolm X's terms: "Brother Malcolm says, in the final analysis all revolutions are fought over the question of land" (Carmichael 1971:197). Land, however, represented more than mere soil to Carmichael, it also represented the potential for resources, technology, and means of production of society.

"It is from the land that we get everything we need for survival. It is from the land that we get our clothes, in the form of cotton. It is from the land that we get our food and the animals we take meat from. It is from the land that we get the mineral resources necessary for the development of a technological society. So we see that if we're talking about revolution, and if we're talking very seriously about revolution, we must be talking about land. Brother Malcolm is absolutely correct."   (Carmichael 1971:197–98)

But even more, land represented to Carmichael a claim to nationhood past and present. Accordingly he argued that blacks had to revitalize their ties to Africa. In fact he contended, "The highest political expression of Black Power is Pan-Africanism. Black Power means that all people who are black should come together, organize themselves and form a power base to fight for their liberation. That's Black Power" (Carmichael 1971:202).

He dismissed as naive and utopian the notion that white America would allow blacks to convert several states of the Union into the land base for their nation. Furthermore, he continued, even if blacks were able to seize such territories in the South, they would not provide the kind of industrial economy to survive in the modern world. "If we seized the land, if we held this land, we would have an agricultural society. From what would we produce our tanks, airplanes, and guns – those things that are necessary to fight imperialism? An agricultural nation could never defeat an industrial society" (Carmichael 1971:203). According to Carmichael, the long-term objective for blacks was therefore to return to their homeland, Africa. "'Are you saying we should all go back to Africa?' No, I am not saying we should all go back to Africa at this point. *We all have to go back there sooner or later though* [author's italics]" (Carmichael 1971:206).

In the interim, Carmichael insisted that American blacks had to move on two fronts. First was the front of the black ghetto. They had to convert it into a bastion of black nationalism or, as we have already said, into a quasi-nation-state with full control of its institutions and with a full flowering of black culture and pride. Second was the front of solidarity with Africa in its struggle for liberation: "we must begin to understand Africa, not only culturally, but politically, and we must begin to support those movements of liberation that seek to build truly revolutionary states in Africa that will support us" (Carmichael 1971:206).

TWO TYPES OF NATIONALISTIC BLACK POWER: CULTURAL AND REVOLUTIONARY

The nationalistic version of black power, as labeled by Carmichael but spawned by Malcolm X, generated intensified ideological and organizational efforts in the latter half of the 1960s. Their goal was to build racial solidarity and pride and to consolidate control by the black of his institutional domain within the black ghetto in a political framework of alienation and estrangement from the larger white society. This was the common ideological thread that connected those who concentrated their attention almost exclusively on constructing this quasi-nation in the ghetto – as in the case of Baraka and Karenga and the cultural nationalism each espoused – with those who saw the building of racial solidarity as part of a broader revolutionary process that would fundamentally transform the power relations between black and white in the American society. The leading exponent of this revolutionary nationalism was Newton and his Black Panther party (examined in the next section of this chapter).

For the cultural nationalism of Baraka and Karenga, the critical issue was the transformation of blacks from an anomic, dispirited, oppressed mass into a vibrant, self-contained, and self-aware community or quasi-nation, socially and culturally rooted to its African ancestry and charged with a sense of destiny and eventual political nationhood. At the very heart of this community was to be a distinctively black value system based on the seven principles of *Kawaida* as initially formulated by Karenga and subsequently adopted by Baraka. Under these principles blacks were to "Think Black, Talk Black, Vote Black, and Live Black" (Pinkney 1976:141). And through these principles they would revitalize their cultural heritage from both Africa and America, would create a racial awareness and identity for themselves and their children, and would build a strong institutional structure within the ghetto that they would control.

Though antedating Baraka in his espousal of *Kawaida*, Karenga failed to display the kind of organizational and strategic skill and genius that Baraka did. As a result, he remained essentially a provincial west coast leader of the movement while Baraka had a national presence. With his Black Community Development and Defense Organization as a springboard, Baraka organized the African Free School for black children around the doctrine of *Kawaida* and the teaching of black history and culture. From it grew the African Free School class that was incorporated in a Newark public school in 1970. Baraka was also instrumental in organizing pan-African conferences and a national black political convention. His goal was to foster unity among the various segments of the black national community and to create a political presence for them in the system. Perhaps his most signal success was the role he played in the transfer of political power from white to black in Newark with the election of a black mayor and in his subsequent influence on public policy through the Committee for a United Newark.

Both Karenga and Baraka in their early days as cultural nationalists were convinced that until blacks achieved cultural solidarity they would not be ready for the revolutionary onslaught against the dominant white society that would eventually liberate them politically. As Karenga said, "'There must be a cultural revolution before the violent revolution. The cultural revolution gives identity, purpose, and direction'" (Pinkney 1976:147). Accordingly, both were disdainful of those nationalists who sought to precipitate revolutionary political change, particularly under the banner of Marxism. They objected strenuously to the formation of coalitions and alliances along class lines, but not to their formation along racial lines with the Third World. During this period Baraka was even more opposed than Karenga to any form of white involvement in the struggle. Karenga was prepared to accept technical aid and funds from whites, but the most important thing that they could do, he insisted, was to "civilize" their fellow whites by instilling humanitarian values among them.

However, by the mid-1970s both Baraka and Karenga had embraced the basic tenets of revolutionary nationalism and had adopted a Marxist-Leninist stance.* According to Baraka, "We say our ideology is scientific socialism, specifically as practiced and theorized by Marx and Lenin and Mao Tse-tung" (Hunter 1975:57). In the October issue of *Black Scholar*, he identified capitalism, the "creator of racism," as the basic enemy of blacks and said that capitalism could only be defeated if blacks joined with other oppressed people in a revolutionary struggle to establish a socialist society.

> "'Our [black] struggle is ultimately a struggle to destroy capitalism, the creator of racism. Skin nationalism cannot do that. We need to gain a clear knowledge of Socialist theory, and unite with those who really want to build a new world. That is the only criteria. Black liberation is Socialist revolution.'"
>
> (Hunter 1975:57)

In radicalizing their cultural nationalism, Baraka and Karenga moved closer to the ideological position of the Black Panther party which sought during that period to connect the cause of racial solidarity with a larger revolutionary struggle.

The Black Panther party and revolutionary nationalism

INTRODUCTION

Founded in 1966 on the west coast shortly after Carmichael had uttered his black power slogan, the Black Panther Party for Self-Defense was created in the

---

*The defection of Baraka and Karenga has seriously thinned the leadership ranks of the cultural nationalists; in fact, they were the only two Pinkney described in detail as leading cultural nationalists in his most recent book on nationalism. According to Charlayne Hunter in her April 28, 1975 article in *The New York Times*, the mantle is now being worn by several less well-known black intellectuals and literary figures.

ideological image of the black nationalist philosophy of Malcolm X. (The phrase "for Self-Defense" was dropped in 1967.) In fact, Huey P. Newton, cofounder and principal leader of the party, "viewed himself as Malcolm's heir and the Black Panther Party as the successor to his Organization of Afro-American Unity" (Foner 1970:xvi). In its early years the party also paid homage to Carmichael as a major prophet of black power and nationalism and "a true revolutionary guided by a great feeling of love for our people" (Newton 1972:9). It adopted as its symbol what Carmichael and his former organization, the SNCC, had used earlier for the Loundes County Freedom party, the black panther. In its Executive Mandate No. 2, issued in June 1967, the party also drafted Carmichael into its ranks and bestowed on him the post of Field Marshal. Later he was elevated to the rank of Prime Minister. (Carmichael resigned from the party in July 1969 a year after the short-lived merger with the SNCC had collapsed.)

THE ORIGINAL PARTY PLATFORM AND ITS CONSTITUTIONAL UMBRELLA

Striking a militant pose from the very beginning, the party issued a ten-point platform and program that made a series of demands on the dominant white society in the name of the black people. It addressed itself, according to Bobby Seale, cofounder of the party, to "the basic political desires and needs [of blacks] that went back into the history of Black people suffering under the exploitative oppression by the greedy, vicious capitalistic ruling class of America. The Platform and Program is nothing more than the 400 year old crying demands of us Black Americans. They are basic demands of 'What We Want' and 'What We Believe'" (Seale 1969:78).

The platform began with a ringing declaration for black control of the black community: "1. *We Want freedom. We want power to determine the destiny of our Black Community*" (Foner 1970:2). And it ended with Item 10 which first summarized the party's demands: "*We want land, bread, housing, education, clothing, justice, and peace*" and then called for the intervention of the United Nations as Malcolm X had done two years earlier. Only this time the demand was for a plebiscite supervised by the United Nations to determine

> "*the will of black people as to their national destiny.... And as our major political objective, a United Nations-supervised plebiscite to be held throughout the black colony in which only black colonial subjects will be allowed to participate for the purpose of determining the will of black people as to their national destiny.*" (Foner 1970:3–4)

Even as the platform expressed a marked estrangement from the dominant society, it still retained the recurring theme in a number of items that the dominant society had a moral and legal obligation to remedy the racial oppression of blacks. Thus several items called for governmental actions and policies ranging from full employment and decent housing to better education. Another item (3) called on the government to live up to an historical promise it had allegedly made: "We believe that this racist government has robbed us and now we are demanding the overdue debt of forty acres and two mules. Forty acres and two mules was promised 100 years ago as restitution for slave labor and mass murder of black people" (Foner 1970:2). Still another item (9) drew the mantle of the Constitution and the Fourteenth Amendment around the demand for trial by a jury of peers. In elaborating on this demand, the platform stated: "We believe that the courts should follow the United States Constitution so that black people will receive fair trials. The 14th Amendment of the US Constitution gives a man a right to be tried by his peer group." And finally Item 7 demanded *"an immediate end to POLICE BRUTALITY and MURDER of black people,"* and invoked the right of self-defense under the Constitution. "The Second Amendment to the Constitution of the United States gives a right to bear arms. We therefore believe that all black people should arm themselves for self-defense" (Foner 1970:3).

Thus the original manifesto of the party retained a lingering though tentative attachment to the value-normative framework of the dominant society, much in the manner that Malcolm X had displayed earlier. It argued that its demands were both just and legitimate under this framework and in words faintly reminiscent of Myrdal insisted that the disparity between practice and norm be redressed.

Continued failure to redress these inequities and to meet these demands would, according to the platform, have disastrous consequences for the dominant society; it would lead to revolutionary upheaval. Such an upheaval, Newton wrote in a later elaboration of this part of the platform, would be in accord with a fundamental principle of justice that was legitimated by white America for itself in its Declaration of Independence as it fought to overthrow British rule; the right to abolish an oppressive system. Thus even in this section the platform had reference to the normative system of the dominant society; it quoted verbatim in its last two paragraphs the first two paragraphs of the most sacred text of that system: the Declaration of Independence. The platform merely italicized the following two sections which were left unmarked in the original text:

"That, to secure these rights, governments are instituted among men, deriving their just powers from the consent of the governed; that, whenever any form of government becomes destructive of these ends, it is the right of the people to alter or to abolish it, and to institute a new government, laying its foundation on such principles, and organizing its powers in such form, as to them shall seem most likely to effect their safety and happiness.... But when a long train of abuses and

usurpations, pursuing invariably the same object, evinces a design to reduce them under absolute despotism, it is their right, it is their duty, to throw off such government, and to provide new guards for their future security."(Foner 1970:4)

WHITE REPRESSION AND PANTHER REJECTION OF THE CONSTITUTION

Immediately upon the promulgation of its program, the party, as its full name indicated, carved out for itself a mission of active self-defense of the black community and proceeded to act on its seventh demand. Accordingly, its members undertook armed patrols of the Oakland, California ghetto, guided by a set of procedures worked out by Newton, a former law student, from the results of his intensive study of state, federal, and constitutional law on the right of citizens to bear arms. The Black Panthers focused their attention on police activity in the ghetto streets and subjected it to continuous surveillance. They even interceded if a black was stopped by the police to insure that his legal and constitutional rights were protected.* They carried these actions off in a sharply disciplined manner, dressed in distinctive garb with guns at the ready. In a short period of time, they established a forceful presence for themselves in the ghetto.

Almost as soon as the Black Panthers took to the streets, a confrontation with the police took place just outside the Panther headquarters. In this initial encounter, the action of the police was confused and hesitant, and nothing much untoward happened. Nothing much also happened several months later when Black Panthers held at bay police who had come to break up a street rally that they were holding to reveal the results of their investigation of the killing of a young black by police and to exhort the crowd in the virtue of self-defense. However, even as these standoffs were taking place, tension and strain were rapidly

---

*Having staked out a protective function for itself, the Black Panther party soon began to define its role in the ghetto in much broader terms. It began to sponsor a program of community services and activities in order to carry out those parts of its 1966 platform that it labeled its survival program for the blacks. Within a few years, it was involved in a number of different activities. Its most celebrated was the Free Breakfast for Children program that was adopted in virtually every chapter and branch of the party. Other activities directed at the young included Liberation Schools, an accredited institute that was designed as an alternative to regular public schools, campaigns against drug abuse, and the like.

In addition, the party developed a legal aid program. Through this program it not only provided assistance for those blacks in trouble with the law, but it also conducted classes and prepared a pocket manual instructing blacks in their rights and what to do in encounters with the police and the courts. The party also moved into the delivery of health care services in the black community. As such, it established clinics in several communities, a research foundation on sickle cell anemia, and other facilities. It also sponsored a program for the distribution of free shoes and clothing in the ghetto. In sum, *The Black Panther* reported in September 1972 that eleven different services were included in its survival program, with eight others still in the process of development.

mounting between the two. And soon the reaction of the police became less confused and hesitant as they sought more coolly and calculatedly to counter the assertive presence of the Black Panthers.

So began a campaign of intensified harassment. "Police bulletin boards featured descriptions of party members and their cars. On foot or driving around, Panthers would be stopped and arrested on charges ranging from petty traffic violations to spitting on the sidewalk. Newton was stopped almost daily by the police intent on arresting him" (Foner 1970:xxii). In turn, the Panthers stepped up their active surveillance of police activity; they even marched on Sacramento to forestall legislative action on a bill to forbid the carrying of arms.

The kindling point was finally reached in the fall of 1967, and a violent encounter between police and Black Panthers erupted. When the shooting was over, one police officer was killed, another wounded, as was Newton, who was subsequently convicted of voluntary manslaughter, despite his protestations of innocence. With the arrest of Newton, the campaign against the Black Panthers moved steadily from harassment to outright repression, not only in Oakland, but in Chicago, Los Angeles, New York, and in virtually any city in which the Panthers had made any headway. Federal agencies also joined local police forces in these efforts. As a result, by 1970 the leadership cadre of the party had been decimated. Some, such as Hampton and Clark, had been killed; others, such as Newton and Seale, had been jailed; and still others, such as Cleaver, had been forced into exile (later Newton also left the country). In all, according to Newton's defense lawyer, Charles Garry, twenty-eight Panthers were killed during the two-year period from 1967 to 1969. In addition, hundreds more were arrested; of these at least eighty-seven were subsequently released, their charges dropped, though not before they spent days if not months in prison.

So blatant did the campaign against the Black Panthers become that the American Civil Liberties Union felt obliged to acknowledge the campaign's existence and to condemn it as a violation of the constitutional rights of the Panthers. Its news release of December 29 1969 began:

> "'The record of police actions across the country against the Black Panther Party forms a prima-facie case for the conclusion that law enforcement officials are waging a drive against the black militant organization resulting in serious civil liberties violations.... First Amendment and due process guarantees have been breached in numerous instances.... Quite aside from the killing of Panthers and police, which we abhor, ACLU affiliates have reported that the style of law enforcement applied to Black Panthers has amounted to provocative and even punitive harassment, defying the constitutional rights of Panthers to make political speeches or distribute political literature.'"   (Foner 1970:263)

The release then described the various kinds of harassments, entrapments, and other unconstitutional actions taken by law enforcement officials. It also decried the role of federal officials in the matter, although it acknowledged, "'Our reports do not prove a directed national campaign to get the Panthers. However, even if not a concerted program of harassment, high national officials, by their statements and actions, have helped to create the climate of oppression and have encouraged local police to initiate the crackdowns'" (Foner 1970:264).

As the Black Panthers became increasingly the target of repression and of cavalier treatment in the courts, the alienation and hostility that they expressed toward the police from the very inception of the organization soon mushroomed into a wide-ranging condemnation of the administration of law and justice in the society as a whole. They complained repeatedly and bitterly that their constitutional rights, upon which they had pegged crucial demands in their platform, were being systematically and arbitrarily violated in the streets and in the courtroom. These were, they insisted, no random occurrences but deliberate acts by agents of a white capitalistic ruling class that was prepared to resort to fascistic tactics to stamp out dissent and advocacy of the legitimate rights of blacks. According to an article in *The Black Panther*, November 22 1969, bylined Candy, "'As the function of the police is to make sure that the people act according to the needs and wants of the state, their means of reaching this end is through fascism. Terror, intimidation, brutality, and murder have become the order of the day as the police try to keep any progressive or dissenting elements from developing in our communities'" (Foner 1970:36).

As a result, the article continued, this ruling class had distorted the intent and meanings of the Constitution for its own purposes.

> "'Dealing with legitimacy, the Constitution is based upon the idea of the power of the people to enjoy certain "inalienable rights," and exercise these rights. Supposedly it is the people that direct the actions of the government and sanction its authority. Today, the Constitution, has been distorted and we find "Government of a few, for a few, and by a few."'" (Foner 1970:36)

The goals of this ruling class, Seale had observed a month earlier in the paper (October 18 1969), were to maximize and to preserve the benefits of capitalism, racism, imperialism, and colonialism, and to this end it had imposed fascism on the American society. In this regard, he argued, the "oppressive ruling class circles of America" stood at the head of the worldwide forces of capitalistic exploitation "with their imperialistic, fascist, aggressive, colonialistic war mongering, not only abroad, but right here at home in America (Babylon), where hundreds of years of subtle and maniacal racism has been organized and developed by the greedy rich, organized and developed into domestic imperialism – fascism" (Seale 1969:78).

In view of what they perceived as the engulfing tide of fascism, the Panthers argued with increasing intensity that blacks could no longer rely on constitutional guarantees. Early in November 1969 an article by Hilliard in *The Black Panther* took a different tack; it resurrected a line of argument that had lain dormant for a while. It contended that the constitutional guarantees had never been meant to apply to the blacks because America always had been and was a "racist, fascist" country, run by a "slave oligarchy and brigandish criminals" whose "primary interest is capitalism" (Hilliard 1969:122).

By June 1970 the Black Panther party had adopted as its official policy the Hilliard line. In a "Message to America," "Delivered on the 107th Anniversary of the Emancipation Proclamation at Washington, DC, Capital of Babylon, World Racism, and Imperialism" (Foner 1970:267), the party denounced the Constitution as never having "'protected our people or [having] guaranteed to us those lofty ideals enshrined within it.'"

> "'The Constitution of the USA does not and never has protected our people or guaranteed to us those lofty ideals enshrined within it. When the Constitution was first adopted we were held as slaves. We were held in slavery under the Constitution. We have suffered every form of indignity and imposition under the Constitution, from economic exploitation, political subjugation, to physical extermination.
>
> We need no further evidence that there is something wrong with the Constitution of the United States of America. We have had our Human Rights denied and violated perpetually under this Constitution – for hundreds of years. As a people, we have received neither the Equal Protection of the Laws nor Due Process of Law. Where Human Rights are being daily violated there is denial of Due Process of Law and there is no Equal Protection of the Law. The Constitution of the United States does not guarantee and protect our Economic Rights, or our Political Rights, nor our Social Rights. It does not even guarantee and protect our most basic Human Right, the right to LIVE!'" (Foner 1970:269)

The partly climaxed its message with a "'CALL FOR A REVOLUTIONARY PEOPLE'S CONSTITUTIONAL CONVENTION, TO BE CONVENED BY THE AMERICAN PEOPLE, TO WRITE A NEW CONSTITUTION THAT WILL GUARANTEE AND DELIVER TO EVERY AMERICAN CITIZEN THE INVIOLABLE HUMAN RIGHT TO LIFE, LIBERTY, AND THE PURSUIT OF HAPPINESS!'" (Foner 1970:271).

Having publicly dissociated itself from the Constitution in its Message of 1970, the party went a step further two years later. In its 1972 revision of its platform, it deleted all references to the mantle of constitutional guarantees with which it had cloaked its demands in the original platform of 1966. It only retained as its concluding two paragraphs the quotation from the Declaration of Independence which legitimized revolution.

FROM AN IDEOLOGY OF BLACK TO REVOLUTIONARY NATIONALISM

Throughout this period the overall ideology of the Black Panther party was also undergoing significant changes. With Malcolm X clearly its patron saint, the party defined its role in its first year almost exclusively in ideological terms that were steeped in his conception of black nationalism. Its primary mission of self-defense, for example, was clearly borrowed from the legacy of Malcolm X. Newton acknowledged this debt in the second installment of his "In Defense of Self-Defense" that appeared on July 3 1969.

After pillorying the white oppressor and those black spokesmen who, endorsed by the whites, were trying to get the blacks to submit passively to this oppression, Newton went on to say that the black community had resisted these blandishments, for it "realizes that force and brutality can only be eliminated by counterforce through self-defense." Malcolm understood this and became along with Marcus Garvey the only "two Black men of the twentieth century who posed an implacable challenge to both the oppressor and the endorsed spokesmen" (Newton 1972:90).

By pressing the doctrine of collective self-defense, Newton continued,

"Malcolm, implacable to the ultimate degree, held out to the Black masses the historical, stupendous victory of Black collective salvation and liberation from the chains of the oppressor and the treacherous embrace of the endorsed spokesmen. Only with the gun were the Black masses denied this victory; but they learned from Malcolm that with the gun they can recapture their dreams and make them a reality."   (Newton 1972:90)

"The heirs of Malcolm," Newton concluded, the Black Panthers, in particular, were now prepared to take up the challenge.

In similar fashion, the party's platform phrased some of its key demands in the language of black nationalism. As we have already seen, its message was clearly addressed to and on behalf of blacks only. It also called for control and defense of the black community by blacks against the white racist society, it stressed the colonized status of the black, and demanded intervention of the United Nations (as Malcolm X had done earlier) so that the blacks could determine their national destiny. The Executive Mandates issued by Newton in 1967 were likewise replete with nationalistic references; this was particularly true of the encomium to Stokely Carmichael that drafted him into the party with the rank of Field Marshal for his distinguished service "in the struggle for the total liberation of Black people from oppression in racist White America" (Newton 1972:9). The party had earlier adopted Carmichael's slogan of black power in promoting its cause. It presented this pronouncement in the first issue of its newspaper *The Black Panther*, on April

25 1967. "'So Brothers and Sisters, everywhere: righteous BLACK POWER *organized* is where it's at. The *BLACK PANTHER PARTY FOR SELF-DEFENSE* really has something going'" (Foner 1970:12).

Committed as he was to black nationalism, by early 1968 Newton nevertheless drew a line against the obsessive and xenophobic preoccupation of cultural nationalists with their black heritage and Africa. He conceded that blacks "have to have an identity. We have to realize our Black heritage in order to give us strength to move on and progress. But as far as returning to the old African culture, it's unnecessary and in many respects unadvantageous. We believe that culture alone will not liberate us" (Newton 1972:93). The reason for this inadequacy was quite evident.

> "Cultural nationalism, or pork-chop nationalism as I sometimes call it, is basically a problem of having the wrong political perspective. It seems to be a reaction to, instead of an action against, political oppression. The cultural nationalists are concerned with returning to the old African culture and thereby regaining their identity and freedom. In other words, they feel that assuming the African culture is enough to bring political freedom. Many cultural nationalists fall into line as reactionary nationalists."   (Newton 1972:92)

What was needed for black liberation, he insisted, was "some stronger stuff" and that stronger stuff was a revolutionary nationalism which "is a people's revolution with the people in power as its goal" (Newton 1972:92).

> "A good example of revolutionary nationalism was the revolution in Algeria when Ben Bella took over. The French were kicked out, but because it was a people's revolution the people ended up in power. The leaders that took over were not interested in the profit motive or exploiting the people to keep them in slavery. They nationalized the industry and plowed the would-be profits back into the community. That's what socialism is all about. The people's representatives are in office strictly by the consent of the people. The wealth of the country is controlled by the people and they are considered whenever modifications in the industries are made."   (Newton 1972:93)

The Black Panther party, he concluded, stood for this approach to black liberation: "[it] is a revolutionary nationalist group and we see a major contradiction between capitalism in this country and our interests. We realize that this country became rich upon slavery and that slavery is capitalism in the extreme. We have two evils to fight – capitalism and racism. We must destroy both racism and capitalism" (Newton 1972:93).

In relating black nationalism to revolutionary nationalism, Newton was not undergoing any kind of ideological conversion. He was merely bringing together the various threads that had already surfaced in his thinking from the moment he founded the party. Even prior to that, he as well as cofounder Seale had been overwhelmed by Frantz Fanon's *Wretched of the Earth* (1968) and had treated it from then on as a sacred fount of revolutionary wisdom. By mid-1967 Newton had proclaimed in his column in *The Black Panther* a revolutionary role for blacks in America: "It is our belief that the Black people in America are the only people who can free the world, loosen the yoke of colonialism, and destroy the war machine" (Newton 1972:83). A month later in his column on "The Correct Handling of a Revolution," he charged the Black Panther party with the responsibility of molding and directing the revolutionary potential of the blacks. As such, it was to serve as the vanguard party. Its primary task would be "to awaken the [black] people and teach them the strategic method of resisting a power structure which is prepared not only to combat with massive brutality the people's resistance but to annihilate totally the Black population" (Newton 1972:15).

Such a strategy of self-defense, he acknowledged, might increase the repressive brutality of

"the man, [but] . . . the fact is that when the man becomes more oppressive he only heightens revolutionary fervor. So if things get worse for oppressed people they will feel the need for revolution and resistance. The people make revolution; the oppressors, by their brutal actions, cause resistance by the people. The vanguard party only teaches the correct methods of resistance."

(Newton 1972:18)

Such resistance had become increasingly essential, Newton had argued a month earlier, because white America had in the final analysis denied to the black the same right it reserved for itself during its own revolution and in its Declaration of Independence: the right to abolish or even to speak of abolishing an oppressive system.

As the Black Panther party was articulating its doctrine of revolutionary nationalism in 1968, it took a decisive step that virtually severed its remaining ties with the cultural and orthodox black nationalists. It entered into an alliance with a California-based Peace and Freedom party, a radical white political group that ran on the platform of opposition to the Vietnam War and of support for black liberation. Cleaver subsequently became the party's candidate for President of the United States in the national election of 1968. One of the immediate consequences of the alliance was the rupturing by summer 1968 of the coalition with the SNCC that had just been gingerly forged a few months earlier. Carmichael, formerly of the SNCC and the one who was instrumental in developing its all-black policy, protested the alliance but remained with the Panthers for one more year before he too resigned over the issue of coalition with whites.

In *The Black Panther* on October 26 1968, the party defended its alliance in part on pragmatic grounds, such as the need for aid in the campaign to "Free Huey" from prison, and in part on the grounds of revolutionary nationalism:

> "'The Black Panther Party (or any Black liberation force) cannot be successful without the complete support of the people. All power comes from the people. But we often hear that a certain segment of the general population has all of the power because it has the largest concentration of money or weapons. This is not true. Without people, both money and weapons are useless....
>
> The people are the ultimate source of power. Let's unite and give more power to the Black Panthers, so that the Panthers will liberate all the power for "the people."'" (Foner 1970:23–4)

But whichever were the grounds mentioned during this period, Newton left no doubt that he and his fellow blacks were to exercise the leadership in any such arrangement. For, he argued, blacks were of necessity on the front lines of the revolutionary struggle because exploitation and racism were part of their daily reality. By contrast, he declared, "white mother-country radicals," many of whom were the offspring of the exploiters, merely knew of oppression from the distance; it was just an abstraction to them. This was the gist of his answer to a question he addressed to himself in May 1968: "The Black Panther Party has had considerable contact with White radicals since its earliest days. What do you see as the role of these White radicals?" (Newton 1972:94–5).

FROM REVOLUTIONARY NATIONALISM TO MARXISM-LENINISM

By the fall of 1969 the Black Panther party had undergone another ideological transformation. It had reshaped its belief in revolutionary nationalism into a hyphenated version of Marxism-Leninism and identified itself as a Marxist-Leninist party. As a result, its defense of the policy of coalition shifted to the need for international solidarity among the oppressed proletariat of the world, non-white and white. This defense was stressed by Cleaver in his effort to counter Carmichael's blistering attack on the coalition policy when he resigned from the party the pervious summer.

> "We are a Marxist-Leninist Party, and implicit in Marxist-Leninism is proletarian internationalism, and solidarity with all people who are struggling and this, of course, includes white people. So that since his [Carmichael's] main object is non-alliance with whites, and turning one's back on whites and having no policy

toward them at all, just to ignore them, he has come down heavy on both of those points [the other point was the alleged dogmatism of the Party] in order to maintain his position. And we consider this position to be racist."

(Cleaver 1969:110)

This ideological enlargement of the category of those with whom solidarity was to be won was permanently imprinted in 1972 in the platform of the party. Not only were the demands of the revised platform made in the name of blacks, but added to the blacks were "oppressed people," "poor oppressed people," or "oppressed communities." Item 1 now read: "1. WE WANT FREEDOM. WE WANT POWER TO DETERMINE THE DESTINY OF OUR BLACK *AND OPPRESSED* COMMUNITIES [author's italics]. We believe that Black and oppressed people ..." In effect, the policy of coalition had become transmuted into a basic dictum of the party.

What had attracted the Black Panther party to Marxism-Leninism, Cleaver explained in another withering rejoinder to Carmichael a month earlier was its desire to develop a link with the ideological movement that had been more successful than nationalism in leading the revolutionary struggle of the colonized people of the world:

"You [Carmichael] are peeved because the Black Panther Party informs itself with the revolutionary principles of Marxism-Leninism, but if you look around the world you will see that the only countries which have liberated themselves and managed to withstand the tide of the counter-revolution are precisely those countries that have strong Marxist-Leninist parties. All those countries that have fought for their liberation solely on the basis of nationalism have fallen victim to capitalism and neo-colonialism, and in many cases now find themselves under tyrannies equally as oppressive as the former colonial regimes."

(Cleaver 1969:107)

A year later in a speech at Boston College, Newton offered a more theoretical explanation for the party's conversion to Marxism-Leninism. He stated that even as the Black Panther party was moving from black nationalism to revolutionary nationalism, it was continually searching for a theoretical framework and methodology that would enable it to analyze objectively changing societal conditions much as an empirical scientist would, to apply the results of this analysis to a valid understanding of the unfolding character of society, and finally to interpret the meaning and significance of all this for the attainment of the party's revolutionary goals. The party had finally found what it was looking for, Newton continued, in the dialectical materialism of Marx and was particularly impressed with the way Lenin applied the dialectical methodology to the specific historical conditions of Russia in 1917. Because of this, he declared, the Black Panthers became a

Marxist-Leninist party. ("The Black Panther Party is a Marxist-Leninist party because we follow the dialectical method and we also integrate theory with practice" (Newton 1972:25).)

In adopting a Marxist-Leninist methodology, the party never intended, Newton insisted, to take over the historical and substantive baggage and the ideological dogma that had accumulated under and encrusted over the names of Marx and Lenin:

> "We are not mechanical Marxists and we are not historical materialists. Some people think they are Marxists when actually they are following the thoughts of Hegel. Some people think they are Marxist-Leninists but they refuse to be creative, and are, therefore, tied to the past. They are tied to a rhetoric that does not apply to the present set of conditions. They are tied to a set of thoughts that approaches dogma – what we call flunkyism."   (Newton 1972:25–6)

Marx himself would reject such use of his method, Newton contended in another part of his speech, for "he was not a dogmatist. Once he said, 'One thing I'm not, I'm not a Marxist.' In those words, he was trying to tell the Progressive Labor Party and others not to accept the past as the present or the future, but to understand it and be able to predict what might happen in the future and therefore act in an intelligent way to bring about the revolution that we all want" (Newton 1972:29).

In view of this, Newton argued, Marx intended his methodology to be used for a dynamic understanding of the transformations that evolve as society moves from one stage of development to another. Thus,

> "Marx attempted to set up a framework which could be applied to a number of conditions. And in applying this framework we cannot be afraid of the outcome because things change and we must be willing to acknowledge that change because we are objective. If we are using the method of dialectical materialism we don't expect to find anything the same even one minute later because 'one minute later' is history. If things are in a constant state of change, we cannot expect them to be the same. Words used to describe old phenomena may be useless to describe the new. And if we use the old words to describe new events we run the risk of confusing people and misleading them into thinking that things are static."   (Newton 1972:26)

To apply this method today, Newton elaborated, required the reformulation of a fundamental premise of orthodox Marxist doctrine. That is to say, the industrial workers or proletariat no longer carried the potential for revolution that they once did at certain stages of capitalism. Today the revolutionary vanguard was the lumpenproletariat; they would "carry the people of the world to the final climax of the transformation of society" (Newton 1972:26). This had come about because "[capitalist] technology is developing at such a rapid rate that automation will progress to cybernation probably to technocracy" (Newton 1972:27). As a result, only a small cadre of technocrats, "too specialized to be identified as a proletariat" (Newton 1972:29), would be needed to run the productive machinery of society. As this happened, an increasing number of the industrial proletariat would be dispossessed from their labor, much as the petite bourgeoisie were dispossessed from their property in the early days of capitalism, and would join the ranks of the unemployed, or in other words the ranks of the lumpenproletariat.

Much of this was yet to happen, Newton admitted, but it would be the inevitable outcome of the present working of the dialectical process. Thus the lumpenproletariat, though a minority today, would become the majority tomorrow. The Black Panther party, however, "will not wait until the proletariat becomes the lumpenproletariat to educate him. Today we must lift the consciousness of the people" (Newton 1972:30). In this way the party would seek to realize the revolutionary potential in the evolving situation and speed up the process of transforming society.

Still another major premise of orthodox Marxism that Newton reformulated in his speech had to do with the withering away of the state that Marx in the Communist Manifesto had predicted would happen after socialism evolved into communism in the post-revolutionary period. Newton insisted that the condition of a "non-state" was already present in the world but not in the manner Marx had forecast. According to Newton, America had created this condition throughout the world by "being transformed at the hands of the ruling circle from a nation to an empire" (Newton 1972:30). As an empire, America had brought the full weight of its advancing technology, its firepower, and its control of mass media to bear on nation-states throughout the world and had destroyed their independence and integrity. "Their self-determination, economic determination, and cultural determination has been transformed by the imperialists and the ruling circle. They were [sic] no longer nations [nation-states]" (Newton 1972:31–2). With the breakdown of their independent institutional and state structures, Newton continued, "*nations have been transformed into communities of the world*" which were presently under the domination and control of the ruling circles of America. In this manner, then, "the ruling reactionary circle, through the consequence of being imperialists, transformed the world into what we call 'Reactionary Intercommunalism.' They laid siege upon all the communities of the world, dominating the institutions to such an extent that the people were not served by the institutions in their own land" (Newton 1972:32). Newton concluded that the "non-state" which Marx had predicted for the future "has already been accomplished, but it is reactionary" (Newton 1972:33).

The goal of the Black Panther party, Newton declared, was "to reverse that trend and lead the people and communities of the world into the age of 'Revolutionary Intercommunalism.' This would be the time when the people seize the means of production and distribute the wealth and the technology in an egalitarian way to the many communities of the world" (Newton 1972:32). And thus, the world would move toward the kind of "non-state" that Marx had envisioned. However,

"after the people possess the means of production we will probably not move directly into communism but linger with Revolutionary Intercommunalism until such time as we can wash away bourgeois thought, until such time as we can wash away racism and reactionary thinking, until such time as people are not attached to their nation as a peasant is attached to the soil, until such time as that people can gain their sanity and develop a culture that is 'essentially human,' that will serve the people instead of some god."   (Newton 1972:37–8)

At that point, he concluded, "we" will have united "as one community" and have transformed "the world into a place where people will be happy, wars will end, the state itself will no longer exist, and we will have communism" (Newton 1972:37).

Less than two weeks after his speech at Boston College, Newton used his version of Marxism as the ideological springboard from which he renewed the Black Panthers' call for "a new constitution for a new world" (Newton 1972:43) at the Revolutionary People's Constitutional Convention in Washington, DC. He did so after a succinct analysis of the dialectical process which he insisted obliged the oppressed communities of the world to unite in their revolutionary struggle for liberation. Three months earlier the party had not attempted such a theoretical approach in its initial call for a new constitution. It had confined itself almost exclusively to a bitter denunciation of the United States as a fascist country and to a categorical repudiation of the American Constitution.

The "Marxist-Leninist" revisions of Newton and other Black Panthers soon came under attack from more orthodox Marxists. Patterson, for example, in a relatively mild rebuke labeled some of the Panthers as Left sectarians. Particularly offensive to many was the emphasis by the Black Panthers on the lumpenproletariat as the vanguard of the revolution. As Draper says in sharp tones:

"No other 'Marxist-Leninists' have ever identified themselves with the *Lumpenproletariat*, the most rootless and degraded elements in capitalist society, whom Marx and Engels regarded as a 'dangerous class' whose conditions of life destined it to play a reactionary role. The peculiar 'amalgam,' [the Black Panther ideology] as Trotsky would have called it, of bits and pieces from Frantz Fanon, Malcolm X, Mao Tse-tung, Ernesto Che Guevara, Regis Debray, and others, is typical of the kind of do-it-yourself Marxism-Leninism that has come into vogue. It is especially characteristic of movements which have invited themselves into the Marxist-Leninist tradition from the outside, bringing with them their own national or particularist folkways, and shopping among all the current versions of the doctrine for those features or formulas which happen to suit or please them the most."   (Draper 1970:102–03)

As we have already seen, Newton never professed to be an orthodox Marxist; he had merely said he was adapting Marx's dialectical method to the analysis of evolving societal transformations. Thus, he readily acknowledged his debt to other revolutionary writers from Fanon to Debray. In fact, his substantive version of Marxism shows a markedly close parallel to the ethno-Marxism of Fanon, including the role of the lumpenproletariat in the revolution. As a result, the ideology of Newton and the Black Panther party has a hybrid quality derived from a variety of sources. Pinkney describes these various sources:

"The ideology of the Black Panther party combines revolutionary black nationalism with Third World adaptations of Marxism-Leninism. Aspects of its ideology are from Frantz Fanon (the cleansing force of violence which frees one from despair and feelings of inferiority); from Mao Tse-tung (the power of the gun); from Che Guevara (death with honor, and many Vietnams); from Ho Chi Minh (feed on the brutality of the occupying army); from Al Fatah (terrorize, disrupt, and destroy); from Kim II Sung (autonomy, integrity, and responsibility of the party)."   (Pinkney 1976:106–07)

Though the substantive results were eclectic, Newton had hoped that the application of Marx's method would resolve for the party some of the basic ambiguities that were built into its ideological heritage from Malcolm X as the party moved, as Malcolm had before it, from black nationalism to revolutionary nationalism. Instead, the creative reinterpretation of Marx merely brought into sharper focus some of these ambiguities and raised additional questions about the shape and character of the revolutionary process and its outcome. According to the orthodox Marxists, such ambiguities could have been eliminated had Newton chosen to accept their definition of the dialectical process and their delineation of the stages of the revolutionary process. But Newton had already said, to paraphrase his words, that he would not exchange a logically consistent and closed theory of past societal transformations for a dynamic and evolving theory of present and future transformations. However, despite this conviction, he never advanced his revolutionary theory of "intercommunalism" and "lumpenproletariat" beyond the stage of broad assertion and general speculation. He never showed, for example, in unambiguous and clear terms how his theory would work through the dialectical process and produce revolutionary transformations on the macro level of the world at large or even in America itself, but he continued to reject the Republic of New Africa's vision of a purely racial upheaval for America with the subsequent carving out of territory from the United States for a sovereign black state, just as he had long ago repudiated the "back to Africa" solution of other black nationalists. In other words, he remained convinced that only the united revolutionary assault of black and white members of the lumpenproletariat, with the blacks and the Black Panther party playing a leading role, could successfully transform the "white mother country," (Cleaver's favorite expression for the United States). But whether such a revolutionary assault could be confined to the United States or would have to be part of a world-wide struggle, remained unanswered just as did many other questions of when, how, and under what circumstances.

THE RETURN TO THE MICROCOSM OF THE OPPRESSED COMMUNITY

By early 1971 Newton began to question seriously the imminence of any revolutionary transformation of the American society. He complained that the "hook-up with White radicals" had not worked; "[it] did not give us access to the White community because they do not guide the White community" (Newton 1972:51). The defection of Cleaver also made Newton reassess the role of the Black Panther party in the black community. He complained that Cleaver had misled the party into a misplaced sense of revolutionary urgency that caused it to emphasize guns and a paramilitary posture and to lose touch with the people.

Now, he insisted, the party had to return to the oppressed community of the blacks in order to serve its true interests and needs through the use of the dialectical method for a "concrete analysis of conditions" (Newton 1972:49). In other words, the party must realize that "revolution is a process and we cannot offer the people conclusions – we must be ready to respond creatively to new conditions and new understandings" (Newton 1972:57).

In this manner the Black Panther party turned inward once again to the black community and sought to develop and to elaborate its revolutionary ideology on the microcosmic level of the community. Top priority was given to its survival programs, which Newton was convinced would keep the revolutionary flame lit for the long haul. But in the interim he was prepared to compromise with elements of the established system. For example, he shifted his earlier blanket condemnation of black capitalists to selective approval of those who contributed financially to the survival programs; he justified this switch in the revolutionary rhetoric of Marx.

"There is no salvation in capitalism, but through this new approach the Black capitalist will contribute to his own negation by helping to build a strong political vehicle which is guided by revolutionary concepts and serves as a vanguard for the people....

So we will heighten the contradiction between the Black community and corporate capitalism, while at the same time reducing the contradiction between the Black capitalist and the Black community. In this way Black capitalism will be transformed from a relationship of exploitation of the community to a relationship of service to the community, which will contribute to the survival of everyone."

(Newton 1972:107–08)

However, whatever the justification, the fact is that the party made a major accommodation with the present system. In a similar vein, as the party solidified its position in the Oakland community it took an increasingly active part in the political process, even after Newton had to leave the country, and was even instrumental in electing black officials to public office. Here too the actions were justified on revolutionary grounds. And thus we find today an interesting mirror image of the Myrdalian doctrine being played out by the Black Panther party: the disparity between the espousal of revolutionary ideals and the call for the overthrow of the present system with practices that help make the system work.

THE IMPACT OF THE BLACK PANTHER PARTY

Though the fortunes of the Black Panther party had waned by the early 1970s, its effect on the black community should not be underestimated. In its early days, according to Draper, "The Panthers seemed at first little more than another self-appointed local band of black nationalists in an urban ghetto" (Draper 1970:99). But it soon created a deep and abiding impression in the minds of blacks in the ghetto of Oakland with its disciplined self-defense forays and early confrontations with the police. Its popularity zoomed locally with a mass rally at the beginning of 1967 at which it reported the results of its investigation of the death of a black youth by police and spread its gospel of self-defense. This occasion also marked the appearance of the first issue of *The Black Panther Black Community Service* which became the voice of the party. As its other community services and activities further broadened its support in the Oakland ghetto; its reputation began to spread throughout the state of California first, and then throughout the nation.

As a result, from a small cadre of about seventy-five primarily from the Bay area, the party began to grow in size and number, to attract converts of no mean stature such as Eldridge Cleaver, and to take on a national significance and scope. So marked was its success that, to continue with Draper,

"From this unlikely beginning, the Black Panthers have become a formidable national movement. In three years they claimed to have set up about thirty chapters, the largest in the Oakland-San Francisco area and Chicago, which have had a membership of about five thousand at its peak, but this was probably cut to about half or less by the end of 1969 as a result of police persecution. Besides Cleaver, it was able to win over though only for a short time, such well-known figures as H. Rap Brown and Stokeley Carmichael of SNCC. It entered into a coalition with the white-based Peace and Freedom Party, which ran Cleaver for President in the 1968 election. Its program of black nationalism was endorsed by the Students for a Democratic Society in March 1969, and it precipitated the SDS split in June of that same year. It is allied with a new League of Revolutionary Black Workers which has sprung up in the automobile industry and particularly threatens the United Auto Workers Union. It initially provided much of the inspiration, leadership, and program of the black student unions in universities, colleges, and high schools."   (Draper 1970:99–100)

The growth in membership and alliances during this period was just part of its meteoric rise; what was equally impressive was the visibility it attained among the black masses throughout the country and the support they gave it. This is attested to by various opinion surveys conducted during this period. However, as its membership, activities, revolutionary rhetoric, and popularity among blacks expanded, and its revolutionary rhetoric grew more strident, it became increasingly an object of terror and hostility among whites. As a result, the media pilloried it with growing venom, and law enforcement officials, both local and national, intensified their repressive measures. By the end of 1972, these countermeasures had taken their toll. As we have already seen, its leadership had been decimated, and factionalism had broken the fabric of unity. The net result was reorganization of the party, a determination to confine most of its work to the black community of Oakland, and a decision to maintain a low profile on the national scene.

The colonial analogy and the quasi-plural society

INTRODUCTION

Varied as were the versions of black nationalism for which Malcolm X was the germinal source and black power the symbolic representation, all shared a common axiomatic premise which served as the cornerstone for this distinctive brand of nationalism. All black nationalists viewed the status of blacks in America, both past and present, as that of colonial subjects whose experience in the North as well as in the South was qualitatively different from that of the white immigrant but parallel to that of the subject peoples of the nonwhite Third World. Both sets of experiences were seen as the product of the same historical process: the colonialist and imperialist expansion of white Europeans that began centuries ago.

As we shall see, this colonial interpretation of the black encounter with America resonates in significant ways with the "plural society" formulation that we have been using. But the interpretation differs from our general view of this encounter in being treated as its sole explanation. We have argued that another model based on the American creed must also be taken into account for a fuller measure of understanding of this encounter. In this section we shall examine the colonial interpretation in detail and assess the extent to which it does indeed account fully for the black experience in America.

BLAUNER AND THE TWO TYPES OF COLONIALISM

While black nationalists invariably allude to the colonial status of the black in America, few have sought to follow through at length with the theoretical meaning and significance of this colonial analogy. One of those who has is the radical white sociologist, Robert Blauner, whose book, *Racial Oppression in America* (1972), sets forth the major outline of this colonial interpretation; another is the black sociologist, Robert Allen, whose book, *Black Awakening in Capitalist America* (1970), emphasizes the neocolonial status of blacks in America.

First let us examine Blauner's treatment of the subject. To begin with, Blauner does not lump all types of colonialism together. He distinguishes the classical or traditional type which "involves the control and exploitation of the majority of a nation by a minority of outsiders" from internal or domestic colonization or colonialism by which a white majority has exploited and controlled racial minorities, particularly the blacks in America. Despite this distinction, Blauner argues, both "developed out of the same historical situation and reflected a common economic and power stratification" (Blauner 1972:83). They are both products of the historic drive by white Europeans for the conquest and domination of peoples of non-Western and nonwhite origins; they also reflect the translation of military and technological superiority into claims of cultural superiority by which racist ideologies have been "elaborated to justify control and exploitation of nonwhite people" (Blauner 1972:84).

Blauner thereby claims that domestic colonialism shares four basic components with traditional colonialism.* The first is mode of entry. Both begin "with a forced, involuntary entry." In traditional colonialism a small invading force of

---

*Actually, Blauner manifestly relates these four components only to the domestic variety, but his discussion until this point focuses on the similarities between the two types of colonialism. It is evident that these four components are at the heart of both systems for Blauner.

whites typically subdues an indigenous nonwhite population; in the internal colonialism of America, blacks are forcibly imported into the dominant white society. The second shared component is "the impact on culture. The effects of colonization on the culture and social organization of the colonized people are more than the results of such 'natural' processes as contact and acculturation. The colonizing power carries out a policy that constrains, transforms, or destroys indigenous values, orientations, and ways of life" (Blauner 1972:84). In traditional colonialism missionaries are particularly charged with spreading the white man's values and beliefs and with the stamping out of heathen religions. In domestic colonialism the pulverization of the "colonized" culture and religion can be even more complete; the net result may be pervasive anomie and alienation among the oppressed. "Third is a special relationship to governmental bureaucracies or the legal order. The lives of the subordinate group are administered by representatives of the dominant power. The colonized have the experience of being managed and manipulated by outsiders who look down upon them" (Blauner 1972:84). This is true whether these outsiders comprise a small group of ruling white elite as in the traditional colony or are members of the white majority in the domestic colonial society.

The fourth component is racism. "Racism is a principle of social domination by which a group seen as inferior or different in alleged biological characteristics is exploited, controlled, and oppressed socially and psychologically by a superordinate group" (Blauner 1972:84). The ideology of racism pervades the traditional colonial societies just as it pervades the domestic colonial society of America.

What the white Europeans were after in their conquest of traditional colonial societies was the twofold objective of expropriating and controlling the land and resources of these indigenous populations and of forcing them to labor on behalf of the economic interests of the white colonialists. Both land and labor were also objectives of domestic colonialism in America, according to Blauner; but each of these objectives could only be realized through relations with different racial minorities, not through the same racial group as in traditional colonialism. Thus Blauner turns primarily to relations with the American Indians in describing how land was expropriated and exploited under the American version of colonialism, but he cannot turn to them as participants in the system of forced labor under domestic colonialism. Efforts to use Indians historically in this manner failed. Instead he sees the black slave as the central figure in the system of forced labor that characterized domestic colonialism. In turn, Blauner cannot effectively link the black slave to the several-century history of the frontier and of land expropriation under domestic colonialism; for the black slave had been divested of all claims to land and resources in Africa when he was forcibly brought to America as enslaved labor.

THE LABOR STATUS OF THE BLACK AND INTERNAL COLONIALISM

In an early essay, Blauner at first failed to identify the presence of an unfree labor supply as a crucial component of the parallelism between domestic and traditional colonial societies. He remedied this omission by adding the following footnote to the statement quoted earlier on the four components shared by the two colonialisms: "the separation in labor status between the colonized and the colonizers" (Blauner 1972:84). According to Blauner, the colonized in both types of colonial societies are forced into various forms of unfree labor; the colonizers or whites, whether native-born or immigrant, sell their labor on a free market. The former are therefore much more likely to be victims of exploitation, discrimination, permanent poverty, and coercion; the latter, even though initially poor and disadvantaged, retain a degree of autonomy, mobility, and collective defense that allows them to soften the burden of the marketplace. In a later essay, what was more or less an afterthought in the earlier one becomes the central link between the two types of colonial societies: the status of the subjugated or colonized nonwhite population as a relatively unfree labor force.

By focusing on forced labor, Blauner provides a compelling argument for the colonial analogy during the period of black enslavement. Despite the brief interlude of radical reconstruction, emancipation did not basically alter the status of the black in the South. The reconstitution of southern society along Jim Crow lines forced masses of blacks into the status of sharecroppers and tenant farmers; they became in effect "agricultural serfs little removed from formal slavery" (Blauner 1972:59). Accordingly the colonial analogy continued to have relevance for the South until recent years.

When he turns to the North, Blauner becomes more imprecise and unclear in his presentation and elaboration of the colonial analogy. On the one hand, he continues his labor status thesis by contrasting the relative freedom of the white immigrant in the labor market with the relative unfreedom of the black. He argues that despite the fact that most white immigrants were penniless upon arrival in America, their voluntary entry and status as free labor allowed them greater autonomy, opportunities, and mobility than the blacks had; their status also created a more favorable set of life circumstances and facilitated their assimilation into the American society.

"Because the Europeans moved on their own, they had a degree of autonomy that was denied those whose entry followed upon conquest, capture, or involuntary labor contracts. They expected to move freely within the society to the extent that they acquired the economic and cultural means. Though they faced great hardships and even prejudice and discrimination on a scale that must have been disillusioning, the Irish, Italians, Jews, and other groups had the advantage of European ancestry and white skins....

Thus the entrance of the European into the American order involved a degree of choice and self-direction that was for the most part denied people of color. Voluntary immigration made it more likely that individual Europeans and entire ethnic groups would identify with America and see the host culture as a positive opportunity rather than an alien and dominating value system. It is my assessment that this element of choice, though it can be overestimated and romanticized, must have been crucial in influencing the different careers and perspectives of immigrants and colonized in America, because choice is a necessary condition for commitment to any group, from social club to national society." (Blauner 1972:56)

Obviously the most unfree labor condition for the black was during the centuries of enslavement in America; equally obvious is the fact that this is the kind of black whose status as forced labor is being compared by Blauner to the white immigrant's status as free labor. But what Blauner fails to mention, which would make his thesis more compelling, is the fact that slavery was not confined to the South and had in fact been legitimated by the North as well. Consequently, it can be argued that, to the extent that the North accepted the institution and in fact practiced slavery, to that extent the "colonial analogy" which is built on the edifice of forced labor was implanted in the institutional infrastructure of the North, and despite the early emancipation of the slaves in the North it remained there, not merely as fossilized remains but as a deeply engrained coding for the future.

However, by the time white immigration got under full sway with the coming of the Irish in the nineteenth century, the northern blacks had already been freed, although the southern blacks were still enslaved. Thus Blauner's black-white comparison deals in fact with two groups which were formally free wage earners in the North. However, one of these groups, the blacks, had become by the nineteenth century a *de facto* part of the "indigenous native population," whose occupational preserve was being invaded by alien outsiders, the white immigrants. Handicapped by an unfavorable competitive position in the labor market which derived from the slave and "racist" heritage of the North, the blacks quickly lost most of the occupational gains they had made prior to the arrival of the white immigrant and found themselves virtually excluded from the rapidly expanding industrial sector of the economy. The white immigrant more or less monopolized those jobs for which the black might have competed. As a result, according to Blauner, white immigrants became part of the "free mobile proletariat" whereas the blacks and other racial minorities were confined to traditional and "precapitalist employment sectors."

"In an historical sense, people of color provided much of the hard labor (and the technical skills) that built up the agricultural base and the mineral-transport-communication infrastructure necessary for industrialization and modernization, whereas the Europeans worked primarily within the industrialized, modern sectors. The initial position of European ethnics, while low, was therefore strategic for movement up the economic and social pyramid. The placement of nonwhite groups, however, imposed barrier upon barrier on such mobility, freezing them for long periods of time in the least favorable segments of the economy."
(Blauner 1972:62)

By drawing these contrasts, Blauner in effect shifts the focus from "forced labor" to "racial exclusion from the developing industrial sector of the economy" as the defining characteristic of the nineteenth-century "colonialism" of the North. He could have pursued his colonial analogy further by looking at the occupational concentration of the blacks in the North. Instead of merely saying that the blacks were confined to the precapitalistic sector, he could have shown that most were in fact employed in domestic and personal service. These occupations are natural extensions of the slave role and depict a continuation of the master-slave relationship, despite the formally free status of the black. Rex argues that the role of domestic servant represents a degree of unfreedom in the labor market that contrasts sharply with that of the free wage earner.

"Whereas the free wage worker enters the labour market directly in order to sell his labour and thereby to finance his own household and family, there is another possibility. This is that a man should be a part of his employer's or master's household. This is above all the situation of the domestic servant who stands at one remove from the calculation of market opportunity which, as Weber saw, was the essence of modern society. It is the domestic servant's master who calculates market opportunity. The fortunes of the servant depend as do those of children upon the fortunes of the paterfamilias."
(Rex 1973:78)

Thus if Blauner had taken his argument further he could have identified three features of the labor status of the blacks in the North in the nineteenth century that would have supported his colonial analogy: (1) their concentration in occupational roles that descended directly from their earlier condition of unfreedom as slaves and in which they were still constrained by varying degrees of unfreedom; (2) the invasion of their occupational domain by white immigrants and their loss of occupational gains; (3) their exclusion from the expanding industrial sector of the economy. However, despite this support for the colonial analogy, blacks were so few in number in the North during the nineteenth century that they lacked the mass and critical density that would have given the analogy more than metaphoric significance.

By the second decade of the twentieth century major population changes had occurred in the industrial North. These have important implications for the colonial analogy. White immigrants were no longer entering the country in substantial numbers, and blacks were migrating in increasingly larger numbers from the South to the North. What is more, the blacks were moving *en masse* into basic industries. Thus Blauner could no longer claim that they were excluded from the "proletarianizing" sector of the economy, but we have already seen that within this sector blacks were confined to the most onerous and backbreaking unskilled jobs. Accordingly Blauner shifts the focus of his colonial analogy from racial exclusion from basic industries to racial discrimination within basic industries. This discrimination, he argues, was qualitatively different from that experienced by earlier white immigrants. The whites had only been temporarily at the bottom; the blacks were going to be permanently there. Further, even when white immigrants were supposedly at the bottom in the nineteenth century, they managed to take away jobs from the blacks who were already here, shoving them into positions even lower than the whites. Thus the blacks continued as a racially segmented underclass even as they broke into the industrial sector which formerly had excluded them. Blauner might have also pointed to the continued concentration of blacks in personal and domestic service occupations as further support for his colonial thesis.

However, by overly concentrating on his colonial analogy Blauner fails to take into account a major transformation in the status of the blacks in the North. Overwhelmed by the masses of migrants from the South, the blacks in the North were no longer able to sustain the claim that they were part of the "indigenous native population;" instead blacks generally were viewed as alien outsiders. The whites, including the white immigrant who had by now been in the country a decade or more, felt as though they were the besieged indigenous population whose occupational and residential terrain was being threatened by these outsiders. In many respects the situation came to resemble less what happens to the colonized subject within his colony and more what happens to the colonized subject when he migrates to the metropolitan society.

Rex adopts this point of view in his discussion of the problems that

"arise when people from colonial economies and, more generally, black people, find their way to the cities of metropolitan countries, and seek to enter the roles of industrial worker and citizen.... The type case of such a situation is presented in the cities of Great Britain, France, Holland, Belgium, and Portugal, where immigrants have migrated from former colonial territories. But it may not be stretching our theoretical framework too far, to suggest that similar problems arise in the United States, when the descendants of negro slaves, who worked originally on Southern plantations, have settled in 'the North' and in the urban economy and society."   (Rex 1973:81)

Within these urban centers the colonial immigrant is consigned to "inferior and marginal industrial" jobs. "When there have not been enough jobs, he has taken more than his fair share of unemployment, and, so far as his housing is concerned, he has been assigned to whatever form of accommodation, and whatever part of the city was least attractive in terms of the particular country's values" (Rex 1973:91).

Accordingly, the colonial immigrants form in Rex's terms a substantial part of the underclass which is "a structurally distinct element from the established native working class" (Rex 1973:215). Even within this underclass, they are labeled "a pariah group. This is a group of outsiders who are called upon to perform some task which is either contrary to the values or beneath the dignity of the host society, even though it is essential to the functioning of that society" (Rex 1973:15). Thus, the colonial migrants are grafted as a class of alien newcomers to the underside of the bottom layer of the metropolitan society, are treated as an unassimilable group of undesirables, and are shunted into crowded slums that become their ghettos and compounds.

The mass migration of recent years has produced for most of the European countries their first major encounter with the nonwhite "colonized" inside the borders of the metropolitan society. These colonized had previously been confined to the distant colonies of the metropolitan society. As a result, a scenario of race relations is currently being written in these countries on blank pages of history; for the grafting of these groups onto the metropolitan society has been a "new" experience.

In the United States the mass migration was merely a new version of an old and continuing historical encounter of the North with the black. The migration superimposed the role of black as alien outsider onto an established and traditional structure of subordination and segmentation that treated the black as "colonized insider." Thus the black could be seen as either or both by the northern white. If viewed as an outsider, the black tended to be described in terms of uncivilized barbarism, of immoral and amoral rootlessness, alienation, and violence. If viewed as an insider, the black tended to be described in terms of domesticated civility and timidity. Both views shared the common theme of black inferiority. Few blacks could escape the double jeopardy of this contrapuntal assessment of their presumed inferiority. However, over time the image of the black as unassimilable newcomer superseded that of the black as a long-standing domesticated subservient so that today the historical roots of the black in the North tend frequently to be overlooked by scholars in favor of the view that he was a recent immigrant.

The full significance of the layered complexity of the black's status in the North has yet to be fully understood; however, it is evident that the colonial analogy is not adequate for the task, particularly in the simplistic terms in which Blauner and others present it.

THE COLONIAL ANALOGY AND THE GHETTO

In addition to the labor status of blacks, considerable attention has also been directed by Blauner and others to their territorial status as a fundamental link with traditional colonialism. These scholars accept fully Clark's designation of the black ghetto as a colony.

> "The dark ghetto's invisible walls have been erected by the white society, by those who have power, both to confine those who have *no* power and to perpetuate their powerlessness. The dark ghettos are social, political, educational, and – above all – economic colonies. Their inhabitants are subject peoples, victims of the greed, cruelty, insensitivity, guilt, and fear of their masters." (Clark 1965:11)

According to Carmichael, Hamilton, Clark, Blauner, Tabb, Allen, and others, an essential component of the colonial status of the ghetto is its economic control and exploitation by outside white forces. Carmichael and Hamilton argue that the same kind of economic status has been imposed on the black ghetto as has been imposed on the traditional colonies: "Exploiters come into the ghetto from outside, bleed it dry, and leave it economically dependent on the larger society" (Carmichael and Hamilton 1967:17). Tabb compares the economy of the ghetto with that of underdeveloped nations and says "The economic relations of the ghetto to white America closely parallel those between third-world nations and the industrially advanced countries" (Tabb 1970:22). In such terms a picture is painted of a "colonized" people, exploited by white businessmen and landlords, drained of its resources, and cheated and gouged by a credit system that puts it on a treadmill of debt and garnishees. Caplovitz's work, *The Poor Pay More* (1963), is frequently cited for its bald and ugly description of the "debt bondage" of ghetto residents.

Paralleling the poverty of the residents is the marginal character of the land on which the ghetto stands. Located on what urban sociologists call the "zone of transition," the ghetto stands like a no man's land between the zone of valued commercial property and the zone of substantial white residential neighborhoods. As such, Clark says, "The objective dimensions of the American urban ghettos are overcrowded and deteriorated housing, high infant mortality, crime, and disease" (Clark 1965:11).

Thus it can be concluded that the ghetto contains little of any wealth, property, or resources within its boundaries that are of any significant value to the larger white society. Clark stresses the absence of resources in the ghetto.

"The dark ghetto is not a viable community. It cannot support its people.... Its businesses are geared toward the satisfaction of personal needs and are marginal to the economy of the city as a whole. The ghetto feeds upon itself; it does not produce goods or contribute to the prosperity of the city. It has few large businesses. Most of the businesses are small, with what that implies in terms of degree of stability. Even the more substantial-appearing businesses (e.g. real estate and insurance companies) are, by and large, marginal."   (Clark 1965:27)

Accordingly, only marginal white businessmen are likely to seek to exploit the internal resources of the ghetto. The mainstream white businessmen seek their opportunities outside the ghetto where the main societal wealth, property, and resources are located. In this respect the ghetto differs from the traditional and historic colonies; in those places the internal wealth, property, and resources were the major goals of expropriation. The colonial analogy falters when it is applied literally to the land and resources of the ghetto.

What then does the larger society seek from the ghetto? Tabb answers the question succinctly: "The ghetto is dependent on one basic export – its unskilled labor power" (Tabb 1970:22). Carmichael and Hamilton agree: "The black communities of the United States do not export anything except human labor" (Carmichael and Hamilton 1967:6). Most of the working population in the ghetto leave its boundaries in the morning to work in the homes, factories, stores, and bureaucracies of the larger white society – primarily at the lowest-paid and least-skilled jobs – and return home to the ghetto at night. In effect, the ghetto serves as a dormitory for these people and as a labor compound for the larger white society. This labor compound differs from that of traditional colonialism in that it contains whole families and is their permanent residence. It resembles the African township of South Africa in that it is geographically isolated from the mainstream white society and is located on unproductive land. However, when unemployment rates soar in the ghetto as they have in recent years, increasing numbers of its residents remain virtually imprisoned inside it and rarely venture outside its borders. For them the ghetto takes on the character of an Indian reservation of the West – without, however, the claims to the land the latter has. The ghetto, in effect, no longer resembles a labor compound for the larger society, as the unemployed blacks are shunted into marginal oblivion. In this manner, the colonial analogy comes full circle once again to the labor status of the black. He has neither the land nor the resources that can be exploited as the resources of the traditional colonies were.

To the various writers on the subject, another essential component of the colonial status of the ghetto is its political powerlessness and control by the outside "white power structure." Carmichael and Hamilton contend that "colonial subjects have their political decisions made for them by the colonial masters, and those decisions are handed down directly or through a process of 'indirect rule.' Politically, decisions which affect black lives have always been made by white people – the 'white power structure'" (Carmichael and Hamilton 1967:6 –7). They agree that the same situation applies in relations between ghetto blacks and whites. They are convinced that whatever differences may separate the whites, they unite to promote and to protect their interests against the blacks. The whites are concerned with maintaining the status quo and are prepared to crush the legitimate aspirations of the black community, as the colonial power typically does against its colonized subjects.

According to this line of reasoning, to maintain control the white society imposes on the ghetto a system of direct rule as do many colonial powers on their colonies. In particular, it ships in a "foreign army of occupation – the police – " (Tabb 1970:30) and of administration who perform a custodial function and keep the subject population under surveillance and control.

> "The educators, policemen, social workers, politicians, and others who administer the affairs of ghetto residents are typically whites who live outside the black community. Thus the ghetto plays a strategic role as the focus for that outside administration which in overseas colonialism is called 'direct rule.'"
>
> (Blauner 1972:87)

Carmichael and Hamilton describe even more elaborately the tentacles of direct control and exploitation with which the white society has infiltrated the ghetto.

> "The black community perceives the 'white power structure' in very concrete terms. The man in the ghetto sees his white landlord come only to collect exorbitant rents and fail to make necessary repairs, while both know that the white-dominated city building inspection department will wink at violations or impose only slight fines. The man in the ghetto sees the white policeman on the corner brutally manhandle a black drunkard in a doorway, and at the same time accept a pay-off from one of the agents of the white-controlled rackets. He sees the streets in the ghetto lined with uncollected garbage, and he knows that the powers which could send trucks in to collect that garbage are white."
>
> (Carmichael and Hamilton 1967:9)

According to the various writers, the whites also resort to another favorite technique of traditional colonialists: the indirect rule of the colonized. Thus it is said that the whites coopt a segment of the blacks to do their bidding. This segment, according to Allen, represents the "indigenous forces of conservatism and tradition" (Allen 1970:11). In the past these blacks were drawn from the ranks of the house slaves and preachers; today they are drawn increasingly from the ranks of the educated and acculturated.

> "These acculturated natives can serve as minor functionaries in the ghetto, as they did extensively in the British Empire. They can act as middlemen between other natives and the colonist businessmen who can then reside 'abroad.' Natives who are brought into the system not only directly serve the colonial power but also are examples to others of how working hard within the system can bring advancement." (Tabb 1970:27)

Carmichael and Hamilton enlarge the category of the coopted blacks to include a number of those in professional and managerial occupations. However, they unleash their greatest resentment against the black political leaders who have become part of the white political machine.

> "The white power structure rules the black community through local blacks who are responsive to the white leaders, the downtown, white machine, not to the black populace. These black politicians do not exercise effective power. They cannot be relied upon to make forceful demands in behalf of their black constituents, and they become no more than puppets. They put loyalty to a political party before loyalty to their constituents and thus nullify any bargaining power the black community might develop. Colonial politics causes the subject to muffle his voice while participating in the councils of the white power structure." (Carmichael and Hamilton 1967:10)

In this manner Carmichael and Hamilton compare the political situation in the ghetto with that of a traditional colony. In pursuing this analogy they recognize a significant distinction between the two. "Obviously, the analogy is not perfect. One normally associates a colony with a land and people subjected to, and physically separated from, the 'Mother Country'" (Carmichael and Hamilton 1967:6). They could have gone on to say that the ghetto is not separated from the mother country and is an intrinsic part of it.

However, they dismiss this difference as irrelevant to their thesis for they point to examples where the blacks are part of the mother country and are still treated as colonized subjects, as in South Africa and Rhodesia (before its transformation into Zimbabwe), and to other examples of colonies where blacks are ruled by white representatives from the mother country, as in most colonies. They conclude their argument by saying: "It is the objective relationship which counts, not rhetoric (such as constitutions *articulating* equal rights) or geography" (Carmichael and Hamilton 1967:6).

Even though they try to gloss over this difference, Carmichael and Hamilton have in fact identified a major weakness in their analogy. This weakness does not stem merely from the fact that the black ghetto in America is part of the mother country and not separated from it. Their rebuttal is convincing that geographic distance does not in itself make the colonial analogy invalid as in the case of South Africa and the Rhodesia of several years back. But what they fail to take into account is the critical distinction between the blacks in the northern ghettos of the United States and the blacks in the two African countries. In Rhodesia, for example, the blacks were excluded from membership or citizenship in the mother country, or to put it in the same terms we have employed earlier they were excluded from membership in the People's Domain (national community) of the mother country and were indeed treated like colonized subjects. Now that Rhodesia has become Zimbabwe, they no longer are. In South Africa they are still excluded. The closest approximation to this status in American history, as we have already shown, was in the period of slavery and Jim Crowism in the South. (It is interesting to note that the only substantive support Allen offers for his colonial analogy are these periods in American history.)

However, when we return to the blacks in the northern ghetto, even Carmichael and Hamilton do not deny that they also have claims to membership in the People's Domain of the mother country and that they share certain legal privileges and immunities as citizens with the other members of the national community. Carmichael and Hamilton dismiss these claims and rights as mere rhetoric; they concentrate instead on the factual inequality and oppression that pervades the status of the ghetto black. While no one can deny the latter, the presence of these claims and rights on the American scene makes the status of the ghetto black qualitatively different from that of the colonized subject who historically had none of these claims and rights insofar as they pertained to the mother country. The net result is that there is an institutional linkage and overlap between ghetto and larger society on the American scene which legitimizes the presence of the black and gives him formal rights in both. The colonized subject had no such legitimacy nor linkage in the typical colony, which had much more the character of a closed societal system than has the ghetto.

In order to maintain their colonial analogy Carmichael and Hamilton, however, insist on making the black ghetto in America into a closed enclave. Its residents are not tied into the legal-normative framework of the larger society. Accordingly they have no privileges or immunities in that society but are merely its subjects and pawns. Allen does not go so far. He is willing to recognize the linkage. He is even willing to admit some merit to the argument of those who object to the colonial analogy.

"Their chief argument is that black people more and more are being granted the same political rights as those accorded to whites. The passage of a host of civil rights laws and their enforcement, even though less than vigorous, clearly supports this conclusion, it can be argued.

It must be admitted that there is some merit to this argument. Certainly the situation of black people has changed in recent years. ... blacks have been granted formal equality." (Allen 1970:13, 19)

However, Allen is not willing to give up the colonial analogy. Instead he claims that these changes in the status of the black indicate that

"black America is now being transformed from a colonial nation into a neo-colonial nation – a nation nonetheless subject to the will and domination of white America. In other words, black America is undergoing a process akin to that experienced by many colonial countries. The leaders of these countries believed that they were being granted equality and self-determination, but this has proved not to be the case." (Allen 1970:14)

ALLEN AND DOMESTIC NEOCOLONIALISM

This transformation into domestic neocolonialism, Allen insists was the product of deliberate government and corporate policy and action and was designed by the white power structure "to counter the potentially revolutionary thrust of the recent black rebellions in major cities across the country" (Allen 1970:17). Accordingly, both government and corporate elite invested in programs and activities from community development and poverty programs to job-training and job-development and shifted the emphasis from direct to indirect rule of the ghetto by recruiting a new black elite as agents of white corporate and government control in the ghetto.

"The members of this [new elite] class consist of black professionals, technicians, executives, professors, government workers, etc., who got their new jobs and new status in the past two decades. [Later Allen added the "black capitalist" to this elite.] They were made militant by the civil rights movement; yet many of them have come to oppose integrationism because they have seen its failures. Like the black masses, they denounced the old black elite of Tomming preachers, teachers, and businessmen-politicians. The new black elite seeks to overthrow and take the place of this old elite. To do this it has forged an in-formal alliance with the corporate forces which run white (and black) America.

The new black elite announced that it supported black power. Undoubtedly, many of its members were sincere in this declaration, but the fact is that they spoke for themselves as a class, not for the vast majority of black people who are not middle class. In effect, this new elite told the power structure: 'Give us a piece of the action and we will run the black communities and keep them quiet for you.' Recognizing that the old 'Negro leaders' had become irrelevant in this new age of black militancy and black revolt, the white corporatists accepted this implicit invitation and encouraged the development of 'constructive' black power. They endorsed the new black elite as their tacit agents in the black community, and black self-determination has come to mean control of the black community by a 'native' elite which is beholden to the white power structure."

(Allen 1970:19)

Allen is saying that the new black elite has not only been coopted by the white power structure but is also pursuing its own narrow class interests at the expense of the black masses. But Allen fails to mention that the same thing is happening to an even larger group of blacks who have been recruited in recent years to white collar, technical, professional, and even managerial jobs outside the ghetto, as government and civil rights forces have mounted pressures in the private and public sectors for equal employment and affirmative action. These blacks, however, have no constituencies to represent or to control but themselves, many do not even live in the black ghetto.

Thus in the past several decades a rapidly growing but still small new black middle class has emerged from the cauldron of the civil rights struggle and from the pressure of government policy and action on the public and private sectors of society. Many of this class have found their way into the occupational mainstream of the larger society. Others occupy similar positions within the new bureaucratic structures of the ghetto. Allen would label this entire process neocolonialism, and yet it could be looked at from another perspective. It could be viewed as the delayed operation of a process of cooptation and "assimilation" similar to that which had in earlier days funneled poor white immigrants into the middle-class occupations of the larger societal system. Only for this to happen to the blacks it has required sustained, deliberate, and elaborate intervention of government and corporate policy and not merely the normal workings of the marketplace as was the case for most white immigrants. For only through such intervention could the historically encrusted wall of institutionalized exclusion and discrimination legitimated by the racial creed be breached, and some blacks gain access to the more desirable occupational slots of the dominant society under the legal-normative code of the American creed.

The black masses, however, remain far removed from the workings of the

American creed and have been only indirectly touched by the policies of equal employment opportunity and affirmative action. Instead, they continue to be locked behind the historically frozen walls of poverty and discrimination. If anything their lot is worsening as advancing technology and automation make their unskilled labor service obsolete and cause an increasing number to swell the ranks of the unemployed and unemployable. They clearly comprise the kind of unassimilable and alienated lumpenproletariat about whom Newton wrote. Their concentration in the harsh and impoverished environment of the black ghetto lends credence to that part of the colonial analogy that maintains they are an oppressed people who have been cordoned off from the dominant white society and are subject to its oppressive control.

Wilson and the declining significance of race

THE WILSON INTERPRETATION

Almost eight years after the appearance of Allen's book, Wilson, a black sociologist, rejected the racial thesis of Allen and that of the other neocolonialist theorists, offering another interpretation for the same basic set of facts: the emergence of a new black middle class tied to the corporate and government sectors and the locking-in of the black masses into the low-wage, marginal sector of the economy with a high rate of unemployment. According to Wilson, these were primarily the results of a basic restructuring of the economy that had ushered in the modern industrial age after World War II. "Basic changes in the system of production have produced a segmented labor structure in which blacks are either isolated in the relatively nonunionized, low-paying, basically undesirable jobs of the noncorporate sector, or occupy the higher-paying corporate and government industry positions" (Wilson 1978:15–16).

Access to these higher-paying jobs for the black, he added, was facilitated by government policies, particularly by its affirmative action program. Such policies, however, "are not designed to deal with the problem of the disproportionate concentration of blacks in the low-wage labor market" (Wilson 1978:110). At that end of the occupational spectrum, he insisted, "those in the black underclass find themselves locked in the low-paying and dead-end jobs of the noncorporate industries" (Wilson 1978:16).

Neither labor market, he continued, generates the kind of racial conflict and antagonism that plagued relations between black and white in the economic sector in the earlier periods of the "plantation economy" and "industrial expansion." In each of these earlier periods the black was the target of oppression, exclusion, and discrimination merely because of his race.

In the low-wage sector of the modern industrial era, he declared, "jobs . . . are not in high demand and . . . therefore do not generate racial competition or strife among the national black and white labor force. Many of these jobs go unfilled, and employers often have to turn to cheap labor from Mexico and Puerto Rico" (Wilson 1978:16). In the higher-paying sector of the modern industrial era racial conflict is kept in check because

> "political changes leading, first, to the passage of protective union legislation during the New Deal era and, second, to the equal employment legislation in the early sixties have virtually eliminated the tendency of employers to create a split labor market in which black labor is deemed cheaper than white labor regardless of the work performed, the market that provided for so much of the racial antagonism during the earlier years of the period of industrial race relations."
>
> (Wilson 1978:110)

Wilson conceded that an "imminent potential for racial conflict" may reside in the "affirmative action programs," but he insisted that this threat has failed to materialize because of the rapid growth of the industries in which the programs have had greatest effect.

> "Their major impact has been in the higher-paying jobs of the expanding service-producing industries in both the corporate and government sectors. The rapid growth of these industries has [not only] contributed to the significant gains that talented and educated blacks have made in white-collar positions. [But] both qualified whites and blacks have been easily absorbed into these positions, and the continued expansion of corporate and government industries has kept racial friction over higher-paying corporate and government jobs to a minimum."   (Wilson 1978:110–11)

In addition, Wilson mentioned the "rigorous prerequisites [of these positions] that eliminate the poorly trained and educated regardless of race" (Wilson 1978:110) and therefore reduce the competitive pool from which the personnel can be drawn. Given the segmented nature of the labor market,

> "vastly different mobility opportunities [are available] for different segments of the black population. On the one hand, poorly trained and educationally limited blacks of the inner city, including that growing number of black teenagers and young adults, see their job prospects increasingly restricted to the low-wage sector, their unemployment rates soaring to record levels (which remain high despite swings in the business cycle), their laborforce participation rates declining, their movement out of poverty slowing, and their welfare roles increasing. On the other hand, talented and educated blacks are experiencing

unprecedented job opportunities in the growing government and corporate
sectors, opportunities that are at least comparable to those of whites with
equivalent qualifications."   (Wilson 1978:151)

Having spelled out the importance of educational and class level for a black's
chances in the labor market, Wilson then zeroed in on his central thesis.

"In view of these developments, it would be difficult to argue that the plight of
the black underclass is solely a consequence of racial oppression, that is, the
explicit and overt efforts of whites to keep blacks subjugated, in the same way
that it would be difficult to explain the rapid economic improvement of the
more privileged blacks by arguing that the traditional forms of racial segregation
and discrimination still characterize the labor market in American industries.
The recent mobility patterns of blacks lend strong support to the view that
economic class is clearly more important than race in predetermining job
placement and occupational mobility. In the economic realm, then, the black
experience has moved historically from economic racial oppression experienced
by virtually all blacks to economic subordination for the black underclass. And
as we begin the last quarter of the twentieth century, a deepening economic
schism seems to be developing in the black community, with the black poor
falling further and further behind middle- and upper-income blacks."
                                                         (Wilson 1978:151–52)

Having made his point about the importance of class, Wilson began the very next
sentence with a conditional clause about the declining significance of race in the
economic sector. Later he continued:

"To say that race is declining in significance, therefore, is not only to argue that
the life chances of blacks have less to do with race than with economic
class affiliation but also to maintain that racial conflict and competition in the
economic sector – the most important historical factors in the subjugation of
blacks – have been substantially reduced."   (Wilson 1978:152)

The reduction or racial strife in the economic sector, Wilson accepted, has not
meant its reduction in other areas of societal life, but merely a shift in the
institutional locale for such strife. For "the traditional racial struggles for power
and privilege are now concentrated in the socio-political order." The primary
antagonists in this racial drama, though, are the same as those who confronted
each other in the economic arena during the earlier period of industrial expansion,
"but the issues now [between blacks and the white working class] have more to do
with racial control of residential areas, schools, municipal political systems and
recreational areas than with the control of jobs" (Wilson 1978:121).

The racial battleground is located in the central city,

"[where] both groups have felt the full impact of the urban fiscal crisis. Unlike middle-class whites and blacks, they have been forced by financial exigencies to remain in the central city and suffer the strains of increased crime, higher taxes, poorer services, and inferior public schools. Moreover, unlike the more affluent whites and blacks who choose to remain in the central city, they cannot easily escape the problems of deteriorating public schools by sending their children to private schools. Thus, the racial struggle for power and privilege in the central city is essentially a struggle between the have-nots; it is a struggle over access to and control of decent housing and decent neighborhoods, as exposed by the black-white friction over attempts to integrate the working-class ethnic neighborhood of Marquette Park on Chicago's South Side; it is a struggle over access to and control of local public schools, as demonstrated in the racial violence that followed attempts to bus black children from the Boston ghettoes of Roxbury and Dorchester to the working-class ethnic neighborhoods of South Boston and Charlestown; finally, it is a struggle over political control of the central city, as exhibited in Newark and Cleveland when the race of the mayoralty candidate was the basis for racial antagonism and fear that engulfed the election campaign."   (Wilson 1978:116–17)

THE CRITICS AND WILSON'S RESPONSE

Immediately upon its publication, controversy enveloped the book. Critics found some fault with Wilson's historical analysis of black-white relations in America and with his attempt to fit sequentially the theoretical models of "orthodox Marxism" and of the "split labor-market" to the earlier stages of the American economy. But they reserved their greatest rancor for Wilson's thesis and title of *The Declining Significance of Race* in the modern industrial economy. For example, in its protest to the American Sociological Association for having given Wilson's book the Spivack award, the Association of Black Sociologists condemned the book for having omitted "significant data regarding the continuing discrimination against blacks at all class levels. It misinterprets even facts presented in the volume, and draws inferences that are contrary to the conclusions that other black and white scholars have reached with reference to the salience of race as a critical variable in American society" (The Association of Black Sociologists 1978). In a symposium on the book conducted in *Contemporary Sociology* Pettigrew denounced Wilson's conclusion as "premature at best, dangerously wrong at worst" (Pettigrew 1980:21).

Wilson undertook a spirited defense of his thesis and even published an epilogue in the second edition of his book. In this epilogue he modified some of his arguments and elaborated on others, but basically be reaffirmed his central thesis.

THE "FLAWED" CLASS CONCEPT

Despite Wilson's energetic defense, we contend that his analysis and interpretation of the present and of the past continue to be flawed, though not quite in the ways that Pettigrew and others have argued. One of the major flaws stems from the ambiguous and inconsistent manner in which Wilson uses his construct of class. Even his definition of class, which he admits can be a "slippery concept" and which he says is a modified version of Weber's, suffers from a lack of clarity. For example, the first clause of his definition states "the concept [class] means any group of people who have more or less similar goods, services, or skills to offer for income in a given economic order" (Wilson 1978:ix). Standing by itself this clause fails to distinguish between those who actually offer these goods, services, or skills for sale and those who share the potential for offering them for sale even though they do not or cannot sell them. In short, the clause seems to represent the "claims" of a person to position in the marketplace, whether subsequently realized or not.

The second clause of his definition appears to clarify the matter; it confines a given class membership only to those who actually sell similar skills, services, or goods in the marketplace. But in his analysis, as we shall see later, Wilson seems to include the unfulfilled claims to position as part of his definition of class, particularly when he says that race is more important than class in determining job placement in the early stages of the economy. And the second clause contains still another element that adds to the indeterminacy of his definition. For example, he says "and who therefore receive similar financial remuneration in the market-place" (Wilson 1978:ix), but he never indicates how important the phrase "similar financial remuneration" is for his definition.

These definitional obscurities would be of little moment if it were not for a much more significant analytic problem Wilson faces. Specifically he continually uses class along with race as an interpretive or independent variable to explain changes in his dependent variable, the status of the black in the economic sector. However, for many scholars including Weber and Marx, position in the economic sector (call it occupational or market status, job placement, or what you will) is a major component of their definition of class. It even seems to be for Wilson; in fact it corresponds closely to the second component of his definition of class. Offhand then it would seem that Wilson is engaged in a tautological exercise in which he is studying the effect of class upon an important component of class. And when he says in commenting upon the present stage of industrial development that "economic class is clearly more important than race in predetermining job placement" (Wilson 1978:152), he seems to be veering toward a head-on collision with the stigma of tautology.

However, inspection of the evidence which he cites to support this generalization reveals that the stigma can be avoided. He states,

> "Access to the means of production is increasingly based on educational criteria (a situation which distinguishes the modern industrial from the earlier industrial system of production).... On the one hand, poorly trained and educationally limited blacks of the inner city, including that growing number of black teenagers and young adults, see their job prospects increasingly restricted to the low-wage sector.... On the other hand, talented and educated blacks are experiencing unprecedented job opportunities in the growing government and corporate sectors, opportunities that are at least *comparable to those of whites with equivalent qualifications* [author's italics]."   (Wilson 1978:151)

In short, Wilson is saying that the level of skill, education, and training is highly correlated with the level of job placement for blacks today. Translated in terms of Wilson's definition of class, it means that the two components of his definition are intermeshed in a way they have never been in the past for the blacks and, at the higher levels of skill and education, this intermeshing is comparable to that of the whites with similar qualifications. Thus we conclude that Wilson is in fact correlating the two major dimensions of the construct of class that he defines for himself and not the relationship between class and something else.

In view of the above, we contend that in making his broad generalizations about the relative importance of class and race on placement in the economic sector, Wilson is inadvertently confining his concept of class to the first component of his definition. Thus when he says that class is more important than race in the economic sector today, he is in fact saying that the claims of the black to a given position through training, skill and education are being realized in the marketplace. And when he says that race was more important than class in the earlier stages of the economy, he is in fact saying that the claims of the black to position were not realized in the marketplace and remained an unfulfilled potential.

Our caveats do not apply to Wilson's generalizations about the life chances of the black, which he saw are primarily played out in the socio-political sector of society, though determined by the black's economic class position. By class in this context, Wilson refers to the actual position of the person in the market place and his remuneration derived therefrom; and by life chances, he refers to those bearing on "external living conditions and personal life experiences" (Wilson 1978:ix). Thus his generalization "that class has become more important than race in determining black life-chances in the modern industrial period" (Wilson 1978:150) seems quite clear. It means that the economic resources available to the black today have a greater influence on where he lives and where he sends his children to school than do restrictive racial policies and practices which formerly imposed a virtually impenetrable barrier to his residential mobility and to his children's educational opportunities.

> "Higher-income blacks are not trapped in impoverished ghettos and, although they experience more difficulty than higher-income whites in finding housing, their economic resources allow them more opportunities to find desirable housing and neighborhoods – integrated or not and either in the central city or in the suburbs – than both lower income blacks and lower income whites. However, the lack of economic opportunity for underclass blacks forces them to remain in economically depressed ghettos and to attend inferior ghetto schools."
>
> (Wilson 1980:22–3)

RACE AND THE RELATIONSHIP BETWEEN THE POLITY AND ECONOMIC SECTOR

In his critique of Wilson's book, Pettigrew identified as still another flaw Wilson's "unwarranted assumption" of the "relative independence of economics from the 'socio-political' sectors of life." Pettigrew never specifies how this "unwarranted assumpton" may have distorted Wilson's analysis; he merely says that the assumption was unwarranted in "light of the sociological literature generally and the racial discrimination literature in particular" (Pettigrew 1980:21). Wilson denied the charge in his response. He claimed that his work paid "particular attention to the role of both structural changes in the modern industrial economy and political changes of the state in displacing racial antagonisms from the economic sector to social, political, and community matters," and that it also demonstrated "contrary to Pettigrew's interpretation, the complex relationship between the economic sector and social political order in several chapters in my book" (Wilson 1980:22).

Despite Wilson's rejoinders and his frequent allusions to the relationship between polity and economy, we contend that he has failed to appreciate the inextricable historical linkage between the polity, political action, and the fate of the black in the economic sector. The state and political action, we insist, have played a much more consequential role in determining the status and treatment of the black in the economic and other sectors in all three of Wilson's industrial stages than he is prepared to accord them.

Wilson, we maintain, has sought to explain the fate of the black in the labor markets of the first two stages largely in terms of the internal workings of the economic sector or, as he says, its systems of production. The theoretical models he has applied to each of these stages have accentuated this tendency. The orthodox Marxian model, for example, which he uses to interpret the plantation economy, operates from the basic premise that the state is part of a societal superstructure derived from the underlying system of economic relations. As a result, it alleges that the polity in the plantation economy was entirely under the control of and responsive to the needs of a planter elite who sought to keep the black in perpetual servitude. The split labor-market theory which Wilson uses for interpreting the second stage of industrial development differs from the Marxian model only in that the white working class, not the white planter, occupies the strategic position in the polity:

> "As industrialization altered the economic class structure in the postbellum South, the organizing power and political consciousness of the white lower class increased and its members were able to gain enough control of the political and juridical systems to legalize a new system of racial domination, (Jim Crow segregation) that clearly reflected their class interests.
>
> In effect throughout the preindustrial period of race relations and the greater portion of the industrial period the role of the polity was to legitimate, reinforce, and regulate patterns of racial inequality [generated within the economic sector]." (Wilson 1980:17)

At this point Wilson stops short of fully accepting the basic premises and assumptions of the theories he has just expounded. He considers it "unwarranted to assume that the relationship between the economic and political aspects of race necessarily implies that the latter is simply a derivative phenomenon based on the more fundamental processes of the former." However, instead of demonstrating how this caveat might apply to the two stages he has just discussed, he applies it only to the present, the third stage of industrial development.

> "The increasing intervention, since the mid-twentieth century, of state and federal government agencies in resolving or mediating racial conflicts has convincingly demonstrated the political system's autonomy in handling contemporary racial problems. Instead of merely formalizing existing racial alignments as in previous periods, the political system has, since the initial stage and municipal legislation of the 1940s, increasingly created changes leading to the erosion of traditional racial alignments." (Wilson 1980:17)

He might have added, in both the economic and socio-political sectors of society.

In failing to apply his own caveat to his analysis of the first two stages, Wilson overlooks the kind of active and directive role that the state played during these two stages in supporting and reinforcing the mores and interests of the dominant whites. In neglecting this, Wilson misses the promise in Fanon's liberation of the political factor in his analysis of colonialism from the superstructure of orthodox Marxist doctrine and the promise in Fanon's contention that political conquest and action have played an important, if not decisive, role in imposing and maintaining a given pattern of racial dominance, economic and otherwise, in the colonial setting.

As a result, Wilson fails to give due weight to the fact that the enslavement of the black was an act of political conquest in Africa of which the white European, though not necessarily the actual conqueror, was prepared to take maximum advantage. Nevertheless, upon the black's first arrival in Virginia, as we have seen, ambiguities surrounded his legal status and the nature of his servitude. Over the next four decades only through court decisions and finally through acts of the Virginia legislature was his servitude defined as being in perpetuity and his legal status as property finally clearly established. This political and legal clarification took place while the ruling political and economic elite in Virginia was still the small yeoman planter; only later did the large slave-owning planter elite take over control of the economy and the political system.

However, even as the process of clarification was taking place, blacks comprised only a fraction of those under some form of servitude. As we have already spelled out in Chapter 3, much more widespread was the servitude of the indentured white servant. However, from the very beginning, his servitude was defined as a contractually agreed arrangement between two parties and of temporary duration. Further, the indentured white servant was assured of certain rights and immunities that cloaked him with a protective mantle of sorts during his servitude and whose implementation he could seek through the courts. Upon completion of his indenture, the white servant was accorded membership in the community of the people and endowed with a legal claim for "freedom dues" to facilitate his transition to this status. The black, during the early years of legal ambiguity, apparently shared some of the rights under servitude of the indentured white servant, but never did these rights carry with them the presumption of his eventually becoming part of the people.

Even after the plantation economy – to use Wilson's designation – took firm hold in the South, the state continued to play an important role. It became the primary agency of coercive control of the system of slavery and was responsible for enmeshing the black slave in an ever elaborating system of repression and domination. Though the planter elite were primarily the authors and beneficiaries of these state actions, most of the other whites accepted and acted upon the basic premises of white supremacy and superiority. And so the mores and law of the white South were closely interwoven.

Just as the system of slavery was born through political action and conquest, so it came to its end through political action and conquest, and not through the internal workings of the economic system. In short, the Civil War terminated what many scholars view as a still flourishing slave economy. True, the white Southerner sought to reimpose forced labor on the black shortly thereafter, but that too was ended by political action, this time by the legislative enactments of the Radical Republicans in Congress.

In reconstruction the political factor remained paramount, for its history was essentially that of a struggle for the political control of the state. However, even as this struggle was being waged, with Congress still in favor of extending the rights of the blacks in the People's Domain, actions by another part of the federal government, the United States Supreme Court, began a long process of judicial corrosion of these rights that helped to undermine the forces for reconstruction and thereby opened the door for subsequent political changes, much as the Court's Brown decision did in 1954. Only in the former case the changes reinstituted a racially segmented plural society in the South instead of dismantling one as in the Brown case. These early decisions curbed the reach of the federal government in enforcing the Fourteenth Amendment by reaffirming the right of the individual state to control its internal affairs and the right of the private sector to practice discriminatory behavior. The former proved significant in the South's later construction of a "Jim Crow" society; and the latter, in the North's retention of its own variant of a segmented racist structure. The Court delivered an even more decisive blow in 1883 when it outlawed the protective mantle Congress had thrown around the civil rights of the black in the social order.

Thus once the white Southerner recaptured control of the political structure through legal and extralegal means of persuasion and coercion, the stage was increasingly set for him to reassert legal control over the social realm as well. And with the Supreme Court's approval in 1896 of a Louisiana law, he blanketed all sections of the social and economic realms with Jim Crow legislation that solidified his new variant of a plural society and that pushed the black out of any competitive relation with the white in all sectors of society. In short, he did not limit his exclusionary and discriminatory treatment of the black merely to the economic sector but extended it to all facets of life.

While Wilson contends that the white laboring class was instrumental in building this structure in order to eliminate the competitive threat of the black in the economic sector, it would appear that this class along with most other classes of southern whites shared a horror of the brief political hegemony of the black during reconstruction and were determined not to let this happen again. Ironically they had to use more devious methods to push the black out of the political realm than out of the other realms in order to avoid a direct confrontation with the reconstruction amendments, but here too they eventually succeeded and obtained the stamp of legality from the Supreme Court.

Thus we contend that the Supreme Court as an agency of the political state did more than "legitimate, reinforce, and regulate patterns of racial inequality" (Wilson 1980:17); it also neutralized over time important constraints contained in the great amendments and in the federal legislation of the reconstruction and thereby opened up the option to the white Southerner of building the kind of Jim Crow structure he eventually did. Had the Supreme Court stood firm in these cases, it is unlikely that the executive and legislative branches of the local and state governments in the South could have constructed that kind of formidable, tightly knit and controlled, racially segmented plural structure. Instead the white Southerner might have had to be content with the more permeable variant that had been reaffirmed for the North, in which discriminatory and exclusionary practices by private individuals and groups were sanctioned and could even be enforced by courts as in the case of restrictive covenants.

In sum, we conclude that the political state through its various agencies at the local, state, and federal levels played an active role in shaping the structure of relations between black and white in the first two of Wilson's stages, just as it played an active role in shaping these relations in the third stage. Though the economic character of these relations may have been a major preoccupation of the political state in the first two stages, as Wilson suggests, the state was also very much concerned with the general status and relations of the black to the white society as a whole. In the first stage, for example, the state not only defined and elaborated the legal relationship between slave and master, but also the general relation of the enslaved black to the white society. It built a coercive and formidable web of laws to protect the white society from the threat of insurrection and resistance. Even the freed black was enmeshed, both South and North, in a network of restrictive laws, from a ban on interracial marriage to suffrage which sought to block his access to full membership in the People's Domain of the white society.

In the second stage, the political state in the South, with the benign agreement of the United States Supreme Court, launched a massive assault on the gains that the black made during reconstruction, neutralized his newly won constitutional guarantees, and once more made the People's Domain a monopoly of the white. In the process the state created a "new" plural structure of social and political, not merely of economic, oppression, exclusion, and exploitation on the back of the blacks.

THE THIRD STAGE: FROM NON-DISCRIMINATION TO AFFIRMATIVE ACTION

When we turn to Wilson's present stage of the economy, the political state – or in this case the federal government, to which Wilson concedes an active and autonomous role – initiates and carries through on policies which completely reverse the direction of those which characterized Wilson's first two stages. And as in the second stage, the "new" direction was charted once again by the United States Supreme Court. Through a series of decisions in the 1930s and 1940s, for example, the Court placed constraints on the South's Jim Crow system; and finally in its 1954 Brown decision, it delegitimized the system and its racial creed.

At the same time President Eisenhower reaffirmed the policy of nondiscrimination in government contracts established through executive order in the Roosevelt Administration some twenty years before and modified somewhat the administrative structure set up by Truman. Four years later Congress entered the lists after an eighty-year hiatus and enacted a voting bill in 1957. The web of nondiscriminatory law that was being spun by the federal government literally peaked with the passage of the Civil Rights Act of 1964. And for the first time in the entire history of federal civil rights legislation a section was included which made it unlawful to pursue discriminatory policies and practices in employment (Title VII).

To many congressmen, intellectuals, and public figures, the "colorblind" character of Title VII represented the key to eradicating the discriminatory practices and policies that infested the economic sector. Through vigorous enforcement by the agency created by the law, the Equal Employment Opportunity Commission, they were convinced that race would not only decline in significance but virtually disappear as a factor in the economic sector. In this manner, they believed, the slate of the past would be wiped clean and America would be emancipated from its history of racial inequities and truly become a society of one people under the American creed.

Even as the legislative victory of the policy of nondiscrimination was being hailed and savored, the linear descendant of the executive branch's nondiscriminatory policy in government contracts had already undergone a metamorphosis in program and policy. Established by Johnson's Executive Order 11246 this linear descendant, the Office of Federal Contract Compliance Programs, had assessed the meager accomplishments of its predecessors and concluded that racial inequities could not be effectively remedied by a policy of nondiscrimination alone. It reasoned that these inequities, primarily products of past discrimination, had become so deeply embedded in the institutional machinery of the present in the economic sector that they would still persist even if deliberate policies of discrimination were abandoned, unless a race-conscious policy deliberately aimed at these inequities was pursued. Accordingly, it established the doctrine that government contractors must not only desist from discriminatory policies but must also submit a plan of affirmative action – a phrase first used in President Kennedy's executive order – in which they would commit themselves to energetic and good faith efforts to recruit blacks and other racial minorities for job categories in which they were presently underutilized. Soon the EEOC, despite its origin as the administrative arm of the nondiscriminatory Title VII, took a similar posture; its guidelines on testing and examinations reflected its growing preoccupation with the lingering consequences of past discrimination irrespective of present intent to discriminate. And with legal challenges of the two agencies' actions and policies, the United States Supreme Court also became involved in the matter. In a case-by-case approach, it has ever since shown a measured willingness to affirm the race-conscious policies of affirmative action as a constitutionally lawful way of redressing the continuing effects of past racial discriminatory policies which may no longer be in force.

Although Wilson attributes more of the gain of the new middle-class black to the policy of affirmative action than to the policy of nondiscrimination of the third stage, he fails to make a clear-cut distinction between the origins and development of the two policy orientations. In fact, he erroneously attributes the origin of affirmative action to the civil rights legislation of the 1960s. ("If there is a basis for labor-market conflict in the modern industrial period, it is most probably related to the affirmative action programs originating from the civil rights legislation of the 1960s" (Wilson 1978:16).)

Had he drawn this distinction more clearly, he might have realized that the two policies actually derived from two different sources and reflected two different stages of development. On the one hand, the policy of affirmative action, as we have already seen, rose from the ashes of the nondiscriminatory policy enunciated several decades earlier through presidential executive orders for application to government contractors that proved ineffective. On the other hand, nondiscrimination represented the statement of principle and policy of the civil rights legislation at the time of its passage by Congress in 1964. Ironically once the EEOC sought to implement the nondiscrimination provisions of Title VII it moved increasingly in the direction of the affirmative action type policy.

In other words, the colorblind policy of nondiscrimination which may be seen as having ushered in Wilson's stage three has given way to the more race-conscious policy of affirmative action as administrative agencies have seriously sought to cope with the present effects of past racial inequities. They have done this despite the outcry of legislators, intellectuals, and others that this approach violates the legislative intent of Congress. Thus it is hard to reconcile Wilson's thesis of the declining significance of race in the economic sector with the realities of the experience of middle-class blacks. Their occupational fortunes have been tied, even Wilson admits, to the surfacing of the race-conscious affirmative action policy but, unlike the race-conscious policies of the first two stages, it has been used to facilitate their access to jobs in the economic sector, and not to block their access. Accordingly, we conclude that race has not declined in significance as a factor affecting the fate of the middle-class black in the economic sector; it has merely been *transformed*.

Before we conclude this section, we would like to take the matter one step further. We contend that even after middle-class blacks gain access to desirable jobs in the corporate or government sector, race still does not disappear, as Wilson seems to allege, as a factor affecting their chances within these sectors. There have been enough documented cases of their encounters with the personal and private prejudices of fellow workers, supervisors, and managers to indicate that race continues to operate in their work encounters and in opportunities for promotion and higher position in the organization. However, even in the absence of such prejudice, the various non-rationalities of the merit system mentioned in an earlier chapter also insure that differences in race, not merely in ability, continue to affect chances in the organization. And then there are the results of studies like the one Hudson (1978) did of the blacks in IBM, a corporation that has taken very seriously its affirmative action mandate and the EEOC guidelines on testing. Hudson found that the rate of promotion and status of blacks in the organization were highly correlated with the lightness or darkness of their skin. Thus it would seem that despite the formal policy of an organization and its determination to implement the policy, race may still affect the circumstances and opportunities of the black within the organization.

THE SOCIO-POLITICAL SECTOR AND RACE

Just as Wilson fails to highlight the race-conscious character of the policy of affirmative action in the economic sector, so does he neglect to point to it as a major issue of controversy in the socio-political sector which he asserts has become the central arena for the playing out of "traditional patterns of racial competition for power and privilege" (Wilson 1978:116). The policy has evoked emotional outcries of "quotas" and "reverse discrimination," and for almost a decade has been the issue probably more than any other that has divided the former coalition of middle-class liberals and intellectuals along ethnic and racial lines. Obviously some of this controversy has had to spill over into the economic sector, but the battleground there has been the more orderly arena of the courtroom instead of the streets. And every time an "affirmative action case" reaches the Supreme Court the controversy flares up anew, and the antagonists glare at and malign each other in the media and through *amicus* briefs in the courtroom. Wilson barely comments upon the combustible nature of the affirmative action issue; he merely alludes to the possibility that it could become "a basis for labor-market conflict in the modern industrial period" (Wilson 1978:16).

Wilson also contends that most of the racial struggles in the socio-political sector pit the key actors of the second stage against each other: the working-class white versus the black. It is essentially a struggle between "have-nots," he contends, who are seeking to gain some control over space, residence, services, and political office in the areas and neighborhoods in which they live. But he fails to see the parallel between the struggle over public schools and busing among these lower-class racial actors and the struggle over affirmative action among the middle-class racial actors. Both matters reflect the application by agencies of the federal government, including the courts, of race-conscious policies to deal with past inequities, and both link the socio-political with the economic sectors. We have already shown this in the case of affirmative action; as for schooling, many lower-class blacks recognize that it provides the only effective channel for their children to escape from being locked into the same hopeless economic position that they are.

THE BLACK UNDERCLASS AND RESTRUCTURING THE ECONOMY

As further evidence of the declining significance of race, Wilson points to the fact that the black underclass has been locked into a "situation of marginality and redundancy" in the labor market which it cannot break out of and which brings it into competition with relatively few whites in the economic sector.

> "In view of these developments, it would be difficult to argue that the plight of the black underclass is solely a consequence of racial oppression, that is, the explicit and overt efforts of whites to keep blacks subjugated.... In the economic realm, then, the black experience has moved historically from economic racial oppression experienced by virtually all blacks to economic subordination for the black underclass." (Wilson 1978:151–52)

There is a ring of casuistry in Wilson's argument. What he seems to be saying is that past racial oppression forced the black masses into this situation of marginality and redundancy; but now that they are there and no longer pose a challenge to whites for better jobs because of the way the economy has been transformed, whites do not find it necessary to oppress them further in the economic sector. And yet, as we have seen, when the black underclass seeks a way out for their children by gaining, in Wilson's words, "access to and control of local public schools" through such things as busing (Wilson 1978:116), whites are likely to oppose them, for at that level there is something to struggle about.

Though we question whether the experience of the black underclass supports Wilson's thesis of declining significance of race, we find little fault with the solution he proposes for dealing with its basic problem.

"In the final analysis, therefore, the challenge of economic dislocation in modern industrial society calls for public policy programs to attack inequality on a broad class front, policy programs, in other words, that go beyond the limits of ethnic and racial discrimination by directly confronting the pervasive and destructive features of class subordination."   (Wilson 1978:154)

Wilson elaborates on this thesis in his epilogue to his second edition.

However, we would put the issue in an even broader societal context. To deal frontally with the basic problems of the black masses, the American society will have to do more than merely implement a government policy that opens up doors to various institutional environments; it will also have to come to grips with the fundamental problems of poverty and unemployment. This will in turn necessitate a basic reordering of priorities in the allocation of resources and funds in the system, greater dependence on government intervention and planning than on the workings of the marketplace, and an ever greater emphasis on affirmative action policies and programs for the foreseeable future.

Whether such a fundamental challenge can finally be met by a capitalist society, no matter how egalitarian its legal-normative code, remains to be seen. But failure to meet this challenge will mean the persistence of a molten core of anger, hatred, and frustration in the very heart of many American cities. Periodically the combustible forces in this molten core may explode in riots and mass looting as they have in the past. Perhaps the siphoning off of any emerging leaders into the new black middle class by the working of the American creed and its capillary process will prevent the molten mass from developing a sustained and disciplined revolutionary direction and focus.

But what may well happen, should such violence erupt with any frequency and should the molten mass expand dramatically, is that the dominant white society may expend ever more resources and manpower on securing and patrolling the boundaries between itself and the ghetto, and in the name of law and order create an even more insidious and terrible version of the plural society than in the past. This version might eventually gobble up the American creed and the People's Domain, and America would then become what the Black Panthers have said it already has become, a fascist society. But even if this nightmare fails to materialize, the fact nevertheless remains that as long as the smoldering mass exists it will perpetuate the North's heritage as a *de facto* plural society, even as a small segment of blacks do become absorbed into the major institutional environments of the People's Domain.

BOOK THREE

THE EXTENSION OF DUALITY
AND THE ENCOUNTERS OF
OTHER RACIAL MINORITIES

Book Three deals with the extension of America's duality to its governmental policies on the entry of "new people" and on the acquisition of "new lands" to the United States – matters that were not officially imprinted with this duality prior to the establishment of the New Nation. The extension to "new people" took place within two years of the formation of the New Nation though its full impact was not felt for another eight or nine decades or until the arrival of the immigrant from Asia. The extension of duality to "new lands" did not stamp government policy until the acquisition of Puerto Rico 110 years after the formation of the New Nation.

Duality and the immigrant from Asia

By 1790, then, the First Congress encompassed the immigrant within the sway of America's duality. It decreed in its first naturalization act that only the white alien could gain access to membership in the People's Domain and become citizens. The nonwhite foreign-born was to remain forever in the then undefined role of alien under the direct administrative control of the federal government. Within this uncharted Plural Terrain, he was to carve out his way of life as a permanent stranger in the land without the full and immediate benefit of the legal-normative shield of rights and immunities that protected the citizen. In time, though, the courts extended some of these rights to the nonwhite alien. They also granted his native-born children membership in the People's Domain by virtue of birth while he remained on the outside looking in.

Almost ninety years elapsed before the full impact of this racial restriction was felt in the flow of immigration. It revitalized America's historic duality at a time when the vestigial effects of the first period of reconstruction were still muting it. It spun a web of duality around a new category of nonwhites, the immigrant from Asia, particularly from China and later from Japan – a web from which he only recently escaped.

The web differed markedly from that which enmeshed the blacks and Indians. For, brutal and repressive as was much of the historical encounter of white America with blacks and Indians, rarely – despite periodic advocacy of a colonization movement for blacks – were doubts expressed by whites about the right of presence of blacks or Indians within the territorial limits of the United States. They were, however, denied access to the People's Domain with its attendant rights and immunities of citizenship and were forced to stay within a terrain of plural segmentation in which they were treated as the subjects or objects of the dominant white society and exposed to its control and exploitation. As a result, the border between the People's Domain and the Plural Terrain became the stage upon which the historical drama between the two racial minorities and whites was enacted, with the black and the Indian seeking continually in one way or another to counteract the pressures of the whites along this line.

For emigrants from Asia, this border had virtually no historical relevance in their encounter with white America during almost the entire first century of their migration. They were only remotely concerned with entry into the People's Domain, from which they were barred anyway. Much more to the point was their preoccupation with sheer survival in the Plural Terrain, as white America soon sought to force them out of it or into submarginal areas within it and to cut off the flow of additional emigrants like themselves into the Plural Terrain. Thus, the border between the Plural Terrain and the territorial limits of the American society became the setting for the historic struggle between the migrant from Asia and white America – a setting significantly different from that which the black and Indian had to face.

The drama began in the frontierlike atmosphere of a California, which by the mid-nineteenth century had just become a state in the Union and was in the throes of an explosive population growth as hordes of white Americans and foreign migrants, including the first wave from Asia (the Chinese), poured into the state in search of opportunity and gold. The structure of discrimination and exclusion that eventually engulfed the immigrants from Asia was built upon the foundations of a racial creed rooted in white America's repressive response to the black and the Indian. However, in less than a decade, a structure had evolved that was explicitly directed against first the Chinese and later the Japanese; in time it became legitimized as in accord with the law of the land through congressional action and judicial decision. In this manner, the label "transient alien" was stamped on the first generation of these immigrants no matter how long they lived in the United States; they had no vested rights of residency and could be expelled at any time. While resident in America, however, the Supreme Court decided, they were to come under some of the protective features of the reconstruction amendments.

All this took place against the backdrop of the imperial interests of the United States government in the Far East and in its relations with the government of China and then of Japan. As such, the issue of the immigrant was caught in the complex entanglements of international affairs and of the position of each country on the world stage. As a result, the respective responses of the Chinese and Japanese governments became part of the unfolding dramas, first within California and then in the national arena of America.

In Part One we examine the interplay of these various internal and external forces and actors as it bore on the treatment and status of the Chinese immigrant. In Part Two we undertake a similar analysis for the Japanese immigrant.

Duality and the annexation of Puerto Rico

With the acquisition of Puerto Rico, the United States came full circle to the point of its beginnings. Originally the product of the duality exported from the colonial power, England, it now became a colonial power in its own right with its own distinctive brand of duality to export to its political dependencies. This was legally an entirely new role for the United States. Until Puerto Rico, it had treated new lands as colonist extensions of itself and granted them territorial status with the assurance of eventual incorporation into the Union as a state. Their people in the meantime were to be protected by most of the rights and immunities of the Constitution. The model for relations with these infant states had been set 110 years earlier with the reaffirmation of the Northwest Ordinance by the First Congress, one year after the formation of the New Nation. The only significant change during this interval was the addition to the model of an even more democratic third stage of territorial governance.

During this period, the United States did confront dualities in its new territories, but these were byproducts of its own "colonist-colonialist" past. For example, in retaining control of policy toward the Indian the United States government in its new acquisitions pursued and elaborated the particular kind of dualism that was set by the British government before the formation of the New Nation. In addition, the United States had to deal with the dualities imported by the American settlers into these new territories. The most significant was the duality based on black slavery.

Although Congress barred slavery from the Northwest Territory in 1879, it did not interfere for the next thirty years with the extension of slavery into new territories, particularly those south of the Mason-Dixon line. However, in 1818 the balance between free and slave states became a preoccupation of a Congress that was divided between the two and worried lest one side or the other become the predominant power in the setting of government policy on a national level. Congress subsequently passed the Missouri Compromise, which drew the equivalent of a Mason-Dixon line west of the Mississippi River. North of this line slavery was to be barred from any territory entering as a state in the Union. South of this line slavery was to be permitted. For thirty years Congress monitored carefully the entry of new states according to the Missouri principle. But in 1854 it disrupted its own accommodation through the Kansas-Nebraska act. Three years later the Supreme Court drew the protective mantle of the Constitution around the extension into new territories of the duality based on slavery. In his opinion for the Court, Chief Justice Taney declared that Congress had no constitutional right to ban slavery in any territory as it had done through the Missouri Compromise. The issue was to be left entirely up to the settlers in the territory. However, in approximately a decade the Taney opinion became moot as the enactment of the Thirteenth Amendment banned slavery in both the territories and states of the Union.

With the passage of the Foraker Act in 1900, the United States was no longer merely acting out its own historical past. It officially joined the ranks of the colonialist powers and created its own version of duality to be exported to its political dependency, Puerto Rico. Unlike the old version that was instrumental in the founding of America and of other nations in the New World, the new version did not involve the colonization and settlement of large numbers of Americans in the new dependency and the creation by them of an entirely new political society in their image. In fact, of the relatively few Americans who migrated to the island, only a small handful ever settled there permanently. Most came to Puerto Rico as colonial administrators for the American government and as managers for the absentee sugar corporations. They functioned as the kind of sojourner elite described in Chapter 2. However, unlike the sojourner elite who longed for their homeland but who remained permanently perched atop the colonial plural society, the American elite were frequently rotated; most remained for a relatively short period of time on the island.

The new version, then, had little to do with the American settler; instead it had to do with the people of the island and with Puerto Rico as a political entity. In effect, the United States in enacting the Foraker bill had devised an entirely new legal relationship with a newly acquired land. As a colonial dependency of the United States, Puerto Rico could not look to eventual incorporation into the Union as a state, and its people did not gain automatically the protective shield of the Constitution. The island and people were instead placed under the complete domination and control of the United States Congress. But in implementing this novel status, Congress sowed confusion and ambiguity as it vacillated between granting the people of Puerto Rico, individually and collectively, some of the rights reserved for membership in a territorial society as typified in the Northwest Ordinance, and retaining for itself the authoritarian control of a colonialist power over the political destiny of a dependency. As a result, Congress imprinted a duality and spawned paradoxes in its control and treatment of the Puerto Rican as an individual and of Puerto Rico as a collective whole. Part Three is devoted to an examination of both as they have unfolded over time.

PART ONE

THE CHINESE-AMERICAN
AND THE BOUNDARIES OF THE
PLURAL TERRAIN

13

CALIFORNIA AND
THE CHINESE IMMIGRANT

Introduction

Just about the time that the first immigrants from China were stepping foot onto its soil, California was undergoing a tumultuous transformation from being a Department of Mexico, to being an American possession and then to being a State in the Union. Control of this transformation rested in the hands of the newly ascendant white Americans, many of whom had just arrived in California themselves. They were intent upon building a political society in their own image, but in the process they imprinted on the various legal and political structures they created the kind of duality that characterized the States from which they came. In this chapter we shall examine how the immigrant from China first got caught in this duality and how later he became its principle target in California.

From a Mexican department to an American possession

By 1841 – twenty years after the Mexican revolution from Spain – California had developed into a relatively peaceful and stable but sparsely populated outpost of Mexico. It was dominated by a ranchero elite who were supported by a small but active commercial class of foreigners, many of whom had absorbed the ranchero way of life. At the bottom was a large mass of Indian peons who did the work; many of them had been christianized, domiciled, and made subservient on what were formerly the mission lands of the church.

Previously restive under the distant rule of Mexico City and on occasion given to open defiance, the California elite seemed finally to stabilize their tenuous relations with the capital through the constitution of 1836, a product of the revolt, which gave them greater home rule and equal status with other departments of Mexico. For five years California then enjoyed a relatively enlightened and prosperous rule under the now Governor Alvardo who promoted a republican form of government in which the military was to be kept out of civilian affairs; he also pursued a "policy of secularization, encouraging private ownership of former mission-held lands" (Hansen 1960:30).

The arrival of the first group of overland white immigrants from America – specifically from Missouri – in late 1841 signaled the beginnings of a new period of tension and stress. As additional wagon trains moved in from Missouri and elsewhere, the Mexican government became increasingly fearful that what had happened to Texas was going to happen to California: namely, that migration of Americans into California would be but a prologue to efforts by the United States government to take over California itself. That its fears were not without historical foundation was attested to by the fact that, beginning with President Jackson, each succeeding president had entertained plans for buying or for conquering the area. Thus by 1842 the Mexican government was seeking to control if not curtail the flow of immigration and to solidify its hold on the instruments of political and military power and governmental authority in California. In so doing, it moved away from home rule to centralized authority and replaced Alvardo with a governor who once again combined military and civil authority and had at his disposal a newly expanded military force of modest proportions and competence.

These governmental actions tempered somewhat the flow of American immigrants. By 1845 Americans still numbered only an estimated 700 persons in comparison with 7000 native Californians, 10,000 domesticated Indians, and 200 Europeans, mostly English and Scotch-Irish. However, the governmental actions also fanned the anger of the American immigrant and government, while at the same time intensifying the unhappiness of the native Californians who resented the withdrawal of home rule. In the meantime the US government and individual Americans such as Fremont engaged in a series of provocative acts. By 1846 tensions had escalated, and incidents of actual fighting had occurred. But when war finally broke out between the United States and Mexico the precipitating incident had less to do with California than with America's annexation of Texas. Within a year the war was over, and in 1848 Mexico ceded to the United States in the Treaty of Hidalgo most of its territorial possessions in what was to become southwestern America, including California.

Even as the treaty was being signed, gold was discovered at Sutter's Mill. Almost overnight California, particularly its northern region, exploded into a feverish, burgeoning turbulence and was transformed into the crude brutality of an open frontierlike society. Within a year the population had quadrupled as seekers of opportunity and gold poured in from other parts of the United States and of the world. An estimated 42,000 came overland in 1849, and another 39,000 arrived by sea.

So compelling was the pressure of men and events, so divergent their mix, and so obsessed with the lust for gold, that the residues of legal and normative stability inherited from California's ranchero and Mexican past were soon overwhelmed and a fragmented, anomic disarray prevailed. To add even more perplexity and confusion to the situation, California at this juncture was also adrift in a sea of legal ambiguities and sovereign uncertainty. It was a kind of legal and civil no man's land between two nations. The treaty had finally and irrevocably severed Californian ties with Mexico, but the United States Congress remained paralyzed in its efforts to grant California territorial status within the United States: northern and southern legislators were at loggerheads over the issue of slavery in new states and territories.

As a result, California continued under the rule of a relatively benign military governor through 1849. He sought to keep matters reasonably peaceable, but he was nevertheless unable to construct or to enforce the kind of legal and judiciary machinery needed for the conduct of the evolving civil affairs and for the regulation of the abrasive, raw, and frequently violent competitive struggle for mining stakes and claims. Consequently, the miners took matters into their own hands. They treated the region of the diggings as public land, "moved in on it freely and without asking anyone's permission" (Caughey 1948:227) staked their various claims to the land. In the process they developed a code of claim ownership and regulation that was adopted in most camps. They also devised in the various camps a machinery of self-government to maintain order, to settle claims, and to punish those who committed crimes against the community. A number of scholars point with pride to the democratic and egalitarian character of these machineries of governance and in many respects they resembled the town meetings of New England. But even at this stage, membership in these growing communities tended to be confined to white Americans; others were not accorded the same rights and immunities.

However, it soon became evident that this self-regulatory machinery, which not only developed in the camps but in the cities as well, could not meet the need for a uniform framework of law, justice, and government. It all too frequently became an instrument of arbitrary moblike violence and injustice, directed against alien and strangers. As a result, pressures mounted inexorably for a resolution to the stalemate over California's sovereignty. By mid-1849, the military governor acceded to the growing demand for an election of delegates to a constitutional convention for California.

The constitutional convention of 1849

In the fall of 1849, 48 delegates assembled at Monterey (25 others failed to show) to draft a constitution for submission to the United States Congress that would allow California to bypass the status of territory and to enter the Union directly as a state. "Of the forty-eight delegates, nine had been residents of the state for less than one year. The average residence in California for all forty-eight members was about two years. Seven of the members were born in California; five were foreign-born; eight had Spanish surnames; sixteen came from slave states; and twenty-one came from free states" (Heizer and Almquist 1971:95).

All of those who were born in California had Spanish surnames; only four of those with anglicized names had lived ten years or more in California. The average age of the delegates was 37: the oldest being 52 and the youngest 25. Most of the delegates were lawyers (15), farmers (10), or businessmen (9). Three others were from the military; two were from each of the following occupations: engineering, medicine, and printing. In short, the convention was numerically dominated by a group of relatively young, geographically and socially mobile white men who were by and large newcomers to the California scene.

From the very beginning these delegates did not act as though they were new arrivals or as if California had a past. Instead they started from the dual premise that the history of California was just beginning and that they were there to create a political society in their image with their version of the American creed from the *tabula rasa* that they had decreed to exist. As such they sought to anchor the new society to the sovereignty of the people. This was eloquently expressed in an early phase of the deliberations by one of the delegates who had come to California from Virginia just sixteen months before:

"All power is in the hands of the people, whether they have delegated it to others or not. The government is subservient to the Constitution, and the ministers of that government are the servants of the people. They have no power except what they derive from the people. All the power committed to their hands is delegated to them through the Constitution. If it does not come through the Constitution, it does not come [at] all. The Constitution is the message of the people to their servants, and what they do not grant in that way they do not grant at all."

(Browne 1850:52)

Accordingly, the delegates used as their model the United States Constitution and those from various states, notably Iowa, New York, and Virginia, and they clearly enunciated this commitment in Section 1 and 2 of the *Declaration of Rights* that comprised Article I of their constitution.

"Sec. 1. All men are by nature free and independent, and have certain inalienable rights among which are those of enjoying and defending life and liberty, acquiring, possessing, and protecting property; and pursuing and obtaining safety and happiness.

Sec. 2. All political power is inherent in the people. Government is instituted for the protection, security, and benefit of the people; and they have the right to alter or reform the same, whenever the public good may require it."

(Browne 1850: Appendix III)

However, even as these vaulting tributes to the people were being made and secured in the first two sections of Article I, it became immediately apparent that not all persons were to be included as part of the people of California. The first inkling of this came in the rambling and confused discussion that followed the introduction of the provision on disfranchisement by the chairman of the committee on the constitution: "Sec. 3. No member of this State shall be disfranchised, or deprived of any of the rights or privileges secured to any citizen thereof, unless by the law of the land, or the judgment of his peers" (Browne 1850:34).

The chairman acknowledged in the ensuing discussion that this provision had been borrowed verbatim from the New York State constitution, but he was unable to assuage the fears of many delegates that this provision could be used to extend rights and immunities of citizenship to categories of persons to whom many delegates obviously had no intention of extending such rights. Nevertheless the chairman contended that the provision was merely intended to extend the protection of the law to "inhabitants of the States" and to foreigners and not only to citizens. Much more prevalent, however, was the view of a delegate who had come to California six years before from Ohio. He argued,

"Whether it is designed or not, the adoption of this section of the bill of rights would secure to certain classes, Indians and Africans (if Africans are ever introduced here,) precisely the same rights that we ourselves enjoy. There is no clause in relation to the introduction of slaves or any other class of men. If you provide that no member of this State shall be deprived of the rights and immunities of a citizen, it is to be presumed that such member enjoys those privileges and immunities. If you declare that no man shall be decapitated for a certain crime, it may reasonably be presumed that he has a head."

(Browne 1850:35)

Worried about this provision's implied inclusion of Indians and blacks as part of the people, the delegates decisively defeated it.

What had been merely implied in the earlier provision became explicitly stated less than a week later when the standing committee on the constitution brought in its first recommendation under Article II on the *Right of Suffrage*: Only white male citizens of the United States, age twenty-one years or older, who resided in California for six months or more, were to be allowed to vote in any election. Almost immediately one of the youngest delegates, a printer, who had migrated from New York two and a half years before, moved to enlarge the pool of eligible voters by including "every male citizen of Mexico, who shall have elected to become a citizen of the United States, under the treaty of peace, exchanged and ratified at Queretaro, on the 30th of May, 1848" (Browne 1850:61). He argued that such a provision was in accord with the obligation that the United States government had assumed in the treaty with Mexico and therefore had to be included in the constitution; otherwise the United States Congress might reject the constitution for failing to meet this treaty commitment.

Few delegates disputed this argument, but most were opposed to the wording of the amendment. They feared that it would open the door to a vote for the Indian. Therefore before they voted on the amendment they sought to determine the citizenship status of the Indian under Mexican law. Despite the absence of a clear-cut answer, most nevertheless concluded that the Indian had such a status (it is probable that Indians with property could vote).

Determined to prevent this from happening in California, the delegates modified the amendment so that Indians and blacks were excluded from those who might be deemed eligible to vote as a result of the treaty. They inserted into the penultimate version of the amendment the parenthetic phrase "(*Indians, Africans, and descendants of Africans excepted*) (author's italics)" after the words: "Every white male citizen of the United States and every male citizen of Mexico" (Browne 1850:74). By the final version, of Article II *Right of Suffrage*, however, the delegates expressed openly what they had in mind all along. Only whites were to be the people, whether they had Mexican or American origins; however, a loophole for individual Indians was retained.

"Sec. 1. Every white male citizen of the United States and every white male citizen of Mexico, who shall have elected to become a citizen of the United States, under the treaty of peace exchanged and ratified at Queretaro, on the 30th day of May 1848, of the age of twenty-one years, who shall have been a resident of the State six months next preceding the election, and the county or district in which he claims his vote thirty days, shall be entitled to vote at all elections which are now or hereafter may be authorized by law: Provided, that nothing herein contained, shall be construed to prevent the Legislature by a two-thirds concurrent vote, from admitting to the right of suffrage, Indians or the descendants of Indians, in such special cases as such a proportion of the legislative body may deem just and proper." (Browne 1850: Appendix V)

Whereas exclusion from the People's Domain was all that the delegates intended with respect to the Indian, they seemed intent on imposing even greater constraints upon the black. They wanted to go so far as to bar him from the territorial confines of California itself, whether as a slave or as a freedman. Thus the delegates had little difficulty with the issue of slavery, despite the number who were formerly from the South and border states. They voted unanimously to include a ban on slavery and involuntary servitude as Section 18 of Article I: "Sec. 18. Neither slavery, nor involuntary servitude, unless for the punishment of crimes, shall ever be tolerated in this State" (Browne 1850: Appendix V).

This action was not taken out of any special regard for the blacks. As expressed by a delegate who had only a year before migrated from Kentucky, blacks were just not welcome in California. This is the substance of Section 19, which he wanted to have follow Section 18 on slavery:

"Sec. 19. The Legislature shall, at its first session, pass such laws as will effectually prohibit free persons of color from immigrating to and settling in this State, and to effectually prevent the owners of slaves from bringing them into this State for the purpose of setting them free." (Browne 1850:48)

He subsequently agreed to withdraw his motion from consideration under Article I for later deliberation in another part of the constitution. A week later he reintroduced his proposition while the convention was sitting as a committee of the whole on another part of the constitution. After a lengthy discussion, his proposal was passed. Two weeks later though, the convention reversed itself and turned the proposition down in its final consideration of the various parts of the constitution. This did not stem from any basic change in the convention's sentiments toward a black presence in California. It stemmed from a growing concern that inclusion of the proposition within the constitution might cause the United States Congress to delay California's application for statehood as had happened earlier in the case of Missouri. As a result, most delegates thought it best to have the matter dealt with later by the California legislature, when statehood was no longer an issue.

In opposing the entry of blacks, the delegates had been obsessed with the presumably destructive effects of the black upon the white worker and his "rightful" control of and place in the labor market – an obsession that was to be resurrected in full fury less than ten years later against the Chinese. According to the various delegates, California was fortunate in attracting an energetic and intelligent labor force of whites from all over the country, not only to dig its gold but also to build its industry. In the words of a delegate who had arrived from Wisconsin less than five months before:

> "Here are thousands upon thousands of enterprising, able, and intelligent young men, leaving their homes and coming to California. They cannot all devote themselves to digging gold in the placers here; they will be compelled to turn their attention to other branches of industry; and if you do not degrade white labor there will not be the slightest difficulty in obtaining white men to labor. But there will be difficulty if they are to work with negroes. Men, sir, who are every way competent to sit in the halls of this Convention, to assist in forming laws for California, are now working in the placers. There are men of intelligence and education, laboring there with the pick and shovel – men who, at home, were accustomed to all the refinements of life. No new State in the Union has ever had a population of so enterprising and intelligent a character. They are working willingly, and they do not consider it a degradation to engage in any department of industry which will afford an adequate remuneration."
>
> (Browne 1850:144)

Protecting the "right to labor" of this white work force, according to another delegate who had come four months earlier from Louisiana though born in Ohio, should be a prime responsibility of any delegate, for in this lies the path to the greatness of the working man and of California itself.

> "This right is not only valuable, but it is a holy commandment – 'by the sweat of thy brow shall thou earn thy daily bread.' I wish to inculcate this command, and encourage labor. I wish, so far as my influence extends, to make labor honorable; the laboring man is the *nobleman* in the true acceptation of the word; and I would make him worthy of his high preprogative, and not degrade him by placing him upon a level with the lowest in the scale of the family of man. I would remove all obstacles to his future greatness, for if there is one part of the world, possessing advantages over another, where the family of Japhet may expect to attain a higher state of perfectability than has ever been attained by man, it is here, in California. All nature proclaims this a favored land."
>
> (Browne 1850:49)

All this would be destroyed, most delegates were convinced, and white labor would be "degraded" (a favorite term of theirs) if the blacks, freed as well as enslaved, were allowed to enter California. Some delegates even reminded the convention that this was the primary reason why they had voted earlier against slavery. They had heard reports that white owners were using their slaves as an involuntary work force to compete unfairly with the individual white miner and were even staking claims to mines in the names of their slaves so that they, the owners, could get more property than they were legally entitled to. Now, these delegates insisted, they had heard other reports of white owners who were prepared in view of the proposed ban on slavery to manumit formally their slaves before coming to California on condition that these slaves agree to work for the white owner for as much as three years without recompense.

Such machinations, the delegates concluded, were bound to have a negative effect on the life circumstances of the white worker. To make the situation even more intolerable, some delegates declared, blacks – even though they might escape the wiles of their past or present white owners – would still become the tool of the capitalist, because the black was an inferior being "adapted for servitude." In the words of the delegate formerly of Louisiana, "It would appear that the all-wise Creator has created the negro to serve the white race. We see evidence of this wherever they are brought in contact; we see the instinctive feeling of the negro is obedience to the white man, and, in all instances, he obeys him, and is ruled by him" (Browne 1850:49).

As a result, he continued, the blacks would soon come under the domination of the capitalists; and "the capitalists will fill the land with these living laboring machines, with all their attendant evils. Their labor will go to enrich the few, and impoverish the many; it will drive the poor and honest laborer from the field, by degrading him to the level of the negro" (Browne 1850:49). This would be so because, in the words of another delegate who had migrated from Wisconsin just four months before, the whites "would be unable, even if willing, to compete with the bands of negroes who would be set to work under the direction of capitalists. It would become a monopoly of the worst character. The profits of the mines would go into the pockets of single individuals. The labor of intelligent and enterprising white men who, from the want of capital, are compelled to do their own work would [not get] adequate remuneration" (Browne 1850:144).

So it was that most of the convention believed that whites would be forced to labor for less and live in degraded life circumstances, demeaned by the presence of the black. But above and beyond the degradation of the individual white worker would be the degradation of the white society; for, according to the previously quoted delegate, blacks are "too depraved to be governed by ordinary laws." As evidence of this, he continued, "when negroes are free, they are the freest of all human beings; they are free in morals, free in all the vices of a brutish and depraved race. They are a most troublesome and unprofitable population.... I have always lived in a free State, sir, and I have always seen that, of all classes of population, the free negroes are the most ignorant, wretched and depraved" (Browne 1850:144).

The delegate formerly of Louisiana then concluded:

"That the negro race is out of his social sphere, and becomes a discordant element when among the Caucasian race, no one can doubt. You have but to take a retrospective view, and you need not extend your vision beyond our own land to be satisfied of this fact. Look at our once happy republic, now a contentious, antagonistical, discordant people. The Northern people see, and feel, and know, that the black population is an evil in the land, and although they have admitted them to many of the rights of citizenship, the admixture has acted in the political economy as a foreign, poisonous substance, producing the same effect as in physical economy – derangement, disease, and, if not removed, *death*. Let us be warned – let us avoid an evil of such magnitude."

(Browne 1850:50)

Even though the state legislature subsequently failed to pass laws to prevent the emigration of free negroes and persons of color, despite attempts to do so in 1850 and 1851, it nevertheless continued to erect additional barriers against access by the Indian and black into the People's Domain, as these barriers had been staked out by the constitutional convention. For example, an indenture act was passed in 1850 that enabled whites to place Indians in virtual labor bondage; in 1852 a fugitive slave law was passed which required the return of runaway black slaves to their owners. But representing the baldest expression of exclusion from the People's Domain was the passage of criminal and civil codes which barred black and Indian from jury service and from testifying as witnesses against whites in civil and criminal actions.

Thus, by 1851 California had created its own version of a plural society. On the one side of the racial divide were the whites who comprised the people of the People's Domain – guaranteed the rights and immunities of the Constitution and control of the political society and its economic resources. On the other side of the racial divide were the blacks and Indians, neither formally enslaved nor factually freed. They shared none of the rights and immunities of the People's Domain and were anchored instead to a Plural Terrain where they were subject to the coercive control and naked exploitation of the whites.

Entry of the Chinese and their linkage to the Plural Terrain

Even as this plural structure was being hammered into shape by the white society, the Chinese began their trek to California, first in a trickle – perhaps in the hundreds through 1849 – and then in a quickening surge. In 1850 for example, an estimated 4000 arrived. By 1852 the numbers had mushroomed to 20,000 then declining to 4000 in 1853. The figures went up dramatically to 16,000 in 1854 and finally subsided to an annual average of 5000 for the next decade. These pioneering Chinese came to California for much the same reason as most of the white Americans and other foreigners had come: to strike it rich in the goldfields and then to return home in comfort and style. As a result, they too were almost exclusively young males but, unlike the others, most were married with family obligations at home.

According to various scholars, the pioneering Chinese escaped for several years the full impact of the coercive plural structure that the white society was building. They did so by avoiding any direct confrontation with the whites in the goldfields – largely confining their mining to played-out fields already abandoned by the whites. They also helped meet the burgeoning demand of various labor markets sorely distended by the exodus of a white work force gone to the goldfields. Coolidge in particular argues that these pioneering Chinese were treated reasonably well as an exotically different but useful people.

> "They were highly valued as general laborers, carpenters and cooks; the restaurants established by them in San Francisco and in the mines were well kept and extensively patronized; they took to pieces the old vessels that lay abandoned in the channel of the Golden Gate; they cleared and drained the rich tule lands, which the white miners were too busy to undertake.... Whatever the white man scorned to do the Chinese took up; whatever white men did, the Chinese could learn to do; he was a gap-filler, doing what no one else would do, or what remained undone, adapting himself to the white man's tastes, and slipping away, unprotestingly, to other tasks when the white man wanted his job." (Coolidge 1969:21–2)

On occasion though – even in these early days – the interests of an individual Chinese and a white American collided as in the case of disputed claims to a mine, disagreements over a debt, and the like. In such situations, the Chinese bumped up against the repressive plural structure and felt firsthand its iron might. In effect, whatever rights he claimed for himself were summarily dismissed by the white society, and he was indeed fortunate if he escaped with his life.

However, much more on a collision course during this period were the white Americans and other foreigners, particularly the Latin American, the Mexican, and the Frenchman. They competed much more directly for claims in the goldfields, and their disputes were much more likely to erupt into open conflict. But it was an uneven conflict. The Americans viewed these foreigners as interlopers and as unprotected by the rights and immunities of the People's Domain despite one clause in the Constitution. As a result, the white Americans became increasingly convinced that the foreigners had transgressed the sacred domain of their rights. Xenophobia grew in virulence, and finally the Americans brought their monopoly of the legal and coercive instruments of the state to bear on these aliens. In 1850, for example, they passed a Foreign Miners License Tax Law, which failed as a revenue measure but which succeeded in driving many of the foreigners from the goldfields. By the end of 1851 these foreign populations had been sizably reduced.

According to Coolidge and others, the year 1852 was a turning point for the Chinese. By then they had become "the largest single body of unnaturalized foreigners in the State" (Coolidge 1969:31). This significantly increased the visibility of their presence; no longer were they merely another element in a medley of aliens. But they were forced into the spotlight of public attention even more by the introduction of what came to be called Senator Tingley's Coolie Bill. This bill would have provided for the enforcement by the courts of labor contracts made in China for work in California. After bitter debate, the bill was defeated, but not before germinating politically and publicly the charge of involuntary servitude against the Chinese which blossomed into full flower several years later. According to this charge, the Chinese were bound to service for a number of years under terms of a "coolie labor contract" which made them virtually slaves. As such, a parallel tended to be drawn in the press between the status of the black and of the Chinese.

Once having surfaced, anti-Chinese sentiment found public and private expression in most segments of the white society, particularly in the mining communities. The veneer of tolerance of the first years collapsed almost overnight. This revealed the infrastructure of prejudice and discrimination that had always been there, having been masked until then by the more intense hostility toward other aliens. The Chinese rapidly replaced the other foreigners as the primary target of public and private opprobrium. This mood obviously played a part in the renewal of the Foreign Miners' License Tax in 1852, though no explicit mention of the Chinese was made in the law. It also dominated the legislative deliberations during the following year's more stringent version of the license law; in fact the legislature voted to have the 1853 law printed in Chinese.

In addition, the legislature passed an act in 1852 that required the posting by the ship owner and captain of a $500 bond for each foreign passenger brought to California. (The act was never enforced and was later declared unconstitutional.) Further, "in 1854 concurrent resolutions were passed by the senate and the assembly instructing the California congressmen to attempt to secure passage in Congress of an act to legalize imposition of a head tax, to be paid by owners or masters of vessels, on each Chinese and Japanese on board with the intention of debarking" (Heizer and Almquist 1971:160).

In this manner California signified a legislative intent to restrict access of the Chinese to the dominant society and ultimately to force him out of direct and fair competition with the whites. The broader implications and meaning of this intent became clear toward the end of 1854 when another branch of government, the state supreme court, inextricably linked the Chinese with the plural structure that had already been constructed for the black and Indian. It did so in the name of this legislative intent. Thus, in the case of People v. Hall, the court extended to the Chinese the legislative ban against black or Indian bearing witness against whites in criminal or civil actions.

In his opinion for the court, Chief Justice Murray followed two lines of argument that converged at the end in a general statement on the need to exclude from the People's Domain the "genetically inferior" nonwhite races, including the Chinese. For his first line of argument, the Chief Justice introduced "data" from history and physical anthropology to support his contention that the word "Indian" had always been used as a generic racial term to include the Mongolian race as well as the aborigines of North America. This usage, he insisted, began with Columbus, who thought he had landed in the Indies and thereby named the natives of the New World Indians. "'From that time, down to a very recent period, the American Indians and the Mongolian, or Asiatic, were regarded as the same type of human species'" (Heizer and Almquist 1971:230). Ethnologists and physical anthropologists had even entertained the theory, he continued, that the ancestors of the American Indians migrated from Asia across the Aleutian Islands into North America and were therefore of a common racial stock with the Mongolians.

But, he added, this theory was now being questioned; some scientists were insisting "'that the Aborigines are a distinct type, and as such claim a distinct origin'" (Heizer and Almquist 1971:231). Even if this were proved to be a valid scientific conclusion, the Justice insisted,

"'this would not, in any degree, alter the meaning of the term, and render that specific which was before generic.

We have adverted to these speculations for the purpose of showing that the name of Indian, from the time of Columbus to the present day, has been used to designate, not alone the North American, but the whole of the Mongolian race, and that the name, though first applied probably through mistake, was afterwards continued as appropriate on account of the supposed common origin.

That this was the common opinion in the early history of American legislation, cannot be disputed, and, therefore, all legislation upon the subject must have borne relation to that opinion.

Can, then, the use of the word "Indian," because at the present day it may be sometimes regarded as a specific, and not as a generic term, alter this conclusion? We think not; because at the origin of the legislation we are considering, it was used and admitted in its common and ordinary acceptation, as a generic term, distinguishing the great Mongolian race, and as such, its meaning then became fixed by law, and in construing Statutes the legal meaning of words must be preserved.'"   (Heizer and Almquist 1971:231)

In his second line of argument, the Chief Justice maintained that the legislature in originally enacting the ban did not merely intend to exclude only blacks, mulattos, and Indians but also to exclude all nonwhites in order to "protect the White person from the influence of all testimony other than that of persons of the same caste."

"'In using the words, "No black, or Mulatto person, or Indian shall be allowed to give evidence for or against a White person," the Legislature, if any intention can be ascribed to it, adopted the most comprehensive terms to embrace every known class or shade of color, as the apparent design was to protect the White person from the influence of all testimony other than that of persons of the same caste. The use of these terms must, by every sound rule of construction, exclude every one who is not of white blood.'"   (Heizer and Almquist 1971:232)

This interpretation, he insisted, was consistent with the actions of the constitutional convention and subsequent legislatures of California which confined the rights and immunities of the People's Domain to the white.

"'If the term "White," as used in the Constitution was not understood in its generic sense as including the Caucasian race, and necessarily excluding all others, where was the necessity of providing for the admission of Indians to the privilege of voting, by special legislation.

We are of the opinion that the words "White," "Negro," "Mulatto," "Indian," and "Black person," wherever they occur in our Constitution and laws, must be taken in their generic sense, and that, even admitting the Indian of this continent is not of the Mongolian type, that the words "Black person," in the 14th section must be taken as contradistinguished from White, and necessarily includes all races other than the Caucasian.'"
(Heizer and Almquist 1971:233)

To decide otherwise and to permit Chinese testimony against whites would vitiate the intent of law and constitution and open the door for the Chinese to all the rights and immunities of the People's Domain. "'The same rule which would admit them to testify, would admit them to all the equal rights of citizenship, and we might soon see them at the polls, in the jury box, upon the bench, and in our legislative halls'" (Heizer and Almquist 1971:233).

This, he continued, was not mere idle speculation but

"'an actual and present danger.... The anomalous spectacle of a distinct people, living in our community, recognizing no laws of this State except through necessity, bringing with them their prejudices and national feuds, in which they indulge in open violation of the law; whose mendacity is proverbial; a race of people whom nature has marked as inferior, and who are incapable of progress or intellectual development beyond a certain point, as their history has shown; differing in language, opinions, color, and physical conformation; between whom and ourselves nature has placed an impassable difference, is now presented, and for them is claimed, not only the right to swear away the life of a citizen, but the further privilege of participating with us in administering the affairs of our Government.'" (Heizer and Almquist 1971:233)

The prevention of such contamination of the People's Domain from the alien presence of an inferior race, the Chief Justice concluded, was the obvious intention of the legislature in framing the ban; therefore the court was obliged to extend the ban to the Chinese. This action, in the words of Lucile Eaves, a social economist and specialist in California labor law, "contributed more than the legislative measures to this setting aside of the Chinese in a class to whom all social and political equality was denied" (Eaves 1910:113). Eaves could have gone on to say even more emphatically that this action firmly linked the legal-normative fates of the Chinese with those of the Indian and the black and reaffirmed the ideological and legal inferiority of the three in the plural structure, which had been created by the state constitution but now was fully elaborated and legitimated by the court.

This ruling did more than deny to the Chinese basic legal and political rights in the People's Domain; it also had particularly grave consequences for his work in the goldfields. According to Eaves, it proved "most disastrous for the Chinese. It made it possible for unprincipled whites to commit crimes against them with impunity, so long as there were none but Chinese witnesses" (Eaves 1910:114). In other words, it gave the stamp of legality to practices already firmly embedded in the roughshod treatment by whites of Chinese over mining claims. Yet not content with this ruling, some mining districts passed laws expelling Chinese; others never allowed them to enter in the first place, and still others forbade sales of claims to them. In short, the grass-roots white miners in most districts were convinced that only they had the free and untrammeled right to labor in the goldfields and to stake their claims of ownership. The Chinese and other aliens were there only on sufferance without rights and claims.

By the mid-1850s pressures grew even greater to drive the Chinese out of the mining areas or at least to place them in a disadvantageous competitive position. A particularly onerous mining tax was passed that proved too cumbersome to enforce. Toward the end of the decade a more moderate version was passed; it even included an exemption for foreigners who had declared their intention to become citizens – a provision obviously of no value to the Chinese who could not become citizens even if they wanted to.

Occupational spread and mounting Sinophobia

In many respects then, mining became the first major economic battleground in which the whites sought to impose severe and varied legal and coercive constraints on the workings of the free labor market in order to handicap if not cripple the competitive position of the Chinese. From that time on they showed increasing determination to plug access to this one institutional mechanism of the People's Domain still apparently available to the Chinese. But their task proved far from easy, for California was still during this period – despite its evolving plural structure – a relatively new and open society. As such its expanding economy and industries had a virtually insatiable appetite for labor. The whites who monopolized the instruments of power and control had not been in the state long enough to build and to sanctify a set of institutional traditions and norms that would carve up the labor market into one for whites and the other for nonwhites as had happened in the North (the south being still dependent on unfree labor).

To complicate matters even more, the Chinese proved to be a versatile, adaptive, effective, and easily exploited work force with remarkably low subsistence needs in virtually every industry they entered. As a result, they showed an amazing capacity to survive despite the institutional and economic handicaps imposed upon them. Even in the mining industry – despite the mounting pressure to force them out – many continued to find work, some in the played-out placers and others as hired help for mining companies in the quartz mills. Their numbers, declined by 30 percent from 1860 to 1870, but the overall work force declined even more during this period, by about 60 percent, as some mines petered out and mechanization took hold in the others. As a result, despite their declining numbers, the Chinese ironically became proportionately a larger part of the mining work force: from 29 percent in 1860 to 57 percent in 1870.

Even during the halcyon days of mining, a substantial minority of Chinese found employment elsewhere. Coolidge estimates that before 1862 as many as two out of five Chinese were involved in "trade (chiefly among themselves), truck gardening, farm labor, washing and household service, fishing and common labor; less than one percent were engaged in manufacturing" (Coolidge 1969:342). By the mid-1860s these figures were stepped up as increasing numbers of Chinese drifted out of mining into other fields of employment; as a result, by 1870 only a minority was left in mining.

The building of the intercontinental railroad during this period provided the Chinese with a major opportunity for jobs, after the initial misgivings of white employers were allayed. Soon, however, the Chinese were being hired in increasing numbers to lay track, to do other construction work, to cook, and to launder clothes until an estimated 8000 to 10,000 were working on the railroads. One white man in particular, Charles Crocker, came to depend almost exclusively on the Chinese. He praised them for their dedication, efficiency, and discipline. However when they finally went on strike for pay that would approximate what white workers were getting, he broke the strike expeditiously and mercilessly, though he continued to depend on them afterward for his work force at their lower rates of pay.

Even as the railroads were employing a number of Chinese, many other Chinese continued to leave the mining areas for the cities, primarily San Francisco but also Sacramento and San Jose. Their numbers were swelled in the mid-1870s by the thousands who lost their jobs once the railroads were built. In the urban areas they moved into a variety of occupations. Many continued to fill the occupational gaps that whites were still reluctant to fill, such as laundering, domestic service, and common labor, but others spread into new areas of work from truck farming and fishing to jobs in light industry. By the 1870s they became an important force in three new struggling industries: cigars and tobaccos, woolens, and boots and shoes. They accounted for 9 out of 10 employees in the first, for 6 out of 10 in the second, and for 2 out of 10 in the third.

Lyman describes the wide range of occupations and industries in which the Chinese came to be employed in this period:

"The variety of work in which Chinese immigrants engaged has been rarely noted in literature on the subject. Not only did Chinese work in abandoned goldfields, build railroads, and wash clothes in America, but they also labored in many areas of mineral extraction; several kinds of fishery and cannery work; a number of different types of construction; the cigar, woolen, shoe, boot, and slipper industries; and garment manufacture. Chinese workers were employed in making bags, brooms, cordage, matches, candles, soap, bottles, pottery, and whips. A considerable amount of the reclamation work in the early West was done by Chinese. In the rural areas of California and other western states Chinese were employed in digging irrigation ditches, underground wine cellars, and reservoirs; in picking grapes, apples, peaches, cherries, pears, and olives; in growing cabbages, pumpkins, celery, and asparagus; and in building stone bridges, rock walls, and paved roads. A Chinese brought fellow Chinese workers to Monterey to pick wild mustard. Others discovered artifical methods of egg hatching, while still other Chinese developed the extensive truck gardening and flower growing industries of the West. In the towns and cities Chinese restaurateurs provided a menu of exotic cuisine for Occidental palates, artisans from Canton carved jade, and Chinese adolescents and old men worked as waiters, busboys, butlers, and domestics wherever service industries and wealthy patrons demanded them."   (Lyman 1974:73–4)

As the Chinese spread into occupations other than mining – as laborers or entrepreneurs – they soon faced barriers similar to those they were already facing in mining. Efforts were mounted by whites – piecemeal at first but later on a broader sustained front – to place the Chinese at a competitive disadvantage, if not to drive them out completely from the various occupations. Some of these efforts took legislative form. In 1860, for example, a monthly tax was levied on Chinese engaged in fishing; failure to pay meant seizure of fish, boat, and/or other property. Though repealed in 1864, the law was only the beginning of a whole series of legal regulations, ostensibly neutral on their face, that served to drive the Chinese from the fishing industry within several decades.

In 1862 the legislature broadened its assault by passing "An Act to Protect Free White Labor against Competition with Chinese Coolie Labor." This act levied a monthly capitation tax, called the Chinese Police Tax, on Chinese adults. Failure to pay the tax would subject the person to severe penalties, the most severe being the seizure of personal property for sale at public auction. (This act was later declared to be in violation of congressional power to regulate commerce with foreign nations.)

These legislative efforts were not only intended to drive the Chinese out of various labor markets, but also to discourage immigration. By 1870 the legislature tried to meet the issue frontally as it had in its abortive efforts of 1855. It passed a law purportedly to protect Chinese women from being forced into white slavery but actually intended to cut down the immigration of Chinese women generally. Each woman entering the state was obliged to prove that she was coming voluntarily and that she was also "a person of correct habits and good character" (Heizer and Almquist 1971:164). A companion law was passed for males in the same year. Ostensibly enacted "'to Prevent the Importation of Chinese Criminals and to Prevent the Establishment of Coolie Slavery'" (Heizer and Almquist 1971:165), the law sought to confine immigration to the Chinese male who "'has come into the state voluntarily and is a person of moral habits and good character'" (Heizer and Almquist 1971:166).

According to Sandmeyer,

"these acts were never enforced, due to the passage of the [federal] Civil Rights Act. But four years later a similar act was passed. The Commissioner of

Immigration was required to satisfy himself as to whether any passengers on incoming ships, who were not citizens of the United States, were lunatic, idiotic, or likely to become a public charge, or a criminal, or 'a lewd or debauched woman.'"

(Sandmeyer 1973:52–3)

Several years later this law too was declared unconstitutional.

What provided the major impetus to these legislative moves was the intensifying and proliferating anti-Chinese sentiment among the white working class. Already manifested in the mining regions, this sentiment spread rapidly and violently as Chinese moved into occupations and areas where they became visible to the white workers. Coolidge claims that the Chinese even in these years served as gap-fillers. Rarely were they in direct competition with the white workers, but the white workers of the period saw it differently. They were convinced that the Chinese posed a serious competitive threat. As the expansive optimism of the early gold mining period gave way to the cold reality of business downturns, they became virtually obsessed with this preoccupation.

The white workers let their convictions and anger be known through words and action. Their growing organized strength transformed them into a potent political force in a state almost evenly divided between the Republican and Democratic parties. As a result, they gained a pivotal role in shaping the political agenda for the parties. By 1867, according to Sandmeyer, "the Chinese question attained a position of outstanding importance in state politics, a position it was destined to maintain for almost forty years" (Sandmeyer 1973:45). At the same time, violence broke out in a number of communities. By the mid-1870s the anti-Chinese campaign had escalated into a political crusade among the organized white working class. It reached its fullest expression in the form of the Workingmen's party, organized in 1877 under the leadership of Denis Kearney. Growing out of the labor unrest of the day, the party also espoused a strong anti-capitalist line and inextricably linked the two issues together. For example, its leaders "proposed to take the government out of the hands of the rich and place it in those of the people, to rid the country of cheap Chinese labor, to destroy land monopoly and the money power of the rich, to provide for the poor and unfortunate, to elect none but workingmen and their friends to office, and to secure the discharge of all Chinese employed in the state" (Sandmeyer 1973:65).

In the final analysis, these leaders were convinced that the threat of the Chinese to the white working class stemmed from the conspiratorial efforts of the capitalist to undermine the solidarity and economic status of the white working class. In other words, the Chinese were being used as tools by the capitalist for the purpose of "degrading" the white proletariat – an argument that had already been used almost thirty years before against entry of freed or enslaved blacks into California.

In time the anti-capitalism of the party became muted as shrill Sinophobia became an obsessive preoccupation. This is evident in Kearney's "manifesto."

> "'We have made no secret of our intentions. We make none. Before you and before the world we declare that the Chinaman must leave our shores. We declare that white men, and women, and boys, and girls, cannot live as the people of the great republic should and compete with the single Chinese coolie in the labor market. We declare that we cannot hope to drive the Chinaman away by working cheaper than he does. None but an enemy would expect it of us; none but an idiot could hope for success; none but a degraded coward and slave would make the effort. To an American, death is preferable to life on a par with the Chinaman.'" (Sandmeyer 1973:65)

The meteoric rise of Kearney and his Workingmen's party was balanced by their rapid descent into oblivion within a few years, but in this relatively short span of time they contributed mightily to the burgeoning expansion of Sinophobia. So widely had this sentiment spread throughout California by the end of the decade that, in a referendum authorized by the state legislature, 96 percent of the 160,000 who cast ballots voted to prohibit Chinese immigration, 3.5 percent abstained, and only one-half of 1 percent voted in favor of continuing the immigration. Critics of the referendum contended that the wording of the resolution and its location on the ballot biased the results. Even though their charge had merit, it is unlikely that an unbiased version of the question would have dramatically reversed the direction or even the near unanimity of the results.

The constitutional convention of 1878

With such a climate of opinion, California was prepared to take a dramatic step in its drive against the Chinese. Accordingly, in the fall of 1878 it authorized through a statewide election the convening of delegates of the people to rewrite the state constitution. The express purpose of this convention was to leaven the new constitution with prohibitions against the Chinese. In its opening days the convention established a standing committee on the Chinese and referred to it the more than twenty anti-Chinese resolutions made by delegates from the floor.

In dealing with the Chinese, however, the convention could not merely incorporate them into the plural framework erected at the convention of 1849. The inclusion of the Fourteenth and Fifteenth Amendments as part of the Federal Constitution by 1870 prevented that. It even undermined seriously the underpinnings of that legal framework. (Even though California had refused to ratify these amendments, it was now bound by their incorporation into the federal Constitution.) In fact, the convention felt obliged to dismantle significant supports for that earlier framework. For example, it deleted the word *white* from the Article on suffrage and thereby brought it into accord with the Fifteenth Amendment – while retaining, however, the crucial requirement of citizenship for the exercise of this right (a requirement now met by the blacks by virtue of the Fourteenth Amendment). In another section of the constitution, Article I, Section 17, the convention even extended the property rights of native-born citizens to foreigners of African descent, rights that had previously been extended only to foreigners of Caucasian descent. The key reservation in each case, however, was that these foreigners – white or black – be "eligible to become citizens of the United States under the naturalization laws" (California Constitutional Convention of 1878–79 III:1491).

However, in rolling back this plural framework the convention was confident that the rights and immunities of the People's Domain that were being extended to the blacks would not have to apply to the Chinese as well; for, it had already been established by treaty and court decision that the Chinese were not eligible for citizenship. As a result, the convention felt no inhibition in denying them any of these rights and immunities. In fact it explicitly forbade the Chinese along with "[any] idiot, insane person,... person hereafter convicted of the embezzlement or misappropriation of public money ..." from ever exercising the right of suffrage (California Constitutional Convention of 1878–79 III:1495).

The convention was much less sanguine about the extent and kinds of constraints that it could legally impose on the mere "presence" of the Chinese – occupationally as well as territorially – in the state. Specifically, it was unable to agree on the limits that treaties and the federal Constitution set on the exercise of state authority on this matter, but it agreed almost to a man that something had to be done about the Chinese "presence" in California.

The split manifested itself early in the deliberations of the fifteen-member committee on the Chinese and was clearly evident in its chairman's report to the convention. In elaborating upon the resolutions recommended by the committee for an article on the Chinese, the chairman lamented the fact that – despite its unanimous conviction that "Chinese immigration was an evil" – the committee could not agree on a single plan of state action "for remedying this evil" (California Constitutional Convention of 1878–79 I:628). As a result, he remarked, the nine sections of the article reflected three separate – even contradictory – strategies, each of which represented a shifting majority decision.

One strategy rejected any fetters, constitutional or otherwise, on the sovereignty of the state and on its right to act on the matter. As argued by the author of one proposal, the state had the "broad and inalienable right ... to protect itself from injury, and to promote the welfare of its people. The police powers of a State are only limited by the character and extent of the evils which may be inflicted upon it from within, or which may threaten it from without" (California Constitutional Convention of 1878–79 I:635).

According to this committee member, the unrestricted immigration of the Chinese constituted such an evil. They were a race

"that can never be digested into the body of the people; one which no process of education or contact can cause it to assimilate with us politically, socially, or morally; one which, in the lapse of centuries, should it unfortunately remain with us, would be the same as to-day, and prove an insoluble and heterogeneous element in our population; one which, by its peculiar composition, has the undoubted faculty to supplant our own people and become the conquerors of our State by a process which is more potent and irresistible than the march of victorious armies through our territories, or the successful invasion of our shores by hostile fleets."

(California Constitutional Convention of 1878–79 I:635)

To meet this evil, he proposed a constitutional ban on "all further immigration to this State of Chinese ineligible to become citizens of the United States under the naturalization laws thereof" (Section 4) (California Constitutional Convention of 1878–79 I:629). He argued that this step would be fully in accord with the power of the state

"to protect its people from moral and physical infection from abroad;... [for] if, under its police and quasi-commercial powers, it can shut its ports to smallpox and contagious fevers, to leprosy, and elephantiasis, to foreign convicts and foreign paupers, why, I ask you, has it not the power to deny the hospitality of its territory to a race who are slowly, but surely and insidiously, substituting themselves for our own people? Is it within the line of logical reasoning that a State can protect its people from disease, but yet not the power to save them from annihilation? Are the institutions of the country founded on so flimsy a basis that States may invoke the highest and exercise the most sweeping powers to quarantine a few unfortunate passengers afflicted with disease, but that they cannot deny the entrance to their ports of swarms of Asiatics, whose presence in their midst is fraught with evils compared with which a plague is the acme of blissful visitation?"

(California Constitutional Convention of 1878–79 I:627)

Another section of the article (Section 5) extended the ban to migrants who might enter California from adjoining states: "No person who is not eligible to become a citizen of the United States shall be permitted to settle in the State after the adoption of this constitution" (California Constitutional Convention of 1878–

79 I: 627). Proponents of this measure also contended that it was phrased in a style that was in accord with earlier court decisions.

> "That section [5] has a precedent in this Convention of Illinois that existed up to some fifteen years, when the Fifteenth Amendment was adopted, prohibiting mulattoes and negroes settling in that State. The State of Indiana prohibited negroes and imposed a fine upon them, which was used for the purpose of taking those from the State that were found in the State. That provision in the Constitution had been sustained by the Supreme Court as applicable to the negroes, and it certainly would sustain it as applicable to persons ineligible to become citizens of the United States."
>
> (California Constitutional Convention of 1878–79 II:660)

Not content with merely banning future immigration, a delegate offered a resolution from the floor that would require "all Mongolians within this State" to remove themselves from the state within four years after the adoption of the constitution. Failure to do so would result in forced seizure and sale of their property to defray the cost of their forcible removal from the state. The preamble to the resolution paid lip service to the

> "paramount authority of the United States of America to regulate commerce and intercourse with foreign nations, and all treaty obligations, . . . [but] the People of California . . . demand, as they possess the inalienable privilege of controlling their domestic affairs to the end that serfdom in every form may be abolished, and themselves protected from a vicious, non-assimilating population, incapable of the duties of American citizenship. As intelligent citizenship must be the reliance of representative government, so must the presence of large numbers of persons, incapable of such citizenship, be its perpetual menace."
>
> (California Constitutional Convention of 1878 II:691–92)

Despite its professed intent to brazen out a collision with federal authority over immigration, the convention backed away from such a direct confrontation by the time it settled on its final version of the article. Only Section 5 survived until the penultimate draft; the other two were eliminated almost immediately. What finally remained in the final version of the article was an introductory sentence to Section 4 that merely proclaimed: "The presence of foreigners ineligible to become citizens of the United States is declared (herein) to be dangerous to the well-being of the State, and the Legislature shall discourage their immigration by all the means within its power" (California Constitutional Convention of 1878–79 III:1493).

The second strategy that ordered the recommendations of the committee on the Chinese avoided the issue of immigration but devised a multi-pronged attack on making life for the Chinese untenable and thereby forcing them to leave California. Its central focus was the cutting off of access to various job and labor markets. Section 3, for example, declared that "no alien ineligible to become a citizen of the United States shall ever be employed on any State, county, municipal, or other public work in this State after the adoption of this Constitution." Section 6 denied them "the right to catch fish in any of the waters under the jurisdiction of the State;" it also forbade the granting of licenses to them "to carry on any business, trade, or occupation in this State." In addition, the committee recommended severe penalties for those white citizens who employed Chinese or, as more euphemistically phrased, aliens not eligible for citizenship. As such, Section 2 threatened any corporation, incorporated under the laws of California, with forfeiture of its franchise and all legal rights if such people were on its work force. Section 8 would remove public officials from office for similar action; and Section 9 would deny employers of Chinese generally the exercise of their right of suffrage (California Constitutional Convention of 1878–79 I:627–28).

Not only did the committee seek to shrivel the employment opportunities of the Chinese, but it also sought to strip them of any rights of property and of any protection of the law. Specifically, Section 6 denied them the right "to purchase, own, or lease real property in this State; and all contracts of conveyance or lease of real estate to any such foreigner shall be void" (California Constitutional Convention of 1878–79 I:628). It also deprived them of the "right to sue or be sued in any of the Courts of this State, and any lawyer appearing for or against them, or any of them, in a civil proceeding, shall forfeit his license to practice law" (California Constitutional Convention of 1878–79 I:627). And as a final touch, the committee provided in Section 7 "for their exclusion from residence or settlement in any portion of the State . . . " (California Constitutional Convention of 1878–79 I:628). Accordingly, it gave local authorities the power to legislate the removal of the Chinese from their incorporated limits.

In presenting these proposals for the committee, the chairman characterized them as "a plan of starvation by constitutional provision. If the Chinese are not to be employed by anybody, are not permitted to labor, they cannot live. Because by labor all must live, and if you deprive them of the right to labor, they must starve. That is the logical sequence of the position assumed by the advocates of this prohibition against the labor of these people" (California Constitutional Convention of 1878–79 I:630). He thereupon declared his personal opposition to these proposals and argued that this strategy "is indefensible, for it deprives the prohibited people of the right of life. I hold that the right to labor is as high and sacred a right as the right to live" (California Constitutional Convention of 1878–79 I:630).

A major supporter of this strategy did not deny the charge of the chairman, but he insisted that the state had no other recourse but to use its reserved power of internal regulation to prevent the Chinese from settling there – being that the state could not legally keep them from crossing its borders. And by using this power, he continued, "we can prevent them [the Chinese] from engaging in business, from being employed by corporations, from earning a living, and prevent their settling by starving them out. That, sir, was admitted by the gentleman who was the Chairman of the Committee on Chinese. He says we can starve them; and that is what we desire to do, if we cannot get rid of them in any other way" (California Constitutional Convention of 1878–79 II:712).

Pervasive as this sentiment was among the delegates, many were nevertheless troubled by some of the constitutional ramifications of these proposals. Particularly troublesome were those resolutions that imposed penalties on the People's Domain for employing Chinese. In the words of the chairman of the committee, this "strikes at the liberty of the citizens of the United States, who, as citizens, have the right to employ whoever they choose. I hold that you cannot abridge that right. It is one of the inalienable rights of American citizens" (California Constitutional Convention of 1878–79 I:630).

As a result of this concern, the convention made short shrift of Sections 8 and 9, which imposed sanctions on public officers who employed Chinese and denied the right of vote to any other employers of the Chinese. It also deleted the first two sentences of Section 6 depriving the Chinese of the right to sue and to obtain business licenses. And it modified Section 2 so that the penalty imposed on corporations for employing Chinese was to be spelled out by the legislature in the future, and not to be an automatic forfeiture of franchise and legal rights.

The built-in dilemma for the supporters of this strategy can be seen in the sarcastic response of one delegate to another delegate's resolution, which was subsequently defeated as a replacement for the original Section 8 struck down earlier.

"If the proposition of the distinguished gentleman from Los Angeles is correct, we have a solution of this vexed question; and if the distinguished gentleman can show us that he is right, legally, we shall certainly be under infinite obligations to him, because it affords us an easy and complete, absolute, and radical solution of the whole question. We can get rid of the Chinaman, because we can tax him out of his rights, and out of his boots; and we would do it, too, but the trouble is, that we do not understand that the gentleman from Los Angeles is correct in his legal interpretation of the power with which we are invested. But I heartily and sincerely desire that he may be able to convince us that we have this exclusive power of taxation. For my part, I am unable to see that we have any such power."   (California Constitutional Convention of 1878–79 II:728)

However, not until the second reading of the entire article did the convention have second thoughts on a key section of the first draft. By a narrow margin of 55 to 52, it struck out the provision that "no aliens ineligible to become citizens of the United States shall be permitted to catch fish in any waters under the jurisdiction of this State; nor to purchase, lease, own, or hold any real property in this State, and all contracts of conveyance or lease of real property to any such aliens shall be void" [Section 5] (California Constitutional Convention of 1878–79 III:1429).

This time the argument that the section was in violation of the federal Constitution treaty provision prevailed. Also heard was the cry that

"It would be a disgrace to our State to pass it [the section]. . . . It is contrary to the most enlightened spirit of the age, and would be a disgrace to our boasted American civilization. And, sir, for one, I utterly reject the idea that a section of that kind would meet or remedy the evil we labor under. It would turn all civilized people against us everywhere. It would show to the world that we are below these very people we would proscribe, in point of civilization; these people whom we call heathens. If we cannot control our own prejudices and feelings enough to act in a civilized manner, we are incapable of making a Constitution. I am as anxious to get rid of the Chinese as any man in the State of California, but I will not vote to deprive them of the means of procuring the necessaries of life, or add to the great wrong inflicted upon us by being ourselves in the wrong. Besides this, it will injure the very cause we are trying to promote. It would have a marked effect on public sentiment in the East. Imagine a Senator or Representative in Congress, when the question of Chinese immigration is under debate, getting up and reading section five now under consideration. I want to know what Senator or Representative would not denounce it as being opposed to the spirit of our civilization. It would array against us a prejudice that we are not entitled to have arrayed against us, and that we should seek to avoid."   (California Constitutional Convention of 1878–79 III:1429)

In the final analysis then, only two provisions from the original draft survived virtually intact in the final version of the article: the sections that deprived the Chinese of employment by corporations incorporated in the state and by government agencies (Section 2 and 3 in the final version). Also retained was the portion of Section 7 that gave authority to local governments to eject the Chinese from their borders.

However, a week after deliberations began on the Chinese issue, an amendment to Section 7 was offered from the floor that captured the attention and support of the convention. Despite slight modifications, it survived the various voting tests and was incorporated in the final version of the article as part of Section 4. The amendment addressed itself to the question of coolieism and in its final form it stipulated that "Asiatic coolieism *is* a form of human slavery, *and* is forever prohibited in this State; and all contracts for coolie labor *shall be* void.... All companies or corporations, whether formed in this country or any foreign country, for the importation of such labor, shall be subject to such penalties as the Legislature may prescribe" (California Constitutional Convention of 1878–79 III:1493).

As the discussion on the amendment got underway, it soon became evident that most delegates lacked any interest in defining precisely the term coolieism. Instead they were using it ubiquitously as a label for branding as a form of slavery or peonage virtually any and all kinds of labor arrangements by which the Chinese entered California. In addition, the delegates were self-righteously convinced that in banning coolieism they were engaging in a lawful activity which even the federal Constitution would support. As one delegate pontificated,

"I pity the gentlemen who have not yet found out that if we ever succeed in ridding ourselves of the curse, so called, of cheap Chinese labor, it must be upon the ground that it is slave labor, and to that it must come. You cannot exclude him because he is a Chinaman; nor because he smokes opium; nor because he eats rice; but you can exclude him because he is essentially a slave ... we have a right to protect ourselves against slave labor, and upon that we have authorities." (California Constitutional Convention of 1878 II:712)

He then quoted a Supreme Court decision.

Even the author of the amendment was convinced that his provision

"would at least cover three-fourths of the Chinamen in this State who are held here under a form of slavery; and we would be able to get rid of these, and prevent any more of that class coming to this State. I believe that in that way we can prevent the evil in a measure, if we cannot wholly remove it from the State. I think the committee should agree upon that amendment, and I do hope and trust that it will become a part of the Constitution of this State." (California Constitutional Convention of 1878–79 II:726)

Though several delegates, including the chairman of the committee on the Chinese, pressed for a precise definition of the term coolieism and the kind of labor arrangement to which it would apply ("I would like the gentleman [the author of the amendment] to explain what he means by coolieism") (California Constitutional Convention of 1878–79 II:724), their queries were drowned in a quagmire of rhetoric, as the convention moved inexorably to a lopsided approval of the amendment.

The third strategy that gave shape to the recommendations of the committee proceeded, in the words of its chairman, "upon the theory that the State has not within itself the power to prohibit Chinese immigration." Under the Constitution as interpreted by the Supreme Court, "there is above and beyond the State a national sovereignty which deals with all these subjects, treaties between nations, intercourse with foreign nations, foreign commerce, and navigation" (California Constitutional Convention of 1878–79 I:628). Further, he argued in a later part of his address, the state also had no constitutional or moral authority to pursue "a plan of starvation by constitutional provision" against the Chinese who were within its borders (California Constitutional Convention of 1878–79 I:630).

But, he concluded, the state – though prohibited by the federal Constitution from proceeding categorically against the Chinese – had the authority to use its reserved police power to protect itself against certain segments and classes of Chinese once they had landed and had "become part of our population and subject to the laws of the State." In other words,

> "the State has the power to protect itself against foreign and wellknown dangerous classes – classes that are admitted by all people to be dangerous and detrimental to the wellbeing of the State, such as paupers, vagrants, criminals, persons suffering from contagious or infectious diseases, and we hold that the State has power to exclude these under the law of self-preservation, which is the first law of the State. That it does not interfere with foreign commerce to exercise this power. We propose, under this section [Section 1], that the Legislature shall have power to enforce the details for executing this plan. We propose that tribunals shall be established, such as the established Courts, before whom persons alleged to be paupers or criminals may be brought for trial. If it shall be found upon examination that they belong to any one of these classes, we propose that a place shall be established in San Francisco for the safe keeping of those persons until they can be removed from the State. We propose, as to the criminal classes of Chinese, that, instead of being incarcerated in prison at the expense of the State, upon conviction, the Legislature shall empower the Courts to remand them to this place, to be afterwards removed from the State. In some sense, it is a system of banishment of these people, as a punishment for crime."   (California Constitutional Convention of 1878–79 I:628)

In this manner the state would have the authority to rid itself of the undesirable elements among the Chinese, not by jailing them but by shipping them out of California to China or to other states, which would then have the problem too. The chairman estimated that about 5000 Chinese would be gotten rid of annually in this fashion.

He then went on to urge the adoption of the Section with a vigor and intensity that he failed to express for any of the other sections of the article. He reminded the convention that it had to operate within the legal framework of the federal

Constitution and treaties and therefore had only the kind of limited option which Section 1 provided it. But he also let it be known in no uncertain terms that his concern about the lawful treatment of the Chinese had nothing to do with any sympathy for them. In fact he considered them an evil presence in California and expressed his passionate opposition to them at the end of his presentation of the committee report. At that point he launched into a lengthy pseudo-scientific disquisition – blending elements of Malthus and Darwin – about the terrible threat that the engulfing waves of Chinese posed to the American civilization. This threat, he insisted, stemmed from the fact that these Chinese were survivors of a struggle for sheer existence that had lasted for thousands of years in China, in which overpopulation of Malthusian proportions had pressed relentlessly against increasingly limited means of subsistence. Thus the Chinese of today, he declared,

"bears with him the heredity of poverty and unrelenting toil for food through thousands of years. His physical organs have become adapted to insufficient food. There has been a process of selection going on in China under which the heavy feeders have fallen out, and under the law of the 'survival of the fittest' none but those who can practice the most rigid self-denial as to food remain. They have also been trained by centuries of incessant toil to procure the maximum of subsistence from the soil.

The result of this life is a sinewy, shriveled human creature, whose muscles are as iron, whose sinews are like thongs, whose nerves are like steel wires, with a stomach case lined with brass; a creature who can toil sixteen hours of the twenty-four; who can live and grow fat on the refuse of any American laborer's table. Capable, as a later writer says, 'of driving the vulture from its prey, which he consumes, and then devours the unclean bird itself.' He is a human creature without sympathy; supremely selfish, for his struggle with nature has kept him busy with himself. Without aspirations, for hope of better things fled from his race centuries ago."   (California Constitutional Convention of 1878–79 I:633)

Against such a species, the chairman continued, the white man had little chance in the field of labor, unless he was prepared to give up what made his civilization so distinctive and unless he was prepared to give up his way of life and his culture. In the final analysis, he would have to "live as the Chinaman lives; work as the beast works; there can be no recreation, no rest, nothing but toil."

"The white man cannot compete in the field of labor with such a being as that – he cannot until he becomes such as the Chinaman is. To compete with the Chinese our people must give up their homes, abandon the family altar, tear down their school houses, blot out their civilization, and adopt the Chinese mode of life. If the white man is to compete with the Chinaman he must adopt a cheaper style of dress, he must inure himself to the cold, he must labor in the night; sleep shall not come to his pillow until the midnight bell tolls the solemn hour. He must arise at the first gray streaks of dawn and at his work. Then what shall be his food? No longer the savory meats, the pure, white bread made by willing hands. No! He must live as the Chinaman lives; work as the beast works; there can be no recreation, no rest, nothing but toil."

(California Constitutional Convention of 1878–79 I:633)

The ultimate outcome, according to the chairman, would be a Mongolization and mongrelization of the American society. "The fittest is he who can survive, that is all there is of the doctrine; not he that is the highest type of man. Turn out your finest thoroughbred horses to roam the plain with mustangs, or your best or purest strain of Durhams to graze with the broad-horned beast of Mexico, and see the operation of the law of the survival of the fittest" (California Constitutional Convention of 1878–79 I:633).

To prevent this from happening, the chairman concluded, immigration had to be stopped, but only Congress had the authority to stop it. As a result California had to mobilize its energies to get Congress to do something about it. In the meantime, California could enact provisions like Section 1, which were well within the state's jurisdiction, and not fritter its energies away on unconstitutional enactments.

The debate on Section 1 was lively and extended; the only opposition expressed was that it did not go far enough. But once convinced that other prospective sections of the article on the Chinese were more restrictive, opposition disappeared, and it was passed without difficulty.

The nine sections of the original article on the Chinese, therefore, were finally whittled down to four sections in the definitive version, Article XIX. This article, along with the rest of the constitution, was formally adopted by the convention on March 3 1879 and ratified several months later by the people of California. However, less than two years later, three of the four sections were overturned through court challenges. First to be declared void was Section 2 which prohibited corporations from employing Chinese. In his opinion for the US Circuit Court on In Re Tiburcio Parrott, Judge Hoffman rejected the state's contention that corporations were creatures of the state and therefore subject to any rules that the state might wish to impose upon them, including whom they shall employ. He insisted that the state had exceeded its constitutional authority in seeking to amend the general law on corporations by enacting Section 2; in addition it had violated the constitutional and treaty rights of the Chinese.

In a separate opinion, Judge Sawyer stressed the right to work as among the inalienable rights of man, next in importance only to the right to live. He also drew the protective mantle of the Constitution and Burlingame Treaty around this right for the Chinese. (This treaty will be examined more fully in the next chapter.)

"As to by far the greatest portion of the Chinese, as well as other foreigners who land upon our shores, their labor is the only exchangeable commodity they possess. To deprive them of the right to labor is to consign them to starvation. The right to labor is, of all others, after the right to live, the fundamental, inalienable right of man, wherever he may be permitted to be, of which he cannot be deprived, either under the guise of law or otherwise, except by usurpation and force. Man ate and died. When God drove him 'forth from the Garden of Eden to till the ground, from whence he was taken,' and said to him, 'in the sweat of thy face shalt thou eat bread, till thou return unto the ground.' He invested him with an inalienable right to labor in order that he might again eat and live. And this absolute, fundamental, and natural right was guaranteed by the National Government to all Chinese who were permitted to come into the United States under the treaty with their government."

(US Circuit Court, 9th District, California 1880:26)

Shortly thereafter, Section 3 which banned employment of Chinese on public works was rendered invalid by a court decision on a similar law passed by the Oregon legislature. In that case, Judge Deady stated:

"'The only legal remedy for the evils, real or fancied, of Chinese or other immigration, is by an appeal to the national government, in whom the power over the subject is exclusively vested. But the fact is, the anti-Chinese legislation of the Pacific coast is but a poorly disguised attempt on the part of the state to evade and set aside the treaty with China, and thereby nullify an act of the national government. Between this and "the firing on Fort Sumter," by South Carolina, there is the difference of the direct and the indirect – and nothing more.'"

(Sandmeyer 1936:207–08)

And finally, three laws that were passed by the legislature in 1880 to implement Section 4 of the state constitution were declared void. One authorized local authorities to expel Chinese from their borders; the other two barred the Chinese from obtaining licenses for business and occupational purposes and from engaging in commercial fishing. In finding the fishing law violative of the Burlingame Treaty and the Fourteenth Amendment, Judge Sawyer stated:

"'Like other privileges he enjoys as an alien by permission of the state, he can only enjoy so much as the state vouchsafes to yield to him as a special privilege. To him it is not a property right, but, in the strictest sense, a privilege or favor. To exclude the Chinaman from fishing in the waters of the state, therefore, while the Germans, Italians, Englishmen, and Irishmen, who otherwise stand upon the same footing are permitted to fish *ad libitum*, without price, charge, let, or hindrance, is to prevent him from enjoying the same privileges as are "enjoyed by the citizens or subjects of the most favored nation;" and to punish him criminally for fishing in the waters of the state, while all aliens of the Caucasian race are permitted to fish freely in the same waters with immunity and without restraint, and exempt from all punishment, is to exclude him from enjoying the same immunities and exemptions "as are enjoyed by the citizens or subjects of the most favored nation."'"   (Sandmeyer 1936:207)

What finally remained as lawful in Article XIX was Section 1, as the chairman of the committee had earlier forecast. In short, the courts were prepared to recognize the police power of the state to regulate undesirable elements within its borders; nevertheless, they dealt summarily with a number of municipal ordinances, ostensibly based on this section, which they deemed as unduly discriminatory of the Chinese as a racial category. Particularly vulnerable to court challenge were measures enacted in San Francisco to regulate laundries.

In effect, Article XIX of the constitution of 1879 was gutted by four major constraints imposed by the courts on anti-Chinese legislation at that time; before 1868 only one of these constraints was in effect. That one derived from the United States Supreme Court decision on the Passenger Cases of 1849, which determined that Congress had the exclusive right to regulate foreign commerce and immigration under the commerce clause of the federal Constitution. In 1868 the second impediment arose with the signing of the Burlingame Treaty with China, which provided citizens and subjects of each country with the mutual right of migration from one to the other. The other two barriers were the products of the reconstruction period: the Fourteenth Amendment and the Civil Rights Act of 1875, both of which afforded the Chinese with a degree of protection under their "equal treatment" and "due process" clauses. The net result was that by the end of the 1870s most state laws and municipal ordinances directed against the Chinese, and not merely Article XIX of the new constitution, were rendered inoperative.

This did not prevent state and local authorities from continuing to pass laws and ordinances against the Chinese; the last major state legislation was passed in 1891. But even the diehards among them became increasingly resigned to the fact that they could do little themselves to stem the flow or to control the situation. For, despite all their efforts, Chinese immigration had continued to grow markedly during the 1870s, averaging 10,000 to 15,000 per year in contrast to 5000 per year in the early 1860s.

The federal government importuned by California

Within a few years after the arrival of the first Chinese in California, state officials began to look to the federal government for help in meeting its – at that time –

nascent Chinese problem. In 1852, for example, "the state assembly committee on mines recommended in its report that a resolution be sent to Congress declaring that importation by foreign capitalists of large numbers of Asiatics, South Americans, and Mexicans (referred to as 'peons' and 'serfs') was 'a danger to the tranquility of the mining regions,' and that speedy action was required to correct the evil" (Heizer and Almquist 1971:155).

Several years later the state senate and assembly passed concurrent resolutions importuning Congress to legalize a head tax to be collected from owners and masters of vessels for each Chinese or Japanese who intended to debark from their ships. However, without waiting for congressional action which never did come, the state legislature passed its own version of a capitation tax, only to have it declared unconstitutional almost immediately.

And so it went. California state legislators would make speeches and occasionally pass resolutions to alert the nation to the Chinese threat. Its congressmen in Washington would repeatedly seek to place the Chinese issue on the national agenda. Not until 1876 did these discrete and individual efforts give way to a coordinated legislatorial approach to the matter. At that time the state senate of California appointed a committee, first of five members then of seven, to inquire:

"1. As to the number of Chinese in this State, and the effect their presence has upon the social and political condition of the State.
2. As to the probable result of Chinese immigration upon the country, if such immigration be not discouraged.
3. As to the means of exclusion, if such committee should be of the opinion that the presence of the Chinese element in our midst is detrimental to the interests of the country.
4. As to such other matters as, in the judgment of the committee, have a bearing upon the question of Chinese immigration."
(California State Senate Special Committee on Chinese Immigration 1877:3)

Upon the conclusion of its inquiry, the committee was to "prepare a memorial to the Congress of the United States, which memorial must set out at length the facts in relation to the subject of this inquiry, and such conclusions as the committee may have arrived at as to the policy and means of excluding Chinese from the country" (California State Senate Special Committee on Chinese Immigration 1877:3). To insure adequate nationwide publicity for its memorial, the committee was also

"authorized and directed to have printed, at the State Printing Office, a sufficient number of copies of such memorial, and of the testimony taken by said committee, to furnish copies thereof to the leading newspapers of the

United States, five copies to each member of Congress, ten copies to the Governor of each State, and to deposit two thousand copies with the Secretary of State of California for general distribution."
(California State Senate Special Committee on Chinese Immigration 1877:3)

The committee heard 60 witnesses, 42 of whom were white. One half the white witnesses were public officials and policemen from San Francisco or Sacramento, almost all of whom had strong anti-Chinese feelings. The rest were drawn from such sundry occupations as farmer, journalist, clergy, and a captain and a mate of an English ship carrying Chinese immigrants. Only nine either had traveled or had lived in China. The Chinese witnesses included the presidents of the Six Companies in San Francisco, one geologist, two interpreters, and eight laborers.

The hearings were heavily biased against the Chinese. Not surprisingly in view of this, the committee's answers to the questions addressed to it in the senate's opening charge were clear and unambiguous. It declared in its memorial to Congress, which was also its report to the state senate, that the Chinese posed a serious and abiding threat to the social, economic, and political stability and wellbeing of the People's Domain. The threat, it insisted, was threefold.

First, the Chinese were of such low moral and psychological character that the men comprised a disproportionate part of the criminal and deviant population, and the women were "almost without exception, of the vilest and most degraded class of abandoned women" (California State Senate Special Committee on Chinese Immigration 1877:5). As a result, the report continued, the people of California had had to bear the cost of incarcerating these criminals and deviants and of patrolling their vice-ridden areas. But even more, these Chinese threatened to undermine the probity of the judiciary system of the People's Domain.

"Our ignorance of the Chinese language, the utter want of comprehension by them of the crime of perjury, their systematic bribery, and intimidation of witnesses, and other methods of baffling judicial action, all tend to weaken the authority of our laws and to paralyze the power of our Courts."
(California State Senate Special Committee on Chinese Immigration 1887:4)

The second and direst threat of all, according to the committee, stemmed from the "fact" that the Chinese represented slave labor.

"The Chinese in California are substantially in a condition of servitude. Ninety-nine one-hundreths of them are imported here by large companies under contracts to repay to the importers out of their labor the cost of their transportation and large interest upon the outlay, and these contracts frequently hold their subjects for long periods. During the existence of these contracts the Chinese are, to all intents, serfs, and as such are let out to service at a miserable

pittance to perform the labor that it ought to be the privilege of our own race to perform."
(California State Senate Special Committee on Chinese Immigration 1877:5–6)

In this fashion, the committee accepted without qualification the "coolie labor contract" theory – drawing no distinction whatsoever between it and the "credit-ticket" arrangement which in fact characterized most Chinese immigration to California. But further, the committee insisted that the Chinese were not merely serfs by labor contract but

"by the very constitution of their nature, by instinct, by the traditions of their order for thousands of years, serfs. They never rise above that condition in their native land, and by the inexorable decrees of caste, never can rise. Servile labor to them is their natural and inevitable lot. Hewers of wood and drawers of water they had been since they had a country, and servile laborers they will be to the end of time. Departure from that level with them is never upward; the only change, apparently, is from servitude to crime."
(California State Senate Special Committee on Chinese Immigration 1877:6)

Such slave labor, the committee concluded, posed a serious threat to the life circumstances of the people of California and to their position in the labor market. For free white labor could not be expected to compete with unfree Chinese labor without being degraded to its level. "Even were it possible for the white laborer to maintain existence upon the wages paid to the Chinese, his condition nevertheless becomes that of an abject slave, for grinding poverty is absolute slavery. The vaunted 'dignity of labor' becomes a biting sarcasm when the laborer becomes a serf" (California State Senate Special Committee on Chinese Immigration 1877:6).

The memorial went on to comment that the earnings of the Chinese were not invested in homes, capital, and land in California, but were instead sent back to China. As a result,

"fertile lands that scarcely require tillage to produce a harvest, are lying idle, partially because the laborer that would purchase and improve them can earn nothing above a bare support wherewith to buy, while the Chinese, who can by their habits of life practically subsist on nothing and save money, export their savings instead of here accumulating property. What the one hundred and eighty millions of solid gold shipped from California to a foreign country would produce, if retained here by white labor and invested in the soil, in the homes and firesides of our own race, requires no illustration or argument. California, instead of being a State of cities, might be a State of prosperous farms; instead of

being in a condition (considering her extraordinary natural advantages) of wonderful yet healthy progress, we find her so retarded in her growth as to amount almost to retrogression."
(California State Senate Special Committee on Chinese Immigration 1877:5)

What then, the report asked rhetorically, were

"the benefits conferred upon us by this isolated and degrading class? The only one ever suggested [referring obliquely to testimony at the hearings] was 'cheap labor.' But if cheap labor means white famine it is a fearful benefit. It cheap labor means not only starvation for our own laborers, but a gradual, yet certain, depletion of the resources of our State for the enriching of a semi-civilized foreign country, it is a benefit hitherto unknown to the science of political economy. If cheap labor means servile labor, it is a burlesque on the policy of emancipation. And if this kind of cheap labor brings in its train the demoralization consequent upon the enforced idleness of our own race, the moral degradation attendant upon the presence in our midst of the most disgusting licentiousness, and the absolute certainty of pestilence arising from the crowded condition and filthy habits of life of those who perform this so-called cheap labor, it were well for all of us that it should be abolished."
(California State Senate Special Committee on Chinese Immigration 1877:7)

The third threat posed by the Chinese, according to the committee, was to the stability and tranquility of the social and institutional fabric of the People's Domain. This threat stemmed from the "fact" that the Chinese comprised an unassimilable body of foreign nationals "incapable of adaptation to our institutions." They came from a country whose

"national intellect ... has become decrepit from sheer age. It has long since passed its prime and is waning into senility. The iron manacles of caste which prevail in that Empire are as cruel and unyielding as those which chain the sudras in Hindostan [sic] to a hereditary state of pauperism and slavery. As an acute thinker has sagaciously observed, the Chinese seem to be antediluvian men renewed. Their code of morals, their forms of worship, and their maxims of life, are those of the remotest antiquity. In this aspect they stand as a barrier against which the elevating tendency of a higher civilization exerts itself in vain. And, in an ethnological point of view, there can be no hope that any contact with our people, however long continued, will ever conform them to our institutions, enable them to comprehend or appreciate our form of government, or to assume the duties or discharge the functions of citizens."
(California State Senate Special Committee on Chinese Immigration 1877:6–7)

Small wonder, the memorial continued, that such persons had never become part of the People's Domain of California nor absorbed into its institutional life. In short,

> "during their entire settlement in California they have never adapted themselves to our habits, modes of dress, or our educational system, have never learned the sanctity of an oath, never desired to become citizens, or to perform the duties of citizenship,* never discovered the difference between right and wrong, never ceased the worship of their idol gods, or advanced a step beyond the musty traditions of their native hive. Impregnable to all the influences of our Anglo-Saxon life they remain the same stolid Asiatics that have floated on the rivers and slaved in the fields of China for thirty centuries of time."
> (California State Senate Special Committee on Chinese Immigration 1877:7)

As a result, the committee lamented, California could not develop into the kind of cohesive and tranquil society of the people that it might have in the absence of such an alien and inferior racial presence.

What had made the threefold threat of the Chinese take on an even more ominous meaning, according to the committee, was the fact that they had already become one-sixth of the population of California and were on the way to outnumbering the whites of the state. At that time, "white labor will be unknown, because unobtainable, and then how long a period will elapse before California will, nay must, become essentially a State with but two orders of society – the master and the serf – a lesser Asia, with all its deathly lethargy?" (California State Senate Special Committee on Chinese Immigration 1877:7–8).

The committee concluded that action must be taken at once to suppress Chinese immigration and, because the federal government through treaty and law had protected this immigration in the past, it must withdraw this protection. In this vein, the committee ended its memorial with an entreaty to Congress to abrogate all treaties with China† that permitted the "emigration of Chinese to the United

---

*This is one of several "catch-22" type statements contained in the committee's report. In this instance, the committee criticized the Chinese for their unwillingness to perform duties of citizenship and yet the committee was part of a state government that had categorically refused to grant the Chinese the right to perform these duties. In another instance, the committee complained that the Chinese male immigrants lacked the stability of family life and were not married (neglecting to mention that most had wives in China); at the same time the state government was doing all in its power to prevent the entry of Chinese women and had also forbidden intermarriage with non-Chinese women.

†To give its memorial an international tone, the committee also addressed an appeal "to the Government of Great Britain to cooperate with our own government in the absolute prohibition of this trade in men and women" and asked it to join with America in abrogating treaties with China "permitting the emigration of Chinese to the United States" (California State Senate Special Committee on Chinese Immigration 1877:9).

States." Until this happened, the memorial continued, "we earnestly recommend legislation by Congress limiting the number of Chinese allowed to be landed from any vessel entering the ports of the United States to, say, not more than ten" (California State Senate Special Committee on Chinese Immigration 1877:9).

Approximately a year and a half later another memorial was submitted to Congress in the name of the people of California. This one was prepared by the Committee on the Chinese at the behest of the constitutional convention of 1878. Its first version was returned to the committee by the convention as inadequate; its second and final version was adopted in mid-December 1878.

This memorial stressed even more than did the first the near unanimity of opinion among the people of California that something had to be done to stop the Chinese immigration.

> "If it be supposed, as has been often said, that the hostility to Chinese immigration is confined to a small and ignorant class of our people, we protest against such an assumption. The discontent from this cause is almost universal. It is not limited to any political party, nor to any class or nationality. It does not spring from race antipathies, nor alone from economic considerations, nor from any religious sentiment, nor from low hatreds, or mercenary motive."
>
> (California Constitutional Convention of 1878 II:739)

The memorial also highlighted the impatience and dismay of the people of California "at the long delay of appropriate action by the National Government toward the prohibition of an immigration which is rapidly approaching the character of an Oriental invasion, and which threatens to supplant Anglo-Saxon civilization on this coast" (California Constitutional Convention of 1878 II:739).

So preoccupied was the committee with the imminence of this "invasion" and with the "dreadfulness" of its consequences that these concerns served as an underlying refrain in four of the five arguments offered in the memorial for opposing immigration. Two of these arguments were also elaborations of themes already stressed in the earlier memorial: namely the inability of the Chinese to be assimilated and their slave-like labor.

With respect to the former, the memorial came down even harder than the earlier memorial on the debased character of the Chinese, on the threat they posed to the health, peace, and safety of the white society, and on the secret political society they presumably built to undermine the political authority of the People's Domain:

> "The Chinese bring with them habits and customs the most vicious and demoralizing. They are scornful of our laws and institutions. They establish their own tribunals for the redress of wrongs and injuries among themselves,

independent of our Courts, and subject the victims of such tribunals to secret punishments the most barbarous and terrible. In our cities they live crowded and herded like beasts, generating the most dangerous diseases. They introduce the ancient, infectious, and incurable malady called leprosy, the germs of which, when once distributed, can never be eradicated, but fasten themselves upon the people as an eternal consuming rot. They poison our youth in both mind and body. They build no homes. They are, generally, destitute of moral principle. They are incapable of patriotism, and are utterly unfitted for American citizenship. Their existence here, in great numbers, is a perpetual menace to republican institutions, a source of constant irritation and danger to the public peace."   (California Constitutional Convention of 1878 II:739)

With respect to the second theme, the memorial substituted the phrase "quasi-slave labor" for the "slave labor" concept of the first memorial; otherwise it retained the earlier emphasis on the destructive consequences of competition by the Chinese on white labor.

"The system of labor, which results from their presence, is a system which includes all, or nearly all, the vices of slavery, without the conservative influence which is incident to the domestic or paternal relation between master and slave. It degrades labor to the standard of mere brute energy, and thus excludes the labor of free white men who will not and cannot endure the degradation of competition with servile labor. Chinese labor is, therefore, substituted for the labor of free white men, and the State is afflicted with a quasi-slave system, under which Chinese population supplants white American citizens, and drives them to other fields or to starvation."
                          (California Constitution Convention of 1878 II:739)

In its final paragraph, this memorial eschewed the implied threat of public violence if nothing was done, unlike the earlier memorial. In fact it contained a conciliatory statement – reflecting no doubt the sentiment of the chairman of the committee – that promised "to avoid all conflict with the national authority, and to limit our action to the exercise of the police power of the State." But the memorial made an even more demanding request of Congress than did the first one. It asked for a total ban, not for the near total ban of the first memorial, "on immigration of Chinese coolies or laborers into the American ports of this coast" (California Constitutional Convention of 1878 II:739).

To strengthen even more its hand in Washington, the convention also addressed memorials to the governors of neighboring states and territories, asking them to join in the drive to pressure Congress and the President to act on the issue.

Thus, by the end of the decade both the officials and people of California reluctantly conceded that they had reached the limits of their authority to deal with the Chinese problem. They even recognized that court decisions since 1870 had narrowed these limits. And so they mounted a campaign with greater determination than ever to place the issue on the agenda of the national government in Washington, D.C.

14

THE FEDERAL GOVERNMENT, CHINA, AND THE EXCLUSION ACTS

Introduction

The reticence of the federal government to come immediately to the aid of California as it began to clamor increasingly for such assistance in the early 1870s had little to do with any sympathy for the Chinese immigrants nor any regard for the reconstruction amendments that had just been passed. Instead, this reticence had to do with the imperial interests of the federal government that collided at that moment of history with the interests of the state of California. The government was deeply involved in working out its relations with China and had just completed negotiations for the Burlingame Treaty.

In time the attack on the treaty, which was orchestrated by the congressional delegation from California, became the springboard for placing the Chinese immigrant problem on the national agenda. Once on the agenda, Congress pushed for ever more restrictive legislation and honed an administrative machinery that perfected procedures for eliminating virtually any immigration from China.

In this chapter we shall examine the interplay between America's relations with, and imperial interests in, China with the tightening of the legal and bureaucratic noose around the Chinese immigrant.

The United States and treaties with China

IMPERIAL INTERESTS AND THE TREATIES OF WANGHIA AND TIENTSIN

America's imperial interests in China first began to unfold in the early 1840s as western Europe and the United States resolved to open up the country to overseas trade, engaged though it had been for centuries in a flourishing trade with its overland neighbors. Spearheading the drive, England had overwhelmed the Chinese government by 1842 in the infamous Opium War, had forced it to abandon its traditional trade arrangement of tribute which symbolically ritualized the superiority of Chinese culture and civilization, and had imposed upon it the one-sided terms of its first treaty arrangement with another country, the Treaty of Nanking. This treaty compelled the Chinese government "for the first time, to give express sanction to foreign trade at certain ports, to fix the conditions under which this trade should be carried on, and to give British traders certain rights of residence in the Chinese Empire" (Willoughby II 1966:726–27).

Fearful that Britain meant to monopolize trade with China, President Tyler prevailed upon Congress to underwrite a mission to China which Caleb Cushing came to head. "Stripped of all verbiage, Cushing's instructions required him to perform one supreme task – to negotiate a treaty with China whereby the same privileges as had lately been acquired by the British would be secured for the American merchants. All other items were quite secondary in importance" (Kuo 1933:35). The result was the Treaty of Wanghia, signed in 1844, which provided even more favorable terms for America than had the earlier treaty for the British.

Although Article 1 talked of "peace" and "sincere and cordial amity," the treaty spelled out in the rest of its articles a grossly unequal set of rights and obligations for the two countries and focused exclusively on their relations with each other within the territorial limits of China. The treaty forced important concessions from the Chinese government: it curtailed, for example, the exercise of China's sovereign right of jurisdiction over its own territory. In doing this, the treaty extended the legal and protective jurisdiction of the American government to its citizens in China and authorized it, not local authorities, to try them for crimes committed on Chinese soil (other than the smuggling of contraband goods) and to take part in the adjudication of disputes between Chinese subjects and American citizens. In addition, the treaty granted American citizens a broad range of rights and immunities in the pursuit of their commercial activities and interests in five ports.

The Treaty of Wanghia signified a decisive departure in America's foreign policy. "The United States was in the Treaty of Wanghia putting on for the first time some of the garments of imperialism" (Dennett 1963:170), but it soon found that it had not "grown up" enought to fit "such ample vestments."

Twelve years later, however, the United States took another long but firmer step along the path of imperialism as it renegotiated the earlier pact in 1858 as the Treaty of Tientsin. Once again the United States benefited from a British military victory over the Chinese government that constricted the sovereignty of China even more severely than had its earlier victory. This time the treaty was not confined to five ports but to all those that might be opened to foreign trade. But like its predecessor, this treaty had nothing to do with relations between the two countries within the territorial limits of the United States, despite the fact that by 1858 almost 40,000 Chinese nationals were in California and California had not only become a state but was actively legislating against these Chinese immigrants.

Concentrating therefore exclusively on the situation in China, the treaty went far beyond the earlier one by devoting a number of articles to establishing official channels of correspondence and communication for the American minister and consular officials with their counterparts in the Chinese government, from the highest level of authority downward. "It was officially recognized for the first time in the Treaty of Tientsin that the American diplomatic representative, minister, or commissioner, had the right to correspond with the highest officials of the Chinese Government on terms of perfect equality" (Ma 1970:19). American war vessels were also given certain rights to protect United States merchant ships in the coastal waters of China and to pursue pirates preying on this shipping.

The treaty reaffirmed the rights and immunities of American citizens in China to engage in commercial activities as provided in the earlier treaty; it even widened their scope and spelled them out in greater detail. By adding Article 29, the treaty drew its protective mantle around still another category of American: the Christian missionary. It stipulated that

> "The principles of the Christian religion, as professed by the Protestant and Roman Catholic churches, are recognized as teaching men to do good, and to do to others as they would have others do to them. Hereafter those who quietly profess and teach these doctrines shall not be harassed or persecuted on account of their faith. Any person, whether citizen of the United States or Chinese convert, who according to these tenets, peaceably teach and practice the principles of Christianity shall in no case be interfered with or molested."
>
> (US Statutes at Large 1863 12:1029)

The final article that was added to the treaty accorded to the American government and its citizens "the most-favored-nation treatment in case any rights or privileges not specified in this treaty were granted to any other nation" (Ma 1970:20).

By 1860 then, the United States had moved a considerable distance from the fumbling beginnings of its imperialistic venture in China. It had carved out a growing sphere of influence, institutionalized its claim to extraterritoriality, and held its own in competition with England and other European powers. Further, its trade with China was flourishing, and almost 100 missionaries were practicing actively in China. Finally, Congress itself was beginning to pay more attention to the need for competent personnel and adequate funds for work in China.

Throughout the period the United States government sought to maintain a formally correct and respectful demeanor in its negotiations with the Imperial Court and to preserve the illusion of equality. For example, President Tyler wrote in his letter that Cushing was to deliver to the Chinese Emperor: "'Now my words are, that the governments of two such great countries should be at peace. It is proper, and according to the will of Heaven, that they should respect each other and act wisely'" (Dennett 1963:141).

In its formal relations, the United States government also sought to play on an image of China that, according to a number of scholars, had resonated favorably in the western world during the seventeenth and early eighteenth centuries. (In fact, Harold Isaacs calls this period the "Age of Respect" for China.) The image was that of a country "of ancient greatness and hoary wisdom: the China of Confucius" (Miller 1969:11).

By mid-nineteenth century, however, such references were largely confined to ceremonial and ritualistic occasions, as unfavorable references to China gained increased currency in public discussions and various media of communications. (Isaacs calls the period from 1840 to 1905 the "Age of Contempt.") Miller contends that the primary bearers of this negative imagery were traders, missionaries, and diplomats. Traders in particular negatively stereotyped the Chinese. They did so virtually from the moment they were allowed to step foot in China. Diplomats were likely to emphasize the same negative themes as the traders but with greater moral indignation over the alleged political, social, and moral depravity of the Chinese. This is evident in the words of a doctor who took part in a diplomatic mission in the mid-1830s.

> "'They [the Chinese] are a people who destroy their own tender offspring; a nation wherein the most infamous crimes are common;... where the merchant cozens his fellow-citizen and the stranger; where a knowledge of the language is the remotest boundary of science; where a language and a literature, scarcely adequate to the common purposes of life, have remained for ages unimproved; where the guardians of morals are people without honor or probity; where justice is venal to an extent unexampled on the face of the earth; where the great legislator Confucius, so much revered, is unworthy of perusal, unless we excuse the poverty of his writings in consideration of the ignorance of the times in which he lived; where a chain of beings, from the emperor to the lowest vassal, live by preying upon one another.'"
>
> (Miller 1969:55–6)

Most contemptuous of all, according to Miller were the Protestant missionaries. They were inclined to see the handiwork of Satan in the heathen and pagan culture and behavior of the Chinese. They talked of "orgies of idolatry" where other observers saw none. And, "in contrast to both the trader group and the diplomat-authors, the Protestant missionaries were disdainful of Confucius and his philosophy" (Miller 1969:63) and were instrumental in corroding his reputation in the West.

These threads, however, were scattered throughout the various media from magazine to textbook, until the Opium War of 1840 brought China into center stage of public and media attention and "served as an important catalyst in popularizing the anti-Chinese themes developed and polished by diplomats, traders, and missionaries over several decades" (Miller 1969:112). Espousal of these themes did not necessarily mean that most Americans had lined up with the British in the struggle. True, some did, but most others expressed "traditional anglo-phobia" and "fear of an English monopoly in China" (Miller 1969:105) and even some moral indignation at the opium traffic. Yet even the severest critics of the British action did not show much sympathy for China itself; they would continually allude to its semi-barbarousness, despotism, and military sham and weakness.

Once the United States government itself became actively involved in the affairs of China by the early 1840s, the media began to assert an intensely nationalistic point of view toward relations with China, to take umbrage at any real or imagined insult to national honor and dignity, to ridicule China's pride and claim of superiority for its traditional culture and civilization, and to call for a more aggressive response than actually taken to any "perfidious" action on the part of China. As a result, by the time of the military confrontation between England and China, most of the media had begun to acclaim Britain's "gunboat diplomacy," some even to lament the American government's reliance on diplomacy to achieve what Britain had gained by force of arms, and to renew the charge against China of being a cruel, treacherous, despotic, and "senile" country.

THE BURLINGAME TREATY AND RECIPROCITY

The American Civil War shunted China from the forestage of public and governmental attention in America and, except for a brief flurry at the final defeat of the Taiping rebellion in 1864, China elicited relatively little comment and discussion in the various media. But the United States government did seek to maintain formal relations with the Chinese government during the war with the appointment of Anson Burlingame as its minister from 1861 to 1867.

China itself during this period was experiencing a revitalization of its ruling establishment in what Wright called the "last stand of Chinese conservatism" (Wright 1967). On the one hand, the ruling class sought to breathe fresh life into the government bureaucracy by rejuvenating traditional Confucian principles and procedures for the recruitment and selection of personnel. On the other, the

Chinese government sought to leaven its deeply engrained distrust and contempt for the western treaty-making process by gaining enough skill and competence in it to offset the mounting inequities of the process. For by the mid-1860s the Chinese government was becoming very restive at the one-sided character of these treaties.

As a result, the Chinese government planned to press for revision of the treaties when they were due for renegotiation in 1868. Accordingly, it began to prepare well in advance its case for these revisions. As a major step in this direction, it circulated a letter to eighteen high provincial officials in which it

> "pointed out that the barbarian question was one of long standing; that China had made one mistake after another until it was now obvious to all that the situation was critical. The barbarians, once weak and remote, had become strong through superior weapons and were now near neighbors as a result of improved communications. In 1860, the yamen continued, China's position had been so desperate that it had been necessary to accept the treaties of Tientsin as a last resort. Many points in them had been unsatisfactory, but the only possible policy had been to observe the treaties in good faith while seeking a means of controlling the foreigners. The times were difficult, but China's present problems could not be solved by empty talk of the Way and its Power (*tao-te*) or by idle tears. It was easy enough, the yamen thought, to point out things that should never be allowed to happen; the problem of the moment was to suggest realistic means to keep them from happening." (Wright 1967:272)

The letter then asked the officials for their opinions on six major issues that were likely to be topics in the forthcoming negotiations. Even before replies were received from the officials, the Chinese government acted on one of the topics. It decided to send for the first time a Chinese mission to foreign countries. It made this decision on two grounds: "(1) it was necessary to study the behavior of the enemy, and (2) by appealing directly to foreign governments, China might persuade them of the justice of her case" (Wright 1967:273).

In seeking a head for the mission, the government concluded that no Chinese was experienced or familiar enough with western ways to be able to present effectively China's case abroad. As a result, it decided to take advantage of its study of western diplomatic practices which showed "that envoys were not necessarily nationals of the countries they represented" (Wright 1967:277), and to ask Anson Burlingame to lead the Chinese mission abroad.

The choice of a foreigner as head of the delegation took the western world and many Chinese by surprise, but to the Chinese government and others the specific choice of Burlingame made a great deal of sense. Ever since his arrival as an American envoy, he had impressed the government with the fairness of his dealings, his sympathetic understanding of the Chinese, his support of a policy of cooperation between the western powers and China, and his admiration for the traditions and history of Chinese culture and civilization. As a result, within several years of his arrival he had already been defined as a "true friend" of the Chinese. He was addressed in this manner by Prince Kung, the *de facto* ruler of China and brother of the Emperor, in a conversation in March 1865 during which the Prince had expressed his concern at Burlingame's imminent departure for the United States. After being reassured that it would be just a temporary visit to America, the Prince replied, "'We wish you to pledge yourself to return to us. If you are willing to resume your mission, you will join me in draining a glass in token of consent. (Mr Burlingame, after a brief pause, takes the glass.) The covenant is ratified; friends are not allowed to forget a promise sealed by a glass of wine'" (Clyde 1964:70).

With the approval of the United States government, Burlingame resigned the post of minister to China and assumed the post of minister for China. Scholars disagree as to the extent to which Burlingame himself was instrumental in engineering the appointment. Some say he had nothing to do with it; others have put forth a conspiratorial theory in which Burlingame and Secretary of State Seward were the arch manipulators. But whatever may have been Burlingame's role, the fact is that he was deeply impressed with his charge of representing the ancient civilization of China. This is evident in the message he sent to Secretary of State Seward in December 1867.

"I may be permitted to add that when the oldest nation in the world, containing one-third of the human race, seeks, for the first time, to come into relations with the west, and requests the youngest nation, through its representative, to act as the medium of such change, the mission is one not to be solicited or rejected."

(US Foreign Relations 1868:494)

The arrival of Burlingame and the rest of his mission in the United States was greeted with widespread acclaim throughout the country. Even on the west coast, the mission was showered with ceremonial ado and banquets. They were also invited to appear on the floor of the House of Representatives and later on the floor of the Senate where flowery compliments were exchanged. Wherever the mission was greeted, the theme of the American hosts was almost always the same. They wanted a marked expansion of commercial and international intercourse with China to be high on the agenda for the treaty revision. Even in San Francisco the message completely overshadowed for the time being any restlessness over the mounting Chinese immigration. In pressing this theme, the Americans seemed to forget for one brief historical moment all their earlier reservations about China. They transformed the image of China from that of a decadent and senile society into that of a vibrant ancient civilization that was prepared to move into the modern world under the tutelage of America. Burlingame was lionized in the press as the one chosen to lead the way for a resurgent China.

Burlingame used the various platforms to promote an even more favorable public and governmental response to China. In San Francisco he stressed the value to America of knowing more about the meritocratic character of the Chinese empire that had allowed it to survive for so long a period. In Washington, DC he addressed the House of Representatives with a plea for greater understanding and appreciation of the Chinese culture and civilization. He also called for equality of negotiation and treatment "'without which nations and men are degraded. We seek not only the good of China, but we seek your good and the good of all mankind'" (Ma 1970:41).

Two weeks later in New York City Burlingame entered an even stronger plea for China. He called for the safeguarding of her autonomy and independence and the application of "principles of eternal justice" and of equal treatment in dealings with her. He denounced those who would use force against her and "'who say that China is not fit to sit at the council board of the nations, who call her people barbarians, and attack them on all occasions with a bitter and unrelenting spirit'" (Clyde 1964:82).

China, Burlingame argued,

> "'is a great, a noble people. It has all the elements of a splendid nationality. It is the most numerous people on the face of the globe; it is the most homogeneous people in the world; it has a language spoken by more human beings than any other in the world, and it is written in the rock. It is a country where there is greater unification of thought than any other country in the world. It is a country where the maxims of great sages, coming down memorised for centuries, have permeated the whole people, until their knowledge is rather an instinct than an acquirement; a people loyal while living, and whose last prayer, when dying, is to sleep on the sacred soil of their fathers.'"   (Clyde 1964:82)

And what was more, he continued, China recognized that she had lost ground in her long period of isolation from the western world and was now prepared to come out of her shell.

> "'She finds that she must come into relations with this civilization that is pressing up around her, and feeling that, she does not wait but comes out to you and extends to you her hand. She tells you she is ready to take upon her ancient civilization the graft of your civilization. She tells you she is ready to take back her own inventions, with all their developments. She tells you that she is willing to trade with you, to buy from you, to sell to you, to help you strike off the

shackles from trade. She invites your merchants, she invites your missionaries.
She tells the latter to plant the shining cross on every hill and in every valley. For
she is hospitable to fair argument.'"   (Clyde 1964:83)

But, Burlingame added in an earlier part of his speech, China

"'asks you to forget your ancient prejudices, to abandon your assumptions of
superiority, and to submit your questions with her, as she proposes to submit
her questions with you – to the arbitrament of reason. She wishes no war; she
asks of you not to interfere in her internal affairs. She asks of you not to send
her lecturers who are incompetent men. She asks you that you will respect the
neutrality of her waters and the integrity of her territory. She asks, in a word, to
be left perfectly free to unfold herself precisely in that form of civilisation of
which she is most capable. She asks you to give to those treaties which were
made under the pressure of war a generous and Christian construction.'"
                                                                            (Clyde 1964:81)

He then concluded with the trenchant advice:

"'Let her alone; let her have her independence; let her develop herself in her
own time and in her own way. She has no hostility to you. Let her do this, and
she will initiate a movement which will be felt in every workshop of the civilised
world. She says now: "Send us your wheat, your lumber, your coal, your silver,
your goods from everywhere – we will take as many of them as we can. We will
give you back our tea, our silk, free labor, which we have sent so largely out into
the world.". . . All she asks is that you will be as kind to her nationals as she is
to your nationals. She wishes simply that you will do justice. She is willing not
only to exchange goods with you, but she is willing to exchange thoughts. She is
willing to give you what she thinks is her intellectual civilisation in exchange for
your material civilisation.'"   (Clyde 1964:83)

The full measure of Burlingame's commitment to his charge from the Chinese
government became even more apparent in the negotiations for a treaty that
ensued shortly thereafter. However, no matter how deep his commitment, the
results might have been much less than he would have wished if the principal
American negotiator, Secretary of State Seward, did not define America's national
interest in terms that allowed agreement with Burlingame on certain fundamental
issues.

Seward, for example, ever since becoming Secretary of State in 1861, had
advocated an expansionist role for America and the building of

"an empire which would not be acquired haphazardly but would develop along
carefully worked out lines. The empire would begin with a strong consolidated

base of power on the American continent and move into the way-stations of the Pacific as it approached the final goal of Asia. Each area would have its own function to perform and become an integrated part of the whole empire. Seward prophesied that the battle for world power would occur in Asia 'commerce has brought the ancient continents near to us.'"   (LaFeber 1963:26–7)

Not until the end of the Civil War, however, was Seward able to begin to implement his design. First he promoted the continental base of power through policies of cheap labor, high tariff, a cross-continent railroad, and the selling of public lands at low prices. And second he sought to pursue a policy of amity and peace with China so that America might be seen as her special friend – thus the readiness with which he supported Burlingame's role as envoy for China.

The negotiations for the treaty provided Seward with the opportunity to bring together the internal and external threads of his policy of empire. He could get the Chinese immigrant as a cheap source of labor and at the same time foster America's commercial and natural interests in China. As such, his version of America's expansionist needs and interests resonated with the value framework that Burlingame sought to apply in pressing the demands of the Chinese government. The outcome of this anomalous situation – two Americans negotiating with each other for a pact between their own country and another – was a treaty that came close to redressing some of the one-sided excesses of the earlier ones and stood as a model of "reciprocity" and "fairness" never again reached in relations between the United States and China during the rest of the nineteenth and early twentieth centuries.

Even in this treaty America did not abandon its claims toward extraterritoriality and "imperialistic" concessions in China (in fact, the pact was treated as supplemental to the Treaty of 1858), but it recognized the sovereignty of China in a way it had not before or would not perhaps ever again, and it agreed to the right of the Chinese government to impose limits upon the exercise of these "imperialistic" claims.

One of the articles introduced an entirely new dimension into a treaty with China. Instead of just dealing with the situation in China, it gave the Chinese government the reciprocal right to do on American soil some of the things that the United States government was already doing on Chinese soil. Specifically, Article III authorized the Emperor of China "to appoint Consuls at ports of the United States" just as the Treaty of 1858 authorized the United States to do so within ports of China (US Statutes at Large 1871 16:740).

Four other articles extended this principle of reciprocity to the nationals of both countries. For the first time in any treaty, Chinese subjects in the United States were to be accorded rights and immunities similar to those given to American citizens in China (except for the crucial extraterritorial right of being tried by the laws of your own country – a right which remained intact for Americans in China). In Article IV, for example, this meant extending the right of religious freedom to Chinese subjects in America to match the provision of the Treaty of 1858 that had already extended this right to Christian citizens of the United States in China. The article also stated that

> "citizens of the United States in China, of every religious persuasion, and Chinese subjects in the United States, shall enjoy entire liberty of conscience, and shall be exempt from all disability or persecution on account of their religious faith or worship in either country. Cemeteries for sepulture of the dead, of whatever nativity or nationality, shall be held in respect and free from disturbance or profanation."   (US Statutes at Large 1871 16:740)

In the other three articles, additional spheres of rights and immunities were carved out for both nationals, areas that had been at best only casually sketched in the earlier treaties for American citizens in China. Thus, Article VII provided for reciprocal access to the public educational institutions under the control of each government. It also stipulated that "the citizens of the United States may freely establish and maintain schools within the Empire of China at those places where foreigners are by treaty permitted to reside, and, reciprocally, Chinese subjects may enjoy the same privileges and immunities in the United States" (US Statutes at Large 1871 16:740).

But none of these relatively virginal areas contained the explosive potential that was to be found in the remaining two articles dealing with the reciprocal rights of migration and residence in each country. The tone of mutuality and equality was set in the first sentence of Article V which pledged the reciprocal right of free and voluntary access to each country:

> "The United States of America and the Emperor of China cordially recognize the inherent and inalienable right of man to change his home and allegiance, and also the mutual advantage of the free migration and emigration of their citizens and subjects, respectively, from the one country to the other, for purposes of curiosity, of trade, or as permanent residents."
>
>   (US Statutes at Large 1871 16:740)

Article VI extended this reciprocity to travel and residence:
> "Citizens of the United States visiting or residing in China shall enjoy the same privileges, immunities, or exemptions in respect to travel or residence as may there be enjoyed by the citizens or subjects of the most favored nation. And, reciprocally, Chinese subjects visiting or residing in the United States, shall enjoy the same privileges, immunities, and exemptions in respect to travel or

residence, as may there be enjoyed by the citizens or subjects of the most
favored nation."   (US Statutes at Large 1871 16:740)

Even as the Senate was considering the treaty for ratification, uneasiness was
expressed over these two articles. Article V caused less apprehension because its
last two sentences forbade involuntary migration and therefore seemed to apply to
the "coolie trade."

"The high contracting parties, therefore, join in reprobating any other than an
entirely voluntary emigration for these purposes. They consequently agree to
pass laws making it a penal offense for a citizen of the United States *or Chinese
subjects* [author's italics] to take Chinese subjects either to the United States or
to any other foreign country, or for a Chinese subject *or citizen of the United
States* [author's italics] to take citizens of the United States to China or to any
other foreign country, without their free and voluntary consent, respectively."
                                                    (US Statutes at Large 1871 16:740)

As a result, the original version was amended only to the extent of adding the
italicized phrases in the above quotation.

Article VI, however, caused a greater flurry among the California senators.
They dropped their objections after one of them succeeded in having the Senate
add the following sentence to the end of the original article: "But nothing herein
contained shall be held to confer naturalization upon citizens of the United States
in China, nor upon the subjects of China in the United States" (US Statutes at
Large 1871 16:740). Through this amendment the senator from California was
convinced that he had at least forestalled permanently the right of citizenship and
membership in the People's Domain for the Chinese, even though the treaty
granted them free and voluntary access to the territory of the United States. (The
Senate modified two other articles of the original draft of the treaty. It struck out
the original Article VII which called for unity of money, weights, and measures
and transformed the last paragraph of the original Article VIII into Article VII
after confining its provisions to public educational institutions.)

Why there was no greater outcry from the California press, public, and
congressmen against these articles during the ratification proceedings remains a
puzzle. As we have seen, more than 65,000 Chinese were already in California and
strenuous but uncoordinated efforts were being made by the people and government of the state to stop this flow. Perhaps the "anti-coolie" clause in Article V
and the non-citizenship clause in Article VI allayed their worst fears and lulled
them into a sense of relative inaction. In 1867, for example, naturalization of the
Chinese was a leading issue in a California election and led to the defeat of a
Republican candidate who allegedly favored it or had not spoken out loudly

enough against it. Perhaps Californians did not have enough time to digest fully the ramifications of the terms of the treaty; it was concluded on July 4 and ratified by the Senate on July 24 – a period of three weeks. And perhaps the mystique of national pride at Burlingame's role, already evident at his arrival with the mission in San Francisco, together with the greedy anticipation by businessmen of expanded commercial profits and favored treatment in China, so enshrouded the entire matter that even the Californian saw the treaty largely in terms of what it meant to America and to the American in China rather than what it meant to China and to the Chinese in America.

But what looms as the greatest puzzle of all is the phenomenon of the Burlingame Treaty itself. It was written at a time when Radical Reconstruction was getting under way and the question arises: To what extent is its apparent aberrant character linked to the particular moment of history in which it was created? Did the emerging reconstruction "idealism" of equality affect the atmosphere in which the treaty was being written? Does this help explain why the treaty expresses an ideal of equality and reciprocity between nations and between foreign nationals that not only belied the factual inequality of naked power and of treaty provisions still in effect from 1858 between the two countries, but also ran counter to the principle of coercive power that manifestly organized relations between China and the United States before this period and did so once again after the period was over?

Further, the preoccupation with reciprocal rights of foreign nationals – half the articles of the treaty were devoted to these rights – was more an American than a Chinese preoccupation. It is worth remembering again that the negotiators for both sides were American, so they were able to put a greater stamp on the normative tone of the document than they would have as only one party to the negotiations. This may well have been the case with respect to the articles on foreign nationals, though less so with respect to the articles on the jurisdiction of the Chinese government in its own territory. In its survey of provincial officials, the Chinese government placed high priority on the issues dealing with its own sovereignty; as such, these articles reflect in all likelihood the explicit instructions that the Chinese government gave to its American negotiator, Burlingame. There is little evidence to support any vital concern on the part of the Chinese government with its nationals in America. In fact, almost until that moment of time the government had forbidden foreign travel for its subjects; it had not even sought to protect its subjects in America in the Treaty of 1858. Thus it would seem that even in 1868 the Chinese government had at best mixed feelings about its policy toward these immigrants, despite the filtering back to China of news of their maltreatment in America. The Chinese government probably relied on the initiative of the American negotiators on the issue.

Secretary Seward, as would be expected, propounded the American view on these articles. As a result, he saw in them (IV through VII) an opportunity for elaborating and securing more firmly than before the rights of American nationals in China. But perhaps even more significantly, as a person dedicated to the expansion of American industry and power, he favored the immigration articles because America would gain access to a major source of cheap labor. However, the rhetoric he used in drafting these articles (which he presumably did in fact do) was not that of a capitalist exploiter but that of an advocate of the American creed and radical reconstruction.

In turn, Burlingame presumably placed top priority on the interests and needs of the nationals of the country he was representing, China, yet the normative context and language in which he framed these interests appears to be that of a New England Yankee imbued with the American creed. He demanded equality, reciprocity, and fairness of treatment for the individual Chinese in America. Being conversant with the American scene, he was well aware of the discriminatory treatment Chinese nationals were being subjected to in California. He alluded to this in a message to Bismarck written in Berlin, January 4 1870:

> "'The treaty concluded with the United States recognizes broadly the right of China to the jurisdiction of its own affairs and offers substantial protection to the Chinese in California. It was this latter consideration which led to the adopting of the more solemn form of a treaty in the United States. A treaty being the supreme law of the land overrides the obnoxious local legislation against the Chinese immigrants.'"   (Dennett 1963:540 fn)

In the final analysis, it would appear that the Burlingame Treaty's articles on foreign nationals were couched in the normative framework of the day with its conceptual keystones of freedom and equality. And yet despite this, the treaty – being merely supplemental to the Treaty of 1858 and not a substitute for it – retained a fundamental cornerstone of inequality: the extraterritorial rights of the United States in China. An American citizen in China had the right to be tried under American law and courts. A Chinese national in America, however, had no such equivalent right; he had to be tried under American law and in American courts.

DISENCHANTMENT WITH THE BURLINGAME TREATY AND EMERGING SINOPHOBIA

Within two years after the signing of the treaty, Anson Burlingame was dead in Moscow; he succumbed while negotiating for China a pact with Russia. His eulogies in America were etched in the same heroic terms as were the paeans that greeted him in 1868. The Chamber of Commerce of New York, for example, expressed its wonder and admiration at his having been chosen by the Chinese government as its representative:

"The wonder to Europe and America was how our countryman was able to so win the confidence of that always mysterious and proverbially exclusive, suspicious and insulated government, as to induce it to confide any such mission to anybody, even to a score of its own most trusted and patriotic mandarins – and especially by what charms or magic he had succeeded in causing it to exalt him, a zealous American and genuine Yankee, to the degree of a mandarin of the first class, and bestow upon the representative of a Republic, which the masses of the Chinese knew not even by name, the power to negotiate treaties in the name of the Brother of the Sun and Moon with the 'outside barbarians' of the uttermost parts of the earth." (Cowdin 1870:6–7)

But even by the time these words were spoken, doubts and second thoughts about the Burlingame Treaty had long since spread throughout California. In fact, almost as soon as the ink was dry, rumblings against the treaty began to be heard. One California senator denounced it "as the most one-sided, unnecessary and injurious treaty ever negotiated" (Coolidge 1969.128). And from the first "spectacular" demonstration in 1870, abrogation of the treaty or at the least of its articles on immigration became a rallying cry for the mounting protest against the Chinese. It became an important plank in the platform of the evolving white working-class movement. From "the first Workingmen's Convention ever held" (Sandmeyer 1973:47) in August 1870, through the People's Protective Alliance in 1873, to Kearney's Workingmen's Party of California of the late 1870s, the message of abrogation was conveyed.

As we have already seen in the last chapter, the call for abrogation of the treaty received the official stamp of legislatorial approval by 1877 and was one of the two formal recommendations made by the Senate of California in its memorial to the United States Congress. A year and a half later another and even more urgent call for abrogation of the treaty was made in the name of the people of California at the constitutional convention of 1878 as the convention forwarded another memorial to the United States Congress. So intent was the convention in demonstrating the importance that Californians of all classes from working to business attached to this demand that it declared in its memorial that California was prepared to forego the commercial benefits of the treaty – which it acknowledged redounded more favorably to it than to any other state – in order to show the depth and sincerity of its opposition to the Chinese immigration and to the treaty.

Early opposition to the treaty came from still another quarter: American officials and others with vested interests in China condemned the treaty for restoring too much sovereignty to the Chinese government over its own territory. A spokesman for this point of view was the man who replaced Burlingame as the United States minister to China, J. Ross Browne. Four months after the signing of the treaty he sought to disabuse Secretary Seward of the notion that

> "'the Government of China is peculiarly friendly to our country, and that great advantages to our commerce are about to accrue from this preference. Enthusiastic expectations are entertained that the Empire, so long isolated from the world, is on the eve of being thrown open to American enterprise; that important concessions will soon be made granting special privileges to our citizens.
>
> I need scarcely say these anticipations are without foundation. The Government of China may have preference; but it has no special regard for any foreign power. The dominant feeling is antipathy and distrust towards all who have come in to disturb the administration of its domestic affairs. But little difference is recognized between one power and another. The concessions obtained by force of arms have been accepted by all.'"   (Clyde 1964:93)

Six months later he addressed a series of questions about the Burlingame Treaty to the Inspector General of the Chinese Imperial Maritime Customs. Obviously annoyed at the generally favorable responses he received, he wrote a sharp rebuttal to the Secretary of State. In that rebuttal he argued that the non-interference policy of the treaty would allow China to sink back into its age-old isolation and posture of sullen resistance to change, would shore up its dilatory practices of only minimally fulfilling its treaty obligations, and would breathe new life into its dream of eventually driving the foreigner from its soil. As a result the treaty would make it virtually impossible to get China to introduce the kinds of improvement that should be introduced if China were to attain "progress" and were to become a "progressive civilization."

Browne's open disdain of the Chinese government resulted in his recall to the United States only a little more than a year after he took over his post, but his views were shared by many of the missionaries and traders stationed in China. They were convinced that the United States had been, in the words of a missionary, "bamboozled by the Yankee Chinaman without a tail [Burlingame]'" (Miller 1969:133) into submitting to China's demands, and in doing so it had given up the one thing that could make China live up to its treaty obligations: the force of arms. Most of them urged the return to "gunboat diplomacy" so that China could be transformed into a Christianized and progressive civilization whose markets and resources could be exploited by the American.

In the eastern part of the United States the euphoric response to the Burlingame Treaty and mission persisted for a while, but then events in China began to cast a pall over it. Particularly significant was the Tientsin Massacre of 1870, which resurrected in the eastern press the older image of China as a xenophobic, anti-Christian, and barbaric country. In short, the first major loss of the Burlingame mission's gains was the refurbished image of China that had been a significant byproduct of the mission's success. Reports of other atrocities against foreigners and Christian churches in the early 1870s compounded the re-ignited editorial anger of the press until force and "gunboat diplomacy" became widely advocated once again as the way to deal with a country so apparently incapable of abiding by international law and decency and of living up to treaty obligations.

Even as these events were unfolding in China, others were taking place along the East Coast that brought the issue of Chinese immigration more closely home to residents of the eastern United States. The critical event, according to Miller, was the importation of Chinese to work in a shoe factory in North Adams, Massachusetts. This unleashed "angry headlines, emotional editorials, and strong protest meetings in Boston, New York, Philadelphia, Rochester, Albany, Troy, Astoria, Newark, and as far away as Hamilton, Ohio" (Miller 1969:175). Fears were expressed that this handful of Chinese, about seventy-five in all, was but an advance guard of an invading horde soon to reach the East. When reports circulated that Chinese workers were being recruited in other parts of the East, the fears were seen as being realized.

> "The year 1870 was a crucial one in crystallizing anti-Chinese sentiment on the East Coast. While editors in this section had expressed considerable anxiety over the nature of Chinese immigration, they were, in the main, content with restricting the Celestial, to the Pacific slope, denying them citizenship, and encouraging them to return to China after having filled their economic function here. Following the Burlingame Treaty, a Darwinian optimism ran high in many eastern newspapers, whose editors were confident that the Anglo-American stock would best the Chinese in any racial contest. In such a mood, these editors were willing to let the Chinese migrate anywhere in the United States and mix freely with the Caucasian population. But this mood shifted rapidly with the arrival of Chinese workers in Massachusetts in June 1870, and a number of eastern editors began to call for Chinese exclusion."   (Miller 1969:194)

As enough Chinese filtered into New York, Boston, and Philadelphia to establish "miniature Chinatowns" by the middle of the decade, that too added fuel to the growing anti-Chinese mood in the East. Stories of decadence, white slavery, and moral degradation circulated much in the same manner as they had already circulated on the West Coast.

Toward the end of the decade, then, the East shared many of the prejudices against the Chinese that California already had, though those of the latter were much more virulent and widespread. Sinophobia had, in short, become a national, not merely a regional, phenomenon. The way was now paved for congressional actions which culminated finally in the Chinese exclusion acts. Miller concludes,

"to view the policy of exclusion simply as a victory for the obsessive prejudice of Californians is neither accurate nor fair. Although that state unquestionably catalyzed and spearheaded the movement for exclusion, there were much more potent national and historical forces at work than the mere accident of evenly balanced political parties. Not even a very enthusiastic tail of such small dimensions could have wagged a dog that was less than willing to be wagged."

(Miller 1969:191)

SUMNER AND NATURALIZATION: THE "UNFINISHED" BUSINESS OF RECONSTRUCTION

Even before the Burlingame Treaty was formally proclaimed by President Grant in early 1870, congressmen from California were actively seeking to water down if not eliminate its various provisions. They introduced bills that would abrogate the immigration articles but leave intact the articles on commerce, that would forbid the making of any kind of labor contracts with Chinese emigrants by Chinese or other companies, and that would allow states to protect themselves against "injury from filthy habits, degrading vices or customs practised by Chinese residents" (Ma 1970:61). Nothing came of these initial efforts; in fact, none of these bills ever came to the floor for a vote in either house.

However, before their drive could gather any additional momentum, it was almost dealt a mortal blow by an "unfinished" piece of reconstruction legislation that Charles Sumner of Massachusetts forced on the attention of the Senate on July 2 1870. This piece of legislation was neither directed at Chinese immigration *per se* nor at the treaty itself; yet, had it been enacted – and for a brief moment it seemed it would be – it would have had profound consequences for them both. Specifically, it would have reaffirmed the rights of the Chinese under the treaty. Even more, it would have breached the restrictive barrier in the treaty that excluded the Chinese from citizenship and membership in the People's Domain.

The setting for this confrontation was the Senate's deliberation of a bill to eliminate and to punish fraudulent practices in naturalization proceedings. Sumner took this opportunity to introduce an amendment that would delete the word *white* from "all acts of Congress relating to naturalization: ... *And be it further amended*, That all acts of Congress relating to naturalization be, and the same are hereby, amended by striking out the word 'white' wherever it occurs, so that in naturalization there shall be no distinction of race or color" (The Congressional

Globe 1870 41:2:5121). Benefiting from an earlier unanimous agreement among the senators to curtail debate in order to expedite action on sections of the bill that night, Senator Sumner was able to get a quick vote on his amendment. It won 27 to 22 with 23 absent.

Almost immediately the senators from California and other opponents of Chinese immigration began to worry about the implications of what had just taken place. They were aware that the amendment would require a change in the first sentence of the Naturalization Law of 1802 then still in effect ("That any alien, being a free white person, may be admitted to become a citizen of the United States, or any of them, on the following conditions"), but they feared even more that the amendment would render as moot the restrictive clause of the Burlingame Treaty.

As a result, they marshaled almost overnight their forces and succeeded on July 4 in getting the action reconsidered by a vote of 27 to 14, with 31 absent. Now there was an extensive debate on the issue, and Sumner became the central target for the opposition.

His critics complained that by offering his amendment he had violated an agreement among the senators to confine deliberations to naturalization procedures only and to avoid any discussion or action on matters of substance or questions of eligibility. Some even suggested that he withdraw his amendment for future consideration. Sumner rejected this complaint with the terse comment that he had been trying for three years to get the amendment before the senate, only to have it bottled up in committee. Now that he had it on the floor he would keep it there and not risk having it bottled up once again.

Sumner then went on the attack in support of his amendment. He agreed that Congress had jurisdiction over the question of naturalization under the Constitution. ("I am not prepared to say that Congress may not shut down the gates and refuse to naturalize anybody.") But once Congress enacted naturalization legislation, he insisted, "the law must be in harmony with the requirements of the Declaration of Independence." (He included the Constitution in a later part of the speech.) He then stated in no uncertain terms: "I consider the Declaration of Independence as paramount law, not to be set aside or questioned in any respect – sovereign, absolute, irreversible, and which we are all bound to respect" (The Congressional Globe 1870 41:2:5156).

Sumner argued that the Declaration of Independence proclaimed unequivocally

"that all men are created equal [and] that they are endowed by their Creator with certain inalienable rights [and] ... the great, the mighty words of this clause are that these great, self-evident, inalienable rights belong to 'all men.' It is 'all men,' and not a race or color that are placed under protection of the

Declaration; and such was the voice of our fathers on the 4th day of July, 1776. Sir, such was the baptismal vow of this nation. According to this vow *all* men are created equal and endowed with inalienable rights. But the statutes of the land assert the contrary; they declaring that only all white men are created equal.

Now, sir, what better thing can you do on this anniversary than to expunge from the statute that unworthy limitation which dishonors and defiles the original Declaration? It is in your power to make the day more than ever sacred."   (The Congressional Globe 1870 41:2:5155)

In this manner Sumner brought to bear the same inexorable logic that he had applied several years before in the debates on the Fourteenth and Fifteenth Amendments. Only then he was intent upon bringing the Constitution in line with the Declaration of Independence, and not as now the statutes of Congress in line with both.

The opposition in the meantime constantly raised the specter, if Sumner's amendment was allowed to stand, of hordes of Chinese inundating and over-whelming the People in their Domain by gaining control of its various institutions and by subverting the ideals of the Domain. In addition, the "coolie labor" of these immigrants, the opposition claimed, would degrade the white workingman to the animal level of the Chinese.

Sumner finally addressed himself to the Chinese issue although it was obvious that he preferred to discuss the matter on the abstract level of principle. He argued that under his amendment some Chinese would probably still come only to labor. These, he said, would pose no problem for they would return home to China soon. Others would come for citizenship, and these too would pose no problem.

"If they come for citizenship, then in this desire do they give a pledge of loyalty to our institutions, and where is the peril in such vows? They are peaceful and industrious; how can their citizenship be the occasion of solicitude?

We are told that they are imperialists; but before they can be citizens they must renounce imperialism. We are told that they are foreigners in heart; but before they can take part with us they must renounce their foreign character. Therefore do I say if they come for citizenship there is no peril; while if they come merely for labor, then is all this discussion and all this anxiety superfluous?... [He climaxed with the ringing declaration that] the greatest peril to this Republic [was not from the prospective influx of Chinese, but] from disloyalty to its great ideas."   (The Congressional Globe 1870 41:2:5155)

Despite the eloquence of his pleas, Sumner's amendment lost upon being reconsidered: 14 to 30 with 28 absent. He tried once again when the naturalization bill reached the Senate floor for final action, but here too his amendment lost: 12

to 26 with 34 absent. The debate over the issue, however, was not entirely in vain, for during its course another amendment was offered (not by Sumner) that called for the breaching of the all-white restriction for one group of aliens: blacks from the Caribbean and elsewhere. "*And be it further enacted*, That the naturalization laws are hereby extended to aliens of African nativity and to persons of African descent" (The Congressional Globe 1870 41:2:5177).

Even those most opposed to the Chinese found some kind words to say about the black; the Chinese had replaced the black on the lowest rung of the racial ladder. As one senator said,

> "If the Senate desires to naturalize a few colored people who are civilized, and who desire to be naturalized, I have no objection to that at all. They are of our own language and of our own religion. They have friends here in America who are republicans. I mean republicans in the sense of loving republican institutions, not in a partisan sense. But when a Chinaman comes here he does not come to Democratic friends or Republican friends; that is, those who believe in republican institutions. He has not any of those. He comes to his Chinese master and gets his order to work." (The Congressional Globe 1870 41:2:5151)

Yet despite these sentiments, the amendment barely survived its first test. It was passed by only one vote, 21 to 20 with 31 absent. It picked up some additional support in the final vote and won 20 to 17 with 35 absent. In this fashion, it became Section 7 of the bill – the only wedge into the racial barrier for naturalization. In Sumner's last attempt to get his amendment through, one of his supporters pleaded with his colleagues to be consistent; they had just passed the amendment on the black aliens and now he asked them

> "not [to] act so inconsistently as to vote down this [Sumner's] amendment. I ask Senators to look at the position in which we are placing ourselves. We have now by a distinct vote placed upon this bill a provision that any person of the African race or of African descent may be naturalized. We have struck the word 'white' out of the naturalization laws so far as it applies to the Hottentot, to the pagan from Africa. Now, is it proposed to deny the right of naturalization to the Chinaman?" (The Congressional Globe 1870 41:2:5177)

His plea, however, failed

Congress and the acts of exclusion

THE JOINT COMMITTEE ON CHINESE IMMIGRATION

Momentarily stunned by Sumner's near victory, the senators from California soon recovered their composure and along with their colleagues in the House began to press once again for abrogation of the Burlingame Treaty and for restrictive legislation against the Chinese. For the next five years their efforts at a frontal assault on the treaty failed to get beyond the various committees of Congress. They did succeed, though, in having the treaty prohibition against coolie trade incorporated in the supplementary immigration act of 1875. The law called for fines and penalties against American citizens who transported "to or from the United States any subject of China, Japan, or any Oriental country, without their free and voluntary consent for the purpose of holding them to a term of service" (US Statutes at Large 1875 18:3:477). The law also forbade "the importation into the United States of women for the purposes of prostitution" (US Statutes at Large 1875 18:3:477) and authorized inspection of ships by the collector of the port to prevent the coming ashore of these women as well as aliens "who are undergoing a sentence for conviction in their own country of felonious crimes other than political or growing out of or the result of such political offenses, or whose sentence has been remitted on condition of their emigration" (US Statutes at Large 1875 18:3:477).

By 1876, however, the national climate of opinion changed perceptibly. The country, in the midst of a nationwide depression, seemed in a receptive mood for more direct action. In that year, for example, both Republicans and Democrats, facing a hotly contested presidential race, adopted anti-Chinese immigration planks in their party platforms. And in Congress, the California contingent once again renewed their assault against the treaty. The one that moved furthest through the labyrinth of Congress was introduced by Senator Sargent. On April 20 he offered the following resolution for consideration by the Senate "at such time as will least interfere with its business."

> "*Resolved*: That the Senate recommends to the President that he cause negotiations to be entered upon with the Chinese government to effect such change in the existing treaty between the United States and China as will lawfully permit the application of restrictions upon the great influx of Chinese subjects to this country."   (US Congressional Record 1876 44:1:2639)

On May 1 Sargent undertook a lengthy defense of his resolution. In this defense he acknowledged the protective mantle cast by the Fourteenth Amendment over persons already in the United States. ("The prejudice of race cannot be considered when persons already among us appeal for protection.") But he took full advantage of the failure of the Senate to pass Sumner's amendment which would have cast a similar mantle over the Chinese immigrant: "But when the question is as to the introduction of large numbers of people into the country whose admission is not a matter of right, but of policy, then we ought to consider whether they are a disturbing element, and whether exclusion is not the best and surest prevention against disorders which are difficult to cure when once fastened upon us" (US Congressional Record 1876 44:1:2850). He then went into an extended discussion of the reasons "why the immigration of these [Chinese] people at present . . . will work harm to this country" (US Congressional Record 1876 44:1:2851) and why this justified governmental action to exclude them from the country. The litany of reasons had by now a ring of familiarity; it ranged from unassimilable ghettoization and degradation of white labor to quasi-slavery, moral decadence, and criminality.

Taking heed of some of the reservations raised during the debate, Sargent modified his resolution when deliberations resumed six days later:

> "*Resolved*: That in the opinion of the Senate negotiations should be entered upon with the governments of China and Great Britain to effect such changes in existing treaties as will tend to check the great influx of Chinese coolies and criminals to this Country."   (US Congressional Record 1876 44:1:4418)

When queried by a fellow senator how his resolution would affect the "ordinary citizen from China," he responded that few would get in because "nine out of ten are coolies, and ninety-nine out of one hundred of the females imported are for immoral purposes, are reduced to a condition of slavery, worse than that of the poorest dog in the meanest household" (US Congressional Record 1876 44:1:4418).

As he pressed for action, the senator from California was confronted by a growing uneasiness among his colleagues. In the words of one senator, "It [the resolution] is a subject too important and too difficult in some of its aspects, it appears to me, for the Senate to decide upon it with precipitancy and without the usual and careful examination of the committee that has matters of that kind in charge." Accordingly, he proposed to have the resolution referred to the Committee on Foreign Relations. Sargent objected strenuously for fear of its being bottled up there: "I object because it has been under the consideration of the Committee on Foreign Relations before this time without action" (US Congressional Record 1876 44:1:4418). However, he accepted the proposal of the senator from Indiana that an *ad hoc* committee be appointed to investigate the matter. The Senate agreed then unanimously to the following resolution:

> "*Resolved*: That a committee of three Senators be appointed to investigate the character, extent and effect of Chinese immigration to this country with power to visit the Pacific coast for that purpose, and to send for persons and papers, and to report at the next session of Congress."
>   (US Congressional Record 1876 44:1:4421)

Eleven days later the House voted to appoint three representatives to join the Senate in the investigation.

The chairman of the joint committee was Senator Morton of Indiana, a relative moderate on the issue, but he was too ill to exercise active leadership at the hearings or to participate in the drafting of the final report. As a result, the two members of the committee from California played a major role in conducting the investigation and in shaping the final report, which was in fact written by Senator Sargent.

Before the joint committee went to San Francisco for its hearings, it already had before it the report and memorial prepared by the State Senate Committee of California. The committee held hearings for over two weeks in San Francisco, listened to 130 witnesses, and prepared a six-page report from over 1200 pages of testimony.

Although the committee, according to its report, professedly set up an impartial framework for the hearings, the atmosphere in the committee room, according to other observers, was cold and hostile to witnesses who had anything favorable to say about the Chinese and warm and friendly to those with unfavorable things to say. Yet despite its obvious bias, the hearings evoked to an extent nowhere approached in the earlier state senate hearings testimony favorable to the Chinese.

"The pro-Chinese witnesses included all the clergymen, diplomats, manufacturers and men connected with railroads, navigation and foreign trade. The anti-Chinese witnesses included nearly all the officials, journalists, and workingmen; of those recently engaged in politics or dependent for their positions upon political favor, two only out of twenty-four were in the least favorable to the Chinese. Of the forty-four witnesses who had been in China or associated with the Chinese in business or as teachers or large employers, only six were anti-Chinese; and of the sixteen who had lived or traveled in China, only seven."
(Coolidge 1969:97–8)

The report contained some of these favorable comments, most notably that bearing on the role of the cheap and docile Chinese labor in building the economy of California:

"The resources of California and the Pacific coast have been more rapidly developed with the cheap and docile labor of Chinese than they would have been without this element. So far as material prosperity is concerned, it cannot be doubted that the Pacific coast has been a great gainer."
(US Senate Report No. 689 (1877) 44:2:IV)

The special beneficiaries of this labor, the report emphasized, were "the capitalist classes. If the inquiry should stop there; if it should be satisfied by the certainty that money is made out of the present condition of things, and not look to the present or future moral or political welfare of our Pacific States, it must be conceded, at least, that many enterprising men find their profit in Chinese immigration, and the general resources of the Pacific are being rapidly developed by means of Chinese labor."

(US Senate Report No. 689 (1877) 44:2:IV)

The report also recorded the opposition to restricting Chinese immigration "among religious teachers, who testified before the committee that the presence of Chinese among us imposes a duty and gives an opportunity of christianizing them" (US Senate Report No. 689 (1877) 44:2:IV).

Virtually all the other classes in California, the report continued, opposed further immigration of the Chinese. This was particularly true of laboring men and mechanics, but "in the testimony will be found that of lawyers, doctors, merchants, divines, judges, and others, in large numbers, speaking of their own observation and belief, that the apparent prosperity derived from the presence of Chinese is deceptive and unwholesome, ruinous to our laboring classes, promotive of caste, and dangerous to free institutions" (US Senate Report No. 689 (1877) 44:2:IV).

Once having started, the report then painted an unrelentingly bleak and negative picture of the impact of the Chinese on the society and institutions of California. It repeated with somewhat less emotional intensity the major themes already emblazoned in the earlier address and memorial of the California senate. Particularly prominent was the theme that Chinese labor, though docile and industrious, threatened to degrade white labor because of its competitive effectiveness and its capacity to live on such low wages. But of ever greater significance for the future of the debate on Chinese immigration was the report's elaboration of a theme that had been treated in a mere fragmentary fashion in the earlier address but was to loom larger in the future as an argument against the Chinese.

According to the report, the Chinese showed no inclination to assimilate and to adopt American institutions and its way of life.

"The testimony seemed to be concurrent that the Chinese are non-assimilative with the whites; that they have made no progress, during the quarter of a century in which they have been resident on the Pacific coast, in assimilation with our people; that they still retain their peculiar costume and follow their original habits in food and mode of life; that they have no social intercourse with the white population; that they work for wages which will not support white men and especially white families; that they have no families of their own in this country, or very few of them...."

It further appears from the evidence that the Chinese do not desire to become citizens of this country, and have no knowledge of or appreciation for our institutions. Very few of them learn to speak our language. They do not desire the ballot.... [They have constructed a] *quasi* government among themselves independent of our laws, authorizing the punishment of offenders against Chinese customs, even to the taking of life."

(US Senate Report No. 689 (1877) 44:2:VI–VII)

In short, to translate the conclusion of the report into our terms, the Chinese had become an independent plural sub-society or segment built outside the People's Domain. Nowhere did the report mention, however, that this arrangement was anything but the product of voluntary choice and action by the Chinese. It failed to mention the massive and impenetrable barriers to the People's Domain erected by the white society against the Chinese that effectively generated and solidified the plural framework that subsequently developed.

The report alluded to this only obliquely when it conceded that the Chinese had been deprived "of the only adequate protection which can exist in a republic for the security of any distinctive large class of persons" (US Senate Report No. 689 (1877) 44:2:V). (Namely, access to the rights and immunities of the People's Domain.) However, the report continued, "the safety of the State demands that such power shall not be so placed." For if they had these rights, such as suffrage,

"there is danger that ... their 'head-men' would control the sale of it in quantities large enough to determine any election. That it would be destructive to the Pacific States to put the ballot in their hands was very generally believed by the witnesses. Their want of knowledge of our language and institutions would prevent an intelligent exercise of suffrage; while their number in California at the present time is so great that they would control any election if the ballot was put into their hands. The number of adult Chinese is, at the present time, as great as that of all the voters in the State, or nearly reaching that number, and they increase more rapidly than the other adult population of the State. To admit these vast numbers of aliens to citizenship and the ballot would practically destroy republican institutions upon the Pacific coast, for the Chinese have no comprehension of any form of government but despotism, and have not the words in their own language to describe intelligibly the principles of our representative system."   (US Senate Report No. 689 (1877) 44:2:VII)

Even without this access, the report argued, the plural sub-society that the Chinese had built threatened the stability of the People's Domain and the well-being of the white American. In time it could take over the Pacific coast because of its competitive advantage in the labor markets, and the numbers who entered could finally force the white American out and destroy his institutions.

The report concluded, that something had to be done about the situation. Accordingly, "the committee recommends that measures be taken by the Executive looking forward a modification of the existing treaty with China, confining it to strictly commercial purposes; and that Congress legislate to restrain the great influx of Asiatics to this country" (US Senate Report No. 689 (1877) 44:2:VIII).

When Sargent submitted the report of the joint committee to the Senate on February 27 1877, the chairman of the committee, Senator Morton, who had been unable to assist in the preparation of the report, requested permission from the Senate to file his own analysis of the testimony at a later date. He remarked that "while I agree in great part with what is contained in the very able report of the Senator from California, yet I do not altogether concur in the views which have been taken in regard to the evidence, and I desire to present my views upon the subject" (US *Congressional Record* 1877 45:1:1961). Unfortunately he died before he could finish his report though, his notes were published after his death.

In 1969 Coolidge compared his conclusions drawn from the testimony and those of a Professor Becker who had matched the testimony with the conclusions in the committee's report and offered the following judgment: "A tabular view of the conclusions of Senator Morton and of Professor S.E.W. Becker compared with published reports reveals the intentional perversion of the testimony [by the committee] in order to produce the desired anti-Chinese campaign document" (Coolidge 1969:104).

CONGRESSIONAL ACTION: THE PROLOGUE TO EXCLUSION

Within a year, Sargent's voluntaristic "plural sub-society" theme became the theoretic fulcrum of his next major legislative move in the Senate. In March 1878 he used a central element of it for his preamble to a resolution which called upon the President "to open correspondence immediately with the governments of China and Great Britain with a view of securing a change or abrogation of all stipulations in existing treaties which permit the unlimited immigration of Chinese to the United States" (US Congressional Record 1878 45:1:1544). In the preamble he emphasized the "voluntary rejection" by the Chinese of membership and participation in the People's Domain of the American society.

"Whereas it appears that the great majority of immigrants are unwilling to conform to our institutions, to become permanent residents of our country, and to accept the rights and assume the responsibilities of citizenship; and
    Whereas they have indicated no capacity to assimilate with our people."
(US Congressional Record 1878 45:1:1544)

This "voluntary rejection," Sargent contended in his subsequent defense of his resolution, reflected the fact that the Chinese had constituted themselves into a "quasi- political" society. They had in effect become "an indigestible mass in the body-politic, alien in habit, thought and feeling [who] are governed by their own tribunals which inflict penalties even to the taking of life for the infraction of their ordinances" (US Congressional Record 1878 45:1:1549). As evidence of this, he quoted frequently from the testimony of the joint committee. In fact he relied heavily on the leading role he played in the investigation to establish his position as Senate expert on matters Chinese.

This is evident in his response to another senator's query about the desire for naturalization on the part of individual Chinese:

"I have observed them there in California for a quarter of a century. I have visited every part of their quarter; I have talked with them from their Chinese merchants down to the cooly; I have talked with men who are best posted in all the details in regard to the matter, and I sat patiently every moment of time, for I think over a month that was occupied by the Joint Committee on Chinese Immigration, where this and all matters connected with them were canvassed, and I yet have to find an instance where there was an expression of desire on the part of a Chinaman to become an American citizen. The whole theory of their immigration is to the contrary."   (US Congressional Record 1878 45:1:1551)

So impressed was the senator with Sargent's response and with his apparent empirical and theoretical command of the data that he gave voice to the fear that the Chinese might indeed be evolving into an alien plural sub-nation within the territorial limits of America. And he declared: "I do not conceive that it is the policy of this country to build up within this nation any foreign nation or to invite immigrants to this country except those who show a desire to assimilate with our country" (US Congressional Record 1878 45:1:1551).

Sargent, however, did more than construct a political and social version of the Chinese "reality" in America; he anchored the structure of this "reality" to the system of unfree labor. ("This Chinese labor is the new slavery in America" (US Congressional Record 1878 45:1:1552).) In short, he incorporated the coolie labor argument of old into a large theoretical statement of "reality." He saw the unfree labor as organically linked to the various other "elements of an independent and antagonistic civilization" that distinguished the Chinese from an American civilization based as it was on free labor.

In the final analysis, he argued, "the contest is between two grades of civilization," but the battleground was the competitive struggle between the two forms of labor. This was the juncture in which the People's Domain of white America faced its greatest challenge and threat. "Like the old slavery, it [the new slavery] will drive out free labor; like the old slavery it will reduce the free labor of this country to its level; like the old slavery, it will admit of but two classes, to wit, capitalists and servile laborer" (US Congressional Record 1878 45:1:1552). The final outcome could be the ultimate destruction of the People's Domain and the survival of a plural society consisting of a racially segmented stratum of menial and degraded labor and a small dominant class of white capitalists.

Sargent's resolution was turned over to the Committee on Foreign Relations. In May, the committee offered a revised version to the Senate which called for the modification of "the provision of the existing treaty between the Empire of China and the United States allowing the unrestricted emigration to this country from China, . . . so as to subserve the best interests of both governments; and the attention of the Executive is respectfully invited to the subject" (US Congressional Record 1878 45:2:3226). The Senate adopted the resolution on May 25; the House on June 17.

Six months later in the absence of any word from the President, the Committee on Education and Labor took matters into its own hands and reported to the House of Representatives a bill to restrict immigration of Chinese to the United States which had been referred to it by a congressman from Nevada a year before. Section 1 of the bill made it illegal for any master to take on board his ship more than fifteen Chinese passengers, male or female, whose destination was any port in the United States. Failure to comply would subject the master to a fine and/or imprisonment of not more than six months. To monitor compliance, the bill stipulated that masters would have to provide under oath a separate listing of all Chinese passengers to the collector of the district at which their ships were docked.

Aware that its bill risked being bogged down in a constitutional quagmire, the committee focused its report on the question: "Can Congress repeal or modify a treaty?" Its answer was an unqualified yes. In defense of its position it cited judicial precedents for treating statute law as the equal of treaty law. Few congressmen questioned this argument; whatever discussion there was centered on the urgent need for the bill's passage. As a result, it was passed in the House after only a single day's debate by a vote of 155 to 72 with 60 not voting.

The same was not true in the Senate; there the debate lasted three days. Opponents of the measure were preoccupied with the impact of the bill on the treaty obligations of the United States toward China. They questioned the wisdom of Congress legislating directly on matters covered by a treaty. Some based their argument on the ground that formal treaties had a higher constitutional authority as law of the land than did statutes. Others based their argument on the ground that such actions would break down the fabric and the integrity of international law and thereby disrupt the fragile balance of relations between nations. One senator even chastized the Senate for its shortsightedness. He claimed that the United States benefited much more from the overall treaty than did China. He therefore concluded that America should not "abrogate a treaty upon a little point while we are the beneficiaries in the great and substantial points" (US Congressional Record 1879 45:3:1302).

Supporters of the bill sought to bypass the constitutional issue. They insisted that the nation had a right to protect itself, and they repeated the House argument that statute law was the equal to treaty law. Most of their attention was paid to elaborating the "plural segmentation" thesis. One senator in particular argued that "the meeting of two civilizations [and races] antagonistic in every form and feature in a struggle for existence in the *same country* [author's italics] cannot be other than an event of momentous historical importance" (US Congressional Record 1879 45:3:1270). He then went on to declare,

> "No more difficult problem is ever encountered by any Government than the administration of a common system of laws over diverse races. It is a problem that is never peacefully solved. If the lessons of human experience are worth anything it never can be so solved. If the difficulty be great under a government whose theory is force, it is insurmountable under the theory of voluntary obedience. No types of character can be conceived more diverse, more antipodal than the American and Chinese. They represent the newest and the oldest. That they should voluntarily unite in a homogeneous society is inconceivable. In every American city or town where there is any considerable Chinese population, there is a Chinese colony, with customs, manner, laws, language of its own. Its inhabitants repay our antipathy with antipathy, scorn with scorn, contempt with contempt. The darkest passages of human history have been enacted when alien races have been brought into contact."
>
> (US Congressional Record 1879 45:3:1271)

Thus was elaborated a theory of the plural society that would have done justice to the theory developed seventy years later by Furnivall (1956) and Smith (1965).

Sargent repeated his by now familiar litany that the Chinese wanted to huddle in their plural enclave and had no interest in becoming citizens or participating in American institutional life.

> "They do not come as ordinary colonists; they do not come to be citizens; and the experience of over twenty-five years in California with these people shows that they are an indigestible element in our midst, a cold pebble in the public stomach which cannot be digested. They are, they remain men of China, without any aspirations for American citizenship, without any adaptability to become citizens."   (US Congressional Record 1879 45:3:1265)

Several senators, however, questioned this sojourner thesis. They expressed the fear that many Chinese had abandoned the temporary status of sojourner and expected to stay permanently in the United States. As one senator declared, "In the earlier years of Chinese immigration they all came as mere denizens, expecting to return, dead or alive, to China. And they did return in due season if they lived and if they died their ashes were returned to their native land. Now they come to stay, to make their homes here, and even to seek their graves here" (US Congressional Record 1879 45:3:1271).

Many of the Chinese, he continued, hoped in time to gain access to the People's Domain. "They all expect to become citizens of the States and voters and to share protection of voters under the fifteenth amendment against all discrimination on account of race, color, or previous condition" (US Congressional Record 1879 45:3:1272). To prevent this from happening, he concluded, the bill had to be passed; for, in the final analysis the white race had to protect itself from the racially inferior Chinese.

Only a senator from Ohio retained a vestige of the kind of normative concern that Charles Sumner had brought to the issue at the turn of the decade. He scoffed at the argument that America would collapse under the influx of the Chinese. He insisted that America was of a more robust nature: "that this was a land and a country which could safely welcome to its shores the outcasts of every other clime, that its powers of digestion and assimilation were such that the very evils which afflicted mankind elsewhere would be taken up into the blood and circulation of this people and convey nutriment and health and strength to every limb and part of our economy" (US Congressional Record 1879 45:3:1275).

However, instead of using the Declaration of Independence as his normative framework for relations between races as had Sumner, this senator relied on Christianity and its principle of brotherhood.

> "It is simply to apply in politics, in our social economy, in our personal intercourse, in the institutions of society, wherever human action is called into being, the Christian rule, the law of divine benevolence, and of human brotherhood, and all the difficulties of caste and creed, and all the conflicts which spring up from the apparently irreconcilable and adverse interests of men disappear, vanish away like the mist and the morning dew in the presence of the warm and bright and health-giving influences of the rising sun."
>
> (US Congressional Record 1879 45:3:1275)

His argument failed to persuade his colleagues, for on February 15 the bill was finally passed 39 to 27 with 9 absent, but only after an amendment by Sargent was added to Section 7 of the bill. The amendment stipulated that the President was to give immediate notice to the government of China of the abrogation of Articles 5 and 6 of the Burlingame Treaty. The House subsequently went along with this proviso.

Two weeks later President Hayes returned the bill to Congress with a veto message. He argued that passage of the bill, particularly with its amendment to Section 7, would mean the end not only of the Burlingame Treaty but also of the Treaty of 1858, being that the former was merely a supplement to the latter. If this were to happen America would suffer grievous consequences in as much as "the treaty of 1858, to which these articles are made supplemental, provides for a great amount of privilege and protection, both of person and property, to American citizens in China" (US House of Representatives Executive Document No. 102 (1879) 45:3:4).

Further, the President declared, Congress might have the authority to terminate an entire treaty, but it could not constitutionally seek to modify only part of a treaty: "As the power of modifying an existing treaty, whether by adding or striking out provisions, is a part of the treaty-making power under the Constitution, its exercise is not competent for Congress" (US House of Representatives Executive Document No. 102 (1879) 45:3:5). As a result Congress' action could be interpreted by China as an abrogation of the whole and not merely part of the treaty.

This he insisted would be unacceptable:

"Whatever urgency might, in any quarter or by any interest, be supposed to require an instant suppression of further immigration from China, no reasons can require the immediate withdrawal of our treaty protection of the Chinese already in this country, and no circumstances can tolerate an exposure of our citizens in China, merchants or missionaries, to the consequences of so sudden an abrogation of their treaty protection."

(US House of Representatives Executive Document No. 102 (1879) 45:3:6)

The President, however, kept the door open in his message for future consideration of Chinese immigration. He proffered the suggestion that this issue might properly become the subject of negotiations between China and the United States and thereby lead to a basic revision of the Burlingame Treaty.

"It may well be that, to the apprehension of the Chinese Government, no less than our own, the simple provisions of the Burlingame Treaty may need to be replaced by more careful methods securing the Chinese and ourselves against a larger and more rapid infusion of this foreign race than our system of industry and society can take up and assimilate with ease and safety."

(US House of Representatives Executive Document No. 102 (1879) 45:3:4)

THE TREATY OF 1880

Within two months after the veto, the American minister to China began to make inquiries of the Chinese government about restricting the flow of Chinese to America. These restrictions, however, were to apply only to coolie laborers, criminals, lewd women, and diseased persons. Approximately a year later, the American government lost interest in this approach and dispatched instead a commission of three to negotiate a broader-gauged restriction of Chinese immigration.

One of the arguments that the commission developed in its early discussions was that the treaty was patently unfair, for it extended its privileges and immunities "to all Chinese subjects throughout the whole territorial integrity of the United States [while] the citizen of the United States is only entitled to the limited hospitality of a few open ports, and in them only for the purpose of trade, travel, or residence" (US Foreign Relations 1881:172). The Chinese government countered with the argument that the treaties of 1858 and 1868 had provided a trade-off for the two countries: extraterritoriality for the American citizen in China and unrestricted immigration for the Chinese subject in the United States.

"Since the establishment of treaty relations between the two countries, citizens of the United States in China have not been relegated to the jurisdiction of the Chinese authorities. China has accorded this privilege to the United States. Chinese subjects have been permitted to go and come at their pleasure. The United States has granted this concession to China. At the ratification of this treaty, the people of both sides of the Pacific Ocean leaped, shouted, and clapped their hands with joy and pleasure, friendly relations were firmly established, divisions were obliterated, the people could come and go as they chose, and the governments only heeded the wishes of the people. All this was eminently just and honorable in the highest degree to the United States"

(US Foreign Relations 1881:174)

The commission also insisted that the Chinese immigrant had taken unfair advantage of treaty provisions that were meant to protect the rights of those who sought permanent, not merely temporary, residence in America. As a result, these sojourning immigrants had erected distinctive plural communities in America when they were supposed to seek membership in the People's Domain and become assimilated to the American way of life as had been true of immigrants from other nations.

"A class of Chinese subjects immigrating to the United States without the purpose of changing their allegiance and intending only a temporary residence, claims all the privileges and exemptions provided by express treaty stipulations for 'permanent residence.' This same class, consisting entirely of laborers, coming in great numbers, with the avowed intention of early return, and concerted arrangements for a new supply, with the almost absolute exclusion of all family and domestic relations in their association, and jealously preserving their peculiar nationality in dress, language, creed, and habits, claims that it is entitled to all privileges of the subjects and citizens of the most favored nation; although the immigration from no other nation at all resembles this in its purpose, its methods, or its consequences. All other immigrants come to the United States with the express purpose of changing their allegiance, with their wives and children, to be in the course of a generation completely incorporated into the country of their adoption."   (US Foreign Relations 1881:172)

Because of their sojourning intention and their lack of families, these immigrants had competed unfairly with the American worker in the marketplace for jobs and had degraded the status of these workers to the extent that their capacity "to discharge those social and political duties which the Government of the United States expects from every one of its citizens [had been disabled]. This competition engenders popular discontent and raises questions which, if left unsettled, may disturb the friendly relations of the two countries" (US Foreign Relations 1881:172).

No mention was made by the commission of the discriminatory plural structure that white America had already erected against the Chinese which prevented even those who might so wish from seeking membership in the People's Domain and from becoming in time like other American workers and citizens. This line of argument was also absent in the Chinese government's rebuttal, although it did make the observation that restriction of Chinese immigration would stand in "contradiction with the Constitution of the United States and existing treaties" (US Foreign Relations 1881:174). The government focused instead on the beneficial effects of Chinese labor for the American economy. "In the many years of Chinese emigration to California a hundred lines of enterprise have arisen, and commercial activity has developed to an immense extent. The Chinese have given a large amount of their labor to your people, and the benefits of that labor to your country have certainly not been few" (US Foreign Relations 1881:173). This was equally true today, the government continued, even though "the rabble [American workers] are making complaints, . . . because the Chinese do good work for small remuneration. . . . [Thus,] since the amount paid to the laborer is small, the employer is able to save more, and hence the benefit still inures to the citizen of the United States. This would seem to be fair reasoning the world over" (US Foreign Relations 1881:173–74).

Within a week, the American commission presented to the Chinese government a draft of a new treaty. Its nub was Article 2 which gave the United States government the authority when it deemed its interests were at stake to "regulate, limit, suspend, or *prohibit* [author's italics]" the immigration of Chinese laborers – a category which included all but those whose purpose in coming was "teaching, trade, travel, study and curiosity." The other two articles were intended to make Article 2 more palatable to the Chinese government. Article 1, for example, reaffirmed the right of those exempted from the ban to enjoy the "privileges, immunities, and exemptions which are granted by either country to the citizens and subjects of the most favored nation." Article 3 guaranteed Chinese subjects presently in the United States "all the protection, rights, immunities, and exemptions to which they are now entitled under the provisions of said treaties" (US Foreign Relations 1881:178).

The Chinese government objected strongly to the wording of the second article; it took particular exception to the word "prohibit." It also raised questions about the inclusiveness of the category, Chinese laborer. As such, it declared firmly that "at the moment, we are only prepared to negotiate for a mode of limitation, having in mind the interests of both governments" (US Foreign Relations 1881:178).

Within a week the Chinese government submitted its own version of a treaty. It would impose, for example, a temporary limitation on the immigration of Chinese laborers, defined solely as unskilled workers and not artisans too. Article 4 stated:

> "The number of immigrants allowed by the regulation, will not be excessively small, nor the terms of years excessively long. Such regulations will apply only to Chinese laborers at work for and employed by American citizens. All other classes may go and come to and from the State of California, and their servants and employees, whether accompanying them or following them, shall not be included in the limiting regulations."   (US Foreign Relations 1881:187)

In addition Article 2 stipulated that Chinese immigrants, including laborers, destined for other parts of the United States would "be allowed to go of their own free will and accord" (US Foreign Relations 1881:186).

The American commission rejected summarily the Chinese version and submitted its own draft. This draft excluded the offending word, "prohibit," of the first draft but retained the phrase "regulate, limit, or suspend," and kept artisans as part of the laboring class to be regulated. It also retained the two other articles of the first draft but added a fourth article which stipulated that "the Government of the United States will communicate to the Chinese Government the legislative measures adopted by it in accordance with the provisions of the foregoing articles, and in case such measures work unexpected hardship to Chinese subjects, will give the fullest consideration to such representations as the Government of China may see fit to make in the premises" (US Foreign Relations 1881:187). Further negotiations resulted in minor editorial modifications of this version; agreement on the treaty was finally reached on November 17 1880.

Even as the American commission was pressing the Chinese government to yield on immigration, it was also renegotiating a treaty on "commercial intercourse and judicial procedure," which was also signed on November 17. The first three articles of this treaty maintained the illusion of reciprocity. Article 3, for example, stipulated that duties on commercial imports to and on exports from either country should be no greater for the ships of the subjects or citizens of the other than for the ships of the natives of that country or of any other country. However, the only significant commercial traffic at that time was between American citizens and China and not between Chinese subjects and America. Article 4, however, clearly reaffirmed the extraterritorial rights of Americans in China even in legal controversies involving the subjects of China, provided the American was the defendant in the case. According to the article,

"[such controversies] shall be tried by the proper official of the nationality of the defendant. The properly authorized official of the plaintiff's nationality shall be freely permitted to attend the trial and shall be treated with the courtesy due to his position. He shall be granted all proper facilities for watching the proceedings in the interests of justice. If he so desires, he shall have the right to present, to examine and to cross-examine witnesses. If he is dissatisfied with the proceedings, he shall be permitted to protest against them in detail. The law administered will be the law of the nationality of the officer trying the case."

(US Senate Document No. 357 (1910) 61:2:240)

Both treaties were ratified by the Senate in May 1881 and formally proclaimed by President Arthur in October.

THE EXCLUSION ACTS OF 1882 AND 1884

Two months later, Senator Miller of California introduced a bill in the Senate that was "to execute certain treaty stipulations relating to Chinese;" it was referred to the Committee on Foreign Relations of which he was chairman. One month later he reported to the Senate a modified version of the bill on behalf of the committee. The major provision of this bill was that sixty days after its enactment, later amended to ninety days, the immigration of Chinese laborers, skilled as well as unskilled, was to be suspended for twenty years. This provision, however, did not apply to any Chinese already in the United States by the deadline. Should any of these Chinese seek subsequently to return home and then to re-enter the United States, they would have to register at a customs house in America before departure and, would have to show the certificate of registration, properly stamped by the American consul, upon their return.

Chinese eligible to enter the United States under the act were obliged to obtain a passport with pertinent facts about themselves attached to it in English. Upon arrival in the United States, these Chinese were to register at a customs house.

> "Entry shall be made in such books of the name of every such Chinese, and his proper signature, or, if signed by his mark, attested by a competent witness, his place of birth (giving town or district), date of birth, last place of residence before coming to the United States, place of residence in the United States, if any, names and residences of his parents, if any, date and place of arrival in the United States, employment or business, height, and physical marks or peculiarities by which he may be identified."
>
> (US Senate Executive Document No. 148 (1881) 47:1:34)

In turn, the collector of customs was to issue these Chinese a certificate of registration setting forth all the relevant personal data. Only diplomatic and other officers of the Chinese government on official business were to be exempted from the passport and certification requirements, their government credentials being deemed sufficient.

To insure that only eligible Chinese entered the country, the bill required that a master of a ship submit a list of Chinese passengers aboard his ship at the time of docking. Before going ashore, these passengers would be interviewed and their papers checked by the collector of customs or his deputy. Masters of any ship, no matter their nationality, who knowingly had aboard a Chinese laborer would be deemed guilty of a misdemeanor and subject to a fine and imprisonment of one year or less, their ship subject to seizure. Penalties would also be exacted from the illegal Chinese laborer and from anyone else seeking to aid him to enter America illegally.

Senator Miller followed his presentation of the bill with a long and fervent speech urging its immediate passage. In his speech, he repeated many of the by now familiar anti-Chinese themes. Of particular note was the important and elaborate treatment he gave to the thesis that Chinese and white Americans could never merge into a single societal and normative framework. They could at best comprise merely antagonistic segments in an unstable plural society, until one drove the other out and thereby established its unchallenged hegemony in that society.

Senator Miller anchored this thesis to a "theoretical" premise of inevitable and inexorable historical conflict and struggle that was almost a mirror image of what Marx had said several decades earlier. Only to Miller, the historical struggle was between races; to Marx, between classes.

"In truth, the history of mankind is for the most part descriptive of racial conflicts and the struggles between nations for existence. By a perfectly natural process these nations have evolved distinct civilizations, as diverse in their characteristics as the races of men from which they have sprung. These may be properly grouped into two grand divisions, the civilization of the East and the civilization of the West." (US Congressional Record 1882 47:1:1483)

As a result,

"the two civilizations which have here met [in America] are of diverse elements and character, both the result of evolution under different conditions, radically antagonistic, and as impossible of amalgamation as are the two great races who have produced them. The attempt to merge them must result, as both reason and experience teaches, in the displacement of one or the other. Like the mixing of oil and water, neither will absorb the other."

(US Congressional Record 1882 47:1:1483)

Proof of this was to be seen in the failure of the Chinese to modify their ways in the least despite their having been on the Pacific Coast for a quarter of a century. This was not surprising, according to Miller.

"It is a fact of history that wherever the Chinese have gone they have always taken their habits, methods, and civilization with them; and the history fails to record a single example in which they have ever lost them. They remain Chinese always and everywhere; changeless, fixed, and unalterable. In this respect they differ from all other peoples who have come to our shores. The men of every other race or nation who go abroad, sooner or later, adopt the civilization of the people by whom they are surrounded, and assimilate with or are absorbed in the mass of humanity with which they come in constant contact. The Chinese are alone perfectly unimpressible.... An 'irrepressible conflict' is now upon us in full force, and those who do not see it in progress are not so wise as the men who saw the approach of that other 'irrepressible conflict' which shook the very foundations of American empire upon this continent....

If we continue to permit the introduction of this strange people, with their peculiar civilization, until they form a considerable part of our population, what is to be the effect upon the American people and Anglo-Saxon civilization? Can these two civilizations endure side by side as two distinct and hostile forces? Can these two forces abide in such close relation without conflict? Is American civilization as unimpressible as Chinese civilization? When the end comes for one or the other, which will be found to have survived? Can they meet half way, and so merge in a mongrel race, half Chinese and half Caucasian, as to produce a civilization half pagan, half Christian, semi-oriental, altogether mixed and very bad?" (US Congressional Record 1882 47:1:1483)

The answers to these questions, Miller insisted, could be catastrophic for the American civilization; for the Chinese had already morally contaminated its cities, degraded its labor, and transformed many white Americans into hoodlums. But this should not be surprising:

"History teaches no lesson with greater clearness or persistence than this: that nations once powerful have degenerated and gone into decay, generally, in consequence of, and in proportion to, the admission and incorporation into their bodies-politic of inferior or heterogeneous races; and this we may apply with peculiar fitness to a nation like ours, whose government is a government of the people. Debase the people and you degrade your sovereign."

(US Congressional Record 1882 47:1:1487)

Thus the survival of the People's Domain and the dominance of the white in America was at stake:

"There can be no stability to . . . institutions and government unless based upon one civilization. Government is the product of civilization. It is evolved from the civilization of the people who ordain it. Free government cannot be maintained permanently in any country in which there exist two diverse and antagonistic civilizations of nearly equal strength. They operate as antagonistic hostile forces, and one or the other must have the ascendancy. . . .

[To preserve the] American Anglo-Saxon civilization without contamination or adulteration with any other this bill must be passed, [its provisions enforced] to the letter. . . . China for the Chinese! California for Americans and those who will become Americans!"   (US Congressional Record 1882 47:1:1487)

Opponents of the measure concentrated their argument on the bill's being in conflict with the Treaty of 1880. They were particularly upset with its twenty-year provision, which they claimed violated in letter and spirit the treaty's refusal to prohibit immigration. Their effort, however, to reduce the period from twenty to ten years through an amendment to the bill failed by one vote.

Relatively few opponents concentrated their fire on the bill's being contrary to the American creed. Only one, again a senator from Massachusetts, resurrected in full the Charles Sumner argument of a decade before that the Declaration of Independence, the Constitution, and the great amendments of radical reconstruction forbade the exclusionary and discriminatory treatment directed against the Chinese in the bill. Only then Senator Sumner had been seeking to gain membership for the Chinese in the People's Domain; now Senator Hoar was fighting against the effort to bar them from merely entering the territory of the United States. No longer was the Sumnerian preoccupation a real issue. In fact, as a final nail in that coffin, an amendment was added to the bill which clearly stipulated "that hereafter no State court or court of the United States shall admit

Chinese to citizenship; and all laws in conflict with this act are merely repealed" (US Senate Executive Document No. 148 (1881) 47:1:36).

Undaunted, Senator Hoar sought to rekindle the issue by bringing into focus the ideals of the past, particularly as they were restated and revitalized in the Radical Reconstruction. He asked dolefully, "What has happened within thirteen years that the great Republic should strike its flag? What change has come over us that we should eat the bravest and truest words we ever spoke?" (US Congressional Record 1882 47:1:1517).

He then linked the historic fates of the Chinese and the blacks in America: "What argument can be urged against the Chinese which was not heard against the negro within living memory?" (US Congressional Record 1882 47:1:1518). They were, he said, considered to be "savages, heathens, wild beasts." But, he continued,

> "Who now [is] so bold as to deny the colored race fitness for citizenship? Twenty years have not passed by since the children of the African savage were emancipated from slavery. In that brief space they have vindicated their title to the highest privileges and their fitness for the highest duties of citizenship. These despised savages have sat in the House and in the Senate. I have served with them for twelve years in both branches. Can you find an equal number, chosen on any principle of selection, whose conduct has been marked by more uniform good sense and propriety?" (US Congressional Record 1882 47:1:1519)

He predicted the same destiny for the Chinese if they were given the chance because, he said, they showed the potential for developing "every quality of intellect, art, character, which fits them for citizenship, for republicanism, for Christianity" (US Congressional Record 1882 47:1:1523). He concluded, "I believe that the immortal truths of the Declaration of Independence came from the same source with the Golden rule and the Sermon on the Mount. We can trust Him who promulgated these laws to keep the country safe that obeys them. The laws of the universe have their own sanction" (US Congressional Record 1882 47:1:1523).

Despite his efforts the measure was passed by an almost two to one margin. The House adopted the bill two weeks later by an even larger margin. However, despite the obvious sentiment of Congress, President Arthur vetoed the bill on April 4. In his veto message to Congress, the President reiterated as his principal objection to the bill the argument earlier voiced by its opponents in Congress. He declared that the twenty-year suspension of Chinese immigration was tantamount to barring them permanently from entering this country, an action which was explicitly forbidden by the Treaty of 1880. The treaty itself, he argued, had been written with America's interests as a paramount consideration.

"This treaty is unilateral, not reciprocal. It is a concession from China to the United States, in limitation of the rights which she was enjoying under the Burlingame Treaty. It leaves us by our own act to determine when and how we will enforce those limitations [on the immigration of Chinese laborers]. Chinese may therefore fairly have a right to expect that in enforcing them we will take good care not to overstep the grant and take more than has been conceded to us."   (US Senate Executive Document No. 148 (1881) 47:1:2)

In view of this, the President continued, "I regard this provision of the act [the twenty-year suspension] as a breach of our national faith; and being unable to bring myself in harmony with the views of Congress on this vital point, the honor of the country constrains me to return the act with this objection to its passage" (US Senate Executive Document No. 148 (1881) 47:1:4). The President also objected to the provision in the bill that imposed the dual requirement of personal registration upon arrival in the United States and the taking out of a passport before departure from China by those "classes of Chinese who still enjoy the protection of the Burlingame Treaty." He complained that this imposed constraints on the Chinese which no other foreigners entering the United States had to experience. Further, he added, "without expressing an opinion on that point, I may invite the attention of Congress to the fact that the system of personal registration and passports is undemocratic and hostile to the spirit of our institutions. I doubt the wisdom of putting an entering wedge of this kind into our laws" (US Senate Executive Document No. 148 (1881) 47:1:4).

Despite these objections, the President proclaimed in no uncertain terms that he remained "deeply convinced of the necessity of some legislation on this subject" (US Senate Executive Document No. 148 (1881) 47:1:4), and that he hoped Congress would write a bill that he could sign. A month later Congress passed another bill which met the principal objection of the President; it reduced the period of suspension from twenty to ten years. The bill also reduced the double registration requirement of the earlier bill to only one for those Chinese eligible to enter the United States. They now had to obtain before departure a certificate from the Chinese government upon which were written relevant personal data in English. No longer was it required that they undergo a similar registration process upon arrival in this country. Other than these modifications, the bill was substantially the same as the vetoed bill. This time the President signed it.

The immediate impact of the law was dramatic. According to the Secretary of the Treasury in a letter to the Senate Committee on Foreign Affairs dated January 16 1884, the number of Chinese entering San Francisco from August 4 1882 to November 9 1883 was 2652 – a mere fraction of the number who entered a year before. Even more significant was the number who left during that period, 14,186, of whom 12,181 held return certificates. Another estimated 3500 entered San Francisco in transit for places outside the United States.

However, even as the act produced these results, it soon became evident that efforts to translate the law into operational procedures and practices had opened up a Pandora's Box of administrative ambiguity, confusion, and arbitrariness. Problems surfaced almost immediately that had not been anticipated by Congress. So obsessed did the opponents of Chinese immigration become with these problems that they persuaded Congress within two years of the enactment of the law to plug some of the more glaring deficiencies and loopholes. Thus in the Henley Act of 1884, Congress suspended the immigration of Chinese laborers from any country, not merely from China. It expanded the category of laborer to include huckster and peddler and tightened the certification procedures for those Chinese eligible to enter the United States.

In revising the law of 1882, Congress did not solve many problems. In fact it greatly enlarged the administrative and judicial morass that had already engulfed the process of certifying those eligible to enter or to return to the United States. Even as the debate on the Henley bill was taking place, courts were clogged with 300 cases of Chinese whose eligibility to enter the country had been challenged by customs officials. After enactment of the bill, the number of challenges increased almost geometrically. Particularly hard hit were the many Chinese merchants who were subjects of China but who resided in another country. They could not obtain certificates because the law prescribed certificates only for those who came directly to the United States from the country of which they were subject or citizen. As a result, they found themselves summarily sent back to the country of origin by customs officials who refused even to honor *ad hoc* procedures devised by the State Department to deal with the problem. The Chinese government protested the discriminatory treatment of these merchants, and President Cleveland sent a message to Congress to redress this inequity.

Within several years another kind of certification problem moved onto center stage of governmental and administrative concern. This had to do with the certification of Chinese laborers, already in the United States at the time of the passage of the law of 1882, who subsequently wished to visit China and then to return to the United States. In a report to Congress, a special agent for the Treasury Department estimated that, by August 1885, 35,235 certificates had been issued at all Pacific ports, 14,726 of them had been returned and the rest, 20,509, were still outstanding. So important had this certifying procedure become by August 1885 that, of the 15,460 Chinese laborers who entered San Francisco from the inception of the law until then, 11,452 carried certificates.

The certification process was extremely cumbersome and time-consuming and was becoming increasingly so as more and more layers of bureaucratic red tape were superimposed upon the process, presumably to reduce fraud and deception. But even so, peremptory and arbitrary challenges of the authenticity of the certificates were frequently made; many of these further clogged the court calendars. Relatively few challenges stood up in court, and at least 1000 Chinese laborers were allowed to re-enter the United States after such a challenge.

While its efforts to prove fraud in court were not overly successful, the Treasury Department nevertheless alleged that a widespread market existed for the illicit sale and purchase of certificates in China. Laborers upon their return to China, for example, presumably sold or gave their certificates to someone else who would then enter the United States as a returnee. To forestall this, the Treasury Department expanded the number of distinguishing physical features, such as moles and so on, that were to be listed on the certificate prior to the departure of a laborer from the United States. Upon his return, the laborer would be examined to see if this list matched his appearance. In addition, the report alluded to charges of corruption among customs officials who allegedly sold certificates to ineligible Chinese. Several suspected officials were transferred to other duties, but no official charges were leveled against them.

Even as the administrative difficulties were being compounded, the situation in the West became increasingly explosive. Violence erupted against the Chinese in California, Wyoming, Oregon, and Washington. In Rock Springs, Wyoming alone, 28 Chinese were killed, 15 wounded, and approximately $150,000 in property was destroyed. The Rock Springs incident evoked a bitter protest from the Chinese government. In a message to the Secretary of State, the Chinese ambassador demanded that the United States live up to the terms of its treaty with China by providing full protection for Chinese subjects and by punishing the guilty. He also insisted that the victims should be indemnified for their loss of life and property. While conceding that opinions might differ on the right of indemnification under domestic and international law and treaties, he nevertheless insisted that he was merely asking for Chinese subjects in America what the United States government had earlier demanded and received for American citizens in China: namely, indemnification for losses incurred during mob violence or lawless acts by Chinese, despite the absence of treaty or legal right to claims such as indemnification. It was difficult, he concluded, for him to believe "that the United States would so far violate the spirit of the 'golden rule,' incorporated by it in one of its treaties, or the 'usages of national comity' ... as to require of China that which under similar circumstances it would not concede to China in reciprocity" (US House of Representatives Executive Document No. 102 (1886) 49:1:9).

Three months later President Cleveland sent a message to Congress in which he took cognizance of the Chinese ambassador's letter. In the message, he deplored the violent outrages and reaffirmed the right of Chinese subjects "to the same measure of protection from violence and the same free forum for the redress of their grievances as any other aliens" (US House of Representatives Executive Document No. 102 (1886) 49:1:2). But he denied that the United States had any reciprocal obligation whether by treaty or by international law to indemnify Chinese subjects in America; however, he continued,

> "In view of the palpable and discreditable failure of the authorities of Wyoming Territory to bring to justice the guilty parties or to assure to the sufferers an impartial forum in which to seek and obtain compensation for the losses which those subjects have incurred by lack of police protection; and considering further the entire absence of provocation or contribution on the part of victims, the Executive may be induced to bring the matter to the benevolent consideration of the Congress, in order that that body in its high discretion, may direct the bounty of the Government in aid of innocent and peaceful strangers whose maltreatment has brought discredit upon the country; with the distinct understanding that such action is in no wise to be held as a precedent, is wholly gratuitous, and is resorted to in a spirit of pure generosity toward those who are otherwise helpless."
>
> (US House of Representatives Executive Document No. 102 (1886) 49:1:3)

Even as Congress was debating this request, additional incidents of violence in Alaska and California further deteriorated relations between China and America. As a result, in August 1886 the Chinese government informed the American ambassador of its intention to curb unilaterally the flow of Chinese laborers to the United States because of the cruel treatment they were receiving. The following January the Chinese minister expanded this proposal to include a ban on those Chinese laborers who wished to return to America after having gone back to China, provided they had neither family nor property of value in America. In exchange for this ban, the Chinese minister demanded that the United States live up to the rest of its treaty obligations: particularly its obligation to protect the Chinese already in the Untied States. He also mentioned its obligation to facilitate the certification of exempt classes under the treaty.

THE ABORTIVE TREATY OF 1888

Shortly after this the Secretary of State proposed that the two countries should enter into negotiations instead of dealing with the issue unilaterally. He also offered a draft for a proposed convention. At first, the Chinese minister refused to enter into negotiations. He claimed that until the issue of indemnity was settled such negotiations would be premature. Within two months, however, he responded to the draft and offered a series of counter-proposals for a renegotiated treaty. In his reply, he emphasized the voluntary character of the proposed ban and therefore rejected as unnecessary the thirty-year period fixed in the American draft. He placed special importance on the protection of Chinese subjects in America and offered a series of specific recommendations which would give the federal government the same kind of cardinal responsibility in the matter as the Chinese imperial government had in the protection of American citizens in China. He also repeated the demand for indemnification for "the losses and damages sustained by the Chinese in all the cases of cruel outrage against them in past years" (US House of Representatives Executive Document No. 1 Part 1 (1889) 50:2:369). He called for reaffirmation of the right of the exempted classes of Chinese to come and go of their own free will, and for continuation of the right of transit of Chinese laborers across territorial America on their way from one country to another.

The American response in its next draft was to reduce the period of the treaty from thirty to twenty years during which time no Chinese laborer could enter or re-enter the United States, except if he already had a family or property valued at $1000 in America. The draft also reaffirmed the previously defined treaty rights of officials, teachers, students, merchants, and travelers for curiosity or pleasure and retained the transit privileges of Chinese laborers. The United States government, however, rejected the various recommendations that would have it play a pivotal and distinctive role in the protection of Chinese laborers as not being in accord with the Constitution or with any treaty provision. On the other hand China, it insisted, was obliged to play such a role in the protection of American citizens in China because of treaty stipulations. Accordingly, it concluded, "the American minister and consuls, in calling upon the Chinese Government to perform those stipulations, have simply requested China to execute the treaty in conformity with her own institutions. China's call on us is to revolutionize our institutions. This proposition it is unnecessary to discuss" (US House of Representatives Executive Document No. 1 Part 1 (1889) 50:2:374). Finally, the response also parried the request for indemnification by stating that Congress would have to examine the merits of each claim separately.

Negotiations continued for almost another year and the final version contained several additional articles and clauses to meet at least in part some of the more serious objections of the Chinese government. Article IV, for example, stipulated that all Chinese in America, whether laborers or not, "shall have for the protection of their persons and property all rights that are given by the laws of the United States to citizens of the most favored nation, excepting the right to become naturalized citizens. And the Government of the United States reaffirms its obligation, as stated in said Article III, to exert all its power to secure protection to the persons and property of all Chinese subjects in the United States" (US Foreign Relations 1888:394). Article V indemnified the losses and injuries suffered by Chinese subjects in America to the extent of $276,000; it called the action a humanitarian gesture by the American government, not its legal obligation. In addition, Article III eased the certification process for merchants and other members of the exempted classes. They could obtain certificates from the government of the country where they last resided, not merely from the government of the country where they were subjects or citizens. Article II, however, added a provision which restricted the right of eligible laborers to return to the United States to no more than two years from departure from the United States.

The treaty was signed by the two countries on March 12 1888 and sent to the Senate where it was ratified, but not before two amendments were appended to the treaty. The first amendment extended the ban on immigration of laborers in Article I to "the return of Chinese laborers who are not now in the United States, whether holding return certificates under existing laws or not" (US Foreign Relations 1888:398). The second amendment was appended to Article II and stated that "no such Chinese laborer shall be permitted to enter the United States by land or sea without producing to the proper officer of the customs the return certificate herein required" (US Foreign Relations 1888:399).

The amended treaty was then sent to China for ratification. Although it had earlier expressed informal approval to the treaty's original terms, the Chinese government began to have second thoughts. It was particularly concerned about the impact of the amendments on the 20,000 laborers still in China who had certificates of return to the United States. Fears were expressed that the amendments would bar their return. As a result, the Chinese government took its time in considering the matter.

THE SCOTT ACT OF 1888

Anticipating favorable action by the Chinese government, Senator Dolph of Oregon introduced a bill in July 1888 that would have put most of the terms of the treaty into effect following ratification by the Chinese government. The bill was passed by the end of August and signed by the President early in September. However, just as the bill passed Congress, rumors were rife that China was going to reject the treaty. This would have nullified the Dolph Act whose implementation depended upon China's approval of the treaty.

The reaction of Congress to these rumors was instantaneous and furious. On September 3 Representative Scott of Pennsylvania introduced a bill whose few provisions virtually obliterated the limits still retained in the Dolph Act to an unrestricted ban on immigration of Chinese laborers and on the re-entry of any who had returned to China. This bill was defined as a supplement to the Exclusion Act of 1882 which in turn was labeled "'An act to execute certain treaty stipulations relating to Chinese'" (US Statutes at Large 1889 25:504). As such it based its ultimate authority on the Treaty of 1880 – a claim that few congressmen challenged despite the obvious incompatibility and contradictions between the sweeping provisions of the Scott Act and the more narrowly defined terms of the treaty.

The bill not only reaffirmed the ban of the older act on any new immigration of Chinese laborers to America, but also extended the ban to the return to America of any Chinese laborer who had gone back to China.

"That from and after the passage of this act it shall be unlawful for any chinese laborer who shall at any time heretofore have been, or who may now or hereafter be, a resident within the United States, and who shall have departed or shall depart, therefrom, and shall not have returned before the passage of this act, to return to, or remain in, the United States."

(US Statutes at Large 1889 25:504)

The bill also provided that no certificates of identity were to be issued any longer under Sections 4 and 5 of the older bill "and every certificate heretofore issued in pursuance thereof is hereby declared void and of no effect, and the chinese laborer claiming admission by virtue thereof shall not be permitted to enter the United States" (US Statutes at Large 1889 25:504).

As the bill was being debated in the Senate, authoritative word came that China had not rejected the Treaty of 1888 but was still actively considering it. This information did not deter the Senate from rushing through its approval, as the House had done earlier. The President signed the bill on October 1. The reaction from the Chinese government was immediate and vigorous. In a message to the State Department in January 1889, it declared the Scott Act to be a flagrant violation of the Treaty of 1880 which guaranteed free exit and return to Chinese laborers already residents of the United States. It also expressed keen disappointment in the failure of the President to fulfill his promise to veto any legislation that violated treaty provisions. Finally, it expressed regret that Congress acted when negotiations were still in progress on a new treaty.

The American government made no immediate response to the basic charge of treaty violation and promised an extended answer later. (In fact it never did respond to this charge despite the repeated urgings of the Chinese government over the next year and a half.) It offered feeble rejoinders to the other charges. It said, for example, that the President had never made such a promise and insisted that China's protracted consideration of the new treaty was tantamount to a rejection of it.

Fourteen months later the Chinese ambassador backed up his government's expression of concern with a detailed inventory of the intense hardships experienced by Chinese subjects as a result of the Scott Act. He claimed, for example, that 600 Chinese laborers who were *en route* to San Francisco when the act was passed were turned back when they reached San Francisco despite the fact that they had legal certificates of return. In addition,

> "the tens of thousands of Chinese subjects who temporarily left the shores of the United States, armed with the signed and sealed assurance of this Government of their right to return, and relying upon its good faith, in almost every case left behind them in this country property, business, families, relatives, obligations, or contracts, which have been imperiled, broken up, or in some shape injuriously affected by their unexpected and unwarranted exclusion.... [Further, the many Chinese] who were in the United States at the time of the passage of the act of 1888 had come here under the guaranty of solemn treaty stipulations, which allowed them 'to go and come of their own free will and accord' and on the solemn assurance that they would be maintained in this privilege against 'legislative enactment;' and under this act, if they should visit their native land, drawn thither by the ties of family, patriotism, or business, they must sacrifice and abandon all their interests and property in the United States; they must choose between a complete breaking up of long established business relations here, and a perpetual banishment from their native land by a continuous residence in this country."   (US Foreign Relations 1890:212)

In addition to these hardships, the ambassador continued, rights of transit of Chinese were being abrogated through administrative orders and "Chinese merchants who have been established in the United States, as well as those in China or in foreign nations who have trade relations with this country, have encountered much harsher treatment and increasing embarrassment during the past year and a half from the customs authorities; and it has become much more difficult than formerly for them to carry on commerce in and with the United States" (US Foreign Relations 1890:213).

In such ways, he continued, had the United States flagrantly violated its treaty obligations to Chinese subjects in America. Yet it had aggressively insisted that the Chinese government do more than live up to its treaty obligations to American citizens in China, which the Chinese government had willingly done. This had been particularly true in the case of missionaries who had been a troublesome presence in China. They had been granted by the Imperial government at the insistence of the United States certain vested rights of residency and ownership of real estate which exceeded the treaty obligations of the Imperial government. Even the American merchants in China had been given preferred treatment in contrast to the harassment accorded the Chinese merchants in America.

"Such, Mr. Secretary are some of the contrasts in the observance and enforcement of treaty rights between the two nations. Can you wonder that the Imperial Government is growing restive and impatient under such dissimilarity of treatment, and is urging me to obtain from you some satisfactory explanation of the conduct of the American authorities in the past and some assurance of the course to be pursued in the future?"   (US Foreign Relations 1890:216)

Failure to redress these wrongs, the ambassador declared, might cause the Imperial government to reconsider its position.

"The public law of all nations recognizes the right of China to resort to retaliation for these violated treaty guaranties, and such a course applied to the American missionaries and merchants has been recommended to the Imperial Government by many of its statesmen; but its long-maintained friendship for the United States, and its desire to observe a more humane and elevated standard of intercourse with the nations of the world, point to a better method of adjustment. Conscious that it has religiously kept faith with all its treaty pledges towards your country, my Government is persuaded that America will not be blind to its own obligations, nor deaf to the appeals made to it on behalf of the Chinese subjects who have been so grievously injured in their treaty rights by the legislation of Congress."   (US Foreign Relations 1890:217)

Nothing came of this threat and so unmoved by it was the American government that the Chinese minister was still complaining six months later that it had failed to answer his first message on the Scott Act fourteen months earlier.

In the meantime, Congress became increasingly obsessed with the notion that Chinese perfidy and fraudulent behavior were defeating the purposes of the exclusion laws, including the Scott Act, and were allowing the Chinese to come into the United States as before. As a result, Congress directed the Secretary of the Treasury to give it information on what was happening. Early in April the Secretary reported that most allegations of unlawful traffic of Chinese laborers referred to the use of fraudulent certificates, to smuggling across the northern and southern borders, and to the existence of an underground railway which presumably brought Chinese laborers into the country. But relatively few of these allegations had been documented by proof. The Secretary also said that his agency had uncovered no instance of a Chinese in transit who had not actually departed the country. He admitted, however, that his agency might not have uncovered all cases of fraud or deception because enforcement of the law, particularly along the

Mexican and Canadian borders, had proved to be extremely difficult with the limited manpower available to the agency.

Overall, according to the Secretary, the entry into San Francisco of new immigrants without legal certificates had dropped off sharply in the past seven years, from 6701 in 1883 to 118 in 1899; the number of returnees with certificates had risen sharply in the same period, from 644 in 1883 to 4900 in 1884 and 9062 in 1889. The number of Chinese in transit had hovered at about the 2000 mark for most of these years.

In general then, approximately 78,500 Chinese had arrived in San Francisco over the seven-year period ending June 30 1889. Of these, about 18,880 were in transit which meant about 60,000 were going to stay in America. Another 88,500 Chinese had left the country over the same period, leaving a net outflow of over 28,500.

Instead of being reassured by the findings of the Treasury Department, the more vigorous opponents of Chinese immigration seized upon the figure of 60,000 as showing that the law had not succeeded in preventing the influx of Chinese. They also remained convinced that widespread chicanery and fraud were being practiced by the Chinese; they supported this belief by transmuting rumors of deception into "facts."

THE GEARY ACT OF 1892

As a result, the opponents of Chinese immigration pressed for even more restrictive legislation. What gave their efforts a sense of compelling urgency was the approaching end of the ten-year time limit on the exclusion acts of 1882 and 1884. As their strategy unfolded, they skillfully blunted legislative efforts that would merely have extended the earlier laws and succeeded in introducing the most repressive legislation ever experienced by the Chinese in America, the Geary Act of 1892. In its original version, the bill would have extended the immigration ban on laborers to all of the previously exempted classes except for the diplomatic and consular officers accredited to the United States government. In its final version, this feature was struck out despite the plea of Geary that most of the exempted classes, particularly the merchants, were really coolies in disguise. Other harsh features, however, were retained. For example, the law did more than extend the proscriptions and distinctions of the earlier laws for another ten years. It also added a qualitatively new dimension.

While earlier laws addressed themselves merely to Chinese laborers who were in some sort of migratory state either as new arrivals into the United States or as returnees, this law extended its coverage to include Chinese laborers who were currently residing in the United States, whether they intended to return to China or not. It stipulated that such Chinese had "to apply to the collector of internal revenue of their respective districts, within one year after the passage of this act, for a certificate of residence" (US Statutes at Large 1893 27:25). These certificates were to contain "the name, age, local residence and occupation of the applicant, and such other description of the applicant as shall be prescribed by the Secretary of the Treasury," who was charged with the administrative responsibility of executing the law (US Statutes at Large 1893 27:26). Failure of the Chinese resident to comply would subject him to arrest and to eventual deportation back to China. Thus the threat of forcible removal from the United States was now introduced as a constraint on Chinese laborers who may have had no intention of leaving.

The law also added a provision that further restricted the procedural rights of new arrivals and returnees to challenge through the courts the administrative decisions that prevented them from landing. It denied them bail on an application for a writ of habeas corpus. They had to remain incarcerated until their case was heard.

Even as the bill was being debated, the Chinese ambassador registered a strong protest over the original Geary version as violating "every single one of the articles of the treaty which was negotiated in 1880" (US Foreign Relations 1892:147). He urged the Secretary of State to seek to dissuade Congress from acting on the bill. Following the passage of the modified version in May, he sent another urgent appeal. This time he called on the Secretary to seek a presidential veto of the measure, because "this bill does even worse injury [to Chinese subjects] than the Scott Law" (US Foreign Relations 1892:149), against whose passage he had raised such a hue and cry several years earlier. In his appeal he focused on the hardships that the certification process would impose on Chinese laborers, particularly on those who had been in the United States a long time. He also condemned the denial of bail as a gross violation of fundamental principles of justice.

Six months later the ambassador sent another forceful protest against the Geary Act as the latest in a series of unfair, unjust, and discriminatory laws against the Chinese. He was particularly upset at the discriminatory character of the penalties prescribed by the act for non-compliance with the certification requirement which he declared was "equivalent to banishment from the United States" – a punishment "applicable only to my countrymen" (US Foreign Relations 1892:154). This was particularly shocking to the Imperial government inasmuch as

"it has been proclaimed throughout the world for over one hundred years that the United States was an asylum for the people of all nations of the earth. In my surprise I naturally exclaim, is this a step backward from progress, civilization, freedom, and liberty? I can not find words to express my regret or the regret of the Imperial Government at the enactment of such a law, which is applied solely and personally to the Chinese, a large majority of whom are unquestionably lawfully within the United States, engaged in the legitimate pursuits of life, and entitled to the protection of the Constitution and laws, instead of the imposition of such punishment as it is attempted to inflict upon them by the last Congress; and the surprise must be greatly enhanced when it is considered that such obnoxious and unenlightened punishment is an unwelcome salute from one friendly and favored nation to another, which has at all times and under all circumstances made amity, honesty of intentions and purposes, and the sacred preservation of its treaty stipulations the chief object in its relations with the United States Government."   (US Foreign Relations 1892:154–55)

To redress the situation, he concluded, the law should be repealed and until then its enforcement abandoned. Four days later he followed up this message with an elaborate critique of the Geary Act conducted by the Chinese Foreign Office.

At long last, the United States government broke its three years of silence and deigned to answer China's protests of the Geary Act. In an arrogant manner, the Secretary of State sought to place the blame for the Scott and Geary laws on the shoulders of the Chinese government for their having failed to ratify the treaty of 1888. He also contended that the Chinese in America were not being treated any worse than were the Americans in China. Conveniently forgetting the extra-territorial rights of Americans in China, he declared that "it would not be difficult to show that from the outset, the position of the foreigner in China has been one of isolation and exclusion, his rights being limited under treaties to certain specified objects within the narrow limits of the treaty ports, and extended only at the will of the Chinese Government to residence and travel in the interior" (US Foreign Relations 1892:158). In addition, he argued, Americans in China had also been victims of mob violence as had the Chinese in America.

According to the Secretary of State, the basic problem was the "inherent immiscibility of the Mongolian and Caucasian races. As are all Europeans to the native Chinese communities, so are the Chinese to the communities of European blood – a people apart, not willing to be engrafted upon the national life, and dwelling under the special license of an artificially created necessity" (US Foreign Relations 1892:159). This fundamental racial incompatibility belied the claim of the Chinese government in its earlier protests

"that the status of Chinese subjects with respect to the body politic of the United States is on the same footing as that of all other aliens of whatever nationality. Neither in the light of international reciprocity nor in that of municipal sovereignty can these assumptions hold good. The restrictions upon foreigners in China are special and onerous as to vocation, residence, and travel, and are based on the natural barriers which seem to forbid the assimilation of the foreign element with the native Chinese race. This condition of immiscibility is likewise as forcibly present in the case of Chinese in the United States as it is generally absent in regard to aliens of the same race and blood as our own."

(US Foreign Relations 1892:159–60)

Each state, the Secretary continued, had the inherent right "to take cognizance of such imcompatibilities and to provide special conditions for the toleration of the unassimilable elements in the national community" (US Foreign Relations 1892:160). In short, China had the right to employ this racial creed as national policy in the plural segmentation it had imposed on Americans and other racially alien foreigners in China; just as the United States had a similar right to elaborate this creed into a national policy of exclusion and restriction as it applied to the immigration and naturalization of Chinese in America.

But, the Secretary insisted, the new law had a different purpose with respect to Chinese subjects actually residing and laboring in the United States. It was meant to confirm "their right to remain and enjoy the privileges of residence stipulated in the existing treaties ... by an orderly scheme of individual identification and certification. The statute as completely aims to protect the persons and rights of all Chinese persons entitled to residential privileges as it does to prevent their fraudulent enjoyment by those not entitled thereto" (US Foreign Relations 1892:159).

Events soon revealed how grossly the Secretary had misrepresented – deliberately or otherwise – the impact of the Geary law and how justified the fears of the Chinese government were. For instead of throwing a protective shield around the resident Chinese as the Secretary said it would, it promised to become a legally effective way for getting rid of large numbers of them as the Chinese government feared it would. This became evident in a letter prepared by the Secretary of the Treasury for the Senate, approximately sixteen months after the enactment of the law. According to his letter, only 13,243 of 106,688 Chinese had registered under the act, leaving 93,445 unaccounted for. "Assuming that about 10 per centum of these would be entitled to exemption as merchants, students, actors, and others of the exempt class, there would remain, say 85,000 liable to deportation under the law" (US Senate Executive Document No. 13 Part 1 (1893) 53:1:1–2). In other words, 80 percent of the resident Chinese were in danger of being sent out of the country under the terms of the Geary Act.

The Secretary's letter then went on to estimate what the cost would be to deport the Chinese.

"The lowest cost for transporting Chinamen from San Francisco to Hong Kong is $35 per capita. Other expenses incident to the arrest, trial and inland transportation would average not less than $35 per capita. If, therefore, all of those above referred to who are not registered should be transported to China, the cost involved would aggregate in round numbers, say $6,000,000. This, in my opinion, would be a moderate estimate of the amount required to carry out the provisions of said act."

(US Senate Executive Document No. 13 Part 1 (1893) 53:1:2)

He then went on to estimate that 10,000 could be deported during the remainder of the fiscal year at a cost of $700,000. A week later, in another letter, the Secretary stated that the cost of steerage passage had risen from $35 to $51 per capita; thus his earlier estimate of costs of transportation had to be raised to $7,360,000.

The prospect of mass deportations greatly alarmed not only the Chinese government but also the Chinese in America. They had received no solace from a Supreme Court decision announced after the year's registration period had expired. (The case of Fong Yue Ting v. United States will be discussed at the end of this chapter.) However, nothing much happened during the year in which the constitutional challenge was still in the courts. "In a report made by Marshal Gard, of the Southern district of California, to the Department of the Treasury on September 15, 1893 concerning the arrests and deportations of Chinese in California, it was found that 62 warrants had been issued under the Geary Act, 45 arrests had been made, and 20 Chinese had been sentenced to be deported" (Ma 1970:101). But in fact only one Chinese had been deported under the act during its year of life, while 152 others had been deported for other reasons during the same period of time, some under the Scott Act, many others for crossing the borders illegally.

⌄

THE MCCREARY AMENDMENT OF 1893

As the scope of the problem became more and more evident, a number of lawmakers began to have second thoughts about what they had wrought and they rallied to the support of a bill to amend the Geary Act introduced into the House by McCreary of Kentucky in October 1893. The primary purpose of the bill was to extend the registration period for six months. McCreary was convinced that many Chinese had failed to register under the Geary Act merely because they were awaiting the Supreme Court decision; now he believed they would because of the adverse ruling.

Without such an extension, he said the country would have to face the enormous task of mass deportations with only $25,000 available to do the job. Further, he continued, most of the 85,000 Chinese would probably seek legal redress once they faced deportation and this would tie up the courts for twelve to fifteen years. But above and beyond the enormity of the task and its costs, he said, was the moral opprobrium that the United States would bring upon itself, for in all of modern history no nation, except perhaps Russia, had perpetrated a similar act of barbarism against a minority in its midst.

> "If we fail now to pass the bill allowing six months additional time for Chinese persons to register what will be the result? Eighty-five thousand human beings will be expelled from our country, most of whom have resided here for years.
>
> There is no parallel for such action in modern history. If you go way back, centuries ago, you will find that Spain drove out the Moors; that in the days of Edward I, in 1290, six centuries ago 15,000 Jews were expelled from England; that in the days of Louis XIV in France, which I believe, if my memory serves me aright, was in 1685, the Huguenots were driven out of France. But in all the history of England since the days of the Magna Charta, in all the history of any other country in modern times, you find no such condition and no such barbarity save and alone in the history of Russia, and her banishment of the Jews has aroused the indignation of all Christendom."
>
> (US Congressional Record 1893 53:1:2424)

The amendment also defined in greater detail the category of "laborer." It was to include those engaged in skilled and unskilled labor and those "employed in mining, fishing, huckstering, peddling, laundrymen, or those engaged in taking, drying, or otherwise preserving shell or other fish for home consumption or exportation" (Section 2). The amendment also tightened the definition of the term merchant: "A merchant is a person engaged in buying and selling merchandise, at a fixed place of business which business is conducted in his name, and who during the time he claims to be engaged as a merchant, does not engage in the performance of any manual labor, except such as is necessary in the conduct of his business as such merchant" (Section 2). Further, the law also required proof from any returning Chinese merchant that he did indeed fit this category before he left the United States (US Statutes at Large 1895 28:8).

Grateful that the deportation proceedings under the Geary Act were to be stopped, the Chinese government nevertheless expressed keen disappointment on the eve of the passage of the McCreary Amendment that it merely extended the deadline for registration. It feared that the same threat of mass deportation would loom once again in six months. As a result, it belabored the American government with expressions of these fears for the next half year. In March 1894 it complained that red tape and lack of facilities were slowing down the registration process. In April it conveyed anxiety over the information it had received: only 24,000 Chinese had allegedly registered out of 70,000 living in California.

The Commissioner of Internal Revenue sought to allay these fears on behalf of the United States government. He insisted that the Treasury Department was expanding the facilities and making more flexible the procedures for registration. He also contended that almost twice as many Chinese had registered in California than were reflected in the Chinese government's figures – in fact, he insisted three out of five had already done so. Added to this were applications from other parts of the country which brought the grand total to 60,000. In sum, he expressed full confidence that most Chinese would indeed be registered by the deadline.

Not merely content with prodding the American government into expediting registration, the Chinese government resorted to still another strategy in its efforts to head off the threat of mass deportation. It reminded the American government at the time of the adoption of the McCreary Amendment that only a temporary respite had been bought with the amendment and that a long-term solution required negotiations between the two countries "to the end that all the existing difficulties between such nations may be permanently settled, and their honor, dignity, and friendship maintained and preserved" (US Foreign Relations 1893:25).

THE TREATY OF 1894

By March 17 1894 the two countries completed a new treaty but, unlike the earlier Treaty of 1888, China joined the United States in formally ratifying it by December. The first four articles of the treaty were literally carbon copies of the earlier abortive treaty, except the latter was to last for twenty years, this one for ten years. In addition, Article I deleted one of the two Senate amendments that had made the earlier treaty unacceptable to China: the ban on the return of any Chinese laborer to the United States was lifted, thereby scuttling a major provision of the Scott Act of 1888. But the absolute prohibition of new immigration of Chinese laborers was reaffirmed. The second offending amendment of the 1888 treaty, however, was retained in Article II, but the article still provided for the right of a certain kind of laborer to come back to the United States: "any registered Chinese laborer who has a lawful wife, child, or parent in the United States, or property therein of the value of one thousand dollars, or debts of like amount due him and pending settlement" could obtain a certificate establishing his "right to return" within a circumscribed time period (US Statutes at Large 1895 28:1210–211).

Also reaffirmed were the rights enjoyed by the exempted classes "of coming to the United States and residing therein," and the "privilege of transit" accorded in the earlier treaties to Chinese laborers in their journey to other countries (Article III) (US Statutes at Large 1895 28:1211). And finally, Article IV retained the guarantee of legal protection to the person and property of Chinese in America first enunciated in the Treaty of 1880.

In exchange for the protective mantle thrown about its various subjects in America, China reluctantly agreed in Article V to the registration of Chinese laborers within the limits of the United States, but not before the purpose of this registration was restated in the positive terms "of affording them [the laborers] better protection" (US Statutes at Large 1895 28:1212) and not in the negative terms implicit in the Geary Act of controlling or getting rid of them. In turn, the Chinese government demanded and received the reciprocal right "to enact and enforce similar laws or regulations for the registration, free of charge, of all laborers, skilled or unskilled (not merchants as defined by said Acts of Congress), citizens of the United States in China, whether residing within or without the treaty ports" (US Statutes at Large 1895 28:1212).

To facilitate such registration, the United States agreed to supply annually to China "registers or reports showing the full name, age, occupation and number or place of residence of all other citizens of the United States, including missionaries, residing both within and without the treaty ports of China, not including, however, diplomatic and other officers of the United States residing or travelling in China upon official business, together with their body and household servants" (US Statutes at Large 1895 28:1212).

Initially of symbolic significance only, since China had no policy of registration at the time of the treaty, this provision soon became a troublesome problem for American officials in China as the Imperial government sought to implement it. Within several years the American ambassador was complaining bitterly to the State Department about the difficulty he was having in getting Americans in China to register and therefore was demanding legislation to compel them to do so. His request was rejected as impractical. However, he received solicitous advice on how to gain greater cooperation from the Americans in China, many of whom bridled at the demeaning act of registration.

THE EXPANSION OF ADMINISTRATIVE AUTHORITY AND THE BUREAUCRATIZATION OF ENFORCEMENT

With the ratification of the Treaty of 1894, Congress did not enact any other significant legislation against the Chinese until the turn of the century. The Treasury Department, which had the difficult task of administering and enforcing the laws, instead became the principal actor in the drama. In 1894 Congress even enhanced the authority of the department by making the decision of its immigration or customs officer final, subject only to an appeal to the Secretary of the Treasury; in other words, no longer could the Chinese immigrant seek redress through the courts.

In turn, the department sought to wend its way through an increasingly dense thicket of legal and practical complexities by creating a patchwork of rulings and of arbitrary decisions – all pointing to a narrow and literal interpretation of the laws that even the most exclusionist of congressmen could not fault. At the center of this administrative morass stood the immigrant officials, at the local ports of entry, particularly those in California, who basked in their enhanced authority. They frequently indulged in an excess of capricious and arbitrary action, often voiding, for example, a valid certificate for entry on some specious technical ground. Not only were returning laborers subjected to such tactics, but even more vulnerable were the merchants, students, and other members of the exempted class as officials at the various levels of authority sought to restrict their access too. This piecemeal, *ad hoc* hacking away of individual members of the exempted classes was overshadowed in 1898 by an administrative ruling from the Secretary of the Treasury. It shrank the size of the exempted classes to only those who were explicitly mentioned in Article III of the Treaty of 1894: namely, officials, teachers, students, merchants, or travelers for curiosity or pleasure. All other gainfully employed Chinese, even though they were not manual laborers, skilled or otherwise, were henceforth to be denied admission. This was to include Chinese in such varied professional white-collar and entrepreneurial occupations as "salesmen, clerks, buyers, bookkeepers, accountants, managers, storekeepers, apprentices, agents, cashiers, physicians, proprietors of restaurants, etc" (US Foreign Relations 1901:72).

This drastic shift to a denotative definition of the exempted class was justified by the Secretary as being in accord with the true intent of Congress as indicated by the laws it passed in the past. This argument was repeated by the Attorney General in his legal opinion reaffirming the Secretary's interpretation: "It may be stated, comprehensively, that the result of the whole body of these laws and decisions thereon is to determine that the true theory is not that all Chinese persons may enter this country who are not forbidden, but that only those are entitled to enter who are expressly allowed" (US Foreign Relations 1901:72). Eight years later, the same reasoning was used to justify the priority this regulation had come to play in the codified rules and regulations governing the admission of the Chinese.

Thus in one fell swoop an administrative decision transformed the category of the excluded from Chinese laborers to *all* Chinese but those in a limited number of occupational and avocational categories. In effect, what Geary had sought to attain in the original version of his act six years earlier was now attained by administrative fiat.

The Chinese government was deeply and visibly upset by this decision. Already embittered at the demeaning and harsh treatment accorded individual teachers, students, merchants, and other members of the exempted class, it now became angered – its language, though, tempered by diplomatic etiquette – at what it considered to be a gross and provocative violation of treaties from Burlingame to the present. Its indignation far exceeded that vented in the earlier controversy over the exclusion of Chinese laborers; for these laborers constituted, even to the Chinese government, the lower order of society – a stratum of little social, political, and even economic consequence in Imperial China. But the groups under challenge were of the better and more privileged classes, and to degrade and to demean them was to impugn the honor, integrity, and dignity of Imperial China. The Chinese government let this be known in a series of protests to the State Department. What added to its chagrin was the extension of the exclusion acts to the newly acquired territories of the Philippines and Hawaii by order of a general in the former (1898) and by congressional enactment in the latter (1900). In each place a fairly sizable indigenous population also became subject to the registration requirement.

By the end of 1901, the Chinese government made one last major effort to blunt the increasingly repressive administrative controls and to head off the threat of another extension of the exclusion laws. In a carefully drawn and documented report, the highly respected Chinese ambassador reviewed the history of America's flagrant abandonment of the ideals of the Burlingame Treaty and of China's accommodative patience that had continually sought to calm the situation. He recounted the hardships imposed on the laborers and with special bitterness described the difficulties and degradations visited on the more privileged classes. He argued that despite these controls America had gained little for its domestic economy and had in turn lost ground in its commercial relations with China. In fact, he insisted, these relations stood in further jeopardy;

> "[for] it is also quite certain that if the present laws shall be reenacted, the two Governments cannot have the cordial and harmonious intercourse which should be maintained, neither can the commercial relations be as extensive, as intimate, and as profitable as the economic conditions of the two countries demand and justify. Can the Government of the United States afford to pay the high price which it will cost to maintain laws which, I think, I have shown are contrary to the spirit and intent of the treaties, to the recognized principles of jurisprudence, and to the spirit of amity and fair dealing which should control the conduct of nations?" (US Foreign Relations 1901:91)

The ambassador's entreaties were to no avail, and within a year the exclusion acts were extended for an indefinite period of time. Within two years after that the Chinese government gave up hope that anything more would ever be done to redress the iniquitous treatment afforded the privileged and laboring classes of Chinese in America. Accordingly, it decided in 1904 to withdraw the mantle of legitimacy which was draped around this treatment by the Treaty of 1894 and formally announced its intention to terminate the treaty. One year later, resentment against America's policies erupted in the form of a boycott of American goods in China. Led by students and merchants, it spilled over into San Francisco where support was widespread among the Chinese population. The boycott cut into American trade and evoked expressions of concern on the part of congressmen who represented various American commercial interests in China. The boycott lasted only a short time, and its significance rested more in its being a symbolic expression of emerging national pride and anger, which had been conspicuously absent during the decades of corrosion of Chinese rights in America, than an effective protest against American policies. By the end of the boycott, it became evident that America's legislative efforts directed against the Chinese had ended; their fate now rested in the administrative machinery that had been created and honed during the decades of legislative enactment.

Even the last two legislative efforts of any import added nothing substantially new to the overall policies on certification and exclusion contained in the earlier acts. The first one, the Act of 1902, merely extended their major provisions indefinitely to mainland America and to the island territories of Hawaii and the Philippines. At the same time, the act strengthened immeasurably the power of the administrative authority in executing and interpreting the law. For example, the Act of 1892 had merely authorized the Secretary of the Treasury to make such rules and regulations as might be necessary for the efficient execution of this act (Section VII). The Act of 1902, however, empowered him "to make and prescribe and from time to time *change* [author's italics] such rules and regulations not inconsistent with the laws of the land as he may deem necessary and proper to execute the provisions of this Act and of the Acts hereby extended and continued" (Section II). The only limitation on his authority was that imposed by the Treaty of 1894.

In short, through its action, Congress implicitly endorsed the broad powers of policy and interpretation that the administrative authority had already preempted for itself in its earlier rulings on exempted classes. This power took on an even broader sweep with the repudiation of the Treaty of 1894 by China for, in its subsequent Amendment of 1904, Congress merely deleted references to the treaty and to the limitations it imposed on the exercise of authority. A year earlier, in 1903, Congress had also strengthened the organizational structure of the administrative authority by transferring the Bureau of Immigration from the Treasury Department to the newly created Department of Commerce and Labor and by giving the Commissioner-General of Immigration greater control over the personnel and activities involved in the machinery of enforcement.

Even with this enhanced authority, the Commissioner-General still complained in his report in 1906 that the exclusion laws continued to be "among the most difficult on the statute books to enforce" (US House of Representatives Document No. 847 (1906) 59:1:5). He offered as one reason for this the fact that a "certain element of the citizenship of this country has never believed in the exclusion policy, being actuated either by strictly interested motives or by the missionary spirit, and the persons forming that element are never willing to assist, and are often ready and glad to oppose, the enforcement of the law" (US House of Representatives Document No. 847 (1906) 59:1:5–6). Another reason was "that the laws relate to a people who, according to all recognized authorities, are deficient in a sense of the moral obligation of an oath, and who in their political views hold caste in higher esteem than law, and are 'clannish' to the highest degree" (US House of Representatives Document No. 847 (1906) 59:1:6).

To the perfidy of the Chinese and the misguided humaneness of citizens could be added in the past an ineffective machinery of enforcement. There was "divided responsibility, due to the disconnected official agencies through which the laws were administered, and it was not possible to effect the organization and systematization necessary for even a reasonably thorough enforcement of the laws" (US House of Representatives Document No. 847 (1906) 59:1:5).

Now, the Commissioner-General insisted, this deficiency was being effectively remedied, and despite the unpopularity of the exclusion laws among segments of the citizenry, the bureau was honing a finely tuned instrument of bureaucratic control. As evidence of this, he pointed to the systematic codification of rules and regulations that had just been completed to replace the more sketchy rules of the past. Repeating his words of the previous year, he concluded, "In no branch of its widespread activities does the Bureau believe that it has so thoroughly succeeded in carrying into effective operation the purpose of the laws committed to its charge as in the exclusion of Chinese of the classes which it is the professed desire of both this Government and Empire of China to keep out of the United States." To perform in this manner in the face of the "many serious obstacles, both in the circumstances to be dealt with by administrative officers and in the opposition of many citizens of this country to the policy of selecting the Chinese alone as subjects for exclusion," the Bureau had had to demonstrate "a degree of vigilance and resourcefulness unexampled, it is believed, in the administration of any other legislation on the statute books" (US House of Representatives Document No. 847 (1906) 59:1:21). In short, the Commissioner expressed a special sense of pride in the claim that his Bureau was being converted into an efficient and depersonalized bureaucratic instrument of social policy, despite the fact that this policy was, in the eyes of many, inhumane, inequitable, and cruel in its treatment of hapless human beings.

Despite the prideful response of the Commissioner, the fact remained that the Bureau never attained the level of routinized uniformity and impersonal efficiency that he espoused. Too much discretionary power remained at the lower rungs of the organizational ladder for this to happen; local immigrant officials at the port of entry, for example, could decide with impunity and idiosyncratically on their own who would be allowed in and who would be kept out. As a result, an arbitrary capriciousness characterized many of their decisions, which worked cruel hardship on many Chinese and against which they had little redress inasmuch as the top officials tended to back their own.

Aware of their strategic role as gatekeepers, a number of these officials soon took advantage of the situation in which so much was at stake for the Chinese, particularly the merchants. They extorted bribes and engaged in other corrupt practices. Compounding these problems, according to Coolidge (1969), was the fact that many of these officials were drawn from California with its pathological dislike of the Chinese. As a result, they resorted to technicalities to reject the credentials of Chinese, detained many others unnecessarily while their credentials were being checked, and demanded payoffs from still others.

Even if he had had greater control at all levels of the bureaucracy, the Commissioner would still have been pressed to perfect the bureaucratic instrumentality he desired. The problems were too chronic and too big and would have required the allocation of resources and personnel too vast to contemplate. The borders, for example, were too long to patrol; efforts to conduct a census among Chinese to better effectuate their certification proved abortive; disruptive counterploys were developed by the Chinese and their sympathizers for virtually every ploy the government developed. As a result, the operation was continually being engorged by red tape that fouled the pipelines, increased the costs, and further victimized the Chinese. From 1901 to 1905, for example, of approximately 6300 Chinese arrested for failing to have the proper credentials, about one-half were eventually deported at the cost of approximately $10,500 each, excluding the additional cost for making the arrest and for trying the Chinese.

To complicate matters even more, the Bureau was beset by an increasingly serious administrative problem at the turn of the twentieth century. By then, a generation of Chinese had been born in America who could rightfully claim American citizenship by virtue of the Fourteenth Amendment and could therefore refuse to go through the certification process. By 1907, 30 percent of those seeking admission claimed to be American citizens. The Bureau developed complicated procedures for validating the claims; a number of those whose claims were challenged subsequently won their cases in court.

By 1907, few students, teachers, travelers, and officials were seeking admission; they comprised less than 5 percent of the total for that year. The largest single category was that of merchants and their families, who comprised approximately 42 percent of the total; returning laborers were 21 percent of the total. In that year, for every 12.6 Chinese who were admitted, one was rejected; roughly the same ratio held for 1908 and 1909, but in 1910 it was reduced by almost a half; for every 6.1 admitted, one was rejected; by 1910 the ratio had risen somewhat to 7.4 to 1.

In the meantime, the number of Chinese seeking to enter or re-enter the country dropped markedly so that, for each year of the first decade of the twentieth century, they rarely exceeded 3000 a year in contrast to close to a million European immigrants coming in each year. Even the Japanese exceeded by multiples of five or more the number of Chinese entering during this period. Thus the bureaucratic behemoth that had been created over the years to control and to exclude the Chinese began to have less and less fodder to feed its maw. The flow of immigrants declined. In time the total number of Chinese in America also shrank until relatively few were left by the 1920s.

The Supreme Court and the legal status of the Chinese: a permanently transient alien

The various exclusion acts etched in bold legal detail two major boundaries of and in the American society that the emigrant from China was to find increasingly difficult if not impossible to cross. The first boundary defined the territorial limits of America, and as time went on fewer and fewer Chinese were able to cross it lawfully. Initially, for example, only laborers – skilled and unskilled – were prevented from doing so. By 1888, even those laborers who had once been allowed in were forbidden from entering a second time despite the fact that they might have had legal certification to do so. By 1898 the pool of the banned was further enlarged to include a large segment of the privileged non-manual occupational classes. Only a few explicitly designated occupations were to be exempt from the ban and allowed to cross the territorial threshold of America. Thus by the early twentieth century, most Chinese were barred from America to an extent and in a manner that no other immigrant had had to face until then.

Even if they managed to cross the territorial boundary, Chinese immigrants were still not able to move about freely in the institutional life of the American society. They faced yet another formidable boundary which none ostensibly was allowed to cross because all were categorically denied the privilege of naturalization and citizenship. As a result, they could not gain access to or participate in the People's Domain as fully-fledged members of the American society.

Court challenges were continually being mounted by Chinese immigrants against their treatment at the territorial boundary in particular but, with the exception of occasional instances of individual redress, they failed to budge the basic policies and practices of the government. Some of these challenges reached the Supreme Court. A few even became benchmark cases which opened up new avenues of judicial interpretation, but almost invariably the outcome of these cases was to cloak government policy with the mantle of constitutional legitimacy and to anchor it in a set of fundamental legal-normative principles.

In the case of Chae Chan Ping v. United States, for example, a Chinese laborer who had resided in San Francisco for twelve years returned to China in 1887. He had in his possession a certificate for re-entering the United States as required by the law of 1884. One year later he decided to go back to the United States and was on his way when Congress passed the Scott Act of 1888 which annulled the kind of certificate he had and thereby abrogated his right to land. Accordingly, Mr Ping was not permitted to go ashore; in his response, he petitioned to have the decision reversed. The lower court denied his petition and on May 13 1889 the United States Supreme Court reaffirmed the lower court's ruling.

In his opinion for the Court, Justice Field declared that "jurisdiction over its own territory . . . is an incident of every independent nation. It is part of its independence" (130 US 1889:604). Accordingly, he continued in a later part of his opinion, the "highest duty of every nation" was "to preserve its independence, and give security against foreign aggression and encroachment." This was true no matter in

"what form such aggression and encroachment come, whether from the foreign nation acting in its national character or from vast hordes of its people crowding in upon us. The government, possessing the powers which are to be exercised for protection and security, is clothed with authority to determine the occasion on which the powers shall be called forth; and its determination, so far as the subjects affected are concerned, are necessarily conclusive upon all its departments and officers."   (130 US 1889:606)

Thus if the United States government through its legislative branch deemed "the presence of foreigners of a different race in this country, who will not assimilate with us, to be dangerous to its peace and security," it had the right to exclude them even though "there are no actual hostilities with the nation of which the foreigners are subjects. The existence of war would render the necessity of the proceeding only more obvious and pressing. The same necessity, in a less pressing degree, may arise when war does not exist, and the same authority which adjudges the necessity in one case must also determine it in the other" (130 US 1889:606).

The case at hand did not deal merely with someone who was trying to get into the United States for the first time, but with someone who had already been here. Accordingly, the judge took cognizance of the fact that the appellant claimed a vested right to return on the grounds of earlier treaty commitments made by the

United States and of a "contractual arrangement" made with the appellant under the laws of 1882 and 1884.

Justice Field then "conceded that the act of 1888 is in contravention of express stipulations of the treaty of 1868 and of the supplemental treaty of 1880," but insisted, "it is not on that account invalid or to be restricted in its enforcement. The treaties were of no greater legal obligation than the act of Congress. By the Constitution, laws made in pursuance thereof and treaties made under the authority of the United States are both declared to be the supreme law of the land, and no paramount authority is given to one over the other." Under such circumstances, he concluded, "the last expression of the sovereign will must control" (130 US 1889:600); in short, the law of 1888 had precedence over the earlier treaties.

Justice Field then dismissed the second claim of the appellant, that the government was "contractually" obligated to let him in under the terms of the laws of 1882 and 1884. He argued,

> "the power of exclusion of foreigners being an incident of sovereignty belonging to the government of the United States, as part of those sovereign powers delegated by the Constitution, the right to its exercise at any time when, in the judgment of the government, the interests of the country require it, cannot be granted away or restrained on behalf of any one. The powers of government are delegated in trust to the United States, and are incapable of transfer to any other parties. They cannot be abandoned or surrendered. Nor can their exercise be hampered, when needed for the public good, by any considerations of private interest. The exercise of these public trusts is not the subject of barter or contract. Whatever license, therefore, Chinese laborers may have obtained previous to the act of October 1, 1888, to return to the United States after their departure, is held at the will of the government, revocable at any time, at its pleasure." (130 US 1889:609)

In the final analysis then, the Chinese immigrant – no matter how long he was in the United States – had no vested right of return once he left this country and could be barred from re-entry by an act of Congress as could any first arrival.

In 1898, however, an important constitutional limit was imposed on the right of the government to bar the return of a Chinese person. Specifically, in United States v. Wong Kim Ark, the Supreme Court ruled that a young Chinese male could not be denied re-entry inasmuch as he was able to demonstrate that he had been born in the United States. According to the Court,

> "A child born in the United States of parents of Chinese descent, who, at the time of his birth, are subjects of the Emperor of China, but have a permanent

domicil and residence in the United States, and are there carrying on business, and are not employed in any diplomatic or official capacity under the Emperor of China, becomes at the time of his birth a citizen of the United States, by virtue of the first clause of the Fourteenth Amendment of the Constitution, 'All persons born or naturalized in the United States, and subject to the jurisdiction thereof, are citizens of the United States and of the State wherein they reside.'"

(169 US 1898:649)

By deciding as it did, the Supreme Court not only opened a door through the territorial wall barring the re-entry of Chinese into the United States; it also drove a slim wedge into the legal barrier that kept the Chinese from membership in the People's Domain. Some could now claim the right of citizenship by virtue of birth. Relatively few Chinese benefited from this ruling, given the relative absence of family life and the presence of a low birth rate in America. (As we shall see in the next chapter, the Japanese benefited much more from this ruling.)

In general then, most Chinese found themselves uncomfortably ensconced between one boundary they could not cross even if they wanted to and another they might not be allowed to recross once they crossed. Thus, many resigned themselves to settling permanently in the Plural Terrain between these boundaries as alien residents. Much to their dismay they discovered in 1893 that just as they had no vested rights to return to the Plural Terrain once they left, so they had no vested rights to stay there, even if they never left.

The principle was enunciated by the Supreme Court as it ruled against three Chinese who had failed to obtain a certificate of residence as required under the Geary Act of 1892. Even the government conceded that all three had lived in America for years and showed every sign of continuing to do so in the future; in fact, they considered themselves permanent residents. Two of the three, however, had neglected to get the required certificate and the third was rebuffed by the collector in his effort to obtain one on the ground that he had failed to produce the required white witness. As a result, all had been arrested and were being held for deportation to China pending the outcome of the Court decision.

In his opinion for the Court in Fong Yue Ting v. United States, Justice Gray built on the earlier Court rulings including that of Chae Chan Ping v. United States which affirmed the right of Congress to exclude aliens. He quoted the following from an earlier decision:

"It is an accepted maxim of international law, that every sovereign nation has the power, as inherent in sovereignty, and essential to self-preservation, to forbid the entrance of foreigners within its dominions, or to admit them only in such cases and upon such conditions as it may see fit to prescribe."

(149 US 1893:705)

If a nation had the inherent right to exclude aliens, he continued, then it also had the right to expel them once they are within its borders, for "the right of a nation to expel or deport foreigners, who have not been naturalized or taken any steps towards becoming citizens of the country, rests upon the same grounds, and is as absolute and unqualified as the right to prohibit and prevent their entrance into the country" (149 US 1893:707).

Thus "the right to exclude or to expel all aliens, or any class of aliens, absolutely or upon certain conditions, in war or in peace ... [is] an inherent and inalienable right of every sovereign and independent nation, essential to its safety, its dependence and its welfare ... " (149 US 1893:711).

The only question before the Court was "whether the manner in which Congress has exercised this right in section 6 and 7 of the act of 1892 is consistent with the Constitution" (149 US 1893:711). His answer was that it definitely was. He concluded, "Congress, having the right, as it may see fit, to expel aliens of a particular class, or to permit them to remain, has undoubtedly the right to provide a system of registration and identification of the members of that class within the country, and to take all proper means to carry out the system which it provides" (149 US 1893:714).

In ordering deportation under certain conditions, Justice Gray insisted, Congress was not subjecting the Chinese to cruel and unusual punishment or violating any of their rights under the Constitution.

"The order of deportation is not a punishment for crime. It is not a banishment, in the sense in which that word is often applied to the expulsion of a citizen from his country by way of punishment. It is but a method of enforcing the return to his own country of an alien who has not complied with the conditions upon the performance of which the government of the nation, acting within its constitutional authority and through the proper departments, has determined that his continuing to reside here shall depend. He has not, therefore, been deprived of life, liberty or property, without due process of law; and the provisions of the Constitution, securing the right of trial by jury, and prohibiting unreasonable searches and seizures, and cruel and unusual punishments, have no application."   (149 US 1893:730)

In a vigorous dissent, Justice Brewer argued that the three appellants were lawfully residing within the limits of the United States at the time of their arrest. They had come to America at the "invitation" (149 US 1893:736) of the Burlingame Treaty of 1868 and had "lived in this country, respectively, since 1879, 1877, and 1874 – almost as long a time as some of those who were members of the Congress that passed this act of punishment and expulsion" (149 US 1893:734). As such, they were entitled under international law to the rights of domicile and even to the rights of a denizen, being that they had been invited into this country by treaty. "But," he continued, "whatever rights a resident alien might have in any other nation, here he is within the express protection of the Constitution, expecially in respect to those guarantees which are declared in the original amendments" (149 US 1893:737). For these guarantees were addressed to all persons lawfully within the territory of the United States and not merely to citizens of the United States.

> "If the use of the word 'person' in the Fourteenth Amendment protects all individuals lawfully within the State, the use of the same word 'person' in the Fifth must be equally comprehensive, and secures to all persons lawfully within the territory of the United States the protection named therein; and a like conclusion must follow as to the Sixth."   (149 US 1893:739)

Accordingly, to deport the three appellants under Section VI of the Act of 1892 would be to deprive them of "life, liberty, and property without due process of law" and to impose "punishment without a trial, and punishment cruel and severe" (149 US 1893:740). It would in effect deny them basic constitutional guarantees, "especially those found in the Fourth, Fifth, Sixth, and Eighth Articles of the Amendments" (149 US 1893:733). The Justice then went on to scoff at the contention of the majority that an order of deportation was not an act of punishment: "It needs no citation of authorities to support the proposition that deportation is punishment. Everyone knows that to be forcibly taken away from home, and family, and friends, and business, and property, and sent across the ocean to a distant land, is punishment; and that oftentimes most severe and cruel" (149 US 1893:740).

Under the Constitution, he continued, "punishment implies a trial: 'No person shall be deprived of life, liberty, or property, without due process of law.' . . . But here, the Chinese are not arrested and . . . [held] for trial, but arrested and, without a trial, punished by banishment" (149 US 1893:741). In addition they were being subjected to capricious and arbitrary actions by the administrative officials and, in having to carry their certificates with them all of the time, they were being treated like the "ticket-of-leave" (149 US 1893:743) convicts under Australian law who must have their tickets in their possession as they go-at-large to earn their livelihood. In this, he concluded, the Chinese were being denied their basic constitutional rights.

To argue that the government could do all this because of the power inherent in sovereignty was "both indefinite and dangerous."

> "Where are the limits to such powers to be found, and by whom are they to be pronounced? Is it within legislative capacity to declare the limits? If so, then the mere assertion of an inherent power creates it, and despotism exists. May the courts establish the boundaries? Whence do they obtain the authority for this?

Shall they look to the practices of other nation to ascertain the limits? The governments of other nations have elastic powers – ours is fixed and bounded by a written constitution. The expulsion of a race may be within the inherent powers of a despotism. History, before the adoption of this Constitution, was not destitute of examples of the exercise of such a power; and its framers were familiar with history, and wisely, as it seems to me, they gave to this government no general power to banish. Banishment may be resorted to as punishment for crime; but among the powers reserved to the people and not delegated to the government is that of determining whether whole classes in our midst shall, for no crime but that of their race and birthplace, he driven from our territory."   (149 US 1893:737)

The same constitutional limitation, he conceded, did not apply to the exclusion of immigrants as in the Chae Chan Ping case:

"The Constitution has no extraterritorial effect, and those who have not come lawfully within our territory cannot claim any protection from its provisions. And it may be that the national government, having full control of all matters relating to other nations, has the power to build, as it were, a Chinese wall around our borders and absolutely forbid aliens to enter. But the Constitution has potency everywhere within the limits of our territory, and the powers which the national government may exercise within such limits are those, and only those, given to it by that instrument."   (149 US 1893:738)

Justice Field, who had always been a strong advocate of Chinese exclusion and had even authored the majority opinion in the Chae Chan Ping case, joined the ranks of the dissenting minority. In his separate opinion, he reaffirmed his earlier position that the United States government had the sovereign right as had other nations to exclude foreigners and even to deny them any vested right of return, but he insisted as Justice Brewer had before him that

"between legislation for the exclusion of Chinese persons – that is, to prevent them from entering the country – and legislation for the deportation of those who have acquired a residence in the country under a treaty with China, there is a wide and essential difference. The power of the government to exclude foreigners from this country, that is, to prevent them from entering it, whenever the public interests in its judgment require such exclusion, has been repeatedly asserted by the legislative and executive departments of our government and never denied; but its power to deport from the country persons lawfully domiciled therein by its consent, and engaged in the ordinary pursuits of life, has never been asserted by the legislative or executive departments except for crime, or as an act of war in view of existing or anticipated hostilities."

(149 US 1893:746)

Nor was such a power to be found in the powers delegated to the United States government by the Constitution.

Both judges ended their opinions with prescient statements about the potential harm contained in the Court's legitimation of the Geary Act of 1892. According to Justice Brewer, "it is true this statute is directed only against the obnoxious Chinese; but if the power exists, who shall say it will not be exercised tomorrow against other classes and other people? If the guarantees of these amendments can be thus ignored in order to get rid of this distasteful class, what security have others that a like disregard of its provisions may not be resorted to?" (149 US 1893:743).

Justice Field foresaw the possibility of harmful consequences for naturalized citizens in the future.

"The decision of the court and sanction it would give to legislation depriving resident aliens of the guaranties of the Constitution fills me with apprehensions. Those guaranties are of priceless value to every one resident in the country, whether citizen or alien. I cannot but regard the decision as a blow against constitutional liberty, when it declares that Congress has the right to disregard the guaranties of the Constitution intended for the protection of all men, domiciled in the country with the consent of the government, in their rights of person and property. How far will its legislation go? The unnaturalized resident feels it today, but if Congress can disregard the guaranties with respect to any one domiciled in this country with its consent, it may disregard the guaranties with respect to naturalized citizens. What assurance have we that it may not declare that naturalized citizens of a particular country cannot remain in the United States after a certain day, unless they have in their possession a certificate that they are of good moral character and attached to the principles of our Constitution, which certificate they must obtain from a collector of internal revenue upon the testimony of at least one competent witness of a class or nationality to be designated by the government." (149 US 1893:760–61)

Despite the forebodings of the dissenting judges, the Supreme Court nevertheless saw fit to create an inherently unstable legal status for the Chinese who lawfully resided in the Plural Terrain. They were henceforth to be defined as permanently transient aliens who had no vested rights of domicile and who could be deported at the pleasure of the government. They had no vested right of return once they left the Plural Terrain; in addition, they could never enter the People's Domain as citizens. In this manner the Court branded them institutionally as perennial sojourners, at a time when most had given up any sojourning inclination and had sunk their roots into the American society.

Even as the Court carved out this transient alien status for the Chinese residents, it retained the mantle of constitutional protection afforded by its decision seven years earlier in Yick Wo v. Hopkins, Sheriff to the Chinese while they were still living in the Plural Terrain. In that case the Court overturned the conviction of a Chinese laundry owner who had been arrested for violating a municipal ordinance that prescribed the kind of buildings in which laundries could be located and vested broad licensing authority with a board of supervisors. The Court ruled that the ordinance, though fair on its face, had been administered in an arbitrary and discriminatory manner by the board against the Chinese. As such, the Court decided that the board's action violated the equal protection and due process clauses of the Fourteenth Amendment.

> "These provisions [of the amendment] are universal in their application, to all persons within the territorial jurisdiction, without regard to any differences of race, of color, or of nationality; and the equal protection of the laws is a pledge of the protection of equal laws.... The questions we have to consider and decide in these cases, therefore, are to be treated as involving the rights of every citizen of the United States equally with those of the strangers and aliens who now invoke the jurisdiction of the court."   (118 US 1886:369)

In accepting the Yick principle, the Court insisted in its later Fong Yue Ting ruling that "the question there was of the power of a State over aliens continuing to reside within its jurisdiction, not of the power of the United States to put an end to their residence in the country" as in the present case (149 US 1893:725). In his dissent, Justice Brewer called this dichotomous approach a constitutional anomaly, for he contended that if the Chinese were entitled to protection as persons under the Fourteenth Amendment, so were they equally entitled as persons lawfully residing within the territory of the United States to protection from arbitrary and capricious deportation under the Fifth and Sixth Amendments as well.

Subsequent decisions of the Court solidified this dualism in the treatment of the Chinese. The Ting principle was extended in rulings which enhanced the power of executive officials in deportation proceedings and constricted the rights of the alien to fight the proceedings. In turn, the Yick principle was extended to protect the Chinese alien from being held "to answer for a capital or other infamous crime, unless on a presentment or indictment of a grand jury," or from being "deprived of life, liberty or property without due process of law" (163 US 1896:238).

This dualism continued to plague the fates of the Chinese and later the Japanese aliens for almost the next half century and symbolized still another manifestation of the biformous character of America's response to its racial minorities. For example, the Ting principle reflected the further corrosion of the status of a nonwhite minority in the Plural Terrain of America; its first-generation settlers could not claim the right to stay there permanently no matter how long they were in the country. By contrast, the Yick principle permitted some of the rights and immunities of the People's Domain to spill over to the Chinese as long as they were ensconced in the Plural Terrain. And finally under the Wong Kim Ark ruling the second-generation Chinese could shed their transient alien status in the Plural Terrain for the status of "citizen" in the People's Domain by virtue of birth.

PART TWO

THE JAPANESE-AMERICAN: FROM PLURAL TERRAIN THROUGH THE CONCENTRATION CAMPS TO THE PEOPLE'S DOMAIN

15

CALIFORNIA ACTS AGAINST THE JAPANESE IMMIGRANT AND JAPAN SEEKS REDRESS

Introduction

Even though the Chinese were the manifest target of the restrictive and exclusionary policies and practices adopted first by the state of California and then by the nation as a whole, the plural structure thereby created had an inherently flexible design and a generic mold that allowed it in time to be applied to the Japanese and other immigrants from Asia. This was particularly true of the edifice built in California. As early as 1854, for example, when the state supreme court, in People v. Hall, linked the Chinese for the first time to the plural structure that had already been built to exclude the blacks and Indians from the People's Domain, Chief Justice Murray did not confine his remarks to the Chinese. Instead, as we saw in Chapter 13, he talked about the Mongolian race and the American Indian's presumed biological linkage to it. As a consequence of this linkage, he declared that the law forbidding Indians (and blacks) from testifying against a white man had to apply to any member of the Mongolian race, not merely the Chinese.

During the same year, the California legislature importuned Congress to legalize the imposition of a head tax not only on Chinese but on Japanese as well. Four years later it passed an "Act to prevent the Further Immigration of Chinese or Mongolians to this State." Four years after that the legislature enacted what it labeled as a Chinese Police Tax to be levied "on each person, male and female of the Mongolian race." And in 1870 it passed an "Act to Prevent the Kidnapping and Importation of Mongolian, Chinese, and Japanese Females for Criminal or Demoralizing Purposes." In short, almost from the very moment that the plural structure was erected against the Chinese in California, legislative and judicial actions manifested a strong intent on the part of white California to subsume the

Japanese as well as other Asians under the legal-normative structure of this Plural Terrain.

By the turn of the century the fate of the Japanese immigrant was explicitly and emotionally linked with that of the Chinese immigrant in the Plural Terrain as the numbers of Japanese immigrants increased and agitation mounted against both. Within five years, however, the onslaught against the Japanese immigrant took center stage in California, and for the next several decades he became the primary target of repressive and discriminatory policies and legislation. The action of the San Francisco School Board in 1906 signalled this turn of events.

The board's action also transmuted what had been essentially a local problem into a national and international problem as a concerned Japanese government expressed alarm over the action to a worried United States government that had become wary of a Japan that had just achieved the stature of a world power. (The ideological significance of this wariness will be scrutinized in the next chapter.) Thus began a series of discussions and negotiations that produced the Gentlemen's Agreement of 1907 which in turn became the framework for continuing diplomatic exchanges that extended over nearly two decades.

In this chapter we shall examine the unfolding drama in which the Japanese immigrant became a pivotal figure in the local, national, and international arenas. We shall be particularly interested in the role of the Gentlemen's Agreement as a protective shield for the immigrant and in the unrelenting drive by California to neutralize this shield and to force the Japanese immigrant into an increasingly untenable position in the Plural Terrain.

Early days in California

JAPANESE MIGRATION

During most of the nineteenth century, there were too few Japanese in California to collide head-on with this latent plural structure that was already in place for them. By 1870 the Unted States Census recorded only 55 in the country as a whole; by 1880 the figure had reached a mere 148, of whom 86 were in California. In addition, none of these early Japanese was the kind of laborer that the Chinese had already become. According to Daniels, a majority were students; others were educated, multilingual "gentlemen of refinement and culture in their own country" (Daniels 1970:3); some even sought to establish an ill-fated agricultural colony in California. They were viewed more as an exotic presence than as a competitive threat by white California – a response similar to that allegedly accorded the earliest of the Chinese immigrants. In support of this thesis, Daniels claims to have found not "a single [recorded] word of protest against these early immigrants" (Daniels 1970:3).

By the mid-1880s the number of immigrants – though still small – increased significantly. According to Kawakami (1912), the average for the first five years of the 1880s was approximately twenty per year; the number jumped to 200 by 1886, 400 by 1888, 700 in 1890. For the first years of the 1890s, according to the US Commissioner-General of Immigration, the figure averaged well over 1000 per year; in 1898 and 1899 it jumped to 2230 and 2844 respectively. As a result, Petersen estimates that by 1900, 24,000 Japanese were residing on the mainland of the United States (Petersen 1971).* The occupational status of the immigrants also began to change by then. They were much less likely to be students and of the more affluent classes than in the past and much more likely to be from the laboring classes. According to Ichihashi (1932), of those who applied for passports to the mainland United States in the years 1886–1908, merchants, students, and laborers predominated (each was more than 20 percent of the total), with the agriculturists and fishermen together making up only 14.1 percent. Once here, the immigrants found employment in agriculture, on railroads, and "in the canneries, in logging, and in the mining, meatpacking, and salt industries" (Kitano 1969:15).

The increases in immigration were triggered by the passage of Japan's first emigration law in 1885. Prior to that, emigration was forbidden for all but students who were encouraged to study abroad. However, so stringent were the terms of this law and so heavy the financial burden on the individual emigrants, most of whom were impoverished, that emigration companies found it profitable to underwrite the expenses of the emigrant and to smooth his way through the bureaucratic labyrinth in his quest for a passport. In 1896 this relationship was brought under the control of the government in its Emigrant Protection Law, which also included a provision that each emigrant should have a responsible guarantor at home who could provide for his care during sickness and if necessary for his return.

In this manner, the emigrant companies were legally required to make provisions for assisting the emigrant abroad, for providing security for his care abroad, and for his return in case of sickness and indigence, and "In performing these various services, including the negotiation of contract labor in countries where that was allowed, the companies charged each emigrant fees, ranging from 10 to 20 yen" (US House of Representatives Document No. 686 (1900) 56:1:5).

---

* Another 56,000 were residing in Hawaii which by 1898 had been annexed by the United States; the role of Hawaii in the two-step flow of Japanese from Japan to mainland United States merits at least a mention, though it will not be developed in our discussion.

The companies were therefore not merely profit-making enterprises but also paternalistic surrogates of the national government. According to US Commissioner-General of Immigration Rice, who had gone to Japan in 1899 to investigate the subject of Japanese immigration to the United States,

> "the Japanese Government has acted upon the theory that the character of the Japanese abroad will be taken as an index of the character of the nation at home. Hence, these regulations provide for the careful inquiry into the character of those going abroad and also require that provisions shall be made for the return of the emigrant, in the event that he becomes sick, or a public charge in a foreign country, before passports are granted."
>
> (US House of Representatives Document No. 686 (1900) 56:1:4–5)

(Rice lamented that these noble intentions were frequently sabotaged by local officials and emigration companies who were more interested in making money than in scrupulously following the law.)

ANTI-JAPANESE AGITATION AND THE ASIATIC EXCLUSION LEAGUE

As the numbers gradually increased, anti-Japanese sentiments began to surface. The first public stirrings occurred, according to Buell, when a shipowners' association in San Francisco manned several of its ships with Japanese in 1888 and when a businessman proposed in 1891 to bring several thousand Japanese to the mainland from Hawaii – a proposal vigorously protested by the Trades Council of the city. In several other instances, violence erupted. Ichihashi, (1932), for example, recounts an assault that took place in San Francisco in 1890 by members of a shoemakers' union against fifteen Japanese cobblers employed by a shoe factory. He also describes another assault by members of a cook and waiters' union against a Japanese restaurant in 1892.

By 1900 these sporadic expressions of anti-Japanese feeling began to take a definite shape. At first they were closely linked to the anti-Chinese agitation that was once again in ascendance as the expiration date for the various acts of Chinese exclusion drew near. Fearful that Congress might allow the acts to lapse, white Californians, particularly those in the various labor unions, mounted a shrill and intense campaign to get them extended indefinitely. This time, however, they wanted the ban to include Japanese and other Orientals, not merely the Chinese. At a mass meeting called by the San Francisco labor council in May 1900 to demand reenactment of the Chinese exclusion acts, speaker after speaker also caviled against the perils of unlimited Japanese immigration. As a result, the meeting not only adopted a resolution in favor of the acts but also one demanding their expansion to include the Japanese.

Six months later the governor made a similar appeal in his biennial message to the California legislature. After declaring that "the peril from Chinese labor finds a similar danger in the unrestricted importation of Japanese laborers," he called upon the legislature to pass resolutions "instructing our Senators and requesting our Representatives in Congress for the immediate institution of all proper measures leading to a revision of the existing treaties with China and Japan, and the passage of all necessary laws and resolutions for the protection of American labor against the immigration of Oriental laborers" (US Senate Document No. 633 (1911) 61:2:168).

Shortly thereafter the legislature adopted such a joint resolution. The San Francisco Board of Supervisors soon followed suit with a similar resolution. Samuel Gompers, president of the American Federation of Labor, joined the chorus in 1902 with a pamphlet in which he rehashed the by now familiar Chinese coolie-labor litany and also linked the Japanese to it. (In response to this agitation, the Japanese government began to restrict by 1900 the flow of Japanese laborers to the continental United States.)

Congress' extension of the Exclusion Act in 1902 did much to mute the clamor against the Chinese, whose immigration had by then been reduced to the mere trickle of 1500 per year. However, Congress' failure to extend the ban to the Japanese forced the issue of their immigration to the center stage of public scrutiny and discussion. The visibility of the issue was enhanced by an annual flow of Japanese from Japan to the mainland of approximately 5000 to 6000 per year with several thousand more coming each year from Hawaii, Mexico, and Canada. In this manner the Japanese, no longer in the shadows of the "Chinese problem," became the primary lightning rod for organized labor's opposition to the "Oriental invasion" and the heirs to the stereotypic baggage earlier bestowed on the Chinese. At its annual convention in 1904, the American Federation of Labor took cognizance of the fact that "the menace of Chinese labor [is] now greatly allayed by the passage and enforcement of the Chinese Exclusion Act, . . . [but, it] has been succeeded by an evil similar in its general character, but much more threatening in its possibilities to wit: the immigration to the United States and its insular territory of large and increasing numbers of Japanese and Korean laborers" (Asiatic Exclusion League 1907:7–8). This immigration, it concluded, had to be stopped, as was that of the Chinese, on grounds similar to those used against the Chinese:

"[namely] (1) that the wage and living standards of such [Japanese and Korean] labor are dangerous to and must, if granted recognition in the United States, prove destructive to the American standards in these essential respects; (2) that the racial incompatibility as between the people of the Orient and the United

States represents a problems of race preservation which it is our imperative duty to solve in our own favor, and which can only be thus solved by a policy of exclusion." (Asiatic Exclusion League 1907:8)

To accomplish this result, the American Federation of Labor called once again on Congress to extend the provisions of the exclusion acts to the Japanese and Koreans. This resolution was reaffirmed at its 1905 and 1906 conventions.

By 1905, Japanese immigration had become a volatile and inflammable political and public issue in San Francisco and in the rest of California. A local newspaper fanned the flames in a series of provocative articles in February. By May the various threads and forces of opposition coalesced into the formation of the Japanese and Korean Exclusion League (changed to the Asiatic Exclusion League in 1907). The League drew much of its support from segments of organized labor, particularly in the San Francisco area. Of 231 affiliated organizations in 1908, for example, 84 percent were labor groups; another 13 percent, fraternal and civic organizations.

The League saw its mission as more than protecting the interests of the working man. It was even more preoccupied with defending the American society against contamination from an "unassimilable and inferior race." It was convinced, as were the opponents of Chinese immigration before it, that two or more unassimilable races could not even constitute a stable plural society, let alone become amalgamated into a common People's Domain. The inevitable conflict between the racial segments would disrupt the moral and economic fabric of the People's Domain because the inferior race would "destroy our standard of living and, consequently, undermine our civilization" (Asiatic Exclusion League 1907:4). As a result the dominant society must seek to protect itself by not even permitting the unassimilable race to land on its soil. This view of the primordial antagonism between the races is clearly depicted in the preamble to the League's constitution:

"Two or more unassimilable races cannot exist peaceably in the same territory. This action between such races results in the extermination of that one which, by reason of its characteristics, physical and mental, is least adapted to the conditions of life originating in the given territory.

The conditions of life are, in the last analysis, determined by the conditions of labor; consequently the question of adaptability as between two unassimilable races must be resolved in favor of that race the characteristics of which most nearly conform to the conditions of labor.

The labor of today in North America is a machine, as distinguished from a manual process. That race, therefore, which by its nature is best suited to complement the machine as the essential factor of production is in that respect the superior race, and therefore best adapted to the conditions of American industrial life.

The Caucasian and Asiatic races are unassimilable. Contact between these races must result, under the conditions of industrial life obtaining in North America, in injury to the former, proportioned to the extent to which such contact prevails. The preservation of the Caucasian race upon American soil, and particularly upon the west shore thereof, necessitates the adoption of all possible measures to prevent or minimize the immigration of Asiatics to America."   (US Senate Document No. 633 (1911) 61:2:169–70)

In the kind of struggle for survival and self-preservation that this confrontation presumably involved, the League was prepared to take a leading role.

"With these principles and purposes in view we have formed the Asiatic Exclusion League of North America, to the end that the soil of North America be preserved to the American people of the present and all future generations, that they may attain the highest possible moral and national standards, and that they may maintain a society in keeping with the highest ideals of freedom and self-government."   (US Senate Document No. 633 (1911) 61:2:170)

Accordingly, the League established branches throughout California and in neighboring western states, but only the one in San Francisco maintained a high level of organization and activity. By 1908 the League claimed a membership of 110,000 in California.

THE SAN FRANCISCO SCHOOL BOARD CRISIS AND PRESIDENT ROOSEVELT

Within six months after its formation, the League began a systematic campaign to breathe life into a local issue that subsequently blossomed into an incident of international significance. The issue was the action taken by the San Francisco Board of Education just a week before the League was organized. Already infected by the mounting sentiment against the Japanese, the board had on that day taken advantage of an old state law that gave boards of education discretionary power to establish segregated educational facilities for Chinese, Indian, and Mongolian children. Assuming without question that the Japanese were subsumed under the category of Mongolian, the board justified its action on the grounds of "relieving the congestion at present prevailing in our schools" and also of achieving "the higher end that our children should not be placed in any position where their youthful impressions may be affected by association with pupils of the Mongolian race" (US Senate Document No. 147 (1906) 59:2:3).

The earthquake of 1906 with its widespread devastation sidetracked any effort to implement the resolution, but the disruption in civil order that followed in its wake brought to a head violent assaults against Japanese persons and property, the most famous of which was the attack against a Japanese scientist. By the fall the Exclusion League resumed its campaign against the Japanese in public schools; it adopted a resolution instructing its executive committee to press the board of education on the policy of separate schools. One year later the board responded to the pressures generated by the League and many white parents by reaffirming its earlier policy. It adopted a resolution directing principals "to send all Chinese, Japanese, or Korean children to the Oriental Public School situated on the south side of Clay Street ... on and after Monday, October 15, 1906" (US Senate Document No. 147 (1906) 59:2:3). The board justified its action on three grounds: (1) the Japanese were crowding the whites out of the public schools; (2) too many Japanese students were adults; and (3) many of the latter were guilty of immoral and undesirable behavior. (All of the charges proved without merit in a subsequent investigation.)

Even as the October resolution was being considered, the Japanese government expressed concern. Its consul complained about the proposed action. After its adoption, he lodged a formal written protest and actively sought to have the board rescind its order, but to no avail. In the meantime, news of the order had begun to filter back to Japan from affected parents and officials of such organizations as the Japanese Association of America. Within a week and a half, the issue became a cause célèbre in the newspapers throughout Japan. Most viewed the board's action as an insult to national honor and pride. Some called for strong retaliatory measures by the Japanese government, even of a military nature. The *Mainichi Shimbum*, for example, wrote:

> "'The whole world knows that the poorly equipped army and navy of the United States are no match for our efficient army and navy. It will be an easy work to awake the United States from her dream of obstinacy when one of our great Admirals appears on the other side of the Pacific ... the present situation is such that the Japanese nation can not rest easy by relying only upon the wisdom and statemanship of President Roosevelt. The Japanese nation must have a firm determination to chastise at any time the obstinate Americans.'"
>
> (Bailey 1964:50)

Other newspapers reacted less emotionally. They blamed the local San Francisco authorities for the outrage and looked to the federal government and President Roosevelt for signs of a continuing regard for Japan and the Japanese people. The volcanic explosion in the media subsided somewhat within several weeks but not to the extent that the issue disappeared from public concern. It retained a chronically festering and smoldering quality that increasingly contaminated treatment of America in the Japanese newspapers.

To underscore the seriousness with which Japan viewed the school affair, the Japanese ambassador met with the Secretary of State on October 25 to make known his government's displeasure over the matter. He refrained from lodging a formal protest because of Japan's past history of friendliness with the United States, but, in the words of the New York correspondent of the *London Times*, "'[the ambassador] made no attempt to minimize the gravity of the present anti-American agitation in Japan'" (Bailey 1964:62).

Disturbed by the outbursts in Japan, the American government sought to reassure the Japanese government even before the meeting with the Japanese ambassador that the school incident was local "and not indicative of American feeling generally." In a telegram to the American ambassador in Japan two days before the meeting with the Japanese ambassador in Washington, the Secretary of State asked him to convey to the Japanese government the contents of the telegram, which pledged the American government to equitable treatment of Japanese subjects in America and to a full investigation of the school incident.

> "'You may assure the Government of Japan in most positive terms that the Government of the United States will not for a moment entertain the idea of any treatment towards the Japanese people other than that accorded to the people of the most friendly European nation, and that there is no reason to suppose that the people of the United States desire our Government to take any different course.
>
> The President has directed the Department of Justice to make immediate and full investigation and take such steps as the facts call for, to maintain all treaty rights of Japanese subjects in the spirit of the friendship and respect which our people have so long entertained. The purely local and occasional nature of the San Francisco school question should be appreciated when the Japanese remember that Japanese students are welcomed at hundreds of schools and colleges all over the country.'"   (Bailey 1964:59–60)

A day after the meeting with the Japanese ambassador President Roosevelt announced that Secretary of Commerce and Labor Metcalf would go to San Francisco to investigate the school incident. The speed with which the President made this announcement reflected his growing concern about the dangerous potential of the situation. In a letter to a senator written within several weeks of the school board action, he expressed the fear that the incident could lead to war between the United States and Japan or at the least to a serious deterioration in their relations.*

"If these troubles in California merely affected our internal arrangements, I should not bother you with them; but of course they may possibly bring about war with Japan. I do not think that they will bring it about at the moment, but even as to this I am not certain, for the Japanese are proud, sensitive, warlike, are flushed with the glory of their recent triumph, and are in my opinion bent upon establishing themselves as the leading power in the Pacific.... I do not pretend to have the least idea as to Japan's policy or real feeling, whether toward us or toward anyone else. I do not think that she wishes war as such, and I doubt if she will go to war now; but I am very sure that if sufficiently irritated and humiliated by us she will get to accept us instead of Russia as the national enemy whom we will ultimately have to fight; and under such circumstances her concentration and continuity of purpose, and the exceedingly formidable character of her army and navy, make it necessary to reckon very seriously with her."

(Roosevelt 1952, 5:474)

The President's announcement about Metcalf helped defuse the situation. It convinced many segments of the Japanese press and government that the American government, President Roosevelt in particular, was indeed sincerely trying to resolve the matter; they accordingly took a more patient and calm view of the crisis.

Metcalf began his mission by seeking to persuade the school board to rescind its

---

* The President's expression of deep concern about Japan's response to the school board action was but one indication of how far Japan's status had changed in world affairs. Just a little more than a half century before, Commodore Perry had sailed into Tokyo Bay and forced the Japanese Shogunate to abandon its two-centuries old policy of seclusion for the first of a series of unequal treaties, initially with the United States and then with the other western powers. The harshest of these treaties was imposed upon Japan in 1866 by the western powers after they had successfully fended off an attempt by several clans to "expel the barbarians." The convention reaffirmed the terms of earlier treaties, particularly those bearing on extraterritorial rights. It forced a commercial and tariff structure on Japan akin to that already in operation in China and levied staggering indemnities on the country.

Yet despite the one-sided character of treaties such as this Japan escaped the fate of becoming a colonial dependency or having its sovereignty impaired to the extent of a China. As Norman comments, "the danger of Japan becoming subject to some one or more of the Western Powers was very real. Internal and social economic decay had reached so advanced a stage that it is pardonable to be puzzled as to how Japan avoided the fate of China" (Norman 1940:43).

Two years later, in 1868, the Shogunate collapsed, and the Imperial government was "restored." Thus began a fifty-year odyssey that changed Japan into a modern industrial nation and freed it from the unequal treaties. Japan's victory over Russia in 1905 completed this transformation and thrust it onto the international stage as a formidable world power.

order. The board refused, claiming that the state law barred such action once a school board had voted to have segregated facilities. Failing in this, Metcalf undertook an intensive two-week study of the matter. He interviewed officials and ordinary people in the white community of San Francisco. He visited the Japanese district and talked to its leaders and others, some of whom had suffered indignities from whites. He even went to the newly established Oriental school.

At the end of November he submitted his report to the President. In it he contended that the issue of older Japanese males attending public schools was at the inflammable center of the entire controversy. Such males comprised a mere handful of students as shown in the following statistics. Within the entire school system of San Francisco at the time of the school order, for example, there were only 93 Japanese pupils distributed among 23 primary schools. Of these, 25 were born in the United States and were roughly of the same ages as the American children in the various classes. A number of the remaining 68 born in Japan were older than the American children. In the eighth grade, for example 9 were over 17 years of age or older, but in the first and second grades only 1 in each grade was 10 years of age.

Though the numbers were small, Metcalf conceded that parental concern about the matter was understandable. The solution to the problem, he argued, did not require the extreme act of excluding all Japanese from white public schools, merely the establishment of an age limit which would apply to children of all racial and nationality groups, not only to those of oriental descent.

He warned that to persist in the present policy of exclusion would make it impossible for a number of Japanese children to attend school. They were living too far from the newly established Oriental school. Thus, contrary to the board's charge that Japanese children had been driving white children from overcrowded schools, Metcalf argued that Japanese children were being driven out by the board's policy. In addition, he dismissed in one sentence the board's charge of immoral behavior by Japanese students: "All of the teachers with whom I talked while in San Francisco spoke in the highest terms of the Japanese children, saying that they were among the very best of their pupils, cleanly in their persons, well behaved, studious, and remarkably bright" (US Senate Document No. 147 (1906) 59:2).

In the rest of his report Metcalf proceeded to describe the various other types of indignities Japanese experienced in San Francisco, from boycotts of their restaurants to physical assaults on their persons and property. He concluded with a strong denunciation of such action and called for better police protection of the Japanese. If "the police power of San Francisco is not sufficient to meet the situation and guard and protect Japanese residents in San Francisco, to whom under our treaty with Japan we guarantee 'full and perfect protection for their persons and property' then, it seems to me, it is clearly the duty of the Federal Government to afford such protection" (US Senate Document No. 147 (1906) 59:2:17).

The President responded very favorably to the report in a letter to Metcalf, but he did not release its contents to the public at that time. However, he soon entered the controversy in a manner that transformed what had been an explosive international issue into an explosive domestic one. He did this in his annual message to Congress on December 4 1906.

In the section entitled "International Morality," he called for fair and just treatment of all strangers and "immigrants who come here under the law."

> "It is the sure mark of a low civilization, a low morality, to abuse or discriminate against, or in any way humiliate such stranger who has come here lawfully and who is conducting himself properly. To remember this is incumbent on every American citizen, and it is of course peculiarly incumbent on every Government official, whether of the nation or of the several State.... [He felt] prompted to say this by the attitude of hostility here and there assumed toward the Japanese in this country. This hostility is sporadic and is limited to a very few places. Nevertheless, it is most discreditable to us as a people, and it may be fraught with the gravest consequences to the nation."
>
> (US Congressional Record 1906–07 59:2:31)

He then described in the most glowing terms the phenomenal growth and development of Japan in the past half century. "During that fifty years the progress of the country in every walk of life has been a marvel to mankind, and she now stands as one of the greatest of civilized nations; great in the arts of war and in the arts of peace; great in military, in industrial, in artistic development and achievement." He stressed repeatedly Japan's military prowess and the patriotism of its people. In general, he concluded, so great had their achievements been, that "the Japanese have won in a single generation the right to stand abreast of the foremost and most enlightened peoples of Europe and America; they have won on their own exertions the right to treatment on a basis of full and frank equality" (US Congressional Record 1906–07 59:2:31).

Most Americans recognized this:

> "In almost every quarter of the Union the stranger from Japan is treated as he deserves; that is, he is treated as the stranger from any part of civilized Europe is and deserves to be treated. But here and there a most unworthy feeling has manifested itself toward the Japanese – the feeling that has been shown in shutting them out from the common schools in San Francisco, and in mutterings against them in one or two other places, because of their efficiency as workers.

To shut them out from the public schools is a wicked absurdity, when there are no first-class colleges in the land, including the universities and colleges of California, which do not gladly welcome Japanese students and on which Japanese students do not reflect credit."

(US Congressional Record 1906–07 59:2:31)

It was to American national interest, Roosevelt continued, to have good relations with Japan, to treat their people as fairly and justly as America would have it treat hers, and where a small body of American citizens acted badly, they should be held accountable for their actions.

"Where the Federal Government has power it will deal summarily with any such. Where the several States have power I earnestly ask that they also deal wisely and promptly with such conduct, or else this small body of wrong-doers may bring shame upon the great mass of their innocent and right-thinking fellows – that is, upon our nation as a whole. Good manners should be an international no less than an individual attribute. . . .

[Unfortunately, the national government has limited authority] to protect aliens in the rights secured to them under solemn treaties which are the law of the land. I therefore earnestly recommend that the criminal and civil statutes of the United States be so amended and added to as to enable the President, acting for the United States Government, which is responsible in our international relations, to enforce the rights of aliens under treaties. . . .* [But] even as the law now is something can be done by the Federal Government toward this end, and in the matter now before me affecting the Japanese, everything that is in my power to do will be done, and all the forces, military and civil, of the United States which I may lawfully employ will be so employed. There should, however, be no particle of doubt as to the power of the National Government completely to perform and enforce its own obligations to other nations."

(US Congressional Record 1906–07 59:2:31)

The reaction of the Japanese press and people, both in Japan and in America, to the President's message was instantaneous and enthusiastic. The Japanese ambassador even made a personal call upon the President to express the gratitude of his

---

*Whereas this recommendation is logically and intrinsically connected to the flow of the President's message on international morality, another recommendation made in this message seems to have been grafted on as an afterthought; certainly he failed to follow through on it in later negotiations with the Japanese government when it wanted it to be included in the treaty. In fact, negotiations on the treaty foundered precisely on this point. What Roosevelt said in his message was, "I recommend to the Congress that an act be passed specifically providing for the naturalization of Japanese who come here intending to become American citizens" (US Congressional Record 1906–07 59:2:31).

country for what he had said. Just as the message placated the Japanese, it agitated and aroused the citizens of San Francisco. Suddenly the school issue took on an urgency and saliency that it had not had before, and the people of San Francisco rallied around the board of education in a strong show of support for its position. The primary target of their swelling anger was not so much the Japanese as it was President Roosevelt. His call for the use of force if necessary to protect the rights of the Japanese and for their naturalization particularly infuriated the people and press of San Francisco. Much of this antagonism to the President's message was shared by other Californians and the tide of opposition spilled over into the other western states as well.

> "The strongest support of Roosevelt's message came from the East, where it was widely applauded for its courage and for its chastisement of a people who seemed bent upon forcing the entire country into war. Nevertheless, considerable uneasiness was voiced by those who observed throughout the entire document, and not merely in Roosevelt's treatment of the San Francisco situation, a tendency to encroach upon the rights of states and to demand greater centralization of power." (Bailey 1964:108)

The states rights' theme was echoed throughout the South and was central in its opposition to the President.

As an immediate aftermath of the President's message, the Senate, on a resolution sponsored by Senator Flint of California, sought to force release of the Metcalf report which had not yet been made public. Finally, acceding to its wish, the President submitted the report on December 18 and attached a message to it. Announced as an even more vigorous defense of the Japanese than his earlier speech to Congress, the message turned out to be primarily a temperate restatement of Metcalf's findings:

> 'I call your [the Senate's] special attention to the very small number of Japanese children who attend school, to the testimony as to the brightness, cleanliness, and good behavior of these Japanese children in the school, and to the fact that, owing to their being scattered throughout the city, the requirement for them all to go to one special school is impossible of fulfillment and means that they cannot have school facilities. Let me point out further that there would be no objection whatever to excluding from the schools any Japanese on the score of age. It is obviously not desirable that young men should go to school with children. The only point is the exculsion of the children themselves. The number of Japanese children attending the public schools in San Francisco was very small. The Government has already directed that suit be brought to test the

constitutionality of the act in question; but my very earnest hope is that such suit will not be necessary....

[He reiterated his intention to use] the entire power of the Federal Government within the limits of the Constitution ... promptly and vigorously to enforce the observance of our treaty, the supreme law of the land, which treaty guaranteed to Japanese residents everywhere in the Union full and perfect protection for their persons and property; and to this end everything in my power would be done, and all the forces of the United States, both civil and military, which I could lawfully employ, would be employed."

(US Senate Document No. 147 (1906) 59:2:1-2)

Release of the Metcalf report rekindled the somewhat abating fury of the San Franciscan people and press. Metcalf, a native Californian, was now treated as a renegade and joined Roosevelt as the enemy of California. By January 1907 the opposition of the San Franciscans had so hardened that it became evident to President Roosevelt that an impasse had developed. At the same time, the Japanese government began to show signs of restlessness at the delay in resolving the school issue. Accordingly the President decided to try a new approach.

What most Californians failed to realize was that, even before the delivery of his message to Congress, Roosevelt had come to view sympathetically the white Californian's desire to bar the immigration of Japanese laborers. In his November letter to Metcalf in which he expressed satisfaction with the report, he recalled, for example, that in an earlier discussion with the Japanese ambassador he had told the ambassador that

"in my judgment the only way to prevent constant friction between the United States and Japan was to keep the movement of the citizens of each country into the other restricted as far as possible to students, travelers, businessmen, and the like; that inasmuch as no American laboring men were trying to get into Japan, what was necessary was to prevent all immigration of Japanese laboring men – that is, of the coolie class – into the United States; that I earnestly hoped his Government would stop their coolies, and all their working men, from coming either to the United States or to Hawaii."   (Roosevelt 1952,5:510)

A month later, in another letter, Roosevelt expressed agreement with the opposition of American working men to the immigration of Japanese laborers.

Despite this sympathetic regard, Roosevelt was determind not to back down on the school issue; however, he decided to try a more subtle and less explosive approach. Accordingly, he conferred with a number of Californians and at the end of January 1907 held a meeting with the entire congressional delegation from California. At the end of the amicable meeting, the delegation expressed optimism that the issue could be resolved and sent two telegrams: one to the superintendent of schools in San Francisco and the president of the board of education inviting them to meet with the delegation and the President in Washington, and the other to the governor of California requesting that all legislative action against the Japanese be deferred until the conference was over. The governor and legislative leaders agreed to this request. After further negotiations, the two school officials as well as the rest of the school board and the mayor of San Francisco arrived in Washington on February 8.

For the next two weeks the delegation from San Francisco met with Roosevelt and the Secretary of State in a series of conferences. During the exchange of views the Californians were apprised of Roosevelt's sympathetic regard for their views on Japanese immigration. He informed them that he was prepared to try and do something about immigration, but he could do little because the school board's policy prevented him from gaining Japan's cooperation on the matter. The obduracy of the school board was preventing him from achieving what was really the goal of the Californians: the exclusion of Japanese laborers from the state. Further, he added, the action of the school board also endangered America's relations with Japan and kept alive the danger of war. As evidence of this, he referred to a "war scare" that had just recently flashed across the headlines of eastern newspapers.

In stressing these themes, Roosevelt provided the basis for a compromise to which the school board finally and reluctantly agreed on February 15. Under the terms of the compromise the school board was to rescind its order for all Japanese children who met the following requirements. (These requirements were to apply to all children of alien parentage, not merely to those of Japanese parentage.)

> "'Second [section]. That no child of alien birth over the ages of ten, eleven, twelve, thirteen, fourteen, or sixteen years shall be enrolled in any of the first, second, third, fourth, fifth, sixth, seventh or eighth grades, respectively.
>
> Third [section]. If said alien children shall be found deficient in their ability to speak, or deficient in the elements of the English language, or unable to attend the grades mentioned in Section 2 by reason of the restrictions mentioned therein such children shall be enrolled in special schools or in special classes established exclusively for such children and in the manner the Board of Education shall deem proper and most expedient.'"   (Kawakami 1912:312)

The board was also given the authority to examine "'children of alien races who speak the English language in order to determine the proper grade in which they may be enrolled [First section]'" (Kawakami 1912:312). In turn, the federal government would withdraw its lawsuit against the board then in the courts and would strive to put an end to the entry of Japanese laborers into California.

As the first step in carrying out the federal government's part of the bargain, the President acted to obtain legislative authority to plug up the increasingly large flow of Japanese from Hawaii and places other than Japan. Accordingly, he submitted to Congress a provision to be added to the immigration bill then under consideration

"that whenever the President shall be satisfied that passports issued by any foreign government to its citizens to go to any country other than the United States or to any insular possession of the United States or to the Canal Zone are being used for the purpose of enabling the holders to come to the continental territory of the United States to the detriment of labor conditions therein, the President may refuse to permit such citizens of the country issuing such passports to enter the continental territory of the United States from such other country or from such insular possessions or from the Canal Zone."

(US Congressional Record 1907 59:2:2809)

The President informed the California delegation that he would not, however, implement this provision or enter into negotiations with Japan to stop the direct flow of laborers until the school board rescinded the order.

Upon its return to San Francisco, the board was greeted by a chorus of derision and protest which made it even more reluctant than it already was to live up to its end of the compromise. As a result, it dallied. In the meantime the California legislature became restive and sought to enact various discriminatory measures against the Japanese. These ranged from "Jim Crow" laws on public transportation to a bill to exclude Japanese children over ten years of age from public schools attended by white children.

Alarmed and angered by this turn of events, President Roosevelt addressed the first of four letters to Governor Gillett of California in which he stated unequivocally that unless efforts to enact discriminatory laws against the Japanese already resident in this country were halted, the entire compromise would fall through and the Californians would never get the exclusion of Japanese laborers they professed to want. He blamed extremists for this and wondered whether, despite their loud and vocal protestations for exclusion, they really wanted to sabotage efforts to achieve it so that they would not lose a political football.

"The whole trouble in securing the exclusion of Japanese laborers has come from the attitude of the violent extremists in San Francisco who profess to have this very object in view. They themselves have been and now are the obstacles in the way to the accomplishment of their profest purposes. This is so obvious that I am inclined to think that many of them do not really wish to secure the exclusion of Japanese laborers, because they feel that to do so would be to take away one of their political assets, and that they prefer to prevent the accomplishment of their nominal purpose so that they may continue to use the question to secure notoriety and temporary influence. It cannot be too strongly stated that this is the central difficulty in the situation."

(Roosevelt 1952, 5:608–09)

In his second letter he argued in even stronger terms the case against discriminatory legislation aimed at the Japanese. At the same time he reassured the governor that "the Administration is as earnestly and eagerly desirous of standing for Calfornia's needs as for the needs of every other section of the country." With this in mind, he continued, he had worked out the compromise solution with the board.

"[But] this peaceful and honorable solution, which secures every object that California desires, is threatened only by the unwise acts of certain Californians. Should these acts become effective, so as to bring to naught what has been done, all solution of the matter will be indefinitely delayed. If the agreement is carried out, all immigration of Japaness laborers will stop forthwith. If by the action of certain Californians themselves we are prevented from carrying it out, this immigration will go on unchecked."   (Roosevelt 1952, 5:613)

Roosevelt's entreaties proved effective, for the governor actively intervened with the legislature and helped put a damper on all legislative efforts. And as a fitting climax, a reluctant school board finally rescinded the order on March 13 still protesting though that this action was in violation of state law. The President acknowledged these efforts in his fourth letter to the governor in which he said, "'I congratulate not only the United States but especially California upon the wisdom of her Legislature and her Governor in this matter; and I congratulate the City of San Francisco upon the wisdom of her School Board.'" Now, he stated, "'I am in the position of being able whole heartedly to champion California's interest'" (Bailey 1964:174). According, the President moved to dismiss the court action then underway and issued an executive order based on the provision that he had incorporated in the Immigration Law of 1907.

The Gentlemen's Agreement of 1907

THE ABORTIVE NEGOTIATIONS FOR A TREATY

By the middle of December 1906 Roosevelt decided to press for an agreement with Japan on the mutual exclusion of each other's laborers. He recognized that the "'Japanese may be reluctant to enter into such an agreement'" (Bailey 1964:153).

Within several months, however, he expressed an increased sense of urgency in working one out. He feared that hostility toward the Japanese laborer and toward Japan was mounting throughout the country, not only in California. At the same time he became convinced that he had devised a formula for making such an agreement palatable to Japan. He would accord to those Japanese eligible to come to this country all the rights and immunities of the People's Domain, including those of the franchise and schooling. This point of view was elaborated in a letter he wrote to Lyman Abbott on January 3 1907.

"Whether we like it or not, I think we have to face the fact that the people of the Pacific slope, with the warm approval of the labor men throughout our whole country, will become steadily more and more hostile to the Japanese if their laborers come here, and I am doing my best to bring about an agreement with Japan by which the laborers of each country shall be kept out of the other country. I want to make things so pleasant for Japan, if I possibly can, that with entire self-respect they can propose or assent to such a proposition. Of course I may fail. Personally, my view is that it does no possible good to deprive those who are here of the franchise. On the contrary, I think that we should studiously give the franchise and school facilities to, and in other ways treat as well as possible, all the Japanese that come, but keep out all the laboring class. I think that thereby we would avoid injuring Japanese self-respect and keep the relations of the two countries good, and would avoid a certainty of race trouble. I have not the slightest sympathy for big men who want to bring in cheap labor, whether Japanese, Chinese, or any other. We cannot afford to regard any immigrant as a laborer; we must regard him as a citizen."

(Roosevelt, 1952, 5:536–37)

The initial response of the Japanese government to these overtures was cool. For example, it parried the request of the United States government that it extend to Hawaii the same policy of restriction that it had voluntarily imposed on the flow of laborers from Japan to mainland America since 1900. As a result, most Japanese laborers continued to come from Hawaii – albeit illegally – and not from Japan itself. By February 1, however, the Japanese government withdrew any objection to having the United States government proceed on its own through legislation to stop the flow of laborers from Hawaii to the mainland. This relieved President Roosevelt of the concern that had made him delay any such action until then. He had feared that to have acted earlier might have been misconstrued by the Japanese as another insult like that of the school board. With that concern out of the way, the President pushed through Congress the amended Immigration Law of 1907, not to be implemented, though, until the school board crisis was finally resolved.

Despite this concession, the Japanese government continued to balk at the kind of formal treaty proposed by the United States; it remained convinced that there was no *quid pro quo* in a treaty reciprocally banning each other's laborers "since no American laborers desired to go to Japan." To agree to such an "obviously one-sided arrangement," the foreign minister had argued earlier would "subject his administration to severe criticism" at home (Bailey 1964:158).

Within a week, however, the Japanese government reconsidered its position and offered a counterproposal to the United States. This proposal was conveyed by the Japanese foreign minister to the American ambassador on February 6:

> "'I hasten to inform you that I have referred the matter to the Cabinet meeting held yesterday and that I am now able to state that this government sharing the desire of your government to remove the feeling of irritation arising from the immigration of Japanese cooly labor in the Pacific coasts will be prepared to enter into some agreement on the subject. Such an arrangement however can only be concluded after the San Francisco school question has been satisfactorily solved and it is proposed that the restriction of Japanese cooly laborers (as distinguished from the settled agriculturist) should be made conditional upon the most favored nation treatment to be accorded to Japanese subjects in the United States in the matter of naturalization.'" (Bailey 1964:161)

In making this proposal, the Japanese government was convinced that relatively few of its subjects would opt for naturalization. Nevertheless, it felt that this provision would balance the equities in any such treaty and help still the outcries in Japan against a one-sided treaty. Further, it believed that it was proposing nothing new. It was merely taking at face value what the President of the United States had recommended earlier in his message to Congress and in various private and public utterances.

The response of the American government was prompt and unequivocal. It would not consider any proposal for naturalization. In the words of the Secretary of State who wired these instructions to the American ambassador in Japan: "'It is wholly useless to discuss the subject of naturalization at the present time. If right exists under act of June twenty-ninth nineteen hundred six discussion unnecessary. If not it is clear that no statute could be passed or treaty ratified now extending Japanese rights beyond the limits of their contention regarding the schools'" (Bailey 1964:162).

In effect, the political and institutional realities in America had made short shrift of the wistful allusions of the President of the United States. The institutionalized exclusion of nonwhite races from the People's Domain was not going to be tampered with even in the interest of international amity and justice at this juncture of American history.

With this as the official American stance, the Japanese government gradually lost interest in negotiating a treaty which it believed had perforce to be under these circumstances one-sided. It subsequently expressed satisfaction with the solution to the school crisis worked out by the President. It was even sympathetically inclined to America's request that it continue to withhold from laborers passports to mainland United States, though not to Hawaii, but it resisted the blandishments of the United States government that these matters become the basis of a new treaty between the countries.

The impasse was finally broken after months of negotiations, with the decision by Japan to proceed voluntarily and unilaterally on the matter. As a result, in consultation with the United State government it worked out a set of procedures that it would follow in issuing passports. The procedures, though, would not be codified as part of a treaty. In this manner, the Gentlemen's Agreement of 1907 was promulgated and put into effect in 1908. The exact terms of the agreement have never been publicly divulged, though the voluminous correspondence between the two countries leading to it was made public in 1924. The United States Commissioner-General of Immigration, however, offered the following summary of the Agreement in his annual report for 1908.

"An agreement was reached with Japan that the existing policy of discouraging the emigration of its subjects of the laboring classes to continental United States should be continued and should, by cooperation of the governments, be made as effective as possible. This understanding contemplates that the Japanese government shall issue passports to continental United States only to such of its subjects as are nonlaborers or are laborers who, in coming to the continent, seek to resume a formerly acquired domicile, to join a parent, wife, or children residing there, or to assume active control of an already possessed interest in a farming enterprise in this country; so that the three classes of laborers entitled to receive passports have come to be designated 'former residents,' 'parents, wives, or children of residents,' and 'settled agriculturists.' With respect to Hawaii, the Japanese government of its own volition stated that, experimentally at least, the issuance of passports to members of the laboring classes proceeding thence would be limited to 'former residents' and 'parents, wives, or children of residents.' The said government has also been exercising a careful supervision over the subject of the emigration of its laboring class to foreign contiguous territory."   (US Commissioner-General of Immigration 1908:125–26)

At the request of the United States, the Japanese openly reaffirmed their commitment to the agreement through a declaration added to the treaty of 1911 three years later.

"In proceeding this day to the signature of the [1911] treaty of commerce and navigation between Japan and the United States the undersigned, Japanese ambassador in Washington, duly authorized by his Government has the honor to declare that the Imperial Japanese Government are fully prepared to maintain with equal effectiveness the limitation and control which they have for the past three years exercised in regulation of the emigration of laborers to the United States. (February 21 1911)"   (US Foreign Relations 1911:319)

In turn, the Japanese government prevailed on the United States to delete from the treaty the last paragraph of Article II of the Treaty of 1894 that seemed to reserve for the United States the right to enact discriminatory legislation against Japanese immigration.

"It is, however, understood that the stipulation contained in this and the preceding Article [I] do not in any way affect the laws, ordinances, and regulations with regard to trade, the immigration of laborers, police and public security which are in force or which may hereafter be enacted in either of the two countries."   (US Statutes at Large 1897 29:849)

In this, the Japanese government made manifest its continued determination to maintain control of the flow of its subjects to the United States, and to do what was needed to avoid their being made the targets of statutory discrimination as were the Chinese. The Japanese ambassador reminded the Secretary of State of this in a memorandum written thirteen years later to protest a section of the Immigration Act of 1924 which was then being considered by Congress and whose subsequent passage effectively and unilaterally terminated the Gentlemen's Agreement.

"In agreeing to the terms of the so-called Gentleman's Agreement [sic], which were arranged in deference to the suggestions and wishes of the United States Government, and in concluding the Commercial Treaty of 1911, one important object of which for Japan was, it will be remembered, to avoid such discriminatory legislation as that now under consideration, the American Government showed that it fully understood and appreciated the Japanese opposition to any form of discrimination against Japanese people as such, and virtually assured the Japanese Government that, in return for these sacrifices, made in order to preserve the self-respect of their nation, the United States Government will see to it that there shall be no discriminatory legislation on the part of the United States against Japanese people as such."   (US Foreign Relations 1924 II:335)

EARLY ASSESSMENTS OF THE EFFECTIVENESS OF THE GENTLEMEN'S AGREEMENT

Intent upon demonstrating its good faith in implementing the agreement, the Japanese government elaborated and codified a set of administrative procedures that tightened and centralized the issuing of passports. It now required much more information and documentation from applicants. As stated in a memorandum from the Japanese ambassador to the Secretary of State, "The form of the passport is so designed as to omit no safeguard against forgery, and its issuance is governed by various rules of detail in order to prevent fraud." The Japanese government even accepted some of the administrative and other suggestions from the American government, including "the definition of 'laborer' as given in the United States Executive Order of April 8, 1907" (US Foreign Relations 1924 II:370).

Once the agreement began to run smoothly in all its details, which was not until June 1908, the results were both dramatic and quick. During that month, for example, total immigration to continental United States and Hawaii shrank to only 35 percent of what it had been for the same month a year before. And, for the first complete fiscal year of operation, ending on June 30 1909, the total figure had dropped to 3275 from 16, 418 for the fiscal year of 1908; 30,824 for that of 1907, and 14,243 for that of 1906. In 1910 the figure fell even lower to less than 3000; but in 1911 it rose to somewhat over 4000.

The response of the United States Commissioner-General of Immigration to the working of the agreement during these early years was highly favorable. In his annual report for the fiscal year ending June 30 1908, the Commissioner-General, even though he only had the results of the first month of its full operation, praised the agreement.

> "[The findings from the statistical] tables and comments furnished constitute a striking illustration of what far-reaching and desirable results may be expected to ensue when two equally interested countries cooperate in good faith toward their accomplishment. All that is necessary is that there shall exist a clear conception of the object sought by each country, a working understanding of the field to be covered and the administrative details to be carried out and general good faith upon the part of all concerned."
>
> (US Commissioner-General of Immigration 1908:128)

By his 1910 report, he was prepared to pronounce this "experiment in immigration control" as a great success.

> "It's now possible to supply detailed figures and to reach at least fairly accurate conclusions with regard to the operation of the experiment in immigration control. The experiment has, with the cooperation of the Japanese Government,

quite satisfactorily accomplished the exclusion of 'Japanese laborers,' as defined in the regulations putting the arrangement into effect."

(US Commissioner-General of Immigration 1910:124)

Throughout this period he expressed pleasure at the degree of vigilance the Japanese government showed in issuing passports. He was impressed with the extent to which Japanese with passports were viewed as being entitled to them by American officials who checked them at the ports of entry. As for those who were not so entitled, he placed the blame on them, not on the passport officials: "It is reasonable to assume that the passport officials of Japan were deceived as to their status, and that most, if not all of them, produced evidence to show that they were proceeding to this country to join immediate relatives or were the possessors of interests in farms located here (US Commissioner-General of Immigration 1909:122). He was also pleased with the agreement between the two countries in the figures they reported: "It is both interesting and gratifying to observe how nearly the figures covering departures from Japan kept by the Japanese officials agree with those kept by the officials of the Bureau, the difference being too slight to call for particular notice" (US Commissioner-General of Immigration 1909:125). A similar comment appears in the other reports. And finally he was delighted at the care the Japanese government was showing in issuing passports to neighboring countries. In his 1910 report he stated,

> "With the lapse of additional time, the effectiveness attending the regulation of Japanese immigration by agreement between the two countries interested becomes more forcibly demonstrated. Japanese applications for admission to Mexican border ports are now confined almost wholly to transits, bona fide residents of Mexico, or domiciled residents of the United States returning, and the few surreptitious entries represent merely the straggling rearguard of the Japanese who entered Mexico in much larger numbers three or four years ago."

(US Commissioner-General of Immigration 1910:299)

In his next year's report he returned to the subject: "The Japanese Government has continued to exercise a careful supervision over the emigration of its laboring class to Canada and Mexico" (US Commissioner-General 1911:133).

Standing in sharp contrast to the way the Gentlemen's Agreement was working out, the US Commissioner-General declared, were the difficulties that his Bureau was continuing to experience in enforcing the Chinese exclusion acts for which it had sole administrative responsibility. Widespread violations still persisted despite the enforcement machinery and administrative codes built up over the twenty-five-year life of the acts. In his 1909 report he stated, for example, "Every plan adopted by the government is promptly met by a counter plan to defeat it" (US

Commissioner-General 1909:128). In his 1910 report he elaborated on this theme and placed part of the blame on the law itself and the red tape that clogged the efforts of his bureau.

> "No one can read the foregoing and study the statistics without some appreciation of the difficulties that must constantly be overcome in enforcing the law with even reasonable effectiveness. In fact, as has repeatedly been stated in the Bureau's reports, systematic and thorough violation of the law has become so prevalent, methods of overturning every statutory barrier have been so perfected by those who amass fortunes out of the business of smuggling that it would be the grossest of untruths to assert that the purpose of the law is ever literally carried out. The law itself is antiquated, incomplete and clumsy: indeed is so ill adapted to the purposes in view when enacting it that it needs revision from the bottom up."   (US Commissioner-General of Immigration 1910:133)

Thus he concluded that the Gentlemen's Agreement was doing a much better job in excluding Japanese laborers than were the exclusion acts in keeping out Chinese laborers. He first made this comparison in the 1909 report:

> "The experiment [Gentlemen's Agreement] has certainly, with the cooperation of the Japanese government, much more completely accomplished the exclusion of 'Japanese laborers,' as defined in the regulations putting the arrangement into effect, than have the Chinese-exclusion laws ever operated to prevent the immigration of 'Chinese laborers,' as defined in such laws, and is working at this moment with a greater degree of relative success."
> (US Commissioner-General of Immigration 1909:121)

He repeated this comparison in his 1910 report, this time stressing even more strongly and vividly the contrasting effectiveness of the two: "The easy effectiveness with which the Japanese coolie labor problem has been met throws into still sharper contrast the cumbersome, ineffective Chinese exclusion law with which our officers are daily struggling in an effort to secure a satisfactory enforcement" (US Commissioner-General of Immigration 1910:299).

PROTECTING THE EXEMPTED CLASSES

In scrupulously abiding by the Gentlemen's Agreement, the Japanese government was not only prepared to deny passports to its laborers, but was equally determined to issue passports to those who were certified after careful scrutiny as being entitled to them under the agreement. Its protection of the rights of the exempted classes contrasted strongly with the dramatic whittling away of these rights of the exempted classes among the Chinese through legal and administrative action by the American government. The Japanese government consistently sought to protect the rights of Japanese, laborer and non-laborer alike, to return to the United States if they had established residence here prior to the date of the Gentlemen's Agreement. We find that approximately 30 percent of those admitted to continental United States from 1909 to 1912 fell into this category. For the next eight years it averaged 40 percent, and from 1921 through 1924 it exceeded 50 percent. The percentage was initially lower for those returning to Hawaii from Japan. It was less than 20 percent until 1911 and 25 percent until 1914. Then the figure rose steadily to 40 percent by 1919; after that the figure exceeded 50 percent until it peaked at 70 percent in 1923 and 1924.

The character of the returnees differed significantly between the mainland and Hawaii during the early years of the agreement. For example, for the first eleven years of the agreement, that is until 1919, approximately 60 percent or more of the returnees to the mainland were in the non-laboring class. Contrastingly, at least seven out of ten of the returnees to Hawaii were of the laboring class until 1914; from 1915 to 1920 the laboring class comprised 60 percent of the returnees. The turning point for the mainland occurred in 1920 when a doubling of the returning laboring class from the year before increased their proportionate representation to approximately one-half of all returnees. This figures remained relatively constant for the next four years with the exception of 1922 when it dipped once again. An exactly opposite trend occurred in Hawaii as of 1921. Until then returnees were primarily of the laboring class, but in that year the non-laboring class comprised for the first time the majority of the returnees (54 percent in 1921 and 55 percent in 1922). By 1923 and 1924 the non-laboring class had expanded its representation to three out of five of all returnees. Thus a dramatic reversal had occurred in the composition of the returnees to the mainland and to Hawaii from the beginning to the end of the Gentlemen's Agreement.

Throughout this period, despite the changing character of the returnee, Japan sought to maintain uniform and equitable application of the rules of return. It plugged in the process loopholes in procedures that permitted any semblance of subterfuge and fraud. This evenhanded treatment had special significance for the Japanese laborer whom the American government was particularly anxious to keep out despite any right of return. And yet throughout the period of the Gentlemen's Agreement the American government challenged only three-quarters of 1 percent of those who were issued passports by Japan and kept them from landing. In the meantime, the returning laborer came to comprise at least one out of five of all Japanese admitted to Hawaii from 1912 to 1916; and at least one out of four from 1917 to the end of the agreement. The percentage for the mainland was less for most of this period although by 1913 it began to approximate one out of five, which it reached and exceeded by 1920. In fact, in 1923 and 1924, it exceeded one out of four. Thus, throughout the entire Gentlemen's Agreement approximately 36,700 Japanese laborers were allowed to re-enter the United States in order to resume their residency.

The Chinese laborer, whose fate was almost entirely in control of the American authorities, fared much worse. As we have already seen in Chapter 14 the Scott Act of 1888 forbade any Chinese laborer, no matter how long he may have been in this country, from returning to it once he left for China. Although the treaty of 1894 lifted this across-the-board ban, rigid rules and arbitrary decisions by immigration officials kept the numbers down. Thus for the years from 1909 to 1924 (the period of the Gentlemen's Agreement) the returning Chinese laborer rarely comprised more than 15 percent of all Chinese admitted to the United States. This was as true at the beginning as at the end of the period.

Interestingly this figure was only a few percentage points higher in the early years of this period than for the Japanese, despite the fact that the pool of Chinese in China who had been to the United States earlier was larger by many multiples than the comparable pool of Japanese in Japan. As a result, only 14,500 Chinese laborers were able to gain re-entry into the United States during this period: a ratio of one for every 2.5 Japanese laborers. In addition, they were almost twice as likely to be debarred than were the Japanese laborers once they reached the American shores.

Another distinctive feature of Japan's performance throughout the duration of the Gentlemen's Agreement was the relatively unchanging character of the occupational criteria it used in defining the "non-laboring classes" to which passports of entry and re-entry could be issued under the original terms of the agreement. Japan rejected the kind of redefinition of the category that American officials had imposed upon the Chinese in 1898. As we have seen, these officials collapsed the category of the exempt non laboring class to include only those occupations explicitly mentioned in Article III of the Treaty of 1894. These included government officials, teachers, students, merchants, and tourists. All others were arbitrarily consigned to the banned category of the laboring class. This redefinition persisted throughout the entire period despite the fact that by 1909 the US Commissioner-General of Immigration complained openly in his annual report over the narrowness of the definition – though he justified it as having been valid for a past period.

> "There is no reason why there should be any more objection to the entry to this country of a real physician or chemist of the Chinese race than to the entry of a merchant. Yet at the time the treaty and laws were adopted and enacted it was thought that 'officials,' 'teachers,' 'students,' 'merchants,' and 'traveling for curiosity or pleasure' were the only classes needed to be or ought to be regarded

as nonlaborers, and the laws have necessarily been so construed, both administratively and judicially. Now with the advancement of western learning and
customs in China, there are Chinese who occupy nearly every occupation or
profession that exists in this country, and embarrassment is constantly met and
overcome only with difficulty [in preventing them from entering the United
States.]"   (US Commissioner-General of Immigration 1909:129)

As a result of this differential definition and treatment of the nationals from the
two countries, the occupational spread among the entering Japanese non-laboring
class exceeded that of the more narrowly circumscribed non-laboring class of
Chinese from the very beginning of the agreement. In the first two years the
difference was not that great. For example, more than three out of five of the
non-laboring Japanese who entered continental United States and whose specific
occupation was known to the authorities fell into the four occupational categories
designated for the Chinese – virtually all of these being either merchants or
students. The remaining two out of five were either actors, clergymen, clerks,
hotel keepers, or other professionals, with the last three occupational roles
predominating.

By 1912 the occupational spread for the Japanese had so broadened that the
Bureau of Immigration had to add a whole new set of occupational categories to its
tables. In fact, it revised its general presentation of the statistical data, reorganizing
the materials under three major headings: Professional, Skilled, and Miscellaneous.
(It retained these headings in its statistical reports until the termination of the
agreement, in the process dropping the category of students.) In that year,
professionals accounted for 10 percent of all Japanese with occupations who
entered the United States. Of these, only two out of five were teachers or officials.
At least three percent of the remaining professionals were in each of the following
categories: actors, clergy, editors, literary and scientific persons, physcians, and
engineers, with the latter comprising almost 20 percent of the total professional
group.

For the next twelve years, the percentage of Japanese immigrants who were
professionals remained fairly constant until 1922 when it reached 20 percent and
declined to 15 percent in 1924. Among the professionals, the most frequent role
was that of government official; its percentage hovered between the 20 and 25
percent mark until the end of the second decade. By 1921 the proportion of
government officials had jumped to 35 percent and peaked with 55 percent in
1922, only to recede to two out of five for the next two years. Engineers and
teachers were next in popularity throughout this period, with physicians perhaps
showing the most striking growth, doubling from 5 percent in 1912 to 10 percent
in 1924.

Within the miscellaneous category, the occupational roles were so varied that it is difficult to find any common basis for comparison. However, throughout this period in the miscellaneous category, persons coming to continental United States connected with agriculture, either as farmer or laborer, predominated; they comprised on the average 40 percent of the miscellaneous category. (The percentage was almost 10 percent higher for those going to Hawaii.) Ranking next in importance in the non-laboring miscellaneous category were merchants and dealers. Their percentage rose from approximately 15 percent during the early part of the second decade to over 20 percent by its end and into the early 1920s. In addition, such other non-laboring miscellaneous occupations as bankers, agents, hotel keepers, the latter in particular, showed a modest growth during this period. Thus, by the termination of the Gentlemen's Agreement a pattern of occupational variation had been firmly established if not enlarged among the entering non-laboring classes from Japan, contrary to the narrow constraints imposed upon their Chinese counterparts. How many were able to pursue their chosen occupations once in America is an interesting but open question, though not particularly relevant for our purposes. The large outflow of these people back to Japan during and after this period, about which we shall talk later, suggests that many failed in their mission and either returned home or sought other occupational pursuits once they landed in America.

THE PICTURE BRIDES AND DISENCHANTMENT WITH
THE GENTLEMEN'S AGREEMENT

The effusive enthusiasm that the US Commissioner-General of Immigration expressed during the first years of the Gentlemen's Agreement began to curdle by the fourth year. In his annual report of 1912, for example, we find the first mention of a complaint that loomed larger with the years until it became a virtual obsession of American authorities and helped sour their attitudes toward the agreement as a whole. The complaint had to do with the trouble immigration officials were having with that feature of the agreement which stipulated that parents, wives, or children of residents had the right to receive passports of entry to America.

By 1911, according to the Commissioner-General's report, one-half of all Japanese admitted to continental United States fell into this category from the somewhat more than a third of the total they comprised in 1909. The figure for Hawaii remained fairly stable during this period – approximately three-fourths of all admitted. As would be expected, women comprised the lion's share of this category. Both in Hawaii and the mainland they approximated four out of every five so designated. Some women were also admitted for other reasons, such as having been former residents of the United States. They comprised an additional 4 to 6 percent of all admitted during this period.

While the fact that women immigrants had more than doubled during these few years obviously disturbed the commissioner in his 1912 report, he concentrated most of his criticism on the kind of women who were entering, the "proxy" or "photograph" brides, to use his exact words. These are women, he explained, "who have been married, under a custom existing and recognized as legal in Japan, to men living in this country whom in many instances they have never seen, the marriages being arranged between the heads of the families of the bride and bride-groom." Accordingly, he continued, "passports are given these women [by the Japanese government] on the ground that they are coming to continental United States to join a husband" – an arrangement in line with the Gentlemen's Agreement according to the Japanese government (US Commissioner-General of Immigration 1912:16).

Although the commissioner did not dispute this interpretation in his report, he nevertheless argued that "these 'proxy' or 'photograph' marriages would not, of course, be recognized as valid in any of the States of this country." Accordingly, he continued, his bureau had established the regulation that "the men to whom the women [the proxy brides] are going are required to meet them at a seaport and go through a ceremony of marriage legal in the United States" (US Commissioner-General of Immigration 1912:16).

The "performance of this ceremony," he insisted, not only legitimized this arrangement under American law, but it also "reduces to a minimum the chances that the women will become public charges and to a certain extent tests the good faith of the men involved in the transaction" (US Commissioner-General of Immigration 1912:16). Behind these words lurked the belief held by immigration officials that many of the proxy brides were being brought to the United States for immoral purposes and would soon find themselves in houses of prostitution. In other words, the officials were convinced that the same fate awaited these women as that already thought to have beset most Chinese women who had come to the United States earlier.

The commissioner of immigration from Seattle, for example, called on the Commissioner-General in his 1914 report to authorize an investigation into the validity of this belief, but he left no doubt as to what he thought the finding would be.

"I would recommend that competent officers who understand the Japanese language make investigations occasionally in order to ascertain whether or not these 'proxy' wives are living with their husbands. They might also investigate as to the occupations of recent female arrivals. I believe the results would be somewhat surprising." (US Commissioner-General of Immigration 1914:305)

Though the immorality theme was part of the hidden agenda of his annual report of 1912, the Commissioner-General did not rely on it in articulating his concern about the photograph brides. Instead he focused his attention on the presumed economic consequences of this immigration. These brides would in all likelihood, he argued, enter the unskilled labor market and become competitors with American workers for jobs – something which the agreement was presumably designed to prevent.

> "The practice of furnishing the passport to these women and admitting them on the basis of the passport and a marriage performed at the port opens the way for the introduction into continental United States of large bodies of common laborers – females it is true, but none the less competitors of the laborers of this country."   (US Commissioner-General of Immigration 1912:16)

In addition, he called attention to the large number of children who would probably be born from such unions – children who would be American citizens by virtue of birth but who would still be viewed as Japanese subjects by the Japanese government and by their parents who could not themselves become American citizens.

> "This practice [of letting photograph brides in] must necessarily result in constituting a large, native-born Japanese population, persons who, because of their birth on American soil, will be regarded as American citizens, although their parents cannot be naturalized, and who, nevertheless, will be considered (and probably will consider themselves) subjects of the Empire of Japan under the laws of that country, which hold that children born abroad of parents who are Japanese subjects are themselves subjects of the Japanese Empire."
> (US Commissioner-General of Immigration 1912:17)

In this manner he raised the specter of dual citizenship and the fear of a "primordial" loyalty to Japan by such children.

The annual report of 1913 repeated verbatim the indictment in the report of 1912 against the photograph brides but, in a footnote appended to the indictment, the new US Commissioner-General who had just taken over the office expressed disagreement with the accommodation worked out by his predecessor to these "proxy marriages." Using the third person in his comments, the new commissioner let it be known that

> "the writer desires, however, to state that he does not agree with the notion that any such marriage is binding upon the United States in the administration of immigration laws; and also that there is no treaty with Japan, or other

arrangement whatsoever, that provides for the recognition by the United States of the so-called marriage of a woman in Japan with a man who may be in the United States at the alleged date of the same."

(US Commissioner-General of Immigration 1913:fn.22)

After offering several reasons for his opinion, the new commissioner concluded the footnote with the statement: "Further comment on this, as well as other matters connected with Japanese immigration, is deferred owing to his brief incumbency" (US Commissioner-General of Immigration 1913:fn.22).

By the annual report of 1915, the new commissioner had something more to say, but this time in somewhat more subdued tones. After paying brief homage to various arrangements under the agreement "which in many respects have operated to the satisfaction of the Governments involved in regulating the influx of Japanese laborers to the country," he complained that they "contain so many exceptions in favor of members of families, and these exceptions are of such a constantly broadening nature, that the purpose in view is not being fully accomplished" (US Commissioner-General of Immigration 1915:18).

By 1915, he contended, women numbered 3487 of the 9029 Japanese admitted to the mainland from Japan. (He failed to mention that this figure constituted in fact a slight decline in the proportionate share women comprised of all those admitted to the mainland.) Most of these women were photograph brides – "young women coming to this country to join 'husbands' with whom a so-called marriage had been contracted in Japan by arrangement between their respective families, often without the parties ever having seen each other" (US Commissioner-General of Immigration 1915:18–19). In addition to questioning implicitly the legality of these marriages, the Commissioner-General concluded with the very explicit complaint that 'in a large majority of cases these women themselves are laborers who enter the fields and factories and work alongside their husbands. They are laborers in exactly the same sense and to practically the same extent as the males with whom they work" (US Commissioner-General of Immigration 1915:19).

However, despite the Commissioner-General's elaborating criticism and the opinion he had expressed as early as the 1913 annual report, the Bureau of Immigration continued to abide by the accommodation it had devised to meet the issue of the photograph brides. They were still to be allowed to enter the country if they underwent a marriage ceremony with their husbands present at the American port of entry in accordance with the laws of the United States. The importance the Bureau attached to this step is evident in the Commissioner-General's annual report of 1919. "This [ceremony], in effect, allowed such a bride, while in an immigration station at a United States port, to qualify as the wife of a resident of the United States in order to become admissible under our immigration law" (US Commissioner-General of Immigration 1919:57).

By insisting on this ceremony, the Bureau was thereby able to bypass its own nagging and persistent doubts about the legality – even under Japanese law – of the marital status of the photograph brides prior to the American ceremony. However, the Bureau never liked this accommodation according to the Commissioner-General. ("This practice was not satisfactory either to the department or to the bureau" (US Commissioner-General of Immigration 1919:57).) The reason was that it was "something not contemplated either by its [the current immigration law's] spirit or letter. In other words, a woman, no matter whence she might come, arriving at one of our ports without possessing the qualifications required by our law for entry, might qualify by being permitted to do *after* arrival that which as one of the necessary elements for admission should have been a fact *before* arrival" (US Commissioner-General of Immigration 1919:57).

Early in 1917, however, the accommodation was brought into question by an act of Congress that in and of itself was not manifestly aimed at the accommodation. In February of that year, Congress finally overrode a presidential veto after failing in two earlier attempts that extended over a three-year period. It passed an immigration law that included a provision for a literacy test. This provision stipulated exclusion for "'all aliens over sixteen years of age, physically capable of reading, who cannot read the English language, or some other language or dialect, including Hebrew or Yiddish.'" The provision contained an important exception to this literacy requirement: "'any admissible alien, or any alien heretofore or hereafter legally admitted, or any citizen of the United States, may bring in or send for his father or grandfather over fifty-five years of age, his wife, his mother, his grandmother, or his unmarried or widowed daughter, if otherwise admissible, whether such relative can read or not; and such relative shall be permitted to enter'" (Garis 1927:130).

With the passage of this law, the Bureau could no longer avoid an answer to the question it had skirted with its accommodation. What was the legal status of the photograph bride (now increasingly called the picture bride in official correspondence), prior to her reaching America? Was she truly a wife and therefore exempted from the literacy requirement, or was she still an unmarried woman (who happened to become a wife after the American ceremony) and therefore subject to the requirement?

The answer required a knowledge and familiarity with the laws and customs of Japan of which the Bureau had little and a level of policy decision higher than the Bureau itself. As a result, the Department of Labor, of which the Bureau was part, took the matter over and initiated a series of inquiries of the Japanese government with the United States Department of State as intermediary.

The reply of the Japanese government through its ambassador in Washington was quick and clear. Such marriages were in accord with the law of Japan where

"it is provided that marriage is complete and takes effect immediately upon its being notified either in writing or orally to the registrar by both parties with the participation in the act of at least two witnesses of full age and its being accepted by him; that if a document is employed for such notification it must be personally signed and sealed by the parties and the witnesses, but it is not necessary that the parties personally appear before the registrar; that if the notification is made orally both the parties and their witnesses must personally appear before the registrar."   (US Foreign Relations 1917:849–50)

In the last paragraph of his reply, the ambassador added "that the marriage system of Japan being as herein before stated, it would be inappropriate to use the phrase 'marriage by proxy' in relation to the subject under consideration" (US Foreign Relations 1917:850).

The Department of Labor accepted the explanation. On May 5 1917 it announced that immigration officials would henceforth recognize the validity of these marriages, unless the Japaness man was a native-born citizen of the United States and therefore under the jurisdiction of American laws (the regulation that was to apply to him will be discussed later) and would discontinue the second marriage ceremony performed by American ports. To establish proof of her marital status, the department continued, the picture bride would have to show to immigration officials a certified copy of the family record of the registrar and a certified copy of the original notification to the registrar by the man of his intention to marry.

Although the latter requirement was waived for picture brides then *en route* to the United States, it almost immediately became the topic of an extended exchange between Japanese and American authorities. In the ensuing correspondence, the Japanese ambassador argued that the Japanese Department of Justice which had jurisdiction over the family registry affairs had "never before been required to issue the copy of the original notification in order to certify the legal validity of a marriage, the copy of the record of the family registry part of which forms the conclusive proof of acceptance by the local registrar of the notification of marriage, either verbal or written, having always been held as the only necessary document for that purpose" (US Foreign Relations 1917:853).

This argument failed to move the Department of Labor until another letter by the Japanese ambassador dated July 25 gave the fullest and most detailed account of Japanese marital practices and their relation to the law that had yet been made. In the course of his explanation, the ambassador showed that the department had misunderstood both the form and substance of the original notification of marriage under Japanese law and its availability as a separate document. To abide by the department's requirement, the Japanese government would have to institute a new set of administrative procedures which it would be prepared to do if the department insisted.

In a letter dated almost a month later, the Secretary of Labor thanked the Japanese ambassador for the detailed letter and admitted that the department had misunderstood how closely interlocked the notification process was with the accepted legal practice in Japan. He assured the ambassador that no new administrative procedures would have to be set up by his government and that henceforth all the wives would have "to furnish to the immigration officers at ports of entry of this country, as evidence of their marriage, [was] a certified copy of so much of the record of the family (called in Japanese the *Koseki-tohon*) of each of the parties to the marriage as contains the items recorded by reason of the occurrence of the marriage" (US Foreign Relation 1917:871).

> "These seem to be documents which it is customary to issue in Japan, so that no new system would have to be inaugurated; moreover, they seem to be the most complete documentary evidence that can be furnished under all the circumstances, as they contain a record, properly authenticated, of the fact that the registrar has received notification from or on behalf of the parties concerned and that the record of the marriage, and therefore the marriage itself has been completed in accordance with Japanese law."   (US Foreign Relations 1917:871)

In his concluding paragraph the Secretary of Labor expressed his department's appreciation for the ambassador's full explanation which helped clear up the various misunderstandings which could have led to "embarrassment in the enforcement of the immigration law generally." He added in his final sentence,

> "It is especially gratifying that the full and free discussion thereof has produced a situation under which the nomenclature that has grown up – the use of the expression 'picture brides,' 'photograph brides,' 'proxy marriages,' etc. – may now be abandoned, since the explanations and assurances of the Japanese government show that the marriages in question are authorized and recognized by the former Government, which fact has led to their full recognition by the United States Government, so that the marriages involved are now to be considered by all concerned as in no sense distinguishable from marriage generally, and the women can be, and ought to be, referred to simply as wives."
>
> (US Foreign Relations 1917:872)

Despite the assurances of the Secretary of Labor and the warmth of his reply, instructions were never issued to modify the earlier guidelines; they still retained the requirement of a certified copy of notification of marriage by the man in

America to the woman in Japan. Why these guidelines were never modified as promised in the letter or what administrative steps the Japanese government had to take to meet this requirement are unclear. But it is highly probable that the Commissioner-General and his Bureau of Immigration played a major role in dissuading the Secretary from issuing any new instructions. For they never came to share the sentiments expressed by the Secretary in his letter. For example, they never stopped calling the women married under these circumstances "proxy," "photograph," or "picture brides." In his annual report the US Commissioner-General admitted that the solution he was hoping would come out of the earlier discussions with Japan had less to do with any interest in clarifying the legal status of the brides than in finding ways of keeping them out of the country – hence his expression of disappointment that their numbers had increased from 1919 to 1920.

> "As stated in the bureau's last annual report, the practice then obtaining as to admission of proxy brides as alleged wives of Japanese in this country was not satisfactory either to the department or the bureau, and the result of conferences on the subject as then set forth was the new rule then adopted which promised a solution of the question with its promulgation by the department. Contrary to this expectation, the number of arrivals of such wives increased from 3189 in 1919 to 3816 by 1920."   (US Commissioner-General of Immigration 1920:18)

The fact is that while the absolute numbers of immigrant women in the general category of "wives, children, and parents of residents" increased somewhat from 1917 to 1920 for the mainland, it had declined for the same period for Hawaii. In both cases, however, the proportion such women constituted of all immigrants admitted annually remained remarkably stable during the period. It hovered around three out of ten for the mainland and four out of ten for Hawaii until 1920 when it declined to approximately one out of three. In fact, these proportions had remained relatively constant for the mainland since 1915, two years before the legal clarification, and for Hawaii since 1916 one year before the clarification.

Thus, despite the friendly exchange between the Secretary of Labor and the Japanese ambassador of August 1917, it soon became evident that the picture bride issue had far from disappeared. Not only did the Bureau fail to alter its regulations of May 5 1917, but it also cracked down on Japanese men born in the United States who wished to take advantage of the picture bride clarification. The Bureau ruled that even though they were still considered nationals of Japan by the Japanese government and therefore subject to laws of Japan, they were in fact American citizens and subject to the jurisdiction of American law. Accordingly, if they married by proxy under Japanese law, their picture brides would be treated as unmarried women under American law and would be subject to the literacy test upon arrival in America. The Bureau refused to resurrect the dockside marriage ceremony it had used prior to 1917 to legalize the union under American law. It insisted "that such a woman cannot be admitted as the wife of a Japanese-American citizen unless the latter proceeds to a place where both he and his intended wife will be under the jurisdiction of the country in accordance with the laws of which the marriage is contracted" (US Foreign Relations 1917:876).

By 1919 the picture bride issue had become so alive that it was at the center of the mounting anti-Japanese campaign in California. (We shall examine this in the next section.) In addition, the Bureau had again reopened the question of the legal status of such marriages: Did the fact that the husband was in residence in the United States at the time of the marriage ceremony bring the ceremony under the jurisdiction of American law? And finally, a senator from California had begun a move to amend the Immigration Law of 1917 by excluding "absolutely Japanese of the laboring class, thus substituting an Act of Congress in place of the arrangement with the Japanese Government" (US Foreign Relations 1919 II:416). The Chief of the Far Eastern Division of the State Department offered the picture bride situation as an explanation for the senator's action in a memorandum dated November 19 1919: "The main objection to the present arrangement, according to letters from Senator Phelan, lies in the admission of the 'picture brides'" (US Foreign Relations 1919 II:416).

In view of the mounting public, political, and administrative pressures, the State Department sought to reopen the issue once again with the Japanese government. In a meeting with the Japanese ambassador in Washington on November 20, the Secretary of State "informally" advised him that

> "in order to avoid the adverse effects on the relations between Japan and America which would result either from a holding that such marriages are illegal or from the enactment of legislation such as has been proposed ... it would be wise for Japan to prevent abuses of this system and I answered affirmatively his informal inquiry whether it would have a good effect if the Japanese Government were to prohibit the entrance of the picture brides into the United States."
> (US Foreign Relations 1919 II:417–18)

One day later the Secretary sought to impress the American ambassador in Japan with the urgent need for immediate action: "Since Congress reconvenes on December 1 and it is probable that the bill now pending will be pushed rapidly, haste is necessary if legislation on this point is to be averted" (US Foreign Relations 1919 II:418).

Under the combined prodding of American officials and the Japanese ambassador in Washington the Japanese government finally acted. Again insisting that it exercise control over the matter, it sent the following announcement to the American government through its ambassador:

"The Japanese Government, placing supreme importance upon the promotion of friendly relations between Japan and the United States, and having carefully examined in that spirit the situation created by the question of the so-called 'picture brides' have decided to adopt measures for the prohibition of such brides from proceeding to the Continental United States."

(US Foreign Relations 1919 II:419)

The Japanese government rejected the suggestion that the prohibition become effective immediately. Instead it set February 29 1920 as the last day for issuing passports to picture brides and September 1 as the last day such passports would be deemed valid.

According to the Commissioner-General's annual report of 1921, "This decree of the Imperial Government of Japan has had the effect of stopping the coming to mainland ports of the United States of 'proxy' brides" (US Commissioner-General of Immigration 1921:10). It did not stop the coming of other women who continued to be protected by the category, wives, children, and parents, but it dramatically reduced the proportion that women in this category comprised of all those admitted under the agreement. Whereas such women constituted one out of three of those admitted during the fiscal year ending June 1920 to both the mainland and Hawaii, by the end of fiscal year 1921 they comprised only one out of four and for the last two years of the Gentlemen's Agreement, 1923 and 1924, one out of five.

Though the flow of picture brides came to a halt by late 1920, it had already done much, along with the influx of other women, to alter the sex ratio of Japanese in America for the decade from 1910 to 1920. Whereas women comprised only 12.5 percent of the total Japanese population in continental United States in 1910, the percentage had almost tripled by 1920, reaching 34.5 percent. In short, in 1910 there were approximately seven men to every woman; by 1920 the ratio was less than two to one. (The total population had increased over 50 percent from 72,000 in 1910 to 111,000 in 1920.)

In the final analysis, then, controversial as the picture bride issue became in America for most of the second decade of the twentieth century, the United States could do little to control this flow unilaterally. The Gentlemen's Agreement clearly protected the right of wives, children, and parents of residents to enter the country and gave Japan the authority to issue passports to them which it did scrupulously according to the laws of Japan. The net result was a substantial increase, both relative and absolute, of the number of Japanese women in America by 1920.

The fate of Chinese women was quite different. Their influx was directly under the control of the United States government – a control which, we have already seen, it exercised with an almost unrelenting vigor until early in the twentieth century. Then it somewhat relaxed its stringent control by officially authorizing admission of "wives and minor children of domiciled merchants," but even so it remained suspicious that many of the women so labeled were actually being brought to America for purposes of prostitution; and the young boys labeled as sons, for purposes of common labor. Accordingly, the US Commissioner-General of Immigration called for constant vigilance in screening people in this category.

> "This is a class [wives and minor children of domiciled merchants] the admission of which has to be carefully guarded because the guise of wife or minor daughter is so easily availed of when some one of the numerous secret societies desires to import a prostitute or slave girl, and that of the minor son can be employed to an unlimited extent for introducing young laborers. The attempts in both of these respects have been numerous during the past year, but it is hoped that the majority at least of the 46 'wives' and 345 'minor children' shown by Table 1 (p. 78) to have been admitted as members of this class have been the actual wives and minor children of real merchants."
>
> (US Commissioner-General of Immigration 1906:86)

As a result of these stringent controls, the number of Chinese women in America remained remarkably constant from 1870 to 1910. At each census count taken during this period, they averaged 4500 with a slight decline in 1890 to fewer than 4000. During the same period, the number of Chinese men varied considerably. The number rose steadily from 1870 until it peaked in 1890 at 103,620; then it declined consistently and markedly. As a result, changes in the proportionate representation of women in the total Chinese population were primarily a function of the variations among men and not among women. Despite this, by 1910 they only comprised 6.5 percent of the Chinese population; in 1900 the figure was 5 percent and in 1890 3.6 percent. In short, by 1910, there were fourteen men for every woman among the Chinese.

The modest relaxation of controls plus the increase in number of native-born Chinese increased the number of women in America by 1920; at the same time the male population continued to decline. But even so, women comprised only 12.6 percent of the population – almost three times less than the figure for the Japanese. The sex ratio declined markedly by 1920, seven men for every woman – a figure, though, that the Japanese had already reached by 1910. In addition, because of the decline in the number of men, the total Chinese population decreased almost 14 percent from approximately 71,500 in 1910 to 61,600 in 1920 – almost half of what the Japanese totaled in 1920, though both were about equal in numbers in 1910.

Thus by 1920 the different immigration policies and controls had clearly and decisively etched their imprint on the character of the two populations. The

Chinese constituted by and large a declining and aging population of single men; few had the chance for a relatively normal family life. Contrastingly, the Japanese comprised an expanding younger population in which women were becoming an increasingly significant part. As a result, a substantial number of Japanese men – albeit still a minority – were able to establish and to live relatively normal family lives.

California and the anti-alien land laws

THE ABORTIVE ATTEMPTS

Hardly had the school crisis been resolved and the final touches put on the Gentlemen's Agreement when rumblings in California threatened to undo what President Roosevelt had worked out with the Japanese government. For, once again, anti-Japanese agitation had surfaced and found expression in the deliberations of the state legislature. At its opening session in January 1909, for example, a number of bills (Ichihashi estimated seventeen) had been placed in the legislative docket. By mid-January, one, an alien land bill, had already been reported upon favorably by the assembly judiciary committee. This measure stipulated that aliens acquiring title to lands in California would have to become citizens within five years or dispose of their holdings, obviously a condition the Japanese could not legally meet.

Upon reading of this action in the newspapers, Roosevelt immediately wired Governor Gillett of California to delay action and followed it with a letter which began, "I am greatly concerned over the anti-Japanese bills which are apparently going thru or are on their way thru the California legislature. They are in every sense most unfortunate." He then went on to describe how well the Gentlemen's Agreement was working after he had such difficulty in getting it in place. "At last we have in first-class working order the arrangement which with such difficulty we succeeded in getting thru two years ago" (Roosevelt 1952, 6:1477).

So well was the agreement working, he continued, that "during the six months ending October 31, last, the total number of Japanese who have come to the mainland of the United States has been 2074, and the total number who have left has been 3181. In other words, the whole object nominally desired by those who wish to prevent the incoming of Japanese laborers has been achieved. More Japanese are leaving the country than are coming in (Roosevelt 1952, 6:1477–488).

"There is therefore, no shadow of excuse for action which will simply produce great irritation and may result in upsetting the present agreement and throwing open the whole situation again. These agitators have themselves to thank if trouble comes from what they do, if there is a fresh influx of Japanese hither. They hamper the National Government in what it has now so efficiently accomplished – the agreement by peaceful means, and thru the friendly initiative of the Japanese Government, to keep Japanese immigrants out of the United States save as Americans themselves visit Japan. Is it not possible to get the legislature to realize the great unwisdom from the standpoint of the country at large, and above all from the standpoint of California, of what is being done?"

(Roosevelt 1952, 6:1478)

In order to mobilize public opinion behind him, the President released three days later the text of the letter to the press as he later did most of the other correspondence on the issue. Initially the impact was slight. On January 22 another anti-Japanese bill was introduced into the California legislature, reviving the San Franciso School Board plan of segregation. However, three days later the governor joined forces with the President and was instrumental in blunting the drive toward enactment of anti-Japanese legislation. He sent a strongly worded message to the legislature and generally persuaded its leaders to shelve or to defeat the bills. The President sent to the governor a telegram of congratulations two days later.

For a week matters seemed under control. Then an attack on a Japanese student on the Berkeley campus of the University of California by what later turned out to be white hoodlums from the town, not students, opened up the issue once again. By February 4 the assembly had resurrected and overwhelmingly passed the anti-Japanese school bill.

Upon hearing this, the President dispatched a telegram immediately to the governor in which he protested: "This is the most offensive bill of all and in my judgment is clearly unconstitutional and we should at once have to test it in the courts. Can it not be stopt in the legislature or by veto?" (Roosevelt 1952, 6:1502). Once again the governor sent a special message to the legislature, but only the intervention of Speaker Stanton of the assembly helped reverse the tide. In a speech he alluded in a mysterious manner to the dire consequences that passage of such a bill might produce – consequences which he was not at liberty to divulge. Accordingly he urged his colleagues to reconsider and table the measure "'until the governor will be in a position to explain more fully the reason for the Federal government's request for delay" (Roosevelt 1952:fn.1502). The assembly heeded his advice and voted to reconsider and to table the measure. Both the President and the governor wired congratulations to the Speaker shortly thereafter.

This ended any real threat of legislative action against the Japanese during the 1909 session of the California legislature, although Roosevelt was still somewhat worried about such action after the school law confrontation. In a letter to his son on February 6, he wrote, "I have spent my usual lively week; but the troubles I have with Congress don't count at all when compared with the trouble I am having with California over Japan. I have been vigorously holding the lid down for the last three weeks, with varying success. I think I shall succeed but I cannot be sure" (Roosevelt 1952, 6:1506). By February 13 Roosevelt was able to write President-elect Taft that everything was now under control: "Since you have been away I have had a very serious time over the Japanese business in the California Legislature. The Republican machine finally came to my help in fine shape and we got the thing all right" (Roosevelt 1952, 6:1519). However, as a face-saving gesture the California legislature passed a resolution importuning Congress to expand the Chinese exclusion act to include all Asiatics and ordering the state labor commissioner to prepare a report on the Japanese in California.

Though Roosevelt fought as hard at the end of his presidential term in February 1909 as he did in his mid-term of 1906 to prevent or to reverse legislative or other actions against the Japanese by California, he had come by then to adopt the basic ideological premises of his opposition. As we have already noted, he no longer advocated as he did in 1906 naturalization for Japanese who wished to become citizens, with their subsequent absorption into the People's Domain. Instead he had become convinced by 1909 that an unbridgeable *racial* gulf separated the Japanese from white Americans. He stated this unequivocally in a letter dated February 4 1909. "Our line of policy [toward Japan and the Japanese] must be adopted holding ever in view the fact that this is a race question, and that race questions stand by themselves. I did not clearly see this at the outset; but for nearly three years I have seen it and thruout my treatment of the question have shaped my course accordingly." As such, he continued, "the one important point is that the Japanese should, as a race, be excluded from becoming *permanent inhabitants of our territory* [author's italics], they in return excluding us from becoming permanent inhabitants of their territory" (Roosevelt 1952, 6:1503).

To do otherwise at the present time and to permit "racial intermingling," he concluded, would be to court "disaster:" "in the present stages of social advancement of the two people, whatever may be the case in the future, it is not only undesirable but impossible that there should be racial intermingling, and the effort is sure to bring disaster" (Roosevelt 1952, 6:1503). This ban on permanent settlement, he insisted, should even apply to non-laboring classes of Japanese, though he would continue to allow them to visit this country.

"Let the Japanese and American visit one another's countries with entire freedom as tourists, scholars, professors, sojourners for study or pleasure for purposes of international business; but keep out laborers, including agricultural laborers, men who want to take up farms, men who want to go into the small trades or even in the professions where the work is of a noninternational character: that is, keep out of Japan those Americans who wish to settle and become part of the resident working population, and keep out of America those Japanese who wish to adopt a similar attitude."   (Roosevelt 1952, 6:1503)

To achieve this objective, he continued, the American government must continue to avoid giving offense to the Japanese.

"[As] a people [they are] very sensitive and at the same time very self-confident in their warlike strength.... In such circumstances the wise policy is to insist on keeping out Japanese immigration; but at the same time to behave with scrupulous courtesy to Japan as a nation and to the Japanese who are here; and also to continue to build up and maintain at the highest point of efficiency our navy. This three-fold policy is precisely the policy of the administration for the past two years."   (Roosevelt 1952, 6:1503)

He then expressed his keen anger at the California legislature whose bills were threatening to disrupt the successful workings of this policy, particularly as expressed in the Gentlemen's Agreement.

"These laws do not prevent the Japanese from coming in, and so they totally fail in accomplishing anything that goes to the root of the difficulty; but they irritate profoundly all the Japanese who are here, and they give great offense in Japan itself. In other words, they accomplish nothing whatever of the object really desirable to attain, and at the same time they jeopardize the public peace. My object is to show the maximum efficiency in doing away with the race problem by excluding immigration, and at the same time cause the minimum of disturbance in the relations between the United States and Japan. These people of whom I complain combine the minimum of efficiency as regards attaining their object and the maximum of insult."   (Roosevelt 1952, 6:1504)

In the final analysis, then, Roosevelt did not disagree with the exclusionist goals of the California legislature, merely with the way it was seeking to achieve them. For he had come to share with them the conviction that the Japanese could never become part of the people of the American society and would always remain a separate, racially unassimilable, quasi-society, oriented toward their mother country and an ever-present threat to the people of the United States. But he also knew that exclusion of the Japanese could not be accomplished by the harsh and clumsy actions of a California legislature but only by a policy of layered delicacy and tact such as his. As can be seen in his final letter to the incoming Secretary of State of the new administration of February 8, he never lost his respect for the military prowess of Japan or took lightly its quest for equality for its nationals in western countries.

> "She [Japan] is a most formidable military power. Her people have peculiar fighting capacity. They are proud, very warlike, very sensitive, and are influenced by two contradictory feelings, namely, a great self-confidence, both ferocious and conceited, due to their victory over the mighty empire of Russia; and a great touchiness because they would like to be considered as on a full equality with, as one of the brotherhood of, Occidental nations, and have been bitterly humiliated to find that even their allies, the English, and their friends, the Americans, won't admit them to association and citizenship, as they admit the least advanced or most decadent European peoples."
>
> (Roosevelt 1952, 6:1511)

THE ANTI-ALIEN LAND ACT OF 1913

Even after Roosevelt left office, the anti-Japanese forces were unable to mount an effective legislative campaign in California for the next four years, despite abortive efforts to do so. They were kept at bay in part by pressure from President Taft similar to that exerted by Roosevelt earlier as he sought to negotiate the Treaty of 1911. In addition, they were forced to contend with the potent opposition of the Panama Pacific International Exposition Company, which wanted to delay any anti-Japanese legislation until after the exposition was held in 1915 in San Francisco. The company feared such legislation would alienate Japan, whose participation was deemed a key to the success of the exposition by its sponsors. And finally, the urban labor groups, centered particularly in San Francisco, that had been the backbone of the anti-Japanese movement had lost some of their drive as the Japanese threat became defined increasingly as rural in nature. (Although proportionately more Japanese lived in rural than in urban areas in 1900 than in 1910, 67 percent to 55 percent, their numbers had tripled over the decade. As a result, they were even more visible in 1910 than in 1900, particularly since they concentrated in relatively few countries.)

By 1912, the anti-Japanese forces had regrouped, primarily in the counties of Japanese concentration. Their voice found full expression in the platform of the Democratic party of California. The state central committee also distributed widely a card which had printed on one side the statement solicited from Woodrow Wilson during the presidential primary of that year: "'In the matter of Chinese and Japanese coolie immigration I stand for the national policy of exclusion. The whole question is one of assimilation of diverse races. We cannot make a homogeneous population out of a people who do not blend with the

Caucasian race'" (Hichborn 1913:fn.213). On the other side was printed a list of the "pro-Japanese actions" taken by President Roosevelt including his recommendation to the 59th Congress that "'an act be passed specifically providing for the naturalization of Japanese who come here intending to become American citizens'" (Hichborn 1913:214).

Though the Democratic party failed in its bid to capture the governor's seat and to win the state for Wilson in the presidential election, it showed considerable strength in both race and, what is more, Wilson's victory gave it a national presence. Accordingly, the stage was set for still another assault by the anti-Japanese forces on the state legislature.

Sensing this, the exposition officials launched an intense campaign to head off the introduction of anti-Japanese bills into the legislative hopper. They caucused with legislators from each party and pleaded for a delay in anti-Japanese legislation until the exposition was over. Their efforts, however, proved of little consequence. They had to face the fact that at the very beginning of the session a number of bills were introduced from both Democrats and Republicans and that by the end of the session over thirty measures had been placed in the legislative hopper. Many of these were directed against ownership of land by aliens. Some confined the proscription to Asiatic aliens alone; others extended the proscription to "all aliens, Europeans as well as Asiatic" (Hichborn 1913:221).

The alien land measures were referred to the judiciary committees of the respective houses. At the final hearing on these bills held jointly by the two committees, the directors of the exposition made a strong and – according to Hichborn – a "Madison Avenue-like" appeal for delay, but they were no match for the small farmers who pleaded for societal and economic survival against Japanese competition and for racial purity. In the words of one such farmer,

"'All about us the Asiatics are gaining a foothold. They are setting up Asiatic standards. From whole communities the whites are moving out. *Already the blood is intermingling. At present the problem is comparatively easy and can be snuffed out. But let it go even a little longer and it cannot be snuffed out.*

We farmers are interested in the Exposition. We will do all that we can for it. But there is one thing that we cannot and will not do for it. We will not jeopardize our race'"   (Hichborn 1913:231)

Such testimony effectively neutralized the directors' pleas, and the hearings (according to Hichborn who does little to conceal his bias in favor of the alien land measure) proved to be "the exposition's last stand" (Hichborn 1913:227).

Within days each committee reported favorably on an anti-alien measure distilled from the morass of bills each had received earlier. The assembly's version as originally proposed by the subcommittee of its judiciary committee was clearly intended to apply to all aliens.

> "It [the bill] did not discriminate against the Japanese or other Asiatics except as they were stockholders in corporations. It included all aliens within its provisions. Under it, no alien could acquire land and hold it for a longer period than one year. The measure contained a leasing clause, however, permitting of aliens holding real property under lease for a period not to exceed five years."
>
> (Hichborn 1913:236–37)

In the deliberations of the judiciary committee, however, a discriminatory section was added which barred ownership of land to corporations owned by aliens, now defined as those "who are ineligible to become citizens of the United States."

> "*Section 8 – Every corporation, the majority of the issued capital stock of which is owned by aliens who are ineligible to become citizens of the United States under the naturalization laws thereof, shall be considered an alien within the meaning of this act.*'"
>
> (Hichborn 1913:237)

Despite efforts to amend it, this modified version passed the assembly by the overwhelming vote of 60 to 15 on April 15.

The senate's version as initially worked out by the subcommittee of its judiciary committee retained a consistent definition of the term alien throughout all of its sections. Unlike the house version it did not restrict the term in its section on corporations only to those ineligible for citizenship. In sum, "the Senate bill applied to all aliens alike, individuals as well as corporations controlled by aliens, Europeans as well as Asiatics" (Hichborn 1913:242).

Once the provisions of the bill became known, powerful opposition developed against its section on corporations from chambers of commerce and from European and Canadian financial and industrial interests. As a result, the Senate amended the section so that, like the assembly's version, it applied to Asiatics only. Both bills had become alike in their discriminatory character. Initially inclined to support the original senate version, President Wilson now felt obliged under pressure from the Japanese government to protest the passage of these bills. In a telegram to Governor Johnson on April 22, a day after the Senate passed its revised version, he stressed as did Roosevelt before him the difficulties and embarrassment such legislation would cause the federal government in its dealings with Japan.

> "'I speak upon the assumption, which I am sure is well founded, that the People of California do not desire their representatives – and that their representatives do not wish or intend – in any circumstances to embarrass the Government of

the United States in its dealings with a nation with whom it has most earnestly and cordially sought to maintain relations of genuine friendship and good will, and that least of all do they desire to do anything that might impair treaty obligations or cast a doubt upon the honor and good faith of the nation and its government.

I, therefore, appeal with the utmost confidence to The People, the governor, and the Legislature of California to act in the matter now under consideration in a manner that cannot from any point of view be fairly challenged or called in question.'" (Hichborn 1913:fn.246)

In his reply the governor denied any intention upon his or any state official's part to embarrass the federal government. In fact, he claimed, they had explicitly sought to stay within the framework of any treaty obligation.

"'I think I may assure you that it is the desire of the majority of the members of the Legislature to do nothing in the matter of alien land bills that shall be embarrassing to our own Government or offensive to any other. It is the design of these legislators specifically to provide in any act that nothing therein shall be construed as affecting or impairing any rights secured by treaty although from the legal standpoint, this is deemed unnecessary.'" (Hichborn 1913:fn.247)

Confused by the governor's reply and the turn of events in the state senate, the President expressed this uncertainty in wires to the governor and to each house of the legislature and requested that the Secretary of State be allowed to meet with them "'for the purpose of counseling with the members of the Legislature and cooperating with them in the framing of a law which would meet the views of the people of the State and yet leave untouched the international obligations of the United States'" (Hichborn 1913:fn.248–49).

Whereas four years earlier the legislature had vociferously balked at "interference" from Washington, now it agreed to the request without objection though it let the President know in no uncertain terms that it was fully committed to "'the right of the Legislature of the State of California to legislate on the subject of land ownership within the State'" (Hichborn 1913:fn.249). In his reply the governor also agreed to the consultation, but he protested in his message to the President "'against the discrimination to which California has been subjected in the assumption that action which has been accepted without demur when taken by other states and by the nation is offensive if even discussed by California'" (Hichborn 1913:fn.252). As examples, he cited Washington and Arizona, which had laws forbidding ownership of lands to aliens ineligible to become American citizens. Further, he argued, "the United States has determined who are eligible to citizenship. The nation has solemnly decreed that certain races, among whom are the Japanese, are not eligible to citizenship. The line has been drawn not by California, but by the United States" (Hichborn 1913:fn.253).

And yet, he continued, because Japan had taken exception to what the California legislature was discussing,

> "'forthwith it is demanded that we cease even discussion, and upon us, if we do not cease calm and dispassionate consideration of that which is desired by a great portion of our people, and which we have the legal and moral right to do, is placed the odium of bringing possible financial disaster and even worse upon our nation: What a situation for a greater State and a great people!...
>
> [He promised, however, that] this State will not willingly do anything to which there could be just objections, national or international.... [But] it does resist being singled out on matters which pass unprotested when they happen elsewhere.'"
>
> (Hichborn 1913:fn.254)

Upon his arrival in California, Secretary of State Bryan went almost immediately into an executive session with members of both legislatures and the governor. He conveyed the President's wishes that action should be delayed. But if that were not possible, he asked that "'whatever the form of the law that no words be used intended to draw a distinction between those eligible to citizenship and those ineligible'" (Hichborn 1913:256). According to the governor the Secretary said little else, for in a subsequent letter to Theodore Roosevelt, the governor commented sarcastically:

> "'After sitting all day, Mr. Bryan presented absolutely nothing that could not have been transmitted within the limits of a night letter, without using all of the allotted words, and at the conclusion of the first consultation, there was a feeling among the legislators not only of disappointment, but that they had been decoyed more or less into a postponement without any real reasons, and that their time in consultation and conference had simply been frittered away.'"
>
> (Daniels 1970:114)

Despite a week of intensive lobbying, the Secretary failed to make much headway. However, he did leave the legislature with the impression that greater care was needed in the writing of a land law that would skirt some of the more obvious points of embarrassment for the federal government in its relations with Japan.

While Bryan was still in California, another version of a land measure began circulating among the legislators which seemed to anticipate some of his objections. Originally conceived by Francis J. Heney, a state senator, and subsequently redrafted by the state's attorney general, U.S. Webb, the measure skillfully avoided any semblance of conflict with treaty obligations of the United States toward Japan. In fact, Section 2 specifically stipulated that aliens not included in

Section 1, namely those ineligible to citizenship under the laws of the United States "may acquire, possess, enjoy and transfer real property, or any interest therein, in this state, in the manner and to the extent and for the purposes prescribed by any treaty now existing between the Government of the United States and the nation or country of which such alien is a citizen or subject and not otherwise" (US Foreign Relations 1913:627).

What the authors of the bill had shrewdly perceived was that the Treaty of 1911 between Japan and the United States made explicit reference only to protecting the rights of citizens and subjects of each country "to own or lease and occupy houses, manufactories, warehouses and shops,... to lease land for residential and commercial purposes" (Article I). The treaty, they insisted, said nothing about owning or leasing land for agricultural purposes. As a result, they contended, their bill could deny Japanese the right to purchase or even to lease agricultural land without violating the terms of the treaty.

All other aliens who were eligible to become citizens under the laws of the United States, they agreed should be permitted to "acquire, possess, enjoy, transmit and inherit real property, or any interest therein, in this state, in the same manner and to the same extent as citizens of the United States, except as otherwise provided by the laws of this state" (US Foreign Relations 1913:627). A similar distinction was made for corporations owned by the two kinds of aliens. In this manner, the authors sought to meet the objections voiced against the corporate provisions of some of the earlier anti-alien land measures.

Once the bill reached the floor of the senate, it encountered the resistance of some Democratic senators who called on the body to defer to the request of the President for delay on passage of any discriminatory legislation that might embarrass his negotiations with Japan. The governor commented in his letter to Roosevelt on the ironic twist of events. The Democrats had lambasted the Republicans and Roosevelt during the 1912 presidential campaign for being "soft" on the Japanese issue and now, with a Democratic president in office, they were counseling delay while the Republicans were pushing ahead with a "hard line" on the issue.

To block the countermove of the Democrats and uncertain of their own strength, the authors of the bill agreed to an amendment that would permit aliens not eligible to citizenship to "lease lands in this state for agricultural purposes for a term not exceeding three years." In short order, proponents of the amended bill decisively defeated efforts of opponents to give priority to a resolution calling for support of the President's request for delay. On May 2 the state senate passed the Heney-Webb bill by the overwhelming majority of 35 to 2.

The assembly responded in kind the next day. It expedited consideration of the bill by labeling it an emergency measure through a 57 to 5 vote. After rebuffing an effort similar to that defeated in the senate which would have deferred action on any land measure, the assembly passed the bill by an even greater margin than did the senate, 72 to 3.

Persuaded by the President to delay signing the bill until its provisions could be communicated to and considered by the Japanese government, Governor Johnson nevertheless rejected the President's request transmitted in a communications by Bryan on May 11 that he defer action entirely on the bill for the present session and "'allow time for diplomatic efforts.'"

> "'The nations affected by the proposed law are friendly nations – nations that have shown themselves willing to cooperate in the establishment of harmonious relations between their people and ours. If a postponement commends itself to your judgment, the President will be pleased to cooperate in a systematic effort to discover and correct any evils that may exist in connection with land ownership by aliens.'" (Hichborn 1913:fn.273)

In his reply, the governor repeated the major arguments propounded by the authors of the bill. He stated unequivocally that the bill violated no treaty rights. In fact, he insisted, it reaffirmed these rights: "'the right of Japanese to own real property for the purposes described [in the Treaty of 1911] is absolute in our State, and we seek to deal only with our agricultural lands. We embody the treaty in our law and we add to it permission to lease our agricultural lands, for the period of three years'" (Hichborn 1913:appendix iv).

There was thus absolutely no merit in the accusation that California had violated a treaty or trespassed on the sovereignty of the federal government.

> "'Where such extraordinary care has been exercised to preserve honor and good faith, in the very words of the contract made by the protesting nation with our own, and to do more by authorizing leases of agricultural lands, it would seem that we ought not to be open to any accusation of violation of treaty rights, or desire to entrench upon that which belongs alone to the National Government, or which might become a matter of international policy.'"
>
> (Hichborn 1913:appendix iv)

The governor then took up the charge that the act was "offensive and discriminatory" and repeated the same argument that he had made earlier in defense of alien land laws generally.

> "'If invidious discriminations ever were made in this regard, the United States made it when the United States declared who were and who were not eligible to citizenship, and when we but follow and depend upon the statutes of the United

States, and their determination as to eligibility to citizenship, we cannot be accused of indulging in invidious discrimination.'"

(Hichborn 1913:appendix iv)

In addition, he reiterated his earlier argument that other states (now three instead of the two he had mentioned before) had enacted laws similar to the California statute, "'without objection or protest. That the protest is now made in respect to California but emphasizes the acuteness of the problem confronting California, and demonstrates that California is differently viewed than other States of the Union, and that if discrimination exists it is discrimination against California" (Hichborn 1913:appendix v).

"'And so,'" he concluded, "'with all respect and courtesy, the State of California feels it its bounden duty to its citizens to do that which the interests of its people demand; that which the conscience of its people approve; that which violates no treaty rights; that which presents no discrimination, and that which can give no just cause for offense '" (Hichborn 1913:appendix v). And with this flourish of rhetoric the governor signed the bill on May 19.

At the time the land laws were being considered in 1913, the Japanese Association and the *Japanese-American Yearbook* estimated that 26,707 acres were owned by Japanese farmers, and another 254,980 acres were leased for a total of 281,687 acres under Japanese control in 1913. In 1910 the total acreage under their control was 194,799, of which they owned 17,035 (Ichihashi 1969:193). Much of this increase over the three years has been attributed by Millis (1915), Ichihashi, and others to the growing fear among Japanese of possible enactment of alien land laws, agitation for which had already begun in the legislature of 1909.

Despite this increase – the size of which Millis* has disputed – the Japanese holdings, whether owned or leased, constituted only a small fraction of the total improved farm land in the state. Under the following subheading: *"There was no Real Problem of Land Ownership by Japanese in California in 1913"* Millis concluded, "The totals of Japanese holdings and values were insignificant. Moreover, in only three counties of the state were as many as twenty farms owned by them, the largest number 31, being found in Fresno. In only three counties did their combined holdings aggregate a thousand acres. In Fresno County they

---

* Millis was primarily responsible for the preparation of the report on the Japanese for the States Immigration Commission of the United States Senate in 1909; his figures for 1912 were generally drawn from the state assessment rolls and were generally lower than those from the Japanese Association. He explained the discrepancy by stating that "it would appear that there were some contracts for purchase where the property had not been transferred and was still assessed in the name of non-Japanese [and therefore would not appear as Japanese on the assessment rolls]. It is in this way, no doubt, that the figures given by Japanese authorities, always somewhat larger than those obtained from the assessment lists, are explained" (Millis 1915:216).

owned 4776 acres, in Tulare County, 1053; in Merced. 1049" (Millis 1915:216).

However, by 1913 the Japanese had become important producers of such items as strawberries, sugar beets, green vegetables, and fruits and nuts on their small holdings on which they practiced intensive farming. Most had started as farm laborers, from which they moved to contract arrangements, then to share cash tenancy, and finally some emerged as owners of land. They were prepared to pay high rental values for the high prices for their land, either as rentals or purchases – a matter which became a sore point in competition with whites – but according to the Immigration Commission study of Japanese farming in 1909, "where their acreage has been added to that productively used in the community it has generally been devoted to growing crops not extensively grown by white farmers" (US Senate Document No. 633 (1911) 61:2:87).

THE RESPONSE OF THE JAPANESE GOVERNMENT: PROTESTS AGAINST RACIAL DISCRIMINATION AND TREATY VIOLATION

As the legislative drama unfolded in California from the opening gavel of the 1913 session, the Japanese government expressed to the American government an ever-increasing concern about the proceedings. Only a few days after President Wilson had taken office in March 1913, the Japanese ambassador had already conveyed to him his government's unhappiness with what was going on in the legislatures of California and of other Pacific states and relayed its urgent request that he do something about it. The President assured the ambassador that he would, within the limits of the constitutional separation of state and federal governments.

As the anti-alien land measures began to take definite shape in April, the Japanese government became even more alarmed and made further vigorous representations through personal meetings of its ambassador with the President and the Secretary of State. As a direct consequence of these representations, the President sent to the governor the various messages that we have already discussed and even had his Secretary of State go out to California to meet with the governor and the legislature.

The passage of the Heney-Webb Act by the California legislature early in May convinced the Japanese government that ever stronger measures were needed. Accordingly, it lodged its first formal protest on the matter with the American government on May 9. In its "urgent and explicit protest," the Japanese government declared that the Heney-Webb act was "essentially unfair and discriminatory" and "prejudicial to the existing rights of Japanese subjects." In addition, the protest continued, the act is "inconsistent with the provisions of the treaty actually in force between Japan and the United States, and is also opposed to the spirit and fundamental principles of amity and good understanding upon which the conventional relations of the two countries depend" (US Foreign Relations 1913:629). The protest then delineated the various ways the act particularly its Article I, violated the Treaty of 1911.

Secretary of State Bryan forwarded the protest to Governor Johnson along with the presidential request of May 11 that Johnson veto the bill to allow more time for diplomatic negotiations to resolve the land issue. In his reply, as we have already seen, the governor rejected the contention that the bill violated any treaty and on May 19 signed the bill.

On the same day, the Secretary of State sent a reply to the Japanese protest of May 9. In it he expressed regret that the Japanese government "should regard this legislation as an indication of unfriendliness toward their people." He then recounted the efforts he and the President had exerted to dissuade the California legislature from such legislation, but "under the constitutional arrangement of the United States we could do no more than that."

> "We feel that the Imperial Government has been misled in its interpretation of the spirit and object of the legislation in question. It is not political. It is not part of any general national policy which would indicate unfriendliness or any purpose inconsistent with the best and most cordial understanding between the two nations. It is wholly economic. It is based upon the particular economic conditions existing in California as interpreted by her own people, who wish to avoid certain conditions of competition in their agricultural activities."
>
> (US Foreign Relations 1913:631)

He rejected the Japanese contention that the California law violated treaty stipulations which protected vested rights of property. In fact, he stated, the opposite was true. The law purported "to respect and preserve all rights under existing treaties. Such is its declared intent" (US Foreign Relations 1913:631). And even if this were not so the constitutional protection of treaty rights provided any alien with a channel of judicial recourse of redress: "in this respect the alien enjoys under our laws a privilege which to one of our own citizens may not be in all cases available, namely, the privilege of suing in the Federal courts" (US Foreign Relations 1913:632).

He concluded the note with the same theme with which he began. The United States treasured friendly relations with the Japanese government, and "there is no reason to feel that its policy in such matters would be embarrassed or interfered with by the legislation of any State of the Union. The economic policy of a single State with regard to a single kind of property cannot turn aside these strong and abiding currents of generous and profitable intercourse and good feeling" (US Foreign Relations 1913:632).

The Japanese government expressed keen disappointment with the Secretary's reply in its own response conveyed by the Japanese ambassador on June 4. In his message the ambassador emphasized that in view of America's sympathetic attitude his government had expected the United States to show a greater willingness to have the issue negotiated between the two countries. Instead, all that was offered as a channel of redress were the courts of the United States. While the individual Japanese would be encouraged to seek judicial relief, "the question at issue is a question between the Government of Japan and that of the United States, as to the true extent and meaning of their existing treaty, and the extent to which the rules and principles of fair and equal treatment may, in comity and good conscience, be invoked in the present case. The wrong complained of is directed against my countrymen as a nation" (US Foreign Relations 1913:634).

In view of these circumstances, "it becomes my duty, under instructions from my Government, to announce to you that the Imperial Government are compelled, much to their regret, to maintain, in its integrity, the protest contained in my previous note on this subject" (US Foreign Relations 1913:634).

Before reaffirming the protest, the ambassador repeated the charges of his earlier note that the California law violated provisions of the treaty and the principle of fair and equal treatment in international relations. In addition, he elaborated in explicit detail a charge that had been only inferentially made in his earlier note: namely, that the law was "unfair and *intentionally racially discriminatory* [author's italics]." This was the only conclusion that his government could come to in view of the fact that

> "the persons prejudicially affected by the enactment complained of are expressly limited to those aliens who are not eligible to citizenship. Considering that Japanese subjects are, as a nation, apparently denied the right to acquire American nationality, that they are the principal sufferers from that enactment, and that the avowed purpose of the law was to deprive my countrymen of the right to acquire and to possess landed property in California."
>
> (US Foreign Relations 1913:633)

At the end of his message he returned to the matter of naturalization. He declared that his government had not raised the issue until now, though

> "the provisions of law, under which it is held that Japanese people are not eligible to American citizenship, are mortifying to the Government and people of Japan, since the racial distinction inferable from those provisions is hurtful to their national susceptibility.... [However,] the question of naturalization ... is a political problem of national and not international concern, [and] so long, therefore, as the distinction referred to was employed in relation to rights of purely political nature the Imperial Government had no occasion to approach

the Government of the United States on the subject. But when that distinction is made use of, as in the present case, for the purpose of depriving Japanese subjects of rights and privileges of a civil nature, which are freely granted in the United States to other aliens, it becomes the duty of the Imperial Government, in the interest of the relations of cordial friendship and good understanding between the two countries, to express frankly their conviction that the racial distinction, which at best is inaccurate and misleading, does not afford a valid basis for the discrimination on the subject of land tenure."

(US Foreign Relations 1913:635)

Before he reached this final conclusion, the ambassador had also taken direct aim at the Secretary of State's claim that economic factors were the sole reason for the California law. He argued that "the number of my countrymen actually affected by the discriminatory legislation complained of is small, and the quantity of landed property actually held by them, both as owners and leaseholders, is very inconsiderable" (US Foreign Relations 1913:634). Further, the Gentlemen's Agreement had even reduced the number of Japanese in the United States. Thus "if the object of the legislation in question was wholly economic, then the conclusion is natural, it seems to the Imperial Government, that the apprehensions upon which the enactment was based were unjustifiable and without sanction of good reason" (US Foreign Relations 1913:634). In short, he was saying in the language of diplomacy that no rational person could take seriously the economic explanation of the Secretary.

A month later the Japanese government submitted an *aide-mémoire* to the Secretary of State which offered detailed support for the ambassador's two notes of May 9 and June 4. One of its major themes was that the United States government had taken in the past a stand similar to that taken by the Japanese government in its dealings with foreign nations, most notably Mexico, Brazil, and Russia; now it was being inconsistent in its dealings with Japan.

Secretary of State Bryan was quite "pained" by the Japanese government's reply to his message of June 4. In another message dated July 16, he told the Japanese ambassador that he was particularly dismayed at the ambassador's government's rejections of his claim that the California law was the product of economic conditions and not racial antagonisms: "I cannot help feeling that in the representations submitted by your excellency the supposition of racial discrimination occupies a position of prominence which it does not deserve and which is not justified by the facts." He conceded, however, that "all differences between human beings – differences in appearance, differences in manner, differences in speech, differences in opinion, differences in nationality, and differences in race – may provoke a certain antagonism." But he insisted that "none of these differences is likely to produce a serious result unless it becomes associated with an interest of a contentious nature such as that of the struggle for existence" (US Foreign Relations 1913:641). He further agreed that these economic cleavages may frequently parallel racial divisions; nevertheless, he insisted that the conflict generated was primarily a function of the economic struggle, the racial division serving merely as a symbolic expression of this struggle.

> "In this economic contest the division no doubt may often take place on racial lines, but it does so not because of racial antagonism but because of the circumstance that the traditions and habits of different races have developed or diminished competitive efficiency. The contest is economic; the racial difference is a mere mark or incident of the economic struggle."
>
> (US Foreign Relations 1913:641)

Because of this inevitable competitive struggle between racial groups, the Secretary continued, they could not unite in a cohesive society and constitute a common People's Domain.

> "All nations recognize this fact, and it is for this reason that each nation is permitted to determine who shall and who shall not be permitted to settle in its dominions and become a part of the body politic, to the end that it may preserve internal peace and avoid the contentions which are so likely to disturb the harmony of international relations."   (US Foreign Relations 1913:641)

In short, the Secretary expressed what can be labeled as a quasi-Marxist theory of plural societies, in which the economic struggle for survival generates conflict and antagonism between racial groups which can neither amalgamate with nor assimilate to each other but must remain separate and distinctive entities, segments, or societies.

Even the Japanese accepted this principle, the Secretary continued, in its ordinance to bar the immigration of Chinese laborers. Furthermore, the United States did not impute "to the Imperial Government in its enforcement of the ordinance a design to make a racial discrimination. On the contrary, the [State] Department assumes that the question with which the Imperial Government were seeking to deal was in its essence economic, and racial only incidentally" (US Foreign Relations 1913:642).

The Secretary then rejected as he had in his earlier note the charge that the California law violated the "letter and spirit" of the treaty. This time, however, he adopted Governor Johnson's argument that the treaty made no reference to the ownership of agricultural land. In addition, the Japanese government seemed to have consented to this omission in the drafting of the treaty because "the Imperial Government desired to avoid treaty engagements concerning the ownership of land by foreigners and to regulate the matter wholly by domestic legislation" (US Foreign Relations 1913:643). In a further exchange of notes, he continued, the Japanese government seemed to have established by 1911 the policy of reciprocity in land ownership "in the sense that citizens of the United States coming from States in which Japan might not be permitted to own land, were to be excluded from the reciprocal privilege in Japan" (US Foreign Relations 1913:643). This he said was "perfectly understood and accepted" (US Foreign Relations 1913:644).

The Secretary concluded his note with a broadening of the channels of redress for any Japanese whose existing property rights might be impaired by the California law. He declared that the federal government "would stand ready to compensate him for any loss which he might be shown to have sustained, or even, in order to avoid any possible allegation of injury, to purchase from his lands at their full market value prior to the enactment of the statute" (US Foreign Relations 1913:644).

Along with his message the Secretary forwarded an *aide-mémoire* to the Japanese government as an answer to the one the latter had sent several weeks earlier. For example, while agreeing that the United States had taken a position in the Mexican dispute similar to that which the Japanese government now took on the California matter, the memorandum stated that it was to no avail. "The [Mexican] law ... remained unaltered" (US Foreign Relations 1913:648).

Still dissatisfied with the replies of the Secretary of State, the Japanese government lodged a third protest on August 26. In its note the major charges were repeated once again. Displeasure was particularly expressed over the invidious distinction created by the act which deprived Japanese of the right to own land but bestowed this right on aliens with whom the United States had no treaty relations.

Once again the Japanese government rejected an economic explanation for the law and insisted "it is clearly indicative of racial antagonism" (US Foreign Relations 1913:651). The note also stated flatly that the reason for the omission of the land ownership clause in the Treaty of 1911 was that "neither contracting party desired at that time such a stipulation, the United States equally with Japan" (US Foreign Relations 1913:652). But, it added,

"the laws of Japan on the subject of alien land tenure are not illiberal, but, in any case, they contain no provisions discriminating, in any manner whatever, against the citizens of the United States. On the contrary, in all that relates to land ownership, as well as in the matter of all other civil rights, the American citizens, without distinctions and without conditions, are accorded in Japan full and complete most favored nation treatment, and there is no desire on the part of the Japanese administration to modify this state of things. What Japan claims is nothing more than fair and equal treatment." (US Foreign Relations 1913:653)

The note then took issue with the Secretary's emphasis on the problems of incorporating alien races into the body politic. The question, it stated, was not immigration of Japanese laborers to the United States. That was being dealt with adequately by the Gentlemen's Agreement, which had resulted in more Japanese laborers leaving the United States than entering it over the past three years. Instead,

> "the present controversy relates exclusively to the question of the treatment of the Japanese subjects who are lawfully in the United States or may hereafter lawfully become resident therein consistently with the existing regulations. So far as such subjects are concerned, the Imperial Government claim for them fair and equal treatment, and are unable either to acquiesce in the unjust and obnoxious discrimination complained of, or to regard the question as closed so long as the existing state of things is permitted to continue."
>
> (US Foreign Relations 1913:653)

Following this note, the United States entered into negotiations with Japan to attempt to write a convention that would resolve the issue. Almost a year later the Japanese foreign minister, who had just taken office, decided that the negotiations were going nowhere. Accordingly, in a note to his ambassador, a copy of which was delivered to the Secretary of State the next day, June 10, he reaffirmed the stand of his predecessor on the issue, but as to the negotiations he declared: "the project as it stands at the present time, instead of composing existing misunderstandings, would, I fear, tend to create new difficulties" (US Foreign Relations 1914:426-27).

Accordingly, he instructed his ambassador to inform the Secretary of State "that the Imperial Government are disinclined to continue the negotiations looking to the conclusion of a convention on the lines of the project which has been under discussion." Instead, the government would prefer resuming "the correspondences which were interrupted by the ineffective negotiations, and that they will now look for an answer to the note which you handed to Mr. Bryan on the 26th August last, hoping that in a renewal of the study of the case a fundamental solution of the question at issue may happily be found" (US Foreign Relations 1914:427). Further, the foreign minister added, the Imperial government would like to make public all the correspondence on the issue.

Two weeks later the Secretary of State informed the ambassador by note that the United States agreed to these requests. He added that he too felt that his own note of July 26th had not been adequately answered because of the advent of secret negotiations on a convention. Now, he continued, that the Imperial government had expressed the desire "to reopen the study of the question and in view of the reservation made in your excellency's note of August 26, 1913," the United States government would like a "detailed answer to my note and *aide-mémoire* of July 16, 1913, in order that this Government may be fully advised as to those contentions and arguments advanced by it, to which the Imperial Government take exception" (US Foreign Relations 1914:428). The Secretary could not refrain from adding a comment of substance in his conclusion to a note otherwise preoccupied with procedural matters. Once again he complained that the Japanese government was laying too much emphasis "on the element of racial discrimination in this discussion. I desire in behalf of my Government to repeat the assurance made in the previous correspondence that the legislation of which your Government complains rests upon an economic basis" (US Foreign Relations 1914:428).

Five months later the Japanese ambassador submitted a detailed reply to the Secretary of State's message of July 16 1913. In it the ambassador repeated the charges of his earlier notes but in a more detailed fashion. Once again he emphasized that the law was a "manifestation of racial antagonism" and "a local policy of discrimination" – and not indicative of a national discriminatory policy nor "the emanation of economic conditions." As evidence of this he quoted President Wilson's telegram to the governor of California on April 22 1913 when the alien land laws were being considered by the California legislature.

He informed the Secretary that the Imperial ordinance mentioned in the note of July 16 was not enacted to keep out Chinese immigrants from Japan but in fact was enacted to extend various rights and privileges to them and "therefore in this respect the law is quite the reverse to that of the California statute, which deprived Japanese subjects of rights hitherto possessed" (US Foreign Relations 1914:430). He then elaborated on the charge that the law violated the letter and spirit of the Treaty of 1911. In so doing he declared that no explicit provision on alien land tenure was made in the Treaty of 1911 because

"such a situation as has been created by the California legislation was never anticipated, and no arrangement was made to meet the exigencies of the case, so that, we are now confronted with a question for which there are no adequate provisions.... [But] although neither nation was then desirous of entering into a categorical treaty stipulation on this subject, the absence of such an agreement was certainly not intended to accord to either party an opportunity to enact laws, the effect of which would be incompatible with the aim and design of the treaty itself, Japan entirely relying in this respect upon the justice and impartiality of the United States."   (US Foreign Relations 1914:431)

Once again, as in his earlier notes, he mentioned the question of naturalization, which he conceded that by itself "should no doubt be considered as a political problem which concerns each individual nation, but when, as in the present case, the question is employed as a means of enforcing a discriminatory measure practically directed against one particular nation it must necessarily assume an international aspect" (US Foreign Relations 1914:431).

After rebutting several other points made in the Secretary's communication of July 16, he summarized his government's position in the following manner:

"It is a matter of great regret to the Imperial Government that they are compelled to own their sense of disappointment to find in the communications so far received from the United States Government, little that appears to answer in a fundamental manner to the main complaint of the Imperial Government, so as to shake their original convictions which dictated the present protest, namely, that the new California statute is invidiously discriminatory against the Japanese nation, that it is contrary to the letter as well as spirit of the existing treaty, and that it is incompatible with the sentiment of amity and friendship which always characterized the intercourse between our two nations. The question at issue, although of a serious and far reaching nature, is not, in its essential aspect, of an intricate character, and the Imperial Government are satisfied that the case has been fully set forth in their notes to the United States Government, and they deem it unnecessary to elaborate their representations to a greater extent than they have already urged."   (US Foreign Relations 1914:433)

He then stated that his government appreciated the offer of the American government to compensate any Japanese subject "whose property rights might have been impaired by the operation of the statute" and to tender its "good office to secure the prompt and efficacious determination of his suit" should he initiate litigation in the courts of the United States.

"Unfortunately, however, the present question is one which affects the people of Japan as a nation, so that, quite independently of the facilities and privileges which individual members of the Japanese community in California may enjoy, they must naturally look to the central administration authorities of the two governments for the adjustment of the question, as it concerns them in its international aspect. The Imperial Government are compelled to consider that the courses suggested by the United States Government would neither be adequate nor meet the exigencies of a case such as the present one, and they deem it their duty once again to assert their view that in questions of this nature the diplomatic channel is the only proper course through which a satisfactory solution of the controversy may fitly be attained."
                    (US Foreign Relations 1914:433–34)

His government, he concluded, terminated negotiations for a convention because it was convinced "that the project, as it then stood, would compose in no wise the existing misunderstandings.... It is, therefore, the earnest hope of the Imperial Government that a response to this note may be forthcoming in which the United States Government will express their concurrence with the views herein contained and will advocate a course which may have the effect of relieving the difficulties. Meanwhile the Imperial Government deem it to be a matter of grave importance that no efforts on their part as well as that of the United States Government should be spared to meet the question with entire rectitude, and to prevent any possible future complications which might arise and result in perplexing the situation and aggravating the susceptibilities of the two nations."

(US Foreign Relations 1914:434)

The note by the Japanese government was never answered by the state department. It became "the last formal communication between the two Governments on the Alien Land Law adopted in California in 1913" (US Foreign Relations 1921 2:332).

RENEWAL OF ANTI-JAPANESE AGITATION AND THE STATE CONTROL BOARD REPORT

During the next five years agitation for further legislative action against the Japanese subsided in California. The outbreak of World War I created a demand for farm produce that brought prosperity to virtually all segments of the agricultural sector, white and Japanese alike. The war also brought Japan and America together as allies on the same side in the war. In addition, Japan's decision to participate in the Panama-Pacific Exposition in San Francisco, despite the earlier provocative action by the California legislature, helped to ease even more the tension in California. "This act of good-will was properly appreciated by thoughtful Californians, many of whom had opposed the Alien Land Law" (Treat 1928:281). What made this act stand out as much as it did was the fact that "the World War had caused most of the European belligerents to abandon their exhibits, so that of Japan was the most elaborate national contribution to the exposition" (Treat 1928:280-81).

By the end of the war, however, anti-Japanese agitation began to resurface. In 1919 alien land bills were once again introduced into the legislature. But in a repeat of past history, the Secretary of State again intervened. This time he cabled the legislature to defer action, lest such action jeopardize the delicate negotiations then underway at the Peace Conference in Versailles in which Japan and the United States were participating.

Acting more like it did in 1909 and 1911 than in 1913, "California," in the words of Governor Stephens, "patriotically acceded for the good of the whole country" (California State Board of Control 1922:12), but the legislature passed a resolution which instructed the State Board of Control "to make a thorough investigation and prepare an accurate, detailed and comprehensive report" upon "the leasing of land in the state to persons ineligible to citizenship" (California State Board of Control 1922:19).

In June 1920 the State Board issued its report which was later revised and dated January 1922. Although the report presumably dealt with the Chinese and Hindus as well as the Japanese, it concentrated primarily on the latter, who possessed 84 percent of all the acres owned by the three and 72 percent of all the acres under lease or crop contract. The total value of the crop raised by the Japanese grew at an even faster rate than did total acreage over the ten-year period; it increased 976.8 percent.

Data for the two years were derived by the State Board from two different sources: the State Bureau of Labor Statistics for the 1909 figure and the Japanese Agricultural Association of California for the 1919 totals. This provoked serious objections from Kiichi Kanzaki, general secretary of the Japanese Association of America. He took particular aim at the figure used for 1909. In a pamphlet published in 1921, he argued that "ten years ago there was no authentic official estimate of farms operated by Japanese. Figures of the Bureau of Labor Statistics, upon which the calculation of the Board of Control is based, are not accurate" (Kanzaki 1921:74). Accordingly he proposed using the figure for 1909 from a Japanese source similar to the one used by the board for its figure for 1919. This figure was almost two and a half times larger, 195,948 to 83,253. Using this figure as a base, Kanzaki continued, "the increase in the past ten years is 117 percent instead of the Board's 412 percent" (Kanzaki 1921:75).

He offered no comparable revision of the board's estimate of percentage increase in total value of crops raised by the Japanese, but he did comment that "out of the total of $67,145,000, representing the value of Japanese production [for 1919], 35 percent goes to landowners as rents, 45 percent to labor in the form of wages, leaving only 20 percent to Japanese tenants or contractors" (Kanzaki 1921:75).

What Kanzaki was saying was that most of the crop produced by the Japanese was being produced under some leasing or contracting arrangement in which Japanese shared only part of the return. This was reflected in the figures that the State Board reported for 1919. The Japanese owned only 74,769 of the 458,056 acres they cultivated. What Kanzaki, and oddly the State Board, failed to mention is that, according to data from Japanese sources, ownership had more than doubled from 1913 to 1919. It had increased from 10 percent of all land cultivated by Japanese in the earlier period to 16 percent in the latter.

Even as the Japanese were expanding their control of land, the State Board declared they were also obtaining strangleholds on the production of certain crops. Citing data from the Japanese Agricultural Association of California, the board asserted that the Japanese produced 80 to 90 percent of all tomatoes, onions, cantaloupes, asparagus, berries, and celery grown in California in 1917. In a rebuttal, included as an appendix in the board report, Chiba, managing director of the Japanese Agricultural Association of California, explained that Japanese dominance in the production of these crops stemmed from the fact they "all require a stooping posture, great manual dexterity and painstaking methods of work which other laborers with long legs unsuitable for stooping can not endure. Not only this, but this is a kind of farming which Americans and immigrants from Europe dislike to follow. Hence it is perfectly clear that if the Japanese had nothing to do with this kind of farming the output of such products in California would be reduced more than half" (California State Board of Control 1922:243). He then described the intolerable conditions of heat and dust under which cantaloupes were grown.

For the State Board, however, the monopolization of certain crops was but further evidence of the fact that the Alien Land Law of 1913 had failed to achieve its purpose of restricting Japanese access to and control of agricultural lands. It attributed the marked increase in ownership to subterfuges that the Japanese had devised with the connivance of certain California attorneys to circumvent the intent of the law. As an example it cited the fact that first-generation Japanese whose ineligibility for citizenship prevented them, under the law, from purchasing land, bought land in the name of their American-born children who could not be deprived of the right of purchase. However, since few of these children were of legal age, a guardian or trustee tended to be appointed – frequently the ineligible alien parent himself – to act on behalf of the child.

An even more popular form of evasion, according to the State Board, was the formation of corporations which were required by law to have a majority of their stock held by American citizens. "To overcome this provision, 51 percent of stock is issued to an American citizen, usually the attorney for the corporation or some employee in his office, who acts as trustee for the real owner of the stock who may be an ineligible alien or a minor child, American born, of alien parents" (California State Board of Control 1922:69).

The board lamented, "It is a source of deep regret that there are attorneys in the state who despite their oath to support the constitution and the laws of this state, nevertheless sell their legal talent in aiding this breach of the spirit and purpose of the Alien Land Law" (California State Board of Control 1922:69).

The board also expressed its concern over the even greater growth of leasing arrangements which under the 1913 law were legal for periods of three years. These arrangements, according to the board, were even more responsible than increased ownership of land in the growing monopolization by the Japanese of the production of certain crops. What gave the Japanese an edge in these arrangements were credit practices that discriminated in their favor.

The board did not confine its remarks to the working of the Alien Land Law. It also reopened the question of the legality of the marital status of picture brides and leveled an attack against the Gentlemen's Agreement, which it claimed had failed to stem the influx of Japanese to this country. "The real ground for complaint would seem to rest rather on what appears to have been a collapse of American diplomacy in consenting to the adoption of the Gentlemen's Agreement, and in the subsequent failure of the United States immigration officials to make full use of even the few safeguards that did exist under the Gentlemen's Agreement" (California State Board of Control 1922:175).

THE ALIEN LAND LAWS OF 1920 AND 1923

Even before the State Board formally submitted its report to the governor in June, an initiative petition was circulating in California to remedy the "defects" of the 1913 law. It won a place on the November ballot and was approved by the margin of 668,483 to 222,086. As put into effect in December 1920, the measure eliminated the leasing provision of the 1913 law. It also banned the appointment of an alien who was ineligible for citizenship as guardian of the estate of an American-born minor that consisted of property which such alien was "inhibited from acquiring, possessing, enjoying or transferring by reasons of the provisions of this act" (Section 4). In addition, the measure set up strict reporting procedures for "trustees" of property belonging to an alien ineligible for citizenship or his minor children "if the property is of such a character that such alien is inhibited from acquiring, possessing, enjoying, or transferring it" (Section 5) (California State Board of Control 1922:63). It also forbade the holding or transfer of real property by trustees or guardians of such property "if the conveyance [of the property] is made with intent to prevent, evade or avoid escheat [to the state]" (Section 9) (California State Board of Control 1922:65).

These restrictions applied to any individual and to any company, association, or corporation "if the memberships or shares of stock therein held by aliens [ineligible for citizenship]..., together with the memberships or shares of stock held by others but paid for or agreed or understood to be paid for by such aliens, would amount to a majority of the membership or the issued capital stock of such company, association or corporation" (Section 9b) (California State Board of Control 1922:65). Violators of the law were not only threatened with the escheat proceedings of the 1913 act, in which their property would revert to the state, but also with imprisonment of up to two years and a fine not exceeding $5000.

Two years later the law was further amended to curtail even more any abiding tie between the Japanese who engaged in farming and the land they cultivated. Virtually any conceivable kind of connection between the Japanese and the land (no longer called agricultural land as in the 1920 law but labeled real property) was delineated and declared illegal. This was most clearly evident in the revised version of Section 7 (Section 11 in the 1923 act): "Nothing in this act shall be construed as a limitation upon the power of the state to enact laws with respect to the acquisition, *possession, enjoyment, use, cultivation, occupation, transferring, transmitting, or inheriting*" (this language was "holding or disposal" in the 1920 law) "by aliens of real property in this state" (Mears 1928:483). In order to make this intent even more manifest, the revised 1923 law spelled out in Section 8 that the restrictions against leasing arrangements or other interest in real property of the 1920 law included "*cropping contracts which are hereby declared to constitute an interest in real property ...*" (Mears 1982:481).

The amended act of 1923 sought to bring to fruition what had only been intimated in the act of 1913. Then the goal was to restrict any further purchase of land by Japanese. Once that was realized with the enactment of the law of 1920, the goal shifted to severing any vestigial tie to the land of other Japanese, whether through leasing or cropping agreements.

Almost immediately after the passage of the two laws, total acreage under Japanese control declined significantly from the high of 458,056 in 1920 to 304,966 in 1925 – a decrease of a third. Ownership of land declined even more over the five-year period – a drop of 44 percent; however, the percentage it comprised of all forms of land tenure remained fairly constant over these years – 16 percent in 1920 and 14 percent in 1925. The most dramatic drop occurred in leasing; it declined 60 percent during the five-year period. Sharing and cropping agreements, however, remained relatively constant during the period – the law of 1923 having as yet not worked out its full effects.

By the mid-1920s then, Japanese aliens who engaged in farming but did not own their land faced a serious dilemma in California. They could stay and become part of an agricultural proletariat which sold its labor services to Japanese and American farmers, or they could migrate to an urban area in California, or they could take up stakes entirely and leave California for Japan or elsewhere.

Relatively few chose the last alternative in as much as the total number of first-generation Japanese declined by less than 3000 from 1920 to 1930 (a figure that would be even smaller if those who died – an unknown number – were subtracted from it). A much larger number chose the second alternative. As a result, the percentage of foreign-born Japanese in rural areas of California declined from 53 percent in 1920 to 42 percent in 1930. The figure remained constant for 1940. The largest number, though, decided to stay where they were. They became what almost all were at the beginning: farm laborers for hire.

THE IDEOLOGICAL JUSTIFICATION FOR THE LAND LAWS

In spearheading the drive to promote alien land legislation, once the State Board's report was in, Governor Stephens of California did not play up the theme of economic competition or mute the thesis of racial differences as had his predecessors and Secretary of State Bryan. Instead, as articulated in his letter of June 19 1920 to Secretary of State Colby, which served as the introduction to the State Board's report, he reversed priorities and said that at the very heart of the matter was the unbridgeable biological and cultural gulf between the yellow and white races that made it impossible for them to assimilate and to become part of a homogeneous and consensual society and People's Domain. This, he proclaimed, had always been true: "history does not show any material fusion of either blood or ideas between these peoples [of the Orient and Occident]," or any instance where "blood fusion of the Occident and the Orient has ... ever successfully taken place" (California State Board of Control 1922:10).

Mindful however of the sensibilities and strength of the Japanese nation, the governor hastened to insist that the unbridgeable difference between races did not at all imply any innate racial superiority of one over the other.

"We [white Californians] assume no arrogant superiority of race or culture over them [the Japanese people]. Their art, their literature, their philosophy, and, in recent years, their scientific attainments have gained for them a respect from the white peoples in which we, who know them so well, fully share. We have learned to admire the brilliancy of their art and the genius that these people display. We respect that deep philosophy which flows so placidly out of that wonderful past of theirs and which has come down through ages that antedate our Christian era. We join with the entire civilized world in our admiration of the tremendous strides which the Japanese nation itself has made in the last two generations unparalleled as its career is in the history of nations. We respect the right of the Japanese to their true development and to the attainment of their destiny."   (California State Board of Control 1922:9)

However, in coming to California in increasing numbers, the governor continued, the Japanese had clustered together in unassimilable "colonies" on agricultural lands which frequently exceeded in size the surrounding white population.

"The Japanese, with his strong social race instinct, acquires his piece of land and, within an incredibly short period of time, large adjoining holdings are occupied by people of his own race. The result is that in many portions of our state we have large colonies of Japanese, the population in many places even exceeding the white population."   (California State Board of Control 1922:8)

In addition, he declared, the Japanese had also proved to be formidable and "crushing" competitors to the white rural populations, not so much because they worked for lower wages but because they worked longer hours and their families joined them in the field. As a result, they had expanded their land holdings and had gained control over the production of certain essential food products. They had come to pose a serious threat to the stability and survival of white California, and

> "California views with alarm the rapid growth of these people within the last decade in population as well as in land control, and foresees in the not distant future the gravest menace of serious conflict if this development is not immediately and effectively checked. Without disparaging these people of just sensibilities, we cannot look for intermarriage or that social interrelationship which must exist between the citizenry of a contented community....
>   The people of California are determined to repress a developing Japanese community within our midst. They are determined to exhaust every power in their keeping to maintain this state for its own people. This determination is based fundamentally upon the ethnological impossibility of assimilating the Japanese people and the consequential alternative of increasing a population whose very race isolation must be fraught with the gravest consequences."
>   (California State Board of Control 1922:9–10)

With white California determined to erect and to maintain "social and race barriers" against the Japanese, the governor expressed his fear over what the Japanese might do in response.

> "The Japanese, be it said to their credit, are not of servile or docile stock. Proud of their traditions and history, exultant as they justly are at the extraordinary career of their country, they brook no suggestion of any dominant or superior race. Virile, progressive and aggressive, they have all the race consciousness which is inseparable from race quality."
>   (California State Board of Control 1922:17)

In this, he was not merely referring to the resentments Japanese in America would express but also the response of the Japanese government and nation, for whose military prowess he had great respect. But, he nevertheless felt hopeful that, if such a showdown took place, America would not back down:

> "In extending to them [the Japanese] the just credit which is theirs, the thought does not occur to our people that because the Japanese come from a puissant nation, whose achievements on the field have brought it renown, that therefore

our attitude would be moulded by pusillanimity or temporary expediency. We have faith in the willingness and power of our common country to protect its every part from foreign danger."   (California State Board of Control 1922:13)

He was confident, however, that such a showdown would not have to take place, because the Japanese government would finally realize the validity of his theory of plural societies: "the inherent desire of every race and type of people to preserve itself" in its own distinctive political society. "We wish to impress most earnestly upon them [the Japanese government] the entire absence of every feeling that can betoken ill-will or be in the slightest degree disparaging" (California State Board of Control 1922:13). In fact, he contended, if each race was behind the boundaries of its own distinctive society, then both would profit greatly by it. For, with the Pacific Ocean becoming "one of the most important highways of commerce on this earth [a]mity and concord and that interchange of material goods as well as ideas, which such facilities offer, will inevitably take place to the benefit of both" (California State Board of Control 1922:10).

> "The people of California only desire to retain the commonwealth of California for its own people; they recognize the impossibility of that peace-producing assimilability which comes only when races are so closely akin that intermarriage within a generation or two obliterates original lines. The thought of such a relationship is impossible to the people of California, just as the thought of intermarriage of whites and blacks would be impossible to the minds of the leaders of both races in the southern states; just as the intermarriage of any immigrant African would not be considered by the people of the Eastern States."   (California State Board of Control 1922:15)

However, he continued, California could do little by itself to bring this state of affairs about. "The [initiative] measure, if adopted, will exhaust the State's power in dealing with this great race problem. The bill, however, does not and will not, because the State legally cannot, prevent Japanese control of our soil nor can it stop further immigration" (California State Board of Control 1922:13).

As a result, he concluded, the federal government must undertake negotiations with Japan for a basic change in the Gentlemen's Agreement; however,

> "the full solution of this question cannot be had short of an exclusion act passed by Congress.... The exclusion act should, in my opinion, provide for the full exclusion of all Japanese, saving certain selected classes; it should further provide for the registration of all Japanese lawfully within the United States at the time that the act is passed; and further provide that the burden should be

upon every Japanese within this country of proving his right to be here by the production of a certificate of registration. In this manner only do I believe that completely effective remedies can be found."

(California State Board of Control 1922:14)

THE UNITED STATES SUPREME COURT AND THE LEGITIMATION OF THE ALIEN LAND LAWS

Passage of the 1913 anti-alien land act brought forth litigation which the courts not infrequently decided in favor of the Japanese. None of the litigation, however, provided a serious challenge to the constitutionality of the law or reached the level of the United States Supreme Court. Instead it primarily reflected efforts of the state attorney general to escheat property on the grounds that the Japanese alien had circumvented the intent of the law by transferring the property to his American-born children.

The court generally took a jaundiced view of this position declaring, as for example in the Harada case argued in the California Superior Court, that

"the actions of Harada were precisely what the actions of an American-born father would have been had the latter wished to make a gift to his minor children. He would have paid the purchase money, he would have provided for the improvements, he would have attended to the negotiations and would have taken care of the papers. It can be confidently stated, that the children of American parents could not have their title attacked under such circumstances on the theory of a trust resulting in favor of the parent, where such parent had repeatedly under the solemn obligations of an oath, disclaimed any interest in the property, but had reiterated that it was a gift to his children. If this is true, such a theory can not obtain here, as the political rights of American citizens are the same no matter what their parentage."

(Japan Consulate General of San Francisco 1925 II:733–34)

Even the efforts to restrict the rights of Japanese aliens to guardianship of their children in the act of 1920 proved vulnerable to judicial decision on the state level. Thus in the Yano Guardianship case, the California Superior Court declared,

"it needs no argument to demonstrate the proposition that a law which gives to one person the right or privilege of becoming the guardian of his child and withholds it from another, both being alike competent in all respects, is not equal as between the two persons. The person from whom it is withheld is not in such a case accorded the protection of equal laws. In this respect the initiative act of 1920 is clearly a violation by this state of the guarantee contained in the

Fourteenth Amendment, that no state shall deny to any person the equal protection of its laws."

(Japan Consulate General of San Francisco 1925 II:546-47)

Subsequent decisions in California courts frequently circumvented this opinion by attacking the initial transfer of property from parent to child as fraudulent, thereby making moot the appointment of the parent as guardian. In addition, the Supreme Court of the State of Washington, in a decision that came after several United States Supreme Court opinions were handed down, took an exactly opposite position from that of the California court and upheld the state legislature's ban on guardianship for alien Japanese. It branded the California decision as being too academic; its own, it said, took practical considerations into account.

By early 1923 four anti-alien land cases had reached the United States Supreme Court and on November 12, decisions were handed down on two cases. The first, Terrace v. Thompson, dealt with a Washington state law that forbade aliens from owning and leasing land who had not declared their intention to become citizens, despite being eligible, or who could not declare their intention because they were ineligible. The second case, Porterfield v. Webb, dealt with the California land law of 1920 that banned aliens who were not eligible for citizenship from leasing or owning land; aliens, eligible for such citizenship, escaped the ban, whether or not they had declared their intention.

In the Terrace case, Justice Butler, in the opinion for the Court, declared that "the State has wide discretion in determining its own public policy and what measures are necessary for its own protection and properly to promote the safety, peace and good order of its people." Accordingly, the state also, "in the absence of any treaty provision to the contrary, has power to deny to aliens that right to own land within its borders" (263 US 1923:217).

The state even had the power, on the question of ownership and leasing of lands to distinguish between aliens who had declared their intention to become citizens and those who had not or could not because of ineligibility, without violating the equal protection clause of the Fourteenth Amendment. The state could do this because its discretion or "classification is based on eligibility and purpose to naturalize" which Congress had established. "Eligible aliens are free white persons and persons of African nativity or descent." And Congress's right to do so was untrammeled: "it may grant or withhold the privilege of naturalization upon any grounds or without any reason, as it sees fit. But it is not to be supposed that its acts defining eligibility are arbitrary or unsupported by reasonable considerations of public policy. The State properly may assume that the considerations upon which Congress made such classification are substantial and reasonable" (263 US 1923:220).

Justice Butler did not offer any explanation why Congress saw fit to exclude the Japanese and other Orientals from naturalization, but the lower court in its earlier ruling on the case did. In his opinion for the court, Judge Cushman propounded the theory of an unbridgeable gap between the two civilizations or plural societies expressed symbolically by the racial difference which made the individual Oriental unsuited for membership in the People's Domain if he should emigrate to America.

"The yellow or brown racial color is the hallmark of the Oriental despotisms, or was at the time the original naturalization law was enacted. It was deemed that the subjects of those despotisms, with their fixed and ingrained pride in the type of their civilization, which works for its welfare by subordinating the individual to the personal authority of the sovereign, as the embodiment of the state, were not fitted and suited to make for the success of a republican form of government." (Japan Consulate General of San Francisco 1925 II:25)

In acknowledging this fact, Judge Cushman continued, Congress undoubtedly recognized "that it was of the essence of its duty to insure the perpetuation of our own type of civilization" by "withholding the right to citizenship from these Oriental races" (Japan Consultate General of San Francisco 1925 II:25). Even the court had a responsibility in this matter:

"[Its duty is] to hold impregnable the barrier erected by Congress to preserve, in its purity, our own type of civilization. The more homogeneous its parts, the more perfect the union. It may be that the changes wrought in the Orient in the last fifty or seventy-five years now warrant a different policy; but there is no law or treaty that yet has said 'the twain shall meet,' or that, if citizenship be accorded these Orientals, the danger is part of our becoming a 'mechanical medley of race fragments.'"
(Japan Consulate General of San Francisco 1925 II:25-6)

In protecting the sanctity of the People's Domain from incursion by subjects of an alien civilization, Judge Cushman continued, the state also had the power to prevent the valued land and resources of the People's Domain from falling into the hands of these subjects.

"It is obvious that one who is not a citizen and cannot become one lacks an interest in, and the power to effectually work for the welfare of the state, and, so lacking, the state may rightfully deny him the right to own and lease real estate within its boundaries. If one incapable of citizenship may lease or own real estate, it is within the realm of possibility that every foot of land within the state might pass to the ownership or possession of non-citizens. Such a result would leave the foundation of the state but a pale shadow, and the structure erected thereon but a Tower of Babel from which the tenants in possession might, when the shock of war came, bow themselves out because they were not bound as citizens to defend the house in which they lodged."

(Japan Consulate General of San Francisco 1925 II:26)

In other words, the state and People's Domain would crumble, particularly in time of war, if, in the words of the State Attorney General, such aliens were "permitted to obtain control of a thing so vital to the political existence of a State as is the land" (263 US 1923:210). In his opinion for the United States Supreme Court, Justice Butler accepted the above argument of Judge Cushman and quoted it verbatim in his opinion.

Before concluding, Justice Butler dismissed rather quickly the appellant's charge that the state law was in conflict with the treaty between the United States and Japan. He adopted the argument first put forth by Governor Johnson of California that the treaty said nothing about agricultural lands and offered as evidence the line of reasoning expressed in Secretary of State Bryan's letter to the Japanese government on July 16 1913. In the final analysis then, Justice Butler affirmed in the name of the Supreme Court the constitutionality of the Washington statute.

In the other ruling handed down on the same day, Porterfield v. Webb, the Supreme Court also upheld the constitutionality of the California Alien Land Law of 1920 restricting the ban on ownership and leasing of land to aliens ineligible for citizenship but, unlike the Washington statute, lifting it from those eligible for citizenship who did not declare their intention to become one. In his opinion for the Court, Justice Butler found this difference between the two statutes as being neither arbitrary nor unreasonable. For, "in the matter of classification, the States have wide discretion. Each has its own problems, depending on circumstances existing there. It is not always practical or desirable that legislation shall be the same in different States" (263 US 1923:233). In all other respects Justice Butler repeated the arguments of Terrace v. Thompson and frequently referred to that decision in his exposition.

One week later the Supreme Court handed down another major decision affecting the California law, in Webb v. O'Brien et al. The major issue before the Court was whether a cropping contract between an American citizen and a Japanese alien was according to the lawyer for the appellees, "in its essence a contract of employment" and did not "constitute a transfer of real property" (263 US 1923:316), or whether it constituted more than an employment contract and conveyed in fact an interest in the land, as argued by the state attorney general. A lower court had ruled earlier in favor of O'Brien and Inouye, and had accordingly concluded that the contract was not banned by the law of 1920. As a result, it enjoined temporarily the state attorney general from enforcing the law against the two.

Acting on an appeal from the state attorney general, the United States Supreme Court subsequently reversed the lower court decision. In his opinion Justice Butler declared,

"The term of the proposed contract, the measure of control and dominion over the land which is necessarily involved in the performance of such a contract, the cropper's right to have housing for himself and to have his employees live on the land, and his obligation to accept one-half the crops as his only return for tilling the land clearly distinguish the arrangement from one of mere employment.... We are of [the] opinion that it is more than a contract of employment; and that, if executed, it will give to Inouye a right to use and to have or share in the benefit of the land for agricultural purposes. And this is so, notwithstanding other clauses of the contract to the effect that the general possession of the land is reserved to the owner, that the cropper shall have no interest or estate whatever in the land, that he is given one-half of all crops grown as compensation for his services and labor, and that division of the crops is to be made after they are harvested and before their removal from the land....

The practical result of such contract is that the cropper has use, control and benefit of land for agricultural purposes substantially similar to that granted to a lessee. Conceivably, by the use of such contracts, the population living on and cultivating the farmlands might come to be made up largely of ineligible aliens. The allegiance of the farmers to the State directly affects its strength and safety. *Terrace v. Thompson, supra.* We think it within the power of the State to deny to ineligible aliens the privilege so to use the agricultural lands within its borders."   (263 US 1923:323-24)

However, Justice Butler introduced an important reservation earlier in his opinon. If the contract were merely that of employment in common occupations, then it would be protected by the Fourteenth Amendment as in the benchmark case of *Truax v. Raich.* For, "a denial of it [the right to make and carry out cropper contracts such as that before the Court] does not deny the ordinary means of earning a livelihood or the right to work for a living" (263 US 1923:324). In short, the right of the Japanese to become part of an agricultural proletariat was upheld, but they could have no vested interest in the land upon which they toiled.*

---

*The ruling on the fourth case was also handed down that day. It denied the right of aliens ineligible for citizenship to own stock in corporations set up to work agricultural lands (Frick v. Webb).

THE DIPLOMATIC EXCHANGE AND THE PROPOSED TRADEOFF

The first glimmerings of the initiative petition movement brought forth as early as March 13 1920 inquiries and expressions of concern from the Japanese government to the American ambassador in Japan. As the initiative movement gained momentum, it became evident that the alien land issue that had remained dormant since the breakoff of correspondence in 1914 was quickly being revived as a major source of strain and of diplomatic exchange between the two governments.

By the summer of 1920 the Japanese government brought pressure on the American government to intervene and to head off the burgeoning initiative movement. In a conversation with the Japanese ambassador in late August, the Secretary of State, Colby, "explained to him the constitutional limitations which made it inexpedient and impracticable for the Federal Government to interfere in the initiative legislation now presented to the people of California" (US Foreign Relations 1920 III:15). However, he did express the United States' regret "that the voluntary action of Japan in refusing hereafter to issue passports to 'picture brides' had not served as the Department had at one time hoped to prevent the initiation of amendments to the California land law" (US Foreign Relations 1920 III:14). He recommended that, as a way of avoiding the impending confrontation, the two governments should pursue the two courses of action proposed by the American ambassador to Japan, Morris, in conversations with the Japanese ambassador a month earlier in Washington.

In that conversation, Ambassador Morris informed Ambassador Shidehara that his recent trip to California had convinced him that the initiative measure would undoubtedly pass and "that any effort on the part of the Japanese residents or the Federal Government to prevent its passage by propaganda or otherwise would only serve to accentuate the present antagonism" (US Foreign Relations 1920 III:12).

Behind the initiative sentiment, the American ambassador argued, was "practically a unanimous determination on the part of the people of California to prevent all Asiatic immigration to California." The reason for this determination "was not primarily economic but ... arose from the fear of the people of California that the presence of a large body of unassimilable people would threaten them with a serious and persistent race problem" (US Foreign Relations 1920 III:12). This fear was increasingly exacerbated by the failure of the Gentlemen's Agreement over the past ten years to stem the flow of immigration.

However, he added, "if we could allow two or three generations to pass without adding by immigration to that number we would then know how Japanese had blended into the economic and social structure of California life." He acknowledged that "there was a division of sentiment among those who had studied the question whether the Japanese people ever could assimilate with Western civilization." But, he insisted that the answer to "this question could only be determined by the test of experience and I saw in the California conditions a peculiar opportunity for such a test;" at the least the climate of opinion toward the Japanese might improve. Accordingly, "if arrangements could be made to provide for total exclusion in the future, . . . we would thus establish the foundation for better treatment by California towards Japanese already there" (US Foreign Relations 1920 III:12). (The Secretary of State echoed this opinion a month later in his conversation with the Japanese ambassador: "I ventured the opinion that the people of California were prepared to accord fair treatment to Japanese residents provided they could be assured for the future of an effective total exclusion beyond that now provided by the terms of the Gentlemen's Agreement" (US Foreign Relations 1920 III:15).)

To implement this plan, Ambassador Morris recommended that the two countries "begin immediate discussion of amendments to strengthen the 'Gentlemen's Agreement' so that it would hereafter operate totally to exclude all Japanese" (US Foreign Relations 1920 III:13). The two countries should also pursue court tests of the constitutionality of the 1913 act "so that we know whether we were discussing a real or fictitious situation" with respect to discriminatory treatment of Japanese aliens already in California (US Foreign Relations 1920 III:12).

The Japanese government responded favorably to these suggestions. Before long intense but unofficial conversations began to be conducted between the two countries. As a result, by November 2, the day of the initiative vote, the state department announced publicly that discussions were taking place and concluded the announcement with the statement that "it is believed he [the Japanese ambassador] thoroughly realizes, as we have sought to make clear, that no outcome of the California movement will be acceptable to the country at large that does not accord with existing and applicable provisions of law, and what is equally important, with the national instinct of justice" (US Foreign Relations 1920 III:17).

Despite this effort by the state department to take some of the sting out of the expected victory of the initiative, newspapers in Japan expressed their contempt and disdain for the measure. (The language of most was fairly moderate; they were hopeful that the successful conclusion of the discussions between the two countries might resolve the issue.) The Japanese government also took strong exception to the passage of the initiative measure. In a memorandum dated approximately one month after the measure went into effect, the Japanese ambassador reminded the American government

"that the California enactment of 1913 gave rise to a formal protest of the Japanese Government, as being in its manifest intent repugnant to all principles of fairness and justice, and disregardful of the letter as well as the spirit of the existing treaty between Japan and the United States. These objections apply to the new law of 1920 with still greater force and cogency, and the Japanese Government are unable to conceal from themselves the sad disappointment with which they view the adoption of that measure."

(US Foreign Relations 1921 II:319–20)

The ambassador then went on to assure the American government of his government's "unwavering faith in the supreme importance which they attach to the maintenance of the traditional relations of good understanding between the two nations." Convinced that these views were shared by the American government, his government was gratified with the "frank and exhaustive discussions of an informal character" then in progress between the ambassadors of the two countries "in an earnest effort to compose the difficulties in question. It is the sincere desire of the Japanese Government that these discussions will soon be brought to a happy conclusion, and that both Governments will be able forthwith to examine and approve plans of adjustment to be recommended by the two Ambassadors" (US Foreign Relations 1921 II:320).

Worried lest the ambassador's memorandum might anger the American government and "prejudice the successful outcome of the negotiations," the Japanese Vice-Minister for Foreign Affairs assured the American government less than a week later that the memorandum was not meant to constitute a formal protest, though such a protest might be forthcoming in the future if the talks were to fail.

Despite this reassurance, the state department was clearly annoyed by the ambassador's memorandum and, in a memorandum of its own issued two weeks later, the department repeated its arguments of 1913 and 1914. It stated unequivocally: "This Government remains firm in the conviction expressed by it at that time, that nothing in the treaty affords a basis for the contention that the California land legislation is in violation either of the letter or the spirit of any treaty obligations which this Government has assumed towards the Government of Japan" (US Foreign Relations 1921 II:322).

In addition, the memorandum continued, the American government had informed the Japanese government in its correspondence of 1913 and 1914 that individual Japanese subjects had

"recourse to judicial determination of such injuries to private rights and interests as might be contended to have been suffered in consequence of the legislation adopted by the State of California.... Yet so far as the Department of State has been made aware, no case involving this issue has been adjudicated by any of the higher courts since the original California land law of 1913 went into effect. In view of this fact, the Department of State cannot but feel that Japanese subjects resident in California can scarcely have found in the operation of that statute such occasion for complaint on the ground of violation of their treaty rights, as had been alleged by the Japanese Government."

(US Foreign Relations 1921 II:322)

Though the purely legal aspects of the question were still to be determined, the memorandum continued,

"the Government of the United States is not unmindful of the feeling with which the Japanese Government and people have viewed the enactment of measures which they esteem to be discriminatory in character; and fully sharing with the Government of Japan the consciousness of the supreme importance to be attached to the maintenance of the traditional relations of good understanding between the two nations, this Government is with like forbearance envisaging the difficult problem of which one aspect is presented by the question of the ownership of land in California, and looks hopefully to the possiblity of a satisfactory adjustment consistent with the honor and true interests of both nations." (US Foreign Relations 1921 II:323)

Accordingly, the department proposed to continue the informal conversations then underway, with the hope that they would in time provide the framework for a negotiated treaty.

On January 25 the American ambassador submitted to the Acting Secretary of State a report on the informal discussions with the Japanese ambassador and a draft of a proposed treaty. These discussions were conducted under two topical headings: "Immigration" and "Japanese citizens resident in the United States." For each topic the ambassadors had prepared, after extensive discussions, a set of recommendations for a new arrangement and treaty.

Under the first topic, the American ambassador described how he and his Japanese counterpart had sought to reconcile the conflicting interests and concerns of the two governments. The American government, for instance, was convinced that the Gentlemen's Agreement in its present form had failed, despite the best intention and efforts of Japan; too many Japanese were still entering the country. The major reason it had failed was because

"it provides no method by which the Government of the United States can exercise any effective control at the ports of entry. This creates an anomalous and dangerous situation. It gives rise to suspicion and resentment among our own people and to exaggerated and unjust charges of bad faith. All the evidence I have been able to examine indicates that the Japanese Government has endeavored in the face of considerable pressure to carry out the letter of the

Agreement. But I submit it is almost too much to expect that any Government will enforce rigorously against its own people a self-denying regulation which is wholly in the interest of another people. It should not be required to do so."

(US Foreign Relations 1921 II:335)

The only remedy for this was legislative action by the American government to enforce any proposed regulation on immigration.

"[However] the Japanese Government is most sensitive in the matter of racial discrimination. It would keenly resent the passage by our Congress of an exclusion law similar to the Chinese Exclusion Act. But my conferences with Baron Shidehara have convinced me it would not seriously object to the enforcement by our Federal Government of discriminatory measures imposed by the Japanese Government on its own people . . . [inasmuch as] for centuries, the Japanese Government has enforced rigid regulations controlling, and even totally prohibiting, emigration from Japan. . . . [Thus] it would find little difficulty in continuing such regulations."

(US Foreign Relations 1921 II:335–36)

The answer to the problem then, the ambassador concluded, was to "retain the form of the 'Gentlemen's Agreement'" but to include a provision for "its legal enforcement [by the United States government] at our own ports" (US Foreign Relations 1921 II:335).

This became the nub of the recommendation hammered out by the two ambassadors under the rubric "Immigration." They also agreed to tighten considerably what had seemed to be loopholes in the old agreement. Passports to the mainland, for example, were to be issued only to families of government officials and under special circumstances to families of non-laboring classes but no longer to families of laboring classes. The right of re-entry to the United States from Japan was to extend for one year only. Much more substantial proof of identity was to be required of exempt classes, and they would in addition have to meet a means test "to insure their not becoming laborers while remaining in the Continental United States and Hawaii" (US Foreign Relations 1921 II:345).

With respect to the second topic, the two ambassadors recommended a convention that would supplement the Treaty of 1911. Its primary, if not sole purpose, would be to avoid the effects of the California alien land law by extending to Japanese subjects lawfully resident within any state or territory of the United States the same legal rights without discrimination accorded to citizens or subjects of other countries in these areas "with regard to the acquisition, possession, enjoyment, disposition, transmission, or inheritance of any real or personal property, or any interest therein, other than public lands, either Federal or State." These would also apply "to the exercise of industries, occupations, or other lawful pursuits" (US Foreign Relations 1921 II:346). In addition, American citizens would reciprocally have the two sets of rights in Japan.

After presenting the draft of the convention, the American ambassador expressed his misgivings about its effectiveness in dealing with the discriminatory treatment accorded Japanese aliens and offered as his solution something that he had proposed in passing in earlier dispatches: the privilege of naturalization for Japanese aliens.

> "My investigations have convinced me personally that the only thoroughly satisfactory method to provide against discriminatory treatment of Japanese aliens would be by Congressional action granting peoples of the Yellow race the privilege of naturalization. I wish that the Congress might feel justified in taking such action. Its effects as I have already pointed out elsewhere would be limited to one generation, and yet in so doing, we would totally change the existing spirit of irritation and resentment which now characterizes our contact with the Orient. We would remove from the peoples of China and Japan the stigma that is placed upon them in thus removing the racial discrimination, and we could the more vigorously enforce restrictions on immigration as an economic protection to our own people. As early as 1906, President Roosevelt seeing as he did so clearly throughout his entire public life the international value of the closest friendship and understanding with Japan, in his annual message to Congress said: 'I recommend to the Congress that an act be passed specifically providing for the naturalization of Japanese who come here intending to become American citizens.' I recognize, however, that this is a question which properly belongs to the legislative department of our Government, and I mention it merely to emphasize my belief that the Treaty as submitted is not a permanent solution or fundamental solution of the issue, although it will allay the present increasingly acute conditions."
>
> (US Foreign Relations 1921 II:347–48)

Even as the draft of the treaty was being prepared for submission to the Secretary of State, Senator Hiram Johnson of California mounted a major campaign against it. In fact, one week before it was given to the Secretary, he presented to the United States a joint resolution passed by the California legislature which memorialized the President and Secretary of State to cease negotiating the kind of treaty they were presumed to be negotiating with Japan. The resolution's chief demand was "that any attempt by the treaty-making power of the United States to nullify the . . . 'alien land law' or to confer upon the subjects of Japan the right to acquire, own, or possess lands within this State, in violation of our State laws, should be opposed as destructive of State's rights reserved under the Constitution of the United States" (US Congressional Record 1921 66:3:1541). The resolution also came out flatly against "any treaty being made between the United States and Japan whereby the right to citizenship shall be extended to the subjects of Japan" (US Congressional Record 1921 66:3:1541).

In the face of such opposition, the Secretary of State let the draft of the treaty lie fallow and never sent it to the Senate for consideration.

16

THE YELLOW PERIL AND
THE END OF THE
GENTLEMEN'S AGREEMENT

Introduction

The care and restraint with which the United States government engaged in the diplomatic conversations and conducted the negotiations with Japan that were discussed in the last chapter illustrates graphically the status in world affairs Japan had attained with its military defeat of Russia in 1905. It had become respected as a military power and its expressions of national concern, whether about its subjects in the United States or its national interests in the Far East, could not be lightly dismissed or cavalierly rebuffed by the US government, as happened frequently in America's relations with China. However, with the growing respect, the attitude of the American government underwent a significant change. From the friendly benevolence that had characterized its treatment of Japan throughout the latter part of the nineteenth century once it had forcibly breached Japan's wall of seclusion, it became more suspicious and distrustful as Japan staked its claim to equality, began to compete with the United States in the Far East, and openly expressed its concern over treatment of its nationals in America. Japan too expressed its growing wariness of America's national aims and purposes. As a result, with each instance of acute tension and strain, fears mounted that relations between the two countries were about to deteriorate to the point of open hostilities. Even President Roosevelt who respected and was in turn respected by the Japanese government gave vent to these concerns.

Caught in the middle of the growing wariness was the Japanese immigrant who was increasingly labeled a fifth-column agent of the Japanese government. In this manner the double-edged yellow peril theme surfaced early in the century and retained a vitality thereafter.

By the 1920s the California proponents of the yellow peril theme carried their fight to end the Gentlemen's Agreement and immigration from Japan onto the nation's capitol. They gained supporters from members of congress who were themselves locked in an ideological battle: should immigration quotas be set to protect the purity of the Anglo-Saxon "race" from contamination by the Southern and Eastern Europeans? The outcome was the Immigration Act of 1924 which enshrined the racial creed as the regnant legal-normative code for controlling the entry of aliens into the United States.

In this chapter we shall examine the deeply-rooted linkage between Japan and the Japanese immigrant in the image of the yellow peril and the flourishing of this image through the first quarter of the twentieth century. In addition, we shall look at the interlocking relationship between the image and the racialist ideology that undergirded the enactment of the Immigration Act of 1924.

The double-edged yellow peril: Japan and the Japanese immigrant

THE EARLY WAR SCARES

The first major example of the growing wariness between the United States and Japan, as we have already noted, was the San Francisco school board crisis; however, this crisis had barely been settled and diplomatic exchanges begun that eventually culminated in the Gentlemen's Agreement when in May 1907 riots erupted in San Francisco against the Japanese immigrant. Once again the specter of war was raised, as the jingoist press of Japan responded with a call for defense of national honor. Rumors of impending war also spread to segments of the American and European press. Even President Roosevelt took a worried view of the situation and so informed Cecil Rice in a letter on July 1: "The San Francisco mob bids fair, if not to embroil us with Japan, at any rate to arouse in Japan a feeling of rankling anger toward us that may at any time bear evil result; and the Japanese Jingoes are in their turn as bad as ours" (Roosevelt 1952,5:699).

He then declared that he was moving on two fronts to meet the new crisis – the kind of two-pronged approach that he had initially forged in the school board confrontation and that became his trademark in relations with Japan. On the one hand, he was seeking to redress the injustice done to the Japanese in San Francisco. ("I am doing everything I can to meet the just grievances of the Japanese, to atone for and remedy any wrong.") On the other, he was also preparing to meet any threat of military intervention by Japan. ("I am also doing everything I can to keep the navy at the highest point of efficiency!" (Roosevelt 1952, 5:699).)

As a further expression of the first prong, he threatened local San Francisco authorities with the use of federal troops if they failed to maintain law and order. He also pressured them to join the federal government in an official expression of regret to the Japanese government and to accept liability for damages incurred by the Japanese during the riots. As a result, "the affair soon ceased to be a diplomatic incident, and it was left to the courts to decide the exact amount of damages" (Bailey 1964:199).

Even as this incident was being resolved, another contaminated relations between the two countries. Specifically, toward the end of June, the Board of Police Commissioners of San Francisco refused to grant licenses for employment bureaus to six Japanese. Once again the federal government intervened and finally succeeded through indirection in having the order rescinded by December.

Worried about the level of tension between the two countries and concerned lest Japan misconstrue the American government's intervention in local affairs as a sign of fear and weakness, President Roosevelt decided to make a major move on the second prong by July 1907. He would send the American fleet on a world cruise manifestly as a gesture of international goodwill, but in fact, as conveyed in his letter to Secretary of State Root on July 13, as a show of strength to Japan.

"I am more concerned over this Japanese situation than almost any other. Thank Heaven we have the navy in good shape. It is high time, however, that it should go on a cruise around the world. In first place I think it will have a pacific effect to show that it can be done; and in the next place, after talking thoroughly over the situation with the naval board I became convinced that it was absolutely necessary for us to try in time of peace to see just what we could do in the way of putting a big battle fleet in the Pacific, and not make the experiment in time of war." (Roosevelt 1952, 5:717)

Even as President Roosevelt made his announcement, his worries were compounded by a series of reports he received about the rumors and predictions of war between the United States and Japan that were circulating in various European capitals. For example, early in July the American consul-general at Shanghai, then on a visit to Germany, relayed the message that French and German officials were expecting a war between Japan and the United States within a few years and were laying odds of 5 to 4 on a Japanese victory. Shortly thereafter the American ambassador to Germany confirmed these impressions in a more detailed dispatch to Washington. In addition, the President received word that a retired American military officer had overheard at a dinner in St Petersburg the boasting of a Japanese diplomat that Japan planned to take the Philippines, Hawaii, Alaska, and the Pacific Coast.

Roosevelt responded to these various reports with skepticism, though he did not dismiss them as being totally absurd. Instead he used them to underscore the importance of his call for preparedness and for the world cruise: "My own judgment is that the only thing that will prevent war is the Japanese feeling that we shall not be beaten, and this feeling we can only excite by keeping and making our navy efficient in the highest degree. It was evidently high time that we should get our whole battle fleet on a practice voyage to the Pacific" (Roosevelt 1952, 5:725).

To add to his woes, from his friend the German ambassador Roosevelt received the warning passed on by a German agent in Mexico that thousands of Japanese military personnel were migrating to Mexico disguised as civilians, presumably to await orders from Japan about future military action against the United States. Roosevelt took note of this warning but in his reply to the ambassador expressed his disbelief. "It seems simply incredible that the Japanese should go to Mexico with any intention of organizing an armed force to attack us from the Mexican border in the event of war with Japan. Such an attack could have no permanent effect save one of extreme irritation and anger" (Roosevelt 1952, 5:720). (In a later letter, Roosevelt explained to the ambassador that he had heard that most of these men were not agents of Japan but merely disillusioned ex-soldiers looking for a better life.)

Roosevelt went on to describe his two-pronged strategy in dealing with Japan, including the sending of the fleet. In view of this strategy, he concluded, "I do not believe that there will be trouble, and I am taking all the steps possible for me to take both to prevent it and to prevent its being disastrous if it should come." But he admitted, nevertheless, that "of course the situation gives me some concern; for the Japanese are a formidable military power and have unknown possibilities both as regards their power and as regards their motives and purposes" (Roosevelt 1952, 5:721).

The rumors of war continued to mount during the next month and reached their peak, according to Bailey, "late in September or early in October, 1907" (Bailey 1964:258), only receding when the results of the goodwill mission sent to Japan by Roosevelt became known. Even then Roosevelt continued to get disquieting reports, particularly from Germany, but for all intents and purposes the war scare of 1907 was over.

The departure of the fleet in mid-December revived the forecast of war in the capitals of Europe; Germany in particular continued to be the source of disturbing news. In January, for example, the rumor of the thousands of marching Japanese in Mexico was revived, and the Kaiser was reported as being absolutely convinced that Japan intended to initiate hostilities against the United States soon.

Though openly skeptical of these reports, Roosevelt nevertheless continued to cast a wary eye on the international scene. For example, "in a conversation with the British ambassador in February the President stated that he did not himself think that the Japanese could mean to provoke war. Nevertheless, Roosevelt asserted, anything might happen with the public mind on both sides of the Pacific inflamed as it was. There might be a riot on the Coast in which a Japanese might be killed; there might be an outbreak in Japan aroused by the passing of American exclusion legislation." (Bailey 1964:269–70)

These rumors and suspicions were largely laid to rest in mid-March with the Japanese government's formal invitation to the fleet to visit Japan and with the American government's prompt acceptance of this invitation. However, despite the sudden brightening of the international scene, Roosevelt remained somewhat apprehensive. In mid-April, for example, in a letter to Root he alluded to the information received from a number of different sources: namely, "that many of the Japanese generals and of the military party generally accept as a matter of course the view that they would land a strong army on the Pacific Slope." The persistence of this report made it

"an act of the most one-sided folly for this country not to make the military preparations, and especially naval preparations, sufficient to put a stop to all thoughts of an aggressive war on the part of Japan. I think that the probabilities are that that war will not take place; but there is a sufficient likelihood to make it inexcusable for us not to take such measures as will surely prevent it. If we have adequate coast defenses and a really large navy, the war cannot take place."

(Roosevelt 1952, 6:1010)

Two days later, he elaborated on this concern in a letter to his son following Congress' refusal "to give me four battleships." In a tone even more foreboding than that of his earlier letter, he declared,

"I cannot give in public my reasons for being apprehensive about Japan, for of course to do so might bring on grave trouble; but I said enough to put Congress thoroughly on its guard, if it cared to be on its guard. I do not believe that there will be war with Japan, but I do believe that there is enough chance of war to make it eminently wise to insure against it by building such a navy as to forbid Japan's hoping for success. I happen to know that the Japanese military party is inclined for war with us and is not only confident of success, but confident that they could land a large expeditionary force in California and conquer all of the United States west of the Rockies. I fully believe that they would in the end pay dearly for this, but meantime we would have been set back at least a generation by the loss of life, the humiliation, and the material damage."

(Roosevelt 1952, 6:1012–13).

What contributed greatly to Roosevelt's apprehensiveness during this period was the set of early reports he had received which seemed to show that the Gentlemen's Agreement had failed to stem the flow of Japanese laborers into the United States. In late March, for example, he complained to the Secretary of State that over 150 Japanese laborers had entered the United States in February. "It is certainly to be regretted that as large a number come in. Even without them, there are more Japanese coming to America than I like to see, having in view the future good relations between Japan and the United States" (Roosevelt 1952, 6:984). Somewhat over a month later, he complained even more bitterly to the Secretary about the continued flow of Japanese laborers and threatened to push for an exclusion law if it continued: "This dispatch from O'Brien shows that over a thousand steerage passengers left Japan for the United States and Hawaii in April. The Japanese might as well be given to understand that if this thing goes on an exclusion law will be past [*sic*]" (Roosevelt 1952, 6:1002).

By July 1908, as we have already seen, the administrative machinery for the Gentlemen's Agreement was finally fully operational in Japan; accordingly the results, began to please the President. He expressed his satisfaction in a letter to a Japanese official in which he stated "'the number of Japanese who left the United States much exceeds the number who remained here'" (Bailey 1964:279). The following month he received a reassuring letter from his Secretary of State attesting to the sincerity of the Japanese government in implementing the Gentlemen's Agreement and to the reasonableness of the length of time needed to make the administrative machinery work. From that time on, President Roosevelt never complained again that the Gentlemen's Agreement was unworkable; in fact as we have already seen the United States government, including the Commissioner-General of Immigration, expressed enthusiasm for the agreement for at least the next several years.

While the success of the Gentlemen's Agreement helped reduce some of the lingering strain between Japan and the United States, the smashing success of the fleet's visit to Japan in October cleared the air of any residual tensions between the two governments. All thoughts of war virtually evaporated. According to Bailey, "the ensuing reception in Japan dispelled all war clouds and paved the way for a diplomatic *rapprochement* which, a year before, had been thought impossible" (Bailey 1964:301).

YELLOW JOURNALISM AND THE YELLOW PERIL

The reduction in tension between the two governments, however, did not serve to abate the shrill attack against the "yellow peril" that had been mounting in intensity in the California press and in other forms of print. Focused initially in the late nineteenth century on the competitive economic threat of the Chinese "invasion of California," the attack shifted with the Russo-Japanese war to the peril of Japan as a military threat to the national interests and aims of the United States government. It was later enlarged to include the Japanese immigrant as a fifth-column threat to the political stability of California and so to the United States at large. By 1910 the economic threat theme had resurfaced as pressure for an anti-alien land law mounted; this time the theme was directed against the Japanese and not the Chinese.

Spearheading this campaign in the California press were the Hearst newspapers, particularly the *San Francisco Examiner*, which had begun its campaign against Japan and the Japanese from the mid-1890s. In the bold print of a two-page advertisement appearing in *Business Week* in 1945, the Hearst organization boasted, "For more than 50 years, the Hearst Newspapers kept warning America about Japan" (*Business Week* September 1 1945:34–5). The Hearst newspapers first became obsessively concerned with the menace of Japan at the time of its victory over Russia. In the words of the advertisement: "the Hearst Newspapers published the startlingly prophetic cartoon reproduced at left, at the signing of the Treaty of Portsmouth which ended the Russo-Japanese War" (*Business Week* September 1 1945:34–5). The cartoon showed a Japanese soldier with rifle at alert standing athwart Korea and casting a shadow across the Philippines and the United States.

The school board crisis turned the attention of the Hearst newspapers to the Japanese immigrant. Their special contribution to the burgeoning anti-Japanese agitation was the fifth-column theme. According to the Hearst newspapers, the Japanese immigrants were in fact military men in disguise. Once having sounded these two themes of the yellow peril, the Hearst newspapers spent the next four decades moving back and forth between them.

Even as Hearst was sharpening his attack on the military menace of Japan, others were prophesying an Armageddon-like collision between Japan and the United States. One of the earliest prophets of doom was Richmond Pearson Hobson, a naval hero of the Spanish American War. He saw the two countries as being drawn into a war and by 1907 had sketched a blueprint of what such a war would be like. He also castigated Americans for not taking the threat seriously and suggested that failure to heed his warning to prepare for the inevitable might result in the loss of the Pacific coast to Japan.

Shortly thereafter, H.G. Wells joined the ranks of the prophets with the publication of his novel *War in the Air*, as did the French historian, Flack. So ominous had the forecasts become and so formidably had the military prowess of Japan been portrayed that *The Nation* magazine sought in its January 1908 issue, to calm the growing anxiety and to bring into more human proportions the capabilities of Japan and the Japanese. Under the heading "The Superhuman Japanese," the magazine tried to deflate the rumors that were then rife: namely, that the Japanese soldier was a superman, that a large fifth column of men with military experience was clandestinely drilling in the Philippines, in Hawaii, and on the Pacific coast awaiting the inevitable war that was soon to engulf the United States and Japan.

Despite such reassurances, the voices of the purveyors of catastrophe were not stilled. In fact, the most celebrated of them, Homer Lea, did not publish until 1909 his compelling tome on the imminent confrontation between the two countries, *The Valor of Ignorance*. In that same year, E.H. Fitzpatrick published his imaginative fictional account of the outbreak and dramatic unfolding of such a war (Fitzpatrick 1909). Fitzpatrick depicts it as the product not of the clash of national interests in the Far East, but of the mounting tension between Japanese immigrants and white Americans in California. The backdrop for the war is the emergence once again of a school question in the California legislature. The immediate precipitant, however, is the bloody altercation between a Japanese waiter and an American sailor in a restaurant in San Francisco leading to a rampage of violence by the whites and a protest demonstration by the Japanese. These Japanese immigrants are not ordinary civilians; as revealed by subsequent events, they are in fact a clandestine "army" of disciplined military personnel.

This first becomes evident in the violent encounter between law officers and Japanese protesters who are demonstrating against the earlier mob action by the whites. Under attack by the combined force of police and militia, the Japanese reveal through their response their true identity. In the words of Fitzpatrick, "on perceiving the peril of such an attack the Japanese, under the direction of some one apparently in authority, displayed themselves in regular military formation and met the bayonet charge of the militia with a well directed fire from their concealed small arms" (Fitzpatrick 1909:28). So effective is their counteraction that they virtually annihilate the militia.

Once news of this debacle leaks out, white California "clamoured in revenge for the extirpation of the Japanese throughout the Pacific States. The Japanese, however, divining their danger, congregated as if by some preconcerted plan into bodies of hundreds and thousands, and quickly formed a military organization. Rifles and even quick firing guns seemed to have been mysteriously produced. From all parts of the Pacific slope organized bodies of armed Japanese moved towards a common center, San Francisco" (Fitzpatrick 1909:29–30).

Thus is unleashed a series of events that culminate in a declaration of war by the United States against Japan: "No sooner, however, had war been declared against Japan, when whole regiments of Japanese sprang as it were, out of the ground in the Pacific states, fully accoutered and equipped for war. The Japanese Government, foreseeing the possibility of such a rupture taking place, had previously sent over an army of fifty thousand soldiers disguised as coolies" (Fitzpatrick 1909:32).

In addition, the powerful Japanese fleet brings in reinforcements and supplies which virtually assume flood proportions after the defeat of the American fleet in a major sea battle. In this manner the Japanese gain mastery of the Pacific Slope and drive out the native whites. Yet despite these catastrophic events, the Americans eventually rally and drive the Japanese from American soil, assisted by the defeat of the Japanese navy by a combined British-American force.

Thus were combined in one dramatic scenario all the major components of the yellow peril: the almost "superhuman" military prowess of Japan and the fifth-column presence of Japanese immigrants in California, really disguised military personnel. In this 1909 fictional version of the yellow peril, Fitzpatrick depicts the Japanese military man, whether in Japan or California, as essentially a person of integrity and decency, closely bound by the samurai code of honor and loyalty. Even the actions of the fifth column in California are not sneakily provocative but are instead responses to either expected or real attacks from the whites, as in the violent confrontation with the militia in San Francisco that precipitates the war.

THE MAGDALENA BAY AFFAIR

Two years later, the fictional yellow peril of Fitzpatrick's fertile immagination gave way to an apparently more threateningly real yellow peril as the Magdalena Bay affair began to take shape. The affair started innocently enough. An American syndicate had been trying unsuccessfully for several years to sell some or all of the property that it had been granted by the Mexican government in Lower California. Finally it received in 1911 an offer from a group of Japanese from San Francisco to purchase some of its property, if the group could also obtain the fishing concession in the area.

Desirous of clearance from the government in order to neutralize the expected public outcry that would greet any announcement of such a sale, the lawyer for the American syndicate requested such approval in a letter to the Secretary of State on August 9 1911. Approximately a week later, the Secretary wrote an ambiguous reply that focused on the expected public outcry.

"It is difficult for me categorically to answer the inquiries you make, but I ought not to disguise the fact – very likely fully realized by you – that such a transfer would be quite certain to be interpreted in some quarters in a manner to cause a great outcry. Such a result would be so obviously a cause of regret to the Government of the United States that it appears unnecessary for me to make further comment in response to your request to know the feeling of the Federal Government in the premises." (US Senate Document No. 694 (1912)62:2:4)

Seeking clarification for some of the more ambiguous wording, the lawyer met with the Secretary and approximately three months later sent him another letter, which he hoped would meet any further objections to the sale. In the letter, he proposed that Americans would retain control of the property with a majority of the board of directors, the Japanese being permitted "to purchase a 35 percent interest in the company, with an option for a further 15 percent interest" (US Senate Document No. 694(1912)62:2:4). The Japanese were in full accord with this plan because they wanted "to avoid doing anything which would in any way incite any feeling or animosity among the citizens of the Pacific coast" (US Senate Document No. 694(1912)62:2:5). In addition, he asserted, he had received the assurances of a Japanese member of parliament that the Japanese government would have no connection with this purely commercial enterprise and would not attempt to establish any coaling station for its navy in Magdalena Bay. However, he admitted the syndicate would have to rely on a Japanese work force, which would presumably be small, to get things going, for such a work force is "more accustomed to such conditions as obtain in Lower California" (US Senate Document No. 694(1912)62:2:5).

Two weeks later the Secretary of State alluded generally to the modified plan in his reply but went on to say, "the department has nothing to add to the suggestion made to you in my letter of August 17, 1911" (US Senate Document No. 694(1912)62:2:5). A last desperate effort by the lawyer to have the department respond to the changed terms of the proposed sale failed to budge it, for in the last official letter on the subject dated December 28, the assistant Secretary of State replied to the lawyer as follows:

"Your intimations of changes in the project and of an intention that the foreign interest shall be a minority one neither persuade the department to add anything to its letter of August 17 nor make it feel called upon to say whether or not it might at any time see reason to disfavor such a project. The foregoing are the only remarks the department is now in a position to make and are the sole conclusions which should be drawn from the official correspondence or the interviews on this subject." (US Senate Document No. 694(1912)62:2:6)

By the end of February the matter took on a more insidious character when Senator Lodge brought it obliquely to the attention of the Senate in a debate on proposed arbitration treaties favored by the Taft administration. Opposed to these treaties, Lodge offered what seemed to be going on in Magdalena Bay as a hypothetical example of how America's hands would be tied by such treaties.

"Suppose, for example, some great Eastern power should directly or indirectly take possession of a harbor on the west coast of Mexico for the purpose of making it a naval station and a place of arms. I am using no imagination in suggesting such a case. It is not very long since an indirect movement was begun, and it is apparently still on foot, to obtain possession for a foreign power of Magdalena Bay, so I may fairly suppose that such a case might arise. If it did, we should immediately intervene. We should declare that this was a violation of our constant policy known as the Monroe doctrine."

(US Congressional Record 1912 62:2:2603)

If such treaties as proposed by the administration were in effect, he continued, the other nation could forestall direct action by the United States by throwing the matter into arbitration. This might take years; meanwhile the other nation would be strengthening its position in the bay area.

Despite the vigorous denial by the Japanese ambassador who clearly understood to which country the oblique utterance referred, Senator Lodge would not let go of the issue. On April 2, he introduced and successfully piloted through the Senate a resolution that called on the President "to transmit to the Senate any information in possession of the Government relating to the purchase of land at Magdalena Bay by the Japanese Government or by a Japanese company" (US Congressional Record 1912 62:2:4170).

On May 1 a report was submitted by the Secretary of State to the Senate. In it he recounted the state department's reaction to the proposed sale and informed the senators that the prospective Japanese purchaser had also been rebuffed by the Japanese government which refused to give its support to the project "unless assured that the transaction would be unobjectionable to the Government of the United States" (US Congressional Record 1912 62:2:5660). The Secretary concluded his report with "an unreserved and categorical denial by the Japanese ambassador of the rumored purchase of land at Magdalena Bay by the Imperial Japanese Government or by a Japanese company." The ambassador had labeled the rumor "as entirely sensational and utterly without any foundation whatever, the Japanese Government having never directly or indirectly attempted or contemplated the acquisition of any land at Magdalena Bay for any purpose" (US Congressional Record 1912 62:2:5660).

Senator Lodge did not dispute what the report had to say about the Japanese government's behavior or about the stalemate in negotiations. But he insisted that nevertheless Japanese subjects had expressed an interest in buying property that had no commercial or industrial value at the present time.

"Its military and strategic value, however, is very great indeed. It lies there, a fine bay, at a point on the coast nearly midway between San Francisco and

Panama – I am not sure of the distances, but it is approximately midway. Nobody would think of buying that property at Magdalena Bay at the present time and of paying a large sum for it except for its military value as a coaling station and naval base."   (US Congressional Record 1912 62:2:5660–661).

In addition, he argued at a later point in the debate, "There is no question that there was a plan of establishing a Japanese colony or a Japanese settlement, or whatever you may wish to call it, on Magdalena Bay" (US Congressional Record 1912 62:2:5661). The potential danger was "that under the possession of a company owned in whole or in part by the citizens or subjects of a foreign power, a colony of their people can establish at Magdalena Bay a coaling station and can acquire possession of a bay, under the title of the company from whom they buy, which would be of enormous military value [to the Japanese Government]." For, he added somewhat later, "I think it would make very little difference from a strategical view whether the coaling station was established by the Government or whether the coaling station was established by a Japanese company which the Government could use if it chose. The danger if it would come would be in the fact, not in how it was done" (US Congressional Record 1912 62:2:5662).

Fortunately, he concluded, the danger had passed and "the situation now is harmless." But, he emphasized, it was incumbent on the American government for its own protection to prevent this from happening in the future. Accordingly, he advised the Senate to consider whether this might not fall under the protective mantle of the Monroe Doctrine. The entire matter was then referred to the Committee on Foreign Relations of which Lodge was chairman, but not before a senator from Maryland had complained about intruding the Monroe Doctrine into the domestic affairs of a neighboring country and had objected to the constant cry of war with Japan.

> "What right have we to interfere with the industrial development in Mexico by foreigners, if the laws of Mexico permit it? I want to stop, if I can, this constant cry of war with Japan. I have never thought for a moment that there is the slightest danger of war. This mad fancy that Japan intends to control and dominate the Pacific Ocean is the most absurd proposition I think that ever crossed the vision of a bewildered brain. Every time a subject of Japan buys a strip of land in Mexico or goes fishing upon the coast of Mexico there is a cry of war."   (US Congressional Record 1912 62:2:5663)

In the middle of May another resolution was passed at the behest of Lodge. It requested from the Secretary of State the complete file of all correspondence on the Magdalena Bay negotiations. The file was delivered by the end of the month.

Eventually on July 31, Senator Lodge submitted to the Senate the final report and accompanying resolution from the committee. According to the report, though no foreign government was directly involved in the negotiations with the American syndicate over lands and the bay, which had "some national value to a foreign nation ... as distinct from any commercial value" (US Congressional Record 1912 62:2:9923), a syndicate or corporation of foreign subjects was involved. This was a matter of some concern to the committee, which accordingly proposed a resolution to cover the problem – a resolution that came to be known as a "corollary to the Monroe Doctrine." As amended somewhat from the floor, the resolution stated:

> "*Resolved*, That when any harbor or other place in the American continents is so situated that the occupation thereof for naval or military purposes might threaten the communications or the safety of the United States, the Government of the United States could not see, without grave concern, the actual or potential possession of such harbor or other place by any Government, not American, as to give that Government practical power of control for naval or military purposes." (US Congressional Record 1912 62:2:10046)

In opening the debate on the resolution, Lodge repeated many of the arguments he had made earlier. Most pointedly he said, "It [this resolution] has been made necessary by a change of modern conditions, under which, while a Government takes no action itself, the possession of an important place of the character I have described may be taken by a corporation or association which would be under the control of the foreign Government" (US Congressional Record 1912 62:2:10045). Thus, he concluded, the Monroe Doctrine, which applied merely to actions by foreign governments, must be modified to include acts by corporations which might be disguised instruments of government policy. The Senate then went into executive session for three hours for further debate and, when it emerged into the open, it passed a slightly amended version of the resolution by the overwhelming vote of 51 to 4.

Even as Lodge was first making a public issue of the affair early in 1912, the Hearst newspapers pounced on it and renewed their long term, though momentarily dormant, campaign to convince America that Magdalena Bay was vital to its security. On April 1 the Hearst Los Angeles paper printed a dispatch from Tokyo which purportedly revealed "practical completion of plans for establishment of a big Japanese colony at Magdalena Bay" (Chamberlin 1955:354) and construction of a coaling station there. Two days later the *San Francisco Examiner* reported that a colony on the bay area had increased three and a half times until it now reached 75,000, most of whom were soldiers, and even more were swarming in each day. Thus, according to the newspaper, the yellow peril had truly arrived at Magdalena Bay.

Despite emphatic denials by Mexican and Japanese officials and the publication in the *New York Times* of a statement from the Japanese premier, the Hearst press called the denials evasive and persisted in its attempt to depict what was going on in Magdalena Bay as a threat to the United States. It even sent newsmen to the bay who found only two Japanese there. This did not prevent them from distorting the words of one of the two into an "authoritative" statement of plans by the Japanese government for a large-scale colony of a quasi-military nature in the future.

The Lodge committee's report and resolution helped dampen the press campaign and bring the matter to a temporary lull, but the issue never really died. In 1917 it surfaced again with a report of "thousands of Japanese fishing all the morning at Magdalena Bay, Mexico and drilling all the afternoon and such wonderful drilling you never saw in all your life – perfect – and . . . they had modern rifles" (Gulick 1917:26). Again the rumors were deflated only after causing an agitated flurry in the press. Two years later the matter hit the press in a somewhat different version, only to be deflated once more.

The response of the Japanese government to the 1912 version of the Magdalena Bay affair was that of dismay and controlled anger. It was particularly appalled at the reluctance of Congress and of the American press to accept its denials at face value. The Japanese press was even less temperate in its response than was the government. Only the death of the emperor helped mute what otherwise threatened to become a constant barrage of vituperation and hostility.

With the passage of the Lodge resolution, Magdalena Bay drifted off the front pages of the nation's press and virtually disappeared as a lightning rod for tension and strain between the two countries. However, before relations could reach any semblance of normalcy, the anti-alien land agitation had erupted in full force in California and had swept through the legislature a law highly discriminatory to the Japanese. As we have already seen in the previous chapter, relations between Japan and the United States took a dramatic turn for the worse with a flood of messages between the two governments and with mass meetings in Tokyo. Once again Japan and the United States seemed on the verge of a military confrontation. According to Josephus Daniels, Secretary of the Navy, "We were near war with Japan in May 1913" (Daniels 1944:161). Even President Wilson came to share reluctantly this conviction after an interview with the Japanese ambassador over the issue. "'It never occurred to me that war could be possible between the two countries,' said Wilson, 'until I observed the manner of the Japanese Ambassador, who was very nervous and gave evidence that his country looked for war'" (Daniels 1944:161).

In the midst of the President's efforts to reassure Japan of his friendship, of his lack of sympathy for the action of California, and of his desire to reduce tensions between the two countries, he was embarrassed at the public disclosure that, unbeknownst to him, part of his administration seemed to be preparing for war with Japan. Obviously meant to apply pressure on him, a story had been leaked to the New York press that the Joint Army and Navy Board had unanimously recommended at a meeting on May 13 1913 that the army and navy be redeployed in order to strengthen the American forces in the Philippines and Hawaii for the purpose of meeting the increasingly "grave" threat of Japan over the "land issue."

Angered at this effort to force his hand, the President dissolved the board and promptly sought to reassure the Japanese government that the board's recommendations had no official standing in his administration – at least as long as peace negotiations were on. Though the President's actions placated the Japanese government, they did not still the support for the board's plan among the American military, particularly those in the navy. According to Daniels, a number of these officers were virtually obsessed with the threat of the yellow peril and constantly sought to convert him to their side. Even Franklin D. Roosevelt, then a newly appointed assistant secretary of the navy, shared this conviction. He strongly supported the board's recommendation and endorsed Rear Admiral Fiske's secret memorandum, "Possibility of War with Japan." Years later, after he had modified his opinion somewhat about the inevitability of war with Japan following the successful Washington Disarmament Conference in 1923, Roosevelt justified the military's preoccupation with the yellow peril by saying that it was a "perfectly natural attitude of Army and Navy officers whose duty it has been in the past to prepare the country against the 'most probable enemy'" to single out Japan as their target (Neumann 1953:150).

WORLD WAR I AND THE YELLOW PERIL

With Japan actively on the side of the allies and with the United States benevolently neutral toward them until 1917, World War I served to mute some of the outstanding issues between the two countries, most notably that bearing upon Japanese immigration. Even the twenty-one demands made by Japan against China after the Imperial government's conquest of the German leasehold on the Shantung Province early in 1915 disturbed only momentarily the aura of goodwill then enveloping relations between the two countries – though it nourished the seeds of future distrust. Much more symbolic of the atmosphere of the period were the Lansing-Ishii Notes of 1917 which reaffirmed friendliness between the two countries and sought to dispel mutual distrust of each other's motives in the Far East. While reiterating an "open door policy" for the Far East, the notes contained a clause that later came home to haunt Secretary of State Lansing. Critics insisted that the clause endorsed Japan's imperialistic aims in China. The Secretary countered with the argument that the clause "merely recognized Japan's special interests in China because of her geographic propinquity and were no concession to imperialistic aims" (Tupper and McReynolds 1937:122).

Despite the evident relaxation of tensions between the two countries, the yellow peril theme did not disappear, as the German propaganda machine and the Hearst press made up in part for the slackening of agitation on the part of indigenous exclusionist groups in California. Only after the war was over was the extent of Germany's efforts to spread anti-Japanese propaganda in America revealed through a congressional investigation. For example, a memorandum from an American correspondent, "a minor cog in the German propaganda machine" (Daniels 1970:75), to Captain von Papen written early in 1915 stated that the purpose of these efforts was to exploit the "natural" anxieties and antipathies of Americans to the Japanese "by fomenting a war scare between the United States and Japan; at the present time this is not dangerous [to do], for the United States Army and Navy men believe that war between America and Japan is inevitable" (US Senate Document No. 62 II (1919) 66:1:1457).

To accomplish this he recommended a concerted and systematic campaign "through the mediums of creating public opinion – that the English have used so well – the newspapers, the theatre, the thousands of moving picture shows and the church." He singled out the Hearst newspapers for a leading role in this campaign, because "an examination of the files of the Hearst newspapers will show their bitterness toward Japan. No chance has been passed by them to warn the people against the Japs and to foment trouble in California. Let there develop trouble in California – and presently we shall show it can easily be made – and the Hearst papers will lead in the attack on the Japs." He also mentioned a number of other newspapers and periodicals as likely supporters of the cause, in particular he referred to an editor whose "sympathies have been entirely with Germany since the outbreak of the war." He proposed the production of a play "in New York, Chicago, San Francisco and Los Angeles that will send its audiences out of the theatres heated to the fever point against the Japanese. There should be one-act plays sent over the big vaudeville circuits creating the same effect. There should be a moving picture production anti-Japanese, and put on all the circuits. It should be shown in weekly installments that synchronize with a continued story to be syndicated in the same cities the pictures appear" (US Senate Document No. 62 II (1919) 66:1:1458).

Once the public mind was prepared, he would then "play the trump card" by creating street disturbances and riots on the Pacific coast. "The thugs who engineered the escape of Harry Thaw from Mattewan will do anything for $1,000 a piece. Rioting in San Francisco, etc., against a few Japanese would be child's play for them. The riots against the Japanese begun. The asiatic Exclusion League, the anti-Japanese organization of the Pacific Coast, enters the plan. Its president has served a term in jail; he will do anything made worth his while" (US Senate

Document No. 62 II (1919) 66:1:1458–459). To insure the success of this venture, he would then "get every California clergyman behind it. Ministers in this country love to see their names in the newspapers. They would rush to denounce the Japanese – especially if some outrages against women were planted. It would be an easy matter . . . to use some young and 'innocent' prostitutes to the detriment of the Japs" (US Senate Document No. 62 II (1919) 66:1:1459).

Though few of these activities ever materialized, the German propaganda machine did grind out countless pamphlets. The German agent Vierick, for example, claimed to have distributed by May 1915 alone a third of a million copies of one pamphlet on the yellow peril. Dozens of similar pamphlets found their way into the public domain from then until America's entry into the war.

But perhaps the most powerful ally of the German machine was Hearst, who needed neither persuasion nor cajolery to intensify his yellow peril campaign. Though the congressional investigation failed in its efforts to prove that Hearst was in the pay of the German government, it nevertheless revealed that the previously quoted correspondent was in the employ of Hearst supplying many pro-German and anti-Japanese articles for his newspapers, that the German propaganda machine and the Hearst newspapers seemed to follow parallel courses in their yellow peril campaign, and that Hearst had produced the kind of scurrilous film-play recommended in the correspondent's memo. So outraged was President Wilson when he first saw the movie "Patria," that he pressured the producer into revising it. In the new version, the villains were given Mexican names – though they continued to wear Japanese uniforms.

POSTWAR CONFLICT OF NATIONAL POLICIES AND INTERESTS

The aura of goodwill generated by being on the same side during the war soon dissipated as the war ended. From then on, "wherever Japanese and Americans met, they seemed to take opposite sides on whatever issue was at stake" (Tupper and McReynolds 1937:124). This was particularly evident at the Peace Conference in Paris in 1919 where the American and Japanese delegations clashed on a number of vital issues. Perhaps the most bitter had to do with the disposition of the German leasehold on the Shantung province and of the islands it had possessed. Japan came to the conference fully expecting to inherit these rights, but its claim to the Shantung province was vigorously opposed by China and the United States, both of whom wanted the province returned to China. The conference agreed that Japan had legal rights to the province and awarded the leasehold to it; Japan in turn agreed orally to return the province eventually to China. The decision by the conference evoked great moral indignation in the American press and Congress; the Senate passed a resolution condemning the transfer of the German rights to Japan.

The disposition of the North Pacific German islands, including the island of Yap, also produced a direct confrontation between Japan and the United States. Although Japan had hoped for full possession of these islands, it accepted the mandatory principle set down by the conference early in its proceedings and agreed to a mandate over the islands instead of ownership. The United States, however, objected strenuously to the inclusion of Yap in the Japanese mandate. It argued to no avail that the cable station on Yap provided communications services of inestimable value to American commercial interests, which would be threatened with disruption if political control of the island fell to the Japanese. (Several years later America and Japan worked out an agreement on the matter.)

The third issue of dispute between the two countries had nothing to do with the disposition of territorial rights, as had the first two, but focused instead on the rights of alien nationals in any country to just and equitable treatment without regard to race or nationality. This proposal was presented by the Japanese delegation as an amendment to two articles dealing with civil and religious rights of minorities. The Chinese delegation, which had opposed the Japanese delegation on virtually every other issue, responded with an enthusiastic endorsement of the proposal. The United States and other western powers saw in this proposal a threat of unlimited immigration from Asia and strenuously opposed it. Yet despite their opposition, the League of Nations Commission approved the proposal overwhelmingly, 11 or 12 to 5, only to have President Wilson, who was in the chair of the commission at that time, rule that the proposal required unanimous consent and was accordingly defeated. Once again America and Japan stood on opposing sides: America may have won the parliamentary victory, but Japan emerged as the moral leader of Asians in their struggle for equal treatment.

Even as Japan and the United States were clashing in Paris, events elsewhere were further exacerbating the strains between them. For example, a rebellion had erupted in Korea against the Japanese in the spring of 1919 and was put down harshly by the Japanese government. This evoked a cry of public indignation in America, particularly among missionary circles which had been extremely active in Korea. The American peace delegation used the reports of the rebellion as an argument against Japan's demand for the German rights in Shantung. Eventually the outcry died down as the rebellion was suppressed, and Japan began to show more of a velvet glove than an iron fist in its treatment of the Koreans.

Another event that exacerbated relations was the joint occupation of Siberia by a relatively small American force and a much larger Japanese force ostensibly to rescue retreating Czecho-Slovak troops. Within a year the American force withdrew, but the Japanese force remained for several years. Both sides accused the other of deception, and the American press, particularly Hearst's, had a field day in castigating the Japanese occupation.

Closer to home, the explosive resurgence of anti-Japanese agitation in California, that manifested itself in the initiative movement for an anti-alien land law, fueled to almost white heat tensions between the two countries. Many demonstrations broke out in Tokyo against the discriminatory legislation.

As a result of these accumulating tensions, "by the summer of 1921 a very dangerous state of mind had developed on both sides of the Pacific" (Treat 1928:258). War talk once again became fashionable. What added to the strain were reports of a mounting arms race in which each country was trying to outdo the other in the building of battleships.

At this juncture, the United States took a decisive step. It invited the major powers, including Japan, to a conference in Washington for the dual purpose of establishing limits on armament and of discussing Pacific and Far Eastern questions. At first reluctant to accept, Japan finally joined seven other invitees at the first session of the conference in November 1921. So successful was the conference that within four months six treaties were signed in addition to two others affecting three member states.

The results of the conference were both immediate and far reaching. It effectively removed the "lowering cloud of suspicion and alarm which had hung over the Pacific" (Treat 1928:263). According to Tupper and McReynolds, "the Conference did much to stabilize conditions in China; it created an understanding in the Pacific; it stopped further competition and suspicion; it ended the Anglo-Japanese Alliance; and it showed a practical way to settle differences" (Tupper and McReynolds 1937:166). Enthusiasm for the accords was widespread. Even such hardliners as Franklin D. Roosevelt saw a chance for a real *rapprochement* with Japan. They were even more impressed by the diligent efforts of the various signatories to put the terms of the agreement into effect by 1923.

A turning point seemed to have been reached in relations between Japan and the United States, only to be proved illusory within two years: "This almost ideal state of affairs lasted for two years, and then was rudely broken by the Exclusion Act of 1924.... The Act endangered the peace of the Pacific; it blighted the bud of international good feeling; and it temporarily ruined the hopes of an even closer co-operation between the United States and Japan" (Tupper and McReynolds 1937:166–67). (We shall examine the Exclusion Act of 1924 in a later section of this chapter.)

JAPAN: "THE GERMANY OF ASIA" AND "ITS PEACEFUL PENETRATION OF THE UNITED STATES"

The post-war collision of national interests and policies between Japan and the United States breathed new life into the yellow peril theme, which had lost some of its urgency during the war despite the efforts of the German propaganda machine and Hearst. The collision molded an even more threatening version of Japan as a fearsome and formidable military power. This version was graphically portrayed and written in a series of aricles published in the *Sacramento Bee* in 1919 by V.S. McClatchy, publisher of the *Bee*. (The series was later combined into a pamphlet in 1920.) According to McClatchy, Japan had taken over the militaristic and imperialistic identity and purpose of the country which had long served as its model in its drive for modernization and westernization. As such, Japan had become "the Germany of Asia, with an ambition somewhat similar to that of her model, but limited possibly to Eastern Asia, instead of the world, while her methods are just as relentless and unscrupulous" (McClatchy 1920:4). Accordingly, McClatchy argued, Japan had been rapidly extending its control over China under the guise of "peaceful penetration" but in fact through the force of arms. It had cruelly suppressed the Korean independence movement and tightened its grasp on the country. It also watched with covetous eyes the independence movement in the Philippines, confident that independence, once achieved, would bring the Philippines into its orbit of influence. In all this, McClatchy proclaimed in the subtitle to his pamphlet, Japan "Threatens the Cause of Justice, the Interests of the United States and the Peace of the World" (McClatchy 1920:1).

So ideally did the label "Germany of Asia" seem to fit the Japan of the renascent yellow peril threat that it was soon widely adopted and used with increasing frequency in the revitalized campaign against Japan and the Japanese. McClatchy himself constantly referred to it in his public utterances and written statements.

To McClatchy, however, "the Germany of Asia" was more than a threat to American interests in Asia. It was an even greater threat to the security of America itself in as much as Japan wanted to secure "a place in this favored land for an unlimited number of her people, and ultimately, to obtain through them absolute control of the country" (McClatchy 1920:46). To achieve this goal, McClatchy continued, Japan eschewed the policy of force that it used in pursuit of its imperialistic aims in Asia for a policy of "peaceful penetration."

This *lebensraum* thesis was repeated by other anti-Japanese spokesmen until it became an important ideological link for connecting the national policy of Japan with the Japanese immigrant into a domestic variant of the yellow peril theme. Chambers, Controller of the State of California, wrote in this vein approximately two years after the McClatchy articles.

"Japan must expand, as one of her editors has declared, or smother. This side of the Pacific is far more inviting than the other, to say nothing of the fact that she has already seized every available opening.... Japan now dominated the Orient, and by force. She seeks the eventual domination of the American side through her policy of peaceful penetration, the 'bloodless struggle' of conquest by colonization. Her purpose is obvious." (Chambers 1921:28)

In this manner then, the Japanese immigrant came to be defined as a tool for a national policy of *lebensraum* imperialism. No longer was he necessarily a military man in disguise as in the pre-war image fostered by Fitzpatrick and Hearst; instead he was just an ordinary tiller of soil or hewer of wood who never gave up his ties to Japan.

LOYALTY TO JAPAN AND DUAL CITIZENSHIP

Not surprisingly, then, the question of ties to Japan of the ordinary Japanese in America became an increasing preoccupation of yellow peril ideologues by the end of the war. Earlier in the century the issue had had little relevance. Virtually all Japanese in America had been born and reared in Japan, had not been allowed to become naturalized citizens of the United States, and were therefore expected to view themselves as loyal subjects or citizens of Japan. But by the end of the second decade an increasing number of Japanese were born in America and therefore entitled to American citizenship. Accordingly, the question of their continuing ties to Japan became a focal concern of the ideologues.

They made much of the fact that, under Japanese law, a child of a Japanese father was considered to be Japanese, no matter where his birth might take place, whether in Japan or elsewhere. As such, he was subject to all the rights and obligations of Japanese citizenship, including military service. They made even more of the fact that few American-born Japanese took advantage of the Law of Expatriation passed by the Japanese government that slightly modified this provision in 1916. The new law allowed a foreign-born Japanese, domiciled in a foreign country, to drop his Japanese citizenship under certain restricted conditions. For example, an application for expatriation had to be filed with the Japanese government before the child reached seventeen, the age at which he was subject to military service, or after he had satisfied his military requirements. If the Japanese government accepted the application, the applicant then became an expatriate. According to the Japanese vice-consul in San Francisco, less than a dozen American-born Japanese had filed for expatriation by 1920, and none had as yet been accepted by the Japanese government (California State Board of Control 1920:183).

The yellow peril ideologues saw behind all this a sinister ploy by the Japanese government to retain the loyalty and devotion of its subjects, even those born abroad. They viewed the small number of applications for expatriation as evidence of how successful the government was in retaining this loyalty. These results, the ideologues claimed, were not accidental. They insisted that the Japanese government had spread its tentacles into the Japanese-American communities. In this manner, "Japan not only claims as her citizens all Japanese born on American soil, but she also takes great care that they grow up really as Japanese citizens, with all the ideals and loyalty of the race, untouched by the notions prevalent in this country, which would weaken that loyalty" (McClatchy 1921:31).

Japan had succeeded in doing this, McClatchy insisted, by compelling Japanese children born under the American flag

"to attend Japanese schools, usually after the public school hours, where they are taught the language, the ideals and the religion of Japan, with its basis of Mikado worship. Here they are taught by Japanese teachers, usually Buddhist priests, who frequently speak no English, and who almost invariably know nothing of American citizenship. The text books used are the Mombusho series, issued under the authority of the Department of Education at Tokio. These schools are located wherever there are Japanese communities, and teachers in the American public schools testify that the Japanese children frequently are studying their Japanese lessons in their public school hours."

(McClatchy 1921:31–2)

In addition, he continued, a number of these children were being sent back to Japan for further education where they were "being thoroughly instructed in the religion and ideals of Japan; so that when they return here they may serve, not as American citizens, but as loyal subjects of the Mikado, to do his will and serve his interests" (McClatchy 1921:32–3).

To the Controller of the State of California, Chambers, the Japanese government did not merely influence the educational and cultural environment of the Japanese community in America. It also extended its control to the organizational life of the community and in the process had created a state within the state of California. As evidence of this, he quoted from a Professor Kuno of the University of California:

"'that the Japanese in this state have a government within a government, that they hold their own legislature, with bodies corresponding to our State Assembly and our State Senate; that the numerous local Japanese organizations are tied to a few central Japanese associations, and these, in turn, are tied to the Japanese consuls at San Francisco and Los Angeles, who, in turn, are tied to the Japanese Government itself. Dues are collected from all members, and the enormous sums thus obtained are used largely for propaganda purposes.'"

(Chambers 1921:27)

In creating a society within a society, the ideologues insisted, the Japanese government had succeeded in building a wall between its people, even those born in this country, and the larger American society. As a result, Japanese in America had come to prefer their isolation, even those born in the United States:

> "They do not assimilate! The melting pot does not affect them as it does in time the most refractory of the European races. They remain always Japanese. They maintain their racial purity more jealously than any other race which comes to our shores. They preserve their ideals, their customs, their language, their loyalty to Japan, even when born here, partly because Japan never ceases to hold them as Japanese citizens, and partly because they are taught in Japanese schools by Japanese teachers who frequently speak no English, and have no sympathy with American ideals. It is a dangerous experiment to attempt to make good American citizens of such material!" (McClatchy 1920:44)

In this manner, McClatchy and others expanded the category of nonassimilable to the American-born Japanese who, unlike their parents, could not be deprived of American citizenship and therefore had the chance of becoming part of the American society and its People's Domain. Yet despite this opportunity, according to McClatchy *et al*, they had voluntarily rejected becoming Americanized and had opted instead for remaining loyal subjects of the emperor.

In elaborating the postwar version of the yellow peril threat, a number of these ideologues had little difficulty in linking it with the call for tighter legal controls on acquisition of land by first- or even second-generation Japanese. But unlike other supporters of such legislation, they did not base their approval merely on the grounds that continued acquisition of land by Japanese posed a serious competitive economic threat to white farmers. Instead they opposed acquisition primarily on the grounds that it threatened the political survival of California and other states of the Pacific slope. They were convinced that such acquisition was part of a diabolical scheme by the Japanese government to gain indirect control of the wealth and resources of the various Pacific states for future conquest.

Variations of this theme were central to the plots of two novels that gained nationwide popularity after the war: Wallace Irwin's *Seed of the Sun* (1921), and Peter B. Kyne's *Pride of Palomar* (1921). In Irwin's novel, for example, the heroine who has been forced to sell her farm recounts to a friend a conversation she has had with Baron Tazumi, a suave, educated, and dedicated agent of the Emperor whom she had earlier rejected as a suitor.

> "'He [the Baron] said he was sorry about the trouble on my farm, and that he would have made things easier for me if I had told him. He said that all the Bly [the heroine's] region had to be Japanese; that my farm was a keystone to an

arch of land that had to be held solidly together. He said that the Japanese were moving in America, just as they were moving in Manchuria and Siberia, to gain control of the land that was to make them a great people upon earth. He said that he, as Tazumi, was merely an agent in the hands of a divine power and that divine power was the Emperor.'" (Irwin 1921:348)

THE RESPONSE OF THE JAPANESE-AMERICAN

Disturbed by the growing postwar criticism of their countrymen in California, the Japanese Association of America addressed a memorial to President Wilson in September 1919, almost a year before the initiative movement for alien land legislation was in full swing. In its memorial, the association vigorously denied the charge of nonassimilability of the Japanese. It insisted that

"the Japanese in California are assimilated to a degree unrecognized by anti-Japanese Americans. The native born Japanese are one hundred percent American, while foreign born Japanese are at least fifty percent American in spite of the many obstacles put in their way. Their spiritual attitude toward, and material contributions to, the various enterprises of the late war eloquently testify to this effect." (California State Board of Control 1920:211)

The association then described its program for "Americanizing" the Japanese immigrant.

"The origin of our more or less organized movement for Americanization can be traced back to 1900. We first directed our effort to what we called social education and economic development. We tried to impart to our fellow countrymen elementary facts of American civilization so that they could better fit themselves for American life. We tried to teach them that assimilation was the first step for their success. Then we tried to convince them that by contributing to the national interests of America they could attain their own economic development.

In 1918 when the American government laid down the general plan of the 'Americanization campaign,' we made it the foundation of our work. In fact, we joined the movement." (California State Board of Control 1920:213)

The association then delineated the various Americanization activities of its various branches, from lectures to courses on a variety of topics about America and on learning the English language. "We are helping to organize classes for women and children newly arrived and securing proper teachers for them. We are also helping them to select textbooks so that they can learn the language, and, at the same time, become familiar with America. Such is the nature and scope of our

Americanization campaign" (California State Board of Control 1920:214).

The association also touched on the schools in which Japanese language was taught. "They are primarily for the study of the Japanese language and are not intended to perpetuate the traditions and moral concepts of Japan" (California State Board of Control 1920:215).

The Exclusion Act of 1924

THE CALIFORNIA COALITION AND CONGRESS

Having successfully engineered the impressive victory of the initiative on the alien land law, the leaders of the anti-Japanese coalition in California were determined to press their cause onto the national stage. They were convinced that only governmental action at the federal level could complete the task they had started. This position was foreshadowed by the governor of California as he transmitted his State Board of Control report to the United States Secretary of State on June 1920. In his covering letter, he stated "The [initiative] measure, if adopted, will exhaust the state's power in dealing with this great race problem" (California State Board of Control 1920:13). Confident that the measure would be overwhelmingly adopted (as it subsequently was), he went on to say that his next step would be to bring this "great race problem" before the nation at large; only Congress could do fully what California could do partially. In short, only Congress could vote total exclusion of the Japanese.

In making this national appeal, he conceded that California was primarily concerned with its own selfish interest. But, he insisted, what was good for California today would be good for the rest of the nation tomorrow inasmuch as California "stands as one of the gateways for Oriental immigration into this country. Her people are the first affected, and unless the race ideals and standards are preserved here at the national gateway the condition that will follow must soon affect the rest of the continent" (California State Board of Control 1920:15).

To formulate and to implement its Washington strategy, the coalition was restructured under the mantle of a new group, the Japanese Exclusion League of California; its president, State Senator Inman. "Inman, however, soon proved to be a figurehead; the real power in the organization devolved into the hands of Valentine Stuart McClatchy, its volunteer special representative, who devoted full time to what he felt was a holy cause" (Daniels 1970:91). McClatchy was the retired publisher of the *Sacramento Bee*, a man of independent means and widespread professional and personal contacts among public and political figures in California and Washington. He soon teamed up with Hiram Johnson, California's senior senator, and the two of them "formed what might be called the general staff of the exclusionist forces" (Daniels 1970:91). Even the league's demise as a membership organization in 1922 did not deter McClatchy or Johnson from their efforts.

Toward the end of 1920 the exclusionist forces launched their nationwide campaign to publicize the California position. It was expounded in articles in national periodicals and its postwar version of the yellow peril theme was stamped with the credibility of repetition in the public media. As a result, McClatchy's label of "Germany of Asia" stuck to Japan, as did the fifth-column label of "once a Japanese always a Japanese" to the second- as well as to the first-generation immigrant. In addition, the exclusionist forces quickly neutralized the modest gains made by the pro-Japanese forces led by Dr Sidney Gulick during the war years.

In Washington itself the evolving climate in Congress boded well for the eventual success of the exclusionists. Congress was already in a state of alarm and worry about rumors of a postwar flood of immigration from southern and eastern Europe. As a result of this fear, Representative Albert Johnson of the state of Washington, chairman of the House Immigration and Naturalization Committee, had introduced a bill into the House in December 1920 that would suspend immigration temporarily (for fourteen months as amended) until Congress could work out a permanent policy on immigration. Debate on the measure revealed the extent and depths of concern and despair over the numbers and kinds of immigrants who were threatening to engulf the United States. The chairman of the committee offered a typical expression of these sentiments when he stated. "The immigration coming now is the most undesirable that ever came to the United States" (US Congressional Record 1920 66:3:227).

Overwhelmingly approved in the House, 296 to 42, the measure was sidetracked in the Senate as the chairman of the Senate Committee on Immigration, William P. Dillingham, substituted an entirely different measure. The substitute bill introduced a quota system based on the nationality of the foreign-born: Section 2. "That the number of aliens of any nationality who may be admitted under existing statutes to the United States in any fiscal year shall be limited to 5 percent of the number of foreign-born persons of such nationality resident in the United States as determined by the United States census [of 1910]" (US Congressional Record 1921 66:3:3443).

Senator Dillingham defended his substitute measure as encouraging the desired immigration from northern and western Europe, which the House measure would cut off. It would also reduce the undesirable immigration from southern and eastern Europe, which an "escape clause" in the House version would encourage by permitting relatives of citizens to enter without regard to the ban.

Although neither bill explicitly mentioned immigrants from Asia, they were obviously included in the ban on immigration in the House version. The Senate measure excluded them from the quota provisions on the grounds that they were either "aliens coming from countries immigration from which is now regulated in accordance with treaties or agreements" or "aliens coming from the so-called Asiatic barred zone as described in section 3 of the immigration act of February 5, 1917" (US Congressional Record 1921 66:3:3443). This meant that all Asians, except the Japanese, were to continue to be barred from the United States; the Japanese were still to garner the protection of the Gentlemen's Agreement.

The substitute bill was overwhelmingly approved by the Senate and in a subsequent conference with representatives from the House was accepted by the conferees: the only change being that the 5 percent figure was dropped to 3 percent. The conference report was accepted without debate in the Senate, and with some debate in the House, but in neither case was any mention made of the implied endorsement of the Gentlemen's Agreement in the bill. Both houses finally approved the measure overwhelmingly, only to have it suffer a pocket veto from President Wilson.

Undismayed, Chairman Johnson introduced a slightly modified version of the same bill in the House on April 18 1921 and, with the passage of a privileged resolution on April 20, was able to bring the measure up for immediate consideration. However, unlike the earlier deliberations, the issue of the Gentlemen's Agreement came up at least obliquely. A representative from Tennessee moved to strike out the words "or agreements" from the clause that exempted "aliens from countries immigration from which is regulated in accordance with treaties or agreements relating solely to immigration" from the quota provisions of the bill. In the ensuing debate, no explicit mention was made either of Japan or of the Gentlemen's Agreement. Johnson, for example, in opposing the amendment emphasized the temporary nature of the measure as a whole and mysteriously suggested that the clause was designed "to find out whether we do force the agreement to be actually recognized or not" (US Congressional Record 1921 67:1:571), but he mentioned neither Japan nor the Gentlemen's Agreement. The representative from Tennessee was equally vague and general in his support of the amendment. There seemed to be little doubt, through, that everyone knew which specific agreement and country was the target of the amendment. Despite this, the amendment was rejected, 77 to 40.

Two days later the bill passed the House but not before an amendment to make the 1920 census and not the 1910 census the base year for the quotas was placed before the House. Proponents of the 1920 census wanted to give immigrants from southern and eastern Europe a larger population base for determining their quotas. The amendment was defeated overwhelmingly 72 to 25.

Subsequently the Senate opted for the virtually identical version of the

Dillingham bill it had passed the year before. At a conference to reconcile the differences between the two bills, its delegates succeeded in persuading the House delegates to forgo most of the revisions the House had added to its version of the bill. As a result, both houses of Congress passed on May 13 the virtually identical version of the bill that President Wilson had vetoed, but this time President Harding signed it. Due to expire on June 30 1922, the bill was subsequently extended for two more years.

Despite the Dillingham bill's implied recognition of the Gentlemen's Agreement, the California delegation had apparently decided to avoid any direct confrontation on the issue during the legislative debate on the bill. Instead its leaders, most notably Hiram Johnson, were busy building a foundation of congressional support for the future. They were particularly confident of obtaining the cooperation of the chairman of the House Immigration Committee, Albert Johnson. In addition, Hiram Johnson and McClatchy were still hopeful that the treaty negotiations then in progress between Japan and the United States would produce the results they wanted. They soon lost their optimism and helped abort the negotiations.

By mid-1921 they began in earnest to organize congressional support for exclusion. They set up a bipartisan committee of congressmen and senators from each of the western states to coordinate action and policy on the issue. In addition, they mounted a sustained public campaign. As time went on it became increasingly evident that McClatchy had virtually taken over management of the movement, with Hiram Johnson playing an increasingly pivotal role in Congress.

THE EXCLUSION OF THE JAPANESE FROM THE PEOPLE'S DOMAIN LEGITIMATED BY THE SUPREME COURT

As the exclusionist forces girded for battle, their cause was bolstered by a Supreme Court decision in November 1922 that laid to rest any constitutional doubts about denying membership in the People's Domain to the first-generation Japanese. Exclusionists could now without fear of legal challenge designate these Japanese as "aliens ineligible for citizenship" and be fully confident that any legislation directed against such aliens would *ipso facto* apply to the Japanese.

In delivering the opinion for the unanimous Court in Takao Ozawa v. United States, Justice Sutherland conceded that Mr Ozawa "was well qualified by character and education for citizenship."

"Including the period of residence in Hawaii, appellant had continuously resided in the United States for twenty years. He was a graduate of the Berkeley, California High School, had been nearly three years a student in the University of California, had educated his children in American schools, his family had attended American churches and he had maintained the use of English language in his home." (260 US 1922:189)

Despite his obvious qualifications, the Justice maintained Mr Ozawa was ineligible for citizenship under terms of the naturalization law first set down in 1790 and continually reaffirmed to 1870. Under these terms only "a free white person" (260 US 1922:195) was eligible for the privilege of naturalization, but the Justice argued, the original framers of the law did not merely have in mind a skin color test; they had a racial test in mind. They meant, in other words, to make the privilege of naturalization available only to persons of the Caucasian race.

In doing this, he continued, the framers obviously excluded

"the black or African race and the Indians then inhabiting this country. It may be true that these two races were alone thought of as being excluded, but to say that they were the only ones within the intent of the statute would be to ignore the affirmative form of the legislation. The provision is not that Negroes and Indians shall be *excluded* but it is, in effect, that only free white persons shall be *included*. The intention was to confer the privilege of citizenship upon that class of persons whom the fathers knew as white, and to deny it to all who could not be so classified. It is not enough to say that the framers did not have in mind the brown or yellow races of Asia.... It is not important in construing their words to consider the extent of their ethnological knowledge or whether they thought that under the statute the only persons who would be denied naturalization would be Negroes and Indians. It is sufficient to ascertain whom they intended to include and having ascertained that it follows, as a necessary corollary, that all others are to be excluded." (260 US 1922:195–96)

In 1870, he added, the naturalization laws were "'extended to aliens of African nativity and to persons of African descent'" (260 US 1922:195), but to no other nonwhite race.

THE RESOLUTE ADOPTION OF EXCLUSION BY THE HOUSE OF REPRESENTATIVES

By 1923 exclusionist forces had made significant progress in the House. Even Johnson, the chairman of the House Immigration and Naturalization Committee, had openly joined their ranks. Whereas he had sought to skirt the Japanese issue in the debate on the immigration law in 1921, early in 1923 he went so far as to introduce a general bill to limit immigration of aliens into the United States. This bill included a clause that would bar admission of immigrants not eligible to citizenship. Two weeks later his committee reported the bill favorably to the House as an amendment to a senate bill (S.4092) that was merely concerned with admission into the United States of certain refugees from the Near East. The amended bill was to be called The Immigration Act of 1923. However, "by reason of the rush during the closing months of the Sixty-seventh Congress," in the words of Representative Raker of California, an influential member of the committee, "S.4092, with this House amendment, died a natural death on the calendar." He emphasized, "this is the first time any bill from a committee carrying this or similar provision excluding aliens ineligible to citizenship was ever reported to either House or Congress" (US Congressional Record 1924 68:1: 8639). (He might also have added that the committee's report (US House of Representatives Report No. 1621 (1923) 67:4) offered most of the grounds and rationale that were used to justify the basic provisions for the immigration bill finally enacted by the house in 1924.)

Undaunted, the chairman of the committee reintroduced substantially the same bill (now called H.R. 101) on the third day of the first session of the newly convened Sixty-eighth Congress; two other bills, also based on the earlier measure, were thrown into the House legislative hopper that day, including one by Raker of California. All were referred to the Committee on Immigration and Naturalization which held extensive hearings on the bills from the end of December through January 1924.

Finally on February 9, the chairman presented to the House (H.R. 6540) "a bill to limit the immigration of aliens into the United States and for other purposes" and a report signed by 14 of the 17 committee members in favor of the bill. In its report, the committee emphasized "the immediate and urgent need for enactment of immigration legislation" with the pending expiration of the "3 per cent law" of 1921 on June 30 1924. The committee warned that "if the 3 per cent law is permitted to expire, and if no other legislation is enacted, the movement to our shores of the largest migration of peoples in the history of the world may be expected to begin on July 1, 1924" (US House of Representatives Report No. 176 (1924) 68:1:2).

This inundation, the committee feared, would bring in increasing hordes of aliens and nonassimilable peoples from the countries of "the new immigration" in southern and eastern Europe. Accordingly, the committee felt that it was important

"to slow down the streams of the types of immigrants which are not easily assimilated. Naturalization does not necessarily mean assimilation. The naturalization process cannot work well with the continued arrival in large numbers of the so-called *new immigration* [author's italics]. The new type crowds in the larger cities. It is exploited. It gains but a slight knowledge of America and American institutions. It has grown to be a great undigested mass of alien thought, alien sympathy and alien purpose. It is a menace to the social, political and economic life of the country. It creates alarm and apprehension. It breeds racial hatreds which should not exist in the United States and which need not exist when the balance shall have been restored."

(US House of Representatives Report No. 176 (1924) 68:1:3–4)

To prevent this flood of undesirables, the committee proposed to reduce the 3 percent quota of the 1921 act to 2 percent plus a small base quota for each country and to shift the quota base year from the census of 1910 to the census of 1890. Once again, immigration from Asia was to be excluded from the quota provision of the bill, not, as in the 1921 measure, because it was presumably covered by other treaties and agreements, but because the Asian immigrant was an alien ineligible for citizenship in the United States. Thus Section 12b of the bill stipulated that "no alien ineligible to citizenship shall be admitted to the United States unless such alien…" and then several minor categories of exemption were delineated.

With this stipulation the Japanese joined the other Asians in being barred from entering the United States. No longer were they to be protected by the Gentlemen's Agreement. In making this recommendation, the committee maintained that it was merely making the immigration policy of the United States consistent with the recent ruling of the Supreme Court in the Ozawa case.

"The Supreme Court of the United States has decided that the nationals of oriental countries are not entitled to be naturalized as citizens of the United States under our naturalization laws…. Clearly there should not come to the United States, beyond the exemptions necessary, persons who cannot become citizens and who must continue in the United States to owe allegiance to a foreign government."

(US House of Representatives Report No. 176 (1924) 68:1:14–15)

The committee recognized that its recommendations ran counter to the terms of the Gentlemen's Agreement, but it made light of the standing of the agreement as an international commitment: "The 'gentlemen's agreement' has not been published. It is an exchange of letters…. The provisions of HR 6540 will end in a satisfactory manner a troublesome problem" (US House of Representatives Report No. 176 (1924) 68:1:15).

Six days later the minority of three committee members submitted its own report to the House. It bitterly assailed the majority's labeling of the "new immigrant" from southern and eastern Europe as undesirable and nonassimilable. Accordingly, it opposed the change of the base year from 1910 to 1890 for the quotas and protested the reduction of the quota from 3 to 2 percent. The minority also complained about other features of the bill, but nowhere did it raise explicit objections to Section 12b and its implicit barring of immigration from Japan, despite the Gentlemen's Agreement.

However, the minority did append to its report a letter from the Secretary of State to the chairman of the committee, dated February 8. This letter raised such an objection, and the minority in an oblique reference seemed to find support for its own position from this letter. "The minority at all times contended that the proposed bill based upon the census of 1890 was discriminatory against certain nationalities and is in violation of our treaties with foreign countries" (US House of Representatives Report No. 176 Part 2 (1924) 68:1:13).

In his letter Secretary Hughes complained that the new bill violated Article 1 of the 1911 Treaty between Japan and the United States in failing to exempt from the exclusion clause Japanese subjects who "enter, travel and reside" in America "to carry on trade, wholesale and retail, . . . upon the same terms as native citizens." In addition, he questioned the wisdom of Section 12b of the new law, the exclusion clause.

> "There can be no question that such a statutory exclusion will be deeply resented by the Japanese people. . . . The Japanese are a sensitive people, and unquestionably would regard such a legislative enactment as fixing a stigma upon them. . . . [Such a law] would largely undo the work of the Washington Conference on Limitation of Armament, which so greatly improved our relations with Japan, [and would undo the beneficial effects on Japanese opinion that] American interest and generosity [had] in providing relief to the sufferers from the recent earthquake disaster in Japan. . . .
>
> The question is thus presented whether it is worthwhile thus to affront a friendly nation with whom we have established most cordial relations and what gain there would be from such action . . . [particularly when such legislative action] would seem to be quite unnecessary even for the purpose for which it is devised. . . . If the provision of subdivision (b) of Section 12 were eliminated and the quota provided in Section 10 of the proposed measure were to be applied to Japan, there would be a total of only 246 Japanese immigrants entitled to enter under the quota as thus determined."
>
> (US House of Representatives Report No. 176 Part 2 (1924) 68:1:16)

Further, he added, the Gentlemen's Agreement also assured the United States of the "active cooperation by the Japanese authorities in the granting of passports and immigration certificates" and "in scrutinizing and regulating immigration from Japan to American territory contiguous to the United States." Such an arrangement, he concluded, would give "a double control over the Japanese quota of less than 250 a year [and] would accomplish a much more effective regulation of unassimilable and undesirable classes of Japanese immigrants than it would be practicable for us, with our long land frontier lines on both North and South to accomplish by attempting to establish a general bar against Japanese subjects to the loss of cooperation with the Japanese Government in controlling the movement of their people to the United States and adjacent territories."

(US House of Representatives Report No. 176 Part 2 (1924) 68:1:17)

The third major objection of the Secretary was to the "adoption of the Census of 1890 as the basis of quota restriction. This has evoked representations from European countries, and especially from Italy, which regards the choice of such a basis as a discrimination against her." (Ten days later, he informed the committee of a protest from Rumania.) The Secretary did not offer any specific remedy but merely asked the committee to "examine these representations attentively" (US House of Representatives Report No. 176 Part 2 (1924) 68:1:17). The rest of the letter pointed to various difficulties that would be encountered in administering the law as drawn and offered various recommendations for dealing with these difficulties. (Ten days later the Secretary, in still another letter, criticized other administrative features of the bill.)

As a result primarily of the Secretary's criticisms, the bill was returned to committee for further consideration and revision, particularly with respect to the administrative features to which the Secretary objected. Somewhat over a month later the committee was prepared to resubmit the bill. In the words of its report, "this revision has occasioned so many changes in lines and paragraphs (mostly technical, or relating to detail) that it has been deemed advisable to reintroduce the bill [formerly HR 6540] which now becomes HR 7995" (US House of Representatives Report No. 350 (1924) 68:1:2).

On March 24 the committee placed the bill and another report before the House; this time 15 of the 17 committee members signed it. In addition to changes in various administrative procedures, the committee also sought to meet the Secretary's charge that the earlier bill violated the Treaty of 1911 by adding the following as another class of those exempt from the exclusionary clause 12 (b): "(6) An alien entitled to enter the United States solely to carry on trade under and in pursuance of the provisions of a present existing treaty of commerce and navigation."

The committee turned down the Secretary's suggestion that this exemption should also apply to all aliens entering the United States under a treaty or agreement dealing with immigration. The committee argued that it was prepared to honor any trade or commercial agreement that brought aliens temporarily into the country, but not agreements that in effect usurped Congress' control over immigration generally.

> "The treaty of 1911 is by title and intent a treaty of commerce and navigation. If there be a provision therein regulating immigration, it is improperly there, since regulation of immigration is a prerogative of Congress, and there cannot be reasonable objection to Congress exercising such prerogative notwithstanding a provision erroneously inserted in such treaty."
>
> (US House of Representatives Report No. 350 (1924) 68:1:6)

Though willing to compromise with the Secretary on the trade issue, the committee flatly rejected his dual suggestion of giving Japan a quota and of retaining the Gentlemen's Agreement as an additional mechanism of control. With respect to quotas, the committee repeated its earlier argument that it felt obliged to bring immigration laws and policies into accord with the ruling of the Supreme Court in the Ozawa case. It also added forcefully, "All must agree that nothing can be gained by permitting to be built up in the United States colonies of those who can not, under the law, become naturalized citizens, and must therefore owe allegiance to another government" (US House of Representatives Report No. 350 (1924) 68:1:6). In addition, the committee argued later in the report that such a quota "would also discriminate in favor of the Japanese as against all other Asiatic races ineligible to citizenship" who were already legally barred from entering the United States (US House of Representatives Report No. 350 (1924) 68:1:9).

Unacceptable as such a quota was, the committee found even more unacceptable the Secretary's suggestion that the Gentlemen's Agreement be continued. The committee questioned as it had earlier its validity as a binding international obligation since Congress had not acted upon it. Yet in the agreement, "the congressional prerogative of regulating immigration from Japan has been surrendered to the Japanese Government" (US House of Representatives Report No. 350 (1924) 68:1:7). In addition, the committee expressed itself as being mystified over what the provisions of the agreement actually were. "It consists of correspondence between Japan and our Department of State which has not been made public and access to which cannot be had by this committee without permission of Japan, as explained in the letter of the Secretary of State" (US House of Representatives Report No. 350 (1924) 68:1:7). As a result, even the Department of Labor which was in charge of immigration did not possess a copy of the agreement and "never has been supplied with same."

In addition to its dubious legality, the committee continued, the agreement had also failed to do what it was purportedly set up to do: namely, keep out the Japanese immigrant. Even Roosevelt, the report insisted, had this in mind when he accepted the agreement; but over the years the Japanese population in America had increased materially "partly by direct immigration and partly by birth, and doubtless also partly by surrepititious entry ... and while not questioning her [Japan's] good faith [in implementing the agreement], we are concerned in the result. In certain portions of the Pacific coast the white race confronts the very conditions foreseen by Roosevelt" (US House of Representatives Report No. 350 (1924) 68:1:8).

Finally the committee addressed itself to the criticism by the Secretary and by its own minority of basing the quotas on the 1890 census. In its rebuttal, it disclaimed calling the "new immigrant" undesirable; it merely called them "nonassimilable or slow of assimilation." It insisted that "the United States desires to assimilate those here and to take them into full citizenship." But it added, "We cannot do it if we continue to add great numbers to their own stock. Our viewpoint must be for the good of the United States" (US House of Representatives Report No. 350 (1924) 68:1:13).

To allow the continued arrival of great numbers of "new immigrants" would "upset our balance of population" and threaten the institutional framework of America.

"Since it is an axiom of political science that a government not imposed by external force is the visible expression of the ideals, standards, and social viewpoint of the people over which it rules, it is obvious that a change in the character or composition of the population must inevitably result in the evolution of a form of government consonant with the base upon which it rests. If, therefore, the principle of individual liberty, guarded by a constitutional government created on this continent nearly a century and a half ago, is to endure, the basic strain of our population must be maintained and our economic standard preserved....

[This strain cannot be maintained] if immigration from southern and eastern Europe may enter the United States on a basis of substantial equality with that admitted from the older sources of supply, [for] it is clear that if any appreciable number of immigrants are to be allowed to land upon our shores the balance of racial preponderance must in time pass to those elements of the population who reproduce more rapidly on a lower standard of living than those possessing other ideals." (US House of Representatives Report No. 350 (1924) 68:1:13–14)

To prevent this from happening, the committee argued, immigration would have to be based on a policy of "equitable apportionment between the emigration originating in northwestern Europe and in southern and eastern Europe, respectively" (US House of Representatives Report No. 350 (1924) 68:1:14), so that this apportionment did not alter the proportions that persons from these two stocks presently comprise of the total American population. This would be better accomplished, the committee insisted, by basing immigration quotas on the census of 1890 and not that of 1910.

> "The present quota law [based on the 1910 census] gives 44.6 per cent of our total quota immigration to the countries of southern and eastern Europe, including Asiatic Turkey and Palestine – an amount vastly in excess of what they could claim on any theory of proportional representation by nations or races, with reference to the racial or various national elements in our present population.
>
> Southern and eastern Europe, including Asiatic Turkey and Palestine, have according to the last census about 11.7 percent of the total population of the United States. HR 7995 [based on the 1890 census] gives these great geographical divisions about 15.3 percent of the total quota immigration."
> (US House of Representatives Report No. 350 (1924) 68:1:16)

The Committee might have added that to continue to base immigration on the 1910 census would materially increase the 11.7 percent figure in time whereas quotas based on the 1890 census would keep the percentage relatively constant.

Inasmuch as population proportions would thereby remain approximately the same,

> "the use of the 1890 census is not discriminatory. It is used in an effort to preserve, as nearly as possible, the racial status quo in the United State. It is hoped to guarantee, as best we can at this late date, racial homogeneity in the United States. The use of a later census would discriminate against the descendants of those who founded the Nation and established and perpetuated its institutions."   (US House of Representatives Report No. 350 (1924) 68:1:16)

Three days later, the minority, consisting this time of two instead of the earlier three members, submitted its own report. Once again it hammered away at the discriminatory character of an immigration policy based on the 1890 and not the 1910 or 1920 censuses. "It is to admit a minimum of immigrants from eastern and southern Europe and a maximum from northern and western Europe" (US House of Representatives Report No. 350 Part 2 (1924) 68:1:3). The reason for this discriminatory policy, "however much it may now be disavowed, is the adoption of an unfounded anthropological theory that the nations which are favored are the progeny of fictitious and hitherto unsuspected Nordic ancestors, while those discriminated against are not classified as belonging to that mythical ancestral stock. No scientific evidence worthy of consideration was introduced to substantiate this pseudoscientific proposition. It is pure invention and the creation of a journalistic imagination" (US House of Representatives Report No. 350 Part 2 (1924) 68:1:4). The report proclaimed all were human beings and then went on to describe their contribution to the American society.

Only three paragraphs of the relatively extensive report had anything to say about the Japanese issue. "Believing that there is no excuse for giving offense to foreign governments with which only a few years ago we were associated in a common cause" (US House of Representatives Report No. 350 Part 2 (1924) 68:1:24), the minority expressed regrets over the failure of the majority to accept all of the Secretary of State's recommendations on the matter instead of merely his least important recommendations, particularly since only a "negligible number of persons" would be involved if the quota principle were applied to Japan.

Furthermore, the minority continued, the majority had misrepresented the problem.

> "Reading the majority report one would suppose that our country was being overrun with Japanese immigrants, when, as a fact, during the present fiscal year, the total number of those classified as immigrants arriving here was 2716, while during the same period there were 1349 emigrants. The net immigration from Japan was, therefore, only 1367, the greater part of which under the terms of the gentlemen's agreement must have consisted of merchants and others who were not laborers."
>
> (US House of Representatives Report No. 350 Part 2 (1924) 68:1:24)

The report concluded with the earlier letters of the Secretary of State as an appendix.

As soon as the bill reached the House floor on April 4, debate focused on its provisions bearing on immigration from Europe. Led by Sabath of Illinois, author of the minority report, and a congressman from New York, a frontal attack was launched against 1890 as the base year for quotas. Such a base year, it was argued, would lead to grossly discriminatory treatment against southern and eastern Europeans and was anchored in a spurious racial theory that labeled such people inferior and unassimilable. Either 1910 or 1920 should be taken as the base year. Supporters of the bill denied the charges of implied inferiority but repeated the charge that these immigrants were unassimilable. In addition, they argued, 1890 as the base year was fairer to those who comprised the predominant American stock; any other year would produce results discriminatory to them.

During the first and most of the second day virtually nothing was said about the Japanese issue. Finally toward the end of the second day, MacLafferty of California complained that the western representatives suffered from a disadvantage of numbers in comparison to those from the East. As a result, they had been shunted aside and their case against the Japanese was not being heard. Consequently, "if we from the Pacific coast are going to be heard we must make somewhat of a noise" (US Congressional Record 1924 68:1:5680). He then launched into an elaborate exposition of the yellow peril theme. Japan, he argued, was under intense population pressure, but it refused to control its birth rate for "that is not along their plan of national greatness, because the Japanese woman knows her chief function is the bearing of children."

"As a result, Japan has had to expand beyond its boundaries. Now, Japan in figuring on her future believes that her people are to occupy the shores of the Pacific. That is the plan of elder statesmen of Japan that sometime within 200 years, and it matters not when, this shall come to pass. Let me remind you, gentlemen, that for 2500 years one dynasty has sat upon the throne in Japan in unbroken succession, so what is 200 years? It may be 50, it may be 75, or 100, or 200 years, but Japan believes the time is coming when she will have the shores of the Pacific peopled with her nationals, and you never saw a Japanese in this country – I realize there are exceptions to all rules – who was not just as much ruled from Tokyo as if he lived in Tokyo; and if he does not obey the mandate and dictates of his home Government, his people will be punished because he does not."   (US Congressional Record 1924 68:1:5680)

He then delineated the ways in which the Japanese were undermining the stability of the white society economically and politically. And he concluded with a ringing declaration:

"every Japanese believes that he is a child of the sun goddess, that the world belongs to Japan, and that Japan can possess any part of the world rightly by any means she may see fit to take. That is their belief. From little childhood it is taught them. And so I say that the American Congress must help us in protecting the Pacific coast; must help us who are so willing to come here and help on other problems not so closely our own. When you come to consider this bill I say [you] must protect us and so protect America. [Applause]"
                              (US Congressional Record 1924 68:1:5681)

After he finished, a mild exchange developed between him and several congressmen; he was asked, for example, why he opposed a modest quota for Japanese immigration and why he failed to recognize the contribution of the Japanese to the agricultural economy of California. But before this mild questioning by the several congressmen could blossom into full-scale argument against the Californian, Sabath of Illinois, who was the leader of those who wanted a more "liberal" bill for the immigrant from Southeastern Europe, rose and in one sentence broke the back of any nascent opposition to Japanese exclusion. He proclaimed "I may say that all the committee [on immigration and naturalization] are in favor of exclusion of the Japanese" (US Congressional Record 1924 68:1:5681).

At that point debate on the Japanese issue stopped. After a complimentary remark made to Sabath by Raker of California, one of the leaders of the exclusionist forces ("After the splendid statement of my friend from Illinois" (US

Congressional Record 1924 68:1:5681)), the discussion turned to immigration from Europe and the pros and cons of 1890 as base year for the quotas occupied center stage. Not until much later in the debate that day did the issue of Japanese exclusion come up again, this time in the general context of the need to keep the nonassimilable immigrant out of America. The added fillip as this theme was applied to the Japanese was as follows: "Clearly there should not come to the United States persons who cannot become citizens and who must continue while in the United States to owe allegiance to a foreign country" (US Congressional Record 1924 68:1:5699).

By the the second day of the debate, it had become evident that the theme of nonassimilability had inextricably linked Japanese exclusion with minimal quotas for southern and eastern Europeans in the eyes of those who favored migration from northern Europe and the 1890 base year. A number repeated the refrain voiced by the congressman from Oklahoma. "We must restrict immigration. We must assimilate those who are here and Americanize them before admitting others. If they want to become Americans and believe in our institutions, let them show their good faith by becoming naturalized and obeying our laws" (US Congressional Record 1924 68:1:5867).

This hope, however, applied only to the southern European. The Japanese immigrant was seen as beyond redemption, in part because, as stated by some, he was ineligible for citizenship. Others saw no hope in either type of immigrant. Both were perceived as threatening the stability of America as reflected in the words of a congressman from Arkansas.

> "We have admitted the dregs of Europe until America has been orientalized, Europeanized, Africanized, and mongrelized to that insidious degree that our genius, stability, greatness, and promise of advancement and achievement are actually menaced.... [Accordingly,] I should like to exclude all foreigners for years to come, at least until we can ascertain whether or not the foreign and discordant element now in what many are pleased to term 'our great melting pot' will melt into real American citizens."
>
> (US Congressional Record 1924 68:1:5865)

In a much more intractable diatribe, a congressman from Maine first spoke in glowing terms of America as a nation

> "God-intended, I believe, to be the home of a great people. English-speaking – a white race with great ideals, the Christian religion, one race, one country, and one destiny [Applause].... It [America] was a mighty land, settled by northern Europe from the United Kingdom, the Norsemen, and the Saxon, the people of a mixed blood. The African, the orientals, the Mongolians, and all the yellow

races of Europe, Asia, and Africa should never have been allowed to people this great land."   (US Congressional Record 1924 68:1:5868)

He traced the contaminating influence of these "alien races of alien blood" to the unrestricted immigration policies of the past which

> "have thrown open wide our gates and through them have come . . . alien races, of alien blood, from Asia and southern Europe, the Malay, the Mongolian, the oriental with their strange and pagan rites, their babble of tongues – a people that we can not digest, that bear no similarity to our people, that never can become true Amercians, that add nothing to civilization, but are a menace to our form of government. . . .
>
> The hour has come. It may be even now too late for the white race in America, the English-speaking people, the laborer of high ideals, to assert his superiority in the work of civilization and to save America from the menace of a further immigration of undesirable aliens. [Applause]. . . . [To accomplish this] I wish it were possible to close our gates against any quota from southern Europe or from the orientals, the Mongolian countries and the yellow races of men."
>
>   (US Congressional Record 1924 68:1:5868–869)

Congressmen from the West Coast, particularly from California, spent little time on the issue of immigration from southern Europe. Their restrictionist sentiments were readily apparent; instead they concentrated their attack on Japanese exclusion. In the process they bore down heavily on the Gentlemen's Agreement: its questionable legal validity, its vagueness, and presumed ineffectiveness. Throughout most played on the theme of the yellow peril. One congressman even warned that the pressure of overpopulation and the quest for land might lead to a race war in the future with Japan at the head of the "colored race."

Congressmen who opposed the 1890 base year sought mightily to counter the image of the southern European as unassimilable or undesirable. They constantly alluded to the strong drive of these immigrants to become Americanized. They also referred to the contributions made by them to the American society and identified some who had become outstanding Americans in their capacities as judges, congressmen, and the like. Some also emphasized the ideals that had shaped America. In the words of a congressman from New York,

> "it was a divine inspiration that guided the mind and hand of the creator of the emblem of our country. Why the idea of a grand galaxy of stars in Old Glory if not to typify to the world a land where the brotherhood of man should be realized? As we gaze at that emblem you see a star for he who, or whose ancestors, came from Poland, a star for him from Russia, England, France, Germany, Belgium, Italy – a star for every nation on the face of the earth. Can

any of you say which of the stars of the flag shines brightest upon the history of our country, on our advancement or our civilization, or on our struggles?"

(US Congressional Record 1924 68:1:5850)

Yet despite their ardent advocacy of the cause of the southern European immigrant, none of these congressmen came out in defense of the Japanese immigrant. In fact, Sabath, author of the minority report that had opposed the 1890 base year, dissociated himself even further from any defense of the Japanese immigrant during this day's debate. Several days earlier, as we have already seen, he had cut off further argument on Japanese exclusion by announcing to the House that all members of the immigration committee, even the minority which he headed, favored exclusion. At one point in this day's debate, he announced that he and his fellow minority members on the committee had deferred to the four members of the committee from the West Coast on the Japanese issue because they "are from that part of our country confronted with the Japanese situation, and were better informed as to the conditions than we, [accordingly] we of the minority have agreed to their views. Therefore there is no question as to the Japanese and Chinese proposition to-day" (US Congressional Record 1924 68:1:5893). He then took an oblique swipe at Japan and the Gentlemen's Agreement ("We of the minority also resent interference on the part of any foreign nation or any foreign people."). He went on to boast of the help he provided in eliminating the picture bride practice.

Having made his position clear on this issue, he hastened to condemn the tendency of some of his congressional colleagues to label as "foreigners" those born here with foreign-sounding names. "These people, though of foreign parentage, and those naturalized have, under the Constitution, the same rights and the same privileges, I believe, as American citizens whose parents might have been born of so-called Nordic parents" (US Congressional Record 1924 68:1:5893). In short he would deprive the Japanese immigrant of the right to enter the territory of the United States, but he would fight to protect the right of the southern and eastern European to gain access to the People's Domain.

In this manner the pattern of debate was set until the final day, April 12. The only truly controversial issue was the base year for setting quotas for immigration from European countries. On the final day a congressman from Massachusetts introduced another option, a quota system based on national origins of the total American population, not merely the foreign-born, which he said had originated in the Senate and was being seriously considered there. It was turned down by the House. (We shall see shortly how it fared in the Senate.)

On that day too the House was read letters from the Secretary of State and the Japanese ambassador which sought to clarify the terms of the Gentlemen's

Agreement and to block legislative approval of Japanese exclusion. (The content and significance of these letters, particularly the one from the Japanese ambassador, will be discussed later in this chapter.) All that resulted from these belated efforts was an abortive attempt by a congressman from Brooklyn to slip into a section of the bill bearing on administrative procedures an amendment that would have reaffirmed the Gentlemen's Agreement: "Nothing in this act shall affect the validity of the 'gentlemen's agreement' of 1907 between the United States and Japan concerning immigration from Japan, which agreement is hereby reaffirmed" (US Congressional Record 1924 68:1:6231).

In addition, the letters produced the first address in defense of the Japanese by a congressman from Ohio who read the letters to the House. Speaking obviously in behalf of the Secretary of State, he opened his speech by opposing the exclusion clause as offering "an unnecessary affront to a great and friendly people." He agreed that there was need for restrictive laws against Japanese immigration, and he even echoed the "plural race" theory of the exclusionist as grounds for such a restrictionist policy: "They are of a different race and in a measure uncongenial to our civilization; they have a different form of government; they have different traditions and ideals, reaching back through thousands of years, and they have a different standard of living" (US Congressional Record 1924 68:1:6249).

But, he said, such restriction "can be obtained in a less offensive and more effective way [than by the exclusion clause], namely, by a recognition of the present situation and by dealing with them under the general provisions of this bill." Under the pending quota bill based on 2 percent of the foreign-born residing in this country in 1890, "only 46 immigrants would be admitted from Japan into the United States per year. That number certainly is not dangerous." In addition, the Gentlemen's Agreement insured the assistance of Japan in excluding Japanese immigrants of certain classes and in regulating the entry of others. "Now, if you wipe out that agreement you have lost the cooperation of the Japanese in preventing immigration into this country, and the condition which would be created would be much worse than the present" (US Congressional Record 1924 68:1:6249). He then offered the messages from the Secretary of State and Japanese ambassador as providing a more elaborate and complete statement of the dual theses he was trying to make.

He wound up his speech with the statement that he was not going to ask for a vote on the Gentlemen's Agreement or the exclusion clause.

"This question is pending in the Senate. The Senate has a larger share in our foreign relations; they are in closer touch with this question; and I am not intending to ask for a vote for striking out of this [exclusion] section, but I do wish to utter here most emphatically my protest against this offensive section;

and before this measure becomes a law and goes to the President for his approval I trust either this whole section will be stricken out or that it may be modified so as to relieve it of its objectionable features."

(US Congressional Record 1924 68:1:6251)

As this last threat to the exclusion section sputtered out, the House returned to the last-ditch efforts of opponents of the 1890 base year to change it, or at least to expand the non-quota immigrant section so that a larger number of persons, many of whom would be southern European, could come in under this rubric. All of these amendments failed, even the one that would have recommitted the bill to the committee with instructions to substitute 1910 for 1890 wherever that date occurred. Finally the Johnson bill (HR 7995) was voted on and passed by the overwhelming margin of 323 to 71 with one answering present and 37 not voting.

THE SENATE AND THE CIRCUITOUS ROUTE TO EXCLUSION

Whereas eventual House approval of Japanese exclusion was never in doubt once the matter reached the Committee on Immigration and Naturalization, such was not the case in the Senate. The future of exclusion was problematic from the moment the Senate Committee on Immigration began to consider the bills to restrict immigration that were introduced in the first session of the Sixty-eighth Congress.

The first bill had been introduced by Senator Lodge of Massachusetts four days after the Senate began its new term. Two months later Senator Watson of Indiana threw another bill into the legislative hopper and on February 20 1924, two weeks after the Watson bill, Senator Reed of Pennsylvania introduced his bill "to limit the immigration of aliens into the United States and for other purposes."

All three bills were referred to the Committee on Immigration. Unlike the House committee, the Senate committee was not under the domination numerically or otherwise of congressmen from the West Coast. Only Hiram Johnson, the senior senator from California, was from the West Coast, though his influence far exceeded his lonely position on the committee. In addition, many members, including the committee chairman, were mindful of the foreign policy implications of their actions and were accordingly responsive to the appeals of the state department and less restrictive than their House counterparts in their approach to immigration.

Aware of the general sentiment in the committee, exclusionist forces threw their biggest guns into the battle, seeking thereby to make a strong impression on the senators. Accordingly, of thirteen days of hearings on the Senate bills that ran from the middle of February through the first week of April, four days were devoted exclusively to the Japanese issue. This contrasted sharply with the only occasional mention of the Japanese issue in the more than two weeks of hearings in the House. The "California position" was most forcefully presented by V.S. McClatchy who stressed the yellow peril theme in its various forms under the general caveat that "of all the races ineligible to citizenship under our law, the Japanese are the least assimilable and the most dangerous to this country" (US Senate Committee on Immigration, Hearings (1924) 68:1:5).

Despite the efforts of the exclusionist forces, they found themselves facing a committee that was seriously split on advocating an immigration policy that would be more restrictive than that already enacted in 1921. Committee members struggled mightily over the issue of European immigration, and by a 6 to 5 vote decided to lower the quota from 3 to 2 percent while retaining 1910 as the base year. So split was the committee "on many of the details of the bill" that its chairman stated, in reporting the bill to the Senate on April 2, "that no consensus was arrived at, we all reserved the right to express our own opinions [or to move for any amendments] on the floor of the Senate. We desired to report the bill as soon as possible, and I am free to say that for myself I voted against the reduction to 2 percent" (US Congressional Record 1924 68:1:5412).

The same absence of a decisive committee recommendation, the chairman continued, applied to the provision in the bill on Japanese immigration. In this case though, he remarked, a subcommittee of the committee had decided to retain a revised version of the 1921 exemption. Accordingly, Section 3 now stipulated that one of the seven exceptions to the definition of the term immigrant as used in the bill and thereby exempted from quota restrictions would be "(7) An alien entitled to enter the United States under the provision of a treaty or an agreement relating solely to immigration." However, the chairman added that it was his recollection that the whole committee had not voted on this provision out of deference to Senator Hiram Johnson of California who was away. "We did not desire to dispose finally of this paragraph until he should be present and state his position in the matter" (US Congressional Record 1924 68:1:5415). He concluded that the committee "preferred to let it [the provision] come up on the floor of the Senate" (US Congressional Record 1924 68:1:5416).

As it stood, the present text of this bill

"would leave the Japanese question about which we have heard so much, exactly in its present condition, excepted out of the quota law. Those classes of aliens also who come here under treaties as traders are excepted out of the quota law. In other words, so far as the text of this bill is concerned, we have left the Japanese question to be settled by diplomacy; and if Japan has construed the gentlemen's agreement too liberally, it was the view of many members of the committee that at least before repealing that agreement she should be consulted in the matter." (US Congressional Record 1924 68:1:5415)

Even before the chairman had a chance to finish his presentation two senators proposed amendments to the bill. The senator from Mississippi, a member of the committee, wanted to substitute 1890 for 1910 as the quota base year. Shortridge, the junior senator from California, wanted to insert a provision similar to that of the House bill that would deny immigration into the United States for aliens ineligible to citizenship.

Both amendments were set aside, as the committee's own measure came up for discussion; in time each section and committee amendments to the sections were to be considered. In turn, Shortridge succeeded in having the Senate delay action on the committee's Section 3 (7) provision until the return of Hiram Johnson. For the next five days, no discussion of the Japanese issue took place as other features of the bill were brought up, particularly those bearing on the base year and the percentages for quotas. The only significant statement on the Japanese issue was made by Senator Reed of Pennsylvania on April 3. He prefaced his remarks with the comment "I would prefer to postpone what I have to say on the [the question of Japanese exclusion] until the matter is argued by some one who wants to offend the Japanese and to put the exclusion sections into the bill." (He was obviously referring to Hiram Johnson.)

"[However,] the committee was unanimous, as far as it was in attendance, in leaving out those sections, because it regarded them as an unnecessary affront to a friendly nation, because we think the amount of immigration now coming in from Japan is negligible, and because we feel that the preservation of the gentlemen's agreement more effectually keeps down Japanese immigration than any exclusion law we could possibly adopt."

(US Congressional Record 1924 68:1:5475)

On April 7 Shortridge of California could no longer contain himself and launched a lengthy speech. In it he first informed the senators of his preference for the House bill and reminded them of his own proposed amendments. He proceeded into a scholarly disquisition on America as a republic, "the highest form of civilized government where the rights of men are held in value" and on the need to maintain the sanctity and viability of its People's Domain by "preserving in American a certain type of citizenship drawn from certain races of the human family."

"In order to assure the stability, in order to make certain the future strength and righteousness of the Nation, we must strive for homogeneity among the citizenship. Therein lies the strength of a republic. As nearly as we can, we should seek for and have racial homogeneity; but assuredly we should have homogeneity in the sense of common belief, common aspirations, common devotion. We should seek to have even more than we have today, one people – one people, not many peoples."   (US Congressional Record 1924 68:1:5742)

The Founding Fathers, he continued, were aware of this; "[they] recognized that there were some races peculiarly fitted to participate in this Republic." Accordingly they established "a national policy as to who should become citizens. I seek to impress this upon the minds of all: That we have had a fixed, well known policy since 1790 to this hour as to naturalization" that has "excluded from citizenship practically one-half of the human race" as it applies only to the "free white person" (US Congressional Record 1924 68:1:5742). The senator then alluded to "an ambitious Empire" as having "sought to disturb and break in upon that policy," only to be foiled by the Supreme Court in the case of Ozawa v. United States.

With this as settled national policy, he asked rhetorically "why should we admit into this country for permanent residence people who may never become citizens of the Republic? That is the question; and that question embraces, so to speak, the amendments which I have offered to this bill" (US Congressional Record 1924 68:1:5743). He then responded to his own question.

"It is unwise to admit into our country to reside permanently, in mass, races of people who may never become citizens of the Republic.... There are racial reasons why that is. There are certain races which will not assimilate. They are foreign to each other. There are certain laws of Nature which it is not desirable for man to undertake to suspend. There are different races of men, with different characteristics, with distinct and separate views of life and of death. There are different races of men upon the earth who, living apart, may live in peace and prosperity and happiness, but when brought together to live on the same soil the result is friction, hostility, trouble, sometimes growing into civil contention or civil war. There are different races where there should not be social intercourse or intermarriage....

The strength of a nation – not to speak of its progress, its honor, its glory – the very strength of a nation lies in the oneness of its people. I have only to invite the thoughts of men to travel over the earth and see those races which have maintained their nationality, their institutions, and it will be perceived that those nations which were unified, knit together have survived, while those made up of divergent interests, divergent races, hostile races, unsympathetic races have either fallen by virtue of dangers from within or have become an easy prey to dangers from without. So that from a social or a racial point of view it is not desirable to admit into our Republic a people or any peoples who will not assimilate, or cannot assimilate or who may never become citizens of the Republic." (US Congressional Record 1924 68:1:5743)

He then brought up the competitive economic threat of orientals to whites along the Pacific coast and the widespread opposition to oriental labor by American workers, both organized and unorganized; and he concluded his speech with a plea for exclusion "from America [of] races that are not eligible to citizenship" (US Congressional Record 1924 68:1:5743).

Barely had he finished uttering these words when Shortridge was brought down from the lofty heights of his rhetoric by a series of sharp and critical questions about details. Leading the attack was the senator from Tennessee who in no way challenged Shortridge's general theory but who nevertheless needled him with a variety of pointed and sarcastic queries about the specifics of his proposed amendments and their presumed effect. Paul (1936) suggests in his prize-winning essay that the senator from Tennessee was seeking revenge for Shortridge's stand on an entirely different issue and was therefore seeking to make him squirm on an issue with which they were both in basic agreement. (This became evident several days later when he joined the exclusionist forces.) Shortridge floundered in his responses to the senator. When pressed for statistics to support his argument, he was unable to supply them. Obviously embarrassed, he sought refuge in piling general assertion upon general assertion.

The next day Shortridge arrived with a battery of statistics to answer the Tennessee senator's questions of the day before and then in an obvious shift in strategy launched into an extended attack on the Gentlemen's Agreement and its failure to achieve President Roosevelt's alleged goal of limiting Japanese immigration. Quoting extensively from Roosevelt's letters, the senator purported to show that even Roosevelt had expressed support of exclusionist legislation if the agreement were to fail. And the time was now long overdue for such legislation. Although his attack on the Gentlemen's Agreement elicited some support from his fellow senators, his return to a demand for complete exclusion evoked a critical response from a number. He was particularly pressed on the issue of why he rejected a quota for Japan, particularly when such a quota might involve no more than 46 to 100 Japanese annually and would also satisfy the state department and the Japanese government. As one senator said:

"My thought was that perhaps the Senator from California would not want to overrule the viewpoint of the State Department and disturb or threaten with disturbance the amicable relations that now exist between this Government and Japan, merely to prevent the admission of 46 or 100 Japanese annually into the United States. I am interested in the Senator's viewpoint."

(US Congressional Record 1924 68:1:5809)

In reply, Shortridge offered the beginnings of a "foot-in-the-door" thesis that was to be developed with greater sophistication in coming days:

> "In the large sense we are opposed to the placing of these peoples upon the quota, for that is but a step along the line of their ambition. If placed upon the quota at all it is a law subject to change, subject to annulment, subject to be added to or taken from."   (US Congressional Record 1924 68:1:5809)

In the quickening tempo of the exchanges, Shortridge crossed swords with the man who had already taken over leadership from the chairman of the immigration committee in shepherding the bill through the Senate, Reed of Pennsylvania. After biding his time, Reed came down hard in opposition to Shortridge's exclusion amendment and in support of the committee's bill:

> "If the bill passes in the form in which it has left the committee, the inflow of Japanese will be restrained by these two factors: First, the gentlemen's agreement, which will remain in effect; and, next, the quota system. We will have a double check, and it will operate as a check not only to the lawful arrival of Japanese immigrants but as a check to the smuggling across the Canadian and Mexican borders and through Cuba. I say, therefore, that the present system is effective and will be made more effective by the adding of this quota law."
>   (US Congressional Record 1924 68:1:5810)

Reed offered still another reason for his opposition to the Shortridge amendment: the need to continue the positive results from the Washington conference and from Amercia's largesse to Japanese earthquake victims that had transformed relations between the two countries from tense and bellicose to warm and friendly. And finally Reed shredded the exclusionist argument about the imperialistic designs of Japan.

> "The fact remains that with the passage of this bill as it stands the number of Japanese is bound to diminish. The Japanese government does not wish to colonize the United States and does not wish to force her emigration into our ports. But they are a proud people, everybody knows that, and they would resent an exclusion law, just as we would resent an exclusion law passed by Japan. They would resent it particularly because they realize as we must that there is no sense in it, that we do not need an exclusion law in order to keep down the number of Japanese in this country. They would resent it finally because it is the same as saying to them that they do not keep their plighted word with this country, when I think and the Secretary of State says that they have kept their agreement and kept it faithfully."
>   (US Congressional Record 1924 68:1:5810)

Displeased by this heavy barrage, Shortridge sought to pick flaws in Reed's arguments only to retreat defensively into a corner. No one came to his defense and his amendments seemed destined to ultimate defeat, although no one rose to challenge his basic thesis.

The Senate then turned to other business and did not return to the immigration bill until later in the day. It then engaged in a desultory and relatively unfocused discussion on various features of the bill. Finally the committee put before the Senate its proposal to exempt from the definition of immigrant, Section 3 (7) "an alien entitled to enter the United States under the provisions of a treaty or an agreement relating solely to immigration." Almost immediately the climate in the Senate chilled, and the committee, which just hours before had fended off so easily Shortridge's assault on quotas for the Japanese, now found itself on the defensive. Leading the attack was Swanson of Virginia. First, he asked whether "people can be admitted under the so-called Roosevelt gentlemen's agreement, and not counted in the quota?" He was assured by Reed that all but "the excepted classes of government officials, temporary visitors, and so forth, is to be counted in under the quota, and the quota will be only a few hundred" (US Congressional Record 1924 68:1:5828).

The senator from Virginia then repeated a complaint that had already been voiced by many congressmen:

> "I have inquired and tried to ascertain, and have listened to this debate, and I have never seen anybody yet who could define to me what the gentlemen's agreement is, about which we hear so much. It seems to me it is as indefinite as vapor. Am I to understand that it will be left to the discretion of the Government officials to determine what that agreement is if this bill is passed?"
> (US Congressional Record 1924 68:1:5828)

The senator then pressed home the point that Japan maintained control over which Japanese received passports to America and accordingly "the question of immigration and the enforcement of it and the judgment as to it is left entirely to Japan." Once having set the stage, the senator warmed to the attack: "Immigration is a domestic question," he declared, and he would never support a provision that would "permit a domestic question to be administered outside this country. As I understand it, this agreement was that passports should be controlled abroad, and it is a practical agreement that this domestic question shall be administered outside of the United States" (US Congressional Record 1924 68:1:5829). The senator then launched into a general philosophical statement about the matter.

> "I feel toward immigration as a man feels toward his own home. I might give you permission to enter my home, but when your entrance into my home has

ceased to be desirable, I stop it. I am not willing to give anybody the power to put in the statute a provision that I cannot control admission to my own home. This is as much a domestic question as any question possibly can be. It seems to me that if we insert this provision in this bill we will actually ratify a method by which the solution of a domestic question can be enforced outside of the United States. I am not impeaching the integrity or the honor of Japan, but I am simply defending an inherent right in this Nation to treat this question precisely as an individual would treat a question relating to his own home."

(US Congressional Record 1924 68:1:5829)

At that point the senator from Colorado entered the fray and questioned the propriety of the Senate's endorsing a contract or agreement made solely by the executive government which had in substance the effect of a treaty, without, however, having been submitted to the Senate for ratification as required by the Constitution.

Obviously discomfited by the onslaught, Reed of Pennsylvania lamely suggested that the Senate had already done so in the quota law of 1921. "We exempted countries with which we had agreements relating solely to immigration. We exempted them entirely from the operation of that act" (US Congressional Record 1924 68:1:5829). Pressed even harder on whether Senate approval of the committee's provision would stamp the agreement with the legitimacy of a treaty, Reed conceded that it would. With that comment he began to backtrack on support of the committee's provision and the Gentlemen's Agreement that he had so lavishly given earlier. Then he had proclaimed that both the agreement and quotas would give America a "double check" on Japanese immigration, particularly since the agreement, he insisted, had been so effective; now he professed to find little use in the provision which was inserted in this bill, he maintained, "at the suggestion of the State Department. For myself, I never saw much use in them, and I think the bill will be equally effective if they are left out. I imagine that the reason the State Department suggested them was that they felt that it was giving us dignity to class this gentlemen's agreement along with treaties and that was their motive in making the suggestion" (US Congressional Record 1924 68:1:5829).

He sought to dissociate himself still further from the committee's provision after the senator from Virginia renewed his attack. "As I understand, nobody knows what this agreement is. Nobody will have authority to interpret it except the foreign ministers of Japan and of the United States. Are we willing to leave our immigration laws subject to their interpretation?" (US Congressional Record 1924 68:1:5829).

Reed agreed that there was much to what the senator from Virginia had to say but reminded him that he should have said it in 1921 as well. Reed then retreated even more ignominiously by suggesting that the committee had not really given much thought to the matter.

> "What we have done has been to copy, parrot-like, at the suggestion of the State Department, the same words that were in the old quota act, and, as I said before – and I think my colleagues on the committee agree with me – I do not think it makes very much difference whether these words go in or stay out."
>
> (US Congressional Record 1924 68:1:5829)

Colt, chairman of the committee, disagreed and said it would make a difference. But he made no strenuous defense of this position. While acknowledging that the senator from Virginia had raised a serious issue, he nevertheless maintained that the United States "did enter into this agreement, and my objection is that if the United States makes any kind of agreement with another nation, before repealing that agreement, whether it is a treaty or a simply agreement, we ought to consult that nation" (US Congressional Record 1924 68:1:5829).

Emboldened even more by the weak and vacillating responses of the leaders of the committee, the senator from Virginia leveled his heaviest barrage of the debate.

> "I am tired of the State Department entering into agreements fixing the foreign policy of this country except by treaty. The Constitution determines how the foreign policy of this country shall be fixed. I am tired of people making understandings of the force and effect of treaties and committing us in foreign matters so as to avoid coming to the treaty-making power. I am certainly opposed to it. I am especially opposed to surrendering a domestic question to the secretaries of the foreign departments. Immigration is a domestic question, to be settled by the law of the United States, and not by Cabinet officers. It is time for Congress to let it be understood, both here and abroad, that the matter of immigration is a domestic question and to be determined by the people of the United States."
>
> (US Congressional Record 1924 68:1:5829–830)

At that juncture the senator from Mississippi rose, expressed his support for the stand of the senator from Virginia, and proclaimed his sympathy for California. He then asked the Senate to postpone until the next day further discussion of the provision so that the senior senator from California who had just returned to Washington could participate in the debate. The Senate then moved on to other minor items in the committee's bill.

The next day Hiram Johnson lent his powerful voice to the growing opposition to the Gentlemen's Agreement.

> "For some reason that I never had been able wholly to fathom, the United States Government yielded its right to determine the character of its immigra-

tion from the Japanese Empire as it has yielded it in the case of no other nation. In respect to every other country our Government not only has tenaciously held to the right but has jealously guarded the right of determining who could come, in what numbers, and in every other particular has insisted that our Government alone should be the sole judge; and as a fundamental proposition it will be obvious that a nation must guard this right, or a nation yields at once its jurisdiction and its control over that which peculiarly is its own province.... We have relinquished our sovereignty in this regard to only one country – that is, Japan."

(US Congressional Record 1924 68:1:5952)

Not merely content with opposing the committee's provision, he sought to breathe new life into the Shortridge amendment and repeated most of Shortridge's arguments, though in a less flamboyant style.

Shortly thereafter – following an interlude of debate on general features of the immigration bill – the senator from Tennessee who had baited Shortridge so sarcastically the other day announced that he too was opposed to the committee's amendment on the Gentlemen's Agreement. Having never been ratified by the Senate, he argued, the agreement

"has not been constitutionally made; it has not been legally made. We ought not to give it any force. Not a Senator in this Chamber has ever seen that agreement. We do not know what it provides; but here we are proposing to put ourselves into the indefensible position of violating our Constitution and upholding an agreement at which not a single Senator has ever looked in his life. Such action would be indefensible. I take it that the Senate will never agree to the amendment proposed by the committee."

(US Congressional Record 1924 68:1:5957)

Having recovered his equilibrium somewhat from the previous day, Reed of Pennsylvania reminded the Senate that the law of 1921 gave implicit approval to the agreement.

"[However,) the present law will expire on the 1st of next July, and we have to do something. What we want to do is to continue the present stituation, except to put on an additional restraint by means of a quota. At the present time the law of 1921 would give Japan a quota if it were not for the 'gentlemen's agreement.' [Furthermore,] it is worthwhile for the Senate to remember that while the 'gentlemen's agreement's was made by Mr. Roosevelt it was observed throughout the Taft administration, throughout both the first and second Wilson administrations, when the administration of the opposite party had plenty of opportunity to terminate it if they did not like it, and has been observed ever since and no administration has criticized it."

(US Congressional Record 1924 68:1:5950)

The senator from Tennessee replied that "it makes no difference what administrations accepted it, I have never known a better time to put an end to it." Furthermore, he declared that he was unequivocally opposed to any quota for Japan, even one as low as 246.

"Whenever we permit a quota of 246, we have established a principle by which in the future Japanese can come in here as the subjects of other nations come in. To that I am opposed. I am opposed to it not because I do not believe the Japanese are a great people, for they are a great people, but because we can never assimilate that race of people with ours, and if we should attempt to do so it would result in injury to both races, and in my judgment ought not to be thought of for a moment by American citizens."

(US Congressional Record 1924 68:1:5958)

In this manner, the senator from Tennessee revealed that he was in complete accord with the sentiments of the two senators from California and probably always had been, though a few days before he had taunted the junior senator from California mercilessly.

Other senators echoed the Tennessean's disdain for the Gentlemen's Agreement, only one senator sought to defend it, and by the end of the day's debate it was evident that the committee's amendment was in deep trouble.

THE EFFORTS OF THE AMERICAN AND JAPANESE GOVERNMENTS TO SALVAGE THE GENTLEMEN'S AGREEMENT

Two days later a letter from the Japanese ambassador to the Secretary of State and the latter's reply were read into the record of the Senate, just as they were to be read into the record of the House of Representatives a day later. The letter from the ambassador was the latest expression of concern by the Japanese government which had been maintaining a close vigil since the inception of congressional deliberations on the immigration bill. As early as a week after the Johnson bill was introduced into the House of Representatives in December 1923 the Japanese ambassador informed the Secretary in a face-to-face meeting of his government's apprehension about the exclusion provision of the bill. He stressed its evident conflict with the Treaty of 1911 and the Gentlemen's Agreement.

Approximately a month later the Japanese government submitted to the state department a memorandum in which these worries were more fully elaborated. Taking note of the Supreme Court's decision in the Ozawa case, the Japanese government stated that the Johnson bill's exclusion of aliens not eligible to American citizenship

> "means an open declaration on the part of the United States, that Japanese nationals as such, no matter what their individual merits may be, are inadmissible into the United States, while other alien nationals are admissible on certain individual qualifications equally applicable to them all. It is not easy to understand that this would not be an arbitrary and unjust discrimination reflecting upon the character of the people of a nation, which is entitled to every respect and consideration of the civilized world. Nor does it seem to harmonize with the well-known principles of America's foreign policy, which stands for international justice and is opposed to discriminations against American nationals." (US Foreign Relations 1924 II:334–35)

The memorandum then went on to remind the American government of the *quid pro quo* in concluding the Gentlemen's Agreement and the Treaty of 1911 with its appended provision.

> "[On the one hand,] the sole desire of the Japanese Government was to relieve the United States Government from the painful embarrassment of giving offence to the just national pride of a friendly nation, which is ever so earnest and has spared no effort in preserving the friendship of the United States.... [On the other hand, in making these arrangements, the Japanese government wished] to avoid such discriminatory legislation as that now under consideration, and the American Government showed that it fully understood and appreciated the Japanese opposition to any form of discrimination against the Japanese people as such, and virtually assured the Japanese Government that, in return for these sacrifices, made in order to preserve the self-respect of their nation, the United States Government will see to it that there shall be no discriminatory legislation on the part of the United States against Japanese people as such." (US Foreign Relations 1924 II:335)

The provision of the new bill, the memorandum continued, violated these understandings and "is mortifying enough to the Government and people of Japan. They are however exercising the utmost forbearance at this moment, and in so doing they confidently rely upon the high sense of justice and fair-play of the American Government and people, which, if properly approached, will readily understand why no such discriminatory provision as above-referred to should be allowed to become a part of the law of the land" (US Foreign Relations 1924 II:336).

The memorandum then assured the state department,

"it is not the intention of the Japanese Government to question the sovereign right of any country to regulate immigration to its own territories. Nor is it their desire to send their nationals to the countries where they are not wanted.... To Japan the question is not one of expediency, but of principle. To her the mere fact that a few hundreds or thousands of her nationals will or will not be admitted into the domains of other countries is immaterial, so long as no question of national susceptibilities is involved. The important question is whether Japan as a nation is or is not entitled to the proper respect and consideration of other nations. In other words the Japanese Government ask of the United States Government simply for that proper consideration ordinarily given by one nation to the self respect of another, which after all forms the basis of amicable international intercourse throughout the civilized world."

(US Foreign Relations 1924 II:336)

Responding to the entreaties of the Japanese government, the Secretary of State raised several basic objections to the House bill in a letter to Congress on February 8. As we have already seen, the House Committee on Immigration and Naturalization responded favorably to one of these objections and modified the bill accordingly. But it stood fast on the exclusion clause and on its opposition to the Gentlemen's Agreement.

On March 24 the committee returned the revised bill to the House floor under a new title, HR7995 accompanied by a new report, HR Report 350. Three days later the Secretary of State and Japanese ambassador met to discuss their mounting concern over the misinformation and ignorance that Congress seemed to display about the agreement. The secretary recommended to the ambassador a course of action to meet the dual charge that the agreement was a secret arrangement and that it had proved ineffective. He suggested that the voluminous correspondence from which the agreement emerged should be abridged into a relatively brief but authoritative memorandum and that the ambassador should write a letter highlighting the mutual understanding between the two governments with respect to the purposes and practices of the agreement and demonstrating the agreement's effectiveness.

After several more discussions, a memorandum was prepared by the state department and transmitted to the Japanese government on April 8. And two days later the Japanese ambassador submitted his letter to the state department. In his letter he stressed that the agreement was "in no way intended as a restriction on the sovereign right of the United States to regulate its immigration" (US Foreign Relations 1924:370). Instead, he insisted, it was an understanding arrived at with the United States after extensive and friendly discussions "by which the Japanese government voluntarily undertook to adopt and enforce certain administrative measures designed to check the emigration to the United States of Japanese laborers." This was done to forestall enactment of "discriminatory immigration legislation on the part of the United States [which] would naturally wound the national susceptibilities of the Japanese people ... [and offend] the natural pride of a friendly nation" (US Foreign Relations 1924:370).

He assured the Secretary that his government had "most scrupulously and faithfully carried out the terms of the Agreement, as a self-imposed restriction." He quoted statistics to prove the effectiveness of his government's efforts. He also insisted that his government was prepared to continue to implement the agreement, even to amend or modify some of its terms so that it might become more restrictive. But his government objected to legislation which singled out its subjects to discriminatory treatment.

He then questioned the necessity of the exclusionary clause, Section 12 (b) of the House Immigration bill, particularly since

> "the Gentlemen's Agreement is, in fact, accomplishing all that can be accomplished by the proposed Japanese exclusion clause except for those 146. It is indeed difficult to believe that it can be the intention of the people of your great country, who always stand for high principles of justice and fair-play in the intercourse of nations, to resort – in order to secure the annual exclusion of 146 Japanese – to a measure which would not only seriously offend the just pride of a friendly nation, that has been always earnest and diligent in its efforts to preserve the friendship of your people, but would also seem to involve the question of the good faith and therefore of the honor of their Government, or at least of its executive branch."   (US Foreign Relations 1924:373)

He closed his letter with a sentence that came back to haunt him mercilessly and that was used by various senators to pervert the overriding friendliness of his correspondence:

> "Relying upon the confidence you have been good enough to show me at all times, I have stated or rather repeated all this to you very candidly and in a most friendly spirit, for I realize, as I believe you do, *the grave consequences* [author's italics] which the enactment of the measure retaining that particular provision would inevitably bring upon the otherwise happy and mutually advantageous relations between our two countries."   (US Foreign Relations 1924:373)

FROM "GRAVE CONSEQUENCES" TO EXCLUSION

Although the letter from the Japanese ambassador elicited no significant comment when it was first read on the Senate floor April 11, three days later it became the target of an explosive response when debate resumed on the committee's amendment on the Gentlemen's Agreement. Whereas the amendment was already under heavy siege from the debates of April 9, now it faced certain annihilation as the Senate prepared to rise to the fullness of its patriotic fervor in order to repulse the "grave" threat from the "yellow peril." No sooner had the Senate turned to the committee's amendment, when Senator Lodge rose to request a closed door session inasmuch as the amendment pertained to "foreign relations with other peoples."

Approximately an hour later, the doors were reopened and soon the intense patriotic indignation expressed in the secret session began to trickle to the Senate floor. No longer suffering from a feeling of defensive isolation the junior senator from California mounted a long-winded attack on the amendment and a strong plea for his amendment. He even revived the yellow peril theme in a matter-of-fact statement about Japan's imperialistic goals.

> "She wants to expand. She seeks other lands. She says her people are over-crowded, wherefore she looks abroad and seeks those countries agreeable to her people and where she may settle permanently, where she may permanently reside. First, she wants more land. She wants expansion. Second, she wants permanent residence in these other lands. Third, she wants the ownership of other lands." (US Congressional Record 1924 68:1:6305)

While Shortridge's comments were received with a tolerance they had not been shown before, the first really significant sign that the amendment was going to be stumped to death was when Senator Lodge rose to say publicly what he had said privately in the executive session. He first professed a lifelong friendship for the Japanese people and an abiding concern for their sensibilities in matters of legislation, forgetting of course his chronic obsession with the yellow peril as seen in his role in the Magdalena Bay affair. However, he continued, the letter from the Japanese ambassador contained a "veiled threat" and "the United States cannot legislate" under the duress of such "veiled threats."

> "Owing to this, what we are now doing assumes the character of an international precedence; and I think it should be understood, and understood by the whole world, that the United States alone is to say who shall come into the United States to form part of its citizenship. What our country determines as to its immigration is neither a just cause of offense nor a subject for war or threats of war. It is an undoubted sovereign right and nothing else."
> (US Congressional Record 1924 68:1:6305)

Lodge was then interrupted by the senator from New Hampshire who asked him "why he repeatedly uses the words 'veiled threat?' The Senator knows perfectly well that in the composition of diplomatic communications the two words 'grave consequences' are not veiled. They are well known in their implication" (US Congressional Record 1924 68:1:6305).

Lodge agreed, saying that "they are just as well known as the phrase 'the United States could not regard with indifference' the violation of the Monroe doctrine. Everybody knows that 'cannot regard with indifference' means. Both phrases are the well-recognized language of diplomacy." Under the circumstances, he concluded, he could not support the committee's amendment, for "I never will consent to establish any precedent which will give any nation the right to think that they can stop by threats or by compliments the action of the United States when it determines who shall come within its gates and become part of its citizenship. That is a decision which belongs to the United States alone, and from that decision there can be no appeal" (US Congressional Record 1924 68:1:6305).

Whatever were the remaining doubts about the fate of the amendment after Lodge spoke, they evaporated when Reed of Pennsylvania, the *de facto* floor manager of the bill, rose to address the Senate. Reverting to the defensive posture he had assumed earlier in the debate and once again explicitly dissociating himself from authorship of the amendment, he meekly put forth the committee's reasons for advocating both the Gentlemen's Agreement and quotas for Japan.

"It was our feeling that that would be more effective than such an exclusion section as has been offered by the Senator from California. It was a choice of methods. To our mind one was a friendly method and the other was at least open to the charge of being an unfriendly method, involving some racial discrimination. It was with that thought that the committee offered the amendment."   (US Congressional Record 1924 68:1:6305)

Now, he continued, the situation had changed and no longer was the relevant issue that of selecting a more desirable method of restricting immigration.

"The letter of the Japanese ambassador puts the unpleasant burden upon us of deciding whether we will permit our legislation to be controlled by apprehensions of 'grave consequences' with other nations if we do not follow a particular line of legislative conduct."

(US Congressional Record 1924 68:1:6305)

On account of that veiled threat he would vote against the committee's amendment.

"[But he would do so] with deep regret, because I believe that this action, which is forced upon us, means the waste of much of the results of 20 years of excellent diplomacy. It means the waste of much of the good feeling that followed the ratification of the four-power treaty, and it means a loss of part of the good relations that followed the prompt and friendly action of America after the Japanese earthquake of last year. When I vote against the committee amendment I expect to do so with a sad heart." (US Congressional Record 1924 68:1:6305)

With the two leading senators sounding the clarion call, the stampede was on. Many echoed variations on the theme of the "veiled threat". Those who had already expressed opposition in the earlier debate merely repeated what they had said before, but with a tinge of "I told you so." Only the senator from South Dakota, a member of the committee, rose to the defense of the amendment. He scoffed at interpreting the Japanese letter as a threat and protested at using the letter as a pretext to defeat the amendment. Instead he said the issue should be faced on its own merits, and the amendment accordingly supported. The chairman of the committee had little to say other than to remind his fellow senators at one point during the debate that the amendment merely replicated what was already in the law of 1921: "The act of 1921 recites the exact language which is in the present bill now before the Senate" (US Congressional Record 1924 68:1:6307).

As the debate wound down, the Democratic senator from Alabama could not refrain from taunting the Republican leaders with the charge that their outburst of patriotic indignation over the ambassador's letter was but a smokescreen for the ignominious retreat they were forced to take on a position they held as late as the past week. Even before the letter they found themselves facing defeat on the amendment. As a result, "when Republican leaders discovered that they were whipped, and whipped to a frazzle, they had a hurried conference, had it this morning, and now they come in and say that they take offense at something that a Jap ambassador has written upon the subject" (US Congressional Record 1924 68:1:6314). He then went into a diatribe against the Republican leaders and the Gentlemen's Agreement.

The vote on the committee's amendment showed how complete the rout had become. Only the senator from South Dakota and the chairman of the immigration committee, Colt, held their ground and voted for the amendment. Seventy-six others, including Reed and Lodge and all the other members of the immigration committee voted against it; eighteen senators did not vote.

Throughout the day's debate on the amendment, senators argued as though two issues were before them, not one. A vote against the amendment, they claimed, would not only abrogate the Gentlemen's Agreement but also deny Japan an immigration quota under the bill. Even Reed of Pennsylvania repeated this claim in his own recantation. In so doing, he conveniently forgot that less than a week before he had met the first concerted attack on the amendment by lamenting its inclusion in the bill. At that time he implied that action on the Gentlemen's

Agreement was not necessary to insure any quota for Japan.

Soon after the vote on the amendment, Reed apparently become aware that this was indeed the case; the two issues were separate. Accordingly he met with the two senators from California and other exclusionist leaders and on the very next day, April 15, brought to the floor of the Senate an amendment "identical in its effect" to the provision already passed by the House. It began as did the other "No alien ineligible to citizenship shall be admitted to the United States unless such alien." The amendment was passed without any recorded vote; however, on the next day Reed called for a reconsideration of that vote. He explained that he wanted to redeem his promise to two senators who had favored the committee amendment that no action would be taken on the exclusion amendment while they were absent. The second vote showed that the two senators were joined by only two others in opposition to the exclusionary amendment; 71 others favored it and 21 did not vote.

SENATOR REED AND THE NATIONAL ORIGINS PROVISION

With the battle over the Japanese exclusion ended, the Senate turned its attention to another major struggle still in progress: the base year for the quotas. The issue had already been joined between those who favored the committee's base year of 1910 and those who wanted the base year of 1890. In addition, Reed had also thrown into the legislative hopper a third alternative which would go into effect, if enacted, several years later. He proposed a quota system based on the national origins of the total population, not merely the foreign-born, as counted in 1920. He conceded that the results of his plan would be similar to those obtained from the quotas based on the 1890 census. But the 1890 method gave the "illusion" of being unfair to southern and eastern Europeans whereas the 1910 was "in fact" unfair to the northern and western Europeans and therefore discriminated against those who comprised most of the American stock. His approach, he argued, avoided both problems because it would be based on the way America was actually constituted. Thus, "if we can determine the national origins of all our people, foreign born and native born, then the fairest thing and the wisest thing to do is to make our immigration an exact cross section of our present population" (US Congressional Record 1924 68:1:5943). His proposal, however, excluded "descendants of such persons as were involuntary immigrants into the territory now included therein" (US Congressional Record 1924 68:1:6471).* He had

---

*Senator Reed's recommendation that descendants of "involuntary immigrants" should be excluded from the population base from which immigration quotas were to be determined is yet another expression of America's historic duality. This will be examined more fully at the end of this chapter.

justified this exclusion earlier by saying "they the American blacks do not want, and we do not want, to allow great immigration from African sources. This is self-evident to all of us" (US Congressional Record 1924 68:1:5468). Aware, though, that the 1870 modification of the naturalization laws permitted citizenship for immigrant blacks, he replied later that they could come under national quotas. For example, blacks from the British colonies in the Caribbean "would be charged, if they came at all against the British quota. We want to hold down the immigration that has begun to spring up among the negroes, of the West Indies" (US Congressional Record 1924 68:1:5945).

On April 16, the Senate passed a modified version of this amendment. It called upon the Secretaries of State, Commerce, and Labor to make a joint estimate by March 4 1926 of the "several national origins of the persons who in 1920 comprised the whole population of continental United States, excepting the descendants of such persons as were involuntary immigrants into the territory now included therein." The revised amendment also provided that after July 1 1927, instead of the original July 1 1926, total annual immigration should not exceed 150,000, reduced from the original 300,000, and "the annual quota of each nationality shall bear the same ratio to said maximum total number of immigrants as the number of inhabitants of the United States having that national origin shall bear to the whole number of inhabitants other than the descendants of involuntary immigrants" (US Congressional Record 1924 68:1:6471).

To fill the transitional gap, the Senate rejected the committee's proposal that immigration quotas be based on 2 percent of the foreign-born population counted in the 1910 census and after complicated parliamentary maneuvering opted for 2 percent of the 1890 census.

Finally on April 18 the Senate ended deliberations on the immigration bill and decided by 62 to 6 with 28 not voting to append its bill (S. 2576) as an amendment to the House bill (HR7995), after all the text of the latter was deleted following its enacting clause. Also upon the urging of Reed, the Senate asked for a conference with the House of Representatives over the two versions of the bill and instructed its conferees to insist upon the Senate's version. The differences between the two, Reed insisted, were significant.

In an earlier debate on the two versions, for example, Reed had boasted that the Senate bill was more restrictive than was the House bill, particularly since it did not provide for a non-quota category of immigrants who could enter the United States without being counted in the quota for their country. (Most of these immigrants were relatives of American citizens.) In its original committee version, though, the Senate bill had been much more liberal than the House bill. Thus, the Senate bill had rotated 180 degrees around the House bill from its first to its final version.

THE REPORT OF THE CONFERENCE AND THE SIGNING
OF THE BILL INTO LAW

During the conference on the bill, the Coolidge administration made a desperate effort to soften the severity of the Japanese exclusion section; it prevailed on the conferees to insert a provision delaying implementation of the section for eight months or until March 1 1925, before which time the President would be requested to negotiate with the Japanese government in relation to the abrogation of the present arrangement on this subject.

Aware that such a delay would not be well received by their colleagues, the House conferees justified it in the name of proper foreign relations. They wrote in their report,

> "this provision gives eight months beyond the time provided in the original House draft in order to adjust our diplomatic relations on this subject in a friendly way and to provide reasonable time for notice through proper diplomatic channels that Congress has enacted legislation which brings to an end at a date certain the present understanding with Japan. This provision does not invite the making of a treaty, the exclusion being effective on March 1, 1925, or in other words bringing exclusion into full force and effect before the expiration of this Congress."
>
> (US House of Representatives Report No. 688 (1924) 68:1:21)

During the eight-month period, "Japanese immigration will be limited to 80 persons by the quota provision of the immigration bill, in addition to those who may come under the exemptions provided for students, ministers, and teachers of all countries" (US House of Representatives Report No. 688 (1924) 68:1:21).

The conference also decided in favor of "the quota plan of the House – 2 percent based on the 1890 census (with a minimum quota of 100)" (US House of Representatives Report No. 688 (1924) 68:1:20) as a transitional measure for three years until the Senate's national origins scheme could become operational. Approving a "rewritten and perfected" national origins plan, the conference enlarged the category of those who were not to be counted as "inhabitants in continental United States." In addition to the already excluded "descendants of slave immigrants" were added "aliens ineligible to citizenship or their descendants," and the "descendants of American aborigines" (US House of Representatives Report No. 688 (1924) 68:1:7). In short, only whites were to be defined as inhabitants in continental United States for the purpose of allocating immigration quotas, according to national origins; nonwhites were summarily excluded. (Also excluded was a significant subcategory of non-quota immigrants who were eligible to enter the United States anyway.)

In general however, the conference accepted a greater part of the House bill than of the Senate's. As such, it was less restrictive than the latter. For example the non-quota feature of the House bill was retained, though its provisions were tightened and "the definition of an 'immigrant' is reduced from the Senate proposal to the original House provision" (US House of Representatives Report No. 688 (1924) 68:1:20). In the end two of the five House conferees refused to sign the conference report; all five Senate conferees signed.

One of the two, Raker of California, let it be known unequivocally in the subsequent debate in the House that he refused to sign the report because of the March 1925 provision, which he complained had been virtually forced down the committee's throat by the President. The reasons for the refusal of the other House conferee, Sabath of Illinois, were apparently more complex. For example, no sooner had the conference report been read to the House when he rose to challenge the provision that would delay for eight months the implementation of the exclusion section. He argued that the conferees had exceeded their authority in supporting this delay and asked for a ruling to that effect from the speaker of the House. Overruled on his point of order, Sabath did not dwell on the Japanese issue in the subsequent debate, other than to scoff at reports by exclusionists that America would be swamped by a quarter of a million Japanese if the delay were granted. Instead he concentrated on other provisions of the bill "which from my point of view, I believe, are of greater importance to America and to us than the Japanese provision" (US Congressional Record 1924 68:1:8230).

Calling the bill "unreasonably harsh," Sabath criticized the shrinking of the non-quota category, which effectively eliminated the clause in the original House bill that identified parents of American citizens as non-quota immigrants. However, he leveled his greatest attack against the national origins provision which he said had been defeated earlier on the floor of the House. He argued that the bill was so discriminatory that "Great Britain will receive under the national origin more than three-fifths of the entire immigration, and that is not taking into consideration Canadian immigration" (US Congressional Record 1924 68:1:8231). Other representatives, particularly from New York, joined him in condemning the conference bill for deleting the more "humane features" of the original House bill. Finally Sabath made a simple motion; he moved "to recommit the report to the committee of conference" (US Congressional Record 1924 68:1:8247).

In the meantime, Raker of California had taken command of the exclusionist forces to whom the provision of delay was anathema. They made short work of Johnson's defense of the delay as "gracefully" notifying Japan of Congress's intention to abrogate the Gentlemen's Agreement ("But we want Japan to be gracefully notified as to the decision of Congress" (US Congressional Record 1924 68:1:8229)). So intense and bitter was their assault on the provision that Johnson chastized one of its partisans at one point in the debate with "Well, does the gentleman want to be kind and decent to another nation, or just hit him on the head?" (US Congressional Record 1924 68:1:8228). Not content however with Sabath's simple motion to recommit, Raker speaking for the exclusionists moved to amend the motion to include

> "instructions to the conferees on the part of the House not to agree to the proviso reported in the bill submitted by the conference committee, beginning on line 2, page 24, and reading as follows: '*Provided* That this subdivision shall not take effect as to exclusion until March 1, 1925, before which time the President is requested to negotiate with the Japanese Government in relation to, the abrogation of the present arrangement on this subject!'"
>
> (US Congressional Record 1924 68:1:8249)

A coalition of exclusionists who would brook no delay in implementation of the exclusion clause and liberals who were disenchanted with the "harsh inhumaneness" of the conference report prevailed by a vote of 192 to 171 with 69 not voting and the bill was sent back to conference on May 9.

One week later on May 15 the second conference report was read to the House; the provision to delay implementation of the exclusion clause had been deleted. In addition, several other minor changes had been made in provisions about alien seamen. Other than these modifications the second conference bill was identical to the first; none of its "inhuman and harsh features" had been touched. Dismayed at the results and still unwilling to sign the conference report, Sabath launched an attack on the bill as soon as it reached the floor and moved to have it recommitted once again. This time he added instructions to the House conferees in his motion. They were "to strike out the national origins scheme that has been voted down by the House and inserted by the conferees;" they were to expand the category of non-quota immigrants along the line of the original House version; and finally they were "to strike out the alien-seamen provision and insert in lieu thereof two new sections which have the approval of all those whose sympathies are with the seamen of America and the world" (US Congressional Record 1924 68:1:8634). Other "liberals," particularly from New York, spoke out strongly in support of the motion. But deserted by the exclusionists who now liked the bill (Raker, their leader, had even signed the second conference report), they were disastrously defeated 33 to 246 and the conference bill won overwhelmingly 308 to 62 with 63 not voting.

In the Senate, the second conference report reached the floor on the same day; two of the conferees who had signed the first report failed to sign the second. One of the two, King of Utah, explained in the ensuing floor debate that he opposed the modifications in the alien seamen provision. Although he did not mention the deletion of the delay provision as a reason, the fact that he signed the first conference report and did not vote for the exclusion clause or against the Gentlemen's Agreement clause of the original Senate bill suggests that he was also unhappy about the deletion of the delay provision. This was in all likelihood the reason why Sterling of South Dakota also failed to sign the second report. Though he did not enter the debate on the second conference report, he had signed the first report probably because the delay provision was in it. He too had refused to support the exclusion clause or to vote against the Gentlemen's Agreement provision of the original bill.

Debate on the second conference report focused primarily on the seamen's provision and secondarily on the complaint that the conference bill was less restrictive than the original Senate bill: the provision for non-quota immigrants was particularly disputed. Unlike Sabath of the House, no one rose to challenge the conference bill as being too inhumane or harsh. Advocates of a "humane bill" on the Senate Committee of Immigration, particularly its chairman, Colt of Rhode Island, had apparently given up the struggle completely. Despite the flurry of complaints, the Senate overwhelmingly passed the second conference bill 69 to 9 with 18 not voting, on the same day as did the House, May 15.

On May 17 the bill was sent to President Coolidge. Before he decided on his course of action, he requested an advisory opinion from Secretary of State Hughes. In his reply dated May 23, Hughes singled out three provisions of the bill which he said were "of special interest to the Department of State." Of the first, its administrative provision, he said that he had no objections because they "have been framed in consultation with representatives of the Department of State" (US Foreign Relations 1924 II:391). He also had no objection to the second provision – the use of the census of 1890 as the basis for determining the immigration quotas from the various countries. He considered the choice of the year as within the discretionary power of Congress, even though some foreign countries complained that quotas derived from 1890 were discriminatory against their nationals.

The third provision, Secion 13(c) providing for the exclusion of aliens ineligible to citizenship, was an entirely different matter, he argued. Aimed particularly at the Japanese, it undercut an understanding with Japan that had been in operation since 1908, the Gentlemen's Agreement. "Through this arrangement this Government has had the benefit of cooperation with Japan in excluding such immigrants [laborers]. It is believed that Japan has faithfully performed her voluntary undertaking" (US Foreign Relations 1924 II:391–92). He then quoted a number of statistics to show that the net increase in Japanese immigrants over fifteen years was minimal, once figures for departures were taken into account.

In addition, he continued, "the Japanese Government has expressed its readiness to discuss with this Government modifications of the Gentlemen's Agreement." Also, under the bill the Japanese quota would have merely been 100, if it were not for Section 13(c). "And even the admission of this small number would be controlled by the operation of the Gentlemen's Agreement." Thus, "the exclusion provision of Section 13(c) is entirely unnecessary, and indeed, by the loss of the cooperation of Japan through the abrogation of the Gentlemen's Agreement, it will probably facilitate the surreptitious entry of Japanese so that the result of the provision of the bill will probably be to increase rather than to diminish the actual Japanese immigration" (US Foreign Relations 1924 II:392).

Furthermore, not only was the exclusion clause unnecessary, but

"it unquestionably will be resented by Japan. The Japanese Government has not questioned the sovereign power of the United States to control immigration but has sought to attain the desired result through cooperation and friendly arrangements with our Government. It is most unfortunate, from the standpoint of our foreign relations and especially in view of the attitude taken by Japan at the Conference on the Limitation of Armament held at Washington, and the spirit of friendship and mutual confidence then evoked, that the question of immigration of Japanese should not have been left to be dealt with by satisfactory mutual agreement, which could have been entered into without derogating in the slightest degree from our full authority to act if any exigency requiring such action should at any time arise. . . .

[Under the circumstances,] if the exclusion provision of Section 13(c) stood alone I should unhesitatingly recommend its disapproval, [but since it is only a part of a comprehensive immigration measure and since] it is necessary for you to consider the policy represented by the bill as a whole, the necessity of an immigration measure to take the place of the existing law which expires on June thirtieth, and also the preponderant sentiment expressed in Congress . . . I return the bill without recommendation."   (US Foreign Relations 1924 II:393)

Three days later the President echoed the basic sentiment of the Secretary in the body of a public statement he issued along with his decision on the immigration bill: "If the exclusion provision stood alone I should disapprove it without hesitation." In the first sentence of his statement he also expressed "regret [over] the impossibility of severing from it [the bill] the exclusion provision which, in the light of existing law, affects especially the Japanese." Despite this shortcoming, he nevertheless felt obliged to sign the bill "which in its main features I heartily approve."

"This Bill is a comprehensive measure dealing with the whole subject of immigration and setting up the necessary administrative machiney. The present Quota Act, of 1921, will terminate on June 30th next. It is of great importance that a comprehensive measure should take its place, and that the arrangements for its administration should be provided at once in order to avoid hardship and confusion. I must therefore consider the Bill as a whole, and the imperative need of the country for legislation of this general character. For this reason the Bill is approved."　　　　　　　　　　　　　　　　(US Foreign Relations 1924 II:396)

In order to make his decision more palatable to the Japanese government and people, he reassured them

"that the enactment of this [exclusion] provision does not imply any change in our sentiment of admiration and cordial friendship for the Japanese people, a sentiment which has had and will continue to have abundant manifestation. The Bill rather expresses the determination of the Congress to exercise its prerogative in defining by legislation the control of immigration instead of leaving it to international arrangements."　　　　　(US Foreign Relations 1924 II:396)

He then pointed to the various exemptions allowed despite the exclusion clause. However, he continued, he would have preferred to rely on the long-term

"understanding with Japan [He refused to call it the Gentlemen's Agreement, though the Secretary of State had.] by which the Japanese Government has voluntarily undertaken to prevent the emigration of laborers to the United States . . . in view of this historic relation and of the feeling which inspired it, it would have been much better in my judgment, and more effective in the actual control of immigration, if we had continued to invite the cooperation which Japan was ready to give and had thus avoided creating any ground for misapprehension by an unnecessary statutory enactment. That course would not have derogated from the authority of the Congress to deal with the question in any exigency requiring its action."　　　(US Foreign Relations 1924 II:396)

Then the President made the significant revelation that he did not necessarily disagree with Congress' goal of restricting, if not excluding Japanese immigration, his argument was merely with the way Congress chose to accomplish its goal: "There is scarcely any ground for disagreement as to the result we want, but this method of securing it is unnecessary and deplorable at this time" (US Foreign Relations 1924 II:396).

THE CHILLING OF RELATIONS BETWEEN THE UNITED STATES AND JAPAN

The virulent reaction of the Senate to his phrase "grave consequences" both surprised and distressed the Japanese ambassador. He expressed his great chagrin in an informal meeting with the head of the US State Department's Far Eastern

Division on April 15, one day after the explosive session in the Senate, and in a letter to the Secretary of State two days later he was still puzzled by the response to the two words:

"Frankly, I must say I am unable to understand how the two words, read in their context, could be construed as meaning anything like a threat. I simply tried to emphasize the most unfortunate and deplorable effect upon our traditional friendship which might result from the adoption of a particular clause in the proposed measure. It would seriously impair the good and mutually helpful relationship and disturb the spirit of mutual regard and confidence, which characterizes our intercourse of the last three quarters of a century and which was considerably strengthened by the Washington Conference as well as by the most magnanimous sympathy shown by your people in recent calamity in my country....

In using these words, which I did quite ingenuously, I had not thought of being in any way disagreeable or discourteous, and still less of conveying 'a veiled threat.' On the contrary it was in a spirit of the most sincere respect, confidence, and candor that I used these words, which spirit I hope is manifest throughout my entire letter, for it was in that spirit that I wrote you. I never suspected that these words, used as I used them, would ever afford an occasion for such comment or interpretation as have been given them."

(US Foreign Relations 1924 II:381–82)

The ambassador reiterated his concerns and dismay in a private meeting that day with the Secretary of State. Hughes sought to reassure the ambassador that he was aware that the ambassador had not intended to convey any sense of threat in that phrase and that he "was very sorry that such a construction had been placed upon his language" (US Foreign Relations 1924 II:382). In a formal response to the ambassador's letter of April 17, the Secretary wrote the next day,

"it gives me pleasure to be able to assure you that reading the words 'grave consequences' in the light of their context, and knowing the spirit of friendship and understanding you have always manifested in our long association, I had no doubt that these words were to be taken in the sense you have stated, and I was quite sure that it was far from your thought to express or imply any threat. I am happy to add that I have deeply appreciated your constant desire to promote the most cordial relations between the peoples of the two countries."

(US Foreign Relations 1924 II:383)

Thus ended the friendly exchange of letters between Secretary and ambassador on the explosive phrase "grave consequences" which Republican leaders in the Senate had used so effectively to abandon their increasingly beleaguered administration position on the Gentlemen's Agreement. In Japan the initial press response to the turn of events in the Senate seemed relatively restrained, according to the American ambassador in Tokyo because the Japanese were still hopeful that something could be done to remedy the situation. The ambassador concluded however with the caveat that the situation could change overnight: "it would be entirely erroneous to assume that Japan is already resigned to the situation or to underestimate the bitterness of the feeling of her resentment over an act which rankles all the more because it is realized that if this exclusion legislation is enacted, there is no recourse or redress" (US Foreign Relations 1924 II:384). A week later, almost as a partial fulfillment of his prophesy, he reported "the Embassy has been receiving numerous protests from all over Japan by telegraph, letter, delegation and personal visit against the pending Japanese exclusion bill. These protests come from groups and organizations of varied character, educational, religious, social, political, commercial, industrial, financial, et cetera" (US Foreign Relations 1924 II:385).

As the immigration bill went into conference between the two houses, the Japanese government sought to derail the exclusion clause by opening up negotiations with the American government based on the Morris-Shidehara treaty draft that was aborted in 1921. This course of action seemed promising as President Coolidge had prevailed upon the conferees to add an eight-month delay to the exclusion clause in their first conference report. But with the torpedoing of the delay provision by the House, this approach appeared doomed. And when the second conference report deleted the delay provision, the Secretary of State wrote to the American ambassador in Tokyo that "no [treaty] arrangement on the basis of the Morris-Shidehara draft could be expected to receive the necessary ratification of the Senate" (US Foreign Relations 1924 II:390). And so this avenue of heading off exclusion was blocked.

The last hope for the Japanese government was in prevailing upon President Coolidge to veto the bill. But this hope too was dashed. Three days before the bill was signed, the Secretary of State sought to soften the impact of the pending approval by requesting a private meeting with the Japanese ambassador. In the conversation he reminded the ambassador of "the efforts which he had made and which the President had made to secure elimination or modification of the provision relating to the exclusion of aliens ineligible for citizenship." But, he continued, Congress was intent on asserting its authority on matters of immigration and passed the provision for this reason and not out of "lack of friendship on the part of the American people toward the Japanese people" (US Foreign Relations 1924 II:393).

Despite this congressional sentiment, he added, the President would "unhesitatingly disapprove" of the exclusion provision if it were "before him as a separate matter," but it was "part of a comprehensive immigration bill" which the country needed to replace the expiring law and for which there was very strong sentiment in the country. Accordingly, "the President felt in view of all these considerations that he could not properly disapprove the Bill" (US Foreign Relations 1924 II:394). But he desired that the Japanese government should know that his approval of the bill did not imply any change in his sentiment with regard to this provision or any lack of cordial feeling toward Japan. The President had fully endorsed the position the Secretary had taken.

The ambassador replied that he could appreciate the Secretary's view and even "the Foreign Office might appreciate the difficulties of the situation," but he added in somber tones that "he was quite sure that the Japanese people would not understand it and would be greatly disappointed. The Japanese people were now basing their hope upon the President's action and if the President approved the Bill it would cause the keenest disappointment. The ambassador hoped there would be no disorder but feared that there would be violent manifestations of that disappointment" (US Foreign Relations 1924 II:395).

Five days after the President signed the bill, May 31, the Japanese government lodged a "solemn protest" with the Secretary of State. It expressed deep concern at the discriminatory character of the Immigration Act of 1924 "which is manifestly intended to apply to Japanese. Neither the representations of the Japanese Government, nor the recommendations of the President and of the Secretary of State were heeded by the Congress, and the clause in question has now been written into the statutes of the United States" (US Foreign Relations 1924 II:398).

The note complained that the basis of the discrimination was racial, which was even more unwelcome than purely economic discrimination "to the principles of justice and fairness upon which the friendly intercourse between nations must, in its final analysis, depend."

> "The Immigration Act of 1924, considered in the light of the Supreme Court's interpretation of the naturalization laws, clearly establishes the rule that the admissibility of aliens to the United States rests not upon individual merits or qualifications, but upon the division of race to which applicants belong. In particular, it appears that such racial distinction in the Act is directed essentially against Japanese, since persons of other Asiatic races are excluded under separate enactments of prior dates, as is pointed out in the published letter of the Secretary of State of February 8, 1924, to the Chairman of the Committee on Immigration and Naturalization of the House of Representatives."
>
> (US Foreign Relations 1924 II:399)

The protest then addressed itself to the argument that Japanese immigrants were not assimilable.

"It will however be observed, in the first place, that few immigrants of a foreign stock may well be expected to assimilate themselves to their new surroundings within a single generation. The history of Japanese immigration to the United States in any appreciable number dated but from the last few years of the nineteenth century. The period of time is too short to permit of any conclusive judgment being passed upon the racial adaptabilities of these immigrants in the matter of assimilation, as compared with alien settlers of the races classed as eligible to American citizenship." (US Foreign Relations 1924 II:399)

The note complained that America had through law and policy excluded the Japanese immigrants from the People's Domain and in so doing seriously impeded their chances to become assimilated into the American society. "It seems hardly fair to complain of the failure of foreign elements to merge in a community while the community chooses to keep them apart from the rest of its membership. For these reasons the assertion of Japanese nonassimilability seems at least premature, if not fundamentally unjust" (US Foreign Relations 1924 II:399).

The note then outlined a brief history of the negotiations between the two countries that culminated in the Treaty of 1911. The Act of 1924, it declared, "is an entire disregard of the spirit and circumstances that underlie the conclusion of the Treaty" (US Foreign Relations 1924 II:400), as well as specific provisions of the Treaty. The note also lamented the breakdown of the Gentlemen's Agreement.

"An understanding of friendly cooperation reached after long and comprehensive discussions between the Japanese and American Governments has thus been abruptly overthrown by legislative action on the part of the United States. The patient, loyal, and scrupulous observance by Japan for more than sixteen years, of these self-denying regulations, in the interest of good relations between the two countries, now seems to have been wasted."
(US Foreign Relations 1924 II:401)

Before concluding with its statement of solemn protest, the note declared,

"It is not denied that, fundamentally speaking, it lies within the inherent sovereign power of each state to limit and control immigration to its own domain, but when, in the exercise of such right, an evident injustice is done to a foreign nation in disregard of its proper self-respect, of international understandings or of ordinary rules of comity, the question necessarily assumes an aspect which justifies diplomatic discussion and adjustment."
(US Foreign Relations 1924 II:401)

On June 16, the Secretary of State replied officially to the Japanese notes of May 31. In his letter he repeated the President's statement that enactment of the exclusion provision "does not imply any change in our sentiment of admiration and cordial friendship for the Japanese people, a sentiment which has had and will continue to have abundant manifestation." He then went on to speculate that with all the exceptions allowed by the bill, it "does not differ greatly in its practical operation, or in the policy which it reflects, from the understanding embodied in the Gentlemen's Agreement under which the Japanese Government has cooperated with the Government of the United States in preventing the emigration of Japanese laborers to this country" (US Foreign Relations 1924 II:404–05).

The only "substantial difference" between the two, he argued, was that the Immigration Act "has expressed, as the President has stated, 'the determination of the Congress to exercise its prerogative in defining by legislation the control of immigration instead of leaving it to international arrangments'" (US Foreign Relations 1924 II:405). The Secretary then sought to supply evidence that this was indeed in the mind of the American government throughout its negotiations with Japan. Even the Treaty of 1911 was concluded "with the distinct understanding that it was without prejudice to the inherent sovereign right of either country to limit and control immigration to its own domains or possessions" (US Foreign Relations 1924 II:407). The same applied to the Gentlemen's Agreement.

Under the circumstances, he continued, the Japanese government need no longer abide by the terms of the Gentlemen's Agreement "inasmuch as the abstention on the part of the United States from such an exercise of its right of statutory control over immigration was the condition upon which was predicated the undertaking of the Japanese Government contained in the Gentlemen's Agreement of 1907–08 with respect to the regulation of the emigration of laborers to the United States." He concluded his note with a conciliatory statement:

> "I desire once more to emphasize the appreciation on the part of this Government of the voluntary cooperation of your Government in carrying out the Gentlemen's Agreement and to express the conviction that the recognition of the right of each Government to legislate in control of immigration should not derogate in any degree from mutual goodwill and cordial friendship which have always characterized the relations of the two countries."
>
> (US Foreign Relations 1924 II:408)

That the Secretary's explanation did not satisfy the Japanese government was evident in a speech delivered by the Foreign Minister to the opening session of the Japanese Diet on July 1st.

> "Our protest against the exclusion clause is based upon the conviction that a discriminatory treatment, as laid down in that clause, is contrary to the dictates of justice and fairness, and is imposed upon us in disregard of the ordinary rules

of international comity. The legislation is now an accomplished fact in the United States, but we can by no means concede that the question is closed. Until our just contentions shall have been given satisfaction, we shall maintain our protest, and shall use our best possible endeavors to seek an amicable adjustment of the question and to ensure forever the traditional friendship between the two nations."   (US Foreign Relations 1924 II:410)

Both houses of the Diet then passed a joint resolution condemning the Immigration Act of 1924 as discriminatory.

Discussions on the matter continued between the two governments for the next six months when the Foreign Minister announced in the Diet late in January 1925 that "it is obvious ... that the continuance of discussions between the two Governments at this time will not in itself serve any useful purpose" (US Foreign Relations 1924 II:411), and broke off further talks on the subject with the United States.

Public furor over the act, however, did not readily subside in Japan. Even as the bill was being considered in April, fifteen leading newspapers in Tokyo joined in a public declaration labeling the bill as "inequitable and unjust." After the President signed the bill, the press denunciations grew even more bitter and intense. Leading organizations and citizens of Japan protested the law. A few anti-American demonstrations and boycotts – soon aborted – erupted in some cities; several suicides were also reported. However, the government sought to discourage any outbreaks of violence. In a prescient statement, the American ambassador in Tokyo cautioned the American government not to misread the relative absence of violence as indifference to the Act.

"Due to the attitude of the Government ... there have been no popular anti-American outbreaks but this does not signify that there has been any lessening of deep-seated resentment and bitterness throughout Japan. The nation can be considered to be behind the Government in any protest they may make at Washington and it would be a mistake to interpret their protest as actuated by mainly domestic political urgency."

(US Foreign Relations 1924 II:402–03)

Even in his address of protest to the Diet on July 1, the Foreign Minister sought to discourage outbreaks of public passion by offering some pacifying pieces of information about the bill.

"No intimation has lately been made, even by the exclusionists, of any inferiority of the Japanese race. Their contention is in effect that the Japanese are to the Americans what oil is to water. Neither oil nor water can be said to be superior or inferior to the other, but the fact is that in no case can oil dissolve and merge in water. In other words, they say, Japanese are unassimilable to American life, and the introduction of such alien elements will prove a source of danger to the United States.... It should, however, be pointed out that the plea of Japanese unassimilability is no more than an arbitrary presumption unsupported by any evidence of facts.... It has always been consistently maintained by the United States, that the liberty to limit and control immigration is one of the essential attributes of the inherent sovereign rights of each nation. The same argument was repeatedly invoked with special emphasis in the discussion of the exclusion clause. We understand that the importance placed on this point by the United States is due to the special conditions of that country. But we have no intention of calling this doctrine in question."

(US Foreign Relations 1924 II:409–10)

And finally he expressed appreciation for the fact "that the President and the Secretary of State of the United States have from the outset shown their opposition to the exclusion clause, and have made all possible efforts to have it eliminated from the Act" (US Foreign Relations 1924 II:410). Despite citing these ameliorating circumstances, he nevertheless ended his speech with a strong indictment of the bill.

To underscore the government's efforts to prevent all doors from being shut on the matter, Japan passed an amendment to the Law of Nationality in mid-July which attempted to solve "the question of dual nationality in which Japanese who have acquired foreign nationality by reason of birth are involved" (US Foreign Relations 1924 II:412). Under the new law, "all children born to Japanese parents in the United States and certain other countries after December 1, 1924, shall be regarded as citizens of these countries unless their parents, within fourteen days after birth, reserve Japanese citizenship for them by registering their names at a Japanese Consulate" (US Foreign Relations 1924 II:413). The American ambassador in Japan reported in late March 1925 "that according to press statements not one of the forty children born to Japanese parents in Hawaii since December first has been registered at the Japanese Consulate General" (US Foreign Relations 1924 II:413).

Despite these conciliatory gestures of the Japanese government, however, resentment and indignation against the immigration law was widely and intensely expressed. The Japanese ambassador Harihara quietly resigned over the matter and only broke his silence in a speech at the farewell dinner for the American ambassador in 1930. He expressed keen disappointment at being made a scapegoat by the exclusionists for his injudicious remarks, particularly since his reputation for being warm and friendly to the United States was well known. In addition, he stated, "the Secretary of State's categorical assurance to the contrary was brushed aside by that accusing party." And then he described the long-term – virtually permanent – injury that this had inflicted on Japanese-American relations. "Naturally the Japanese Government and people deeply resented this, and that resentment is felt now as it was then. Nor will it ever die out so long as the wound inflicted remains unhealed. Friendship once marred in this manner can with difficulty resume its wholesome growth unless some effective remedy is administered" (Ichihashi 1969:367).

THE REACH OF THE RACIAL CREED AND THE NONWHITE ALIEN

Overall the Immigration Act of 1924 represented the complete triumph of the racial creed as the regnant legal-normative code for controlling the entry of aliens into territorial United States and into its institutional domains. As early as the founding days of the Republic the creed had determined which aliens had access to citizenship and to the People's Domain; only free white persons were granted the right of naturalization in 1790. This restriction was untouched by the Civil War and the great amendments of reconstruction. In the residual fervor of radical reconstruction, though, an exception was made; black aliens were granted the right of citizenship. All other nonwhite races were excluded. This applied with particular vengeance to aliens of the yellow race. Their exclusion from the People's Domain was reaffirmed and legitimated as the law of the land by the Supreme Court in 1922.

By 1924 Congress was determined to extend the reach of the racial creed from merely barring entry of nonwhite aliens into the People's Domain to barring their entry into the territory of the United States itself. The particular target was the Japanese alien. All other Asians already suffered from this double disability; the black alien too (as we shall shortly see) did not escape unscathed from this effort.

The logic of the exclusionists in Congress was seductively simple and seemingly impeccable: Why not bring immigration policy into consonance with the naturalization statutes? In short, why should aliens ineligible to citizenship be permitted to enter a country that they could not hope to be a part of? For, if they were allowed in, such aliens became a nonassimilable plural subsociety that ensconced itself in the normatively ill-defined institutional and geographic terrain lying between the People's Domain and the territorial limits of the country. There, the congressional exclusionists insisted, these aliens stood in antagonistic competition to the people of the People's Domain and posed at the least an economic threat to the stability of the Domain. If they were aliens from Japan, they were an even more serious political threat; for their loyalty and ties to Japan made them a potent fifth column carrying out the imperialistic designs of their homeland.

As a result, once such ineligible aliens were in, the congressional exclusionists contended, the only recourse for the people was to build a wall between the aliens and themselves and to use force if necessary to prevent the aliens from gaining access to and possession of the resources of the People's Domain. But this method of dealing with the problem had certain limits imposed upon it. The exclusionists were fully aware, for example, that such an alien, once he was within the territorial limits of the United States, derived some benefit from the fundamental paradox that had historically characterized the legal-normative system of America: namely, the dialectical tension and struggle between the opposing racial and American creeds that generated contradictory cues with reference to the treatment of anyone, even an alien, residing in territorial America. As such, the racial creed might have deprived the ineligible alien of membership in the People's Domain, but the American creed, as interpreted by the Supreme Court, had come to provide him with a modicum of protection from the normative code that prevailed in the People's Domain. For example, the Supreme Court had spread in some of its rulings the protective umbrella of the due process and equal treatment clauses of the Fourteenth Amendment over the alien. In addition, the racial creed might have prevented the alien from owning land as in the alien land laws of California, but the American creed had protected his constitutional right to work as decided by the Supreme Court in Truax.

Congressional exclusionists also recognized that limited though the protective mantle was for such an alien, it became much more encompassing for his American-born children. No longer could the racial creed operate constitutionally to deny them membership in the People's Domain. The Fourteenth Amendment as interpreted by the Supreme Court decreed that all such children born in America were to have the right of citizenship. As citizens these children could not be deprived of the right to own property as their parents were under the racial creed. In short, the children of aliens ineligible to citizenship could themselves claim all the rights and immunities of membership in the People's Domain and bask under the protective mantle of the American creed as spelled out in the Constitution and Declaration of Independence.*

This situation was viewed as an abomination by the congressional exclusionists, particularly as it applied to the Japanese alien and his offspring; for they saw the children as no better than the parent. Both were presumably dedicated and loyal subjects of the Emperor. This notion was reinforced by Japanese laws on citizenship which, as we have seen, made expatriation an extremely complicated and difficult task. (Japan dramatically dropped its claims on these children as it

---

*Actually this is an overstatement; for, as we have seen in earlier chapters, the Plessy-Ferguson decision had relegitimized the racial creed and helped create a plural structure segmented along racial lines within the social realm of the People's Domain. In a benchmark case in 1927 the Supreme Court labeled the Chinese, hence all Asians, as nonwhite and therefore subject to the same Jim Crow restrictions in Mississippi as were the blacks.

revised its citizenship laws in mid-1924. This was too late to affect the deliberations on the Immigration Act of 1924, which had already been passed by Congress and signed by the President.)

Accordingly, the congressional exclusionists were convinced that the only way to avoid the normative paradox of America and the problem of American-born offspring was to construct an impermeable wall around the territorial limits of America, thus preventing immigrants ineligible to citizenship from even stepping foot on American soil.

As the exclusion clause was formulated in the Act of 1924, it was obviously aimed against the Japanese. But what many scholars fail to realize is that the bill also sought to curtail, if not eliminate, immigration of the black alien as well, the only other nonwhite who showed any inclination to come to America. Protected as they were by the heritage from reconstruction which gave them the right to become citizens, black aliens could not be kept out of the United States on the same basis as the Japanese. However, the author of the national origins section of the bill, Senator Reed of Pennsylvania, conceived of an ingenious scheme that would make relatively few black aliens eligible to enter this country. And if the numbers could be kept down, few would be in a position to take advantage of their inheritance from the past.

His scheme becomes evident once we deal with his fundamental category of inhabitants in the continental United States which was to serve as the population base from which immigration quotas were to be devised for the various nations. Included as "inhabitants" were the foreign- and native-born, aliens as well as citizens. He added one major exception to his original bill. He denied the identity of "inhabitant" to "descendants of such persons as were involuntary immigrants into the territory now included therein" (US Congressional Record 1924 68:1:6471). With virtually all blacks being thereby excluded from the population base, Reed assured his colleagues that there would be few immigrants "from African sources" (US Congressional Record 1924 68:1:5468). When the bill reached its final form, the phrase was changed to read "the descendants of slave immigrants" (US Statutes at Large 1925 43:159). In addition, "aliens ineligible to citizenship and their descendants" and "the descendants of aboriginal Americans," euphemisms for yellow men and red men, were also excluded from the category (US Statutes at Large 1925 43:159). That only left the white race as "inhabitants in continental United States." (In keeping with the tradition set in the writing of the Constitution, no explicit references to race were made in the bill, but no one could miss the meanings of the various euphemisms.)

Thus, even in its first effort to deal comprehensively with immigration, America could not avoid the duality of its historic past. It created once again a plural structure along racial lines. On the one said of the racial divide were the whites. They comprised the "inhabitants in continental United States" upon whom immigration quotas were to be based. On the other side of the divide were the nonwhites. Once again, as in earlier encounters with dominant America, they were denied any identity. As such they might be called the "non-inhabitants in continental United States" and, through endowing them with this invisibility, Congress hoped they would contribute nothing to the immigrant flow into America.

Even with racial lines clearly drawn in the bill, most senators and representatives were not finished in this effort to purify and homogenize the flow of immigration into the United States. For example, they looked askance at the flow of new immigrants from southern and eastern Europe. They continually referred to these immigrants as nonassimilable or difficult to assimilate and frequently called them undesirable. In sum, these immigrants were seen as a contaminating influence on a society that had been built and maintained by the northern European who still constituted the majority of the American population.

Some congressmen accounted for the negative qualities of the new immigrants in purely cultural terms. Many others resorted to racial terms; they perceived the new immigrants as of an inferior racial stock to that of the northern European. And some even saw them as no more desirable biologically than those of the yellow and black races. But virtually no one was prepared to rule them out of the white race, despite whatever inferiorities and undesirablenesses they were branded with. In addition, no one could find any constitutional basis for declaring them ineligible for citizenship, or any historic ground for considering them involuntary immigrants, or any grounds for calling them aboriginal Americans or any other equivalent masking device to label them. In short, no one could find any grounds for treating them as Congress had treated the nonwhite races.

As a result, the new immigrants had to be counted among the "inhabitants in continental United States," and quotas had to be assigned to the countries from which they came. In other words, the solution that was used to avoid giving quotas to nonwhite races was not available for dealing with the "inferior sub-races of whites." The alternative solution finally tailored for them was to base the quotas first on the census of 1890 and then on the national origins of the "inhabitants in continental United States" as recorded in 1920. In each instance, the quotas were very much lower for immigrants from southern and eastern Europe than for immigrants from northern and western Europe. The solution, therefore, was discriminatory treatment for the undesirable subraces of whites in contrast to the exclusionary treatment for the nonwhite races. In sum then, both groups were treated unfairly but with a qualitative difference in the unfairness of the treatment that can be translated into numerical terms. The nonwhite races were treated as a cipher, a zero; and the "new" white European immigrants were given some numerical value, though much less than that assigned to the more favored "old" white European immigrant.

17

WORLD WAR II AND THE CONCENTRATION CAMPS

Introduction

With the passage of the immigration act, blatant anti-Japanese agitation and violence subsided for the rest of the 1920s; and the anti-Japanese coalition of labor unions, farm and patriotic organizations split apart, though each organization continued to pass anti-Japanese resolutions at its annual meeting.* The period of relative quiet was disrupted in the 1930s with the onset of the worldwide depression and the rise of an ultranationalistic military elite in Japan. Almost immediately the double-edged theme of the yellow peril sprang to renewed life and was in fairly full bloom by the eve of the attack on Pearl Harbor. Coupled with the belief in military necessity, it provided the "grounds" for uprooting the Japanese immigrant and his American-born offspring from the Plural Terrain of the West Coast and herding them into concentration camps for the duration of World War II.

In this chapter we shall examine the durability of the double-edged theme of the yellow peril and how it contaminated the "reality" in which military and government officials acted in World War II and led them "inexorably" to legitimize a policy of mass evacuation and internment. In addition, we shall look at the way the policy was carried out and how it reaffirmed America's historic duality.

*The structural core of the coalition, the Japanese Exclusion League, which had been dormant since 1922, was, however, resuscitated and given the new title of California Joint Immigration Committee under the leadership of V.S. McClatchy. One of its major tasks during this period was to head off the modest groundswell of sentiment to modify the exclusion clause.

Prelude to the war

A VENEER OF RELATIVE CALM

Despite the relative tranquility of the 1920s, even Mears (1925) recognized that not far from the surface of public consciousness in California lay a deeply embedded set of beliefs and stereotypes about the Japanese immigrant "established through three decades ... and no longer dependent for its existence upon the prodding of 'pressure groups'" (ten Broek, Barnhart, and Matson 1968:66). The beliefs that surfaced most frequently during this period viewed the Japanese immigrant as a shrewd and dishonest businessman.

> "It is a common opinion among thousands of people, especially on our Pacific Coast, that the Japanese are fundamentally dishonest in their business dealings. I have heard from intelligent men stories of how Japanese business men attempt to cheat American firms, just as one hears from the lips of the common workman how shrewd the 'Jap' is in worming his way into better economic status." (Young 1929:10)

In addition, Mears (1925) claims that a less rabid version of the yellow peril theme was also present. For example, the loyalty of even the second-generation Japanese continued to be questioned as allegations were made about the great numbers who supposedly returned to Japan for education. Also alleged was that control was exercised by the Imperial government over community organizations and that it practiced warlike activities in such places as Magdalena Bay.

In a study conducted among high school seniors and college freshmen from Santa Clara County in 1927, C.N. Reynolds found that they were one and a half times more likely to mention undesirable than desirable traits of Japanese. Chief among the undesirable traits mentioned were "Take unfair advantage; dishonest, tricky, treacherous (55); ruinous, hard or unfair competitors (10)." Reynolds (1927) commented on the stability of these unfavorable stereotypes; they seemed to be the same ones "made against the Japanese during the anti-Japanese agitation of the Alien Land Law campaigns" (Strong 1934:128–29).

In many respects relations between Japan and the United States during the last part of the 1920s mirrored this relative calm. For example, both countries met with Britain in Geneva in 1927 to widen the controls on naval shipbuilding established at the Washington Conference of 1922; other signatories to the conference refused to attend. They even found themselves on the same side on certain issues. After the conference broke down, "the press of Japan and the United States found some agreement in putting the blame for failure on Britain" (Neumann 1963:172). Three years later they also met with other signatories at a conference in London which was somewhat more successful. "London in 1930 saw the last of the naval limitations conferences in which the conferees parted in substantial agreement, and it was the last Japanese-American negotiation to be conducted without mutual recriminations" (Neumann 1963:175).

During the mid-1920s the United States and Japan also confronted similar problems in the face of resurgent militant nationalism on the Chinese mainland. "Both countries were affected unfavorably by China's increasing hostility to foreign residents and interests; their common difficulties soon contributed to more harmonious exchanges" (Neumann 1963:179). They responded with a foreign policy of moderation and of measured military response to the situation.

And finally an effort was made in America toward the end of the decade to undo the damage of the exclusion act by giving Japan an immigration quota – a modification of the law which even Congressman Albert Johnson of Washington, author of the exclusion act, supported. This effort failed due to the bitter opposition of the exclusionists and to the changed world circumstances in the early 1930s. As a result, the exclusion act continued to contaminate relations between the two countries despite the drift toward normalcy during the late 1920s.

THE DETERIORATING RELATIONS DURING THE 1930S

The world economic crisis that followed the stock market crash of 1929 had a traumatic impact on the domestic situation inside the United States and Japan. It dramatically reshuffled the internal political forces in each country, with a profound effect on their subsequent relations to each other and to the world outside. In Japan, for example, ultranationalistic military leaders challenged the authority of the moderate civilian government. With the successful incident at Mukden in September 1931, sparked by an attack on Chinese forces by subordinate military officers of the Kwantung Army, they gained ascendancy in the conduct of foreign affairs.

The Mukden incident and Japan's subsequent attack on Manchuria seriously threatened the veneer of calm. The ferocity of its later response to Chinese riots and boycotts in Shanghai in January 1932 completely demolished the veneer and revived almost overnight one edge of the double-edged yellow peril theme that had lain fallow for a brief period of time. The American press almost as a single voice condemned the barbarity of the Japanese response, labeling it immoral and illegal. The press also expressed renewed concern about Japan's long-term imperialistic aims and reminded its readers of Japan's militaristic history and character. Only a few papers, however, called for drastic economic or military retaliation by America against Japan, though a section of the sensationalist press highlighted the doomsday notion of an impending Armageddon between Japan and the United States.

The Hoover administration, preoccupied as it was by the burgeoning domestic problems, could nevertheless not refrain from expressing moral outrage at Japan's action. It also authorized the dispatch of an observer to attend the League of Nations' deliberations on China's appeal. In addition, Secretary of State Stimson, using the highly moralistic and legalistic language for which he was generally known, promulgated a non-recognition policy which warned Japan that "the United States does not intend to recognize any situation, treaty or agreement which may be brought about by means contrary to the Pact of Paris" (Borton 1970:379). Dismayed by the lack of response from other nations, Stimson sought to apply even greater moral pressure on Japan through an open letter to William E. Borah, Chairman of the Senate Foreign Relations Committee.

> "The text of the letter reviewed the importance of the Open Door policy, the Nine Power Treaty of 1922, and the Kellogg-Briand Pact and without naming Japan specifically it made clear that these principles of American policy were being violated. An appeal was made to other nations to follow the non-recognition doctrine and thus place a 'caveat' on Japan's gains which would effectively bar the legality of any titles or rights acquired. Further American action was hinted at in the suggestion of reconsideration of the 1922 limitations on American battleship construction and on the fortification of Guam and the Philippines."
> (Neumann 1963:195)

The Borah letter drew an angry response from the Japanese government, which insisted that it was merely pursuing legitimate national interests and seeking to create a stable order from the disorder in Manchuria. A similar line of argument was used in its rejection of the League's Lytton report and in its subsequent walkout from the League of Nations.

As the military clamped even firmer control over the Japanese government and an outbreak of war with China once again loomed, the other edge of the yellow peril theme – that of the subversive threat of the Japanese immigrant – came increasingly into focus. Although the Hearst papers had never really relinquished it, this sub-theme resurfaced at the official level of a congressional hearing held in August 1934 by the Dies Committee in Los Angeles. At that hearing a witness testified that fishing boats operated by alien Japanese were in fact disguised naval vessels that had high-power radio transmitters and could be converted instantaneously into minelayers and torpedo boats. A transcript of that hearing was entered into the record of the hearings on the "Americanization of Fisheries" five years later.

> "Changing it [the vessel] from a fishing boat to a potential enemy minelayer and torpedo vessel can be accomplished in the high seas without going to a shipyard,

in a period of from 3 to 6 hours, including the loading of the mines and installing the torpedo tubes and stowing the torpedoes."
(US House of Representatives Committee on Merchant Marine and Fisheries 1939 76:1:5)

By 1935 enough commotion had once again been raised about the subversive nature of the Japanese immigrant that Carey McWilliams wrote an article in *The Nation* seeking to rebut the various charges. Entitled "Once Again the 'Yellow Peril, '" his article condemned the anti-Japanese drive that had apparently gained renewed life. He complained that numerous bills had been introduced in the current session of the California legislature. Most of these were aimed at driving Japanese from the fishing business, presumably on patriotic grounds. For, according to rumors being spread by the various anti-Japanese sources, most notably the California Joint Immigration Committee, most of the Japanese fishing boats had been built in Japan to be instantly converted into minelayers and torpedo boats and were being "manned by Japanese naval officers disguised as fishermen" (McWilliams 1935:735). McWilliams also referred to the charges made "in the present session of Congress [by] various California irresponsibles, assured of powerful press support,... that there are 500,000 armed Japanese in the United States and 2000 trained Japanese naval officers operate fishing boats off the coast of California" (McWilliams 1935:736).

McWilliams then sought to refute each of the rumors and charges by offering evidence to the contrary. For example, he derided the 500,000 figure by saying that according to the 1930 census fewer than 140,000 Japanese were in continental United States. He ridiculed the 2000 figure by saying only 680 Japanese were licensed fishermen in California.

"The 'naval officers' legend has this slender factual basis: in order not to be arrested should they ever return to Japan, all male Japanese between certain ages must register each year that they are 'not available for active military service,' being absent from their country. So registering, they are listed by Japan as 'reserves;' hence, technically, the 676 alien fishermen may be considered part of the potential military forces of Japan."   (McWilliams 1935:736)

He concluded his article with the statement:

"Unlike other alien groups the Japanese are members of a race which is, by popular legend, the future enemy of the United States. Every disturbance in trade between Japan and America, every recrudescence of the 'yellow peril' for campaign stuff, will affect the resident Japanese. They have emerged from the status of menials, but without full realization of their position they are unwitting pawns in the great game now being played in the Pacific."
(McWilliams 1935:736)

For the next four years the fishing menace issue was kept alive in the state politics of California. Finally in 1939 it moved to the national stage of Washington. There Kramer, congressman from California who had headed the UnAmerican Committee hearings in Los Angeles in 1934, introduced two bills in the House of Representatives:

> "one to amend section 166 of the immigration laws, to restrict certain alien seamen from landing in the United States; the other to amend section 221 of the Shipping Act barring certain aliens to participate in benefits thereof ... both of these bills pertain particularly to the Japanese seaman whose activities were brought to my attention during the investigation of which I served as chairman of the subcommittee to investigate un-American activities [in 1934]."
>
>   (US Congressional Record 1939 76:1:4411)

He then summarized the testimony of that date and added the additional charge that many of these seamen were military personnel in disguise, including secret agents who were landing at will in the United States.

> "This massing of Japanese naval and military men as seamen off the Pacific coast to fish is really for the purpose of fishing, but they are not fishing for fish. They have reached a point where they are absolutely dangerous to the safety of this country, and the time has come when we must protect our shores against any such operations as are now going on."
>
>   (US Congressional Record 1939 76:1:4412)

The congressman repeated his charges at hearings on his bill held by the Committee on Merchant Marine and Fisheries on June 13 1939. Seven months later he expressed impatience at another hearing over the committee's delay in acting on his bills. At this hearing the chairman raised doubts about the effectiveness of such a bill to eliminate espionage of the American fleet: "If we had the most rigid legislation under high heaven, what would prevent some people, if they wanted to conduct espionage on the fleet from going to Mexico or some of the neighboring states and doing it" (US House of Representatives Committee on Merchant Marine and Fisheries 1940 76:3:4). Later he added "If Japan or any other nation wants to conduct an espionage campaign to see what the navy is doing, how can they do it any more effectively with men going out from our shores than with men going out, say from Mexico or some nearby nation?" (US House of Representatives Committee on Merchant Marine and Fisheries 1940 76:3:5).

In addition, the acting president of the Seafarers' International Union (AFL) expressed the opposition of his union to the bill "because we feel that it imposes a hardship on certain people who cannot become citizens, those who are legally admitted into this country, but who cannot become citizens due to the fact that they were born in the Orient" (US House of Representatives Committee on Merchant Marine and Fisheries 1940 76:3:11). After identifying those born in the Orient as Japanese, he continued,

> "All of these people have been in the country a period of 30 to 35 years. They came in here before the Oriental Exclusion Act went into effect. The Japanese were the first out there in the sardine industry down there on the coast, and also the Italians. Now, these people have raised families and their kids are Americans. The kids grow up and they follow in their fathers' footsteps on the fishing boats down there. There are about 450 Japs in the fishing industry who cannot become citizens and they are not spies. All they are interested in is to be able to catch enough sardines to make a living."
>
> (US House of Representatives Committee on Merchant Marine and
> Fisheries 1940 76:3:11–12)

Asked about their ages, he answered "Some of the fishermen around California are 40, 50, 60, and 70 years olds." He then addressed himself to the spying charges.

> "There are about 33 boats down there in California owned by the Japanese, small fishing boats. There are 20 of them under 5-ton capacity, 10 between 5 and 10 tons capacity, and three between 10 and 20 tons. They only go outside and get sardines and come back in again. They are not speedy enough to follow the maneuvers of the Navy anyway, and if they wanted to spy on the American Navy they can just go across the border down to Mexico. There is all kinds of opportunity for any foreigners to get down there. The restrictions on immigration in Mexcio are very easy. They can operate a few miles below the border.... They [the spies] can easily operate out there in fast boats following the fleet, but these fishermen live in a community of their own there and they raise kids and the kids are American citizens, and they own their own homes, and if this bill goes through without giving a little bit of leeway to those people they will be in the bread line."
>
> (US House of Representatives Committee on Merchant Marine and
> Fisheries 1940 76:3:12)

He then read a formal statement in behalf of his union that elaborated on the various points he had already made and which stated unequivocally:

> "Lots of propaganda has been published in newspapers and magazines about spying by the Japanese fisherman. This is nothing less than ridiculous. Any person can go into the offices of the United States Geological Survey and get charts which give the depths and conditions of any harbor in any locality in the

United States. These Japanese fishermen are not interested in trying to duplicate the marine cartography of the United States Geological Survey. These men are fishermen, engaged exclusively in their trade. They are not spies."
(US House of Representatives Committee on Merchant Marine and Fisheries 1940 76:3:15)

The committee made a modest concession to the union leader's plea in the final draft of the provision that required fishing vessels to be wholly owned by citizens of the United States. It exempted from this provision "any vessel of less than 5 net tons built in the United States which is engaged solely in the fisheries" even though owned by an "alien (whether or not eligible to become a citizen of the United States) who has been a resident of the United States continuously since July 1, 1925, and who shows to the satisfaction of the Secretary of Commerce that he is a law abiding resident of the United States of good repute" (US Congressional Record 1940 76:3:12855). However, the President could cancel this exemption in "the interests of the national defense." The bill was finally passed by the House of Representatives on September 30 1940 and sent to the Senate where it was bottled up by the Commerce Committee. Undaunted by this roadblock, the California legislature passed its own version of the bill.

THE EVE OF PEARL HARBOR AND THE YELLOW PERIL THEME

By 1940 relations between the United States and Japan had deteriorated to such an extent that the United States abrogated the Commercial Treaty of 1911 and was on the verge of moving from a moral to an economic embargo of Japan. In turn Japan was making military moves against French and British possessions in the Far East and was about to announce a formal alignment with the other Axis powers. Under these circumstances the press, particularly on the West Coast, abounded with stories of Japanese spies and the yellow peril theme was reenergized to its full fury.

In one of the most spectacular displays of "investigative" fervor, John L. Spivak wrote a series of "exposés" on Japanese espionage in America in the New York-based weekly magazine, *Friday*. The initial installment was published with a picture on the cover of a sinister-looking Japanese with a dangling cigarette in his mouth and a hat pulled down over much of his face and was entitled "They Spy in America." Spivak resurrected many of the familiar features of the Magdalena Bay stories. For example, he wrote that colonies of Japanese, military men in disguise, were strewn along the coast just below San Diego:

"One of these colonies, in Ensenada on the west coast of Lower California, has some 300 fishermen. Most of them speak excellent English, and are obviously well educated. Many were imported from Japan by a San Diego fishing company operated by Japanese aliens. In the desert regions, where so large a number would promptly attract attention, the colonists are found in groups of twenty to sixty." (Spivak 1941:5)

These colonies, Spivak went on, were found "only in areas of strategic military importance," and many of these Japanese were in the process of gathering strategic information about the area. For example, "they photograph every lane and cowpath leading through the mountains to the thinly populated villages in the interior of Lower California" (Spivak 1941:5). Further, he continued, until a year ago when Mexico finally banned them, Japanese fishing boats paraded in and out of the bay ostensibly to go fishing,

"[but] Mexicans who had served in the Mexican Navy were impressed by the extraordinary feature of most of the Japanese fishing boats. They were made of steel, had cruising ranges up to 6000 miles, and were so made that they could be easily converted into mine layers. On the decks of some of these ships were emplacements for machine guns and small cannon.... Their methods of catching fish are even stranger. The crews are always taking soundings of the coastline, bays, harbors, inlets, and then photographing the entire area. Some of these boats went to sea and remained two or three months, returning without enough shrimp in their bins for their crew's salad." (Spivak 1941:7)

Now, he said, there were other kinds of espionage activities conducted by secret agents who slipped in and out of the United States disguised as American residents. This espionage extended to the San Diego waterfront itself where a Japanese-American "fishing concern" set itself up next door to a shipbuilding company that was "reconditioning two ships for the United States Navy" (Spivak 1941:10).

To give a sense of conspiratorial authenticity to the entire matter, the article included a map of Mexico and lower United States on which were written in barely legible script the various sites for the conspiratorial activities. The second article delved into the "strange affairs of Dr O.H. Warner" whose "ships fly US flags but are run by Japanese." And so through innuendo and rumor spiced by an aura of mystery and conspiracy, Spivak painted a picture of widespread skulduggery and conspiracy which brought into full play the double-edged theme of the yellow peril.

Caught in the wake of the mounting maelstrom of suspicion and doubt were the Nisei, the American-born children of the Japanese alien, many of whom were at least eighteen years of age. Already Americanized in much of their lifestyle, they tried feverishly to demonstrate their loyalty to America. The culminating expression of these efforts was a Nisei mass meeting at the Hollywood Legion Stadium in May 1941 endorsed by the American Legion and other patriotic organizations. Despite such valiant efforts, the Nisei could not shake the dual-citizenship label and the charge of primordial loyalties to Japan. They had few opportunities to refute these charges in the mass media. Occasionally their plight did receive national attention in mass-circulation publications. One such instance was the publication of an article by Magner White in *The Saturday Evening Post* of September 30 1939 called "Between Two Flags."

The article portrayed in a sympathetic light the quest of the Nisei for acceptance in America. It contrasted their Americanized lifestyle to the traditional old country style of their foreign-born parents.

> "It is said around Los Angeles that the Isseis are 'more Japanese than the Japanese themselves;' in this country the old folks have clung desperately to the mores of the old, unaware that modern Japan had moved on. But their children have gone to school and on into American colleges and, in a single generation, have jumped from the Middle Ages ideas of their fathers to somewhere near next month's calendar." (White 1939:14)

At the same time the article referred repeatedly to the white Californian's countercharge to the acculturative response of the Nisei: "American outside, Japanese inside." It even quoted the head of the national defense committee of a California American Legion Post who regaled an audience of Nisei at a meeting of the Japanese American Citizen League in 1939 with the following words: "'If we ever have war with Japan and I have anything to say about it, the first thing I'll do will be to intern every one of you'" (White 1939:15).

Somewhat more than a year later – just after Japan had formally joined the Axis – *Life Magazine* spread an extensive layout of pictures before the American public that showed just how Americanized the Nisei had become. In one picture a beauty queen was being crowned; in another, couples were ballroom dancing; in yet another, a baby contest was being held; and in still others, baseball fans, a church choir, and a wild west drama were depicted. In this manner the Nisei were shown in Americanized garb, engaged in a variety of Americanized activities, and performing them with an Americanized flair.

However, the text of the picture layout cast an ominous shadow over the light and airy portrayal of the second-generation Americanized Japanese.

> "The shadow of the treaty by which Japan joined Germany and Italy in military alliance fell no more darkly over Washington last week than it did over the flowered fields and coastal cliffs of Southern California. To Americans in the West it sounded a summons for increased watchfulness over the big Japanese

minority dwelling in their midst. To the Nisei – second-generation Japanese-Americans – it meant more trouble, more discrimination, more work to survive.

For many a month suspicious Californians have disliked the spectacle of Japanese farmers tending fruit and flowers amid oil fields, near airports and aircraft factories. Civilians and naval authorities alike have looked askance on Japanese fishing boats cruising near US warships during maneuvers. Why, they asked, were Japanese fishermen and canners permitted to live on Terminal Island, within gunshot of the naval operating base at San Pedro? There were rumors that on outbreak of a US-Japanese war, the 141,000 Japanese-Americans in this country would sabotage oil wells and bomb factories, that the familiar Pacific tuna fleet would turn overnight into a flotilla of fast torpedo boats, that Japanese fishermen would mine California harbors. Why did Japanese-Americans cross the ocean by hundreds each year to visit their ancestral home? Why did so many radio masts sprout from Japanese homes in California?"

(*Life Magazine* 1940:75)

The article then described the attempts by the Nisei to answer these various charges:

"Last week the Nisei sought to answer some of the questions white Americans were asking. They declared that most of the land they tilled had been farmlands long before drillers tapped the oil stores underneath. They pointed out that their slow old fishing boats had been locally built, were physically unable to carry the heavy air-compression machinery required to discharge torpedoes. They insisted they loved America and were ready to fight in its defense."

(*Life Magazine* 1940:75)

But the article ended on a note of doubt: "But many Californians still wondered" (*Life Magazine* 1940:75).

Thus by the eve of America's entry into World War II, the deeply embedded theme of the yellow peril had become once again refurbished and revitalized, particularly on the West coast. Its two branches were already in fairly full bloom when the Japanese struck at Pearl Harbor.

Pearl Harbor and the anti-Japanese campaign

INTRODUCTION

The attack on Pearl Harbor confronted American military leaders with the prospect of an imminent assault of an indeterminate magnitude against the West

Coast by Japanese forces. To meet this potential threat, on December 11 General Marshall upgraded the Western Defense Command, under the command of General DeWitt, to a theater of operations and began a rapid reinforcement of its ground and air defense.

> "[However] by the third week in December, as the pattern of Japanese operations and the disposition of Japanese naval forces became known, apprehensions about an imminent and serious attack on the west coast subsided. The Western theater continued to have a high priority for equipping its air and antiaircraft units, but the flow of material for its other forces suddenly dropped off.... In instructions to his subordinate commanders issued on the last day of 1941, General DeWitt himself recognized that there was no longer any immediate danger of an invasion in force. By then the principal external threat to the Western theater appeared to be from the air, and maximum air defense was therefore most important."   (Conn, Engelman, and Fairchild 1964:84)

From then on the military command in Washington never again took seriously the threat of an armed invasion of the West Coast, though it continued to expect sporadic hit and run raids by submarines and planes. General DeWitt, however, was never quite sure; he never abandoned completely fears of an invasion.

But the threat of an invasion seemed real enough immediately after Pearl Harbor. As a result, an air of foreboding pervaded the West Coast; no one knew quite what to expect or even what was happening. As a result, ominous rumors spread quickly and frighteningly. The apprehensions of civilian and military authorities, for example, were "fanned in the first few days of war by a series of false reports of Japanese ships and planes on the very doorsteps of the Pacific states" (Conn, Engelman, and Fairchild 1964:82). "It was [even] whispered that the entire Pacific fleet had been destroyed; that every reinforcing ship sent out from the mainland had been sunk off the coast by Japanese submarines" (ten Broek, Barnhart, and Matson 1968:69). As news continued to percolate from the war to the homefront of an ever deteriorating situation in the Pacific, fears mounted among the coast population and press that an invincible enemy would soon be ready to pounce on a vulnerable coastline.

At the same time rumors grew rife about subversive activities of Japanese living in California. On December 10, for example, a Treasury agent reported to the Western Command that "an estimated 20,000 Japanese in the San Francisco metropolitan area were ready for organized action" – a report subsequently repudiated by the local FBI chief who "scoffed at the whole affair as the wild imaginings of a discharged former FBI man" (Conn, Engelman, and Fairchild 1964:117). In addition, "a whispering campaign suggested that Japanese truck farmers in California were inoculating their produce with poison in order to dispose of their customers. The Los Angeles Times on December 11 captioned an article: 'Vegetables Found Free of Poisons' and labeled 'rumors of possible sabotage of California through poisoning or other means' as 'simply malicious and unfounded,' stating that more than 2000 samples of Japanese-grown produce had been chemically analyzed and found to be pure. At a later date chemical analysis disproved a rumor that Japanese canned crab in stock in the markets had ground glass in it. The Seattle Post Intelligencer of December 11 carried the Headline: 'Fifth Columnists Set Plane Beacon Fires Near Pt. Angeles,' and described flaming arrows pointing toward Seattle that had presumably been planted by 'fifth columnists seeking to guide Japanese air invaders.' On an inside page of the same edition was a small item in which the Assistant Governor stated that the fires had been set by white men who were clearing the land of brush and that the arrow shape of the beds of coals was in all probability coincidental. Everywhere on the West Coast, brush fires, flashes of light of any description, and stray gleams in a blackout were given sinister construction. Both officials and ordinary civilians saw signs and portents with increasing ease."

(War Relocation Authority 1946b:99–100)

To compound these anxieties, Secretary of Navy Frank Knox returned from an inspection of Pearl Harbor with the words that "the most effective fifth column work of the entire war was in Hawaii, with the possible exception of Norway" (War Relocation Authority 1946b:100). (Three months later he sharply curtailed his sweeping generalization in a letter to the Tolan Committee; and no evidence was ever forthcoming of the subversive activities he alleged took place.) "Newspaper headlines on the Knox report generally stressed this aspect: 'Secretary of Navy Blames Fifth Columnists for the Raid,' 'Fifth Column Prepared Attack,' 'Fifth Column Treachery Told'" (ten Broek, Barnhart, and Matson 1968:70). Thus within a few weeks of the outbreak of the war, the double-edged yellow peril theme – already activated before the war – began to grow even stronger and to sprout ever new tentacles.

During this period, however, treatment of the Japanese residents remained in relatively low key. Voices were even raised in their behalf. For example, three congressmen from the Pacific coast went on record in support of the Japanese-Americans. They asked Americans not to tar these Japanese with the responsibility and guilt of perfidious Japan and to afford them the protection of the Constitution and the Bill of Rights. In his study of 112 California newspapers, Grodzins found that favorable editorials about resident Japanese outweighed unfavorable ones from Pearl Harbor to the end of December 1941; letters to the editor also showed a similar slant during this period (Grodzins 1949).

THE DEPARTMENT OF JUSTICE AND SELECTIVE CONTROL
OF ENEMY ALIENS

In addition, the federal government did not rush pellmell into a campaign of across-the-board repression and restraint against the Japanese. It undertook a selective and relatively limited program of control confined exclusively to the Japanese alien; his American-born children were left untouched. This was reflected in the public proclamation issued by President Roosevelt on the day of the Pearl Harbor attack under the statutory and constitutional authority bestowed on his office during time of war. It stipulated that "all natives, citizens, denizens, or subjects of the Empire of Japan being of the age of fourteen years and upwards who shall be within the United States or within any territories in any way subject to the jurisdiction of the United States, and not actually naturalized" would be liable to be apprehended, restrained, secured, and removed as alien enemies if they failed to follow regulations as promulgated and or were dangerous to the public peace or safety of the United States. Included in the regulation was a list of contraband the alien was not to possess and the proscription against entering any area designated as prohibited for reasons of public safety and national security. The Attorney General was charged "with the duty of executing all the regulations hereinafter contained regarding the conduct of alien enemies within continental United States, Puerto Rico, the Virgin Islands and Alaska" (US House of Representatives (1942) 77:2:294). The President issued similar proclamations against German and Italian aliens during the next two days.

In implementing the proclamations, the Attorney General first turned his attention to enemy aliens who were deemed "dangerous to the public peace and safety." Leadership in a Japanese organization and even donation to a national cultural society was enough to include the Japanese alien in the roundup conducted by the FBI. As a result within four days of the proclamation 1500 Japanese aliens were interned, almost all of whom were from the Pacific coast. Somewhat more selective criteria were used in picking up German and Italian aliens. Their combined total in the early days equaled that for the Japanese, despite the fact that the latter had been in America on the average much longer than had the others and were therefore more likely to have deeper roots in the United States.

Despite the obvious tilt of implementation against the Japanese, the Attorney General sought to assure all enemy aliens that "*at no time . . . will the government engage in wholesale condemnation of any alien group*" (Grodzins 1949:233).

Throughout the period the Attorney General sought to keep faith with this promise. "Every notice issued to his staff testified to the desire that there should be no vigilante action, that the Japanese should be treated courteously and fairly, and that federal officials should have full control" (Godzins 1949:234).

To General DeWitt of the Western Defense Command the pace of implementation by the Attorney General was much too slow. Egged on by the army's provost marshal general, he prodded the justice department into further action. By the end of December, partially in response to this prodding, the justice department issued its first regulations on the surrender of contraband goods by enemy aliens. Dissatisfied with these regulations and with the general "laxity of enforcement," the General requested a meeting with representatives of the Attorney General in San Francisco "for the purpose of mapping a new program 'on the ground'" (Grodzins 1949:236).

From this series of meetings early in January 1942 emerged a set of agreements between the army and justice department that marked a real turning point in the department's approach to enforcing the presidential proclamations. Its top priority was to be the expeditious and effective discharge of all of its responsibilities under the proclamations with much less regard than before for the fairness of this implementation for the individual alien:

"The Department of Justice agreed to expand immediately the list of contraband goods to include all the articles prohibited by the presidential proclamations of December 7 and 8. In the second place, the department agreed that it would 'automatically accept' military recommendations for restricted areas, from which all enemy aliens would be evacuated. In the third place, less cumbersome methods for the search and seizure of contraband in premises occupied by alien enemies were agreed to. The question of probable cause will be met only by the statement that 'an alien enemy is resident in such premises.' No prior Washington approval for the issuance of such warrants would be necessary. In the fourth place, the Department of Justice agreed to conduct an alien enemy registration in the Western Theater of Operations at an early date. In the fifth place, the department expressed its willingness to conduct 'spot raids' on alien enemies, so long as such raids were confined to premises 'controlled by enemy aliens or where enemy aliens are resident.' Finally, the Department of Justice would determine how far it 'would proceed as a matter of law and policy' in making more flexible the procedures for raids on localities 'particularly . . . in which radio transmitters are probably to be found.'"   (Grodzins 1949:237)

The department however balked at the army's request for mass raids on enemy aliens for contraband. The Attorney General even went so far as to say that he would ask the President to transfer authority from the justice department to the army in the Western Theater of Operations if his position on mass raids were overruled by the President.

Placated though not enthused by the agreement, the General considered it a "great step forward," but he was still unhappy at the restrictions imposed on "mass raids." He also expressed reservations about limiting the regulations to aliens only. Control of the American-born Japanese, he insisted, remained a perplexing problem still to be solved.

> "He asked 'what methods exist or what steps are in contemplation looking toward the control of (1) dual citizens, (2) disloyal, subversive citizens (where there has been no overt act detected);' he also inquired to what extent a 'responsible Military Commander in a theatre of operations' might 'contravene normal processes to take necessary action in an emergency in order to provide for the internal as well as the external security of his theatre,' and to what extent the Department of Justice itself was able to take similar measures."
>
> (Grodzins 1949:239)

Almost immediately the expanded contraband regulations were announced and the new search procedures put into effect; however, the first large-scale "spot raids" did not take place until early in February. In addition, on January 14 the President authorized the Attorney General in Proclamation No. 2537 to register all enemy aliens and to provide them with certificates of identification. This was done early in February in the Western Defense Command and later in February in the rest of the country. It took much longer than expected to put into operation what General DeWitt considered the most important provision of the new control program; the barring of all enemy aliens, German and Italian as well as Japanese, from certain designated prohibited areas. Not until January 21 did the General submit his initial recommendations for California.

> "[It] called for the exclusion of enemy aliens from eighty-six Category A zones and their close control by a pass and permit system in eight Category B zones. Many of the Category A areas were uninhabited or had no alien population, but the execution of this recommendation nevertheless would have required the evacuation of more than 7000 persons. Only 40 percent of these would have been Japanese aliens, and the majority would have been Italian."
>
> (Conn, Engelman, and Fairchild 1964:119–20)

The Attorney General agreed in principle to the General's recommendations. On January 29 he designated in a public pronouncement the first two prohibited areas in California from which all alien enemies were to be excluded on or about February 15 1942. Two days later he designated another fifteen areas. The Attorney General left little doubt in his last announcement that he was taking this action in large measure because of pressure from the army: "This brings to 86 the total of such areas which the Attorney General, on the recommendation of the War Department, has declared to be prohibited to German, Italian, and Japanese aliens" (US House of Representatives Report No. 2124 (1942) 77:2:306).

In his first announcement the Attorney General showed a concern for the alien that was a vestigial reminder of his earlier concern. Thus he justified the exclusion of aliens from the designated area not only as an aid to national defense but also as a form of protection for the aliens themselves. In addition, he sought to guard against the vigilante actions of local officials and populations by emphasizing that "in the interests of an efficient and speedy solution of the problem, local officials and the public at large should leave this complicated program in the hands of the Federal Government and should not take conflicting action which might impede the program" (US House of Representatives Report No. 2124 (1942) 77:2:302). He also announced that Thomas Clark, recently appointed as coordinator of the alien enemy control program for the Western Defense Command, would be in charge of implementing the plan.

Serious strains began to develop between the General and the justice department as he sought to designate ever larger areas as prohibited to enemy aliens (Category A).

> "Justice officials balked at accepting the very large Category A areas he recommended for Washington and Oregon, since they included the entire cities of Seattle, Tacoma, and Portland. The execution of this recommendation would have required the evacuation of about 10,700 additional enemy aliens and, as in the case of California, only about 40 percent of these would have been Japanese. As a practical matter the Department of Justice would have found it extremely difficult to supply either the manpower or the internment facilities that a compulsory evacuation of 17,000 or 18,000 enemy aliens would have required."
> (Conn, Engelman, and Fairchild 1964:129–30)

In view of these considerations, the Attorney General announced on February 4 a more modestly delineated list of prohibited areas for Washington (7) and for Oregon (24) which enemy aliens were to leave by February 15.

By then the General had also begun to consider seriously calling for the designation of Los Angeles and San Diego as prohibited areas. In the interim the Attorney General designated as a "restricted area" for all enemy aliens the California coastline from its northern border "to a point approximately 50 miles north of Los Angeles, and extending inland for distances varying from 30 to 150 miles." In this area aliens would be subjected to a curfew and "at all other times during the day they must be found only at the place of residence or employment indicated in their certificates of identification, or going between those two places, or within a distance of not more than 5 miles from the place of residence" (US House of Representatives Report No. 2124 (1942) 77:2:310).

By Friday 7 the General finally acted; he recommended blanket Category A coverage for the two cities. Five days later he called for the same designation for almost all of the San Francisco Bay area. "If all of General DeWitt's recommendations for Category A areas through 12 February had been accepted, it would have made necessary the evacuation of nearly 89,000 enemy aliens from areas along the Pacific coast – only 25,000 of whom would have been Japanese" (Conn, Engelman, and Fairchild, 1964:130). (Given the greater concentration of German and Italian aliens near strategic points, "General DeWitt's Category A recommendations would have affected nine-tenths of the west coast German alien population and nearly three-fourths of the Italian aliens, but less than two-thirds of the Japanese aliens" (Conn, Engelman, and Fairchild 1964:130).)

With his February 7 designation of eighteen prohibited areas in Arizona, the Attorney General issued no further regulations; it was evident that an impasse had been reached in his relations with the General. In a letter to the Secretary of War dated February 9, he wrote after making several other comments,

"that if, as he had been informally advised, all of Los Angeles County was going to be recommended as a Category A area, the Department of Justice would have to step out of the picture because it did not have the physical means to carry out a mass evacuation of this scope. In conclusion, he stated that the Department of Justice was not authorized under any circumstances to evacuate American citizens; if the Army for reasons of military necessity wanted that done in particular areas, the Army itself would have to do it."

(Conn, Engelman, and Fairchild 1964:131)

THE MOUNTING REACTION AGAINST THE WEST COAST JAPANESE

As the new program of control was being implemented in January, the war in the Pacific was going from bad to worse for America. Manila had fallen and Japanese troops were advancing on a broad front throughout Southeast Asia. Even Australia seemed threatened as island after island in the Southern Pacific fell to Japan. The west coast of America too appeared to be under siege as reports persisted that ships were constantly being attacked by enemy submarines. In a letter to the Attorney General the Secretary of War commented, "A few days ago it was reported by military observers on the Pacific coast that not a single ship has sailed from our Pacific ports without being subsequently attacked. General DeWitt's apprehensions have been confirmed by recent visits of military observers from the War Department to the Pacific Coast" (Conn, Engelman, and Fairchild 1964:120). (These reports proved to be unfounded, but DeWitt never doubted them.)

With the war in the Pacific going as badly as it was, fears, apprehension, and anger grew to such proportions among residents of the West Coast that they soon began to spill over into attitudes toward the Japanese living there. Within short order popular sentiment turned dramatically against these Japanese. Aware that this evolving situation provided them with "a natural opportunity to further their long-term aims" (Grodzins 1949:19), a number of organizations from the old exclusionist coalition revived their anti-Japanese campaign and embroidered it with old and new versions of the yellow peril theme. As would be expected, the California Joint Immigration Committee was at the center of this rejuvenated drive. In the words of one of its officers, "'This is our time to get things done that we have been trying to get done for a quarter of a century'" (Grodzins 1949:20).

In its first news release since the outbreak of the war, the committee started by telling the American people how right the committee had always been in proclaiming that the Japanese were a national problem, and not merely a problem for California. "'The United States suddenly awakens to find in its western coast, congregated in vital defense areas and occupying some of the most fertile valleys of California, a Japanese population in excess of 90,000'" (Grodzins 1949:44). Much of the animus of the news release was not directed at the Japanese alien *per se*, but at his American-born children, almost three out of four of whom, the committee claimed, were still "'Japanese citizens, liable under that citizenship to be called to bear arms for their emperor, either in front of, or behind, enemy lines'" (Grodzins 1949:44). In this manner, the loyalty of the "dual-citizen" Nisei came under sharp attack. The committee complained in its release of January 2 that "'Congress has been derelict in not making dual citizenship impossible for Americans, and in not correcting a condition under which American citizens, through enforced alien teachings, are weaned from their allegiance. Perhaps the savage blow inflicted at Hawaii may cause us to awaken. It is time'" (Grodzins 1949:44).

The issue became a major item on the agenda of the committee at its first meeting after the outbreak of the war. On February 7 one of the keynote speakers called for a program to "'educate the people of the United States to the whole problem of dual citizenship.... We have a chance now that we never have had. If we go ahead and hammer at this thing week after week and day after day, we will change the attitude of what is practically the whole of the United States except the northern end of California. We are the only people here who have been wise to the menace'" (Grodzins 1949:45). The basic purpose of this program was to pressure Congress into enacting a constitutional amendment against dual citizenship.

In addition, by the time of its meetings, leading members of the committee had dusted off and brought up to date the exclusionist stand by which its progenitor organization had successfully gotten Congress to ban the entry of Japanese immigrants to the United States. Now it called for the forcible evacuation of the Japanese citizen and alien from the West Coast. At the meeting backers of exclusion moved to displace dual citizenship as the priority issue of the committee.

One of the most prestigious members of the committee argued that it should continue to oppose dual citizenship but not to divert its energies toward a constitutional amendment. Instead it should spend its efforts on the more pressing national problem of removing Japanese, whether aliens or American citizens, from the West Coast. This opinion was seconded by another prestigious leader. He claimed that the dual citizenship matter involved a too cumbersome political approach, whereas evacuation of Japanese could be obtained by urging "'the military command in this area to do the things that are obviously essential to the security of this State'" (Grodzins 1949:47).

The challenge was successful, and on February 13 the committee expressed its new set of priorities in the following resolution, offered in its testimony before the US House of Representatives Select Committee Investigating National Defense Migration (the Tolan Committee).

> "'IT IS RESOLVED that the entire Pacific Coast to such extent landward as may be required to insure safety should be declared a combat zone, and ... that the Japanese, including Japanese citizens of the United States, be removed as quickly as possible from said zone, and ... that where like dangers exist in the interior, other combat zones be established and like removals made therefrom.'"
>
> (Grodzins 1949:48)

In its rebirth, the committee soon refurbished the linkage that its progenitor had forged with charter members of the organizational coalition in the earlier struggle over exclusion. In particular, the California Department of the American Legion actively entered the fray, its state legion adjutant being chairman of the committee as well. On January 5, for example, the War Council of the department passed a dual citizenship resolution that mirrored the one advocated by the committee; however, it went further than the committee did at that juncture. It also demanded "'that all Japanese who are known to hold dual citizenship ... be placed in concentration camps [along with enemy aliens]'" (Grodzins 1949:39). By the middle of January the national commissions of the Legion at a meeting in Washington, DC called on the government to evacuate and intern immediately all enemy aliens and nationals in combat zones such as the Pacific coast. To delegates from the coast this was freely translated to mean Japanese only, both aliens and American citizens; they were little concerned with evacuating German or Italian aliens. By the middle of February, the War Council reaffirmed its call for internment of enemy aliens and other persons suspected of subversive activities, but now it added a demand that the military take over control of the matter.

Another charter member of the old coalition, the Native Sons of the Golden West, renewed with even greater fury than before its attack on the Japanese in the first three post-December 7 issues of its official publication, *The Grizzly Bear*.

In a strident I-told-you-so tone it charged in its January issue that if its historic advice had been followed America might have been spared the horrors of Pearl Harbor.

> "'Had the warnings been heeded – had the federal and state authorities been "on the alert" and rigidly enforced the Exclusion Law and the Alien Land Law; had the Jap propaganda agencies in this country been silenced; had the legislation been enacted ... denying citizenship to offspring of all aliens ineligible to citizenship; had the Japs been prohibited from colonizing in strategic locations; had not Jap-dollars been so eagerly sought by White landowners and businessmen; had a dull ear been turned to the honeyed words of the Japs and the pro-Japs; had the yellow-Jap and the white-Jap "fifth columnists" been disposed of within the law; had Japan been denied the privilege of using California as a breeding ground for dual citizens (nisei); – the treacherous Japs probably would not have attacked Pearl Harbor December 7, 1941, and this country would not today be at war with Japan.'"
>
> (Grodzins 1949:48)

Even as its official organ was restating its historic mission against the Japanese, the organization's leaders were already calling for evacuation of Japanese aliens and their American-born children and finally on February 14 the central executive board of the organization endorsed the "policy of forced mass evacuation for all resident Japanese, regardless of citizenship status" (Grodzins 1949:50).

Joining the chorus of mounting denunciations by the traditional exclusionist organizations were a number of relatively new recruits to the movement; they also began to clamor for evacuation. Many were agricultural organizations that saw in the growing din against the Japanese a once-in-the-lifetime chance to get rid of them as competitors by driving them from the land.

Though the anti-Japanese fervor of segments of the old exclusionist coalition was reborn phoenix-like in full vigor by early January, not too many public figures had as yet joined anything like a crusade against the Japanese residents. One exception, Congressman Ford of California, transmitted early in January to the Secretary of State a telegram he had received from one of his constituents, a movie actor, calling for evacuation of Japanese. By mid-January he peppered various government officials with the message

> "'that all Japanese, whether citizens or not, be placed in inland concentration camps. As justification for this, I submit that if an American born Japanese, who is a citizen, is really patriotic and wishes to make his contribution to the safety and welfare of this country, right here is his opportunity to do so, namely, that

by permitting himself to be placed in a concentration camp, he would be making his sacrifice and he should be willing to do it if he is patriotic and is working for us. As against this sacrifice, millions of other native born citizens are willing to lay down their lives, which is a far greater sacrifice, of course, than being placed in a concentration camp.'" (Grodzins 1949:65)

In a later communication he added "if American citizens of Japanese ancestry were not 'loyal enough' to accept internment, 'they ought to be placed in a camp anyhow'" (Grodzins 1949:65).

Despite these various rumblings, the real turning point in the climate of opinion occurred, according to the Tolan Committee, with the publication in late January of the report by the commission appointed by the President to investigate and report the facts relating to the attack made by Japanese armed forces upon Pearl Harbor on December 7, 1941 (the Roberts Report). ("Following the appearance of the Roberts report on January 25, the public temper changed noticeably" (US House of Representatives Report No. 1911 (1942) 77:2:2).) The report stated categorically that "prior to December 7, 1941 Japanese spies [were] on the island of Oahu. Some were Japanese consular agents and others were persons having no open relations with the Japanese foreign service. These spies collected, and, through various channels transmitted, information to the Japanese Empire respecting the military and naval establishment and dispositions on the island" (US Senate Report No. 159 (1942) 77:2:12).

The report subsequently asserted "that the center of Japanese espionage in Hawaii was the Japanese Consulate at Honolulu." So successful was its operation that "it is now apparent that through their intelligence service the Japanese had complete information. They evidently knew that no task force of the United States Navy was anywhere in the sector northeast, north, and northwest of the Hawaiian Islands" (US Senate Report No. 159 (1942) 77:2:13).

Nowhere in the report did the commission directly accuse the Japanese residing in Hawaii, whether alien or American-born, of any sabotage. It did suggest that some "persons having no open relations with the Japanese foreign office" may have engaged in espionage. But more significantly the commission saw the resident Japanese as the underlying reason for the commanding general's inaction in breaking up the espionage ring. Specifically his concern, the commission declared flatly, with their sensibilities kept him from ordering in the summer of 1941 the arrest of the more than 200 consular agents in Hawaii

"for failing to register as agents of a foreign principal as required by the statutes of the United States. In conferences respecting this question [with FBI and military intelligence officers], the commanding general, Hawaiian Department, objected to the arrest of any such persons at least until they have been given notice and an opportunity to register, asserting that their arrest would tend to thwart the efforts which the Army had made to create friendly sentiment toward the United States on the part of Japanese aliens resident in Hawaii and American citizens of Japanese descent resident in Hawaii and create unnecessary bad feeling. No action was taken against the agents."

(US Senate Report No. 159 (1942) 77:2:13)

What the commission merely implied (espionage) or failed even to mention (sabotage) became transformed into proven facts as the press and radio hammered home the thesis that the disaster at Pearl Harbor was aided, if not actually caused, by the fifth-column activities of Japanese aliens and their American-born offspring in Hawaii. Such subversion and sabotage, many pundits forecast, were bound to happen on the West Coast. Congressman Dies of the House Unamerican Committee added to the transformed atmosphere by declaring on the House floor that in three days after the report was issued "'a fear of displeasing foreign powers and a maudlin attitude toward fifth columnists was largely responsible for the unparalleled tragedy at Pearl Harbor.'" A document to be issued by his committee, he continued, would "'disclose that if our committee had been permitted to reveal the facts last September the tragedy of Pearl Harbor might have been averted.'" He then called for "'an immediate end to this suicidal policy of coddling the tools and dupes of foreign powers.'" He concluded ominously "'unless this Government adopts an alert attitude toward this whole question there will occur on the west coast a tragedy which will made Pearl Harbor sink into insignificance compared with it'" (Grodzins 1949:84–5). Dies' much-heralded report was not made public until a month later. In the interim he released frightening tidbits which he said would be documented by his report. For example, he said that Japanese organizations were a haven for spies and fifth columnists; the power and water systems of Los Angeles were mapped in detail by these spies and fifth columnists, and so on.

The arrests and spot raids by the justice department at the end of January and early February seemed to lend credence to the most ominous of the rumors and suspicions. Even the most apprehensive of the various prophets of doom had to admit, though, the absence of evidence of sabotage or fifth-column activities by local Japanese. But in one of the more remarkable circumlocutions of the war even this was transmuted into evidence of the gravity of the problem. In his testimony before the Tolan Committee on February 21 1942, Earl Warren, Attorney General of California, repeated what by now had become a standard argument for him and many other officials, including General DeWitt. He declared that the absence of sabotage and fifth-column activities on the West Coast merely showed how disciplined the resident Japanese really were. They were merely biding their time to strike a well-planned and devastating blow synchronized with an attack by the armed forces from Japan.

"I take the view that that [the absence of sabotage and fifth column activities] is the most ominous sign in our whole situation. It convinces me more than perhaps any other factor that the sabotage that we are to get, the fifth column activities that we are to get, are timed just like Pearl Harbor was timed and just like the invasion of France, and of Denmark, and of Norway, and all of those other countries.

I believe that we are just being lulled into a false sense of security and that the only reason we haven't had disaster in California is because it has been timed for a different date, and that when that time comes if we don't do something about it, it is going to mean disaster both to California and to our Nation. Our day of reckoning is bound to come in that regard. When, nobody knows, of course, but we are approaching an invisible deadline."
(US House of Representatives Select Committee Investigating National Defense Migration (1942) 77:2:11011–1012)

In responding as he did, Warren joined the two strands of the yellow peril theme (attack from without and subversion from within) into a single doomsday image of a Pearl Harbor for the West coast. As the seemingly invincible Japanese war machine rolled on in Southeast Asia and the South Pacific, those for whom this image had gained increased credibility became obsessed with the subversion strand of the yellow peril theme.

Even the eminent newspaper columnist Walter Lippman bought the Pearl Harbor image. As evident in a column he wrote on February 12 called "The Fifth Column on the Coast," he proclaimed "the Pacific Coast is in imminent danger of a combined attack from within and without.... It is a fact that the Japanese navy has been reconnoitering the coast more or less continuously'" (Daniels 1971:68). He expressed his concern that the Japanese in America might seek to help this invasion.

With anxieties of external and internal threats galvanized anew, the Japanese on the West Coast soon found themselves engulfed in an increasingly repressive atmosphere of suspicion, distrust, and hatred. The yellow peril theme was hoisted aloft ever higher and more prominently as the symbol of a cruel, deceitful, and disloyal enemy. As this orgy of ugliness spread from coast to coast, both the public and the media expressed first impatience and then anger at the slow pace and selective nature of alien control by the justice department and at Attorney General Biddle's nonevacuation policy. They called for mass removal of the Japanese, alien and citizen alike. Even Lippman joined this chorus of criticism: "'There is an assumption [in Washington] that a citizen may not be interfered with unless he has committed an overt act.... The Pacific Coast is officially a combat zone; some part of it may at any moment be a battlefield. And nobody ought to be on a battlefield who has no good reason for being there. There is plenty of room elsewhere for him to exercise his rights'" (Daniels 1971:68).

As the tide of public and press opinion turned, local and state officials became increasingly outspoken. Attorney General Warren, for example, made his first public reference to a West Coast Pearl Harbor on January 30. He called for evacuation of the Japanese residents. This stance was supported three days later by district attorneys and sheriffs throughout California at a meeting convened by Warren. At the same time he asked the district attorneys of counties with a Japanese population to prepare a map showing the relationship between the residence of Japanese and strategic installations. After obtaining the results, he commented,

"Such a distribution of the Japanese population appears to manifest something more than coincidence. But, in any case, it is certainly evident that the Japanese population of California is, as a whole, ideally situated, with reference to points of strategic importance, to carry into execution a tremendous program of sabotage on a mass scale should any considerable number of them be inclined to do so."
(US House of Representatives Select Committee Investigating National Defense Migration (1942) 77:2:10974)

For the next several weeks Warren advanced various facets of the yellow peril theme – particularly those bearing on the loyalty of the Japanese aliens and American-born. By February 7, he advocated that the military take over control of the situation. "'We are fighting an invisible deadline. There is only one group in the last analysis that can protect this State from the Japanese situation and that is the armed forces of this government'" (Grodzins 1949:96). He pressed his point of view on various government officials, including General DeWitt.

Even those officials who had uttered favorable comments about the Japanese residents in December joined the bandwagon. The mayor of Los Angeles, for example, who had urged tolerance of Japanese-Americans in December, called for their mass evacuation by early February. By then he had also accepted the Pacific Coast Pearl Harbor thesis with its day of Armageddon in which a coordinated internal and external attack by Japanese forces would be mounted. By mid-February he was openly advocating the transfer of authority for control of the problem from the justice department to the military. Three days later he supported a constitutional amendment which would deal "with the question of dual citizenship."

The governor of California had also called for fair and tolerant treatment of the Japanese in December and had even vouched for the loyalty of most American-born Japanese. By late January he no longer voiced these opinions. He began to urge more effective control, lest the people of California take matters into their own hands. But he was unwilling even as late as mid-February to support a policy of forced mass evacuation; instead he continued to explore the possibilities of a much more limited program of evacuation. Other state and local officials had no such initial misgivings about intolerant treatment of the Japanese to live down. At a very early stage they espoused a policy of evacuation. By mid-February 30 percent of California's counties had passed formal resolutions calling for mass evacuation of Japanese residents from coastal to inland areas. The likelihood of passing a resolution depended on the number of Japanese in the county. Thus, "fifty-four percent of the California counties with 100 or more Japanese per 10,000 total population urged evacuation or passed restrictive measures against Japanese in the pre-evacuation period; 21 percent with less than 100 Japanese per 10,000 population took the same type of action" (Grodzins 1949:115).

By the end of January misgivings and anxieties similar to those expressed by the local and state officials on the West coast began to find increasing expression among the West coast congressmen and senators in Washington as well. Although Congressman Ford seemed even then to be the only visible articulator of these anxieties on the congressional stage, others were already meeting privately to see what could be done to prod the justice department into faster action and to advance the cause of mass evacuation. In early February these informal interactions took on a formal structure at a conference of congressmen and senators from three Pacific states called by Senators Johnson of California and Holman of Oregon. Two committees were set up, one on alien nationality and sabotage and the other on defense. Both took testimony from government officials and others, some of which ran counter to what the committees wanted to hear. For example, the committee on defense heard from naval and army authorities that the Japanese armed forces might be capable of sporadic raids on the West Coast, but that '*it would be impossible for the enemy to engage in a sustained attack on the Pacific Coast at the present time*" (Grodzins 1949:72). This testimony was pointed to by the chief of the alien enemy control unit of the justice department in his own appearance before the second committee as undermining the basic argument of proponents of mass evacuation "that an organized fifth column could spring up at the point of an enemy attack" (Grodzins 1949:73). He recorded the angry response of the committee to his statement in subsequent notes to himself.

"'The congressional hotheads ignored the opinion. They said Army and Navy authorities were jackasses, that they had been proved wrong at Pearl Harbor, that there was no reason to accept their testimony, and that the California congressmen were not going to wait for another Pearl Harbor in Los Angeles.'"

(Grodzins 1949:73)

The committee was also irritated by Attorney General Biddle's continued refusal to support the evacuation of citizens of Japanese extraction, and by his insistence that "the sole duty of the Department of Justice was to apprehend those [aliens] believed to be dangerous, and it was wholly up to the Army to say whether a region as a whole must be cleared of citizens and aliens alike" (Grodzins 1949:74).

In mid-February the two committees wound up their work and formally adopted in joint session a recommendation that made no mention of the testimony they did not want to hear. They called for "'the immediate evacuation of *all persons of Japanese lineage* and all others, aliens and citizens alike, whose presence shall be deemed dangerous or inimical to the safety of the defense of the United States from all strategic areas'" (Grodzins 1949:77). They then sent the recommendation to the President in a letter stressing "the seriousness of the Japanese menace along the entire Pacific Coast" (Grodzins 1949:78). They also appointed a committee to discuss the recommendation with the President. However, before arrangements for the meeting were completed, President Roosevelt had issued Executive Order 9066 which made the entire matter moot.

As the demand for mass evacuation became a virtual obsession for most of the congressional delegation from the West, only a handful of congressmen from the rest of the country shared their intense sentiments. The most ardent of these supporters were Congressmen John Rankin of Mississippi, Martin Dies of Texas, and Senator Tom Stewart of Tennessee, all from the South.

Evacuation and internment

THE TAKEOVER BY THE ARMY

Aware of the growing public sentiment against the Japanese on the West Coast and impatient with the normative constraints imposed by the Department of Justice in the implementation of its alien control program, General DeWitt responded to the pressure from California government officials by expressing at the end of January his willingness to assume responsibility for the enemy alien program if authority for it were transferred to him by the President. Two days later his aide repeated the statement before a congressional delegation from the West. At this juncture, however, the General was not quite sure what his overall plan would be if he were in charge. He seemed sympathetic to the California governor's plan for a limited voluntary resettlement of Japanese aliens within California. At the same time the Secretary of War and his assistant were toying with the idea of military reservations being established around strategic installations with some sort of licensing system for entering and leaving the area. Both were against mass evacuation and were "pretty much against interfering with citizens unless it can be done legally" (Conn, Engelman, and Fairchild 1969:125). As we have already seen, they had even had senior military officers testify before the committees of the Pacific coast congressional caucus that an attack from Japanese forces was unlikely against the West coast.

Distressed at this turn of events, the Provost Marshal and his deputy complained that the governor's plan "savors too much of the spirit of Rotary and overlooks the necessary cold-bloodedness of war" (Daniels 1971:60). Encouraged by the ever mounting public pressure for concerted action, they and their allies in the Western Command decided to redouble their efforts for a policy of mass evacuation of the Japanese. Within a week they succeeded in turning matters around by persuading the General to endorse once again mass evacuation in the name of military necessity. They even gained the enthusiastic support of the assistant Secretary of War, though the Secretary still needed some convincing. However, nothing could be done to implement their scheme; final authority for alien control was still vested in the Department of Justice, which continued to oppose such a plan despite a policy of cooperating with the Western Command. And on February 9 relations between the department and the Western Command came to a complete impasse as the Attorney General "formally advised the Secretary of War, by letter, that he could not accept the recommendation of the Commanding General [of the Western Defense Command] for the establishment of a zone prohibited to enemy aliens in the States of Washington and Oregon of the extent proposed by him." The Attorney General complained that this would require "a mass evacuation of many thousands" which the Department of Justice was not "physically equipped to do . . . only the War Department has the equipment and personnel to manage the task." He concluded his letter with the statement that the Department of Justice only had legal authority under the various proclamations to apprehend and to evacuate alien enemies, not "American citizens of the Japanese race." "If they have to be evacuated, I believe that this would have to be done as a military necessity in these particular areas. Such action, therefore, should in my opinion, be taken by the War Department and not by the Department of Justice" (US Army, Western Defense Command and Fourth Army 1943:7−8).

In this manner, the patchwork of interdepartmental cooperation was rent; and the issue of final authority, joined. The war department articulated its bid for taking over control in a memorandum which raised a series of questions to be addressed to President Roosevelt.

"'(1) Is the President willing to authorize us to move Japanese citizens as well as aliens from restricted areas?

(2) Should we undertake withdrawal from the entire strip DeWitt originally recommended, which involves a number of over 100,000 people, if we included both aliens and Japanese citizens?

(3) Should we undertake the intermediate step involving, say, 70,000 which includes large communities such as Los Angeles, San Diego, and Seattle?

(4) Should we take any lesser step such as the establishment of restricted areas around airplane plants and critical installations, even though General DeWitt states that in several, at least, of the large communities this would be wasteful, involve difficult administrative problems, and might be a source of more continuous irritation and trouble than 100 percent withdrawal from the area?'" (Conn, Engelman, and Fairchild 1964:131)

On February 11, the Secretary of War Stimson raised these questions with the President by phone and received his full approval to do anything he thought necessary. In the words of the assistant Secretary of War, "'we talked to the President and the President, in substance, says go ahead and do anything you think necessary ... if it involves citizens, we will take care of them too. He says there will probably be some repercussions, but it has got to be dictated by military necessity, but as he puts it, "Be as reasonable as you can"'" (Daniels 1971:65). He also expressed the belief that the President was prepared to sign an executive order giving the war department the authority to do whatever it wished to do.

Ironically a day later General Mark Clark, who had been asked earlier by General George C. Marshall to prepare an official report on the advisability of mass evacuation, submitted his memorandum which came to the opposite conclusion, also in the name of military necessity. He decried the cost in military manpower and energy that total evacuation would require.

"'I cannot agree with the wisdom of such a mass exodus for the following reasons:

(a) We will never have a perfect defense against sabotage except at the expense of other equally important efforts. The situation with regards to protecting establishments from sabotage is analogous to protecting them from air attack by antiaircraft and barrage balloons. We will never have enough of these means to fully protect these establishments. Why, then, should we make great sacrifices in other efforts in order to make them secure from sabotage?

(b) We must weigh the advantages and disadvantages of such a wholesale solution to this problem. We must not permit our entire offensive effort to be sabotaged in an effort to protect all establishments from ground sabotage.'" (Daniels 1971:66)

Instead General Clark wanted to concentrate on protecting crucial installations, including the evacuation of all enemy aliens from their immediate environs. He would have relied on civilian police and the FBI to monitor and control the situation and would also have resorted to internment of ringleaders and suspects. His recommendations, whatever their merits, had come too late. The forces advocating mass evacuation under the guise of military necessity were now in saddle.

On February 14, three days after the President's approval, General DeWitt submitted to the Secretary of War his final recommendation for evacuation of Japanese and other subversive persons from the Pacific coast. He prefaced his recommendation with two "estimates of the situation." First, he warned that the Pacific coast might be the target of "possible and probable enemy activities," including naval attacks on shipping in coastal waters and on coastal cities and vital installations, air raids on vital installations, particularly within two hundred miles of the coast, and sabotage of vital installations throughout the Western Defense Command.

> "Hostile Naval and air raids will be assisted by enemy agents signaling from the coastline and the vicinity thereof; and by supplying and otherwise assisting enemy vessels and by sabotage.
>
> Sabotage (for example, of airplane factories), may be effected not only by destruction within plants and establishments, but by destroying power, light, water, sewer, and other utility and other facilities in the immediate vicinity thereof or at a distance. Serious damage or destruction in congested areas may readily be caused by incendiarism."
>
> (US Army, Western Defense Command and Fourth Army 1943:33)

As his second estimate of the situaton, he warned that all Japanese residing on the Pacific coast, whether born in Japan or America, could not be trusted and were "potential enemies." The primordial ties and loyalties of race could not be denied, despite any veneer of "becoming Americanized."

> "In the war in which we are now engaged racial affinities are not severed by migration. The Japanese race is an enemy race and while many second and third generation Japanese born on United States soil, possessed of United States citizenship, have become 'Americanized,' the racial strains are undiluted.... That Japan is allied with Germany and Italy in this struggle is no ground for assuming that any Japanese, barred from assimilation by convention as he is, though born and raised in the United States, will not turn against this nation when the final test of loyalty comes....
>
> It, therefore, follows that along the vital Pacific Coast over 112,000 potential

enemies, of Japanese extraction, are at large today. There are indications that these are organized and ready for concerted action at a favorable opportunity. The very fact that no sabotage has taken place to date is a disturbing and confirming indication that such action will be taken."

(US Army, Western Defense Command and Fourth Army 1943:34)

He than described the proximity of Japanese in the states of California, Washington, and Oregon to various strategic installations, both military and civilian.

Given his estimates of the situation, the Commanding General then went on to recommend

"that the Secretary of War procure from the President direction and authority to designate military areas in the combat zone of the Western Theater of Operations (if necessary to include the entire combat zone), from which, in his discretion, he may exclude all Japanese, all alien enemies, and all other persons suspected for any reason by the administering military authorities of being actual or potential saboteurs, espionage agents, or fifth columnists."

(US Army, Western Defense Command and Fourth Army 1943:36)

He then requested that the Secretary of War be empowered to requisition the services of all agencies of the federal government which would be obliged to respond to such requisitions and "to use any and all federal facilities and equipment, including Civilian Conservation Corps Camps, and to accept the use of State facilities for the purpose of providing shelter and equipment for evacuees" (US Army, Western Defense Command and Fourth Army 1943:36).

The memorandum then went on to recommend the evacuation of Japanese aliens, Japanese-American citizens, and alien enemies other than Japanese from military areas designated as those areas in California, Oregon, and Washington that the General had earlier requested to be so labeled by the Attorney General. This was to be "initiated on a designated evacuation day and carried to completion as rapidly as practicable" (US Army, Western Defense Command and Fourth Army 1943:36). The memorandum spelled out the various procedures that could be followed, stating that "all arrangements [should] be accomplished with the utmost secrecy" and "adult males (above the age of 14 years) [should] be interred separately from all women and children until the establishment of family units can be accomplished" (US Army, Western Defense Command and Fourth Army 1943:37). The memorandum estimated that approximately 133,000 persons would be involved in the evacuation, of whom approximately 112,000 would be Japanese.

Interestingly, two years later the Commanding General was still trying to justify his estimates of the situation which led to his recommendation that Japanese and other subversive persons be evacuated from the Pacific coast. In his final report he asserted that his first estimate had been proved right by subsequent events: "there were hundreds of reports nightly of signal lights visible from the coast, and of intercepts of unidentified radio transmissions. Signaling was often observed at premises which could not be entered without a warrant because of mixed occupancy" (US Army, Western Defense Command and Fourth Army 1943:8). (Several authorities doubt the authenticity of many of these alleged reports despite the General's statement that "following the evacuation, interceptions of suspicious or unidentified radio signals and shore-to-ship signal lights were virtually eliminated and attacks on outbound shipping from west coast ports appreciably reduced" (US Army, Western Defense Command and Fourth Army 1943:fn.8).)

The General also sought to justify his second estimate by emphasizing the location of Japanese near strategic installations:

"Whether by design or accident, virtually always their communities were adjacent to very vital shore installations, war plants, etc.... It could not be established, of course, that the location of thousands of Japanese adjacent to strategic points verified the existence of some vast conspiracy to which all of them were parties. Some of them doubtless resided there through mere coincidence. It seemed equally beyond doubt, however, that the presence of others was not mere coincidence.... In any case, it was certainly evident that the Japanese population of the Pacific Coast was, as a whole, ideally situated with reference to points of strategic importance, to carry into execution a tremendous program of sabotage on a mass scale should any considerable number of them have been inclined to do so."

(US Army, Western Defense Command and Fourth Army 1943:9–10)

(Various authorities point to the fact that the Japanese resided and worked in most of these areas long before the strategic installations were built.)

In addition he argued that most Japanese organizations "followed a line of control from the Japanese government, through key individuals and associations to the Japanese residents in the United States" (US Army, Western Defense Command and Fourth Army 1943:10).

"In his estimate of the situation, then, the Commanding General found a tightly-knit, unassimilated racial group, substantial numbers of whom were engaged in pro-Japanese activities. He found them concentrated in great numbers along the Pacific Coast, an area of the utmost importance to the national war effort. These considerations were weighed against the progress of the Emperor's Imperial Japanese forces in the Pacific."

(US Army, Western Defense Command and Fourth Army 1943:17)

He then described the deteriorating situation on the Pacific warfront at that time and three isolated instances of enemy submarine shellings of the Pacific coast.

"In summary, the Commanding General was confronted with the Pearl Harbor experience, which involved a positive enemy knowledge of our patrols, our naval dispositions, etc., on the morning of December 7th; with the fact that ships leaving West Coast ports were being intercepted regularly by enemy submarines; and with the fact that an enemy element was in position to do great damage and substantially to aid the enemy nation. Time was of the essence.

The Commanding General, charged as he was with the mission of providing for the defense of the West Coast, had to take into account these and other military considerations. He had no alternative but to conclude that the Japanese constituted a potentially dangerous element from the viewpoint of military security – that military necessity required their immediate evacuation to the interior. The impelling military necessity had become such that any measures other than those pursued along the Pacific Coast might have been 'too little and too late.'"

(US Army, Western Defense Command and Fourth Army 1943:18–19)

Once General DeWitt submitted his memorandum of February 14 1942, the civilian heads of the war department took over the task of preparing an executive order for the President authorizing the mass evacuation. Their representatives met with those from the justice department to discuss a draft that had been written. Although several of his subordinates were distressed at the prospects of mass evacuation, Attorney General Biddle raised no objection and was prepared to assist them in refining it. He therefore gave his blessing to the transfer of authority from the justice to the war department. Without so much as a whimper of protest, he backed a policy of mass evacuation to which he had objected all along.

In this manner the justice department joined the war department in presenting to the President an executive order which he signed on February 19. In this order (E.O. 9066) the President authorized the Secretary of War and military commander whom he may from time-to-time designate

"to prescribe military areas in such places and of such extent as he or the appropriate Military Commander may determine, from which any or all persons may be excluded, and with respect to which the right of any person to enter, remain in, or leave shall be subject to whatever restrictions the Secretary of War or the appropriate Military Commander may impose in his discretion."

(US House of Representatives Report No. 2124 (1942) 77:2:314)

The order also placed authority in the hands of the military "to enforce compliance with the restrictions applicable to each Military area herein above authorized to be designated, including the use of Federal troops" (US House of Representatives Report No. 2124 (1942) 77:2:314). The war department, however, had second thoughts about having to shoulder full responsibility for enforcing the military restrictions under the order and for punishing violations. Accordingly it drafted and sent to Congress a bill with the approval of the President and with the concurrence of the justice department that would empower federal courts to treat as a misdemeanor punishable by fine and/or imprisonment not to exceed one year any "violation of restrictions or orders with respect to persons entering, remaining in, or leaving military areas or zones which the War Department recommends to be enacted into law" (US Congressional Record 1942 77:2:2722).

In seeking congressional approval, the war department was doing more than merely seeking to shift the responsibility for enforcement from the military to the courts. It was also seeking to broaden and to strengthen the legal and constitutional basis for the President's executive order by having Congress give legislative sanction to it.

Thus the Secretary of War sent to both houses of Congress on March 9 a draft of the proposed statute with an identical covering letter. It was immediately referred to the military affairs committee of each house. During the closed hearings of remarkably short duration, the law was amended by the war department to include penalties for acts committed within the military areas, such as violation of curfews. No opposition to the potentially sweeping nature of the bill developed in either committee. Even the fact that these regulations were also to be imposed on American citizens of Japanese descent evoked virtually no comment and certainly no concern in the Senate committee. In the few instances where it was mentioned, the matter was dismissed with the offhand remark that after all they were "dual citizens" and the regulations should apply. In the House hearings, the citizenship issue was explicitly mentioned, but it raised no eyebrows and evoked no criticism. And so both committees unanimously endorsed the bill and sent it to their respective houses.

Professing military urgency the chairman of the House Military Affairs Committee rushed the bill through the House despite the protest of one member who wanted more time for deliberation on a bill that so profoundly affected "the rights of citizens." In the Senate, Chairman Reynolds of the Military Affairs Committee launched into a long and rambling speech as he opened debate on the bill. He emphasized that

"without exaggeration one of our most important fronts is the American front, and without the proper control of aliens [whom he estimated numbered five millions] and enemies of this Government we can hardly expect to be successful in other areas of the world unless we first provide protection for American citizens on the American front, where we must guard carefully our great munitions and manufacturing structures engaged in the production of war materials." (US Congressional Record 1942 77:2:2722)

As evidence of the kind of threat that America faced from within, he offered the litany of fifth-column activities before and during the attack on Pearl Harbor that had by then come to be accepted as the gospel truth. But he admitted that since Pearl Harbor, "enemy activity on the Pacific coast has quieted;" however, he repeated what had by then become part of the military catechism:

> "This lull itself leads our officials to suspect perhaps further blows, and evidences the fact that enemy groups of saboteurs are under excellent control by their leaders. Air and submarine attack from the sea, for example, could be coordinated with sabotage on land by dynamiting dams, power plants, oil fields, refineries, and defense factories. Japanese settlements often are near these vital areas." (US Congressional Record 1942 77:2:2723)

The major fifth-column threat, he continued in agreement with his colleague from Iowa, was the American-born Japanese. Though United States citizens by birth,

> "they are also held to be subjects of Nippon unless they specifically renounce the Emperor. Few renunciations have been made and all citizens may be conscripted into the Japanese service.... Japanese consuls, Buddhist priests, and other leaders have been propagandizing the children of their countrymen for years right here beneath the shadows of the American flag, right here in continental United States. We learn that from translations of essays written by Japanese high-school students in southern California to celebrate the twenty-six hundredth anniversary of the Empire. These students have expressed and do express pride in their dual citizenship and approval of Japanese ambitions in Asia." (US Congressional Record 1942 77:2:2723)

As he proceeded, Reynolds subsumed the fifth-column threat of the Japanese into a more general discussion of the threat from Axis powers generally, and Nazi Germany specifically. He read aloud newspaper headlines to show how real the threat was. He called for suspension of "all naturalization for the duration of the war." He also chided his colleagues for their failure to support legislation he advocated in 1936 which "would have excluded from the United States a mass of people, among them them spies, saboteurs, and agitators of sedition and subversion, who now are a source of unending anxiety to the military authorities of this Nation" (US Congressional Record 1942 77:2:2724).

He finally returned to the bill at hand "which will confer broad powers on the military authorities charged with the protection of certain zones in our country.

We well know that the necessities of our situation are such that these powers must even extend to the control of persons who are citizens of the United States" (US Congressional Record 1942 77:2:2724).

He ended his speech by reading his committee's strong endorsement of the bill. "It is the opinion of the committee that immediate passage of this bill is a military necessity not only with respect to the Pacific coast region but also with respect to any other part of the United States or its possessions in which it is desirable to create military areas under Executive Order No. 9066 or other Executive orders" (US Congressional Record 1942 77:2:2725).

In the ensuing debate, several senators expressed concern about the vagueness of the bill, about the broad sweep of power it gave the military. Senator Taft acidly summarized these concerns when he said:

> "Mr. President, I think this is probably the 'sloppiest' criminal law I have ever read or seen anywhere. I certainly think the Senate should not pass it. I do not want to object, because the purpose of it is understood.... I have no doubt that in peacetime no man could ever be convicted under it, because the court would find that it was so indefinite and so uncertain that it could not be enforced under the Constitution."   (US Congressional Record 1942 77:2:2726)

Despite his disdain for the bill, Taft did not try to block its consideration, and it was passed without any further ado that day, March 19.

With passage of the bill, Congress draped the mantle of statutory legitimacy over the military to do what it would with evacuation of the Japanese, alien and American citizen alike, just as the President had cloaked it earlier with executive legitimacy. Still to come was the mantle of constitutional legitimacy which was bestowed by the Supreme Court at a later date (we shall discuss this in a later section of this chapter).

PHASE ONE: VOLUNTARY EVACUATION

Even before Congress was brought into the act, General DeWitt issued his first public proclamation under the authority of the President's executive order and in the name of military necessity. The proclamation established two military areas. Number 1 included the coastal halves of the states of California, Oregon, and Washington, and southern Arizona. Number 2 included the rest of the four states. The proclamation then warned in general terms that "'such persons or classes of persons as the situation may require will by subsequent proclamation be excluded from all of Military Area No. 1'" and from selected zones in Military Area No. 2; the rest of Area No. 2 was presumably to be free of "'any prohibition or regulation or restrictions'" (ten Broek, Barnhart, and Matson 1968:117). An accompanying press release let it be known in no uncertain terms "which persons or classes of persons" the General had in mind. The Japanese, whether born in Japan or in America, would be the first to be excluded by future proclamation; then perhaps German and Italian aliens and others.

In making the proclamation public, the General hoped that the Japanese in Military Area No. 1 would take the hint and start to leave the area of their own accord. As such, he sought to encourage them openly to depart. All that was required was that they make out a change of residence notice; after Proclamation 3 the notice served as an official travel permit. After that they were free to locate themselves wherever they wanted within non-prohibited areas. To facilitate this movement, the General proposed to build centers at Manzanar, California and Parker, Arizona to serve as "'resting points from which the Japanese, once there, could proceed further eastward once they had secured jobs and community acceptance'" (ten Broek, Barnhart, and Matson 1968:118). By March 21 2000 Japanese had "voluntarily" congregated in Manzanar. Several thousand more sought to make it on their own, most of these attempting to relocate within interior California. But as these new arrivals entered the various interior communities they were greeted by an explosive antagonism from the citizenry and law officials alike that had been building since February when rumors spread that the coastal Japanese were to be "dumped" on other areas.

> "Those who attempted to cross into the interior states ran into all kinds of trouble. Some were turned back by armed posses [sic] at the border of Nevada; others were clapped into jail and held overnight by panicky local peace officers; nearly all had difficulty in buying gasoline; many were greeted by 'No Japs wanted' signs on the main streets of interior communities; and a few were threatened, or felt that they were threatened, with possibilities of mob violence." (Daniels 1971:84)

Forebodings of this had already been expressed at the San Francisco hearings of the Tolan Committee late in February. For example, the regional director of the Office of Defense, Health, and Welfare Services testified: "I have seen resolutions of the governors, the chambers of commerce and all the hospitality centers west of the Rocky Mountain States. They don't want them either." He then went on to comment "May I say that all they are talking about is Japanese. We have had telegrams from all the towns in California protesting" (US House of Representatives Select Committee Investigating National Defense Migration 1942 77:2: 11054). Even the national secretary of the Japanese American Citizens League called for the discouraging of voluntary evacuations at the hearings "in view of the alarming developments in Tulare County [California] and other communities against incoming Japanese evacuees" (US House of Representatives Select Committee Investigating National Defense Migration 1942 77:2:11137).

So loud had these protests become by the end of March that General DeWitt decided to put an end to what he had labeled as Phase One: Voluntary Evacuation. Accordingly he issued on March 27 Public Proclamation No. 4 which, in a complete about face from Proclamation No. 1, forbade any persons of Japanese ancestry to leave Military Area No. 1 "until and to the extent that a future proclamation or order of this headquarters shall so permit or direct" (US House of Representatives Report No. 2124 (1942) 77:2). On the same day his Public Proclamation No. 3 clamped down hard on the Japanese in Military Area No. 1 and selected zones in Area 2. It established in these areas a curfew from 8 pm to 6 am for all enemy aliens and persons of Japanese ancestry and required that "at all other times all such persons shall be only at their place of residence or employment or traveling between those places or within a distance of not more than five miles from their place of residence" (US House of Representatives Report No. 2124 (1942) 77:2:330).

For two days Japanese could still leave the areas voluntarily, for Proclamation No. 4 did not go into effect until January 29. But after that date they were constrained from leaving the areas and severely limited in what they could do in them. Violators of either or both proclamations were to be prosecuted under terms of the public law passed by Congress just a week before.

According to Daniels, the proclamations, more notably No. 3, "affected the daily lives of Japanese Americans [in Military Area No. 1 and selected zones of Area No. 2], and created for them alone, the closest thing to a police state ever seen in the United States" (Daniels 1971:85). These proclamations did not have the same effect on Italian or German aliens, because they were white and not as easily detected. In addition most of their fellow countrymen were citizens and beyond the reach of the law; under these circumstances many of these aliens might have been able to pass as citizens.

PHASE TWO: MASS EVACUATION

Even before Phase One had officially ended, a dress rehearsal for Phase Two was about to take place. On March 24, three days after passage of Public Law No. 503 for which he had been waiting, General DeWitt issued his first civilian exclusion order: "All persons of Japanese ancestry, including aliens and non aliens [were to] be excluded from that portion of Military Area No. 1 described as 'Bainbridge Island,' in the State of Washington, on or before 12 o'clock noon, PWT, of the 30th day of March 1942" (US House of Representatives Report No. 2124 (1942) 77:2:333). Prior to that date persons could receive permission to leave the island and take up residence under the provisions of the voluntary evacuation program of

Phase One that was still in operation. All of the others would have to report to the Civil Control Office for forcible evacuation to an assembly center. However, whichever choice they made, "a responsible member of each family, preferably the head of the family" was to report to the control office on March 25 for further instructions.

Those opting for the assembly center were provided with a list of personal property and utensils they could take with them; larger items were to be stored at government expense. On the designated day 257 Japanese were taken to the assembly center at Manzanar, California, the one in Washington not having been completed as yet.

Phase Two was to involve the compulsory evacuation of Japanese to assembly centers, a transitional move to be followed by Phase Three in which the evacuees would be sent from the assembly center to the permanently constructed relocation centers. In designing Phase Two, General DeWitt stated unequivocally in his final report that "no precedents existed in American life." And whereas in Europe precedents existed, these "were unsatifactory for many reasons." And then in a surge of apparent pride he proclaimed that "the Army was [therefore] faced with the problem of designing a new type of civilian evacuation which would accomplish the mission *in a truly American way* [author's italics]" (US Army, Western Defense Command and Fourth Army 1943:77).

What he meant by an American way was in part reflected by some of the guidelines set up to implement the evacuation. For example, family units and communities were not to be split up if at all possible. In addition financial losses were to be minimized by having the Federal Reserve Bank of San Francisco and the Farm Security Administration provide evacuees with advice and assistance. The General sought, in effect, to introduce a touch of the American way in Phase Two by infusing an element of "compassionate regard" for people being forcibly evacuated. He also sought to inject the American emphasis on efficiency. As a result, areas were to be evacuated in order of their relative military importance, and evacuation was to be accomplished with as minimal a number of active military units as possible. Further, evacuees were to be moved to assembly centers as close as possible to their places of former residence in order to expedite matters and to reduce initial travel.

Once the dress rehearsal was successfully completed, the army began to evacuate systematically and sequentially Japanese from a total of 108 specially designated exclusion areas, each of which contained approximately 1000 Japanese. Initially only those exclusion areas located in Military Area 1 of California, Oregon, and Washington were evacuated. As a result, approximately 10,000 were moved into assembly centers from March 24 to June 6 1942. But by mid-year General DeWitt had gone back on his promise in Public Proclamation No. 1 not to move persons from Military Area 2. He ordered the removal of 9000 Japanese from Military Area 2 of California. This took place between July 4 and August 11.

In each instance, the evacuation from a given exclusion area was preceded by a civilian exclusion order that gave the Japanese about seven days to be registered, processed, and moved out. As in the dress rehearsal, they were allowed to take minimal possessions with them. With so little time to dispose of their holdings, many suffered staggering losses in income and property despite the protection they were presumably to get from federal agencies. One estimate of their total loss exceeded one-third of a billion dollars.

At the beginning of the evacuation only Manzanar was able to accommodate evacuees. By the end of the first week in May fifteen others had been built, one each in Oregon, Washington, and Arizona and the rest in California. (After June 1 Manzanar was converted from an assembly center to a relocation center.) Many of these centers were formerly race tracks, fairgrounds, and livestock exhibition halls. "The living quarters, especially at the race tracks, were exceedingly small and bore the atmosphere of their former use" (ten Broek, Barnhart, and Matson 1968:126). In other words, they smelled. The United States Public Health Service found that sanitation was bad in these centers, though the army insisted that conditions were good. Surrounding the centers were barbed wire fences with military police patrolling the perimeter. "Guard towers were spotted at frequent intervals and searchlights were installed. The evacuees were warned by one of the first bulletins circulated in the centers that they must obey the commands of the sentries" (ten Broek, Barnhart, and Matson 1968:126).

Control of these centers was firmly in the hands of the military which laid down the rules and regulations, though efforts were made to encourage educational and recreational activities among the residents. By August 11, 110,000 Japanese had been forcibly removed from their homes and businesses to be placed in transitional "concentration camps" before they were finally relocated into more permanent ones.

THE WAR RELOCATION AUTHORITY AND THE CENTERS

The decision to separate evacuation from relocation had been reached as early as March 1942, several weeks after the President's executive order had been issued in February. At that time the Departments of Justice and War and Bureau of the Budget opted, each for its own reasons, for the establishment of a civilian agency to assume responsibility for the supervision and relocation of evacuees once the army completed their removal from the military areas and placed them in assembly centers. Milton Eisenhower of the agricultural department was called in to assist in the formulation of plans for the proposed agency. He worked informally with the various parties for several weeks, until the President officially established the War Relocation Authority under Executive Order No. 9106 on March 18 and named him its first director.

Under the terms of the order, he was given broad powers "to accomplish all necessary evacuation not undertaken by the Secretary of War or appropriate military commander, provide for the relocation of such persons [evacuees] in appropriate places, provide for their needs in such manner as may be appropriate, and supervise their activities" (US House of Representatives Report No. 2124 (1942) 77:2:316). However, he was to obtain prior approval of the military for any evacuation activities he wished to undertake in military areas and in general to work closely with it. He was also given the broad directive of providing, "insofar as feasible and desirable, for the employment of such persons at useful work in industry, commerce, agriculture, or public projects." And he was charged with the responsibility of prescribing "the terms and conditions of such public employment" and of safeguarding "the public interest in the private employment of such persons" (US House of Rerepresentatives Report No. 2124 (1942) 77:2:36). To facilitate these efforts the order provided for the establishment of a War Relocation Work Corps within the War Relocation Authority.

Once in office, Eisenhower and his aides began to formulate plans that would make the WRA into a conduit for relocation and not into a custodian of relocation. Accordingly, they envisioned a threefold function for the agency, two of which would facilitate the movement of Japanese into communities outside the military areas. For example as part of the voluntary migration program of Phase One then in effect, the agency would provide "financial aid for Japanese required to move out of the military area but unable to do so because of lack of funds." In addition, the agency "would establish a group of waystations, possibly as many as 50 holding from 1000 to 1500 people to serve as dispersion points from which evacuees could relocate to jobs in urban centers or on farms." And as a third function, the agency "would establish a great many small work camps similar to Civilian Conservation Corps camps and scattered through the States west of the Mississippi River with the employable population living in camp and working chiefly on farms in the surrounding neighborhood" (War Relocation Authority 1946a:5).

No sooner had the WRA opened its first regional office in San Francisco when it became evident that the voluntary migration program of Phase One was in serious trouble. So many protests poured into the office from law and other public officials of the inland communities to which the Japanese were migrating that by the end of March the agency recommended that the General discontinue the voluntary evacuation program and with the end of the program the financial function as outlined above became virtually stillborn.

The two other functions fared an even worse fate. This was the unexpected result of a conference of governors of western states convened by the WRA early in April in Salt Lake City for the manifest purpose of calming their anxieties about evacuation and of gaining support for the WRA's resettlement program. Despite the appeals of Eisenhower and his warning that failure to treat the Japanese evacuees equitably might evoke reprisals from Japan in its treatment of interned Americans, the governors passionately opposed the proposed WRA program. They objected to Japanese having access to property, jobs, businesses, or any part of their communities and warned of a violent reaction by the people of their community. They denied that Japanese born in America had any civil or other kinds of rights. In general they were convinced that "the type of program best suited to the situation was one of concentration camps with workers being farmed out to work under armed guards. Some representatives advocated out and out detention camps for all Japanese" (War Relocation Authority 1946a:7). Even the colonel representing the Western Defense Command attacked the WRA plans. "He advised that the guarding by the Army of small camps, such as might be provided by former CCC camps, would be impractical from a military standpoint, and that the Army would not undertake to guard centers housing less than 5000 persons" (War Relocation Authority 1946a:7).

The debacle at Salt Lake City completely unraveled the initial plans of the WRA; henceforth the agency was to move increasingly toward a custodial role for evacuees with certain "humane trimmings." Even as the WRA was reshaping its basic program, it was in the process of working out its relationship with the military as stipulated in the President's executive order. Finally on April 17, a memorandum of agreement was signed between the WRA and the war department. The agreement reaffirmed the primacy of the military in the evacuation process. Thus Item 1 stated "The evacuation of combat zones is a military necessity and when determined upon must not be retarded by resettlement and relocation. In other words, the timing of evacuation is a military function which War Relocation Authority will do all in its power to accommodate" (US Army, Western Defense Command and Fourth Army 1943:239).

Despite this constraint, a distinct area of autonomy was carved out for the WRA. It was, for example, to assume responsibility for selecting the sites for the relocation centers, subject to war department approval, and was to have full responsibility for their operation once they came into existence. At the same time, the war department would be responsible for acquiring the sites selected by the WRA. It would also be charged with constructing the initial facilities at the centers and with procuring and supplying their initial equipment. The WRA, in turn, would have to maintain and replace the equipment and construct any additional facilities.

In addition, the war department would provide for the transport of evacuees to assembly centers, which would continue to be operated by the department, and from assembly center to relocation center under military guard. And finally the military was to be charged with protecting the security of the relocation site. In order to implement this provision, the military issued civilian restrictive orders which designated the perimeters around the sites as War Relocation Project areas to be patrolled by military police. The military was also to control ingress and egress into the areas so that only authorized persons could enter or leave. It delegated to the WRA the authority for determining who the authorized persons would be.

With the signing of the agreement, the WRA took over the selection of ten sites for war relocation centers with the approval of the war department. One, Manzanar in California, was used originally as an assembly center and transferred to the WRA as a relocation center in June. The other nine merely functioned as relocation centers: one was in California, two in Arizona, two in Arkansas, and one in Colorado, Idaho, Utah, and Wyoming respectively. Delays in the selection and construction of these centers meant that evacuees stayed longer in the assembly centers than expected. In late May the transfers from assembly centers began, first to the Tule Lake relocation center and the Colorado River center, and then to the other centers as they were completed; the last to receive evacuees was Jerome in Arkansas which opened in October 1942. Only in the case of Manzanar did evacuees stay put as it was transformed from assembly to relocation center. By the end of October approximately 110,000 Japanese had been relocated at these centers. The smallest at Granado, Colorado accommodated approximately 8000; the largest at Colorado River, Arizona held approximately 20,000; the rest averaged approximately 10,000 (after the segregation process was completed in December 1944, Tule Lake Center had the largest number of evacuees).

The centers stayed in operation for an average of 1160 days. The Jerome center was the first to close: its closing date, June 30 1944. The last to close was Tule Lake on March 20 1946. The rest closed in October or November 1945. A substantial percentage of the evacuees stayed in these centers until almost the very end. For example, approximately 45 percent of the evacuees in centers that closed either October or November 1945 did not leave the centers until there were fewer than three months left to closing. Their average stay corresponded to the average length of time their centers were in operation. Other evacuees began to leave the camps on indefinite leaves and terminal departure almost as soon as the camps opened; 900, for example, left the relocation centers on indefinite leave by the end of 1942; approximately 10,000 had left by the middle of 1943; another 9000 by its end. And so it went. Despite these egress figures, approximately 70 percent of the evacuees were still at the centers by the end of 1944; and well over half by the middle of

1945. Those who left were primarily the young adults and young childless couples (some went back to college; others volunteered or were inducted into the armed services). As a result by the end of the period of incarceration evacuees consisted primarily of the very young and the very old with families.

Overall, then, by the end of 1942 over 110,000 Japanese had been ripped from the social fabric of their normal life, deprived of both legal and human rights, subjected to severe economic loss, and shipped off to concentration camps located in desolate and isolated places. For well over 90 percent of the evacuees these camps were their home for at least a year, and for over 50 percent their home for two and a half to three years. In the camps the evacuees were forced to come to terms with a strange and forbidding environment, to adapt to a barracks-style life at great personal discomfort and inconvenience, and to submit to a bureaucracy that set the terms of adaptation, forged patterns of dependency, and despite its self-image of benevolence could and would exercise its authority to coerce compliance. However, according to Daniels,

> "there were no torture chambers, firing squads, or gas ovens waiting for the evacuated people. The American concentration camps should not be compared, in that sense, to Auschwitz or Vorkuta. They were, in fact, much more like a century-old American institution, the Indian reservation, than like the institutions that flourished in totalitarian Europe. They were, however, places of confinement ringed with barbed wire and armed sentries. Despite WRA propaganda about community control, there was an unbridgeable gap between the Caucasian custodians and their Oriental charges; even the mess halls were segregated by race. Although some of the staff, particularly those in the upper echelons of the WRA, disapproved of the racist policy that brought the camps into being, the majority of the camp personnel, recruited from the local labor force, shared the contempt of the general population for 'Japs.'"
>
> (Daniels 1971:105)

No other ethnic or racial group residing in America during World War II suffered such indignities or were treated in this cavalier and categorical manner. Even the enemy aliens from Germany and Italy fared immeasurably better. For despite the President's proclamation of December 8 and General DeWitt's expressed desire to evacuate German and Italian aliens from Military Area No. 1, nothing like this *en masse* treatment happened. The war department overruled him, so Italians and Germans continued to be treated on an individual basis. In fact, by fall of 1942 Italian aliens were virtually relieved of all restrictive regulations promulgated by the Departments of Justice and War; controls on German aliens were also subsequently relaxed.

Only Japanese aliens were treated *en masse* as enemies of the United States, and yet over half of the Japanese had been in America thirty years or more, much longer than the average German or Italian alien. But what makes the scope of the injustice to the Japanese even more overwhelming is the fact that two out of three evacuees were not even aliens. They were American-born citizens.

ALIENATION AND THE QUESTION OF LOYALTY

Small wonder that a number of evacuees and scholars have challenged the image of harmony and cooperation by which some officials of the WRA and Japanese American Citizens League (JACL) have sought to characterize the response of the evacuees to their new life in the camps. Instead they have insisted that, in the early days of evacuation, tension and anomie permeated the atmosphere of most centers as the response of the residents ranged from hostile alienation to apathetic resignation. Over time, some of these critics have conceded, the Issei may have developed a degree of internal cohesion and accommodated themselves to life in and to the bureaucracy of the centers. But the young, the Nisei, they argued, grew increasingly divided and factionalized. A declining number followed the JACL line of accommodation and harmony. Those who did tended to be relocated early. The rest grew increasingly restless and resentful of the life in the center. A number, including the Kibei (the American-born Japanese educated in Japan), expressed their intensifying alienation from America by identifying with Japanese nationalism, some to the extent of seeking repatriation. Others rejected Japanese nationalism and articulated their resentment in the ideological terms of the American creed and Constitution, arguing that as American citizens they had been unlawfully deprived of their constitutional rights.

Evidence of the volatility of the situation was apparent almost as soon as the transfer from assembly to relocation centers had been completed. Protest demonstrations erupted in the Colorado River center over the arrest of two residents in November. Two weeks later an arrest of a resident at the Manzanar center in California also evoked protest demonstrations that were finally quelled by the military police. Whereas the Colorado incident merely reflected tensions between administration and evacuees, the Manzanar incident reflected ugly cleavages that had begun to split the evacuees into factions.

These isolated incidents offered merely fragmentary evidence to the authorities of the growing alienation of the young; soon they were confronted with a more general expression of it. This was a byproduct of the Secretary of War's decision to recruit an all-Nisei volunteer combat team primarily from the evacuees in the camps. Backed by a public statement from the President that began "'No loyal citizen of the United States should be denied the democratic right to exercise the responsibilities of citizenship, regardless of his ancestry'" (Daniels 1971:112), the Secretary sent to the centers teams of American officers, who, with the cooperation of the WRA, were to interview all male Nisei of draft age and to have them fill out questionnaires designed among other things by the military to test the loyalty of the Nisei respondents. Despite their best efforts, "the compaign for volunteers was disappointing to the Army; only 1181 Nisei cnrolled as volunteers – 6 percent of the 19,963 male American citizens of Japanese ancestry between the age of 17 and 37 – although 3500 had been expected to do so" (ten Broek, Barnhart, and Matson 1968:168). Eventually only 805 were actually accepted into the service.

In the meantime the WRA was able to link its need for loyalty data in planning a leave clearance program with that of the army's. As a result, it submitted a roughly comparable questionnaire to that of the army's to the rest of the population of the centers, specifically female Nisei and Issei of both sexes, seventeen years of age or older. Of particular interest to both the army and the WRA was the response to Question 28. Originally it was phrased: "Will you swear unqualified allegiance to the United States of America and faithfully defend the United States from any or all attack by foreign or domestic forces, and foreswear any form of allegiance or obedience to the Japanese emperor, or any other foreign government, power, or organization?" Later it was revised to read as follows: "Will you swear to abide by the laws of the United States and to take no action which would in any way interfere with the war effort of the United States?" (War Relocation Authority 1946c:162–63).

The results were not overwhelmingly reassuring to the War Relocation Authority. Overall approximately 4 percent of the evacuees refused to register at all so that they could be questioned. Among those who registered 12.4 percent failed to answer the question with an unqualified yes. The least likely to answer yes were the male Nisei (approximately one out of four refused to do so); next were female Nisei (15 percent); Issei, both male and female, were most likely to answer yes (only 3.5 percent of each failed to do so).

The negative responses were not spread evenly throughout all the relocation centers. One, Tule Lake, accounted for most. There, 42 percent refused to register or failed to answer Question 28 with an unqualified yes; for all the other centers combined the figure was 12 percent. Within Tule Lake an interesting difference characterized the responses of Nisei and Issei of both sexes. The Issei were less likely to register than were the Nisei, with the Issei male the least likely of all (41 percent), and the Nisei male the most likely (only 21 percent failed to do so). Differences were small between the females, though here again the Issei were the less likely to register (29 percent to 26 percent respectively). But among those who registered, virtually all of the Issei, both men and women, answered yes to Question 28 (99 percent for both). Nisei males were least likely to say yes (only 65 percent) with Nisei females in between (78 percent).

POLICY OF SEGREGATION

Once the results of the loyalty question became public, pressure was intensified on the WRA to segregate the loyal from the disloyal evacuees. This pressure had begun to be exerted from almost the moment the relocation process had been completed. General DeWitt, in particular, had urged its adoption and in December 1942 he even submitted a list of those whom he would have segregated in one of the camps. Another officer argued that all the Kibei should be segregated. As time went on, even the administrators of the various centers began to voice approval of separating out the "troublemakers" in the camps. However, the central administration of the WRA resisted these efforts as "precipitous action," though it continued to study the matter throughout the period.

The results of the questionnaire weakened the agency's stance for cautious action, particularly since a Senate subcommittee used them to hammer home the need for segregation. When the Senate passed a resolution on July 6 1943 recommending segregation, the pressure on the WRA grew irresistible, and nine days later the WRA announced a policy of segregating those persons who "by their acts have indicated that their loyalties lie with Japan during present hostilities or that their loyalties do not lie with the United States" (ten Broek, Barnhart, and Matson 1968:161).

Under the policy five classes of evacuees were to be segregated at Tule Lake, already labeled as a haven for dissidents from results of the questionnaire and other incidents. They included foreign- and American-born Japanese who had applied for removal to Japan; those who had answered the revised loyalty question in the negative or had refused to answer and had not changed their mind despite a hearing; those who had been denied a leave clearance by the WRA for "loyalty reasons," and finally parolees from internment and detention camps. During the fall of 1943 transfers were made from the various centers to Tule Lake. The net result was a total of 18,000 residents – two-thirds of whom were American-born.

As might be expected, Tule Lake became an even greater trouble spot than before. For a time the army had to run it under military discipline and control. It became the center for fervent Japanese nationalism and was under the control of "patriotic zealots" who imposed an authoritarian regime of orthodoxy and coercion on others. "Eventually more than a third of those at Tule Lake formally applied for repatriation to Japan after the war" (Daniels 1971:116). Of these almost two-thirds were American-born and, of the American-born, almost two out of five had never been to Japan in their life.

Renunciation of American citizenship was made relatively easy by an act of Congress in 1944. And 6000 evacuees, mostly from Tule Lake, soon applied to give up their citizenship. The Department of Justice began almost immediately to take steps to send them all to Japan after the war and succeeded in fact in deporting 2000.

RENUNCIANTS AND THE STRUGGLE TO REGAIN AMERICAN CITIZENSHIP

By war's end many renunciants had second thoughts about returning to Japan and began a twenty-five-year legal struggle to regain their citizenship. Early in the struggle, three Japanese women born in the United States regained their citizenship on the grounds that their renunciations were "not as a result of their intelligent choice but rather because of mental fear, intimidation, and coercions, depriving them of free exercise of their will" (176 Federal Reporter, Second Series 1949:953). In his opinion for the US Court of Appeals, Ninth Circuit on Acheson v. Murakami *et al.*, delivered August 26 1949, Chief Judge Denman lashed out at the role the United States government played in creating an atmosphere of tension and duress that was bound to lead "to a condition of mind and spirit of the American citizens imprisoned at Tule Lake Center, which make the renunciations of citizenship not the free and intelligent choice of appellees." He referred particularly to

> "the unnecessarily cruel and inhuman treatment of these citizens (a) in the manner of their deportation for imprisonment and (b) in their incarceration for over two and a half years under conditions in major respects as degrading as those of a penitentiary and in important respects worse than in any federal penitentiary, and (c) in applying to them the Nazi-like doctrine of inherited racial enmity, stated by the Commanding General [DeWitt] ordering the deportations as the major reason for that action."
>
> (176 Federal Reporter, Second Series 1949:954)

He was particularly upset by the General's elaboration of his racial doctrine in his final report and in testimony before the House Naval Affairs Committee. And in biting words, he thundered,

> "The identity of this doctrine with that of the Hitler generals towards those having blood strains of a western Asiatic race as justifying the gas chambers of Dachau must have been realized by the educated Tule Lake prisoners of Japanese blood strain. The German mob's cry of 'der Jude' and 'the Jap is a Jap' to be 'wiped off the map' [a statement made by General DeWitt] have a not remote relationship in the minds of scores of thousands of Nisei, whose constant loyalty has at last been recognized, though the map referred to may have been the area of exclusion."
>
> (176 Federal Reporter, Second Series 1949:958)

Important as the federal government may have been in creating the conditions of duress for the three women, the Chief Judge continued, the prime culprits were the pro-Japanese nationalists who had virtually captured control of the communal life at the Tule Lake center. He then discussed in vivid detail the atmosphere of terror, intimidation, and pressure that prevailed at Tule Lake as the pro-Japanese leaders sought to coerce residents at the center to renounce their citizenship. He offered details on how each of the women experienced this oppressive and threatening environment and decided under duress to renounce her citizenship. As he said of one, "she lived in an atmosphere of pressures, compulsions, influences, and coercions which deprived her of any voluntary willingness to renounce her citizenship. Being subject to and living daily in such an atmosphere caused her to renounce her citizenship" (176 Federal Reporter, Second Series 1949:965).

Thus he concluded, "since the purported renunciation of the plaintiffs ... was not as a result of their free and intelligent choice but rather because of mental fear, intimidation, and coercions depriving them of the free exercise of their will, said purported renunciations are void and of no force of effect" (176 Federal Reporter, Second Series 1949:965–66).

One year and a half later, Chief Judge Denman drew back from any automatic application of the principle spelled out in the Murakami case. Speaking for the Appeals Court, he severely curbed the ruling of a lower court in the Tadayasu Abo case. This ruling would have restored citizenship to Japanese renunciants in a class action primarily on grounds that the oppressive atmosphere at Tule Lake center, coupled with "parental pressure by alien parents on citizen children to prevent family break up and avoid draft induction" and other factors "cast the taint of incompetency upon any act of renunciation made under their influence by American citizens interned without Constitutional sanction, as were the plaintiffs" (77 Federal Supplement 1948:808).

Chief Judge Denman insisted that even in this environment the decision to renounce American citizenship was not always the result of coercion as in the Murakami case, but the result of voluntary choice. Thus, "the burden of proof is on each [adult plaintiff] to show that he was brought to a condition of mind by his treatment while interned which destroyed his free action in renouncing." But the plaintiff could use the known oppressiveness of his imprisonment in Tule Lake as providing a "rebuttable presumption" that his act of renunciation was involuntary. Accordingly, to rebut this presumption, the government would have to furnish evidence to show his renunciation was voluntary. "When such evidence is introduced the presumption disappears, but the fact of the coercive conditions remains as part of each plaintiff's showing to support his individual burden of proof" (186 Federal Reporter, Second Series 1951:773). The judge concluded that individual hearings would have to be held for the plaintiffs to determine the character of their renunciation. Those mentally incompetent at the time of the original renunciation were exempted from the ruling as were fifty-eight others who had gone to Tule Lake merely as family members of those already incarcerated there.

In a companion decision on the same case, Barber v. Tadayasu Abo *et al.*, the Appeals Court stayed the hand of the District Director of Immigration from deporting the renunciant to Japan. The District Director had offered the dual citizenship argument as grounds for his proposed action; now that the applicants had renounced their American citizenship they were solely citizens of Japan. This contention, Chief Judge Denman declared in behalf of the Court, could only be determined in a court action, for "mere renunciation of one citizenship does not of itself create another. It is only by the law of the nation of the successor citizenship that the renunciant may attain it" (186 Federal Reporter, Second Series 1951:777). Whether this accorded with the laws of Japan, he concluded, "is a fact to be determined by the trial court" (186 Federal Reporter, Second Series 1951:778). And with this he ordered the applicants released from custody to await further proceedings.

Thus, in one day the Court of Appeals of the Ninth Circuit created a novel status for the renunciant. On the one hand, renunciants had to await Department of Justice hearings to determine whether their citizenship status would be restored. On the other hand, they could not automatically be deported to Japan as an enemy alien or citizen of Japan. To remedy this anomalous situation, the lower court literally invented a new status; these renunciants were non-deportable native-born Americans without a country. "All that the expatriation statute . . . purports to effect is termination of American citizenship. It in no way fixes or determines any particular alien nationality for the expatriate" (76 Federal Supplement 1947:667).

Not until 1968 was the last case of renunciation heard, but by the end of the 1950s, with citizenship restored to 4978 of 5409 renunciants, the Department of Justice changed its original position that most renunciations were voluntary. Now, according to the Assistant Attorney General, the government was prepared to assume,

> "'unless the contrary was indicated, that the renunciations were not free and voluntary acts but were accomplished under duress and we have given the benefit of the doubt in favor of citizenship restoration. . . . The only applications which we have denied are those where reliable evidence of disloyalty to the United States was found. Most of these were Kibei. . . . We will vigorously defend our adverse determination of these comparatively few cases in the courts where the renunciants are entitled to have our decision reviewed.'"
>
> (Girdner and Loftis 1969:453–54)

By then 65 per cent of the 2031 renunciants who had actually repatriated to Japan had gotten their American citizenship back.

The Supreme Court and legitimation of the curfew and exclusion

The human effects of the evacuation and internment policy lingered for decades beyond the closing of the last relocation center. By the end Americans at all levels had begun to see the experience in an entirely different light and, as we have already seen, even the courts developed second thoughts about the matter.

The fact nevertheless remained that during the war 70,000 American citizens were treated by the American government and its people in a manner never before experienced by any other group of people, citizen or non-citizen. Not even the Indian removal policy of the 1830s had the same profound ramifications. For not only were the numbers of Indians involved smaller but the Indians had not yet gained entry as had the Nisei into the People's Domain and were not thereby entitled to its rights and immunities.

What compounded the injustice was the fact that all branches of the federal government were parties to the policy of evacuation. The executive branch through the President had issued the order establishing the policy and had provided the agency personnel for carrying it out. Congress had given its approval to the executive order and passed a law that gave teeth to the implementation of the policy. And finally in 1943 the Supreme Court gave legitimacy to the policy and, as in its earlier Jim Crow decisions, provided white America with another way of legally forcing a racially distinct nonwhite category of American citizen out of the People's Domain into the Plural Terrain. There, they were incarcerated in concentration camps and their identity transmuted from citizen to "native American aliens" or "racial enemies" of white America.

The first major step the Court took in legitimizing the treatment of the Japanese was its ruling in June 1943 in Hirabayashi v. United States. In that case, Hirabayashi, a Nisei, had been convicted of a misdemeanor under the congressional act of March 1942 for violating the curfew imposed by General DeWitt's Public Proclamation No. 3 on Military Area No. 1 pursuant to the authority granted to him under Executive Order No. 9066. Hirabayashi had also been found guilty of violating Civilian Exclusion Order No. 57 by failing to report to a Civil Control Station. Both sentences for a misdemeanor were being served concurrently.

In his appeal Hirabayashi contended that the proclamation and order constituted an unconstitutional delegation of legislative authority by Congress to the military commander and also violated his constitutional rights under the Fifth Amendment. In his opinion for the unanimous Court, Chief Justice Stone rejected both contentions of the defendant, as they bore on the curfew conviction. Having decided that, the Chief Justice continued, the Court did not rule on the second conviction because the defendant faced no additional punishment for the second conviction, inasmuch as the sentences for both were to be served concurrently.

With respect to the curfew, Chief Justice Stone declared, the Court had determined the military commander had acted lawfully in promulgating the orders and proclamation. Both the President in his Executive Order No. 9066 and Congress in its act of March 21 1942, which "ratified and confirmed Executive Order No. 9066" (320 US 1943:91), had knowingly delegated to him the authority to promulgate curfew orders. The larger question was whether Congress and the President had the constitutional authority to impose such restrictions in the first place as an emergency war measure. He answered this rhetorical query emphatically in the affirmative:

"Since the Constitution commits to the Executive and to Congress the exercise of the war power in all the vicissitudes and conditions of warfare, it has necessarily given them wide scope for the exercise of judgment and discretion in determining the nature and extent of the threatened injury or danger and in the selection of the means for resisting it.... Where, as they did here, the conditions call for the exercise of judgment and discretion and for the choice of means by those branches of the Government on which the Constitution has placed the responsibility of war-making, it is not for any court to sit in review of the wisdom of their action or substitute its judgment for theirs." (320 US 1943:93)

In view of the conditions that prevailed in the early months of 1942, he continued, such as the advance of Japan in the Far East, the continuing threat to Pearl Harbor and even the West Coast, it could not be doubted "that reasonably prudent men charged with the responsibility of our national defense had ample ground for concluding that they must face the danger of invasion, take measures against it, and in making the choice of measures consider our internal situation." Thus the curfew and other "challenged orders" could be justified as "defense measures for the avowed purpose of safeguarding the military area in question, at a time of threatened air raids and invasion by the Japanese forces, from the danger of sabotage and espionage" (320 US 1943:94–5).

Chief Justice Stone then turned to the second charge by the appellant: that the curfew, if it were indeed lawful and necessary, should have been imposed on all citizens within the military area or on none. To impose it merely on citizens of Japanese ancestry violated their constitutional rights under the due process clause of the Fifth Amendment.

The Chief Justice dismissed the two options proffered by the appellant as demanding too much of the country "in a case of threatened danger requiring prompt action." The first option would inflict "obviously heedless hardship on the many." The second would involve the great risk of "sitting passive and unresisting in the presence of the [enemy's] threat." There had to be a third option, he declared. "We think that constitutional government, in time of war, is not so powerless and does not compel so hard a choice if those charged with the responsibility of our national defense have reasonable ground for believing that the threat is real" (320 US 1943:95).

The Chief Justice devoted most of the rest of his opinion to "showing" why General DeWitt was "reasonable" in confining his orders to citizens and aliens of Japanese ancestry. First, he described the importance for the war effort of the various industrial and military installations in Military Area No. 1 and the ever-present "danger to our war production by sabotage and espionage in the area." He then repeated the "canard" from the Roberts Commission about the fifth-column activities of Japanese during the Pearl Harbor attack. Under the circumstances, he concluded, "at a time of threatened Japanese attack upon this country, the nature of our inhabitants' attachments to the Japanese enemy was consequently a matter of grave concern" (320 US 1943:96), particularly since most of the Japanese in America lived in Military Area No. 1 and close to these installations.

The Chief Justice then went through most of the familiar items on the yellow peril agenda that had long been used to question the loyalties of citizens, let alone aliens of Japanese ancestry. He referred to their nonassimilability to, their Japanese language schools which "are generally believed to be sources of Japanese nationalistic propaganda, cultivating allegiance to Japan" (320 US 1943:97), to the dual citizenship of many American-born Japanese, to the numbers sent back to Japan for schooling, and to the close connection of the Japanese consulates with organizations in the Japanese community and so forth.

In view of these "facts," he continued, it was reasonable for the military authorities, Congress, and the President to conclude that the loyalty of many citizens of Japanese ancestry to Japan made them potential fifth columnists. In as much as their "number and strength could not be precisely and quickly ascertained," it was understandable why the "war-making branches of the Government" worried "that in a critical hour such persons could not readily be isolated and separately dealt with, and [that they] constituted a menace to the national defense and safety, which demanded that prompt and adequate measures be taken to guard against it" (320 US 1943:99). Accordingly, it was reasonable for them to want to deal with all persons of Japanese ancestry, even citizens, in a categorical manner; no other group of American citizens constituted a similar threat.

"The fact alone that attack on our shores was threatened by Japan rather than another enemy power set these citizens apart from others who have no particular associations with Japan.... We cannot close our eyes to the fact, demonstrated by experience, that in time of war residents having ethnic affiliations with an invading enemy may be a greater source of danger than those of a different ancestry." (320 US 1943:101)

Thus, he concluded, the military authorities and Congress were well within the boundaries of the war power authorized by the Constitution in placing "citizens of one [racial] ancestry in a different category from others." ("We need not now attempt to define the ultimate boundaries of the war power.") However, he conceded that under ordinary circumstances,

"distinctions between citizens solely because of their ancestry are by their very nature odious to a free people whose institutions are founded upon the doctrine of equality. For that reason, legislative classification or discrimination based on race alone has often been held to be a denial of equal protection.... We may assume that these considerations would be controlling here were it not for the fact that the danger of espionage and sabotage, in time of war and of threatened invasion, calls upon the military authorities to scrutinize every relevant fact bearing on the loyalty of populations in the danger areas." (320 US 1943:100)

Accordingly, the appeal of Hirabayashi was denied by the Court and his conviction reaffirmed.

In his concurring opinion, Justice Rutledge took exception to the Chief Justice's statement

"that the courts have no power to review any action a military officer may 'in his discretion' find it necessary to take with respect to civilian citizens in military areas or zones, once it is found that an emergency has created the conditions requiring or justifying the creation of the area or zone and the institution of some degree of military control short of suspending habeas corpus." (320 US 1943:114)

He acknowledged the wide discretion the Constitution allows the officer in time of war, "but it does not follow there may not be bounds beyond which he cannot go and, if he oversteps them, that the courts may not have power to protect the civilian citizen" (320 US 1943:114). This case, he concluded, did not go beyond these bounds.

Although concurring in the Court's decision, Justice Murphy was even more unhappy than was Rutledge with the Chief Justice's statement. He declared in no uncertain terms,

"it does not follow, however, that the broad guaranties of the Bill of Rights and other provisions of the Constitution protecting essential liberties are suspended by the mere existence of a state of war. It has been frequently stated and recognized by this Court that the war power, like the other great substantive powers of government, is subject to the limitations of the Constitution.... We give great deference to the judgment of the Congress and of the military authorities as to what is necessary in the effective prosecution of the war, but we can never forget that there are constitutional boundaries which it is our duty to uphold."   (320 US 1943:110)

He took issue with the Chief Justice's claim that the curfew imposed by General DeWitt on citizens of Japanese ancestry was well "within the boundaries of the war power" endorsed by the Constitution. Instead he argued, "in my opinion, this [action] goes to the very brink of constitutional power."

"Distinctions based on color and ancestry are utterly inconsistent with our traditions and ideals. They are at variance with the principles for which we are now waging war. We cannot close our eyes to the fact that for centuries the Old World has been torn by racial and religious conflicts and has suffered the worst kind of anguish because of inequality of treatment for different groups. There was one law for one and a different law for another. Nothing is written more firmly into our law than the compact of the Plymouth voyagers to have just and equal laws....

Today is the first time, so far as I am aware, that we have sustained a substantial restriction of the personal liberty of citizens of the United States based upon the accident of race or ancestry. Under the curfew order here challenged no less than 70,000 American citizens have been placed upon a special ban and deprived of their liberty because of their particular racial inheritance. In this sense it bears a melancholy resemblance to the treatment accorded to members of the Jewish race in Germany and in other parts of Europe. The result is the creation in this country of two classes of citizens for the purposes of a critical and perilous hour – to sanction discrimination between groups of United States citizens on the basis of ancestry. In my opinion this goes to the very brink of constitutional power."   (320 US 1943:110–11)

However, he conceded that the critical military situation on the Pacific coast might have justified the curfew order, but he added the following caveat that clearly foreshadowed his stance a year and one half later in the Korematsu case.

"In voting for affirmance of the judgment I do not wish to be understood as intimating that the military authorities in time of war are subject to no restraints whatsoever, or that they are free to impose any restrictions they may choose on the rights and liberties of individual citizens or groups of citizens in those places which may be designated as 'military areas.' While this Court sits, it has the inescapable duty of seeing that the mandates of the Constitution are obeyed. That duty exists in time of war as well as in time of peace, and in its performance we must not forget that few indeed have been the invasions upon essential liberties which have not been accompanied by pleas of urgent necessity advanced in good faith by responsible men....

Nor do I mean to intimate that citizens of a particular racial group whose freedom may be curtailed within an area threatened with attack should be generally prevented from leaving the area and going at large in other areas that are not in danger of attack and where special precautions are not needed. Their status as citizens, though subject to requirements of national security and military necessity, should at all times be accorded the fullest consideration and respect. When the danger is past, the restrictions imposed on them should be promptly removed and their freedom of action fully restored."

(320 US 1943:113–14)

Violation of an exclusion, not a curfew, order was the central issue in the Korematsu case, which reached the Supreme Court more than a year after Hirabayashi. The petitioner, a Nisei, had been found guilty of remaining in a designated military area, "contrary to Civilian Exclusion Order No. 34 of the Commanding General of the Western Command, US Army, which directed that after May 9, 1942, all persons of Japanese ancestry should be excluded from that area" (323 US 1944:215–16). He was appealing his conviction on the grounds that his constitutional rights had been violated not only because he was being forced to leave the designated area but also because he was required to report to and to remain at an assembly or relocation center if he left the areas.

The Court, no longer unanimous as it was in Hirabayashi, rejected the petitioner's efforts to link exclusion with detention and did what it had done earlier in the Hirabayashi case. It limited consideration to the specific or primary charge on which the petitioner was convicted. In Hirabayashi, it was violation of the curfew; in Korematsu, violation of exclusion. In justifying the separation of the two charges, Justice Black in the majority opinion for the Court stated that the petitioner had never even gotten to an assembly center. He had merely been apprehended for not wanting to leave the designated area.

"[Therefore] we cannot say either as a matter of fact or law that his presence in that center would have resulted in his detention in a relocation center. Some who did report to the assembly center were not sent to relocation centers, but were released upon condition that they remain outside the prohibited zone until the military orders were modified or lifted. This illustrates that they pose different problems and may be governed by different principles. The lawfulness of one does not necessarily determine the lawfulness of the others. This is made clear when we analyze the requirements of the separate provisions of the separate orders. These separate requirements were that those of Japanese ancestry (1) depart from the area; (2) report to and temporarily remain in an assembly center; (3) go under military control to a relocation center there to remain for an indeterminate period until released conditionally or unconditionally by the military authorities. Each of these requirements, it will be noted, imposed distinct duties in connection with the separate steps in a complete evacuation program. . . .

  Since the petitioner has not been convicted of failing to report or to remain in an assembly or relocation center, we cannot in this case determine the validity of those separate provisions of the order. It is sufficient here for us to pass upon the order which petitioner violated."   (323 US 1944:221–22)

Having narrowed the issue to exclusion, the Court then gave general applicability to what it had insisted in the Hirabayashi case had only a particular relevance to that case. That is, in Hirabayashi the Court had said it was deciding nothing more than the issue of curfew: "We decide only the issue as we have defined it" (320 US 1943:102). But in Korematsu it used its curfew decision in Hirabayashi as a model for its decision on exclusion. It justified joining the two, in the words of Justice Black, because

"exclusion from a threatened area, no less than curfew, has a definite and close relationship to the prevention of espionage and sabotage. The military authorities, charged with the primary responsibility of defending our shores, concluded that curfew provided inadequate protection and ordered exclusion. They did so, as pointed out in our *Hirabayashi* opinion, in accordance with Congressional authority to the military to say who should, and who should not, remain in the threatened areas."   (323 US 1944:218)

Thus, the Court applied to Korematsu in literal fashion the principles and grounds it had used in Hirabayashi. As a result Justice Black repeated in summary fashion the yellow peril litany of the earlier case. It was once again used as the "factual framework" which made reasonable the judgement of the military authorities to order an evacuation of Military Area No. 1 and placed their action well within the boundaries of the war powers authorized by the Constitution. Seeking to reassure his colleagues who would have preferred linking exclusion with detention and not with the curfew, he stated that "it will be time enough to decide the serious constitutional issues which petitioner seeks to raise when an assembly or relocation order is applied or is certain to be applied to him, and we have its terms before us" (323 US 1944:222). Obviously defensive at the charges the dissenters would hurl at the majority's decision, Justice Black complained,

"It is said that we are dealing here with the case of imprisonment of a citizen in a concentration camp solely because of his ancestry, without evidence or inquiry concerning his loyalty and good disposition towards the United States. Our task would be simple, our duty clear, were this a case involving the imprisonment of a loyal citizen in a concentration camp because of racial prejudice. Regardless of the true nature of the asembly and relocation centers – and we deem it unjustifiable to call them concentration camps with all the ugly connotations that term implies – we are dealing specifically with nothing but an exclusion order. To cast this case into outlines of racial prejudice, without reference to the real military dangers which are presented, merely confuses the issue."

(323 US 1944:223)

In his dissenting opinion, Justice Roberts argued that the Court erred in making the issue of exclusion and curfew indivisible, when it should have made the issue of exclusion and detention indivisible.

"This is not a case of keeping people off the streets at night as was *Hirabayashi v United States*, 320 US 81, nor a case of temporary exclusion of a citizen from an area for his own safety or that of the community, nor a case of offering him an opportunity to go temporarily out of an area where his presence might cause danger to himself or to his fellows. On the contrary, it is the case of convicting a citizen as a punishment for not submitting to imprisonment in a concentration camp, based on his ancestry, and solely because of his ancestry, without evidence or inquiry concerning his loyalty and good disposition towards the United States. If this be a correct statement of the facts disclosed by this record, and facts of which we take judicial notice, I need hardly labor the conclusion that Constitutional rights have been violated."   (323 US 1944:226)

In effect, he continued, the petitioner was caught in the crossfire of two conflicting orders. One forbade him from leaving the area (Public Proclamation No. 3); the other (Civilian Exclusion Order No. 34) forbade him from staying "unless he were in an Assembly Center located in that zone." As a result, "he dare not remain in his home, or voluntarily leave the area, without incurring criminal penalties . . . the only way he could avoid punishment was to go to an Assembly Center and submit himself to military imprisonment" (323 US 1944:23).

In view of the fact that detention was the only legal way for the petitioner to leave the area, Justice Roberts added,

"this case cannot, therefore, be decided on any such narrow ground as the possible validity of a Temporary Exclusion Order under which the residents of an area are given an opportunity to leave and go elsewhere in their native land outside the boundaries of a military area. To make the case turn on any such assumption is to shut our eyes to reality. . . . [For,] the two conflicting orders, one which commanded him to stay and the other which commanded him to go, were nothing but a cleverly devised trap to accomplish the real purpose of the military authority, which was to lock him up in a concentration camp. The only course by which the petitioner could avoid arrest and prosecution was to go to that camp according to instructions to be given him when he reported at a Civil Control Center."   (323 US 1944:232)

In another biting dissent, Justice Murphy pursued with vigor the line of reasoning already foreshadowed in his concurring opinion on the Hirabayashi case. There, he agreed to uphold the curfew on the grounds that the military command should have a fairly wide range of discretionary action in wartime, but even there, he insisted its actions must also face the constitutional test of reasonableness and necessity. In making the curfew applicable to only one racial group, the military was reaching the "very brink of [its] constitutional power" (320 US 1943:111), but at least the curfew bore "some reasonable relation to the removal of the dangers of invasion, sabotage and espionage" (323 US 1944:235). However, in going beyond setting a curfew and ordering the "exclusion of 'all persons of Japanese ancestry, both alien and non-alien,' from the Pacific Coast area on a plea of military necessity in the absence of martial law" as in the Korematsu case, the military command had taken action that "goes over 'the very brink of constitutional power' and falls into the ugly abyss of racism" (323 US 1944:233).

> "The exclusion, either temporarily or permanently, of all persons with Japanese blood in their veins has no such reasonable relation [to the removal of the dangers of invasion, sabotage, and espionage]. And that relation is lacking because the exclusion order necessarily must rely for its reasonableness upon the assumption that *all* persons of Japanese ancestry may have a dangerous tendency to commit sabotage and espionage and to aid our Japanese enemy in other ways. It is difficult to believe that reason, logic or experience could be marshalled in support of such an assumption."   (323 US 1944:235)

To support his contention that "this forced exclusion was the result in good measure of this erroneous assumption of racial guilt rather than bona fide military necessity" (323 US 1944:235–36), Justice Murphy offered evidence from General DeWitt's final report and from the General's voluntary testimony before a House Naval Affairs Subcommittee in 1943.

> "'I don't want any of them [persons of Japanese ancestry] here. They are a dangerous element. There is no way to determine their loyalty. The west coast contains too many vital installations essential to the defense of the country to allow any Japanese on this coast.... The danger of the Japanese was, and is now – if they are permitted to come back – espionage and sabotage. It makes no difference whether he is an American citizen, he is still a Japanese. American

citizenship does not necessarily determine loyalty.... But we must worry about the Japanese all the time until he is wiped off the map. Sabotage and espionage will make problems as long as he is allowed in this area.'" (323 US 1944:fn.236)

Nowhere, Justice Murphy continued, did the General offer any reliable evidence that the Japanese were indeed generally disloyal "or had generally so conducted themselves in this area as to constitute a special menace to defense installations or war industries, or had otherwise by their behavior furnished reasonable ground for their exclusion as a group" (323 US 1944:236).

Instead the General justified the exclusion "mainly upon questionable racial and sociological grounds not ordinarily within the realm of expert military judgment" (323 US 1944:236–37). The Justice listed the various "beliefs" about the Japanese that the General had transmuted into "facts." In doing so the Justice catalogued the major ideological components of the yellow peril theory that had not originated with the General but which he had used to validate his order. He then offered his conclusion.

"A military judgment based upon such racial and sociological considerations is not entitled to the great weight ordinarily given the judgments based upon strictly military considerations. Especially is this so when every charge relative to race, religion, culture, geographical location, and legal and economic status has been substantially discredited by independent studies made by experts in these matters....

[This was not to deny] that there were some disloyal persons of Japanese descent on the Pacific Coast who did all in their power to aid their ancestral land. Similar disloyal activities have been engaged in by many persons of German, Italian and even more pioneer stock in our country. But to infer that examples of individual disloyalty prove group disloyalty and justify discriminatory action against the entire group is to deny that under our system of law individual guilt is the sole basis for deprivation of rights. Moreover, this inference, which is at the very heart of the evacuation orders, has been used in support of the abhorrent and despicable treatment of minority groups by the dictatorial tyrannies which this nation is now pledged to destroy. To give constitutional sanction to that inference in this case, however well-intentioned may have been the military command on the Pacific Coast, is to adopt one of the cruelest of the rationales used by our enemies to destroy the dignity of the individual and to encourage and open the door to discriminatory actions against other minority groups in the passions of tomorrow....

No adequate reason is given for the failure to treat these Japanese Americans on an individual basis by holding investigations and hearings to separate the loyal from the disloyal, as was done in the case of persons of German and Italian ancestry.... It is asserted merely that the loyalties of this group 'were unknown and time was of the essence.' Yet nearly four months elapsed after Pearl Harbor before the first exclusion order was issued; nearly eight months went by until the last order was issued; and the last of these 'subversive' persons was not actually removed until almost eleven months had elapsed. Leisure and deliberation seem to have been more of the essence than speed. And the fact that conditions were not such as to warrant a declaration of martial law adds strength to the belief that the factors of time and military necessity were not as urgent as they have been represented to be....

I dissent, therefore, from this legalization of racism. Racial discrimination in any form and in any degree has no justifiable part whatever in our democratic way of life. It is unattractive in any setting but it is utterly revolting among a free people who have embraced the principles set forth in the Constitution of the United States. All residents of this nation are kin in some way by blood or culture to a foreign land. Yet they are primarily and necessarily a part of the new and distinct civilization of the United States. They must accordingly be treated at all times as the heirs of the American experiment and as entitled to all the rights and freedoms guaranteed by the Constitution."   (323 US 1944:240)

On the same day that the Court reaffirmed the right of the military to exclude the citizen of Japanese ancestry from Military Area No. 1 in Korematsu, it also decided in the Endo case to limit the custodial control of the WRA over American citizens of Japanese ancestry whose loyalty to the United States had been established. In this case, Mitsuye Endo had been granted a leave clearance in August 1943 by the WRA. This meant that she had met the WRA's requirements, including certification of her loyalty, for applying for an idefinite leave from the relocation center that would allow her to resettle in any community other than those in prohibited military areas. Instead of applying for an indefinite leave, Ms Endo petitioned the district court for a writ of *habeas corpus* claiming "that she is a loyal and law-abiding citizen of the United States, that no charge has been made against her, that she is being unlawfully detained, and that she is confined in the Relocation Center under armed guard and held there against her will" (323 US 1944:294).

In opposing her petition, the WRA and Department of Justice agreed that she was "a loyal and law-abiding citizen," and that no charge had been made against her of disloyalty. They even conceded "that it is beyond the power of the War Relocation Authority to detain citizens against whom no charges of disloyalty or subversiveness have been made for a period longer than that necessary to separate the loyal from the disloyal and to provide the necessary guidance for relocation" (323 US 1944:294–95).

However, they insisted "that detention for an additional period after leave clearance has been granted is an essential step in the evacuation program" (323 US 1944:295). They stressed that the opposition of "interior states" to "an uncontrolled Japanese migration" had made the WRA abandon its earliest plans for relocation and resettlement and develop its present program.

> "[The development of] such a planned and orderly relocation [process] was essential to the success of the evacuation program; that but for such supervision there might have been a dangerously disorderly migration of unwanted people to unprepared communities; ... unsupervised evacuation might have resulted in hardship and disorder; ... the success of the evacuation program was thought to require the knowledge that the federal government was maintaining control over the evacuated population except as the release of individuals could be effected consistently with their own peace and well-being and that of the nation." (323 US 1944:296–97)

Thus the government concluded, "supervised relocation, as the chosen method of terminating the evacuation, is the final step in the entire process and is a consequence of the first step taken" (323 US 1944:297).

In his opinion for the Court, Justice Douglas rejected the argument of the Department of Justice and the WRA. He stated that the various executive orders of the President and the congressional act of 1942 were war measures.

> "Their single aim was the protection of the war effort against espionage and sabotage.... Neither the Act nor the orders use the language of detention.... And that silence may have special significance in view of the fact that detention in Relocation Centers was not part of the original program of evacuation but developed later to meet what seemed to the officials in charge to be mounting hostility to the evacuees on the part of the communities where they sought to go....
>
> [Now] if we assume (as we do) that the original evacuation was justified, its lawful character was derived from the fact that it was an espionage and sabotage measure, not that there was community hostility to this group of American citizens. The evacuation program rested explicitly on the former ground not on the latter as the underlying legislation shows." (323 US 1944:300–02)

Even though the various executive orders and law were silent on the question of authorizing detention, it could be assumed to have been legitimate in the early days of the relocation centers before the loyalty of evacuees was established.

> "[However,] the authority to detain a citizen or to grant him a conditional release as protection against espionage or sabotage is exhausted at least when his

loyalty is conceded.... [For] a citizen who is concededly loyal presents no problem of espionage or sabotage. Loyalty is a matter of the heart and mind, not of race, creed or color. He who is loyal is by definition not a spy or a saboteur. When the power to detain is derived from the power to protect the war effort against espionage and sabotage, detention which has no relationship to that objective is unauthorized." (323 US 1944:302)

If the Court were to hold otherwise, he insisted, "we would transform an espionage or sabotage measure into something else. That was not done by Executive Order No. 9066 or by the Act of March 21, 1942, which ratified it. "What they did not do we cannot do" (323 US 1944:302). To say that they did, "would be to assume that the Congress and the President intended that this discriminatory action should be taken against these people wholly on account of their ancestry, even though the government conceded their loyalty to this country. We cannot make such an assumption" (323 US 1944:303–04). Thus, he concluded, "Mitsuye Endo is entitled to an unconditional release by the War Relocation Authority" (323 US 1944:304).

Justice Murphy concurred with the opinion of the Court, but he then repeated the main theme of his dissent in the Korematsu case:

"I am of the view that detention in Relocation Centers of persons of Japanese ancestry regardless of loyalty is not only unauthorized by Congress or the Executive but is another example of the unconstitutional resort to racism inherent in the entire evacuation program. As stated more fully in my dissenting opinion in *Korematsu v United States, ante*, p. 233, racial discrimination of this nature bears no reasonable relation to military necessity and is utterly foreign to the ideals and traditions of the American people." (323 US 1944:307–08)

Although he concurred with the results, Justice Roberts ridiculed the Court's efforts to deal with the Endo case as though it merely involved the bureaucratic overzealousness of the WRA in exceeding its statutory or legal authority in developing its detention program for loyal citizens. He argued that the President and Congress knew about the detention program and approved it, despite the absence of any mention of it in the various executive orders or law of March 1942. He concluded, therefore, that the issue before the Court was not that of excessive zeal by a subordinate agency, but that of the constitutional responsibilities of the major agencies of government, the executive and legislative, in condoning the denial of certain rights to American citizens.

"[Accordingly] the court is squarely faced with a serious constitutional question, – whether the relator's detention violated the guarantees of the Bill of Rights of the federal Constitution and especially the guarantee of due process of law.

There can be but one answer to that question. An admittedly loyal citizen has been deprived of her liberty for a period of years. Under the Constitution she should be free to come and go as she pleases. Instead, her liberty of motion and other innocent activities have been prohibited and conditioned. She should be discharged."

(323 US 1944:310)

Mass evacuation and the two myths

The decision on the Endo case marked a turning point in the relocation program. In anticipation of an adverse decision not only in the Endo but also in the Korematsu case (which of course did not materialize), the army announced the revocation of the West Coast mass exclusion order effective January 2 1945. A day later the WRA announced the closing of all relocation centers by the end of 1945 and the liquidation of the entire WRA program by mid-1946. These deadlines were more or less met on time and so, by the middle of 1946, with the exception of the renunciants whose fates were still being decided, what the American Civil Liberties Union called "'the worst single wholesale violation of civil rights of American citizens in our history'" (Biddle 1962:213) drew to a close.

What made the wholesale violation take on a particularly Kafkaesque quality was its having been a consequence of governmental policies that were based on "collective representations" transmuted into propositions of truth and fact. The beliefs that had been used to construct the reality of the policy-makers, particularly the military, were the myth of military necessity and the myth of the yellow peril.

The latter myth, which we have painstakingly sought to expose in this chapter, had been deeply embedded in the "collective conscience" of the people of California and the cadre of military and civilian officials of the national government since the turn of the century. Each edge of the yellow peril found particular resonance in one of the two circles. Japan as a fearsome military power with whom America was likely to do battle at some point in time had been a preoccupation of the military for decades as President Roosevelt himself conceded in describing the crisis of 1913. The people of California, especially their political leaders, had long made known their fifth-column suspicions of the Japanese immigrant – a belief they used with telling effect in the drive for alien land laws in the second decade of the century.

Each edge – though of differing priority to each circle – was inextricably linked with the other in a historically coherent manner. Perhaps if Japan had not played such a consistently active role in protesting treatment of its nationals in America and if the dual citizenship issue had not been so readily available for extending the attack against the loyalty of the Japanese immigrant to that of his children, then the linkage between Japan as a nation and the Japanese immigrant as an alien might have been less clearly perceived or perpetuated. But reality seemed to reinforce belief, and together they forged a strong connection between the two aspects of the yellow peril.

As a result, whichever aspect was immediately highlighted by the events of the day, the other was sure to vibrate with attention before too long. And since Japan and the Japanese immigrant were continually relevant parts of America's foreign and domestic environments for the four decades prior to the attack on Pearl Harbor, small wonder that the two edges of the yellow peril were continuously being honed at the center of public and governmental attention during much of this period.

The attack on Pearl Harbor, despite its having caught America by surprise, was then like the long-awaited but dreaded fulfillment of a Delphi-like prophesy that had been made decades before but which had left unsettled the exact time it was to happen. With victory after victory for the Japanese forces in the Pacific during the early months after the attack, the image of "superpower" that had already been sketched by Fitzpatrick at the beginning of the century (Fitzpatrick 1909) was dusted off and brought up to date as the frightening picture of what the enemy was like. As a result, the traditional image and the present reality of defeats combined to make Japan seem more like an invincible foe than merely a formidable one.

As events in the Pacific seemed to confirm the awesomeness of Japan's military prowess, the second edge of the yellow peril – momentarily quiescent – began to revive and to find expression first among the committed exclusionists. With the publication of the Roberts report it blossomed into full fury and became an obsessive preoccupation of many, even to the extent of affecting the flow of intelligence to the military policy-makers on the coast and of contaminating their interpretation of this intelligence. The contaminating influence of this image reached the peak of absurdity when the absence of incidents of sabotage and espionage was taken by the military policy-makers as "proof" of the organized fifth column designs of the Japanese on the coast. In this manner the yellow peril image reached Goliath-like proportions on the West Coast and became the prism through which the military command perceived the world of reality in which it had to act.

This prism did more than distort the perceptions of the policy-maker; it also fed into and fueled his sense of urgency that something had to be done about the yellow peril. As such it breathed vitality and drama into the second myth without which action against the yellow peril could not have been taken: the myth of military necessity.

In the early days following the attack on Pearl Harbor, it is understandable why military authorities in California and Washington were apprehensive about the intentions of the Japanese armed forces toward the Pacific coast. Were they preparing some sort of assault, large or small? Accordingly, military necessity seemed to dictate the build-up of men and equipment; even the naming of the Western Defense Command as a theater of operations seemed a reasonable move or precaution. However within a month, as we have seen, the military command in Washington became convinced that no large-scale assault was imminent, only sporadic raids. They never changed this assessment. As a result, the command reduced the flow of men and equipment for the active defense of the Pacific coast, though support for air defense retained some sort of priority. Despite this reassessment the command neglected to withdraw the label of theater of operations from the area.

Even as Washington was playing down the military threat to the Pacific coast, General DeWitt and his staff remained convinced of its seriousness. They raised to the level of fact every report and rumor of enemy action and came to believe what they wanted to believe. In short, they remained convinced that enemy action posed a grave threat to American shipping and might even be a prelude to a large-scale attack in the future.

Sure that the external attack would materialize at some point in time, the General and his staff became increasingly uneasy about the internal threat of sabotage and subversion. Having swallowed the yellow peril thesis in its entirety, they were adamant in their insistence that the Japanese in America were merely biding their time before showing their dedication and loyalty to the homeland through subversive action. As a result, not even the absence of incidents could jar their faith in the internal threat of the yellow peril. To them the faith in the myth was itself sufficient proof of its own validity. They were certain that sabotage and subversion were bound to happen in the future, given their conviction of the undying fealty of the Japanese alien and his children to the Emperor of Japan.

To wait passively for what was predestined to happen would mean, according to them, risking military disaster for the country; thus military necessity required decisive action against something certain to happen in the future. In this manner, the myth of military necessity was spawned phoenix-like from the myth of the yellow peril. Each fertilized the other and germinated still a third myth: that mass evacuation of aliens and citizens of Japanese ancestry was essential to the security and survival of the western theater of operations.

General DeWitt and his staff therefore embraced the policy of evacuation.* As

---

*Ironically, in Hawaii the "fact" of military necessity operated to put a damper on the pressures for mass evacuation of the Japanese that were generated by the Roberts report. Goaded by Secretary of Navy Knox, its prime mover, and by other military and governmental officials in Washington

evidence of its effectiveness, they cited the absence of incidents of sabotage and subversion. Thus, the same datum was used both as an indication of the need for the policy, and later as a sign of how successfully the policy had met the need – an exercise in tautological reasoning if ever there was one.

---

including the President, General Emmons reluctantly developed plans to evacuate 20,000 Japanese from Oahu to the mainland. He and his staff successfully countered the original suggestion from Washington that 150,000 be evacuated to outlying islands.

The reluctance of the General did not stem from any basic regard for the Japanese or even rejection of the premises of the yellow peril, although his independent investigation showed virtually no merit in the Roberts commission's report of subversion by resident Japanese. Instead he was worried about the effect that mass evacuation of the Japanese would have on the island's economy, inasmuch as they comprised the bulk of the island's skilled labor force. In addition, he objected to the quantity of shipping and other resources and personnel that would have to be diverted from more pressing military needs to carry out the evacuation.

His arguments eventually persuaded the higher echelon in Washington, who also had became concerned about "the difficulty of providing enough suitable facilities for relocating the Japanese on the mainland, and 'the political repercussions on the West Coast and in the United States generally to the introduction of 150,000 more Japanese'" (Conn, Engelman, and Fairchild 1964:211).

As a result, despite continuing pressure from other sources, the General kept scaling down the number of Japanese who were to be evacuated; in the final analysis only 1875 were eventually sent to the United States. And "on 2 April 1943 the War Department instructed General Emmons to suspend evacuation to the mainland until and unless the number of his internees exceeded the capacity of the Hawaiian Department's own facilities for internment, which never happened" (Conn, Engelman, and Fairchild 1964:214).

As recapitulated by an army spokesman in a statement to the Honolulu press when evacuation ended, the plan for mass evacuation was finally defeated by the fact of military necessity: "The shipping situation and the labor shortage make it a matter of military necessity to keep most of the people of Japanese blood on the island" (Conn, Engelman, and Fairchild 1964:214).

18

POSTWAR METAMORPHOSIS: FROM CONCENTRATION CAMP TO THE PEOPLE'S DOMAIN

Introduction

The closing of the camps did not end the travail of the first-generation Japanese and their children. They had to face the loss of their property and wealth, and a number of those who returned to the West Coast were greeted with hostility and violence. However, within a few years the climate of opinion changed. They were increasingly hailed in the halls of congress and elsewhere for their loyalty during the war and for the heroism of their sons who had died in battle for the United States. The federal government even sought to make amends through a modest evacuation claims program. These amends were an expression of regret for the consequences of the policy of evacuation – their suffering – and not for the policy itself. In time the barriers to citizenship and immigration were also lifted.

In this chapter we shall examine the paradoxical character of a duality that for over a half a century had confined the Japanese to the Plural Terrain and even impounded them in concentration camps but later lifted the barriers and allowed them to gain access to and membership in the People's Domain.

The return of the evacuees and white resistance

With the lifting of the mass exclusion orders, evacuees began to drift back to their homes on the West Coast. A number were greeted with harassment and even violence by the people in some of the communities to which they returned.

"In the first half of 1945 there were more than thirty incidents of violence in California, thirty-nine by February of 1946, after which they almost entirely ceased. Twenty of these were shootings, the rest arson and other assaults. Shots were often fired into the air to frighten rather than to kill or maim, but sometimes people narrowly escaped with their lives. Hundreds of less serious incidents occurred, including the burning of a housewife's laundry on the line, which were nevertheless often traumatic to the individuals involved. February, March and April of 1945 were the worst months, when agitators and hoodlums apparently felt if they frightened the first evacuees who came back, the rest would stay away." (Girdner and Loftis 1969:399–400)

Their efforts were only partially successful, fewer than half of the evacuees who were in California in 1940 failed to return there. In some of the areas of greatest resistance, relatively few evacuees returned: only one out of four returned to Salinas. In other areas the results were minimal. For example, over nine out of ten returned to Fresno and Madera Counties and two out of three, to Placer and Sacramento Counties. The rest of the evacuees moved elsewhere. Of the 30,000 who left the relocation camps before January 1 1945 and were forbidden to return to areas on the Pacific coast, approximately one-half settled in the Midwest, and well over a third in the Plains States and the West. Fewer than one out of ten went as far as the East coast. After January 1 1945, as restrictions eased on the Pacific coast, two out of three returned to the Pacific coast, all but one of ten of these going to California. The Midwest and West attracted only about one out of ten respectively, with only one out of twenty going to the East Coast.

Physical coercion was not the only threat evacuees had to face in returning to the Pacific coast. Many also faced the threat of expropriation of their property through fraudulent practices by whites. (In fact, those who stood to gain by blocking the return of evacuees were frequently behind the efforts at physical coercion.)

"It has been estimated that at least one-third of American Japanese truck farmers were ruined by relocation – their farms run down or foreclosed, their machinery stolen, rusted, or seized for debts. Sometimes the agents entrusted with property, whether bankers, lawyers respectable business men or mere speculators were reluctant to let go of the profitable enterprises they were engaged in on a temporary contract basis or verbal agreement. It was easy to take advantage of legal technicalities or to renege on verbal agreements."

(Girdner and Loftis 1969:417)

The scope of the fraud and vandalism perpetrated against the evacuee and his property was also described in a letter from the Secretary of Interior to the Speaker of the House of Representatives on March 1947.

"Private buildings in which evacuees stored their property were broken into and vandalized. Mysterious fires destroyed vacant buildings. Property left with 'friends' unaccountably disappeared; goods stored with the Government some-times were damaged or lost. Persons entrusted with the management of evacuee real property mulcted the owners in diverse ways. Tenants failed to pay rent, converted property to their own use, and committed waste. Prohibited from returning to the evacuated areas even temporarily to handle property matters, the evacuees were unable to protect themselves adequately."

(US House of Representatives Report No. 732 (1947) 80:1:2)

Even the state government of California sought to take advantage of the situation. Egged on by the state legislature which appropriated several hundred thousand dollars for the purpose, Attorney General Kenny reluctantly moved ahead on escheat proceedings. (Apparently he and Governor Warren had had second thoughts about overly rigid enforcement of the alien land laws, which the governor had so passionately advocated when he was attorney general.) Despite his personal misgivings. Kenny filed a number of cases, almost four times as many as had been filed during the previous three decades. (According to statistics derived from the California Attorney General's office, 80 percent of the seventy-three escheat proceedings against Japanese since the inception of the alien land laws in 1911 were started after the attack on Pearl Harbor.) These efforts were labeled by the returning Nisei as "legal intimidation . . . an attempt to prevent the return of the evacuee farmers to the State's agricultural industry" (Girdner and Loftis 1969:430). An even more turgid comment was made by a Nisei spokesman in 1946. He declared that "one of the biggest land grabs in history is in California," and "the Great Golden State, now one of the richest, proudest and most populous in the nation, is in the uncomfortable position of being the grabber" (Girdner and Loftis 1969:429). (The two other West Coast states of Oregon and Washington also tightened enforcement of their land laws, as did thirteen other western states. All sought to carve up in one way or another Japanese property through escheat proceedings.)

Not content with merely squeezing the Japanese out of their land holdings, California sought to use its power of licensing to discriminate against them. For example, the State Board of Equalization decided in mid-1945 that persons of Japanese descent would have to get a written recommendation from military authorities before the board would grant them a sales tax permit essential to carrying on a retail business. Under the combined indifference of the military authorities and advice by the Attorney General that it had no such discretionary power, the board retreated to tactics of delay in order to discourage Japanese applicants. But perhaps the most potent use of the power of licensing was effected by the state legislature. It enacted in 1945 a provision that banned the granting of commercial fishing licenses to aliens ineligible to citizenship; prior to 1943 any qualified person could obtain such a license "without regard to alienage or ineligibility to citizenship" (334 US 1948:413).

The judicial wedge into the wall of resistance

Confronted by this combined assault on the rights of property and of employment of the returning evacuees, the Japanese American Citizens League (JACL) abandoned its policy of passive accommodation and launched a battle in the courts. Its more aggressive stance was hammered out at its first postwar convention held in the spring of 1946. The league's initial legal target was the alien land law of California. The first case to reach the United States Supreme Court was Oyama *et al.* v. California argued before the Court on October 22 1947. In this case the Japanese petitioners sought to quash escheat proceedings which had been brought by the state of California against them on the grounds that the Issei father, Kajiro Oyama, had fraudulently given his Nisei son, Fred, two small parcels of land in violation of the alien land law of California. Petitioners contended that the state's action was illegal because the alien land law was unconstitutional. They pressed their attack against the law on three fronts:

> "first, that it deprives Fred Oyama of the equal protection of the laws and of his privileges as an American citizen; secondly, that it denies Kajiro Oyama equal protection of the laws; and, thirdly, that it contravenes the due process clause by sanctioning a taking of property after expiration of the applicable limitations period."
> (332 US 1948:635)

In its ruling on January 19 1948, the Court reversed the decision of the California Supreme Court and found on behalf of the petitioners. In his opinion for the Court, Chief Justice Vinson declared that the son had been deprived

> "of the equal protection of California's laws and of his privileges as an American citizen. In our view of the case, the State had discriminated against Fred Oyama; the discrimination is based solely on his parents' country of origin; and there is absent the compelling justification which would be needed to sustain discrimination of that nature [as in the Hirabayashi case]." (332 US 1948:640)

Fred Oyama, the Chief Justice argued, had to bear burdens of proof which no other minor citizen had to. For example,

> "for most minors California has the customary rule that where a parent pays for a conveyance to his child there is a presumption that a gift is intended; there is no presumption of a resulting trust, no presumption that the minor takes that

land for the benefit of his parent.... Thus the burden of proving that there was in fact no completed bona fide gift falls to him who would attack its validity.

Fred Oyama, on the other hand, faced at the outset the necessity of overcoming a statutory presumption that conveyances financed by this father and recorded in Fred's name were not gifts at all. Something very akin to a resulting trust, *was* presumed and, at least *prima facie*, Fred *was* presumed to hold title for the benefit of his parents." (332 US 1948:641–42)

By being "saddled with an onerous burden of proof which need not be borne by California children generally," the Chief Justice continued, "Fred Oyama lost his gift, irretrievably and without compensation, solely because of the extraordinary obstacles which the State set before him." These obstacles were set before him because of the "fact that this father was Japanese and not American, Russian, Chinese, or English. But for that fact alone, Fred Oyama, now a little over a year from majority, would be the undisputed owner of the eight acres in question" (332 US 1948:644).

Accordingly, the Chief Justice declared, the Court upheld the petitioners' first contention that the escheat proceedings deprived the son of his rights as a citizen under the Fourteenth Amendment. And it was therefore unnecessary for the Court to deal with the question of the constitutionality of the alien land law as it applied to the right of the father, as an ineligible alien, to equal protection of the laws and to due process of law.

In his concurring opinion, Justice Murphy lamented the fact that the Court had failed to address itself to the constitutional question.

"To me the controlling issue in this case is whether the California Alien Land Law on its face is consistent with the Constitution of the United States. Can a state prohibit all aliens ineligible for American citizenship from acquiring, owning, occupying, enjoying, leasing or transferring agricultural land? Does such a prohibition square with the language of the Fourteenth Amendment that no state shall 'deny to any person within its jurisdiction the equal protection of the laws'?" (332 US 1948:650)

Having raised this rhetorical question, Justice Murphy then answered in the language of his Hirabayashi, Korematsu, and Endo opinions:

"The negative answer to those queries is dictated by the uncompromising opposition of the Constitution to racism, whatever cloak or disguise it may assume. The California statute in question, as I view it, is nothing more than an outright racial discrimination. As such, it deserves constitutional condemnation.

And since the very core of the statute is so defective, I consider it necessary to give voice to that fact even though I join in the opinion of the Court."

(332 US 1948:650)*

Six months later California suffered still another reversal at the hands of the United States Supreme Court. Its 1945 statute which denied commercial fishing licenses to aliens ineligible to citizenship was declared unconstitutional. In his opinion for the Court, Justice Black declared that Takahashi who had been a fisherman from 1915 to 1942, during which time he had no problem obtaining a license, had been arbitrarily deprived of his means of livelihood. Citing the Court's earlier decision on Truax as the basic precedent,† Justice Black argued that the California statute failed to meet the test that would have allowed an exemption from the Truax principle: namely, the presence of a special public interest. In so doing, he dismissed the state's claim that the statute was primarily a fish conservation measure which sought to reduce the number of fishermen by excluding alien Japanese. He also rejected California's claim that because the people of California owned the tidewaters and fish in them, they had the right to protect themselves from competitors by excluding whomever they wished. Finally he dismissed California's contention that "because the United States regulates immigration and naturalization in part on the basis of race and color classifications, a state can adopt one or more of the same classifications to prevent lawfully admitted aliens within its borders from earning a living in the same way that other state inhabitants earn their living" (334 US 1948:418–19). The federal government had "broad constitutional powers" to do what it did, but the individual states were generally bound to accord legally admitted aliens equality of treatment under the Fourteenth Amendment. As a result, "the power of a state to apply its law exclusively to its alien inhabitants as a class is confined within narrow limits" (334 US 1948:420); the alien land laws, for example, fell within these narrow limits, but the licensing of commercial fishing did not.

In his concurring opinion, Justice Murphy hammered home his by now familiar thesis that laws such as the licensing one were a "direct outgrowth of antagonism toward persons of Japanese ancestry. Even the most cursory examination of the background of the statute demonstrates that it was designed solely to discriminate against such persons in a manner inconsistent with the concept of equal protection of the laws. Legislation of that type is not entitled to wear the cloak of

*Although the United States Supreme Court never acted on the constitutionality of the alien land laws, the Oregon Supreme Court declared its state's statute unconstitutional in 1948; the California Court in 1952 (the latter on the ground that the law violated the United Nations Charter).

†The significance of the Truax decision was discussed in Chapter 15.

constitutionality." He then went on to illustrate how "the statute in question is but one more manifestation of the anti-Japanese fever which has been evident in California in varying degrees since the turn of the century" (335 US 1948:422). He emphasized the close connection between the yellow peril theme, in the minds of Californians, and the Japanese as fishermen. He concluded that the statute "is a discriminatory piece of legislation having no relation whatever to any constitutionally cognizable interest of California" (334 US 1948:427).

The evacuation claims program and re-legitimizing the situs of the Japanese

The Supreme Court's decisions were not the only wedges being driven into the wall of resistance against the Japanese evacuees. Even as it was being phased out, the WRA sought to ease the transition of the evacuees and published pamphlets attacking the anti-Japanese prejudices of West Coasters. Voluntary local groups also sought to mediate the transition; even state officials, including Governor Warren, sought to maintain law and order in the various areas. Convinced, however, that the answers to the evacuees' problems could only be worked out in the nation's capitol, the JACL began a serious lobbying effort in Washington as part of its rejuvenated aggressiveness. Some top government officials, including President Truman and the Secretary of Interior as well as former officials of the WRA, proved sympathetic to the league's cause as did several legislators. The first issue on which headway was made almost immediately was compensation to the evacuees for losses they had sustained, estimated at $400,000,000 by the Federal Reserve Bank of San Francisco.

At the end of April 1946, the Secretary of Interior sent to Congress the draft of a bill establishing an Evacuation Claims Commission for the purpose of adjudicating "claims of persons of Japanese ancestry against the United States for losses arising out of the evacuation or exclusion of such persons by the War Department from the west coast, Alaska, and Hawaii during World War II" (US House of Representatives Report No. 2679 (1946) 79:2:3). The losses they sustained were heavy, though a final estimate of actual financial and property losses was yet to be made. "Some lost everything they had; many lost most of what they had" (US House of Representatives Report No. 2679 (1946) 79:2:3). The reason was that "the evacuation orders gave the persons affected desperately little time in which to settle their affairs" (US House of Representatives Report No. 2679 (1946) 79:2:4).

The people, he implied, deserved this consideration because they had been generally loyal to the United States during this ordeal. As evidence, he cited a fact which just a few short years before had been used by General DeWitt to "prove" the opposite and therefore to justify their incarceration. The fact that he alluded to was the absence of any "case of sabotage or espionage by Americans of Japanese ancestry during the entire war," according to "the records of the intelligence agencies" (US House of Representatives Report No. 2679 (1946) 79:2:4). In addition, he pointed to "the outstanding record of our 23,000 Japanese Americans who served in the armed forces, in both the European and Pacific theaters" (US House of Representatives Report No. 2679 (1946) 79:2:3).

In applauding the behavior of the Japanese-Americans the Secretary could not help but focus attention on the underlying bankruptcy of the DeWitt policy of evacuation and incarceration; nowhere did he question its wisdom. He merely stated in matter-of-fact terms:

"The chief military justification for the removal of these 110,000 persons was the possibility of the existence of a disloyal element in their midst, the critical military situation in the Pacific which increased uneasiness over the possibility of espionage or sabotage, and the lack of time and facilities for individual loyalty screening."   (US House of Representatives Report No. 2679 (1946) 79:2:3)

After commenting on a number of features of the proposed bill such as that the maximum award would be $2500, renunciants would be excluded from filing any claims, and the like, he concluded his letter with the statement: "As a matter of fairness and good conscience, and because these particular American citizens and law-abiding aliens have borne with patience and undefeated loyalty the unique burdens which this Government has thrown upon them, I strongly urge that the proposed legislation be enacted into law" (US House of Representatives Report No. 2679 (1946) 79:2:5).

The bill was thrown into the legislative hopper of both houses and, while it was still being considered by the House Judiciary Committee, President Truman wrote a strong letter of endorsement to its chairman. In it he stressed the loyalty and patriotism of most Japanese-Americans.

"The fears which impelled the Government to adopt the harsh expedient of excluding Americans of Japanese ancestry from strategic military areas have, most happily, proved largely groundless. An overwhelming majority of our Japanese-American population has proved itself to be loyal and patriotic in every sense. Those of them, and there were many, who entered the armed services have acquitted themselves with great distinction. It would, in my opinion, be a tragic anomaly if the United States were, on the one hand, to acclaim and decorate with honors the brave Nisei troops who fought so valiantly and at such sacrifice overseas, while, on the other hand, it ignored and left unredressed the very real and grievous losses which some of them, together with their families, have suffered as a result of Government action in the midst of the same war."(US House Representatives Report No. 2679 (1946) 79:2:1—2)

Both bills were unanimously approved by the Committees on the Judiciary of both houses. The Senate version reached the floor on July 24 and after being amended somewhat was passed unanimously with virtually no debate. The House version reached the floor on July 26 1946. "It failed of passage in the House, due principally to the fact that it reached the floor of that body so shortly before the adjournment sine die of the Congress that a quorum could not be mustered to secure a vote on the measure, objection having been made to its passage by consent" (US House of Representatives Report No. 732 (1947) 80:1:4).

Eight months later the Secretary of Interior sent to the Speaker of the House a letter virtually identical with the one he had sent earlier. Again he enclosed a draft of the proposed legislation of the past year and again he urged passage of the legislation in terms similar to those of the past letter. Again it was referred to the judiciary committees of both houses, but this time it was reported back with certain significant modifications.

For example the House Judiciary Committee proposed that the administration of the program be placed with the Attorney General and not with a separate commission under the supervision of the interior department. It justified this change by claiming that the justice department "is perhaps more adequately equipped in specialized personnel more familiar with the disposition of claims against the Government than the Department of Interior, and is better able to absorb such functions, partaking as they do of its normal phase of operations, than other governmental agencies more remote in skills" (US House of Representatives Report No. 732 (1947) 80:1:1).

The revised bill tightened the eligibility provisions of the original but it retained the $2500 maximum award and the eighteen-month period for filing claims. However, it reduced the attorney's fees from 20 to 10 percent of the award. The committee estimated that the total cost would be $10,000,000.

Again the committee gave voice to the highly laudatory testimony it heard about the Japanese, both alien and American-born citizens:

"The committee was impressed with the fact that, despite the hardships visited upon this unfortunate racial group by an act of the Government brought about by the then prevailing military necessity, there was recorded during the recent war not one act of sabotage or espionage attributable to those who were the victims of the forced relocation. Moreover, statistics were produced to indicate that the percentage of enlistments in the armed forces of this country by those of Japanese ancestry of eligible age exceeded the Nation-wide percentage. The valiant exploits of the Four Hundred and Forty-second Regimental Combat Team, composed entirely of Japanese-Americans, and the most decorated combat team in the war, are well known. It was further adduced that the Japanese Americans who were relocated proved themselves to be, almost without exception, loyal to the traditions of this country, and exhibited a commendable discipline throughout the period of their exile."

(US House of Representatives Report No. 732 (1947) 80:1:4)

And it closed its report by saying it rejected the argument that

"the victims of the relocation were no more casualties of the war than were many millions of other Americans who lost their lives or their homes or occupations during the war.... The argument was not considered tenable, since in the instant case the loss was inflicted upon a special racial group by a voluntary act of the Government without precedent in the history of this country. Not to redress these loyal Americans in some measure for the wrong inflicted upon them would provide ample material for attacks by the followers of foreign ideologies on the American way of life, and to redress them would be simple justice."   (US House of Representatives Report No. 732 (1947) 80:1:5)

Speaker after speaker fell over each other in complimenting the committee on its work. They called the bill "meritorious," "excellent," "just and fair," and "grounded in honor and in justice." And in the words of a congressman from Massachusetts:

"In this bill we are attempting to redress a wrong which has been suffered by these persons of Japanese ancestry by reason of an action of our Government which was entirely unique in our history. Never before had there been a forced evacuation of this sort....

At this particular time when there are those seeking every effort to attack ideologies and American principles, it seems to me that if we pass this bill we are putting ourselves in very good position to resist those attacks, because this will show to the world that when our Government by voluntary action of its own affecting a special racial group brings about a situation where these individuals suffer loss of their property, even though the act of the Government is caused by military necessity we are ready, willing, and anxious to go forward with remedial legislation and attempt to redress those wrongs and do the right thing in the interest of simple justice."   (US Congressional Record 1947 80:1:9872)

Despite his effusive support of the measure, the congressman from Massachusetts saw no reason to fault the evacuation order that brought on the suffering. Another congressman was even more insistent that assurances be given that this "worthwhile" measure not be taken as even an implicit criticism of General DeWitt, "an able and efficient officer, now retired." He reminded his colleagues that the President, Congress, and Supreme Court all supported the evacuation order.

Anticipating such a reaction, the chairman of the subcommittee declared: "There is no disposition on the part of the committee or anyone so far as I know to question the good faith of the people who made that order. It appeared they were acting then in a patriotic spirit and exercising their best judgment on the evidence as it appeared at the time." He added benignly, "fortunately, their fears were groundless; there was no sabotage" (US Congressional Record 1947 80:1:9871). In general this was the sentiment of the congressmen; only one, Walter of Pennsylvania, was prepared to say that perhaps the evacuation order should never have been given. "This bill in a small way will make whole those people who were the innocent victims of an order that probably should never have been issued" (US Congressional Record 1947 80:1:9872).

Following the brief flurry of encomiums to the committee for its work coupled with a testy defense of the evacuation order itself, the House passed the bill unanimously. Almost a year later it passed the Senate in slightly amended form without debate. The House agreed to the amendment and finally on July 2 1945 President Truman signed it into law.

Almost immediately it became evident that sponsors of the program had vastly underestimated the total amount of the claims that were going to be filed. By January 1950, the statutory deadline for filing returns, approximately 24,000 claims had been submitted with a total value of nearly $133 million, thirteen times greater than the original estimate of $10 million. Approximately 61 percent of these claims were for $2500 or less, and 17 percent, for $2501 to $25,000.

In addition to being overwhelmed by the number and total value of the claims, the Japanese Claims Section, established in the Department of Justice in accordance with the law, was bogged down in the red tape of formal adjudication proceedings as required by the law. As a result, the processing of claims was excruciatingly slow and administratively expensive. In 1949, with much of the year devoted to setting up complicated procedures and opening regional offices, a mere 21 claims were processed; and in 1950 only 210 were adjudicated. The administrative cost for each claim was well over $1000.

Aware that at that rate the processing of all the claims would take at least a century or more, the Attorney General returned to Congress for modifications in the original bill. He proposed that the law be amended to permit informal compromise settlements for claims of $2500 or less instead of the more arduous adjudication proceedings. The proposed amendment sailed through both houses without debate and was signed into law by the President on August 17 1951.

Almost immediately claims began to be processed at the rate of 1000 per month. By 1955 virtually all claims under $2500 were compromised, and awards were made with administrative costs substantially lowered. Approximately 22,000 cases were closed, of which 92 percent were compromised, 3 percent adjudicated, and 5 percent dismissed. The total amount awarded was $25,500,000, one-third of the total amount asked for.

This left 2077 claims still to be processed at a total value of $55,000,000; 59 percent of these claims were for $10,000 or more. "On a dollar basis, they represent substantially all of the larger claims and under the present law, since they are too large to be compromised, they can only be settled by adjudication" (US House of Representatives Report No. 1809 (1956) 84:2:6).

To expedite the process and to modify other procedures, the Attorney General turned once again to Congress. He requested that the ceiling be lifted on claims that could be settled through informal compromise. A bill that passed the House without debate incorporated this recommendation. The Senate, however, insisted upon limiting the amount to $100,000. Claims in excess of that were to be handled either by the Court of Claims or by a vote of Congress. The House subsequently accepted this amendment. This bill also permitted any claimant who was dissatisfied with the Attorney General's decision to go to the Court of Claims for adjudication of his claim.

In addition, the revised bill did not confine claims merely to persons of Japanese ancestry as did the other bills. It permitted claims to be submitted by corporations, partnerships, charitable organizations, church congregations, and so on, both profit and nonprofit, the majority of whose members or stockholders were of Japanese ancestry. The bill also validated seventy-five claims which were mailed but not received by the deadline set in the orginal bill. And finally the bill validated the claims of detained or interned persons who had been deprived of this right under the alien enemy law or Trading with the Enemy Act.

Although the amended bill quickly passed the House without debate, several senators rose to speak their piece, though none in opposition to it. Most noteworthy was the comment by Magnuson of Washington state. He declared that the evacuation order may indeed have been a mistake, though perhaps an understandable one – a declaration that only one other congressman had been willing to make in earlier discussion of the claims bill and its subsequent amendments. "After the attack on Pearl Harbor many Japanese were taken from their homes. I think it turned out that *we made a mistake* [author's italics], but I can understand that the better part of caution was to take action" (US Congressional Record 1956 84:2:10565).

He then put in the record a portion of a statement he had made earlier; it declared categorically that the bill "has the support of all the west coast delegation in Congress on a non-partisan basis. It is noncontroversial and certainly meritorious in the tradition of democracy's ability to make up for its mistakes" (US Congressional Record 1956 84:2:10565). In much the same spirit, Dirksen of

Indiana concluded his plea for the bill with the following statement: "I, as a member of the Committee on the Judiciary to which HR 7763 was referred, urge my colleagues to approve this vital and meritorious legislation which would help in part to mitigate the wartime property losses suffered by one loyal segment of our population" (US Congressional Record 1956 84:2:10565).

In this climate of sweetness and light, the bill was passed by the Senate unanimously. The House subsequently concurred with the Senate amendment, and the bill was finally signed by President Eisenhower on July 9. Although passage of the bill permitted settlement of the remaining claims, it still took nine more years before the last one was settled. That one involved the payment of one third of a million dollars to surviving members of a family whose original claim was for four times the amount.

The significance of the claims program was perhaps more symbolic than remedial. In practice it provided only partial restitution at the rate of less than ten cents for every dollar lost, if the Federal Reserve Board figures are to be taken at face value. Few Japanese evacuees recovered anything near what they had lost. But perhaps more significantly the program signified that four years after Americans had uprooted them from their homes and herded them into concentration camps, the Issei had been accorded once again "the right of situs" in the Plural Terrain of the American society and the Nisei "the right of situs" in its People's Domain. In relegitimizing their presence, the United States government expressed its regret for their suffering and made some amends for their losses but it denied its responsibility for implementing a policy of evacuation that turned out to be both unnecessary and unjust. Congress, for example, persisted in reaffirming the myth of military necessity as justifying the policy. However, it did not defend the myth as having been validated by "subsequent facts" as General DeWitt had insisted in his final report written just two years before the claims program was first broached in Congress. Instead, it defended the myth as having been a "reasonable expectation" that reasonable men would have had during the period the policy was implemented, though the passage of time "fortunately" proved the expectation to be in error. And so now Congress was willing to make some amends for the "necessary suffering." Only a few congressmen were prepared to call the suffering unnecessary and the policy a mistake.

The House and its abortive efforts to grant citizenship to the Issei

Once the legitimacy of their fellow ethnics' presence in their respective domains had been restored, the Japanese American Citizens League was in a better position to pursue one of its major postwar objectives: that of gaining access to the People's Domain for the Issei by dismantling the legal barriers to their naturalization. And so in the late 1940s it pressed its suit with renewed vigor, in 1948 gaining an important ally, President Truman. In his celebrated Civil Rights Message to Congress on February 2 1948, he included the provision "all properly qualified legal residents of the United States should be allowed to become citizens without regard to race, color, religion or national origin." He reminded Congress that, as a wartime courtesy to wartime allies, it had already removed the bars to naturalization of persons from China, the Philippines, and India. Now, he continued, "I urge the Congress to remove the remaining racial or nationality barriers which stand in the way of citizenship for some residents of our country" (US Congressional Record 1948 80:2:929).

Even before the President's statement, the House of Representatives had already begun to show signs of wanting to do something about the matter. For example, five months before the President's message, it had passed a bill (HR 3555) granting citizenship to the parents of men who were wounded or died in World War II. This provision was obviously directed at the Issei, parents of Nisei sons who died or were wounded. The judiciary committee's report on the bill placed great weight on a letter from a major official of the Veterans of Foreign Wars. The letter stressed the valor of Nisei fighting in Italy.

> "I am confident that the devotion to duty and country of the men who made up these units cannot be surpassed by that of any other group fo men. We must, therefore, feel that the Gold Star Mothers and Fathers of over 500 of these boys who fell in battle for this country have tangible stake in the America for which their sons died. It is the least that a grateful republic might offer – this tendering to them the opportunity of becoming citizens of the United States."
>
> (US House of Representatives Report No. 595 (1947) 80:1:2)

The Senate, however, never acted on this bill.

Within two months of the President's message, Judd of Minnesota introduced a bill into the House that was in accord with the President's recommendation; it provided "the privilege of becoming a naturalized citizen of the United States to all immigrants having a legal right to permanent residence." The bill also went one step further. It would "make immigration quotas available to Asia and Pacific peoples." Hearings were held in the spring of 1948, and they furnished remarkable evidence that the climate of opinion toward the Japanese in America was undergoing a dramatic metamorphosis. A congressman from California, for example, lauded the Issei as people who are "law abiding, believe in higher education for their children, and contribute generously to such community projects as the Red Cross, Community Chest, and other local drives." He then praised lavishly their loyalty to the United States and the services they performed during the war: "Their real loyalities were with the United States and they helped defeat the country to which they owe technical allegiance." He concluded his testimony with the comment that "Certainly people like these who have lived in the United States for almost half century should be allowed to become citizens of the land they love so well" (US House of Representatives Report No. 65 (1949) 81:1:3). High military officials also testified to the valor of the Nisei in Italy and other warfronts. Even the wartime Undersecretary of War, who had been so instrumental in persuading the Secretary of War to support mass evacuation, endorsed the bill. Without expressing any remorse over the role he had played, he stressed the cooperation and loyalty of the Issei in the camps and the valor of the Nisei on the battlefields.

Despite the highly favorable testimony, the committee failed to act on the bill for the rest of the session. In the opening days of the Eighty-first Congress, Judd resubmitted an identical version of his bill (HR 199) to the House. This time the judiciary committee unanimously brought the bill to the floor of the House with a highly favorable report, slightly more than a month after it had been resubmitted. In its report the committee reminded the House that three-fourths of the previously ineligible inhabitants of Asia had already been extended the privilege of citizenship through special legislation, as in the case of those from China, India, and so on. All the present bill would do, therefore, would be to extend a policy already in operation to the other fourth. The Issei in America has earned this privilege, the report continued, quoting extensively from the earlier hearings. Again the dual theme of loyalty of the Issei in the camps and elsewhere and the valor of the Nisei on the battlefields was stressed. The report concluded, "in this record of outstanding devotion to the highest principles of Americanism, the committee finds conclusive grounds for admission of the qualified members of this small group to the priceless privileges of United States citizenship. It is a matter of simple justice to do so" (US House of Representatives Report No. 65 (1949) 81:1:5).

With respect to immigration from Asian countries, the committee created an entirely new construct,

"a so-called Asia-Pacific triangle which embraces that section of the world which hitherto has not been included in our immigration scheme. A special quota for this section has been provided for. The increase effects a horizontal level merely, for a special quota will be obtained by subtracting small amounts from the now extant eligibility lists of other countries. Racial barriers will no longer exist in United States immigration policy."

(US Congressional Record 1949 81:1:1676)

Each country within this triangle was given a specific quota based on the population figures for the 1920 census; Japan's was larger than that of any other Asian country.

Floor discussion of the bill revealed broad consensus. Even congressmen from California supported the measure; they described how their constituents were impressed with the military valor of the Nisei and the loyalty of the Issei. Several telegrams were read into the record from constituents and resolutions from various organizations. One was from the Los Angeles Board of Supervisors. (A congressman from Idaho read a whole series of telegrams into the record too, some from local chapters of the JACL, all in support of the measure.)

One congressman from California waxed so rhapsodic about the bill that he literally repudiated the racial theories that his colleagues had used so effectively in 1924 and again in the early days of World War II. However, he only perceived the bill as a rejection of the racism of Hitler and the Japanese warlords, not of that of his colleagues. "This bill is opposed to the theory advanced by Hitler's Germany and the war lords of Japan, and accepts the American theory of equality" (US Congressional Record 1949 81:1:1685).

Another congressman from California, equally rhapsodic, proclaimed that the bill finally accorded Japanese and other Asians the privilege of being treated as human beings and of being considered a part of the people of the People's Domain.

> "By this legislation we are recognizing that this group of people are human beings just as we are. They are human beings just like the Germans, the Italians, the Scandinavians, and the Irish, who came to America and who have had a big part in making America what it is." (US Congressional Record 1949 81:1:1688)

With such consensus on the dual issues of naturalization and immigration quotas for the Japanese* the measure was adopted overwhelmingly by voice vote on March 1 and sent to the Senate Committee on the Judiciary, which once again failed to act.

Apprised by the Senate Judiciary Committee that it had deferred action on the two House measures, HR 3555 and HR 199 "pending the preparation of all-inclusive legislation to be introduced at an indefinite date in the future" (US House of Representatives Report No. 634 (1949) 81:1:2), the House Judiciary Committee began to consider the way out of the legislative morass proposed by a committee member, Walter of Pennsylvania. He introduced House Joint Resolu-

---

*The only sour note in the entire deliberation was the complaint by several congressmen that the bill imposed a quota of 100 on the British West Indies where no such quota existed before; however, efforts to restore the earlier situation failed.

tion 238 that would reaffirm the naturalization law of HR 199: "to provide without racial restriction the privilege of becoming a naturalized citizen of the United States to all immigrants having a legal right to permanent residence." This resolution avoided taking a stand on the issue of immigration quotas.

During the deliberations, the committee received a strongly worded letter of support for the resolution from Masaoka, the National Legislative Director of the Japanese American Citizens League, who had made such a favorable impression during the committee's hearings in April 1948. In his letter the director left no doubt that the right of naturalization for their parents had top priority for the Nisei members of the organization. In an eloquent plea, he stated,

> "These alien Japanese in the main are our parents who have done their best to rear us to be exemplary American citizens. With the complete approval of our parents, most of us served in the armed forces of the United States, some in Europe and others in the Pacific. We believe our war record speaks not only for itself but also for the training of our parents who taught us to live, and if necessary, to fight for our America."
>
> (US House of Representatives Report No. 634 (1949) 81:1:3)

After asking for "no special favors or privileges for them," he declared "Our parents are growing old. In the twilight of their lives as useful individuals we desire that they be permitted to share our American citizenship with us, their children" (US House of Representatives Report No. 634 (1949) 81:1:3). He then expressed regret that the Senate subcommittee had blocked the immigration provision of HR 199 and hoped that it would be enacted in the future. But he emphasized "Although we recognize the importance of the immigration features of HR 199, our primary interest, as we testified before your committee in April 1948, is naturalization for our alien parents. Thus, we can endorse this resolution sincerely and wholeheartedly" (US House of Representatives Report No. 634 (1949) 81:1:3–4).

On May 19 the committee reported to the House full agreement on the resolution that would delete from Section 303 of the Nationality Act of 1940, as amended, all racial restrictions to the right of naturalization. Accordingly Section 303 would now read:

> "The right to become a naturalized citizen of the United States shall not be denied or abridged because of race: Provided, that no alien who, under law existing immediately prior to the enactment of this Act, would have been ineligible to immigrate to the United States because of race shall become eligible for immigration to the United States by reason of the adoption of this resolution."　　(US House of Representatives Report No. 634 (1949) 81:1:4)

On June 6 the resolution was passed by voice vote without debate and sent the next day to the judiciary committee of the Senate.

Four months later the Senate committee acted favorably on the resolution. Although its report lacked the enthusiasm of the House committee's, it nevertheless repeated similar reasons for its favorable response. In view of these reasons the committee continued, it was "satisfied that the evidence of their fitness to become citizens of the United States is overwhelming" (US Senate Report No. 1167 (1949) 81:1:2). The report concluded with what might be construed either as an apology for the Senate's tortoise-like pace or as a rebuke to the House's hare-like haste.

"There are pending in the [Senate] Committee on the Judiciary, bills upon which would in addition to removing racial ineligibility to naturalization, also remove racial ineligibility from the immigration laws. These bills involve a number of complicated issues including the problem of a complete new formula for allocation of quotas. The committee, without at this time expressing its views on these bills, is of the opinion that these bills should be considered in conjunction with the over-all study and investigation of our entire immigration and naturalization system which is presently in progress and which is expected to result in a complete revision of the immigration and naturalization laws."

(US Senate Report No. 1167 (1949) 81:1:3)

The resolution reached the Senate floor in the middle of October, but consideration of it was delayed eight months due to the objection of Russell of Georgia. On June 8 1950, he rose to complain that the House resolution, though primarily intended for the Japanese alien, was written so that it opened the door to naturalization to many other aliens as well. Accordingly, he proposed to amend the resolution so that it explicitly applied to the alien for whom the original resolution was presumably intended: "Japanese persons and persons of Japanese descent who (i) entered the United States (including the Territory of Hawaii) prior to July 1, 1924 (ii) have resided continuously in the United States (including the Territory of Hawaii) since such entry, and (iii) are not subject to deportation" (US Congressional Record 1950 81:2:8285). McCarran, chairman of the judiciary subcommittee that considered the resolution, agreed with Russell's interpretation. And so the amendment passed the Senate by voice vote.

Neither house was prepared to accept the other's version of the resolution; as a result the matter went to conference. But at the conference the issue proved a smoke screen, for the Senate conferees readily gave up their version in exchange for approval by the House conferees of an entirely new section, which apparently the Senate conferees wanted all along and which would amend Section 305 of the Nationality Act of 1940. This "new" section would bar from naturalization anyone who advocated or taught opposition to all organized governments or their violent overthrow and/or who was affiliated with groups espousing such doctrines as the Communist party, Communist-front organizations, or other totalitarian parties or organizations. In addition, any person could be stripped of his citizenship if he joined such organizations within five years of his naturalization.

With the tradeoff arranged, the conferees returned to their houses and won quick approval of the conference report without more than a murmur of disapproval. However, they ran into a presidential veto. In his veto message, Truman expressed regret that the original House version did not stand alone. He had long favored its naturalization provisions as evidenced by his civil rights message of 1948. "It represents a positive response by the United States to a proper demand of justice and human brotherhood. By this means we can give concrete assurance to the peoples of Asia that no resident of the United States will fail to qualify for citizenship solely because of racial origin" (US House of Representatives Document No. 702 (1950) 81:2:1).

However, he continued, the new section was reprehensible and "the language of this second section is so vague and ill-defined that no one can tell what it may mean or how it may be applied The result might be to weaken our naturalization laws rather than strengthen them. The result might also be to jeopardize the basic rights of our naturalized citizens and other persons legitimately admitted to the United States." The five year provision he feared would create "a twilight species of second-class citizens, persons who would be deprived of citizenship on technical grounds, through their ignorance or lack of judgment" (US House of Representatives Document No. 702 (1950) 81:2:2). Accordingly, he urged Congress to preserve the first section and to delete the second.

Within three days of receiving the message, the House overwhelmingly overrode the President's veto. McCarran and other leaders of the Senate apparently became worried that the added section would weaken another bill then under consideration so they let the matter die.

Two months later, the House tried once again to press for action on the substance of its original resolution. This time, though, the House passed it as a bill (HR 9780) and not as a resolution. In the Senate, the bill got further along than did several of its predecessors. It received the approval of the judiciary committee, only to be blocked on the floor of the chamber.

Three weeks later, the House made its final attempt to pass legislation similar to that which it had tried for three years previous and identical to the last two attempts which were devoted exclusively to the rights of naturalization. Once again the legislation faltered in the Senate and disappeared, never to be acted on.

The McCarran Act and delegitimation of the racial creed in naturalization

Finally the Senate was prepared to act on its own. On January 29 1952 McCarran unveiled to the Senate on behalf of the judiciary committee a monumental omnibus bill on immigration, naturalization, and nationality (S2550) which, in the words of the report he authored, "involves an undertaking which has never before been accomplished, namely the revision and codification of all the immigration and naturalization laws" (US Senate Report No. 1137 (1952) 82:2:2). The bill had its origins five years before in Senate Resolution 137 which authorized a subcommittee of the judiciary committee to investigate the entire immigration system. Two and a half years later in 1950, an exhaustive report entitled, "The Immigration and Naturalization Systems of the United States" was filed with the Senate. Simultaneously McCarran introduced an omnibus bill into the Senate (S3455) that was referred to the judiciary committee. And for the next two years the bill nestled in the committee, as it underwent two revisions and transformations much like a larva in a cocoon, to emerge in full bloom on the Senate floor as S2550.

In certain basic respects, despite all the effort that had gone into it, the bill did not break new ground but merely reaffirmed and elaborated on the old. For example, it retained the national origins quota system of the 1924 act. It kept 1920 as the base year for allocating immigration quotas and even continued to exclude "descendants of slave immigrants" and "all original Americans" from the category of total inhabitants of the United States. However, it substituted

> "a mechanically simplified formula for determining the annual quota for each quota area (the term 'quota area' is substituted for the term 'nationality' as being more appropriate) which provides that the quota for each quota area will be one-sixth of 1 percent of the number of inhabitants in the continental United States in 1920 attributable by national origin to that quota area. It is specifically provided that the number of inhabitants in the United States in 1920 attributable to a particular quota area shall be the same number which was previously determined in establishing the national origin quotas under Section II of the Immigration Act of 1924, thereby precluding the necessity for any redetermination of that number."   (US Senate Report No. 1137 (1952) 82:2:14–15)

The McCarran bill did not merely stop there. It abandoned the exclusionism of the 1924 act and brought Japan and other Asian countries into its scheme. Accordingly it adopted the concept "Asia-Pacific triangle," first used by the House Committee on Judiciary in 1949, and computed quotas for areas within the triangle with the stipulation that the total for the triangle was not to exceed 2000. Japan's quota was to be pegged at 185 while most of the others were to have minimum quotas of 100. Unlike any other quota area however, immigrants to the United States whose ancestry comprised at least 50 percent of peoples indigenous to the triangle would be charged to the quota for the triangle. In all other cases, the immigrant was to be charged to the quota of the country from which he actually emigrated. To compensate in part for this discriminatory treatment, a special quota of 100 was set aside for the triangle as a whole.

In still another radical departure from the 1924 act, McCarran and his subcommittee finally articulated in their bill what the House had been espousing in vain for about four years. They dropped all racial barriers to naturalization after testimony had persuaded them that the time had come for delegitimizing the racial creed, which they now saw as an "un-American" way of blocking access to citizenship and to the People's Domain.

> "The testimony before the subcommittee which submitted the comprehensive report on the immigration and naturalization systems (US Report 1515, 81st cong) was overwhelmingly to the effect that racial bars to naturalization and immigration should be removed. The committee feels that denial of naturalization based solely on race is an outmoded and un-American concept and should be eliminated from our statutes."   (US Senate Report No. 1137 (1952) 82:2:40)

In most other ways, the McCarran Act was fully in accord with the direction and patterns set by earlier immigration laws, particularly that of 1924 and those of Chinese exclusion. It increased the power of the administrative bureaucracy to make binding policies and decisions on immigration and vested final authority in the Attorney General, while playing down the possibility of judicial review. It also sought to tighten administrative procedures. The most significant of these reflected the subcommittee preoccupation with subversives.

> "More thorough screening especially of security risks is provided.... Structural changes are made in enforcement agencies for greater efficiency.... The exclusion and deportation procedures are strengthened.... Naturalization and denaturalization procedures are strengthened to weed out subversives and other undesirables from citizenship."   (US Senate Report No. 1137 (1952) 82:2:3)

As part of its preoccupation with subversion, the subcommittee expanded the categories of excludable deportable aliens to include those who belonged or had belonged to subversive organizations. However, the Attorney General could exempt an alien from this provision if he found "that the alien's membership or affiliation has ceased; that he has, for the past 5 years, been actively opposed to the doctrine, program, principles, and ideology of the subversive organization of which he was a member or affiliate, and that the issuance of the visa and the admission of the alien would be in the public interest" (US Senate Report No. 1137 (1952) 82:2:10).

In addition, the bill created new classes of excludable aliens. These included aliens convicted of two or more offenses that involved more than five years of confinement, those coming to America "solely principally or incidentally to engage in any immoral sexual act," and narcotic law violators and such like. The bill also redefined the nonquota classes. Perhaps the most significant change was the dropping of professors from that status on the grounds that they could either get into the country under the provision of the bill that "allocates 50 percent of each quota to aliens of exceptional ability whose services are needed in this country or the one which provides for the temporary admission of such aliens" (US Senate Report No. 1137 (1952) 82:2:18).

Approximately six weeks later, four senators from the judiciary committee submitted a minority report that took strong exception to the bill and urged the Senate to turn it down. Though lauding the staff and chairman of the subcommittee on immigration for their hard work and dedication, the four regretted that the judiciary committee had acted before receiving the final reports on S2550 from the state and justice departments and before it examined a new omnibus bill on immigration being prepared by a group of senators, including the four (the Humphrey-Lehman bill).

The minority report complained that the majority's bill violated basic tenets of the American creed and ran "counter to our democratic traditons of justice and equity" (US Senate Report No. 1137 Part II (1952) 82:2:1). It did this by retaining some of the worst features of the 1924 act. For example, it continued to discriminate against southern and eastern European immigrants in favor of those from northern and western Europe. It also allowed unused quotas to lie fallow. The minority report reserved its most serious criticism for the majority's seeming obsession with subversion. It bitterly assiled S2550 as assuming "every alien is a suspicious character whose every activity must be circumscribed and who may be called upon not once but again and again to prove the innocence of his beliefs" (US Senate Report No. 1137 Part II (1952) 82:2:9).

With respect to the majority bill's treatment of Asians, the minority report conceded that "the proposed measure takes a most important step forward by making all peoples, regardless of race, eligible for immigration [and natiraliza-tion]" (US Senate Report No. 1137 Part II (1952) 82:2:5).But the report complained that the 50 percent ancestry rule discriminated against the Asians and should be abandoned; all aliens should be chargeable to the quota of their country of birth, regardless of race.

The Humphrey-Lehman bill and the struggle for
Asian-American support

A day before the minority report was submitted to the Senate, the new omnibus bill to which it referred had already been introduced into the Senate by Hubert Humphrey and referred to the judiciary committee. Speaking in behalf of the twelve other sponsors of the bill, among whom were three of the four signers of the minority report, Humphrey requested that a joint statement and summary of the bill be printed in the Congressional Record. The statement began with the simple declaration: "We are today introducing an omnibus immigration and naturalization bill which codifies, simplifies, and humanizes our immigration and naturalization laws" (US Congressional Record 1952 82:2:2141). It then went on to pinpoint the basic deficiencies, inequities, and the undemocratic and arbitrary character of the McCarran bill (S2550), much as the minority report was to do. For example, it condemned the McCarran bill for adopting "the arbitrary procedures of the police state in handling aliens who have just escaped tyranny and are seeking entry to the home of the freedom. Many of the deportation procedures of S2550 are of a like nature" (US Congressional Record 1952 82:2:2141).

The statement then proceeded to show how provisions of the new bill (S2878), labeled the Humphrey-Lehman bill, would meet these defects; these provisions were much in line with the recommendations of the minority report. Thus, the base year for the quota system would be 1950, not 1920; unused portions of the quotas would be pooled and reallocated for religious and political persecutees and escapees from behind the Iron Curtain and such like; even reformed totalitarians would be admitted. As such, administrative procedures would be humanized and made more just and responsible with review and appeal provisions built into the structure.

The new bill would also do things which the minority report failed to mention; it would include "the descendants of slave immigrants" as part of the total American population for computation of immigration quotas; it would also grant nonquota status "to all natives of the Western Hemisphere, including persons born in Western Hemisphere colonies" (US Congressional Record 1952 82:2:2142).

In short, the Humphrey-Lehman bill, according to the statement, was determined to weed out all the racially restrictive and discriminatory features that still remained in the McCarran bill, despite its claim of being racially nondiscriminatory. For Japanese and other Asians, this meant that the discriminatory McCarran 50 percent "nationality-by-origins" provision was to be replaced in S2784 by a universal "by birth" criterion in determining against which country's quota an immigrant was to be charged. In addition, the Japanse and other Asians would never have to worry about reaching some time in the future the 2000 ceiling imposed on immigrants from the Asia-Pacific triangle.

However, even the sponsors of S2784 were not prepared to claim, in their statement, that the Japanese would receive a larger quota in their bill. In fact, estimates computed by the Bureau of the Census showed the opposite. Fewer would be eligible to come in under the Humphrey-Lehman bill than under the McCarran bill, 185 to 250 respectively. In addition, the sponsors were not prepared to claim that the Japanese or other Asians would benefit appreciably by the 'pooling' of the unused quotas. In fact, the statement declared, "The so-called 'pooling' of the unused quotas would be of special benefit to otherwise qualified persons from the following countries and areas: Italy, Poland, Greece, Holland, Czechoslovakia, Hungary, Germany, Austria, Yugoslavia, Venezia Guila, the Middle East – especially refugees" (US Congressional Record 1952 82:2:2141). And finally, the Humphrey-Lehman bill merely reaffirmed what the McCarran bill already offered the Japanese and other Asians in America: the privilege of naturalization.

The difference between the two bills, therefore, did not seem very great with respect to treatment of Japanese and other Asians. In other areas the differences were indeed substantial. And these differences were at the center of the sponsors' attention when they characterized the Humphrey-Lehman bill as being much more liberal, humane, democratic, just, and equable than the McCarran bill.

The sponsors of the Humphrey-Lehman bill realized they faced an uphill battle to obtain any kind of legislative attention for their bill, in view of the fact that the formidable chairman of the subcommittee on immigration, McCarran, had his own bill in place which he could say was the product of years of painstaking work and thought. To counter this, the Humphrey-Lehman sponsors let it be known that their bill had also taken at least a year of preparation. As a further stratagem in this campaign, Humphrey brought to the attention of the Senate on April 23 "expressions of support which we have received from many public-spirited individuals and organizations representing practically every area of religious and nationality life in the United States" (US Congressional Record 1952 82:2:4247). He then unveiled a press release issued after a meeting with officials from various Catholic organizations. He also made public a letter being mailed by the Friends Committee on National Legislation to its constituents and a letter opposing the McCarran Act which was signed by representatives of thirteen national organizations. Some of these groups were Jewish, at least one was Italian, Polish, or Czechoslovakian, and the rest were politically liberal, such as the Americans for Democratic Action, the American Veterans Committee, the Association of Immigration, and Nationality Lawyers. Further he read messages from other Jewish, Catholic, and Protestant organizations. In short, he showed that an imposing array of white ethnic, and politically liberal groups were aligned on his side.

This stratagem failed to budge the judiciary committee. Several weeks later Humphrey returned to the Senate floor with the complaint that the committee had failed to grant his bill, which was to be offered as a substitute for McCarran's, a hearing which he insisted "the Committee on the Judiciary owes us" (US Congressional Record 1952 82:2:4777) and which another co-sponsor of the bill labeled "a just, fair, and reasonable request" (US Congressional Record 1952 82:2:4779).

Two days later, Lehman renewed the appeal for a public hearing for the bill (S2842) and requested delay in considering the McCarran bill (S2550) as the Senate moved to consider the latter. He complained,

"I assure the acting majority leader that my protest comes from the heart and represents a deep feeling of concern on my part and on the part of my colleagues with respect to the manner in which the Humphrey-Lehman bill (S2842) has been treated, which is a much more important consideration than the manner in which we personally have been treated, even though we do not believe that that kind of treatment should have been accorded to us."

(US Congressional Record 1952 82:2:4890)

In this manner the battle lines between the two sides were drawn. After several preliminary skirmishes the real debate began on May 13. McCarran opened the proceedings with a long and spirited defense of his bill. He stressed its long painstaking preparation. He also countered the Humphrey strategy with communications from public supporters of his bill. He began with the reading of a resolution "unanimously adopted by the American Coalition, which is composed of 93 patriotic, civic and fraternal organizations representing a membership of several million persons" (US Congressional Record 1952 82:2:5090). The clerk then read the list of organizations in which the words loyal and patriotic were prominent parts of the names of many. In addition, a telegram of endorsement was received from the national executive committee of the American Legion and The National Society, Daughters of the American Colonists.

In order to show that his bill was not merely being supported by conservatives, restrictionists, and nationalists, he then threw in as his piéce de résistance telegrams from the Japanese American Citizens League. One was from Mike Masaoka, the league's National Legislative Director, others were from chapters in San Mateo and Cleveland. All praised the McCarran bill for removing the dual discrimination under which Japanese and other Asians had long suffered. In the words of Masaoka, "The elimination of these racial prohibitions, as provided by your bill, is not only a matter of long-deferred justice but will have an enormously salutary effect upon our international relations" (US Congressional Record 1952 82:2:5092). Also read into the record was a resolution of support passed unanimously by 1728 delegates of the Filipino Federation of America at a special convention.

Later that day, Lehman responded in kind by reading into the record a list of the ethnic, religious, and politically liberal groups that supported his bill. He also added a list of approximately sixty-five prominent individuals who had signed a New York Times advertisement condemning the McCarran bill and supporting the Humphrey-Lehman bill. Throughout the entire list of organizations and individuals, however, only one Asian name could be found. The organization that was listed was the Chinese-American Citizens National Association; the individual who had signed the advertisement was its president.

Two days later, McCarran rejoined the battle of the endorsements. He read into the record a telegram of hearty support from what purported to be "the only nationally organized group of American citizens of Chinese descent in this country" (US Congressional Record 1952 82:2:5207), the Chinese-American Citizens Alliance – an obvious slap at the Chinese organization which had endorsed the other side.

Perturbed by the seemingly solid support for the McCarran bill from Asian organizations, Lehman and Humphrey sought to convince them of its discriminatory nature. However, the only issue they were able to hit hard at was the 50 percent "nationality-by-origins" provision. Humphrey did seek to make the general point that the McCarran bill was based on the notion of Anglo-Saxon superiority in which all other races including the "oriental people" were to be treated as second-class citizens. None of the efforts seemed to make any headway among the Japanese or other Asian groups. The next day, McCarran read into the record a telegram of endorsement from the Midwest Chinese-American Civil Council of Chicago. To offset this, the Humphrey forces brought to the Senate's attention a letter from the National Congress of American Indians, opposing the McCarran bill, primarily on the grounds of being excluded from the population base for allocation quotas from the 1920 census.

Finally, on May 19, the first major skirmish between the opposing forces was joined. Humphrey moved that the McCarran bill be recommitted to the judiciary committee with instructions to hold hearings on the Humphrey-Lehman bill. His motion was beaten decisively by vote of 28 for recommitment, 44 against, and 24 not voting; and so the Humphrey-Lehman forces lost the first major skirmish in the battle over immigration.

Immediately after the vote, Lehman rose to offer on behalf of fourteen other senators an amendment in the nature of a substitute for the McCarran bill. He later identified it as really being S2343, for which S2842 had been "a prototype." The substitute differed from S2842 in one fundamental respect. The base year for allocation of quotas was to remain 1920 as in the 1924 act and not 1950 as in S2842. Lehman explained this retreat as necessary in order to gain additional support from senators who may have approved of S2842 in principle but who disliked the additional number of immigrants (estimated at 100,000) who would have been eligible to enter the United States because of population growth from 1920 to 1950. He insisted, however, that the pooling of unused quotas and their reallocation as retained from S2842 would compensate for the ethnic and racial inequities built into quotas based on the 1920 census. Other major provisions of S2842 were also retained. For example, Section 1 (a) stipulated that "no person shall be denied the right to become a citizen of the United States or the privilege to enter the United States as an immigrant solely on the ground of his race, nor shall any applicant for admission be assigned to a quota solely on the basis of his race" (US Congressional Record 1952 82:2:5427).

Debate resumed with the same intensity as before. And Humphrey tried again to appeal for support of the Asian-American. However on May 21, McCarran virtually ended the contest for Asian support by reading into the record a telegram from the national presidents of four major Asian organizations, the JACL, Chinese American Citizens Alliance, Filipino Federation of America, and Korean National Association. It stated that,

> "four national organizations representing 90 percent American citizens of Asian ancestry strongly oppose substituting Humphrey-Lehman bill for McCarran omnibus bill. Humphrey-Lehman substitute ill advised, impractical, and not in the best interest of persons of Asian ancestry.... We endorse unqualifiedly McCarran-Walter bill as fairest and most realistic possible approach to immigration and naturalization problems at this time."
>
> (US Congressional Record 1952 82:2:5624)

Ironically this telegram was read after McCarran made a passionate plea against the substitute bill for its "opening of the gates to a flood of Asiatics." He insisted that a nonquota status for persons born in the Western Hemisphere would make an estimated 600,000 orientals who were natives of nonquota countries of the Western Hemisphere eligible for immediate immigration to the United States, and the large number of Asians would overwhelm Western Europe in competition for the pooled unused quotas. Yet despite these utterances the Asian support for the McCarran bill did not falter.

After this tirade, McCarran continued with a more dispassionate critique of the substitute bill and its shortcomings. One of his major points was that the pooling of unused quotas would undermine and destroy the basic national origins concept of immigration quotas. Before the day was over the Humphrey-Lehman forces suffered their second major defeat. The substitute bill lost by an even larger margin than did the recommittal vote: 27 yes, 51 no, and 18 not voting.

Efforts to amend the McCarran bill continued even after the defeat. Several technical amendments passed, but all those derived from specific sections of the substitute bill were beaten. In the course of the debate, McCarran repeated his "flood gate argument," though always mentioning at the same time the support he had received from Asian-American organizations. Finally, on May 22 the battle was over; the McCarran Act won handily in the Senate.

Conferees were appointed to meet with those of the House to iron out differences between the versions of the bill each had passed – the House version having passed a month before without the controversy experienced in the Senate. The conferees sought to allay some of the fears about the arbitrary and capricious exercise of power by immigration authorities. Accordingly, they "refined the language so as to make it emphatically clear that the Attorney General may not (as has been erroneously charged) capriciously deport an alien solely on the basis of inconsequential, unwitting infraction of the law" (US Congressional Record 1952 82:2:6986). In addition, greater flexibility was built into those provisions of the bill that applied to persons who were persecuted for racial, religious, and political reasons. Other minor differences were also ironed out and the conference report and revised bill returned to each chamber. After brief debate, both houses passed the bill by overwhelming margins, the House on June 10, the Senate on June 11.

Presidential veto: a historical replay in reverse of presidential action in 1924

Despite the overwhelming defeat of the Humphrey-Lehman liberal forces in Congress, they had one more front on which the battle could still be won; that is, at the level of the President. And the President did not disappoint them. He vetoed the McCarran Act and returned it with a message to Congress on June 25 1952. In his message, he cited two basic reasons for his action. He strongly opposed the national origins quota system which he said perpetuated the myth built into the 1924 immigration act "that Americans with English or Irish names were better people and better citizens than Americans with Italian or Greek or Polish names" (US House of Representatives Document No. 520 (1952) 82:2:3–4). This concept of Nordic superiority

"is utterly unworthy of our traditions and our ideals. It violates the great political doctrine of the Declaration of Independence that 'all men are created equal.' It denies the humanitarian creed inscribed beneath the Statue of Liberty proclaiming to all nations, 'Give me your tired, your poor, your huddled masses yearning to breathe free.'"

(US House of Representatives Document No. 520 (1952) 82:2:4).

He added that this discriminatory policy would keep out precisely those people from Eastern and Mediterranean Europe whom America should be helping in the struggle with Communism – refugees and defectors.

The second major reason was the capricious and arbitrary power lodged in the hands of administrative authority by the bill, particularly as these applied to exclusion and deportation. He was particularly upset with the provision which

"would empower the Attorney General to deport any alien who has engaged or has had a purpose to engage in activities 'prejudicial to the public interest' or 'subversive to the national security.' No standards or definitions are provided to guide discretion in the exercise of powers so sweeping. To punish undefined 'activities' departs from traditional American insistence on established standards of guilt. To punish an undefined 'purpose' is thought control.... These provisions are worse than the infamous Alien Act of 1798, passed in a time of national fear and distrust of foreigners, which gave the President power to deport any alien deemed 'dangerous to the peace and safety of the United States.' Alien residents were thoroughly frightened and citizens much disturbed by that threat to liberty."

(US House of Representatives Document No. 520 (1952) 82:2:6)

The President went on to mention other objectionable features of the bill, but he stated categorically that he favored those provisions of the bill in which "all racial bars to naturalization would be removed, and at least some minimum immigration quota would be afforded to each of the free nations of Asia." In fact, he continued, "I have long urged that racial or national barriers to naturalization be abolished. This was one of the recommendations in my civil-rights message to the Congress on February 2, 1948. On February 19, 1951, the House of Representatives unanimously passed a bill [HR403] to carry it out" (US House of Representatives Document No. 520 (1952) 82:2:2). He left no doubt that, had HR403 reached his desk, he would have gladly signed it into law (he even ended his message with a plea to Congress to pass the bill).

"[But] this most desirable provision comes before me embedded in a mass of legislation which would perpetuate injustices of long standing against many other nations of the world, hamper the efforts we are making to rally the men of the east and west alike to the cause of freedom, and intensify the repressive and inhumane aspects of our immigration procedures. The price is too high and, in good conscience, I cannot agree to pay it."

(US House of Representatives Document No. 520 (1952) 82:2:2)

Accordingly, he vetoed the bill, hoping that "all our residents of Japanese ancestry, and all our friends throughout the Far East" (US House of Representatives Document No. 520 (1952) 82:2:2) would understand why he had to do what he did. Thus, as in 1924, once again the interests of persons of Japanese ancestry were sacrificed in the name of some broader national purpose or good. In 1924 President Coolidge said he would have vetoed the exclusion clause against the Japanese had it stood alone but, in the broader interests of maintaining America's national heritage and stability, he felt obliged to approve the omnibus immigration bill of which it was part. Now in 1952, in a historical replay in reverse, President Truman insisted he would have enthusiastically approved the removal of naturalization and immigration bars to persons of Japanese or Asian ancestry had the provisions stood alone but, in the broader interests of the American creed and justice he felt obliged to veto the omnibus immigration bill of which these provisions were part. In short, despite their constrasting definitions of what constituted the national good, both presidents viewed the interests of the Japanese alien or immigrant as expendable to the realization of that good, for that historical moment at least. Truman, however, was not as successful as Coolidge. His veto was overridden, so that the higher national good he and the liberal forces in Congress quested lost to the view of the national good consistent with that which Congress and Coolidge had espoused in 1924. In both years the liberal immigration forces were decisively defeated. By comparison persons of Japanese ancestry suffered an even worse defeat than the liberals in 1924, but were better off in 1952. A least they managed to snatch a victory.

Liberals and Japanese-Americans at cross purposes: 1924 and 1952

In still another major respect, the legislative drama of 1952 was like a historical replay, again in reverse – a negative afterimage – of the legislative drama of 1924. Then, as we have seen, Congressman Sabath and other liberal congressmen seeking to reduce discriminatory quotas against the southern and eastern Europeans failed to make common cause with those who wanted to keep the door open – or at least slightly ajar – for Japanese immigration. In fact, as we have seen, they completely abandoned the Japanese immigrant. Some did it perhaps for racist reasons, inasmuch as they shared the yellow peril conviction of the exclusionists. Others like Sabath did it for reasons of political expediency and convenience (witness Sabath's complete about-face on the issue in 1946 and 1952). They thought they would thereby win the support of the exclusionists for their cause. But they gained nothing from this act of dissociation; they were badly defeated in the final showdown.

By 1952, however, the liberal congressmen including Sabath had repudiated the approach of 1924. They no longer sought to detach themselves politically from persons of Japanese ancestry. In fact the liberals actively sought to woo them and to persuade them of an identity of ideological and political interests. Accordingly, the liberals pressed hard on the theme that the Humphrey-Lehman bill was a much better vehicle for the satisfaction of these mutual interests than was the "reactionary" McCarran bill.

This time, however, the shoe was on the other foot. The leaders of the American-Japanese community, most notably those from the Japanese American Citizens League, as well as leaders of other Asian-American communities, were unresponsive to these pleas. They continued their resolute support of the McCarran bill, even after President Truman's veto. A number of reasons can be readily adduced for this adamant stand. On the most immediate and pragmatic level certain facts stand out. From the point of view of the JACL, the Humphrey-Lehman bill gave persons of Japanese and Asian ancestry nothing of any real significance at that moment of historical time that the McCarran bill did not also give them. Inasmuch as naturalization for the Issei was its top priority, the JACL was not overly concerned with the 50 percent ancestry rule, nor with the significance of a 2000 limit on immigration from the Pacific triangle, particularly when the actual quotas Japanese immigrants would obtain in the immediate future were even higher in the McCarran than in the Humphrey-Lehman bill. In addition, the JACL and kindred Asian organizations had just gone through three to four years of legislative experience in which the House of Representatives had repeatedly passed the naturalization bill they wanted, only to have it blocked in the Senate. The pivotal figure in this scenario they recognized was McCarran. Only he had the kind of legislative clout that could break the logjam. So, in the name of real politick, they joined forces with him and thereby gained their immediate political objective.

In view of the pragmatic political situation, the only thing that might have placed the JACL on the side of the liberals would have been a history of shared political and ideological commitment and experience. But as we have seen there was no such history. Leaders of the JACL must have been well aware of the fate their progenitors had faced in the Congress of 1924 and also of the readiness with which liberals swallowed the yellow peril myth in World War II to march in the vanguard of the crusade for mass evacuation. After all the greatest spokesman for liberalism of that period, President Franklin D. Roosevelt, had signed the order that herded the Japanese into concentration camps.

Thus liberal congressmen and leaders of the Japanese community, most of whom were Nisei by 1952, operated at cross purposes during this historical period. They had different agendas and spoke for constituencies who had qualitatively different needs and interests in the area of naturalization and immigration. On the one hand, the liberal congressmen in 1924 and 1952 had taken up the cudgel for white minorities from southern and eastern Europe, most of whom were already part of the people of the Peoples's Domain. Thus naturalization posed no problem for them; instead they were pressing for a more equitable immigration policy that would allow proportionately even more of their countrymen to enter the United States and to become part of the People's Domain after five years than were presently allowed.

On the other hand, Nisei leaders of the Japanese community were primarily speaking by 1952 in behalf of the first-generation Issei who were ensconced in the Plural Terrain of America and legally forbidden from becoming part of the people of the People's Domain. Gaining the privilege of naturalization and access to the People's Domain for these Issei – their parents – had top priority for these leaders. Only secondarily were they concerned about the immigration of their kin from Japan. Even there the struggle for the Japanese immigrant differed strikingly from that for the eastern European immigrant. The door was shut tight for the former and had to be pried open; for the latter the door was already ajar and merely needed to be opened wider.

Convergence of interests in 1965: Japanese-American and liberal

Once the battle for naturalization and for immigration quotas had been won, the interests of the Japanese community began to converge with those of the liberals and white ethnic minorities on the issue of immigration. Ideologically their positions grew closer as they assailed the discriminatory allocation of quotas under the McCarran Act, but even here the focus still differed. The national origins feature of the act was an anathema to the liberals and progeny of eastern European immigrants; whereas the Asia-Pacific triangle was an anathema to the Japanese-Americans. Finally, in 1965 they joined forces to help bring about a radically new immigration law (HR2580) that abolished both features of the McCarran Act.

In a letter to Senator Kuchel of California, Masaoka of the JACL, who had strongly backed the McCarran Act in 1952, urged the senator to vote for the bill (HR2580) which sought

"to provide greater immigration opportunities, within numerical limitations, to members and close relatives of American citizens and resident alien families, to those whose professions, skills, or work will benefit the economy, welfare or culture of the Nation, and to refugees from political or religious persecution or catastrophic nature calamity, all without regard to race, ancestry, national origin, religion, or color.... [These worthy objectives would be accomplished] by substituting a new immigration system based on specified preference priorities for the existing national origins quota system and the special Asia-Pacific triangle 'ancestry' discrimination."

(US Congressional Record 1965 89:1:24502)

In short, Masaoka no longer talked as though he were representing aliens and outsiders who wanted to gain access to the People's Domain. That, he reminded the House Judiciary Committee in testimony on HR2580, was his and the JACL's lot in 1952 and the reason for their stand on the McCarran Act "in spite of its deficiencies." Now he talked as a representative of a racial and ethnic group that had become part of the People's Domain, was living in accordance with the American creed, and had the credentials to prove it.

"No group of Americans is more law abiding. Japanese Americans spend more time for education, including the college level, than the average American. More are in the professions than the average. More own their own homes, and operate their own business enterprises. The average income, individual and family, as well as urban and rural, are higher than their non-Japanese counterparts. They are more community and civic minded, contributing more on the average to such charities as the Community Chest, Red Cross, etc. At the same time, they remain off of relief rolls and generally refuse other government aid of relief nature. They bought more war bonds, and buy more Government savings bonds.

By almost any legitimate criterion of exemplary citizenship and Americanism, Japanese Americans are an assimilated, integrated, and accepted part of the communities in which they live and of the Nation to which they owe allegiance." (US Congressional Record 1965 89:1:24504)

Now that the Japanese in America had finally been accepted into the People's Domain and accorded the rights and immunities of the American creed and equality of treatment under the law and Constitution, he argued, why not extend the same principles of equality and equity to America's policy of immigration and to its external relations with the nations of the world. Passage of the immigration bill (HR2580) would accomplish this, because

"it would bring our immigration law into conformity with our civil rights and other such statutes dealing with the internal opportunities of our citizens;... it would bring our practices closer to our preachments of equality and equity; [and] ... it would demonstrate that our concern for the peoples and nations and problems of Asia are equal to our concerns for Europe."

(US Congressional Record 1965 89:1:24504)

To Masaoka and others, the enactment of the 1965 bill represented the final step in the abolition of the racial creed as the established principle guiding America's historic policy of immigration. ("It would complete the objective of eliminating race as an accepted principle and practice in our immigration law" (US Congressional Record 1965 89:1:24504).) Thus by the mid-1960s, with the enactment of HR2580 and the other civil rights acts of 1964 and 1965, America had finally delegitimized the racial creed as part of its legal-normative code for regulating treatment of nonwhite minorities in any of their varied statuses, as potential or actual immigrant, as alien, or as citizen. Only the American creed and its axiomatic premise of equal treatment was henceforth to be the regnant legal-normative code for all.

The aftermath

Once the constraints of the plural society were lifted and the concentration camps closed down, the second generation Japanese-Americans (Nisei) rose rapidly in the world of occupations. In their study of the socio-economic mobility of three generations of Japanese-Americans, Levine and Montero report that seven out of ten Nisei male college graduates who entered the labor market from 1953 to 1966 joined the ranks of professionals. And "fully 85% of the men who undertook graduate work took up professional duties" (Levine and Montero 1973:44). In sharp contrast only one out of ten of their counterparts who entered the labor force before World War II could find professional jobs. Another two out of ten served in managerial posts; the latter figure included those employed in family enterprises. (Equally striking is the percentage in each labor cohort who earned at least a college degree: 47 percent in the former and 9 percent in the latter.)

Sowell paints an even more glowing picture of the postwar mobility of the Japanese-Americans. He reports that in 1959 the income of mainland Japanese-Americans was slightly less than that of the whites. "By 1969, the average personal income of Japanese Americans was 11 percent above the national average, and average family income was 32 percent above" (Sowell 1981:175). Sowell is convinced that the internment experience had no "permanently negative effect" on the Japanese-Americans. As evidence, he points to the higher rate of mobility for those from the mainland than for those from Hawaii. He even goes so far as to offer the internment experience as a partial explanation for the success of the mainland Japanese-Americans – albeit he couches his explanation in gingerly phrased words. "Perhaps it [the internment] even had a positive effect – in narrowly economic terms – by freeing the *Nisei* from the restrictive bonds of parental expectations, particularly as regards taking over the family business rather than pursuing new fields. In this regard, many Japanese Americans themselves – including Senator S.I. Hayakawa – have credited the internment experience with improving their long-run mobility" (Sowell 1981:176).

Sowell's conjecture may or may not have sociological merit; only a carefully designed study can answer that question. But his assertion that "many Japanese Americans" perceive their internment experience as having had positive consequences for themselves flies in the face of compelling evidence to the contrary – Senator Hayakawa's comment notwithstanding. A tangible expression of this evidence can be seen in the outpouring of overwhelming support of Japanese-Americans of all generations individually and collectively through their organizations for several bills introduced into Congress in 1979. (The Japanese American Citizens League, in particular, played an important role in getting the legislative machinery moving on the bills as did Nisei in Congress who were among their chief sponsors in each house.) As finally enacted on July 31, 1980, the bill proposed to "establish a Commission to gather facts to determine whether any *wrong* [author's italics] was committed against those American citizens and permanent resident aliens affected by Executive Order Numbered 9066, and for other purposes" (US Statutes at Large 1980 94 Pt 1, 96:2:964).

As a result of the hearings and debates in Congress and the coverage by the media, it became increasingly apparent that, in the words of Senator Matsunaga of Hawaii, who, though a Nisei, was spared internment because he was from Hawaii: "It [the internment experience] remains the single most traumatic and disturbing event in the lives of many Nisei. Some, now middle-aged and older, still weep when they think about it. Some become angry. And some still consider it such a degrading experience that they refuse to talk about it" (US Senate Committee on Governmental Affairs 1980 96:2:9–10). In even more personal and poignant terms Congressman Mineta of California, who was interned as a young child along with his parents, is quoted by a newspaper reporter as having said, "It [the internment experience] was like being the victim of a rape . . . you don't want to talk about it, but you can't forget it. You know that you are the innocent victim, but all of a sudden you become the guilty one" (Strobe 1980:35).

What most of the Nisei said they wanted from the bill was to have America finally confront itself on what Congressman Bauman of Maryland labeled in a subsequent debate "one of the greatest denials of civil liberties to ever occur in peacetime or wartime in our history" (US Congressional Record 1980 96:2: H6211) and to have America expunge from the historical record the stigma many felt they were still bearing. For, according to Senator Matsunaga of Hawaii "their children have started to ask questions about the internment of their parents and grandparents. Why didn't they 'protest'? Did they commit any crimes that they are ashamed of? If the Government was wrong, why hasn't the wrong been admitted and laid to rest forever?" (US Senate Committee on Governmental Affairs 1980 96:2:10).

Thus, contrary to what Sowell suggests, the searing experience of the past remains a puzzling and disturbing part of the present for most Japanese-Americans whatever their present level of material well-being. An older Nisei woman who testified before the Senate committee expressed succinctly these sentiments: "there will always be a shadow over the history pages of the United States of America unless immediate steps are taken to remedy this great injustice" (US Senate Committee on Governmental Affairs 1980 96:2:251). What she and others have yet to come to full agreement about is what constitutes an appropriate redress for this injustice.

PART THREE

PUERTO RICO:
FROM COLONIAL DEPENDENCY
TO COMMONWEALTH STATUS

19

PUERTO RICO AS
AN UNINCORPORATED TERRITORY:
THE EARLY YEARS
AND THE STRUGGLE OVER
AMERICAN CITIZENSHIP

Introduction

With the passage of the Foraker Act in 1900, the United States created a second model for its relations with newly acquired lands that departed dramatically from the model in operation ever since Congress reaffirmed the Northwest Ordinance a year after the formation of the New Nation. Under that model the New Nation treated new lands as colonist extensions of itself and granted them Territorial status with the assurance of eventual incorporation into the Union as a State. Their people in the interim were to be protected by most of the rights and immunities of the Constitution.

For several years before enactment of the Foraker Act, there seemed little reason to doubt that Puerto Rico would be accorded a similar status. The military governor seemed to expect it, the President seemed to infer it in his message to Congress, and the first draft of the Foraker Act that was introduced into the Senate in January 1900 seemed to confirm it. However, within less than a month's time, the bill had been drastically changed; and Puerto Rico's status, transformed into one that was unique in American history. The island was to become the first legally defined unincorporated territory without any promise of statehood or protection of the Constitution. This launched an odyssey through uncharted political and legal waters for the island and Congress that continues to buffet and to confound their relations to this day.

In this chapter we shall examine the sequence of events that led to this transformation and the significance and meaning of this transformation as Congress created, in effect, the first colonial dependency of the United States. In addition, we shall look at the confusion and controversy that this "novel" status generated during the next several decades over the issue of American citizenship.

Military conquest and occupation

Three months after the formal declaration of war against Spain on April 25 1898, American military forces landed on the coast of Puerto Rico and seized one of its ports. Within three days of the landing, Major General Miles issued a proclamation inviting the people of Puerto Rico to join the Americans in the struggle against the Spanish oppressor. He assured them that the Americans "come bearing the banner of freedom, inspired by a noble purpose to seek the enemies of our country and yours, and to destroy or capture all who are in armed resistance. They bring you the fostering arm of a nation of free people whose greatest power is in justice and humanity to all those living within its fold." Accordingly, he promised them relief from the oppression they had been suffering under the Spanish rule and the full measure of protection and "blessings of the liberal institutions of our government." He added, "it is not our purpose to interfere with any existing laws and customs that are wholesome and beneficial to your people so long as they conform to the rules of military administration, of order and justice." And he ended his proclamation with the ringing declaration that "this is not a war of devastation, but one to give to all within the control of its military and naval forces the advantages and blessings of enlightened civilization" (US House of Representatives Document No. 2 (1900) 56:2:19–20).

The response of the Puerto Rican people to the proclamation, according to American military officials, was extremely positive. In the words of a Puerto Rican physician at a Senate hearing conducted several years later "under these promises the Puerto Ricans rallied under the American flag, abandoned the Spaniards, left them isolated to their own fate, and fought together with the American Army to be delivered and to receive the blessings of enlightened civilization, as General Miles had offered" (US Senate Document No. 147 (1900) 56:1:109).

Within three weeks of the initial landing, American forces, encountering light resistance, occupied one-third of the island, but by then Spain had sued for peace. A peace protocol was accordingly signed between the two countries on August 12, providing for the immediate end to hostile military operations and for the evacuation of all Spanish military forces from the island. Within somewhat more than two months the evacuation was completed under the supervision of a joint evacuation commission. Thus, on October 18 1898, 390 years of Spanish rule ended on the island.

"[On that date] the military control of the whole island of Porto Rico and its adjacent islets and keys passed from Spain to the United States, and the command of the troops, by assignment of the President, devolved upon Major General John R. Brooke, US Army who had also been the president or

chairman of the American evacuation commission, and who, by virtue of such assignment, became the military governor of Porto Rico."
                    (US House of Representatives Document No. 2 (1900) 56:16–17)

Despite America's *de facto* control of the island, the Spanish Crown retained, under international law, nominal sovereignty over it until a treaty of peace was formally ratified by the two countries.

> "During this second period of the military government of Porto Rico, the United States had the status of a belligerent nation, in legal possession and control through hostile occupation, of a colony of Spain. In pursuance of obligations imposed by international law, the United States, having dispossessed and overthrown the former government, was called upon to take every step in its power to reestablish and secure public safety and social order. This obligation is particularly enjoined upon military forces by the laws of war."
>   (US House of Representatives Document No. 2 (1900) 56:2:23)

Accordingly, the military governor came to rely heavily on military commissions and a provost court to mete out justice in crimes perpetrated by or against the American army personnel. He allowed civil affairs to run fairly much as they had run under the Spanish authorities with the obvious provision that loyalties were to shift from Spanish to American authorities. In January 1899 the military authority was ordered by the President to collect customs duties on imports from the United States; these tariffs continued to be levied even after ratification of the treaty.

On December 10 1898 the United States and Spain took a major step toward ending the state of hostilities between them; they signed the Treaty of Paris. Under its terms, Spain was to cede to the United States Puerto Rico, Guam, and the Philippines. Spanish subjects in these territories were permitted to retain their allegiance to the Spanish Crown if they should declare their intention to do so before public authorities within a year of ratification of the treaty; otherwise they would be deemed to have renounced that allegiance "and to have adopted the nationality of the territory in which they reside" (Article IX) (US Statutes at Large 1899 30:1759). The treaty also guaranteed "the free exercise of their religion" to inhabitants of these territories (Article X) and the right to retain their property (Article VIII) (US Statutes at Large 1899 30:1759–760). But perhaps the treaty's most potent provision, which had a far-reaching effect on the political fate of the inhabitants of Puerto Rico, as well as those of the Philippines, was the article that stipulated "the civil rights and political status of the native inhabitants of the territories hereby ceded to the United States shall be determined by the Congress" (Article IX) (US Statutes at Large 1899 30:1759).

With the ratification of the peace treaty by both countries on April 11 1899, the legal status of the United States in Puerto Rico underwent a change. "The Army of the United States in Porto Rico, was no longer a belligerent, for there was no public enemy, and there could no longer be a hostile occupation and control" in this "third period" of military occupation, according to Brigadier General Davis.

> "It was no longer possible to use the military commission as an instrumentality for administering the laws of war when hostilities had ceased absolutely. The laws of the land were thereafter executed by the courts of the country, the personnel of which was appointed by the military governor, who, as chief executive, possessed the power of mitigation or pardon in criminal cases."
>
> (US House of Representatives Document No. 2 (1900) 56:2:23–4)

Other than this change, however, "the responsibility or power" of the military governor was in no way "altered, changed or limited" by higher governmental authority in Washington with the ratification of the treaty.

> "[As a result] during the third period of military government he [the military governor] proceeded to legislate respecting change and substitution of obnoxious codes with the same freedom that had characterized his action during the first and second periods of such government.... [In addition] the commanding general was without instructions to regulate his administration of civil affairs according to any theory of the extension or denial to Porto Rico of the constitutional guarantees."
>
> (US House of Representatives Document No. 2 (1900) 56:2:26)

Under the circumstances the military governor developed his own policy on the matter. In a circular published in the Puerto Rican press in August 1899, he set forth the policy and philosophy of government that he was pursuing. He was, he insisted, seeking to prepare Puerto Rico for the governmental status of a territory.

> "Judging from the past, [this is the form of civil government which] Congress may be expected to enact for Porto Rico. The changes that have already been made, and those now intended, should supply for the island, until otherwise provided by Congress, a form of government resembling, as respects the superior branches, the Territorial form heretofore applied in the United States to those portions of the national domain in transition stage or one preparatory to full statehood and membership in the National Union."
>
> (US House of Representatives Document No. 2 (1900) 56:2:28)

He then delineated the kind of territorial government that might be organized by Congress. He pointed out that some of the statutes in force in Puerto Rico were rooted in the Spanish code of law, in conflict with this territorial model and the American Constituton.

"[Accordingly,] it has been found to be necessary to modify or repeal some of those Statutes, and this has been done by the order of military commander of the island as representing the President of the United States; but the changes have never been made without the fullest consideration, and always on the advice of leading Porto Ricans, irrespective of party.... Every step taken by the commanding general in changing the existing order of things has for its ultimate, and indeed its primary object, the adaptation of the laws and administration to suit the change that may soon come and which all desire: that is complete territorial autonomy."

(US House of Representatives Document No. 2 (1900) 56:2:28)

Throughout his circular, the General seemed to hedge somewhat. Though he fully expected Congress to enact territorial status for Puerto Rico, he nevertheless kept the conditional form in his writing. For example, after listing twelve of the more important orders he had promulgated, he concluded: "The effect of the orders issued and of the changes resulting therefrom tends directly to harmonizing the existing system, and that to come with territorial autonomy, *should it be enacted by Congress* [author's italics]" (US House of Representatives Document No. 2 (1900) 56:2:29).

The President and territorial status for the island

The General's statement of August 1899 appeared to be by December a remarkably perspicacious forecast of what the official United States policy toward governance of Puerto Rico was about to become. For example, in his message to Congress on December 5, President McKinley recommended that Congress enact a temporary governmental structure for Puerto Rico similar to that set for Alaska, which he explicitly identified as having been accorded the legal status of territory since 1884. "The time is ripe for the adoption of a temporary form of government for this island; and many suggestions made with reference to Alaska are applicable also to Puerto Rico" (US Congressional Record 1900 56:35). Both structures, the President proposed, were to be patterned after what Blair has called the first grade of territorial government as originally set down in the Northwest Ordinance in 1787 and later modified to fit the requirements of the Constitution in 1789 (Blair 1903). This meant that both territories were to be governed by officials appointed by the President and confirmed by Congress; neither was to have an elected legislative body, which would presumably be added once they reached the second grade of territorial government as prescribed by the Northwest Ordinance.

In the case of Puerto Rico, the President recommended

"the appointment by the President, subject to confirmation by the Senate, of a governor and such other officers as the general administration of the island may require, and that for legislative purposes upon subjects of a local nature not partaking of a Federal character a legislative council, composed partly of Porto Ricans and partly of citizens of the United States, shall be nominated and appointed by the President, subject to confirmation by the Senate, their acts to be subject to the approval of the Congress or the President to going into effect."

(US Congressional Record 1900 56:1:36)

In making this recommendation, he departed from the pattern in effect since 1800. From that date no territory but Michigan had had to start with the first grade of territorial governance; instead each started with the second grade and after 1854 with a third grade of governance. The latter provided for popular elections to both houses of the legislature and elimination of the veto power of Congress over territorial legislation.

The President justified his failure to recommend an elective legislative body for Puerto Rico or the immediate adoption of the second grade of governance on the grounds that he doubted Puerto Ricans were ready for self-government. He expected them to become ready in a short period of time and thereby qualify for the second grade of governance.

"I have not thought it wise to commit the entire government of the island to officers selected by the people, because I doubt whether in habits, training, and experience they are such as to fit them to exercise at once so large a degree of self-government; but it is my judgment and expectation that they will soon arrive at an attainment of experience and wisdom and self-control that will justify conferring upon them a much larger participation in the choice of their insular officers."

(US Congressional Record 1900 56:1:36)

To expedite the achievement of this level, he proposed the adoption of a system of modern and free education for the island. "Systems of education in these new possessions founded upon common-sense methods, adapted to existing conditions and looking to the future moral and industrial advancement of the people, will commend to them in a peculiarly effective manner the blessings of free government" (US Congressional Record 1900 56:1:36).

In the meantime, he proposed that basic constitutional guarantees be extended to the inhabitants of Puerto Rico.

"The guaranties of life, liberty, and of civil rights should be faithfully upheld; the right of trial by jury respected and defended. The rule of the courts should assure the public of the prompt trial of those charged with criminal offenses, and upon conviction, the punishment should be commensurate with the enormity of the crime." (US Congressional Record 1900 56:1:36)

He also addressed himself to the increasingly depressed state of Puerto Rico's economy, which had become even worse under American tutelage. He attributed the situation in part to the devastation wrought by a hurricane in August 1899, but primarily he blamed the loss of the island's principal markets on the withdrawal of Spanish sovereignty from the island.

"The markets of Spain are closed to her products except upon terms to which the commerce of all nations is subjected. The island of Cuba, which used to buy her cattle and tobacco without customs duties, now imposes the same duties upon these products as from any other country entering her ports. She has therefore lost her free intercourse with Spain and Cuba without any compensating benefits in this market." (US Congressional Record 1900 56:1:36)

Even as Puerto Rico had lost these markets, America continued to impose tariffs on it as though it were still under Spanish sovereignty. This, he insisted, must be remedied. "The markets of the United States should be opened up to her products. Our plain duty is to abolish all customs tariffs between the United States and Puerto Rico and give her products free access to our markets" (US Congressional Record 1900 56:1:36).

In his message the President also dwelt at length on the situation in the Philippines. He complained that rebel Filipino leaders were continuing hostilities against American forces, despite the peace treaty with Spain. He denounced their "sinister ambitions," and he rejected their claim that they had been promised independence for their assistance in the war against Spain. Until they were finally defeated and the islands pacified – at least one already was – they would have to continue under military occupation. At present, "it does not seem desirable that I should recommend at this time a specific and final form of government for these islands. When peace shall be restored it will be the duty of Congress to construct a plan of government which shall establish and maintain freedom and order and peace in the Philippines" (US Congressional Record 1900 56:1:34).

In the meantime, he concluded, the United States should begin a program of reconstruction.

"We should not wait for the end of strife to begin the beneficent work. We shall continue, as we have begun, to open the schools and the churches, to set the courts in operation, to foster industry and trade and agriculture, and in every way in our power to make these people whom Providence has brought within our jurisdiction feel that it is their liberty and not our power, their welfare and not our gain, we are seeking to enhance. Our flag has never waved over any community but in blessing. I believe the Filipinos will soon recognize the fact that it has not lost its gift of benediction in its worldwide journey to their shores."   (US Congressional Record 1900 56:1:35)

The President also addressed himself to the situation in the Hawaiian islands. Since Hawaii's annexation in 1898, many complicated legal issues had not been resolved because Hawaii had as yet no structure of governance. Accordingly, he urged Congress to pass the bill prepared by a commission set up for that purpose which would confer territorial status on the Hawaiian islands and a design for government "under the Federal Constitution." Interestingly, five months later, on April 30, such a law was passed. It provided for a third grade of territorial government and, according to Blair, it was the most democratic of all governance structures for territories established to the date of the publication of his work.

"Not only are most of the officers of the government elected directly by the people, but all of those who are appointed by the president must be citizens of the island. In no other territory of the United States has the power of the president to appoint officers for a territorial government been limited to citizens of the territory."   (Blair 1903:65)

The original Foraker and Payne bills: territorial status for the island

Approximately a month after the President's message, January 9, Foraker of Ohio introduced a bill in the Senate "to provide a government for the island of Puerto Rico and for other purposes'" that was read twice and referred to the Committee on Pacific Islands and Puerto Rico of which he was Chairman (S2264 A Bill 1900 56:1:1). The bill contained many of the recommendations proposed by the President and, though it did not explicitly label the island a territory, its provisions left no doubt that the bill intended to confer such a status on Puerto Rico. For example, all inhabitants except those who elected to retain their allegiance to Spain were to be deemed "citizens of the United States;" and together they were to "constitute a body politic with governmental powers as hereinafter conferred, and with power to sue and be sued in the courts of the United States in the name of the 'Island of Puerto Rico' in all cases which such courts have jurisdiction where one of the parties is a State or Territory of the United States" (Section 3) (S2264 A Bill 1900 56:1:2).

In addition judicial and legal proceedings and processes conducted by this body politic "shall run in the name of 'The United States of America, island of Puerto

Rico,' and all [of its] criminal or penal prosecutions shall be conducted in the name and by the authority of 'The United States of America, island of Puerto Rico'" (Section 13) (S2264 A Bill 1900 56:1:5). The bill also set the American Constitution as the basic legal-normative framework for the island; it as well as "all the laws of the United States locally applicable ... was to have the same force and effect in the island of Puerto Rico as elsewhere in the United States" (Section 10) (S2264 A Bill 1900 56:1:5).

> "The laws and ordinances now in force in the island of Puerto Rico shall continue in full force and effect ... so far as the same are not inconsistent or in conflict with the Constitution and laws of the United States locally applicable, or the provisions hereof, until altered, amended, or repealed by the legislative authority hereinafter provided for the island or by Act of Congress of the United States." (Section 4) (S2264 A Bill 1900 56:1:2)

Further, Section 29 stipulated that legislation enacted by the legislative assembly of the island of Puerto Rico, United States of America should not "be inconsistent with the Constitution of the United States" (S2264 A Bill 1900 56:1:13).

The bill also established a set of general policies on revenues and taxation that conformed closely to the President's recommendations. For example, Section 8 eliminated any tariffs on merchandise flowing between the island and the United States as the President requested. However, a tariff rate structure consistent with that used by the United States was to be levied against all imports from other countries (Section 6). And finally,

> "all the internal-revenue taxes imposed under the provisions of the Revised Statutes elsewhere in the United States in so far as the same are locally applicable, and all the provisions of the laws of the United States providing for internal-revenue taxation and the collection thereof not locally inapplicable shall be and remain in force within the island of Puerto Rico until otherwise provided by Congress." (Section 7) (S2264 A Bill 1900 56:1:4)

The bill did depart markedly from the President's recommendation with respect to the governance structure it proposed. It scrapped his suggestion for a first-grade territorial government as described in the Northwest Ordinance in favor of a second-grade structure. Thus, the government was not merely to consist of presidential appointees, but also of a popularly elected house of delegates. At the peak of the governmental structure was to be a governor who was to be appointed for a four-year term by the President, with the advice and consent of the Senate. He was to have "all the powers of governors of the Territories of the United States that are locally applicable" (Section 14) (S2264 A Bill 1900 56:1:6).

In addition, a number of other officials were also to be appointed by the President with the advice and consent of the Senate for a period of four years.

"[These were to include] a secretary, an attorney-general, a treasurer, an auditor, a commissioner of the interior, and a commissioner of education, each of whom shall reside in the island during his official incumbency and have the powers and duties hereinafter provided for them, respectively, and who, together with the governor and five other persons of good repute, to be also appointed by the President, by and with the advice and consent of the Senate, from the native inhabitants of the island, shall constitute an executive council."

(Section 15) (S2264 A Bill 1900 56:1:7)

In addition to the administrative responsibilities held by various members of the council, the council as a whole was to serve as one of the two houses of the local legislative authority. The other, the House of Delegates, was "to consist of thirty-five members elected biennially by the qualified voters of the island, as hereinafter provided; and the two houses thus constituted shall be designated 'the legislative assembly of the island of Puerto Rico, United States of America'" (Section 24) (S2264 A Bill 1900 56:1:9–10).

The bill set forth the legislative process and the qualifications of prospective candidates for the House of Delegates. It also stipulated suffrage for all citizens of the island "who possess the qualifications of voters under the laws and military orders now in force in the island, subject to such regulations and restrictions as to registration and otherwise as may be now provided, or as may be prescribed by the executive council" (Section 26) (S2264 A Bill 1900 56:1:10–11).

In addition, the bill reaffirmed another feature of the second-grade territorial governmental structure; namely, the biennial election by qualified voters of the island of "one Delegate to the House of Representatives of the United States, who shall be entitled to a seat, but not to a vote, in that body, on the certificate of election of the governor of the island" (Section 36) (S2264 A Bill 1900 56:1:18). And finally the bill also elaborated a judiciary system for the island that also conformed to the territorial model.

Ten days after the Foraker bill was presented to the Senate, Payne introduced a bill in the House of Representatives "to extend the laws relating to customs and internal revenue over the island of Puerto Rico ceded to the United States" (HR6883 A Bill 1900 56:1:1). It was referred to the Committee on Ways and Means, of which he was chairman. The bill elaborated even further the close territorial link between the island and the United States that had already been set by the Foraker bill. For example, the island was to constitute a single customs collection district with San Juan as the port of entry and six other locations as sub-ports of entry (Section 2). In addition the President was "authorized to establish an internal-revenue collection district to embrace all the said islands, or in his discretion to annex said islands to some other internal-revenue collection district of the United States" (Section 3) (HR6883 A Bill 1900 56:1:2).

The revised bills: a "novel" legal status for Puerto Rico

After several weeks of committee hearings, each bill was reported back to its respective house early in February 1900. By then neither bore much resemblance to the bill that had originally been introduced into it. The House bill, for example, had been so completely revamped that even its number was changed from HR6883 to HR8245. And though the Senate bill retained its number (S2264), it was so substantially amended that the legal status of Puerto Rico vis-à-vis the United States had become completely transformed. (Even its name was changed from Puerto Rico to Porto Rico.) No longer was the island to be considered a territory incorporated into the United States as set forth in the original version but a new kind of legal entity unique in American history. The Committee on Pacific Islands and Puerto Rico added a few more elements defining the "novel" status of the island and its inhabitants during the next month and a half. By the March 31 version of the revised bill,* all the elements that are discussed in this section were in place. All were subsequently enacted into law; the section numbers, however, were changed. Approximately a year later the Supreme Court invented a new legal category for this uniqueness.

The transformation is clearly evident in the critical changes made between the two versions of the Senate bill. For example, all inhabitants, excluding those who elected to retain allegiance to Spain, were no longer to be identified as "citizens of the United States" (Section 3) (S2264 A Bill 1900 56:1:2) but were to be labeled instead as "citizens of Porto Rico, and as such entitled to the protection of the United States". Even their children were to be citizens of Puerto Rico and not of the United States, despite the Fourteenth Amendment. And as "citizens of Porto Rico" the inhabitants were to "constitute a body politic under the name of The People of Porto Rico, with governmental powers as hereinafter conferred, and

---

* By this date however, S2264 A Bill had in fact become HR8245 An Act. For, on March 1 Senator Foraker had reported to the Senate that the Committee on Pacific Islands and Puerto Rico decided to insert its revised version of S2264 as a substitute for HR8245 which had just been favorably acted upon by the House of Representatives. As a member of the committee stated, "We simply struck out the entire House bill and agreed to report what we have already heretofore considered and reported (namely the revised S2264)" (US Congressional Record 1900 56:1:2438). Accordingly, the source for the quotations from the revised version of the Senate bill in this section will be HR8245 An Act, March 31 1900.

with power to sue and be sued as such" (Section 6) (HR8245 An Act 1900 56:1:7). They were not to constitute a body politic of American citizens which could "sue and be sued in the courts of the United States in the name of the 'Island of Puerto Rico' in all cases in which courts have jurisdiction where one of the parties is a State or Territory of the United States" (Section 3) (S2264 A Bill 1900 56:1:2). In the same way, all judicial and legal processes and procedures were no longer to be run or conducted under the rubric "The United States of America, island of Puerto Rico," as in the original version. In the revised version "all judicial process shall run in the name of 'United States of America, ss: the President of the United States,' and all criminal or penal prosecutions in the local courts shall be conducted in the name and by the authority of 'The people of Porto Rico'" (Section 14) (HR8245 An Act 1900 56:1:11).

The revised version also deleted all references to the American Constitution as the basic legal-normative framework for the islands. It cast no protective mantle around the rights and immunities of the people of Puerto Rico nor served as a standard by which the legitimacy of local laws could be assessed. The only standard that was to be applied was the "statutory laws of the United States not locally inapplicable" (Section 12) (HR8245 An Act 1900 56:1:10). The only place the word Constitution was retained was in the section specifying the conditions under which writs of error or appeals from court decisions in Puerto Rico might be taken to the United States Supreme Court. Thus expunged from virtually all provisions that had contained it in the original version, the Constitution was mentioned in a completely new stipulation contained in the revised version: "all officials authorized by this Act shall before entering upon the duties of their respective offices take an oath to support the Constitution of the Untied States and the laws of Porto Rico" (Section 14) (HR8245 An Act 1900 56:1:11).

Just as the revised bill completely altered the legal status of Puerto Rico, so did it do an about-face on the revenue and taxation provisions of the original bill. At the very hub of this change was the abandonment of free trade between Puerto Rico and the United States for a system of tariffs and duties on articles imported into one from the other. (This will be dealt with in detail when we examine the revised House bill which more fully explicates the change.)

Finally, despite the change in the legal status of the island, the revised bill retained virtually intact most of the governance features of the original bill. In effect, Puerto Rico was to be governed by a territorial governmental structure of the second grade, even though it had been stripped of the legal status of being a territory. To add to the anomalous situation, the revised bill retained the phraseology that the governor of Puerto Rico was to have "all the powers of governors of the Territories of the United States" (Section 15) (HR8245 An Act 1900 56:1:12). The attorney general, to "have all the powers and discharge all the duties provided by law for an attorney-general of a Territory of the United States"* (Section 19) (HR8245 An Act 1900 56:1:14) and "writs of error and appeals from the final decisions of the supreme court of Porto Rico and the district court of the United States shall be allowed and may be taken to the Supreme Court of the United States in the same manner and under the same regulations and in the same cases as from the supreme courts of the Territories of the United States" (Section 33) (HR8245 An Act 1900 56:1:22 – 3). In still other respects, the revised version conformed even more closely to the second-grade territorial structure than the original version by explicitly adding the provision "that all laws enacted by the legislative assembly shall be reported to the Congress of the United States, which hereby reserves the power and authority, if deemed advisable, to annul the same" (Section 29) (HR8245 An Act 1900 56:1:19).

However, the symbolic references indicating the territorial status of Puerto Rico in the original version were strikingly altered. Thus the two houses of the legislature no longer constituted "'the legislative assembly of the island of Puerto Rico, United States of America'" (Section 24) (S2264 A Bill 1900 56:1:10). Instead they became "'The legislative assembly of Porto Rico'" (Section 25) (HR8245 An Act 1900 56:1:16). And the enacting clause of laws was no longer going to read "'Be it enacted by the legislative assembly of the island of Puerto Rico, United States of America'" (Section 26) (S2264 A Bill 1900 56:1:11). Instead it would be phrased "'Be it enacted by the legislative assembly of Porto Rico'" (Section 27) (HR8245 An Act 1900 56:1:17).

But beyond these largely symbolic modifications, the bill as finally enacted deprived Puerto Rico of a major right granted to territorial governments of the second grade: the right to elect "one Delegate to the House of Representatives of the United States, who shall be entitled to a seat, but not to a vote in that body" (Section 36) (S2264 A Bill 1900 56:1:18). Instead it was granted the right to elect "a resident commissioner to the United States, who shall be entitled to official recognition as such by all Departments, upon presentation to the Department of State of a certificate of election of the governor of Porto Rico, and who shall be entitled to a salary, payable monthly by the United States, at the rate of five thousand dollars per annum" (Section 37) (HR8245 An Act 1900 56:1:26).

Unlike the Senate bill, the revamped House bill contained none of the features of its original version. For example, Puerto Rico was no longer to be part of the system of customs and taxation that tied the United States and its territories together. It was to function instead outside of this system. As such, it was to receive none of the general benefits of the free flow of goods between states and territories. It would be obliged to pay tariffs on duties on all merchandise shipped

*As finally enacted, the law substituted *attorney* for *attorney-general*.

to the United States and its territories, just as the United States would have to pay duties on all goods shipped to Puerto Rico. These tariffs were to be assessed at only 25 percent (later lowered to 15 percent) of the duties ordinarily levied on the articles, but they would nevertheless have to be no lower than the rate and amount of the internal revenue tax imposed upon the same articles of merchandise being manufactured domestically in either country.

In addition, Puerto Rico was obliged to impose the same tariffs, customs, and duties upon all articles of import that came "from ports other than those of the United States which are required by law to be collected upon articles imported into the United States from foreign countries" (Section 2). And finally,

"the customs duties collected in Puerto Rico in pursuance of this Act, less the cost of collecting the same, and the gross amount of all collections of customs in the United States upon articles of merchandise coming from Puerto Rico shall not be covered into the general fund of the Treasury, but shall be held as a separate fund, and shall be placed at the disposal of the President, to be used for the government and benefit of Puerto Rico until otherwise provided by law."

(Section 4)* (US House of Representatives Report No. 249 (1900) 56:1:16)

The committee reports and justification of the transformation

In seeking to justify what they had done, both committees pointed in their reports to their respective houses (US House of Representatives Report No. 249 (1900) 56:1; US Senate Report No. 249 (1900) 56:1) to the decision to forego free trade in favor of tariffs as the key to the profound changes. They insisted that this was done with the welfare of Puerto Rico in mind. In fact the Senate committee gave the impression in its report that this was the only consideration that influenced its decision. The House committee was much more circumspect in its claims; it said that the welfare of Puerto Rico was only "one of the reasons."

According to both, their hearings and other testimony demonstrated how truly devastated the economy of the island was and how extensive were the financial requirements of the island to build schools, roads, bridges, buildings, and the like and to perform necessary government functions and services.

Given this testimony, both committees then determined that funds obtained from the internal revenue tax provisions of the original bill would not have been adequate for these needs.

*In the March 31 version of HR8245, Puerto Rico had been changed to Porto Rico. Another change was the substitution of *duties and taxes* for *customs*.

"With all these facts and considerations in mind, the [revised] bill has been framed with a view to establishing a defined local government with sufficient revenues to defray all ordinary expenses and to inaugurate a system of education, undertaking needed public improvements, providing safeguards for necessary franchises, the substitution of American for Porto Rican coins, and to bring about a restoration of prosperity by opening markets on conditions that will stimulate production and bring quick and satisfactory results."

(US Senate Report No. 249 (1900) 56:1:3)

And so the decision to rely on import duties was made. To show that they were sincere in their efforts to help Puerto Rico, both committees supported the provision that all customs duties collected in Puerto Rico from the United States and in the United States from Puerto Rico would be placed into a separate fund for use by the President "for the government and benefit of Puerto Rico." The House Committee in particular felt that this was the least Congress could do.

"We are compelling the Puerto Ricans to pay this sum to get into our market, a discrimination which we make against no other portion of the territory belonging to the United States where the inhabitants are not in a state of insurrection. We think it but just, therefore, that they should have the benefit of this revenue for the purposes, among other things, of planting an American schoolhouse in every community on the island."

(US House of Representatives Report No. 249 (1900) 56:1:6)

Despite this mild expression of guilt, the House had nevertheless become so entangled in the convoluted logic of its newly articulated position and benevolence that it even put forth the claim that the tariffs would benefit the agricultural sector of Puerto Rico – a factor of overriding importance since "the most urgent demand from Puerto Rico is that a market be provided for its surplus crops [coffee, sugar and tobacco]" (US House of Representatives Report No. 249 (1900) 56:1:2). According to the committee, markets for these products in the United States were bound to expand because the tariff rates would be lower on sugar and tobacco than those imposed on similar products from other countries. As a result, the committee boasted "that under this substitute [bill] the great bulk of it [the three products] will find a market in the United States" (US House of Representatives Report No. 249 (1900) 56:1:4).

As we have already seen, the Senate committee sought to convey the impression that the internal well-being of Puerto Rico was its major, if not sole, consideration in adopting tariffs. However, even it had to admit that during the hearings the committee was put under intense pressure to eliminate free trade by the domestic producers of the kinds of major crops raised in Puerto Rico, sugar and tobacco and coffee already being on the duty-free list. Their major objections to free trade were threefold:

> "1 It was in violation of the policy of protection.
> 2 It was inimical to the interests of the United States with which Puerto Rican products would come in competition.
> 3 It would be a precedent that would have to be followed in other cases [such as the Philippines] that might hereafter arise where the competition resulting might be still more injurious to American interests."
>
> (US Senate Report No. 249 (1900) 56:1:6–7)

In reporting these objections, the committee sought to rebut each one and ended with the declaration that it had disregarded the objections in making its decision. Yet despite these efforts to play down the influence of the pressure from domestic interests, debate must have been very heavy within the Senate committee. Two members felt strongly enough to submit a minority report, even though the committee's decision on tariffs was in the direction domestic interests favored. The two members complained that the committee had not gone far enough: its tariff rates were too low. They expressed the fear that Puerto Rico and later the Philippines, if the same rates were to apply to them, would have a competitive advantage in the domestic markets of the United States.

The House committee was more forthright than the Senate committee in acknowledging the influence that domestic interests had on its deliberations. It conceded that the interests of domestic manufacturers of cigars and spirits had been taken into account in the clause stipulating that tariffs on Puerto Rican goods to America had at least to equal the internal revenue tax imposed on domestic manufactures. "The last provision is necessary in order that our manufacturers of cigars and spirits may be at no disadvantage on account of the low tariff between Puerto Rico and the United States, on account of our internal revenue laws" (US House of Representatives Report No. 249 (1900) 56:1:1–2).

The committee also took notice of the fears expressed by a representative of the beet-sugar industry that the no-duty provision on sugar of the original bill "might be regarded as a precedent for free sugar from the Philippine Islands, and eventually from Cuba." The committee's report sought to calm his fears by saying that even the substitute bill with its tariff provision "establishes no precedent." And it went on to declare that "surely the [political] party which had the courage to provide adequate protection in 1897 for this new industry can be safely trusted to foster it, now it has passed beyond the stage of experiment and is an assured success" (US House of Representatives Report No. 249 (1900) 56:1:3).

Though the House committee's majority report took greater cognizance than did the Senate committee's report of the pressure of domestic interests for tariffs against Puerto Rican products, it nevertheless still sought to play down the influence of this pressure on the committee's decision to favor tariffs. Not so however the six minority members of the committee, five of whom were Democrats (only one Democrat signed the majority report) and the other the sole member of the Silver Party. In a special report they expressed dismay and mystification at the sudden reversal of policy from free trade to tariffs:

> "We do not know why these sudden changes have occurred. We cannot believe that the President has been converted from the opinion he so lately expressed, or that he now admits the unwisdom of the solemn advice he so recently gave to Congress. We are not advised that his opinion was hastily formed and that he had not maturely considered the subject upon which he was advising us."
> (US House of Representatives Report No. 249 (1900) 56:1:19–20)

Instead they placed the blame at the doorstep of special interests and on the Republican party's responsiveness to these interests. As such they protested "earnestly against the adoption of a robber policy."

> "We do not believe the people of this land, ardently attached as they are to our free institutions, can be brought to favor a policy which oppresses the inhabitants of territory owned by the United States anywhere, and over which the flag of the Republic floats, even if such a policy should serve in a degree to enrich some citizens of the Union. We protest earnestly against the adoption of a robber policy which makes this Republic take the place of the ruthless monarchy, Spain, in despoiling Puerto Rico, now a portion of the United States." (US House of Representatives Report No. 249 (1900) 56:1:20)

In this manner the first utterance was sounded of what was to become the rallying cry of those who opposed the tariff provisions of the revised bill, not only in the House but in the Senate as well.

Once the two committees had decided on a tariff policy for Puerto Rico, they had to come to terms with a provision of the Constitution that forbade any such duty on the goods that flowed between parts of the United States. Thus Article 1 Section 8 of the Constitution stipulates: "All duties, imposts and excises shall be uniform throughout the United States."

So important did each committee deem this issue to be that they devoted almost two-thirds of their respective reports to arguing that Congress had the authority to levy the duties the committees recommended despite the clause in the Constitution. For example, both committees agreed that the Constitution was operative and was the supreme law of the land among the various states of the United States: "The limitations of the Constitution are upon the Federal corporation called the United States, and are upon the States, respectively, that constitute that nation" (US House of Representatives Report No. 249 (1900) 56:1:6); "the term 'United States,' as used in the Constitution, has reference only to the States that constitute the Federal Union and does not include Territories" (US House of Representatives Report No. 249 (1900) 56:1:16).

But the committees insisted that the Constitution was not extended *ex proprio vigore* with the mere acquisition of new land or with the mere granting of territorial status to such land unless Congress declared it to be so extended. For, in the capitalized words of the Senate report, "THE ORGANIZATION AND GOVERNMENT OF TERRITORIES IS NOT A CONSTITUTIONAL RIGHT, BUT SOLELY A QUESTION OF EXPEDIENCY WITHIN THE DISCRETION OF CONGRESS" (US Senate Report No. 249 (1900) 56:1:10).

> "It is clear that Territories are not created, organized, or supervised under the Constitution as a constitutional right, but that they are on the contrary created, organized and supervised by Congress by virtue of both inherent and constitutional power with which Congress, as the political department of the Government, is vested, to rule and regulate the Territories of the United States; and the rights, power, privileges, and immunities granted to the inhabitants of the Territories, whatever they may be, are all given by Congress and do not flow from the Constitution beyond what Congress may declare. In other words, the provisions of the Constitution do not operate beyond the States, unless Congress shall so enact.... There is no guaranty in the Constitution that a Territory shall even have a republican form of government or that the civil and political status of the inhabitants of a Territory shall be of any particular character."   (US Senate Report No. 249 (1900) 56:1:10–11)

The first time Congress extended the Constitution to a territory, the report declared, was with the formation of a territorial government for New Mexico in 1850. Since then it had done so fairly regularly although Congress still retained "the constitutional power ... to either extend or withhold the Constitution in all such cases, as may deem advisable" (US Senate Report No. 249 (1900) 56:1:6).

Even if Congress decided not to extend the Constitution to a territory, the Senate committee insisted, its legislative power over the territory was neither unlimited nor absolute, for it must abide by constraints imposed by the Constitution on what Congress may legislate generally.

> "They [these constraints] operate for the benefit of all for whom Congress may legislate, no matter where they may be situated, and without regard to whether or not the provisions of the Constitution have been extended to them; but this is so because the Congress, in all that it does, is subject to and governed by those

restraints and prohibitions.... [For example,] Congress shall make no law respecting an establishment of religion, or prohibiting the free exercise thereof; no title of nobility shall be granted; no bill of attainder or ex post facto law shall be passed; neither shall the validity of contracts be impaired, nor shall property be taken without due process of law; nor shall the freedom of speech or of the press be abridged; nor shall slavery exist in any place subject to the jurisdiction of the United States." (US Senate Report No. 249 (1900) 56:1:11)

But the matter of uniform imposts was not deemed one of the legislative enactments prohibited by the Constitution.

The House committee seemed to view the power of Congress over territories as much more absolute and unlimited than did the Senate committee: "The power of Congress with respect to legislation for the Territories is plenary" (US House of Representatives Report No. 249 (1900) 56:1:16). But it acknowledged that congressional legislation did have to abide by certain constitutional restraints. The only such example it offered was "the thirteenth amendment to the Constitution, which prohibits the existence of slavery in any place over which the United States has jurisdiction" (US House of Representatives Report No. 249 (1900) 56:1:10).

Both committees agreed that another restraint limiting the legislative power of Congress over territories was the agreed-upon terms of a treaty. The House report declared:

"In all of the [earlier] treaties, save that relating to Alaska, provision has been made that the territory acquired should be incorporated into the Union as soon as possible, and that in the meantime the civil rights of its inhabitants should be guaranteed. In the treaty with Russia whereby Alaska was acquired no provision was made for the incorporation of the Territory into the Union, but provision was made that the inhabitants should have the immunities of citizens of the United States and protection in the enjoyment of their liberty, property, and religion. Had not these terms been made in the treaties, the territory acquired would have become subject to the legislation of Congress under its power to make all needful rules and regulations respecting it, which is without limitation." (US House of Representatives Report No. 249 (1900) 56:1:10)

As the Senate report pointed out, no such limitation was to be found in the Treaty of Paris. In fact the treaty explicitly provided for Congress to determine the civil rights and political status of the inhabitants of Puerto Rico and the other ceded territories. The report emphasized, "No such clause as this [one in the Treaty of Paris] has ever before been found in any treaty ceding territory to the United States. Its effect is, therefore, to be considered now for the first time. There is no ambiguity about it; neither can there be any controversy as to its effect" (US Senate Report No. 249 (1900) 56:1:12).

Despite their confidence that neither of the above two restraints applied to their recommended action on Puerto Rico, the two committees apparently were worried that a third type of restraint might rise to plague them. For, "while [the] power of Congress to legislate for newly acquired territory does not flow from, and is not controlled by, the Constitution as an organic law of the Territory, except when Congress so enacts" (US Senate Report No. 249 (1900) 56:1:11), the committees were worried that once Congress explicitly extended any kind of constitutional protection to the territory, it would be obliged to extend the entire protective umbrella of the Constitution. Congress would then lose the right to levy tariffs on products of the territory, given the constitutional requirement of uniform imposts. To avoid this hazard, both committees decided to delete in their revised bills all references to the Constitution as the legal-normative framework for the laws of Puerto Rico.

The minority members of the House committee took strong exception to the statement that Congress had the plenary power over territories that the majority claimed. In their report, they claimed that the Constitution was meant to apply to all of the United States which, in opinions delivered by Chief Justices Marshall and Taney, included both states and territories. To hold otherwise as the majority did, the minority report continued, was to give Congress such arbitrary and absolute power as had "never before [been] claimed in our land."

> "It is wholly inconsistent with the theory and form of our Government. The exercise of such power is pure and simple imperialism, and against it we enter our most solemn protest. We never have held and can not hold territory as a political dependency and subject to unequal taxation. No Congressional enactment nor treaty stipulation can make such provision. Our Union is one of the States with a common interest and a common destiny. The blessings of free government rest alike upon all of our people, whether in the thirteen original States or in the youngest member of the Union, or in the newest acquired territory. It does not matter in which form territory is acquired, it is to be held under our Constitution with the object of finally being admitted into the Union as a State."   (US House of Representatives Report No. 249 (1900) 56:1:18)

Though concurring with the minority report, Newlands of Nevada submitted a separate opinion in which he offered a more detailed exposition of the view "that the prohibitions and limitations of the Constitution apply to the powers of Congress in all legislation, and that the Constitution, ex proprio vigore, applies to all territory belonging to the United States" (US House of Representatives Report No. 249 (1900) 56:1:20). In his statement he argued that "the entire history of the framing of the Constitution indicates that the purpose of its makers was to organize a union of States; to permit the admission of new States, and to permit the acquisition of territory for the purpose of organizing new States, and that over the entire country, both the States and the infant States, the Constitution was to be the organic law, the charter of their liberties governing and controlling the action of the Federal Government."

(US House of Representatives Report No. 249 (1900) 56:1:22)

Newlands relied heavily on the Dred Scott decision to bolster his contention that "Territories" were "infant States." He concluded with the categorical statement that "the weight of authorities sustain the proposition that the Constitution, *ex propio vigore*, controls the action of the Government created by the Constitution wherever it operates, whether in States or Territories" (US House of Representatives Report No. 249 (1900) 56:1:29).

But perhaps the most compelling indictment of the revised bill came from the one Republican who opposed the revised bill but who had refused to join the Democrats in their minority report. In a separate statement he warned of the "disaster to a free people of throwing aside their free institutions" by not applying the Constitution to the newly acquired island "in order to exercise despotic power."

"I recognize our full duty to do our utmost to secure the welfare and happiness of the people of our new possessions. But I regard it as a most inauspicious omen that our first legislative act should be framed on the theory that freedom does not follow the flag, but that the latter goes to those islands unattended by the great principles of liberty which have made it glorious. Who can measure the evils that will result from a denial of the fundamental muniments against oppression with which our Constitution surrounds the individual? If even in this country, and with all these safeguards, the citizen is not always secure against official exaction or the rapacity of those who are more powerful than he, what can be expected without this protection in islands that are separated from us by 10,000 miles of sea. Is it not clear that at the outset there is danger that we may pave the way for a more hideous extortion and robbery than ever disgraced India?"

(US House of Representatives Report No. 249 (1900) 56:1:31–2)

Articulated as was the rationale of the two committees for bypassing the Constitution once they decided to impose tariffs on trade between Puerto Rico and the United States, it is not very clear why they also felt obliged to withdraw the legal status of territory from their revised bills. One reason can be inferred from the Senate committee's reply to a charge made by various lobbyists that free trade between the United States and Puerto Rico would be "in violation of the policy of protection."

> "They [the committee members] do not think, for instance, that there is in the [free trade] proposition any departure from the policy of protection, because that policy has always been maintained only as between the United States and the rest of the world, while within our own jurisdiction, among all our States and Territories, there has always been free trade. Now that Porto Rico has become a possession of the United States, it would be an application of the same policy to establish free trade between the two countries. It would be but treating this territory as no longer foreign, but American."
>
> (US Senate Report No. 249 (1900) 56:1:7)

Thus, in reassuring the lobbyists that the policy of protection remained intact between the United States and the rest of the world, the committee also reaffirmed as traditional and universal the policy of free trade between states and territories. As a result, in the name of historic continuity and consistency, the committee would have had to extend the same policy to Puerto Rico if the island were granted territorial status. To avoid this historic obligation so that tariffs could be imposed, the committee chose to deny in its revised bill the status it gave the island in its original bill.

Almost as an afterthought, the Senate committee offered still another reason for denying territorial status to the island and its inhabitants. It stated in its report that Puerto Ricans, an "illiterate" population "of [a] wholly different character" and history, were "unacquainted" with the self-governing traditions of the People's Domain and were therefore "incapable of exercising the rights and privileges guaranteed by the Constitution."

> "If we should acquire territory populated by an intelligent, capable and law-abiding people, to whom the right of self-government could be safely conceded, we might at once, with propriety and certainly within the scope of our constitutional power, incorporate that territory and people into the Union as an integral part of our territory, and, by making them a State as a constituent part of the United States, and extend to them at once the Constitution of the United States; but if the territory should be inhabited by people of wholly different character, illiterate, and unacquainted with our institutions, and incapable of exercising the rights and privileges guaranteed by the Constitution to the States of the Union, it would be competent for Congress to withhold from such people the operation of the Constitution and the laws of the United States, and, continuing to hold the territory as a mere possession of the United

States, so govern the people thereof as their situation and the necessities of their case might seem to require." (US Senate Report No. 249 (1900) 56:1:8–9)

In view of this statement, it would seem reasonable to assume that the Senate committee had rethought in its revised bill not only the territorial status of Puerto Rico but also its structure of governance, and accordingly made the island even more subject to direct rule by the United States. However, this was not the case, for the revised bill retained virtually intact the second-grade structure of territorial government, thereby creating an anomalous situation. According to the committee, Puerto Rico was not qualified enough to be granted territorial status; yet qualified enough to be granted significant self-governing provisions of that status.

No effort was made by either Senate or House committee to explain this apparent paradox, but behind it, as perhaps a hidden item on the agenda, lay a pulling back on the part of both committees from allowing a people so culturally and racially different from the white American to become an incorporated part of the United States first as a territory and then as a state.* Obviously, none of the Democrats on the House committee made this an issue in their minority report. They were certainly not going to oppose the majority position on the grounds that it was culturally and racially discriminating against the people of Puerto Rico. Four of the five Democrats were from the South and obviously in favor of the Jim Crowism burgeoning in their region against the black. They did lament, though, the breaking of a promise to the people of Puerto Rico of self-government.

"In passing this [revised] bill Congress is setting out to act in bad faith toward the people of Puerto Rico. Why was it the people of that island so gladly welcomed General Miles and the armies of the United States in July, 1898, when they invaded their territory and struck down the power of Spain? Was it not because they believed that as the shackles of Spain were stricken from them they were to be admitted to the immunities and blessings of our liberal institutions as well as our enlightened civilization? We were told our soldiers were hailed as redeemers." (US House of Representatives Report No. 249 (1900) 56:1:19)

Congressional debate: A colonial dependency?

The chairman of the House committee, Payne, reported his revised bill back to the House on February 8. On February 19 debate began and for the next nine days

---

*As we shall see later, Justice Brown made quite manifest this hidden item on the agenda and gave it great prominence in his opinion for the Supreme Court in the Insular Cases, which upheld the Foraker Act and the constitutional right of Congress to make Puerto Rico "a territory appurtenant and belonging to the United States, but not a part of the United States" (182 US 1901:287).

waxed heavy almost entirely along party lines. The chairman led the Republicans and vigorously pursued the line that tariffs would benefit Puerto Rico whereas the internal revenue provisions of his original bill would have ruined the island's industries and would have been a failure as a revenue raiser.

> "Mr Chairman, the taxation would simply have destroyed these [island] industries and would have not have given us any appreciable revenue, no money for schools, no money for highways, no money for anything except the hard, stern realities of governing those people. So as a revenue raiser the bill which I first introduced was a failure."   (US Congressional Record 1900 56:1:1942)

Further, the revenue plan as originally introduced would have only benefited the planter and the merchant of sugar and tobacco. Little would have filtered down to the laborers and even with the reduced tariffs the same classes would benefit. Under these circumstances, "would it not be fair that these people who get the greatest benefits should pay the expenses of the government?" (US Congressional Record 1900 56:1:1943). The burden of an internal revenue taxation plan, he concluded, would have to be borne by the laboring classes.

The Democrats *en masse* ridiculed Payne's argument that the tariffs were merely for the welfare of Puerto Rico. They insisted that they were primarily introduced to protect the interests of the beet-sugar, tobacco, and other trusts and industries in the United States, both at home and abroad, and were therefore, in the words of a congressman from Tennessee, "the baldest form of imperialism." As such, he continued, "the opposition to this bill plants itself upon this ground. The measure is imperialism itself" (US Congressional Record 1900 56:1:1947). Later in the debate he developed his views.

> "The policy we are asked to pursue here will without doubt further impoverish the island. It may serve to enrich some of the corporations and syndicates, and perhaps a few individuals, but I do not believe it will benefit our people as a whole.... The policy proposed is a robber policy, and will inevitably lead to a hatred of this country by the people of Puerto Rico as bitter and unrelenting as they ever could possibly have entertained toward the monarchy from which they have been wrested by us."   (US Congressional Record 1900 56:1:1952)

The Republicans became increasingly defensive at this line of attack and in the main sought to ignore it, but Payne of Ohio conceded early in the debate that he and his fellow Republicans were indeed protectors of domestic industries: "the beet-sugar industry has been something of a pet of mine since I have been in Congress." He also admitted that "if they [beet-sugar factories] get incidental protection against the future out of this bill, I am glad of it" (US Congressional Record 1900 56:1:1944).

Payne also saw the tariff provisions as a warning to Cuba, the Philippines, and other countries "that we propose to protect this industry when it comes to the question of admitting the 1,000,000 tons that will come from Cuba. So I was glad to bring in this substitute, this new bill, that we might assert this principle, that we might give them incidental protection against a threatening future." He admitted he had added a provision to the revised bill to protect domestic cigar-makers, and that he had added a relatively high duty on rice which, he said to his Democratic opponent from Georgia, would "benefit your Georgia planters in raising rice. We did not have to do it. We did not get a vote from your side by reason of doing it. But out of our national spirit we put it on and forced you to take this tariff" (US Congressional Record 1900 56:1:1944).

Even as the question of who would benefit by the tariffs was being debated, another threaded its way through the discussion until it became the focus of the debate. Did Congress have the authority to levy tariffs in view of the uniformity requirements of the Constitution? Almost all of the Republicans answered in the affirmative. Their argument followed the line already set down by the majority report. They insisted that Congress had plenary power to rule newly acquired territories and to set up governance structures for them. As a result, it could do anything it wanted except for certain constitutional constraints that limited its authority to act generally on certain matters.

Almost all the Democrats disagreed: their line of argument generally followed that of the minority report. They insisted, for example, that the Constitution followed the flag *ex proprio vigore* into any newly acquired land and that therefore congressional action even in such lands must be in accord with constitutional dictates. In the words of the congressman from Tennessee:

> "It is monstrous to suppose that Congress is not restrained by the Constitution from passing laws imposing customs duties on the minerals and ores of the Territories of Arizona and New Mexico, the furs and fish of Alaska, the lumber of Oklahoma, and of all products of these Territories when imported into any of the States of the Union, and also upon all importations of products of every kind into the Territories from the States, or any of them. If the action it is proposed to take by this bill in respect to Puerto Rico can be taken, it must inevitably follow that Congress can pass laws imposing customs duties affecting all the Territories as indicated above."
>
> (US Congressional Record 1900 56:1:1949)

Each side spent hours citing judicial, statutory, and common law precedents for their arguments. On the one side, Republicans relied heavily (as did the majority report) on what Chief Justice Marshall had said in cases dealing with the territorial status of Florida and Louisiana. On the other side, Democrats opted (as did the minority report) for what Chief Justice Taney had said in the Dred Scott Case of 1857 in declaring the Missouri Compromise unconstitutional, thereby opening up the territory for slavery under the Constitution (see Appendix B).

Once the constitutionality of the House bill became a focal concern, debate was no longer confined to the issue of tariffs – which was actually the sole concern of the House bill. Instead it soon addressed itself to the question of governance. Democrats, apparently aware of the revised Foraker bill in the Senate, insisted that the Constitution required that Puerto Rico be accorded territorial status. What the Republicans were proposing, they argued, was to make Puerto Rico into a colonial dependency of the United States.

> "Does it [the Republican majority] propose to revive in the government of Puerto Rico the long-exploded eighteenth-century colonial system? Does it mean to say that, having acquired Puerto Rico in the interest of humanity and in the cause of liberty, we shall govern it in the interest of beet sugar and in the cause of Connecticut fillers?" (US Congressional Record 1900 56:1:2067).

A congressman from Virginia was even more forceful in his condemnation of the bill, "one of the most dangerous bills that we have ever been offered in Congress since the formation of our government."

> "It will end the history of the Republic and open the history of the empire. It dethrones the Goddess of liberty and elevates the demon of power. It destroys constitutional government and creates a Congressional despotism. It is but the forerunner of countless other bills to follow in order to inaugurate the new imperialistic regime. It is antagonistic to all the traditions of our country, to all the principles of our Government, and will, I believe, be the commencement of much disgrace and much disaster (Applause)."
>
> (US Congressional Record 1900 56:1:2011)

Thus the terms colony, colonial dependency, imperial government, empire, and despotism were used by Democrats to characterize the kind of political structure undergirding the Republican bill. In supporting such a structure, various Democrats argued, the Republicans were guilty of bad faith to the Puerto Ricans who had openly welcomed the American army in anticipation of the economic gains of free trade as a territory of the United States under the political and legal blessings of the Constitution and American creed.

In turn, the Republicans had great difficulty in identifying exactly what the political and legal status of Puerto Rico would be under their bill. They were fully aware that the island was to be denied territorial status, but they were unwilling to accept the Democratic label of "colonial dependency." Finally, a congressman from Massachusetts made a valiant effort to clarify the political status of Puerto

Rico, which he insisted could really be traced back to the Treaty of Paris' stipulation that Congress alone would provide for the civil rights and political status of the inhabitants of Puerto Rico. "It [the Treaty] created a separate political community with a citizenship of its own, though the community and its citizens owe a paramount allegiance to the United States." And then he made the point, "We have not far to seek to find a political relationship exactly like this. The Indian in his tribal relations is subject to the jurisdiction of his tribe, but owes a paramount allegiance to the United States" (US Congressional Record 1900 56:1:2097). Thus in his desire to avoid the term "colonial dependency" the congressman identified the political status of Puerto Rico with that of an Indian tribe. Both were in effect, if we adopt the phraseology of the United States Supreme Court *circa* 1831, "Domestic Dependent Nations."

Interestingly race never really surfaced as an issue in the debate over the status of Puerto Rico. Obviously the Democrats, most of whom were from the South, were not inclined to oppose the discriminatory features of the Republican bill in view of their own support of Jim Crow discrimination against the black in the South. By the same token Republicans were not prepared to concede publicly that their bill was discriminatory, partly since they argued that it was for the welfare of the island as a whole and also in view of their historic commitment to "racial equality." As a result both sides generally avoided the issue but, in the few instances it was mentioned, its potential for creating confusion in the ranks of each side was clearly evident. For example, a Democratic congressman from Kentucky opposed the Republican bill, not because he favored territorial status for the island but precisely because he opposed territorial status. In a circumlocutive fashion, he explained that the Supreme Court was bound to declare the Republican bill unconstitutional and thereby give Puerto Rico a territorial status through the back door "and in a few years some political party will clamor to make them citizens and voters." This would also be the inevitable result of the imperialistic policy being pursued by the Republicans. ("I am opposed to this whole imperial policy, even if there were no constitutional objections. No empire ever civilized any people in the world's history.")

"I am opposed to increasing the opportunities for the millions of negroes in Puerto Rico and the 10,000,000 Asiatics in the Philippines of becoming American citizens and swarming into this country and coming in competition with our farmers and mechanics and laborers. We are trying to keep out the Chinese with one hand, and now you are proposing to make Territories of the United States out of Puerto Rico and the Philippine Islands, and thereby open wide the door by which these negroes and Asiatics can pour like the locusts of Egypt into this country."   (US Congressional Record 1900 56:1:2172)

The Kentucky congressman would instead set both Puerto Rico and the Philippines adrift.

In another example of explicit racial reference, a Republican from Massachusetts, one of the few of his party opposed to the bill, raised the banner of radical reconstruction and the specter of the Dred Scott decision in which the Supreme Court stated "that a black man had no rights which a white man was bound to respect." As a result of that decision, he continued, "this country was deluged with blood to wash that decision from our laws." Now Congress was setting the stage for the same kind of court decision in the case of Puerto Rico.

> "Now, we are asked to lay the foundation for a moot case with the weight of Congress behind it and ask for another decision that the white men and brown men of Puerto Rico are merely our chattels, and that the commonest constitutional right secured to the meanest black man that treads American soil does not belong to them although they are under the flag."
>
> (US Congressional Record 1900 56:1:2091)

Unimportant as race was in the debate over Puerto Rico, it became a central issue in the frequent references to what would be the probable fate of the Philippines. Insisting that what was done for Puerto Rico would also have to be done for the Philippines, the Republicans pointed to the large number of different tribes and races "differing in language, differing in customs, and differing in civilization" (US Congressional Record 1900 56:1:1952) that the report by the Philippine commission said comprised the island. According to a Republican congressman from Pennsylvania, "If there is anything in the world clear it is that these eighty-four tribes require different modes of government, different kinds of laws, different treatment adapted to their respective needs" (US Congressional Record 1900 56:1:1953). The Republican bill allowed the United States to assume the white man's burden of giving them "peace and order, education, civilization" (US Congressional Record 1900 56:1:1952). To grant them territorial status would be inconceivable and an "amazing proposition."

The Democrats readily conceded that the Philippines consisted of a medley of races and cultures. Their disdain for them was evident in the comments of a Democratic colleague from Illinois. "We are told that the reason for extending this imperial system to the Philippines is because they are a lot of savage tribes, semi-barbarians, incapable of self-government" (US Congressional Record 1900 56:1:2162). The solution for the Philippines, many Democrats agreed, was neither the dependent colonial status proposed by the Republicans, nor the territorial status proposed by the Democrats for Puerto Rico; instead the United States should hold the islands in trust and in time grant them independence. In the words of a congressman from Kentucky, "if that Malayan, Oriental civilization threatens to be an injury to the institutions of this country, then I say, let those islands go for the interest of our people, because I love this Anglo-Saxon race on this continent better than any other on God's earth" (US Congressional Record 1900 56:1:2403).

No matter what the Democrats said, some Republicans remained distrustful of their motives; they had difficulty reconciling the Democrats' commitment to racialism in America with their espousal of territorial equality for Puerto Rico and presumably for the Philippines. Accordingly, they were convinced that the Democrats were merely trying to maneuver the Republican party to reaffirm its original commitment to territorial status for both. And once this happened, these Republicans were convinced the "true colors" of the Democratic party would surface. The Democrats would condemn the Republican party for granting citizenship to so many different "semi-civilized" races. In the words of a Republican congressman from Ohio,

> "They [the Democrats] will be saying [in the approaching political campaign].... 'Why, these bloody Republicans annexed 10,000,000 Malays. ...' They will tell you all about the monstrosities of those people in religion and habits and everything of that kind, and they will say 'The House of Representatives voted that those people were citizens and entitled to all the rights of citizens.' And then they will pick out those men to do this thing, and will say, 'Why, look at that fellow. He helped us to get into this fix.'... That vote is going to be a vote upon this dogma as directly as a vote was ever cast upon a legal propostion."   (US Congressional Record 1900 56:1:2080)

Finally, after nine days of debate, the House, voting almost entirely along party lines, narrowly passed on February 28 the revised bill, 172 to 162 with 20 not voting and 1 merely answering present.

One day later the bill (HR8245) reached the Senate and almost immediately, even without holding a formal meeting, the committee on Pacific Islands and Puerto Rico, as we have already seen, decided to offer its own revised version as a substitute for HR8245. (Its substitute included the basic revenue provisions of the House's bill, although tariff rates were reduced from the House's 25 percent to 15 percent.) Almost a week later, the Senate began serious debate on the substitute bill; the debate lasted on and off for almost a month.

Although the revised Senate bill covered the entire range of governance and only a small part of it was devoted to tariffs and revenues, the latter matter loomed large in the debate. The Democrats charged once again that domestic trusts were behind the demand for tariffs. The Republicans once again denied the charge and insisted tariffs were to be imposed for the welfare of the Puerto Ricans. In fact, Foraker of Ohio insisted that no territory had ever been treated as generously as Puerto Rico would be under the bill; for Puerto Rico was to receive all the revenues collected from the tariffs in Puerto Rico as well as those collected on Puerto Rican goods sent to the United States. The Democrats scoffed at this argument, claiming money was merely being taken from one pocket and put into another under the bill.

During the debate Foraker was hard-pressed by the Democrats to define the kind of legal-political entity that he had created with his "People of Porto Rico" now that the island was to be denied territorial status and the protective umbrella of the Constitution. He was asked, for example, by a senator from Nebraska, "what is to be the character, if any, of the government of Puerto Rico? What is to be its classification? Is it to be a district, a colony, a Territory, a State, or a mere province or dependency?" All Foraker would say in response was: "It is not by the language of this bill given any name except the name of Puerto Rico.... That is to say, it is not called a district; it is not called a Territory; it is not called any particular kind of a political subdivision" (US Congressional Record 1900 56:1:3038).

When asked by the senator whether this absence of classification "was the result of accident or design," Foraker answered, "it was the result of design." The senator then protested vigorously.

> "We ought not to run away from the question of settling the political status and the classification of that island. I doubt if there can be found in the history of the United States a bill drawn exactly as this bill has been drawn. The island is to be a political entity known as the people of Puerto Rico. What relation do these people hold to the United States? What is the island of Puerto Rico; that is, what is its relation to the United States?" (US Congressional Record 1900 56:1:3038)

Foraker refused to answer this question; he insisted that the Senate had other business on hand.

Earlier in the debate, Foraker had come close to defining the political status of the island as a colonial dependency (a phrase he and his fellow Republicans in the Senate were reluctant to adopt, as were their colleagues in the House).

> "I regard Puerto Rico as a dependency belonging to the United States, and not as a part of the United States in any integral sense [as is a Territory].... [Thus] Puerto Rico is not a part of the United States within the meaning of the Constitution, but is a dependency of the United States and, being a dependency of the United States, we have a right to legislate for it as a possession belonging to the United States, but not as a country that is a part of it."
>
> (US Congressional Record 1900 56:1:2654–655)

Foraker was equally vague when he was pressed to tell what the clause, citizen of Puerto Rico and as such entitled to the protection of the United States, meant in the revised bill. After hemming and hawing for a while, Foraker replied that "the word citizen implies nothing more, when used in its political sense, than that the person who is the citizen owes allegiance to the government under which he belongs as a citizen, and that government owes him protection in return. Now, I understand the people of Puerto Rico do owe us allegiance and that we owe them protection; therefore, they should of right be declared citizens." When a senator from Georgia remarked that this definition would apply "to a subject as well as a citizen," Foraker merely shrugged and replied "Well I suppose it would. That shows the unimportance of the term" (US Congressional Record 1900 56:1:2474). A week later a senator from Kentucky denounced Foraker's definition and declared that citizenship also meant the various rights and immunities of the Fourteenth Amendment and the Bill of Rights.

As in the House, a considerable portion of the debate was devoted to the constitutionality of the revised bill. And as in the House, Republicans were aligned almost solidly behind the argument that Congress had plenary power over governance of acquired lands, in the absence of constraints imposed by treaty and as long as Congress did not act in ways inherently forbidden by the Constitution In turn, Democrats were almost solidly opposed to them. They argued that the Constitution went with the flag; therefore the revised bill's denial of territorial status and the protection of the Constitution to Puerto Rico violated the basic law of the land as did the tariff imposts. Each side cited judicial and political precedents with Chief Justice Taney's opinion given top billing by the Democrats.

As in the House, race never really surfaced as a major issue in the debate over Puerto Rico; however the question of hypocrisy did emerge as an issue in a spirited exchange between a senator from South Carolina and one from Wisconsin. According to the senator from South Carolina, the Republican party had flaunted the slogan of racial equality in the South during the period of reconstruction after the Civil War. Now it was supporting a policy of racial inequality in the Philippines and Puerto Rico, and a Republican committee even introduced in the Senate "a provision upon the Hawaiian bill by which contract slaves in that island were to be governed under a similar black code to that which we enacted in South Carolina and in other Southern States [immediately after the Civil War]" (US Congressional Record 1900 56:1:3218). Both policies, he contended, represented nothing more than the selfish interest of the Republican party. During reconstruction it reflected "a desire to perpetuate the domination of the Republican party in the United States." Even more, "there was first a desire of revenge by putting the ex-slaves in control of the Southern States and putting white necks under black heels" (US Congressional Record 1900 56:1:3218). Now the Republican party was merely concerned with satisfying the commercial and industrial interests of its supporters, and the various trusts.

The Republican senator from Wisconsin vigorously denied these charges. He upheld the idealism of the Republican party during reconstruction and its compassion for the Puerto Rican in the present bill. In turn, he lashed out at the hypocrisy of the Democratic party generally and the senator from South Carolina specifically. At the very moment the South Carolina senator was shedding crocodile tears for territorial and constitutional equality for the Puerto Ricans, he declared, the South Carolinan's state was disfranchising blacks and reimposing the vise of inequality on them. Soon the heated exchange dribbled away to various desultory comments as others entered the discussion.

As words gave way to voting, Republicans repeatedly defeated efforts by various Democrats to restore the basic features of the original bill. Finally on April 3 they passed the revised bill by the relatively narrow margin of nine votes: 40 to 31 with 16 not voting. Eight days later the House accepted the Senate version by a 16 vote margin: 158 to 142 with 38 not voting and 12 answering merely present. The next day President McKinley signed the bill into law.

The curb on economic imperialism: the 500-acre limit on corporate land acquisitions

With the final passage of the Foraker Act, a number of House Republicans, particularly in the Committee on Insular Affairs, began to share misgivings with the Democrats that the unique political status they had bestowed on Puerto Rico would open up the island to unrestrained economic imperialism and exploitation by American corporations and trusts. Even the minimal curbs built into a territorial governance structure were absent. Accordingly, they looked for an opportunity to do something about it. This arose almost a week later, April 18, when President McKinley sent an identical message to both houses. In this message the President pointed to the imminence of the deadline, May 1, imposed by the Foraker Act for the transfer of governance from military to civilian authority and to his need for more time to recruit civilians for the various administrative posts. Accordingly, he requested passage of a joint resolution by Congress that would allow military personnel to continue to serve temporarily in their administrative posts after May 1 without losing their commissions.

Senator Foraker, chairman of the Committee on the Pacific Islands and Porto Rico, took up the President's cause immediately and secured passage the next day of a joint resolution (SR116) that would allow military personnel to serve in the government of Puerto Rico for three months beyond the deadline without losing their commission. During the brief debate, Tillman, Democrat from South Carolina, twitted Foraker by asking him the necessity for the resolution under the Foraker Act.

> "Porto Rico is not under the Constitution of the United States, we have been told. It therefore is not subject to any laws of the United States except those which we enacted in the bill last week for its government. I should like the Senator to tell me whether, under the act for the government of Porto Rico, there is any requirement which would prohibit Army officers from continuing to hold these places for the time being."
>
> (US Congressional Record 1900 56:1:4406)

Foraker delayed for a time but then finally answered the question in the following manner.

> "It is not a constitutional provision that makes this legislation necessary in that respect, but a statute of the United States. The law providing for a civil government expressly extends to Porto Rico all the statutory laws of the United States not locally inapplicable, and a statute which prohibits an officer of the United States Army from holding and exercising the duties of a civil office would be locally applicable in Porto Rico as prescribed in that statute."
>
> (US Congressional Record 1900 56:1:4406)

The following day the resolution was sent to the House of Representatives where it was referred to the Committee on Insular Affairs, which was then deliberating on its own version of a resolution. In reporting to the House the next day, the committee expressed its approval of both resolutions, but it attached to each the same two amendments. The first amendment stipulated that "all franchises, privileges, or concessions mentioned in Section 32 of said [Foraker] act shall be approved by the President of the United States," and not by the governor and executive council of Puerto Rico alone (US House of Representatives Report No. 1105 (1900) 56:1:1).

The second amendment severely curbed the activities of private corporations whether chartered in Puerto Rico or elsewhere. It forbade them from issuing stocks or bonds except in actual exchange for cash or property at a fair evaluation. In addition, it placed an almost complete ban on their involvement in agriculture and real estate.

> "No corporation shall be authorized to conduct the business of buying and selling real estate, or issuing currency, or of engaging in agriculture, or permitted to hold or own real estate, except such as may be reasonably necessary to enable it to carry out the purposes for which it was created.

Banking corporations, however, may be authorized to loan funds upon real estate security, and to purchase real estate when necessary for the collection of loans, but they shall dispose of all real estate so obtained within five years after receiving the title."

(US House of Representatives Report No. 1105 (1900) 56:1:1)

After successfully fending off a challenge to the relevancy of the amendments through a solomon-like decision of the presiding officer, the chairman of the committee, a Republican from Wisconsin, insisted that the two amendments were meant "to remedy defects, and they are very serious and obvious defects, to the original act" (US Congressional Record 1900 56:1:4616). For example, the Foraker Act gave to the governor and executive council of Puerto Rico, consisting of eleven men only five whom had to reside in Puerto Rico, unrestricted power to grant all franchises on the island. "There is no State in this Republic which would consent for one moment to grant to any six men or any eleven men, with or without the consent of the President of the United States, the absolute disposition of the franchises in that State" (US Congressional Record 1900 56:1:4616). The exercise of this sweeping power could easily lead to excesses and abuses, which the first amendment sought to control by requiring presidential approval for the granting of franchises.

The second amendment, he declared, merely sought to curb irresponsible behavior on the part of corporations which the original act seemed to permit.

"Corporations are necessary institutions in business affairs, and we want them to go to Porto Rico as quickly as they can for the benefit of that island itself; that is, the corporations who will deal properly and justly with the people when they get there.... [But] we do not want any balloon enterprises, which will take the people into the clouds and then burst and drop them. We want business men, strong, safe, solvent corporations, to undertake the business of the island, and there is no restriction in that amendment which would prevent the going there of corporations of that character as soon as the civil government is established in the island. And these restrictions were made by the amendments to this bill to remedy possible abuses if they should occur. Of course, we all know that there are abuses in many cases in the management of corporations."

(US Congressional Record 1900 56:1:4617)

A congressman from Connecticut, who had failed in his challenge of the relevancy of the amendments, rose to oppose vigorously the chairman's arguments and the amendments. He leveled his harshest criticism against the ban on real estate and agricultural holdings by corporations and against the requirement that banks divest themselves of such holdings in five years.

"I am not one of those who believe that the whole American people are a set of rascals and scoundrels who would go to Porto Rico and plunder it. I believe that the businessmen of this country are entitled to some confidence even in the House of Representatives, whether organized as trust companies, savings banks, or as sugar planters in Porto Rico. I believe that if this bill goes into effect you will prevent corporate capital of great amounts, or small amounts of aggregated capital, engaging in the cultivation in Porto Rico of sugar and fruit . . . by saying that any such company shall not buy any of the lands, you will have absolutely put a damper on the island of Porto Rico from which it will not recover in twenty-five years."   (US Congressional Record 1900 56:1:4618)

The spokesman for the Democratic minority on the Insular Committee, a congressman from Virginia, then offered a spirited defense of the amendments. In doing so, he expressed the collective disdain of the minority for the Foraker Act and the need to sustain the efforts of the committee "if we do not want to leave the people of Porto Rico in a position which, in all probability, will result in the loss of their lands and homesteads, and make slaves of them too" (US Congressional Record 1900 56:1:4619). For failure to bar corporate activity in real estate and agriculture would mean

"that within the shortest period possible after the government provided for in the act of April 12 has been organized and put into operation the great corporations of this country will own every single acre of the sugar and tobacco lands of this most fertile island. And if that shall become the case, then the condition of the population will, I believe, be reduced to one of the absolute servitude. The people of Porto Rico will be driven to cultivate these lands for these corporations at whatever daily wage they choose to pay them."
                    (US Congressional Record 1900 56:1:4619)

Further, the unrestricted power of the executive council to grant franchises would magnify these evils. Such power "has never before been conferred in any Territorial act passed by Congress since the establishment of our Government" (US Congressional Record 1900 56:1:4619). In making this statement, the Democratic congressman obviously went beyond what the Republican chairman had said earlier about states never having allowed such unlimited power.

From that point on, the debate was dominated by Democratic congressmen, most of whom repeated their opposition to the Foraker Act in their opening comments and all of whom elaborated on various features of the arguments made by their spokesman. One Democratic congressman from Georgia even compared the probable fate of Puerto Ricans to that of the American Indians, if the corporations had their way. "It would be but a few years when all of this population in that thickly settled island would become paupers, just as in many instances we find with the Indians within our own territory here" (US Congressional Record 1900 56:1:4620).

Finally the debate was over. On April 24 the amended resolution was passed by voice vote and sent to the Senate. There it was quickly rejected, largely through the urgings of Foraker, and a conference was called to reconcile the differing versions of the resolution.

A week later, April 30, Foraker submitted a conference report to the Senate that reflected agreement on a watered-down version of the House's amended resolution. For example, instead of having the President approve all franchises, privileges, or concessions granted under the Foraker Act, he would merely approve those for railroads, street railways, telegraph, and telephone; all others would continue to be granted exclusively by the governor and executive council.

The most significant changes were the lifting of the total ban on corporate holdings in agriculture and the granting to corporations of the privilege of owning and controlling land that was not in the excess of 500 acres:

> "Every corporation hereafter authorized to engage in agriculture shall by its charter be restricted to the ownership and control of not to exceed 500 acres of land; and this provision shall be held to prevent any member of a corporation engaged in agriculture from being in any wise interested in any other corporation engaged in agriculture."   (US Congressional Record 1900 56:1:4851)

The other controls on corporate activity in the amended House version were more or less retained.

Despite obvious misgivings over the House amendments to his simple resolution, Foraker nevertheless took satisfaction in his report to the Senate at having modified the House's stance on these several issues, particularly its ban on corporate holdings in agriculture. But he insisted that unless Congress agreed immediately to the conference report, Puerto Rico would be without a legally constituted government the next day. And so, under the gun of the deadline, the conference report was passed with minimal debate in the Senate and with no debate in the House on April 30.

The Supreme Court and Puerto Rico as an unincorporated territory of the United States

Six months after the Foraker Act went into effect, its tariff provision was challenged by a firm that brought an action "against the collector of the port of New York, to recover back duties to the amount of $659.35 exacted and paid under protest upon certain oranges consigned to the plaintiff at New York, and brought thither from the port of San Juan in the Island of Porto Rico during the month of November, 1900" (182 US 1901:247). The case, Downes v. Bidwell, was argued in the United States Supreme Court in January 1901, and in May the Court ruled in a five to four split decision that the impost provision of the Foraker Act was constitutional. Even the majority—though agreed on the conclusion—was split on the detailed rationale for its conclusion. Thus Justice Brown, though he delivered the judgment for the Court, wrote an opinion which no other justice endorsed; two justices concurred with Justice White's separate opinion; and a brief opinion was written by the fifth justice.

According to Justice Brown, the basic issue at stake was the following one: "when the Constitution declares that all duties shall be uniform 'throughout the United States,' it becomes necessary to inquire whether there be any territory over which Congress has jurisdiction which is not a part of the 'United States.'" His answer was that only "the *States* whose people *united* to form the Constitution, and such as have since been admitted to the Union upon an equality with them" (182 US 1901:277) comprised the "United States." The rest, territories included, did not, though they were under the jurisdiction of the United States government. As such only the former were subject to the uniformity and other provisions of the Constitution; the latter only to the extent that the United States government through Congress extended these provisions to the territory or acquired land. However, once any provision was extended to these areas Congress could not retract it.

Accordingly, Congress had plenary and virtually unrestricted power in governance over territories. It even had the power "to prescribe upon what terms the United States will receive its inhabitants, and what their *status* shall be in what Chief Justice Marshall termed the 'American Empire'" (182 US 1901:279).

"It is obvious that in the annexation of outlying and distant possessions grave questions will arise from differences of race, habits, laws and customs of the people, and from differences of soil, climate and production, which may require action on the part of Congress that would be quite unnecessary in the annexation of contiguous territory inhabited only by people of the same race, or by scattered bodies of native Indians."   (182 US 1901:282)

As a result, Congress could be expected to exercise considerable caution in granting citizenship to inhabitants of various newly acquired possessions.

"If those possessions are inhabited by alien races, differing from us in religion, customs, laws, methods of taxation and modes of thought, the administration of government and justice, according to Anglo-Saxon principles, may for a time be impossible; and the question at once arises whether large concessions ought not to be made for a time, that, ultimately, our own theories may be carried out, and the blessings of a free government under the Constitution extended to them. We decline to hold that there is anything in the Constitution to forbid such action."   (182 US 1901:287)

Brown conceded that "many eminent men" feared that unrestrained possession of power by Congress could lead to "unjust and oppressive legislation, in which the natural rights of territories, or their inhabitants, may be engulfed in a centralized despotism" (182 US 1901:280). But he said these fears were unjustified for two basic reasons. First, even if Congress did not voluntarily provide a protective constitutional umbrella for a territory, it still faced constitutional prohibitions that "go to the very root of the power of Congress to act at all, irrespective of time or place." As examples, Brown mentioned bills of attainder and titles of nobility. He mentioned the First Amendment, but stopped himself with the comment: "We do not wish, however, to be understood as expressing an opinion how far the bill of rights contained in the first eight amendments is of general and how far of local application" (182 US 1901:277). His second basic reason was that "there are certain principles of natural justice inherent in the Anglo-Saxon character which need no expression in constitutions or statutes to give them effect or to secure dependencies against legislation manifestly hostile to their real interests" (182 US 1901:280).

> "Whatever may be finally decided by the American people as to the *status* of these islands and their inhabitants – whether they shall be introduced into the sisterhood of States or be permitted to form independent governments – it does not follow that, in the meantime, awaiting that decision, the people are in the matter of personal rights unprotected by the provisions of our Constitution, and subject to the merely arbitrary control of Congress. Even if regarded as aliens, they are entitled under the principles of the Constitution to be protected in life, liberty and property."   (182 US 1901:283)

In the meantime, he concluded, "we are ... of [the] opinion that the Island of Porto Rico is a territory appurtenant and belonging to the United States, but not a part of the United States within the revenue clauses of the Constitution; that the Foraker act is constitutional, so far as it imposes duties upon imports from such island, and that the plaintiff cannot recover back the duties exacted in this case" (182 US 1901:287).

In his separate opinion, Justice White agreed with Brown that the crucial question was whether Puerto Rico was part of the United States or, in White's terms, whether it had become incorporated into the United States: "Had Porto

Rico, at the time of the passage of the act in question, been incorporated into and become an integral part of the United States?" (182 US 1901:299). However, unlike Brown, White did not confine his definition of the United States to states alone. Instead he argued that, with the treaty of peace with Great Britain which established America's independence, "all the territory within the boundaries defined in that treaty, whatever may have been the disputes as to title, substantially belonged to particular States. The entire territory was part of the United States, and all the native white inhabitants were citizens of the United States and endowed with the rights and privileges arising from that relation" (182 US 1901:319).

Subsequently, he continued, Virginia ceded part of the land it claimed which became the Northwest Territory.

"[In this cession,] it was expressly stipulated that the rights of the inhabitants in this regard should be respected. The ordinance of 1787, providing for the government of the Northwest Territory, fulfilled this promise on behalf of the Confederation. Without undertaking to reproduce the text of the ordinance, it suffices to say that it contained a bill of rights, a promise of ultimate statehood, and it *provided* [author's italics] that 'The said territory and the States which may be formed therein *shall ever remain a part of this confederacy of the United States of America*, subject to the articles of confederation, and to such alterations therein as shall be constitutionally made, and to all the acts and ordinances of the United States in Congress assembled, conformably thereto.'

... At the adoption of the Constitution, the United States, as a geographical unit and as a governmental conception both in the international and domestic sense, consisted not only of States, but also of territories, all the native white inhabitants being endowed with citizenship, protected by pledges of a common union, and, except as to political advantages, all enjoying equal rights and freedom, and safeguarded by substantially similar guaranties, all under the obligation to contribute their proportionate share for the liquidation of the debt and future expenses of the general government." (182 US 1901:319–20)

In short, with the founding of the New Nation, "We the People" included not only those who lived in the states but also those who lived in the Northwest Territory. All were protected by the various provisions of the Constitution, and the constraints imposed upon the government, including the uniformity requirement for imposts, applied to all within this People's Domain.

Since then, Justice White continued, new land had been acquired under the treaty-making and war-making powers of the Constitution but, contrary to what the plaintiffs contended, provisions of the Constitution did not automatically apply to this new land nor did the land become automatically incorporated into the United States.

"[Instead,] the Constitution has undoubtedly conferred on Congress the right to create such municipal organizations as it may deem best for all the territories of the United States whether they have been incorporated or not, to give to the inhabitants as respects the local governments such degree of representation as may be conducive to the public well-being, to deprive such territory of representative government if it is considered just to do so, and to change such local governments at discretion."   (182 US 1901:289)

Further, Congress had the authority to determine the character of the relationship between the newly acquired land and the United States. It could if it so chose incorporate the land into the United States as a territory with the expectation that it would eventually become a state, or it could bestow on the land another kind of status, as in the case of Puerto Rico. It could also extend provisions of the Constitution or withhold them. And Congress could even refuse to abide by the terms of a treaty which stipulated the rights and status of the inhabitants of the newly acquired land, in as much as these terms were merely promises of future congressional action. Justice White admitted, though, that Congress had never repudiated such terms of a treaty.

However, the justice continued, despite the plenitude of its power Congress did not govern these territories outside of the Constitution, for "every function of the government being ... derived from the Constitution, it follows that that instrument is everywhere and at all times potential insofar as its provisions are applicable" (182 US 1901:289). And "as Congress in governing the territories is subject to the Constitution, it results that all the limitations of the Constitution which are applicable to Congress in exercising this authority necessarily limit its power on this subject" (182 US 1901:291).

In some instances, these limitations involved the withdrawal "of all authority on a particular subject."

"[For example,] undoubtedly, there are general prohibitions in the Constitution in favor of the liberty and property of the citizen which are not mere regulations as to the form and manner in which a conceded power may be exercised, but which are an absolute denial of all authority under any circumstances or conditions to do particular acts. In the nature of things, limitations of this character cannot be under any circumstances transcended, because of the complete absence of power."   (182 US 1901:294–95)

In other instances, they merely "regulate a granted power" (182 US 1901:295) and determined which provisions of the Constitution were to apply and under what conditions. And "when the applicability of any provision of the Constitution is questioned," the crucial issue was the status of a particular acquisition vis-à-vis the

United States (182 US 1901:294). For example, "Congress derives its authority to levy local taxes for local purposes within the territories, not from the general grant of power to tax as expressed in the Constitution," but from its right to govern newly acquired land. As a result, "it follows that its right to locally tax is not to be measured by the provision empowering Congress 'To lay and collect Taxes, Duties, Imposts and Excises,' and is not restrained by the requirement of uniformity throughout the United States" (182 US 1901:292). However, once Congress had bestowed territorial status on the acquired land and had thereby incorporated it into the United States,

> "the power just referred to, as well as the qualification of uniformity, restrains Congress from imposing an impost duty on goods coming into the United States from a territory which has been incorporated into and forms a part of the United States. This results because the clause of the Constitution in question does not confer upon Congress power to impose such an impost duty on goods coming from one part of the United States to another part thereof, and such duty besides would be repugnant to the requirement of uniformity throughout the United States."   (182 US 1901:292)

This constitutional restraint did not apply to Puerto Rico, Justice White insisted, because Congress had decided to withhold territorial status from the island and had refused thereby to incorporate it into the United States. Even the Treaty of Paris had failed to promise such a status to Puerto Rico. As a result, "whilst in an international sense Porto Rico was not a foreign country, since it was subject to the sovereignty of and was owned by the United States, it was foreign to the United States in a domestic sense, because the island had not been incorporated into the United States, but was merely appurtenant thereto as a possession" (182 US 1901:341–42).

Justice White conceded that this was the first time since the Articles of Confederation that such a status had been accorded to a land formally ceded to the United States: "There has not been a single cession made from the time of the Confederation up to the present day, *excluding the recent treaty with Spain* [author's italics], which has not contained stipulations to the effect that the United States through Congress would either not disincorporate or would incorporate the ceded territory into the United States" (182 US 1901:318–19).

As a result, Puerto Rico was the first to occupy the novel status of an unincorporated territory of the United States.

> "As a necessary consequence [of this status], the impost in question assessed on merchandise coming from Porto Rico into the United States after the cession was within the power of Congress, and that body was not, moreover, as to such

imposts, controlled by the clause requiring that imposts should be uniform throughout the United States; in other words, the provision of the Constitution just referred to was not applicable to Congress in legislating for Porto Rico."

(182 US 1901:342)

In articulating his position, Justice White inadvertently showed how shrewdly prescient Senator Foraker had been. Had the senator merely deleted mention of the Constitution in his revised bill, it would have been enough for Justice Brown to sustain the constitutionality of the tariff, but evidently not enough for Justice White and the two colleagues who endorsed his opinion. Their support was contingent upon the additional deletion of any direct or indirect reference to territorial status for Puerto Rico. Only then apparently were they prepared to say that the island was not part of the United States and therefore not subject to the uniformity clause of the Constitution. And had they not voted as they did, the Foraker Act would have been declared unconstitutional.

In his dissenting opinion with which Justices Harlan, Brewer, and Peckham concurred, Chief Justice Fuller exposed even more graphically than did White the fundamental weakness of the Brown argument. He hammered home the thesis that the United States comprised both states and territories and that the uniformity provision of the Constitution was applicable to both as were its other provisions. In a separate set of observations, Justice Harlan added a new dimension to the argument. He took issue with the Brown contention that "the National Government is a government of or by the States in union, and that the prohibitions and limitations of the Constitution are addressed only to the States." This assumed that "the present government is a mere league of States, held together by compact between themselves" when in fact

"it is a government created by the People of the United States, with enumerated powers, and supreme over States and individuals, with respect to certain objects, throughout the entire territory over which its jurisdiction extends. If the National Government is, in any sense, a compact, it is a compact between the People of the United States among themselves as constituting in the aggregate the political community by whom the National Government was established. The Constitution speaks not simply to the States in their organized capacities, but to all peoples, whether of States or territories, who are subject to the authority of the United States." (182 US 1901:378)

Justice Harlan also assailed the Brown argument that Congress had unrestricted power to govern the territories and could introduce the Constitution into their governance at will. To allow that position to stand, "we will, in that event, pass from the era of constitutional liberty guarded and protected by a written constitution into an era of legislative absolutism" (182 US 1901:379). In the final analysis, "it [Congress] is the creature of the Constitution. It has no powers which that instrument has not granted, expressly or by necessary implication" (182 US 1901:382).

Harlan ridiculed Brown's notion that the Anglo-Saxon character and its presumed commitment to natural justice served as a curb to congressional absolutism.

"[The Founding Fathers] well remembered that Anglo-Saxons across the ocean had attempted, in defiance of law and justice, to trample upon the rights of Anglo-Saxons on this continent and had sought, by military force, to establish a government that could at will destroy the privileges that inhere in liberty. They believed that the establishment here of a government that could administer public affairs according to its will unrestrained by any fundamental law and without regard to the inherent rights of freemen, would be ruinous to the liberties of the people by exposing them to the oppressions of arbitrary power. Hence, the Constitution enumerates the powers which Congress and the other Departments may exercise – leaving unimpaired, to the States or the People, the powers not delegated to the National Government nor prohibited to the States." (182 US 1901:381)

Although the Brown thesis lent itself to a devastating and overwhelming attack by the dissenting judges, particularly Harlan, the more sophisticated White thesis required a more subtle set of distinctions to which Chief Justice Fuller addressed himself. He launched a two-front attack on the White thesis. First, he rejected as did Justice Harlan the distinction that both White and Brown had made between constitutional restrictions "which regulate a granted power and those which withdraw authority on a particular subject" (182 US 1901:295).

"The concurring opinion recognizes the fact that Congress, in dealing with the people of new territories or possessions, is bound to respect the fundamental guarantees of life, liberty, and property, but assumes that Congress is not bound, in those territories or possessions, to follow the rules of taxation prescribed by the Constitution. And yet the power to tax involves the power to destroy, and the levy of duties touches all our people in all places under the jurisdiction of the government." (182 US 1901:373)

In effect, the Chief Justice was calling the distinction spurious. Justice Harlan used even stronger words.

"I cannot accept this reasoning as consistent with the Constitution or with sound rules of interpretation. The express prohibition upon the passage by Congress of bills of attainder, or of *ex post facto* laws, or the granting of titles of nobility, goes no more directly to the root of the power of Congress than does the express prohibition against the imposition by Congress of any duty, impost or excise that is not uniform throughout the United States. The opposite theory, I take leave to say, is quite as extraordinary as that which assumes that Congress may exercise powers outside of the Constitution, and may, in its discretion, legislate that instrument into or out of a domestic territory of the United States."   (182 US 1901:383–84)

Secondly, Fuller as well as Harlan expressed mystification over White's concept of incorporation; both viewed it as having some sort of "occult meaning." But to the extent that they claimed to understand what the word meant, both were convinced that the Foraker Act had accomplished just that for Puerto Rico. The governance structure that the act set up for the island, they argued, was tantamount to granting Puerto Rico a *de facto* territorial status, so closely did it resemble the customary second-grade pattern of territorial governance. And merely because Congress failed to use the word "incorporate" it could not hide this similarity or, in the words of the Chief Justice, "Great stress is thrown upon the word 'incorporation,' as if possessed of some occult meaning, but I take it that the [Foraker] act under consideration made Porto Rico, whatever its situation before, an organized territory of the United States" (182 US 1901:373).

Justice Harlan took the argument one step further. He declared that even if Congress had granted explicit *de jure* territorial status to the island, it would not have found it necessary to alter the governance structure created by the Foraker Act:

"Suppose Congress had passed this act: '*Be it enacted by the Senate and House of Representatives in Congress assembled*, That Porto Rico be and is hereby incorporated into the United States as a territory,' would such a statute have enlarged the scope or effect of the Foraker act? Would such a statute have accomplished more than the Foraker act has done? Indeed, would not such legislation have been regarded as most extraordinary as well as unnecessary?"
                                                                 (182 US 1901:391)

Thus, both judges concluded, Puerto Rico had indeed been granted the status of a territory or its equivalent and was therefore protected by the uniformity provision of the Constitution.

Puerto Rico as an unincorporated territory: the early years

THE SUGAR MONOCULTURE AND THE EMERGENT PLURAL SOCIETY

Once Congress had expressed its fears of a corporate takeover of Puerto Rico's agricultural economy through enactment of the 500-acre limit, it moved on to other business. It failed to set up any machinery of control for the resolution or to assign the responsibility for enforcement to any governmental agency. And so the resolution represented little more than a symbolic expression of distrust of corporate power by those who blamed the trusts for the revision of the original Foraker Act. It provided no imperative for action.

What further undermined the intent of the resolution was the open invitation extended by the newly appointed governor and his administration to business investment in Puerto Rico. In addition, Congress' own tariff policies provided a protective umbrella for the production of the one crop on the island that could benefit from large-scale corporate investment. At the same time Congress withheld the kind of protection that Spanish authorities had previously provided for another crop which merely required small-scale holdings.

Thus sugar replaced coffee as the more attractive investment opportunity, much as coffee had replaced sugar in the middle of the nineteenth century "The golden age of the coffee planter was the latter part of the nineteenth century when coffee was the main agricultural export crop and the chief source of income for half the population" (Crist 1948:179).

As evidence of sugar's mounting profitability surfaced, three corporations were organized within four years of the Foraker Act by American interests to exploit the island's sugar resources. Resorting to ill-concealed subterfuges to bypass the acreage limit, these corporations began to buy and lease property to such an extent that within fifteen years the holdings of two of the three, for whom information is available, equalled 71,000 acres. By 1928 the three joined by a fourth American corporation owned, leased, or controlled 170,675 acres, or two-thirds of all acreage devoted to the raising of sugar cane.

In addition, these American-owned companies controlled by the 1930s one-fourth of the largest and most technically sophisticated sugar mills for milling not only their sugar cane but also the cane of small independent colonos. As a result, by 1928, "they milled 436,260 tons of sugar, or more than 58 percent of the entire sugar crop. Fifty percent of the entire crop of 748,677 tons was produced by the American sugar companies alone. In 1930 the American companies again produced 50 percent and the production of all absentee companies was 59 percent of the total" (Diffie and Diffie 1931:53).

So powerful an impact did the encroachment of the American sugar interests have on the agricultural economy of Puerto Rico that sugar rapidly overtook coffee as the single most important agricultural product. In 1898, for example, only 15 percent of land under cultivation was devoted to sugar; 41 percent, to coffee. But by 1908 more acreage was devoted to the growth of sugar than to coffee, and the disparity between the two grew even larger with the years. As a result, by 1909 the export value of sugar was more than four times greater than that for coffee.

As the production of sugar gained dominance, it completely transformed the agricultural sector from what Quintero Rivera called "a semi-feudal hacienda economy to an economy dominated by capitalist plantation agriculture" (Quintero Rivera 1974:196). Under the older system, production, particularly the raising of coffee beans, was organized around relatively small-scale haciendas in which a tradition of paternalism connected the resident owner with his impoverished jibaros. For example in 1899, according to Crist, "of 40,000 plantations 93 percent were operated by owners, i.e., coffee growers, largely resident, who were overseers of a vast submerged amorphous mass of poorly paid, poorly fed, poorly clad *jibaros*" (Crist 1948:180). (In addition, a number of jibaros periodically drifted in and out of the hacienda economy as they engaged in mountain-slope subsistence farming.) Despite these ties, the hacendados did not hesitate in the least during the period of Spanish hegemony to resort to coercion and violence at any sign of restlessness on the part of their jibaros. They also flaunted the superiority of their Spanish identity and culture over the presumably nondescript heritage of the jibaro, many of whom were amalgams of various racial and ethnic groups.

As the fabric of the hacienda economy was being rent asunder by the inexorable advance of the sugar interests, the hacienda elite found themselves sorely pressed by the burgeoning American colonialism. A number gave up. They sold out to the American interests and remained either as a rentier class or went to live in the city as part of the bourgeoisie. Others struggled to hang on. Still others joined the new wave as they shifted from the production of coffee to that of sugar. However, despite this threat to their economic status, the hacendados still sought to reaffirm their claim to elite status.

Much less fortunate were the jibaros who could no longer depend on their ties to the hacendados for subsistence or claims to land. Accordingly they became a propertiless rural proletariat who sold its services for wages to an impersonal absentee corporate landowner whose control of the labor market enabled him to exploit the jibaro mercilessly in the worst tradition of early capitalism. As a result, the jibaros became an even more alienated and anomic mass than they had been before – similar in many respects to that which Furnivall identified in his study of Burma and the East Indies (Furnivall 1956). There too he found that the superimposition of a capitalistic on a traditional economy pulverized the established ties among segments of the indigenous population and thereby created an alienated, anomic, and amorphous plural mass.

However, in time the jibaro as a rural proletariat developed a sense of common economic interest and fate which on occasion was galvanized into collective action. The first recorded strike, for example, was as early as 1901; and by 1917, thirty-two were reported in a Senate document. Most of these strikes were brutally crushed and only a few produced modest gains for the jibaros. In the process, however, some of the rural proletariat became receptive to the words of the socialists who railed against the absentee American capitalist and his Puerto Rican quislings. Also recruited to the ranks of the disaffected were the small independent colonos whose dependence on the large sugar mills made them exceedingly vulnerable to exploitation by corporate interests.

In this manner, American colonialism generated a deep structural "fault" that pitted the Puerto Rican jibaro and colonos against an invisible American capitalist whose interests were looked after in part by a group of managers imported from America. These Americans soon adopted a colonial-type lifestyle that contrasted strikingly with that of the jibaro and colono. In the words of a peripatetic journalist who undertook an eight-month tour of the Caribbean and in the process developed a breadth of vision without losing his American perspective:

> "The calm and neutral observer, neither underfed nor blessed with the task of clipping sugar-stock coupons,... cannot but wonder why the sweat-stained laborers in the cornfields should be seen wearily tramping homeward to a one-room thatched hovel to share a few boiled roots with a slattern woman and a swarm of thin-shanked children while the Americans who direct them from the armchair comfort of fan-cooled offices stroll toward capacious bungalows, pausing on their way for a game of tennis in the company compound, and sit down to a faultless dinner amid all that appeals to the aesthetic senses. Least of all can he reconcile the vision of other Americans, whose only part in the production of sugar is the collecting of dividends, rolling about the island in luxurious touring cars, with the sight of the toil-worn, ragged workers whose uncouth appearance arouses the haughty travelers to snorts of scorn or falsetto shrieks of 'how picturesque.'"   (Franck 1920:277–78)

And so was etched within a few years of America's acquisition of Puerto Rico the broad outlines of a plural society so deeply divided along class and ethno-racial lines that it seemed to spring as a construct not only from the pen of Furnivall but also from the pen of Marx. This ethno-Marxist variant of a plural society was in the process of pushing from center stage the colonial estate arrangement that had built ties of tradition and paternalism between jibaro and the hacendado during the days of Spanish hegemony.

At the top of the structure was the American. He occupied the key positions in the economy as a managerial class for the corporations and in the government as part of the appointed administrative elite structure. Influential as they became, Americans comprised a very small, self-contained group on the island. Over a thirty-year span from 1900 on, according to census reports, they never numbered more than 2000 or more than two-tenths of 1 percent of the population. In the government, though, they comprised by 1909 somewhat over 10 percent of the administrative bureaucracy of 3000, according to a presidential report to Congress.

As a result, the American corporations and government had to depend upon a large number of Puerto Ricans to keep the administrative machinery going. Some served as "middlemen at the service of North American corporations: specifically, managers, corporation lawyers, and so on down the corporation bureaucratic hierarchy to foremen. Some of these managers and lawyers gradually became shareholders in the companies, and by the late twenties and thirties were among the wealthiest families on the island" (Quintero Rivera 1974:200–01). Others became part of a rapidly growing merchant class "that became tied to the US market. Since the island was now under the tariff system of the United States, the merchants who flourished during the first decades of the century were those dealing with trading houses in New York, Baltimore and Philadelphia, and not the old merchant group that had controlled the trade between the island and Spain" (Quintero Rivera 1974:201). And finally there was a group of professionals: "doctors, engineers, federal employees and a small group of white-collar workers. Their interests as a social group were centered around the development of a modern, professionalized and bureaucratized way of life in which they would play a central role" (Quintero Rivera 1974:201).

In short an entire middle stratum of Puerto Ricans emerged whose interests and life circumstances directed them toward an identification with the colonial power. The process resembled much of what had happened during the centuries of Spanish hegemony, but the groups involved differed significantly. In many instances those groups who benefited under Spanish rule, such as coffee growers and so on, were now the outsiders, replaced by a new occupational category.

In neither instance did this intermediate group relate itself to or identify with the interests of the rural or urban working classes. It remained as a floating class of intermediaries who became obsessed with their class relations to the mainland. Even those who had lost out in the struggle for "anointment" were equally obsessed. A major consequence was that the forces and factions unleashed in the political arena by the American structure of governance concentrated almost exclusively on these relations: the politics of status became their primary preoccupation.

"The unnatural concentration upon the status issue, however justified it may have been by the inescapable reality of American colonialism, was at the same time a useful device for maintaining the status quo in Puerto Rican society and politics. It helped to rationalize the rule of the classes over the masses. It presented an ideal excuse for sacrificing social and economic issues to political and constitutional issues."   (Lewis 1963:115)

THE POLITICS OF RELATIONS WITH THE MAINLAND: A PERENNIAL ISSUE

The issue of political status did not prove divisive in the early days of the American occupation. Even the crystallization of the political forces into the two parties that came into being in rapid succession in 1899 – first the Puerto Rican Republican party and then the Federal party – did not disturb the climate of opinion. Both parties shared the expectation that America would treat the island justly and would set up a governance structure that would grant it territorial status and self-governing provisions at least matching those wrested from the Spanish when both were part of the autonomist tradition and party.

The Foraker Act shattered these illusions and thereby gave the status issue a renewed sense of urgency and importance. Both parties expressed their disappointment with the act and reaffirmed their commitment to enlarged self-governance for the island. However, they still defined the solution as incorporation of the island into the United States, first as a territory and then as a state.

Within four years, after several sweeping electoral victories by the Republican party for seats in the House of Delegates, the programs and policies of the two parties began to diverge markedly. The Republican party drew even closer to an American identity. It was incorporated into the national Republican party and granted the right to send delegates to the party's presidential conventions. In the process it reaffirmed its drive for ultimate statehood.

In the meantime the Federal party was replaced by a more broadly based political party called the Unionists. It attracted to its ranks those who had already become disaffected and alienated from American rule. Accordingly, it did more than reaffirm the Federal party's call for statehood. It added as an equally legitimate alternative to its platform: independence.

"The creation of the Unionist Party in 1904 ... marked the turning point [in the honeymoon idyll with the United States], for its endorsement in its program of that year of political independence as one feasible status, among others, for the island was the first declaration by a political group that a separatist status could be viewed as a possible solution to the problem."
                                                                   (Lewis 1963:104)

Within nine months of its birth, the Unionist party faced its first election and won handily, as it did for the next twenty years. In short, it retained control of the House of Delegates for the next two decades – frequently by an overwhelming majority.

Thus the stage was set for a prolonged debate over the status of the island among political parties within the House of Delegates and for a prolonged struggle over the status of the island between the predominant party in the House and American authorities, both on the island and in Washington.

> "The politics of this period were, in fact, simply a never-ending variation upon the theme of status. . . . One result of this was to create a vested interest in exploiting the status issue, in milking from it as much political credit as possible, on the part of the *criollo* political leadership. . . . This is why, too, so much of the political history of the period was an elaborately executed ballet wherein the active parts were played by an elite group of professional politicians around the narrow and sterile but dramatic status theme, switching membership from one group to another as the interests of the moment dictated, engineering party splits and mergers, issuing sonorous *pronunciamientos* in which the plangent rhetoric only faintly disguised the single enduring motive of political preferment."
>
> (Lewis 1963:114)

The chronic ferment over the issue was continually in evidence even in Washington as bills were regularly introduced into Congress. In addition, Congress was literally besieged with memorials from the House of Delegates over the issue. Finally in 1909 the issue was seemingly brought to a head by the refusal of the House of Delegates to act on any appropriation bill. This brought the flow of governmental funding to a halt in Puerto Rico. The House justified its action by arguing that the governor and his appointed executive council were continually thwarting its will by rejecting the various reforms it proposed. At the end of the legislative session, it complained in a report to Congress and the President "about the 'unjust Organic Law which makes it impossible for the people's representatives to pass the laws they desire'" (Ribes Tovar 1973:410).

Angered by the House of Delegates' action, President Taft sent a message to Congress in which he belabored the House of Delegates for its "irresponsible" behavior. This, he insisted, was also evident in the narrow self-interested bills the House had passed which incurred the executive council's veto. In addition, he chided the House for failing to recognize that "Porto Rico has been the favored daughter of the United States."

> "In the desire of certain of their leaders for political power, Porto Ricans have forgotten the generosity of the United States in its dealings with them. This

should not be an occasion for surprise, nor in dealing with a whole people can it be made the basis of a charge of ingratitude. When we, with the consent of the people of Porto Rico, assumed guardianship over them and the guidance of their destinies, we must have been conscious that a people that had enjoyed so little opportunity for education could not be expected safely for themselves to exercise the full power of self-government; and the present development is only an indication that we have gone somewhat too fast in the extension of political power to them for their own good."

(US House of Representatives Document No. 43 (1909) 61:1:6)

To bring the House of Delegates in line, he recommended that Congress amend the Foraker Act by "providing that whenever the legislative assembly shall adjourn without making the appropriations necessary to carry on the government, sums equal to the appropriations made in the previous year for the respective purposes shall be available from the current revenues and shall be drawn by the warrant of the auditor on the treasurer and countersigned by the governor" (US House of Representatives Document No. 43 (1909) 61:1:3).

American citizenship and the Jones Act

THE TAFT COMMISSION AND SELECTIVE CITIZENSHIP

Having achieved his legislative objective, the President sent the Secretary of War to Puerto Rico by late December to get a firsthand view of the situation. In the words of the Secretary, who was accompanied by two other military men, he was "to learn the present state of the island administration, political, economic and hygienic, and to report the results of my impressions to you [the President] with such recommendations of changes in the organic law as the conditions in my judgment required" (US House of Representatives Document No. 615 (1910) 61:2:2).

After an eight-day tour of the island during which the three spoke to officials and ordinary persons, he reported

"a general and almost universal desire and demand of all classes, interests, and political parties for American citizenship for all the people of Porto Rico as a whole; for an elective upper house so that, with no check but a veto by the governor, full legislative power shall be lodged in American citizens, who are likewise citizens of Porto Rico, elected by male voters whose only qualifications shall be age and citizenship; and for a separation of executive and legislative functions...."

[But] many men, both Americans and Porto Ricans, of such education, character, and general knowledge of affairs in the island as to make their judgment entitled to great weight, are of the opinion that such a system would be disastrous to the health and economic and political welfare of the island, would jeopardize investments, retard healthy development, and would eventuate in forcing the United States in the not distant future to withdraw power improvidently granted, and set back, on account of having traveled too fast, the realization of local self-government. They represent that it was unwise to grant general suffrage to a people a vast majority of whom have neither the education to vote intelligently nor the property interests to make them deeply concerned in the administration of public affairs."

(US House of Representatives Document No. 615 (1910) 61:2:4)

Accordingly, this elite favored citizenship for only a select few. Expressing basic agreement with their sentiments, the Secretary stated categorically "I do not favor conferring citizenship collectively" (US House of Representatives Document No. 615 (1910) 61:2:4). He proposed that citizenship be accorded voluntarily and individually upon application to the courts. Further he proposed that suffrage should no longer be universal. Instead he recommended that it be confined to those who qualify and become American citizens and "are able to read and write" or own real-estate property or have been a taxpayer not less than six months before an election.

A month later the President sent the Secretary's report to Congress with his endorsement, and six weeks later the Committee on Insular Affairs sent a bill to the House floor that contained most of the Secretary's recommendations. Although in its report the committee suggested it was granting citizenship collectively to the Puerto Ricans, it in fact required that each Puerto Rican would have to go through a legal process individually. The bill also set up the restrictive qualifications for suffrage recommended by the Secretary and adopted his proposal for the senate. It reduced however the 5000-acreage limit he had proposed to 3000 acres. In short, the committee virtually rubber stamped the administration's proposal.

These recommendations were scored in a minority report issued by six members of the committee two weeks later. Bearing the imprint of Congressman Jones of Virginia, the minority report declared that "the people of Porto Rico, through their accredited representatives, have expressed their opposition to many of the features of this proposed legislation. Rather than accept the bill which has the approval of the committee they prefer that the Foraker Act as it has been amended from time to time shall continue to constitute the organic law of Porto Rico" (US House of Representatives Report No. 750 Part 2 (1910) 61:2:2).

"Especially obnoxious to the Porto Rican People ... and ... in conflict with the progressive ideas and liberal principles of this enlightened age" (US House of Representatives Report No. 750 Part 2 (1910) 61:2:2), the report continued, were the bill's provisions on citizenship and on a senate. The former, according to the report, should be granted collectively and instantly by Congress and not individually through the courts. The latter should be entirely elective and should not be composed of an appointed majority. The report also criticized other provisions of the bill that would concentrate even more authority in the hands of appointed officials. It rejected the projected increase in acreage and said the interests of the small sugar planter could only be protected by keeping the 500-acre limit. Despite its plea for expanded self-governance, the report failed to take issue with the restrictive suffrage requirements written into the original bill.

Almost a week after floor debate began, Jones, leader of the minority, announced that the majority and minority had resolved several of their major differences. First, the original bill was to be amended to provide for the granting of American citizenship collectively by an act of Congress instead of individually through the courts. And second, the bill was to be modified to provide for the gradual change in the composition of the senate from 8 appointed and 5 elected members, to 7 elected and 6 appointed, twelve years hence.

Despite these modifications, the resident commissioner from Puerto Rico was only slightly mollified by the citizenship amendment. He continued to object strongly on the floor of the House to the appointive character of the senate and to the suffrage restriction which remained untouched in the amended bill. He argued that the bill, despite its citizenship provision, was even more retrogressive than the Foraker Act and took away privileges the latter had bestowed on Puerto Rico. Neither, he insisted, lived up to the self-governance provisions given by Spain in the last years of its reign.

These sentiments were echoed in a letter from four leading political figures in Puerto Rico. These leaders included the speaker of the House of Delegates, the chairman of the central committee of the Union Party, and the special commissioner to Washington from the House of Delegates. In their letter they called for the defeat of the revised bill. Though welcoming the citizenship clause, they complained that they would at the same time be "deprived of the right of manhood suffrage that we now possess; our present intervention in the administration of the public health, charities and corrections of the island is taken away from us; our legislative power is curtailed in sanitation and electoral matters; and we are denied the right to elect a senate similar to that of the States and Territories of free America" (US Congressional Record 1910 61:2:7626). Despite these objections, the House passed the amended bill a week later and sent it to the Senate. It died there despite a favorable report from the Committee on the Pacific Islands and Porto Rico.

JONES AND THE ABORTIVE EFFORTS AT COLLECTIVE CITIZENSHIP

A year later Jones revived the issue of collective citizenship and introduced a bill to that effect in the House. This was, he insisted, one of the two things that Puerto Ricans most wanted; his measure, however, avoided any reference to what he called the second most desired thing: self-governance. ("What they [the Puerto Ricans] most desire, and what they have long and earnestly endeavored to secure is, American citizenship accompanied with the right to legislate for themselves in respect to all purely local affairs" (US House of Representatives Report No. 341 (1912) 62:2:2).)

The purpose of his measure, he continued in his report for the Committee on Insular Affairs, was twofold. "It is to settle and definitely fix the civil and political status of the people of Porto Rico, and at the same time to make those at present defined to be citizens of Porto Rico, and certain other natives, citizens of the United States" (US House of Representatives Report No. 341 (1912) 62:2:1).

His bill, he continued, charted no new ground as seen in earlier efforts of the House and was fully in accord with the platforms of both major political parties. Even the Secretary of War had come out forcefully for it in his last annual report, though he hedged his support with the argument that "it is to be carefully remembered that this demand for citizenship must be, and in the minds of Porto Ricans is, entirely dissociated from any thought of statehood. It is safe to say that no substantial [segment of] public opinion in the United States or even in Porto Rico contemplates statehood for the island as the ultimate form of relation between us and Porto Rico" (US House of Representatives Report No. 341 (1912) 62:2:2). This line of argument was repeated by other high-ranking American officials including the President. They insisted that the granting of collective citizenship to Puerto Ricans did not by itself convey the promise of territorial status or future statehood to them as a people.

Most congressmen were persuaded that the issue of citizenship could be divorced from that of statehood. They accordingly expressed their support for the measure in the debate that followed. Some, however, were not convinced and saw the granting of citizenship as an important foot-in-the-door for statehood. In the words of a congressman from Illinois:

"It is as inevitable, in my judgment, as that the sun will rise to-morrow, that when Porto Rico is an organized Territory of the United States and her citizens are made citizens of the United States, they will at once commence to demand admission into the Union with greater force and with better logic than they ask to be made citizens. If they are citizens of the United States with a population such as they have, it is not practicable for any long time to deny their request or demand that they shall remain a State of the Union."

(US Congressional Record 1912 62:2:2795–796)

Two other congressmen picked up this line of argument in expressing their opposition to the measure and in the process unleashed a racial salvo against citizenship that most other congressmen would probably have applauded if the issue had been statehood. For example, a second congressman from Illinois began by agreeing with his colleague. "The gentleman from Illinois . . . has well said this [measure] is but the entering wedge for a demand for statehood." He went on to say, "I question the wisdom of the enactment of this bill into law.... The people of Porto Rico – and I weigh my words when I speak of Porto Rico, because I have been there – do not understand, as we understand it, government of the people, by the people" and were not competent to engage in it. This was due in part to the debilitating effects of living near the equator. "I undertake to say that if you pick up a million people, your kind of people and my kind of people – the Caucasian race – and put them for 100 years or 200 years or 300 years, without any unmixed blood, 20 degrees south of the Equator, I undertake to say, in my judgment, the civilization would decrease in force, in capacity for self-government." Further, the hybrid character of the Puerto Ricans also made them incompetent for self-government. "I am informed by people who are familiar, 75 or 80 percent of those people are mixed blood in part and are not equal to the full-blood Spaniard and not equal, in my judgment, to the unmixed African, and yet they are to be made citizens of the United States" (US Congressional Record 1912 62:2: 2796).

A congressman from Texas then took up the racial cudgel. First he decried the imperialism of Republican administration that brought under the control of the United States racially mixed peoples.

> "We went away from our own shores in search of adventure and by force of arms annexed an incongruous, inharmonious, and entirely unassimilable people, both in the East and in the South, in the Philippines and in the West Indies. In both instances we got a people who can make no contribution to our political institutions, no contribution to our civilization in any way, that we would regard as valuable."
>
> (US Congressional Record 1912 62:2:2796–797)

They and the other nonwhite races "have a right to exist – at least we have no right to say they shall not – and certainly Americans cannot with propriety suggest that they shall not have such political institutions, such forms of government, as they prefer." Despite this right, he insisted, these people were inherently incapable of being ruled under a government of the people and by the people – the superior form of government of the white; instead they required an authoritarian-type regime. If America insisted upon keeping such people in tow, it ran the danger of contaminating itself through political and biological hybridization.

"Political mixing with alien people is as dangerous and unprofitable to the State as physical mixing is sinful and hurtful to us as a people.... We imperil our own free institutions by imitating Imperial Rome when she dealt with colonies. With a fatuity that is really incomprehensible we, a free people, have been tempted to employ the tools of tyranny, and that can never be done without danger. Nations that live by the sword must perish by the sword."

(US Congressional Record 1912 62:2:2798)

To avoid this, he concluded, America should give independence to these people and never allow them to become part of its body politic, either individually as citizens or collectively as a state.

Despite the opposition, the House overwhelmingly passed the bill and sent it to the Senate's Committee on the Pacific Islands and Porto Rico. In its favorable report to the Senate issued almost a year later, the committee stressed that "at the present time these people [Puerto Ricans] are in the anomalous condition of being, in their international relations, a people without a country. They have ceased to be subjects of Spain and have not become citizens of the United States. In traveling abroad they do not have the benefit of the protection due to citizens of the United States" (US Senate Report No. 1300 (1913) 62:3:2).

The report then addressed itself to those who opposed the measure because they feared "that it involves the right of inhabitants of Porto Rico to participate in the government, and ... that it would lead to the agitation of the question of statehood for Porto Rico." After reassuring them that "the grant of citizenship to those described in the bill does not in anyway involve the right of suffrage nor implicate directly or indirectly the question of statehood," the report then went on to say what citizenship would do for the Puerto Ricans.

"Citizenship will give them certain personal legal rights and privileges both in their relations to the local government and in their status abroad; will tend to increase their self-respect and to cultivate and develop a larger capacity for self-government. It will promote contentment and satisfaction among the people with their allegiance to the United States, but does not involve the right to participate in the government nor affect in any particular the question of statehood, any more than the privilege of citizenship to those born within the United States proper gives to them the right of suffrage. The two questions are in no way related, and the latter is mentioned here not for the purpose in any way whatever of expressing an opinion upon it, but simply to emphasize the fact that it is a separate and distinct proposition from the one involved in this bill."

(US Senate Report No. 1300 (1913) 62:3:2)

Despite the favorable report, the Senate quietly buried the bill.

THE UNIONIST PARTY'S DISENCHANTMENT WITH AMERICAN CITIZENSHIP

By the end of 1913 the constant repetition of the theme that citizenship did not mean statehood – tellingly used to drum up a favorable response for the former in Congress and among the American public – had seriously corroded support for citizenship in Puerto Rico. The most graphic display of disaffection took place at the November convention of the ruling Unionist party. There, the party expressed its concern that Congress meant what it said and would never grant statehood to Puerto Rico. Accordingly it voted to eliminate from its platform a pro-statehood plank and to rewrite its pro-independence plank in much stronger language.

> "We declare that the highest ideal of the Union, like that which all strong bodies and all free men have had since the beginning of the world, is the founding of a free country, to be the mistress of her own sovereignty, now and in the future. With this ultimate aim in view, the 'Union de Puerto Rico' proclaims the Constitution of Porto Rico into a Republic, wholly independent, or with the protectorate and friendship of the Anglo-American Republic."
> (US House of Representatives Committee on Insular Affairs (1914) 63:2:56)

In the meantime, the platform continued, the party would be remiss "if, in devoting itself exclusively to the defense of that ideal, it were to neglect or give up the struggle for such other transitory solutions as would assure to the island a form of autonomous government, with full power to regulate its internal affairs in conjunction with the Government of the United States" (US House of Representatives Committee on Insular Affairs (1914) 63:2:56).

The party soon stamped its revised ideological position on the program and agenda of the House of Delegates which it controlled and in a double-barreled approach officially put Congress on notice of this position. On January 14 1913 the House sent a congratulatory message to the Democratic majority of the House of Representatives on their party's recent victory at the polls which enabled the Democrats to gain control of the federal government. In the message it called on the Democratic party to fulfill the principles of Jefferson by giving Puerto Rico the self-governing machinery it wanted and which the Republican party had promised but never delivered.

> "Our people request a new constitution providing for two elective houses, ample legislative powers in all local matters, an executive cabinet composed of bona fide residents of Porto Rico, and other measures of self-government worthy of the high sense of justice of the American people and of the demonstrated capacity and natural right of the people of Porto Rico."
> (US Congressional Record 1913 62:3:1573)

A month later the House of Delegates sent a resolution to the Senate, which still had the citizenship issue before it. The resolution requested that the Senate and Congress "take no action upon this matter without direct consultation and in accordance with the will of the Porto Rican people, because there exist tendencies favorable and adverse to United States citizenship for the Porto Ricans" (US House of Representatives Committee on Inuslar Affairs (1914) 63:2:54).

Even as the Unionist party was beginning to crystallize its opposition to American citizenship, the Free Federation of Workingmen in Puerto Rico made known to the Senate its strong support for American citizenship at a "great mass meeting" held at the end of 1912. ("Citizenship is a substantially unanimous aspiration of all this country constantly requested of Congress during many years by political parties and American Federation of Labor in Porto Rico and the United States.") The federation also protested in its cablegram "against all representations against citizenship by a few reactionary and aristocratic individuals of the monarchic type who are enemies in Porto Rico of the glorious American institutions and obstacles to the progress of the people in accordance therewith" (US Senate Document No. 968 (1912) 62:3:1). Earlier that year the American Federation of Labor had published a separate appeal under the heading of "A People Without a Country" which was presented to the Senate by Borah of Idaho. Four years later, the President of the Free Federation in Puerto Rico, Iglesias, reaffirmed his union's pro-citizenship stand in testimony before the US Commission on Industrial Relations. He explained that he hoped that with citizenship the workingmen of Puerto Rico would "be placed on the same footing as the working men of the United States" (US Senate Document No. 415 (1916) 64:1:11091) and would thereby receive the same kind of legal protection against the exploitation by corporations and capitalists.

THE HOUSE DEBATE ON THE JONES BILL

Despite the rumblings of opposition from Puerto Rico, Jones of Virginia, who was now chairman of the committee with the Democratic victory, was back with another set of measures on Puerto Rico. Unlike the earlier bill it was not confined to the issue of citizenship; instead it was a relatively elaborate measure written to replace the Foraker Act as the organic law for Puerto Rico. In the hearings for one of these bills, the resident commissioner of Puerto Rico, Rivera, elaborated on the reason for his party's request for a delay on the issue of American citizenship. The Puerto Rican people felt, he declared, that action by Congress on the issue now would prejudice their case for independence in the future and would accordingly doom Puerto Rico – in the absence of any chance for statehood – to the perpetual status of a colony or dependency of the United States.

"The sentiments of the Porto Rican people could be condensed into declaring to this committee: 'If you wish to make us citizens of an inferior class, our country not being allowed to become a State of the Union, or to become an independent State, because the American citizenship would be incompatible with any other national citizenship; if we can not be one of your States; if we can not constitute a country of our own, then, we will have to be perpetually a colony, a dependency of the United States. Is that the kind of citizenship you offer us? Then, that is the citizenship we refuse.'"
 (US House of Representatives Committee on Insular Affairs (1914) 63:2:54)

Whereas to continue the present status of Puerto Ricans as the people of Puerto Rico, he added, would not only leave open the option for independence but would also leave open the option for statehood, should that ever become available. Of the two options, he conjectured, Puerto Rican people would probably prefer statehood.

In the report on the bill that finally emerged from the committee, Jones did not make reference to the opposition of the Unionist party to American citizenship. Neither did he highlight the granting of citizenship in the title or first two paragraphs of his report, as he had done in his last report for the bill presented at the last session of Congress. Instead he stressed the liberal governance features of the proposed bill: "It has long been apparent that changed conditions in Porto Rico, as well as the advancement made by its people in the art of civil government, justified, if they did not demand, the substitution of a more permanent and liberal form of government for that which has obtained in the island all these years" (US House of Representatives Report No. 461 (1914) 63:2:1). Jones then revealed, somewhat later in the report, that unlike any earlier bill this one contained a provision for an entirely elective senate composed of nineteen members which would replace the largely appointed executive council of the Foraker Act. In making this proposal, the committee that had unanimously approved of the report expressed confidence in the self-governing capacity of the Puerto Rican people: "experience has shown that the people of Porto Rico may safely be intrusted with the power to elect the members of both branches of their legislature" (US House of Representatives Report No. 461 (1914) 63:2:2).

Despite this vote of confidence, the committee revived in the new bill the onerous restrictions on suffrage proposed by the earlier Olmsted measure.

"There are now no educational or property qualifications imposed upon the exercise of the right of suffrage in Porto Rico. It is provided in this bill that after the date of its approval no person shall be allowed to register as a voter who is not a citizen of the United States over 21 years of age, and who is not able to read and write, or, on the date of registration, shall not own taxable real estate in his own name."   (US House of Representatives Report No. 461 (1914) 63:2:2)

The bill also added several new departments and offices to the executive branch of government and reconstituted the executive council as an advisory body to the governor. Its earlier legislative function was to be taken over by the senate. In this manner the bill proposed "that the legislative branch of the government should be entirely divorced from that of the executive, except insofar as the governor is given the absolute veto power over all legislation" (US House of Representatives Report No. 461 (1914) 63:2:2).

Finally the bill contained a Bill of Rights for the people of Puerto Rico which was conspicuously absent from the Foraker Act. The Bill of Rights in its final form contained most of the protective guaranties of the American Constitution and its Bill of Rights except for two significant omissions. First, the Puerto Rican Bill of Rights failed to stipulate either indictment by a grand jury or trial by jury in criminal cases although it granted other rights of the Sixth Amendment including the right to a speedy and public trial. Second, the Puerto Rican Bill of Rights made no mention of the Seventh Amendment with its right of trial by jury for all civil suits above $20. This measure, though favored unanimously by the Committee on Insular Affairs, never came up for a vote on the floor of the House.

Jones revived the virtually identical measure at the first session of the next Congress, and hearings were held by his committee during the middle of January 1916. At these hearings the governor of Puerto Rico, Yager, sought to play down the importance of the independence movement on the island. He referred to a recent convention of the Unionist party which deferred to an indefinite future the acquisition of independence and gave instead top priority to the enhancing of the machinery of self-government. Accordingly he concluded that American citizenship had once again become popular even among the Unionists.

In his rebuttal, the resident commissioner, Rivera, did not dispute the governor's remarks about the lowering of the priority of immediate independence by the Unionist party. But he insisted that the party still defined independence "as the ultimate status of the island" just as the island's Republican party still favored "statehood as the ultimate regime." Both, he admitted, "appear at the present time to be remote measures," but he added, "no one expects Porto Rico to continue always a colony."

He did dispute the governor's remarks on the issue of American citizenship. He insisted that the Unionist party's stand on the matter continued unchanged:

"We, the Unionists, believe that from the standpoint of American national interest this question of citizenship should be left undecided for the present, in order to prevent a possible embarrassment in the international policies of this country as a result of premature action . . . to declare now American citizenship for the Porto Ricans does not answer any practical purpose, especially when this Congress is about to promise independence to the Filipinos and when a former Congress granted independence to the Cubans. Neither Cuba or the Philippine Islands is superior to Porto Rico as regards the ability to maintain a national life of its own. They are both larger in territory, but not more civilized or wealthier in proportion to their respective areas."

(US House of Representatives Committee on Insular Affairs (1916) 64:1:10)

In the report on the bill that finally emerged on the House floor at the end of January, Jones again made no reference to the opposition from the Unionist party to citizenship. In fact, no mention was made of the citizenship provision at all. The report merely focused on the several differences betwen the new bill and the earlier one, of which this was a virtual copy. Indeed the only significant differences between the two bore on such matters as the allocation of internal revenue taxes and who had absolute veto power over the legislative process, the governor or the President. The revised version also enlarged a proposed public service commission to nine members, two of whom were to be elected.

On the opening day of the House debate, the resident commissioner was given the floor. He launched into a long and stirring plea for his country. He labeled the Jones bill "as a step in the right direction," but he insisted, "This bill can not meet the earnest aspirations of my country. It is not a measure of self-government ample enough to solve definitely our political problem or to match your national reputation, established by a successful championship for liberty and justice throughout the world since the very beginning of your national life" (US Congressional Record 1916 64:1:7471).

In an obvious appeal to the Democratic majority, he likened the status of the Puerto Ricans to that of the Southerner after the Civil War. Both experienced war and conquest, he said, and in the case of the South this "let loose . . . after the Fall of Richmond thousands and thousands of office seekers, hungry for power and authority, and determined to report to their superiors that the rebels of the South were unprepared for self-government [Laughter]." He then declared in measured terms, "We are the southerners of the twentieth century" (US Congressional Record 1916 64:1:7471).

Next he expressed concern that, despite the fully elective legislatures under the bill, Puerto Ricans would still not be able to control their own affairs such as defining the educational policy for the island. He also complained about the suffrage restrictions which would eliminate, he estimated, approximately two-thirds of the registered voters who had already shown their capacity for self-government. He leveled his severest criticism against the imposition of

American citizenship on Puerto Ricans. He insisted that Puerto Ricans were content with the people of Porto Rico designation established by the Foraker Act:

> "We are satisfied with this citizenship and desire to prolong and maintain it – our natural citizenship, founded not on the conventionalism of law but on the fact that we were born on an island and love that island above all else, and would not exchange our country for any other country, though it were one as great and as free as the United States." (US Congressional Record 1916 64:1:7472)

The people of Puerto Rico would opt for American citizenship "without a moment's hesitation" if the island were to disappear through "a geological catastrophe," but "so long as Porto Rico exists on the surface of the ocean, poor and small as she is, and even if she were poorer and smaller, Porto Ricans will always choose Porto Rican citizenship."

He conceded that Puerto Ricans had favored American citizenship earlier, but only as it provided for joining "the fellowship of the American people as a State of the Union." But this ardor had diminished as statehood seemed an impossibility. Thus, "if you deny us statehood, we decline your citizenship, frankly, proudly, as befits a people who can be deprived of their civil liberties but who, although deprived of their civil liberties, will preserve their conception of honor, which none can take from them, because they bear it in their souls, a moral heritage from their forefathers" (US Congressional Record 1916 64:1:7472).

In a final plea he asked the House not to act prematurely on the matter, and he recommended that a plebiscite be conducted on the island to ascertain the true wishes of the Puerto Ricans. As he concluded his speech, Rivera showed that he and his party had not in fact given up their dream of eventual independence for the island:

> "Give us now the field of experiment which we ask of you, that we may show that it is easy for us to constitute a stable republican government with all possible guaranties for all possible interests. And afterwards, when you acquire the certainty that you can found in Porto Rico a republic like that founded in Cuba and Panama, like the one that you will found at some future day in the Philippines, give us our independence and you will stand before humanity as the greatest of the great; that which neither Greece nor Rome nor England ever were, a great creator of new nationalities and a great liberator of oppressed peoples [Applause]." (US Congressional Record 1916 64:1:7473)

Immediately upon the end of his speech, a congressman from Minnesota rose and gave voice to what Rivera and his Unionist party feared would be the outcome of Congress' granting of American citizenship to Puerto Rico: the irrevocable loss of eventual independence. The congressman expressed himself in flag-waving terms:

"If this bill is enacted into law, and I think it will be, it means that the Congress of the United States says to the people of Porto Rico, once and for all, that they are a part of the United States domain and will always remain there: that the agitation for independence in Porto Rico must come to a decided and a permanent end. I do not suppose it is particularly congenial to those interested in political propaganda to put to one side such a splendid topic to talk upon as the independence of any place, but if there is anything that you and I must be agreed upon, it is this: That Porto Rico will never go out from under the shadow of the Stars and Stripes [Applause]." (US Congressional Record 1916 64:1:7473)

The reason for this was quite apparent: the United States needed Puerto Rico to protect the Panama Canal. In addition, "Porto Rico is necessary to the United States as a key to the defense of the whole American continent against aggression from Europe" (US Congressional Record 1916 64:1:7473). Besides, he added, this would be in the interest of the Puerto Ricans themselves. They had already experienced the economic and political beneficence of American rule, and "they have learned to know that liberty does not necessarily mean independence, they have learned that personal liberty and freedom require an interdependence of individuals in order that they may be mutually protected, that citizenship under the sovereignty of the United States means full and complete liberty and freedom. They fully realize that. I say that to their credit" (US Congressional Record 1916 64:1:7474).

The response to his peroration was enthusiastic. That day only a congressman from New York, who proudly labeled himself a "Socialist," fully supported the commissioner's pleas for determination by Puerto Rico of its own citizenship status and for eventual independence if the island so chose. He also denounced the bill's property qualification for suffrage: "Instead of each man being entitled to a vote, you will have property recognized as the legal entity, as the political unit of Porto Rico" (US Congressional Record 1916 64:1:7477). He ended by calling for universal suffrage: "I believe in the principle that every human being [interruption] has the right that any other human being has under the same circumstances and under the same conditions" (US Congressional Record 1916 64:1:7478).

In the ensuing debate confusion reigned for a few moments over the issue of dual citizenship as it existed under the Constitution. A congressman from Ohio precipitated the confusion by his response to another congressman's query as to the status of a Puerto Rican if he should decide not to accept American citizenship under the bill. According to the Ohioan, "it would be a question whether he would be a citizen of Porto Rico or 'a man without a country.' My opinion would be – although I find that it is not the opinion of those who were heard in the hearing – that you do not destroy the citizenship of the place where he lives any more than you destroy my citizenship of Ohio." He then went on to the dual citizenship concept of the Fourteenth Amendment. "I have a double citizenship. I am a citizen of the United States and I am a citizen of Ohio. The man who is in Alaska in a sense has a double citizenship. He is a citizen of the United States and a citizen of Alaska" (US Congressional Record 1916 64:1:7479).

The two forms of citizenship, he elaborated, were inextricably interwoven for those in states and organized territories. Thus a person could not be a citizen of Ohio without also being a citizen of the United States. But he expressed doubt about the compatibility or incompatibility of a dual Puerto Rican and American citizenship.

The discussion of the topic then ceased, never to be returned to again. And as the debate progressed, the House became increasingly convinced that American citizenship would not only be good for the Puerto Rican people, but – contrary to the remarks of the commissioner – would also be widely supported on the island. Some congressmen suggested that passage of the bill would transform Puerto Rico into an organized territory, but most who said this immediately disclaimed that this would mean eventual statehood for Puerto Rico. Several expressed hope, however, that in some distant future this might happen. Those to whom even the thought of this was an anathema repeated their cultural and racial arguments against it and countered with a proposal for eventual Puerto Rican independence similar to that in prospect for the Philippines.

The congressman from Illinois, who had earlier stressed a climatic theory to account for racial differences in competency for self-government, developed in an address he entered into the congressional record a more clearly defined racial theory for his opposition to the present bill. Its passage, he insisted, would lead to eventual statehood for Puerto Rico which he opposed: "the Caucasian race, a term [including] the German, the Scandinavian, the Irishman, the Englishman, the Scotchman, the Frenchman, and others . . . are competent for self-government, . . . and I think they grow in competency from year to year." The other races were not competent and did not become more competent with time, he continued, particularly those from Latin America and Puerto Rico. ("The people of Porto Rico have not the slightest conception of self-government.")

And then to nail down his argument, he advanced the thesis that Puerto Ricans had a large strain of black in them. Their brethren in the United States had "made great advance since servile labor was abolished, attributable to its association with the Caucasian race."

"Porto Rico is populated by a mixed race. About 30 percent are pure African. I was informed by Army officers when I was down there that when the census was taken every man that was a pure African was listed and counted as such, but that there was really 75 to 80 percent of the population that was pure African or had an African strain in their blood. Now, gentlemen, will anybody say that I am abusing the African. I am not any more than I am abusing the Filipinos or the Moros; and I am certainly not abusing the Africans in the United States. The race has made great advance since servile labor was abolished, attributable to its association with the Caucasian race, being one-tenth of our population and living in the north temperate zone."

(US Congressional Record 1916 64:1:appendix1036)

When debate resumed two weeks later, it moved in an unexpected direction. A congressman from Colorado voiced concern over the lot of the workingmen in Puerto Rico and expressed alarm over reports that they were being denied the right to organize into unions by official coercion and action. Accordingly, he introduced an amendment to guarantee workers this right. As evidence for his concern, he read into the record a report from the American Federation of Labor which listed a number of abuses of this right. The report contained a reaffirmation by the Free Federation of Workingmen in Puerto Rico of their position on American citizenship.

"[American] citizenship should be conferred upon the people of Porto Rico, not individually but en bloc, collectively, and thus make for a more complete Americanization of the people of Porto Rico, in full touch, sympathy, and cooperation with the people of the United States. The possessors of capital should be obliged to pay their full share for what the government needs for public education, for sanitation, for roads, and for improvements on the island, as well as the security of justice for all."

(US Congressional Record 1916 64:1:8411)

Various congressmen, including Jones, professed surprise and ignorance of any official attempt to interfere with the right to organize. Accordingly they were convinced that such an amendment was unnecessary. Even the resident commissioner – despite lukewarm support for the amendment – disclaimed any knowledge of official opposition to unions. "In no instance have the officials of Porto Rico opposed the organization of the laboring classes." But then in a telling concession he admitted, "The only fact is that at some times laborers and certain of their leaders have during strikes disturbed the public order and the public peace, and the Governor of Porto Rico has been obliged to compel them to respect order" (US Congressional Record 1916 64:1:8412). In this manner the resident commissioner revealed that the cleavage between his party and the workingmen's organization was rooted in more than an ideological difference over American citizenship inasmuch as it was also expressive of deeply divergent class and economic interests.

After a brief exchange the amendment was decisively defeated, as was that of a congressman from Oklahoma which sought to protect the property rights of entrepreneurs and capitalists from expropriation without compensation.

Upon resumption of debate two days later, Jones felt obliged to reassure some of his colleagues that the bill was not intended to provide complete self-government for Puerto Rico.

'I will say to the gentleman from Wisconsin that he is not quite correct in assuming that this bill is intended to give the Porto Ricans full and complete authority over all of their domestic matters. It is intended, however, to give them the fullest measure of self-government that, in the opinion of the committee, ought to be bestowed upon them, taking into consideration the interests of the United States. For instance, the President appoints the attorney general under this bill, under a section that has already been read, and the President appoints the commissioner of education, while the governor appoints the other four heads of departments."

(US Congressional Record 1916 64:1:8458)

He elaborated on the reason for presidential appointment of the commissioner of education.

"As to the department of education, if the Porto Rican government had complete control over that subject there might be some question as to whether English would be taught in the schools or whether Spanish would be substituted therefor. The committee thought it would be better to have that matter under the control of a commissioner of education appointed by the president, so as to insure the continued teaching of English in the public schools."

(US Congressional Record 1916 64:1:8458)

Subsequently the debate turned to the provision of the bill that set property and literacy qualifications for candidates for the new senate. The "Socialist" from New York, for example, moved to strike this provison from the bill and in his speech he railed against giving the propertied class the right to rule the country.

"You are drawing distinctions which should not exist. You are separating the people. You authorize one portion of the community to rule over the other portion of Porto Rico. It is a dangerous thing, and I do not believe that you should embody it in the law of Porto Rico as reflecting the best judgment of Congress in the year 1916. We can not go back to the theories of those legislators of 100 years ago who did try to create special distinctions for the propertied class.... Why should you now in the year 1916 go back to reactionary principles, to reactionary theories, to theories that have been exploded, to theories which will place property above men? That is where the vice of this thing lies." (US Congressional Record 1916 64:1:8460)

Despite his eloquence his amendment was overwhelmingly defeated. Later an even more varied attack was made on the bill's restrictions on suffrage. Seemingly successful was an amendment to grant the right to vote to women as well as to men. It passed the House on May 22, only to be overturned the next and final day of debate. Even less successful was the effort by the "Socialist" from New York to strike the property and literacy requirements for voting. He reminded the House that it was disfranchising a vast majority of Puerto Ricans who had already used the franchise and were now to be ruled by the propertied classes.

"The people of Porto Rico have been exercising the franchise for 14 years. We are now called upon to confer a new right or a new privilege. We are asked to take away a right that people have enjoyed for 14 years ... and now you attempt to separate the Porto Rican people into two classes. One class is to make the law and the other class is to obey it. One class is to rule, the other class is to be ruled." (US Congressional Record 1916 64:1:8465)

He concluded his speech with a strong declaration: "I challenge your right to endow property with the franchise which you deny to man" (US Congressional Record 1916 64:1:8466).

Similarly unsuccessful was the effort by another congressman to strike the property qualification. And finally a congressman from Wyoming sought to exempt from the restrictive provisions those who had already exercised their right of franchise in earlier elections. But he too failed to persuade the House despite his declaration:

"I doubt if under a republican form of government in a representative government there resides anywhere authority to take the right of franchise from those to whom it has once been granted, except as a punishment for crime. You may modify conditions of franchise with regard to the new voter. We did that in my State when we adopted our State constitution. We provided the qualifications for the elector of the future, but we made no effort to disfranchise those who had been voting up to that time."

(US Congressional Record 1916 64:1:8469)

THE SENATE AND THE JONES BILL

Finally on May 23 the House passed the bill substantially as the committee had reported it and sent it to the Senate. Approximately six weeks later the Committee on Pacific Islands and Porto Rico to which the bill had been referred reported favorably on it with several modest amendments.

In its report, the committee explained that one of its amendments was proposed "as a wise and prudent check for the control of all ordinary disbursements and special funds;" several others were meant "to make clear the intent that all money collected on account of internal revenue shall accrue to the government of the island, applying as well to articles produced elsewhere but consumed in the island." In addition, the committee set up a residence requirement for all appointees of the governor: its purpose was "to give earnest to the people of Porto Rico of the intention of the American Government to extend and make larger the policy of local self-rule. The requirement of residence of one year imposed upon four of the heads of departments is a practical demonstration of our Government's intention in this regard" (US Senate Report No. 579 (1916) 64:1:2).

Perhaps the most important amendment was the committee's effort to soften the property and literacy restrictions on voting by waiving these restrictions for ten years for "all legally qualified electors of Porto Rico at the last general election." In explaining its action, the committee stated:

> "It has been represented to your committee that the provisions of the bill imposing a literacy test or property qualification as a condition of the exercise of suffrage would disfranchise a large number of the residents of Porto Rico who heretofore have participated in the elections. Your committee was of the opinion that such limitation of the franchise was not advisable, and has therefore provided that those who have voted may continue in the exercise of the privilege for 10 years, at the end of which time they will be brought under the operation of the general provisions. It is thought that within the next 10 years those for whom this exception is made will be able to qualify under one of the alternative conditions of voting."   (US Senate Report No. 579 (1916) 64:1:5−6)

The committee did not disturb the property or literacy requirements for candidates for the legislature.

Six weeks after the committee submitted its bill, Chairman Shafroth sought to begin debate on the floor of the Senate, but once again an organic bill on Puerto Rico was shunted aside and destined for another quiet burial.

Seeking to keep the matter alive in his annual message to Congress, President Wilson went beyond the passing reference to Puerto Rico of his previous message to make a strong plea for immediate action on the bill before the Senate. He declared:

> "The present laws governing the Island and regulating the rights and privileges of its people are not just. We have created expectations of extended privilege which we have not satisfied. There is uneasiness among the people of

the Island and even a suspicious doubt with regard to our intentions concerning them which the adoption of the pending measure would happily remove."

(US Congressional Record 1917 64:2:17)

Within a month after the President's address, Shafroth sought once again to bring the measure to the floor of the Senate. Once again he failed to obtain the unanimous consent agreement that was needed. Four days later he tried again. This time he stressed the urgency of the law, for Resident Commissioner Rivera had died in November and Puerto Rico was without representation in Congress. In addition the fall election in Puerto Rico had been delayed pending approval of the bill so that two elections would not have to be conducted so close to each other. But again he failed to get the unanimous consent agreement he requested. Finally, a week later, he succeeded in bringing the bill to the floor by a plurality of only seven votes and debate began.

In his opening remarks, Chairman Shafroth made almost immediate mention of the question of American citizenship and the internal political division on the issue in Puerto Rico. But he insisted opposition to it had apparently diminished and so his committee had now decided to opt for collective American citizenship for Puerto Ricans "unless they protest against it, unless they file with the court a declaration that they want to remain citizens of Porto Rico." He also added that the measure contained a Bill of Rights lacking in the Foraker Act. "This bill, Mr. President, proposes to give them what is termed a bill of rights – certain rights that are usually specified in our State constitutions, and providing considerable guaranties in regard to liberty, the writ of habeas corpus, and other matters of that nature" (US Congressional Record 1914 64:2:1325).

He then proceeded to describe other features of the bill, but once he reached the property and literacy qualifications for candidates for office, a senator interrupted to ask if these qualifications applied to voters too. This led to a short but brief debate. Of particular interest to some congressmen was the property restricton. Defensively Shafroth answered that this was the way the bill had come from the House, though his committee had softened the potential effect of the restriction by its ten year waiver.

Two weeks later debate opened on the various amendments to the bill offered by the committee. During the debate on a 7-percent limitation on public indebtedness, the issue of citizenship arose. Some senators revived the notion of individual citizenship voluntarily obtained through the courts. Others argued that the United States had typically given collective citizenship for all those of territorial status. The response of the senator from Mississippi typified the kind of ambivalence that beset the opinions of most. He said unqualifiedly that insofar as he was "personally concerned, I really think it is a misfortune for the United States to take that class of people into the body politic. They will never, no, not in a thousand years understand the genius of our government or share our ideals of government." He then offered a racial reason for his preference. "I really had rather they would not become citizens of the United States. I think we have enough of that element in the body politic already to menace the Nation with mongrelization." But, he continued, the United States was apparently determined to hold on to the island ("the investments that have been made there by American white men will induce the Government to continue to hold it") and to treat it in accordance with "the Anglo-Saxon disposition in dealing with subject provinces." Thus, "if the Porto Ricans are going to be held against their will, as we are holding them now, then we ought to legislate for their interests. We should make the coercion as palatable as possible" (US Congressional Record 1917 64:2:2250).

At that point a senator from New Mexico interrupted him with a question: "It is our duty to give them some citizenship, is it not?" The senator from Mississippi readily agreed with this suggestion and stated that the collective citizenship provision of the committee's bill did just that. The Senate's failure to accept this recommendation, he warned, would rekindle the dream of independence among Puerto Ricans, most of whom recognized "that independence is impossible" and would "serve to encourage those people to hope for the unattainable."

> "If the question of independence were submitted to them, to choose between being a dependency of the United States or having their independence, I do not believe 1 percent of them would vote to become a part of the United States. If they should do otherwise they would prove themselves utterly unfit for citizenship in a free country, for a man who does not desire to be free and independent has not the elements of manhood in him essential to the making of a desirable citizen of this Republic."
>
> (US Congressional Record 1917 64:2:2251)

The debate continued somewhat longer and then ended for the day.

Almost two weeks later, the chairman placed before the Senate a revised version of the committee's amendment of the House bill's provision on suffrage restriction. Instead of the ten-year waiver of property or literacy requirements for those Puerto Ricans who had voted in 1917 island elections as the committee's initial version stipulated, the revised version made the exercise of suffrage in 1917 as one of the three alternative prerequisites the legislature of Puerto Rico could prescribe as a qualification for voting after the first election. The legislature was also authorized to impose any other qualification it should wish. But the one additional requirement that the legislature was obliged to apply universally after the first election was American citizenship. No one could be qualified as an elector or candidate for office who rejected the collective American citizenship bestowed by the bill.

Led by a senator from New Jersey, opposition to the property and secondarily to the literacy requirement was voiced almost immediately. The dissenters insisted that the property qualification, which was in the form of an annual tax payment of $3, should be dropped, even though it was an alternative, not a universal prerequisite for voting. Supporters of the property restriction insisted that ownership of property showed a person was stable and capable of participating responsibly in self-government even though he could not read or write, "because," in the words of a senator from Georgia, "the man who has accumulated something who has his little farm, even though he does not know how to read and write, has a steadying influence that gives him some standing" (US Congressional Record 1914 64:2:3008).

After several exchanges, the committee beat back efforts to modify its amendment and it was passed unchanged, though the senator from New Jersey did succeed in eliminating any property qualifications for candidates for elected office.

A week later the whole issue was opened up once again by Senator Norris of Nebraska. He informed the Senate that the committee's amendment as it was passed gave the legislature in Puerto Rico authority to fix qualifications for voting in a manner that the Senate had obviously not intended. Instead of being compelled by the amendment to use each of the three stipulations as alternative modes of qualification, the legislature could decide to use only one, to the exlusion of the others.

"As I read it, I do not believe there can be any doubt that the Legislature of Porto Rico will be able to fix the qualifications of the electors in that island as they see fit, provided they come within the limits of this particular part of the law. They can change it from time to time as they desire. They may have a qualification one year which will be entirely of an educational nature, and the next year they can fix it entirely upon the ownership of property.... The next year they can put it in another class, and that class consists of those people who at the election of 1917 were legal voters."

(US Congressional Record 1917 64:2:3469)

The senator then proceeded to describe what might happen if the legislature made the 1917 vote the sole qualification for voting. Eventually this cadre of voters would progressively die out because their numbers would constantly diminish.

"So, if the legislature wanted to confine the voting population of that island to a select few and would provide that they shall all be in class (a), as we have designated them, the electorate would grow less and less, until the island would be controlled entirely by a few people – those who had the qualification to vote because they exercised the right to vote in 1917. Do we want to do that? Are we going to give to the legislature that power? Are we going to say that they shall have the power to provide that no man shall vote in Porto Rico except he has a qualification in the holding of property and provided that he pays taxes every year? It seems to me that we ought to fix more definitely the qualifications of voters, and we ought to do it here." (US Congressional Record 1917 64:2:3469)

So alarmed was the Senate by Norris' argument that it voted immediately to reconsider the provision. And so began the process of rewriting Section 35 from the floor. What finally emerged was a provision that deleted any role for the Puerto Rican legislature in prescribing voter qualifications and that stipulated that after the first election

"voters shall be citizens of the United States and 21 years of age and shall have one of the following qualifications:
(a) Those who at the election of 1917 were legal voters and exercised the right of suffrage.
(b) Those who are able to read and write either Spanish or English.
(c) Those who are bona fide taxpayers in their own name in an amount of not less than $3 per annum." (US Congressional Record 1917 64:2:3472)

After further jockeying on the issue, the Senate voted to strike the property qualification (c) from the bill, but it refused to delete either of the other two qualifications as it voted down decisively the New Jersey senator's substitute motion: "Sec. 35. That qualified electors shall be all males who are 21 years of age and over, and who are citizens of the United States" (US Congressional Record 1917 64:2:3477).

Three days later in a complete reversal, Chairman Shafroth of Colorado offered as a substitute for the approved section a motion that would restore to the Puerto Rican legislature a pivotal role in determining voting qualifications after the first election. The only prescribed requirements for suffrage would be American citizenship and being twenty-one years of age or older; further, the motion proscribed the Puerto Rican legislature from imposing any property qualification on the voter.

"That at the first election held pursuant to this act the qualified electors shall be those having the qualifications of voters under the present law; thereafter voters shall be citizens of the United States, 21 years of age and over, and have such additional qualifications as may be prescribed by the Legislature of Porto Rico: *Provided* That no property qualification shall ever be imposed or required of any voter." (US Congressional Record 1917 64:2:3666)

The only explanation offered by the chairman for this about-face was that now "the Legislature of Porto Rico will only have the power that is given to every State legislature and that has been given to every legislature under a Territorial form of government, and there has been no abuse of the powers thus granted" (US Congressional Record 1917 64:2:3666).

With this troublesome issue finally out of the way, the Senate passed the amended version of the House bill on February 20 1917. The House in turn refused to accept the Senate's amendments and so the bill went to conference.

THE CONFERENCE REPORT AND SUFFRAGE

Within three days the conference agreed on the points under dispute – a striking contrast to the four years it took the Senate to respond to the legislative initiatives of the House in passing a revised organic law for Puerto Rico. In responding to the House bill this time, the Senate had made approximately 95 changes. Of these, according to the conference report, the House conferees acceded to 65 and persuaded the Senate conferees to drop 18. Eleven others involved a compromise reformulation in which the House conferees amended the Senate amendments.

In describing the kinds of amendments they agreed to, the conference managers from the House declared in their statement to the House that "Many of the Senate amendments agreed to by the managers on the part of the House relate to the bill of rights contained in the bill, whilst a number of others merely change the language of the sections to which they relate, without changing their substance. Others relate to matters of detail, and are not very material" (US Congressional Record 1917 64:2:4166).

The House conferees admitted that four other amendments they had accepted were matters of substance. The most important had to do with qualifications for suffrage. In short, they accepted the Senate's ban on property qualifications and on its deletion of literacy requirements for the simple requirements of age and American citizenship and for the pivotal role of the Puerto Rico legislature in prescribing any other qualifications. In addition they dropped the existing qualification for candidates to elective office, although they retained the literacy requirement.

They also accepted the Senate's demand

"that nothing in this act shall be construed as abrogating or in any way changing section 3 of a joint resolution approved May 1, 1900, with respect to real estate holdings [the 500 acre limit], and [which] directs the governor of Porto Rico to have made and submitted to the next regular session of Congress report of all the real estate used for the purpose of agriculture and held either directly or indirectly by corporations, partnerships, or individuals."

(US Congressional Record 1917 64:2:4166)

However they persuaded the Senate conferees to limit the report to holdings in excess of 500 acres.*

When the conference report reached the House floor, a bitterly intense but brief debate erupted over the issue of suffrage. The onslaught was led by a congressman from Minnesota who chastized the House conferees for adopting the Senate provision. He complained that they should have held out for the House version and not buckled so quickly. As a result, he insisted, they had gone against the wishes of "all the people in Porto Rico in responsible positions."

Then noting a smile on the face of the "Socialist" from New York who was obviously pleased with the turn of events, he continued with a forecast of gloom and doom for Puerto Rico. The fate of the island would now be placed in the hands of an "irresponsible" "ignorant" "mob" which would provoke in the future "trouble, revolution and bad government."

"I am not surprised that he smiles; but I want to say that that smile finds no echo amongst the people who stand for something in Porto Rico; and I want to say to him that that smile will stand for revolution and outrage in Porto Rico before the story is completed and told. There are in the island of Porto Rico a limited number of responsible individuals. There are a great many who are irresponsible. They are ignorant; they have no property; they have no ideals; they are a mob. They can be trained and made good and efficient citizens; but when you put in their hands the instrumentality of voting without first giving them a chance to learn the duties of citizenship you are preparing for trouble, revolution, and bad government in the island of Porto Rico."

(US Congressional Record 1917 64:2:4168)

In supporting the Senate's version, he went on, the House would be "repeating the great error our fathers committed when they gave the newly emancipated slaves in this country immediately the right to vote." In this manner he identified Puerto Rican masses with the black. Both required a long period of tutelage and

---

*The fourth amendment of substance accepted by the House conferees was the Gronna amendment.

"[This] declares that one year after the approval of this act it shall be unlawful to import, manufacture, sell, or give away any intoxicating drink or drug in Porto Rico, and prescribes the penalty for a violation of this provision. It further provides, however, that if within five years after the approval of this act the qualified voters of the island shall vote to repeal this provision it shall thereafter not be in force and effect."   (US Congressional Record 1917 64:2:4166)

training by whites before they could acquire the minimal skills of self-government. Instead of doing this, he added, referring to the black,

"we committed a crime against him [the black] and against government when we gave him the right to vote before we gave him training in the way he should exercise it. Those so-called reconstruction days are the darkest in America's history. Infinitely better for the negro, infinitely better for the country if we had extended to him the right to vote only as fast as he became proficient in its exercise. By this bill you are placing the ballot in the hands of men in Porto Rico infinitely less qualified to exercise the responsibilities of suffrage than were the negroes of South Carolina, Georgia, Florida, Mississippi, Texas, if you please, in 1866 and 1867."   (US Congressional Record 1917 64:2:4168)

At this point, Chairman Jones interrupted the congressman with a question: "Is it not true – of course the gentleman knows it is – that they [the Puerto Ricans] have manhood suffrage there now? This [bill] is not changing the situation." The congressman vehemently insisted that suffrage was restricted even now and when pressed for evidence of this, he asserted defensively "that they do not all vote there, and have done it. They have technically the right to vote in Georgia, but they do not vote. They have the right to vote in Virginia, but they do not vote; and the records all disclose that only a limited number in Porto Rico vote to-day" (US Congressional Record 1917 64:2:4168).

Another congressman came to his defense, not by supporting his assertion about the present, but his earlier assertion that "responsible" Puerto Ricans wanted limited suffrage. Rescued from the untenable position in which he had placed himself on the issue of present suffrage, the Minnesota congressman resumed the attack. While admitting that "I have never been in Porto Rico. I have never looked the people over," he nevertheless insisted that even the late resident commissioner was among the "responsible" Puerto Ricans who had advocated limited suffrage before committee hearings.

He then mounted a bitter assault against the conference report's deletion of property qualifications for elected office holders.

"This same vice extends further. The House placed a property qualification upon the senators and representatives in this insular legislature. In order that a man might become a member of the House of Representatives in Porto Rico, under the bill that we passed in the House he had to own some property. He had at least to have a pair of pants, or a cow, or a horse, or a dog, or a garden, or something. Under this conference report he does not need to own anything but a little hair on his back and a purpose in his heart, whatever it may be. He can sit in the house of representatives and decide the fate of the insular government there.

We required that a member of the senate should have property of a certain amount. Under this bill anybody who can get the mob to yell for him can sit in the chambers of the mighty, vote taxes and spend them with a profligate hand, a proceeding of which we are not without some knowledge in this country."

(US Congressional Record 1917 64:2:4168)

Other congressmen expressed regret that at least an educational requirement for suffrage was not retained, but all laughed at the Minnesotan's contention that Puerto Rico did not presently have universal manhood suffrage. One congressman from Texas even went so far as to question "the very defective and miserable memory of the gentleman from Minnesota ... when he says that there was nobody [from Puerto Rico] before the committee asking for universal male suffrage" (US Congressional Record 1917 64:2:4170).

After a brief flurry between the two congressmen in which the Minnesotan taunted the Texan with the question "Do all the colored people in Texas exercise this God-given right [to vote]?" Chairman Jones ended the debate by expressing his sympathy for the position of the Minnesota congressman.

'I agree with much that he has said upon this subject. He knows, of course, that when the bill passed the House it contained both an educational and a property qualification. The gentleman knows too perfectly well what my position was upon this subject; but the sentiment of the Senate, if I am correctly informed, was strongly against either a property or an educational qualification. And if I remember aright, there was not a single dissenting vote in the Senate against the proposition to strike both of these qualifications from the bill. In these circumstances the conferees of the Senate felt obliged to insist upon the Senate propositon, and, in my judgment, this bill could not have been passed by this Congress if the House conferees had held out for either a property or an educational qualification; certainly not if they had insisted upon retaining the property qualification." (US Congressional Record 1917 64:2:4170–171)

And with the chairman having the last word, the House voted to accept the conference report. Three days later the Senate also agreed to it but without any debate. On March 2 1917 President Wilson signed the measure, and it became law.

American citizenship and the reaffirmation of Puerto Rico as an unincorporated territory

Shortly after the bill's passage, it became evident that few Puerto Ricans would take the necessary steps to reject the offer of American citizenship; only an estimated 300 did so, primarily for ideological reasons. Even the Unionist party recognized that passage of the bill made moot the issue of citizenship; therefore, at its next convention it embraced American citizenship. Though it continued to hope for independence at some distant future, it resolved to redouble its energies in the struggle to expand the machinery of self-government. And with America's entry into the war, it sought to rally Puerto Ricans behind the war effort. Accordingly it backed the drive to conserve food and to recruit young Puerto Ricans into the armed forces.

The glow of wartime solidarity even reached the halls of Congress where Resident Commissioner Davila delivered an address on August 20 1918 in which he reminded the House of Representatives of his people's patriotic fervor, which had elicited such widespread admiration from the American press. He reminded the representatives of the contribution Puerto Ricans had played in the food conservation drive. He also quoted from the *New York Herald* on the enthusiastic response of Puerto Ricans to the military draft and the accolades given by military leaders to their enthusiasm and performance as soldiers.

He attributed much of this enthusiasm to the leadership of President Wilson and to the Jones Act.

"It should be understood that an extraordinary movement of sympathy has taken place in the island toward the American Nation since President Wilson initiated his work in our behalf and since this Congress has granted us an organic law more democratic than the one we had. Therefore, President Wilson, who has labored so earnestly in our behalf, and the present Congress, which shaped his wishes into law, are the only personal influences that may have been responsible for the patriotic stand of the Porto Rican people about which so much is now being published."   (US Congressional Record 1918 65:2:9287)

He went on to consider even more important reason for this loyalty.

"This country [the United States] is fighting for the freedom of the world, and Porto Rico, which is a part of the world, has been fighting for freedom for many centuries. Thanks to the efforts of the great American who presides over the destiny of this Nation, and at present over the destiny of the world, the great powers are advocating the liberty and self-determination of small countries, and Porto Rico is a small country. America is fighting for the sake of justice, and that is what Porto Rico needs – justice. So your principles are our principles, your cause is our cause, and our duty as American citizens imposed upon us the obligation of fighting against all the enemies of the United States, no matter what the cause of fighting is. Are not these powerful reasons to unite the island of Porto Rico, small as it is, in a perpetual brotherhood with this great part of the American continent?"   (US Congressional Record 1918 65:2:9287)

He then quoted Wilson's policy of self-determination for small nations, which he argued was also enunciated in the political platforms of both parties. The Puerto Rican people were confident that the President and Congress would apply these principles to Puerto Rico too. "Full justice is yet to be granted to the people of Porto Rico, for we have not been given any voice in the appointment of our governors nor in the appointment of the attorney general, commissioner of education, or justices of the supreme court, yet the executive has the power of absolute veto granted him by this Congress" (US Congressional Record 1918 65:2:9288).

Now, he concluded, the people of Puerto Rico felt that these inequities would be redressed;

> "[they felt] that they have in President Wilson and the American Congress sympathetic friends, and they hope soon to obtain full recognition of their rights. The gratitude of the people of Porto Rico is great and intense for the concessions already made them, and their love for the American people will attain extraordinary proportions when this Congress does complete justice to our people, granting us all the power to which we are entitled in the management of our own affairs."   (US Congressional Record 1918 65:2:9288)

Before long the optimism generated by the idealism of Wilson began to dissipate and within a half year the resident commissioner took an increasingly somber view of the present and future status of Puerto Rico. What particularly jarred him in late January 1919 was the ruling of the United States Supreme Court in the Carlos Tapia case. This case dealt with the arrest of Tapia by legal authorities in Puerto Rico and his being charged with attempted murder. They took this action without seeking either a presentment or indictment from a grand jury, neither of which was required under terms of the Jones Act's Bill of Rights.

Tapia's lawyers in turn sought to quash the charges on the ground that, despite the absence of this requirement in the Jones Act, the act itself with its grant of American citizenship had transformed Puerto Rico from an unincorporated to an incorporated territory and therefore had brought the island under the full protective umbrella of the Constitution in which action by a grand jury was required. Accordingly, they charged that inasmuch as Puerto Rico had become a territory incorporated into the United States, Tapia "could not be legally held for trial without the presentment or indictment of a grand jury." The lower courts sustained their argument but the United States Supreme Court reversed their judgments, offering no opinion for its ruling.

The resident commissioner brought the ruling to the attention of the House of Representatives on February 12. In a dramatic address he declared that once again ambiguity seemed to envelop the status of Puerto Rico. For, contrary to what he and others had thought, the granting of American citizenship under the Jones Act had not changed Puerto Rico into an incorporated territory under the full protection of the Constitution.

"These decisions of the Supreme Court clearly show that the high tribunal considers the position of Porto Rico at present as it was under the Foraker Act, that no change had been operated in our status with the granting of the American citizenship to the citizens of Porto Rico, and that therefore we are yet an unincorporated territory."   (US Congressional Record 1919 65:3:3210)

In short the same questions persisted as had persisted for the "20 years of American domination."

"Are we foreigners? No; because we are American citizens, and no citizen of the United States can be a foreigner within the boundaries of the Nation.... [And yet] are we a part of the Union? No; because we are an unincorporated Territory under the rulings of the Supreme Court. Can you find a proper definition for this organized and yet unincorporated Territory, for this piece of ground belonging to but not forming part of the United States? Under the ruling of the courts of justice we are neither a part nor a whole. We are nothing."   (US Congressional Record 1919 65:3:3210).

Responsibility for this state of affairs to the extent that there was fault "belongs exclusively to the doubtful position adopted by the Congress of the United States." It was about time Congress clarified its position, for the "people of Porto Rico are entitled to know their fate. I think we are entitled to know your views, in order that our people may know what to expect of the American people and what course you are going to follow [Applause]." He went on, "we are asking for a definite solution, and the Congress of the United States must satisfy our wishes as soon as possible, because the policy of the past is inconsistent with the American principles and with the views expounded by the great leaders of the Nation in the present crisis of the world" (US Congressional Record 1919 65:3:3210).

He added that Congress should not try to make its decision alone; it should take into account the opinion of the Puerto Ricans through a plebiscite or referendum on the question of the political status of the country. This should be done because "in my judgment the fate of a country ought not be decided without a proper consultation with the people affected by the decision, in accordance with the right of self-determination, about which so much has been said." At present opinion on the island was very much divided on statehood or independence.

"The Republican Party favors statehood. The Unionist Party which is the majority party, demands self-government at the present and independence in the future, when the people of the United States will think that it is proper to grant independence to the people of Porto Rico, but really I cannot say what is the opinion of a majority of the people of the island. I can not say whether a majority of the people is in favor of statehood or in favor of independence."

                                           (US Congressional Record 1919 65:3:3210)

But, he continued, if Congress foreclosed the option of statehood, so that "we are not allowed to be a part of your organization [then] we must be allowed to be a whole, with our own government and our own flag" (US Congressional Record 1919 65:3:3210). A majority of the people of Porto Rico would agree with this. And so he reached his conclusion:

"If it is not your intention to make of Porto Rico a State of the Union, if you think as the Boston Court of Appeals that we are an insular piece of ground, with a considerable population, far removed from any physical relation with the States and Territories; if you think that on account of our differences in language, ethnology, and habits we can never form a part of the American federation; if we can not be a star in that glorious heaven of blue with its stripes of red and white; if we can not be a vital living part of the Nation we love and want to serve; if that concession can not be granted to us by the land that is always the friend of the helpless and small, then we must demand that the American people give us the freedom that is our God-given right. You have but two alternatives – statehood or independence. It is impossible to arrive at any other conclusion under the American Government."

                                           (US Congressional Record 1919 65:3:3212)

These sentiments were repeated several months later by the president of the Puerto Rican senate, who was also the leader of the Unionist party, in a speech to a delegation of congressmen from the United States. If Puerto Rico could not become a state, he declared, then its only remaining aspiration was independence; "for she could not resign herself to a colonial form of government" (US House of Representatives Committee on Insular Affairs (1919) 66:1:48). He insisted that Puerto Rico was not in any rush to gain its independence. It was prepared to continue its present status for a long time provided Congress expanded the machinery of self-government. At the heart of this expansion should be the election of the governor and greater input by the Puerto Rican legislature on the appointments of administrative heads of the executive branch. At present, he complained as did the resident commissioner, the American-appointed and American-bred officials from governor to department head showed a marked insensitivity to the ways and needs of the Puerto Rican people and displayed a compulsive arbitrariness in seeking to "Americanize" the island.

As a fitting conclusion to these remarks the congressional delegation was then presented with a resolution "adopted by caucus of the Senate, House, and Central Committee of the Unionist Party of Porto Rico on the 15th day of April 1919." Beginning with a preamble that extolled the democratic virtues of the United States and its principle of self-determination, the resolution then made the following declaration:

"Until the final political status of Porto Rico shall have been determined, after having ascertained the will of the people of the island through a plebiscite of their qualified voters, the Congress of the United States be petitioned:

(a) That the Legislature of Porto Rico be vested with power to legislate without restriction on all local matters.

(b) That the governor of the island be elected by the vote of its qualified electors.

(c) That the governor, with the advice and consent of the Senate of Porto Rico, shall appoint all heads of departments."

(US House of Representatives Committee on Insular Affairs (1919) 66:1:52)

Three years after the resident commissioner had sounded the alarm on the floor of the House of Representatives in Washington, the United States Supreme Court gave full expression to his fears, initially generated by its Tapia decision. In the case of Balzac v. People of Porto Rico, Chief Justice Taft declared in his opinion for the Court that Congress had granted American citizenship to Puerto Ricans under the Jones Act primarily to deal with the "anomalous status" they were in as citizens of Porto Rico. The act made explicit, he stated, what had previously been merely implicit to foreign countries: namely that Puerto Rico was under the protection of the United States government. However, in no way did the granting of citizenship transform the island from an unincorporated to an incorporated territory of the United States under the full protection of the Constitution. As a result, the defendant, Balzac, could not invoke the Sixth Amendment as grounds for a jury trial in a misdemeanor case involving libel, being that the local Puerto Rican law only granted such trials in the cases of felony.

The Chief Justice added that in granting American citizenship to Puerto Ricans the Jones Act gave individual Puerto Ricans certain additional rights. "It enabled them to move into the continental United States" and to establish residence in any of the States. Once they became "residents of any State [they could] there ... enjoy every right of any other citizen of the United States, civil, social and political [under the Constitution]. A citizen of the Philippines must be naturalized before he can settle and vote in this country. Act of June 29, 1906.... Not so the Porto Rican under the Organic Act of 1917" (258 US 1922:308).

In short, the Puerto Rican who settled in an American city was protected by the constitutional right of trial by jury.

"In Porto Rico, however, the Porto Rican can not insist upon the right of trial by jury, except as his own representatives in his legislature shall confer it on him. The citizen of the United States living in Porto Rico can not there enjoy a right of trial by jury under the Federal Constitution, any more than the Porto Rican. It is locality that is determinative of the application of the Constitution, in such matters as judicial procedure, and not the status of people who live in it." (258 US 1922:30)

The Chief Justice then proposed a cultural and institutional explanation as the reason for Congress' failure to provide for the right of trial by jury in the organic act of 1917. Although couched in relatively neutral terms, his explanation conveyed the ethnocentric notion of the superiority of Anglo-Saxon institutions and customs which produced in time a mature enough citizenry to assume the responsibility of the jury system.

"The jury system needs citizens trained to the exercise of the responsibilities of jurors. In common-law countries centuries of tradition have prepared a conception of the impartial attitude jurors must assume. The jury system postulates a conscious duty of participation in the machinery of justice which it is hard for people not brought up in fundamentally popular government at once to acquire. One of its greatest benefits is in the security it gives the people that they, as jurors actual or possible, being part of the judicial system of the country can prevent its arbitrary use or abuse." (258 US 1922:310)

People like the Puerto Ricans and the Filipinos, he argued, were "trained to a complete judicial system which knows no juries, living in compact and ancient communities, with definitely formed customs and political conceptions." As a result, Congress was wise in refraining from forcing a jury system on them and in leaving it up to them "to determine how far they wish to adopt this institution of Anglo-Saxon origin, and when" (258 US 1922:310).

The same reasoning lay behind Congress' failure to express

"an intention to incorporate in the Union these distant ocean communities of a different origin and language from those of our continental people. Incorporation has always been a step, and an important one, leading to statehood . . . it is reasonable to assume that when such a step is taken it will be begun and taken by Congress deliberately and with a clear declaration of purpose, and not left a matter of mere inference or construction." (258 US 1922:311)

He concluded,

"On the whole, therefore, we find no features in the Organic Act of Porto Rico of 1917 from which we can infer the purpose of Congress to incorporate Porto Rico into the United States with the consequences which would follow."

(258 US 1922:313)

20

THE QUEST FOR
SELF-GOVERNANCE:
INDEPENDENCE OR
COMMONWEALTH STATUS

Introduction

As it became increasingly evident that the granting of American citizenship to the individual Puerto Rican did not alter the colonial status of the island, the demands for self-governance and further clarification of the political status of Puerto Rico intensified. These demands grew louder and more insistent with the arbitrary "imperial" rule of Governor Reily who repeatedly expressed his determination to "Americanize" the island and with the Supreme Court's Balzac decision in 1922. The resulting ferment produced unusual ideological alignments. The Socialist and working-class party, for example, favored statehood; a major party of the established island elite supported eventual independence.

Not until the late 1940s, however, did Congress approve any significant advances in self-governance for the island. The first noteworthy change was in the right to elect its own governor. The pace quickened perceptibly with the election of Luis Munoz-Marin a year later. Under his prodding, Congress soon gave Puerto Rico authority to write its own constitution, and subsequently endorsed a newly created status of Commonwealth for it.

In this chapter we shall examine the tumultuous political history of Puerto Rico since the 1920s that produced innovative structures of governance which paralleled in many respects those that have traditionally marked the transformation of a Territory into a State in the Union. The island's structures, though, were pioneering ventures in America's Colonial, not in its People's, Domain.

The struggle for an unambiguous political status

GOVERNOR REILY AND THE AMERICANIZATION CRISIS

Even before the Supreme Court's Balzac decision highlighted the stressful ambiguity in the relations between Puerto Rico and the United States, these relations had been thrown into a state of turmoil by E. Mont Reily, the newly appointed governor of the island. In his inaugural address on July 30 1921, he hammered out two policy themes for his prospective administration that proved unpalatable to the leaders of the Unionist party still in control of the legislative government of the island. First he announced his intention to Americanize the island, primarily through changes in the school system.

"I shall not be satisfied until the whole [school] system is greatly improved along the lines of American ideas and American ideals. As Porto Rico is as much a part of the United States as is Ohio or Kentucky, I hope to see the language of Washington, Lincoln, and Harding taught equally with that of Spanish in our public schools, and that all other languages shall be secondary. Therefore English must be taught more and more. This I shall insist upon and the commissioner of education and all his subordinates shall be instructed accordingly."   (US Congressional Record 1922 67:2:4040–041)

Second, he announced his intention to stamp out any agitation for independence, which he had heard was being fomented by foreigners.

"If that be true, I want you to be fully aware that there is no room in Porto Rico for any foreigner who is not willing to support and uphold our established Government.... [This stance was fully supported by President Harding and the Secretary of War, both of whom] are as deeply interested in the Porto Rican people as they are in those of any State in the continental Union. They would be deeply distressed to see any feeling or growing sentiment on these islands tending toward any thought or idea of independence.... [Nor] is there any sympathy or possible hope in the United States for independence for Porto Rico from any individual or from any political party. Let no man or newspaper deceive you. The last two great national conventions held in the United States, Democratic and Republican, declared unanimously against independence for Porto Rico. Neither, my friends, is there any place on these islands for any flag save the flag of our beloved and common country, the Stars and Stripes, and there never shall be. So long as Old Glory waves over the United States it will continue to wave over Porto Rico. Old Glory has come to stay."

(US Congressional Record 1922 67:2:4041)

Using his dual ideological "truths" as a ramrod, the governor sought to Americanize the executive branch of government by replacing those who had been in office for a long time, some of whom were Puerto Ricans, with continental Americans, many of whom were from Kansas. He also sought to remove various members of the judiciary on the grounds of incompetence and to intervene actively in the judicial process. These actions brought him into direct conflict with the Unionist party. The party voted down his candidates for office when their nominations reached the legislature, and it decried publicly his unfolding pattern of arbitrary action.

In turn the governor overruled the legislature and installed his candidates for office notwithstanding. He also launched a bitter public attack against the Unionist party. He zeroed in on its independence plan and insisted that this showed the party was basically concerned with subverting American interests and values on the island for its own nationalistic and separatistic goals. Using this attack as his lever, he systematically sought to undermine the party's influence in the government through arbitrary action and among the people through public statements.

As the struggle gained momentum, the Unionist party met in conference during the late fall of 1921 and decided to eliminate from its platform the independence plank which, though couched in vague terms about some distant future, had proved so vulnerable to attack. At the same time the party vigorously rejected the Americanization or assimilationist doctrine of the governor. Four of its leading members, including the resident commissioner, spelled out in a petition to Congress this objection to assimilation or incorporation which they viewed as synonymous. They even quoted political and scientific authorities to prove that a policy of assimilation "rests upon a purely ideological basis and runs counter to the scientific laws of psychic development" (US Congressional Record 1922 67:2:980).

As an alternative, they proposed an autonomous form of government modeled after the newly created Free State of Ireland.

"[Such a government would] create contentment, enhance the affection and good faith always evidenced by the people of the United States toward the people of Porto Rico, and bring about a closer tie that time will prove indestructible. The United States can be as generous to Porto Rico as Great Britain has been to Ireland. In short, paraphrasing from the pamphlet we reprint, it will be hailed as an honor to this the greatest of all democracies to make a Porto Rico governed by itself, a country where freedom should beget loyalty, and we venture to say that the last hand which will wave the American flag on our island will be that of the Porto Rican."

(US Congressional Record 1922 67:2:980)

Ten days later at their behest, Campbell introduced a bill into the legislative hopper of the House; King followed suit almost a month later in the Senate. Both bills sought to provide an autonomous government for the island and to create the new political status of Associated Free State of Porto Rico. Neither bill was ever reported out of committee.

Despite this flurry of activity, the conflict between governor and Unionist party did not subside. Instead each side grew even more distrustful of the other. The governor, for example, continued to believe the party still favored independence. The party remained convinced that the governor was still intent upon undermining – if not destroying – its influence in Puerto Rico and upon creating an unfavorable image of it in America. So rapidly and badly did their relations deteriorate by March 2 1922 – only seven months after the governor's inauguration – that Resident Commissioner Davila brought the matter formally to the attention of the House of Representatives in Washington. In an impassioned speech on March 2, he rose to fulfill "my sacred obligations to the good people of Porto Rico, who are responsible for my presence in this body, as well as my obligations to the United States" by protesting against and asking relief "from the acts of an unprincipled, un-American, and altogether unfitted administrator, Gov. E. Mont Reily, of Porto Rico. His oft repeated abuse of power and his systematic insults to a friendly people have finally made this man intolerable to the people of the island" (US Congressional Record 1922 67:2:3301).

He then launched into a lengthy attack on the governor in which he made a number of specific charges. Many were leveled against the governor's alleged tampering with the integrity and independence of the judiciary. He also accused the governor of fomenting

"strife and discord among the citizens ... [and of destroying] the cordial relations now so happily existing among the loyal and patriotic people of Porto Rico, by false statements and by wicked and unwarranted accusations in public speeches against men of high character and patriotism who had shortly theretofore been elected by the people to places of honor and high responsibility in the government of Porto Rico.... [In addition,] E. Mont Reily has in his public speeches in utter disregard of the feelings and sentiments of the citizens of Porto Rico denounced the flag of Porto Rico as a 'dirty rag,' [and] has attempted to poison the mind and prejudice the public opinion of the people of the United States by falsely stating in public speeches that prominent leaders of the people of Porto Rico were disloyal and traitors."

(US Congressional Record 1922 67:2:3303)

Accordingly, the resident commissioner concluded,

"[the governor has] since his arrival in Porto Rico launched a campaign against the party in power and the most prominent leaders of the party. We carried the country by an overwhelming majority at the general elections and have the support and backing of the people of Porto Rico. Gov. Reily has declined to recognize the leaders of the majority party, has taken as his advisers belonging to the minority and is guided exclusively by their advice."

(US Congressional Record 1922 67:2:3305)

The next day a Democratic congressman from Mississippi introduced a resolution to investigate the conduct of the governor, but it elicited no debate or discussion and was referred to the Committee on Insular Affairs. Less than a week later, however, most of the commissioner's charges were repeated in a formal resolution presented to both houses of Congress by the resident commissioner from the Puerto Rican senate. Following the preamble, the resolution went on

"solemnly to accuse E. Montgomery Reily before the Congress of the United States of having violated the organic act and other statutes of Porto Rico, and of having done everything possible to discredit in Porto Rico the great Nation which is the cradle of liberty and democracy, by acting not as a true representative of the United States of America but as a vulgar agitator and an irresponsible despot." (US Congressional Record 1922 67:2:3479)

Accordingly, the Puerto Rican senate called on Congress to investigate thoroughly the governor's administration and asked the President to remove him from office.

Ten days later a congressman from Kansas rose in defense of the governor. He insisted that the governor had made considerable progress in realizing his twofold ideological objectives. As evidence, he pointed to the "fact" that "for the four years previous to Gov. Reily's going to Porto Rico as its governor but 1600 flags were sold in Porto Rico, while in the half year that he has been governor over 13,000 American flags have been purchased by the people, and to-day in the schools of Porto Rico the children are taught that there is only one flag and one country – 'Old Glory and America'" (US Congressional Record 1922 67:2:4043).

He also argued that the governor merely sought through his actions to make the executive and judiciary branches of government more effective by weeding out the incompetent and the disloyal. These actions, he contended, were popular with many segments of Puerto Rican society. However, the governor found himself dogged by the implacable enmity of the Unionist party which seemed determined, even before his arrival in Puerto Rico, to destroy him. The Unionist party, he declared, represented a small oligarchic elite who "possess the wealth and the higher education" and who cared little about the interests and welfare of the "masses [who] are poor and without property" (US Congressional Record 1922

67:2:4040). This elite had discouraged the teaching of English in schools and were actively pursuing a nationalistic course of separatism and independence. The governor's successes "in his fight for Americanism in Porto Rico" had forced the Unionist party to eliminate "from their platform the independence plan that it had been carrying for years."

> "[Now] new propaganda has been started in Porto Rico to serve the same purpose which the independence plank of the Barcelo machine was accomplishing – a free State of Porto Rico – which means a government dominated by the Barcello-Coll y Cuchi-Davila machine, with the Old World system of 'government by a few,' and the resultant exploitation of the people. It is unnecessary to add that this would be the end of Americanism in Porto Rico."
>
> (US Congressional Record 1922 67:2:4043)

In his defense of the governor, the congressman threw suspicion on the motives of the resident commissioner. He asked in rhetorical terms whether the governor's "innocent" veto of a $5000 allocation by the Puerto Rican legislature for use of the resident commissioner might not explain the latter's vituperative attack against the governor.

In a vigorous rebuttal several weeks later the resident commissioner denied the charges against him. He renewed his attack on the governor for his arbitrary behavior and for his labeling any quest for self-governance and cultural identity as traitorous and disloyal. If the governor were allowed to continue in this manner, increasing numbers of Puerto Ricans would become alienated from the United States. And instead of being satisfied with an autonomous govenment under the American flag, the people of Puerto Rico would increasingly turn toward independence – a sentiment that "is very old in Porto Rico [and] dates back to the time of the Spanish regime" (US Congressional Record 1922 67:2:5028).

> "The strongest argument in favor of independence in Porto Rico to-day is E. Mont Reily. The greatest obstacle to the advancement of Americanism in the island to-day is E. Mont Reily. The advocates of independence are appealing for new recruits to their cause every day by pointing to E. Mont Reily as a symbol of Americanism. Do you expect to continue to hold the loyalty and respect of the people of Porto Rico when you send to the island as governor an irresponsible despot, who wraps himself within the folds of the Star Spangled Banner and then attempts to rule our people after the fashion of a Roman proconsul? The people of Porto Rico honor and respect the American flag, which is our flag as well as your flag. But I say to you in all seriousness, gentlemen, that the Stars and Stripes is being desecrated when it is made to serve

as a shield to protect the conduct of a bully who wantonly insults our people and then seeks refuge beneath the folds of our sacred national emblem."

(US Congressional Record 1922 67:2:5029)

He concluded his address with another call for a congressional investigation and mentioned in passing that "the grand jury [in Porto Rico] is investigating the expenditure of the public funds appropriated by the legislature for the office of the governor" (US Congressional Record 1922 67:2:5030).

A week later the congressman from Mississippi renewed his call for an investigation of the governor and informed his colleagues "that the grand jury in Porto Rico had [just] made its presentment to the district attorney, with the request that he proceed against the governor for the misuse of public funds" (US Congressional Record 1922 67:2:5410).

Twelve days later the congressman called again for an investigation and belabored the Committee on Insular Affairs, of which he was a member, for its failure to conduct such an inquiry. He claimed that the governor had sabotaged the grand jury proceedings in Puerto Rico by removing the district attorney and by getting a judge whom he had just appointed to dismiss the grand jury. Unlike his earlier discourses on the governor, he made no attempt to disguise his contempt.

"And now we see this Governor of Porto Rico, this counterfeit, this vice of governors, dressed in his little brief authority, cutting such fantastic tricks before high heaven as make the angels weep, walking up and down the earth proclaiming to a trembling world, 'I did it.' [Laughter] I deny that. The flag which the Governor of Porto Rico has raised is not the Stars and Stripes. He pulled down the flag of Porto Rico in the presence of the people there and denounced it as a 'dirty rag,' but the only flag that has been raised there since he came that was not there when he arrived is the flag of mourning."

(US Congressional Record 1922 67:2:5914)

Except for a brief statement in the Senate about the matter almost a month later, nothing further was said until September. At that time the resident commissioner renewed his call for an investigation. He explained that he had been silent for the past four months, because he had been led to believe that the President would remove the governor if the attacks on the latter were to subside. Now, he continued, his patience had been eroded and he would once again resume his appeal for an investigation. He cited further evidence of the governor's abuse of power. And again he raised a series of questions.

"Are you going to allow the confidence that the people of Porto Rico have in this country be destroyed? Are you going to break faith with your fellow citizens of Porto Rico? Are you going to allow a dishonest man to remain governor of the island?... We are merely asking for an investigation. Are you going to refuse it? Is there no justice for the people of Porto Rico? We want the people of America to know what is happening in my country, and the only way to find out the truth is by an impartial investigation of the affairs of the island under Reily's administration. I think that we are entitled to be heard. The American people are not going to deny a forum to the people of Porto Rico."

(US Congressional Record 1922 67:2:13170)

The entreaties of the resident commissioner seemed finally to have been heard by the leadership in Congress. For early in the fourth session of the Sixty-seventh Congress a resolution was introduced in the Senate calling for a joint committee of the Senate and House "to investigate the governmental affairs of Porto Rico during the last 10 years, [and] the conduct of the officials of the insular government." The joint committee was also to do more than just look at the behavior of government officials; it was to investigate "the industrial and economic and living conditions of the people of the island, and to report their findings and recommendations to the Senate and House as speedily as possible" (US Congressional Record 1923 67:4:2148). A similarly broad-gauged resolution was introduced into the House the same day, but before either resolution emerged from its respective committee, President Harding had called for and received the resignation of Governor E. Mont Reily. Thus ended on March 2 the dramatic confrontation between an "Americanization" governor and a local elite intent upon maintaining the national and cultural identity of Puerto Rico under its hegemony.

THE ABORTIVE ATTEMPTS AT AN ELECTIVE GOVERNORSHIP

The cumulative strain between the office of governor and the legislature dissipated with the appointment as governor of Horace M. Turner, formerly chairman of the House Committee on Insular Affairs. He soon developed effective and harmonious working relationships with the legislative leaders. So positive were their reactions to him that by January of the following year he was called by the resident commissioner in a speech on the floor of Congress "one of the best governors the island has ever had. He is a statesman of remarkable ability, a true and honest representative of American principles, and a devoted friend of the people of Porto Rico" (US Congressional Record 1924 68:1:861).

Despite their growing regard for the governor, the legislative leaders decided, four months after his inauguration, to renew their campaign for greater self-governance, including the popular election of the governor. The governor, instead of opposing this move as would have Reily, encouraged and supported it. As a result, on July 24 the legislature unanimously passed a joint resolution creating a commission that would go to Washington to seek changes in the organic act of Porto Rico and to ascertain from Congress and the President their intentions "as regards the final status of our island." The commission was to include representatives from the three major parties in the legislature and also the governor as an ex-officio member. The major modifications in the organic law it was to seek were the following:

"(a) That the Congress, as well as the President of the United States of America, declare the purposes of said authorities as regards the final status of the island of Porto Rico;

(b) That the Legislature of Porto Rico be granted power to legislate without restriction on all local matters;

(c) That the people of Porto Rico shall elect their governor by vote of their qualified electors;

(d) That all appointments now made by the President of the United States, with the approval of the Federal Senate, shall hereafter be made by the Governor of Porto Rico with the advice and consent of the insular senate;

(e) That the island be granted power to legislate on all its financial problems, and to regulate the acquisition of lands, and to levy local excise or internal-revenue taxes to be collected in benefit of the insular Territory, and in general on all such measures as may be demanded by the interests and needs of Porto Rico which are not in conflict with such other measures of the same nature as are of a national character; and

(f) That all such measures of a national character that tend to benefit education, agriculture, and other sources of knowledge or of wealth in the island shall be extended to Porto Rico in the same proportion in which they are extended to all the States of the American Union."

(US Congressional Record 1924 68:1:862)

By the end of the year a commission of ten members was appointed. As it reached Washington in the second week of January, it addressed to the President and Congress a memorial to which it appended the joint resolution. In its memorial the commission called again on the

"authorities of the Republic [for] an authoritative declaration with regard to which is to be the definite status of Porto Rico when it shall be no longer a mere possession of the United States, and when it shall start upon the full enjoyment of a life in consonance with the highest ideals of democracy and justice, a consummation that is expected by both the American and the Porto Rican peoples."   (US Congressional Record 1924 68:1:1470)

The commission also requested "fundamental changes in the organic act" so as to allow greater autonomy for the island.

"It is our belief and claim that our progress during the years in which we have been establishing a free and progressive Commonwealth justifies us in asking for such consideration in the granting of complete self-government as we believe we merit and deserve. It is our belief that we are justified in claiming that the time has come when we, American citizens that we are, may with entire safety assume full responsibility in the management of our own affairs. The work we have accomplished and with which you are familiar should be to you a guaranty that the work we will accomplish in the future for the welfare of our people, such as sanitation, road building, the elevation of labor, the lessening of the burdens of poverty, the wiping out of illiteracy, shall be such as to bring continued credit to ourselves and honor to the other Commonwealths of the Union."
                    (US Congressional Record 1924 68:1:1470)

In his reply President Coolidge was vague about the future; he also made no commitment about the present and merely counseled patience and gratitude.

"You have spoken of desiring to know what may be your condition in the future. In that you have a curiosity common to all of us, and the answer is naturally a common one. Your lot in the future will depend entirely upon your actions in the present.... Your island is prosperous, it is making great progress, it is learning the art of self-government, your people are becoming more and more educated, your living conditions are growing better, and your whole atmosphere is one of prosperity and ought to be one of contentment. The only way to prepare for something better to-morrow is to do well the duties that come to us to-day. In your efforts in that direction I wish you all possible success and happiness."   (US Congressional Record 1924 68:1:1470)

Despite this unpromising beginning, the commission energetically pursued its campaign of lobbying congressmen and heads of the various executive departments. One result was that within a month of its arrival two bills were introduced into Congress, one in each house, that were addressed to the major goal of the commission: namely, the popular election of the governor. The House bill, for example, provided "for the election of the governor in 1928 and the appointment of the heads of departments by the governor, by and with the advice and consent of the senate of Porto Rico" (US House of Representatives Report No. 291 (1924) 68:1:2).

Members of the commission testified at length at the hearings for the bills, and in an impassioned plea the delegate from the island's Republican party declared:

"We ask as Porto Ricans and as American citizens complete self-government. We do not want to be longer a mere possession. We want to be a people in the real sense of the word, a commonwealth, a community of American citizens with all the rights and all the duties that are in the common patrimony and heritage of the American citizenship, so that we may say with the same pride that you do, with the same pride that the Romans of the time of Cicero said, 'We are Romans,' 'We are American citizens.'"

(US House of Representatives Report No. 291 (1924) 68:1:5)

Both committees reported favorably on the bills to their respective houses. However, despite the favorable report, the House version never reached the floor. The Senate version, though, reached the floor by the middle of May. At the behest of the Secretary of War, it was amended so that the popular election of the governor would begin in 1932, not 1928; however, "if at any time prior thereto inquiry by the Census Bureau shows that the percentage of illiteracy shall have been reduced below 30 percent, the election could be held earlier" (US Congressional Record 1924 68:1:8600). (The Senate was informed that the present estimate of illiteracy was 50 percent.) Following a brief debate both the amendment and the original bill were passed and sent to the House Committee on Insular Affairs, from which they never emerged.

Even before this abortive effort reached the Senate floor, most of the commissioners had returned to Puerto Rico. Although virtually nothing was accomplished to change the status of the island, the mission nevertheless produced a marked change in the internal political scene. So well had the two heads of the two major parties worked together that *en route* home they prepared "a manifesto calling for a political and electoral alliance of the Unionist and Republican Parties" (Ribes Tovar 1973:445).

The Alliance was formally established on May 24; its primary objective, "the attainment of self-government within the framework of the American Union" (Ribes Tovar 1973:446). For a large faction of the Republican party, however, the Alliance proved objectionable. As a result, they split from the parent party and set up the Historic Constitutional party in which the platform of statehood for Puerto Rico was reaffirmed. Recognizing their electoral weakness, the new party decided within several months to join forces with the Socialist party which also stressed statehood for the coming election. This coalition was no match for the Alliance in the 1924 election, although the splinter Republican group outpolled its parent body by approximately 4000 votes.

No sooner had the new legislature convened when it renewed efforts to gain a

broader range of self-governance. By the middle of August these efforts coalesced
into the passage of a concurrent resolution which requested "the Congress of the
United States to amend, reenact and add certain sections to the organic act of
Porto Rico" (US Congressional Record 1925 69:1:603). All in all, fourteen
modifications were requested and, as in the joint resolution of a year before, the
pivotal change was to be in the selection of the governor. He was to be chosen by
popular vote beginning with the election of 1928. A second major recommendation was the addition of a section to the organic law which would confirm for
Puerto Ricans the concept of dual citizenship just as it had already been confirmed
for the territories and states of the Union. Having already been designated citizens
of the United States by the Jones Act of 1917, they wanted now to become
"citizens of Porto Rico" too.

Most of the other recommendations were meant to enhance the authority of the
legislature and/or the governor once he was elected. Accordingly the legislature
would assume virtually full control over taxation even to the extent of imposing
tariffs on imports from America. It would also be able to override by a two-thirds
vote presidential veto of any of the laws it passed. Further, the legislature would be
"empowered to enforce the provisions of the joint resolution approved May 1,
1900, with respect to the buying, selling, or holding of real estate;" it would also
be empowered "to impose additional and progressive taxes on all property owned
or controlled in excess of 500 acres by corporations, partnerships, associations,
and individuals, and to provide for the forfeiture of all lands owned or controlled
by corporations in violation of the prohibition established in the aforesaid joint
resolution" (US Congressional Record 1925 69:1:605).

The resolution also proposed that the legislature meet annually instead of
biennially and that its per diem be raised. In addition, it proposed that once the
governor was elected he would assume sole responsibility with the advice and
consent of the senate for the appointment of other top officials. Further, it
recommended that the present department of agriculture and labor be divided into
two separate departments, each with its own head, and that the composition of the
Public Service Commission be changed from the present nine appointed members
to three members, two of whom would be elected while the third, the commissioner, would be appointed by the governor with the advice and consent of the
senate.

The other recommendations had to do with the judiciary. For example,
proceedings would be conducted not only in English as in the past but also in
Spanish. Stricter controls would be imposed on the judges in issuing "interlocu-
tory or preliminary injunction[s] suspending or restraining the enforcement or
execution of any law or statute of Porto Rico" (US Congressional Record 1925
69:1:605).

Finally the resolution authorized the appointment of a commission from the legislature of Puerto Rico by the president of the senate and speaker of the house that would proceed to Washington

"to continue the work left pending by the commission sent to Washington under resolution of the last legislature; and said commission shall have ample powers, which are hereby granted to it, to demand a most complete and absolute self-government permitting our island to develop its economic and social progress to the point of placing itself in condition some day to propound the problem of its final status through a plebiscite of our people to express their sovereign will." (US Congressional Record 1925 69:1:606)

Once again a commission embarked on a mission of persuasion, and once again it met with limited success. The resolution it carried was read to Congress on the first month of the year. In the following spring Butler introduced a bill into the Senate that was reported back favorably by his Committee on Territories and Insular Possessions less than a month later.

Despite the entreaties of the Puerto Rican commission, the bill completely skirted the issue of electing the governor, but it did adopt the resolution's "citizen of Porto Rico" concept. In making this recommendation the Senate committee declared that the provision was "identical with that enacted some years ago for Hawaii" (US Senate Report No. 1011 (1926) 69:1:2). In short, the concept of dual citizenship would henceforth apply formally to Puerto Rico as it already did for the various territories and states of the Union.

Only one other recommendation of the resolution was adopted virtually intact; that which would have the legislature meet annually instead of biennially. Three others were incorporated with major modifications. For example, the legislature would be given certain enhanced powers of taxation but no right to exact tariffs or export duties, and the limits of its authority to assume public indebtedness were clearly set. In addition, compensation for the legislators would be increased but not to the extent that the resolution called for. Finally the Public Service Commission would be reduced to three members, none of whom was to be elected as recommended by the resolution.

Nine other recommendations of the resolution were completely ignored, the most important of which had to do with the election of the governor. The Senate bill, however, contained two provisions that had not been mentioned in the resolution. One had to do with the appointment of an auditor; and the other, with the granting of writs of habeas corpus and of mandamus by the courts.

The bill was briefly debated on the floor of the Senate without any attention being paid to the citizenship provision whatsoever. After being passed at the end of February, the bill was sent to the House, which abandoned its own version of the bill. Without any debate, it passed the House by the first of March and was signed into law by President Coolidge on March 4 1927.

Thus in a matter-of-fact way Congress completed in 1927 what it had started in 1917. Then it had bestowed American citizenship on Puerto Ricans; now it granted them a distinctive Puerto Rican citizenship. In short, Puerto Rico now shared with the inhabitants of states and incorporated territories of the Union the constitutionally defined right of dual citizenship, though Puerto Rico itself continued to remain outside of the Union as an unincorporated but organized territory.

The leaders of the Alliance found little comfort in Congress' lukewarm response to their Concurrent Resolution No. 6 and to the modest "formalistic" gains they made. They were particularly disturbed that the Senate had backed off on a pivotal issue when several years earlier it had taken a stand: namely, the election of the governor. Accordingly, they were convinced that, despite these minor gains of the new bill, their quest for expanded self-governance had been rebuffed by the United States government, if not set back.

THE CONFLICT BETWEEN THE ALLIANCE AND PRESIDENT COOLIDGE: PUERTO RICO AS A "FREE STATE"

As a result the Alliance sought support for their struggle from their fellow Caribbean and Latin American countries, particularly those who shared their Spanish colonial history and whose representatives had gathered in Cuba in January 1928 for the Sixth Pan American Conference. In a cablegram to the presiding officer who was Cuban, Barcelo, president of the Puerto Rican senate, and Tous Soto, speaker of the Puerto Rican house of representatives, asked the conference to endorse "the following cablegram that we have just addressed to the President of the United States of America, Hon. Calvin Coolidge" (US Congressional Record 1928 70:1:6347). The text of the cablegram followed. In it, the two leaders congratulated the President for the inspiring speech he had just made at the conference with its lofty message of "justice and self-determination for all" and urged him to apply to Puerto Rico "the wonderful language of that brave speech, so worthy of a great American" (US Congressional Record 1928 70:1:6347).

They continued,

"Porto Rico feels humiliated because of the inferior condition she is subjected to in spite of the hopes the treaty of Paris awoke in us; in spite of the unfulfilled promises made to our people, and in spite of the repeated legitimate demands in favor of a regime that may enable our island to exercise her own sovereignty over her own internal affairs and to freely solve the grave economical situation she is undergoing."   (US Congressional Record 1928 70:1:6347)

If the United States for a variety of reasons, including

> "different ethnological conditions, can not make of our island but a mere subjected colony, then we ask to be allowed to be constituted as a free State, concerting thus with your great Republic such good and fraternal relations as may be necessary for the mutual welfare of the United States and Porto Rico and to the dignity of our citizens."
>
> (US Congressional Record 1928 70:1:6347)

They then invoked the American creed and Christianity as moral justification for their demands. "Justice and nothing but justice is what we ask as citizens of America, as faithful Christians, and as children of the Almighty God that gave us the same inalienable rights your great Republic knew how to invoke when declaring for independence at the memorable convention at Philadelphia" (US Congressional Record 1928 70:1:6347).

The two leaders also told the President in the cablegram that they were "cabling to Habana asking our sister nations of America now meeting there to join us in making this petition to your excellency." They were resorting to this tactic because "ours is the only Spanish-American country whose voice has not been heard at Habana during the Pan American Conference, for it was not represented there" (US Congressional Record 1928 70:1:6347).

Several days later the two leaders sought to clarify what they meant by 'free state" in another cablegram addressed to the presiding officer of the conference and to the United States Secretary of State. In the cablegram they objected to the interpretation that several news services had placed on the term; it did not refer to "international independence ... but [to] internal sovereignty. We do not ask the conference to intervene in domestic affairs of the American Union, but to express its solidarity and sympathy with aspirations of Porto Rico to full political and financial self-government in harmony with President Coolidge's opening speech" (US Congressional Record 1928 70:1:6348).

Not content with merely garnering international support for their cause, the legislative leaders also sought to exhort the American people through its newly acclaimed hero, Charles A. Lindbergh, who was then on a triumphant tour of the island. In a speech full of the most lavish encomiums, the president of the senate, Barcelo, read the contents of a resolution passed by both houses of the Puerto Rican legislature that rendered "homage to Col. Charles A. Lindbergh." It offered him Puerto Rico's "most cordial welcome," declared him "an illustrious citizen of Porto Rico," awarded him a commemorative gold medal, and made him "the bearer of a message, which will be delivered to him at a joint session of the legislature, from the people of Porto Rico to the people of the United States" (US Congressional Record 1928 70:1:6348).

In this message, a resolution from both houses, the legislature welcomed

Lindbergh in the name of the earlier Spanish explorers from Columbus to Ponce de Leon who had also come to Puerto Rico; all had spread the "message of civilization and progress" from one shore to another: the Spanish explorers from the Old to the New World and Lindbergh from the New to the Old. Now, the resolution continued, the "lone eagle" could be the bearer of another message:

> "to your country and to your people you will convey the message of Porto Rico, not far different from the cry of Patrick Henry, 'Liberty or death.' It is the same in substance, but with the difference imposed by the change of times and conditions. The message of Porto Rico to your people is: 'Grant us the freedom that you enjoy, for which you struggled, which you worship, which we deserve, and you have promised us.' We ask the right to a place in the sun – this land of ours, brightened by the stars of your glorious flag."
>
> (US Congressional Record 1928 70:1:6348)

Taking advantage of still another commemorative occasion, Barcelo and Tous Soto sent virtually identical cablegrams on Lincoln's birthday to the president of the United States Senate. Each offered a unanimous resolution from his respective house that invoked "memorable" words of the "martyred President:" "The Government of the people, by the people, and for the people shall not perish from the earth." The resolutions asked that these words be applied to Puerto Rico by enacting, in the words of the senate resolution, "the bills introduced by your Resident Commissioner providing for the election of the Governor of Porto Rico by the vote of the people at the elections of 1932 and authorizing our people to draft their own constitution" (US Congressional Record 1928 70:1:2939).

One week later, February 20, the Puerto Rican senate affirmed "once more its sentiments and aspirations in favor of full and complete self-government for Porto Rico" in a resolution addressed to the President and Congress of the United States. In the resolution the senate reaffirmed its commitment to the Concurrent Resolution 6 of August 1925, particularly that section bearing on the election of the governor. The senate also ratified as an expression of its own will the cablegrams sent by Barcelo and Tous Soto to President Coolidge about his address to the Pan American Conference. And finally the resolution protested the several bills introduced into the senate "which seek to restrict the powers of the Legislature of Porto Rico in the matter of budgets and appropriations" (US Congressional Record 1928 70:1:4058).

Stung by this onslaught, particularly by the cablegram to the Pan American Congress and by the resolution entrusted to Lindbergh, President Coolidge responded with a long and frequently bitter letter to Governor Towner which he expected to be transmitted to the Puerto Rican legislature. He complained:

"The cablegram and resolution seem to be based largely on a complete misunderstanding of concrete facts. It would not be difficult to show that the present status of Porto Rico is far more liberal than any status of its entire history; that its people have greater control of their own affairs with less interference from without; that its people enjoy liberty and the protection of law, and that its people and its Government are receiving material assistance through its association with the continental United States. The treaty of Paris, of course, contains no promise to the people of Porto Rico. No phrase of that treaty contemplated the extension to Porto Rico of a more liberal regime than existed. The United States has made no promise to the people of Porto Rico that has not been fulfilled, nor has any representative or spokesman for the United States made such a promise. . . .

The Porto Rican government at present exercises a greater degree of sovereignty over its own internal affairs than does the government of any State or Territory of the United States."

(US Congressional Record 1928 70:1:4872)

Later in his letter he sought to explain this last assertion by stating that "the principal difference between the government of Porto Rico and that of the organized and incorporated Territories of the United States is the greater power of the legislature and the fiscal provisions governing Porto Rico, which are far more liberal than those of any of our States or Territories" (US Congressional Record 1928 70:1:4873).

As evidence he pointed to the "fact" that all internal revenues, income taxes, and customs duties collected in Puerto Rico were turned over to its treasury as were the internal revenue taxes collected in the United States on Puerto Rican products; states and incorporated territories received only a fraction of these revenues. Thus he estimated that of the $11,000,000 operating revenues received by Puerto Rico in 1927, the latter would only obtain two millions or less than 20 percent of the amount.

He was particularly upset by the charge in the cablegram that Puerto Rico was a "mere subjected colony."

"Certainly giving Porto Rico greater liberty than it has ever enjoyed and powers of government for the exercise of which its people are barely prepared can not, with propriety, be said to be establishing therein 'a mere subjected colony.' The people of Porto Rico are citizens of the United States, with all the rights and privileges of other citizens of the United States, and these privileges are those which we invoked 'when declaring for independence at the memorable convention at Philadelphia.'"

(US Congressional Record 1928 70:1:4872)

The President went on to describe how bad conditions were in Puerto Rico before America took over. He quoted Spanish authorities to show the dire poverty, degradation, and disease suffered under Spanish rule.

"[In addition] prior to the American occupation the Porto Rican people had received practically no training in self-government or the free exercise of the franchise. While there existed a body of educated, intelligent men, the great mass of the people were without experience or training in self-government, and only a small percentage could qualify as voters under very broad electoral qualifications."   (US Congressional Record 1928 70:1:4873)

All this began to change with the coming of the military government and continued to change with the passage of the two organic acts. As a result, Puerto Rico was much better off now than it had ever been.

"We found the people of Porto Rico poor and distressed, without hope for the future, ignorant, poverty-stricken, and diseased, not knowing what constituted a free and democratic government and without the experience of having participated in any government. We have progressed in the relief of poverty and distress, in the eradication of disease, and have attempted, with some success, to inculcate in the inhabitants the basic ideas of a free, democratic government. We have now in Porto Rico a government in which the participation by Americans from the United States is indeed small. We have given to the Porto Rican practically every right and privilege which we permitted ourselves to exercise. We have now progressed to the point where discouragement is replaced by hope, and while only 30 years ago one was indeed an optimist to see anything promising in Porto Rico, to-day one is indeed a pessimist who can see any reasonable human ambition beyond the horizon of its people."

(US Congressional Record 1928 70:1:4873)

In an expression of unbounded enthusiasm he proclaimed, "Perhaps no territory in the world has received such considerate treatment in the past 30 years as has Porto Rico, and perhaps nowhere else has progress been so marked and so apparent as in Porto Rico. We are certainly entitled to a large part of the credit for this situation" (US Congressional Record 1928 70:1:4873).

As a final embellishment on his pronouncement, the President pointed to advances in health and education made under American tutelage. And he spelled out in somber tones the economic losses Puerto Rico would sustain if it became a "free state" and were excluded from America's umbrella of tariffs. He disclaimed any intention on the part of the American government to thwart "reasonable" aspirations of the people of Puerto Rico. In fact, he insisted,

"The island has so improved and its people have so progressed in the last generation as to justify high hopes for the future; but it certainly is not unreasonable to ask that those who speak for Porto Rico limit their petition to those things which may be granted without denial of such hope. Nor is it unreasonable to suggest that the people of Porto Rico, who are a part of the people of the United States, will progress with the people of the United States rather than isolated from the source from which they have received practically their only hope of progress." (US Congressional Record 1928 70:1:4874)

Obviously upset by the President's letter, the Puerto Rican legislature adopted a concurrent resolution authorizing the presiding officers of each house, Barcelo and Tous Soto, to prepare an official reply. It also requested "the Congress of the United States to appoint a congressional committee to investigate the political, economical, and social conditions of Porto Rico" (US Congressional Record 1928 70:1:5257).

In their official reply routed through the resident commissioner in Washington, the legislative leaders disputed each of the statements made by the President. While acknowledging the "enjoyment of individual liberty and the protection of law" accorded the island by the Jones Act of 1917, they nevertheless insisted that "we can not accept, however, the statement that 'the present status of Porto Rico is far more liberal than any status in its entire history.' The autonomous system of government granted to Cuba and Porto Rico by Spain was more ample, more liberal in many respects, than our present political status." They then quoted from the royal decree of 1897 which established self-government in Cuba and Porto Rico. They conceded that if the United States made the Puerto Rican governor elective and adopted other self-governance measures, then the resulting "republican and representative form of government [would be] superior to the Spanish autonomous character" (US Congressional Record 1928 70:1:6337).

Barcelo and Tous Soto scoffed at the President's notion that "the Porto Rican government at present exercises a greater degree of sovereignty over its own internal affairs than does the government of any State or Territory of the United States." Their rebuttal compared the rights of the people in the states to elect their governors, to write their own constitutions, and to have their legislative representatives override the veto of a governor with the absence of these rights among Puerto Ricans. They conceded that "it is true that Porto Rico disposes of its customshouse and internal revenue receipts, while the States do not. But, surely, no State is willing to change places with Porto Rico and to surrender its internal sovereignty for the sake of receiving all the taxes derived from incomes and excises" (US Congressional Record 1928 70:1:6338).

They took strong exception to the President's claim that the island had gained economically and materially from being under the protective wing of America. The economic gains, they insisted, had gone disproportionately to a small elite group comprised primarily of absentee American capitalists while most Puerto Ricans suffered from economic deprivation and degradation. Even the tariff structure operated to benefit the few: "it increases the production of sugar and tobacco – two-thirds of which are in the hands of continental Americans who have monopolized almost all our best lands – and decreases the production of coffee owned chiefly by Porto Ricans" (US Congressional Record 1928 70:1:6342).

They complained that "in our opinion the hardest financial problem with which the people of Porto Rico are confronted is that of unemployment. Indeed, unemployment affects the Porto Rican home directly, and commerce, the small industries, and even our most insignificant social activities, indirectly" (US Congressional Record 1928 70:1:6342).

They ended their rebuttal with another call on Congress and the President to clarify the island's political status.

"We must say with the utmost frankness that the problem of our definite status after 30 years of American rule has not been given due consideration by the national administration, the political parties, the American statesmen, the press, and the American people as a whole. A community of one million and a half of American citizens, by adoption, who have as a precious heirloom the old and noble culture which sowed the seed of democracy throughout this entire American continent, not excluding the northern section, is certainly entitled to know its future political status, to ask the American people what its place will be in the Union of free Commonwealths forming the glorious American constella-tion."   (US Congressional Record 1928 70:1:6343)

They then proposed an autonomous political status that involved neither complete independence nor statehood.

"[With such an autonomous structure,] Porto Rico would have almost all the rights and privileges enjoyed by the States – except national representation – besides certain additional local powers justified by our peculiar situation. We would be associated with, though not incorporated into the Union. In this way, both peoples would be joined by a common flag, a common sovereignty, and a common citizenship. We would be bound to each other by ties of mutual interest, aspirations, and affection, and Porto Rico would be in a position to constitute the spiritual isthmus between the Americas – the foundation for a bridge of ideals between the two continents, the two races, and the two civilizations of the Western Hemisphere. This is our answer to the question raised by the Chief Magistrate of the Nation."

(US Congressional Record 1928 70:1:6344–345)

A year later the resident commissioner renewed the plea for clarification of the island's political status in a speech at a conference on International Relations in New York State. In doing so, he dramatically illustrated the paradoxical and contradictory status of the island and its people.

"Individually the Porto Ricans are American citizens, both at home and abroad, and enjoy all the rights inherent to American citizenship throughout the United States. But once these individual unities join the Porto Rican family and form a collective body this aggregation composed of American citizens becomes foreign to the United States in a domestic sense."

(US Congressional Record 1929 71:1:183)

And as though to highlight the incomprehensibility of this paradoxical duality, he stated queruously, "It is hard to understand how the citizen of Porto Rico can be *individually domestic and collectively foreign* [author's italics]" (US Congressional Record 1929 71:1:183).

As part of this resurgent expression of concern with cultural and national sensibilities, the Puerto Rican legislation unanimously petitioned Congress in April 1930, a year after Davila's speech, "officially to restore to our island its true name of Puerto Rico in place of Porto Rico as it is now called, because it is considered that full justice will thus be done to our history, our language, and our traditions." In the preamble of its resolution, the legislature complained that the name, Porto Rico, had been imposed upon the island by Congress "immediately following the change of sovereignty ... without justifying reasons." The name itself "is an impure idiomatic compound partly formed of the foreign word porto, which, although of Latin origin, has not yet been adopted into our language, but is here used illegitimately to substitute the word puerto, genuinely Spanish.... There are no reasons either in the history, the language, or the traditions of our people supporting the legitimacy of the foreign term porto" (US Congressional Record 1930 71:2:9922).

Two months later the concurrent resolution was thrown into the legislative hopper of each house of Congress. The Senate passed on it within two weeks, but it was passed over as it reached the floor of the House six months later. The Senate tried once again with the convening of a new Congress at the end of December and passed the resolution, which now had the label SJ Res 36, by the end of April. Three weeks later the House also accepted the resolution, only after eliminating the lengthy preamble, and on May 17 1932 President Hoover signed the name change into law.

Passage of the resolution turned out to be the last congressional victory for the Alliance that had controlled the Puerto Rican legislature since 1924. The resolution's reaffirmation of Puerto Rico's historical, cultural, and national identity was a fitting epitaph to the ideological traditions of the major partner of the Alliance, the Unionist party. For even before the resolution passed Congress, the Unionist party had terminated its alliance with the Republican party, but was denied the right by the Attorney General of Puerto Rico to use its Unionist label or to run candidates under the label on the ground that it had not run as a separate entity in the previous two elections. Finally rebuffed on appeal to the Supreme Court of Puerto Rico, the leaders abandoned the fight and reorganized the party as the Puerto Rican Liberal party. The resulting confusion reduced its popular strength enough to allow for a victory in 1932 by the revitalized coalition of Socialist and Republican parties, which in 1924 included only splinter Republicans but now encompassed the main force of Republicans. As a result of this political change combined with the mounting pressures of the Great Depression, an entirely new list of political and economic priorities was prepared and presented to United States Congress by a new kind of spokesman for Puerto Rico, Santiago Iglesias, leading member of the Socialist party, head of the Free Workingmen's Association, and now the newly elected resident commissioner.

IGLESIAS AND STATEHOOD

In his first major address to the House of Representatives at the end of March 1933, Iglesias pointed to the internal "economic and social conditions prevailing among the masses of producers and workers in Puerto Rico" as "the most vital problem requiring immediate attention." He blamed much of the island's economic ills on the large land holdings dedicated to the production of a single crop, sugar, by absentee owners. As a result there was a high rate of unemployment; "the margin of subsistence is already dangerously narrow for the vast majority of the people" (US Congressional Record 1933 73:1:1003). "In the midst of a land fertile enough to provide the most nutritive and fresh foods, the Puerto Rican is largely dependent on imported foods from United States, his diet consisting mainly of rice, dried fish, and beans" (US Congressional Record 1933 73:1:1005).

Iglesias desired to remedy this situation:

"My work in Congress will be dedicated mainly to ask you for the rehabilitation of the people of the island. The economic program set forth for the people by the President should be extended fully to Puerto Rico.... I propose to work

for the abolishing of the ills that the absent monopolies and financial combinations regulate, contract, and control – social, political, financial, and governmental conditions of life in the island ... [in addition,] we want to intensify
and diversify agriculture, promoting means of work and providing more
practical education ... [and] we have to diversify our occupations, open new
industries and provide work the year round for our people."

(US Congressional Record 1933 73:1:1003)

Although the Socialist party "was and is more interested in the island's economic
problems" and had never been "greatly concerned with the immediate need for
raising the statehood-independence political issue ... its fundamental goal is
permanent association with the people of the United States." But he protested,
earlier in his speech, this association should not be that of a colonial dependency,
but that of an equal member of the American political community.

"We reject all formulas of a colonial government. We consider this formula
disgraceful and not compatible with the civil dignity of our Nation, and
therefore we proclaim the permanent union of the people of Puerto Rico with
the people of the United States to maintain and consecrate socially, politically,
and industrially a democratic community with the same rights and duties as any
community of our Nation. We want and are willing to be recognized as an
integral part of the States of the Union and lead our future in that line."

(US Congressional Record 1933 73:1:1004)

He hoped that Congress would hear this fervent plea and

"that at the earliest opportunity Congress, in considering the economic
reconstruction of Puerto Rico, will make a declaration that the ultimate political
status of the island will be to organize the people of Puerto Rico as a State of the
Union. Having defined this objective Congress should give Puerto Rico
economic cooperation by extending to the island all national measures with
ample freedom of action to work out a program and reach the goal by the own
efforts of its people. The words of hope and action of President Roosevelt
should embrace Puerto Rico as an integral part of our Nation, and I believe he
has in mind this thought....

Puerto Rico is American socially, politically; and its trade, its practices, and
its industry pile and flourish under the American flag. Puerto Rico is proud of
this, economically and sentimentally."

(US Congressional Record 1933 73:1:1005)

Two weeks later this informal request for statehood was codified into a formal
resolution from both houses of the Puerto Rican legislature. As read in the United

States Senate on May 15, the resolution stated "that the people of Puerto Rico desires that Puerto Rico become a State and be admitted to the Union under the same conditions as the States which integrate the same." It also requested legislation from Congress "authorizing the people of Puerto Rico to frame its own State constitution in order to submit it for the approval of the Congress of the United States of America after it is ratified by the electoral body of Puerto Rico to which it shall be submitted through a plebiscite for such purpose" (US Congressional Record 1934 73:2:8816).

In the meantime the resolution continued, "the people of Puerto Rico demands an immediate liberalizing reform, of a political and economic nature, of the autonomic regimen of government which it now enjoys, petitioning the Congress of the United States of America, as it is hereby petitioned, to amend the organic act of Puerto Rico in force in accordance with the following:" The resolution then called for the popular election of the governor, for enlargement of his authority to appoint officials with the consent of the Puerto Rican senate, and also for expanded authority for the legislature whereby it could override any veto of the executive, enact tariffs, exercise control over property, and enforce the 500-acre provision.

A week after the resolution was read in the United States Senate, Luiz Munoz-Marin declared in a letter to Congress that the Liberal party was unalterably opposed to statehood and that its legislative representatives had voted against the concurrent resolution. This stance, he insisted, reflected the sentiment of the average Puerto Rican more than did that of the Republican party, the former having polled 22 percent more votes in the last election than did the only member of the Coalition that truly advocated statehood. He continued:

> "The Socialist Party does not advocate statehood, but its members in the legislature voted for the resolution, thus giving it a majority. The Socialist members also explained officially their reasons for voting the resolution. They voted it because they are allied with the Republican Party because they understand that the resolution contains a request that the people of Puerto Rico be given the opportunity to reject statehood at the polls, and because the resolution also solicits certain economic reforms, such as local tariff-making powers, which the Socialist Party deems beneficial, but which are antagonistic to statehood."   (US Congressional Record 1934 73:2:12181)

He explained that the Liberal party opposed statehood principally for economic reasons.

> "[It] feels that statehood not only would make the economic situation of Puerto Rico more serious than it is, or more than it would be at the moment of granting

statehood – no matter when that moment might be – but would tie the hands of Congress and the Federal Government in perpetuity in its dealings with the economic situation in Puerto Rico.... The Liberal Party stands for the independence of Puerto Rico. There is not unfriendliness towards the United States among 98 percent of the people of my country and much less among the members of the Liberal Party.... The attitude of the Liberal Party both toward independence and toward the American people may be said to be identical with that of the followers of Manuel Quezon in the Philippines."

(US Congressional Record 1934 73:1:12181)

The position of each of the spokesmen was further elaborated late in May and early in June at hearings on a bill that had been introduced into the United States House of Representatives "to enable the people of Puerto Rico to form a constitution and state government and be admitted into the union on an equal footing with the states" (US House of Representatives Committee on Territories (1935) 74:1: title page).

In his testimony Senator Munoz-Marin conceded that statehood might bestow significant political gains on Puerto Rico, ranging from popular election of a governor to two senators and eight or nine representatives in Congress. In turn Puerto Rico would suffer serious economic losses from statehood. First it would lose its customs receipts and a large part of its internal revenues and income tax receipts.

"We could still have local income tax, but having to pay a Federal income tax, and Puerto Rico being such a poor country, the Federal tax having precedence, we would have practically no source of taxation with which to support our government. Even under existing conditions we do not provide as many services as we should provide to our people, because of lack of financial means."

(US House of Representatives Committee on Territories (1935) 74:1:44)

He proceeded with an even more serious objection to statehood.

"It perpetuates the present economic system in Puerto Rico. It is a single-crop system, that crop, being, as you know, sugar cane. It is in the hands of a few large corporations, most of them absentees as demonstrated by their percentage of the total production. Under the high tariff that prevails and is likely to prevail for many years in the United States protecting the sugar of Puerto Rico, it coming in under that privilege, Puerto Rico is bound to continue to be a single-crop country. To continue to develop this absentee economic control enriches a few people in Puerto Rico and a few people in the States, but it impoverishes the whole people of Puerto Rico and makes us a people of landless peons. The overproduction of sugar in Puerto Rico is also bad for Puerto Rico and Puerto

Ricans. It prevents the production of sufficient food and other necessary crops. The overproduction of sugar in Puerto Rico also prevents the development of small industries. The overproduction of sugar prevents the rational development of other branches of agriculture and the use of lands for our people; and statehood would perpetuate that. Under statehood we would always have the sugar situation as we have it now. It would be very difficult to prevent an increase in sugar production. It is not only bad for us, but it is equally bad for all American sugar, for American sugarcane growers and the beet sugar producers of the United States. The big corporations of Puerto Rico will be in favor of the large production of sugar, but they are not Puerto Ricans, the Puerto Ricans have an interest in the development of Puerto Rico. The big corporations are interested in gain for themselves....

[If Puerto Rico does not become a state,] we can develop rationally along other economic lines. We can have the chance to build up and have small industries and make our people self sustaining and develop our agriculture for the raising of foodstuffs, animals, and so forth, an economy of security and justice."

(US House of Representatives Committee on Territories (1935) 74:1:44–5)

In his testimony, Commissioner Iglesias reaffirmed his commitment to statehood for Puerto Rico. He took strong exception to Munoz-Marin's argument that statehood would provide no economic benefits to the people of the island. He insisted that the democratic freedoms of the Bill of Rights and the American creed had served and would continue to serve as an important normative umbrella and influence on the economic struggle by the masses of Puerto Rico against the privileged classes and corporations on the island "who for years have been opposed to the economic and social demands which have been made by the masses of workers year after year."

"[Further,] the institutions of the United States are responsible for much of the wonderful progress made in Puerto Rico. When the American Army landed in Puerto Rico the working classes had no personality, no liberty, and no opportunity to extricate themselves from the miserable state in which they were at the time. The Spanish regime controlled the thoughts, the rights, and the moral integrity of the masses. The masses were poverty stricken, downtrodden; they were without recognition and utterly unable to defend and uplift themselves."   (US Congressional Record 1935 74:1:10351)

At that time only a few children attended school, education being for the privileged classes only.

"And now we have over 250,000 children in schools and the schools admit the poor and humble as well as the rich and socially great.... [In addition,] we had no organization of labor at that time. I, myself, have been incarcerated many times for advancing the philosophy of organized labor. On one occasion, with others, I was sentenced to 4 years and 4 months in the penitentiary because I dared, as they said, to conspire to raise the price of labor, to form illicit societies. The societies were those that represented unions affiliated with the American Federation of Labor, and the conspiracy was to raise the price of labor, representing an increase in the wages for the workers and diminishing the hours of labor. President Roosevelt and the American Federation of Labor were instrumental in freeing me and the workers by their intervention. The old laws of Spanish colonization were repealed and the principles of the Constitution of the United States began to prevail in the island."

(US Congressional Record 1935 74:1:10351)

He agreed that absentee corporate power was a serious problem for the island, but he insisted that the island's ruling elite had contributed to the growth of this power:

"They [the corporations] have had not only the benefits of the tariff, but they have had also the protection and favors of the party that has been in power, to expand and become as strong and powerful as they are now.... It was the Federal Party and the Unionist Party that was in power 29 years. Those things that these gentlemen have mentioned here today are not new to Puerto Rico. We had to come to this country [the United States] in the past years just to ask for help and assistance against social and economic injustices and oppressions."

(US Congressional Record 1935 74:1:10352)

The commissioner expressed pleasure that his political opposition was now prepared to act against this corporate power, perhaps through enforcement of the 500-acre limit. "We can and should remedy our corporation laws and I am very glad that many of the men of intelligence, position, and character have the opportunity to think today that these conditions and laws should be remedied" (US Congressional Record 1935 74:1:10352).

Hearings on the bill ended on June 18 1935. However, the committee never made a report on it to the House and so it quietly died. The issue remained quiescent during the next session of Congress because Commissioner Iglesias' attention was distracted by the surfacing of the independence issue on the floor of Congress. (We shall examine this in more detail shortly.) He was particularly disturbed by the Tydings bill that called for a referendum on the issue. In a speech on the floor of the House four days after the bill was introduced, he charged that the bill did not accord with the wishes of most Puerto Ricans. It broke faith with those who saw the dissemination of the American creed with its promise of statehood as the ultimate salvation for the island.

The following April in the first session of the Seventy-fifth Congress Iglesias offered a much fuller explanation in a speech on the House floor "Why Puerto Rico Does Not Want Independence." He insisted that independence was being sought by only a small number of "rich, or business men, the intellectuals and the 'illustrados' . . . [who] are almost sure that, if Congress would force independence on the island, in the long run they would get control by force of the 'new' regime for their own benefit and glory." There were in addition "a few well-to-do discontented professionals who would like to have the island turned over to them for their personal administration." Such people were to be found in "every community of any size, . . . only our particular group seems to have done an unusually good job of advertising and making a lot of noise through sensational news and other devices" (US Congressional Record 1937 75:1:A809).

In short, he asserted, most Puerto Ricans were opposed to independence.

"[For example,] the masses of the workers of Puerto Rico know that independence for them would mean loss of their freedom and individual rights as citizens and also an inevitable economic catastrophe for the island; it would mean for them that sort of nationalist independence without liberty and without human guaranties of life. The material interests from outside and inside surely will continue to receive ample protection."

(US Congressional Record 1937 75:1:A809)

In addition, he concluded, most of the "honest propertied" classes opposed independence. "For the producing people, independence is not a problem of propertied interests and business alone, but it also is the great problem of keeping freedom and the rights of citizenship, democracy, education, and popular representation in the affairs of the country" (US Congressional Record 1937 75:1:A809).

In the meantime Iglesias resumed his legislative efforts to make Puerto Rico an integral part of the United States, but he scaled down the scope of his goal. He introduced a bill in the early days of the first session of the Seventy-fifth Congress that would merely transform Puerto Rico into an incorporated territory and not into a state immediately. Again the House Committee on Insular Affairs quietly buried a bill of his on the political status of the island despite the support he received from the American Federation of Labor.

A year later, just as the Seventy-sixth Congress convened, Iglesias introduced an identical version of his territorial bill into the House. A month later he urged passage of his bill in a speech to the House in which he repeated his message that the people of Puerto Rico wanted "permanent union ... with the people of the United States to maintain and consecrate socially, politically, and industrially a democratic community with the same rights and duties as any community of our Nation. We want and are anxious to be recognized as an integral part of the States of the Union, to lead our future along that line." And again he rejected "all formulas of a colonial government. We consider this formula disgraceful and not compatible with the civil dignity of our Nation." He also expressed his belief that incorporation would not "necessarily cause the insular government to lose the benefits she now has regarding customs duties, internal revenue, income tax, and other United States taxes from which she has been exempted" (US Congressional Record 1939 76:1:A684).

Approximately five months later, with no action on his bill forthcoming from the committee, Iglesias submitted for the record a memorandum from the Puerto Rican Legislative Joint Committee. The memorandum urged Congress in the name of the concurrent resolution of 1934 to admit Puerto Rico into the Union as a state. Until that status was accorded the island, the memo asked Congress to expand the island's self-governance machinery, including popular election of the governor. A month later Iglesias introduced an identical version of his earlier statehood bill. He even persuaded Burke to introduce a similar statehood bill into the Senate. However, none of these legislative efforts bore any fruit; all were buried in committee.

Iglesias died before he could renew his legislative struggle for statehood. His successor once again introduced to the House out of deference to him Iglesias' statehood bill; once again it was quietly buried. Thereafter his successor placed a higher priority on gaining a wider range of self-governance.

For all his commitment to the issue Iglesias could show few gains in the political status of Puerto Rico during his seven years as commissioner. Such modest gains as there were included broadening the authority of the Puerto Rican legislature to deal with the economic crisis on the island, but the legislature still had to operate within the constraints of the Jones bill. In addition Congress extended the citizenship by birth provision of the Fourteenth Amendment to the island and exempted persons traveling between Puerto Rico and the continental United States from the payment of a stamp tax on steamship tickets.

The most significant initiatives taken in his term of office were on the economic front to meet the devastating impact of the depression on the island. Iglesias strove to have the New Deal social legislation extended to Puerto Rico and to have the Coalition party develop plans for the economic rehabilitation of the island. However, he and his party were outflanked by the Liberal party which gained control of a presidential commission charged with the preparation of such a plan. Under the commission's Chardon plan, the sugar monoculture of the island was to be broken up through the redistribution of landholdings to small farmers, through the operation of a publicly owned sugar mill, and through the diversification of the island's economy. Though Iglesias endorsed the Chardon plan in principle, he complained about the favoritism of the Puerto Rican Reconstruction Administration toward the opposition Liberal party in its recruitment of personnel and in its enunciation of policy.

SENATOR TYDINGS AND INDEPENDENCE

The linkage between the Liberal party leadership and the federal relief and rehabilitation agencies on the island allowed the party to retain a political presence in Puerto Rico which it might have lost in view of its defeats in the 1932 and 1936 elections. The party incidentally explained these defeats as due to fraud and corruption at the polls much in the same manner as the original coalition party had explained its defeat in the 1924 election. But in the 1930s with victory at the polls the coalition denied all such allegations and insisted that the elections had been the fairest and cleanest in the island's history. In turn the coalition expressed deep chagrin at the Liberal party's preferential access to federal funds while maintaining an ideological posture of independence. In the words of a coalition member of the Puerto Rican legislature in an address in 1936,

> "The Liberal Party of Puerto Rico has been playing a shameless game of double-dealing with the Government here in Washington – a game of accepting favors and money with one hand and spreading anti-American propaganda with the other. On their numerous missions to Washington, Liberal Party leaders are loud in their protestations of stout, loyal Americanism; in Puerto Rico, secretly before but openly now, they are anti-American. The best and most convincing proof of the latter is the liberal leader's recent speech at Caguas, PR, in which he exhorted the people to revolution if necessary. Let him explain, if he dares or if he will, honestly, his convictions concerning American institutions, his attitude now and in the past with respect to the American regime. Let him explain his words in the Caguas speech, 'We will go to the extreme of revolution if necessary.'" (US Congressional Record 1936 74:2:8566)

The Liberal party denied any revolutionary intent, though it continued to express its commitment to independence as the ultimate political solution for the island. In stating and restating this theme, the Liberal party enhanced the respectability of independence as an ideological position on the island, but it gave virtually no support to those who wanted immediate realization of this goal, even at the expense of force and violence. This was left to a relatively small fringe group, the

Nationalist party that was organized early in the 1930s and that polled a mere 2 percent of the vote in the 1932 election.

Rebuffed at the polls, the Nationalist party under the leadership of Pedro Albrizu Campos began a more violent and confrontational course of action, including the dynamiting of public buildings and installations. In late 1934 four nationalists were intercepted as they sought entry into the grounds of the University of Puerto Rico, allegedly to plant bombs according to the governor's report; in an exchange of gunfire three of the nationalists were killed. At their funeral the head of the party, Campos, vowed vengeance against the chief of police, Colonel Riggs, a retired army officer; four months later Riggs was shot to death. Sporadic attacks against the police and other public officials continued. Even Iglesias was wounded as he spoke at a political rally in the 1936 election.

Campos and other nationalist leaders were convicted of conspiracy to overthrow by force the authority of the United States government in Puerto Rico and were imprisoned in 1936. This did not lessen the activities of the nationalists. In the infamous "Ponce Massacre of 1937," they paraded in strength through the streets of the two towns despite the cancellation of a permit to parade that had been granted earlier. In the ensuing clash with police, approximately twenty, including two policemen, were killed; and over a hundred, including five policemen, were wounded. An investigation by the American Civil Liberties Union placed the blame for the clash and the killings on the police.

Despite the nationalistic ferment on the island and even despite the Liberal party's reaffirmation of its independence platform, the only significant move for independence during the 1930s came not from the island but from Washington. Its major proponent was Senator Tydings of Maryland, chairman of the Committee on Territories and Insular Affairs. He introduced a bill in late April 1936 that would "give the people of Puerto Rico the option of becoming independent as a result of a national referendum in the island on the question whether they would rather continue under the American flag or have independence" (US Congressional Record 1936 74:2:5925). In presenting his bill the senator admitted that he was less interested in fulfilling the national aspirations of the Puerto Rican than in ridding the United States of an increasingly troublesome presence. He was particularly disturbed by the assassination of the police chief and by the difficulty of gaining convictions against the nationalist in the courts of Puerto Rico. "There have been several murder cases there in which convictions have not been obtained, and as to which a great mass of the people of Puerto Rico think there has been a miscarriage of justice" (US Congressional Record 1936 74:2:5926).

In addition, he complained that the elections had been fraudulent, more people having registered to vote than actually lived in the various regions. He quoted an extensive report from the American official in charge of the Division of Territories and Island Possessions of the Interior Department, which purported to show the extent of the fraud. Matters such as these made "us question the worth of American institutions as being adapted to the people of Puerto Rico and to the conditions under which they live" (US Congressional Record 1936 74:2:5925).

Further, he went on, America had been very generous to Puerto Rico just as it had been to its other island possessions. It had poured millions of dollars of the American taxpayers' money into the island without any visible result; in fact, things had gotten worse.

> "Since we have had the islands, and particularly in recent years, many, many million dollars have been poured into Puerto Rico from the Federal Treasury in all sorts of social campaigns, housing compaigns, W.P.A. and P.W.A. programs; and it seems as if the more we do the worse conditions become in the island. Although this is Federal money, there is a continual quarrel about how the Federal Government shall spend, not the money of the people of Puerto Rico, but the money of the people of the United States of America."
>
> (US Congressional Record 1936 74:2:5926)

He concluded, why should America not do for Puerto Rico what it had already done for the Philippines?

The outcry against the Tydings bill was immediate and loud from the Coalition party. As we have already seen, Iglesias responded vigorously against it, calling it a "cyclone bill" because of its potentially disastrous effect on the island. Another member of the Coalition party commented sarcastically that only the Nationalists and Liberal parties would benefit. Despite this comment, even the Liberal party expressed strong reservations at the precipitous way the Tydings bill would cut off American aid and ties to Puerto Rico once independence was granted.

In view of this intense and widespread reaction, Tydings did not press for action on his bill; instead he introduced a resolution a month later, May 25, calling for the appointment of a committee to study the question of Puerto Rican independence. The seventeen members of the committee were to be drawn from the executive and congressional branches of the federal government and from the four major political parties in Puerto Rico. Four days later an amended version of the resolution was brought to the floor of the Senate by Tydings' Committee on Territories and Insular Affairs. The revised version reduced the total figure to fifteen members, a majority of whom would be selected by Congress and the rest along the lines of the original version. This committee was to

> "study the question of Puerto Rican independence in all its aspects, including the financial and economic relationships best suited to both the United States and Puerto Rico under such independence, and, in general, to inquire into the

present and future relations between the United States and Puerto Rico. Said committee shall render the report to the President of the United States not later than January 20, 1937, and the President shall within 30 days after receipt thereof, transmit said report together with his recommendations thereon to the Congress." (US Congressional Record 1936 74:2:8460)

Three days later the resolution was passed without debate and sent to the House where it was referred to the House Committee on Rules.

Two weeks later the House committee reported out a completely revised version of the resolution that showed the effectiveness of Iglesias' backstage maneuvering. No longer did the resolution call for the appointment of a committee to study the question of independence; instead it called "for the appointment of a Commission to study the social, economic, and political conditions of Puerto Rico" (US House of Representatives Report No. 2965 (1936) 74:2:2). Included in the commission's study was to be an investigation into the "conditions of the working people of the island." In addition, the commission was "to inquire into the present and future political and economic relations between the United States and Puerto Rico" (US House of Representatives Report No. 2965 (1936) 74:2:1), the possibility of statehood not being excluded. Membership was to include the fifteen mentioned in the Senate version, plus three others, one from each of the following organizations: Iglesias' Free Federation Workingmen of Puerto Rico, the Agricultural Association of Puerto Rico, and the Puerto Rico Chamber of Commerce. The House bill also provided "that the Governor of Puerto Rico and the Resident Commissioner of Puerto Rico [Iglesias] shall be members ex officio of said Commission" (US House of Representatives Report No. 2965 (1936) 74:2:2).

No action was taken on the resolution once it reached the House floor. Despite this absence of action, Iglesias expressed satisfaction on the floor of the House several weeks later that at the least the various bills of Tydings had also not been passed by the House.

Not until seven years later did Senator Tydings introduce another bill on independence. The congressional vacuum during the period was filled by Representative Marcantonio's persistent efforts to lay before the House a bill on independence which never left the House Committee on Insular Affairs. Tydings explained the prolonged interruption in his efforts as due to the then pending war in Europe and to the subsequent outbreak of war with Japan. Now, he declared on April 1943, the time was again ripe for consideration of the issue, particularly in view of the recent passage of an independence act for the Philippine Islands which was to become effective in ten years. His proposed bill for Puerto Rico would provide for immediate independence but, unlike his earlier bill, the break between the two countries would not be precipitous or complete. Thus independence would not mean the immediate imposition of full tariff rates on Puerto Rican goods exported to the United States; instead the rates would be increased gradually over a twenty-year period. Further, America would retain military, coaling, and naval stations on the island and would generally assume a protective function for it.

Before independence would be granted, his bill would require the "calling of a convention to frame a constitution for the government of the island of Puerto Rico." This constitution would have to include the various guaranties of the American Constitution and would have to be submitted for ratification by the people of Puerto Rico and for the approval of the President.

Tydings insisted that his bill had been primarily drawn "in the utmost sincerity" to meet the aspirations of the Puerto Rican people. However, he could not resist repeating his earlier theme that America would be well rid of the island. It cost too much to support. "We have spent more than $300,000,000 in Puerto Rico in the past 10 years, and to my certain knowledge, after a very lengthy inspection of the island not many years ago, the results have not justified the expenditures" (US Congressional Record 1943 78:1:2833). Several members of his committee expressed chagrin at Tydings' actions, not because they opposed his bill, but merely because he had presented it without consulting with them and without waiting for the results of a subcommittee's on-the-spot investigation of social and economic conditions on the island. Tydings acknowledged this and claimed sole responsibility for his bill.

The new Tydings bill was introduced into the Senate at a time when the internal political situation in Puerto Rico was being dramatically transformed from that which had prevailed when the senator introduced his first version in 1936. No longer did the Coalition party, the party of federal statehood, dominate the island legislature; for, despite a slim plurality, it lost control of both houses in the closely contested election of 1940 to the newly formed Munoz-Marin Popular Democratic party. All that the Coalition party salvaged was the office of resident commissioner. Thus only in Washington was an official voice still heard that called for federal statehood. And true to his predecessor Iglesias' memory, Commissioner Pagan introduced into the legislative hopper of the House in 1943 once again the latter's statehood bill much as he had done three years earlier at Iglesias' death. Again it never left the committee. But by the end of the 1944 election, even this voice was stilled as Munoz-Marin's party overwhelmed all opposition and even swept out of office the last remnant of the Coalition party's former preeminence.

In early 1943 the Puerto Rican legislature also withdrew its official commitment to statehood of ten years before. In a concurrent resolution it called once again on

Congress to allow as expeditiously as possible the people of Puerto Rico to decide their permanent political status through "special free and democratic elections." The resolution did not specify the desired form for this status, but it did declare in its preamble that continuation of the present colonial system of government was intolerable: "in all political parties and civic and economic sectors of Puerto Rico the unanimous opinion prevails that the colonial system of government should be totally and definitely abolished" (US Congressional Record 1943 78:1:1562).

Thus by the time Tydings introduced his bill in April 1943, he no longer had to face the obstacle of statehood as official policy of the Puerto Rican legislature as he had seven years before. He was also aware that the new president of the senate and leader of the Popular Democratic party had been a staunch advocate of independence when he was still a member of the Liberal party. Tydings was not even disturbed by Munoz-Marin's avoidance of public debate on the actual character of Puerto Rico's permanent political status. He was convinced that the time was now ripe to garner support for his bill on the island itself. As evidence of this gathering support, he read into the record a week after placing his bill in the legislative hopper an Associate Press dispatch that two important newspapers on the island were backing his bill. This showed, he insisted, that Puerto Ricans recognized that his bill "is very fair to the people of Puerto Rico and provides them with an opportunity to achieve independence with a minimum of hardship. Therefore it is gratifying to me to know that the bill has been received in Puerto Rico in the spirit in which it was introduced" (US Congressional Record 1943 78:1:3172). At his committee's hearings on the bill early in May, he also put into the record the telegrams of support he had received from 25 to 30 pro-independence organizations on the island. Support for the Tydings bill peaked at the first Congress for Independence that met in August in Puerto Rico, when 1800 delegates from all parts of the island convened in the midst of an enthusiastic audience that numbered about 15,000.

In Washington the bill met with resistance from administration officials. Secretary of the Interior Ickes, in particular, expressed his opposition. He said it would be a "serious mistake" for both Puerto Rico and the United States to enact the bill, because "the economic dislocations in Puerto Rico incident to the war are very serious. The readjustments not only in the Island but throughout the Caribbean which will take place when it ends may be very widespread." He also complained that the bill offered Puerto Ricans the restricted choice of independence or the continuation of "the present dependency status. Its provisions would not permit them to consider the further alternative of obtaining self-government while remaining under the American flag, through a grant of statehood or commonwealth rights. I strongly feel that whenever the time becomes opportune for permanent determination of the future status of Puerto Rico the people should be given a broader opportunity to express their desires than would be possible under S. 952" (US Congressional Record 1943 78:1:A2539).

In the meantime he favored the granting "to the people of Puerto Rico a constantly increasing measure of real control over their local affairs.... The President has stated that he favors a measure to give the Puerto Ricans the right to elect their Governor... I believe that greater autonomy should be limited to that step at this time" (US Congressional Record 1943 78:1:A2539).

Within Puerto Rico, a Statehood Congress was convened in May 1943, to express its opposition to the Tydings bill and to reaffirm its goal of statehood. In his opening address the Chief Justice of the Supreme Court of Puerto Rico complained that the Tydings bill was divisive and that statehood remained the only logical and meaningful goal for the island:

"To become politically what California or Massachusetts is in the bosom of the most powerful nation, materially and spiritually, is to assure for us and our offspring the blessings of ordered liberty and, therefore, the constant progress of individual dignity and the well-being of the community; this is to tread directly toward the kingdom of heaven on earth."

(US Congressional Record 1943 78:1:A2415)

The Tydings bill never reached the floor of the Senate during either session of the Seventy-eighth Congress despite Tydings' efforts to spark interest in it. On one occasion during the second session, he introduced still another reason for support of his bill.

"Why should not the Puerto Ricans have independence? While they are loyal to our country, of course, they are essentially alien to our language, for ... very few Puerto Ricans speak English fluently. Spanish is the prevailing language, and although they have been under the American flag since 1898, the Puerto Ricans want to retain their Spanish language. If they want to retain it, that is their privilege. But the line of cleavage in culture, speech, and thought is wide as between the Latin on the one hand and the predominant Anglo-Saxon, characterized by the United States, on the other....

Puerto Ricans are basically a proud people. They are basically of the Latin or Spanish culture. They cling to the heritage of their fathers and mothers. I do not mean to say that they are not loyal Americans, for they are. However, by long centuries of thought, philosophy, training, and culture, their roots are in a different environment from those of the people of the United States."

(US Congressional Record 1944 78:2:1669)

Unable to obtain any action in the Seventy-eighth Congress, Tydings reintroduced his bill in the opening days of the Seventy-ninth Congress. In the early March hearings on the bill Tydings received the kind of support he was looking for from the independence movement in Puerto Rico. The first witness, chairman of the first Puerto Rican Pro-Independence Congress and president of the Puerto Rico Independence party, testified on the unanimous endorsement by the congress of Tydings' bill and on the pro-independence declaration of the congress with its 3000 signatures. This declaration proclaimed:

"Puerto Rico eagerly desires to constitute itself as a nation under a democratic system of government; Puerto Rico desires to preserve its historic personality, to develop its culture, to orient its economy, to promote its production, to foster its industry, to raise the working and living standards of labor, to enfore policies of true social justice, and to provide security and welfare for all its citizens. For these reasons, the people of Puerto Rico, throughout all sectors of public opinion, categorically repudiate the colonial regime."

(US Senate Committee on Territories and Insular Affairs (1945) 79:1:25)

Another witness, the president of the Congress for Puerto Rican Independence, elaborated even further on the presumably widespread support for independence. He declared that virtually all members of the Puerto Rican legislature, which was now almost exclusively under the control of the Popular Democratic party because of its smashing victory in the 1944 election, were for independence. He even read into the record Munoz-Marin's manifesto of 1936 which strongly endorsed independence: "In Puerto Rico, independence is not only the ideal of numberless Puerto Ricans, but the destiny of all Puerto Ricans" (US Senate Committee on Territories and Insular Affairs (1945) 79:1:37). He also read into the record two cablegrams, one signed by 11 members of the island's senate and the other by 22 members of the island's house of representatives.

When the hearings resumed six weeks later, testimony in favor of the bill continued to be heard from spokesmen from pro-independence organizations. Some dissenting voices were also heard from the statehood organizations, but the words that did most to put a damper on the generally favorable response to the Tydings bill came on the next to last day of testimony from Munoz-Marin, president of the Puerto Rican senate. He informed the committee that he was appearing as the chairman of a joint legislative commission which was charged with implementing the concurrent resolution unanimously passed by the legislature calling for a referendum on the island's permanent political status. He then read a statement unanimously endorsed by the commission which included members from all the island's major political parties.

The statement declared that "We hold that the colonial form of government which now prevails in Puerto Rico is contrary to the democratic rights of our people and to the democratic tradition of the United States." It then stated "that a prompt and satisfactory settlement should be made democratically on the basis of self-determination. Such is our mandate from the people and the Legislature of Puerto Rico." It requested that Congress conduct a referendum of the people of Puerto Rico. Unlike the referendum proposed by Tydings in 1936, independence would not be the only option available to the voter. The referendum would contain "the different forms of permanent political status that the Congress may be willing to establish in Puerto Rico." The statement then suggested that "in fairness to all sections of opinion in Puerto Rico, . . . all forms of political status that may have some support among Puerto Ricans be submitted. Broadly speaking, the forms of political status that have support in public opinion are independence, statehood, and a form of dominion government based on full and final political rights" (US Senate Committee on Territories and Insular Affairs (1945) 79:1:374).

The statement concluded with the categorical declaration that no matter what political status was chosen, chaos would result unless Congress would agree to meet "certain minimum economic conditions." It then spelled out some of these conditions from free trade to "temporary continuance of other grants and aids to Puerto Rico, these to be discontinued as productivity and commerce reach certain agreed levels." In turn the statement recognized that "if the legitimate interests of the United States are to be fully protected, military establishments and rights must be permanently enjoyed by the United States in Puerto Rico" (US Senate Committee on Territories and Insular Affairs (1945) 79:1:374).

In his testimony, Senator Munoz-Marin declined to reveal his personal preferences, insisting that he had pledged in the name of unity not to take a stand for the present on the issue, but to let the people speak for themselves. The committee received his testimony warmly, and Tydings invited him to propose amendments to the bill.

Within a week Munoz-Marin and the commission returned with a revised version of the proposal they had made earlier to the committee. The new version spelled out in greater detail the "three alternative forms of government" that the people of Puerto Rico were to vote on in a referendum. Tydings and his committee accepted the proposal virtually intact and introduced it into the legislative hopper on May 15 as a new bill. They shelved the bill before them. In a subsequent address, Senator Munoz-Marin described the new bill as containing four titles which offered three alternative forms of government to the people of Puerto Rico.

"Title 1 provides that there shall be a referendum in which the people of Puerto Rico shall decide whether they want independence under certain economic conditions necessary for their survival, or statehood, or dominion status similar to that of Australia or Canada in the British Commonwealth of Nations. Title 2 describes independence. Title 3 describes statehood. Title 4 describes dominion status. If a majority of the people of Puerto Rico vote for independence, then title 2 shall go into effect. If they vote for statehood, then title 3 shall go into effect. If they vote for dominion status, then title 4 shall go into effect. In this manner, if the bill is approved, the people of Puerto Rico themselves will choose their own future, on the basis of an offer by the American Congress, and in choosing it they will have before them the fullest possible picture of what they are voting about." (US Congressional Record 1945 79:1:A2684)

An identical bill was introduced into the House of Representatives by Resident Commissioner Pinero the next day and referred to the Committee on Insular Affairs.

In the middle of October, President Truman threw his support behind the bill. In a letter to both houses of Congress, he urged them to act: "It is now time, in my opinion, to ascertain from the people of Puerto Rico their wishes as to the ultimate status which they prefer, and, within such limits as may be determined by the Congress, to grant them the kind of government which they desire." They were dissatisfied with the present form of government, and debate within the island over the various forms of government had created "uncertainty ... among the people as to just what the future of Puerto Rico is to be. These uncertainties should be cleared away at an early date;" through a referendum conducted by Congress on the various alternatives.

"However, in the interest of good faith and comity between the people of Puerto Rico and those of us who live on the mainland, Congress should not submit any proposals to the Puerto Ricans which the Congress is not prepared to enact finally into law. We should be prepared to carry into effect whatever options are placed before the people of Puerto Rico, once the Puerto Ricans have expressed their preference." (US Congressional Record 1945 79:1:9676).

Despite the entreaties of the President, neither house acted on the referendum bill in the form it had been submitted either in this or any other session of Congress. In the meantime Tydings did not give up the battle completely for his original independence bill; he introduced it in each newly convened Congress until his defeat in 1950 in his race for reelection as a senator.

MUNOZ-MARIN AND COMMONWEALTH STATUS

In resurrecting the dominion or free state status as an alternative form of government for the island, the dominant Popular Democratic party signified its willingness to perpetuate the constitutionally unique and ambiguous mold in which relations between Puerto Rico and the United States had been cast from the passage of the Foraker Act, provided that the mold was capable of a marked expansion in self-rule, political autonomy, and in social and economic experimentation for the island. In its first bid for power in 1940, the party studiously avoided any identification with what then seemed to be the only two options, statehood or independence. Munoz-Marin, however, was not allowed to forget his staunch support of independence as a member of the Liberal party by the opposition Coalition party. And even as his Popular Democratic party won a spectacular though narrow victory, he was pilloried as a secessionist and independent. The rancor generated by the hard-fought and close victory did not disappear once the election was over. His slim margin of control over the two houses of the legislature, and the Coalition party's control of the post of resident commissioner, insured that the struggle would continue. In fact the controversy exploded with renewed vigor with the appointment of Rexford Tugwell as governor. Led by Resident Commissioner Pagan in Washington, the Coalition complained that the newly appointed governor had aligned himself with the "secessionist" Popular Democratic party and was guilty of sponsoring communistic social experiments on the island. Congress was accordingly besieged by resolution and letter not merely from the opposition party but also from Farmer associations and such like calling for the ouster of Tugwell.

In turn the Puerto Rican legislature sent to Congress two memorials in February 1942. One declared that the governor had the most enthusiastic support of the people and legislature. The other called for the repudiation of "all the activities of the Resident Commissioner of Puerto Rico to the United States which tend to create in the United States the false impression that Governor Tugwell, the representative of President Roosevelt in Puerto Rico, does not have the support of this Senate or of the people" (US Congressional Record 1942 77:2:A984).

The following year the Puerto Rican senate sent an even more strongly worded resolution in support of the governor. In addition it took full responsibility or credit for the social legislation and experimentation "blamed" on the governor. It went on to declare that "all the legislation approved was part of the political platform on which the majority of this legislature ... were elected." What was more, it declared, the same held true of the political platform on which "the greater part of the minority of this legislature" (US Congressional Record 1943 78:1:1563) was also elected – meaning the Socialist party.

The controversy exploded in full fury as the new election approached and again the resident commissioner led the attack. He complained bitterly at a news conference in Washington before the election about "the undemocratic and totalitarian administration of Governor Tugwell." He expressed confidence that "the intelligent voters of Puerto Rico will endeavor to eradicate the totalitarian program when they go to the polls this year," but then in a foreboding manner stated "there is no clear chance of a fair, impartial, and decent election in Puerto Rico under Governor Tugwell" (US Congressional Record 1944 78:2:A4235 –236). The smashing victory of the Popular Democratic party at the polls, which included the office of resident commissioner, put an end to the public bickering over the governor.

PRESIDENT ROOSEVELT'S COMMISSION AND RECOMMENDED CHANGES IN THE ORGANIC ACT

Even as the partisan struggle over Tugwell unfolded, both parties joined together to pledge solidarity with the President and the American people in the war against the "totalitarian powers." Both parties also approved of the recommendation that President Roosevelt made to Congress on March 9 1943 that "it consider as soon as possible an amendment of the organic law of Puerto Rico to permit the people of Puerto Rico to elect their own Governor, and to redefine the functions and powers of the Federal Government and the government of Puerto Rico, respectively." He also informed Congress that he had already appointed "a committee composed of an equal number of Puerto Ricans and of continental residents to advise me concerning changes in the organic law" (US House of Representatives Document No. 126 (1943) 78:1:2). Although he approved of the President's recommendation, Resident Commissioner Pagan could not resist linking his favorable response in a news release with a renewed demand for the resignation of Governor Tugwell.

The chairman of the committee was Secretary of Interior Ickes. Also included as continental representatives were Governor Tugwell, Fortas, and Father McGowan. Senator Munoz-Marin, another senator from the Coalition party, a judge, and a former legislator filled the quota from Puerto Rico. Almost as soon as the committee met at its first meeting in July 1943, Munoz-Marin insisted that in view of the committee's charge of redefining basic relations between Puerto Rico and the United States, it was obliged to deal with more than the present. It was also called upon to make recommendations "that will in some way determine the method for working out the future definite and permanent relationship between the government of Puerto Rico and the Federal Government ... [in short] a method for determining [its] ultimate status" (US Senate Subcommittee of the Committee on Territories and Insular Affairs (1943) 78:1:312).

After a brief discussion about whether this matter fell within the jurisdiction of the committee, the matter was put off until near the end of the committee's deliberations. At that time Munoz-Marin proposed that the bill include a section which would authorize "the calling of a constitutional convention in Puerto Rico at the appropriate time ... to allow the people of Puerto Rico, through their constitutional convention, to frame a constitution to be submitted to Congress, which Congress may accept or reject, according to whether it thinks it is harmful to the moral rights of the United States in the premises; if rejected, Congress to present its objections and the constitutional convention to consider them and frame another constitution until Congress and the constitutional convention are in agreement, at which time that constitution would be submitted to the people of Puerto Rico for their approval or rejection or ratification."

(US Senate Subcommittee of the Committee on Territories and Insular Affairs (1943) 78:1:535)

The committee split on the proposal, continental Americans on one side and Puerto Ricans on the other. Finally it decided to handle the issue of ultimate status for the island by recommending the creation of a "Joint Advisory Council for Puerto Rico."

"It shall study and report to the President and the Congress of the United States on necessary or desirable changes in this Act. The Council shall also study and report on proposals with respect to the basic relationships between the United States and Puerto Rico, which proposals shall, when and as approved by Congress, be submitted to the people of Puerto Rico for their decision. The Council shall also study and recommend a comprehensive economic program to be made operative over a period of years, the purpose of which shall be the economic rehabilitation of the Island."

(US House of Representatives Document No. 304 (1943) 78:1:11)

In the discussion committee members left no doubt that the phrase "basic relationship" included "political status," though several objected when one Puerto Rican member said "I was accepting the phrase, 'basic relationship' as synonymous with 'political status'" (US Senate Subcommittee of the Committee on Territories and Insular Affairs (1943) 78:1:540).

Fearful that the President might view the committee's actions as having overstepped the boundaries of its jurisdiction, Secretary of Interior Ickes stressed in his covering letter to the President that

"the Committee has taken the position that its mandate is limited to this one phase of the United States-Puerto Rico relationship [namely, the election of a governor and reinforcement of the machinery of self-government in Puerto Rico] – and has made no recommendation on the question of the so-called ultimate political status of Puerto Rico or on various other amendments to the organic law which have presented themselves in the course of the discussions,

though it has proposed a mechanism [the Joint Advisory Council] to assure constant review of such questions to the end that appropriate measures may be devised and taken to meet other problems and changing needs and conditions."
(US House of Representatives Document No. 304 (1943) 78:1:4)

Obviously the major provision of the proposed bill was the popular election of the governor and the further stipulation "that no further changes in the Organic Act shall be made except with the concurrence of the people of Puerto Rico or their duly elected representatives" (US House of Representatives Document No. 304 (1943) 78:1:7). The powers of the governor were to be "essentially the same as those of the appointed Governor with respect to insular affairs. Certain of the powers now exercised by the Governor are, however, deemed to be appropriate to an official appointed by the President of the United States. Those have been entrusted to a Commissioner General to be appointed by the President with the advice and consent of the United States Senate" (US House of Representatives Document No. 304 (1943) 78:1:4).

The committee had considerable difficulty in working out the precise authority and responsibilities of this commissioner. Puerto Rican members bridled at the suggestion that he would represent "American sovereignty" in Puerto Rico. They were more prepared to see him as representing "executive power in Puerto Rico." Some even objected to the presence of such a link on the island: none existed in any of the states of the Union. In reply they were told by Fortas:

"that Puerto Rico is not a State, nor it is not contemplated that it be a State under this arrangement and under the terms of reference of this Committee.... I point out further, on the substantive side that Puerto Rico is an offshore area, a considerable distance from the United States, and that it is surrounded by areas that are possessions of a foreign government and that will presumably continue to be the possessions of a foreign government.... For those reasons it seems to me that there ought to be a representative of the President in Puerto Rico with considerable dignity and standing."
(US Senate Subcommittee of the Committee on Territories and Insular Affairs (1943) 78:1:381)

Finally the committee agreed to stress the commissioner general's role as coordinator of all federal and civilian functions and activities and to play down somewhat any exercise of authority which might impinge on the insular authority of the governor. The commissioner general would still

"be responsible for the faithful execution of the laws of the United States applicable to Puerto Rico. He may grant respites for all offenses against the laws of the United States until the decision of the President can be ascertained.

Whenever it becomes necessary he may call upon the commanders of the military and naval forces of the United States in the Island to prevent or suppress invasion, insurrection, rebellion, or (upon the request of the Governor) lawless violence."

(US House of Representatives Document No. 304 (1943) 78:1:11)

CONGRESS PIGEONHOLES THE ELECTIVE GOVERNOR BILL

The committee completed its deliberations by the first week of August. Three weeks later Ickes submitted its report and proposed bill to the President. A month later the President submitted the package to Congress. In his covering letter, the President stated:

"Under this bill the people of Puerto Rico would be given an opportunity for the free exercise of the powers of local self-government – executive, legislative, and judicial. There would be reserved to the President the power to veto only such measures passed by the legislature as were beyond the proper field of local self-government. There would be a United States Commissioner General in Puerto Rico upon whom would devolve the responsibility for the execution of the laws of the United States and for the coordination and supervision of the activities of insular agencies. He would also have authority to require reports of all activities of the insular government for transmittal to the President through the Secretary of the Interior. The fiscal relationship of the insular government to the Federal government would not be altered, nor would the ultimate power of Congress to legislate for the Territory. The people of the island would, however, be given assurance of the intention of Congress to obtain the concurrence of the people of the island before imposing upon them further changes in the Organic Act."

(US House of Representatives Document No. 304 (1943) 78:1:3)

The bill was introduced in the Senate as S1407 by Tydings and referred to a subcommittee of the Committee on Territories and Insular Affairs headed by Chavez of New Mexico. Hearings were held on seven days extending from November 16 to December 1 1943. In his opening statement Secretary Ickes commented,

"This bill confers real home rule upon Puerto Rico. By eliminating divided responsibility for the selection of insular officials, it effectively answers the complaint of the Puerto Rican People, whether or not that complaint is justified, that their unsound economic and social conditions are caused by our having appointed officials who, lacking sympathy with the aims of the people, have frustrated their efforts to better themselves."

(US Senate Subcommittee of the Committee on Territories
and Insular Affairs (1943) 78:1:11 – 12)

In answer to a question by a committee member Ickes conceded that an intermediate step to electing the governor might be the appointment of a citizen of Puerto Rico to the office first. He stated further, "As a matter of fact, it has been my hope if and when a vacancy occurs down there I could recommend a Puerto Rican for a Governor." He even called "desirable" the senator's explanation for the intermediate step: "I think it would have been very persuasive if a citizen of Puerto Rico could have been selected as a Governor and demonstrated ... that they were capable and could handle the situation with perhaps more harmony than has been possible with an outsider" (US Senate Subcommittee of the Committee on Territories and Insular Affairs (1943) 78:1:14).

During the course of the hearings, it became evident that certain features of the bill were in trouble. Questions rose particularly about the role of the commissioner general, the Joint Council, and the provision that required approval of the people of Puerto Rico for any changes in the organic law. Even more sweeping complaints of the bill were made by spokesmen for the pro-independence bill. They came out flatly against it because it did not deal with the "ultimate political status of the island" which to them could only mean independence – statehood being out of the question. Some even put in plugs for the Tydings bill.

The Committee on Territories and Insular Affairs presented to the Senate its report and its amended version of the bill during the early days of the second session of the Seventy-eight Congress, February 2 1944. The committee's bill retained most of the basic provisions for attaining two major objectives of the original bill, "(a) Reinforcement of the machinery of self-government; (b) election of Governor" (US Senate Report No. 659 (1944) 78:2:1), though it modified some of the details of these provisions, such as reducing the salary of the governor and other officials.

Other major objectives of the original bill were either deleted or basically transformed. For example, the Senate bill deleted the provision that obliged Congress to gain the concurrence of the people of Puerto Rico or their elected representatives before making any further changes in the organic law. The committee justified its action by saying,

"one Congress cannot bind subsequent Congresses. Therefore, this clause might act as an important factor in creating unfortunate situations and misunderstandings between the people of Puerto Rico and the people of the

United States, should a future Congress, in the exercise of its constitutional prerogatives, disregard such a promise."

(US Senate Report No. 659 (1944) 78:2:2)

The Senate committee's bill also deleted the proposed Joint Advisory Council. The committee explained its action by saying that it felt

"that any studies and any proposals of changes in the basic [political] relationships between the United States and Puerto Rico are of such transcendental importance that they should be handled directly by Congress and that they should not be entrusted to a few individuals or Government officials, however expert or however good their intentions."

(US Senate Report No. 659 (1944) 78:2:11)

And finally the Senate committee's bill curtailed the authority of the proposed commissioner general because it feared that to allow his powers to stand as in the original bill, he "in fact, would turn out to be the real Governor of Puerto Rico." Thus, "the committee felt that if true self-government is going to be granted to the people of Puerto Rico and if they are going to be given the right to elect their own Governor, this should be done without superimposing upon the Governor an official of the United States" (US Senate Report No. 659 (1944) 78:2:9).

The committee agreed to the following, however:

"there should be a Federal official to coordinate the administration of all Federal and civilian functions in Puerto Rico, but this office should be an administrative office with limited and well-defined duties and responsibilities, which would be in consonance with the spirit of the bill and the policy to grant true self-government to the people of Puerto Rico."

(US Senate Report No. 659 (1944) 78:2:9)

Accordingly, the name of the office was changed from commissioner general to coordinator of federal agencies, and its functions spelled out:

"The Coordinator coordinates the administration of all Federal civilian functions and activities in Puerto Rico, but the responsibilities which have heretofore been lodged in other Federal officials representing the Federal Government, such as the United States district attorney, remain with those officials. The committee likewise struck out the power to grant respites and to call upon the military and naval forces of the United States, etc."

(US Senate Report No. 659 (1944) 78:2:9)

During the brief debate on the bill on the Senate floor, Senator Vandenberg of

Michigan asked "on what theory is Puerto Rico to be given an elected Governor when similar privilege is not extended to the ... much older Territories of Hawaii and Alaska." Chavez, the chairman of the subcommittee, replied "on the theory of doing justice. The fact that we are not doing justice to Alaska and Hawaii should not keep us from doing justice to Puerto Rico at this instant." Senator Tydings added that no such request had come from Hawaii; many had come from Puerto Rico. He explained the reason for this:

> "Practically all the Governors of Puerto Rico have not been Puerto Ricans, or residents of Puerto Rico; they have been residents of the United States. Practically all the Governors of Hawaii, on the other hand, have been life-long residents of Hawaii, and many of them have been natives. For that reason there has not been the agitation in Hawaii for the election of a Governor in comparison with the agitation in Puerto Rico ... if the Hawaiians wanted the privilege of electing their Governors, I think the Senate would look with great sympathy upon their request."   (US Congressional Record 1944 78:2:1664)

Senator Vandenberg concluded this exchange with the comment that appointment of a resident to the governorship would seem to be "a perfectly logical intermediate step in the development of greater local autonomy." The senator then asked about the residency qualifications for the elected governor; he was particularly concerned lest the residency requirement permit Governor Tugwell to run for office. Upon being reassured that the committee had set the requirement for a long enough period of time to prevent this from happening, the senator withdrew any further objections to the bill. It was then passed section by section without further debate.

After the bill was passed, a member of the committee rose to express his concern about the political polarization on the island between advocates of statehood and independence. Mindful of the division in the Puerto Rican legislature between Coalition and Popular Democratic parties, he questioned whether anyone would be happy with the proposed bill and whether efforts to torpedo it might not occur in the House of Representatives. Unless the contending factions could come to some sort of agreement on the issue soon, he concluded, he would throw his weight behind the Tydings bill of independence. This gave Tydings an opportunity to deliver a long speech in which he proclaimed that his bill was the only realistic course of action for the island. It had not yet come to pass, he insisted, because of the "selfishness, the greed of a few persons. That is all there is to it. While we are fighting this war for democracy – God save the name – we are willing to keep these people in economic slavery because of a few investments there by persons in this country who are reaping handsome dividends as a result" (US Congressional Record 1944 78:2:1669).

If the issue were put to a vote on the island, he continued, it would win by a "landslide." Puerto Ricans saw themselves as a nation distinct from America – a conception in which they had a great deal of pride. The bill was then sent to the House of Representatives where, as the senator from Washington had feared, it was buried in the Committee on Insular Affairs.

APPOINTMENT OF A PUERTO RICAN AS GOVERNOR AND PASSAGE OF THE ELECTIVE GOVERNOR BILL

The overwhelming victory of the Popular Democratic party at the polls in 1944 did not result in the immediate revival of the issue of elective governor, despite the role that Munoz-Marin had played in the President's commission. Instead the challenge of the Tydings bill was first met and dealt with. Then in July 1946 President Truman took the step that Secretary of Interior Ickes had earlier urged President Roosevelt to take. He appointed the first Puerto Rican to the office of governor as Tugwell's term came to an end. His choice, Jesus T. Pinero, had already achieved a level of popularity in Washington as resident commissioner; the office had become his with his party's victory in 1944. Pinero's appointment to governor was enthusiastically supported by the Puerto Rican legislature. In view of this, an editorial in the Washington Post of July 26 1944 concluded, "there is assurance that there will be harmony and cooperation between the legislative and executive branches of the island government; and this should be a real contribution toward solution of Puerto Rico's difficult economic problems." The editorial then praised Truman,

> "[for providing] a practical application of the liberal colonial policies which this country has preached – and lately practiced. It is an extension of the democratic principle and of the idea for which we have always stood of fostering self-government among dependent peoples. It is a demonstration of good will which will bind Puerto Ricans to us more closely than ever. In making the choice, the President set aside political considerations for those of statesmanship. The decision is as wise as it is generous."
>
> (US Congressional Record 1946 79:2:A4461)

Less than a year later, May 2 1947, the issue of an elective governor was revived as a bill was introduced in the House of Representatives to amend the organic act and was referred to the Committee on Public Lands. Three and a half weeks later, the committee reported out a bill that was confined exclusively to the office of governor and its powers. According to the report,

> "the bill proposes to accomplish the following purposes: (1) to authorize the

people of Puerto Rico to elect their Governor, beginning with the general election in 1948; (2) to authorize the Governor to appoint the heads of all executive departments, except the auditor, with the advice and consent of the Puerto Rican Senate; (3) to provide a line of succession in the event the Governor is temporarily absent or unable to perform his duties; (4) to authorize the Governor to appoint the members of the Supreme Court of Puerto Rico."
(US House of Representatives Report No. 455 (1947) 80:1:2)

The committee also reported that, unlike the division of opinion in hearings on the earlier bill, "there was unanimity of support of the legislation on the part of both Federal and insular government officials, including the Secretary of the Interior and the Governor of Puerto Rico. On the basis of endorsements received from the island, the committee considers this bill to be very satisfactory to an overwhelming majority of the people" (US House of Representatives Report No. 455 (1947) 80:1:2).

The committee insisted, however, that enactment of the bill would not basically

"alter Puerto Rico's political or fiscal relationship to the United States. Congress does not surrender any of its constitutional authority to legislate for Puerto Rico or to review insular laws. Neither would this legislation prove an obstacle to a subsequent determination by the Congress of the permanent political status question. The passage of this bill, however, would stand as an evidence of our good will toward the people of Puerto Rico and as a demonstration to the nations of the world, at a time when territorial administration is a matter of international interest and concern, that the United States practices as well as preaches the doctrines of democracy and self-determination."   (US House of Representatives Report No. 455 (1947) 80:1:3)

When the bill reached the House floor, only Marcantonio of New York rose to speak. He remarked that he would not stand against consideration of the bill because it was of small moment, "an empty gesture. It is not even a realistic reform within the colonial system, but I do not want to deprive the people of Puerto Rico of even this gesture after we have deprived them of so much and so often." However, he expressed the following fear:

"[the bill] will be utilized by imperialist elements in the United States and by opportunists in Puerto Rico as a means by which to evade and postpone the determination of the basic issue – the status of Puerto Rico. This bill is not a reform in any real sense. The mere election of a governor of Puerto Rico does not grant to the people of Puerto Rico any sovereignty. It merely adds an embellishing facade on an ugly and rotten colonial structure. . . .

[Congress must] act on the question of Puerto Rico's status now. The people of Puerto Rico, I sincerely believe, want independence – a free Puerto Rico. I am confident that the American people agree with them. Let Congress therefore not evade or postpone. Congress must keep faith with both the people of Puerto Rico and of the United States by granting to Puerto Rico its freedom now."

(US Congressional Rcord 1947 80:1:7077)

Marcantonio then read into the record a lengthy declaration unanimously approved by the Central Committee of the Independence party of Puerto Rico in May. The declaration repeated much of what Marcantonio had just said. It characterized the bill as unsubstantial and said that only independence would free Puerto Rico from the bondage of colonialism. It had particularly choice words for Munoz-Marin who, it insisted, had sold out the independence movement "for a few crumbs of colonial power, forgetting his promises and violating the mandate he received from the people. This is treason" (US Congressional Record 1947 80:1:7079).

Without further debate, the bill was passed and sent to the Senate where it was referred to the Committee on Public Lands. Within two weeks the committee reported back favorably on the House bill to which it added two new sections. The first resurrected from its earlier bill the post of coordinator of federal agencies in Puerto Rico. The Committee argued that this kind of administrative post was necessary

> "[because] at the present time, there are at least 58 Federal agencies with field offices or branches operating in the island. Many of them are engaged in giving aid to Puerto Rico on bases that seem to be at times conflicting and contradictory. Based on a recent inspection trip by several members of the committee, there seemed to be a need to bring the activities of all these agencies into focus and eliminate unnecessary duplication and waste."

(US Senate Report No. 422 (1947) 80:1:3)

The second section added by the committee stipulated that "the rights, privileges, and immunities of citizens of the United States shall be respected in Puerto Rico to the same extent as though Puerto Rico were a State of the Union and subject to the provisions of paragraph 1 of section 2 of Article IV of the Constitution of the United States" (US Senate Report No. 422 (1947) 80:1:2).

> "The purpose of this addition is to assure that citizens of the United States not residing in Puerto Rico will have the same treatment in Puerto Rico as local residents. This right is guaranteed by the Constitution to citizens of the various states but has been held not to apply to Puerto Rico. Legislation in Puerto Rico has discriminated against nonresident American citizens."

(US Senate Report No. 422 (1947) 80:1:4)

The committee's amended version was adopted without debate approximately three weeks later, July 26, by the Senate. The House concurred with the Senate version on the same day, and President Truman signed the bill into law ten days later, August 5.

Commonwealth status and a constitution

MUNOZ-MARIN: DEFINING A NEW POLITICAL STATUS FOR PUERTO RICO

One year later, Luis Munoz-Marin won a landslide victory as Puerto Rico's first elected governor, and his party strengthened its hold on the legislature and on the office of resident commissioner. In his inaugural address, Munoz-Marin called upon the Puerto Rican people to unite and to forge new political pathways so that they "may, within the smallness of their territory, realize the greatness of their destiny." He cautioned them against seeking to shed "obsolete colonialism," only to be entrapped by the vice of "obsolete" and "archaic nationalism." To settle for nationalism and independence would mean subjecting the society to grievous economic changes "that would be highly damaging in their effect of restricting the integral liberty, in their work, in their commerce, in the betterment of their homes, in security, in the creative dynamism of millions of human beings who could hardly be benefited by a change in my title" (US Congressional Record 1949 81:1:310).

Accordingly, he insisted, Puerto Rico should seek to forge a new creative relationship "in fraternal cooperation with all the people of the United States." For the United States had shown itself capable of extending home rule to its "colonial people" and allowing them to carve out their own future.

> "In what colony, in what part of the world or in what time, has there taken place an act like this? What colony has ever elected, with the free votes of its people, its own legislative and executive government? No greater tribute can be paid to the people of the United States, and particularly to their President and Congress, than recognition of the unprecedented nature of their action. Traces remain of the colonial system in Puerto Rico; but it is evident that colonialism is being abolished rapidly in this community. There is still some distance to travel. Precisely for this reason it should be our concern to see well where we are going, what the objective is ahead of us." (US Congressional Record 1949 81(1:310)

In his inaugural address then, Munoz-Marin explicitly abandoned the notion of independence, just as he had abandoned the notion of statehood much earlier as a viable political status for Puerto Rico. He decried the notion that "[the island was] obliged to believe that there are only two doors through which it can go to meet its future, even if both are mined with destruction. To this it could be said by a habitually superficial school of thought that it is better to go out one of the two doors, even though they are mined, than not to go out at all. The answer to this is that nobody speaks of not going out. Does man perchance not know how to open doors where there are none? Is it not his duty to himself to look for ways of opening new ones when those that there are may be mined for his destruction? Is it not the essence of liberty to have the power to choose from among alternatives? And if intelligence multiplies the alternatives, is it not in that way widening liberty? The people always can, in choosing among many, old and new alternatives, decide for one of the old with the same freedom as for one of the new." (US Congressional Record 1949 81:1:310)

Though he called for a newly creative alternative he did not in the speech give it a label.

Seven months later, July 1949, in a personal report to the House Committee on Public Lands Munoz-Marin alluded again to the new form of government that was being created for Puerto Rico.

"In passing the law allowing the people of Puerto Rico to elect their own Governor for the first time, it is my view that Congress is practically giving shape to a new kind of State. You find no dependency anywhere in the world that elects its own executive and legislative government. The step taken in Puerto Rico is tradition-shattering. It is a completely new departure which does a very high honor to the United States Congress and to the United States President. It does create a new kind of State. It is not an old kind of State, of course, but neither is it a dependency, because it governs itself locally. It is not an old kind of State because it has no voting representation in Congress. Of course, it has no voting representation in Congress because it pays no Federal taxes."

(US House of Representatives Committee on Public Lands (1949) 81:1:4)

However, he continued, something was still missing in the final construction of this "new kind of State" – "something missing which I do not anticipate will be very difficult to correct." The governor then proceeded to enlighten the committee:

"What is missing to make Puerto Rico a new kind of State is that the people of Puerto Rico should have the right to make their own constitution. This is a matter of great importance as a principle. In practice, the constitution would probably be very similar, certainly along fundamental lines, to the one now ruling by Act of Congress."

(US House of Representatives Committee on Public Lands (1949) 81:1:4)

Congress could impose a constitution upon the island, but the people of Puerto Rico knew it would not do that. It would allow them to write their own.

> "The idea of allowing the people of Puerto Rico to draft and approve their own constitution in a manner similar to the way the States do when they are first admitted, would be a tremendous step forward in principle, although in practice the amount of self-government would not be very different, as it is now substantial."
>
> (US House of Representatives Committee on Public Lands (1949) 81:1:4)

CONGRESS AUTHORIZES THE WRITING OF A CONSTITUTION

Less than a year later the governor and his party sought to fill this "missing gap." On March 13 1950 the Resident Commissioner Fernos-Isern placed in the legislative docket of the House of Representatives "a bill to provide for the organization of a constitutional government by the people of Puerto Rico." It was referred to the Committee on Public Lands. In its first section the bill stated "fully recognizing the principle of government by consent, this act is now adopted in the nature of a compact, and so that the people of Puerto Rico may organize a government pursuant to a constitution of their own adoption." The next section outlined the procedures that were to be followed at the various stages of development and approval, including a referendum on the present act itself. The third section stipulated that "the constitution of Puerto Rico shall create a government republican in form and shall include a bill of rights." The next two sections indicated which sections of the organic act of 1917 were to be repealed and which were to be retained with passage of this bill. The organic act was to be henceforth known as "The Puerto Rican Federal Relations Act" (US House of Representatives Committee on Public Lands (1950) 81:1:37).

The next day the resident commissioner offered an extended explanation and justification of his bill. He began with the following declaration:

> "Under the Constitution of the United States there are certain rights and privileges which may not be applicable in a given area. But there are certain rights which are fundamental. American citizens wherever they may live are endowed with them.... [This also refers to] the right to organize a local government, the right to live under a government of the people's choice [which] is expressly recognized in the Constitution of the United States.... There is no question that at the time the Constitution of the United States was adopted the people had and did not relinquish the right to organize their Government. They had already adopted their State constitutions. Later they adopted the Federal Constitution. It is such a simple and elementary right the people of Puerto Rico

wish now to exercise. They wish to adopt a local constitution and reaffirm their station within this Union."

    (US House of Representatives Committee on Public Lands (1950) 81:1:35)

In doing this for Puerto Rico, Fernos-Isern conceded that Congress would be breaking new ground. He acknowledged that only incorporated territories had been in the past authorized to write constitutions which transformed them into states of the Union. No precedent existed for granting unincorporated territories the right to write a constitution but he insisted "the fact that there has been no precedent should not deter Congress; such fact did not deter the Eightieth Congress from authorizing Puerto Rico to elect its governor." The relation of Puerto Rico with the United States had from the beginning "developed in a line parallel but not coincident with that followed by the incorporated territories attaining statehood" (US House of Representatives Committee on Public Lands (1950) 81:1:36).

> "Puerto Rico started in 1900 with a government comparable to that of an incorporated territory. By a series of enactments Congress has brought Puerto Rico to a status today which is way beyond a territorial pattern of government. It is much more comparable to that of a State. What my bill proposes to do is to perfect such status for Puerto Rico. Puerto Rico would have a position parallel to that of a State, although it would not have such participation in the Federal Government as the people of a State have. In other words, we are not asking for the right to vote for presidential electors, we are not asking for the right to elect two senators, we are not asking for the right to elect Members of this House other than a voteless resident commissioner.... We are developing a new pattern of federation, applicable to our circumstances, which do not permit us at the present, nor in the foreseeable future, to develop along the classical lines and the uniform pattern followed by former or present territories in their ascent to statehood."
>
> (US House of Representatives Committee on Public Lands (1950) 81:1:36)

Near the end of his address, the resident commissioner gave a label to the new political status that Puerto Rico would acquire with passage of the bill. No longer an unincorporated territory of the United States, it would become

> "a Commonwealth of American citizens, living within the federation, in accordance with such provisions of the Constitution of the United States as are applicable in the case, living under a local government shaped and organized and functioning with the consent of the people of Puerto Rico, within this great federation. This would not make Puerto Rico a State, but it would make of Puerto Rico a community of American citizens living in the American way. We

would not participate in national elections nor be represented in Congress any more than we now are; but we would have local government as democratically organized as in a State, and, with few exceptions, Federal laws would apply as in a State."
(US House of Representatives Committee on Public Lands (1950) 81:1:35–6)

The next day Governor Munoz-Marin emphasized in a hearing in the House Committee on Public Lands that the proposed bill did not envisage federal statehood for Puerto Rico, though it did not preclude that possibility in the future.

"I would say the door would always be open to statehood, because the Constitution hardly allows it to be shut. But a clear record can be made upon approval of the bill that that is not the present intention of Congress, and that its action should not in any way be interpreted as a promise of statehood, even though a future Congress may do so."
(US House of Representatives Committee on Public Lands (1950) 81:1:22)

The resident commissioner immediately interjected that this bill would set up a structure of self-government for unincorporated territories parallel with the one that already existed for incorporated territories.

"Since Puerto Rico has not been incorporated, not until such a step of incorporation were taken would such promise of statehood be implied. This bill does not change the fundamental situation of nonincorporation in which Puerto Rico is now situated, but it allows Puerto Rico to develop along the lines of self-government in a parallel line with a Territory that develops into statehood. That is the situation under this bill. In other words, it is the development in self-government of a non-incorporated area of the United States."
(US House of Representatives Committee on Public Lands (1950) 81:1:22)

In the meantime the Governor had already stressed the similarity in the structure of self-government in the proposed bill with that of any state of the Union. "The [proposed] Constitution of Puerto Rico should be on the basis of dignity with the States, but still what we are asking for is not statehood. It would not be represented by voting representation in the Congress" (US House of Representative Committee on Public Lands (1950) 81:1:19).

The governor also denied that the proposed structure would incline Puerto Rico toward independence. He explained that the primary reason for proposing the commonwealth structure was to gain certain tax and financial benefits which would not be available if Puerto Rico were a state.

"If Puerto Rico were a Federal State of the Union, the people of Puerto Rico would have to pay in taxes about $50,000,000 or $60,000,000 a year which is practically the whole operating budget of the Puerto Rican government to expand the schools, the hospitals, the public services of all kinds. So it would be just a collapse of all possible hope of the people of Puerto Rico to get out of the economic situation from [which] they are trying to work out by what I call 'operation bootstrap.' Perhaps in the course of a generation that will not be so. That is up to that generation both in Puerto Rico and in the Congress to act upon. For the present time, and for quite sometime after, that is the situation in Puerto Rico."

(US House of Representatives Committee on Public Lands (1950) 81:1:29)

Approximately two weeks later a virtually identical bill was introduced into the Senate by O'Mahoney and Butler and referred to the Committee on Interior and Insular Affairs. It was further amended in the committee so that its procedural steps were even more explicitly drawn than was the House bill. Accordingly the second section stipulated that "this act shall be submitted to the qualified voters for acceptance or rejection through an island-wide referendum to be held in accordance with the laws of Puerto Rico. Upon the approval of this act, by a majority of the voters participating in such referendum, the Legislature of Puerto Rico is authorized to call a constitutional convention to draft a constitution for the said island of Puerto Rico. The said constitution shall provide a republican form of government and shall include a bill of rights." The third section stipulated that once the constitution was adopted by the people of Puerto Rico, the United States President would transmit it to Congress, "if he finds that such constitution conforms with the applicable provisions of this act and the Constitution of the United States" (US Congressional Record 1950 81:2:8321–322). Congress would also have to approve it for it to become effective.

Sections 4 and 5 spelled out the provisions of the Jones Act of 1917, henceforth to be called the Puerto Rican Federal Relations Act, that were to be repealed by this act and those that were to remain in effect.

Hearings were held on both bills for the next several months. The only significant opposition to the bills developed from the "diehards" for statehood or independence. Congressman Marcantonio of New York, for example, delivered a blistering attack on Munoz-Marin and the bill for perpetuating colonialism and standing in the way of independence.

Finally on June 6 the amended Senate bill reached the floor. The House version never left its committee. The Senate report "stated clearly and unequivocally that S3336 is not a statehood bill. Nor is it an independence bill. It does not commit the Congress, either expressly or by implication, to take any action whatever with respect to either. It in no way precludes future determination by future Congresses of the political status of Puerto Rico" (US Senate Report No. 1779 (1950) 81:2:4).

The report also stressed the following points:

"The measure would not change Puerto Rico's fundamental political, social, and economic relationship to the United States. Those sections of the Organic Act of Puerto Rico concerning such matters as the applicability of United States law, customs, internal revenue, Federal judicial jurisdiction in Puerto Rico, representation in the Congress of the United States by a Resident Commissioner, et cetera, would remain in force and effect. Upon enactment of S3336, these remaining sections of the organic act would be referred to as the Puerto Rican Federal Relations Act.

The sections of the organic act which section 5 of this bill would repeal are concerned primarily with the organization of the insular executive, legislative, and judicial branches of the government of Puerto Rico and other matters of purely local concern. These aspects of local self-government would be provided for in any constitution adopted and any government organized by the people of Puerto Rico....

In view of all the evidence presented to the committee, it is the committee's considered opinion that a majority, a very substantial majority, of the people of Puerto Rico do wish the authority to draw up their own constitution and to organize their own insular government under it within the safeguards of the Federal Constitution." (US Senate Report No. 1779 (1950) 81:2:3—4)

The report also included letters of endorsement from the President and the departments of interior and state.

Within two days the bill was passed by the Senate without debate and sent to the House where it was referred to the Committee on Public Lands. Within a week the bill was favorably reported back to the floor of the House. The committee report repeated most of the Senate committee's arguments, but with one significant addition. It added a brief historical account of the linkage between incorporated territorial status with statehood and the absence of such linkage for unincorporated territories.

Eleven days later the bill reached the House floor with an explanation by the resident commissioner, stressing: "This is not statehood. Puerto Rico will continue to be represented in Congress by its Resident Commissioner. This is not independence. Puerto Ricans will continue proudly to be American citizens, in a common loyalty to our common institutions" (US Congressional Record 1950 81:2:9585).

Thereupon an intense and bitter debate broke out, led by Marcantonio of New York. He assailed the bill as a sham of self-governance; it did nothing more than perpetuate the colonial status of Puerto Rico. He denounced Governor Munoz-

Marin for betraying the independence movement which he had professedly led. The congressman read into the record an earlier speech in which he labeled the governor "the Nero of Fortalez" for ostensibly living on a lavish scale while most Puerto Ricans were starving. Only Javitz of New York joined him in any criticism of the bill. Javitz complained about the absence of the alternatives of independence or statehood in any referendum on the island. But when the showdown came on Marcantonio's motion to recommit the bill, Javitz opposed it, leaving Marcantonio's as the only vote in favor of recommitting. The bill accordingly passed the House overwhelmingly by the end of the day. Four days later, on July 3, President Truman signed it, and as its sponsors had hoped it became a statute, Public Law 600, before July 4, Independence Day.

PUERTO RICO WRITES A CONSTITUTION "CREATING" COMMONWEALTH STATUS FOR THE ISLAND

By the end of August 1950, the Puerto Rican legislature passed Act No. 27 which provided for an island-wide referendum on Public Law 600 among qualified voters to be held on June 4 1951; it even provided for a special registration of new voters for the referendum. By early fall most of the major parties had taken a position on Public Law 600 and were campaigning vigorously to influence voters. The Popular Democratic party, for example, went all out for the law and called for its overwhelming approval in the referendum. It argued that the act did not prejudice the future political status of Puerto Rico. It did mean "the organization of a local government on the fully democratic basis of government by consent of the governed, and the continuance of desirable, cultural, political and economic relations with the United States on the basis of consent and in the nature of a compact" (Puerto Rico Constitutional Convention 1952:19). The Socialist party also approved of the act "as conducive to the organization of local political institutions based on the democratic principle of government by consent." The Puerto Rican Independence party, however, came out for an unqualified rejection of the law "which they described as a subterfuge to disguise colonialism and imperialism under the cloak of democratic self-government." It maintained its uncompromising position for a free and independent Puerto Rico. Accordingly, it advised its members to vote against the act or to abstain from voting. Only the Statehood party failed to take a stand on Public Law 600. One faction called for rejection of the act, "on the grounds that its approval would inevitably postpone consideration and final recognition of the right of Puerto Rico to be admitted as a State of the Union" (Puerto Rico Constitutional Convention 1952:20). The other, though disappointed, viewed Public Law 600 as a distinct improvement on the organic act and therefore felt it should be supported.

By the day of the referendum, 777,675 were registered and qualified. Of these only 65 percent actually went to the polls to select one of the two options offered them on a ballot. They could either check the sentence "I vote to accept Public Law 600 of the Eighty-first Congress" or the sentence "I vote against accepting Public Law 600 of the Eighty-first Congress." The Spanish version of Public Law 600 was printed at the bottom of the ballot (Puerto Rico Constitutional Convention 1952:17).

The public law was overwhelmingly approved; 76.5 percent for and 23.5 percent against. Some scholars nevertheless suggest that the strategy of abstention by the Independence party was more effective than has been generally acknowledged; for in fact fewer than half of the eligible voters (49.76 percent) voted for the public law.

Almost immediately the machinery for the election of delegates to a constitutional convention was put into place. Nine delegates were to be elected from each of the eight districts into which Puerto Rico had been divided. No political party, however, could nominate or elect more than seven in any one district. In addition, no more than twenty-three delegates were to be elected at large, with no single party being permitted to nominate or elect more than fourteen. Thus no party could completely dominate the convention, as some minority representation was built into the structure.

Candidates had to possess the dual American and Puerto Rican citizenship, be over twenty-five years of age, literate in either Spanish or English, and with residency of one year in Puerto Rico if a candidate at large or in a district if a candidate was from that district.

Only the Independence party refused to put up any candidates; its grounds were the convention's lack of authority to make Puerto Rico a free and independent republic. The other three parties campaigned actively, each pursuing its own ideological goals. The Statehood party called for election of its slate to make sure that the constitution "would in no manner jeopardize the right of Puerto Rico to become eventually a State of the Union." The Socialists called for support of their candidates "so that they could draft a constitution in such a manner as to protect and advance the rights of workers in their relations with their employers." And the Popular Democratic party adopted an official party program at a special convention which spelled out the principles that would guide it in writing the constitution:

"The people of Puerto Rico shall enjoy powers of self-government within the American Union. Their Constitution shall be amended only by authority of the people of Puerto Rico.

The relations between the people of Puerto Rico and the American Union shall be governed by the principles of voluntary association and of government by consent.

The Constitution shall implement the organization and development of Puerto Rico as a free community of American citizens in voluntary association with the American Union.

(Puerto Rico Constitutional Convention 1952:24)

The entire slate of delegates from the Popular Democratic party won handily in the election of August 27 1951. Only the restriction on the number of candidates from any one party probably prevented it from making a complete sweep of the election. Its 7 candidates from each district and its 14 candidates at large won for a total of 70. Fifteen other delegates were chosen from the Statehood party and 7 from the Socialist party. Of the grand total of 92 delegates, 32 were lawyers; 13, farmers; 11, businessmen; 9, labor leaders; 6, teachers; 4, physicians; 3, journalists; and 14, from other professions and occupations.

The delegates met for the inaugural session of the convention on September 17 and elected Dr A. Fernos-Isern, Resident Commissioner in Washington, as its president. Within a week the convention had been organized into ten permanent committees, each charged with doing the detailed work, such as examining the 330 proposals dropped into the convention's hopper, holding hearings, and drafting proposals and resolutions for consideration by the convention as a whole. During their deliberations, the various committees examined each of the constitutions of the states of the Union as well as that of the federal government and adapted many of their features to the instrument they were writing. After approximately five months of deliberations the convention approved a constitution for the Commonwealth of Puerto Rico on February 6 1952 by a vote of 88 to 3, one delegate being out of the country at the time of the vote.

The constitution consisted of a preamble and nine articles. Whereas much of the document was patterned after the constitutions of various states of the Union, the distinctive political status of Puerto Rico was nevertheless manifest throughout, particularly in the preamble and Article I.

The preamble was a much watered-down version of the Popular Democratic party's program adopted at its constitutional convention. Less manifest in the preamble, though, was the latter's image of Puerto Rico as a virtually autonomous political community with exceedingly loose co-fraternal ties with the United States.

The preamble's first paragraph was virtually a paraphrase of the federal and various states constitutions; its primary emphasis was on the sovereignty of "We the People" with some mention of the autonomy of Puerto Rico as a political collectivity.

"We, the people of Puerto Rico, in order to organize ourselves politically on a fully democratic basis, to promote the general welfare, and to secure for ourselves and our posterity the complete enjoyment of human rights, placing our trust in Almighty God, do ordain and establish this Constitution for the commonwealth which, in the exercise of our natural rights, we now create within our union with the United States of America."

(Puerto Rico Contitutional Convention 1952:31)

Its last paragraph stressed the importance of American citizenship for the Puerto Rican and the loyalty of the commonwealth to the principles of the federal Constitution.

"We consider as determining factors in our life our citizenship of the United States of America and our aspiration continually to enrich our democratic heritage in the individual and collective enjoyment of its rights and privileges; our loyalty to the principles of the Federal Constitution; the coexistence in Puerto Rico of the two great cultures of the American Hemisphere."

(Puerto Rico Constitutional Convention 1952:31)

Article I came even closer to suggesting the "autonomous character" of Puerto Rico with its sovereignty rooted in the people of the island subject only to "the terms of the compact agreed upon between the people of Puerto Rico and the United States of America:"

"SECTION 1. – The Commonwealth of Puerto Rico is hereby constituted. Its political power emanates from the people and shall be exercised in accordance with their will, within the terms of the compact agreed upon between the people of Puerto Rico and the United States of America."

(Puerto Rico Constitutional Convention 1952:32)

Section 2 met the conditions imposed by Public Law 600: "The government of the Commonwealth of Puerto Rico shall be republican in form and its legislative, judicial and executive branches as established by this Constitution shall be equally subordinate to the sovereignty of the people of Puerto Rico" (Puerto Rico Constitutional Convention 1952:32).

The second article consisted of twenty sections that went far beyond any minimal requirement for a Bill of Rights that Congress may have set in Public Law 600. For example it contained the basic political and legal rights of the first Ten Amendments of the federal Constitution and even those of the great Reconstruction Amendments, the Thirteenth through the Fifteenth. Thus Section 1 declared that "the dignity of the human being is inviolable. All men are equal before the law. No discrimination shall be made on account of race, color, sex, birth, social origin or condition, or political or religious ideas. Both the laws and the system of public education shall embody these principles of essential human equality" (Puerto Rico Constitutional Convention 1952:34). In addition, Section 12 declared, "Neither slavery nor involuntary servitude shall exist except in the latter case as a punishment for crime after the accused has been duly convicted. Cruel and unusual punishments shall not be inflicted" (Puerto Rico Constitutional Convention 1952:43).

In addition to basic legal and political rights, the article also recognized basic social and economic rights that had not been part of the traditional definition of the Bill of Rights. Some were drawn from state constitutions of relatively recent vintage; others, from federal and state legislation; and still others of unique derivation, from the Puerto Rican experience. Thus Article II included provisions guaranteeing the right to an education, to choose an occupation freely, to receive equal pay for equal work, "to a reasonable minimum salary, to protection against risks to his health or person in his work or employment, and to an ordinary workday which shall not exceed eight hours" (Section 16) (Puerto Rico Constitutional Convention 1952:45). Further, workers were guaranteed "the right to organize and to bargain collectively with their employers through representatives of their own free choosing in order to promote their welfare" (Section 17) (Puerto Rico Constitutional Convention 1952:46) and also "the right to strike, to picket and to engage in other legal concerted activities" (Section 18) (Puerto Rico Constitutional Convention 1952:47).

Above and beyond these, Section 20 of Article II also pledged someday to have the government fulfill the entire panoply of human rights incorporated in the United Nations Declaration of Human Rights:

"SECTION 20. – The Commonwealth also recognizes the existence of the following human rights:

The right of every person to receive free elementary and secondary education.

The right of every person to obtain work.

The right of every person to a standard of living adequate for the health and well-being of himself and of his family, and especially to food, clothing, housing and medical care and necessary social services.

The right of every person to social protection in the event of unemployment, sickness, old age or disability.

The right of motherhood and childhood to special care and assistance."

(Puerto Rico Constitutional Convention 1952:48)

In order to realize the fulfillment of these rights, the article concluded with this promise:

> "the people and the government of Puerto Rico shall do everything in their power to promote the greatest possible expansion of the system of production, to assure the fairest distribution of economic output, and to obtain the maximum understanding between individual initiative and collective coopera-tion. The executive and judicial branches shall bear in mind this duty and shall construe the laws that tend to fulfill it in the most favorable manner possible."
> (Puerto Rico Constitution 1952:48)

The rest of the constitution spelled out the responsibilities and functions of the various branches of government. Many provisions merely reaffirmed practices and procedures established earlier by the organic law and the various amendments over time to it. Most were modeled in their original or revised formulations after provisions of constitutions from various states of the Union, from those defining the office of the elected governor to those that required "all public officials and employees of the Commonwealth, its agencies, instrumentalities and political subdivisions before entering upon their respective duties, shall take an oath to support the Constitution of the United States and the Constitution and laws of the Commonwealth of Puerto Rico" (Article VI: Section 16) (Puerto Rico Constitu-tional Convention 1952:110).

There were, in addition several innovative structual features in the constitution. One in particular would prevent the total domination by a political party of either or both houses of the legislature. Modeled after Act 1 of 1951, which established a similar principle with respect to the election of delegates to the constitutional convention, Section 7 of Article III provided for an increase in the number of legislators in either or both houses if any party succeeded in electing more than two-thirds of the members of that house. Such legislators, identified as senators or representatives-at-large, would be drawn from minority parties proportionate to their vote in the election. In addition, the constitution retained the 500-acre limit of the Joint Resolution of Congress of 1900 explicitly excluding the government of Puerto Rico from this restriction.

Once the convention approved the draft constitution, it ordered the printing and distribution to voters of over a million copies in Spanish and 30,000 copies in English and published the text in Spanish and English in the four daily newspapers in Puerto Rico. Approximately a month later, March 3, a referendum on the constitution was conducted. Voters were asked on the ballot to select one of the following two sentences: "I vote in favor of the adoption of the Constitution approved by the Constitutional Convention," or "I vote against the adoption of the Constitution approved by the Constitutional Convention." Of the 783,610 eligible voters, 457,562 actually voted and of these approximately 80 percent voted in favor of the constitution (Puerto Rico Constitutional Convention 1952:30).

THE PRESIDENT AND CONGRESS APPROVE THE CONSTITUTION WITH CERTAIN RESERVATIONS

In accordance with Public Law 600, the results of the election and the text of the constitution were forwarded to President Truman for his approval. And in a letter dated April 22, the President notified Congress that "I do find and declare that the Constitution of the Commonwealth of Puerto Rico conforms with the applicable provisions of the act of July 3, 1950, and of our own Constitution" (US House of Representatives Report No. 1832 (1952) 82:2:8). The President summarized the major provisions of the constitution and gave a brief historical account of the various changes in Puerto Rico's political status under American tutelage. He concluded his letter with this stirring declaration:

> "The people of the United States and the people of Puerto Rico are entering into a new relationship that will serve as an inspiration to all who love freedom and hate tyranny. We are giving new substance to man's hope for a world with liberty and equality under law. Those who truly love freedom know that the right relationship between a government and its people is one based on mutual consent and esteem.... The Constitution of the Commonwealth of Puerto Rico is a proud document that embodies the best of our democratic heritage. I recommend its early approval by the Congress."
>
> (US House of Representatives Report No. 1832 (1952) 82:2:10)

On the same day Resident Commissioner Dr Fernos-Isern, who had also presided over the constitutional convention, introduced into the House of Representatives a resolution calling for approval of the Puerto Rican constitution. In turn it was referred to the Committee on Interior and Insular Affairs. A week later the committee reported its unanimous endorsement of the resolution (HJ Res 430) to the House. Its report offered a straightforward account of the step-by-step implementation of the "compact for a Constitution" made between the people of Puerto Rico and the federal government through enactment of Public Law 600. It denied any claims of fraud in the final referendum on the constitution. Its subcommittee, which had been charged with observing the conduct of the referendum, had discounted any such claims through its spot checks on the island.

The report also summarized the major provisions of the constitution and declared,

"The constitution provides the same system of checks and balances as our own Constitution, and contains provisions which will insure the complete independence of the legislative, executive, and judiciary, one from the other.... [Further,] The Constitution of the Commonwealth of Puerto Rico has many features of an unusually democratic nature, such as providing for the suspension of the writ of habeas corpus only by the legislature in the event of riot or rebellion. Another unique feature is one which insures in the legislature a minimum working membership of minority parties in order that an effective opposition may exist at all times."

(US House of Representatives Report No. 1832 (1952) 82:2:7)

But the report repeated the theme emphasized in the Senate Report on Public Law 600 in 1950: "the approval of this constitution by the Congress will not change Puerto Rico's fundamental-political, social, and economic relationship to the United States" (US House of Representatives Report No. 1832 (1952) 82:2:7).

Two weeks later as the House began to consider the resolution, a congressman from Indiana pounced almost immediately on Section 20 of Article II. He complained that provisions in the section "are as different from our concept of the bill of rights as day is from night." Earlier he had contended "The Bill of Rights in the American Constitution was drafted by a people who wanted to protect the liberties and freedom of the individual against the encroachment of government. They did not undertake to set out in the Bill of Rights the things that they demanded that government should do for them, but, rather, they sought to limit the power of the Government over the individual person and to protect him in those human rights." The Puerto Rican constitution, he continued, assured everyone "that it is his right to expect these [social and economic] blessings to somehow flow from others, with no implication whatsoever of individual duties and responsibilities" (US Congressional Record 1952 82:2:5120). This bill of rights was a replay of the United Nations Universal Declaration of Human Rights to which communistic and socialistic countries subscribed, he thundered. Several other speakers joined the congressman in his complaint, and by the end of the debate that day only a few voices were heard in favor of the section.

The debate on Section 20 continued two weeks later. Meanwhile the committee took the matter under advisement and offered to amend the resolution by declaring the Congress approved of the constitution except for Section 20 of Article II. In addition, the committee also expressed concern that Section 5 of Article II might prevent schools administered under nongovernmental auspices from operating on the island. Accordingly, it proposed to amend the section by stating "compulsory attendance to elementary schools to the extent permitted by the facilities of the state as herein provided, shall not be construed as applicable to those who receive elementary education in schools established under non-governmental auspices" (US Congressional Record 1952 82:2:6181).

The committee also declared in its amended resolution that these changes would have to be accepted by the constitutional convention of Puerto Rico in a formal resolution to the governor of Puerto Rico before the constitution could go into effect.

The committee's amended resolution was passed on May 28 and sent to the Senate, but not before it beat back an effort by another congressman to amend the constitution still further. He had expressed concern about the "true" character of the relations established in the constitution between the United States and Puerto Rico. He feared that Puerto Rico was being transformed into a *de facto* state of the Union and that it would be "making an irrevocable delegation of its authority under article IV, section 3, clause 2 of our Constitution. Will it be beyond the power of Congress to review any legislation adopted under the constitution as it now can do? If the Congress passes a law that is in conflict with a law adopted by Puerto Rico, will the law passed by the United States Congress supersede that of the Puerto Rican Legislature?" (US Congressional Record 1952 82:2:6170). To avoid this ambiguity, he proposed the following amendment to the Puerto Rican constitution: "nothing herein contained shall be construed as an irrevocable delegation, transfer or release of the power of the Congress granted by article IV, section 3, of the Constitution of the United States" (US Congressional Record 1952 82:2:6183). The House voted it down.

The day after the House passed the amended version of the constitution it was referred to the Senate Committee on Interior and Insular Affairs. In the meantime the Senate had under consideration its own resolution on the constitution that had been introduced into the legislative hopper by O'Mahoney on April 22, the same day the House bill had been introduced by Dr Fernos-Isern.

Seven weeks later the committee reported out its resolution, which included the various amendments already incorporated in the bill which had passed the House two weeks before. The committee justified exclusion of Section 20, Article II on the following grounds:

"to constitute an effective right there must be a well-founded and enforceable claim with a correlative and enforceable duty upon others to satisfy it. Corresponding enforceable duties to the rights asserted cannot be determined and fixed under section 20, and, therefore it is unrealistic, confusing, and misleading to assert such rights in a constitution which is intended to be a fundamental and clear statement of matters which are enforceable and of the limitations on the exercise of power.... Because of the novelty of the assertion of these so-called human rights as constitutional rights the confusions and uncertainties to which we have referred are not remedied by our judicial precedents and constitutional history."

(US Senate Report No. 1720 (1952) 82:2:1–2)

The report also explained that the amendment to Senate 5 of Article II was meant to clear up any possible misinterpretation of the compulsory educational requirement.

The report emphasized that the constitution of Puerto Rico was meant to regulate internal situations. The island's external relations with the United States were still to be controlled by those provisions of the organic act that remained in force (the Puerto Rican Federal Relations Act). Thus, "within this [constitutional] framework, the people of Puerto Rico will exercise self-government. As regards local matters, the sphere of action and the methods of government bear a resemblance to that of any State of the Union." However, the report continued, "Puerto Rico does not become a member State of the Union under this resolution nor is there any promise of statehood. Its people will not participate in national elections nor do they gain representation in Congress other than they now have" (US Senate Report No. 1720 (1952) 82:2:6–7).

> "Approval of this constitution will make the historic American concept of 'government by consent of the governed' a reality for the 2¼ million American citizens in the American territory of Puerto Rico. This concept is set forth in our Declaration of Independence and has been realized through our State constitutions within the Federal system....
>
> [But] the Commonwealth of Puerto Rico is not a State of the United States. Neither is it an independent republic. It is a self-governing community bound by the common loyalties and obligations of American citizens living under the American flag and the American Constitution and enjoying a republican form of government of their own choosing."

(US Senate Report No. 1720 (1952) 82:2:6–7)

As debate began two weeks later, a senator from South Carolina launched an attack almost immediately on the latitude the proposed constitution offered to Puerto Rico in governing itself. He expressed concern that a governor could assume dictatorial powers under the constitution: "great power is built up in a governor's office. He appoints officials throughout the State, and, in that way he can build up a powerful machine" (US Congressional Record 1952 82:2:7842). After announcing his intention not to be a party to such a state of affairs ("I shall not do anything to contribute to the building up of a dictatorship in Puerto Rico") he proposed an amendment that would limit the governor to one four-year term of office.

Undaunted by his defeat from an opposition that emphasized the absence of such a restriction in most states, the senator then zeroed in on his primary concern: the absence of any apparent constraint on the Puerto Rican legislature from reinstating sometime in the future Section 20 of Article II or any other section which Congress might find objectionable. Accordingly he proposed another amendment that would require the approval of Congress for any proposed amendment or revision of the Puerto Rican constitution: "no amendment to or revision of the constitution of the Commonwealth of Puerto Rico shall be effective until approved by the Congress of the United States" (US Congressional Record 1952 82:2:7848).

Opponents of the amendment argued that no state of the Union faced a similar constraint. The point was made in a set of queries raised by a senator from New Mexico: "If the State of New Mexico, the State of Colorado, the State of Idaho, the State of Michigan, or the State of South Carolina desire to amend their State constitutions do they ask Congress for permission to do so?" The senator from South Carolina accepted the challenge by declaring,

"I answer that question by saying that we are not granting statehood at this time to Puerto Rico. That is something quite different. We are giving them only the right, in a very limited way, to conduct the affairs of their own government in Puerto Rico. We are, under the Constitution of the United States, retaining our rights over Puerto Rico. We cannot get away from that."

(US Congressional Record 1952 82:2:7846)

Opposition to the amendment virtually crumbled when the chairman of the interior committee announced that he and other members of his committee could live with it. As a result it passed handily. After an abortive effort to add an amendment on trial by jury was beaten back, the resolution as amended was passed as a substitute for that already approved by the House.

Before a conference committee met in order to iron out the differences between the two bills, Governor Munoz-Marin sent a strong protest to the Senate against the amendment. In his telegram, he declared:

"People here are dismayed with amendment that nullifies significance of the whole constitutional process.... the amendment adds an obvious colonial touch. The people of Puerto Rico in voting to accept law 600 in the nature of a compact, in which the principle of government by consent was 'fully recognized' certainly had no idea they were consenting to any trace of colonialism. No self-respecting people would. Free men may live under such circumstances but they will certainly not go to the polls and vote that they love and cherish them. I fear that if the matter cannot be remedied in conference great moral harm will be done to our people and some moral harm to the good name of the United States in the world." (US Congressional Record 1952 82:2:7924)

In view of this strong reaction, the Senate's amendment was markedly diluted in the conference between the managers of the two houses. In its report to the House at the end of June, the five managers on part of the House declared that

> "the conference agreement deletes that portion of the Senate amendment making it mandatory that every proposed change in the new Puerto Rican Constitution be approved by the Congress of the United States. The conferees believe that in keeping with the spirit of Public Law 600, Eighty-first Congress, and the purposes of the Puerto Rican Constitution, the people of Puerto Rico should have freedom to change their constitution within the limits of applicable provisions of the United States Constitution, the Puerto Rican Federal Relations Act, Public Law 600, Eighty-first Congress, and House Joint Resolution 430." (US Congressional Record 1952 82:2:8619)

Accordingly, the conferees specified such limits in detail in their amendment.

The House approved the conference report on June 30 without comment once it was read. In the Senate the next day, the senator from South Carolina expressed his reluctant consent to the revised wording of his amendment; but he nevertheless insisted on reading into the record support for his original amendment from the statehood party in Puerto Rico. In turn, an opponent of the senator's original amendment expressed his satisfaction with the revised wording of the amendment. And then the Senate voted agreement with the report. Two days later, July 3, President Truman signed the bill into law, once again in time for an Independence day celebration.

CONCLUSION

And so, after half of a century a "novel" structure of self-governance was finally constructed and legitimated for the first unincorporated territory in American history. This structure was the end product of a process of transformation that paralleled the change from territory to state. However, it was a transformation that took place outside of the People's Domain. Despite its present status, Puerto Rico remains essentially a colonial dependency of the United States, though its people retain the right to enter the People's Domain if they move to the mainland.

For more than a quarter of a century the people of Puerto Rico have lived with this duality. How much longer they will wish to do so is open to question. Discontent with such an inherently unstable arrangement is surfacing. And unless Congress moves to dissolve the duality soon and incorporate the political community of Puerto Rico into the People's Domain as a state in the Union, the pressure for independence may grow irresistible.

POSTSCRIPT

Duality: a framework for comparative analysis

We have now come to the end of our study, which it is to be hoped will be the first of others that will attempt to test and to apply the duality thesis elsewhere. It is our contention that this thesis should apply wherever the expansion of the white European generated the dual processes of colonialization and colonization and produced the socio-political structures we have examined. As we have already suggested, the character of these dual structures, their linkages and relationships, have varied with the national identity of the white European, the racial identity of the nonwhite, the proportions of each race, and the historical circumstances. Accordingly, the way in which duality has been imprinted in the various societies is problematic and merits detailed study.

As we have already seen, the earliest and perhaps most pervasive historical exportation of duality happened during the conquest and settlement of the New World, first by the Spanish, then by the English, and finally by other Europeans. They built their dual societies in South America, Central America, and North America and eventually lost them, as these societies became independent nations still bearing the marks of their dualistic heritage.

In Book One we examined in some detail the duality imprinted by the English in their conquest and settlement of Virginia, but we merely surveyed the dualities of the other twelve colonies. However, they too could have been examined in a fashion similar to that of Virginia. We have already suggested that a distinctive variant appears to have developed in Massachusetts and in other New England colonies. Hopefully, the versions constructed in the different colonies will be compared and contrasted in the future. Such research would add flesh to the skeletal structure of this study and thereby give us a much fuller and more complete description and understanding of the "colonialist-colonist" heritage of the New Nation.

We also look briefly in Appendix A at the duality stamped by the Spanish conquistador on the island of Hispaniola. We conclude – albeit tentatively – that the kind of duality generally imprinted by the conquistador on Spanish America was eventually integrated into a distinctive kind of societal system. Much research remains to be done in order to provide a definitive test of this conclusion. Such a test would take place if the duality thesis were applied to and examined for a variety of societies in Central and South America, including Mexico, Peru, Ecuador, and the like.

By the time the white European moved onto the continents of Asia and Africa, he had become, by and large, a colonialist who was interested in building an imperial system for his home country. Accordingly, he only constructed the kind of racially segmented plural society about which Furnivall wrote (Furnivall 1956), with himself perched at the top as a "sojourner elite." In some places, however, he settled permanently and evolved a colonist society too. As a result, duality resurfaced in such places as South Africa, Zimbabwe (Rhodesia), Australia, and New Zealand.

In Australia and New Zealand the white European overwhelmed an aboriginal population that was pushed to the perimeters of the white society as a racial minority, much as the Indian was in America. In South Africa and Zimbabwe the situation was different. Whites built their own society as a small minority among a vast population of subjugated nonwhites. As might be expected, the dual structures constructed in these societies reflected the marked variations in population proportions of white and nonwhite as well as the different historical circumstances.

Finally, by the middle of the twentieth century, countries like England were no longer able to insulate themselves internally from the duality they had been exporting as colonialist powers for centuries. They began to experience duality within their domestic borders as increasing numbers of nonwhites, their former colonial subjects, entered the metropolitan country. Unprepared for any other kind of relationship with these nonwhites, they tried to reconstruct internally the kind of plural societal arrangements that characterized their colonial possessions abroad. However, the plural arrangements had to be superimposed domestically upon a legal-normative system that advertently or inadvertently bestowed upon the nonwhites certain rights in the People's Domain. As a result, the nonwhites have resisted being confined to the same status as in the colonial plural society and have sought to expand their rights in the People's Domain. In turn, the whites in these countries have exerted pressure to drive the nonwhites from the Domain or at the least to minimize their rights within it. The conflict here is along the borders of the two societal systems and not within the plural structure itself as in the colonies.

It would seem, then, that the duality thesis we have developed apparently has broad applicability as a theoretic and analytic construct. It brings together into a common conceptual framework a variety of historical experiences which share a similar motif. All have been directly or indirectly products of the dual processes of colonialization and colonization generated by the expansion of the white European over a span of five centuries. Thus, America's encounter with its racial minorities has not been the kind of unique historical phenomenon that some scholars continue to treat it as. Instead it can be located theoretically and analytically in the flow of white European expansion as one kind of adaptation of duality, and it can accordingly be compared and contrasted with the adaptations of other countries ranging from Australia and South Africa to those of Latin America.

The existence of this common framework underlies Fredrickson's recent work *White Supremacy* (1981) which is referred to on the book jacket as "the first comparative history of United States and South African race relations." The author denies having used any theoretical model for his analysis. "No preconceived formula or 'model' could be advanced that would do justice to the complex patterns of causation involved" (Fredrickson 1981:xxi). And yet he comes close, in our judgment, to employing a "model" akin to duality as the theoretical frame of reference for studying the variations in race relations between the two countries. In fact, Davis in his highly favorable review of the book ("one of the most brilliant and successful studies in comparative history ever written") declares, "Mr Fredrickson is at his very best when he untangles the complex relationships among political independence, white equality, economic opportunities and the emergence of societies segregated between white and nonwhite races" (Davis 1981:20). To paraphrase Davis, Fredrickson is at his best when he studies the relationships between the kinds of societal arrangements the white built for himself and those he built on the backs of the subjugated nonwhite.

From a dualistic to a monistic society

The comparative framework that we have proposed does more than allow us to contrast the dual structures imprinted in these different societies. It also allows us to compare and to contrast the various ways some of these societies have sought to resolve their duality and to build a monistic society. One of the most interesting efforts is currently taking place in Zimbabwe, which was under the complete domination of a small white minority until recently. Following a "constitutional" transfer of power to the formerly subjugated nonwhite majority, Zimbabwe has been dissolving the plural society of its colonial past and is expanding membership in the People's Domain formerly monopolized by the whites. It is doing this without seeming to deprive these whites of basic rights and immunities in the Domain. The crucial question for the future is: Can Zimbabwe continue on this path and remedy deeply embedded economic and other inequities suffered by the nonwhite majority as a heritage of the colonialist past without resorting to arbitrary policies of expropriation or even of expulsion of the whites?

If Zimbabwe succeeds in these efforts and also succeeds in reconstituting itself as a stable monistic society with a People's Domain open to all, irrespective of race, then it will have demonstrated for all the world to see that a nonwhite majority, once in power, can confront the bitter heritage of its colonial past without redirecting the racist policies of this heritage against the whites. It will, in effect, have pioneered for the future the model of a harmonious multi-racial society built on the legal-normative foundations of equality and justice for all. Phoenix-like, this model will have been constructed upon the still smoldering ashes of the racially unjust and unequal colonialist society.

From reconstruction to redemption: America's unresolved agenda on duality

At the other end of the population spectrum, the United States seemed to have come closer in the 1960s to resolving its historic duality than had any of the other "colonist-colonialist" societies in which the white European had become the numerical majority. It dismantled the legal-normative foundations of its plural society and granted its racial minorities access to and legal equality within the People's Domain. It even began to implement policies that sought to redress the continuing effects of past inequities.

Opposition to these measures, however, mounted dramatically so that by 1981 a historian was able to proclaim that America's second period of reconstruction had given way to a second period of redemption. "In both the 19th and 20th century, a period of turbulent change was succeeded by a desire for 'stability,' followed in turn by an open assault on achievements, enshrined in Federal law and the Constitution that had appeared irreversible" (Foner 1981:23).

Though, as Foner cautions, "History never really repeats itself" (Foner 1981:23), the similarities between the two periods of redemption point to certain common elements. Both brought to an end efforts by America to come to terms with its duality, and both ushered in a period in which the dominant whites fostered the belief that this duality no longer posed a "real" problem for the present.

Tempting as the belief in this illusion may be, the dominant whites have to face a sobering fact. Many of the inequities imprinted from the duality of America's past are still deeply engraved in its institutional arrangements. For the dominant whites to allow these inequities to continue to fester and to contaminate the American society and its People's Domain is to run the grave risk of serious racial disturbances in the future. Should these disturbances erupt and should the response of the white be brutal and repressive, then the threat would be more than to the fabric of America's civil society. It would also be to America's most cherished of traditions, a political society based on "We the People." As Foner concludes, "Between the undoing of [the First Period of] Reconstruction and the modern civil rights movement, the better part of a century elapsed. Today, Americans may not have the luxury of another prolonged failure to come to grips with the legacy of 250 years of slavery and 100 of segregation" (Foner 1981:23).

APPENDIX A

THE SPANISH CONQUISTADOR
IN THE NEW WORLD

Colonial exploitation and the encomienda

Within two decades after Columbus's discovery of the island of Hispaniola, the Spanish conquistador had not only wrested the land and its resources from the Indians but had also imposed upon them a system of forced labor that was to remain in effect in the Spanish colonies for the next several centuries. Under this system of the encomienda, first elaborated and institutionalized by Governor Ovando, the successor to Columbus's successor as governor, Indians were parcelled out to Spaniards in numbers ranging from a few to several hundred. The number any Spaniard received depended on his status and on his role in the conquest of Hispaniola. In the early days of Ovando's rule no Spaniard went without any Indians at all, for the governor had succeeded in extending the rule of Spain over the entire island and in bringing under Spanish control a large number of Indians, many after fierce and vicious battles.

Most of the Indians were employed in the mining of gold and of other precious ores; others, in cultivating foodstuffs for the Spanish conquistador. They had to endure back-breaking manual labor for long hours under intolerable conditions. For them the encomienda was a brutal and coercive system of labor control not unlike slavery. Thus was set in place a colonial system of political control and economic exploitation divided along racial lines.

So harsh were the working conditions that by the end of Ovando's governorship in 1509, the mortality rate among Indians had risen catastrophically. Some scholars have insisted that the rapid rise was not entirely due to the working conditions. They also attribute it to the Indians' vulnerability to the diseases brought to the island by the conquistador. But whatever the reason, many died.

Others did not wait to die; they escaped into the wilderness or fled to nearby islands. As a result, by 1520 the Indian population had declined so markedly that it no longer functioned as an adequate labor supply for the island. Consequently, increasing numbers of Spaniards found themselves without any Indians and without any productive role to play on the island. To make matters worse, the mining industry was in a state of precipitous decline as sources of gold were being depleted.

Fortunately for the stability of the island, the surplus of Spaniards had begun to be drained off by 1520 as the conquest of New Spain got underway. In this fashion Hispaniola became a staging area for the conquest of the mainland; the surplus of Spaniards joined the bands of conquistadores in search of plunder and gold. In addition, the cultivation and milling of sugar cane had begun to challenge the ailing mining industry as the mainstay of the island's economy. The demand for labor for sugar plantations therefore intensified pressures for a new source of labor that would fill the gap created by the dwindling supply of Indians. Thus was erected another colonial edifice of exploitation: this time on the backs of the enslaved black.

Colonization and the aristocratic society

Most of the Spaniards in the early years did not expect to stay permanently in the New World. Instead they saw themselves as adventurers and conquerors who were out to win quick wealth and glory with which they would return home, set themselves up in hidalgo status, and live in a seigniorial manner. Relatively few lived to realize these ambitions. Many more returned home disenchanted and penniless. Some, though, did stay, particularly after significant gold strikes had been made on Hispaniola and after Governor Ovando had formally established the encomienda and stabilized and extended the rule of the Crown. They thereby became the first white European colonists in the New World. These early colonists included "the hidalgos, the peasants who aspired to become hidalgos, and the few letrados; [they] were the essential explorers, conquerors, and populators of Espanola." In their role as settlers, their goal was to re-create on the island an aristocratic way of life modeled after that in Spain. They disdained manual labor and "aspired to the seigniorial status much admired in Spain; [accordingly] they desired a life surrounded by *criados* and serfs and slaves, the display of mansions and lands, and of silk and velvet" (Floyd 1973:69).

In addition, they glorified the role of the military hero and conquistador much as it had been glorified during the reunification and reconquest of Spain.

"The height of seigniorial ambition was to attain a title and coat of arms attesting to military prowess, but on Espanola during this time, none was acquired or possibly even asked for, owing to the apparently easy victories over the Tainos. Only Bartolome Colon was named as adelantado, a title made famous during the reconquest. The letrado-hidalgo class as a whole contented themselves with acquiring coats of arms for their towns in 1508 to commemorate their settlement of the land and in the case of Verapaz, their victory over the Indians. The coat of arms thus became community surrogates for individual vecinos, whose general inclination was toward living out their lives on the island as small, feudal lords." (Floyd 1973:73–4)

Few colonists, however, were able to attain the wealth that would provide them with the Old World baroque splendor they sought. "These few were actual founding fathers of Spanish civilization in the Caribbean. Some of these settlers came with Columbus on his second voyage; others came with Ovando or on some obscure intermediate voyage between these times or after, or on one of the many vessels carrying the Indies trade." At the center of this nascent island aristocracy stood the members of the Columbus family; "they eventually had the most wealth, attained the highest social prestige, and boasted the greatest number of *criados*" (Floyd 1973:77).

The dual societal structures and their linkages

The entire aristocratic structure, though built by the colonists from their Old World antecedents, rested on the uniquely New World foundation of the colonial conquest of the Indian and the exploitation of his labor. This colonialist foundation to the aristocratic society was organized as a racially segmented plural society that reflected the raw exercise of power between conqueror and conquered and generated the labor energy needed to power the aristocratic society.

THE CROWN AND THE LAWS OF BURGOS: A "NORMATIVE" UMBRELLA FOR THE PEACEFUL INDIANS

The intervention of the Crown, in all likelihood, prevented the full realization of the brutalizing and dehumanizing potential inherent in the plural structure. From the earliest days of the encomienda the King and Queen of Spain expressed a continuing concern about the treatment of the Indian. They deplored the excesses and brutalities of the system of forced labor, though they did not question the necessity for the system itself. (They even favored the enslavement of Indians who fought the conquistador.) The King finally gave legal expression to this concern with the enactment of the Laws of Burgos in 1512. In promulgating the Laws of Burgos, the King gave the system of encomienda as designed for the New World a legal standing it lacked before. It was now incorporated into the laws of the Spanish empire and was no longer merely a practice sanctioned by King and local authorities. In addition, the system's axiom that Indians had inherently evil and slothful inclinations which had to be remedied was adopted as a cardinal principle of the legislation itself. In legitimizing the system, the King also surrounded it with normative constraints that were meant to protect the Indians from its more coercive and harsher features. Furthermore, the encomendero was to assume the paternal-like obligations of civilizing and Christianizing the Indians so that they would not only lose their evil and slothful ways but would also in time become "free vassals" of the King.

By casting the encomienda system in this normative mold, the King hoped to impose an organically interlocked status hierarchy, similar to the estate structure in Spain, upon what was essentially a dehumanized colonial system of racial exploitation and forced labor. In doing this, he was prepared to include the Indian in his hierarchic domain of subjects, though initially as wards of the Crown, just as the Church was prepared to include them in its hierarchic domain of souls.

Scholars have disagreed as to the extent the policy of the Crown did indeed shape the practice of the encomenderos. Some have continued to accept Las Casas' argument that the effect was minimal and that the sheer brutality of the system was primarily responsible for the rapid depletion of the Indian population in Hispaniola and in other parts of the Spanish empire. While agreeing that the encomienda system was harsh, other scholars have insisted that the paternalistic features that it developed under the aegis of Crown and Church made it unlikely that it was the kind of graveyard postulated by Las Casas. (As we have seen these scholars attribute the population decline primarily to other causes.) The same concern was not expressed by the Crown, however, for those Indians who were enslaved or later for the African slaves. Their fate was left primarily in the hands of their owners, although the Church retained a continuing interest in their souls.

THE SPANISH CONQUISTADOR AND INDIAN WOMAN

Another link between the dual structures that the colonist forged almost from the moment that the first one set foot on the soil of Hispaniola was with the Indian woman. Primarily young and unattached, many of these men soon developed liaisons with the native women. According to Mörner, "in a way, the Spanish conquest of the Americas was a conquest of women. The Spaniards obtained the

THE SPANISH CONQUISTADOR IN THE NEW WORLD

Indian girls both by force and by peaceful means" (Mörner 1967:22).

So widespread did this practice become that by 1501 the King and Queen of Spain expressed concern in their instructions to Governor Ovando that Indian women were being forced into liaisons with Spanish men. They called upon the governor to send women back to their tribes and to permit only those liaisons to continue into which the woman entered voluntarily. Several years later they encouraged the governor to arrange a number of intermarriages for purposes of government policy, but few Spaniards sought to legitimize their relationships. As a result, interracial unions flourished but relatively few led to marriage.

Thus within two decades of the Spanish conquest of Hispaniola a generation of mestizos began to reach adolescence and early adulthood.

> "As a rule the first generation of mestizos was accepted as 'Spaniards.' This is easy to understand for mestizos born in marriage, but, as we have pointed out, these were not at all frequent. On the other hand, during this early period many mestizos were recognized by their fathers. The process of legitimization seems to have been frequently used at this time both in Spain and Portugal."
>
> (Mörner 1967:27)

Some of these mestizos, however, joined their maternal group, the Indians; and a few even "led a marginal existence between the two groups without being accepted by either. But this phenomenon was to occur on a large scale only later on" (Mörner 1967:29). In short, the mestizo as a distinctive racial category in a colonial status system was yet to emerge.

The Sociedad de Castas and the creole elite

By the eighteenth century miscegenation in Spanish America had produced, according to various scholars, an elaborately refined, hierarchically arranged "Sociedad de Castas." In New Spain, for example, the nomenclatures of "castas" identified 18 different categories; in Peru, 14. They were based on the interracial unions of Spaniards, Indians, blacks, and their mixed offspring of varying racial combinations. The major divisions were "invested with different legal status as well as the strong element of corporate privileges" (Mörner 1967:54). According to another scholar, "there were in fact only three legally and socially definable groups: 'Spaniards,' 'castas,' and 'Indians'" (Mörner 1967:60). Mörner insisted that the legal status of five categories could be distinguished and ranked. At the top were the Spaniards; second were the Indians; third, the mestizos; fourth, the free negroes, mulattoes, zamboes; and last, the slaves. With reference to social status, Mörner retained the same rank order except for the Indians whom he ranked last.

Thus by the eighteenth century the society which King Ferdinand had envisioned seemed to have materialized, but it was not merely a carbon copy of the society which the Crown and the colonists had sought to transport from Spain.

"[It was] a society *sui generis* [created] by transferring to the New World the hierarchic, estate-based corporative society of late medieval Castile and imposing that society upon a multiracial colonial situation. This colonial reality was characterized, first, by the dichotomy between conquerors and conquered, masters and servants and slaves, and, second, by the miscegenation between these opposite groups."   (Mörner 1967:54)

In this manner the dual structures created by the forces of colonization and colonialization in Spanish America appeared to merge into a composite Sociedad de Castas. Its unifying external value framework was provided by the Crown and Church. Its internal system of stratification was organized around a "color" axis into what a Chilean scholar has called a "pigmentocracy." These colonial estate societies and their pigmentocratic status gradients were, however, less likely to emerge in those parts of Spanish America that lost their Indian labor force and had to depend on black slave labor, as in the case of Hispaniola and other islands of the Caribbean. The racial segmentation of the latter plantation societies lacked the organic interconnectedness of the estate societies and resembled the more conflictual and coercive segmentation of the orthodox colonial plural society.

In effect, long before the Spanish colonists had gained their independence, their dual colonist and colonialist heritages seemed to have already joined to create a "novel," institutional, and stratificational framework that carried over into nationhood of each. At the same time there was built into the framework a basic cleavage within the Spanish elite that eventually became the axis around which the struggle for independence revolved.

Almost from the moment the first colonists settled in Hispaniola, conflicts of interest surfaced between the Crown and settlers. As we have already seen, the Crown disagreed with the colonist over his treatment of the Indians, but behind this particular disagreement loomed a fundamental concern of the Crown. It feared that the colonists intended to establish separate feudal-like fiefdoms in the New World, similar to those that King Ferdinand and Queen Isabella had to quash in Spain in order to unify their kingdom. Accordingly, the Crown sought to retain in its hands the reins of political power and authority. It did this by enveloping the colonist with an elaborate governmental and bureaucratic structure that allowed royal authority to reach into the local centers of residence in the New World. In doing this, the Crown co-opted the early cabildos, the centers of local authority frequently established by the leading conquistadores, and made them part of the bureaucratic system. In addition, the Crown sent from Spain persons loyal to it to fill the high offices in the two structures and regularly replaced them with others from Spain so that none could build a private "fiefdom" in the colony; for a similar reason they denied the request of the colonist that the encomienda be made hereditary.

The colonists and their Creole progeny, however, were not without influence and power on the local level. On occasion, for example, they were able to thwart completely the implementation of royal policy. For example, their rebellious response to the New Laws of 1542 forced the King to withdraw his attempt to abolish the encomienda. He subsequently sought to dismantle it in piecemeal fashion; but what really dealt the system its mortal blow was the marked decline in the Indian population in virtually all of the Spanish empire.

In a more regular and routinized manner, the colonists infiltrated the lower and middle levels of the bureaucracy during the Hapsburg era and accordingly blunted the impact of royal policy it deemed contrary to their interests. Lang has offered other examples

"of the kind of *ad hoc* informal systems that emerged throughout the empire, linking together structures of local power and bureaucratic officials in an intricately layered network of cooptation and collusion which attained over the time the force of custom. Mediation between the content of directives and the reality of local conditions occurred at practically every level of bureaucratic administration. Cedulas directed toward the organization of Indian labor, the control of contraband trade, and the collection of taxes had to run the gauntlet of Creole influence. Bureaucratic structures were still crucial reference points for social organization. But this frame-work was susceptible to considerable manipulation by local interests."   (Lang 1975:45)

Despite the manipulative skill the local Creole elite developed in accommodating royal policy to local interest, the constant presence of officials from Spain, the Peninsulars, who monopolized bureaucratic and governmental power and who also viewed themselves as the font of respect and good taste, became a source of irritation and resentment. This resentment did not initially prevent the Creole from patterning his life style after the Peninsular or from retaining his loyalty to the Crown. But in time his resentment became politicized and as he became alienated from the Crown, he formed the vanguard of the forces for liberation and separate nationhood.

THE DRED SCOTT DECISION: TERRITORIAL STATUS AND THE CONSTITUTION

Chief Justice Taney rejected Dred Scott's claim that he and his family should be given their freedom because of their stay in the territory in which Congress had prohibited slavery. He said that Congress had erred in passing the Missouri Compromise. The statute, he insisted, was based on an article in the Constitution that had no application to the territory in question. The reason, he explained was the Congress's power

> "'to dispose of and make all needful rules and regulations respecting the territory or other property belonging to the United States' ... is confined, and was intended to be confined, to the territory which at that time belonged to, or was claimed by, the United States, and was within their boundaries as settled by the treaty with Great Britain, and can have no influence upon a territory afterwards acquired from a foreign Government [like the Louisiana Purchase from France]. It was a special provision for a known and particular territory, and to meet a present emergency, and nothing more." (60 US 1857:432)

The Chief Justice then launched into a lengthy discussion of the historical background of the provision. He contended that it could be linked to a controversy that threatened the unity of the thirteen states from the beginning of the Revolution. The controversy was finally resolved during the period of the Confederation with an agreement on the disposition of large and unsettled territories which were included in the chartered limits of some of the states. These lands were to be ceded for the common good and the proceeds from the sale of the land were to be treated "as a common fund for the common benefit of the States;" a structure of governance was to be devised for them.

At the time the arrangement was worked out under the Confederation, according to the Chief Justice, there was no general government with special and enumerated powers to receive the lands. For, "this Confederation had none of the attributes of sovereignty in legislative, executive, or judicial power. It was little more than a congress of ambassadors, authorized to represent separate nations, in matters in which they had a common concern" (60 US 1857:434).

As a result, the arrangement was tantamount to a treaty signed by thirteen sovereign nations.

> "[They] had a right to establish any form of government they pleased, by compact or treaty among themselves, and to regulate rights of person and rights of property in the territory, as they might deem proper. It was by a Congress, representing the authority of these several and separate sovereignties and acting under their authority and command, (but not from any authority derived from the Articles of Confederation,) that the instrument usually called the [Northwest] ordinance of 1787 was adopted; regulating in much detail the principles and the laws by which this territory should be governed; and among other provisions, slavery is prohibited in it. We do not question the power of the States, by agreement among themselves, to pass this ordinance, nor its obligatory force in the territory, while the confederation or league of the States in their separate sovereign character continued to exist."   (60 US 1857:435)

Once the Constitution was adopted, however, a new form of government was created which "was to be carefully limited in its powers, and to exercise no authority beyond those expressly granted by the Constitution, or necessarily to be implied from the language of the instrument, and the objects it was intended to accomplish" (60 US 1857:435).

> "The new Government was not a mere change in a dynasty, or in a form of government, leaving the nation or sovereignty the same, and clothed with all the rights, and bound by all the obligations of the preceding one. But, when the present United States came into existence under the new Government, it was a new political body, a new nation, then for the first time taking its place in the family of nations. It took nothing by succession from the Confederation. It had no right, as its successor, to any property or rights of property which it had acquired, and was not liable for any of its obligations."   (60 US 1857:441)

Thus, with the dissolution of the league or confederacy of states, he continued,

> "It was obvious that some provision was necessary to give the new Government sufficient power to enable it to carry into effect the objects for which it was ceded, and the compacts and agreements which the States had made with each

other in the exercise of their powers of sovereignty ... it was to place these things under the guardianship and protection of the new Government, and to clothe it with the necessary powers, that the clause was inserted in the Constitution which gives Congress the power 'to dispose of and make all needful rules and regulations respecting the territory or other property belonging to the United States.... It [this clause] applied only to the property which the States held in common at that time, and has no reference whatever to any territory or other property which the new sovereignty might afterwards itself acquire."   (60 US 1857:435–36)

As part of its obligation to implement agreements made by the confederacy of states, the Chief Justice concluded, the new Government reaffirmed in 1789 its commitment to the Northwest Ordinance of 1787, but this too, he insisted, was to apply only to those lands covered by the earlier agreement.

With regard to the acquisition of land outside the original limits of the United States, he continued, the new federal government has the power under the constitution to do so, provided the newly acquired territory is eventually admitted as a State in the Union. In other words, the federal government has no constitutional authority

"to establish or maintain colonies bordering on the United States or at a distance, to be ruled and governed at its own pleasure; nor to enlarge its territorial limits in any way, except by the admission of new States. That power is plainly given; and if a new State is admitted, it needs no further legislation by Congress, because the Constitution itself defines the relative rights and powers, and duties of the State, and the citizens of the State, and the Federal Government. But no power is given to acquire a Territory to be held and governed permanently in that character."   (60 US 1857:446)

The government, he added, does not have to admit immediately the new territory into the Union as a state; it has the discretionary power to delay its admittance "until it [the territory] is in a suitable condition to become a State upon an equal footing with the other States.... It is a question for the political department of the Government, and not the judicial" (60 US 1857:447). Further, Congress as part of this political department has the discretionary power to establish the kind of structure of governance that seems to fit the particular needs of the territory. The examples the Chief Justice used to illustrate his point closely resembled the two grades of governance spelled out in the Northwest Ordinance. But he cautioned, "what is the best form must always depend on the condition of the Territory at the time, and the choice of the mode must depend upon the exercise of a discretionary power by Congress, acting within the scope of its constitutional authority" (60 US 1857:449).

The Chief Justice went on to emphasize that Congress has no discretionary power "over the person or property of a citizen ... under our Constitution and form of Government. The powers of the Government and the rights and privileges of the citizen are regulated and plainly defined by the Constitution itself" (60 US 1857:449). This principle, he continued, also applies to the people of the territory, many of whom may have come from one of the states of the Union. Thus,

"It may be safely assumed that citizens of the United States who migrate to a Territory belonging to the people of the United States, cannot be ruled as mere colonists, dependent upon the will of the General Government, and to be governed by any laws it may think proper to impose. The principle upon which our Governments rest, and upon which alone they continue to exist, is the union of States, sovereign and independent within their own limits in their internal and domestic concerns, and bound together as one people by a General Government, possessing certain enumerated and restricted powers, delegated to it by the people of the several States and exercising supreme authority within the scope of the powers granted to it, throughout the dominion of the United States."
(60 US 1857:448)

As a result, when a territory becomes part of the dominion of the United States, the Chief Justice concluded,

"The Federal Government enters into possession [of the territory]... with its powers over the citizen strictly defined, and limited by the Constitution, from which it derives its own existence, and by virtue of which alone it continues to exist and act as a Government and sovereignty. It has no power of any kind beyond it; and it cannot, when it enters a Territory of the United States, put off its character, and assume discretionary or despotic powers which the Constitution has denied to it. It cannot create for itself a new character separated from the citizens of the United States, and the duties it owes them under the provision of the Constitution. The Territory being a part of the United States, the Government and the citizen both enter it under the authority of the Constitution, with their respective rights defined and marked out; and the Federal Government can exercise no power over his person or property, beyond what that instrument confers, nor lawfully deny any right which it has reserved."
(60 US 1857:449–50)

The Chief Justice then offered various amendments from the Bill of Rights as examples of prohibited areas of legislation by Congress. He maintained that not only are the rights of person protected by the Constitution but so are the rights of private property.

"Thus the rights of property are united with the rights of person, and placed on the same ground by the fifth amendment to the Constitution, which provides that no person shall be deprived of life, liberty, and property, without due process of law.... [Furthermore,] the powers over person and property of which we speak are not only not granted to Congress, but are in express terms denied, and they are forbidden to exercise them. And this prohibition is not confined to the States, but the words are general, and extend to the whole territory over which the Constitution gives it power to legislate, including those portions of it remaining under Territorial Government, as well as that covered by States. It is a total absence of power everywhere within the dominion of the United States, and places the citizens of a Territory, so far as these rights are concerned, on the same footing with citizens of the States, and guards them as firmly and plainly against any inroads which the General Government might attempt, under the plea of implied or incidental powers.... [Accordingly,] if the Constitution recognizes the right of property of the master in a slave, and makes no distinction between that description of property and other property owned by a citizen, no tribunal, acting under the authority of the United States, whether it be legislative, executive, or judicial, has a right to draw such a distinction, or deny to it the benefit of the provisions and guarantees which have been provided for the protection of private property against the encroachments of the Government.... The right of property in a slave is distinctly and expressly affirmed in the Constitution. The right to traffic in it, like an ordinary article of merchandise and property, was guaranteed to the citizens of the United States, in every State that might desire it, for twenty years. And the Government in express terms is pledged to protect it in all future time, if the slave escapes from his owner. This is done in plain words – too plain to be misunderstood. And no word can be found in the Constitution which gives Congress a greater power over slave property, or which entitles property of that kind to less protection than property of any other description. The only power conferred is the power coupled with the duty of guarding and protecting the owner in his rights." (60 US 1857:450–52)

In view of these considerations, the Chief Justice concluded,

"It is the opinion of the court that the act of Congress which prohibited a citizen from holding and owning property of this kind in the territory of the United States north of the line therein mentioned, is not warranted by the Constitution, and is therefore void; and that neither Dred Scott himself, nor any of his family, were made free by being carried into this territory; even if they had been carried there by the owner, with the intention of becoming a permanent resident." (60 US 1857:452)

REFERENCES

Abraham, H.J. (1972) *Freedom and the Court*. NY: Oxford University Press.

Adams, J.T. (1927) *Provincial Society 1690–1763*. NY: The Macmillan Co.

Adorno, T.W., Frenkel-Brunswick, E., Levinson, D.J., and Sanford, R.N. (1950) *The Authoritarian Personality*. NY: Harper and Row.

Allen, R.L. (1970) *Black Awakening in Capitalist America*. Garden City, NY: Doubleday & Co. Inc.

Andrews, C.M. (1934) *The Colonial Period of American History: The Settlements. Vol. I*. New Haven, Conn.: Yale University Press.

Aptheker, H. (1956) *Toward Negro Freedom*. NY: New Century Publishers.

————— (ed.) (1962) *A Documentary History of the Negro People in the United States: from Colonial Times through the Civil War*. NY: The Citadel Press.

Asiatic Exclusion League (1907, reprinted 1977) *Proceedings 1907–1913*. NY: Arno Press.

The Association of Black Sociologists (1978) News Release. September 6 1978.

Association of Citizens' Councils (1954) *The Citizens' Council*. Greenwood, Miss.

Bacon, B.C. (1856) *Statistics of the Colored People of Philadelphia*. Philadelphia: T. Ellwood Chapman.

Bailey, T.A. (1964) *Theodore Roosevelt and the Japanese American Crises*. Gloucester, Mass.: Peter Smith.

Ballagh, J.C. (1895) *White Servitude in the Colony of Virginia*. Baltimore: The Johns Hopkins Press.

Bauer, R.A. and Bauer, A.H. (1971) Day to Day Resistance to Slavery. In J. Braccy and E. Rudwick (eds) *American Slavery: The Question of Resistance*. Belmont, Calif.: Wadsworth Publishing Co. Inc.

Bell Jr., D.A. (1973) *Race, Racism and American Law*. Boston: Little, Brown & Co.

Bemiss, S.M. (ed.) (1957) The Three Charters of the Virginia Company of London. In E.G. Swem (ed.) *Jamestown 350th Anniversary Historical Booklets. No. 4*. Williamsburg, Va.: Virginia 350th Anniversary Celebration Corp.

Bergman, P.M. (1969) *The Chronological History of the Negro in America*. NY: The New American Library.

Berman, D.M. (1966) *A Bill Becomes a Law: Congress Enacts Civil Rights Legislation*. NY: The Macmillan Co.

Bettelheim, B. (1943) Individual and Mass Behaviour in Extreme Situations. *Journal of Abnormal Psychology* **38**:417–52.

Biddle, F. (1962) *In Brief Authority*. Garden City, NY: Doubleday & Co. Inc.

Blair, C.A. (1903) *The Territorial Policy of the United States*. Guthrie, Okla.: The State Capitol Co.

Blauner, R. (1969) Whitewash Over Watts: The Failure of the McCone Commission Report. In R.M. Fogelson (ed.) *The Los Angeles Riots*. NY: Arno Press and The New York Times.

—— (1972) *Racial Oppression in America*. NY: Harper and Row.

Blaustein, A.P. and Ferguson Jr., C.C. (1962) *Desegregation and the Law: The Meaning and Effect of the School Segregation Cases*. NY: Random House.

—— and Zangrando, R.L. (eds) (1968) *Civil Rights and the Black American*. NY: Simon and Schuster.

Bloch, H.D. (1969) *The Circle of Discrimination*. NY: New York University Press.

Boorstin, D.J. (1958) *The Americans: The Colonial Experience*. NY: Random House.

Borton, J. (1970) *Japan's Modern Century: From Perry to 1970*. NY: The Ronald Press Co.

Bracey Jr., J.H., Meier, A., and Rudwick, E. (eds) (1971) *Blacks in the Abolitionist Movement*. Belmont, Calif.: Wadsworth Publishing Co.

Brawley, B. (1921) *A Social History of the American Negro*. NY: The Macmillan Co.

Breitman, G. (1967) *The Last Year of Malcolm X*. NY: Schocken Books.

Brock, W.R. (1963) *An American Crisis: Congress and Reconstruction 1865–1867*. NY: Harper and Row.

Brown, A. (1898) *The First Republic in America*. NY: Houghton, Mifflin Co.

—— (1964) *The Genesis of the United States. Vols I and II*. NY: Russell and Russell Inc.

Browne, J.R. (1850) *Report of the Debates in the Convention of California on the Formation of the State Constitution in September and October 1849*. Washington, DC: J.T. Towers.

Bruce, P.A. (1910) *Institutional History of Virginia in the Seventeenth Century.* *Vols I and II.* NY: G.P. Putnam's Sons.

Brydon, G.M. (1947) *Virginia's Mother Church: and the Political Conditions under which it Grew.* Richmond, Va.: Virginia Historical Society.

───── (1957) Religious Life of Virginia in the Seventeenth Century: The Faith of our Father. In E.G. Swem (ed.) *Jamestown 350th Anniversary Historical Booklets. No. 10.* Williamsburg, Va.: Virginia 350th Anniversary Celebration Corp.

Buckley, J. (1973) What Does Affirmative Action Really Affirm? In *US Congressional Record* **93:1**:16429–6457.

Buell, R.L. (1922) The Development of the Anti-Japanese Agitation in the United States. *Political Science Quarterly* **37(4)**:605–38.

The Bureau of National Affairs (BNA) *Fair Employment Practices Cases.* Washington DC: The Bureau of National Affairs Inc.

───── *Fair Employment Practice Manual.* Washington, DC: The Bureau of National Affairs Inc.

───── (1977) *Labor Relations Reporter* **95**. Washington, DC: The Bureau of National Affairs Inc.

Burgess, J.W. (1902) *Reconstruction and the Constitution 1866–1876.* NY: Charles Scribner's Sons.

Business Week (1945). September 1:34–5.

California Constitutional Convention of 1878–79. *Debates and Proceedings. Vols. I, II, III.* Sacramento, Calif.: State Printing Office.

California State Board of Control (1920) *California and the Oriental.* Sacramento, Calif.: State Printing Office.

───── (1922) *California and the Oriental.* Revision. Sacramento, Calif: State Printing Office.

California State Senate Special Committee on Chinese Immigration (1877) *Memorial of the Senate of California to the Congress of the United States.* Sacramento, Calif.: State Printing Office.

Caplovitz, D. (1963) *The Poor Pay More.* Glencoe, Ill.: Free Press of Glencoe.

Carmichael, S. (1971) *Stokely Speaks.* NY: Random House.

───── and Hamilton, C.V. (1967) *Black Power: The Politics of Liberation in America.* NY: Random House.

Caughey, J.W. (1948) *The California Gold Rush.* Berkeley, Calif.: University of California Press.

Chamberlin, E.K. (1955) The Japanese Scare at Magdalena Bay. *Pacific Historical Review* **24**:345–59.

Chambers, J.S. (1921) The Japanese Invasion. *The Annals of the American Academy of Political and Social Science* **XCIII**: 23–9.

The Chicago Commission on Race Relations (1922) *The Negro in Chicago: A*

Study of Race Relations and a Race Riot. Chicago, Ill.: The University of Chicago Press.

Clark, K.B. (1965) *Dark Ghetto*. NY: Harper and Row.

———— (1966) The Civil Rights Movement: Momentum and Organization. In T. Parsons and K.B. Clark (eds) *The Negro American*. Boston: Houghton Mifflin Co.

Cleaver, E. (1969) Eldridge Cleaver Speaks from Exile. In P.S. Foner (ed.) (1970) *The Black Panthers Speak*. NY: J.B. Lippincott Co.

Clyde, P.H. (1964) *United States Policy Toward China: Diplomatic and Public Documents 1839–1939*. NY: Russell and Russell Inc.

Cohen, F.S. (1942) *Handbook of Federal Indian Law*. Albuquerque, N.M.: University of New Mexico Press.

Collier, J. (1947) *The Indians of the Americas*. NY: W.W. Norton and Co. Inc.

Commager, H.S. (ed.) (1963) *Documents of American History*. Seventh edition. NY: Appleton-Century-Crofts.

———— (ed.) (1968) *Documents of American History*. Eighth edition. NY: Appleton-Century-Crofts.

The Congressional Globe (1870) **41:2.**

Conn, S., Engelman, R.C., and Fairchild, B. (1964) *US Army in World War II: The Western Hemisphere: Guarding the United States and Its Outposts*. Washington, DC: Office of the Chief of Military History, Department of the Army.

The Constitution of the United States of America with the Amendments (1872). Washington, DC: Government Printing Office.

Coolidge, M.R. (1969) *Chinese Immigration*. NY: Arno Press.

Cowdin, E.C. (1870) Tribute of the Chamber of Commerce of the State of New York to the Memory of Anson Burlingame. NY: John W. Ameaman Printer.

Cox, L. and Cox, J.H. (eds) (1973) *Reconstruction, the Negro and the New South*. NY: Harper and Row.

Cox, O.C. (1970) *Caste, Class and Race*. NY: Modern Readers Paperback. First published 1948.

Craven, W.F. (1964) *Dissolution of the Virginia Company: The Failure of a Colonial Experiment*. Gloucester, Mass.: Peter Smith.

Crist, R. (1948) Sugar Cane and Coffee in Puerto Rico. Part I. *American Journal of Economics and Sociology* **7(2):**173–84.

Daniels, J. (1944) *The Wilson Era: Years of Peace. 1910–1917*. Chapel Hill, NC: The University of North Carolina Press.

Daniels, R. (1970) *The Politics of Prejudice*. NY: Atheneum.

———— (1971) *Concentration Camps, USA: Japanese Americans and World War II*. NY: Holt, Rinehart and Winston.

Danzig, D. (1966) In Defense of "Black Power". *Commentary* September 42:41–6.

Davis, A., Gardner, B.B., and Gardner, M.R. (1941) *Deep SOuth: A Social Anthropological Study of Caste and Class*. Chicago, Ill.: The University of Chicago Press.

Davis, D.B. (1981) Black and White: Two Ways. *The New York Times Book Review Section* January 25:1, 20.

Davis, J.A. (1946) Nondiscrimination in the Federal Services. *The Annals of the American Academy of Political and Social Science* 244:65–74.

Declaration of Independence (1776). In *The Declaration of Independence and Constitution of the United States of America*. NY: R. Spalding. Published 1865.

Dennett, T. (1963) *Americans in Eastern Asia: A Critical Study of United States' Policy in the Far East in the Nineteenth Century*. NY: Barnes and Noble Inc.

Diamond, S. (1958) From Organization to Society: Virginia in the Seventeenth Century. *The American Journal of Sociology* LXIII (5):457–75.

Diffie, B.W. and Diffie, J.W. (1931) *Porto Rico: A Broken Pledge*. NY: Vanguard.

Dollard, J. (1949) *Caste and Class in a Southern Town*. NY: Harper and Brothers.

Doyle, B. (1971) *The Etiquette of Race Relations*. NY: Schocken Books.

Drake, S.C. and Cayton, H.R. (1962) *Black Metropolis: A Study of Negro Life in a Northern City*. NY: Harper and Row.

Draper, T. (1970) *The Rediscovery of Black Nationalism*. NY: The Viking Press.

DuBois, W.E.B. (1910) Reconstruction and Its Benefits. In R.C. Twombly (ed.) (1971) *Blacks in White America since 1865*. NY: David McKay Co. Inc.

——— (1935) *Black Reconstruction in America 1860–1880*. NY: The World Publishing Co.

——— (1967) *The Philadelphia Negro*. NY: Schocken Books.

Duncan, O.D. and Duncan, B. (1957) *The Negro Population of Chicago: A Study of Residential Succession*. Chicago: The University of Chicago Press.

Dunning, W.A. (1907) *Reconstruction: Political and Economic 1865–1877*. NY: Harper and Brothers.

Eaves, L. (1910) *A History of California Labor Legislation*. Berkeley, Calif.: The University of California Press.

Elkins, S.M. (1963) *Slavery*. NY: Grosset and Dunlop.

Emerson, T.I., Haber, D., and Dorsen, N. (1967) *Political and Civil Rights in the United States. Vol. II*. Boston: Little, Brown & Co.

Equal Employment Opportunity Commission (EEOC) (1966) *First Annual Report*. Washington, DC.

——— (1968) *Third Annual Report*. Washington, DC.

——— (1970) *Fifth Annual Report*. Washington, DC.

——— (1972) *Seventh Annual Report*. Washington, DC.

———— (1975) *Tenth Annual Report*. Washington, DC.

Erikson, K.T. (1966) *Wayward Puritans: A Study in the Sociology of Deviance*. NY: John Wiley and Sons.

Every, D.V. (1966) *Disinherited: The Lost Birthright of the American Indian*. NY: Avon Books.

Fanon, F. (1968) *The Wretched of the Earth*. NY: Grove Press Inc.

The Federal Convention of 1787. (1911) *The Records of. Vols I, II, III*. New Haven, Conn.: Yale University Press.

Federal Reporter, Second Series: Cases argued and determined in the United States Court of Appeals for the District of Columbia (and) United States Circuit Courts of Appeals. St Paul, Minn.: West Publishing Co.

176 F.2nd 953 (1949) Acheson, Secretary of State v. Murakami *et al.*

186 F.2nd 766 (1951) McGrath, Attorney General *et al.* v. Tadayasu Abo.

186 F.2nd 775 (1951) Barber, District Director v. Tadayasu Abo *et al.*

220 F.2nd 386 (1955) Robert M. Dawson Jr *et al.* v. Mayor and City Council of Baltimore City.

420 F.2nd 1225 (1970) Griggs v. Duke Power Co.

428 F.2nd 144 (1970) US v. International Brotherhood of Electrical Workers, Local No. 38.

431 F.2nd 245 (1970) Jones v. Lee Way Motor Freight Inc.

442 F.2nd 159 (1971) The Contractors Association of Eastern Pennsylvania v. The Secretary of Labor.

471 F.2nd 408 (1973) US v. Wood, Wire and Metal Lathers International Union, Local Union No. 46.

520 F.2nd 420 (1975) Kirkland v. The New York State Department of Correctional Services.

Federal Supplement: Cases argued and determined in the United States District Courts. St Paul, Minn.: West Publishing Co.

76 F.Supp 664 (1947) Ex parte Tadayasu Abo *et al.*

77 F.Supp 806 (1948) Tadayasu Abo v. Clark *et al.*

142 F.Supp 707 (1956) Browder v. Gayle.

280 F.Supp 719 (1968) US v. The Sheet Metal Workers International Association, Local Union No. 36, AFL-CIO.

292 F.Supp 243 (1968) Griggs v. Duke Power Co.

292 F.Supp 413 (1968) Dobbins v. Local 212, International Brotherhood of Electrical Workers, AFL-CIO.

415 F.Supp 761 (1976) Brian F. Weber v. Kaiser Aluminum and Chemical Corp. and United Steelworkers of America AFL-CIO.

Fitzhugh, G (1850) *Slavery Justified, by a Southerner*. Fredericksburg, Tex.: Recorder Printing Office.

Fitzpatrick, E.H. (1909) *The Coming Conflict of Nations or the Japanese-American War.* Springfield, Ill.: H.W. Rokker.

Floyd, T.S. (1973) *The Columbus Dynasty in the Caribbean: 1492–1526.* Albuquerque, N.M.: University of New Mexico Press.

Fogel, R.W. and Engerman, S.L. (1974) *Time on the Cross.* Boston: Little, Brown & Co.

Fogelson, R.M. (1968) Violence as Protest. In R.H. Connery (ed.) *Urban Riots: Violence and Social Change.* Proceedings, The Academy of Political Science, Columbia University, NY. xxix(1):25–41.

―――― (1969) White on Black: A Critique of the McCone Commission Report on the Los Angeles Riots. In R.M. Fogelson (ed.) *The Los Angeles Riots.* NY: Arno Press and The New York Times.

Foner, E. (1981) Redemption II. *The New York Times* November 7.:23.

Foner, P.S. (ed.) (1970) *The Black Panthers Speak.* NY: J.B. Lippincott Co.

Franck, H.A. (1920) *Roaming Through the West Indies.* NY: Century.

Franklin, J.H. (1952) *From Slavery to Freedom.* NY: Alfred Knopf.

―――― (1961) *Reconstruction: After the Civil War.* Chicago, Ill.: The University of Chicago Press.

Frazier, E.F. (1957) *The Negro in the United States.* NY: The Macmillan Co.

Fredrickson, G.M. (1971) *The Black Image in the White Mind: The Debate on Afro-American Character and Destiny, 1817–1914.* NY: Harper and Row.

―――― (1981) *White Supremacy: A Comparative Study in American and South African History.* NY: Oxford University Press.

Freyre, G. (1946) *The Masters and the Slaves.* NY: Alfred Knopf.

Furnivall, J.S. (1956) *Colonial Policy and Practice.* NY: New York University Press.

Garis, R.L. (1927) *Immigration Restriction.* NY: The Macmillan Co.

Genovese, E.D. (1965) *The Political Economy of Slavery.* NY: Random House.

―――― (1968) On Stanley M. Elkin's *A Problem in American Institutional and Intellectual Life.* In A. Weinstein and F. Gatell (eds) *American Negro Slavery.* NY: Oxford University Press.

Girdner, A. and Loftis, A. (1969) *The Great Betrayal: The Evacuation of the Japanese-Americans During World War II.* NY: The Macmillan Co.

Glazer, N. (1975) *Affirmative Discrimination: Ethnic Inequality and Public Policy.* NY: Basic Books.

Glazer, N. and Moynihan, D.P. (1963) *Beyond the Melting Pot.* Cambridge, Mass.: The MIT Press.

Gordon, M.M. (1964) *Assimilation in American Life.* NY: Oxford University Press.

The Governor's Commission on the the Los Angeles Riots (1965) Violence in the

City – an End or a Beginning (Report). In R.M. Fogelson (ed.) (1969) *The Los Angeles Riots*. NY: Arno Press and The New York Times.

Graham, G.S. (1970) *A Concise History of the British Empire*. London: Thames and Hudson.

Greene, L.J. (1968) *The Negro in Colonial New England*. NY: Atheneum.

―――― and Woodson, C.G. (1970) *The Negro Wage Earner*. NY: Russell and Russell Inc.

Grimshaw, A.D. (ed.) (1969) *Racial Violence in the United States*. Chicago, Ill.: Aldine Publishing Co.

―――― (1969) Three Cases of Racial Violence in the United States. In A.D. Grimshaw (ed.) *Racial Violence in the United States*. Chicago, Ill.: Aldine Publishing Co.

Grodzins, M. (1949) *Americans Betrayed: Politics and the Japanese Evacuation*. Chicago, Ill.: The University of Chicago Press.

Gulick, S.L. (1917) *Anti-Japanese War Scare Stories*. NY: Fleming H. Revell Co.

Hansen, W.J. (1960) *The Search for Authority in California*. Oakland, Calif: Biobooks.

Hauser, P.M. (1971) Demographic Factors in the Integration of the Negro. In J.H. Bracey Jr., A. Meier, and E. Rudwick (eds) *The Rise of the Ghetto*. Belmont, Calif.: Wadsworth Publishing Co.

Headley, J.T. (1970) *The Great Riots of New York: 1712–1873*. NY: Bobbs-Merrill Co. Inc.

Heizer R.F. and Almquist, A.F. (1971) *The Other Californians*. Berkeley, Calif.: University of California Press.

Hening, W.W. (ed.) (1823) *The Statutes at Large being a Collection of all the Laws of Virginia from the first session of the legislature, 1619. Vols 1–5*. Philadelphia: Thomas Desilver.

Herndon, M. (1957) Tobacco in Colonial Virginia: "The Sovereign Remedy." In E.G. Swem (ed.) *Jamestown 350th Anniversary Historical Booklets. No. 20*. Williamsburg, Va.: The Virginia 350th Anniversary Celebration Corp.

Hichborn, F. (1913) *Story of the Session of the California Legislature of 1913*. San Francisco: James H. Barry Co.

Higginbotham Jr., A.L. (1978) *In the Matter of Color: Race and the American Legal Process: The Colonial Period*. NY: Oxford University Press.

Hilliard, D. (1969) David Hilliard Speaks. In P.S. Foner (ed.) (1970) *The Black Panthers Speak*. NY: J.B. Lippincott Co.

Hoetink, H. (1967) *The Two Variants in Caribbean Race Relations*. London: Oxford University Press.

Hofstadter, R. (1964) *Anti-Intellectualism in American Life*. NY: Alfred Knopf.

―――― and Wallace, M. (eds) (1970) *American Violence: A Documentary History*.

NY: Alfred Knopf.

Hook, S. (1973) HEW's Faculty "Quotas" Inspire – Semantic Evasions. Reprinted in *US Congressional Record* **93**:1:16437–6438.

Hoover, D.W. (ed.) (1968) *Understanding Negro History*. Chicago, Ill.: Quadrangle Books.

Hudson, R.L. (1978) Factors which Influence Mobility of Blacks in an Elite Corporation: A Case Study of Black Mobility. Unpublished PhD dissertation, Graduate Faculty in Sociology, The City University of New York.

Humphrey, E.F. (1965) *Nationalism and Religion in America*. NY: Russell and Russell Inc.

Hunter, C. (1975) Black Intellectuals Divided over Ideological Direction. *The New York Times* April 28:1, 57.

Ichihashi, Y. (1932) *Japanese in the United States: A Critical Study of the Problems of the Japanese Immigrants and Their Children*. Stanford, Calif.: Stanford University Press.

————— (1969) *Japanese in the United States*. NY: Arno Press and The New York Times.

Isaacs, H. (1958) *Scratches on our Minds: American Images of China and India*. NY: J. Day Co.

Irwin, W. (1921) *Seed of the Sun*. NY: George H. Doran Co.

Jacobs, W.R. (1972) *Dispossessing the American Indian*. NY: Charles Scribner's Sons.

(Japan) Consulate General of San Francisco (1925) *Documentary History of Law Cases Affecting Japanese in the United States, 1916–1924. Vols I, II.*

Jensen, M. (1968) *The Founding of a Nation*. NY: Oxford University Press.

Johnson, C.S. (1928) The Changing Economic Status of the Negro. *The Annals of the American Academy of Political Science* CXL:128–37.

Jordan, W.D. (1974) *The White Man's Burden: Historical Origins of Racism in the United States*. NY: Oxford University Press.

Josephy Jr., A.M. (1973) What the Indians Want? *The New York Times Magazine* March 18.

Kadushin, C. (1974) *The American Intellectual Elite*. Boston: Little, Brown.

Kammen, M. (1972) *People of Paradox*. NY: Alfred Knopf.

Kanzaki, K. (1921) *California and the Japanese*. Pamphlet.

Kawakami, K.K. (1912) *American-Japanese Relations: An Inside View of Japan's Policies and Purposes*. NY: Fleming H. Revell Co.

King Jr., M.L. (1958) *Stride Toward Freedom*. NY: Harper and Row.

————— (1963) I Have a Dream. In P.S. Foner (ed.) *The Voice of Black America. Vol II*. NY: Capricorn Books.

————— (1964) *Why We Can't Wait*. NY: The New American Library.

———— (1967) *Where Do We Go From Here: Chaos or Community?* Boston: Beacon Press.

Kitano, H.L. (1969) *Japanese Americans.* Englewood Cliffs, N.J.: Prentice-Hall.

Knollenberg, B. (1960) *Origin of the American Revolution: 1759–1766.* NY: The Macmillan Co.

Konvitz, M.R. and Leskes, T. (1961) *A Century of Civil Rights.* NY: Columbia University Press.

Kristol. I. (1966) The Negro Is Like the Immigrant Yesterday. *The New York Times Magazine* September 11:50–1.

Kuo, P.C. (1933) Caleb Cushing and the Treaty of Wanghia, 1844. *The Journal of Modern History* 5(1):34–54.

Kuper, L. and Smith, M.G. (eds) (1949) *Pluralism in Africa.* Berkeley, Calif.: University of California Press.

Kyne, P. (1921) *The Pride of Palomar.* NY: Cosmopolitan Book Corp.

LaFeber, W. (1963) *The New Empire: An Interpretation of American Expansion 1860–1898.* Ithaca, NY: Cornell University Press.

Lang, J. (1975) *Conquest and Commerce: Spain and England in the Americas.* NY: Academic Press.

Lea, H. (1909) *The Valor of Ignorance.* NY: Harper and Brothers.

Levine, G.N. and Montero, D.M. (1973) Socioeconomic Mobility among Three Generations of Japanese Americans. *Journal of Social Issues* 29(2):33–47.

Lewis, G.K. (1963) *Puerto Rico: Freedom and Power in the Caribbean.* NY: Monthly Review Press.

Life Magazine (1940) The Nisei: California Casts an Anxious Eye upon the Japanese Americans in Its Midst. October 14.

Lincoln, C.E. (1961) *The Black Muslims in America.* Boston: Beacon Press.

Link, A.S. (1956) *Wilson: The New Freedom.* Princeton, N.J.: Princeton University Press.

Lipset, S.M. (1963) *The First New Nation.* NY: Basic Books.

Litwack, L.F. (1961) *North of Slavery: The Negro in the Free States, 1790–1860.* Chicago, Ill.: The University of Chicago Press.

Lowenthal, D. (1972) *West Indian Societies.* NY: Oxford University Press.

Lyman, S.M. (1973) *The Black American in Sociological Thought.* NY: Capricorn Books.

———— (1974) *Chinese Americans.* NY: Random House.

Ma, W.H. (1970) *American Policy Toward China.* NY: Arno Press.

McClatchy, V.S. (1920) *The Germany of Asia. Sacramento Bee* (Pamphlet).

———— (1921) Japanese in the Melting Pot: Can they Assimilate and Make Good Citizens? *The Annals of the American Academy of Political and Social Science* XCIII:29–34.

McCoy, D.R. and Ruetten, R.T. (1973) *Quest and Response: Minority Rights and the Truman Administration*. Lawrence, Kan.: The University Press of Kansas.

McLaughlin, A.C. (1905) *The Confederation and the Constitution 1783–1789*. NY: Harper and Brothers.

McWilliams, C. (1935) Once Again the "Yellow Peril." *The Nation* **140 (3651)**: 735–36.

Malcolm X (1965a) *The Autobiography of Malcolm X*. NY: Grove Press Inc.

———— (1965b) *Malcolm X Speaks*. NY: Grove Press Inc.

Mears, E.G. (1925) California's Attitudes Towards the Oriental. *American Academy of Political and Social Science Annals* CXXII:199–213.

———— (1928) *Resident Orientals on the American Pacific Coast*. Chicago, Ill.: The University of Chicago Press.

Meier, A. and Rudwick, E. (1967) The Rise of Segregation in the Federal Bureaucracy: 1900–1930. *Phylon* XXVIII(2): 178–84.

Memmi, A. (1965) *The Colonizer and the Colonized*. Boston: Beacon Press.

Merritt, R.L. (1966) *Symbols of American Community*. New Haven, Conn.: Yale University Press.

Miller, K. (date unknown) *Segregation: The Caste System and Civil Service*. Washington, DC: Howard University (Pamphlet).

Miller, L. (1966) *The Petitioners: The Story of the Supreme Court of the United States and the Negro*. NY: The World Publishing Co.

———— (1971) Supreme Court Covenant Decision – an Analysis. In J.H. Bracey Jr., A. Meier, and E. Rudwick (eds) *The Rise of the Ghetto*. Belmont, Calif.: Wadsworth Publishing Co.

Miller, S.C. (1969) *The Unwelcome Immigrant*. Berkeley, Calif.: University of California Press.

Millis, H.A. (1915) *The Japanese Problem in the United States*. NY: The Macmillan Co.

Mitchell, V.P. (ed.) (1970) *Race Riots in Black and White*. Englewood Cliffs, N.J.: Prentice-Hall.

Moreau de Saint-Mery, M-L-E. (1797) Whites in a Slave Society. In L. Comitas and D. Lowenthal (eds) (1973) *Slaves, Free Men, Citizens*. Garden City, NY: Doubleday.

Morison, S.E. (1965) *The Oxford History of the American People*. NY: Oxford University Press.

Mörner, M. (1967) *Race Mixture in the History of Latin America*. Boston: Little, Brown & Co.

Myrdal, G. (1944) *An American Dilemma*. NY: Harper and Brothers.

———— (1974) *An American Dilemma Revisited*. Two lectures at City College of the City University of New York, November 12 and 19.

The Nation (1908) The Superhuman Japanese. **86 (2220)**:51.

The National Advisory Commission on Civil Disorders (1968) *Report*. Washington, DC: Government Printing Office.

Neumann, W.L. (1953) Franklin D. Roosevelt and Japan, 1913–1933. *Pacific Historical Review* **xxii (2)**:143–53.

————— (1963) *America Encounters Japan: From Perry to MacArthur*. Baltimore: The Johns Hopkins Press.

Nevins, A. (1969) *The American States during and after the Revolution, 1775–1789*. NY: A.M. Kelley.

Newton, H.P. (1972) *To Die For the People*. NY: Random House.

Norman, E.H. (1940) *Japan's Emergence as a Modern State*. NY: Institute of Pacific Relations.

Northrup, H.R. and Rowan. R. (1970) *Negro Employment in Basic Industry*. Industrial Research Unit, Wharton School of Finance and Commerce, University of Pennsylvania.

Office of Federal Contract Compliance, US Dept. of Labor (1968) Revision of Chapter 60. Part 60–1: Obligations of Contractors and Subcontractors. *Federal Register* **33(104)**: May 28.

————— (1971) Part 60–2: Affirmative Action Programs (Revised Order No. 4). *Federal Register* **36(234)**: December 4.

————— (1971) Part 60–3: Employee Testing and other Selection Procedures. *Federal Register* **39(192)**: October 2.

————— (1974) OFCC-EEOC Memorandum of Understanding. *BNA FEP Manual* **401**:271–73.

Osgood, H.L. (1957) *The American Colonies in the Seventeenth Century. Vol. I* Gloucester, Mass.: Peter Smith.

Ovington, M.W. (1969) *Half a Man*. NY: Schocken Books.

Park, R.E. (1950) *Race and Culture*. Glencoe, Ill.: The Free Press.

Paul, R.W. (1930) *The Abrogation of the Gentlemen's Agreement*. Cambridge, Mass.: The Phi Beta Kappa Society.

Peck, S.M. (1968) The Economic Situation of Negro Labor. In J. Jacobson (ed.) *The Negro and the American Labor Movement*. Garden City, NY: Doubleday and Co.

Petersen, W. (1971) *Japanese Americans*. NY: Random House.

Pettigrew, T.F. (1980) The Changing – Not Declining – Significance of Race. *Contemporary Sociology* **9(1)**:19–21.

Phillips, U.B. (1968) Southern Negro Slavery: A Benign View. In A. Weinstein and F. Gatell (eds) *American Negro Slavery*. NY: Oxford University Press.

Pinkney, A. (1976) *Red, Black, and Green: Black Nationalism in the United States* NY: Cambridge University Press.

Pottinger, J.S. (1972) Race, Sex and Jobs: The Drive Toward Equality. *Change* 4(8):24, 26–9.

Presidential Executive Order 10925 (1961).

———— 11246 (1965).

The President's Committee on Civil Rights (1947) *To Secure These Rights: a Report*. NY: Simon and Schuster.

The President's Committee on Equal Employment Opportunity (1962) *The First Nine Months: a Report*. January 15. Washington, DC.

———— (1963) Chapter 60: *Federal Register*. September 6. Washington, DC.

———— (1963) *Report to the President*. November 26. Washington, DC.

———— (1964) *Plans for Progress: A First Year Report*. August. Washington, DC.

The President's Committee on Equality of Treatment and Opportunity in the Armed Services.

The President's Committee on Government Contract Compliance (1953) *Equal Economic Opportunity: A Report*. January 16. Washington, DC.

The President's Committee on Government Contracts (1955) *A General Statement Regarding the Implementation of the National Program for Equal Economic Opportunity*. January. Washington, DC.

———— (1958) *Five years of Progress 1953–1958*. Washington, DC.

The President's Committee on Government Employment Policy, Washington, DC.

First Report, May 1956; Second Report, April 1958; Third Report, August 1959; Fourth Report, January 1961.

Prucha, F.P. (1962) *American Indian Policy in the Formative Years*. Lincoln, Neb.: University of Nebraska Press.

Puerto Rico Constitutional Convention (1952) *Notes and Comments on the Constitution of the Commonwealth of Puerto Rico*. Washington, DC.

Quarantelli, E.L. and Dynes, R.R. (1968) Looting in Civil Disorders: an Index of Social Change. In L.H. Masotti and D.R. Bowen (eds) *Riots and Rebellion*. Beverly Hills, Calif.: Sage Publications.

———— (1971) Property Norms and Looting: Their Pattern in Community Crises. In J.A. Geschwender (ed.) *The Black Revolt*. Englewood Cliffs, N.J.: Prentice-Hall.

Quarles, B (1969) *Black Abolitionists*. NY: Oxford University Press

Quintero Rivera, A.G. (1974) The Development of Social Classes and Political Conflicts in Puerto Rico. In A. Lopez and J. Petras (eds) *Puerto Rico and Puerto Ricans*. NY: John Wiley and Sons.

Raab, E. (1973) Quotas by any other Name. *US Congressional Record* **93:1**: 16447–6449.

Race Relations Law Reporter. School of Law, Vanderbilt University.

Raine, W.J. (1970) The Perception of Police Brutality in South Central Los Angeles. In N. Cober (ed.) *The Los Angeles Riots*. NY: Praeger.

Raines, H. (1979) American Indians Struggling for Power and Identity. *The New York Times Magazine* February 11:21.

Reynolds, C.N. (1927) *Oriental-White Race Relations in Santa Clara County, California*. Unpublished PhD thesis, Stanford University.

Record Commissioners of the City of Boston (1883) *Report*. Boston: Rockwell and Churchill, City Printers.

Rex, J. (1970) *Race Relations in Sociological Theory*. NY: Schocken Books.

———— (1973) *Race, Colonialism and the City*. London: Routledge and Kegan Paul.

Ribes Tovar, F. (1973) *A Chronological History of Puerto Rico*. NY: Plus Ultra Educational Publishers Inc.

Ringer, B.B. (1976) Affirmative Action, Quotas and Meritocracy. *Society* 13(2):12, 22–5.

———— (1982) 'Summary of "We the People" and Others'. Unpublished.

Robinson, D.L. (1971) *Slavery in the Structure of American Politics 1765–1820*. NY: Harcourt Brace Jovanovich Inc.

Robinson Jr., W.S. (1957) Mother Earth: Land Grants in Virginia 1607–1699. In E.G. Swem (ed.) *Jamestown 350th Anniversary Historical Booklets. No. 12*. Williamsburg, Va.: Virginia's 350th Anniversary Celebration Corp.

Roosevelt, T. (1952) *The Letters of Theodore Roosevelt*. E.E. Morison (ed.) *Vols 5, 6*. Cambridge, Mass.: Harvard University Press.

Rosenbloom, D.H. (1971) *Federal Service and the Constitution: The Development of the Public Employment Relationship*. Ithaca, NY: Cornell University Press.

Ross, A.M. (1967) The Negro in the American Economy. In A.M. Ross and H. Hill (eds) *Employment, Race and Poverty*. NY: Harcourt, Brace and World.

Rudwick, E.M. (1964) *Race Riot at East St. Louis July 2, 1917*. Carbondale, Ill.: Southern Illinois University Press.

Rustin, B. (1968) "Black Power" and Coalition Politics. In J. Grant (ed.) *Black Protest*. Greenwich, Conn.: Fawcett Publications Inc.

———— (1969) The Watts "Manifesto" and the McCone Report. In R.M. Fogelson (ed.) *The Los Angeles Riots*. NY: Arno Press and The New York Times.

Sandmeyer, E.C. (1936) California Anti-Chinese Legislation and the Federal Courts: A Study in Federal Relations. *The Pacific Historical Review* v(3): 189–211.

———— (1973) *The Anti-Chinese Movement in California*. Urbana, Ill.: University of Illinois Press.

Schurz, C. (1969) *Report on the Condition of the South*. NY: Arno Press and The New York Times.

Seale, B. (1969) Bobby Seale Speaks. In P.S. Foner (ed.) (1970) *The Black Panthers Speak*. NY: J.B. Lippincott Co.

Sears, D.O. and McConahay, J.B. (1970) Riot Participation. In N. Cohen (ed.) *The Los Angeles Riots*. NY: Praeger Publishers.

Seligman, D. (1973) How Equal Opportunity Turned into Employment Quotas. *US Congressional Record* **93**:1:16454–6456.

Silver, J.W. (1966) *Mississippi: The Closed Society*. NY: Harcourt, Brace and World.

Smith, A.E. (1947) *Colonists in Bondage*. Chapel Hill, N.C.: University of North Carolina Press.

Smith, M.G. (1965) *The Plural Society in the British West Indies*. Berkeley, Calif.: University of California Press.

Southern Regional Council (1961) *The Federal Executive and Civil Rights*.

Sowell, T. (1976) "Affirmative Action" Reconsidered. *The Public Interest* **42**: 47–65.

———— (1981) *Ethnic America: A History*. NY: Basic Books.

Spivak, J.L. (1941) The Strange Affairs of Dr. O.H. Warner: His Ships Fly US Flags but are Run by the Japanese. *Friday* **2**(21):June 13.

Stampp, K.M. (1956) *The Peculiar Institution*. NY: Random House.

———— (1972) *The Era of Reconstruction, 1865–1877*. NY: Alfred Knopf.

Stedman, J.G. (1806) A Planter's Day. In L. Comitas and D. Lowenthal (eds) (1973) *Slaves, Free Men, Citizens*. Garden City, NY: Doubleday and Co.

Steinberg, S. (1981) *The Ethnic Myth*. NY: Atheneum.

Stonequist, E.V. (1937) *The Marginal Man*. NY: Charles Scribner's Sons.

Strobe, B. (1980) The Japanese Americans. Is It Time To Say Sorry? *San Jose Mercury News, California Today* May 11. Reprinted in US House of Representatives Subcommittee on Administrative Law and Governmental Relations of the Judiciary (1980) *Hearings* **96:2**.

Strong, E.G. (1934) *The Second-Generation Japanese Problem*. Stanford, Calif.: Stanford University Press.

Subcommittee an Civil and Constitutional Rights, US House Committee on the Judiciary (1981) *Hearings* **97**:1, Serial No. 24, Part 1.

Sumner, W.G. (1940) *Folkways*. Boston: Ginn and Co.

Tabb, W.K. (1970) *The Political Economy of the Black Ghetto*. NY: W.W. Norton and Co.

Taeuber, K.E. and Taeuber, A.F. (1965) *Negroes in Cities: Residential Segregation and Neighborhood Change*. Chicago, Ill.: Aldine Publishing Co.

Tannenbaum, F. (1944) Book Review: An American Dilemma. *Political Science Quarterly* **59**(3):321–40.

———— (1946) *Slave and Citizen*. NY: Vintage Books.

ten Broek, J., Barnhart, E.N., and Matson, F.W. (1968) *Prejudice, War and the Constitution: Causes and Consequences of the Evacuation of the Japanese Americans in World War II*. Berkeley, Calif.: University of California Press.

Thorpe, E.E. (1971) Chattel Slavery and Concentration Camps. In J. Bracey, A. Meier, and E. Rudwick (eds) *American Slavery: The Question of Resistance*. Belmont, Calif.: Wadsworth Publishing Co.

Tocqueville, A. de (1969) *Democracy in America*. Garden City, NY: Doubleday and Co.

Tolchin, M. (1980) Bill to Strengthen Fair Housing Act killed as Senate Closure Vote Fails. *The New York Times* December 10:B8.

Tomlinson, T.M. and Sears, D.O. (1970) Negro Attitudes toward the Riot. In N. Cohen (ed) *The Los Angeles Riots*. NY: Praeger Publishers.

Treat, P.J. (1928) *Japan and the United States 1853–1921*. Stanford, Calif.: Stanford University Press.

Tresolini, R.J. and Shapiro, M. (1970) *American Constitutional Law*. London: The Macmillan Co.

Tupper, E. and McReynolds, G.E. (1937) *Japan in American Public Opinion*. NY: The Macmillan Co.

Turner, F.J. (1920) *The Frontier in American History*. NY: Henry Holt and Co.

US Army, Western Defense Command and Fourth Army (1943) *Final Report: Japanese Evacuation from the West Coast 1942*.

US Circuit Court, 9th District, California (1880) In re *Tiburcio Parrott. Rights of Chinese*. March 22.

US Commission on Civil Rights (1971) *Federal Civil Rights Enforcement Effort: Report*. Washington, DC.

——— (1974) *The Federal Civil Rights Enforcement Effort–1974, Vol. II*. Washington, DC.

——— (1975) *The Voting Rights Act: Ten Years After*. Washington, DC.

US Commissioner-General of Immigration *Annual Report* (1906); (1908); (1909); (1911); (1912); (1913); (1914); (1915); (1919); (1921).

US Congress
Debates and Proceedings (1790).
Debates and Proceedings (1795).

US Congressional Record (44:1, 1876); (45:1, 1877–78); (45:2, 1878); (45:3, 1879); (47:1, 1882); (53:1, 1893); (56:1, 1900); (50:2, 1906–07); (61:2, 1910); (62:2, 1912); (62:3, 1913); (64:1, 1916); (64:2, 1916); (65:2, 1918); (65:3, 1919); (66:3, 1920–21); (67:1, 1921); (68:1, 1924); (69:1, 1925); (70:1, 1928); (71:1, 1929); (71:2, 1930); (73:1, 1933); (73:2, 1934); (74:1, 1935); (74:2, 1936); (75:1, 1937); (76:1, 1939); (77:2, 1942); (78:1, 1943); (78:2, 1944); (79:1, 1945); (79:2, 1946); (80:1, 1947); (80:2, 1948); (81:1, 1949); (81:2, 1950); (82:2, 1952);

(84:2, 1956); (89:1, 1965); (93:1, 1973); (96:2, 1980).

US Department of Labor *Annual Report* (1973); (1974); (1978); (1979).

US Department of Labor, Office of the Assistant Secretary (1969) Memorandum on Order Amending Philadelphia Plan Relating to Minority Group Employment Goals. *Fair Employment Practice Manual.* The Bureau of National Affairs, Inc. Washington, DC.

US Foreign Relations 1868, 1881, 1888, 1890, 1892, 1893, 1901, 1913, 1914, 1917, 1920, 1921, 1924.

US House of Representatives
An Act HR8245(1900) 56:1.

US House of Representatives
A Bill HR 6883(1900) 56:1.

US House of Representatives
Committee on Insular Affairs (63:2, 1914) *Hearings.*
Committee on Insular Affairs (64:1, 1916) *Hearings.*
Committee on Insular Affairs (66:1, 1919) *Hearings.*
Committee on Merchant Marine and Fisheries (76:1, 1939) *Hearings.*
Committee on Merchant Marine and Fisheries (76:3, 1940) *Hearings.*
Committee on Public Lands (81:1, 1949–50) *Hearings.*
Committee on Territories (74:1, 1935) *Hearings.*

US House of Representatives
Document No. 686 (1900) 56:1.
Document No. 2 (1900) 56:2.
Document No. 847 (1906) 59:1.
Document No. 43 (1909) 61:1.
Document No. 615 (1910) 61:2.
Document No. 126 (1943) 78:1.
Document No. 304 (1943) 78:1.
Document No. 702 (1950) 81:2.
Document No. 520 (1952) 82:2.

US House of Representatives
Executive Document No. 102 (1879) 45:3.
Executive Document No. 102 (1886) 49:1.
Executive Document No. 1 Part 1 (1889) 50:2.

US House of Representatives
Report No. 249 (1900) 56:1.
Report No. 1105 (1900) 56:1.
Report No. 750 (1910) 61:2.
Report No. 341 (1912) 62:2.
Report No. 461 (1914) 63:2.

Report No. 1621 (1923) 67:4.
Report No. 176 (1924) 68:1.
Report No. 176 Part 2 (1924) 68:1.
Report No. 291 (1924) 68:1.
Report No. 350 (1924) 68:1.
Report No. 350 Part 2 (1924) 68:1.
Report No. 688 (1924) 68:1.
Report No. 2965 (1936) 74:2.
Report No. 1911 (1942) 77:2.
Report No. 2124 (1942) 77:2.
Report No. 2679 (1946) 79:2.
Report No. 455 (1947) 80:1.
Report No. 595 (1947) 80:1.
Report No. 735 (1947) 80:1.
Report No. 65 (1949) 81:1.
Report No. 634 (1949) 81:1.
Report No. 1832 (1952) 82:2.
Report No. 1809 (1956) 84:2.

US House of Representatives
   Select Committee Investigating National Defense Migration (77:2, 1942)
      Hearings.
   Subcommittee an Administrative Law and Governmental Relations of the
      Committee on the Judiciary (96:2, 1980) *Hearings.*
US Public Statutes at Large I.
US Reports. Cases Adjudged in The Supreme Court. Washington, DC.
   30 US 1 (1831)
      The Cherokee Nation v. The State of Georgia.
   60 US 393 (1857)
      Dred Scott, Plaintiff in Error v. John F.A. Sandford.
   83 US 36 (1873)
      Slaughter-House Cases.
   92 US 542 (1876)
      U.S. v. Cruikshank *et al.*
   100 US 303 (1880)
      Strauder v. West Virginia.
   109 US 3 (1883)
      Civil Rights Cases.
   118 US 356 (1886)
      Yick Wo v. Hopkins, Sheriff.
   130 US 581 (1889)

The Chinese Exclusion Case: Chae Chan Ping v. U.S.
149 US 698 (1893)
Fong Yue Ting v. U.S.
163 US 228 (1896)
Wong Wing v. U.S.
163 US 538 (1896)
Plessy v. Ferguson.
169 US 649 (1898)
U.S. v. Wong Kim Ark.
175 US 528 (1899)
Cumming v. Richmond County Board of Education.
182 US 244 (1901)
Downes v. Bidwell.
211 US 45 (1908)
Berea College v. Commonwealth of Kentucky.
238 US 348 (1915)
Guinn and Beal v. U.S.
245 US 60 (1917)
Buchanan v. Warley.
258 US 298 (1922)
Balzac v. People of Porto Rico.
260 US 178 (1922)
Takao Ozawa v. U.S.
263 US 198 (1923)
Terrace et al. v. Thompson, Attorney General of the State of Washington.
263 US 225 (1923)
Porterfield et al. v. Webb, Attorney General of the State of California et al.
263 US 313 (1923)
Webb, Attorney General of the State of California et al. v. O'Brien et al.
271 US 323 (1926)
Corrigan et al. v. Buckley.
273 US 536 (1927)
Nixon v. Herndon et al.
275 US 78 (1927)
Gong Lum et al. v. Rice et al.
294 US 587 (1935)
Norris v. Alabama.
305 US 337 (1938)
Missouri ex Rel, Gaines v. Canada, Registrar of the University of Missouri.
311 US 128 (1940)

Smith v. Texas.
320 US 81 (1943)
Hirabayashi v. U.S.
321 US 649 (1944)
Smith v. Allwright, Election Judge, *et al.*
323 US 192 (1944)
Steele v. Louisville and Nashville Railroad Co. *et al.*
323 US 214 (1944)
Korematsu v. U.S.
323 US 283 (1944)
Ex Parte Mitsuye Endo.
332 US 463 (1947)
Patton v. Mississippi.
332 US 633 (1948)
Oyama *et al.* v. California.
334 US 1 (1948)
Shelley v. Kraemer.
334 US 410 (1948)
Takahashi v. Fish and Game Commission *et al.*
339 US 282 (1950)
Cassell v. Texas.
339 US 629 (1950)
Sweatt v. Painter *et al.*
339 US 637 (1950)
McLaurin v. Oklahoma State Regents for Higher Education *et al.*
345 US 461 (1953)
Terry v. Adams.
345 US 972 (1953)
Brown *et al.* v. Board of Education of Topeka *et al.*
346 US 249 (1953)
Barrows *et al.* v. Jackson.
347 US 483 (1954)
Brown *et al.* v. Board of Education of Topeka *et al.*
349 US 294 (1955)
Brown *et al.* v. Board of Education of Topeka *et al.*
358 US 1 (1958)
Cooper v. Aaron.
365 US 715 (1961)
Burton v. Wilmington Parking Authority *et al.*
368 US 157 (1961)

Garner *et al.* v. Louisiana.
369 US 31 (1962)
Bailey v. Patterson.
373 US 244 (1963)
Peterson *et al.* v. City of Greenville.
373 US 267 (1963)
Lombard *et al.* v. Louisiana.
378 US 226 (1964)
Bell *et al.* v. Maryland.
401 US 424 (1971)
Griggs *et al.* v. Duke Power Co.
407 US 163 (1972)
Moose Lodge No. 107 v. Irvis *et al.*
431 US 324 (1977)
International Brotherhood of Teamsters v. U.S. *et al.*
443 US 193 (1979)
United Steelworkers of America, AFL-CIO v. Weber *et al.*
US Senate
A Bill S2264 (1900) 56:1.
US Senate
Committee on Governmental Affairs (96:2, 1980) *Hearings*.
Committee on Immigration (68:1, 1924) *Hearings*.
Committee on Territories and Insular Affairs (79:1, 1945) *Hearings*.
US Senate
Document No. 147 (1900) 56:1.
Document No. 147 (1906) 59:2.
Document No. 357 (1910) 61:2.
Document No. 633 (1911) 61:2.
Document No. 694 (1912) 62:2.
Document No. 968 (1912) 62:3.
Document No. 415 (1916) 64:1.
Document No. 62 Vol. II (1919) 66:1.
US Senate
Executive Document No. 148 (1881) 47:1.
Executive Document No. 13 Part 1 (1893) 53:1.
US Senate
Report No. 689 (1877) 44:2.
Report No. 249 (1900) 56:1.
Report No. 1300 (1913) 62:3.
Report No. 579 (1916) 64:1.

Report No. 1011 (1926) 69:1.
Report No. 159 (1942) 77:2.
Report No. 659 (1944) 78:2.
Report No. 422 (1947) 80:1.
Report No. 1167 (1949) 81:1.
Report No. 1779 (1950) 81:2.
Report No. 1137 Parts I and II (1952) 82:2.
Report No. 1720 (1952) 82:2.

US Senate
Subcommittee of the Committee or Territories and Insular Affairs (78:1, 1943) *Hearings*.

US Statutes at Large
(12, 1863); (13, 1866); (14, 1868); (16, 1871); (18, 1875); (24, 1887); (25, 1889); (27, 1893); (28, 1895); (29, 1897); (30, 1899); (43, 1925); (71, 1957); (74, 1960); (78, 1964); (79, 1965); (82, 1968); (94, 1980).

van den Berghe, P.L. (1967) *Race and Racism: A Comparative Perspective*. NY: John Wiley and Sons Inc.

———— (1972) The United States is a "Herrenvolk" Democracy. In P. Rose (ed.) *Nation of Nations*. NY: Random House.

Van Riper, P.P. (1958) *History of the United States Civil Service*. Evanston, Ill.: Row, Peterson and Co.

Vander Zanden, J.W. (1965) *Race Relations in Transition*. NY: Random House.

Wade, R.C. (1965) The Negro in Cincinnati, 1800–1830. In D.W. Hoover (ed.) *Understanding Negro History*. Chicago, Ill.: Quadrangle Books.

War Relocation Authority (1946a) *The Relocation Program*. Washington, DC: US Government Printing Office.

———— (1946b) *Wartime Exile*. Washington, DC: US Government Printing Office.

———— (1946c) *Evacuated People: A Quantitative Description*. Washington, DC: US Government Printing Office.

Washburn, W.E. (1971) *Red Man's Land: White Man's Law*. NY: Charles Scribner's Sons.

Waskow, A.I. (1967) *From Race Riot to Sit-In*. Garden City, NY: Doubleday and Co.

Wax, M. (1971) *Indian Americans*. Englewood Cliffs, N.J.: Prentice-Hall.

Weaver, R.C. (1948) *The Negro Ghetto*. NY: Russell and Russell Inc.

Weiss, N.J. (1970) The Negro and the New Freedom. In A. Weinstein and F.O. Gatell (eds) *The Segregation Era, 1863–1954*. NY: Oxford University Press.

Wertenbaker, T.J. (1957) The Government of Virginia in the Seventeenth Century. In E.G. Swem (ed.) *Jamestown 350th Anniversary Historial Booklets*.

No. 16. Williamsburg, Va: Virginia 350th Anniversary Celebration Corp.

———— (1959) *The Planters of Colonial Virginia.* NY: Russell and Russell Inc.

White, M. (1939) Between Two Flags. *The Saturday Evening Post* **212(14):** September 30.

Williams, E. (1944) *Capitalism and Slavery.* Chapel Hill, NC.: University of North Carolina Press.

Willoughby, W.W. (1966) *Foreign Rights and Interests in China.* 2 vols. Taipei: Ch'eng-Wen Publishing Co.

Wilson, W.J. (1978) *The Declining Significance of Race: Blacks and Changing American Institutions.* Chicago, Ill.: The University of Chicago Press. Second edition 1980.

———— (1980) A Response to Marrett and Pettigrew. *Contemporary Sociology* **9(1):21–4.**

Woodson, C.G. (1922) *The Negro in Our History.* Washington, DC.: The Associated Publishers Inc.

Woodward, C.V. (1957) *The Strange Career of Jim Crow.* NY: Oxford University Press.

Woofter, Jr., T.J. (1928) *Negro Problems in Cities.* Garden City, NY: Doubleday, Doran and Co.

Wright, L.B. (1959) *The Atlantic Frontier: Colonial American Civilization 1607–1763.* Ithaca, NY: Cornell University Press.

Wright, M.C. (1967) *The Last Stand of Chinese Conservatism: The T'ung-Chih Restoration, 1862–1874.* NY: Atheneum.

Young, K. (1929) *The Social Psychology of Oriental-Occidental Prejudice.* American Council Institute of Pacific Relations (Pamphlet).

———— (1944) Book Review: "An American Dilemma." *American Sociological Review* **9(3):326–30.**

Zinn, H. (1965) *SNCC: The New Abolitionists.* Boston: Beacon Press.

NAME INDEX

SUBJECT INDEX